EMANCIPATION

EMANCIPATION

The Making of the Black Lawyer
1844–1944

J. Clay Smith, Jr.

University of Pennsylvania Press

Philadelphia

The Jack and Lovell Olender Foundation made a generous contribution toward the publication of this book so that it could be made available to a wider audience. Willie Leftwich, Esq., provided additional promotional funding, the family of Professor Herbert O. Reid, Sr., made a contribution in his memory for books to be donated to designated historically black colleges and universities and various law schools, and Sanford Cloud, Jr., Esq., made a contribution toward the indexing costs.

Library of Congress Cataloging-in-Publication Data
Smith, J. Clay (John Clay), 1942–
   Emancipation: the making of the black lawyer, 1844–1944 / J. Clay Smith.
     p. cm.
   Includes bibliographical references and index.
   ISBN 0-8122-3181-3
   1. Afro-American lawyers—History.   I. Title.   II. Title: Making of the black lawyer, 1844–1944.
KG299.A35S65   1993
349.73'08996073—dc20
[347.3008996073]   93-3781
                                    CIP

For
PATTI
—my beloved wife

Contents

Please consult the index for references to states not listed on the
Table of Contents.

viii   Contents

Foreword

By Justice Thurgood Marshall

African-American lawyers have played a unique role in American history. Imbued with respect for the rule of law and the responsibility that such belief engenders, these lawyers have used their legal training not only to become masterful technicians but to force the legal system to live up to its creed: the promise of "equal justice under law."

Long before the Civil Rights Movement ever crystallized the plight of African-Americans, Negro lawyers had identified the inequities in the legal order and begun to lay the foundation for social change. In storefront offices, over kitchen tables, and on porch steps, these lawyers worked diligently to protect and expand the rights of African-Americans and to ensure, case by case, that justice would not forever be delayed. Lawyers such as Macon Bolling Allen fought for and gained admission to the bar in 1844, overcoming widespread discrimination among state bar associations and securing for African-Americans an important foothold in the legal structure. Jonathan Jasper Wright became the first African-American justice of a state supreme court prior to 1945, despite resistance among whites. Professors and legal theorists at the nation's African-American law schools, including my mentor at Howard University, Charles Hamilton Houston, worked tirelessly to educate and prepare young students to become skilled professionals and social engineers.

Until now, the important role Negro lawyers have played in American public life has gone largely unrecognized. In his book, *Emancipation: The Making of the Black Lawyer, 1844–1944*, J. Clay Smith, Jr., a professor at Howard University School of Law, traces the history of African-Americans in the legal profession. With painstaking and exhaustive detail, Professor Smith documents the challenges these lawyers faced—both in and outside of the legal community—and the contributions they have made. *Emancipation* is an important and impressive work; one cannot read it without being inspired by the legal acumen, creativity, and resiliency these pioneer lawyers displayed. I commend Professor Smith's comprehensive book. It should be read by everyone interested in understanding the road African-Americans have traveled and the challenges that lie ahead.

Preface

The inspiration to write this book, the research of which began twenty-five years ago, came not only from the black world but from the white world as well. The book is as much about the role that white lawyers and judges played in the history of black lawyers as it is a work about black lawyers themselves. Naturally, my aim was to tell the story of the black lawyer, but heretofore unknown, historically important white lawyers have also emerged in this story, which will provide a clearer appreciation of the interrelationships of American lawyers in general and black American lawyers in particular.

This book is limited to the first one hundred years of the sojourn of the black lawyer in America (1844–1944), for it is this very period of American history that has been studied least by scholars of black legal history, although literature about white lawyers during the same period is far more extensive. The history of such modern legal figures as Justice Thurgood Marshall and of nonlegal civil rights figures can be positioned more properly within a comprehensive history of the black legal pioneers who preceded Marshall to the bar by eighty-nine years, for the foundation in the law and the precedents established by Marshall's predecessors have been spectacular.

The decision as to how to approach this book was difficult. How does one write a book spanning one hundred years that both tries to tell a story and present the truth? I chose to tell the story of the black lawyer in fact. This process was made difficult because of the large number of inaccuracies having to do with the black lawyer that have taken hold in the marketplace of ideas—errors that have taken years to correct. It also was difficult to complete this book because, as W. Augustus Low and Virgil A. Clift, the editors of *Encyclopedia of Black America*, wrote a decade ago, "written references [on black lawyers] are practically non-existent and there is no single adequate reference."[1]

1. *Encyclopedia of Black America* 502 (W. A. Low and V. A. Clift eds. 1981).

I ultimately decided to present this work from an originist perspective. This approach required an investigation of the origins of the black lawyer that followed them from the states of their emancipation to the states in which they, as lawyers, emancipated their people. (Little known is the fact that some of the people these lawyers emancipated were white.) As products of the state, lawyers are educated in the law schools of the states or the District of Columbia, and they are first admitted to the state bar; the history of the black lawyer, like his white counterpart, is also local. There is commonality between black lawyers' and white lawyers' experiences, but it is not all common, as this book proves. The essential differences would have been lost if I had chosen to mirror the history of white lawyers as the experience of black lawyers.

Several books about lawyers served as models for this work's format. I refer to Anton-Hermann Chroust's comprehensive two-volume book, *The Rise of the Legal Profession in America*, published in 1965. This book presents "a general or narrative history of the American legal profession from its earliest colonial beginnings to the middle of the nineteenth century."[2] Chroust, in turn, modeled his book on the masterwork of Charles Warren, who wrote *A History of the American Bar* in 1911. Three other books, which deal with black subjects, also were used as examples for my book: Dietrich C. Reitzes's *Negroes and Medicine*, published in 1958; Geraldine Segal's *Blacks in the Law*, published in 1983; and A. Leon Higginbotham's *In the Matter of Color*, published in 1978. The common thread of all of these books is that they focus on the history of their subjects by telling the story from a local perspective. This approach, which I intend to follow in my work, in no way diminished the national scope of these books, but rather proved the validity of viewing their subjects as integral parts of the American landscape. This approach allows the nation to learn about itself through the heroic deeds of men and women throughout the nation—but, as will be seen, exceptional circumstances contributed in no small measure to the origins of the black lawyer.

Chroust's work was the most important model for my own because it strove to be a comprehensive repository of information; similarly, my book is intended to be the first definitive effort to identify and to portray collectively all that is available about black lawyers. (One readily sees the similarity by comparing my table of contents with that of Chroust's book.) What Chroust and Warren did to present the history of white lawyers (without a single black lawyer mentioned), I have done for the black lawyer (with many white lawyers included).

2. A. H. Chroust, *The Rise of the Legal Profession in America* vii (1965).

The literature on black lawyers is growing. The first known history of black lawyers, *Negroes and the Law*, was written by Fitzhugh Lee Styles in 1937. Since then, Richard Kluger's *Simple Justice* was published in 1975; Walter Leonard's *Black Lawyers* was published in 1977; Genna Rae McNeil's biography of Charles Hamilton Houston, *Groundwork*, was published in 1983; and Gilbert Ware's biography, *William H. Hastie: Grace Under Pressure*, was published in 1984.

Acknowledgments

Over the past twenty-five years, hundreds of people have provided me with information, leads, and tips about black lawyers and white lawyers whose contributions have never been recorded in American law or history. Some of those tips led me to verify facts on the tombstones of black lawyers. Regrettably, when I started this research, I did not note down the names of several people who provided me with information or guidance and deserve to be mentioned: I thank them and others whose direction toward valuable information about their fathers and mothers, aunts and uncles, brothers and sisters, friends and acquaintances, is greatly appreciated.

Institutional support has been enormously helpful and has made me even more aware and appreciative of the role that reference librarians and local historical societies play in the development of scholars and the preservation of rare documents and records. Many of the names of public reference librarians and from historical societies appear in the notes and thus are not mentioned here.

Special acknowledgment is given to Professor Herbert Ordré Reid, Sr., who first taught me that black lawyers had a history during a lecture at Howard University School of Law in 1964. Ollie May Cooper, who had been the law deans' secretary at Howard University for many years, shared with me her scrapbook and papers spanning nearly fifty years, information that was passed on to me by her nephew, Paul Cooper, after her death. The help of Charles Sumner Brown, whose research on black lawyers is a treasure trove, saved me from erroneous conclusions, forced me to verify more facts, and humbled me before a black lawyer who was stalking the history of his peers during the 1950s. I thank Daniel Williams, the archivist of Tuskegee University, for his support in helping me to identify many of the news articles cited in this book.

Other institutions and persons that have helped me to complete this book include the Amistad Research Center, Tulane University; Associated Publishers, Inc.; Atlanta–Fulton County [Georgia] Public Li-

brary; Atlanta University Library Center; Black Heritage Society of
Providence, Rhode Island; Boston University Archives; The Burke
Library, Union Theological Seminary, of New York City; Cambridge
[Massachusetts] City Public Library; Chicago Historical Society; Chi-
cago Public Library; Collins P. Huntington Library, Hampton University; Crittenden County [Vermont] Historical Society; Federal Bar Association; George Washington University Archives; Georgia Historical
Society Library; Great Plains Black Museum; Harvard University Library; Harvard University Law School Archives; Hastings College of
Law; Howard University School of Law Library; Lane College; Library
of Congress; Loyola University Law Library of Chicago; Massachusetts
Supreme Court Archives and Records Preservation; Memorial Libraries, Deerfield, Massachusetts; Minnesota Historical Society; Moorland-Spingarn Research Center, Howard University; Morris Brown
College; National Archives; National Bar Association; National Business League; National Council of Negro Women Historical Develop-
ment Project; National Portrait Gallery; New England School of Law
Library; New York State Library and Archives; New York University
Archives; New York University School of Law Records Office; Oklahoma Historical Society; Savannah State College Library; Schomburg
Center for Research in Black Culture; Sigma Delta Tau Legal Frater-
nity; Smith College Archives; South Carolina State Library; Tuskegee
University Library and Archives; United States Senate Library; United
States Supreme Court Library; University of Chicago Archives; Uni-
versity of the District of Columbia; University of Minnesota Law Re-
view; University of Pennsylvania Law Library; University of Pitts-
burgh; University of Rhode Island; University of Washington Law
Library; Vermont Historical Society; Victoria University of Wellington,
New Zealand; Virginia Historical Society; Virginia Union University;
Washington Bar Association; Washington University School of Law;
Wilberforce University Archives; and Wyoming State Historical Research Division.

Individual support has come from Fay Acker, Edwyna Anderson,
Helen Elsie Austin, Professor Richard L. Aynes, Malik Azeez, Pro-
fessor Betty Bandell, Robert L. Bell, Robert Bender, Professor Mary
Frances Berry, Esme E. Bhan, Barney Bloom, David Blow, Lynnette
Kay Bourne, Elizabeth Bouvier, Edith Jones Boyd, Thomas M. Boyd,
Dean Wiley A. Branton, Sr., Professor John Brittain, Charles Sumner
Brown, Ellen Epps Brown, Erroll Brown, Jacquelyn Y. Brown, Wesley
A. Brown, Professor W. Hamilton Bryson, Scott F. Burson, Bertha Cal-
loway, Virginia Camerman, René L. Campbell, Lisle Carter, Jr., John
E. Cary, Jr., Tanja H. Castro, Erika C. Chadbourn, Professor Ronald

Chester, Prince C. Chambliss, Jr., Professor James P. Chandler, Anna Edith Chaplin, Keith A. Clinard, Luella Coleman, Ollie May Cooper, Mr. and Mrs. Paul F. Cooper, Otis and Marialyce Cowart, Beverly Crawford, James M. Christian, Sr., Congressman George W. Crockett, Jr., Vicki Crompton, John Crump, Betty Culpeper, Robert Roy Dann, Ivy Davis, Charles E. Donegan, Francis R. Doyle, Professor Julian R. Dugas, William L. England, Jr., Ralph B. Everett, Marc L. Fleischaker, Mary Katherine Stewart-Flippin, Jan Flores, Professor John Hope Franklin, Charles Freeney, Kay M. Fullerton, Judge Wendell Gardner, Willard B. Gatewood, Walter A. Gay, Jr., Dean Tom Gerety, Truman K. Gibson, Jr., Watson T. Goffney, Sr., Professor Robert D. Goldstein, Shauna M. Graves, Chester J. Gray, Robert E. Greene, Erwin N. Griswold, John A. Haak, Phoebe A. Haddon, Dorothy M. Haith, Vanne O. Hayes, Judge Margarate Haywood, Leo Hendricks, Linda Henry, Judge A. Leon Higginbotham, Jr., Ruth Hill, Professor Gilbert Holmes, Joseph R. Houchins, Roy C. Howell, Josephine Hughes, Derrick Humphries, Raymond Jackson, Suzanne Jenkins, Bob Irwin, Jerold Jacobs, Charles G. Johnson, Clifton H. Johnson, Henry Lincoln Johnson, Jr., Douglas Jones, Jr., Hilda Jones, Professor James Jones, JoAnne Garland Jones, Samuel B. Jones, Sidney A. Jones, Jr., Vonciel Jones, Wilhelmina Griffin Jones, Casper L. Jordan, Professor Ann Juergens, Drew Kadel, Fritz Kahn, Aline M. Kean, Christine Kehrwald, Charles L. Keller, Becky Kojan, Professor Gil Kujovich, Charles P. Kindregan, Judge Michael Waring Lee, Gerald Bruce Lee, Willie Leftwich, Professor Jethro K. Lieberman, Gaynelle Reed Lewis, Cynthia A. Lewis, William Lewis, Toni Lieteau, Professor Edward J. Littlejohn, Peggy Lopez, Myles V. Lynk, Cynthia Mabry, Fritz J. Malval, Jordan Marsh, Justice Thurgood Marshall, Thurgood Marshall, Jr., Emily V. Smith-Martin, Professor Larry L. Martin, David Maslin, William T. Mason, Jr., William S. Mayo, Shirla R. McClain, Professor Joseph McCormick, Jr., Nancy McCormick, Sara L. McGill, Professor Genna Rae McNeil, Louis Rothschild Mehlinger, W. Leanna Miles, Viola Ollivette Fisher-Minor, Juanita Jackson Mitchell, Thomas W. Mitchell, Phoebe Novotny Nelson, Betty Odabashian, L. John Osborn, Judge Cecil B. Patterson, Jr., Linda V. Parker, Professor Jeanus B. Parks, Jr., Edwin L. Parms, Frank Peatree, Mrs. John G. Pegg, Ambassador Edward J. Perkins, Thelma Ackiss Perry, Professor Randall T. Peterson, Judge Lawrence W. Pierce, Judge Elizabeth Davis Pittman, Mary Platt, Richard Popp, Aaron Porter, James S. Pregraves, David R. Proper, Williard B. Ranson, Marguerite Rawalt, Vincent E. Reed, David Rice, Marie Rine, Bettie J. Robinson, Judge G. Bruce Robinson, Judge Spottswood W. Robinson III, Chris Roggerson, Jr., Salvatore

Romano, Thomas Rouland, Thelma Rutherford, William K. Sahr, Ena St. Louis, John Schmelzer, Mrs. Armond W. Scott, Armond W. Scott III, Geraldine R. Segal, Althea T. L. Simmons, Jessie Carney Smith, Nathaniel H. Speights, Dean Robert A. Stein, Carolyn Hill Stewart, Judge Juanita Kidd Stout, Jill Strickland, Rowena Stuart, Harold K. Stubbs, Jonathan K. Stubbs, Robert J. Swan, Al Sweeney, Judge Jack Tanner, Susan Tatelman, Vannie L. Taylor III, Judge Lucia T. Thomas, Thurlow E. Tibbs, Jr., Judge Edward B. Toles, Arthur L. Tolson, Maria Tracey, U.S. Senator Paul S. Trible, Jr., Raymond F. Trent, Professor Mark V. Tushnet, Wilda Wahpepah, Professor Hanes Walton, Jr., Professor Lynn D. Wardle, Professor Charles D. Watt, Jr., Wendell Webster, Dorothy B. Porter-Wesley, Barbara J. Weston, Ruth Weyand, Dr. Desra White, Cleota Proctor Wilbekin, Leroy Wilson, Jr., Lisa C. Wilson, Mary Wilburn, Frederick D. Williams, Isiah J. Williams III, Lillian S. Williams, Professor Phoebe W. Williams, Raymond Williams, Michael R. Winston, Professor Randall B. Woods, and Janet Simms Woods.

Thanks also goes to my legal assistants in the order of service at Howard University Law School who organized my files, clipped newspapers, and helped to verify facts: C. Lamont Smith, Thomas Deon Warner, Karen Osborn, Richard Mirsky, Michael Todd, John T. Henderson, Jr., Teresa Howie, Kenneth P. McNeely, Nicole Jenkins, Ronald E. Mills, Andrea D. Williams, Michelle J. Harris, Terri L. Hunter, Bernard Haggerty, and Johnine F. Waters. Special thanks to Michelle J. Harris, who also typed the bibliography, Andrea D. Williams, who helped compile the combined census figures on black and white lawyers contained in the appendix, and Terri L. Hunter, who checked the case citations. Responsibility for any errors, of course, is mine.

The support and encouragement I received from my colleagues in the law faculty, its administrative and library staffs, and the research grants from Interim Dean Daniel O. Bernstine, Acting Dean Alice Gresham Bullock, and Dean Henry Ramsey, Jr., of the Howard University School of Law have been most gratifying, helpful, and appreciated. The assistance provided by law school secretaries Betty Washington and Jenifer Harps Hentrel helped to speed the project along. The manuscript was typed by Annabel Collins, whose patience and understanding shall always be remembered.

I could not have completed this book without the support of my wife, Patti Jones Grace Smith, whose love, devotion, and criticism aided me during the lowest moments of this enterprise.

A special thanks to my children, Stager, Michelle, Michael, and

Eugene, who throughout most of their lives have helped me to reach this point; to Timothy R. Clancy, the able associate director of the University of Pennsylvania Press, for his support for and early recognition of the value of this book; and to Mindy Brown, the project editor, whose editorial suggestions greatly enhanced the book.

J. Clay Smith, Jr.
Washington, D.C.
January 1993

Introduction

Compiling this history of the black lawyer has been a tortuous and contentious task. For years it was "a compulsive busyness rather than the study of history" that drove me "to collect records when [I did] not know what to seek,"[1] or where to seek them. After years of wandering in the desert of legal doctrine and theory, I came to recognize what Oliver Wendell Holmes had determined some years ago, that "the life of the law has not been logic: it has been experience . . . it is [not] only the axioms and corollaries of a book of mathematics . . . we must consult history [because] the substance of the law . . . depends very much [on] the study of history."[2]

This book cannot be categorized exclusively as either legal or social history: it is about the black lawyer, whose personhood has never fit neatly into either category. The history of black lawyers as chronicled in these pages, however, should help to establish their essential importance to legal and social history.[3] Because the history of lawyers in American legal history is "a white man's history,"[4] and has been told "as a white man's story,"[5] the literature about the honorable and constructive role that the pioneer black lawyers have played in the law has been scant. *Negroes and the Law*, the first significant book on black lawyers, was written by Fitzhugh Lee Styles, himself a black lawyer, and published in 1937. Another black legal historian, Charles Sumner Brown, wrote the first comprehensive article on the genesis of black lawyers in the *Negro History Bulletin* in 1959, entitled, "The Genesis of the Negro Lawyer in New England." The groundwork established by these two authors and other scholars has provided many clues that contributed greatly to the completion of this work.[6]

The struggle of the black lawyer to emerge from the ashes of slavery to meet "the social exigencies in the professional needs of the masses" has been remarkable.[7] Even before the ratification of the "Negro's charter of liberty,"[8] the Thirteenth Amendment abolishing slavery in 1865, and the Fourteenth Amendment establishing the concept of dual citizenship in the state and the nation in 1868, the black lawyer had already taken his place in society. He also had determined that "democracy is equality, economic, political and . . . social."[9]

It may be surprising to learn that black people had entered the white world of law prior to the Civil War, but blacks were determined to become suitors for their own emancipation and equality. All the more remarkable is the fact that "the young colored man was invited to his calling by no prospect of success, by no example of a daring and courageous forerunner."[10] The admission of Macon Bolling Allen into the legal profession in 1844 presented the first challenge to America's legal community, which then had to contend with the mind of a black man in a white man's profession at a period when the majority of black people were constitutionally enslaved. And negative anecdotes about black lawyers began to surface in 1848, soon after Macon B. Allen was admitted to the bar. One rhyme read,

> I wish de legislature would set dis *darkie free*,
> Oh! what a happy place den de *darkie* land would be.
> We'd have a *darkie* parliament,
> An' *darkie* codes of law,
> An' *darkie* judges on de bench,
> *Darkie* barristers and aw.[11]

In 1844 the black lawyer, unlike the white lawyer, could not look back to a Colonial legal past. Black people were not considered as part of the chartered or proprietary colonies. Nor was the black lawyer driven to reflect on an ancestry rooted in European culture or its common law, as determined by the Privy Council of London. At the same time, black lawyers are not known to have directly introduced African legal doctrines into American law, but it can hardly be assumed that the pioneer black lawyer was unaware of African traditions, which indirectly may have been introduced in the area of dispute resolution.[12] Still, the first black lawyers apparently never challenged the premises upon which the common law was based, perhaps because their ancestors had been for so long uprooted from their African roots that some of the fundamental legal principles of African tribal law and custom had been lost.

The black lawyer entered the legal profession after all the initial debates on nationhood and many individual protections against the national government had been determined; but it is known that black people were qualified and probably voted to ratify the Articles of

Confederation, and they were qualified voters in some states at the time the Constitution was adopted.[13] They entered the legal profession in the North while their mothers, fathers, aunts, uncles, and cousins were slaves in the South, or if free, were considered as mere "sojourners in the land."[14]

In *Democracy in America*, Alexis de Tocqueville observed in 1835, nine years before America's first black lawyer was admitted to the bar, that the "aristocracy . . . occupies the judicial bench and the bar."[15] Once black lawyers were admitted to the bar, they considered themselves as counterpoise to the aristocracy as they discovered that they, like white lawyers, could influence and perhaps "control the democracy"[16] through the courts of law. At times the black lawyer may have sought acceptance as an aristocrat, but the white legal aristocrats excluded him from their ranks. Foreclosed from this opportunity, the black lawyer, always mindful of his slave ancestry, "humble parentage,"[17] and race, viewed himself as an emancipator of his people. And he fought against the Negrophobia that gained prominence in articles such as the following from the Reconstruction era:

The graveyards you have selected, beautiful, and adorned as a resting-place of those you have loved must be desecrated to satisfy the spite of those liberty lovers, and choice places given to the negro, even if it should require the exhuming of friends long buried. You must divide your pew in church, even if your wife and child are forced to sit on the floor, and no complaint must be made should Sambo besmear the carpet you have placed there with juice of tobacco. Your children at school must sit on the back seats and in the cold, whilst the negro's children sit near the stove and on the front seats, and enjoy in every instance the money you toil for, whilst Sambo is sleeping and stealing. Or, as the darky explained to his less posted brother: "We's gwine to ride free on de railroads, smoke in de ladies' car, and put our feet on the percushions of the seats whenever we damn please. We's gwine to be allowed to stop at de hotels, an set at de head of de table, and hab de biggest slice ob de chickens, and lay around in de parlors and spit on de carpets, and make de white trash hustle themselves and wait on us without grumblin'. We's gwine to be allowed to go to de white schools and set upon the platform with de teacher. We's gwine to be buried in italic coffins on top of de white folks, and Gabriel shall call: 'All ob you colored gemmen rise first.' "[18]

As the Reconstruction era began, the need for black lawyers who were "to serve the newly freed black population"[19] was recognized in the South, but "Negrophobia [remained] prevalent,"[20] thwarting the progress of the black lawyer. Still, despite "Negrophobia," black lawyers persevered, and one black lawyer, John Mercer Langston, was even mentioned as a possible vice-presidential candidate in 1888.[21]

The death of Frederick Douglass in 1895 marked the end of one era and the beginning of a new era for the black lawyer, for Douglass had been the primary and most forceful voice of black America heard by the judiciary, even though he was not a lawyer.[22] The writings of Douglass had pled the case against slavery, for the rights of women, and for the general equality of all people.[23] His voice had no doubt been an inspiration to black lawyers and those aspiring to become black lawyers to plow the field of justice that Douglass had claimed for his people.[24] After Douglass died, it was left to the black lawyer to give meaning to his words in all public forums.[25]

Black lawyers were one of the last group of professionals to emerge as a class in the black community. They were given a "high status" in the black community, but they occupied "a less-favored position within the social structure" as a whole.[26] Their presence and their small numbers were not viewed as a significant threat in the legal community because they were only marginally accepted by white lawyers and white clients. Black people often used black lawyers in almost hopeless criminal matters but turned to white lawyers in the more lucrative civil cases.[27]

The black lawyers' status remained viable, but they faced direct competition from the black preacher in terms of prestige and effectiveness: the black lawyer worked in a public forum which he did not control, and over which he had little influence, but the black preacher came closer than any other black professional to serving as an advocate in the public arena. Black preachers had a built-in constituency; black lawyers had to build theirs. But the black preacher was also able to protect the black lawyer when he entered the public arena to plead the black cause, because the white power structure knew that the preachers could stir up the black community and influence their vote. The black lawyer thus often found sanctuary for his public persona in the privacy of the black church.[28]

Black preachers consistently outnumbered the number of black lawyers in the South. In 1930 Alabama had 1,653 black preachers and "four lawyers who cared to struggle against the caste system in the Alabama courts."[29] One million black people in Alabama looked to three or four lawyers to seek justice, but they were doubtful that such a small number of black lawyers could launch a successful attack against the racial policies of the white establishment. During and after the Reconstruction era, then, black people, anchored to the church, remained tied to black preachers rather than to black lawyers as the primary source of leadership in the community.[30] A noted Philadelphia scholar concluded that even black physicians had more opportunities than did black lawyers.

The Negro lawyer does not have the opportunity to succeed that the Negro clergymen and physicians have had. These latter practically have the practice of their people, but not so the Negro lawyer. He is still a pioneer and at a disadvantage, in that his practice is not private, or among his own people, but he must plead before a white judge often against a white lawyer and generally, with a white jury. Yet, there is but little complaint on the part of the Negro lawyers. The average Negro coming from the South and knowing how great a handicap the lawyer of his race suffers in that section, hesitates long before employing a Negro lawyer. There are not more than a third as many Negro lawyers in Pennsylvania as physicians. In Philadelphia there are fourteen; in Pittsburgh five; in Harrisburg, one.[31]

A noted American historian confirms the maltreatment of black lawyers in Rentiesville, Oklahoma, an "all Negro town . . . to which [John Hope Franklin] went after [his] father had been expelled from court by a white judge [and was] told . . . that no black person could ever represent anyone in his court."[32] The discrimination against black lawyers was so severe that many of them left the profession of law and entered teaching or became clerks in stores, barbers, or government workers.[33] Still, though the remaining black lawyers were "often made the butt of jibes and ridicule,"[34] they never dropped the baton passed to them by Frederick Douglass, the baton of emancipation.

Prior to the Civil War, the education of blacks in the North was scattered. According to one report, only "1.7 percent of the Negro population of school age attended school."[35] The systematic education of black people in America did not exist until after the Civil War.[36] A few black slaves were secretly educated before and after the war, with the knowledge of their slave or former slave masters,[37] even though it was a crime to educate slaves in most Southern states.[38] And some blacks, born free or granted their freedom, received some form of education in the North and the West,[39] and at least twenty-eight blacks received college degrees prior to the Civil War.[40]

The public education of southern blacks dates back to 1620 in Virginia, although public institutions for blacks and Indians were soon replaced by private schools operated by various religious groups.[41] According to one source, on September 17, 1861, "the American Missionary Association established at Fortress Monroe, Virginia, the first day school among Freedmen. . . . This school laid the foundation of Hampton Institute," later elevated to one of the nation's first black colleges.[42]

Common schools for blacks in the South supported by public funds began in earnest on March 3, 1865, with Congress's creation of the Freedmen's Bureau, which assisted in establishing thirteen black colleges in seven southern states and the District of Columbia.[43] The purpose of the bureau was "to ease and speed transition from slavery to full citizenship . . . and its initial efforts proved quite beneficial to the former slaves."[44] It invested "over five million dollars into public schools for Negroes, employing 3,300 teachers for 146,581 pupils."[45] One of the black students sent to Richmond, Virginia, to attend the newly opened "Freedmen's School" was James Alexander Chiles, who was six years old when he enrolled in the school. The early opportunity to obtain an education eventually led him to the University of Michigan law school, from which he was graduated in 1889.[46]

Although blacks were introduced to education during their formative years, during the Reconstruction era, many were poorly educated. Yet, most former slaves who had an opportunity to get an education, had "a frenzy for book learning."[47] In fact, blacks, driven by an obsession to learn,[48] surpassed whites "who [had] never been . . . handicapped" by lack of educational opportunity.[49]

After the Civil War, there is little doubt, though there is no definitive study on the point, that blacks, like whites, entered the legal profession with grade-school educations.[50] Likewise, there is no study on the exact number of blacks entering white and black law schools between 1844 to 1945, or the range of their educations. We know that in the 1840s four white colleges admitted such blacks as John Mercer Langston, who later became a lawyer.[51] Between 1914 and 1936, Charles S. Johnson's book, *The Negro College Graduate*, reports that black professionals were concentrated in the fields of medicine (37.0%), dentistry (24.7%), pharmacy (14.0%), and law (12.7%).[52] These graduates received their formative education primarily at black public high schools[53] and from eight private black colleges.[54] Given the existing repressive political and social conditions facing blacks following Reconstruction, one can only surmise why black and white teachers at black high schools and black colleges did not discourage blacks from entering the legal profession. (In fact, they may have.) It is likely, however, that the teachers knew that no definition of fundamental rights—life, liberty, property, and due process of law, for example—could be achieved for blacks unless black lawyers entered the legal arena to fight for their own rights. Hence, black students were drawn to black law schools, such as Howard University, from almost every black college and every significant "public high school for Negroes" in the nation, and from white public and private colleges as well.[55] Most of these students never had had any contact with a black lawyer.[56]

By 1900, black colleges could boast of several black law graduates who had attended black undergraduate colleges.[57] In 1917, seven black and one Indian graduate of Hampton Institute had obtained law degrees.[58] But by 1923, when the American Bar Association and the Association of American Law Schools introduced higher standards for entry into law schools,[59] the number of black students who enrolled in law schools from black public and private high schools and some of the black colleges began to decline significantly. Efforts by publications such as *The Home Mission College Review*, however, continued to encourage black students to enter the legal profession.[60]

Professional Degrees Granted Negroes (1914–36) from Negro and Northern Schools.[61]

Year	Law		Total
	Negro	Northern	
1914	37	4	41
1915	21	6	27
1916	32	4	36
1917	26	5	31
1918	20	13	33
1919	14	1	15
1920	14	12	26
1921	25	6	31
1922	56	18	74
1923	37	33	70
1924	32	15	47
1925	28	25	53
1926	37	20	57
1927	16	21	37
1928	16	20	36
1929	27	20	47
1930	19	25	44
1931	12	1	13
1932	17	2	19
1933	13	8	24
1934	7	1	8
1935	11	0	11
1936	4	0	4
Total	516	268	784

By 1800 persons seeking to enter the legal profession were required to have studied law for a prescribed period "in fourteen out of the nineteen states or organized territories into which the Union was then divided."[62] But by 1840, the prescribed period had been reduced to "not more than eleven out of thirty jurisdictions, or one-third of the total."[63] By 1860, the requirement was for "nine of thirty-nine jurisdictions, or one-fourth of the total number."[64] And by the end of the Civil War, "North Carolina was one of the only southern states and Ohio the only state or territory west of the Alleghanies to retain the requirement even nominally."[65] In many Northern and Southern jurisdictions, a person could be admitted to the bar upon merely showing "good moral character [and] being a voter."[66]

Due to the decentralized admission system existing before 1900, the standards for admission to the bar varied greatly. Local, county, and circuit court judges were very powerful because they appointed the lawyers who examined and determined which applicants were qualified for admission to the bar. The applicant usually was examined on substance and procedure in open court. Members of the bar were called upon to vouch for the education, character, and morals of applicants.[67] The license to practice law in one county did not, in all states, authorize a lawyer to practice in other counties within a state, or even before the state supreme court. This decentralized system, therefore, allowed lawyers to keep others from doing business in their county without a local lawyer's participation.[68]

The founding of the American Bar Association in 1878 began a movement toward centralization of admission standards.[69] By World War I, centralized boards of bar examiners existed in thirty-seven jurisdictions, but "no state . . . required attendance at a law school."[70] Some state legislatures created boards of examiners that recommended that certain applicants be admitted to the lower or appellate state courts but also delegated to such courts the power to deny the admission of any applicant. In other states, the governor was empowered to appoint the board of examiners, who, by law, held the admitting power.[71] While the overall standards of admissions were increased, centralization did not eliminate the politics of admission.

Entry to the bar for the black lawyer, like most of his white counterparts, was accomplished, prior to the founding of the black law school, through the apprenticeship system. For example, in 1844, after he completed apprenticeship, Macon Bolling Allen, America's first black lawyer, was admitted to the bar in Maine.[72] In 1845, the year that Macon Bolling Allen applied for membership to the bar in Suffolk County, Massachusetts, he was ineligible to be admitted without first being examined. Under the prevailing practice in Suffolk County, "persons who had studied in [that state] for three years in the office of a member of the Bar and presented a certificate of good character were entitled to admission. Persons who had not studied the three years in an office of a member of the Bar [were required to] be examined."[73] Allen applied to the Massachusetts bar because of the liberal views of many of its citizens against slavery. Allen may have been unaware that he was qualified to be admitted in thirty other states without examination,[74] subject, of course, to racial restrictions. Perhaps the bar examination was of no concern to him.

By 1870, twenty-six years after Allen's admission to the bar in Maine, new educational standards were required before lawyers might practice. Between 1870 and 1880, efforts were made to increase the educational requirements to qualify for admission to the bar. By 1890, "23 out of 49 states prescribed a period of study and in 1917, 36 out of 49 had such a requirement. In 1921, through the efforts of the American Bar Association, 28 states required three years' preparation."[75] Yet, even with increased standards, often met by blacks, the rules were bent by the bar examiners in favor of white applicants.[76] Occasionally, during the Reconstruction era, "almost white blacks," those with "Anglo-Saxon blood [in] their veins, [were] entitled . . . to study and be admitted to practice law."[77] Such a status was a different kind of favoritism; it favored the progeny of former slavemasters as against pure African descendants.

W. Harold Flowers, Sr., of Arkansas, reports yet another kind of favoritism, evident as late as 1937. A black man "in the good graces of white folks . . . could get admitted,"[78] said Flowers, suggesting that blacks who spoke out against the status quo were not qualified applicants for admission to the Arkansas bar.

During Reconstruction, the opportunity to study law in the South was afforded to blacks who were appointed as clerks of the various courts. In these positions, they could read legal documents, see how technical transfers of property and probate matters were constructed, and learn the techniques of trial advocacy through observation. In this way, John Werles and Lewis J. Winston, both of Mississippi, qualified for admission to the bar of that state.[79] In 1875, a few black lawyers in the North studied law while employed as stenographers in large white law firms or as court criers.[80] Another group of black lawyers took advantage of dual licenses to practice law in lower courts of the state for limited periods prior to passing a bar examination.[81]

As black lawyers were admitted to the bar, their offices and homes became training centers for others who aspired to become lawyers. These lawyers provided students with opportunities to study under their instruction and often offered them their first job and status as partner.[82] However, by 1915, the standards of admission to the bar in both the South[83] and the North had begun to have some impact on the number of blacks practicing, due to the American Bar Association's decision to increase admission standards.[84]

In 1928, Professor Charles Hamilton Houston, soon to become the resident vice-dean of Howard University School of Law, carried out a survey that illustrated the dearth of black lawyers in the South. A letter was mailed to the clerks of courts in several Southern counties inquiring about the black lawyer population. The response to the Houston survey proved dramatically that Southern whites did not want black lawyers in their counties and effectively excluded them from the practice of law. A sampling of the replies follows:[85]

[T]here is no Negro lawyer or Negro in this, Habersham County, Georgia. I never knew or heard of any Negro with nerve enough to come to this County or Court House to practice law from any other county or section.[86]

We havent any Nig Negro,s [*sic*] lawyers in this District.[87]

No Negro lawyer in this county now nor has ever been. A Negro lawyer would be as much out of place here as a snow ball. . . .[88]

No Negro lawyer in this County, Thank God.[89]

Most of the clients of black lawyers during the Reconstruction and Post-Reconstruction eras were illiterate former slaves. In 1860, the year of the last census before the Emancipation Proclamation, nearly four million black people were slaves; nearly 500,000 blacks were free. Most of the slaves were located in thirteen South Atlantic and Eastern South-Central states. The six largest slaveholding states in these regions in 1860 were Virginia, with 490,865; South Carolina, with 402,198; Georgia, with 462,198; Mississippi, with 436,631; Alabama, with 435,080; and Louisiana, with 331,726. The largest number of free blacks among these six states in 1860 was in Virginia, with a total of 58,042; followed by Louisiana, with 18,647; South Carolina, with 9,914; Georgia, with 3,500; Alabama, with 2,690; and Mississippi with 733.[90]

Although the collection of census data on illiteracy began in 1840, four years before Macon B. Allen became America's first black lawyer, illiteracy figures regarding blacks were not specific because blacks were combined with American Indians and Chinese and Japanese data. Because state laws in several states made it a crime[91] to teach slaves to read, these states promoted illiteracy as a virtue associated with servitude. Being a free black did not qualify them for an education. According to the 1850 census, "there was a total free Negro population 20 years of age or over of 219,520. Of this figure, 90,522, or 41.2 percent, were reported unable to read or write, leaving nearly 60 percent in the illiterate class."[92] The high degree of illiteracy among blacks during the Reconstruction era and the Post-Reconstruction era limited blacks to service occupations largely concentrated in categories such as baker, bookkeeper, stenographer, blacksmith, electrician, painter, plumber, tanner, cook, gardener, janitor, molder, motorman, plasterer and galvanizer, teamer, upholsterer, and waiter.[93]

When black Southern plaintiffs, particularly in rural areas, invoked the judicial process for redress of civil wrongs against white defendants, they were "generally regarded as inferior and not entitled to the same rights as any white person . . . and much more so when . . .

charged with a crime by a white person."[94] Many blacks migrated from county to county to find a better life and better educational opportunities, but these talented black men and women, some of whom later became lawyers, left little behind "to stimulate [their] return."[95] As the black lawyer class was inaugurated in the South during the Reconstruction era, they moved "from county to county and from circuit to circuit," from the country to the city, to find places with sizeable black populations and receptive political climates.[96]

It has been argued that "[i]n a non-egalitarian society professionals necessarily reflect the stratification of their clients."[97] With a few exceptions, the clientele of most black lawyers before and after the Post-Reconstruction era were black, even in major cities with large ethnic populations.[98] In fact, some scholars argue that segregation in Northern cities offered black lawyers an opportunity to cash in on "a partial monopoly within the segregated class structure."[99] This statement bears some truth, but only in the context of necessity. The opportunity of black lawyers in the free market was not free. Since the white commercial community hardly ever used the services of black lawyers, the black lawyers never developed wealth or influence in the commercial community.[100]

In commercial law, during the first one hundred years of black legal history, black business was "largely restricted to small retail stores and the service type of establishment, especially to racial enterprises such as barbershops, beauty parlors, and mortuary establishments, where whites did not care to compete."[101] However, even successful small black businessmen were sometimes pressured by their friends to let white lawyers handle their business. For example, in the 1920s P. W. Chavers, who operated a ladies garment factory and founded the first nationally chartered black bank in Chicago, resisted a friend's suggestion that he fire the black lawyers who were representing him in some commercial litigation. The words of Chavers's friend demonstrate the point:

You know, Mr. Chavers, I think you shoulda hired some white lawyers fo' this case . . . I know you believe in usin' your own folks. . . . I hear tell the only way you kin win is to git some white . . . lawyers. . . . Colored lawyers is all right for' crap games . . . bu' this is big time.[102]

Black lawyers survived by necessity, serving a restricted market within the black community which itself often used white lawyers at higher legal fees[103] because they thought that justice could be obtained only in this way. This was particularly the case in many parts of the South where black lawyers were poorly treated and black people knew it, though the situation was the same for some parts of the North as well.

Criminal law was the only area in which black lawyers could be said to enjoy a monopoly, because "the police system was primarily for Negroes."[104] The local police wielded authoritarian power in the enforcement of criminal laws against blacks, and the testimony of black witnesses on behalf of black defendants charged with crimes against whites often fell on deaf ears. Such conditions prompted Isaac Lawrence Purcell, a black lawyer in Jacksonville, Florida, to write that "sheriffs and deputies ought to be honest . . . having the highest regard for the life and liberties of the people . . . but not [using their offices] as a means of revenging personal wrongs or injuries of the people whose color is their only sin."[105] Purcell was not only speaking for his black client but for himself as a black professional.

In the South and the North, the black community expected the black lawyer to defend any black man charged in a capital case, even if there was no money to pay legal fees. This expectation was based on both religious and moral principles which dictated that "to him that is given much, much is expected." The community expected the black lawyer to defend blacks against the police, because "lawyers [were] luxuries" to the black poor, "to be used when the devil catches them." The black lawyers obliged.[106]

The so-called beneficial black monopoly created by segregation also worked its way into the armed forces. Several black lawyers were drafted into or volunteered for the army during World War I.[107] They were assigned to segregated military units and defended black soldiers who were court-martialed. Although not designated as judge advocates, black military lawyers, such as Captain Leroy Godman, a 1905 Howard University law graduate, not only defended black service members before military courts, but also represented black soldiers after they returned to civilian life. In one case, Godman defended a black officer charged with cowardice. Godman discovered that the black unit to which his client was assigned had been sent into battle against German machine guns with no training in the use of grenades. He sought and won "the release and exoneration of the [black] officer."[108]

In the first decade of the twentieth century, black clients were so scarce in some areas that one black lawyer postponed his wedding when a client unexpectedly showed up requesting his services.[109] And in an example of cooperation among the isolated black lawyers, McCants Stewart, a practicing lawyer in Portland, Oregon, wrote in 1905 to James A. Cobb, of Washington, D.C., requesting that Cobb investigate a pension claim of Stewart's client.[110]

Claims of black lawyers' incompetence were leveled from almost the time blacks first entered the legal profession, but these claims intensified during the Post-Reconstruction era.[111] No matter how many court victories black lawyers won in American courts,[112] they were often the object of "unjust criticism."[113] The charge of incompetence slowed the progress of black lawyers, and fed racial stereotypes in the white legal community.[114] "Incompetence" in the eyes of the black community, meanwhile, did not necessarily imply that the black lawyer lacked the technical skills required to conduct a case in a court of law. Black people sometimes understood incompetence in a material way. The black lawyer was supposed to make more money than a bootblack. If he did not, the black community presumed that his lack of material success was due to incompetence. This stigma, often exploited by white lawyers, prompted blacks to use white legal services, despite the criticism this practice drew from the black press, which chided white lawyers for representing people they did not respect. Blacks were urged "not to employ them."[115] In order to compete for clients, black lawyers in the 1890s began to advertise in newspapers and in such professional directories as *The Twentieth Century Union League Directory*. These directories were widely used in such cities as Chicago and Washington, D.C., which had significant black professional populations.[116]

The reputation of the black lawyer was most significant in the area of criminal law, because his expertise there had won white clients, mostly immigrants, prior to World War I in both the North[117] and the South. Even during the Post-Reconstruction era, black lawyers represented whites in the South, especially "foreigners of Southern Europe, who as a class care[d] nothing for the color of the attorney if he [had] capacity and energy to attend to their work promptly and well."[118]

The black lawyer was the best spokesperson for himself. He often took to the pulpit "making some stirring speeches at a number of churches [on such subjects as] 'The Status of the Negro in Courts.'"[119] The pulpit of the black church became a forum for the black lawyer to rebut claims of incompetence, but the real forum to rebut such claims was his performance in the courts. In 1916 Clayton T. A. French, a 1910 graduate of Columbia University's law school, won a case before Judge Otto A. Rosalsky in the New York Court of General Sessions on technical grounds. French was called to the bench by the judge and publicly complimented and praised "on his sound knowledge of legal procedure," a compliment that was reported in a Palatka County, Florida newspaper.[120] Favorable comments made by white judges about the performance of black lawyers in their courts increased the credibility of black lawyers in both the black and white communities.

But the threat of economic reprisal from the white community was another reason that many black people in the South did not utilize the services of black lawyers. When the black lawyer asserted the rights of his people, the white political power structure often found itself in a defensive posture. And as one black lawyer has written, "The man who brings himself into ill-repute with the southern white man because of his fearlessness, daring courage, and intelligent insight, as well as denunciation of practices and customs . . . will soon find that he is feared and distrusted by his own people."[121] The effect of such fear made the expectation of "economic security and reasonable protection for [the black lawyer] and [his or her] family [a] fantasy."[122] With little prospect of economic security, black law graduates in the 1930s avoided going South to practice law.[123] They followed their black clients into the northern cities and into "the heart of the Negro business districts."[124]

Prior to World War I, black lawyers in the North had attempted to develop a "large practice among white people."[125] During the war, as blacks migrated to the North, the influx of blacks "provided the Negro lawyer for the first time with a dependable clientele."[126] In the mid-1930s successful black lawyers could "average about $5,000 a year."[127] The migration of large numbers of blacks to the North offered the black legal profession an opportunity to regain "some of its lost prestige."[128] However, the environment in the court systems in the North was not entirely different from that of many Southern and Western cities,[129] though the political power of blacks had grown significantly in the large Northern cities.[130] The North also saw the emergence of a new breed of progressive, research-oriented, better-trained lawyers who could stand toe-to-toe against the best white lawyers.[131]

In the 1920s, and later, black lawyers struggled to "attain a competitive advantage within a . . . free market," but they remained restricted by the state and "dominant private producers."[132] Generally, the consumer may have valued the services of black lawyers as a matter of principle, but with the dearth of black judges and lawyers, and the absence of blacks on juries in the North, this value became a skewed ideal, and blacks began to perceive that the justice system was politically controlled.[133]

Social stigma also continued to discredit the black lawyer. In 1928 the image of the black lawyer was stereotyped by the "Amos 'n' Andy" radio show. This comedy show, heard by millions of Americans, portrayed the black lawyer as bungling and ill-trained. The nation listened to episodes in which "Kingfish" described "Calhoun," a member of the Mystic Knights of the Sea Lodge, as follows:

Kingfish: He's [Calhoun's] a bucket shop lawyer.
Amos: A bucket shop lawyer? What kind o' lawyer is a bucket shop lawyer?
Andy: Yeh—what yo' mean, he's a bucket shop lawyer?
Kingfish: Well, what I means by dat brothers—I tenk that he got to

be a lawyer widout lookin at any books. I thenk he had a
friend git him past de bar.[134]

The "Amos 'n' Andy" show aired for many years, and the character of
Calhoun, "inept, incompetent and generally dishonest," stigmatized
the black lawyer among both blacks and whites.[135] Yet less than a year
after "Amos 'n' Andy" first aired, Scipio Africanus Jones, a black lawyer
from Little Rock, Arkansas, addressed the law students of Howard University, telling them "that the bugaboo of prejudice against the Negro
lawyer is largely a myth."[136] Perhaps prejudice against Jones in Little
Rock was a myth, but it was not a myth in Oklahoma in 1930, the year in
which Charles Albert Chandler, a Yale University Law School graduate,
was "called [a] 'nigger' in a courtroom."[137] Word of the mistreatment
of black lawyers by whites naturally reached the black community and
caused potential clients to doubt the efficacy of black professionals.

*   *   *

In 1944, the centennial of the entry of the first black lawyer into the
practice of law, the black community saw the black lawyer still fighting
for dignity and respect: "there [were] still many towns, some county
sites, where Negro lawyers [were] not permitted to practice even in
uncontested civil matters."[138] For these black lawyers, barred from
their communities, the chance to demonstrate legal competence bordered on the impossible. Lacking a chance to demonstrate their skills
and denied the opportunity to create a client base, the black lawyer
remained to some only a myth.[139]

Though laboring under a cloud of doubt, black lawyers' efforts to
dismantle the apartheid system in America became their special obligation. They were eager to assume the lead in civil rights litigation, even
without significant financial support. The funding of civil rights litigation was particularly difficult for the pioneer lawyer in the South
because compensation for wrongs done by a white man was beyond the
conception of many black citizens. However, as black lawyers began to
file lawsuits and to speak out in public forums for civil rights, black
people gained courage to use these lawyers to seek redress of their
grievances. In time, the poor quietly began to give small amounts of
money to pay "lawyer's fees," as did some whites "who sympathize[d]
with the fight to gain equal rights for blacks on a variety of fronts."[140]
For years, leading black citizens raised funds to support civil rights
litigation by begging from door-to-door.[141]

Nevertheless, financial support for civil rights litigation was often
slow in coming. Sometimes the money for continuing litigation ran out
during the trial. Very often, when funds were exhausted, the black
community expected black lawyers to bankroll the litigation out of

their own pockets, even when the matter had reached the United States Supreme Court. And in some cases, these lawyers did defray the costs of litigation, because the issues before the court were of such vital interest to millions of black Americans. Black lawyers were also forced to seek funding from blacks outside of their own state when local citizens feared retaliation from the white power structure because of their actual or perceived support of civil rights litigation.[142] In 1904 Wilford H. Smith, perhaps the most celebrated civil rights attorney to appear before the United States Supreme Court at that time, sought financial assistance from Booker T. Washington in raising $1,500 to cover the costs of a civil rights case from the trial level to the United States Supreme Court.[143]

The need to form civil rights organizations capable of planning for and funding lawsuits became evident as black lawyers were admitted to the bar in Northern and Southern states,[144] and as racism continued to isolate the black community. Therefore, it was natural that black lawyers were involved not only in the Niagara Movement, the forerunner of the National Association for the Advancement of Colored People, but also were responsible for the call to establish this historic organization in 1905.[145]

The association of black lawyers with the NAACP, organized in 1909, was to be expected, given the aims of the association.[146] After all, black lawyers had carried the bulk of civil rights litigation, protests, and legislative initiatives to liberate blacks for sixty-five years prior to the formation of the NAACP. But black lawyers experienced a surprise when "black leaders in NAACP themselves emphatically favored using prominent white attorneys"[147] to lead the civil rights assault. This may have been a strategic move, given the hostility of the courts to civil rights litigation, yet the use of white lawyers to fight for black rights made the black lawyer seem incompetent in the eyes of an already doubting black community. Only "highly distinguished white attorneys,"[148] it was thought, could argue the black man's burden before the courts of the land, a policy that later would be questioned by the National Bar Association, a black bar group.[149]

In the meantime, black leaders such as W. E. B. Du Bois criticized black lawyers who refused to turn over their cases to white lawyers at the appellate level. Du Bois and other black NAACP leaders, fearing that critical race cases would be lost if they were argued before the United States Supreme Court by black lawyers, discouraged them from bringing their own cases before the court without the assistance of white lawyers. And perhaps the NAACP's leadership was right, for in at least two instances where black lawyers refused to give up their cases to white lawyers, the black lawyers lost.[150]

The appointment of Charles Hamilton Houston to head the NAACP's legal arm in 1934 was a political and substantive decision. Politically, Houston's appointment assured the black community that one of its own lawyers would play a decisive role in the NAACP.[151] Houston's appointment no doubt brought renewed interest by old members of the NAACP as well as new and potential members. Houston, who had been a professor and dean of Howard University's law school, could also expect the solid support of its graduates, many of whom were practicing in the Southern states. Substantively, Houston's appointment demonstrated the willingness of the NAACP to place the strategy for the modern civil rights movement in the hands of one of the best-trained lawyers in the nation, who happened to be black.[152]

Black lawyers such as Houston were drawn to politics as a matter of necessity because the jury lists were often composed of "political workers," and because black jurors "invariably" were disqualified by white prosecutors in criminal cases.[153] Hence, the participation in politics by the black lawyer was seen as an avenue of power, as a way to influence the court system in the same way the white folks did. Since judges were elected, and since elections were controlled through the political party machinery of the Republican and Democratic parties, black lawyers became active in the party of their choosing in order to influence elections and to benefit from them.[154] With a few exceptions,[155] black lawyers joined the Republican party from 1872 until the election of President Franklin D. Roosevelt.[156] Yet in the South, the Republican, the Democratic, or splinter political parties never fully granted the elective franchise to colored citizens.[157] This was particularly the case during the Post-Reconstruction era. As Wilford H. Smith, a black lawyer reports,

The boldest and most open violation of the Negro's rights under the Federal Constitution, was the enactment of the grandfather clauses, and understanding clauses in the new Constitution of Louisiana, Alabama, the Carolinas, and Virginia, which have had the effect to deprive the great body of them of the right to vote in those states, for no other reason than their race and color.[158]

However, even in the states mentioned by Wilford H. Smith, black lawyers found ways to influence and to participate in local and national politics. For example, in 1912 four black lawyers were delegates to the National Republican Convention.[159] Before World War I, black lawyers won political appointments to the staffs of the United States Attorney's Office in various locations, even though the United States Attorney, who controlled these posts, was sometimes hostile to them.[160]

Between 1917 to 1945, several black lawyers were elected to state legislatures in Ohio, New York, West Virginia, Illinois, and Pennsylvania.[161] To a lesser degree, blacks were elected or appointed to the bench.[162] As a result of the spoils system, there were many more appointments of black lawyers to public offices in the 1900s,[163] and from 1929 to 1939.[164]

The progress of black lawyers lagged in the South. In 1937, Charles Hamilton Houston, who had just resigned his post as resident vice-dean of Howard University's law school, reported that law students from the South were "loathe to return" there because the black lawyer had "no future in . . . politics [and] no voice in determining the officials who administered the law."[165] This condition lasted until 1944, the year in which Thurgood Marshall and William Henry Hastie argued and won *Smith v. Allright*[166] (popularly referred to as the "white primaries case"). After the *Allright* decision, blacks could vote in the primary elections in the South. This decision did not immediately enlarge the voting power of blacks, but it lent legitimacy to the arguments of lawyers such as Thurgood Marshall, who continued to complain to the United States Attorney General about discriminatory voting barriers in the South.[167] In countless instances, when black citizens were mistreated by their elected representatives at the local level or in Congress, they turned to the black lawyer to speak for them as if they were constitutionally ordained to do so.

Black women began to enter into the legal profession in 1872, when Charlotte E. Ray graduated from the Howard University School of Law. She practiced in the District of Columbia in 1872, after passing the bar, but like many of the black women mentioned in this book, Ray soon vanished from the public eye, as did Mary Shadd Carey, an 1883 law graduate of Howard University; Ida G. Platt, who was admitted to the bar in Chicago, Illinois, in 1894; and Lutie A. Lytle, America's fourth black woman lawyer, who became America's first woman law professor in 1897.

Ray, Shadd, Platt, and Lytle, and the black women who followed them to the bar in the United States, laid new foundations for their communities. There is nothing that black male lawyers experienced that black women lawyers, though few in number, did not also experience. They entered a legal world controlled and dominated by white males, judges, and jurors. Black women lawyers, often aided by black male lawyers, faced an uphill battle in a male-dominated profession.

The extent to which black males and black females competed in law school, for clients or for political appointments, is not documented. However, there are several examples in these pages of black women who were superior students in law schools, aggressive forces in their law practices, and savvy political operatives.

The development of black women in the legal profession was blunted by the paucity of their numbers. They had few mentors and were forced to find their own paths to success. From 1872 to 1944, every woman who attended law school and entered the practice of law was a pioneer—the offspring, so to speak, of Charlotte E. Ray. They worked toward a dual goal: the emancipation of black women and the emancipation of their race from the legacy of slavery. The available evidence clearly demonstrates that black women broke new ground, overcame barriers, and disproved the notion that black women could not succeed in all branches of the legal profession.

*   *   *

This book is about the making of black lawyers in the states of the nation between 1844 and 1944. The experience of the black lawyer in each state is represented in the pages that follow.

The first black male lawyers have been identified in forty-three states between 1844 to 1944, and, although they are not named, the United States Census Reports indicate black lawyers in the state of North Dakota in 1900, in Nevada and Wyoming in 1910, and in New Hampshire and Vermont in 1920.[168] The first black women lawyers have been identified in twenty-two states between 1872 and 1945, and, although unidentified by name, black women pioneers are known to have been present in the states of Connecticut, Delaware, Florida, and Texas in 1940.[169] Apparently, only the states of Alaska and Idaho had no black lawyers prior to 1945.

The purpose of this book is to present a history of the black lawyer in America by concentrating on their origins in the states of the nation. The task of locating all the black lawyers between 1844 to 1944 has proven humanly impossible. As a result, the contributions of black American lawyers discussed in these pages may fall short of the scope of their collective genius. However, the common experiences of the black lawyers represented here and the exceptional challenges they faced in their efforts to succeed in the law is probably matched by those of the black lawyers whose names and contributions to the law remained unknown. This volume should prove useful to anyone interested in American history and the significant but little known contributions that black lawyers have imparted to American law. The question is, Did the pioneer black lawyers make a contribution to the evolution of the law or merely demonstrate that they could function in this sphere?[170] There is little doubt that the black lawyer did both.

The first chapter of this book introduces the legal education of blacks in white law schools and in black law schools. Chapter 2 singles out the New England states of Maine and Massachusetts, because the genesis of the black lawyer began in these states.

Chapters 3 through 9 develop the history of black lawyers along the geographical regions (and the states within) established by the American legal system.[171] Hence, the reader should not be confused if a certain state traditionally considered to be part of a different geographical region turns up in an unusual location. These regions have evolved over a long period of time in the American legal system, and whatever their logic, the book does not disturb that system.

Chapter 10 is specific to bar groups that are national and local in nature. The subject matter is presented in a single chapter to capture comprehensively the interplay of black lawyers and the white and black bar movements.

While this book is organized, in part, along established historic and legal geographic lines, its unifying theme deals with the making of the black lawyer in American law and history. This history is unique to the states that granted black lawyers licenses to practice law. It is from these states that admitted black lawyers from 1844 to 1944 that the complete picture of the black lawyers' efforts to emancipate their people emerges.

NOTES

1. J. W. Hurst, *Law and Social Process in United States History* 2 (1987).

2. O. W. Holmes, Jr., "The Places of History in Understanding Law," in *The Life of the Law* 3 (J. Honnold ed. 1964).

3. Boorstin, "Tradition and Method in Legal History," 54 *Harv. L. Rev.* 424, 436 (1941).

4. M. H. Bloomfield, "John Mercer Langston and the Training of Black Lawyers," in W. J. Leonard, *Black Lawyers* 59 (1977). See also, Leonard, "The Development of the Black Bar," 407 *Annals of the American Academy of Political and Social Science* 134 (May 1973).

5. M. H. Bloomfield, *American Lawyers in a Changing Society, 1776–1876*, at 302–3 (1976).

6. F. L. Styles, *Negroes and the Law* (1937); Brown, "The Genesis of the Negro Lawyer in New England," 22 *The Negro History Bulletin* (Part I) 147 (April 1959), and Part II in the May issue, at 171. See also, William H. Hale, "The Career Development of the Negro Lawyer in Chicago" 8 (Ph.D. diss., Univ. of Chicago, Sept. 1949).

7. K. Miller, "The Historic Background of the Negro Physician," 1 *J. of Negro History* 99, 100 (1916).

8. Bernard H. Nelson, "The Fourteenth Amendment and the Negro Since 1920," at 1 (Ph.D. diss., Catholic Univ., 1946).

9. Bruce, "Interest of the Public in Legal Education," Vol. 45 *Report of the Forty-Third Annual Meeting of the American Bar Association* 480, 485 (1920) (quoting Professor William F. Dodd, the University of Chicago Law School).

10. J. M. Langston, *From the Virginia Plantation to the National Capitol* 105 (1894).

11. This rhyme appears in an article written by J. R. Bartlett, "Americanism Pertaining to Afro-Americans," in *Afro-American Encyclopedia; Or, the Thoughts,*

Doings, and Sayings of the Race 339, 340 (J. T. Haley ed. 1895). A note following the rhyme gives its original source as "Ethiopian Melodies" (1848). Stereotypical rhymes and anecdotes about black lawyers would continue to appear in legal publications for years to come. See e.g., "The Judge's Story," 6 *The Green Bag* 360 (1894), 13 *The Green Bag* 412–13 (1901).

12. See, J. H. Wigmore, *A Panorama of the World's Legal Systems* 261 (Hindu Justice in the early 1800s), 627 (Justice in Arabia), 629 (Justice in Africa), 630 (Mohammedan Legal System) (Library ed. 1938).

13. *Dred Scott v. Sandford*, 60 U.S. (19 How.) 393, 537 (Justice McLean, dissenting), 572–73 (Justice Curtis, dissenting) (1857).

14. See e.g., *State v. Clairborne*, 19 Tenn. 331, 335 (1838).

15. A. de Tocqueville, *Democracy in America*, I, at 125 (R. D. Heffner ed. 1963).

16. *Ibid.*

17. C. G. Woodson, *The Negro Professional Man and the Community* 185 (reprint, 1969).

18. W. Gillett, *Retreat from Reconstruction, 1869–1879*, at 217 (1979) (quoting *Richmond (Ky.) Register and The Independent*, Aug. 13, 1874).

19. R. L. Abel, *American Lawyers* 108 (1989).

20. W. Gillett, *Retreat from Reconstruction, 1869–1879*, at 191 (1979); R. Bardolph, *The Civil Rights Record* 84–129 (1970).

21. M. H. Bloomfield, *American Lawyers in a Changing Society, 1776–1876*, at 383, n.35 (1976).

22. See, e.g., Douglass, "A Plea for Free Speech in Boston," in Vol. 5 *The World's Best Orations* 1906 (D. J. Brewer ed. 1899) (Douglass's oration was delivered in Boston in 1860). A Douglass biographer writes "that Douglass . . . might well have found a way to read with an antislavery lawyer and gain admission to the bar. . . . It is fascinating to speculate on how Douglass might have argued alongside . . . [such] civil rights lawyers as Thomas Jefferson Durant for the protection of black Americans under the Fourteenth Amendment." W. S. McFeely, *Frederick Douglass* 205 (1991).

23. *Afro-American Encyclopedia; Or, the Thoughts, Doings, and Sayings of the Race* 381, 383 (J. T. Haley ed. 1895) (statement of William Lloyd Garrison).

24. Smith, "Forgotten Hero," 98 *Harv. L. Rev.* 482 (1984).

25. At the time of Douglass's death, black lawyers were among the number who wrote glowing tributes in his memory. Four such tributes were from lawyers Josiah T. Settle, of Memphis, Tennessee, J. C. Napier, of Nashville, Tennessee, Robert Herberton Terrell, of Washington, D.C., and P. B. S. Pinchback, of New Orleans, Louisiana. See *Afro-American Encyclopedia; Or, the Thoughts, Doings, and Sayings of the Race* 384–91 (Settle), 392–98 (Terrell), 398–402 (Pinchback), 402–3 (Napier) (J. T. Haley ed. 1895).

26. William H. Hale, "The Career Development of the Negro Lawyer in Chicago" 11 (Ph.D. diss., Univ. of Chicago, Sept. 1949), citing E. C. Hughes, "Dilemmas and Contradictions of Status," 50 *Am. J. of Sociology* 353–59 (1944–45).

27. *Id.* at 10, citing Oswald Hall, "The Informal Organization of Medical Practice in an American City" 2 (Ph.D. diss., Univ. of Chicago, 1944).

28. See e.g., E. F. Frazier, *The Negro Church* 43 (1964). The influence of the "Negro Church" would continue for "Negro . . . lawyers and politicians." By 1928, even white lawyers and politicians were in the pulpits of the Negro church, realizing that they could "reach and influence a larger number of

Negroes." Haynes, "The Church and Negro Progress," 140 *Annals of American Academy of Political and Social Science* 264, 265 (Nov. 1928). Black teachers, ministers, physicians, and dentists all preceded black lawyers as recognized professionals in the black community. See also, A. B. Koger, *The Negro Lawyer in Maryland* 1 (1948); R. L. Abel, *American Lawyers* 99 (1989).

29. B. G. Gallagher, *American Caste and the Negro College* 99, 100–2 (1966) (Tables 2 and 3).

30. J. H. Franklin, "The South's New Leaders," in *Black History* 312 (M. Drimmer ed. 1968). Although black lawyers developed as a class after emancipation, the class grew slowly. In 1890 there were only 431 black lawyers in the nation. By 1920, the number of black lawyers had increased to 950, a 120.4 percent increase. Work, "The Negro in Business and the Professions," 140 *Annals of the American Academy of Political and Social Science* 138, 139 (Nov. 1928).

31. R. R. Wright, *The Negro in Pennsylvania* 80 (reprint, 1969); W. E. B. Du Bois, *The Philadelphia Negro* 114–15 (1970). According to a leading black scholar, "the first regularly recognized Negro physicians, of whom there is a complete record, was James Derham, of New Orleans, . . . He began the practice of medicine in New York about 1837," seven years before Macon Bolling Allen became the first black lawyer admitted to practice. K. Miller, "The Historic Background of the Negro Physician," 1 *J. of Negro History* 99, 103–4, 107 (1916); K. Miller, "The Negro's Progress in Fifty Years," 49 *Annals of the American Academy of Political and Social Science* 182 (Sept. 1913): "The [N]egro lawyer has not been so fortunate as his medical confrere. . . . The client's interest are . . . dependent upon the judge and jury white whom the white attorney is sometimes supposed to have greater weight and influence."

32. J. H. Franklin, *Race and History: Selected Essays, 1938–1988*, at 278 (1989).

33. *New York Freeman*, May 16, 1885. This is not to say that black lawyers went underground—they did not. In fact, in 1883 black lawyers were among those who called for a national convention of colored men to meet in Louisville, Kentucky, to formulate a strategy for political and social survival. J. H. Franklin, *George Washington Williams* 166–67 (1985).

34. K. Miller, "The Advocacy of the Negro Lawyer," *Norfolk Journal and Guide*, March 20, 1926.

35. Payne, "Negroes in the Public Elementary Schools of the North," 140 *Annals of the American Academy of Political and Social Science* 224 (Nov. 1928).

36. H. A. Bullock, *A History of Negro Education in the South* 1 (1967).

37. "Letter on Slavery by a Negro," 1 *J. of Negro History* 60, 61 (1916). In 1789 a person identified only as a Free Negro stated, "Ever since an indulgent master rewarded my youthful services with freedom and supplied me at a very early age with the means of acquiring knowledge, I have laboured to understand the true principles, of which the liberties of mankind are founded, and to possess myself of the language of this country, in order to plead the cause of those who were once my fellow slaves, and if possible to make my freedom, in some degree, the instrument of their deliverance."

38. Kenneth S. Tollett, "Universal Education, Blacks and Democracy," in *Race: Twentieth-Century Dilemmas—Twenty-First Century Prognoses* 49, 58 (W. A. Van Horne and T. V. Tonnesen eds. 1989); Tollett, "Black Lawyers, Their Education, and the Black Community," 17 *How. L. J.* 326, 327 (1972); W. L. Fleming, *Documentary History of Reconstruction* (Vol. 1) 243 (P. Smith ed. 1960): "Some kind of legislation for the freedom was necessary in 1865–1866. The slave codes were obsolete. . . . [N]egro education [was] formerly . . . forbidden."

39. *Free Blacks in America, 1800–1860*, at 2 (J. H. Bracey, Jr., A. Meier and E. Rudwick eds. 1971).

40. Kenneth S. Tollett, Universal Education, Blacks and Democracy in *Race: Twentieth-Century Dilemmas—Twenty-First Century Prognoses* 61 (W. A. Van Horne and T. V. Tonnesen eds. 1989); *Negro Year Book 1918–1919*, at 281 (M. N. Work ed. 1919): Monroe Work indicates that during the following decades blacks received college degrees: 1820–1829 (3), 1830–1839 (none), 1840–1849 (7), 1850–1859 (12), 1860–1869 (44). Before 1876, a total of 314 academic and professional degrees were awarded in the United States, 34 of which were law degrees. See also, C. S. Johnson, *The Negro College Graduate* 8 (1938).

41. *Id.* at 259 (*Negro Year Book*).

42. *Id.* at 260 (*Negro Year Book*); H. A. Bullock, *A History of Negro Education in the South* 32 (1967).

43. *Id.* at 261 (*Negro Year Book*). Newbold, "Common Schools for Negroes in the South," 140 *Annals of the American Academy of Political and Social Science* 209 (Nov. 1928) (Common schools for Negroes in the older Southern States were born in a period of political and economic distress).

44. C. L. Weltner, *Southerner* 124 (1966).

45. *Ibid.*

46. W. D. Johnson, *Biographical Sketches of Prominent Negro Men and Women of Kentucky* 28–29 (1897) (Chiles went to Lexington, Kentucky, to practice law after he left Michigan); *General Catalogue of the University of Michigan, 1837–1911*, at 434 (I. N. Demmon ed. 1912).

47. Kenneth S. Tollett, "Universal Education, Blacks and Democracy," in *Race: Twentieth-Century Dilemmas—Twenty-First Century Prognoses* 58 (W. A. Van Horne and T. V. Tonnesen eds. 1989).

48. *Ibid.*

49. C. G. Woodson, *The Negro Professional Man and the Community* 186–87 (reprint, 1969).

50. See, e.g., J. Clay Smith, Jr., "Profile: Howard University Entering Law Students, 1904–1920—Age, Legal Residence and Education" (Dec. 1985) (paper).

51. R. Stevens, *Law School: Legal Education in America from the 1850s to the 1980s* 81 (1983).

52. C. S. Johnson, *The Negro College Graduate* 19 (1938).

53. *Negro Year Book, 1918–1919*, at 321–22 (M. N. Work ed. 1919) (partial listing by state of "public high schools for Negroes").

54. These black colleges include Howard University, Atlanta University, Fisk University, Hampton University, Lincoln University, Morehouse College, Virginia Union College, and Wiley College. Howard University is not included in the 12.7% of legal professionals because it had its own law school. Therefore, the percentage of black students graduating from law school from among the black colleges that Johnson identifies may be slightly higher. C. S. Johnson, *The Negro College Graduate* 92 nn.1–4, 93–98 (1938).

55. Approximately 100 black colleges were represented at Howard University School of Law between 1893–1920 from the schools listed in *Negro Year Book, 1918–1919*, at 321 (M. Work ed. 1919). J. Clay Smith, Jr., "Profile: Howard University Entering Law Students, 1904–1920—Age, Legal Residence and Education" (Dec. 1985) (paper). J. Clay Smith, Jr., "Profile: Howard University Entering Law Students, 1893–1903—Age and Legal Residence (Dec. 1985): approximately 700 students entered Howard University's law

school during this period, mostly from the South. However, between 1869, the year Howard University's law school opened, and 1920, persons from every state in the nation entered its law school, except from the states of Washington, Oregon, Idaho, Montana, Utah, Arizona, North Dakota, Vermont and Maine. The average age of the male and female students entering Howard University from 1893 to 1920 was age 25.08 (male) and age 24.11 (female). J. Clay Smith, Jr., profiles a thousand entering students, some of whom were white and others people of color from foreign countries. See also, C. G. Woodson, *The Negro Professional Man and the Community* 193 (reprint, 1969). In a limited survey of 246 black lawyers, Woodson reports that the average age at graduation in 1928 was 28.7 years. Students attending Howard University Law School also graduated from the following white colleges: University of Chicago, Oberlin College, George Washington University, Denison University, Brown University, University of Michigan, Harvard University, Catholic University, Cornell University, Temple University, Geneva College, Dartmouth College, University of Nebraska, Yale University, Kansas University, Armour Institute, University of Pittsburgh, University of Pennsylvania, Massachusetts Normal Art School, Northfield College, Valparaiso University, Wisconsin University and Bucknell College. See also, Ellis, "The Chicago Negro in Law and Politics," 1 *The Champion Magazine* 349 (March 1917).

56. William E. Taylor, Acting Dean of Howard University School of Law reports that, "the colored child living in the South [in 1930 reached] high school or college without any contact whatever with a colored lawyer and without knowing that a colored person could practice law, or that there is any law school which members of his race may attend. When he learns these facts, he must leave his home and friends . . . [and] travel several hundred miles. . . . The nearest law school which the colored child of southern Florida may attend is more than a thousand miles away, in the District of Columbia or in Pennsylvania. Is it not perfectly natural then that colored children should have but little interest in the legal profession?" Taylor, "The Negro and the Legal Profession," *New York Age,* June 3, 1939.

57. C. S. Johnson, *The Negro College Graduate* 121 (1938) (Table LXIX), citing W. E. B. Du Bois and A. G. Dill, *The College-Bred Negro American* (n.p.) (1910). See also, E. L. Ayers, *The Promise of the New South: Life After Reconstruction* 323 (1992), who reports that without black colleges there would be no black lawyers.

58. Brokenburr, "Hampton Men in Professions and Business," 48 *The Southern Workman* 262, 263 (June 1919).

59. C. S. Johnson, *The Negro College Graduate* 16 (1938).

60. "The Law as a Profession," 2 *The Home Mission College Review* 4 (Jan. 1929).

61. C. S. Johnson, *The Negro College Graduate* 15 (1938) (Table IV). By 1944, Virginia Union University, a black college, reported that Mrs. Urith Barco Josiah had been graduated from St. Johns University School of Law in 1943, and that John Pharr, Jr., and Wesley Williams, Sr., also Virginia Union graduates, had been admitted to practice in New York and Washington, D.C., respectively (see also, XLV *Virginia Union Bulletin* 3 [Nov. 1944]).

62. C. S. Johnson, *The Negro College Graduate* 331 (1938).

63. *Ibid.*

64. *Ibid.* New York was one of the states that established special admissions provisions for students completing twelve to eighteen months of study in a law school. Such students were admitted to the bar generally on the motion of a

member of the law faculty or the dean. Students with law degrees were admitted to the bar without any difficulty (*16th Annual Catalogue, Law School of Columbia College, 1873–1874*, at 29 [1874]).

65. *Ibid.* (*The Negro College Graduate*).

66. A. Z. Reed, *Review of Legal Education in the United States and Canada for the Year 1930*, at 9–10 (1931).

67. Mollison, "Negro Lawyers in Mississippi," 15 *J. of Negro History* 38, 43 (1930).

68. Letter from C. W. Dickerson to Charles S. Brown, July 31, 1958; Alexander, "Blacks and the Law," 43 *N.Y.S.B.J.* 15, 19 (Jan. 1971).

69. "Report of the Committee on Legal Education and Admission to the Bar," Vols. 1–2 *Reports of the American Bar Association* 209, 235 (1878–1879) (recommending, among other things, essential course of instruction); *id.*, Vol. 15, at 317 (1892); *id.*, Vol. 16, at 15–16 (1893); see also, "Report of Committee on Judicial Administration and Remedial Procedure," 31 *Reports of the American Bar Association* 505, 516–517 (1907), for the move to centralize bar examinations in the states.

70. *Law in American History* 459 (D. Fleming and B. Bailyn eds. [1971]).

71. A. Z. Reed, *Review of Legal Education in the United States and Canada for Year 1930*, at 11–12 (1931).

72. Brown, "The Genesis of the Negro Lawyer in New England," 22 *The Negro History Bulletin* (Part I) 147, 148 (April 1959).

73. See Bailey, "Favoritism in Bar Examination and How to Avoid It," vol. 45, *Report of the Forty-Third Annual Meeting of the American Bar Association* 488, 501 (1920), quoting an unidentified member of the Massachusetts bar, who had been admitted in 1844.

74. C. S. Johnson, *The Negro College Graduate* 331 (1938).

75. *Ibid.*

76. See, e.g., Bailey, "Favoritism in Bar Examination and How to Avoid It," vol. 45, *Report of the Forty-Third Annual Meeting of the American Bar Association* 488 (1920).

77. Straker, "The Negro in the Profession of Law," 8 *The A.M.E. Rev.* 178, 179 (1891).

78. Telephone conversation with W. Harold Flowers, Sr., March 15, 1989.

79. Mollison, "Negro Lawyers in Mississippi," 15 *J. of Negro History* 38, 40, 47 (1938).

80. W. P. Dabney, *Cincinnati's Colored Citizens* 206–7, 413 (1926).

81. "E. T. News Editor Now Full Fledged Lawyer," *East Tennessee News*, March 8, 1928.

82. This phenomenon was not limited to the East and the South, where the population of black lawyers was of modest size. It happened in the northwestern states as well. Andrew R. Black, an 1899 Howard University law graduate, was admitted to the Washington State bar in 1901, after first working in the law offices of another black lawyer, John Edward Hawkins. E. H. Mumford, *Seattle's Black Victorians, 1852–1901*, at 98 (1980).

83. See, e.g., *Reminiscences of an Active Life: the Autobiography of John Roy Lynch* 366 (J. H. Franklin ed. 1970), for material about Mississippi in 1900, and Higgins, "The Longest Struggle," in *Tony Brown's Journal* 4, 5 (Jan.-March 1984), concerning Mississippi in 1910.

84. *New York Negro Lawyers* 7 (S. H. Lark ed. 1915).

85. The survey was in the form of a letter signed by H. B. Williams, the

Secretary of Howard University School of Law. It stated, "The Howard University Law School is trying to determine how many Negro lawyers are practicing in the United States, where they are located and how long they have been practicing. . . . Would you . . . give us this information about the Negro lawyers in your jurisdiction, if any?" All of the letters sent to the clerks of courts were identical, with sufficient space at the bottom for reply. The survey was sent to county courts in Alabama (Marion County); Florida (Hillsborough, Duval, Dade, Perry, "Palakis" [sic], and Braidentown counties); Georgia (Laurens, Habersham, Catoosa, and Jefferson counties); Kentucky (Carlisle County); Louisiana (Clacasieu County); Missouri (Lafayette, Howard, Stoddard, and Randolph counties); Texas (Lynn, Throckmorton, Parker, Mills, Panola, Hamilton, and Live Oak counties); Virginia (Dickerson and Page counties). Other counties may have been surveyed, but apparently only the letters to and responses from the above clerks of courts have survived. The survey and replies were obtained from Charles S. Brown, in June 1986.

86. Idus E. Brewer, clerk of court, County of Habersham, Clarksville, Georgia.

87. Ed Yates, clerk of court the Circuit Court, County of Carlisle, Bradwell, Kentucky.

88. James R. Jackson, clerk of Circuit Court, Taylor County, Perry, Florida.

89. J. I. Prichard, District Clerk, Howard County, Texas.

90. *Negro Population in the United States, 1790–1915*, at 57 (S. L. Rogers ed. 1918).

91. According to W. E. B. Du Bois, "the laws on this point were explicit and severe. There was teaching, here and there, by indulgent masters, or by clandestine Negro schools, but in the main, the laws were followed. All the slave states had such laws, and after the Nat Turner insurrection in Virginia [1831], these laws were strengthened and more carefully enforced." W. E. B. Du Bois, *Black Reconstruction in America, 1860–1880*, at 638 (reprint, 1973).

92. *Negro Population in the United States, 1790–1915*, at 405 (S. L. Rogers ed. 1918).

93. *Id.* at 502.

94. W. H. Smith, "The Negro and the Law," in *The Negro Problem* 127, 144 (B. T. Washington ed. 1903): many rural blacks had virtually no access to the services of black lawyers for almost one hundred years after Reconstruction. See also, Hastie, "A Note to the Aspiring Lawyer on His Prospective Profession," 33 *The Fisk Herald* 10 (April 1940); J. Dowd, *The Negro in American Life* 137 (student's ed. 1926). Dowd argues that Southern and Northern justice toward poor blacks and poor whites was the same, but concludes that "in all cases of offenses of white men against Negroes [in the South] the juries are reluctant to bring in a verdict of conviction, except in the mildest form."

95. C. G. Woodson, *The Negro Professional Man and the Community* 185 (reprint, 1969).

96. *Id.* at 107. Woodson concludes that black lawyers migrated "from city to city in the same section [of the country]," in the South. See also, Mollison, "Negro Lawyers in Mississippi," 15 *J. of Negro History* 30, 53 (1930).

97. R. L. Abel, *American Lawyers* 36 (1989).

98. William H. Hale, "The Career Development of the Negro Lawyer in Chicago," 71 (Ph.D. diss., Univ. of Chicago, Sept. 1949).

99. *Id.* at 33. Hale also states "that . . . membership in a minority category (such as the medical profession) greatly limits the volume and kind of clientele

which the individual will be able to attract." This theme is applicable to blacks in the legal profession as well. *Id.* at 9.

100. Other black professionals, such as morticians, did have a monopoly in black communities, as it was unlikely that a white man would select a black funeral director to bury a member of his family. E. Franklin Frazier must have referred to such professionals when he said, "It is the Negro professional . . . who benefit from segregation . . . because they do not have to compete with whites." *Id.* at 33, citing, Frazier, "Human, All Too Human," *Survey Graphic* 74 (Jan. 1947).

101. M. R. Davie, *Negro in American Society* 119 (1949).

102. M. C. Wright, *The Guarantee, P. W. Chavers: Banker, Entrepreneur, Philanthropist in Chicago's Black Belt of the Twenties* 196 (1987).

103. T. C. Walker, *The Honey-pod Tree* 71 (1958).

104. R. R. Wright, *The Negro in Pennsylvania* 143 (reprint, 1969).

105. Isaac L. Purcell, "Is the Criminal Negro Justly Dealt with in the Courts of the South?" in *Twentieth Century Negro Literature* 104 (D. W. Culp ed. 1902); see also, Calvin, "'North Carolina Has Finest Set of Judges,' Says Durham Attorney," *Pittsburgh Courier*, Sept. 1, 1928: "It may naturally be expected that prominent white lawyers and politicians have a larger influence with [the police] than many others." During the Post-Reconstruction era, the North was not much better. In some counties in Indiana, "a major reason for discrimination of justice was the absence of blacks from the police force, the paucity of black attorneys, and the presence of all-white juries." D. E. Bingham, *We Ask Only a Fair Trial: A History of the Black Community of Evansville, Indiana* 57 (1988).

106. William H. Hale, "The Career Development of the Negro Lawyer in Chicago," 38, 41 (Ph.D. diss., Univ. of Chicago, Sept. 1949); M. R. Davie, *Negroes in American Society* 115 (1949).

107. The following black lawyers were commissioned as officers after training at Fort Des Moines, Iowa, in 1919: Francis M. Dent, Jr., Leroy H. Godman, Jesse S. Heslip, Charles Hamilton Houston, Charles P. Howard, Azzie B. Koger, Linwood Koger, Ralph E. Mizell, Louis Rothschild Mehlinger, James M. Stockett, Jr., George Vaughn, Austin T. Walden, and Christopher Wimbish. *History of the American Negro in the Great World War* 119–30 (W. A. Sweeney ed. 1919).

108. A. W. Hunton and K. M. Johnson, *Two Colored Women with the American Expeditionary Forces* 48, 61 (1920).

109. A. Buni, *Robert L. Vann of Pittsburgh Courier* 40 (1974).

110. Letter from McCants Stewart to James A. Cobb, June 21, 1905; letter from Cobb to Stewart, Oct. 24, 1905.

111. T. C. Walker, *The Honey-pod Tree* 71 (1958). Thomas C. Walker, who practiced law in Gloucester County, Virginia, in 1890, states, "Generally speaking, I found the southern white man very skeptical as to the Negro's legal ability."

112. "Atty. Francis Williams in Legal Battle," *The Chicago Defender*, Dec. 14, 1918.

113. "The Colored Lawyers," *Norfolk Journal and Guide*, Oct. 24, 1914. There is some evidence that the black community was concerned about black lawyers' "careless and unmindful" attention to their clients in New York, Baltimore, Maryland, and Chicago. See also, "The Negro Lawyer," *The Atlanta Independent*, Aug. 28, 1915; C. G. Woodson, *The Negro Professional Man and the Community* 190, 193, 225–26 (1934), quoted in "The Legal Needs of Black-Owned Businesses in Los Angeles," 20 *UCLA L. Rev.* 827 (1973).

114. Letter from Clifford Langsdale to Ruth Weyand, July 28, 1943.

115. "The Case of the White Lawyer," *The Dallas Express*, May 19, 1917.

116. *The Twentieth Century Union League Directory* 3, 59–63 (A. F. Hilyer ed. Jan. 1901).

117. K. Kusmer, *A Ghetto Takes Shape: Black Cleveland, 1870–1930*, at 81 (1976). In the early part of the twentieth century, many immigrants from Europe, themselves the subject of discrimination, used black lawyers to advance their economic position. However, by the late 1930s these immigrants had managed to work their way into the white world. Meanwhile, "the intensification of racial prejudice that accompanied the postwar era" made it more difficult for the black lawyer to draw white clients. *Id.* at 191–92, 247. Black lawyers such as Charles S. Sutton filed several civil rights suits in Cleveland. Although Sutton won only two "substantial settlements," these law suits were apparently significant precedents. *Id.* at 130. See also "The Colored Lawyers," *The Washington Bee*, March 6, 1915. It is noted also that prior to World War I, black lawyers in Georgia "depended almost entirely on black patronage and made a modest living dealing in real estate, insurance, and claim collections" (J. Dittmer, *Black Georgia* 37 [1977]). However, after the war the monopoly held by white men in the judicial system drew black clients to white lawyers (*ibid*).

118. "Florida Lawyers," *New York Freeman*, March 12, 1887, at 1, col. 4, quoting Thomas de S. Tucker, a black lawyer.

119. "Thomas L. Jones Makes Speech," *The Indianapolis Freeman*, April 17, 1915.

120. Bruce, "Well-Prepared Young Lawyer," *The Palatka Advocate*, July 10, 1916.

121. Robinson, "Lawyers vs. Democracy," *Norfolk Journal and Guide*, March 2, 1940. There is another view. In 1940 William Henry Hastie, the dean of Howard University's law school, spoke of "a new confidence in the . . . South" in black lawyers' "competent handling of private cases and through litigation of matters of public and community interest." Hastie, "A Note to the Aspiring Lawyer on His Prospective Profession," 33 *The Fisk Herald* 10, 11 (April 1940). See also, Mollison, "Negro Lawyers in Mississippi," 15 *J. of Negro History* 15, 59 (1930): "The Negro lawyer was by reason of the character of his environment naturally handicapped in what practice he had. His was the task of winning cases of Negro clients against white plaintiffs and complaints before a white judge and a white jury, in a community which was hostile and prejudiced and not at all noted for its fair play; in short, in a community where he could not be aggressive in the interest of his client for fear of being the victim of violence."

122. *Ibid.* ("Lawyers vs. Democracy").

123. "Future Cloudy," *New York Times*, Aug. 16, 1937. In 1944 another author stated, "Potentially, there should not be great opportunity for Negro lawyers. So often is the Negro lawyer wronged—in the South at least—and so bitter do most white people understand his plight that there should be a tremendous need for Negro attorneys to assist Negro clients. . . . In 1940 much less than 1% of all lawyers were Negroes. Two thirds of the 1,063 Negro lawyers resided outside the South." A. Rose, *Negro in America* 112 (1944).

124. C. S. Johnson, *The Negro College Graduate* 336 (1938); Mollison, "Negro Lawyers in Mississippi," 15 *J. of Negro History* 38, 68 (1930).

125. *Ibid.* (*The Negro College Graduate*).

126. *Id.* at 335.

127. "Future Cloudy," *New York Times*, Aug. 16, 1937, quoting Raymond Pace Alexander, of Philadelphia. Reportedly, few black male lawyers in the South became prosperous between 1870 and 1915. L. Schweninger, *Black Property Owners in the South, 1790–1915*, at 295–300 (1990). It is not conclusive that this prosperity came solely from the practice of law.

128. C. S. Johnson, *The Negro College Graduate* 335 (1938).

129. Western states, such as Oklahoma, were almost as bad as the worst Southern states in terms of discrimination against blacks. A. W. Dagley, "The Negro of Oklahoma," 133 (M.A. thesis, Univ. of Oklahoma, 1926); J. Greenberg, *Staking a Claim*, 117–18, 121 (1990). Greenberg discusses the racial climate in Oklahoma and the role played by black lawyers. Jim Crow laws and customs in the South also affected the black lawyer's ability to represent black businessmen, who believed that their cases would be "handicapped . . . if they were defended by a Negro attorney against a white one in a court of law." B. J. Davis, Jr., *Communist Councilman from Harlem* 45 (1969).

130. See, e.g., J. Q. Wilson, *Negro Politics* 48–76 (1969); H. Walton, Jr., *Black Politics* 104–20 (1972).

131. C. S. Johnson, *The Negro College Graduate* 337 (1938). In the early days of the black lawyer "the greatest endowment of the budding lawyer was the gift of speech and resounding rhetoric, and without such possessions the public then felt one misplaced who dared enter the profession. The capacity for quiet, persistent, patient and laborious research into the mysteries and principles of the law was regarded as secondary in the equipment of the lawyer, particularly those of our Race." Remarks of Scipio Africanus Jones, from *The National Bar Association Proceedings of the Sixth Annual Convention* 30 (Aug. 7, 1930).

132. R. L. Abel, *American Lawyers* 15 (1989).

133. *Id.* at 18–19; see also, George M. Johnson, "Legal Profession," in *The Integration of the Negro into American Society* 90 (E. F. Frazier ed. 1951).

134. Whitaker, "'Amos 'n' Andy' Set an Image," *Washington Post*, April 11, 1976, at A18, col. 1, quoting from episode 79. Calhoun was portrayed by actor John Cook.

135. *Ibid.* See also, M. P. Ely, *Amos 'n' Andy* 207–8 (1991).

136. "'Study Law' Says Scipio Jones," *Pittsburgh Courier*, Feb. 23, 1929.

137. J. Greenberg, *Staking a Claim* 117 (1990).

138. Stuart, "Negro Lawyers Have Had a Lot to Face, Stiff Race Prejudice," *Pittsburgh Courier*, May 20, 1944.

139. William H. Hale, "The Career Development of the Negro Lawyer in Chicago," 41 (Ph.D. diss., Univ. of Chicago, Sept. 1949).

140. Vol. 5 *The Booker T. Washington Papers, 1899–1900*, at 554 (L. R. Harlan, R. W. Smock, and B. S. Kraft eds. 1976).

141. J. Greenberg, *Staking a Claim* 116–17 (1990), referring to the funding of litigation by Charles Albert Chandler, a black lawyer in Oklahoma, in *Lane v. Wilson*, 307 U.S. 268 (1939), a case striking down discriminatory voting practices.

142. Vol. 5 *The Booker T. Washington Papers, 1899–1900*, at 650 (L. R. Harlan, R. W. Smock, and B. S. Kraft eds. 1976): letter from Giles Beecher Jackson, a black lawyer in Richmond, Virginia, to Booker T. Washington, Oct. 5, 1900.

143. *Id.* at Vol. 7 (1903–4), at 480 (L. R. Harlan and R. W. Smock eds. 1977).

144. In 1898, William R. Morris, a black lawyer in Minnesota established the Afro-American Law Enforcement League. See Vol. 3 *History of Minneapolis* 816–17 (M. Shutter ed. 1923). In 1914, black lawyers in Galveston, Texas,

organized the Anti-Lynching Protecting Association, funded by blacks to protect the rights of their clients charged with crimes. See M. Bloomfield, "From Deference to Confirmation: The Early Black Lawyers of Galveston, Texas 1895–1920," in *The New High Priest* 163 (G. W. Gawalt ed. 1984). In 1917 J. Frank Wheaton co-founded the Equity Congress, a community-based civil rights organization in Harlem, New York. Through this group, Wheaton raised funding for cases that sought to overturn restrictive covenants and to mobilize blacks in Harlem to support black businesses. James C. Thomas, Sr., a co-founder of the Equity Congress, laid the foundation for his lawyer son, James C. Thomas, Jr., to be elected alderman in 1917. Vol. 10, *The Booker T. Washington Papers, 1909–1911*, at 316–17 (L. R. Harlan, R. W. Smock, G. McTigue, and N. E. Woodruff eds. 1981). As late as the 1930s, Leon A. Ransom, a professor of law at Howard University, was asking ministers throughout the South to take up collections in their churches to defend blacks in criminal matters. P. Murray, *Song in a Weary Throat* 161 (1987).

145. W. L. Katz, *The Black West* 302 (1973): W. E. B. Du Bois credits Frederick L. McGhee, a black lawyer in Minnesota, with the idea for the Niagara Movement.

146. R. L. Jack, *History of the National Association for the Advancement of Colored People* 8–9 (1943).

147. Meier, "Attorneys Black and White: A Case Study of Race Relations within the NAACP," 62 *J. of American History* 913, 915 (March 1976).

148. *Ibid.*

149. *Id.* at 943.

150. See, e.g., *Franklin v. South Carolina*, 218 U.S. 161 (1910); *McCabe v. Atchison, Topeka and Santa Fe Railway Company*, 235 U.S. 151 (1914). For the debate on the use of white lawyers in the Franklin case, see, Vol. 10, *The Booker T. Washington Papers, 1909–1911*, at 362–63 (L. R. Harlan, R. W. Smock, G. McTigue, and N. E. Woodruff ed. 1981), and in the McCabe case, see "Annual Meeting Report of NAACP," 10 *Crisis* 135, 137 (Jan. 1915).

151. In 1926, Professor Kelly Miller, a noted and respected black scholar at Howard University, had commented on the use of white lawyers by the black community, comments no doubt directed at groups like the NAACP. Professor Miller said, "However kindly the white lawyer might be, however faithful he may be to the cause which he engages to espouse, with him it is the case, and not the *cause* that is uppermost. Prudence and good judgment may indeed require that we employ white counsel. . . . But in no instance should the Negro lawyer be left wholly out of the equation." Miller, "The Advocacy of the Negro Lawyer," *Norfolk Journal and Guide*, March 3, 1926.

152. M. V. Tushnet, *The NAACP's Legal Strategy Against Segregated Education, 1925–1950*, at 29, 31 (1987). Tushnet says, "The NAACP's leadership believed that a litigation effort directed by black lawyers would be responsive to black concerns, because there would be no need to educate the lawyers on the issue that blacks might be sensitive to, and that black lawyers would show to blacks and whites that white prejudice were unfounded." *Id.* at 29–30. Recent scholarly work has criticized black and white historians who "have slighted the local attorneys . . . that supplied the impetus for the launching of a civil rights campaign in the state and national courts." See, Vibert L. White, "Developing a 'School' of Civil Rights Lawyers: From the New Deal to the New Frontier" 2 (Ph.D. diss., Ohio University, 1988). Recognition of the black lawyer by the NAACP was slow in coming. James Weldon Johnson was the first black lawyer

to receive the coveted Spingarn Medal in 1925, followed by Charles W. Chesnutt in 1928, and William Henry Hastie in 1943. See, M. W. Ovington, *The Walls Came Tumbling Down* 118 (reprint, 1969).

153. C. G. Woodson, *The Negro Professional Man and the Community* 210 (reprint, 1969); Colbert, "Challenging the Challenge: Thirteenth Amendment as a Prohibition Against the Racial Use of Peremptory Challenges," 76 *Cornell L. Rev.* 1, 5–8, 20–24 (1990).

154. See, e.g., H. F. Gosnell, *Negro Politicians: The Rise of Negro Politics in Chicago* 108 (1935).

155. See, e.g., Wynes, "T. McCants Stewart: Peripatetic Black South Carolinian," 80 *South Carolina Historical Magazine* 311, 315 (Oct. 1979); W. J. Simmons, *Men of Mark* 964, 966 (1887).

156. Black lawyers followed the signal from Frederick Douglass in 1872: "The Republican Party is the ship, all else is the sea." W. F. Nowlin, *The Negro in American Politics* 83 (1931).

157. Straker, "The Negro in the Profession of Law," 8 *The A.M.E. Review* 178, 183 (1891).

158. Wilford H. Smith, "The Negro and the Law," in *The Negro Problem* 127, 142 (B. T. Washington ed. 1903).

159. *Negro Year Book, 1918–1919*, at 208–9 (M. Work ed. 1919). The delegates included Scipio A. Jones (fifth district of Arkansas), Joseph E. Lee (at-large, Florida), Perry W. Howard (eighth district, Mississippi), and W. T. Andrews (at-large, South Carolina).

160. Vol. 13 *The Booker T. Washington Papers, 1914–1915*, at 57–58 (L. R. Harlan, R. W. Smock, S. Valenza, and S. M. Harlan eds. 1984).

161. *The Negro Year Book, 1918–1919*, at 55 (M. Work ed. 1919). A. Lee Beatty and Harry E. Davis, were elected in Ohio; Edward A. Johnson, John C. Hawkins in New York; Harry J. Capehart, T. Gillis Nutter in West Virginia; S. B. Turner, Warren Douglas, Adelbert H. Roberts in Illinois; and John C. Asbury in Pennsylvania. See also, "Thirteen Negro American Legislators," 21 *Crisis* 120–21 (Jan. 1921).

162. H. F. Gosnell, *Negro Politicians: The Rise of Negro Politicians in Chicago* 11 (1935).

163. In 1919, L. S. Hicks, of Boston, George W. Ellis, of Chicago, and George H. White, Jr., of Philadelphia, were appointed assistant corporation counsels. In the same year, Franklin A. Denison, of Chicago, was appointed assistant attorney general of Illinois and S. A. T. Watkins, assistant United States district attorney in Chicago. Two other appointments were made in Pennsylvania and Kansas. In Pennsylvania, John W. Parks was appointed assistant to the attorney general and John Q. Sayers was elected county attorney of Graham County, Kansas; *The Negro Year Book, 1918–1919*, at 54 (M. Work ed. 1919).

164. The files of Ollie May Cooper, who was secretary to the dean at Howard University, indicate that Howard law graduates David Grant, Joseph Birch, and Robert Burrell held positions as assistant city attorneys (Grant—St. Louis, Missouri; Birch—Flint, Michigan; Burrell—Buffalo, N.Y.), and that Oliver Hill was elected to the city council of Richmond, Virginia, in 1933.

165. Houston, "Need for Negro Lawyers," 4 *J. of Negro Education* 49, 51 (1935).

166. *Smith v. Allright*, 321 U.S. 649 (1944); *Constitutional Law* 1521 (G. R. Stone, L. M. Seidman, C. R. Sunstein, and M. V. Tushnet eds. 1986).

167. Even after the Allright decision, Thurgood Marshall continued to press the United States Attorney General to investigate the refusal of Southern registrars to permit blacks to register to vote. In fact, Marshall informed the U.S. Attorney General that "discrimination registration practices are even more dangerous than the 'white primary.' " Letter from Thurgood Marshall to Francis J. Biddle, Oct. 3, 1944.

168. See Appendix 1: The First Black Lawyers, 1844–1944; Appendix 2, The Twelfth (1900), Thirteenth (1910), and Fourteenth (1920) Censuses. Although the Fourteenth Census records a black lawyer in Vermont in 1920, Lawrence J. Turgeon, Vermont's state librarian, reported that in 1958, "There are statements about Negro ministers in our history books . . . but no mention . . . of a Negro lawyer. . . . The older men in the Bar [have] never heard of a Negro being admitted to the Vermont Bar." See letter from Lawrence J. Turgeon to Charles S. Brown, May 26, 1958. Similarly, George O. Shovan, clerk, New Hampshire Supreme Court, reported that "we have no record of any Negro ever applying for or being admitted to the bar of this state." Letter from George O. Shovan to Charles S. Brown, May 26, 1958.

169. *Ibid.* Appendix 2, The Sixteenth (1940) Census.

170. C. G. Woodson, *The Negro Professional Man and the Community* 194 (reprint, 1969).

171. See J. M. Jacobstein and R. M. Mersky, *Fundamentals of Legal Research* 58 (3rd ed. 1985) for map of the United States and the historical regional breakdowns followed in this book.

Chapter 1

Black Students in White Law Schools and the Black Law Schools

Blacks in White Law Schools

The history of blacks in legal education in America has been generally ignored.[1] The absence of scholarship on blacks in legal education may result from the perception that blacks played no significant role in the evolution of legal education. This perception is distorted, because it fails to take into consideration the purpose and effect that the nation's racial policies had on the opportunities for black men and women to pursue law as a career.[2]

Starting in the colonial period of American history, a person could enter the legal profession "by his own efforts and through self-directing reading and study [or] work in the clerk's office of some court [or] serve as an apprentice [to] a reputable lawyer [or] enter one of the four Inns of Court in London."[3] Legal education for blacks, as for whites, began under the apprenticeship of an established lawyer or under the preceptorship of a judge. About the time Macon Bolling Allen, who in 1844 became America's first black lawyer, started his apprenticeship in the office of a white lawyer in the state of Maine, "there were . . . nine university-affiliated law schools" in the nation.[4] There is no evidence that any black lawyer was trained in a university prior to 1868, the year in which George Lewis Ruffin enrolled in the Harvard University School of Law.[5]

The apprentice and preceptor systems were not free, nor were they free from racial prejudice. An apprentice was charged a fee for the instruction he received. The period of instruction necessary to qualify for examination varied from state to state, and sometimes from county to county. The basic texts used for the study of law in an apprenticeship included Coke's *Institutes*, French's *Law*, and Blackstone's *Commentaries*.[6]

Several freestanding law schools were in operation in 1850, the year John Mercer Langston became the first known black applicant to an American law school.[7] In 1850, Langston, a resident of Ohio, applied to a law school at Ballston Spa, New York, operated by J. W. Fowler. Langston describes that experience as follows:

[I] wrote frankly and truthfully about [myself] telling who [I] was, all about [my] race, complexion, qualifications and character, assuring Mr. Fowler that [I] could not only furnish all needed recommendations . . . but was able to meet every charge for tuition, board, or other demand, in advance.[8]

Langston was invited to the law school for a "look-see." According to Langston, the invitation was more for Fowler to look at him than for Langston to see the law school. Langston might have been admitted to the law school, but for politics. The year before he applied for admission, Senator John C. Calhoun, of South Carolina, had visited the same law school and promised Fowler that he would encourage young men from his state to attend the law school. Fearing that the enrollment of a black student (though in appearance Langston was far from black, or even brown) would "offend" Senator Calhoun, Fowler denied his application, unless Langston consented "to pass" as a Frenchman or a Spaniard.[9] If Langston had agreed to "pass," he was informed that he would have to sit "apart from the class; ask no questions [and] behave . . . quietly."[10] Langston refused to accept this condition of admission because it required him to "yield [his] American birthright."[11] Langston also was denied admission to another law school, located in Cincinnati, Ohio, operated by Judge Timothy Walker.[12]

Through the account of John Mercer Langston one can witness the first detailed training of a black lawyer under an apprenticeship, which Langston entered into around 1853 under a liberal white probate judge, Philemon Bliss, of Ohio. The study of law under the preceptorship of a judge or in a lawyer's office was very personal. Langston lived near his law teacher. He studied hard, observed courtroom trials, and had access to his teacher's law library. Langston reports that he burned the midnight oil because much "importance was attached at all times, and to every subject of the law, to the accuracy . . . theory and practice" of the law.[13] His curriculum included "exercises in writing on law topics . . . discussions on such subjects [and] moot court,"[14] and he was "at liberty, even urged to ask any question in regard to the general management of a case."[15] The usual period of apprenticeship, though such periods varied from state to state, was a minimum of two years or less, if the applicant could demonstrate the mastery of legal principles to the satisfaction of the local judges. Langston was admitted to the Ohio bar in 1854 after a year's study under Judge Bliss.[16]

Langston's opportunity to study law prior to the Civil War was unique. Given the discrimination against Langston's initial efforts to gain admission to a law school in the North, it is unlikely that blacks were trained as lawyers or admitted to any bar in the South prior to the Civil War. Even after the Civil War, the first generation of black lawyers "can hardly be blamed for not preferring [legal] training which at that time was still more or less an innovation."[17]

During the Reconstruction and Post-Reconstruction eras, the education of a few early black lawyers was sometimes financed by liberal whites. For example, Julia B. Nelson "provided for the education of William Henry Richardson, who later became a professor of law at Howard University."[18] Samuel Clemens, better known as Mark Twain, paid for Warner T. McGuinn's board at Yale's law school in 1887.[19] Tuition at New England law schools was not cheap, a factor that may have discouraged blacks from applying. In 1873, the cost of tuition and fees at Columbia University's law school was over one hundred dollars per year "payable in advance," and board cost "from $5 to $7 a week . . . rooms . . . from $1.50 to $2.00 per week."[20] Cornell law school's tuition was seventy-five dollars per year in 1888 while Yale's was $115 per year in 1906.[21] By 1935, when blacks were being admitted in greater numbers into Northern state law schools, the University of Maryland law school's tuition for its night program was $153 per year. The tuition of the predominately black Howard University School of Law in the 1930s was $135 per year.[22]

Black Americans, like their white counterparts, "saw the birth of land grant colleges" as an opportunity to obtain an education after the Civil War.[23] Although comprehensive data are unavailable, it seems likely that "during the nineteenth . . . centur[y], most law schools taught few or no blacks," except at black law schools.[24] Even though black students were trained at respected high schools and colleges, their credentials may have been questioned simply because they received their education at black schools. White high school graduates received better treatment. At many public and private law schools, "a student could be admitted . . . upon the completion of a high school education" as late as 1920.[25]

It was at the University of South Carolina and the University of Michigan that blacks were first admitted and graduated from publicly supported law schools. Between 1873 to 1877, the University of South Carolina Law School was integrated temporarily. Some scholars have mistakenly referred to the University of South Carolina Law School as a "colored school" because a number of blacks were enrolled there during Reconstruction, causing some white law students to withdraw.[26] In 1877, the University of Michigan graduated its first black law students,[27] followed by the University of Iowa, which graduated its first black law student in 1879.[28] Until the mid-1940s, the University of South Carolina was the only public university in the South that had admitted blacks to a state-supported law school,[29] albeit during the Reconstruction era.

There is little information about the treatment of blacks by white students and white faculty or about opinions by the law faculty regarding the performance of black students as compared to white students. It appears that students and faculty at most law schools welcomed, accepted, or tolerated black students.[30] In some instances, black students were so superior to their white counterparts that they were even revered. In 1868, the year Harvard University's law school admitted George Lewis Ruffin, black law students and the diversity they represented were new experiences for white students and faculty. The students and faculty there had known the black race only as a slave group. Ruffin, who graduated the following year, faced hostility from students who sought to exclude him from the student assembly at Harvard. However, the geographical diversity of the student body at Harvard prevailed over those who considered blacks inferior.[31]

Racism, however, touched black Harvard University law students in the city of Cambridge. In 1894, William Henry Lewis, a black Harvard law student, "was refused service in a barbershop in Cambridge."[32] Lewis sought the assistance of another black lawyer in Massachusetts, and between the two of them they "had the legislature amend [the anti-discrimination] law to include 'barber's shops.'"[33]

Raymond Pace Alexander could not have afforded to attend Harvard's law school without the assistance of a white dean at the University of Pennsylvania, from which Alexander graduated with honors in 1919. Alexander's college dean used his influence to assist him in obtaining a job with Professor Edmund B. Day, chairman of Harvard's Department of Economics. This job enabled Alexander "to study with no financial worries."[34] However, the "social life between the white student body and the blacks was totally non existent."[35] According to Alexander, the students from Southern states "never spoke to black students and even the pleasant and courteous Northern and Western students merely said a quiet 'hello' and no more."[36] During this period, blacks were denied membership in all of the law clubs at Harvard, clubs in which students shared class notes and made lasting and important friendships. Denied membership in such clubs, blacks and Northern Jewish students formed their own club.[37]

Some faculty members, recognizing the talent of black law students, are known to have helped several seek job opportunities. Harvard law dean Roscoe Pound and Professor Samuel Williston attempted to place

Alexander in a prestigious Philadelphia law firm. Arrangements were made to have Alexander interviewed, but no mention was made of his race. Alexander carried letters of recommendation to the interview from Dean Pound and Professor Williston. When Alexander arrived at the firm for the interview he was informed that "there had been a mistake."[38] The mistake was Alexander's race. After graduation, Raymond Pace Alexander hung his Harvard law degree in a rented room in Philadelphia and began to practice law in the "Negro Section."[39]

A Columbia University law professor and former law dean, George W. Kirckwey,[40] encouraged Edith Spurlock Sampson, a black student in the New York School of Social Work, where he taught criminology, to attend law school around 1921. Professor Kirckwey's progressive views about black women entering the legal profession apparently had been influenced by his contact with Gertrude Elzora Durden Rush, the first black woman admitted to the Iowa bar in 1918.[41] Professor Kirckwey "painted a picture in which he portrayed a rosy future for a colored woman lawyer."[42] Indeed, Sampson's future in law was significant. She earned her first law degree from the John Marshall Law School in 1925 and her Master of Laws from Loyola Law School (Chicago), becoming the "first woman of any race awarded a degree from [Loyola]."[43]

Women, both black and white, were equal in their lack of opportunities for gaining admission to Harvard Law School prior to 1953.[44] However, Pauli Murray, a black woman who was about to receive her law degree from Howard University, protested when Professor T. R. Powell, chairman of Harvard's graduate school admissions committee, rejected her application because her "picture and the salutation of your college transcript indicate that you are not of the sex entitled to be admitted to Harvard Law School."[45] Murray's eloquent appeal to A. Calvert Smith, the secretary of Harvard University, fell on deaf ears.[46]

Yale admitted its first black law student, Edwin Archer Randolph, around 1878.[47] The experiences of early black law graduates at Yale remain a mystery. Information about Yale's admissions policy, however, is quite favorable. In 1910, Yale University admitted the first black deaf mute law student, Roger Demosthenes O'Kelly.[48] In 1915, when Nathan B. Young entered Yale, there were two other black law students enrolled and not "much prejudice." Young became one of the first black law students elected to the debating club.[49]

Maryland University's law school, initially a private school until taken over by the state in 1920,[50] admitted two black students, Charles W. Johnson and Harry S. Cummings in 1887. The progress that blacks had made during the Reconstruction era still caused "dissatisfaction . . . among some of the white students and . . . some . . . faculty,"[51] and as the day of graduation approached for Johnson and Cummings, white students balked at the prospect of black students and their parents sitting among their own families. However, "the good judgement . . . and kindly feeling of the majority of white ones" prevailed, perhaps because one of these black students "stood very high in the class."[52]

William Ashbie Hawkins's reception was not as hospitable in 1890, the year he enrolled at Maryland University's law school. Hawkins was forced out of law school during his first year as a result of an "anti-black petition signed by a majority of the student body."[53] It would take a lawsuit filed fifty-five years later by Charles Hamilton Houston and Thurgood Marshall to force the University of Maryland to again open its doors to blacks.[54]

In the North, the Post-Reconstruction era brought other shining lights to legal education, such as Rufus Lewis Milford Hope Perry, one of New York University's first black law graduates.[55] Perry was selected as the class orator in 1891. He was also "the only member of his class to hand in his examination papers for the Bar in Latin."[56] Perry's score on the New York bar exam was so high "that he was asked by the examining officials to pass on the papers of his fellow students."[57]

In the West, blacks had been admitted to the bar for several years before George Marion Johnson entered Boalt Hall School of Law at the University of California in 1926. In fact, there was a total of three other black students in the second and third year classes at Boalt Hall when Johnson was admitted.[58] Two of Johnson's law teachers encouraged him to complete law school. Professor Barbara Armstrong, the only woman on the law faculty, and Professor Roger Traynor, who later would become one of the leading jurists in the nation, were mentors to Johnson during the years he spent at Boalt Hall. Professor Armstrong, concerned about Johnson's work schedule, helped him to borrow money so that he could spend more time studying. She and Professor Traynor encouraged Johnson to pursue a Doctor of Juridical Science degree in tax, which he completed in 1930.[59] Thereafter, Professor Traynor helped Johnson to gain employment on the staff of the California State Board of Equalization.[60]

Tabytha Anderson's experience at Hastings College of Law, located in San Francisco, California, was quite different. Likely one of the first black women admitted to the law school, Anderson "suffered more than the ordinary roughness accorded a freshman in James A. Ballentine's Tort Class. . . . Ballentine's noted Southern-gentleman manners at best fell short of women students and were certainly not color-blind."[61] Anderson left Hastings, enrolled at Howard University's law school in Washington, D.C., and was graduated in 1931.

In the middle section of the United States, blacks were admitted to several law schools. The Detroit College of Law "open[ed] its doors [in 1891] without regard to sex, color or citizenship," admitting William W. Ferguson in 1896.[62] In 1933, at Chicago Law School, Harry Pace, an honor graduate, "was elected by acclamation of his fellow students to preside over the moot court [and] filled absences of various professors and taught classes in Guaranty and Suretyship in addition to classes in . . . Insurance."[63]

An impressive group of black students scored so high in their legal academic work that they were elected to the Order of Coif, the most prestigious academic society for graduating law students. The earliest known black law student elected to Coif was Jasper Alston Atkins, a 1922 graduate of Yale University's law school.[64] William Edwin Taylor was elected to Coif at Iowa University's law school in 1923, as was Richard F. Jones, of the University of Pittsburgh's law school.[65] They were followed by Leon Andrew Ransom, of Ohio State University's law school, Iven McLeod, of the University of Cincinnati's law school, and William Robert Ming, Jr., of the University of Chicago's law school in 1927, 1929, and 1933, respectively.[66]

Perhaps the most overlooked academic achievement of black students in the early days of the twentieth century was their election to the law review. At least a dozen black students made law review between 1922 and 1943. Clara Burrill Bruce at Boston University School of Law was the first black student elected editor-in-chief of a law review in America in 1925.[67] Bruce had been elected to Boston University's law review in 1924. As a member of the review, Bruce published four articles,[68] was a member of the student council, was class day orator in 1926, and "maintained the highest scholastic record for three years."[69] Three students appear to share the honor of being the first blacks elected to other law reviews: Jasper Alston Atkins, of Yale, Charles Hamilton Houston, of Harvard, and William Edwin Taylor, of Iowa, were elected to law reviews in 1921.[70] Yale appears to be the first law school to have two black students, John Francis Williams and Jasper Alston Atkins, on the law review at the same time.[71]

In 1926, Sadie Tanner Mossell Alexander and Robert Burke Johnson became the first black student contributors and associate editors of the *University of Pennsylvania Law Review*.[72] Alexander's election to the law review provoked controversy when "Dean [Edward] Mikell refused to break precedent by permitting a black woman membership on the Board."[73] Philip Werner Amram, the law review editor, however, threatened to resign unless Dean Mikell reversed his decision. Dean Mikell backed down and Alexander remained on the review.[74]

Theodore Moody Berry and Helen Elsie Austin became members of the *University of Cincinnati Law Review* in 1928. Because of illness,

Austin was unable to serve on the review, and Berry became the first black student editor. Berry reports, "After my first year in law school, the law librarian suggested that I apply for law review. I did and I was accepted."[75] During Berry's two years on the law review, he published five student notes and one article.[76] Helen Elsie Austin spent her second year of law school at the University of Colorado and became the first woman and black student on its law review.[77]

At Harvard, William Henry Hastie became a member of the *Harvard Law Review* in 1928,[78] and William Robert Ming, Jr., became a member of and published in the inaugural issue of the *University of Chicago Law Review* in 1933.[79] Between 1934 and 1943, only Harry E. Bonepart, of Ohio State University, R. Lawrence Clay, of Temple University, and Hobart Taylor, Jr., of the University of Michigan, are known to have been members of the law review. Bonepart was the first black student on the *Ohio State Law Review* in 1935.[80] Clay published an article in the *Temple Law Quarterly* in 1941,[81] and Hobart Taylor, Jr., published ten articles in the *Michigan Law Review* between 1942 and 1943, breaking the record of publications by a black student in a law review previously set by Theodore M. Berry at the University of Cincinnati between 1929 and 1930.[82]

Meanwhile, black students were also being admitted to graduate law programs. Michigan University admitted Mason Nelson, a graduate of Howard University's law school, to its master of laws program in 1892, just two years after that program was established. The following year, Nelson was awarded his master of laws degree.[83] The Boston University and New York University law schools also awarded master of laws degrees to blacks in 1893 and 1901, respectively,[84] as did a few other law schools during the Post-Reconstruction era. The Doctor of Juridical Science degree, the research doctorate in the law, was not awarded until 1923, the year Harvard University awarded this degree to Charles Hamilton Houston.[85] Harvard took an early lead in the number of S.J.D. degrees awarded to black men who became distinguished law professors and deans at leading black law schools such as Howard University. Cornell University awarded a juridical science doctorate to a black man, Joseph R. Houchins, in 1934.[86]

Despite the achievements of black law students, their numbers declined between 1930 and 1939 at all law schools except Northwestern, which graduated twenty-five students in the years after the Depression. The graduation in 1944 of Jane Cleo Marshall (Lucas), the first black woman law graduate from the University of Michigan's law school, took place during the centennial of the admission of the first black lawyer in America—a sign, perhaps, that black women would succeed in white law schools.[87]

The Black Law School

Nine years after the founding of Howard University School of Law, the nation's first black law school, the American Bar Association was founded. The ABA established the Committee on Legal Education and Admission to the Bar in 1878, with the purpose of reforming legal education in the United States.[88] In its first report, the committee declared that "education is the parent of public and private virtue,"[89] even though educational institutions, particularly those in the South, excluded blacks. During Reconstruction, the virtue of education for university-trained black law students was first rooted at Howard University School of Law in 1869.

Howard University's law school and other black law schools that subsequently opened would be greatly affected by the regulations of the Committee on Legal Education and Admission to the Bar, and by the Association of American Law Schools (AALS), founded as an auxiliary organization of the ABA in 1900. The purpose of the AALS was to advance the standards of legal education.[90] Since blacks were generally excluded from the ABA until 1943, law professors at Howard University and other black law schools were absent from the public debate on legal educational policy preceding and following the formation of the ABA and the AALS.[91] The exclusion of blacks from the ABA and the AALS is a plausible reason for the fact that black lawyers were not hired as professors by white law schools until 1925, the year that Clarence M. Maloney spent "a review year at . . . Buffalo School of Law."[92] Outside of the black law schools, however, the administration and faculty of the AALS member schools remained predominantly white after 1944.[93]

Between 1890 and 1920, a number of freestanding law schools opened. During this period "there were . . . twenty-one day-and-night schools with 5,164 students and forty-three night schools with 5,570 students."[94] Some of these schools were black law schools. As the number of blacks and other ethnic minorities showed a greater interest in law, both black and white night law schools, mostly in urban areas, offered them an opportunity to obtain a legal education.[95] LaSalle Extension University, the YMCA Law School Association Institute, the International School of Law, and the American Correspondence School of Law in Chicago are some of the schools that fit this category.[96] Other less formal state and private law schools, such as Iowa's Oskaloosa College, appear to have graduated blacks as well.[97]

The demand for a legal education by blacks, poor whites, and other ethnic minorities and the low tuition of freestanding law schools were mutually beneficial. Many blacks were able to enter the field of law who were unable to afford the tuition at local universities, and they could do so while living and working in their communities. A number of these law graduates entered the legal profession and served the bar and black community with distinction. Indeed, many of the black lawyers attending freestanding night law schools became as successful as their counterparts educated in law schools associated with universities.

By the early 1920s, a move was made by the "academic lawyers" to increase the standards for admission into law schools. The ABA moved to close several urban freestanding law schools, which were attended by minorities in significant numbers. The academic lawyers "stressed the need to rid society of the night schools to ensure competent public-spirited and ethical lawyers."[98] Yet the stated objective—increasing the standards of the bar—may not have been the only goal. Some of the ABA's influential members were blunt about their aims: "The legal profession was a means by which Jews, immigrants, and city-dwellers might undermine the American way of life."[99]

Black law schools fell victim to the ABA's new policies. Blacks were adversely affected by the closing of a number of urban law schools.[100] Black lawyers, barred from membership in the ABA, were powerless to argue the adverse impact of this new policy from within the organization. Powerful ABA members who served in important legislative and judicial bodies in their states implemented the new policies.[101] Black law schools that were able to do so promptly complied with the new standards requiring that students admitted to law schools have two years of college and two years of law school to qualify to take bar examinations, and that the law school offer a three-year graded law school.[102] That Howard University was able to establish and support a law school placed it in an enviable position in 1920. By then, as the chairman of the ABA Section on Legal Education said, "we [were] in a law school age."[103]

Howard University opened its law department in 1869, just four years after the abolition of slavery, two years after the first jury composed of black and white citizens was empaneled in a federal court, one year after the ratification of the Fourteenth Amendment, and one year before Christopher Columbus Langdell was appointed dean of Harvard University School of Law.[104] It was at Howard University "that the first class of colored law students ever known in the United States was organized."[105]

In 1868 John Mercer Langston, the first black lawyer admitted to the Ohio bar and one of the first black lawyers to be admitted to practice law in the nation, was summoned to Howard University to organize the law department. Langston was all too familiar with the importance of this summons. In 1850, he had been the first known black in the nation denied admission to a law school.[106] Langston organized the law department with white lawyers. Albert Gallatin Riddle, Henry D. Beam, and Judge Charles Cooper Nott were all respected and learned men who were anxious to be among the first professors to educate former slaves in the law.[107] The nation watched as Howard University did what no other white university or independent law school had done or would do for years to come: it opened a law school with a racially integrated faculty.[108]

During the organizational development of the law school, Langston traveled to various Southern states giving speeches about Howard University's law department and encouraging black men and women to apply for admission.[109] Convincing black freedmen to consider law as a profession was difficult, since they had never heard of or seen a black lawyer. Langston used himself as an example of how blacks could become lawyers, particularly since the ratification of the Thirteenth and Fourteenth Amendments. To Howard University law graduates, Langston no doubt explained, would pass the responsibility to emancipate and to protect the interests of black people and to interpret the newly won rights of black citizens under the amended Constitution.

John Mercer Langston served as dean until 1875.[110] Langston was the first black American to have the title of "law professor"; the title had been conferred on George Wythe, America's first law professor, at William and Mary College in 1779.[111] Six students were admitted the first year of Howard's law program, and classes commenced "in a few rooms on the second floor of the main building on the [Howard] University Campus."[112] By the end of the spring semester, the number of students had increased to twenty-two.[113] By the fall semester, the enrollment had increased to forty-six students.[114]

The aim of Howard University's law school was to train predominantly black male and female students in the principles of law, to aid these men and women in the law knowledge that would allow them to lead the freedmen out from under laws, rules, regulations, and human conduct that denied, negated, or restrained the virtue of liberty. Howard University School of Law "was founded to direct the political life of . . . Negroes,"[115] and no doubt to ensure that the legal profession would not be confined to a privileged group.[116]

The first law commencement at Howard University was considered to be one of the most historic events in American law. Prior to this time, only one law degree had ever been conferred on a black person—George Lewis Ruffin, at Harvard University in 1869. John Mercer Langston's invitation to Senator Charles Sumner to deliver the commencement address on February 3, 1871, was initially returned with regrets. Senator Sumner had already agreed to deliver the third commencement address at Columbian University College of Law (George Washington University), established in 1865, which was scheduled on the same day as Howard University's. But Dean Langston would not take no for an answer from the popular Senator Sumner, and "the case [was] explained, especially . . . that this was the first class of young colored lawyers ever graduated in the world." Dean Langston's plea won over Senator Sumner, who withdrew his acceptance to speak at the Columbian University Law School's commencement.[117]

Perhaps Sumner was persuaded to address the first graduating class because of the presence of other politically significant invited guests. On commencement day, Dean Langston had assembled some of the most important speakers in America. General O. O. Howard, the president of Howard University, Ohio senator John Sherman, Civil War general William Tecumseh Sherman, and Amos T. Ackerman, the attorney general of the United States, were all confirmed guests and speakers at the law commencement exercises.[118] However, it was the remarks of Senator Sumner that were anxiously awaited, because Sumner had been an early opponent of the Fugitive Slave Act of 1850 and long an opponent of slavery. Senator Sumner's speech was uncharacteristically short. He urged the graduates to "always be on the side of human rights,"[119] and further stated that

belonging to a race which for long generations has been oppressed and despoiled of rights, you must be vigilant and sensitive defenders of all who suffer in any way from wrong. . . . No matter who is the offender; whether crime be attempted by political party, by Congress, or by President—wherever it shows itself whether on the continent or on an island of the sea, you must be ready at all times to stand forth, careless of consequences, and vindicate the right. So doing you will uphold your own race in its unexampled trials.[120]

Perhaps sensing the challenges that black lawyers intending to go South would face as they argued for the rule of law, Ackerman, the U.S. attorney general from Georgia, predicted that Howard's first ten law graduates "would hold positions of influence among their race, and use that influence for the good of all men."[121] At Howard University Law School's second commencement, Tennessee senator Horace Maynard's message was unambiguous: "Your future is committed to your own hands."[122] Commenting on these graduates, the *New National Era* said,

These young men go forth into the world, even to be followed by a score in two more from the same university, to give to the false and hate-inspired charge of the black man's natural inferiority a living, forcible and effective denial. Belonging to the race that has been crushed till not a spark of humanity could scarce be expected in them, this graduating class of men has shown [itself to be], by its achievements in acquiring knowledge of one of the highest branches of study . . . the peer of any race.[123]

As dean, John Mercer Langston's role seems to have been almost exclusively administrative. Regrettably, specific information about Langston's leadership in the development of specific academic programs for the new freedman is minimal. However, Dean Langston was competent and deeply devoted to the mission of Howard University's law school and to its students. Langston instituted a law course of study at Howard University comparable to that of other law schools, such as Harvard University's. The first-year students were assigned Walker's *Introduction to American Law*, Blackstone's *Commentaries*, Kent's *Commentaries*, and Smith's *On Contracts*. The second-year students were assigned Greenleaf's *On Evidence*, Hilliard's *On Torts*, Washburn's *On Evidence*, Williams's *On Real Property*, Parsons's *On Bills and Notes*, Stephens's *On Pleading*, Adams's *On Equity*, and Bishop's *On Criminal Law*.[124] Dean Langston was very aware that the inauguration of the law school and the graduation of students of color would affect the world of law and he predicted that, "[in] spite of popular prejudice," Howard University law graduates would be "called to the bench, to the senate, to fields of business enterprise, or the self-sacrificing struggles of reform."[125]

A white professor, Albert Gallatin Riddle, was an outstanding member of Howard University's first law faculty. Riddle, formerly of Ohio, had served in the Ohio state legislature in the 1860s, represented Ohio in the United States House of Representatives, and "had been among the first to advocate the abolition of slavery in the District of Columbia and the enlistment of Negro troops."[126] Professor Riddle's lectures were published in 1873, the first book ever by a faculty member of a black law school. His *Law Students and Lawyers, the Philosophy of Political Parties, and Other Subjects* was based on eight lectures delivered between 1869 to 1873. Professor Riddle emphasized "law [as] the highest and grandest science."[127]

The Riddle lectures reveal important insights into the mission of Howard University's law school, and into the hostile environment Howard graduates would face as pioneer black lawyers. Professor Riddle advised Howard law students to take the bar examination immediately and to open law offices, but warned that the formation of partnerships "may be narrowed . . . on account of race."[128] The law students were informed to go "where there already is, or quite certainly will be, law business."[129] They were directed to "avoid small towns," and to go to places where there was "an atmosphere of law."[130] Professor Riddle invited Howard's law students to go West, because these "men commence on terms more nearly equal."[131] He prepared them to face juries whose "pre-formed judgments would disqualify them from sitting in any other case."[132] Professor Riddle told Howard law students that, faced with great odds against success, they could not afford to fail— "not any of you."[133] He admonished the students that they "must not only equal the average white competitor; [they] must surpass them. . . . [For the] world has already decided that a colored man who is no better than a white man is nobody at all."[134]

In 1877, as the Reconstruction era ended, John Hartwell Cook, a member of Howard University's first graduating law class, was appointed dean. Cook, who was black, had gained a reputation in criminal law in the District of Columbia and was a respected member of the bar, but he was forced to resign the deanship in 1878 due to ill health.[135]

Dean Cook was succeeded in 1878 by Richard Theodore Greener, who had just joined the law faculty. Besides being the first black graduate of Harvard University in 1870, Greener had been a professor of philosophy at the University of South Carolina and was an 1876 graduate of its law school. Greener's deanship lasted for two years. The university did not admit law students in 1876–77 because of a lack of applications.[136] During Greener's short tenure as professor and dean, "he gained a reputation as a spokesman for Negroes when he advocated migration of the freedmen to western states such as Kansas to settle fertile land and escape oppression."[137] It has been speculated that the predominantly white board of trustees at Howard University closed the law school as "a device to get rid of Greener."[138]

In addition to Dean John Hartwell Cook and Richard Theodore Greener, between 1878 and 1930 Howard University's decanal office was held by William F. Bascom (interim dean 1875–77), Warren C. Stone (1880–81), Benjamin Franklin Leighton (1881–1921), Mason N. Richardson (1921), and Judge Fenton Whitlock Booth (1921–30), all of whom were white.[139] The prestige that these lawyers and judges brought to the law school during its early years may have done much to enhance the black law school in a white legal world. As Dean Langston had set the standard for the education of slave progeny in the field of law, deans Stone, Leighton, and Booth laid the foundation for the survival of the law school during its second stage of development.

From its beginning, Howard University drew outstanding white faculty to its law school.[140] However, most of the white professors taught on a part-time basis.[141] Howard also hired several black lawyers to teach, whose scholarly endeavors would mold, in an essential way, the legacy of Dean Langston and Professor Riddle.[142]

In 1890, two black Howard University law students joined the faculty. Professor William Henry Richards had received his law degree from Howard in 1881, while Professor William Henry Harrison Hart had received his in 1887. Both men became master teachers and were greatly admired by their students.[143] Professor Richards became recognized in the areas of real property, pleading and practice, and equity.[144] Professor Hart became recognized in the areas of criminal law, torts, and corporations.[145] Through Hart's political connections, he "secured funds from Congress for Howard's first law building and $10,000 a year to run it."[146]

Professor Hart won the admiration of his students and the civil rights community when he was prosecuted, convicted, and fined for refusing to change to the "colored section" on a train traveling between the District of Columbia and Maryland. Hart, represented by two white lawyers, appealed his case to the Maryland Court of Appeals, which ruled that the conduct of the railroad violated the commerce clause of the constitution.[147] Professor Hart left the law school in 1922, after thirty-two years of teaching; Professor Richards retired from the law school after a record-breaking thirty-eight years.[148]

Denied the possibility of teaching in white law schools, other Howard University law black graduates returned to their law school to teach. James C. Waters, Jr., a 1911 graduate, returned to the law school in 1921 to serve as its secretary, librarian, and professor of law,[149] as did Judge Robert Herberton Terrell, an 1889 graduate who had earned his undergraduate degree from Harvard University in 1884. Terrell, a member of the municipal court of the District of Columbia, joined the faculty in 1910 and taught jurisprudence, pleading and practice in inferior courts, legal ethics, and domestic relations.[150] James Adlai Cobb, a law school classmate of Judge Terrell and fellow municipal court judge, joined the faculty in 1916. Cobb's credentials were impeccable. He had served as a special assistant in the United States Department of Justice and had been in private practice. Terrell served on the faculty until 1925. Cobb, who taught commercial law and constitutional law, was on the faculty through the 1930s, serving as vice-dean from 1923 to 1929.[151]

Charles Hamilton Houston joined Howard's law faculty in 1924. The son of a lawyer, Houston had attended Amherst College, graduating Phi Beta Kappa, and had earned the LL.B. and S.J.D. degrees from Harvard University in 1922 and 1923, respectively.[152] Houston arrived at Howard just a few years after the university trustees had voted "that steps be taken to so advance the School of Law that it may become eligible for membership in the American Association of Law Schools."[153] The board's action was a bold step, because very little had changed in Howard's law curriculum or admission standards since 1869. When Howard's law school opened in 1869, the standard curriculum was designed to accommodate a two-year evening program. All branches of the law were taught, including moot court and a course in ethics, which was taught on Sunday mornings by Dean Langston.[154] All the instructors used "the lecture system of instruction," and each student was required to complete a series of forensic exercises and a dissertation prior to graduation.[155] Great emphasis was placed on legal writing[156] and the importance of preparation of daily course assignments, though it was recognized that most students held full-time day jobs.

At Howard, the students were often informed and reminded of Professor Riddle's admonition that "the study and most of the practice of law is purely intellectual [and] that law is a jealous mistress."[157] Unlike schools such as Harvard and Yale, Howard's law school was still admitting some students with a high school education[158] when Professor Houston joined the faculty in 1924. Yet the law school had progressed with distinction in spite of the absence of rigid admissions requirements, and so had its graduates.[159]

To gain accreditation, the challenge for Howard University was not to remake the law school. After all, Howard lawyers had broken legal ground in a number of states. They also had gained substantial respect in both the white and black worlds with their legal training. Yet because of racism the law school remained outside the legal academy represented by the accrediting agencies of the Association of American Law Schools and the American Bar Association. The challenge facing Howard was to transform the law school into a form acceptable to the accreditation agency that would guarantee its survival. That challenge fell to Professor Charles Hamilton Houston.

Two years after Houston joined the faculty, Howard University elected Mordecai Wyatt Johnson as its first black president. In 1929, Dean Fenton Whitlock Booth retired as dean of the law school, leaving his goal of accreditation unmet. Charles Hamilton Houston succeeded Booth as resident vice-dean of the law school.[160] President Johnson and Resident Vice-Dean Houston both believed that "if Howard were to continue to be a useful and important school for black Americans it had to gain national accreditation and begin to provide for its students a legal education program which was competitive in relation to the highest quality full-time university law schools in the country."[161]

When Houston assumed the resident vice-deanship, its faculty consisted of twelve professors and a clerk of the moot court, who had earned law degrees from Michigan, Harvard, Howard, Columbia, and George Washington universities. The curriculum offering was traditional.[162] The law school was coeducational. Houston's first goal was to increase the admission standards, a move that was highly controversial among students and alumni.[163]

Students were admitted under four classifications: regular students, regular students with advanced standing, special students, and, in the afternoon/evening course, unclassified students. Students admitted were required to be high school graduates and to present evidence of some college training accompanied by written testimonials as to character. A regular student was one who had completed at least two years of college. Students with advanced standing were those who, in addition to the completion of two years of college, had a year of law at another approved law school. Special students were admitted in exceptional cases. These were students who could not meet the educational requirements of the regular students and were required to attend law school for three years. Unclassified students were placed in the afternoon/evening program and were required to take a reduced load of courses; they remained in the law school for up to six years.[164] Houston's new admission requirements may have been too ambitious, because the supply of black applicants did not match the law school's demands. To keep its doors open, the law school was forced to admit more special and unclassified students; this policy troubled Houston because such practices appeared to be instituted solely for purposes of generating revenue.[165]

Dean Houston, with his eye on the accreditation requirements of the American Bar Association and the Association of American Law Schools, and mindful of the expectations of President Mordecai W. Johnson, prepared to close the evening law program and to discontinue the special and unclassified admissions categories.[166] Public outrage followed. Even the white press opposed Houston's changes,[167] but Houston held firm. By 1930, Howard University School of Law had "shifted from the part-time or 'mixed' groups [to] exclusively full-time work."[168] This meant that the law school no longer operated a part-time evening program.

In 1930 the Committee on Legal Education recommended and the American Bar Association approved and elected the Howard University School of Law to membership.[169] The following year, the Association of American Law Schools also reviewed Howard's application for admission and determined that it was "duly qualified for membership."[170] The Howard University School of Law became the sixty-ninth school admitted to the Association of American Law Schools.[171]

With accreditation won, Dean Houston turned his attention to the particular qualitative mission of the law school. Dean Houston believed that the law school should be a rigorous training ground for the future leaders of black and white America.[172] The mission, as Houston saw it, was clear:

If a Negro law school is to make its full contribution to the social system it must train its students and send them [into situations to apply pressure]. This does not necessarily mean a different course of instruction from that in other standard law schools. But it does mean a difference in emphasis with more concentration on the subjects having direct application to the economics, political and social problems of the Negro.[173]

For Houston, it was not enough that the law faculty warn students about hostile juries and race bias against black lawyers. What was needed was an emphasis[174] on the methodology hidden in the juris- prudence so that Howard University law graduates could render ser- vice to "the race as an interpreter" of the law and thereby help to gain their full citizenship by whatever legal means necessary.[175]

Charles Houston resigned from the resident vice-deanship at How- ard in 1935 to assume responsibility for national civil rights planning as special counsel to the NAACP. Although Houston had been at the law school for only eleven years—five years as a professor and six as resident vice-dean—he had transformed the school from a part-time to a full-time law school, established a minimum number of teachers devoted to full-time instruction and research, reduced the outside employment of students (allowing for more time spent in the library), raised admissions standards above the high school level, began efforts to secure a separate building to house the law library, and initiated the first discussions about the need for a new law school building. Houston opened the third phase of the law school's history; his departure chal- lenged his successors to fully implement his program.[176]

Professor William Edwin Taylor succeeded Houston as acting dean. Taylor, a 1923 graduate with honors of the University of Iowa School of Law, had joined the law faculty in 1929. Dean Taylor made great efforts to recruit blacks to the law school from black colleges. Recogniz- ing that other, less expensive and nonaccredited black law schools were wooing students with college training, Taylor's pitch was that "it [was] difficult if not impossible to prepare for a legal career except in ac- credited law schools."[177] In 1939, there were eighty-eight accredited law schools in the nation, thirty-four of which did not admit blacks. The dual accreditation of Howard University's law school by the ABA and AALS and its progressive black university environment made the law school an attractive choice for many. Dean Taylor, recognizing Hous- ton's contributions to the law school, reminded the community that "the present high rating of Howard University School of Law . . . is not the result of an accident. . . . It is the result of a long and eventful history."[178] It is unclear why Taylor was not made the permanent law dean. Perhaps he saw a greater challenge in becoming the first dean at the newly formed black Lincoln University Law School at Jefferson,

Missouri, a product of *Missouri ex rel. Gaines v. Canada.*[179] (This decision forced Missouri to establish a separate but equal law school, or to admit black law students to the all-white University of Missouri School of Law.)

Perhaps the most significant development during Taylor's years as acting dean was the addition of James Madison Nabrit, Jr., to the law faculty. Nabrit, an honors graduate of Northwestern University's law school, had extensive experience with civil rights litigation in Texas, and joined the law faculty in 1936. Professor Nabrit immediately urged the faculty to adopt "the first course in Civil Rights in an American Law School,"[180] which was instituted in 1937. Professor Nabrit, who compiled the course materials, stated that the purpose of the course was, first, "to discover what the law was in respect to minorities in this area of civil rights; second, to develop techniques for raising constitutional questions in respect to disabilities affecting minorities . . . and third, to separate those disabilities for which legislative action would be required for their elimination."[181] The civil rights course at Howard University School of Law, established by a black law teacher and taught to black law students, made the law school the center of modern civil rights methodology, just as Charles Hamilton Houston had envisioned.

William Henry Hastie, judge of the United States District Court of the Virgin Islands, succeeded Acting Dean Taylor on July 1, 1939,[182] two months before the outbreak of World War II. Hastie, a former editor of the *Harvard Law Review* and a 1930 graduate of Harvard University's law school,[183] was no stranger to Howard University School of Law. After his graduation from law school, he joined the Howard law faculty as an instructor. Promoted to lecturer in 1931, he taught part-time at Howard and worked on his Doctor of Juridical Science (S.J.D.) degree at Harvard, which he earned in 1933.[184] In November of 1933, Harold L. Ickes appointed Hastie assistant solicitor of the Department of Interior. There he became an expert on the affairs of the Virgin Islands. This expertise, and the influence of some local leaders in the Virgin Islands, made Hastie President Roosevelt's choice to fill the U.S. District Court vacancy there, a first at the federal level for any black lawyer in America.[185] Hastie served with distinction on the United States District Court from March 24, 1937[186] until he was appointed dean of Howard University's law school.

When Hastie assumed the deanship, he discovered that the number of applicants to the law school was about the same as when he had joined the faculty in 1930. He also discovered that "not many more than two hundred had completed such pre-legal . . . eduation as is now the minimum standards in most parts of the country."[187] In fact, "not more than 15 Negroes with university school training are [annually] entering the practice of law" in the United States, despite the "need for more competent Negro lawyers."[188] In 1939, a total of 1,350 black lawyers served a black population of 13,000,000 people, "a ratio of one [black] lawyer to 10,000 potential clients."[189] Dean Hastie, estimating a critical need to interest black undergraduates in the study of law, personally visited black colleges in the South to recruit talented black students to Howard University.[190]

Dean Houston's groundwork had begun to take hold when Hastie became dean. All but two members of the entering class in the fall of 1939 had earned bachelor's degrees, even though only two years of college satisfied the admissions requirements at the law school.[191] Howard drew law students from at least twenty-seven states and thirty-four undergraduate institutions, making it undisputably a national law school. Sixty percent of Howard University's law students came from historically black colleges located in the South.[192] When Dean Hastie assumed the leadership of the law school, the total enrollment was sixty-one students, down by ten students from the previous year.[193] But Dean Hastie won the admiration and respect of the students and the faculty, who admired "his intellect and marvelous teaching ability."[194]

In 1939, the faculty's teaching experience was noteworthy. It ranged from two years to more than ten years of experience. At no time previously had the law school "had a faculty with so much full-time law-teaching experience."[195] Dean Hastie encouraged two *magna cum laude* graduates of the class of 1939 to join the law faculty. The appointments of Spottswood William Robinson III and James Aaron Washington, Jr., as part-time law instructors were criticized by some because of their inexperience.[196] Yet later both would become deans of Howard's law school.[197] As these new instructors settled in, Professor Bernard Samuel Jefferson, who had published a lead article in the *Boston Law Review* in 1939[198] (likely the first ever by a black professor), took leave from the faculty to work on his S.J.D. degree at Harvard's law school which he completed in 1943.[199] In 1944 Professor Jefferson would become the first black lawyer to publish lead articles in the *Harvard Law Review* and the *Columbia Law Review*.[200] William Robert Ming, Jr., a former member of the Howard University law faculty, would become the first black to publish a lead article in the *University of Chicago Law Review*. He had been appointed to the University of Chicago Law School faculty in 1947.[201]

Besides the important and exciting scholarship by the faculty, Dean Hastie helped to establish a "methodology by which a large volume of civil rights litigation was conducted out of the nexus of the Howard Law School [by] key black [faculty] at the law school . . . [Together Hastie and the faculty] joined ranks to mold legal arguments which would have lasting effect on American law."[202] He also enhanced the academic offerings in the law school with the introduction of courses in administrative law, code pleading, and trial practice.

The success of Dean Hastie's term at Howard's law school, which ended in 1946, was not his alone. Substantial credit for the progress made at the law school between September 1941 and June 1943 was due to the work of Leon Andrew Ransom, a brilliant, hard-working, and dedicated professor who served as acting dean when Dean Hastie was appointed as civilian aide to the Secretary of War. Dean Hastie's appointment came just thirteen months after he took office as dean. He was granted leave to accept what was considered by the university to be an important national post. The nation was at war, racism in the South was rampant, and a black man of Hastie's stature was needed to assure black Americans that a segregated army would treat black soldiers with respect. Dean Hastie soon became a spokesman for the equal treatment of black soldiers: "There can be no excuse for conduct by Americans which subject any member of his Army to humiliation, abuse, or treatment as a despised inferior."[203]

Acting Dean Leon Andrew Ransom, who had joined the law faculty in 1930, was highly regarded by students, faculty, alumni, and the civil rights bar. They all knew that Ransom, a 1927 honors graduate of Ohio State University's law school who had earned his Doctor of Juridical Science degree at Harvard Law School in 1935,[204] was one of the forces behind every major civil rights fight being waged in the South.[205] Ransom had an almost impossible task as acting dean. He had to reverse a decline in enrollment at the law school, which led him south to recruit students at historically black colleges, and to manage a law school whose financial resources were limited. In addition, the absence of Dean Hastie intensified Ransom's teaching load when, due to declining enrollment, the part-time faculty was eliminated.[206] The school's morale suffered even more when the board of trustees extended Dean Hastie's leave of absence for another year. However, Ransom, with inexhaustible energy and commitment to the law school, held on until 1943, when Dean Hastie resigned from the War Department, citing its discrimination against black servicemen, and returned to the law school.[207]

During the war years, enrollment at the 110 approved law schools in the nation "dropped from 28,174 in 1938 to 5,686 in 1943, or 79.8 percent. During the same period, the enrollment at Howard University's law school dropped from 71 to 33, or 53.5 percent."[208] By the fall of 1943, the total enrollment "in the eighty-one active accredited schools was 3,663, so that the average enrollment was only forty-five students." Howard stood thirty-fifth in enrollment among the eighty-one schools.[209] Acting Dean Ransom miraculously held the law school together by reopening the evening law division in 1942.[210] While such an action seemed risky, given the fact that the AALS had approved Howard's accreditation in 1931 on the condition that the evening division would close, ultimately the risk was minimal since most law schools had sought waivers from the AALS to reduce their admissions standards and reopen night programs during the war years.[211]

When Dean Hastie opened the fall term of the law school in 1943, he could boast that enrollment had increased by twenty students and that Howard was "one of the larger American law schools during the war period."[212] However, the war years had taken a toll on the law faculty and a physical toll on Professor Ransom. The professors were teaching an average of four courses in both the day and evening divisions. Even Dean Hastie was forced to teach ten semester hours in addition to his general decanal administrative duties during the 1943–44 school year.[213]

The year 1944 had a dual significance for black American lawyers, because it marked both the seventy-fifth anniversary of Howard University School of Law and the centennial anniversary of the admission of Macon Bolling Allen, the first black lawyer, into the legal profession. In addition to these benchmarks, between 1871 and 1944 the law school had graduated more than one thousand students, many of whom had achieved great distinction, as Dean Langston and Professor Riddle had forecasted.[214]

In addition to being the first American law school to open its doors with both a black dean and a white professor, Howard University's law school was the first to declare a nondiscriminatory policy in 1869.[215] White male and female students were admitted to Howard University from its inception. By 1870, white students were enrolled in the law school.[216] Despite the announced nondiscrimination policy, one black woman and one white woman in 1869 alleged that they were denied admission to the law school on the basis of their sex.[217] Nevertheless, at least seven women, believed to be white, who were barred from attending white law schools were graduated between 1882 and 1904: Emma M. Gillett (1882), Ruth G. D. Havens (1882), Eliza A. Chambers (1886), Marie A. D. Madre (1897), Cynthia E. Cleveland (1899), Clare Greacen (1899), and Evva B. Heath (1904).[218] Although not much is known about the roles these women played in American law, it is known that in 1898 Emma M. Gillett co-founded the Washington College of Law for Women, now known as the American University School of Law. She holds the dual distinction of becoming the first woman graduated from a law school to enter legal education and to become a dean of a law school.[219]

Mary Ann Shadd Carey, a black woman, claimed that she was admitted to Howard University's first law class in 1869; if her contention is true, this makes her and Lemma Barkaloo, who entered Washington University's law school in Missouri in the same year, the first women admitted to an American law school.[220] However, the honor of being the first black woman to receive a law degree and the first to be admitted to the bar in the nation belongs to Charlotte E. Ray, who was graduated from Howard University School of Law in 1872. She became the first black woman admitted to the bar of the District of Columbia.[221] Only three other white women had been graduated from a law school prior to Ray.[222]

At least thirty-five women (seven white, twenty-eight black) were graduated from Howard University's law school between 1896 and 1944: eight women between 1869 and 1900, twenty between 1901 and 1930, and seven between 1931 and 1944. Although white women gravitated to Howard University to study law prior to 1900, thereafter they also applied to white law schools as opportunities for white women widened.[223] White women law students found a home at Howard University because it never adopted the majority view "that women did not possess a 'legal mind.' "[224]

During the 1920s, the number of black women increased enough at Howard University's law school that they formed Epsilon Sigma Iota, the first black legal sorority in the world.[225] The sorority assisted in placing its members in law firms and organized social activities for women law students and graduates.[226] Another legal sorority, Gamma Delta Epsilon, was formed in 1937 at the Robert H. Terrell Law School to forge bonds among all black women lawyers.[227] Ollie May Cooper, a 1921 Howard University law graduate, became a leader in both legal sororities and, because she remained at Howard's law school as secretary to the dean, she became an important force behind them on campus. Virtually all women students joined the legal sororities. As secretary to the law dean of Howard University and as the second black woman to teach law in the nation, "Dean Cooper," as she was affectionately called, became a force for increasing the opportunities of black women in the legal profession.[228]

While there was progress at Howard University's law school in women's advancement into the legal profession, Pauli Murray (who in 1944 was elected as the first woman senior class president in the seventy-five-year history of the school) reports that women students were ridiculed by some professors.[229] Yet, Murray's graduation from law school in 1944 was an important symbol to her "because in 1844, 100 years ago, my grandmother, with whom I lived as a small child, was born a slave. . . . The world can be turned upside down in a century."[230]

The identification of white males and other races and nationalities attending Howard University's law school has proved to be difficult. Several white males are known to have graduated from the law school.[231] George Wesley Atkinson, an 1874 white Howard law graduate, was elected governor of West Virginia in 1897, served in Congress, and became a judge on the United States Court of Claims.[232] The first law degree conferred upon a person of Asian descent was awarded to Tamatsu Fuwa, of Kurami, Japan, in 1898, and at least seven graduates from Puerto Rico and others believed to be Hispanic were graduated from Howard University's law school between 1903 and 1927. Howard awarded law degrees to Seabron F. Hall, of Liberia, and Fred E. Ebito, of Nigeria, in 1923 and 1927, respectively.[233]

At the close of the first one hundred years of black lawyers in America, Howard University School of Law had established itself as the legal capstone for all races and women in the nation,[234] but the "critical shortage of Negro lawyers throughout the country" remained.[235]

Between 1870 and 1880, five other black law schools were founded. Of these five law schools, only one would survive beyond the Reconstruction era. Straight University College of Law and Lincoln University School of Law were established in 1870.[236] Straight University's law school was founded by the American Missionary Association, and it graduated its first law class in 1876.[237] Like Howard University's law school, Straight operated on an interracial basis from its inception.[238] Its graduates were routinely admitted to the Louisiana Supreme Court. The school remained interracial until 1886, when white students bypassed Straight University to attend Tulane University's law school.[239] Complying with the state's Jim Crow laws, "Tulane . . . refused to admit blacks to any of its schools."[240] Straight University's law school "closed in 1887 without explanation," after graduating a number of black students, including Louis A. Martinet, its "first Negro graduate of distinction."[241]

In 1870, the Board of Trustees of Lincoln University established a law school in Oxford and West Chester, Pennsylvania, but the "school did not survive the panic of 1873."[242] No students were graduated from the school, according to university officials.[243] After the school closed, the students transferred to other law schools or studied law with a judge or in a lawyer's office. One such student, Louis Kossuth Atwood, was admitted to the Mississippi bar at Jackson in 1877. Another student, Archibald Henry Grimké, enrolled at Harvard University's law school and received his law degree in 1874.[244]

Wilberforce University, located near Xenia (Greene County), Ohio, opened a law department in 1872.[245] The department was administrated by Roswell F. Howard and John Little, both listed in the university's catalogue as professors of law.[246] Several lawyers served as honorary members of the Board of Trustees of the University, and two were distinguished and nationally recognized black lawyers: Judge Jonathan Jasper Wright and Congressman Robert Brown Elliott. Both men were from South Carolina. Judge Wright was the first black lawyer to serve on a state supreme court (in South Carolina) and Robert B. Elliott, newly elected to the United States Congress, was the first black to represent South Carolina there.[247] Although the law department operated for thirteen years, Wilberforce conferred no law degrees on the three students "put upon the study of law."[248]

Shaw University (now Rust University), located in Holly Springs, Mississippi, was the first black law school in the South to commence a three-year program, in 1878.[249] It was also the first law school in the state of Mississippi to train blacks in the law, as they were barred from attending the University of Mississippi's law school. The Shaw University program closed in 1880 because few students applied, and perhaps because those interested in the law did not believe that a formal education was required, given the liberal certification requirements for lawyers set out by the state at that time.[250]

Central Tennessee College opened the second black law school in the South in 1879, thirteen years after the college was chartered.[251] John Lawrence, a "leading Nashville lawyer," was engaged to develop the law school. Indeed, it appears that Lawrence, who became the law school's first dean, provided all or most of the instruction.[252] Only a few students applied to the law school when it opened, even though the tuition was thirty dollars a term and no college degree was required.[253] Central Tennessee College graduated Joseph H. Dismukes, its first law graduate, in 1883.[254] By 1900, approximately twenty-five black students had been graduated from Central and were "fairly well received by the white lawyers."[255]

Central Tennessee College's law school was quite competitive. Indeed, it was an alternative to Howard's and Straight University's law schools because of its quality faculty, its comparable curriculum,[256] and its convenient location in Nashville, Tennessee.[257] Classes met daily at Central. Its students were required to attend the local courts in Nashville to observe "some important suit in progress, or some instructive debate in the State Legislature, which [met] in this city."[258] The law school did not have a law library. It depended on donations to supplement the readily available course books which could "be bought in the city" either new or "second-hand at reduced prices."[259] The law school's creed required its students to work hard if they were to succeed:

The young men who enter this profession must be well prepared to meet their antagonist in trials, where prejudice is so strong against the color line as it is in most parts of the United States. The crowded condition of the profession, and the ease with which white lawyers can be retained . . . make it quite problematical whether the young colored lawyer may not starve. . . . The [Central Tennessee College Law] department . . . has already proved that the well educated colored attorney, who is wise in his department toward all, and industrious in his preparation can succeed.[260]

Central Tennessee College's first graduate, Joseph H. Dismukes, joined the faculty after he was graduated from the law school and became Tennessee's first black law professor[261] in 1883. George T. Robinson, an 1887 graduate, and J. W. Grant, an 1890 graduate, also joined Central law's faculty. In 1895, J. W. Grant became Central's law dean.[262] Perhaps Central's most significant contribution to American law is that America's fourth black woman lawyer, Lutie A. Lytle, was graduated from the law school in 1897; she joined Central's law faculty, becoming the first black female lawyer in the South and the first female law professor of a chartered law school in the world.[263] In 1900, Central Tennessee College was succeeded by Walden University, which continued the law school until 1921, the year the university closed.[264]

Between 1881 and 1896, five black law schools were established. All but one of these law schools were closed by 1914. In 1881, Allen University, located in Columbia, South Carolina, opened a law department staffed solely by black instructors.[265] David Augustus Straker, an 1871 Howard University law graduate, was appointed its first dean and professor of common law. Dean Straker taught most of the courses and, because of his work, four law graduates were admitted to the South Carolina bar in 1882, as were others in 1884 and 1886.[266] During the first commencement exercise, Dean Straker told the graduates why he could not fail to educate them as lawyers:

In October, 1882, the Law Department of Allen University was opened. I was chosen by the trustees, Dean and Law Professor in this department. I was not wanting in difficulty of my ability to perform so herculean a task in which was involved so great responsibilities. My duty was to educate in the law, colored youths of a race declared to be inferior in capacity with all others. If I failed I certified to both you and your incapacity. My responsibility then was, the maintenance of an entire race's fitness and capacity.[267]

A law degree could be earned at Allen University in one-and-a-half years. Allen University law graduates were so well prepared that "the [South] Carolina Supreme Court . . . issued a special commendation" to them.[268] Besides Dean Straker, Robert Adger Stewart appears to be the only other full-time law instructor during the school's early years.

Professor Stewart joined the faculty in 1884, the year he was graduated from the law department. After Dean Straker left the school, Stewart was offered the deanship but refused to accept the position because of the overwhelming racial prejudice in South Carolina, a condition that no doubt influenced his decision to leave the state as well.[269] The law school closed in 1898 after graduating a total of twenty-five students.[270]

In 1888, Shaw University, located in Raleigh, North Carolina, opened a law department to provide "good legal help to colored people who . . . were taken advantage of."[271] Shaw University's first and only law graduate in 1890 was Edward Austin Johnson. Two years later, Johnson was appointed to the faculty and then became dean and professor of legal forms, a position he held for several years. While serving as dean, Johnson also held the post of assistant United States District Attorney in the Eastern District of North Carolina.[272] The full curriculum offerings at Shaw are unknown, but it was the only black law school that had a course in legal shorthand. The course was offered on the premise that such a skill would broaden the opportunities for a black lawyer to work in a "legal firm" in a clerical position or "as an office assistant," should discrimination impede his or her ability to practice law.[273]

Shaw University graduated fifty-seven law students before it closed in 1916.[274] Many of these graduates made significant contributions in the field of law. Edward A. Johnson went to New York and became the first black elected to the New York General Assembly in 1917.[275] James Youman Eaton, an 1894 graduate, was elected by the Vance County Board of Commissions in North Carolina to the post of county attorney. He was subsequently elected in 1898 to the North Carolina State Senate, where he fought against the disfranchisement of black voters. He practiced law in North Carolina for more than twenty-five years.[276] Shaw University graduated fifty-four law students between 1891 and 1914.[277]

In 1875, Nathaniel R. Harper, one of the first black lawyers admitted to the Kentucky bar, opened the Harper Law School in Louisville, Kentucky. Harper trained black lawyers in his privately operated law school until 1890, the year Simmons University opened a law department in the same city.[278] One of Simmons's most distinguished deans was Albert S. White, an 1892 graduate of Howard University's law school.[279] Around 1910, the law department was renamed Central Law School and apparently offered not only a bachelor of laws degree but also a master of laws degree.[280] Central Law School was and remained affiliated with the black Simmons University until 1931. In 1930, there were several signs that the law school may have been in trouble. It reduced its tuition by thirty dollars, its enrollment dwindled to fifteen students,[281] and it was in all likelihood unable to meet the newly imposed standards of the American Bar Association.

In 1896, Morris Brown College, located in Atlanta, Georgia, opened a law department.[282] Perhaps James M. Henderson, who is said to have graduated from the Detroit College of Law and who became the second president of Morris Brown College in 1896, had something to do with establishing the law department.[283] A student could enter the law department at Morris Brown College in his third year at the college. The course of training was three years.[284] Whether any students finished the law program at Morris Brown College is unknown. The law department closed in 1907.[285]

Between 1900 and 1939, eight black law schools were established. By the end of 1944, only two of these law schools remained opened. Lane College of Law was opened in Jackson, Tennessee, in 1900. Not much is known about the law school, except that its lifespan was of short duration. It closed in 1903.[286]

In 1915, the John Mercer Langston School of Law was established in Washington, D.C., by Laudros Melendez King, an 1897 graduate of Howard University's law school. King served as the school's first dean.[287] The law school was actually a department of the Frederick Theodore Frelinghuysen University, headed by Anna J. Cooper.[288] The university and presumably the law school were founded on "the concept that a private institution was needed to educate those students who could not measure up to the higher educational standards required by Howard University."[289] The law school was named after John Mercer Langston, the first black congressman from Virginia and the founding dean of Howard University's law school. The law school did not have permanent quarters when it was opened. Classes were held three evenings a week in the law offices of Zeph P. Moore, one of the part-time black instructors.[290] Fifty students were enrolled in the law school in 1915 and many of these and subsequent admittees were graduated from Freylinghuysen University's John Mercer Langston Law School.[291]

In 1927, the John Mercer Langston Law School and Freylinghuysen University fell on hard times after Congress placed control over education in the hands of the District of Columbia. Like Howard University, John Mercer Langston, a two-year law school, was forced to change its program to three years. It too established a master of laws degree which was awarded after completion of the third year.[292]

After Dean King died, George A. Parker succeeded him as dean. Dean Parker recognized that the all-white District of Columbia School Board might close the university and the law school. He sought to obtain accreditation from the American Bar Association and the American Association of Law Schools to bypass the local standards of the District of Columbia's School Board. This attempt proved futile. In the meantime, "Congress exempted . . . Washington College of Law—primarily for white women—and Southeastern—the YMCA Law School, the least elite of the white schools—from this control."[293] The efforts by Dean Parker to obtain accreditation appear to have been opposed by Frelinghuysen University president Anna J. Cooper. Because of the actions of Congress and the District of Columbia government, and because of run-ins with President Cooper, Dean Parker resigned in 1927. The John Mercer Langston Law School closed shortly after Dean Parker's resignation.[294]

The faculty of John Mercer Langston Law School, mostly composed of Howard University Law School graduates, resigned with Dean Parker. Discussions among the law faculty ensued, and in 1931 seven of the black faculty of the John Mercer Langston Law School founded the Robert H. Terrell Law School, named after one of the first black judges in the District of Columbia.[295] George A. Parker was elected dean. Eighteen students enrolled in the Terrell Law School evening program, which graduated its first student, Leroy Taylor, in June 1934.[296] Taylor subsequently joined the law faculty.[297] In 1935, five Terrell Law School students founded and incorporated Sigma Delta Tau, the first legal fraternity under black control.[298]

The law faculty of Terrell were all respected in the District of Columbia, and the law school was in direct competition with Howard University School of Law. Terrell's reputation was further enhanced because of Arthur Wergs Mitchell, the first black Democrat elected to Congress, who served as a member of the school's board of trustees.[299] Terrell's graduates passed the District of Columbia's bar examination in record numbers.[300]

Like Howard University School of Law, Terrell's law school did not exclude women as students or as members of its faculty.[301] Indeed, the third black woman to teach law in the United States, Helen Elsie Austin, a 1939 graduate of the University of Cincinnati Law School, was appointed to the Robert H. Terrell Law School faculty in 1941.[302] The Terrell Law School continued in existence under the leadership of Dean Parker until it closed in 1945, reportedly graduating some six hundred students.[303]

In 1922 Virginia Union University, located in Richmond, Virginia, opened an evening law school with fourteen students. It was staffed by two black professors: Peter J. Henry, a 1907 graduate of Howard University's law school, and Clarence McDonald Maloney, a 1913 graduate of Dalhousie University Law Department.[304] The law school was opened following "a request from the citizens in Richmond for classes in law."[305] Professor Maloney left Virginia Union's law school in 1925, perhaps involuntarily, because he criticized the "white president of Hampton Institute . . . for telling blacks to be silent on race questions."[306]

In the meantime, Virginia Union's law school continued to enroll black students at an annual fee of $118.50.[307] By 1927, the law faculty had grown to four black instructors: Peter J. Henry, who taught contracts, insurance, partnership and bills, and notes; J. C. Robertson, a graduate of Shaw University law department, who taught legal ethics, constitutional law, and conflicts of law, and was judge of the moot court; Harry M. Green, a 1922 graduate of Howard University's law school, who taught bailments and carriers, damages, banks and banking trusts; and Cyrenius August McKenzie, who read law in New York City and Richmond, and who taught civil procedure, torts, and criminal law.[308] Virginia Union's law department closed in 1931, having graduated only one class of seven students in 1927.[309]

In 1932, Z. Alexander Looby founded the Kent College of Law, located in Nashville, Tennessee,[310] and operated with the approval of the American Bar Association until it closed in 1941. The law school operated five evenings a week under the leadership of Dean Lobby and two law instructors who were both Howard University law graduates.[311] The law school's strength was based on the credentials and legal training of Dean Looby, who earned his Doctor of Juridical Science degree at New York University School of Law in 1925. Kent offered a comprehensive curriculum.[312] Dean Looby, one of the few black lawyers in the South, was committed to keeping the law school open because of the lack of opportunity "for a Negro to get legal training."[313] The ABA was in agreement, but concluded that "it would be far better if it could be carried on under the auspices of [a black college,] such as Fisk University," where the facilities and support might be found to afford a better chance "for a Negro who aspires to be a lawyer."[314] The Fisk University and Kent Law School connection never crystallized. When the Kent College of Law closed in 1914, it had educated only a handful of black students.[315]

Only one other black law school is known to have operated in Tennessee. In 1932, the Keyston College of Technology School of Law opened in Memphis, Tennessee, with an enrollment of twenty-four students. It closed the following year.[316]

In 1939, following the United States Supreme Court's decision in *Missouri ex rel. Gaines v. Canada*,[317] state schools were required to provide equal facilities to train black lawyers if they were excluded from white schools. The decision forced states such as Missouri and North Carolina to establish and fund black law schools. Missouri became the first state to establish a black law school,[318] the Lincoln University School of Law, in Jefferson City, Missouri.[319] The law school consisted of an "all-Negro faculty . . . of three full-time instructors," one part-time instructor, and a small clerical staff.[320] William Edwin Taylor, who was the acting dean of Howard University's law school, became Lincoln University's first law dean.[321]

Lincoln University (Missouri) opened its law school with thirty-four students in 1939 and continued to admit the same number of students until 1943, when it closed temporarily during World War II "for lack of 'properly accredited' students," to reopen the following year.[322] By 1944, the year that Scovel Richardson, a graduate of Howard University's law school, became dean,[323] approximately ten students had been graduated from the law school and nine of these students had been admitted to the Missouri bar.[324] The law school remained open for several years.

North Carolina Central School of Law, located in Durham, North Carolina, was the second public law school to open as a result of the *Gaines* decision. In 1939, the North Carolina General Assembly authorized the creation of a law school at North Carolina Central University, a black state-supported university.[325] The "first efforts to set up a Negro law school at North Carolina College . . . ended in failure"[326] due to the dearth of student enrollment. Since blacks were barred from attending any of the state's public or private law schools, efforts were renewed to create a black law school at North Carolina Central.[327] In 1940, North Carolina Central's law school reopened under the leadership of a white law dean, M. T. Van Hecke, who was also the dean of North Carolina University's law school. Dean Hecke assembled a white law faculty to operate the school, which was soon turned over to Dr. Albert L. Turner, the law school's first black dean in 1942.[328]

Summary

Blacks, like their white counterparts, entered the legal profession by teaching themselves the law, by working in the judicial system, through on-the-job training, through observation, and by working under the tutelage of lawyers or judges.

In 1850, John Mercer Langston became the first known black to apply to and be denied entry to a law school, though he could have been admitted if he, a light-skinned man, had denied his black heritage. As this chapter and others in this book reveal, law was the last profession blacks entered. Many entered through the doors of American law schools; George Lewis Ruffin, for example, holds the dual distinction of being the first black to be graduated from Harvard

University School of Law (in 1869) and from any university-affiliated law school in the nation.

Private law schools, such as those at Yale and Columbia universities, opened their doors to a few black students early on, as did public universities such as South Carolina University, which graduated its first black law students during Reconstruction, in the 1870s. After the universities of Michigan and Iowa graduated their first black students in law in 1877 and 1879 respectively, other state universities also slowly opened their law schools to blacks.

Black Americans' early experiences in white law schools were often difficult. They faced racism and fought against it, often with the support of key faculty members and deans. In some cases, white professors may have tested the racism of the white legal establishment by recommending black students to major law firms, most of whom were rejected because of their race.

The black law students broke ground in white law schools and excelled despite doubts by some about their abilities to compete. However, compete they did, and a black woman, Clara Burrill Bruce, was elected editor-in-chief of the *Boston University Law Review* in 1925 and was graduated with honors. Other black students graded on other law reviews at Iowa, Yale, Harvard, Michigan, and the University of Chicago in the 1920s and 1930s, and were admitted to the Order of the Coif, an academic honor society.

But the black law schools would be the source of the largest numbers of black law graduates in the nation between 1871 and 1944, particularly Howard University's law school (founded in 1869). Howard University's law school, in part, was founded to direct the political life of black people, though the school was racially integrated from its inception. It was the first American law school to open its doors to an integrated faculty, to admit women of all races, and to graduate a black woman, and it was one of the first law schools to confer a master of laws degree on a white woman graduate. During Reconstruction, white women gravitated to Howard University's law school because the school never doubted the capacity or the appropriateness of women in law. White males also attended Howard University's law school during and after the Reconstruction era. One of Howard University's law graduates, George Wesley Atkinson, became the tenth governor of West Virginia in 1897.

Howard University School of Law became a stable and important institution due in part to its ability to attract competent instructors, black and white, and because it offered a curriculum similar to that of the white law schools. Its graduates, mostly poor and from the rural South, were admitted for years with little more than high school educations. However, the law school, using traditional and exceptional methods of instruction (and both students and faculty were aware that their role, indeed, their obligation was to emancipate their people) defied the odds by succeeding, turning the law inside out to emancipate blacks from racist laws.

Howard University School of Law was one of nineteenth black law schools formed between 1869 and 1939. The importance of these black law schools to legal education is inestimable. They produced a cadre of law professors who assumed the role of legal interpreters for black people. It is unfortunate that much of the scholarship of these black and white professors has been lost.

Many of the black law schools closed before 1945, but not before they had made a gallant effort to keep their tuition down, to pay their faculties a decent salary, and to satisfy the standards established by the American Bar Association and the Association of American Law Schools, the accrediting agencies. Prior to their demise, the black law schools, mostly located in the South, produced black men and women who made and influenced history. Among them was Central Tennessee College of Law's Lutie A. Lytle, an 1897 law graduate who joined Central's faculty in the same year. Professor Lytle became the first woman law professor in American law at a chartered law school.

The history of blacks in legal education in both white and black law schools and those trained in various Inns of Court in London are detailed in the pages that follow.

NOTES

1. *Law in American History* 406, n.5 (D. Fleming and B. Bailyn eds. 1971). Two recently published books have short passages on blacks in legal education, but they do not cover the subject in detail: R. Stevens, *Law School: Legal Education in America from the 1850s to the 1980s* 317 (1983); R. L. Abel, *American Lawyers* 391 (1989). But see, Tollett, "Black Lawyers, Their Education, and the Black Community," 17 *How. L.J.* 326, 328 (1972).

2. George Marion Johnson, "Legal Profession," in *The Integrating of the Negro into American Society* 90 (E. F. Frazier ed. 1951).

3. D. K. Weisberg, *Women and the Law* 231 (1982).

4. *Law in American History* 419 (D. Fleming and B. Bailyn eds. 1971).

5. W. T. Davis, Vol. II *Bench and Bar of Massachusetts* 565 (1895).

6. Brown, "The Genesis of the Negro Lawyer in New England (Part II)," 22 *The Negro History Bulletin* 171, 176 (May 1959).

7. J. M. Langston, *From the Virginia Plantation to the National Capitol* 109 (1894).

8. *Id.* at 106.

9. *Id.* at 107–8.

10. *Id.* at 108.

11. *Ibid.*

12. *Id.* at 110. Professor Timothy Walker was a law teacher at the University of Cincinnati, which was formed in 1834. He was the "guiding spirit of the law school," but a spirit that excluded Langston from its reach. For more on Walker, see Carrington, "Teaching Law in the Antebellum Northwest," 23 *U. of Toledo L. Rev.* 3, 21 (1991); Carrington, "Butterfly Effects: The Possibilities of Law Teaching in a Democracy," 41 *Duke L. J.* 741, 796 (1992).

13. *Id.* at 122 (*From the Virginia Plantation to the National Capitol*).

14. *Ibid.*

15. *Id.* at 123.

16. W. Cheek and A. L. Cheek, *John Mercer Langston and the Fight for Black Freedom* 227 (1989).

17. Mollison, "Negro Lawyers in Mississippi," 15 *J. of Negro History* 38, 49 (1930).

18. "$20,000 Bequeathed to Washington Lawyer," *The New York Age*, Jan. 7, 1915.

19. McDowell, "From Twain, A Letter on Debt to Blacks," *Washington Post*, March 14, 1985, at 1, col. 1.

20. *16th Annual Catalogue, Law School of Columbia College, 1873–1874*, at 28 (1874).

21. Lukingbeal, "Cornell Law Students—Change and Continuity," *Cornell Law Forum* 33 (1988 Centennial Issue); *Law in American History* 444, n.10 (D. Fleming and B. Bailyn eds. 1971), for information about Yale.

22. *Pearson v. Murray*, 169 Md. 478, 486, 182 A. 590, 593 (1936).

23. *Law in American History* 427 (D. Fleming and B. Bailyn eds. 1971).

24. R. L. Abel, *American Lawyers* 99 (1989).

25. "The University of Detroit Law School," 12 *Univ. of Detroit L. J.* 6 (1948).

26. A. Z. Reed, *Training for the Public Profession of the Law* 152 (reprint, 1986), referring to the University of South Carolina as a "colored school." But see, J. S. Reynolds, *Reconstruction in South Carolina, 1865–1877*, at 234 (reprint, 1969): white students also were enrolled in the law school.

27. Brown, "The Initial Admission of Negro Students to the University of Michigan," 2 *The Michigan Quarterly Rev.* 233 (Autumn 1963); *General Catalogue of the University of Michigan, 1837–1911*, at 401 (I. N. Demmon ed. 1912), for information about Albert Burgess and Thomas Ralph Crisup.

28. Letter to author from Professor Gregory H. Williams, Iowa University College of Law, Nov. 9, 1988.

29. See *Wrighten v. Board of Trustees of University of South Carolina*, 72 F. Supp. 948 (E.D.S.C. 1947). In 1901 the Maryville College of Law "closed the one . . . loophole that permitted interracial education" in Tennessee. L. C. Lamon, *Black Tennesseans, 1900–1930*, at 4 (1977). Basically, blacks were shut out of white higher education in the law in the South prior to the 1950s. See George Marion Johnson, "Legal Education," in *The Integration of the Negro into American Society* 90, n.12 (E. F. Frazier ed. 1951).

30. Three rare letters written in 1896 that express the opinions of Professor Harvey Hurd (Northwestern University School of Law) and deans Thomas A. Moran (Chicago College of Law) and Marshall D. Ewell (Kent College of Law) about "colored men as [law] students and lawyers" shed light on the ability of blacks in law. Professor Hurd, who observed and taught "a considerable number of students, most of whom graduated," saw no differences between the performance of black students and white students. The two deans shared

essentially the same views. The letters were appended to Bradwell, "The Colored Bar of Chicago," 29 *Chi. Legal News*, Oct. 31, 1896, at 75, 78.

31. W. J. Leonard, *Black Lawyers* 110 (1977).

32. G. B. Robinson, "Robert Morris, John S. Rock, William H. Lewis, and Edgar P. Benjamin," *Occasional Paper No. 4*, Afro-American Studies Program, Boston University, 1975, at 57.

33. *Id.* at 69.

34. Alexander, "Blacks and the Law," 43 *N.Y.S.B.J.* 15 (Jan. 1971).

35. *Id.* at 16.

36. *Ibid.*

37. *Ibid.*

38. *Id.* at 16–17.

39. *Id.* at 17.

40. For information about Dean George W. Kirckwey, see J. Goebel, Jr., *A History of the School of Law Columbia University* 186, 211 (1955). Kirckwey served as dean from 1901 to 1910, but remained a member of the law faculty for a number of years after his deanship ended.

41. Brooks, "Edith Sampson Cracked Sex Bias to Win Success," *Chicago Defender*, Sept. 4, 1943.

42. *Ibid.*

43. *Who's Who in Colored America* 450 (G. J. Fleming and C. E. Burckel eds. 7th ed. 1950).

44. *Women at Harvard Law School, 1953–1987, Alumnae Directory*, foreword (N. Lictenstein and R. W. Tate eds. 1988).

45. P. Murray, *Song in a Weary Throat* 239 (1987); letter to Pauli Murray from Dorothy K. Clark, secretary, Graduate School of Arts and Science, Radcliffe College, June 21, 1944.

46. Letter from Pauli Murray to A. Calvert Smith (undated), likely sent to Harvard University following Murray's graduation from Howard's law school in June, 1944.

47. *Biographies of Graduates of the Yale Law School, 1824–1899*, at 404 (R. W. Tuttle ed. 1911).

48. "N. C. Has Only Deaf Mute Lawyer of Race in America," newspaper clipping source unidentified, July 31, 1926 (author's files). A few years later Ohio State University graduated, D. J. Murray, one of the first black blind lawyers in the nation. See G. R. Segal, *Blacks in the Law* 145 (1983).

49. Chambers, "At 95, He's a Model for All Lawyers," *National Law Journal*, April 24, 1989, at 13, col. 4.

50. *Pearson v. Murray*, 169 Md. 478, 481, 182 A. 590, 591 (1936). The University of Maryland Law School remained private until 1920, when it merged with the Maryland State College of Agriculture.

51. Elaine K. Freeman, "Harvey Johnson and Everett Waring—A Study of Leadership in the Baltimore Negro Community, 1880–1900," at 59 (M.A. Thesis, George Washington University, 1968), quoting J. Brackett, "Notes on the Progress of the Colored People of Maryland Since the War," 8 *Johns Hopkins University Studies in Historical and Political Science* 11–12 (1890). See also, Bogen, "The First Integration of the University of Maryland School of Law," 84 *Maryland Historical Magazine* 39, 41 (Spring 1989).

52. *Ibid.* ("Harvey Johnson and Everett Waring").

53. *Ibid.*, quoting R. Logan, *The Negro in American Life and Thought: The*

Nadir, 1877–1901, at 235 (1954); see also *The Marcus Garvey and UNIA Papers* 392 (R. Hill and B. Blair eds. 1987).

54. *Pearson v. Murray*, 169 Md. 478, 182 A. 590 (1936); M. V. Tushnet, *The NAACP's Legal Strategy Against Segregated Education, 1925–1950*, at 58 (1987).

55. Letter to author from Yvette M. Garcia, research assistant, New York University Archives, Dec. 11, 1990; *New York University General Alumni Catalogue* 113 (W. J. Maxwell ed. 1916).

56. Vol. 1 *Who's Who in Colored America* 156 (J. J. Boris ed. 1927). James Henry Hilton, also black, was graduated from New York University's law school in 1898; see *New York University General Alumni Catalogue* 134 (W. J. Maxwell ed. 1916). Neither Perry nor Hilton appeared to have practiced law for sustained periods. Perry became a successful writer of Hebrew books and acted as a correspondent for the French newspaper, *Courier des Etats-Unis*. At the time of Hilton's death in Richmond in 1916, he worked for the post office as a letter carrier. See "James Hilton Dead," *Chicago Defender*, Feb. 12, 1916.

57. Vol. 1 *Who's Who in Colored America* 156 (J. J. Boris ed. 1927).

58. G. M. Johnson, *The Making of a Liberal* 12–13 (1985), bound manuscript. Johnson reports that he "was invited to join two different study groups, but could not accept because of employment conflicts."

59. *Id.* at 14–16. Johnson reports that he preferred to do his doctoral work in civil rights, but feared that if he did so his academic achievement "might be discounted" and would interfere with his future efforts to move into "more lucrative litigation areas."

60. *Id.* at 17–19.

61. T. G. Barnes, *Hastings College of the Law: The First Century*, 169–70 (1973). In 1943, the year Thomas Berkley finished his studies at Hastings College of Law, he was the only black in the law school; he reports that "there hadn't been a black in the school for 20 years. And there was no place where you could stay on the campus." "Were Those the Days?" *The National Law Journal* S10, April 30, 1990.

62. *Detroit College of Law Announcement, 1891–1892*, at 5 (1892); *id.* at 24 (1896–1897).

63. "Harry Pace Finishes Law School," *Pittsburgh Courier*, July 15, 1933, at 2, col. 1.

64. "Yale Man," *Pittsburgh Courier*, Feb. 16, 1929.

65. Taylor, "Howard's Law School," *Howard University Alumni Journal* 13, Sept. 1935. The alumni journal incorrectly states that Taylor was "the first man elected to the Order of Coif," although he was surely the first black student at the University of Iowa Law School to win this honor. See G. R. Segal, *Blacks in the Law* 181–82 (1983), concerning Richard Jones.

66. "A Young Negro Soldier," *Chicago Defender*, June 18, 1927 (Ransom); interview by author with Theodore M. Berry, June 9, 1989 (McLeod); "Brilliant Career of Young OPA Lawyer Halted by War," *Chicago Defender*, Oct. 9, 1943, on Ming. Other law schools, such as New York University School of Law, permitted black students to join the Epsilon Tau Chi legal fraternity in 1937. See "Lawyer Butts Admitted to Appeals Court," *Norfolk Journal and Guide*, Oct. 9, 1937.

67. 5 *Boston L. Rev.* 242 and 6 *Boston L. Rev.* 36, 121, 183 (1925), listing her as head of the law review. Her actual title was "Chairman of the Review." Bruce's achievement was noted in *The Negro Year Book, 1931–1932*, at 177 (M. N. Work ed. 1931); see also, W. B. Gatewood, *Aristocrats of Color* 328 (1991).

68. 4 *Boston L. Rev.* 270 (1924), on circumstantial evidence; 5 *Boston L. Rev.*

116 (1925), on Bills and Notes; 5 *Boston L. Rev.* 263 (1925), on workman's compensation. See also, 5 *Boston L. Rev.* 41, 112, 186 (1925); Vol. 1 *Who's Who in Colored America* 29–30 (J. J. Boris ed. 1927).

69. "Along the Color Line," 36 *Crisis* 14 (Jan. 1929). Bruce also was awarded the Robinson Prize and the Woolsack key; letter to author from William Schwartz, dean, Boston University School of Law, Aug. 19, 1987.

70. See 30 *Yale L.J.* 161, 280, 395, 501, 607, 732, 845 (1921), 31 *Yale L.J.* 73, 183, 299, 408, 514, 635, 747, 869 (1922), on Atkins; 35 *Harv. L. Rev.* 68, 319, 450, 593, 743, 859, 950 (1921–1922), on Houston; 7 *Iowa Law Bulletin* 46, 100, 162, 250 (1921); 8 *Iowa Law Bulletin* 47, 92, 177, 245 (1922), on Taylor.

71. See 31 *Yale L.J.* 31, 73, 183, 299, 408, 514, 635, 747, 869 (1922). Both Atkins and Williams served on the Board of Editors. See also, "Last Rites Held for Lawyer Jack Atkins, 81"; *Jet*, Aug. 9, 1982; *Yale Alumna Directory* 16 (1949); "Alexander Takes New Office," *Pittsburgh Courier*, Oct. 9, 1926, on Williams.

72. See 75 *U. of Penn. L. Rev.* 61, 154, 247, 349, 447, 554, 646, 760 (1926–1927). For more about Johnson, see "Young Negro Lawyer Gets Berth," *Gary American*, Jan. 17, 1931.

73. Bloom, "Sadie Alexander Is School's 1st Black Woman Graduate," 7 *The Law Alumni Journal* 19 (Winter 1972).

74. *Ibid.* Nevertheless, Alexander studied alone and had few opportunities to socialize. Fortunately, she could discuss the law with her Harvard-trained husband, Raymond Pace Alexander. See Sadie T. M. Alexander, "The Best of Times, the Worst of Times," 12 *The Law Alumni Journal* 19, 20 (Spring 1977). Other black women have reported racial and sexual discrimination as well. Viola F. Minor (not a member of the law review) reports that "a 'bigot teacher' to whom [she] directed a question [at the Portia Law School, New England School of Law] re voting in the South (still a matter of debate) [gave her a] Zero [that] affected [her] four year average of magna" (letter to author, Sept. 15, 1988). In 1926, Jama A. White, another black student at Portia Law School, was expelled from the law school under dubious circumstances. White purchased coal and groceries from a dealer and a store without informing them that she "was living apart from her husband," who was under court order to provide for her support. Relying on her knowledge of the law, White refused to pay for these goods, presumably because she expected her husband to do so. Word spread in the law school that Jama White "was making improper use of knowledge acquired in law school." After she refused to pay for the goods, the dean of the law school declined to allow White, whose grades were very high, to enroll for her senior year. She retained Clement Garnett Morgan, a black lawyer who had been practicing law since 1893 (the year he was graduated from Harvard's law school) and sued Portia Law School. After the Massachusetts Supreme Court ultimately ruled against her claim and acting as her own attorney (*pro se*), she petitioned the United States Supreme Court to hear her case, which it declined to do. Whether White became a lawyer is unknown, but she is no doubt the first black law student to sue a law school alleging "unfair discrimination" and perhaps the first woman to file a petition in the United States Supreme Court *pro se* to argue her own case as a woman. See, "Says School Expelled Her, Negress Sues," *Boston Advertiser*, April 23, 1929; "Ask for Reinstatement in Hub Law School," *Courier-Citizen*, April 24, 1929; "Seeks $20,000 for Expulsion," *Boston Herald*, April 23, 1929. *White v. Portia Law School*, 274 Mass. 162, 174 N.E. 187 (1931), *cert. denied*, 288 U.S. 611 (1933). See also, R. Chester, *Uneasy Access: Women Lawyers in a Changing America* 29 (1985).

Jama A. White's historic petition before the United States Supreme Court is as important as the appearance of another black laywoman, Luce Terry Bijah Prince, before a member of the court around 1796. According to George Sheldon, a Massachusetts historian, "Luce Bijah gained a national reputation" during a series of lawsuits for ejectment, trespass, or to quiet title to certain land deeded to Bijah, her husband, and located in the city of Guilford (Windham County) and/or the city of Sunderland (Bennington County), Vermont, prior to statehood in the 1760s. Bijah would have received his grant around the time of "the order of the King-in-Council of 1764, which . . . established the eastern boundry of Vermont" that was used when Congress adopted resolutions favoring Vermont's statehood in 1791. *Vermont v. New Hampshire*, 289 U.S. 593, 598, 613–14, 619 (1932).

During the court proceedings, Prince was granted permission to address the court and was thus the first woman ever to do so. See K. B. Morello, *The Woman Lawyer in America: 1638 to the Present—The Invisible Bar* 8 (1986). George Sheldon is specific: "The Court was presided over by Hon. Samuel Chase of Maryland," who at the time, like other members of the United States Supreme Court "rode circuit" to hear cases outside of the nation's capital. Prince was represented by two white Vermont lawyers, who "managed the case of Bijah and Luce." Sheldon reports that Luce Prince "argued the case at length before the court convened in Vermont. Justice Chase said that Luce made a better argument than he had heard from any lawyer at the Vermont bar" (Sheldon, "Negro Slavery in Old Deerfield," 8 *New England Magazine* 54, 56–57 [March 1893]). Eli Bronson was the moving party against the Princes. Bronson and the Princes were citizens of Vermont.

Samuel Chase was appointed to the United States Supreme Court by President George Washington in 1796. George Sheldon's report about Luce Prince's argument before Justice Chase, though as yet unearthed in official court records, is supported by the more contemporaneous report on this event in the second volume of Josiah Gilbert Holland's *History of Western Massachusetts* 360 (1855). Some confusion exists in the literature as to whether Dudley Chase, a lawyer in Vermont and later chief justice of the Vermont Supreme Court, heard the Princes' case instead of Justice Samuel Chase. But this is unlikely because Dudley Chase, the uncle of Salmon P. Chase, who succeeded Roger Brooke Taney as chief justice of the United States Supreme Court, did not become a judge in Vermont until 1817. See "The Vermont Bench and Bar," in Vol. 5, W. H. Crockett, *History of Vermont* 86 (1923). See also, Leon Friedman, "Salmon P. Chase," in Vol. 2, *The Justices of the United States Supreme Court, 1789– 1969: Their Lives and Major Opinions* 1113 (L. Friedman and F. L. Israel eds. 1969) and Irving Dilliard, "Samuel Chase," in *id.*, Vol. 1, at 185, 194.

The case involving the land claims of the Princes and others was likely heard before Vermont's only federal district judge, Samuel Hitchcock, who was appointed to the bench on September 3, 1793. The Vermont District Court was in the Second Federal District and was added to the Eastern Circuit by act on March 2, 1791. See Book 1, *The Federal Cases Comprising Cases Argued and Determined in the Circuit and District Courts of the United States, 1780–1800*, at xi, xxvii (reprint, 1988). However, such courts in federal circuits then also consisted "of one Supreme Court Judge" under Federal legislation adopted on March 2, 1793. C. Warren, Vol. 1, *The Supreme Court in United States History* 89 (rev. ed. 1926). Justice Samuel Chase is known to have "sat at . . . one session of court in Vermont while on circuit, at Bennington May 1796, which is the time period when the [Prince] litigation would have taken place" (Letter to author from David R. Proper, librarian, The Memorial Libraries, Deerfield, Massachusetts, Dec. 31, 1991; document of Circuit Court designation, dated May 12, 1796, provided to author by Stanley P. Tozeski, National Archives—New England Region, Jan. 26, 1992).

Since grants of land, sometimes duplicative, were made to Vermont grantees by the governors of New Hampshire, New York, and Massachusetts, it is reasonable to conclude that a land grant to Bijah in the 1760s, thirty years before Vermont became a state, might be the subject of litigation after its statehood. This is particularly likely due to the complicated land lease system that existed in Vermont before statehood. In fact, Guilford, of which Sheldon reports Bijah was a charter grantee, was established by grant from the governor of New Hampshire under this system, see W. T. Bogart, *The Vermont Lease Lands* 33, n.28 (1950). Land disputes arising under the land grant system would have to be decided under the jurisdiction of federal courts as the court's power extended to controversies "between Citizens of the same State claiming Lands under Grants of different States." See Article III, sec. 2, U.S. Constitution. The same language is codified in Section 12, Judiciary Act of 1789. See also, *The Judicial Code and Rules of Procedure in Federal Courts* 705–6 (D. J. Meltzer and D. L. Shapiro, compilers, 1991). It is certainly possible that either Eli Bronson or the Princes claimed title to land granted to each by different states during this period, e.g., Massachusetts, New York, and New Hampshire; W. T. Bogart, *The Lease Lands* at 5, 24 (1950). It is plausible that Luce Terry Prince did argue her family's land rights before Judge Hitchcock and Justice Samuel Chase or before Chase, sitting alone, in 1796. Until the reports of Massachusetts historians Holland and Sheldon are discredited, Luce Terry Bijah Prince and Jama A. White, two black laywomen, must be viewed as groundbreakers in the history of the United States Supreme Court. See also, B. Katz and J. Katz, *Black Women: A Fictionalized Biography of Luce Terry Prince* (1973) and "Luce Terry Prince: Vermont Advocate and Poet," in *The Black Presence in the Era of the American Revolution 1770–1800*, at 209, 211 (Smithsonian Institution 1973).

75. Interview with Theodore M. Berry, June 8, 1989.

76. See, e.g., "False Imprisonment—Arrest Without Warrant," 3 *U. Cincinnati L. Rev.* 479 (1929), followed by "Municipal Corporations—Licenses—Reasonableness of Amount," "Contract—Mutual Promises as Consideration, and Internal Revenue," in 4 *U. Cincinnati L. Rev.* 102, 239, 390 (1930), and "Municipal Corporations—Streets Construction and Repair," 5 *U. Cincinnati L. Rev.* 241 (1931). See also, Vols. 2–5 of the *U. Cincinnati L. Rev.* at Vol. 2/458 1929), Vol. 3/57, 203, 359, 467 (1930) and Vol. 5/84 (1931), listing Berry.

77. See 1 *Rocky Mountain Law Rev.* 47 (1928). Austin published an article, "Evidence—Examination of Jurors on Voir Dire—Questions of Interest in Insurance Companies (Montana)," 1 *Rocky Mountain L. Rev.* 67 (1928). See also, "Elsie Austin Wins Honors," *The Boulder Colorado New Herald*, n.d., no page, from Austin's scrapbook.

78. See 42 *Harv. L. Rev.* 103, 248, 410, 550, 676, 930, 1064 (1928–1929).

79. 1 *U. of Chi. L. Rev.* 110 (1933); "Constitutional Law—Validity of Party Resolution Depriving Negro Rights to Vote in Party Primary," 1 *U. of Chi. L. Rev.* 142 (1933): Ming may be the first black student on law review in the nation to publish an article directly on a black issue.

80. Bonepart published an article, "Augmentation of Assets by Means of Cash Items," in 1 *Ohio State Student Bar Association Law Journal* 128 (1935); see *Who's Who Among Negro Lawyers* 5 (S. T. M. Alexander ed. 1945).

81. See 16 *Temple L.Q.* 62 (1941), listing Clay, and "Equity—Jurisdiction—Multiplicity of Suits—Patents," *id.* at 98.

82. See notes, "Administrative Law—Right of Persons Aggrieved by Orders to Review by Appellate Courts," 42 *Mich. L. Rev.* 157 (1943); "Constitutional Laws—Due Process Limitations in Statutes Regulating Extrastate Contracts," 42 *Mich. L. Rev.* 159 (1943); "Constitutional Law—Right to Impose a License Tax upon Dissemination of Religious Literature," 42 *Mich. L. Rev.* 163 (1943); "Parties—Lack of Controversy Where Parties Represent Same Interests," 42 *Mich. L. Rev.* 170 (1943); "Powers—Testamentary Power—Enforceability of Contract to Exercise," 42 *Mich. L. Rev.* 72 (1943); "Taxation—Special Assessment—Due Process—Requirement of Notice for Repair of Existing Improvements," 42 *Mich. L. Rev.* 177 (1943); "Constitutional Law—Freedom of Religion—Compulsory Flag Salute," 42 *Mich. L. Rev.* 319 (1943); "Court's—Federal Courts—Diversity of Citizenship Requirement—Person Evacuated to Other State by Government Order," 42 *Mich. L. Rev.* 321 (1943); "Future Interests—Charities—Validity of Accumulation for Charity When Impracticable to Accumulate Desired Amount," 42 *Mich. L. Rev.* 323 (1943); "Municipal Corporations—Constitutional Law—Exemption of Homestead from Taxation for State Purposes," 42 *Mich. L. Rev.* 326 (1942), and "Comment, Judicial Notice by Appellate Courts of Facts and Foreign Laws Not Brought to the Attention of the Trial Court," 42 *Mich. L. Rev.* 509 (1943). See also, 42 *Mich. L. Rev.* 128, 307, 480 (1943).

83. *General Catalogue of the University of Michigan, 1837–1911*, at 524 (I. N. Demmon ed. 1912).

84. Bradwell, "The Colored Bar of Chicago," 5 *Mich. L.J.* 385, 395 (1896): James E. White, an 1893 Howard University law graduate, was awarded a master of laws degree from Boston University in International Law; E. H. Mumford, *Seattle's Black Victorians, 1852–1901*, at 98 (1980). Andrew R. Black was an 1899 law graduate of Howard University.

85. *Harvard Law Quinquennial* 221 (F. S. Kimball ed. 1948).

86. *Id.* at 202 (William Henry Hastie, 1933), 360 (Andrew Leon Ransom, 1935), 232 (Bernard Samuel Jefferson, 1943). See also, Carter, "William Henry Hastie: Jurist, Scholar, Friend," 79 *Harv. Law Record* 3 (Nov. 30, 1984); "Future Cloudy," *New York Times*, Aug. 16, 1937, for discussions of black S.J.D. degree holders Houston and Hastie. See also, *Cornell Directory of Alumni and Chronicle* 102 (1988). Houchins never taught law in a law school. After graduating from Cornell University's law school, he went to Texas and was admitted to the bar. He taught at Wiley College, a black school, and later became a member of the "Black Cabinet" of the Roosevelt Administration. Interview with Frankie Houchins (his wife), Oct. 28, 1991.

87. Taylor, "The Negro and the Legal Profession," *New York Age*, June 3, 1939. Although there appears to be a decline in the number of black lawyers admitted to law schools between 1930 and 1945, St. John's Law School, the University of Southern California Law School, Loyola Law School (Los Angeles), Indiana University Law School, Boston College of Law, and Cornell University Law School appear to have admitted black students in modest numbers. See "To Practice Law Here," *Amsterdam News*, June 18, 1930: St. John's University graduated Horatio Boxill, Ernest A. McKenzie, and Simon

Hilliman, all of the British West Indies and South America. Edward Lucius Jefferson was graduated from the University of Southern California Law School in 1931 (letter to author from Lori Putman, registrar, University of Southern California, April 17, 1987). H. Claude Hudson was the first black law graduate of Loyola Law School (Los Angeles) in 1931; see "Faculty Approves Scholarship to Honor the Memory of H. Claude Hudson," 7 *Loyola Lawyer* 1, 11 (Spring 1989). John Morton Finny, the son of a former slave, completing his legal training at the University of Indiana in 1935 (Terry, "It's Such a Pleasure to Learn," *Washington Post Parade Magazine* 10–11, March 18, 1990). Harold Arnoldus Stevens was Boston College of Law's first black graduate in 1936. See Navarro, "Judge Harold Stevens, 83, Dies; First Black on Court of Appeals," *New York Times*, Nov. 11, 1990, at 40, col. 1; letter to author from Professor Richard G. Huber, Nov. 3, 1987. The records of Cornell University indicate that Eugene K. Jones was one of its first black students in 1936. Lunkingbeal, "Cornell Law Students—Change and Continuity," *Cornell Law Forum* 38, n.3 (1988). By the end of World War II, Akron Law School (affiliated with the Cleveland Law School) would begin to train students such as Alexander Young Russell, who "placed second out of 600 in the state who took the bar examination . . . in 1944." Callaghan, "Alex Mixes Lessons and Laughter," *Akron Beacon Journal*, July 7, 1963; letter to author from Richard L. Aynes, Associate Dean, Akron University Law School, July 25, 1991. Jane Cleo Marshall (Lucas) confirmed that she graduated from the University of Michigan, the first black woman to do so (interview on May 12, 1992).

88. "Report of the Committee on Legal Education and Admission to the Bar," Vol. 1 *Report of the American Bar Association* 209, 225–226 (1879).

89. *Id.* at 209.

90. Hepburn, "Organized Co-operation for the Ideals of Legal Education," in Vol. 45 *Report of the Forty-Third Annual Meeting of the American Bar Association* 467, 471 (1920). Charles M. Hepburn was chairman of the ABA Committee on Legal Education and Admission to the Bar.

91. *Law in American History* 456 (D. Fleming and B. Bailyn eds. 1971).

92. W. H. Bryson, *Legal Education in Virginia, 1779–1979*, at 401 (1982). Professor Maloney, a 1913 graduate of Dalhousie University Law Department in Halifax, Nova Scotia, went to Buffalo's law school after being one of the founding law instructors at Virginia Union University Law School, a black school located in Richmond, Virginia, in 1921. See *Virginia Union University Catalogue, 1921–1927*, at 7 (1927). Denied a position on the law faculty at Boalt Hall at the University of California in 1930, George Marion Johnson, who had earned an S.J.D. degree there, was recruited to Howard University's law faculty. See G. M. Johnson, *The Making of a Liberal* 24 (1985). It was easier for Goddfredo Manuel Gasten, who apparently attended Harvard University's law school, to teach law at the University of Puerto Rico in 1937. "Appointed Law Professor in Puerto Rico," *Washington Tribune*, Sept. 25, 1937. In 1939 John Marshall Law School, located in Chicago, Illinois, hired Euclid Louis Taylor to give a series of lectures on extradition. Taylor had previously served as a lecturer on the faculty of the Chicago Law School for two years. Huff, "Negro Lawyer to Lecture at John Marshall Law Inst.," *Oklahoma Black Dispatch*, June 3, 1939.

93. George M. Johnson, "Legal Profession," in *The Integration of the Negro into American Society* 96 (E. F. Frazier ed. 1951).

94. *Law in American History* 429 (D. Fleming and B. Bailyn, eds. 1971).

95. M. S. Goldman, *A Portrait of the Black Attorney in Chicago* 35 (1972). In 1917, "only seven states did not have law schools within their borders. . . . By 1917, fifty-nine percent of the cities [with populations] over 100,000 had law schools: Chicago had nine, Washington eight, New York five, and St. Louis and San Francisco four each." *Law in American History* 428 (D. Fleming and B. Bailyn, eds. 1971).

96. Elmer W. B. Curry of Ohio and Sidney P. Dones of California attended LaSalle Extension University School of Law (Chicago). Curry became a successful lawyer and Dones a businessman. Vol. 1 *Who's Who in Colored America* 50 (J. J. Boris ed. 1927); "The Sidney P. Done Co.," *The California Eagle*, Dec. 5, 1914, at 1, col. 1. Forrest B. Anderson was graduated from the YMCA Law School (associated with Northeastern University) in Boston, Massachusetts, in 1913 and became a successful lawyer in Kansas. See Vol. 1 *Who's Who in Colored America* 5 (J. J. Boris ed. 1927). William S. Henry received his law degree from the International School of Law in 1908 and became a claims adjuster in Indiana. *Virginia's Contribution to Negro Leadership* 29 (W. Cooper ed. 1937) (mimeo).

97. Louis C. Taylor received a law degree from Oskaloosa College, located in Mahaska County, Iowa, in 1922 and became a magistrate in Okfuskee County, Oklahoma, in 1923. *Who's Who Among Negro Lawyers* 34 (S. T. M. Alexander ed. 1944).

98. *Law in American History* 463 (D. Fleming and B. Bailyn eds. 1971).

99. *Ibid.* Anticipating a change in standards requiring two years of college to qualify for admission to law school, the ABA's plan was denounced by Charles R. Carusi as "dangerous, uncalled for, unnecessary and un-American" ("Proceedings of the Section of Legal Education and Admissions to the Bar," Vol. 46 *Report of the Forty-Fourth Annual Meeting of American Bar Association* 662 [1921]).

100. R. Stevens, *Law School: Legal Education in America from the 1850s to the 1980s* 193–95 (1983).

101. Hepburn, "Organized Co-operation for the Ideals of Legal Education," in Vol. 45 *Report of the Forty-third Annual Meeting of the American Bar Association* 467, 471 (1920).

102. Hastie, "A Note to the Aspiring Lawyer on His Prospective Profession," 33 *The Fisk Herald* 10 (April 1940): *Law in American History* 454 (D. Fleming and B. Bailyn, eds. 1971).

103. Hepburn, "Organized Co-operation for the Ideals of Legal Education," in Vol. 45 *Report of the Forty-third Annual Meeting of the American Bar Association* 467, 473 (1920), for information on Charles M. Hepburn.

104. The Thirteenth Amendment was promulgated on December 18, 1865; the Fourteenth Amendment was promulgated on July 28, 1868. S. P. Weaver, *Constitutional Law and Its Administration* xxxiv, nn.21–22 (1946); *Law in American History* 426 (D. Fleming and B. Bailyn eds. 1971); "The First Integrated Jury Impaneled in the United States, May, 1867," 33 *Negro History Bulletin* 134 (Oct. 1970), quoting *The Richmond Enquirer and Sentinel*, May 10, 1867, at 1, col. 1, and listing names of the black jurors who either were members of the grand jury that indicted or were to determine the guilt or innocence of Jefferson Davis, the ex-president of the Confederacy. However, the case against Jefferson Davis was *nolle prosequi* (dismissed) on February 26, 1869. Davis was never tried. Nichols, "United States v. Davis," 31 *Am. Historical Rev.* 266, 284 (1926). Although the law school was a "department" in the university, it is not known exactly when it was elevated to a "school," although it is speculated that it was

around 1912. R. Logan, *Howard University: The First One Hundred Years* 151, 628 (1968). Throughout this book, the author refers to the law school as Howard University School of Law.

105. J. M. Langston, *From the Virginia Plantation to the National Capitol* 303 (1894).

106. *Id.* at 104, 106. Langston "was refused admission to several law schools, and was earnestly advised by his friends not to attempt the study [of law] as it would doubtless prove too intricate . . . for a colored man; but he persevered." Letter of Mary J. Safford, M.D., New York, April 5, 1869, printed in the *National Anti-Slavery Standard*, April 7, 1869, at 3, col. 3.

107. *Id.* at 298, 303 (*From the Virginia Plantation*). W. Dyson, *Howard University: The Capstone of Negro Education, 1867–1940*, at 219–20 (1941). Regarding Charles Cooper Nott, see M. T. Bennett, Vol. 1 *The United States Court of Claims: A History*, Part I, 39 (1976).

108. Another white law faculty member was Reuben D. Mussey, a former general in the Union Army during the Civil War. General Mussey's home, which was near the courthouse, became the second site of Howard's law school. Taylor, "Howard's Law School," *Howard University Alumni Journal* (Sept. 1935), at 13.

109. Straker, "The Negro in the Profession of Law," 8 *The A.M.E. Church Rev.* 178, 179 (1891).

110. The year 1869 was designated as the official date of the founding of the Howard University School of Law on September 15, 1932, when the law faculty voted to have a new seal of the law school produced with a "date year of 1869" (Minutes of Faculty, Sept. 15, 1932). See also, Johnson, "The Law School," 1 *How. L.J.* 86 (1955), in which Dean George Marion Johnson referred to January 1869 as the date the law school "began operations."

111. *Law in American History* 414 (D. Fleming and B. Bailyn eds. 1971); E. N. Griswold, *Law and Lawyers in the United States* 38 (1985); A. Z. Reed, *Training for the Public Profession of the Law* 193 (reprint, 1986).

112. Taylor, "Howard's Law School," *Howard University Alumni Journal* (Sept. 1935), at 13.

113. A. M. Daniel, "The Law Library of Howard University," 1867–1956, 51 *Law Library Journal* 202, 203–4 (1958).

114. *Howard University Law Department* 3, 7 (1871).

115. Data from Professor William H. Richards, compiled by Ollie May Cooper, July 16, 1935.

116. See also, A. Z. Reed, *Review of Legal Education in the United States and Canada for the Year 1930*, at 5 (1931).

117. J. M. Langston, *From the Virginia Plantation to the National Capitol* 304 (1894).

118. *Howard University Law School Bulletin* 10–15 (1871).

119. *Id.* at 14.

120. *Id.* at 15.

121. *Ibid.* The graduates of Howard University's law school would certainly face challenges as lawyers in the South: ten months after they were admitted to the bar, the United States Supreme Court held that a state law barring a "negro, or Indian" from giving testimony against whites was constitutionally permissible. *Blyew v. United States*, 80 U.S. 581, 592 (1871). This decision would greatly limit the role black lawyers played in challenging racist actions of the state or proving tort or contractual liability against white wrongdoers, because

the claim would have to be established by the testimony of whites, without the aid of corroborative testimony from black witnesses, whose testimony was barred. Likewise, a white person charged with a crime witnessed only by a black person would go free because the law prohibited testimony by blacks against whites in a criminal case. In *Blyew*, Amos T. Ackerman, the attorney general of the United States who had addressed the first graduating law class of Howard University, argued that the "condition of things in Kentucky under its law excluding the evidence of blacks where white persons have committed crime [was] disgraceful to a Christian community." *Id.* at 588, 589.

122. *Id.* at 8. Senator Maynard's remarks were made on Feb. 27, 1872. On Feb. 4, 1871, Professor Albert G. Riddle moved the local supreme court of the District of Columbia to admit nine Howard University law graduates: A. W. Shadd (Pennsylvania), John H. Cook (Ohio), Lewis A. Bell (Mississippi), John A. Johnson (Missouri), Thomas B. Warrick (Virginia), John H. Williams (Ohio), Wathal G. Wynn (Virginia), George D. Johnson (Pennsylvania), and Charles N. Thomas (Pennsylvania). The tenth graduate, George L. Mabson, was admitted to the North Carolina bar in 1871. Two of the graduates, A. W. Shadd and Louis A. Bell, also petitioned for admission to the Louisiana Supreme Court, but their petitions were denied because local rules permitted the admission of only out-of-state applicants who had previously been admitted to a "state court." The District of Columbia did not qualify. Shadd communicated his denial of admission to the Louisiana Supreme Court to Professor Riddle. Professor Riddle, incensed at the treatment of his former students and perhaps sensing a racial motive, moved the local court of the District of Columbia not to recognize the admission of members of the Louisiana bar to the bar of the District of Columbia, a motion that was granted (Minutes of the General Term of the Supreme Court of the District of Columbia, May 4, 1863, to October 9, 1871; see Rules of Practice of the Supreme Court of the District of Columbia, adopted Jan., 1869).

123. *New National Era,* Feb. 9, 1871.

124. *Howard University Law School Bulletin* 4 (1871).

125. From handwritten commencement address by Dean John Mercer Langston, who was then also vice-president of Howard University, at pp. 4, 6, circa 1873. Langston himself had recently been called to public service by President Ulysses S. Grant. In 1871 President Grant appointed Dean Langston to the Board of Health in the District of Columbia. He served as the board's legal counsel until 1877. *Freedom and Citizenship: Selected Lectures and Addresses of Hon. John Mercer Langston* 28 (J. E. Rankin ed. 1883); *Afro-American Encyclopedia; Or, Thoughts, Doings and Sayings of the Race* 230 (J. T. Haley ed. 1895).

126. R. W. Logan, *Howard University: The First One Hundred Years* 48 (1968). Professor Riddle was said to "stand boldly among the few who [were] true to freedom's cause in the dark age of our nation's history." Letter of Mary J. Safford, M.D., New York, April 5, 1869, published in *The National Anti-Slavery Standard,* April 17, 1869, at 3, col. 3. See also, N. Brandt, *The Town that Started the Civil War* 145, 257 (1990).

127. A. G. Riddle, *Law Students and Lawyers: the Philosophy of Political Parties, and other Subjects* 8–9 (1873).

128. *Id.* at 104–5.

129. *Id.* at 109.

130. *Id.* at 110.

131. *Id.* at 111.

132. *Id.* at 41. In 1988, Robert H. Cooley, Jr., a 1937 Howard University law graduate, reported that his law professors—both black and white—prepared their students "to go immediately into a possibly hostile courtroom environment." Lee, Miles, and Smith, "The Black Lawyer in Virginia: Reflections upon a Journey, 1938–1988," 37 *Virginia Lawyer* 29 (Oct. 1988). See also, P. Murray, *Song in a Weary Throat*, 182–83 (1987); women students were taught the same in 1944.

133. *Ibid.* (*Law Students and Lawyers*).

134. *Ibid.*

135. "Death of John H. Cook," *The National Republican*, March 10, 1879.

136. W. Dyson, *Howard University: The Capstone of Negro Education*, 1867–1940, at 229 (1941).

137. R. Logan and M. Winston, *Dictionary of American Negro Biography* 267 (1982).

138. R. Logan, *Howard University: The First One Hundred Years* 86 (1968). During Dean Greener's tenure at Howard, the school was faced with a local school board statute requiring the university to increase its two-year program to three years. This new requirement discouraged already financially strapped black students from applying to law school. During this period, it is also likely that tuition at the law school increased because "Congress announced that none of its appropriation might be used for Howard's professional schools." This is the most plausible explanation for the law school's brief closings in the late 1870s and early 1880s. See R. Stevens, *Law School* 81 (1983). The law school complied with the three-year requirement by adding a third year after which a student would be awarded an LL.M. degree. R. Logan, *Howard University: The First One Hundred Years* 87 (1968). This degree was awarded intermittently from 1882 until 1926. *Id.* at 227, 81 ("No students received degrees from the Law Department between 1877 and 1881").

139. William F. Bascom was a lawyer, but was teaching in the College Department (School of Liberal Arts) when he was named interim dean. Bascom and Professor John Hartwell Cook were the only instructors for twenty-five students between 1875 and 1876. Warren C. Stone's background remains a mystery. Benjamin Franklin Leighton was a well-respected Washington, D.C., lawyer who was president of the D.C. Bar Association 1901 and 1903. He was a trustee of American University during the time he served as Howard University's law dean. Almost seven hundred students, mostly black, were graduated during Leighton's forty years as dean of Howard University School of Law. Dean Leighton taught real property, contracts, constitutional law, and statutory law. Mason N. Richardson joined the law faculty in 1897. He taught commercial law and partnership. He served as dean from February 1921 to November 1921. Judge Fenton Whitlock Booth was an 1892 graduate of the University of Michigan's law school; he "served without pay for seven years as dean of the Howard University Law School in Washington." See M. T. Bennett, Vol. 1 *The United States Court of Claims: A History, Part I* 103, 104 (1976), and *Relief of Professor William H. H. Hart: Papers Relating to the Claim of William H. H. Hart, S. 2233*, 68th Cong., 1st Sess. 412 (1924), for material on Dean Leighton, as well as Marquis, Vol. 1 *Who Was Who in America, 1897–1942*, at 719 (1981) and *The Court-House of the District of Columbia* 209 (1939). On Bascom and Stone, see R. Logan, *Howard University: The First One Hundred Years* 38, 81, 86 (1969); telephone conversation with Paul Coates, Moorland-Spingarn Research Center, Howard University, January 2, 1991, on Dean Richardson.

140. Except for John Mercer Langston's brief tenure as acting president between 1873 and 1875, all of Howard University's presidents were white. Mordecai Wyatt Johnson, Howard's first black president, did not assume office until 1926, fifty-nine years after Howard University was founded. R. Logan, *Howard University: The First One Hundred Years* 64, 81, 243, 247 (1968).

141. It should be remembered that until 1930 Howard University's law school was a night school, and it was classified as a part-time school. All of the white deans taught a course or two. Other known white faculty between 1880 and 1944 included Arthur Alexis Birney, who would later serve as United States attorney in the District of Columbia. Birney taught pleading and practice at law, equity, and equity jurisprudence. Judge R. B. Warder, a former member of the Supreme Court of Ohio, taught at Howard's law school as well. George Francis Williams taught property, domestic relations, and commercial paper. Alfred J. Buscheck, a graduate of the University of Wisconsin Law School and Yale (S.J.D.), taught contracts, corporations, public utilities, business units, and partnership in the 1930s. Nathan Cayton, a graduate of the National University School of Law (George Washington University), was a municipal judge in the District of Columbia from 1920 to 1927 and taught moot court in the 1920s and 1930s. Theodore Cogswell, a Georgetown University Law School graduate, was a part-time lecturer on wills and trusts in the 1930s. Milton Albert Kallis, a graduate of Northwestern University School of Law and Harvard (S.J.D.), was an instructor in legal history, personal property, bills and notes, sales, bankruptcy, private corporations, jurisprudence, municipal corporations, federal jurisdiction, and administrative law. Judge Charles C. Cole, Associate Justice, Supreme Court of the District of Columbia, taught jurisdiction of the federal courts and statutory construction.

Other white professors included Thomas P. Woodward (who taught property); Walter Wheeler, a law graduate of the Institute of Law, John Hopkins University; Charles Vernon Imlay, a law graduate of Harvard University; James Peter Schick, a law graduate of Georgetown University's law school; Edward Stafford, a graduate of George Washington University's law school; and Dale David Drain, a graduate of Columbia University's law school. See *Relief of Professor H. H. Hart: Papers Relating to the Claim of William H. H. Hart, S. 2233*, 68th Cong., 1st Sess. 413 (1924), regarding Professors Birney, Cole, Williams; R. Logan, *Howard University: The First One Hundred Years* 86 (1969), regarding Professors Williams and Warder; *Association of American Law Schools: Directory of Teachers in Member Schools* 29, 33, 36, 74 (1933), on professors Buscheck, Cayton, Cogswell, and Kallis; *Howard University: Prospectus of the Law School 1903–1904*, at 1 (1904), regarding Professor Woodward; *Bulletin and Catalogue of Howard University School of Law* 6–7, July, 1919, regarding Professors Imlay, Schick, Stafford, and Drain. See also, Vol. 5 *The Booker T. Washington Papers, 1899–1900*, at 648 (L. R. Harlan, R. W. Smock, and B. S. Kraft eds. 1976), on Birney; R. Logan, *Howard University: The First One Hundred Years* 86 (1968), on Warder; *id.* at 225, on Williams. Two other white instructors also taught at Howard: James H. Smith and John D. Smith, W. Dyson, *Howard University: The Capstone of Negro Education, 1867–1940*, at 220 (1941).

142. The particular method of instruction at Howard University School of Law was to make the student aware of how the law neutralized and formalized principles so as to limit the enlargement of political power. This method of instruction gave students particular insight into the civil rights litigation they

would encounter as full-fledged lawyers. See J. Greenberg, *Race Relations and American Law* 22 (1950).

143. Professors Richards and Hart often were asked to sponsor former students to the United States Supreme Court. "Colored Lawyers Gaining Recognition in the Highest Courts," *Richmond Planet*, Nov. 25, 1922; D. L. Beasley, *The Negro Trail Blazers of California* 197 (1919). The salaries received by Howard law professors during the early years is somewhat unclear. Professor Hart received $1,500 per year as a law professor from 1890 to 1922. *Relief of Professor H. H. Hart: Papers Relating to the Claim of William H. H. Hart, S. 2233*, 68th Cong., 1st Sess. 412 (1924).

144. *The Echo of '20, Howard University 1919–1920* (unnumbered pages), yearbook.

145. R. Logan and M. Winston, *Dictionary of American Negro Biography* 294 (1982).

146. Jasper, "God's Angry Man," *Washington Afro-American*, Sept. 8, 1956. See also, R. Logan, *Howard University: The First One Hundred Years* 120 (1968). Professor Hart also raised private funds for the law school. In 1895 "the Federal Government began to make an annual appropriation especially for the Law Department." W. Dyson, *Howard University: The Capstone of Negro Education, 1867–1940*, at 223 (1941).

147. *Hart v. State*, 100 Md. 595, 60 A. 457 (1905). See also, A. B. Koger, *The Negro Lawyer in Maryland* 9 (1948) (pamphlet); M. L. Callott, *The Negro in Maryland, 1870–1912*, at 134 (1969). Professor Hart also ran a farm for indigent black children near Fort Washington, Maryland. Hart petitioned Congress to reimburse him for expenditures said to be owed to him from the District of Columbia for taking care of these indigent city children. *Relief of Prof. William H. H. Hart: Papers Relating to the Claim of William H. H. Hart, S. 2233*, 68th Cong., 1st Sess. (1924). The matter was referred to the United States Court of Claims, *Hart v. United States*, 58 Court of Claims 518 (1923).

148. Smith, "Retirement of Herbert Ordré Reid, Sr.," 3 *The Jurist* (Howard law school alumni journal) 18 (Summer 1989).

149. Vol. 1 *Who's Who in Colored America* 215 (J. J. Boris ed. 1927).

150. *The Echo of '20, Howard University 1919–1920* (unnumbered pages), yearbook; R. W. Logan, *Howard University: The First One Hundred Years* 97 (1968).

151. *Id.* at 117–18 (*First One Hundred Years*).

152. G. R. McNeil, *Groundwork: Charles Hamilton Houston and the Struggle for Civil Rights* 33, 53 (1983).

153. R. Logan, *Howard University: The First One Hundred Years* 225 (1968).

154. J. M. Langston, *From the Virginia Plantation to the National Capitol* 301 (1894).

155. *Id.* at 298–99.

156. *Id.* at 299.

157. A. G. Riddle, *Law Students and Lawyers: the Philosophy of Political Parties, and other Subjects* 43, 45 (1873).

158. "Howard U. Law School Shows Progress in First 10 Years," *Norfolk Journal and Guide*, Jan. 30, 1938.

159. R. Stevens, *Law School: Legal Education in America from the 1850s to the 1980s* 81 (1983). Classes at Howard University School of Law were conducted from 5 to 8 P.M., October to June, "with special reference to the needs and opportunities of those who are engaged during business hours of the day in

clinical and other pursuits." Tuition ranged from forty dollars in 1869 to one hundred and thirty-five dollars in 1933. *Howard University Law School Bulletin* 4–5 (1871); A. Z. Reed, *Review of Legal Education in the United States and Canada for the Year 1933*, at 38 (1934). The increase in enrollment between 1894 and 1905 may be attributed to "the fact that tuition was remitted." See W. Dyson, *Howard University: The Capstone of Negro Education* 1867–1940, at 230 (1941). The matriculation fee was ten dollars and the cost of books was thirty dollars a year. "Hart's Howard in 1900," *The Washington Afro-American*, Sept. 8, 1936.

160. R. Logan, *Howard University: The First One Hundred Years* 266–267 (1968).

161. Genna Rae McNeil, "To Meet Group Needs: The Transformation of Howard University School of Law, 1920–1935," in *New Perspectives on Black Educational History* 155 (V. P. Franklin and J. D. Anderson eds. 1978).

162. The law curriculum at Howard University was as rigorous as that of other national law schools in 1929. The first-year curriculum contained the following courses: Agency, Civil Procedure at Common Law, Contracts, Criminal Law, Criminal Procedure, Jurisprudence, Property I, Property II, and Torts. The second-year curriculum included: Bailments and Carriers, Civil Procedure, Court Practice, Equity Jurisprudence and Trusts, Equity Pleading and Practice, Evidence I, Evidence II, Negotiable Instruments, Property III, and Public Service Companies. The third-year curriculum included: Bankruptcy, Conflict of Laws, Constitutional Law, Corporations, Court Practice and Brief Making, Damages, Federal Procedure, Insurance, Partnership, Quasi Contracts, Suretyship, and Wills and Probate Law (*Catalogue of Howard University School of Law* 18–24 [July, 1929]).

163. Smith, "The Forgotten Hero" (book review), 98 *Harv. L. Rev.* 482, 486 (1984).

164. *Howard Law School Catalogue, 1928–1929*, at 6–7, 9–10 (1929).

165. Houston, "Survey of Howard University Law Students" 3–4, Dec. 21, 1927 (paper).

166. Genna Rae McNeil, "To Meet Group Needs: The Transformation of Howard University School of Law, 1920–1935," in *New Perspectives on Black Educational History* 157 (V. P. Franklin and J. D. Anderson eds. 1978).

167. *Id.* at 158.

168. A. Z. Reed, *Review of Legal Education in the United States and Canada for the Year 1930*, at 24, 39, 45 (1931).

169. See George H. Smith, Annual Address of Chairman of ABA Committee on Legal Education," Vol. 56 *Report of the Fifty-fourth Annual Meeting of the American Bar Association* 614, 616, Sept. 17–19, 1931. *Id.* at 611: Howard University's law school was the first "colored school ever considered for rating by the American Bar Association," which then excluded black lawyers from its general membership. See "American Bar Association Approves Howard Law School," *Afro-American*, May 9, 1931.

170. *Handbook of the Association of American Law Schools and Proceedings of the Twenty-ninth Annual Meeting* 8, Dec. 28–30, 1931.

171. "Recognition is Given Howard," *St. Louis Argus*, Jan. 8, 1932. In 1933, Howard University's law library became the first library associated with a black law school to be admitted to the American Association of Law Libraries. W. Dyson, *Howard University: The Capstone of Negro Education*, 1867–1940, at 226 (1941). Allen Mercer Daniel, a lawyer and the acting law librarian at Howard, "was the first [black law librarian] admitted to the Association."

172. McNeil, "Charles Hamilton Houston," 3 *Black L.J.* 123, 124 (1975).

173. Houston, "Need for Negro Lawyers," 4 *J. of Negro Education* 49, 51 (1935).

174. The Howard University law faculty included such men of distinction as William Henry Hastie, William Robert Ming, Jr., Leon Andrew Ransom, George E. C. Hayes, James Madison Nabrit, Jr., and Vice-Dean Houston. Each of these legal scholars, as teachers and as interpreters of the law, would lay the foundation to remake old law into new law. Genna Rae McNeil, "To Meet the Group Needs: The Transformation of Howard University School of Law, 1920–1935," in *New Perspectives on Black Educational History* 164 (V. P. Franklin and J. D. Anderson eds. 1978).

175. *Id.* at 49; McNeil, "Charles Hamilton Houston," 3 *Black L.J.* 123, 125 (1975); Genna Rae McNeil, "To Meet the Group Needs: The Transformation of Howard University School of Law, 1920–1935," in *New Perspectives on Black Educational History* 165 (V. P. Franklin and J. D. Anderson eds. 1978).

176. Smith, "Forgotten Hero," 98 *Harv. L. Rev.* 482, 492 (1984); "Howard U. Law School Shows Progress in First 10 Years," *Norfolk Journal and Guide*, Jan. 30, 1938. Dean Houston's life would later be captured in *The Road to Brown*, a video newsreel directed by Mykola Kulish and reviewed by Donald G. Nieman in 35 *The Am. J. of Legal History* 333 (July 1991).

177. "Howard University Dean Cites Need of Trained Lawyers," *Nashville Globe*, June 2, 1939.

178. Taylor, "Howard's Law School," *Howard University Alumni Journal* 13 (Sept. 1935).

179. 305 U.S. 337 (1938). Ironically, this case had been handled by Vice-Dean Charles H. Houston and Leon Andrew Ransom, a member of Howard's law faculty.

180. J. M. Nabrit, Jr., *Cases and Materials on Civil Rights* i (1949) (mimeo).

181. Ibid.

182. *Annual Report of the President of Howard University to the Secretary of the Interior* 53, June 30, 1939. Actually, Taylor did not leave Howard University until the fall of 1939. Taylor and Dean Hastie may have had irreconcilable differences. See letter from Taylor to president of Howard University, Sept. 23, 1939.

183. G. Ware, *William Hastie: Grace Under Pressure* 29–34 (1984).

184. *Id.* at 48; see also *Directory of Teachers in Member Schools of the Association of American Law Schools* 64–65 (1933) and *Harvard Law Quinquennial* 202 (F. S. Kimball ed. 1948).

185. *Id.* at 81–85 (*Grace under Pressure*).

186. Vol. 1 *Virgin Island Reports* XI (1917–1939) (R. L. Anderson, reporter).

187. Hastie, "A Note to the Aspiring Lawyer on His Prospective Profession," 33 *The Fisk Herald* 10 (April, 1940).

188. *Annual Report of the President of Howard University to Board of Trustees for Fiscal Year* 51, June 30, 1940.

189. *Annual Report of Howard University Law School* 7, June 30, 1941.

190. Letter from H. Listin to Dean William H. Hastie, Nov. 22, 1939.

191. *Annual Report of the President of Howard University to Board of Trustees* 51, June 30, 1940.

192. *Report of the Acting Dean for the [Howard University] School of Law* 1–3, June 30, 1939.

193. *Annual Report of the President of Howard University to Board of Trustees* 51, June 30, 1940.

194. Robinson, "William Henry Hastie—The Lawyer," 125 *U. of Pa. L. Rev.*
8 (1976); Smith, "The High Mountain of William Henry Hastie as Witnessed
from Howard University School of Law," 19 (commemorative symposium at
Harvard Law School, Nov. 16, 1984).

195. *Report of the Acting Dean for the [Howard University] School of Law* 5, June
30, 1939.

196. "Rumor of Howard Law Student Unrest Denied," *Washington Afro-
American*, Oct. 7, 1939; 24 *Howard University Bulletin, School of Law* 20, Dec. 1,
1939. Washington, supported by Dean Hastie, went to Harvard University Law
School to work on his master of laws degree. Letter to James M. Landis, dean of
Harvard Law School, from William Henry Hastie, Jan. 8, 1940. Hastie wrote
that he was "confident [that James Aaron Washington, Jr.] can do satisfactory
work." Washington received his master of laws degree in 1941. *Harvard Law
Quinquennial* 456 (F. S. Kimball ed. 1948).

197. *Annual Report Howard University School of Law, 1959–1960* (1960): Washington served as acting dean for one year. R. W. Logan, *Howard University: The
First One Hundred Years, 1867–1967*, at 378 (1969): Robinson was dean from
1960 to 1962.

198. Jefferson, "Race Discrimination in Jury Service," 19 *B.U.L. Rev.* 413
(1939).

199. Professor Jefferson received his LL.B. from Harvard University's law
school in 1934. *Harvard Law Quinquennial* 232 (F. S. Kimball ed. 1948). For a
retrospective on Professor Jefferson's legal career, including his student days at
Harvard and his teaching days at Howard, see, "Oral History: Justice Bernard
S. Jefferson," 14 *Hastings Constitutional L.Q.* 225, 235–241 (1987).

200. Jefferson, "The Supreme Court and State Separation and Delegation
of Powers," 54 *Colum. L. Rev.* 1 (1944); Jefferson, "Declarations Against Interest: An Exception to the Hearsay Rule," 58 *Harv. L. Rev.* 1 (1944); *Annual
Report of the Acting Dean of the School of Law* 16, June 30, 1941. Professor
Jefferson received the Doctor of Juridical Science degree from Harvard in
1943. *Harvard Law Quinquennial* 232 (F. S. Kimball ed. 1948).

201. Ming, "Racial Restrictions and the Fourteenth Amendment: The Restrictive Covenant Cases," 16 *U. of Chi. L. Rev.* 203 (1949). Professor Ming
joined Howard University's law faculty in 1937. He left the faculty in 1942. He
taught the following courses: Property I, Domestic Relations, and Administrative Law. 27 *Howard University Bulletin, School of Law, 1937–1938*, at 15, 16, 17
(1937). See, P. Murray, *Song in a Weary Throat* 182 (1987): Pauli Murray, a
student at Howard University's law school during Hastie's years as dean, listed
William Robert Ming, Jr., Leon A. Ransom, George E. C. Hayes, James Madison Nabrit, Jr., James Aaron Washington, Jr., and Spottswood W. Robinson III
as distinguished members of the faculty. (Letter to author from Elizabeth
Sage, Archives, University of Chicago Library, Dec. 6, 1990, for material on
Ming.)

202. Robinson, "William Henry Hastie—The Lawyer," 125 *U. of Pa. L. Rev.*
8, 9 (1976). The uncompensated legal services rendered by the faculty focused
upon "litigation challenging racial salary discrimination in the compensation
of public school teachers, decisions of the United States Supreme Court concerning unlawful practices in the obtaining of confessions, and efforts to obtain
for the Negro in the South opportunities for graduate and professional training in state universities." *Annual Report of the President of Howard to Board of
Trustees* 52, June 30, 1940.

203. Speech by William Henry Hastie at the dedication ceremonies of the Anacostia Leave Camp, Anacostia, Washington, D.C., Sept. 20, 1941, at 1.

204. *Harvard Law Quinquennial* 360 (F. S. Kimball ed. 1948).

205. R. Kluger, *Simple Justice* 127 (1975).

206. For example, Professor George Marion Johnson was "commandeered by the federal government to serve as assistant executive secretary to the President's Committee on Fair Employment Practices." *Annual Report of the Acting Dean of the Law School* 13, June 30, 1942.

207. G. Ware, *William Hastie: Grace Under Pressure* 124–130 (1984); Hastie, "Negro Officers in Two World Wars," 12 *Journal of Negro Education* 312 (1943). Dean Hastie's resignation was widely reported by the black press and word of his resignation reached Charles E. Wyzanski, Jr., a Harvard University law school classmate and at that time a U.S. Federal District Judge in Boston. Judge Wyzanski wrote, "I have read with some interest such items as appeared in the press regarding your resignation from the War Department. From my limited knowledge, it seemed to me that you acted with justification." Letter from Judge Charles E. Wyzanski, Jr., to Dean William Henry Hastie, Oct. 11, 1943. See also, *Annual Report of the President of Howard University to the Administrator, Federal Security Agency* 61, Feb. 24, 1942 and *Annual Report of the Acting Dean for the School of Law* 13, 15, June 30, 1942. Hastie's resignation from the War Department became effective on January 3, 1943. His extended leave from the law school was due to expire on June 30, 1943. Hastie did not return to his official duties at the law school until after he co-argued *Smith v. Allwright*, 321 U.S. 649 (1944) in November 1943 (a case that ultimately declared white primaries unconstitutional).

208. *Annual Report of the President of Howard University* 60, May 1, 1944. The evening program at Howard University's law school was beneficial to black women who "worked in Washington in the day, and attend[ed] the law school at night in 1944." Letter to author from Veva L. Young, August 15, 1990: Young attended law school at Howard University because "Tennessee, [her] home state, did not allow [blacks] to attend the professional schools." *Ibid.*

209. *Annual Report of the Dean, Howard Law School, 1943–1944*, at 1, July 8, 1944.

210. *Ibid.*

211. R. Stevens, *Law School: Legal Education in America from the 1850s to the 1980s* 199 (1983).

212. "Hastie Returns to Howard U.," *Pittsburgh Courier*, Sept. 4, 1943.

213. *Annual Report of the Dean, Howard Law School, 1943–1944*, at 8, July 8, 1944. One of the courses Dean Hastie taught during 1943–1944 was Contracts. He may also have taught Conflicts, a course he had taught when he first joined Howard's faculty (14 *Howard Law School Bulletin* 17, Dec. 1, 1944).

214. See R. W. Logan, *Howard University: The First One Hundred Years* 94 (1968), table 2.

215. The first Howard University Law School bulletin stated that "[in] the admission of students no discrimination is made on account of color or sex, and the advantages of the Department are free to all." *Howard University Law School Bulletin* 4, 6 (1871).

216. Letter of Mary J. Safford, M.D., New York, April 5, 1869, printed in *National Anti-Slavery Standard*, April 17, 1869, at 3, col. 3.

217. Robinson, "Women Lawyers in the United States," 2 *Green Bag*, 10, 28 (1890).

218. *Id.* at 28, on Havens and Chambers. Louise V. Bryant is mentioned as a white graduate.

219. *Id.* at 10, 228. See also, "Only Woman Law Dean Is Howard Graduate," *New York Age*, Aug. 19, 1922, at 1, col. 4. White "middle-class women," such as Emma Gillett, attended the "Negro law school" to "the discomfort of their families." R. Stevens, *Law School* 90 n.79 (1983); R. Chester, *Unequal Access: Women Lawyers in a Changing America* 12 (1985). Emma Gillett was graduated from Howard University Law School, admitted to the District of Columbia bar, and entered into private practice in 1882. She became the first woman appointed notary public in the District of Columbia; she co-founded the Washington College of Law in 1898 and became dean in 1913. Jean S. Schade, "The College of Law—A History from the Founding of the College Until Its Merger with American University, 1896–1949," at 13 (M.A. Thesis, Catholic University, 1969). Blacks were barred from attending this law school, but it soon opened its doors to white men. Saunders, "Founded by Feminists," *The American [University] Law School Jurist* 12, 13 (March 1991). The Washington College of Law for Women merged into what is today the American University Law School. When the American Bar Association lifted its gender restrictions in 1918, Emma Gillett became the first active woman in the Section on Legal Education. See D. K. Weisberg, *Women and the Law* 243 (1982) and Riley, "Woman at the Bar," 8 *The Law Student* 7 (Jan. 1931). Grace Hays Riley, dean of the Washington College of Law for Women, reports that "Emma Gillett had studied law at the university for colored students in the [1880s] and she too had engaged in active practice for many years." See also, McNeil, "Justiciable Cause: Howard University Law School and the Struggle for Civil Rights," 22 *How. L.J.* 283, 285, n.14 (1979).

220. Robinson, "Women Lawyers in the United States," 2 *The Green Bag* 10, 13, 28 (1890); R. Stevens, *Law School: Legal Education in America from the 1850s to the 1980s* 13 (1983). In 1873, William Wells Brown described Carey as a native of Delaware who "received a far better education than usually fell to the lot of the free colored people of her native state. . . . Mrs. Carey is resolute and determined. . . . Had she been a man, she would probably have been with John Brown at Harper's Ferry." W. W. Brown, *The Rising Sun; Or, the Antecedents and Advancement of the Colored Race* 539–40 (1873).

221. J. M. Langston, *From the Virginia Plantation to the National Capitol* 303 (1894).

222. The first woman "on record" to graduate from a law school was Ada H. Kepley, an 1870 graduate of the Union Law College of Chicago (Northwestern). Phoebe W. Couzins was graduated from Washington University Law School in St. Louis, Missouri, in 1871, and Sara Kilgore from Michigan's law school in 1871. See Drachman, "Women Lawyers and the Quest for Professional Identity in Late Nineteenth-Century America," 88 *Mich. L. Rev.* 2414, 2429, 2430 (1990), for references to Ada Kepley, Sara Kilgore Wertman, and Emma Gillett. In 1872, the year Charlotte Ray received her law degree from Howard University, Harriet A. Patton received hers from the University of Michigan. R. Stevens, *Law School: Legal Education in America from the 1850s to the 1980s* 82 (1983). Arabella Mansfield, a white woman, was admitted to the Iowa bar in 1869; Lemma Barkaloo, also white, to the Missouri bar in 1870; and J. Ellen Foster to the Iowa bar in 1872. *Id.* at 82. See also, K. B. Morello, *The Woman Lawyer in America: 1638 to the Present—The Invisible Bar* 46 (1986), on Couzins; *General Catalogue of the University of Michigan, 1837–1911*, at 388, on

Kilgore, 390, on Patton (I. N. Demmon ed. 1912); Robinson, "Woman Lawyers in the United States," 2 *The Green Bag* 10, 20 (1890). From listings in Ollie May Cooper's files, other black women followed Charlotte E. Ray to Howard University's law school, and were graduated from that institution: Mary A. Shadd Carey (1883), Caroline E. Hall Mason (1916), Lillian B. Wright Page (1916), Ollie May Cooper (1921), May C. Martin (1921), Willie H. Blount (1922), Zephyr Abrigail Moore Ramsey (1922), Gladys T. Peterson (1922), Lillian E. Skinker Malone (1922), Madeline P. Rogers (1923), Estelle C. Jackson-Jackson (1924), Etta B. Lisemby De Frantz (1924), Shirley C. Williams (1924), Isadora A. Letcher (1925), L. Marian Poe (1925), Anna Roberta Hooper (1926), Elsie T. Jefferson (1929), Alma P. Smith Cornish (1929), Zenobia V. Coleman Hart (1930), Kathleen D. Romer (1930), Thelma D. Ackiss Perry (1931), Tabytha Anderson (1931), Ruby L. Johnson Lowe (1937), Cassandra A. Maxwell Birney (1938), Florrie L. Willis Blackwell (1940), Shirley F. Carter (1943), and Pauli Murray (1944). This information was furnished to author by Ollie May Cooper in 1979. See also, W. Dyson, *Howard University: The Capstone of Negro Education, 1867–1940*, at 237–38 (1941).

223. Although many law schools continued to exclude women after 1900, by 1915 at least forty-one did not. With an increased number of white law schools opened to women, their applications to Howard declined. See R. L. Abel, *American Lawyers* 90 (1989).

224. D. K. Weisberg, *Women and the Law* 235 (1982). The law faculty of Howard University supported the efforts of white women to be admitted to the bar even though they had not attended the law school. For example, Belva Ann Lockwood (a graduate of National University School of Law) was sponsored for admission to the United States Supreme Court by Professor Albert G. Riddle, of Howard University School of Law. On February 13, 1879, history was made when Lockwood became the first woman admitted to the United States Supreme Court. See Proctor, "Belva Ann Lockwood," Vols. 35 and 36, *The Records of the Columbia Historical Society* 192, 197, 215, n.2 (1935).

225. The names of the organizers of Epsilon Sigma Iota Sorority were Willie Hazel Blount, of Texas; Zephyr Abrigail Moore, of California; Gladys Tignor Peterson, of the District of Columbia; and Lillian R. Skinker, of Virginia, the first chief justice of the group. Bledsoe, "History of Senior Class," in *Howard University Yearbook of 1922 (Book V)* (pages unnumbered). Organized at Howard University School of Law, Epsilon Sigma Iota Sorority was incorporated in the District of Columbia on June 17, 1921, by Ollie May Cooper, Bertha C. McNeil, and Gladys E. Tignor. The corporate purpose of the group was "social and educational, and [designed] to induce other women to enter upon the study of law." Certificate of Incorporation, Liber 37, Folio 78, File No. 16192.

226. Official Minutes of Epsilon Sigma Iota Sorority, Jan. 1939–June 11, 1945. The leaders of the sorority throughout the years were Etta B. Lisemby, Pearl Cox, and Ollie May Cooper.

227. Telephone conversation with Ellen Eppes Brown, Washington, DC, Sept. 17, 1985. P. Murray, *Song in a Weary Throat* 183 (1987). Gamma Delta Epsilon, Inc., was incorporated on March 6, 1940, in the District of Columbia, by Arnetta L. Randall, Barbara H. Taplett, and Shellie O. Bacote, three students at the Robert H. Terrell law school. Certificate of Incorporation, Liber 57, Folio 147, File No. 26197. The corporate objective of Gamma Delta Epsilon was to serve "social and educational purposes, and to induce other women to enter upon the study of law." Judge Margaret Haywood, a 1940 graduate of

Terrell law school, confirmed that all three incorporators were black women. Judge Haywood became a member of the legal sorority in 1937. Telephone interview with Judge Haywood, June 4, 1992.

228. "Lawyers Say 'Dean Cooper' Trained Us," *Washington Afro-American*, April 25, 1964, at A–2, col. 8. When Ollie May Cooper retired as secretary to Dean Spottswood W. Robinson III in 1961, the president of Howard University, James Madison Nabrit, Jr., presented her with a citation that states in part, "During the administration of Dean Fenton W. Booth [1921–1930], you were called . . . to . . . teach a one-hour course—without pay and recognition." Citation to Miss Ollie May Cooper, program of the Eighteenth Annual Law School Dinner, June 6, 1961.

229. P. Murray, *Song in a Weary Throat* 183 (1987).

230. Lewis, "From the Editor—Pauli Murray," *P.M. Magazine*, June 14, 1944. In 1944, the number of women at Howard University's law school constituted the largest enrollment in the school's history. There were eleven black women students in the law school. *Annual Report of the Howard Law School* 2, June 30, 1945.

231. R. Stevens, *Law School: Legal Education in America from the 1850s to the 1980s* 81 (1983). Stevens says that in 1887 four out of twelve Howard law students were white.

232. "The Bench and Bar of the Court of Claims to Judge George W. Atkinson on His Retirement," April 17, 1916, 51 Court of Claims Reports XVII (1915); M. T. Bennett, *The United States Court of Claims: a History, Part I*, at 106 (1976); Vol. 1 *The West Virginia Heritage Encyclopedia* 215 (1976).

233. J. Clay Smith, Jr., "The Hispanic National Bar Association and the Need for Hispanic Lawyers," 3, paper presented before the Fifth Annual Convention of the Hispanic National Bar Association, Denver, Colorado, Sept. 12, 1981. Latino, Hispanic, and Puerto Rican graduates from the law school include Manuel de Jesus Boneta (1903), Pedro S. Navedo (1911), Nicolas Silva Mercado (1915), Diego Eugenio Ramas (1915), Pedro Lascot (1918), Tizol Pacheco Benigno, and Domingo A. Lanauge-Rolon (1923), Ramos Delgado (1927). J. Clay Smith, Jr., "Profile: Howard University Entering Law Students, 1893–1903—Age and Residence," (Dec. 1985), paper; *id.*, "Profile: Howard University Entering Law Students, 1904–1920—Age, Legal Residence and Education," (Dec. 1985), paper.

234. Letter to Professor James Madison Nabrit, Jr., from Alexander P. Tureaud, Dec. 8, 1943. See also, Winston, "Howard Law: Open to All Races," *Washington Post*, Nov. 21, 1991, at 22, col. 4.

235. *Annual Report of the President of Howard University* 61, May 1, 1944.

236. A. Z. Reed, *Training for the Public Profession of the Law* 425, on Lincoln; 495, on Straight (reprint, 1986).

237. Tureaud, "The Negro at the Louisiana Bar," 1 (n.d.) (unpublished paper); *ibid.*, on Miller.

238. *Ibid.*; Miller, "Whither the Black Jurist, A Place in American Law," 14 *The Hampton Rev.* 31 (Fall 1988).

239. Tureaud, "The Negro at the Louisiana Bar," 1 (n.d.) (unpublished paper).

240. *Ibid.*

241. *Ibid.*

242. Letter from A. O. Grubb, acting president, Lincoln University, to Charles S. Brown, May 23, 1958.

243. *Ibid.* Another author says that Lincoln University graduated six students in law before it closed. Washington, "History and Role of Black Schools," 18 *How. L.J.* 385, 391 (1974).

244. Letter from A. O. Grubb, acting president, Lincoln University, to Charles S. Brown, May 23, 1958; Mollison, "Negro Lawyers in Mississippi," 15 *J. of Negro History* 38, 42, 46–47 (1930); R. Logan and M. Winston, *Dictionary of American Negro Biography* 271, 272 (1982).

245. A. Z. Reed, *Training for the Public Profession of the Law* 497 (reprint, 1986).

246. *Triennial Catalogue of Wilberforce University for Academic Year 1872–73*, at 5 (1873).

247. Justice Wright commenced his term as associate justice of the Supreme Court of South Carolina on December 9, 1870. Woody, "Jonathan Jasper Wright, Associate Justice of the Supreme Court of South Carolina, 1870–1877," 18 *J. of Negro History* 114, 119–120 (1933). Robert Brown Elliott was sworn in as South Carolina's first black congressman on March 4, 1871. J. S. Reynolds, *Reconstruction in South Carolina, 1865–1877*, at 152 (reprint, 1969).

248. F. A. McGinnis, *History of the A.M.E. Church* 430 (1941). Apparently, law courses were offered and credit was given in other academic departments, if coursework was completed by the student. It remains a mystery why students admitted to the law department were never granted law degrees. *Id.* at 60. Perhaps the objective of Wilberforce University was never to award law degrees, but to offer a higher form of legal training and educational development than students received by pursuing private study law outside of a university. The law course may simply have been one to prepare their students to take the bar examination.

249. A. Z. Reed, *Training for the Public Profession of the Law* 177, 425 (reprint, 1986).

250. Mollison, "Negro Lawyers in Mississippi," 15 *J. of Negro History* 38, 49 (1930). A president of Rust College has written that there is no record indicating that Rust College had a law school from 1878 to 1880. However, he has also acknowledged that "the college did have a fire which destroyed all records in its files in 1940." Letter from W. A. McMillan to author, Nov. 9, 1987. No mention is made about a law department in W. B. Baker's, *History of Rust College*, published in 1924. Ten years before the fire, Irving C. Mollison (author of "Negro Lawyers in Mississippi," cited above), who had been a black lawyer in Mississippi for many years, mentioned the law department at Rust University.

251. There is some uncertainty as to exactly when Central Tennessee College opened its law school. One contemporary source says the law school was established in 1874, but was not organized until 1878. "Central Tennessee College—Its Theological and Law Department," *Indianapolis Freeman*, June 22, 1889, at 1, col. 1. Central Tennessee College, chartered by the Tennessee legislature in 1866, was a Methodist Episcopal school.

252. *Afro-American Encyclopedia; Or, the Thoughts, Doings and Sayings of the Race* 297 (J. T. Haley ed. 1895); A. A. Taylor, *The Negro in Tennessee, 1865–1880*, at 195 (1941). Taylor does not identify Dean Lawrence's race.

253. "Central Tennessee College—Its Theological and Law Department," *Indianapolis Freeman*, June 22, 1889, at 1, col. 1. Central required only that a candidate for admission "give evidence of good moral character, pass a satisfactory examination on all studies up to a high school grade, or bring a certificate or diploma from some reputable school of having completed the English

course." *Catalogue Central Tennessee College, 1896–1897*, at 45 (1897). However, the law school did recommend that applicants "complete, if practicable, a higher course of study than the common English branches, before entering this department" (*ibid*).

254. L. Merriam, *Higher Education in Tennessee* 273 (1893).

255. *Afro-American Encyclopedia; Or, the Thoughts, Doings and Sayings of the Race* 297 (J. T. Haley ed. 1895); Lewis L. Laska, "A History of Legal Education in Tennessee, 1770–1970," at 688 (Ph.D. diss., George Peabody College of Teachers, May 1978).

256. *Catalogue For Central Tennessee College, 1896–1897*, at 44 (1897). According to the catalogue, first-year students used the following texts:

AUTHOR	SUBJECT
Blackstone	Commentaries
Brown	Law and Contracts
Anson	Law of Domestic Relations
Schouler	Law of Nations
Vattel	Law of Pleadings (Civil and Equitable)
Heard	Law of Bills and Notes
Norton	Law of Partnership
Tyler	Law of Evidence
Reynolds	Criminal Law and Procedure
Clark	Moot Court and Debates

Second-year students used the following texts:

AUTHOR	SUBJECT
Cooley	Law of Torts
Desty	Law of Federal Procedure
Boone	Law of Real Property
Bispham	Equity Jurisprudence
Shufman	Pleadings, Common Law
Heard	Equity
Reynolds	Law of Evidence
Cooley	Constitutional Limitations
Boone	Law of Corporations
Boone	Moot Court and Debates

257. Mollison, "Negro Lawyers in Mississippi," 15 *J. of Negro History* 30, 49 (1930).

258. *Catalogue for Central Tennessee College, 1896–1897*, at 45 (1897).

259. *Ibid.*

260. *Afro-American Encyclopedia; Or, the Thoughts, Doings and Sayings of the Race* 294, 297 (J. T. Haley ed. 1895).

261. Lewis L. Laska, "A History of Legal Education in Tennessee, 1770–1970," at 689 (Ph.D. diss., George Peabody College for Teachers, May 1978).

262. *Twentieth Century Negro Literature* 108 (D. W. Culp ed. 1902), on Robinson; H. F. Kletzing and W. H. Crogman, *Progress of a Race* 535 (1901), on Grant.

263. *Topeka Daily Capital*, Sept. 15, 1897. In 1898, three other women, who had been conducting law class in a private capacity, began to teach law when

the Washington College of Law (American University) was organized on April 2, 1898. Jean S. Schade, "The Washington College of Law: A History from the Founding of the College Until Its Merger with the American University, 1896–1949," at 10 (M.A. thesis, Catholic University, April 1969). These women instructors included J. Ellen Foster, Ellen Spencer Mussey, and Emma M. Gillett. *Catalogue of the Washington College of Law (primarily for women)* 3–4 (1898–1899). Charlotte E. Ray and Mary Shadd Carey were graduated from Howard University's law school in 1872 and 1883, respectively; Ida G. Platt and Lutie A. Lytle were graduated from the Chicago Law School and Central Tennessee University's law school in 1894 and 1897, respectively.

264. A. Z. Reed, *Training for the Public Profession of the Law* 497 (reprint, 1986). Reed says that the law school closed in 1917. "Cameron-Trimble Cultural Cradle of Nashville," History 2 (n.d.), author's files.

265. A. Z. Reed, *Training for the Public Profession of the Law* 425 (reprint, 1986); D. A. Straker, "The Negro in the Profession of Law," 8 *A.M.E. Review* 178, 181 (1891).

266. G. R. Richings, *Evidence of Progress Among Colored People* 288 (1904).

267. W. Dyson, *Howard University: The Capstone of Negro Education, 1867–1940*, at 234, n.57 (1941), quoting *First Annual Address of The Law Graduates of Allen University* by Dean D. Augustus Straker, 4 (1885).

268. Harper, "Some Black Lawyers in the Post–Civil War South," *ABA Litigation* 41 (Spring 1977); A. Z. Reed, *Training for the Public Profession of the Law* 171 (reprint, 1986).

269. "Graduates and Ex-Students," 58 *The Southern Workman* 332, 333 (July 1929). Stewart became a clerk in the U.S. Treasury Department in Washington, DC.

270. A. Z. Reed, *Training for the Public Profession of the Law* 425 (reprint, 1986); Washington, "History and Role of Black Law Schools," 18 *How. L.J.* 385, 396 (1974); *Catalogue of Allen University, 1899–1900*, at 3–4 (1900).

271. *Id.* at 385, 394–95 ("History and Role of Black Law Schools"), quoting W. Carter, *Shaw Universe* 44 (1973).

272. Vol. 1 *Who's Who of the Colored Race* 156 (F. L. Mather ed. 1915); *The College of Life or Practical Self-Educator: A Manual of Self Improvement for the Colored Race* 126 (H. D. Northrop, J. R. Gay, and I. G. Penn eds. 1896).

273. Washington, "History and Role of Black Law Schools," 18 *How. L.J.* 385, 394–95 (1974), quoting W. Carter, *Shaw Universe* 44 (1973).

274. Letter to Charles S. Brown from Martha W. Wheeler, Registrar, Shaw University, June 3, 1958, listing names of law graduates by class from 1890 to 1914; Miller, "Whither the Black Jurist, A Place in American Law?" 14 *The Hampton Rev.* 31 (Fall 1988).

275. E. R. Lewinson, *Black Politics in New York City* 59 (1974).

276. *Dictionary of American Negro Biography* 349 (R. Logan and M. Winston eds. 1982).

277. Washington, "History and Role of Black Law Schools," 18 *How. L.J.* 385, 394, 395 (1974).

278. G. D. Wilson, "A Century of Negro Education in Kentucky," 107–8 (rev., 1986) (manuscript).

279. W. D. Johnson, *Biographical Sketches of Prominent Negro Men and Women of Kentucky* 53, 54 (1897).

280. For example, A. J. Slaughter is reported to have received an LL.M. from Simmons University (Central Law School). *Who's Who Among Negro Law-*

yers 32 (S. T. M. Alexander ed. 1945). A. Z. Reed, *Training for the Public Profession of the Law* 429 (reprint, 1986).

281. A. Z. Reed, *Review of Legal Education in the United States and Canada for the Year 1930*, at 41 (1931): issued annually; *id.* at 25 (1932); *id.* at 49 (1934). See also, R. L. Abel, *American Lawyers* 101 (1989).

282. A. Z. Reed, *Training for the Public Profession of the Law* 427 (reprint, 1986).

283. G. A. Sewell and C. V. Troup, *Morris Brown College: The First One Hundred Years* 46, 41 (1981).

284. *Id.* at 46–47.

285. A. Z. Reed, *Training for the Public Profession of the Law* 427 (reprint, 1986).

286. A history of Lane College does not mention the existence of a law school. A. Cooke, *Lane College: Its Heritage and Outreach, 1882–1982* (1987). But see, G. P. Hamilton, *The Bright Side of Memphis* 72 (1908), which mentions that Lane University had a law department and identifies its dean, H. R. Saddler.

287. "Attorney at Law and Examiner in Chancery," *The Washington Bee*, June 22, 1918.

288. L. D. Hutchinson, *Anna J. Cooper, A Voice from the South* 158 (1981).

289. "Terrell Law School Founded on a Dream and a Whole Lot of Knowledge," *The Washington Afro-American*, April 15, 1964.

290. L. D. Hutchinson, *Anna J. Cooper, A Voice from the South* 158 (1981).

291. Vol. 1 *Who's Who in Colored America* 115 (J. J. Boris ed. 1927).

292. For example, John Anderson Landford was graduated from John Mercer Langston Law School in 1920 with an LL.B. degree and received an LL.M. degree in 1921. Vol. 1 *Who's Who in Colored America* 119 (J. J. Boris ed. 1927).

293. R. Stevens, *Law School: Legal Education in America from the 1850s to the 1980s* 195 (1983); R. L. Abel, *American Lawyers* 101 (1989).

294. "John M. Langston Law School Announces Fall Term," *Washington Eagle*, Aug. 13, 1927; L. D. Hutchinson, *Anna J. Cooper, A Voice from the South* 169 (1981); "Terrell Law School Founded on $145, A Dream and a Whole Lot of Know-How," *Washington Afro-American*, April 25, 1964, at A8, col. 5.

295. *Ibid.* ("Terrell Law School Founded on $145"). For more about Robert H. Terrell, see, M. Sammy Miller, "Robert Herberton Terrell, 1877–1925: Black Lawyer and Community Leader" (Ph.D. diss., Catholic Univ., 1977).

296. "Message from Dean George A. Parker," Vol. 1, No. 2 *The Barrister* 1 (1941) (Robert H. Terrell Law School newspaper). The founders of the Terrell Law School included George A. Parker, L. M. Hershaw, Augustus W. Gray, Louis Rothschild Mehlinger, Philip W. Thomas, Chester A. Jarvis, and Benjamin S. Gaskins. "Washington to Open New Law School," *Chicago Defender*, Aug. 22, 1931. The founders invested twenty-five dollars each as capital to open the Terrell Law School. The school soon moved to the YMCA. See "Tenth Anniversary Celebration," *The Barrister*, 1941 (program of Robert H. Terrell Law School from Charles George Johnson's scrapbook).

297. Thomas, "Biographical Bits About Terrell Teachers," Vol. 1, No. 8 *The Barrister* 9 May 2, 1941.

298. Delta Sigma Tau was incorporated in the District of Columbia on April 6, 1935, by Nathan A. Dobbins, J. H. Kirklin Renfro, W. Harold Flowers, Leon A. Jones, and Benjamin F. Hailstorks, Jr. See Certificate of Incorporation No. 23141. Thereafter, a second chapter of Delta Sigma Tau was started at Howard

University School of Law. Telephone interview with Robert L. Bell, chief justice, Delta Sigma Tau, May 22, 1992. The legal fraternity was open to "all male students and attorneys." An objective of the group was "scholarship and professionalism in the study [of law]."

299. "Message from Dean George A. Parker," Vol. 1, No. 2 *The Barrister* 1 (1941); *Black Americans in Congress, 1870–1989*, at 93 (B. A. Ragsdale and J. D. Treese eds. 1990).

300. See e.g., "5 Pass D.C. Bar Examination," *Chicago Defender*, April 22, 1944, noting the bar passage of Terrell's District residents William Sylvester Thompson, Vernon E. Johnson, W. Theophilus Jones, Franklin Green, and Rufus W. Johnson. See also, Greenya, "Golden Lawyers," 5 *Washington Lawyer* 30, 34 (Sept.–Oct. 1990), regarding William Sylvester Thompson. "5 From Terrell and Howard University Pass D.C. Bar," *Washington Tribune*, Aug. 26, 1944.

301. Bessie Samuels Chase, a 1939 Terrell Law School graduate, was first in her class and the only woman out of twenty-one law students. "And She Led the Class," *Washington Afro-American*, 1939 (from the scrapbook of Charles George Johnson). Other Terrell women would follow: Wilhelmina Jackson (Rolark) and Lucia T. Thomas. See "5 From Terrell and Howard University Pass D.C. Bar," *Washington Tribune*, Aug. 26, 1944; telephone interview of Lucia T. Thomas by author, Oct. 3, 1986.

302. See interview by Lucia T. Thomas of Helen Elsie Austin, Vol. 8, No. 2 *The Barrister* 9, 13–14 (May 1941). The only known black women lawyers to precede Professor Austin as law teachers were Lutie A. Lytle (Central Tennessee School of Law) in 1897 and Ollie May Cooper (Howard University School of Law), circa 1925. See Smith, "Patricia Roberts Harris: A Champion in Pursuit of Excellence," 29 *How. L.J.* 437, 447, n.49 (1986), on Ollie May Cooper.

303. Meyer, "'The Only Colored Man . . .' at Justice," *Washington Post*, April 11, 1976, at A18, col. 1.

304. R. Stevens, *Law School: Legal Education in America from the 1850s to the 1980s* 201, n.34 (1983); W. H. Bryson, *Legal Education in Virginia, 1779–1979*, at 283, 399, 761 (1982); *Virginia Union University Catalogue* 7, 65 (1922).

305. *Virginia Union Bulletin Centennial Issue: A Century of Service to Education and Religion* 28 (June 1965).

306. W. H. Bryson, *Legal Education in Virginia, 1779–1979*, at 401 (1982).

307. A. Z. Reed, *Review of Legal Education in the United States and Canada for the Year 1929*, at 59 (1930).

308. W. H. Bryson, *Legal Education in Virginia, 1779–1979*, at 341 (Lewis), 283 (Henry), 549 (Robertson), 391 (McKenzie) (1982); *Virginia Union Catalogue* 7 (1927).

309. *Virginia Union Catalogue* 70 (1927). The following students, all from Richmond, Virginia, received LL.B. degrees in 1927: Joseph St. James Gilpin, Spottswood W. Robinson, Jr., Ernest Briggs, Emmett Carroll Burke, Leslie Franklin Byrd, Leroy Erskine Ragland, and William Henry Stokes. One author believes that the increased standards imposed by the American Bar Association were the real reasons Virginia Union closed its law school. R. L. Abel, *American Lawyer* 101 (1989).

310. "Nashville Gets Law School," *Nashville World*, Sept. 16, 1932.

311. The two law instructors at Kent Law School were Walter S. Walker, a 1926 graduate of Howard University School of Law, and Coyness Ennix, a

native of Nashville, Tennessee and a 1931 graduate of Howard University's law school. *Kent College of Law Bulletin, 1933–1934*, at 2 (1934).

312. *Id.* at 4–5.

313. Horack and Shafroth, "The Law Schools of Tennessee," 15 *Tenn. L. Rev.* 311, 384–85 (1938).

314. *Id.* at 385.

315. One source indicates that the enrollment reached a level of eleven students. Two Kent College law graduates passed the Tennessee bar between 1933 and 1937. R. L. Abel, *American Lawyers* 100 (1989). Another source notes that when the law school closed, it had educated eighty-eight students. Lewis L. Laska, "A History of Legal Education in Tennessee, 1770–1970," at 703 (Ph.D. diss., George Peabody College for Teachers, 1978).

316. A. Z. Reed, *Review of Legal Education in the United States and Canada for the Year 1932*, at 28, n.2, 50 (1933).

317. 305 U.S. 337 (1938).

318. Barksdale, "The Gaines Case and Its Effect on Negro Education in Missouri," 51 *School and Society* 309–11 (April 1940).

319. Letter from William E. Taylor to Martin Popper, in 1 *Lawyers Guild Rev.* 32 (1941). Daniel W. Bowles, a 1911 Howard University law graduate, joined the faculty of Lincoln University's law school. *Who's Who Among Negro Lawyers* 6 (S. T. M. Alexander ed. 1945).

320. McWilliams, "Racial Dialectic: Missouri Style," 160 *The Nation* 208 (Feb. 24, 1945).

321. Dean Taylor became active in the National Lawyers Guild. See 1 *Lawyers Guild Rev.* 32 (1941).

322. McWilliams, "Racial Dialectic: Missouri Style," 160 *The Nation* 208–9 (Feb. 24, 1945). By 1945, with the return of black soldiers from the war, and the accreditation of Lincoln University's law school by the American Bar Association and the Missouri Bar Examiners, the law school was able to move forward. See also, Walker, "Legal Education in Negro Institutions of Higher Learning," 73 *School and Society* 326 (May 26, 1951).

323. "Scovel Richardson, 70, Dies; Judge on U.S. Trade Court," *Washington Post*, April 1, 1982, at C14, col. 1.

324. *Id.* at 209. The Lincoln University School of Law closed in 1955. Barksdale, "The Gaines Case and Its Effect on Negro Education in Missouri," 51 *School and Society* 309–11 (April 1940).

325. Washington, "History and Role of Black Law Schools," 18 *How. L.J.* 385, 399–400 (1974); Walker, "Legal Education in Negro Institutions of Higher Learning," 73 *School and Society* 326 (May 26, 1951).

326. P. Murray, *Song in a Weary Throat* 127 (1987): when the school opened only one student enrolled; his name was Logan Drummond Delany.

327. "N.C. College Has Grade A School for Law Students," *Pittsburgh Courier*, Sept. 5, 1942, at 20, col. 1.

328. *Bulletin of North Carolina Central University, School of Law* 7 (1972–74); Washington, "History and Role of Black Law Schools," 18 *How. L.J.* 385, 399–400 (1974).

Chapter 2

New England: The Genesis of the Black Lawyer

Although the states of Maine and Massachusetts are Atlantic states (the subject of chapter 3), they are here specially treated because the American black lawyer originated in these states.

Maine

The state of Maine has the distinction of admitting the first black American to the bar. His name was Macon Bolling Allen. Through the efforts of General Samuel Fessenden, a white liberal, Allen was sponsored for admission to the courts of Maine in 1844, the same year William Wetmore Story published the first book on contracts in the United States. At that time, any citizen was eligible to be admitted to the bar in Maine who produced a certificate of good moral character. All others were required to pass a written examination. Allen, a native of Indiana, initially failed to qualify for admission because it was determined that he was not a citizen of Maine. But in the same year he applied for admission by examination and passed successfully.[1]

The admission of the first black person into the learned profession of the law was greeted with mixed feelings. The *Daily Eastern Argus*, reporting on Allen's admission, exclaimed, "Vell, Vot of it?"[2] Furthermore, the *Argus* wrote, "is the practice of law so much more respectable than hoeing potatoes that a lawyer can be disgraced by contact with a black man, and not a farmer?"[3] Whether because of the initial reactions to his admission to the bar or because of his desire to relocate to a state with more black Americans, Macon Bolling Allen "never entered upon the practice [of law] in Maine."[4] Within a year of his admission to the Maine bar, he left for Boston, with hopes of being admitted to the Massachusetts bar.[5]

Thirty-five years passed before Maine admitted John H. Hill, its second black lawyer. Hill, a native of West Virginia who apparently had been sent to Maine to attend college, also studied law under a white lawyer. Hill was admitted to the bar of the Supreme Judicial Court of Sagadahoc County on April 11, 1879, by Judge Charles J. Faulkner, Jr.[6] However, like Macon Bolling Allen, Hill did not remain in Maine. He returned to his native state of West Virginia, where he was also admitted to the bar.[7]

There is no evidence that any other blacks studied law or were admitted to practice in Maine before 1913, the year Milton Roscoe Geary was admitted to the bar. Geary entered the University of Maine School of Law in 1911 to take specific courses to qualify for bar admission. He had previously studied in a law office in Marlboro, Massachusetts. Geary was the first black student admitted to the University of Maine law school. After successfully completing his formal studies, Geary was admitted to the bar in February 1913. Unlike the two black lawyers who had preceded him, Geary remained in Maine and opened a law office in the city of Bangor. From all available accounts, Geary, the only black lawyer in Maine, was well received, perhaps because of the dearth of white lawyers in Maine.[8] He built his practice among white clients by "engaging in various civic, religious and cultural community projects and organizations."[9] In 1927, Geary was ordained as a minister in the Northern Baptist Convention, but law remained his main source of income. Geary was the first black member of the Penobscot Bar Association, and he remained the only black lawyer in the state of Maine through the 1940s.

Massachusetts

Macon Bolling Allen, the first black lawyer in the nation, arrived in Boston in 1845. He was admitted to the Suffolk County Bar in Massachusetts on May 3, 1845, earning the dual distinction of being the first black lawyer admitted to practice in Maine and in the Commonwealth of Massachusetts.[10] Allen's admission to the Suffolk County Bar—and his physiognomy—was widely publicized in Boston and in other New England states. Three days after Allen was admitted to the Suffolk County Bar, the *Daily Eastern Argus*, which had previously reported on his admission to the bar in Maine, again saw fit to take up the subject:

In the municipal court of Boston . . . Mr. Macon B. Allen was admitted on a certificate of competency, signed by Judge Merrick [of Maine], to practice as an attorney and counsellor at law. The *Post* says that Mr. Allen is 29 years of age— is a native of Indiana, and his color and physiognomy bespeak a mingled Indian and African extraction, in about equal proportions. He is of medium height and size, and passably good looking. He is indeed a better looking man than two or three white members of the Boston Bar, and it is hardly possible that he can be a worse lawyer than at least six of them, whom we could name. He commenced his legal studies in the Office of General [Samuel] Fessenden . . . and completed them with Mr. [Samuel E.] Sewell [of Maine].[11]

The Liberator, a Boston paper, reported that Allen had "received a classical education and, although a colored person, is, we are informed, a young man of such character and deportment, gentle, unassuming and strictly upright, as must very materially, if not wholly in his case, obviate any of the peculiar consequences attendant upon the circumstances of a similar personal complexion."[12]

If Macon B. Allen moved to Boston hoping to find a receptive clientele, he was to be disappointed. A year after Allen was admitted to practice law, he expressed his disappointment in a letter to John Jay of New York City:

The prospect of my securing an adequate support . . . is certainly not so good as could be desired. Owing to the peculiar custom of the New England people, and especially Boston people, to sustain those chiefly who are of family and fortune, or who have been long established, this is not regarded as the best place for me who can boast none of these requisite appendages. . . . It has been frequently suggested to me that New York, where people greatly differ from our own in this particular I have noted, and with a colored population who themselves, it is reasonable to suppose, have sufficient business which they would give him . . . [could] employ a colored lawyer . . . better than . . . Boston.[13]

Allen's woes were further magnified when he was publicly insulted by an abolitionist at the Boston Town Hall during the heated debates against the United States' expansionist policies during the Mexican War.[14] Fearing that the war with Mexico would expand slavery and enhance the power of recently annexed Texas, abolitionists in 1846 asked New Englanders to pledge not to support the government's war efforts. Allen voiced outrage at the abolitionists' "indecorous" conduct toward him when he refused to sign the pledge "not to sustain the government in any event, in the present war with Mexico."[15] One abolitionist accused him of being unconcerned about the slave conditions existing in the South. Allen wrote to William Lloyd Garrison:

Though not in the habit of declaring what sentiments I entertain, deeming it of little consequence, I trust it will not seem presumptuous if I embrace the occasion . . . to say, that I sympathize as strongly with my brethren in bonds—with whom I am identified in almost every particular, as my nature, not a cold one, enables me to do so, and accordingly to the right that is in me, and my humble ability, am ever ready and willing to do all I can for their melioration. The cause of the Colored man, in whatever section of our country, expressly is really my own cause; and it would be monstrous indeed if I did not so regard it.[16]

Admitted to practice law in Boston, Allen was listed in the Boston City Directory in 1851 as a counsellor-at-law living in Charlestown.[17] His skill as a lawyer and his leadership in the community were no doubt the reasons that Governor George N. Briggs, of the Whig Party, appointed Allen justice of the peace on April 21, 1847, an appointment which was renewed by Governor Emory Washburn, also a Whig, in 1854.[18] Allen's appointment as justice of the peace made him the first black lawyer in the history of the nation to be appointed to a judicial post.

Allen served honorably as a justice of the peace and practiced law in Boston continuously until after the Civil War. With the advent of the Reconstruction era in the South, he left Boston, relocating to Charleston, South Carolina, where he was admitted to the bar, entered politics, and opened a law practice.[19]

Robert Morris, Sr., America's second black lawyer, commenced the study of law in Boston under the tutelage of Ellis Gray Loring, a white man connected with the anti-slavery movement.[20] Loring, an 1827 Harvard University law graduate, hired Morris as a house servant in 1837, when Morris was fifteen years old. Loring also had a white lad in his employ. Robert Morris, Sr., got a chance to study law because the white servant "neglected his duties,"[21] allowing him to move up to "help out by doing copying in Loring's law office."[22] Pleased with the intellect of young Morris, Loring encouraged him to study law.[23] On February 2, 1847, Robert Morris, Sr., was admitted to the Superior Civil Court of Suffolk County and thereafter began to practice law.[24]

Morris was an aggressive and assertive lawyer whose technical skills were recognized by many in the community and by members of the local bar. In 1847, in what may be the first lawsuit filed by a black lawyer on behalf of a client in the history of the nation, a jury in Boston ruled in favor of Morris's client, though the details of the trial are unknown. Morris, however, recorded his feelings and observations about his first jury trial:

There was something in the courtroom that made me feel like a giant. The courtroom was filled with colored people, and I could see, expressed on the faces of every one of them, a wish that I might win the first case that had ever been tried before a jury by a colored attorney in this country. At last my case was called; I went to work and tried it for all it was worth; and until the evidence was all in, the argument on both sides made, the judge's charge concluded, and the case given to the jury, I spared no pains to win. The jury after being out a short time returned, and when the foreman in reply to the clerk answered that the jury found for the plaintiff, my heart pounded up and my people in the courtroom acted as if they would shout for joy.[25]

After his victory in this trial, Morris's popularity soared: A black man had prevailed against a white lawyer. A few months later Robert Morris, Sr., was approached by a group of citizens led by Benjamin F. Roberts and asked to file a lawsuit to desegregate the Boston public school system. Roberts complained that his daughter was precluded from attending a neighborhood school because she was black. Morris accepted the case, and in 1848 he filed, and personally tried, the first civil rights case challenging a segregated public school system in Boston.[26] The name of this celebrated case was *Roberts v. City of Boston*.[27]

The complainants in the lawsuit were Sarah Roberts, a five-year-old black child, and her father, Benjamin F. Roberts. At the trial Morris attempted to prove (without success) that a resolution passed by the local school board in Boston requiring "colored children" to attend "colored schools" was illegal. In this instance, Sarah Roberts was required to travel an additional fifth of a mile from her house than the nearest public primary school. In fact, the nearest public school was nine hundred feet from Sarah Roberts's house, and five schools for white children lay between Sarah's home and her school. But the local court ruled in favor of the local school board, represented by P. W. Chandler, and Morris was required to pay court costs of $51.30.[28] Morris immediately appealed the ruling to the Supreme Judicial Council of Massachusetts, the highest court in the commonwealth, and won the support of Charles Sumner, an abolitionist Boston lawyer who in 1851 would be elected to the United States Senate.

Attempting to overturn the lower court's ruling, Robert Morris and Charles Sumner filed, in 1848, the first civil rights appellate brief ever co-signed by a black lawyer and a white lawyer in any case in America. The brief argued that the constitution and laws of Massachusetts made all persons, without distinction of age, sex, birth, color, origin, or condition, equal before the law. However, the court refused to overturn the lower court's decision, holding that it was reasonable and "practical" to require black children in Boston to travel further distances to attend "colored schools."[29]

Although Morris and Sumner lost this case, their effort helped set in motion a jurisprudence of opposition to segregated public education that would culminate one hundred and five years later in *Brown v. Board of Education*,[30] which held that state-imposed segregation in public school systems was unconstitutional. Robert Morris lost his case before the Supreme Council of Massachusetts but won the respect of the black citizens of Boston.

In 1851, following the *Roberts* case, Robert Morris, Sr., was involved in a case so important that it ultimately reached the desk of the president of the United States. In February of that year, the United States marshal arrested in Boston a black waiter known as Frederick Wilkens, who was named in the warrant as Shadrack, a fugitive slave.[31] His owner, John DeBree, of Norfolk, Virginia, sought the return of Shadrack under the provisions of the newly enacted Federal Fugitive Slave Act of 1850.[32] Robert Morris, Sr., was retained to represent Shadrack after Charles Sumner declined to do so because the case might "effect [his] pending senatorial election."[33]

The arrest of Shadrack shocked the black community in Boston, and on the date of the hearing to determine whether he would be returned to Virginia, the federal courtroom and the streets outside were full of black spectators. When the decision was announced granting Shadrack's owner the right to take him back to Virginia, white witnesses alleged that "Mr. Morris [opened the courtroom door and gave] a signal . . . to the crowd . . . who filled the corridor. . . . The uncontrollable mass swarmed in, heedless of all attempts of the officers to keep them back; the general deputy marshal took refuge under a table and . . . [the people] enveloped [Shadrack] in the cloud which darkened the whole room."[34] Shadrack disappeared and was later heard to be in Canada.[35]

Word of this event reached the president of the United States, Millard Fillmore, who immediately issued a proclamation calling for the prosecution "against all persons, who shall have made themselves aiders and abettors in this flagitious offence."[36] The rescue of Shadrack by black people frightened such national political leaders as former senator Henry Clay of Kentucky. Clay said that "because [Shadrack's] escape had been effected by 'a band who are not of our own people,' [it] raised the question whether the government of white men is to be yielded to a government of blacks."[37]

Morris and several other black Boston citizens alleged to be involved in helping Shadrack to escape were indicted for treason and conspiracy to violate federal law. News of the impending trial drew wide coverage in Massachusetts and beyond. On March 9, 1851, a preliminary hearing was held before a United States commissioner who determined that

the evidence, which is wholly uncontradicted, shows that the defendant who is a counsellor at law, and who in that capacity was acting here in court as the attorney of [Shadrack] combined with a lawless body of men acting together by force and violence to break and resist the laws . . . and enabled [Shadrack] to escape from the process of the law.[38]

Morris and the others pleaded not guilty to all the charges against them.[39] Nevertheless, each defendant was found guilty, a verdict which they appealed to the United States Circuit Court. After reviewing the findings of the United States commissioner and the record of trial, the United States Circuit Court of Appeals reversed the convictions on technical grounds.[40] In October 1851, the court remanded Morris's case to the United States District Court of Massachusetts for a new trial,[41] but this time, on November 11, 1851, Morris was acquitted.[42] Hence, a case that could have ended Morris's legal career instead increased his prestige among his people, the abolitionists, and the bar.

While Morris's acquittal was well received by most citizens, some continued to hold Morris up "to public odium."[43] Still, in spite of Morris's prior criminal indictment for treason, Governor George N. Briggs commissioned him as a magistrate in Essex County, Massachusetts, making him the second black lawyer in the history of the nation to hold a judicial post.[44] His run-in with the federal authorities did not adversely effect his private practice, either. He continued to be retained "[to keep] the books of one of the wealthy railroad companies in Boston, a business almost entirely confined to lawyers."[45]

Robert Morris, Sr., remained a bold and aggressive lawyer in the Commonwealth of Massachusetts, and he called on blacks to continue to resist—even by force—the Fugitive Slave Law of 1850.

Let us be bold, if any man flees from slavery, and come among us. When he's reached us we'll say he's gone far enough. If any man comes here to New Bedford, and they try to take him away, you telegraph to us in Boston, and we'll come down three hundred strong, and stay with you; and we won't go until he is safe. If he goes back to the South, we'll go with him.[46]

After the Civil War ended and freedom was at hand, the law practices of black lawyers picked up in the New England states,[47] and Robert Morris, Sr., "became one of the busiest lawyers practicing criminal law in Boston," representing blacks and, especially, Irish immigrants.[48] In fact, Morris's Irish clients constituted "fully one half of the work" he performed, "mak[ing] him the first really successful colored lawyer in America."[49] By 1882, Morris is said to have earned an annual income of "over $3,000."[50] By 1866, Morris had gained such popularity and stature that he ran for mayor in the city of Chelsea, but was not elected. However, word of his candidacy for mayor was spread as far away as New Orleans, Louisiana, where the local press reported that "[t]hose who believe that a black man is only fit for slavery and the lash, will probably be again shocked by the announcement that the citizens of Chelsea of Massachusetts have run Robert Morris, a Negro lawyer for mayor of that city."[51]

Robert Morris's son, named after his father, also became a lawyer. Robert Morris, Jr., was admitted to the Massachusetts bar on September 8, 1874, becoming the first second-generation black lawyer in the nation.[52] Little is known about the legal career of Robert Morris, Jr. He probably qualified for the bar by reading law in his father's law office. Robert Morris, Jr., died in December 1883, two weeks after his father's death.[53]

On February 2, 1856, Aaron Alpeoria Bradley became the third black lawyer admitted to the Massachusetts bar at Suffolk County.[54] Bradley may also have been a member of the New York bar. One historian critical of Bradley has written that Bradley moved to Boston after serving a two-year sentence in New York for seduction, and that Bradley was "stricken from the rolls of attorneys."[55] The same historian wrote that Bradley was later "removed from practic[ing] in any court in Massachusetts, for contempt of court and malpractice," a claim Bradley denied throughout his political career in Savannah, Georgia, the place to which he moved after the Civil War.[56] While the details of Bradley's alleged disbarment in New England are not conclusive, it is entirely conceivable that he could have been disbarred for impermissible reasons such as race or class.

In May 1861, Edward Garrison Walker became the fourth black lawyer admitted to the Suffolk County bar in Massachusetts, after reading the law and passing a comprehensive bar examination.[57] Walker immediately entered into the law practice of John Q. A. Griffin of Charlestown. His skills as a criminal lawyer were exceedingly advanced, and judges "frequently [assigned Walker] as defense [counsel] in important criminal cases, including several murder cases."[58] It was possibly the notoriety of these cases that brought him name recognition during his successful candidacy for election to the General Court (the Massachusetts legislature) in 1866. Walker's thus became "the first colored man elected to the legislature in the United States."[59] During his legislative career, Walker was known as "one of the pioneers in the woman suffrage movement."[60] In 1886, Walker formed a law firm with James Harris Wolff and Edward Everett Brown in Suffolk County—the first black law firm in the state of Massachusetts.[61]

On September 14, 1861, Dr. John Swett Rock, a black physician, set aside the practice of medicine for the study of law and was admitted to practice before Judge Russell in all the state courts of Massachusetts on motion of T. K. Lothrop, a white Boston lawyer.[62] He entered the private practice of law in Southac.[63] The death in 1864 of United States Supreme Court Chief Justice Roger Brooke Taney (the author of the *Dred Scott* decision,[64] which held that blacks had no rights that a white person was bound to respect), was soon to make it possible for Rock to become the first black lawyer admitted to the United States Supreme Court.

In 1864, after Chief Justice Salmon P. Chase, an anti-slavery lawyer from Ohio, succeeded Chief Justice Taney, Dr. Rock wrote a letter to his United States senator, Charles Sumner, observing that "we now have a great and good man for our chief justice, and with him I think my color will not be a bar to my admission [to the United States Supreme Court]."[65] Senator Sumner agreed, recognizing that the admission of a black lawyer to the United States Supreme Court would have great symbolic meaning. In an apparent attempt to persuade Chief Justice Chase to accept Rock's application for admission to the United States Supreme Court, Senator Sumner advised the chief justice that "the admission of a colored lawyer to the bar of the Supreme Court would make it difficult for any restriction on account of race to be maintained anywhere. Street cars would be open afterwards."[66]

On February 1, 1865, the day President Abraham Lincoln signed the joint resolution (adopted by the U.S. Senate and the House of Representatives) which proposed the Thirteenth Amendment outlawing slavery, John Swett Rock appeared before the United States Supreme Court for admission.[67] The ceremony was a moment of high drama, for Rock's admission to the court was a repudiation of all in which Chief Justice Taney believed.

Twenty-four years after Macon Bolling Allen had become the first black lawyer in the nation, Dr. John Swett Rock became the first black lawyer admitted to practice before the United States Supreme Court, on a motion by Senator Charles Sumner. Chief Justice Chase, "bowing gravely and gracefully," said, "Let Mr. Rock advance to the clerk's desk, and take the oath."[68] The scene was described by Francis W. Bird, editor of *The Boston Commonwealth*, as follows:

Mr. [Francis V.] Balch, [Senator] Sumner's private secretary, was admitted also on [Senator] Sumner's motion. Both gentlemen proceeded to the clerk's desk, and the oath was administered by the clerk. I observed that the clerk [Mr. Daniel Wesley Middleton] studiously averted his face from Mr. Rock, looking only towards Mr. Balch. I do not wonder, for it must have been a bitter pill for a malignant Copperhead to administer the oath, under those circumstances, to a colored counsellor-at-law. . . . How strange and solemn were the thronging memories of that moment. [Justices] Jay, Rutledge, Ellsworth and Marshall looking upon the scene; the perturbed shade of Taney, followed by the black spectra of Dred Scott flitting round the room.[69]

The admission of Dr. Rock to the United States Supreme Court was a momentous event in Washington. Moments after his admission, Congressman John Dennison Baldwin of Massachusetts arranged to have Dr. Rock "received upon the floor of the House of Representatives while it was in session," making him the first black person so honored by a member of Congress.[70] According to John W. Forbes,

Congressman . . . Baldwin . . . escorted Mr. Rock to a seat in the Representatives Hall, where he was cordially congratulated by the leading men . . . for even to them it seemed remarkable that a colored man should know enough law to practice before the Supreme Court. The rank and file of the members simply regarded the visitor as a prodigy in law.[71]

Dr. John Swett Rock had come to Washington, D.C., to be admitted to the United States Supreme Court only to find that, when he attempted to return to Boston, his certificate of admission would be insufficient identification to leave the nation's capital.

After Mr. Rock's admission to the United States Supreme Court [the] scene changed. Mr. Rock applies to the ticket office for a ticket to Baltimore, [Maryland]. The ticket is sold to him, his money is taken, and as he proceeds to the cars, he is stopped and asked for his "pass." His certificate of admission to the Supreme Court will not pass him. He is obliged to go to the enrollment office to see that he is not enrolled in the District. He takes a certificate of that fact to the Provost-Marshal, who gives him a pass, authorizing him to leave the District.[72]

The admission of Rock to the bar of the highest court of the land would have an impact throughout the judicial system. Rock's admission would make it exceedingly difficult for any inferior court to exclude black lawyers from admission solely on account of race; as Charles Sumner wrote, "[it] helped the way for admission of his race to the rights of citizenship, and especially the right to vote."[73]

William Henry Johnson, an ex-slave from Richmond, Virginia, was admitted to the Massachusetts bar in the Bristol Superior Court on March 21, 1865.[74] First hired as a janitor in several lawyers' offices, Johnson "became interested in reading law books."[75] He subsequently "became a regular law student in Francis L. Porter's office."[76] Though Porter explained very little to Johnson, he did give "direction to his reading."[77] Johnson not only studied the law, but he also learned the business and was ultimately encouraged to apply for admission to the bar by another white lawyer, George Marston. Johnson practiced law for several years in various counties in Massachusetts and in Rhode Island, Exeter, New Hampshire, and Brooklyn, New York.[78] He is no doubt the first black lawyer to represent clients in Rhode Island and New Hampshire, though it is uncertain whether he was ever admitted there, except to try a limited number of cases. His practice was diverse. He handled both civil and criminal cases, but his specialty was in the area of administrative law, particularly in the defense of liquor dealers around New Bedford. Yet Johnson was also a leader in the controversial temperance movement, a conflict that seemingly had little effect on his practice.[79] From 1880 to 1881, Johnson served as an elected member of the Common Council of New Bedford.

In 1869 George Lewis Ruffin became the first black lawyer to graduate from Harvard Law School. Prior to his admission to law school, he read law in the offices of Jewell and Gaston while employed as a barber. But Ruffin desired a formal legal education. He was better trained than many blacks, having received a good education in his early years. Ruffin entered Harvard in 1868, "where he distinguished himself by completing the three year course in one year, becoming the first black to be graduated from the law school and the second black to be graduated from Harvard University."[80] He was admitted to the Supreme Judicial Council of Massachusetts on September 18, 1869. Immediately after Ruffin was admitted to the bar, he was elected to the Massachusetts state legislature from Boston's ninth ward in 1870.[81] His popularity increased, and he was elected to Boston's Common Council, where he served from 1876 to 1877.[82] In 1883 Ruffin came to the attention of Governor Benjamin Franklin Butler, who had served as a general in the army during the Civil War. After Butler's efforts to appoint another black lawyer, Edward Garrison Walker, to the bench proved unsuccessful,[83] Governor Butler nominated Ruffin to become a municipal judge in Charlestown, a position to which he was confirmed by the Executive Council of the state legislature on November 7, 1883.[84] This appointment made Ruffin "the first Negro to obtain a judicial office higher than magistrate in the North."[85] He served honorably on the bench until his death in 1886. By 1900, in honor of the contribution George Lewis Ruffin had made in law and politics, civic and professional clubs bearing his name sprang up in the nation as far west as Cincinnati, Ohio.[86]

Ruffin assisted other black lawyers in their practice and vouched for their character when they applied for admission to the bar. One such lawyer was George Washington Williams, who Ruffin vouched for in 1881, the year that Williams was admitted to the Massachusetts bar. Williams started a practice and was soon retained by the Cape Cod Canal Company of Boston.[87] George Ruffin's son, Hubert St. Pierre Ruffin, "who spent two years as a member of the Harvard class of 1881," joined his father's firm after leaving Harvard's law school.[88]

In 1875, three additional black lawyers were admitted to the bar in Massachusetts: James Harris Wolff, John Dunkerson Lewis, and Archibald Henry Grimké. Prior to entering the Harvard University School of Law, James Harris Wolff "studied law under former Massachusetts Congressman Daniel Wheelwright Gouch."[89] Wolff was admitted to Harvard in 1874 and remained there only one year, without taking a degree.[90] On June 26, 1875, he was admitted to the Suffolk County bar and to the Supreme Judicial Council of Massachusetts. Shortly afterward Wolff moved to Maryland and became "the first colored lawyer admitted to practice in the United States Circuit Court [of

Maryland]."[91] It is not known how long Wolff remained in Maryland, but it was probably not long, since Maryland state law did not permit blacks to be admitted to the bar until 1885. However, Wolff returned to Boston prior to 1883, when he was appointed as "a clerk in the Adjutant General's Office by Governor John Davis Long [and resumed the] practice of law."[92] During his legal career, Wolff was twice a judge advocate in the Massachusetts Grand Army of the Republic (G.A.R.), "becoming the first colored man to hold the position"[93] in this veterans' military organization. In 1913, the year James Harris Wolff died, he was said to be "one of the most prominent Negro lawyers in [Massachusetts]."[94]

John Dunkerson Lewis was not as prominent as other black lawyers in Massachusetts. Lewis, like many of his peers, studied law for twenty-five months before he qualified for certification to the Suffolk County Court. He was admitted to that court on November 1, 1875.[95]

In 1872, Archibald Henry Grimké won a scholarship to study law at Harvard Law School. Grimké, the son of white South Carolina lawyer Henry Grimké and a slave mother, was graduated from the Harvard University School of Law in 1874, thereby becoming its second black graduate.[96] After Grimké graduated from Harvard, disagreement erupted in his family as to whether he should practice law in the North or the South. Grimké's family, some of whom had supported his education financially, believed he should practice in the South. But Grimké, who was born in slavery, was not anxious to go south, though several black lawyers from Massachusetts and other New England states had done so.[97] After passing the Massachusetts bar in 1875, he entered into practice for one year with William I. Bowditch, a white lawyer. Grimké became "richer in knowledge"[98] through his association with Bowditch, and in 1876 he formed a partnership with James H. Wolff, and in 1884 with Butler Roland Wilson, a recent black graduate of Boston University School of Law.[99]

Grimké did not find the practice of law very lucrative.[100] In 1887, he turned to journalism and became a prolific writer.[101] (Following the dissolution of the law firm, Butler Wilson opened his own law office. His services were in demand by whites and blacks, especially in the area of criminal defense work.[102]) It is perhaps due to the influence of Grimké's writings, as well as pressure from blacks who protested the lack of black government appointments, that President Grover Cleveland[103] appointed Grimké as United States Consul in Santo Domingo in 1894.[104] Upon completion of this assignment in 1898, Grimké "became one of the leading spirits in the American Negro Academy in Washington, D.C., serving as president . . . from 1903 to 1916."[105]

Clement Garnett Morgan was Harvard University's third black law graduate, following Archibald Grimké by nineteen years.[106] Admitted to the Suffolk County bar in 1893, the year he left Harvard, Morgan entered private practice in Cambridge, Massachusetts. No other black lawyer had practiced law in Cambridge before. Three years out of law school, Morgan was elected to the Common Council of Cambridge "from Ward 2, a predominantly white area."[107] Morgan later served as an alderman in Cambridge from 1898 to 1899.

William Henry Lewis, Sr., was the fourth black law graduate of Harvard University. In 1893, the *Boston Daily Globe* wrote, "if you should visit the library of the Harvard law school at almost any hour in the day you would see the desk [of William Henry Lewis] in the middle of the room, absorbed in his books."[108] During his law days at Harvard University, Lewis also played on the varsity football team; he excelled as both a law student and athlete. He graduated in 1895,[109] the same year in which Frederick Douglass died and Booker T. Washington made his famous "cast down your bucket" speech in Atlanta, Georgia,[110] and one year before *Plessy v. Ferguson*[111] was decided.

Admitted to the bar in Massachusetts in 1895, Lewis began the practice of law in Boston's Barrister's Hall, associating with two white lawyers, Albert A. Bridgham and John L. Dyer.[112] In 1898, Lewis announced his candidacy for the Cambridge Common Council, a post to which he was elected in 1899. He served on the Common Council for two years, after which he was elected to the Massachusetts House of Representatives. Lewis represented the Middlesex District of Cambridge from 1903 to 1906,[113] winning public praise as "a careful, industrious and conservative legislator."[114] During his first term, he served on the joint judiciary committee, which was "an exceptional honor" for a freshman legislator.[115]

Initially a critic of Booker T. Washington's views, especially those expressed in his Atlanta Compromise Speech,[116] Lewis by 1901 had joined Washington's supporters. Perhaps he sided with Washington because of his influence with President Theodore Roosevelt, a Harvard man.[117] Lewis never fully embraced Washington's philosophy, but both men—recognizing Roosevelt's respect for each of them—determined to resolve their public differences for the sake of the race.[118] As Lewis explained:

For a long time after leaving law school I was counted as one of the radicals and agitators, but I found so many good people who approved of Dr. Washington's course and who were just as sincere in their advocacy of human rights as I myself, that I began to ask myself if they were wholly wrong and myself wholly right. I came to believe that they were more right than I, and so decided I should not make the business of my life the pulling down of some other men or slinging mud at a real worker.[119]

The influence of Booker T. Washington, no more so than Lewis's extraordinary credentials, was a factor in Roosevelt's decision to appoint Lewis third assistant United States attorney in Boston in 1903. Henry P. Moulton, the United States District Attorney of Boston, carried out the appointment,[120] which won the praise and support of United States Attorney General Philander C. Knox and of Massachusetts senators, George Frisbie Hoar and Henry Cabot Lodge, Sr. However, Lewis's appointment did not go uncriticized by some local lawyers, who claimed that there was not enough work in the office to keep Lewis busy. This assertion proved to be unfounded.[121] Southern United States senators may have indirectly influenced the appointment of Lewis when they raised questions "as to why no Negro appointments were made in the North."[122] In 1907, Lewis was reappointed assistant district attorney by Charles J. Bonaparte, the United States attorney general. Lewis was assigned to head the new bureau of naturalization upon recommendation of Asa P. French, the United States district attorney of Massachusetts.[123]

With a Harvard University law degree and significant public appointments behind him, William H. Lewis returned to a successful private practice in Massachusetts, arguing cases in all courts, including the Massachusetts Supreme Judicial Council. He drew praise for his legal skills from Judge Oliver Wendell Holmes, then a member of that court.[124] In 1911, amid opposition from Southern senators from Alabama, Georgia, and North Carolina, William Henry Lewis was nominated by President William Howard Taft as assistant attorney general of the United States. The nomination "was confirmed in the most perfunctory manner without debate or a demand for rollcall" on June 14, 1911.[125]

President Taft, in consultation with Massachusetts Senator Henry Cabot Lodge, Sr., had made the appointment of Lewis a campaign plege in 1910. Lewis's appointment was "something of a political move to demonstrate to the Negro voters that President Taft's Administration was not unfriendly to the idea of recognizing colored Republicans."[126] Lewis, the first member of his race to hold a high office in the Department of Justice that required Senate confirmation, was an effective assistant attorney general. While serving in the Department of Justice, he quietly worked to oppose President Taft's appointment of William C. Hook of Kansas to fill the vacancy left by Justice John Marshall Harlan on the United States Supreme Court. Lewis researched the judicial opinions of Judge Hook, who was then a member of the United States Circuit Court in Leavenworth, Kansas, and discovered that his judicial views were racially biased.[127]

Lewis was frequently called upon to give speeches in and outside of

Massachusetts during his term as assistant attorney general of the United States. During a Lincoln Day observance in 1913, Lewis addressed the Massachusetts State legislature and declared that the nation would not have survived without the emancipation of the slave.[128] Speeches such as these no doubt drew more blacks to the Republican Party.

William Henry Lewis remained in office as assistant attorney general until President Taft lost the presidency to Woodrow Wilson in 1912. President Wilson's attorney general, William G. McAdoo, "asked for Lewis's resignation."[129] Lewis returned to Boston and resumed his law practice. Although he had sterling credentials, no apparent efforts were made to lure Lewis to any white law firms. He had simply been born too soon. Lewis was also disappointed when Booker T. Washington was not able to deliver the corporate business of John D. Rockefeller and Andrew Carnegie to Lewis's firm.[130]

In 1916 Lewis and another black attorney, John B. Edwards, defended two black men in a highly publicized murder case in Providence, Rhode Island. The defendants were charged with murdering a white physician. The third person charged in the crime was a suspected accomplice, the wife of the physician. The case, known as the Mohr murder case, was widely reported primarily because of the defense tactics and sheer brilliance of Lewis and Edwards. The press reported that the "defense of the Negroes is being made by . . . able men, one a pure blooded African and the other a mulatto."[131] Edwards, a member of the Rhode Island bar, was "harshly dealt with" by the press covering the trial because "of [his] darker shade."[132] The *New York Age* made an effort to correct some racial stereotypes by stating that Edwards "is not 'big' as described by Dorothy Dix, nor of the 'cottonfield type of darky' as pictured by Mrs. Jacques Futrell."[133] On the other hand, Lewis, the light skinned co-counsel, received much better treatment from the press. Dispatches referred to Lewis as "'the great Lewis,' the 'crafty,' 'shrewd,' 'able,' 'eloquent' Negro lawyer, who so easily eclipses the best the white race has provided for this dramatic event."[134] Such disparate reporting exemplifies the pitfalls darker black lawyers faced in many communities in the nation—North and South—during this period. Lewis and Edwards waged an aggressive defense on behalf of their clients, who were both convicted of murder. The convictions were appealed to the Rhode Island Supreme Court and were ultimately upheld.[135]

Due to the rising number of lynchings of blacks during the presidency of Woodrow Wilson and the president's reluctance to propose legislation making lynching a federal crime, the pressures on Congress to address this issue grew.[136] In 1921, while the Dyer Anti-Lynching

Bill[137] was pending in Congress, William H. Lewis, Sr., and Butler Roland Wilson, both of Boston, and James Adlai Cobb, a law professor at Howard University, provided legal briefs on the constitutionality of Congressman Leonidas C. Dyer's bill. The legal brief was actually prepared to educate and win the support of Senator William E. Borah of Idaho, an influential senator who questioned the constitutionality of the anti-lynching legislation. Southern senators were opposed to the legislation, which would have made lynching in any state a federal crime.[138] Congressman Dyer's proposed legislation never passed. Politics, and questions concerning the constitutionality of the Dyer bill, doomed the anti-lynching legislation.[139] Nevertheless, the request by Senator Borah that black lawyers prepare a legal brief was at least some recognition of their legal acumen. And yet the efforts of William Henry Lewis and other black lawyers to promote the civil rights of black Americans were dashed in 1926 when the United States Supreme Court decided *Corrigan v. Buckley*, which held that restrictive covenants based on race were not violative of the United States Constitution.[140]

William Henry Lewis, Sr., almost sixty years of age, continued to be retained by white defendants to litigate complex cases, some of which reached the United States Supreme Court.[141] In 1930, Lewis successfully argued *United States v. Farrar* before the Supreme Court, which held that the Volstead Act imposed no criminal liability on the purchase of illegal alcohol.[142] James E. Farrar, a white man, retained Lewis and a white lawyer associated with the Liberty League of New York[143] to appeal his case to the highest court. It was said that "Lewis, Boston's noted colored lawyer, made the argument with great ability."[144]

Like his father, William Henry Lewis, Jr., attended Harvard University School of Law, but for only one year, after being graduated from Harvard College. The senior Lewis was not content to have his son attend any school other than Harvard, "because his Harvard training had meant too much to him, not to mention his contribution to Harvard."[145] After his admission to the Massachusetts bar in 1926, the younger Lewis practiced law with his father for several years.

Other lawyers, such as Matthew Washington Bullock, Sr., and Edward Orval Gourdin, both Harvard University law graduates, made exceptional contributions to the law. Matthew W. Bullock, Sr., received his law degree from Harvard in 1907. He first practiced law in Atlanta, Georgia, returning to Boston in 1917. Admitted to the Massachusetts bar in 1921, he was soon appointed special assistant attorney general of Massachusetts, a post he held from 1925 to 1926, whereupon he was appointed to the Massachusetts Parole Board by Governor Alvan T. Fuller. Bullock's talents came to the attention of nine other governors under whom he served in various capacities.[146] Matthew Bullock's son, who was named after his father, graduated from Harvard University in 1943.[147]

Edward Orval Gourdin, a 1924 law graduate of Harvard, was appointed assistant United States district attorney in Boston with the support of President Franklin D. Roosevelt. Gourdin prosecuted many of the smuggling cases of the period, and, by the time of the outbreak of World War II, he had "risen to chief of the legal division" in the United States attorney's office of Boston.[148]

At the turn of the century, the pioneer black law graduates of Boston University also emerged. In 1894, Edgar P. Benjamin was graduated with honors from Boston University School of Law. Benjamin was permitted to sit for the bar examination (which he passed) prior to the date of his graduation.[149] Benjamin entered the private practice of law and became a respected corporation lawyer. He was admitted to practice before the United States Supreme Court in 1906. In 1914, Benjamin reported that he was the "sole counsel for many large firms and corporations . . . many of which are white."[150] The judiciary placed much confidence in Benjamin's legal ability by appointing him "special investigator" when local attorneys sued judges and clerks in mandamus proceedings.[151] Indeed, judges retained Benjamin to represent them when they had run-ins with the law. In 1919, Benjamin gained much notoriety when he represented Judge Albert F. Hayden and Maurice J. O'Connell, clerk of the Roxbury Court, who were indicted for wrongful misconduct.[152]

William Clarence Matthews was graduated from Boston University School of Law in 1907 and admitted to the Massachusetts bar in 1908.[153] He worked his way through law school in the law offices of William Henry Lewis, whose firm he joined after law school.[154] In 1913, President William Howard Taft recommended that Matthews be appointed as special assistant United States attorney of Massachusetts, and he was reappointed to this position in 1925 by President Calvin Coolidge. In 1926, the Department of Justice assigned Matthews to California as special assistant to the attorney general to oversee water adjudication litigation that was pending in federal court.[155]

John W. Schenck attended Boston University law school but completed his studies in the law firm of Matthews and Kittredge. In 1921, Schenck was appointed assistant United States attorney in Boston by President Warren Harding and was retained in that position by President Calvin Coolidge.[156]

After receiving his law degree from Howard University in 1918, Herman Emmon Moore became one of the first blacks to receive a master of laws degree from Boston University School of Law the following year. After completing his graduate training, "he established a reputation as a brief writer for various Boston law firms."[157] He later served as an assistant attorney for the Boston elevated railway, thereby becoming "the first Negro in this post."[158] In 1921 Moore went to Chicago to practice law, after having practiced with William Henry Lewis, Sr., for two years.[159]

Several other black lawyers in Massachusetts made their marks before the close of World War II. G. Bruce Robinson was graduated from Boston University School of Law in 1936. After a short period in private practice, Robinson was appointed assistant attorney general of Massachusetts, a position he held from 1942 to 1945.[160] David Eugene Crawford was admitted to the United States District Court in Boston in 1908. He became a respected member of the bar and was several times appointed master of chancery for Suffolk County. In 1924 Crawford was appointed public administrator of Suffolk County.[161] Robert Morris Stevens conducted his legal studies in a law office and was admitted to practice in Berkshire County, Massachusetts, in 1912. He is distinguished as being "the first man of color to practice law West of Worcester in the State of Massachusetts."[162] Col. John Stanhope Ray Bourne, Julian D. Rainey, and James G. Wolff also made significant contributions to the law. Bourne practiced law both in Cambridge and Boston in 1916.[163] Bourne was an honor graduate of Northwestern University School of Law in 1916 and began to practice law in Cambridge and Boston later that year. In 1920 Bourne authored "a legislative bill for employment of colored conductors and motormen on the Boston Elevated Car system."[164] Julian D. Rainey was the second black lawyer to join the legal staff of the Boston Elevated Railroad Corporation in 1920 and became an assistant corporation counsel in Boston in 1930 at a yearly salary of $5,000.[165] In the same year Rainey joined the legal staff of the city of Boston, a second black lawyer, James G. Wolff, was also hired on the staff.

Suffolk Law School in Boston graduated Thomas Vreeland Jones, perhaps its first black graduate, in 1915.[166] Cyril Fitzgerald Butler followed Jones to Suffolk and was graduated from law school there in 1919. He was the class orator at commencement. In 1919, Butler also was admitted to the bar in Massachusetts; after "two years in the law office of [a] prominent (white) attorney, a congressman from Cambridge, . . . [he] opened his own offices" and later became a member of one of the first local legal committees established by the recently organized National Association for the Advancement of Colored People.[167]

In 1925 Clifton Reginald Wharton, Sr., a member of the Massachusetts bar, was appointed secretary of the American legation in Monrovia, Liberia, having taken the foreign service examination in January 1925 and on March 21, 1925."[168] Upon his return from military service in World War I, Wharton practiced law in Boston from 1920 to 1924. Wharton entered the government services as a clerk in the Veterans Bureau in May 1924. By August 1924, he had become a law clerk at the Department of State at an annual salary of $1,860.[169] And in 1931, John T. Lane became the first black clerk of the Juvenile Court of Boston at a salary of $3,500.[170]

Few women were admitted to the Massachusetts bar prior to 1945, but seventy-nine years after Macon Bolling Allen, Blanche E. Braxton gained admission on March 16, 1923.[171] Braxton engaged in some private practice, but the extent of her success in the law is unsubstantiated.[172] Braxton, however, broke ground on March 21, 1933, when she became the "first colored woman" admitted to practice in the United States District Court in Massachusetts.[173]

Inez C. Fields, a 1922 Boston University law graduate, became the second black woman admitted to the Massachusetts bar, on April 15, 1924.[174] Thereupon Fields returned to Virginia, her native state, and joined her father's law firm. On October 27, 1926, Clara Burrill Bruce became the third black woman admitted to the Massachusetts bar.[175] Bruce was a graduate of the Boston University School of Law, where she was elected editor-in-chief of the *Boston Law Review* in 1925, thus becoming the first black student to head a law review in the history of American legal education. After her graduation, Bruce returned to Washington, D.C., where she managed her husband's real estate business. Bruce's son, Burrill Kelso Bruce, attended law school at Harvard University between 1934 and 1936, making Clara Bruce one of the first black women lawyers whose son also undertook the study of law.[176] In 1927, Viola Ollivette Fisher-Minor was one of five black women graduated from Boston's Portia Law School (New England Law School).[177] Since Fisher-Minor received her law degree prior to her twenty-first birthday, she was required to wait until that age before she qualified to take the bar examination.[178] She remained in Boston and was eventually appointed confidential aide to Governor Leverett Saltonstall in 1939. Another woman, Rowena Easterling Taylor, was admitted to the bar on November 9, 1938, but little more is known about her.[179]

The graduation of Jacqueline Guild from the Portia Law School in 1933 is noteworthy because she appears to have been the first woman in the state to follow her father (Ray Wilson Guild, Sr.) to the bar, and to practice law with him.[180] Admitted to the bar in 1933, she was a successful lawyer during her "thirteen-year association with her lawyer father" in Cambridge, Massachusetts. Thereafter, her progress slowed, probably because of her race and sex, and her continued success in private practice began to wane.[181]

Summary

Because slavery had been abolished in Massachusetts in 1783, it is not surprising that Macon Bolling Allen was admitted to the bar in a New England state. It is a mystery, however, why Allen initially chose to enter the legal profession in Maine, with a population of approximately 1,355 blacks, rather than in Massachusetts, with a black population of 8,669 in 1840. Perhaps Allen went to Maine because of its historical opposition to slavery. What is known is that a liberal white lawyer in Maine tutored Allen until he became competent to win admission to the bar in 1844. Such support, coupled with Allen's brilliant mind, level of education, and personal stamina, all contributed to his ultimate success as a lawyer, and to the success of the legions of black lawyers that followed him to the bar. But even with the history of abolitionist sentiment in Maine, Allen apparently had no opportunity to practice law there, nor was he successful in the law in Massachusetts, to which he returned to become that state's first black lawyer in 1845.

Macon Bolling Allen's opportunity to practice law did not come until after the Civil War. Allen and many other black lawyers—as well as white lawyers, went south to make their fortunes (Allen went to South Carolina). Allen made no fortune, but he did become a respected member of the bar and a judge as well.

Allen's experience in Massachusetts was unlike that of Robert Morris, Sr., who was admitted to the Massachusetts bar in 1847. It was Morris who first demonstrated that a black lawyer could try a case before a white jury on behalf of a white client and win. The nation's first jury verdict at the hands of a black lawyer in 1847 showed black people in Massachusetts that the court *was* a forum for justice.

Black people watched Morris closely when, in 1847, he sued the Boston public school system to desegregate the schools. Morris lost this case at trial, and he and Charles Sumner, who co-filed the first brief ever by a black lawyer and a white lawyer, also lost the case before the Supreme Judicial Council, Massachusetts's highest court. This case, though lost, set the stage for *Brown v. Board of Education*, which held that state-imposed segregation in public schools was unconstitutional. Robert Morris, unlike Macon B. Allen, earned a respectable salary doing legal work—some $3,000 a year—after the Civil War by serving the needs of white immigrants.

Black lawyers like Morris were drawn to politics. Although Morris lost his bid in 1866 to become mayor of Chelsea, Massachusetts, this first mayoralty campaign by a black man challenged the perception among blacks, and no doubt whites, that winning public office was beyond their reach. Other black lawyers, such as Edward Garrison

Walker, proved that blacks could be elected to state office. In 1866, Walker became the first black elected to the Massachusetts legislature.

Allen and Morris made significant strides for black lawyers. However, the admission of John Swett Rock to the United States Supreme Court, followed by his official welcome by congressmen on the floor of the House of Representatives in 1865, brought the black lawyer to the attention of the nation. Such affirmation had never been conferred on the black lawyer, and it became a symbol for the emancipation of the slaves. Rock's admission to the Supreme Court of the United States was the first license granted to a black person by a branch of the national government to argue for his own cause and interpretation of the laws of the nation and the Constitution. Macon B. Allen, Robert Morris, Sr., and John Swett Rock embody the essence of the experience of the first black lawyers in the nation. Yet each of them also experienced racial discrimination that stunted their potential.

Four law schools are principally responsible for the education of black lawyers in Massachusetts: Harvard University, Boston University, Suffolk Law School, and Portia Law School. It was Harvard University that first graduated a black law student in 1869; this graduate, George Lewis Ruffin, would become the first black lawyer to hold a judicial post higher than magistrate in the North in 1883. William Henry Lewis, an 1895 Harvard University law graduate who was discriminated against when a local barber would not cut his hair, effectively urged the Massachusetts state legislature to amend the civil rights law to make such conduct illegal.

Perhaps the most important achievement for Lewis, and for black lawyers and the nation, was his nomination by President William Howard Taft to the post of assistant attorney general of the United States in 1911. The confirmation of the Senate made him the highest-ranking black person in the history of the nation. Other Harvard University law graduates, such as Matthew Washington Bullock, would also serve in important posts in the Department of Justice.

Many black Boston University law graduates became successful and are mentioned elsewhere in these pages, but William Clarence Matthews may be one of Boston University's earliest black law graduates to serve as assistant United States attorney in Massachusetts, a post he was recommended for by the president of the United States, William Howard Taft.

Suffolk Law School graduated its first black student in 1915, while Boston University and Portia Law School (opened for women) were among the first in Massachusetts to admit black women.

The pioneer black lawyers in Massachusetts trained other blacks to become lawyers, many of whom began their legal careers in the offices of their mentors. Thus, black lawyers became employers of other black people, who worked in the offices as secretaries and law clerks. The sons of these lawyers frequently followed their fathers to the same law schools, and two black women joined their father's firms.

Though the first black lawyers, men and women, endured trials and tribulations along the way, they were never deterred from their central objective—the emancipation of their people in the New England states and beyond.

NOTES

1. Brown, "The Genesis of the Negro Lawyer in New Engand" (Part I) 22 *The Negro History Bulletin* 147, 148 (April 1959), citing W. Weeks, *History of the Law, the Courts, and the Lawyers of Maine* 552–53 (1863). Ferguson, "Group Roles in America Legal History—Blacks," 69 *Law Library Journal* 470, 473 (1969). Macon Bolling Allen was born A. Macon Bolling. On January 26, 1844, prior to his admission to the bar in Maine, he had his name changed by act of the Massachusetts legislature. See *Black Abolitionist Papers, 1830–1865*, at 32 (G. E. Carter and C. P. Ripley eds. 1981). See also, G. Gilmore, *The Ages of American Law* 45 (1977). Gilmore reports that "the first American book on contracts" was authored by W. W. Story and entitled, *Treatise on the Law of Contracts Not Made Under Seal* (1844).

2. *The Daily Eastern Argus*, July 15, 1844, at 2, col. 4.

3. *Ibid.*

4. W. Weeks, *History of the Law, the Courts, and the Lawyers of Maine* 552–53 (1863).

5. *Ibid.*

6. Letter from Esther L. Brawn, clerk, Supreme Court—Superior Court, Sagadahoc County, Maine, to Charles S. Brown, June 27, 1958.

7. Brown, "The Genesis of the Negro Lawyer in New England" (Part II) 22 *The Negro History Bulletin* 171, 174 (May 1959).

8. "Only Negro Lawyer in Maine," *Philadelphia North American*, April 23, 1915. The number of white lawyers in Maine declined from 891 in 1900 to 855 in 1910. *The Twelfth Census, Special Report, Occupations* 292, Table 41 (1904); *The Thirteenth Census*, Vol. 4, *Population* 434, Table 7 (1914).

9. Brown, "The Genesis of the Negro Lawyer in New England" (Part II) 22 *The Negro History Bulletin* 175 (April 1959); J. O. Horton and L. E. Horton, *Black Bostonians* 9 (1979).

10. *Dictionary of American Negro Biography* 11 (R. Logan and M. Winston eds. 1982). Letter from Chester A. Dolan, Jr., clerk, Supreme Judicial Court of Massachusetts, to Charles S. Brown, April 29, 1958; letter from Stephen T. Riley, director, Massachusetts Historical Society, to Charles S. Brown, May 27, 1958, quoting the *Boston Daily Advertiser*, May 5, 1845; A. H. Chroust, Vol. 2 *The Rise of the Legal Profession in America* 90 (1965).

11. "That Colored Gentlemen," *Daily Eastern Argus*, May 6, 1845, at 2.

12. *The Boston Liberator*, May 9, 1845.

13. *Black Abolitionist Papers, 1830–1865*, at 32 (G. E. Carter and C. P. Ripley eds. 1981): letter from Macon B. Allen to John Jay, Nov. 26, 1845.

14. D. H. Donald, *Charles Sumner* 143 (1960).

15. *Black Abolitionist Papers, 1830–1865*, at 32 (G. E. Carter and C. P. Ripley eds. 1981): letter from Macon B. Allen to William Lloyd Garrison, June 1, 1846.

16. *Ibid.*

17. Letter from Chester A. Dolan, Jr., clerk, Supreme Judicial Court of Massachusetts, to Charles S. Brown, April 29, 1958.

18. Letter from Kevin H. White, secretary of the Commonwealth of Massachusetts, to Charles Sumner Brown, April 2, 1962.

19. Brown, "The Genesis of the Negro Lawyer in New England" (Part I) 22 *The Negro History Bulletin* 148 (April 1959), footnote omitted. Allen died in Washington, D.C., on October 15, 1894, at age seventy-eight. Letter from Virginia Rugheimer, librarian, Charleston, S.C., Library Society, to Charles S. Brown, Sept. 23, 1958, citing death notice appearing in the *News and Courier*, Oct. 17, 1894: "Internment at Friendly Union Cemetery."

20. W. T. Davis, Vol. 2 *Bench and Bar of Massachusetts* 424 (1895), on Ellis Gray Loring. Some confusion surrounds Robert Morris's name. On several occasions, he signed his name Robert Morris, Jr., and this name appeared in Boston newspapers and on his court pleadings; the confusion has been carried forward by scholars of the period. Technically, however, Robert Morris was not a "Jr" (his father's name was York Morris), and it is not clear why he chose to sign his name in this manner. See Hopkins, "Famous Men of the Negro Race: Robert Morris," *Colored American* 337–38 (Sept. 1901).

21. *Ibid.* ("Famous Men of the Negro Race").

22. *Ibid.*

23. *Ibid.*

24. George A. Levesque, "Black Boston: Negro Life in Garrison's Boston, 1800–1860," at 114 (Ph.D. diss., S.U.N.Y., 1976); "Robert Morris," *The New York Globe*, March 10, 1883, at 1, col. 1.

25. J. Daniels, *In Freedom's Birthplace: A Study of the Boston Negroes* 451 (reprint, 1969).

26. Before Morris filed the initial lawsuit, he demanded that the Boston School Board Committee give blacks due respect, as "the Colored People are unanimous against . . . insult to your honorable body." *Black Abolitionist Papers, 1830–1865*, at 373 (G. E. Carter and C. P. Ripley eds. 1981): letter from Robert Morris, Sr., to Henry Weeden, Aug. 9, 1848.

27. *Roberts v. City of Boston*, Case No. 976, Court of Common Pleas, Suffolk County, Boston, Massachusetts, October 1848.

28. *Id.* This information appears in the record of trial.

29. *Roberts v. City of Boston*, 5 Cush. 198, 59 Mass. 198 (1849). Charles Sumner's eloquent argument before the Supreme Court of Massachusetts was published and widely circulated. *Argument of Charles Sumner, Esq. Against the Constitutionality of Separate Colored Schools, in the Case of Sarah C. Roberts v. City of Boston*, Dec. 4, 1849. There is no evidence one way or another that Robert Morris, Sr., spoke before the court. See also, Smith, "One Lone Kid in Boston, 1849," *Washington Star*, Sept. 5, 1975, at A12, col. 3; Baltimore and Williams, "The State Constitutional Roots of the 'Separate but Equal' Doctrine: Roberts v. City of Boston," 17 *Rutgers Law Journal* 537, 538–39 (1986); A. H. Chroust, Vol. 2 *The Rise of the Legal Profession in America* 90–91 (1965). The role that Robert Morris, Sr., played in the *Roberts* case has been underemphasized by leading historians of the period. See e.g., D. H. Donald, *Charles Sumner* 180–81 (1960); Levy and Phillips, "The Roberts Case: Source of the 'Separate but Equal' Doctrine," 56 *American Historical Review* 510, 512 (1950). Available court

records do not show any appearance by Sumner in the case until the matter reached the Supreme Judicial Council (Massachusetts Supreme Court). Years later, Archibald H. Grimké, Harvard University's second black law graduate, credited the work of Robert Morris, stating that "[Sumner's] argument in favor of equality before the law . . . before the Supreme Court . . . was action against the constitutionality of separate schools in Boston. . . . And a very effective anti-slavery agent he provided, all the more so because of the presence of Robert Morris, a black lawyer, whom he had associated [with] himself as counsel in the case." A. H. Grimké, *The Life of Charles Sumner* 220 (1892).

30. The work of Morris and Sumner paid off in 1855 when the Massa-chusetts legislature overruled the *Roberts* case by statute, a point noted in *Brown v. Board of Education of Topeka, Kansas*, 347 U.S. 483, 491, n.6 (1954); see also, C. Mabee, *Black Freedom* 173 (1970).

31. *Boston Courier*, Feb. 17, 1851.

32. Between 1793 and 1850, two statutes were enacted for the purpose of securing the slave owners their property rights for slaves who had escaped: the congressionally enacted Fugitive Slave Act of 1793 and the Fugitive Slave Act of 1850. Both acts were directed to the enforcement of Article IV, Sec. 2, of the Constitution of the United States, which provided that "persons held to service or labor in one state under the laws thereof [and escaping into another] shall be delivered upon claim of the party to whom such service or labor may be due." The act of 1793 gave the slave owner almost absolute power to seize his alleged property, even if he crossed state lines to do so. Under the acts of 1793 and 1850, a slave owner was required to present the alleged fugitive slave before a federal judge or local magistrate and establish ownership. There was no right to a jury trial. The Act of 1793 was deemed too rigorous for enforcement and was viewed by many as unconstitutional. However, in 1842 the United States Supreme Court upheld the constitutionality of the Fugitive Slave Act, though it left it up to the states whether to provide assistance to federal authorities to enforce the act. *Prigg v. Pennsylvania*, 41 U.S. (16 Pet.) 539 (1842). The aboli-tionists persuaded many state legislators to pass laws prohibiting state officials from assisting federal authorities in the return of fugitive slaves. This in turn caused Southerners to lobby for the passage of the Fugitive Slave Act of 1850. This new act placed enforcement in the hands of federal officials and federal commissioners with jurisdiction concurrent with federal courts. Vol. 9, *The New International Encyclopedia* 333–34 (1925); J. H. Franklin, *From Slavery to Freedom* 151–52, 266 (1967); Cottrol, "Law, Politics and Race in Urban America: To-wards a New Synthesis," 17 *Rutgers Law Journal* 483, 494 (1986).

33. D. H. Donald, *Charles Sumner* 197 (1960).

34. J. Daniels, *Freedom's Birthplace* 62 (reprint, 1969), quoting Thomas Har-low, "a leading member of the Suffolk Bar at that time."

35. *Ibid*; see also, J. H. Pease and W. H. Pease, *They Who Would Be Free* 220 (1974).

36. "Respecting the Rescue of an Alleged Fugitive Slave at Boston," Vol. 9 *United States Statutes at Large* 1006 (G. Minot ed. 1862); "Proclamation of the President of the United States, Washington, Feb. 18, 1851," in the *Boston Courier* Feb. 19, 1851.

37. J. Daniels, *Freedom's Birthplace* 62, n.2 (reprint, 1969).

38. *Boston Courier*, March 10, 1851. During the preliminary hearing an eye witness testified, "I saw Mr. Morris in a cab on Garden Street. . . . One of the men in the cab . . . was Shadrack." *Boston Courier*, March 8, 1851.

39. *Boston Courier*, April 2, 1851. James Scott, Lewis Hayden, Elizut Wright, and Joseph K. Hayes were the other black men indicted.

40. *United States v. Morris*, 26 Fed. (Case No. 15,815) 1323 (Curtis Repts. 23) (1st. Cir. 1851). Morris and the other co-defendants were represented by two friends of Charles Sumner, John P. Hale of New Hampshire and Richard H. Dana, Jr., of Massachusetts, both abolitionists. In 1852, Robert Morris expressed his gratitude to both Hale and Dana on behalf of "our colored citizens . . . for your most able and manly defense of the parties indicted for the rescue of Shadrack." *Black Abolitionist Papers, 1830–1865*, at 373 (G. E. Carter and C. P. Riley eds. 1981), quoting letter from Morris to John P. Hale and Richard H. Dana, Jr., *National Anti-Slavery Standard*, Feb. 5, 1852. For additional information on these men see D. H. Donald, *Charles Sumner* (passim) (1960). By 1859 Morris, and other members of the Committee of Finance of the Vigilance Committee had raised over $6,000 "for the relief of fugitives." *Ibid.*; see also, "Aid to Fugitive Slaves," *Boston Liberator*, Feb. 18, 1859.

41. *Boston Courier*, Oct. 8, 1851.

42. *Boston Courier*, Nov. 13, 1851; B. Quarles, *Black Abolitionists* 205–6 (reprint, 1970); J. Daniels, *Freedom's Birthplace* 62, (reprint, 1969).

43. *Black Abolitionist Papers, 1830–1865*, at 373 (G. E. Carter and P. Riley eds. 1981); see also, "Rescue of Shadrack," *The Liberator*, Nov. 21, 1851, and "The Colored Lawyer and Shadrack," *Voice of the Fugitive Slave*, Dec. 3, 1851.

44. M. R. Delany, *The Condition, Elevation, Emigration and Destiny of the Colored People of the United States* 117 (1852).

45. *Ibid.*

46. Robinson, "Robert Morris, John Rock, William H. Lewis, and Edgar P. Benjamin," *Occasional Paper No. 4*, Afro-American Studies Program, Boston University, at 57, 61 (1975), quoting *The Boston Liberator*, August 13, 1858.

47. The increase in business among black lawyers during this period enabled them to help others pass the bar examination in spite of their overcrowded court calenders and limited resources. For example, Henry A. Brown, who was admitted to the Louisiana bar in 1872 and later licensed to practice in Vicksburg, Mississippi, read law in the Boston law office of Robert Morris, Sr. "Henry A. Brown," *People's Advocate*, April 17, 1880.

48. Robinson, "Robert Morris, John Rock, William H. Lewis, and Edgar Benjamin," *Occasional Paper No. 4*, Afro-American Studies Program, Boston University, at 62 (1975).

49. *Dictionary of American Negro Biography* 454, 455 (R. Logan and M. Winston eds. 1982); J. O. Horton and L. E. Horton, *Black Bostonians* 56–57 (1979).

50. *The New Orleans Tribune*, Dec. 9, 1866.

51. W. T. Davis, Vol. 2 *Bench and Bar of Massachusetts* 527 (1895).

52. *New York Globe*, Jan. 6, 1883.

53. After Robert Morris, Sr., died Edward G. Walker, also a black lawyer in Boston, eulogized Morris, commenting on his efforts to free the slave Shadrack. Walker quoted Morris as saying to the imprisoned Shadrack, "I am one with others of your race that are waiting for the slightest opportunity that may offer to attempt to rescue you from the meshes of this unrighteous [fugitive slave] law." "Robert Morris, [Sr.]," *The New York Globe*, March 10, 1883, at 1, col. 1. According to Pauline E. Hopkins, who interviewed descendants of Robert Morris, Sr., "Robert Morris, Jr., . . . was profoundly educated. He had studied at Oxford, England, in France, in Rome, and at the Harvard Law School. For a time he was French interpreter at the Suffolk bar." Hopkins, "Famous Men of

the Negro Race: Robert Morris," 2 *The Colored American Magazine* 337, 342 (Sept. 1901).

54. Brown, "The Genesis of the Negro Lawyer in New England" (Part I) 22 *The Negro History Bulletin* 151 (April 1959); letter from Chester A. Dolan, Jr., clerk, Supreme Judicial Court of Massachusetts, to Charles S. Brown, April 29, 1958.

55. E. M. Coulter, *Negro Legislators in Georgia During the Reconstruction Period* 38 (1968), quoting *Journal of the Proceedings of the Constitutional Convention of the People of Georgia . . . [1867–68]* at 273 (Aug. 1868).

56. *Ibid.*

57. W. T. Davis, Vol. II *Bench and Bar of Massachusetts* 278 (1895): Davis states that Walker was the "third colored man admitted" to the Massachusetts bar; *Dictionary of American Negro Biography* 623 (R. Logan and M. Winston ed. 1982).

58. "Edwin G. Walker," *Boston Daily Globe*, Jan. 14, 1901.

59. *Ibid.* Walker shares this honor with Charles L. Mitchell, a black man not trained as a lawyer who was elected to the General Court during the same election. But see Nicolosi, "Twilight Mystery," 50 *Yankee* 174 (June 1986), which says that Alexander Lucius Twilight was elected to the Vermont legislature in 1836; it has not been conclusively determined that Twilight was black, however.

60. *Ibid.*

61. "Mass., First Colored Law Firm," *New York Freeman*, May 15, 1886.

62. G. W. Forbes, *John S. Rock* 4–5 (n.d.), typescript biography of John Swett Rock, on file at the Boston Public Library. Rock was also a dentist. F. Kidd, *Profile of the Negro in American Dentistry* 60 (1979).

63. Letter from Chester A. Dolan, Jr., clerk, Supreme Judicial Court of Massachusetts, to Charles Sumner Brown, April 29, 1958.

64. *Dred Scott v. Sandford*, 60 U.S. (19 How.) 393, 407 (1857); Smith, "Toward a Pure Legal Existence: Blacks and the Constitution," 30 *How. L.J.* 921 (1987). Prophetically, a year after Chief Justice Taney's decision in *Dred Scott*, Dr. Rock addressed a meeting in Boston: "Judge Taney may outlaw us . . . and this wicked government may oppress us; but the black man will live when Judge Taney . . . and this wicked government are no more." John Swett Rock, "Address to a Meeting in Boston, Massachusetts," March 1, 1858, *Afro-American History: Primary Sources* 71, 74 (T. R. Frazier ed. 1971).

65. Robinson, "Robert Morris, John Rock, William H. Lewis, and Edgar P. Benjamin," *Occasional Paper No. 4*, Afro-American Studies Program, Boston University 63, n.21, 64 (1975), quoting George W. Forbes.

66. Letter from Charles Sumner to Chief Justice Solomon P. Chase, December 21, 1864, taken from George W. Forbes, "John S. Rock," 7 (n.d.) transcript biography of John Swett Rock, on file at Boston Public Library. Senator Charles Sumner's association fifteen years earlier with Robert Morris, Sr., in *Roberts v. City of Boston*, 5 Cush. 198, 59 Mass. 158 (1849), became one of the supporting bases of his motion before the United States Supreme Court on behalf of Swett's admission. *Id.* at 7 ("John S. Rock").

67. *Id.* at 5 ("John S. Rock"); C. Warren, Vol. 2 *The Supreme Court in United States History, 1836–1918*, at 411–12 (1926); Contee, "The Supreme Court Bar's First Member," *Supreme Court Historical Society Yearbook* 82 (1976); Levesque, "Boston's Black Brahmin: Dr. John S. Rock," 26 *Civil War History* 326, 335 (1980); J. M. McPherson, *Battle Cry of Freedom* 840–41 (1988).

68. Bird, *The Commonwealth*, Feb. 4, 1865.

69. *Ibid.* The account of Dr. Rock's admission to the United States Supreme Court is also mentioned in the works of Charles Sumner. C. Sumner, Vol. 9 *The Works of Charles Sumner* 227 (1874).

70. Forbes, "John S. Rock," 10 (n.d.), typescript biography of John Swett Rock, on file at Boston Public Library.

71. *Ibid.*

72. *Ibid.*

73. C. Sumner, Vol. 9 *The Works of Charles Sumner* 232 (1874).

74. "William Henry Johnson," *The Evening Standard*, Dec. 19, 1896.

75. *Ibid.*

76. *Ibid.*

77. *Ibid.*

78. Brown, "The Genesis of the Negro Lawyer in New England" (Part II) 22 *The Negro History Bulletin* 171 (April 1959).

79. "William Henry Johnson," *The Evening Standard*, Dec. 19, 1896; *New Orleans Tribune*, April 12, 1865.

80. Brown, "The Genesis of the Negro Lawyer in New England" (Part II) 22 *The Negro History Bulletin* 173 (April 1959); W. T. Davis, Vol. II *Bench and Bar of Massachusetts* 565 (1895).

81. W. J. Simmons, *Men of Mark* 741 (1887).

82. W. J. Leonard, *Black Lawyer* 110 (1977).

83. Brown, "The Genesis of the Negro Lawyer in New England" (Part II) 22 *The Negro History Bulletin* 173 (April 1959); see also, Webb, "The Heights of Glory," *Washington Post*, Feb. 18, 1990, at B1, col. 1, a comprehensive essay about General Butler during and after the Civil War. Governor Butler appointed Ruffin, his second choice, to the bench instead of Edward G. Walker because the Republican-dominated legislature would not confirm Walker, who for a period had "become a Democrat [because] he felt the Republican Party had been unfair to Blacks." W. J. Leonard, *Black Lawyers* 113 (1977).

84. W. J. Simmons, *Men of Mark* 741 (1887).

85. Brown, "The Genesis of the Negro Lawyer in New England" (Part II) 22 *The Negro History Bulletin* 171, 173 (May 1959).

86. W. P. Dabney, *Cincinnati's Colored Citizens* 121–22 (1926).

87. J. H. Franklin, *George Washington Williams* 138 (1985).

88. E. J. West, "Harvard and the Black Man, 1636–1850," in *Variety of Black Experience at Harvard* 1, 12 (W. Sollors, T. A. Underwood, and C. Titcomb eds. 1986); *Dictionary of American Negro Biography* 535, 536 (R. Logan and M. Winston ed. 1982).

89. Letter from Kimball C. Elkins, senior assistant, Harvard University Archives, to Charles S. Brown, May 10, 1961; W. T. Davis, Vol. II *Bench and Bar of Massachusetts* 417 (1895).

90. "James H. Wolff Dies in Hospital," *Boston Herald*, May 5, 1913.

91. "Wolff Will Lead," *Boston Record*, Feb. 14, 1905.

92. "James H. Wolff Dies in Hospital," *Boston Herald*, May 5, 1913.

93. *Ibid.*

94. *Ibid.*

95. Letter from Thomas Stanton, assistant clerk, Suffolk County Court, to Charles S. Brown, May 2, 1961.

96. *Dictionary of American Negro Biography* 271, 272 (R. Logan and M. Winston eds. 1982); K. P. Lumpkin, *The Emancipation of Angelina Grimké* 221 (1974).

97. A. W. Grimké, "A Biographical Sketch of Archibald H. Grimké," 3

Opportunity 44, 46–47 (Feb. 1925). Archibald Henry Grimké's decision not to return to the South may have been influenced by prevailing opinions, like those of his father's brother, Frederick Grimké. Frederick Grimké "believed that the Negro was racially inferior to the white man and could never measure up to the responsibilities of middle-class democracy." M. H. Bloomfield, *American Lawyers in a Changing Society, 1776–1876*, at 263 (1976). See also, Carrington, "Teaching Law in the Antebellum Northwest," 23 U. of Toledo L. Rev. 3, 11 (1991), for more on Frederick Grimké.

98. *Ibid.* ("Biographical Sketch of Archibald Grimké").

99. Vol. 8 *The Booker T. Washington Papers, 1904–6*, at 93 (L. R. Harlan, R. W. Smock, and G. McTigue eds. 1979). In the same year Butler R. Wilson was admitted to the bar, another black lawyer, Edward Everett Brown, was also admitted. Letter from Chester A. Dolan, Jr., clerk, Supreme Judicial Court of Massachusetts, to Charles S. Brown, April 29, 1958. Brown was admitted to the Massachusetts bar on July 8, 1884.

100. *Dictionary of American Negro Biography* 271, 172 (R. Logan and M. Winston ed. 1982). In order, perhaps, to subsidize their law practice, both Archibald H. Grimké and his law partner, Butler R. Wilson, edited *The Hub*, a Boston newspaper devoted to the welfare of black people. *Dictionary of American Biography* 632 (A. Johnson and D. Malone eds. 1931). Butler Roland Wilson attended Harvard University's law school for one year (1917–18); see *Directory of Black Alumni/ae Harvard Law School* vi (June 1989).

101. Grimké writings include "Right on the Scaffold, or The Martyrs of 1822" (1901), a sympathetic account of the life of Telemaque (Denmark) Vesey, leader of the Charleston slave uprising in 1822; "The Ballotless Victim of One-Party Governments" (1913), a protest against race-discrimination at the ballot box; and "The Sex Question of Race Segregation" (1915), which treats issues involving discrimination and women. *Dictionary of American Biography* 632, 633 (A. Johnson and D. Malone eds. 1931).

102. Mr. Wilson's skills and legal acumen were instrumental in his appointment as master of chancery, an appointment made by the court to assist its fact-finding in complex cases. Such an appointment boosted the image of the black lawyer throughout New England. *Dictionary of American Negro Biography* 662 (R. Logan and M. Winston eds. 1982).

103. *Dictionary of American Biography* 632 (A. Johnson and D. Malone eds. 1931).

104. B. Brawley, *Negro Genius* 165 (1937).

105. *Id.* at 166.

106. Vol. 1 *Who's Who of the Colored Race* 198 (F. L. Mather ed. 1915); *Dictionary of American Negro Biography* 462 (R. Logan and M. Winston eds. 1982).

107. *Id.* at 452 (*Dictionary of American Negro Biography*).

108. "Center Rush Lewis, Colored Virginian Whom Harvard Men Admire," *Boston Daily Globe*, Dec. 12, 1893; "Candidate for the House," *Boston Daily Globe*, Oct. 15, 1901.

109. See "Brains, Not Color," *Boston Daily Globe*, Aug. 16, 1903. Though he was one of the most popular students in the law school, Lewis was twice denied service at a Harvard Square barbershop because of his race. S. R. Fox, "W. Monroe Trotter at Harvard," in *Varieties of Black Experience at Harvard* 53 (W. Sollors, T. A. Underwood, and C. Titcomb eds. 1986).

110. See Smith, "Forgotten Hero" (book review of G. R. McNeil, *Charles*

Hamilton Houston and the Struggle for Civil Rights), 98 *Harvard Law Review* 482, 483 (1984).

111. *Plessy v. Ferguson*, 163 U.S. 537 (1896), affirmed the separate but equal doctrine.

112. Brown, "The Genesis of the Negro Lawyer in New England" (Part II) 22 *The Negro History Bulletin* 173 (April 1959).

113. *Who's Who in the Colored Race* 177 (F. L. Mather ed. 1915). During his second term on the Common Council, Lewis successfully led a movement to establish "Washington Elm Day." "W. H. Lewis, Lawyer, Dies," *Boston Herald*, Jan. 2, 1949.

114. "Good Legislator," *Cambridge Tribune*, Nov. 1, 1902.

115. *Ibid.*

116. L. R. Harlan, *Booker T. Washington: The Making of a Black Leader, 1856–1901*, at 312 (1972).

117. Theodore Roosevelt graduated from Harvard College in 1880. He was also the first president to publicly acknowledge that he had dined with a Negro, Booker T. Washington, at the White House. W. F. McCaleb, *Theodore Roosevelt* 132–33 (1931). L. R. Harlan, *Booker T. Washington: The Wizard of Tuskegee* 16–17, 42–43 (1983).

118. L. R. Harlan, *Booker T. Washington: The Wizard of Tuskegee* 16–17, 42–43 (1983).

119. Robinson, "Robert Morris, John Rock, William H. Lewis, and Edgar P. Benjamin," *Occasional Paper No. 4*, Afro-American Studies Program, Boston University 57, 70 (1975), quoting J. Daniel, *In Freedom's Birthplace: A Study of the Boston Negroes* 128 (1914).

120. "Brains, Not Color," *Boston Daily Globe*, Aug. 16, 1903; "William H. Lewis Appointed," *Springfield Republican*, Jan. 13, 1903; Vol. 6 *The Booker T. Washington Papers, 1901–2*, at 614 (L. R. Harlan, R. W. Smock, and B. S. Kraft eds. 1977); *id.* at Vol. 11, at 216, *id.* at Vol. 12, at 225.

121. "Brains, Not Color," *Boston Daily Globe*, Aug. 16, 1903; Vol. 6 *The Booker T. Washington Papers, 1901–2*, at 614 (L. R. Harlan, R. W. Smock, and B. S. Kraft eds. 1977); *id.* at Vol. 11, at 216; *id.* at Vol. 12, at 255.

122. "Lawyers Not Pleased and Say No Assistant Was Required," *Boston Herald*, Jan. 13, 1903. During his first term as assistant United States attorney, Lewis appeared before the federal courts on several occasions. See e.g., *Curley v. United States*, 130 F. 1, 2 (1st Cir. 1904), a criminal case involving conspiracy to defraud the United States; *Betts v. United States*, 132 F. 228, 229 (1st Cir. 1904), a criminal case involving the use of the mails to defraud; *McInerney v. United States*, 143 F. 729, 730 (1st Cir. 1906), a criminal case on appeal involving evidentiary matters; *Gallagher v. United States*, 144 F. 87 (1st Cir. 1906), a criminal case involving uttering false national bank notes.

123. "Appointed Head of a New Bureau," *Boston Herald*, May 21, 1907. Lewis handled several important cases under the newly formed naturalization office and argued several important cases before the federal courts. See *O'Leary v. United States*, 158 F. 796, 797 (1st Cir. 1907), the first major case Lewis handled in his new capacity as assistant United States attorney in charge of the Bureau of Naturalization in Boston; *Dickinson v. United States*, 159 F. 801 (1st Cir. 1908), a criminal case involving conversion of funds; *Sullivan v. United States*, 161 F. 253 (1st Cir. 1908), a criminal case involving perjury; *In re Rustigian*, 165 F. 980 (D. R.I. 1908), on immigration and naturalization; *United States v. Simon*, 170 F. 680, 681 (D. Mass. 1909), an immigration and naturaliza-

tion case in which Lewis was designated by the attorney general of the United States to represent the United States Department of Justice; *United States v. Dwyer*, 170 F. 686 (D. Mass. 1909), also on immigration and naturalization.

124. "Lewis Is Confirmed," *Boston Transcript*, June 15, 1911.

125. *Ibid.* Some credit for Lewis's confirmation is said to be due to efforts by Booker T. Washington and his lieutenant, Emmet Scott, who "headed off threatened opposition by some Southern senators." L. R. Harlan, *Booker T. Washington: The Wizard of Tuskegee* 349 (1983); Vol. 10 *The Booker T. Washington Papers, 1909–11*, at 426 (L. R. Harlan, R. W. Smock, and N. E. Woodruff eds. 1981).

126. "Lewis Is Confirmed," *Boston Transcript*, June 15, 1911. Lewis also won the support of Senator Elihu Root of New York, one of the most distinguished members of the Senate. See "Lewis at Last Confirmed," *Boston Advertiser*, June 15, 1911. Lewis was paid $5,000 a year. *Boston Advertiser*, March 1, 1911.

127. L. R. Harlan, *Booker T. Washington: The Wizard of Tuskegee* 353 (1983).

128. "Lewis Reviews Emancipation," *Boston Globe*, Feb. 13, 1913, at 11, col. 4.

129. L. R. Harlan, *Booker T. Washington: The Wizard of Tuskegee* 406 (1983).

130. *Ibid.*

131. "Mohr Testimony," *New York Age*, Nov. 21, 1916.

132. "Wm. H. Lewis and John B. Edwards Dominant Figures in Famous Mohr Murder Trial," *New York Age*, Jan. 27, 1916.

133. *Ibid.*

134. *Ibid.*

135. See *State v. Brown*, 40 R.I. 527, 102 A. 65 (1917), reversing conviction of defendant Henry H. Spellman, represented by John B. Edwards, and reversing conviction of Cecil Victor Brown, represented by William H. Lewis; *State v. Brown*, 45 R.I. 9, 119 A. 324 (1923): Spellman died in prison before the completion of his retrial and appeal. Brown's conviction was upheld. The final appeal was handled solely by John B. Edwards. It should be noted, as these cases point out, that Elizabeth F. Mohr, the wife of the murdered physician who was indicted and tried with Brown and Spellman as an accessory before the fact, was acquitted.

136. For example, "At the 1921 meeting in San Francisco the American Bar Association resolved 'that further [*sic*] legislation should be enacted by Congress to punish and prevent lynching and mob violence.'" J. H. Chadbourn, *Lynching and the Law* 117–18 (1933).

137. For text of the Dyer bill see House Rep. 71, 68 Cong., First Sess., at 16.

138. The anti-lynching legislation was named for its author, Congressman Leondias C. Dyer of Missouri. J. W. Johnson, *Along This Way* 362 (1933); R. L. Jack, *History of the National Association for the Advancement of Colored People* 32, 40, 91 (1943).

139. *Id.* at 367 (*Along This Way*); J. H. Chadbourn, *Lynching and the Law* 118 (1933).

140. *Corrigan v. Buckley*, 271 U.S. 323 (1926); the white lawyers representing the NAACP included Louis Marshall, Moorefield Storey, James P. Schick, Arthur B. Spingarn, Herbert K. Stockton; the black lawyers were James Adali Cobb and Henry E. Davis.

141. Lewis continued an active practice, arguing a major case before the United States Supreme Court in 1922. Ironically he lost the case under the pen of William Howard Taft, then chief justice of the United States Supreme

Court, who had also appointed Lewis as the nation's first black assistant attorney general. See *Ponzi v. Fessenden*, 258 U.S. 254 (1922). *Ponzi* involved the authority of the federal government to permit its prisoners to be turned over to a state for prosecution.

142. *United States v. Farrar*, 281 U.S. 624 (1930). Lewis argued this case with James A. Cresswell.

143. James A. Cresswell was also associated with the Liberal Civic League of Massachusetts.

144. "Lewis Wins Big Case Before Supreme Court," *The Guardian*, May 31, 1930. See also, "Former U.S. Attorney Wins Notable Case," *Amsterdam News*, June 4, 1930; "Boston Attorney Wins Rum Case Before U.S. High Court," *Chicago Defender*, June 7, 1930.

145. R. P. Alexander, "Voices from Harvard's Own Negroes," in *Varieties of Black Experience at Harvard* 93 (W. Sollors, T. A. Underwood, and C. Titcomb eds. 1986); *Harvard Law Quinquennial* 270 (F. S. Kimball ed. 1948). William Henry Lewis, Jr., attended Harvard University's law school between 1925 and 1926. He was admitted to the bar in 1926 and practiced law in Boston. Other than Archibald Henry Grimké, whose father was white, William Henry Lewis, Jr., was one of the first second-generation black lawyers to *attend* Harvard Law School. William Henry Lewis, Sr., received his A.B. degree from Amherst College in 1892. The Lewises, father and son, practiced law in Boston for nearly ten years before the senior Lewis died in 1949. In 1940, they filed a brief in *Palmero v. United States*, 112 F.2d 922 (1st Cir. 1940), involving the Narcotic Drug and Export Act. William Henry Lewis, Jr., was an outstanding lawyer in his own right, taking criminal appeals to federal appeal courts, as his father had done before him. See *Deacon v. United States*, 124 F.2d 352 (1st Cir. 1941), a case concerning criminal conspiracy to transport lottery tickets; and *Thierry v. Gilbert*, 147 F.2d 603 (1st Cir. 1945), a rent increase case under the Office of Price Administration during World War II. William Henry Lewis, Sr., continued to litigate cases even as he approached a senior status at the bar. See *Wilson v. Lanagan*, 99 F.2d 544 (1st Cir. 1938), a matter involving habeas corpus; *Rottenberg v. United States* and *Yakus v. United States*, 137 F.2d 850 (1st Cir. 1943), *aff'd*, 321 U.S. 414 (1944), a case involving the interpretation of the Emergency Price Control Act.

146. Vol. 1, *Who's Who in Colored America* 30–31 (J. J. Boris ed. 1927); H. Elsie Austin, "Pioneering—All the Way: Matthew W. Bullock, Sr." 4 (mimeo, n.d.); "Bullock to Open Law Office," *The Guardian*, Oct. 13, 1917. There were other black Harvard University law graduates prior to 1920, among them Aiken Augustus Pope, who received his law degree in 1918. He later practiced law in New York City. R. P. Alexander, "Voices from Harvard's Own Negroes," in *Varieties of Black Experience at Harvard* 95 (starred footnote) (W. Sollors, T. A. Underwood, and C. Titcomb eds. 1986); *Harvard Law Quinquennial* 352 (F. S. Kimball ed. 1948).

147. *Harvard Law Quinquennial* 77 (F. S. Kimball ed. 1948).

148. *Dictionary of American Negro Biography* 264 (R. Logan and M. Winston ed. 1982); "Mr. District Attorney," *Ebony* 82, 83 (March 1951).

149. Robinson, "Robert Morris, John Rock, William H. Lewis, and Edgar P. Benjamin," *Occasional Paper No. 4*, at 4, Afro-American Studies Program, Boston University 73 (1975).

150. *Id.* at 74.

151. Vol. 1 *Who's Who in Colored America* 12 (J. J. Boris ed. 1927).

152. "Colored Attorney Defends Roxbury Judge," *The Guardian*, May 16, 1919.

153. Two other black lawyers were graduated from Boston University's law school during this same period: Lucius Sumner Hicks and Charles Lyke Raysor. Hicks was graduated in 1908 and admitted to practice in Massachusetts in 1909. Vol. 1 *Who's Who of the Colored Race* 136 (F. L. Mather ed. 1915). Raysor was graduated in 1911 and admitted to practice in Massachusetts in the same year. Both men entered private practice. *Id.* at 227.

154. Vol. 1 *Who's Who in Colored America* 140 (J. J. Boris ed. 1927); *Marcus Garvey: Life and Lessons* 408 (R. A. Hill and B. Bair eds. 1987).

155. *Ibid.* (*Who's Who in Colored America*).

156. "Negro Born in Charlotte Slave Hut Wins High Post," *Charlotte Observer*, Jul. 29, 1927.

157. "Transfer Slip Is Memento of Island Judge," *Chicago Tribune*, Jan. 14, 1940.

158. *Ibid.*

159. "Heads Lawyers of Cook County," *St. Louis Argus*, Feb. 7, 1930.

160. Telephone interview with G. Bruce Robinson on Sept. 3, 1988. "Boston Lawyer Is Given High Post," *Chicago Defender*, Aug. 22, 1942, at 3, col. 4.

161. *Virginia's Contribution to Negro Leadership* 18 (W. Cooper ed. 1937) (mimeo); Vol. 1 *Who's Who of the Colored Race* 80 (F. L. Mather ed. 1915); Vol. 1 *Who's Who in Colored America* 48 (J. J. Boris ed. 1927).

162. Vol. 1 *Who's Who in Colored America* 192 (J. J. Boris ed. 1927).

163. "Boston Lawyer Makes Good," *The Guardian*, Feb. 1, 1919.

164. Vol. 1 *Who's Who in Colored America* 18 (J. J. Boris ed. 1927).

165. *Ibid.* The involvement of both Rainey and Wolff in local political groups may have played a part in their appointments. During the 1920s, Rainey was the national director of the Colored Division of the National Democratic Committee and Wolff was connected with the Equal Rights League.

166. D. L. Robbins, *Suffolk University: A Social History* 1, 10 (1981); "Suffolk University: The Law School, 1906–1981," *The Advocate* 11 (1981).

167. Vol. 1 *Who's Who in Colored America* 32 (J. J. Boris ed. 1927).

168. "New Secretary Sails," *Afro-American*, April 11, 1925; J. C. Miller, *The Black Presence in American Foreign Affairs* 38, 60 (1978); Smith, "Clifton Wharton, 90, Dies; 1st Black Career Ambassador," *Washington Post*, at D6, col. 1, April 26, 1990.

169. "New Secretary Sails," *Afro-American*, April 11, 1925.

170. "Young Negro Lawyer Appointed Clerk of Boston Court," *New York Age*, Nov. 7, 1931. Similar administrative appointments were received by other black lawyers in the years that followed. For example, Ray Wilson Guild was appointed assistant director of civil defense of Massachusetts in 1942. "Boston Lawyer Is Given High Post," *Chicago Defender*, Aug. 22, 1941, at 3, col. 4.

171. Letter to author from Richard J. Rouse, clerk, Supreme Judicial Court, March 20, 1991, verifying date of admission.

172. Telephone interview with Luella Coleman, Nov. 16, 1988.

173. "Mrs. Blanche Braxton," *Boston Chronicle*, March 25, 1933.

174. Letter to author from Richard J. Rouse, clerk, Supreme Judicial Council of Massachusetts, Feb. 22, 1991, verifying date of admission.

175. Letter to author from Richard J. Rouse, clerk, Supreme Judicial Council of Massachusetts, March 20, 1991, verifying date of admission. The records

of the court establish that Bruce was not the "second Negro woman" admitted to the Massachusetts bar as reported in Vol. 1 *Who's Who in Colored America* 29–30 (J. J. Boris ed. 1927) and W. B. Gatewood, *Aristocrats of Color* 331 (1991).

176. *Harvard Law Quinquennial* 75 (F. S. Kimball ed. 1948).

177. Letter from Viola F. Minor to author, Sept. 15, 1988.

178. "'Too Young' For Law Degree: Gets Certificate 'Til 21," *Pittsburgh Courier*, June 18, 1927.

179. Letter to author from Richard J. Rouse, clerk, Supreme Judicial Council, March 20, 1991, verifying date of admission; Alexander, "Women Practitioners of the Law in the United States," 1 *Nat'l B.A.J.* 56, 64 (July 1941), listing Rowena E. Taylor. Other local references in Cambridge, Massachusetts, that list Taylor as "the second woman attorney" are in error. See Guild, *Cambridge's Colored Citizens* 8 (Nov. 9, 1938). This pamphlet is a reprint of an article by Ray W. Guild, Sr., in the *Cambridge Chronicle-Sun* (n.d.).

180. R. Chester, *Unequal Access: Women Lawyers in a Changing America* 27 (1985).

181. *Id.* at 29.

Chapter 3

The Atlantic States

The Atlantic states include Connecticut, Delaware, the District of Columbia, Maryland, New Jersey, Pennsylvania, and Rhode Island.

Connecticut

In contrast to their peers in many other states, the first black lawyers admitted to practice in the state of Connecticut were formally trained. Edwin Archer Randolph was admitted to the Superior Court in New Haven, Connecticut, in 1880, the year he graduated from Yale University's law school.[1] He was Yale's first black law graduate and the first black person admitted to practice in Connecticut. Randolph, however, never practiced in Connecticut, returning instead to practice in his native state of Virginia.[2]

Walter J. Scott "entered [Yale Law School] and at the same time entered the office of [former] Judge Joseph Sheldon."[3] With this dual instruction, Scott was graduated from Yale University's law school in 1881, the "only colored man in his class."[4] Scott was admitted to the Superior Court in New Haven in 1881, on the motion of J. T. Platt, a member of the Yale University law faculty, and to the Supreme Court of Connecticut in 1882.[5] After being admitted to the bar, Scott remained in Connecticut to practice law, becoming the first black lawyer to do so. In Connecticut, a Yale University law degree placed Scott in a distinct class of lawyers. He remained in the law offices of Judge Sheldon, who took Scott to court and taught him how to try a criminal case. Scott's defense work in the Vroman murder case in 1881 is considered the first case ever tried by a black lawyer in Connecticut.[6] But Scott did not remain in Connecticut for long. In 1882, he relocated to Petersburg, Virginia, a city with a larger black population. He associated with

A. W. Harris, a prominent black lawyer and Howard University law school graduate who was also a member of the Virginia legislature.[7]

In 1897, Walter Scott Miller and George W. F. McMechen were graduated from Yale University. Both men were admitted to the Superior Court in New Haven. Miller remained in Connecticut, but McMechen went to Baltimore, Maryland, "where he spent most of his active life."[8] Miller later joined his classmate in Maryland to form a law firm.[9]

George Williamson Crawford, a 1903 graduate from Yale University's law school, was one of the first black lawyers to practice law in Connecticut for a sustained period of time.[10] Crawford won the coveted Townsend Oration award during his senior year at Yale.[11] After Crawford's graduation, he was admitted to practice in 1904 and immediately hired as a clerk in the New Haven Probate Court, a position he held until 1907.[12] Thereafter, Crawford entered private practice in New Haven. Crawford tried many lawsuits in Connecticut throughout his career, but one protracted litigation stands out as demonstrating his legal skills and the respect accorded him by the bar. In 1937, seventeen political leaders of Waterbury, Connecticut, were criminally charged with breach of the public trust. All of the defendants were white. Crawford was initially retained by four of the defendants. So great were his skills, however, that by the end of the nine-month trial he represented thirteen of the defendants, who were all acquitted.[13]

Harry Griffy Tolliver followed George W. Crawford to Yale University's law school. Tolliver completed his legal studies at Yale in 1908. Admitted to the bar in the same year, he entered the private practice of law. In 1922, he was elected as an alderman in New Haven, a position he held for four years. Later, in 1926, Tolliver was appointed assistant corporation counsel for the city of New Haven.[14]

Between 1922 and 1925, three other black lawyers, all formally trained at law schools outside of Connecticut, were admitted to the bar there. W. Arvey Wood, a Howard University honors law graduate, was admitted to the bar in 1923, and he practiced in Hartford. In 1923, he was selected to serve as a grand juror. He held this post until 1926, the year he became one of the first black lawyers to be elected justice of the peace. After serving one year in that post, Wood entered the private practice of law. In 1925 he was one of the first lawyers to join the newly organized association of black lawyers, the National Bar Association.[15] Howard P. Drew, a 1920 graduate of Drake University School of Law, was admitted to practice in Iowa in 1920 and in Hartford, Connecticut, in 1921. Drew, like W. Arvey Wood, was one of the first black lawyers to join the National Bar Association in 1925.[16] During Drew's legal career in Connecticut, he was elected justice of the peace and served as acting judge in the Hartford police and city court. He thus became the first black lawyer in the state to hold a judicial post above justice of the peace.[17] In 1930, Drew published an article in the *Hartford Courant* describing "the history of the white people's attitude toward the Negro in Connecticut from . . . 1639, when the first slaves were brought into the state until [1930], when most white people . . . [felt] that there [were] no other Negroes but domestic servants, common laborers, and an indigent class afloat."[18] After 1930, the number of black lawyers in Connecticut diminished from six to three.[19]

Although the Sixteenth Census (1940) records the existence of three black women lawyers in Connecticut, their identities remain a mystery.[20]

Delaware

Louis Lorenzo Redding chose Harvard law school because he believed that it was "the best law school in the country."[21] In 1923, during Redding's second year at Harvard, he observed a trial in his home town of Wilmington, Delaware. At that time, black citizens could only sit on one side of the courtroom, but Redding elected to sit in the white section. Asked to move to the black section of the courtroom, Redding refused, causing the bailiff to "yank" him out of the courtroom. Redding returned to Harvard and pledged that he would return to that very courtroom as a lawyer.[22]

When Louis L. Redding graduated from Harvard University's law school in 1928, he applied for admission to the Delaware bar. At that time no other black lawyer was known to have qualified for admission to the bar, although some had applied.[23] One of the drawbacks for blacks was that in Delaware an applicant for admission had to be sponsored by a preceptor, a process thought to be designed "to keep out blacks and other 'undesirables.'"[24] Redding wrote several letters to lawyers asking them to sponsor him to the bar. He received several negative responses. One white lawyer wrote,

You doubtless know that a colored man has never been admitted to the Bar of Delaware. For many years there was a settled prejudice against women, Jews and Negroes. Women and Jews have broken in, but as yet, the Negroes have not because of a wholly unjustifiable racial prejudice, which I do not share in my more lucid intervals.[25]

Redding got the message and ended his attempts to study under this lawyer. Instead, he applied to Daniel O. Hastings, a former municipal court judge who was serving as the United States senator from Delaware.[26] Senator Hastings was probably persuaded to sponsor Redding because of the political clout of Redding's father, who was influential in the Delaware Republican Party. Nevertheless, Senator Hastings would not allow Redding to study in his local office, as did other applicants to the bar whom he had sponsored. Despite such treatment, Redding "spent all his time in the law library studying on his own, determined not to fail the bar exam."[27] In 1929, Louis L. Redding became Delaware's first black lawyer and entered private practice. For twenty years following his admission to the bar, Redding, the only black lawyer identified in the state, was "excluded . . . from the [Delaware] Bar Association, the state's legal fraternity."[28]

District of Columbia

George Boyer Vashon was admitted to the bar of the District of Columbia on motion of A. K. Browne on October 26, 1869, becoming the first black lawyer admitted to practice there.[29] Vashon immediately entered the federal civil service in the District of Columbia. In 1870 he was hired by the census office of the Department of Interior, where he worked for three years. In 1873 Vashon left Washington to take a professorship in mathematics at Alcorn State University in Lorman, Mississippi.[30] In spite of his extraordinary legal talents,[31] Vashon probably chose to leave the District of Columbia because there were no other blacks to practice with and the newly freed black population could not afford lawyers.

The year in which Vashon was admitted to the bar in the District of Columbia, Howard University opened its law department. On January 6, 1869, under the deanship of John Mercer Langston, who two years earlier had become the second black lawyer admitted to practice before the United States Supreme Court,[32] and Professor Albert Gallatin Riddle, a white law teacher, Howard established a law curriculum, recruited students, and seated its first class. Dean Langston was the main student recruiter for the law school. It was his responsibility to convince the slave progeny that law was a profession in which they could succeed. Dean Langston recruited in the South as well as in Northern cities looking for students interested in the formal study of law. He used the Freedman's Bureau, with which he was affiliated, to identify persons interested in becoming lawyers. Among Langston's recruits were veterans of the Civil War. In Ohio he found Milton M. Holland, a Congressional Medal of Honor winner who had recently been discharged from the army. Recommended by Ohio governor Rutherford Birchard Hayes and Civil War general B. F. Butler, under whom Holland had served, he "secured a clerkship in the U.S. Treasury Department in Washington, [D.C.,] at a salary of $1,200 per annum."[33] This job enabled Holland to underwrite his legal education at Howard, which conducted evening classes.

Dean Langston was well respected in the legal community of the District of Columbia. Indeed, he had been considered for appointment to the district's Supreme Court when General John M. Oliver, formerly of Arkansas, was rejected for the post.[34] Dean Langston's reputation in American law was established on February 4, 1871, when the first class of black students to graduate from an American law school received their law degrees from the Department of Law at Howard University.

The Supreme Court of the District of Columbia and the war claims commissions, which heard various disputes for property damage arising out of the Civil War, were the legal forums in which Howard University law graduates made their first court appearances, sometimes with the assistance of Professor Riddle. After Charles N. Thomas was graduated from Howard University's law school in 1871, he worked in Riddle's law office. Curiously, Thomas handled claims before the Southern Claims Commission, representing "Southern loyalists against the government for . . . supplies taken or furnished the U.S. Army during the rebellion."[35] In 1873 Thomas, with the assistance of Riddle, handled the first criminal case ever tried by a black lawyer in the District of Columbia. The case involved Sam Rainey, who was charged with the murder of J. A. Tucker, and it received wide coverage by the press, which noted Thomas's skillful performance.[36] Thomas's closing argument at the trial was reported as "legal, able and convincing."[37] So able and persuasive was Thomas's closing argument that prior to the verdict, the prosecuting attorney agreed to reduce the murder charge to manslaughter in what was clearly a "triumph for the defense."[38]

John A. Moss, a contemporary of Thomas, quickly became known as "common-law John" because of his litigation skills and his familiarity with legal principles in the Supreme Court of the District of Columbia. Moss, an 1873 graduate of Howard University's law school, came to the attention of President Rutherford B. Hayes, who appointed him to the post of justice of the peace. As such, he became the District of Columbia's first black judicial officer.[39] He was reappointed justice of the peace by presidents James A. Garfield and Grover Cleveland, and was the only "colored man" to ride in President Cleveland's inaugural procession in 1885.[40] Moss gained further notoriety during his legal career when he defended a mounted policeman who had been charged with murder in Anacostia (a section of Washington, D.C.). His diligence resulted in the policeman's acquittal, and he won the esteem of the police force.[41]

John Patterson Sampson left the publishing business to attend the

National University Law School (George Washington Law School). He was graduated and admitted to the bar of the District of Columbia in 1873. Sampson entered the private practice of law and became prominent in local politics.[42] Two years out of law school, he was appointed to the position of justice of the peace by President Rutherford B. Hayes. In 1876 he was listed as a magistrate,[43] and as such he was the first black lawyer to serve in a judicial capacity in the District of Columbia above the office of justice of the peace.

Other pioneer graduates of Howard University's law school, like David Augustus Straker, started their legal careers in the local courts of Washington, D.C. In 1874, Straker made his first appearance in court before Justice David C. Humphreys, a native of Alabama. Straker defended Alexander Williams, who was charged with burglary and larceny. Williams was convicted, but three days later Straker defended Robert Johnson on similar charges and won his client's acquittal.[44]

The practice of law in Washington, D.C., during the pioneering days of the black lawyer required "a combination of moral strength, mental resourcefulness and physical completeness."[45] A lawyer worthy of public esteem in the District of Columbia had to appear to be successful, and so it was with the black lawyer.[46] The local black press played an important role in presenting the black lawyer as an aggressive and honorable person. For example, in 1871, the year Howard University graduated its first law class, the *New National Era and Citizen*, edited by Frederick Douglass, ran the following advertisement about Charles N. Thomas:

We call the attention of our readers in the South to the advertisement in another column of Charles N. Thomas, Esq. Mr. Thomas is prepared to prosecute the claims of any against the government; we can recommend him as an energetic and highly trustworthy lawyer. Colored men of the South having claims against the government can do no better than to put their affairs in his hands. We will gladly accept through our offices any charges to be entrusted to Mr. Thomas.[47]

At the close of the Reconstruction era, a number of other extremely talented black lawyers emerged in the District of Columbia to set the pace and level of competition for black clients. These lawyers not only associated with each other to try complex legal cases, but also generally became advocates for the rights of the descendants of the slave population.

One of the most skillful lawyers to practice in the District of Columbia during this period was Emanuel D. Molyneaux Hewlett, an 1877 graduate of Boston University School of Law.[48] Hewlett was admitted to the Supreme Court of the District of Columbia in 1883 and "appeared in a number of notable cases during his career."[49] He was one of at least six black lawyers actively practicing law in the city in 1885.[50] In 1888, Hewlett and another black lawyer, James M. Ricks, publicly defended black citizens, who were frequently portrayed by the press as being prone to criminal conduct. Hewlett, described as "a prominent colored lawyer,"[51] stated that "more than a third of the cases made against colored people were unjust [and] that police made arrests to keep up their record."[52] Hewlett claimed that blacks convicted of crimes by the court "did not have real trial[s], because the Negroes had no means to engage a lawyer."[53] James M. Ricks, an 1886 law graduate of Howard University's law school, agreed with Hewlett's views, adding that the crimes committed by blacks in the District of Columbia were caused "because of influences under which they lived."[54] Hewlett often joined with other lawyers, like Milton M. Holland, to serve as defense attorneys in highly publicized murder cases.[55]

Hewlett's reputation as a lawyer came to the attention of President Benjamin Harrison, who in 1890 appointed him justice of the peace in the District of Columbia, a position to which he was successively reappointed by presidents Grover Cleveland, William McKinley, and Theodore Roosevelt.[56] When "Judge Hewlett," as he was called, died in 1929, the Supreme Court of the District of Columbia adjourned out of respect for Hewlett, an honor reserved for the most respected members of the bar.[57]

The black law firm was born in the District of Columbia, in 1892, when William Lepré Houston was graduated from Howard University's law school.[58] The Houston firm became an institution in the District of Columbia and lasted for nearly seventy-five years.[59] Houston's son, Charles Hamilton Houston, who greatly benefited from his father's influence, financial support, and power, later became the resident vice-dean of the Howard University law school and the architect of the modern legal civil rights movement.[60] William Lepré Houston, and a few black lawyers before him, can be credited with diversifying their interests in areas of other than the criminal law, and it was this diversification that led Houston to apply for admission to the United States Court of Claims in 1914 on motion by Belva Ann Lockwood, a white female lawyer.[61] As early as 1887, other black lawyers, such as John Wesley Cromwell, had branched out into civil and administrative law areas, instead of concentrating solely in criminal law.

John Wesley Cromwell was graduated from Howard University's law school in 1874, and William C. Martin graduated from the same school in 1886. On December 15, 1887, seven months after Congress created the Interstate Commerce Commission, Cromwell and Martin became the first black lawyers to litigate a case before it. They represented the

Reverend William H. Heard, who had been required to pay the same fare as whites on the railroad coaches but received unequal accommodations on the Georgia Railroad Company because he was black. The representation of Reverend Heard by Cromwell and Martin established that the conduct of the Georgia Railroad Company had subjected their client to "undue prejudice and disadvantage in violation of the [ICC Act]."[62] The appearance of Cromwell and Martin before the ICC set the stage for the participation of black lawyers before the ICC and other federal regulatory commissions. Once there, these lawyers were able to prosecute claims based upon racial discrimination by carriers and other regulated industries doing business in interstate commerce.

William Lepré Houston appeared before the ICC in 1920 on behalf of several thousand "colored railway employees," and he established the right of his clients to be classified as station agents, among other things. This victory generated business from the Order of Railroad Station Agents, a white organization whose members were distributed over the entire nation and had claims similar to those of blacks. Houston thus became the first black lawyer to represent white clients before the ICC.[63] William Houston broke further ground for black lawyers in 1937 when Homer S. Cummings, the attorney general of the United States, appointed him special assistant in the Anti-trust Division of the Department of Justice. Houston retired from the division in 1942.[64]

In 1902 James Adlai Cobb, an 1899 graduate of Howard University's law school, formed a partnership with Louis G. Gregory, who had graduated from the same school in 1902. Cobb's association with Gregory lasted only four years. Gregory left the firm for a more secure job in the United States Treasury Department.[65]

By 1914, the private practice of law for black lawyers in the District of Columbia was almost exclusively in the criminal defense area. During this time, Fountain Peyton, Harry L. Tignor,[66] Emanuel D. Molyneaux Hewlett, and Thomas L. Jones were the leading black criminal defense lawyers in the city.[67] In 1914, Tignor, Hewlett, and Peyton won acquittals for several clients charged with forgery, assault with dangerous weapons, and depreciation of property.[68] According to a 1915 account, Thomas L. Jones, an 1892 graduate of Howard University's law school, was considered "one of the best known criminal lawyers at the bar."[69] Out of thirty-five or more murder cases, the press reported that no client of Jones was ever hung.[70]

But criminal law was not the only area of practice for black lawyers. Thomas Junius Calloway,[71] Thomas L. Jones, and Laudros Melendez King[72] were black lawyers who were dubbed as "kings" of the civil practice of law in the District of Columbia. Jones had "a very large equity practice"[73]; Calloway was the vice-president and general manager of the Lincoln and Improvement Company, and Laudros Melendez King, a 1897 graduate of Howard University's law school, practiced both criminal and civil law, and won significant cases in both areas. King also served, by appointment of the Municipal Court of the District of Columbia, as an examiner in chancery from 1911 to 1930.

Black graduates from a majority of law schools were barred from working in white law firms in Washington, D.C., prior to 1945 and for thirty years thereafter. When Louis Rothschild Mehlinger graduated with honors from Howard University's law school in 1921, there were "no offers from . . . prestigious law firms. . . . Solo practice for most black lawyers wasn't much better."[74] Other Howard University law graduates, such as William Benson Bryant, encountered financial obstacles to private practice in 1936, as many black clients were unable to pay legal fees. This fact alone "was a disincentive to the pursuit of a legal career."[75] Poverty left many black citizens unrepresented in criminal matters and without the resources to prosecute legitimate civil claims. So great was the need for legal representation of blacks in the District of Columbia that, in 1939, the Federation of Civic Associations, a group of black social organizations, proposed to employ attorneys to counsel the poor on ways to avoid "the snares of loan sharks."[76]

The white bar at this time was not supportive of the needs of the black lawyer. Black lawyers were systematically barred from using the District of Columbia Bar Association law library, even though it was located in the United States Court House.[77] Without the means to furnish their law offices with all the necessary law books, and with limited access to the public law libraries in the city, legal mistakes and shortcuts often flawed the pleadings of black lawyers. Such errors brought them before the bar association's grievance committee, which was controlled by white lawyers and actively excluded any black members. Caught in a virtual catch-22, the black lawyers were oftentimes disbarred from practice as a result of their presumed misconduct.

The exclusion of black lawyers from the grievance committee become a major issue in the city. In 1943, Nathan A. Dobbins was charged by the grievance committee with an alleged ethics infraction. His lawyers, George E. C. Hayes and James A. Cobb, both black, successfully argued that the systematic exclusion of black lawyers from the committee violated the United States Constitution.[78]

Perhaps because of the increased risk of disbarment and because of the need to pool their limited resources in order to provide better client services, James A. Cobb, Perry W. Howard, and George E. C. Hayes formed a partnership in 1935. The firm was unique because it was composed of lawyers who were all politically connected to the Republican Party.[79] This allowed the firm to broaden its legal practice beyond criminal law to the more lucrative area of municipal law.

By the beginning of World War II, the black lawyer in the District of Columbia was well on his way to demonstrating that law was a profession in which blacks could succeed. However, racial prejudice still plagued them in the courtroom, for few blacks were chosen to serve on juries. The dearth of black citizens called to serve on jury duty forced black lawyers to use racial stereotypes as a technique to aid their clients, as the following account attests:

In making his final appeal to the jury in a case involving a Negro accused of murder, a Negro lawyer in the middle of an emotional appeal to the jury stopped dramatically, turned to the bench and said, "Your Honor, I pause to get a glass of water." The white bailiff arose and started toward the water cooler. . . . The attorney, however, raised his hand and said to the bailiff, "No, sir, not you." He then turned to the Negro court messenger nearby, pointed his finger at him and said "Boy, *you* get me that water." The white jury acquitted the Negro lawyer's Negro client.[80]

A second episode also describes how a black lawyer successfully used custom and racial separation to obtain an acquittal for his client:

A Negro lawyer was defending a Negro for assault and robbery of a white man. When the white prosecuting witness was under cross-examination he admitted that the robbery and assault took place in a barroom. He [was] further asked whether . . . he had gone in this place to get a drink. He replied in the affirmative. He admitted that he had been in this barroom on other occasions. He was finally asked: "isn't" this place a Negro barroom? Upon his admission this was a Negro barroom and he was a white man associated with Negroes the jury acquitted the defendant.[81]

The proximity of black lawyers to the national government in the District of Columbia provided a greater opportunity for employment, although this work was often menial. Many black lawyers in Washington worked in non-legal federal jobs during the day in order to earn enough money to open a practice or to subsidize an evening law practice.

Federal employment gave some black lawyers a start. For example, after Milton M. Holland was graduated from Howard University's law school in 1872, he continued his employment as a clerk in the United States Treasury Department until 1887, when he opened a law practice.[82] Albert Pierre Albert joined the government as a pensions examiner during his law school days, and after graduating from Howard University law school in 1885, he continued to work in the government for forty years.[83] Lafayette McKeene Hershaw, an 1892 Howard University law graduate, was classified as an "executive" in the civil service.

Hershaw later became one of the founders of the Niagara Movement, the forerunner of the National Association for the Advancement of Colored People.[84] Robert Herberton Terrell was appointed auditor in the Fourth Auditor's Office at the Department of the Navy, a position he held from 1889 to 1893.[85]

But by the close of the Spanish-American War in 1898, jobs for black lawyers in government had significantly diminished. For example, the Collections Division of the Internal Revenue Service decreed that "none but lawyers might qualify for the Law Division,"[86] but when Huver I. Brown and William T. Wilson, both black lawyers working in other divisions, applied for jobs in the law division, they lost their jobs.[87]

Despite the decline of black lawyers working in the federal government at the beginning of the twentieth century, Louis George Gregory managed to gain employment in the law division of the Treasury Department.[88] Still, the employment of black lawyers in federal jobs in Washington, D.C., remained spotty. Race placed a great part in the hiring practices of the federal government, and its failure to hire black lawyers continued for decades. In 1940, William Henry Hastie, dean of Howard University's law school, reported that between 1930 and 1940 "of [Howard's] one hundred and three [law] graduates . . . only one man is employed on a legal staff of a federal agency" in Washington, D.C.[89]

There were, however, some breakthroughs in agencies created under the New Deal. For example, Arthur J. Christopher, Jr., a 1944 graduate of Howard University's law school, was in 1946 the first black lawyer hired at the National Labor Relations Board, although his efforts to gain employment at NLRB began the year he graduated.[90] William Robert Ming, Jr., left a law professorship at Howard University to head the court review-worthy branch of the Office of Price Administration, where he managed a staff of twelve lawyers.[91]

As in Boston and other major cities in the nation, in the District of Columbia several black lawyers were elevated to the rank of United States district attorney and to higher posts as well. Perhaps the first black lawyer appointed special United States district attorney for the District of Columbia was William Henry Harrison Hart. Hart graduated from Howard University's law school in 1887 and received his appointment in 1889.[92] James Adlai Cobb was appointed special assistant to the attorney general of the United States in 1907 by President Theodore Roosevelt, making him the highest-ranking black lawyer in the history of the Department of Justice. Cobb served at this post with distinction until 1915, when he joined the Howard University law faculty on a full-time basis.[93] Cobb's years of service as special assistant to the attorney general helped strengthen his knowledge of federal law. Cobb was an active federal lawyer and made frequent appearances in complex cases on behalf of the United States before federal courts in the District of Columbia.[94]

Perry W. Howard also served from 1921 to 1928 as special assistant to the United States attorney general by appointment of President Warren G. Harding. He left this position after he was indicted—but not convicted—for "selling federal jobs."[95] While Howard held the position of special assistant to the attorney general, he was responsible for hiring a fellow-Mississippian, Louis Rothschild Mehlinger, to a professional staff position at the "lily-white" Department of Justice.

Mehlinger, whose father was Jewish and mother black, was a light-skinned man, but declared himself to be of the "colored race." People in the federal government and in the general public were offended and shocked when Mehlinger, a black lawyer, called upon them to discuss cases. In 1931, Mehlinger, representing the Department of Justice, went to Ithaca, New York, to meet a United States claims commissioner on a case. When the commissioner met Mehlinger, he asked why the department had sent a messenger.[96]

Mehlinger's broad command of federal law was so comprehensive that he was assigned to represent the United States government before the United States Court of Claims. He traveled throughout the nation conducting fact-finding investigations and preparing cases to argue before the United States Court of Claims. Mehlinger was always especially careful when traveling to the South because of the dangers facing blacks, of which he knew firsthand: his brother had been lynched in Mississippi. The anticipation of such danger led Mehlinger to book railroad reservations for a day after he was expected to leave or appear in court. He then routinely "left a day earlier than his reservations date as he feared that if he had left on the scheduled day he might be taken off the train by Ku Klux Klan elements once the train came to a rural area."[97] Mehlinger's careful and thorough legal arguments were frequently upheld by the United States Supreme Court.[98]

Other black lawyers appointed to the post of assistant United States district attorney included Thomas L. Jones (who was selected as most qualified from a list of fifteen by Peyton Gordon, United States Attorney for the District of Columbia) in 1925[99] and Andrew H. Howard in 1943.[100]

Robert Herberton Terrell was the first black lawyer appointed to a judgeship above justice of the peace or magistrate in the District of Columbia in 1902. Terrell had graduated from Howard University's law school in 1889 and earned a master of laws degree from Howard in 1893, the same year he was admitted to the District of Columbia bar. In

1896 Terrell formed a law partnership with former congressman John Roy Lynch, under whom he had worked in the federal government in the administration of President Benjamin Harrison.[101] Terrell received his first judicial appointment in 1901 from President Theodore Roosevelt, to the post of justice of the peace in the District of Columbia. He had been aided by the behind-the-scenes influence of Booker T. Washington.[102] President Roosevelt reappointed Terrell in 1906.[103] In 1909, when Congress reorganized the court system in the District of Columbia, President William H. Taft appointed Terrell to one of the judgeships on the municipal court of the District of Columbia.[104]

This appointment brought praise from prominent blacks such as Armond W. Scott, himself a lawyer.[105] Judge Terrell's competence and the respect he had gained from judges, from the bar, and from the public was thought to make it virtually impossible for President Woodrow Wilson to fail to renew Terrell's appointment after the presidential election of 1912. The issue of Judge Terrell's reappointment to the bench was one of President Wilson's first major decisions in 1913. Despite his superlative qualifications, his appointment was opposed by Senator James K. Vardaman of Mississippi, a steadfast foe of black citizens, and by other Southern senators solely on account of Terrell's race. However, members of the all-white District of Columbia Bar Association and other men of power remained steadfast supporters of Terrell. The impressive support of the local bar no doubt influenced Wilson, and Judge Terrell was nominated to a fourth term.

The Senate fight that ensued was carefully watched by blacks nationwide. Would the Republicans withdraw their support for Terrell in the face of the Southern opposition led by Senator Vardaman? Black citizens viewed the Terrell nomination as a litmus test on the Republican Party's loyalty to them and to the conciliatory philosophy of Booker T. Washington, which still influenced the political views of prominent blacks in the nation. Black lawyers, led by Thomas L. Jones, rallied behind President Wilson's nomination of Terrell. In fact, Jones wrote President Wilson that the "90,000 colored population of [the] District [of Columbia] deserved to have a person of color on the bench."[106]

The white press was split on the Terrell nomination. The black press was solidly behind it. The race issue boiled over when the *Washington Evening Post* suggested that a black judge could not define the law for white men.[107] Fortunately, the racist sentiments against Judge Terrell's appointment did not prevail. The United States Senate confirmed Terrell's appointment with the support of Northern and Western senators by a vote of 39 to 24.[108] He was sworn into office on April 28, 1914, and won a fifth term on the bench in 1918.[109]

James Adlai Cobb succeeded Judge Terrell on the municipal court of the District of Columbia in 1926, the year President Calvin Coolidge nominated him for that post. Cobb, like Terrell, was well qualified to be a judge. He had served as special assistant to the attorney general of the United States from 1907 to 1915[110] and had the solid backing of black citizens despite his close ties with Booker T. Washington (who had lost support among blacks in the District of Columbia). While the elevation of Cobb to the bench was significant, it "deprive[d] the race of its most promising civil rights advocate," according to Kelly Miller, a leading Howard University scholar.[111] However, Cobb's appointment afforded an opportunity for a black law student to gain a clerkship with a black judge.[112] In 1926, Judge Cobb hired Frank W. Adams, a 1925 Howard University law graduate, as his clerk.[113]

Judge Cobb was fearless on the bench, even during the year he was being considered for reappointment. In 1930 Cobb ordered United States Senator Cole Blease of South Carolina to pay a $186 note to a South Carolina bank. Ten days after Judge Cobb's ruling, Senator Blease "made an attack upon 'n. . . .r' judges on the floor of the Senate."[114] Nevertheless, President Herbert Hoover reappointed Judge Cobb to the bench in 1930, and he held the position until his term expired in 1936.[115] Armond W. Scott, a successful lawyer in the District of Columbia, succeeded Judge Cobb on the Municipal Court by appointment of President Franklin D. Roosevelt in 1936. Scott, a 1904 graduate of Shaw University School of Law, quickly won national praise from the black press for his "just interpretation" of the laws.[116]

A year after the Scott appointment, President Roosevelt appointed William Henry Hastie to the United States District Court of the Virgin Islands, making Hastie the first black lawyer appointed to a federal district court in the history of the nation.[117] Hastie was exceptionally qualified for this appointment. He had graduated from Harvard University School of Law in 1930, was a member of the *Harvard Law Review*, taught at Howard University's law school, and had served as assistant solicitor under Harold L. Ickes, secretary of the interior. Hastie's appointment was not without some opposition, however, although this opposition was veiled in a different cloth. Senator William H. King of Utah, chairman of the subcommittee of the Senate Judiciary Committee, claimed that the black inhabitants of the Virgin Islands did not want a "colored man" as their judge and questioned Hastie's lack of trial experience.[118] Senator Millard E. Tydings of Maryland also opposed the Hastie nomination. With the assistance of several black lawyers, including Thurgood Marshall and Leon A. Ransom, and with the support of the National Bar Association, the NAACP, and, particularly, the political power of Congressman Arthur Wergs Mitchell, the only black representative in Congress,[119] Hastie won confirmation on March 19, 1937.[120]

A legal education was often used by black lawyers as a springboard into business, government, and other professions, or in civic and related areas in the District of Columbia. Andrew Franklin Hilyer, one Howard graduate, not only practiced business law in the District of Columbia, but also invented and patented two hot air register attachments.[121] John H. Butler used his legal training in banking in the District of Columbia and later in Charleston, South Carolina.[122] Mortimer Melbourne Harris became a very successful real estate lawyer.[123] Archibald Henry Grimké was appointed United States Consul to Santo Domingo by President Grover Cleveland, a position in which he served from 1894 to 1898.[124] James F. Bundy served on the school board of the District of Columbia and assisted in drafting the constitution of the board.[125] Other prominent black lawyers, such as Charles Hamilton Houston and Benjamin L. Gaskins, also later served on the Board of Education.[126]

Black lawyers in Washington, D.C., led fights in several areas of civic concern. Allen Mercer Daniel fought to have blacks nominated to attend West Point Military Academy.[127] Daniel, a professor of law at Howard University, also led a protest when Leo Frank, a Jew accused of murdering a white girl in a pencil company in Georgia, was lynched. He called for federal legislation against mob violence.[128] Daniel called the murder of Frank a "fiendish crime,"[129] and used the lynching to bring attention to the discrimination against Asians, Indians, and Africans in other parts of the world.[130]

In 1939, black lawyers actively participated in the Second National Conference on the Problems of the Negro and Negro Youth held in Washington. The conference, chaired by Mary McLeod Bethune, a member of President Roosevelt's "Black Kitchen Cabinet," was called to blueprint a course of action for the president in several areas of concern to black citizens. Many black lawyers were among the delegates to this conference,[131] during which James Madison Nabrit, Jr., a member of the Howard University law school faculty, recommended a constitutional amendment to strengthen black voting rights.[132] Charles Hamilton Houston attacked the testing policies of the Civil Service Commission and the exclusion of blacks from jobs in the Tennessee Valley Authority.[133]

The greater visibility brought about by such conferences, the advent of World War II, and the increasing criticism blacks leveled at the War Department to protest its discriminatory and exclusionary recruitment policies may have been behind the decision of the National Broadcasting Company (NBC) to consult with William Henry Hastie for public service programming advice.[134] Hastie was requested to review NBC's "policies . . . plans . . . [and] accomplishments in the public service field . . . every six months."[135]

Charlotte E. Ray became the first woman admitted to the bar in the District of Columbia in 1872, the same year she graduated from Howard University's law school (where she was also the first woman to do so) and three years after the admission of George Boyer Vashon, the District of Columbia's first black lawyer. Described as "a dusty mulatto, possessing quite an intelligent countenance," Ray was the first black woman in the United States to practice law. She was only the fifth woman in the United States admitted to the bar of any state.[136]

Like her male counterparts, Ray entered the private practice of law as a sole practitioner and advertised her availability as a lawyer in the *New National Era and Citizen*.[137] The number of years that she practiced law in the District of Columbia is unknown, but it is certain that Ray was the first black lawyer and first woman lawyer to specialize in corporate law. In 1893, Ray's "special envisionments" were said to "make her one of the best lawyers on corporations in the country."[138] She was described as eloquent, "for her sex," in the courtroom.[139] White women, denied admission to other state bars on the basis of sex, pointed to Ray's admission to practice in the District of Columbia as a legal precedent for their own admission before state supreme courts.[140] Though Ray had exceptional abilities, her practice failed to attract sufficient clients "on account of prejudice."[141] Before the beginning of the twentieth century, Ray gave up her practice, moved to Brooklyn, New York (where she married a man whose last name was Fraim), and began to teach school. The date of her death is uncertain. One source infers that she died in 1897 while others say that she died at age sixty in 1911.[142] Other women who completed law school and, like Ray, faced race and sex discrimination, chose to pursue different professions.[143]

Discrimination may have played a role in the exclusion of black women from the bar in the District of Columbia. Lillian R. Skinker-Malone, a 1922 honor graduate of Howard law school, reported that

I sat for the D.C. bar after I was graduated from Howard law school. I noticed that when I turned my paper in the examiner turned one of the covers of the examination. He did this only when blacks turned in their examinations. I didn't pass.[144]

In 1926, Ollie May Cooper, a 1921 graduate of Howard University's law school, was admitted to practice after she successfully passed the bar examination. Cooper was the first black woman admitted to the

District of Columbia by examination,[145] an achievement noted even by the German-American press.[146] In 1929, Cooper and Isadora A. Jackson Letcher, a 1925 law graduate of Howard University, formed the first law partnership in America composed solely of black women.[147] Later, in 1932, Thelma Davis Ackiss asked that Ollie May Cooper move for her admission into the District of Columbia Court of Appeals, because Cooper was the only black woman admitted to practice before that court. By so doing, Cooper became the first black woman lawyer in the District of Columbia to move for the admission of another black woman lawyer to the highest court in the District of Columbia.[148] In 1936 Ackiss became the first black woman to write a comprehensive review of United States Supreme Court decisions relating to black Americans.[149]

Helen Elsie Austin, who had been a former assistant attorney general of Ohio, came to Washington, passed the bar, and was appointed legal adviser to the Recorder of Deeds Office in 1939.[150] Subsequently, Austin became in 1942 the first black woman lawyer hired at the Office of Price Administration, where she shared an office with Richard Milhous Nixon.[151] In 1940 Lucia T. Thomas, who had graduated from Terrell Law School that year, joined the law firm of George A. Parker, becoming one of the first black women to associate with a black male lawyer in the District of Columbia.[152] Soon thereafter Thomas relocated to Chicago, Illinois, to practice law.

Maryland

Edward Garrison Draper was the first black person ever to receive a certificate to practice law from a Maryland court. Draper studied law at a firm in Baltimore, Maryland, under Joseph Jones Gilman, a respected member of the bar. Unable to be certified in Maryland because the state did not recognize blacks as citizens, Draper requested to be examined so that he could carry a certificate of competence to Africa, where he emigrated to practice law.[153] In 1857, Draper was examined by Judge Zachias Collins Lee of the Superior Court of Baltimore, who certified as follows:

Upon the application of Charles Gilman, Esq., of the Baltimore bar, I have examined Edward G. Draper, a young man of color, who has been reading law under the direction of Mr. Gilman, with the view of pursuing . . . practice in Liberia, Africa. And I have found him most intelligent and well informed in his answers to the questions proposed by me, and qualified in all respect to be admitted to the bar in Maryland, if he was a free white citizen of this state. . . . This certificate is . . . furnished to him . . . with a view to promote his establishment and success in Liberia at the bar there.[154]

Blacks were *personae non grata* in Maryland's jury system and were excluded from legal practice by state law for several years after the passage of the Fourteenth Amendment, which affirmed the state and national citizenship of black Americans.[155] The Reconstruction era, the zenith for the entry of blacks into the legal profession in many Southern states, did not loosen the rigid exclusionary practice that barred blacks from admission to the bar in Maryland.[156]

At the close of Reconstruction, Charles S. Taylor went to Baltimore to practice law. He was well qualified and had previously been admitted to the bar of Massachusetts. After securing an office in Baltimore, he "presented his credentials as to his character and upon motion of the Hon. Archibald Stirling, Jr., . . . a . . . very liberal district attorney, was admitted to the Federal District Court as the first Negro lawyer . . . within the confines of Maryland."[157] Believing that his admission to the Federal District Court in Maryland would satisfy Maryland state law, Taylor applied for admission to the state bar in Baltimore. However, Taylor's application was rejected because of his color. Undaunted in his desire to practice in Maryland, Taylor filed a petition in the Maryland Court of Appeals, the highest court in Maryland, for admission to the bar. He argued that Maryland's law qualifying only white male citizens of Maryland to be admitted to the bar was a violation of the Fourteenth Amendment. His argument fell on deaf ears. In 1877 the Maryland Court of Appeals upheld the right of the state to bar the admission of blacks to the legal profession as a matter of state right.[158] Taylor, "discouraged and defeated, . . . returned to Massachusetts."[159]

Seven years later a bill was introduced in the Maryland legislature to override the precedent announced in Taylor's case. The legislation was never passed.[160] The *Baltimore Sun* was critical of the legislature's failure to overrule the precedent. The law, the paper said, interfered with a black lawyer's "right to . . . earn his bread in any honest way [the Negro] saw fit."[161]

Disappointed by the Taylor case, a group of black citizens organized the Colored Equal Rights League, which was determined to see that blacks were seated on juries and admitted to the bar.[162] The league received support from a group of black ministers led by the vociferous Reverend Harvey Johnson. The ministers formed an adjunct group called the Brotherhood of Liberty, which was organized to crusade against denial of liberty according to race. High on the list of race restrictions to be opposed was the state law prohibiting blacks from becoming members of the Maryland bar.[163] Reverend Johnson was the pastor of Union Baptist Church in Baltimore. In 1884, he assembled the Brotherhood of Liberty at his home and outlined a plan of action to challenge the law.[164] The members of the Brotherhood of Liberty

pooled their funds and retained Alexander Hobbs, a white attorney, to
assist them in their cause. Charles S. Wilson, a black member of the
Massachusetts bar and a teacher in Maryland, was persuaded to test the
law excluding blacks from bar membership, as Charles S. Taylor had
done before him.[165]

On February 7, 1885, Wilson applied for admission to the Supreme
Bench of Baltimore City.[166] His application drew much public attention, and a huge crowd was present at the hearing on the day the court
considered the petition for admission. Hobbs argued that Wilson was
fit and otherwise qualified to practice law in the state of Maryland. He
used the same argument that Charles Taylor had used in his unsuccessful effort to gain admission to the Maryland bar. This time the
result was different. On March 19, 1885, "the Supreme Bench of
Baltimore City, in a unanimous opinion . . . held . . . that . . . color alone
would never bar a person from receiving justice within its limits and
jurisdiction."[167]

The Brotherhood of Liberty had won the battle but not the war, for
Charles S. Wilson was found not qualified for admission to the bar for
reasons other than race.[168] The Brotherhood of Liberty, determined to
have a black lawyer admitted in Maryland, "hurried . . . to Howard
University School of Law" and persuaded Everett J. Waring to apply to
the Maryland bar after graduation. On October 10, 1885, a few months
after his graduation, Waring "presented himself to the Supreme Bench
of Baltimore City and was admitted to the bar, becoming the first
Negro lawyer admitted to practice in the courts in Maryland."[169] Waring's admission was followed in 1886 by that of Joseph S. Davis, an
1884 Howard University law graduate.[170]

The Brotherhood of Liberty lost no time in their pursuit of justice.
They retained Everett J. Waring to test "the court's infringement of the
rights of colored people."[171] Waring's first real challenge was to test the
legality of the Bastardy Act, a law which established the rights of white
women, but not black women, to seek financial support when testifying
against the father of an illegitimate child. The discriminatory application of the law was viewed by Waring as unconstitutional. On the day of
the hearing, the courtroom was filled with lawyers and laymen who
crowded in to witness the first legal argument by a black lawyer in
a Maryland courtroom. Accounts of the argument indicate that the
"youthful advocate did not disappoint those who had pinned their
faith in him."[172] When Waring concluded his argument, "remarks of
congratulations were audible from his brother members of the bar, as
to his knowledge of law."[173] The court ruled against Waring's client, but
"to Baltimore's Negroes the mere presence of Waring as counsel made
the event seem a major victory."[174]

A high moment in American law came in 1890, when Waring entered the chambers of the United States Supreme Court to argue *Jones v. United States*.[175] Not since the admission of John Swett Rock to the United States Supreme Court in 1865 had the nation witnessed such a historical event at the nation's highest court.[176] The *Jones* case, popularly referred to as the "Navassa Island Case," concerned over one hundred mistreated and underpaid black laborers who were allegedly lured to the unclaimed Navassa Island to mine guano deposits.[177] The violence that ensued resulted in the death of one of the officers of the Navassa Phosphate Company. The accused men were taken to Baltimore, Maryland, to stand trial for murder. Black leaders in Baltimore retained Everett J. Waring and Joseph S. Davis to defend the three black men charged with murder, a crime that Waring argued could not be constitutionally tried in any American court. Waring's oral argument, touching on technical international and constitutional law issues, was superb. The *New York Age* reported that Waring "elaborated each and every one of his points [being] interrupted by questions from the bench."[178]

The United States Supreme Court affirmed the conviction of Waring's clients, who had been sentenced to be executed. Ultimately, however, the three defendants were not executed. Everett Waring and other leaders in the community were successful in persuading President Benjamin Harrison to commute the death sentences to life in prison.[179] In sum, if not in all regards, the fact that black lawyers had appeared before the highest court in the land representing black people was viewed by the blacks as a "grand step forward."[180]

After Waring appeared before the United States Supreme Court, his popularity in Baltimore increased. Both whites and blacks sought his services. In fact, he came under severe criticism from local black leaders for representing "some white youths charged with assaulting a young colored woman."[181] Claims that Waring had betrayed his race by representing the white defendants exemplify the conflicts sometimes suffered by black lawyers in more affluent urban areas who depended on the black community for their living.[182]

Waring's admission to the Maryland bar in 1885 may have prompted the University of Maryland Law School to admit three black students between 1887 and 1890. Harry Scythe Cummings and Charles S. Johnson completed the three-year law course in two years, graduating in 1889.[183] William Ashbie Hawkins was forced out of the Maryland Law School during his second year when strong anti-black sentiments were voiced by the student body. He enrolled in Howard University's law school and graduated in 1892.[184]

Within weeks of their graduation and admission to the Baltimore bar, Charles S. Johnson and Harry S. Cummings were defending blacks charged with raping and assaulting two white girls. So dramatic were the defenses and courtroom manners of Johnson and Cummings that the *New York Age* described their court appearances as being "like romance—like a dream."[185] They also broke new ground in civil rights actions by seeking monetary damages as a remedy for the violation of basic rights instead of merely asking the court to order the termination of illegal conduct. This approach proved much more effective, because it touched the pocket of the wrongdoer.[186]

The exceptional legal skills demonstrated by the partnership of Charles Johnson and Harry S. Cummings ended with Johnson's untimely death in 1896.[187] Thereafter, Harry Cummings shifted part of his professional attention to politics and was elected to the Baltimore City Council, a first for a black in Maryland.[188] But the fact that Cummings lived in a ward with a sizable black population did not help him win reelection in 1892, when he lost to a white Democrat. Nor did his legal credentials help to elect him in 1895, when he lost to a black dentist, Dr. J. Marcus Cargill.[189] Nevertheless, Cummings recaptured his seat on the Baltimore City Council in 1897, and he held it, at the expense of his law practice, until 1915.[190]

Among Cummings's many accomplishments, two significant political episodes stand out. In 1904, he was selected as one of the delegates to the Republican National Convention to give a speech seconding the nomination of Theodore Roosevelt for president,[191] and in 1905, while a member of the Baltimore City Council, he led a successful fight to defeat the Poe Amendment, a legislative measure that would have disenfranchised black voters in Maryland.[192]

The artful advocacy of William Ashbie Hawkins in the area of civil rights had a direct impact upon segregated Baltimore in the closing days of the nineteenth century. Upon graduation from Howard University law school in 1892, Hawkins formed a partnership with another black Baltimore lawyer, George W. F. McMechen, an 1897 law graduate of Yale University. The stability of the firm and the long association of McMechen and Hawkins made these lawyers a force to be reckoned with, both by the establishment and by other black lawyers.[193] When William Ashbie Hawkins was admitted to the Maryland bar, he reported that "it took the severest courage and self-sacrifice to withstand the studied insults and cruel indifference which was the common lot to endure by us all."[194] However, Hawkins and other pioneer black lawyers in Baltimore endured, until "the Negro lawyer . . . [was] no longer an experiment."[195]

Six years after his graduation from Howard University's law school, Hawkins was arguing civil rights cases before the Maryland Court of

Appeals, the highest court in Maryland. In 1898, the Maryland Court of Appeals rejected Hawkins's claim that it was unconstitutional for a private mechanical arts school under contract to the city to deny admission to a black youth sponsored by a member of the Baltimore City Council.[196] But Hawkins's theory—that the exclusionary conduct, based on race, by a private party using public property violated the Fourteenth Amendment—would later become the law of the nation.[197] The decision of the Maryland Court of Appeals did not discourage a determined Hawkins from using the courts to redress the grievances of his people; given the inability of blacks to be elected to the Maryland General Assembly, he believed that "the courts were the 'final arbiter of [the] rights [of blacks].'"[198]

William Ashbie Hawkins participated in almost every major civil rights case in Maryland during the first quarter of the twentieth century, including the litigation of civil rights claims before the Interstate Commerce Commission.[199] He authored pamphlets on the relationship between blacks and the courts and on the duties and responsibilities of the black lawyer.[200] In 1920, Hawkins ran unsuccessfully as an independent candidate for the United States Senate, a first for a black citizen of Maryland.[201]

Warner T. McGuinn, an 1887 graduate of Yale University's law school, arrived in Baltimore in 1890 after a brief stay in Kansas City, Kansas. McGuinn practiced with Harry Scythe Cummings and Charles S. Johnson from 1893 to 1895. Thereafter, he practiced alone. By 1896, McGuinn had been appointed commissioner of liquor and licenses in Baltimore, a position that he held until 1900.[202] At the same time, Malachi Gibson, an 1891 Howard University law graduate, was appointed secretary of the Judiciary Committee of the Maryland State Legislature.[203] Later, McGuinn and William L. Fitzgerald were elected to the Baltimore City Council, in 1918 and 1919, respectively.[204]

Between 1885 and 1922, forty-two black lawyers were admitted to the bar in Maryland. By 1944, fifty-nine years after the first admission, a total of seventy lawyers had been admitted to practice in the Maryland courts.[205] This was a significant period for these lawyers because their presence and performance dispelled the notion that the legal profession was one in which blacks could not succeed. And succeed they did. Hugh Mason Burkett became the "first colored man licensed as [a] real estate broker in Maryland."[206] Beginning in 1917 black lawyers, concerned about the quality of judges being elected or appointed to the bench, began to rate white lawyers who were campaigning to become judges.[207] Ephraim Jackson, an 1899 graduate of Howard University's law school, made several innovative inroads into the criminal law area, and by 1920 he had tried more murder cases "than any colored member of the bar."[208] Josiah F. Henry, Jr., a 1923 University of Michigan law graduate, and William A. C. Hughes, Jr., a 1930 graduate of Boston University's law school, blazed new trails in civil rights to enlarge opportunities for black citizens in Maryland.[209]

The role of advocate in Maryland was more difficult for some black lawyers than for others. Criminal defense lawyers had an especially difficult time. In some instances black criminal lawyers had to take extraordinary steps to protect the interests of their clients from the power of the state. In 1918 Philip B. Perlman, an assistant attorney general of Maryland, filed a scathing answer to a mandamus action filed by George L. Pendleton, a black lawyer who claimed that the board of corrections had refused to allow him access to his imprisoned clients. Pendleton instituted a suit against the state for damages because of Perlman's conduct.[210] Pendleton's reputation as a lawyer was later sullied on what some called trumped-up ethical charges brought by the attorney general of Maryland.[211]

In 1933 Thurgood Marshall returned home to Baltimore to practice law after graduating from Howard University School of Law. The private practice of law must have been difficult for Marshall, especially since many of the clients for whom he brought civil rights actions could not afford to pay him. Perhaps this is one reason Marshall went to New York to join the staff of the National Association for the Advancement of Colored People in 1936. The NAACP guaranteed Marshall a monthly salary of $150.00, thus allowing him to give full time and attention to civil rights.[212] Thurgood Marshall left Baltimore, but not before he, Charles Hamilton Houston, and William I. Gosnell, all black, had successfully sued the state of Maryland to gain the admission of Donald G. Murray to the University of Maryland Law School. Murray was the first black admitted since anti-black sentiment forced William Ashbie Hawkins to leave the law school in 1890.[213] Four years after his victory in the Murray case, Marshall returned to Maryland, this time as an NAACP lawyer, to sue the board of education of Anne Arundel County for wage discrimination in its practice of awarding higher salaries to white teachers. Marshall, joined by Howard University law professor Leon Andrew Ransom and Howard's dean, William Henry Hastie, persuaded the court on constitutional grounds that the disparity in wages for black public school teachers was unconstitutional.[214]

Looking back over the first half century of black lawyers at the bar in Maryland, Azzie Briscoe Koger wrote:

The Negro has come to regard the Negro lawyer as the champion of his rights before these courts and looks constantly to the Negro lawyer to lead him, as a sort of legal Moses, to the land of freedom and promise. . . . The Negro lawyer accepts this challenge and very seriously regards the responsibility of leadership in this field. . . . He has proved [his] ideals above temporal values. The Negro lawyer has sought to bring to members of our group a fuller view of a finer and richer life.[215]

Prior to 1945, no black women were admitted to the Maryland bar.[216]

New Jersey

George Jackson was one of twenty-six applicants examined for admission to the bar before the Supreme Court of New Jersey in 1893. A resident of Camden, New Jersey, Jackson was "the first colored man admitted to the bar of the State of New Jersey."[217] At the time George Jackson was admitted to the bar, the only paper required to be filed under the New Jersey bar's admission rules was a certificate from a counsellor-at-law to authenticate a clerkship in a law office. Jackson filed two such certificates. One was signed by Samuel H. Patterson of Asbury Park, New Jersey, certifying that Jackson had served a clerkship in his office from February 25, 1886, to July 1, 1887. The other certificate was filed by John W. Swartz of Freehold, New Jersey, who certified Jackson's clerkship in his office from October 1, 1887, to October 1, 1889.[218] Little more is known about George Jackson, except that he subsequently left New Jersey in 1906 and went to St. Paul, Minnesota, where he was admitted to the bar.[219]

Immediately after being graduated from Howard University's law school in 1893, George A. Douglass became "the second colored man to be admitted as a New Jersey lawyer," though he had already been admitted to the District of Columbia bar.[220] When Douglass applied for the New Jersey bar, he "brought letters from the Chief Justice of the Supreme Court of the District of Columbia [Edward F. Bingham], the United States District Attorney of the District of Columbia and from Wheeler H. Peckham of New York."[221] Examined by E. Q. Keasby, Thomas Anderson, Oscar Keen, John A. Miller, and Halsey M. Barrett, Douglass "proved to be extremely well prepared, both in law and practice."[222]

Only two other black lawyers are known to have been admitted to the New Jersey bar before the turn of the twentieth century: Alfredo Bonito Cosey and Traverse Spraggins.[223] Little is known about Spraggins, but Cosey, an 1899 Howard University law graduate, was quite a scholar. He published several books, including *American and English Law of Title of Record, 1535–1911* (1914). This was one of the first law books of its kind ever published by a black lawyer.[224] Cosey's legal career was not as bright as his scholarly life, however. In 1914, he was charged with criminal extortion, a charge he denied.[225] Nevertheless, in 1916 the New Jersey Supreme Court "direct[ed] that Cosey's name be stricken from the rolls . . . of New Jersey."[226]

James A. Garfield Lightfoot, a 1907 graduate of Howard University law school, clerked in the office of a white ex-judge, John J. Crandall, from 1910 to 1912. He was admitted to the New Jersey bar in 1912 and was certified as a counsellor in 1922.[227] After his admission to the New Jersey bar, Lightfoot associated with another black lawyer, Isaac Henry Nutter. Their firm was successful in criminal defense matters, especially murder cases. Around 1915 Lightfoot also published the *Atlantic City Advocate*, which had "a circulation of ten thousand."[228]

Isaac Henry Nutter, a 1901 Howard University law graduate, was admitted to the New Jersey bar in 1905 and soon associated with John J. Crandall.[229] Nutter established a good reputation as a criminal defense lawyer. Because of his extraordinary talents, from time to time the local New Jersey court's assigned him to prosecute criminal cases. Between 1905 and 1919 Nutter handled approximately thirty murder cases, "one of which [resulted] in [a] second degree" murder conviction. The other cases resulted in four manslaughter convictions and twenty-five acquittals.[230] In 1934, Nutter prosecuted a criminal case against a defendant represented by his former partner, James A. Garfield Lightfoot. In 1934 it was not unusual to have two black lawyers opposing each other in either a criminal or civil matter in New Jersey. Lightfoot's defense was so compelling that "it took the jury just seven minutes . . . to acquit."[231]

Isaac H. Nutter's performance as a criminal lawyer and community leader came to the attention of New Jersey governor Walter E. Edge who, during the National Business League's annual meeting in 1918, stated that "Mr. Nutter is doing wonderful work for the Negro race [and] is preaching the doctrine of equal opportunity and the elimination of prejudice."[232] However, praise from the governor did not immunize Nutter, an ardent civil rights advocate, from trumped-up claims of ethics violations. In 1920, he was charged with receiving stolen goods. An indictment followed.[233] Nutter, asserting his innocence, stated "that a week [earlier] he had been told by [a minister] that he would be indicted if he appeared at Trenton, [New Jersey,] to speak in favor of the passage of the equal rights bill," then pending in the state legislature.[234] Nutter established that he had been framed "for political purposes" and the charges against him were dropped.[235]

Robert S. Hartgrove, a 1908 graduate of Boston University School of Law, was admitted first to the Massachusetts bar in 1908 and subsequently to the New Jersey bar. In 1915, Hartgrove was appointed master in chancery in New Jersey and later an assistant attorney general of New Jersey (the first black to receive such an appointment).[236]

Hartgrove was one of the first black lawyers to argue a case before the New Jersey Supreme Court. In 1933, he won an important civil rights case involving black children who had been denied swimming privileges in the public schools because of their race. Hartgrove's persuasive argument drew the following language from the court: "To say to a lad, 'You may study with your classmate, you may attend gymnasium with them, but you may not have swimming with them because of your color,' is unlawful discrimination."[237]

Robert Queen, a 1915 graduate of Howard University's law school, passed the District of Columbia bar in 1918, then went to Norfolk, Virginia, as a War Department demobilization clerk for troops returning from overseas at the end of World War I.[238] In 1919, Queen resigned from government service and opened a law office in the District of Columbia with Zeph Moore, a black attorney. He later relocated to New Jersey and was admitted to the bar there in 1921. In 1922, Queen opened a law office in Trenton and worked part-time for the city in tax foreclosures and part-time for the housing authority.[239] In 1943, Queen and Frank H. Wimberley, a 1922 graduate of Howard University's law school, defended Clarence Hill, a black soldier charged with the murder of six people in Mercer County, New Jersey, and four shotgun attacks in Bucks County, Pennsylvania. These murders were popularly referred to as the "Duck Island Murders,"[240] and public outrage called for the death penalty. Through the skill and legal acumen of Queen and Wimberley, the soldier was convicted on only one of the murder indictments and was sentenced to life imprisonment.

Perhaps Queen's most significant and lasting service as a lawyer was his argument before the New Jersey Supreme Court in 1944. He persuaded the court to strike down the separate but equal doctrine in public education in the state of New Jersey.[241]

William A. Dart, a 1918 graduate of Boston University School of Law, passed the Massachusetts bar in 1919, the South Carolina bar in 1920, and the New Jersey bar in 1921.[242] Dart's performance as a private practitioner reached the attention of New Jersey governor Harold G. Hoffman, and Dart was appointed to the post of deputy attorney general of New Jersey in 1935, becoming the highest-ranking black ever appointed to the office of the New Jersey attorney general.[243]

By 1944, two other "firsts" had been achieved by the black lawyers in New Jersey: Robert Burke Johnson, a 1927 graduate of the University of Pennsylvania Law School, had been appointed to the Camden, New Jersey, board of education,[244] and Roger M. Yancey, a 1928 graduate of the University of Newark Law School (Rutgers), had been appointed special assistant to Francis Biddle, the United States attorney in charge of the civil division of New Jersey. Yancey was appointed with the endorsement of Senator William H. Smathers.[245]

The experience of black women lawyers in New Jersey before 1945 is unknown.

Pennsylvania

Black lawyers' efforts to gain admittance to the bar in Pennsylvania began in 1845. In that year, George Boyer Vashon commenced the study of law in the office of Walter Straton Forward, "a prominent figure in Pennsylvania politics."[246] When Vashon completed his studies in 1847, he applied for admission to the Allegheny County bar, which rejected his application: under state law only white men were eligible for admission to the bar.[247] In fact, to be examined for admission to the bar, Vashon was forced to file a "show cause suit before Judge Walter H. Lowrie of the District Court."[248] After all legal procedures were exhausted, Vashon left for the Republic of Haiti. The *Pittsburgh Telegraph* reported that Vashon had been "driven from home, friends, and family by the bitter, vulgar, and unnatural prejudice against color." Prior to leaving the United States for Haiti, Vashon was admitted to the New York Bar in 1848.[249]

Vashon did not apply for admission to the Allegheny bar again until 1867, after the Civil War. Even though he had been a member of the New York bar since 1848, Vashon's application for admission to the Allegheny bar was again rejected by the three-judge Court of Common Pleas, but this time on the technical ground that he had not submitted two character references with his application.[250] However, the words of one of the presiding judges, "that blacks and whites ought to be entirely separated,"[251] certainly made it appear that black lawyers were unwelcome in Pennsylvania. Though denied the privilege of practicing law in his native state, Vashon applied for and was admitted to practice before the United States Supreme Court on April 6, 1868,[252] becoming the third black lawyer in the nation's history to achieve that honor. A year later Vashon became the first black lawyer admitted to practice in the District of Columbia.

Jonathan Jasper Wright returned to his native state of Pennsylvania to study law after being graduated from Lancasterian University in Ithaca, New York, in the late 1850s. Wright initially studied law for two years in Montrose (Susquehanna County), Pennsylvania, in the law offices of Bently, Fith, and Bently, while teaching school to pay for his law books and tutoring.[253] He subsequently moved to Wilkes-Barre, Pennsylvania, to study law for an additional year under Judge O.

Collins. Wright's first attempt to take the bar examination in the early 1860s failed, presumably because of racism.[254]

Wright left Pennsylvania and settled in Beaufort, South Carolina, until slavery was abolished by the Thirteenth Amendment in 1865. He then returned to Montrose, Pennsylvania, "demanded an examination,"[255] and was admitted to the bar on August 13, 1865.[256] Shortly thereafter, Wright, "the first colored man admitted to practice law" in the state,[257] left Pennsylvania permanently to practice law in Beaufort.[258] He later became a member of the South Carolina Supreme Court.

In 1874, John Daniel Lewis graduated from Columbia University School of Law and later moved to Philadelphia, Pennsylvania, to practice law.[259] Admitted to practice by the Pennsylvania Supreme Court on February 9, 1876,[260] Lewis established "quite a lucrative practice."[261] As a private practitioner, Lewis ran into trouble in 1882 when he was criminally indicted and tried for charging his client an illegal fee for securing a pension. Lewis's acquittal on this charge brought relief to the community. The local press reported that the government had "misled . . . some ignorant colored people into instituting this suit."[262] Lewis was so committed to the principles of equality for his race that when he died in 1891, he willed one thousand dollars for the creation of "the Lewis Protective Bureau of civil rights . . . to protect, and secure . . . colored citizens in the United States."[263] According to the national press, Lewis's death reduced the number of active black lawyers in Philadelphia to two: Theophilus J. Minton and Jeremiah Howard Scott.[264]

Thomas T. Henry studied law in John Daniel Lewis's law office for two years and was admitted to Philadelphia's Court of Common Pleas and Orphan's Court on December 31, 1881. While a law student in Lewis's office, Henry waited tables at the St. Elmo Hotel. A guest in the hotel took an interest in Henry and purchased for him his law books.[265] Henry became the first black lawyer to pass the examination for admission to the bar, which was administered by the newly created Board of Examiners.[266]

In 1888, the University of Pennsylvania graduated its first black student, Aaron Albert Mossell, Jr.[267] During his senior year in law school, Mossell wrote a brilliant paper challenging the constitutionality of state anti-miscegenation laws. Mossell argued that such laws were unconstitutional under the Fourteenth Amendment to the United States Constitution. Mossell posed two questions regarding the government's right to interfere with mixed marriages which would not be answered by the Supreme Court for seventy-nine years: "What can be the freedom, of that government, whose liberty of thought, feeling and action, is hampered by arbitrary law? How can [blacks or whites] pursue [their] own good in [their] own way; subject only to the rights of others, not their opinions, tastes or prejudices?"[268] After graduating from the University of Pennsylvania's law school, Mossell practiced law in Philadelphia for a short period before moving to Lockport, New York. Prior to his admission to the New York bar, Mossell studied in the law offices of Brown and Lewis to prepare for the examination. Mossell, described as a "brilliant young colored lawyer," was admitted to the federal court in Lockport on November 17, 1892.[269]

As the nineteenth century drew to an end, there were only "ten practicing Negro lawyers" in Philadelphia.[270] According to W. E. B. Du Bois, only two were considered "successful practitioners."[271] Three others were described as having difficulty "earning a living" in their attempts to practice before the criminal courts.[272] The other five black lawyers were described as "having little or no practice."[273] The ability of the black lawyer, however, was not at issue. The barrier facing black lawyers was that neither white nor black citizens of Pennsylvania used their services, because whites controlled all the systems of justice.[274] Despite the fact that an influential Philadelphian, John Wanamaker, said that he "would [n]ever mark a man down . . . as a NEGRO lawyer,"[275] other businessmen of Wanamaker's influence are not known to have spoken up for the black lawyer. There is no evidence that Wanamaker, a successful businessman, ever retained a black lawyer.

The racist attitude toward black lawyers in Pennsylvania thawed somewhat in 1891. In that year, J. Welford Holmes and William M. Randolph were admitted to the bar in Pittsburgh, and William Henry Ridley became the first lawyer of his race admitted to the bar in Media, Pennsylvania.[276] The admission of these lawyers laid the foundation for the subsequent admission in Pittsburgh of Walter E. Billows in 1892 and of William Henry Stanton and Frank R. Stewart, both in 1895. Each of these lawyers "were active and respected practitioners."[277] After 1895, admission to the Pittsburgh bar slowed until P. J. Clyde Randell and George H. White, Jr., were admitted in 1918 and 1919, respectively.[278]

Charles L. Brooks, an 1892 Howard law graduate, was also admitted to the Pennsylvania bar in that year.[279] Brooks spent several years in the real estate business and became counsel to the Cherry Building and Loan Association of Ardmore and Montgomery counties in 1902. During Samuel W. Pennypacker's term as governor of Pennsylvania, Brooks was appointed a notary public.[280]

William Justin Carter, an 1892 graduate of Howard University law school, first taught school in Annapolis, Maryland, before relocating to

Harrisburg, Pennsylvania, in 1894. In 1895, Carter was admitted to the Dauphin County bar and appointed assistant district attorney for Dauphin County, a position he held until 1896.[281] Thereafter, he handled many important criminal cases as a private practitioner. He represented white and black defendants. In one case, Carter represented an Italian-American named Martin Santora, who was charged with murder. Carter's defense of Santora was so effective that he "was presented with a bouquet of flowers by the jury that heard the case,"[282] a distinction held by few lawyers in American law. Carter later became counsel to several white business establishments.[283] He served as secretary to Pennsylvania lieutenant governor Edward Beidleman from 1920 to 1923.[284]

After John Stephens Durham completed a term as minister-in-residence and consul-general to the Republic of Haiti, he studied law privately and was admitted to the Pennsylvania bar in 1893.[285] Two years later, he was appointed assistant attorney to the Spanish Treaty Claims Commission in Cuba by a United States Navy Department official, J. Martin Miller. Durham's assignment was "to evaluate damage occasioned by the volcanic eruptions of Mount Pelée in Martinique."[286]

William Henry Stanton, admitted to the bar in Pittsburgh in 1895, read law in the law office of Charles F. McKenna, a former United States district court judge.[287] Stanton was the "first lawyer in Western Pennsylvania, white or colored, appointed by the court to defend a pauper charged with murder and to be paid [a fee] by the county for [his] services."[288] Stanton handled many murder cases and had an excellent acquittal record. He also represented the Douglass Loan and Investment Company and the Knights of Pythias, a black fraternal group.[289]

Several dramatic occurrences at the turn of the century signaled, for a time, the upward mobility of black lawyers in Pennsylvania. In 1899, James B. Raymond became the first black lawyer in Pennsylvania to serve in a judicial capacity on the Aldermanic Court in Altoona, Pennsylvania.[290] In 1902, Temple Law School graduated George Edward Dickerson, who passed the Pennsylvania bar in 1901 "with an average of over 94."[291] Dickerson served for several years as assistant solicitor for the city of Philadelphia and was considered one of the most outstanding criminal lawyers in Philadelphia.[292] In 1919, Dickerson gained notoriety by defending several blacks charged in the riots that "broke out along the Gray's Ferry Section as a result of a scarcity of housing facilities."[293] Dickerson not only defended blacks but "sued and received damages against the county for the loss of property destroyed by the mob, and brought to trial the officers who [murdered a black man]."[294]

Dickerson also gained notoriety in a celebrated case involving Frederick Brown, a black fugitive wanted for murder in South Carolina who had fled to Philadelphia. South Carolina governor Coleman L. Bease objected to the Pennsylvania authorities' refusal to return Brown to South Carolina without formal extradition, a procedure Dickerson insisted was required by the Constitution and the laws of Pennsylvania. Dickerson's artful advocacy drew a "To hell with the Constitution" response from Governor Bease and the claim that he "would lead a mob to lynch a Nigger myself."[295]

Robert Lee Vann, a 1909 graduate of Western University School of Law (University of Pittsburgh), was admitted to the bar in 1910, at the same time George Edward Dickerson was admitted. After graduating from law school, Vann's first goal was to organize what would become a major black newspaper, *The Pittsburgh Courier*. He served as editor and legal counsel for the *Courier* for nearly forty years.[296]

Vann, one of a handful of lawyers in Pittsburgh, also entered private practice. He decided to become a criminal lawyer and was tutored in this field by William H. Stanton.[297] Vann won the respect of the black community by winning the acquittal of a black man who had been charged with murdering a white man fourteen years earlier.[298] But Vann's business slowed as blacks continued to gravitate to white lawyers.[299] Vann, "like most black attorneys . . . [sought] out ways to supplement his income, turning to the newspaper business and politics."[300]

In 1918, Vann was confirmed as fourth assistant city solicitor in Pittsburgh and gained prominence in Republican Party circles. His appointment was "the highest position a black had ever received in [Pittsburgh]."[301] Although Vann was a Republican, he supported Franklin D. Roosevelt for president in 1932, and this won him an appointment as special assistant to Homer S. Cummings, attorney general of the United States. Vann's appointment was hailed as a demonstration that the Democrats, who had never appointed a black to such a high position in the Department of Justice, recognized black legal talent.[302] Vann's appointment was almost a complete disaster. He arrived in Washington expecting to be accorded the respect of a special assistant to the attorney general, but was instead treated like a legal clerk. Vann had no office, no desk, and no stenographer assigned to him for at least six weeks. After Vann was assigned stenographers, "they often refused to take dictation because he was black."[303] Attorney General Cummings never met with him.

Vann worked "in the Lands Division, investigating and verifying titles for the Resettlement Administration and Reforestoration Program, for future post office sites and for Indian schools."[304] He was named to two advisory committees on "colored affairs" and chaired various interdepartmental matters involving the Department of Labor and the Department of Agriculture. He was also named to the Virgin Island Advisory Council. These duties played well in the black press, but had little effect on national policy. Vann, unhappy with his role, left the Department of Justice in 1936. He was succeeded by another black Pennsylvania lawyer, Theron B. Hamilton.[305]

The year after Robert Vann left the Department of Justice, he won national attention by opposing the appointment of Alabama senator Hugo Black to the United States Supreme Court. Vann criticized Senator Black for refusing to support anti-lynching legislation. After Senator Black was confirmed, Ray Sprigle, a reporter for the *Pittsburgh Post-Gazette*, "broke the story that Black had been a member of the Ku Klux Klan in 1923 and had been given a life membership in the Klan." Vann called for Black's resignation.[306] Vann himself was considered, but never seriously, for the United States Supreme Court when Justice George Sutherland retired in 1938.[307] When Vann died in 1940, he was mourned by the whole nation, and the Liberty Ship *Robert L. Vann* was launched in his honor.[308]

Around the time that George Edward Dickerson and Robert Lee Vann were admitted to the bar in Pennsylvania, Harry W. Bass, an 1896 graduate of the University of Pennsylvania Law School, became, in 1910, the first black citizen elected to the Pennsylvania House of Representatives.[309] Despite the fact that blacks had newly won political power in the Pennsylvania state legislature, the courts of Philadelphia admitted no black lawyers between 1910 and 1920, possibly because the highly visible criminal and civil rights victories of the ten or so black lawyers admitted to the bar before that time made it seem that some measure of parity had already been achieved.[310]

Between 1922 and 1926, black graduates from Yale and Harvard University law schools relocated to Philadelphia. In 1922 John Francis Williams, an editor of the *Yale Law Journal*, graduated from Yale's law school and joined a railroad company in Pennsylvania. Despite Williams's distinction as a member of Yale's law journal, no law firm would hire him.[311] In 1923, Raymond Pace Alexander graduated from Harvard University's law school and went to work in the law office of a black lawyer, John R. K. Scott, of Philadelphia.[312] Alexander's task as a lawyer was a difficult one, for black people still did not call upon black lawyers to represent them. But Alexander "succeeded in winning the confidence of the public by his . . . untiring efforts in behalf of every client."[313] Alexander's dedication and attention to detail brought him several court-appointed cases.[314] Alexander was also an innovative law office manager. Rather than undertake the details of negotiating all realty transactions, he trained his law clerks to do so, thereby freeing himself to concentrate on more complicated matters.[315]

Black people in Philadelphia quickly came to know that Alexander was an advocate for their rights. In 1924 he sued and successfully enjoined the Chestnut Street Theatre from excluding blacks from a production of *The Ten Commandments*[316] and later won large damage awards against the Pennsylvania and Reading Railroads and the Philadelphia Rapid Transit Company for racial discrimination and other tortious conduct.[317] But the success that would have brought stature to Alexander's white counterparts instead brought "repressive treatment" against him.[318] Whites "just could not stand seeing a well trained, well groomed, courteous, well maintained but strong-willed black lawyer . . . appearing before . . . all white juries and winning cases."[319] Even more irritating to his white counterparts was the fact that white clients flocked to Alexander because of his superlative litigation skills.[320] Alexander's reputation was further enhanced when he obtained the acquittal of Louise Thomas, a defendant accused of murder, after securing a reversal of her conviction by the Pennsylvania Supreme Court. It was an acquittal that saved Thomas from the death penalty.[321]

Alexander's law firm provided opportunities for other talented Harvard University law graduates, such as Maceo William Hubbard,[322] for they "[found] no large and well established law firms of the white race" that would accept them.[323] The legal talent Alexander recruited to his law firm assisted him in a variety of cases, including one that won the vindication of two black golfers who had been unfairly treated by whites. He also pressed for equal educational opportunities for black children in the public school system.[324]

Sadie Tanner Mossell married Raymond Pace Alexander just about the time he graduated from Harvard Law School. Possessing the second Ph.D. degree ever awarded to a black woman in the nation's history, Sadie Alexander in 1927 entered, and became the first black woman to graduate from, the University of Pennsylvania Law School, thirty-nine years after her father, Aaron A. Mossell, Jr., received his law degree from the same school.[325]

Alexander's matriculation at the University of Pennsylvania Law School was not without conflict, even though she ultimately graduated with honors.[326] Her election as a member of the *Pennsylvania Law Review* was almost foiled when Edward Mikell, the dean of the law school, opposed her election by the student-run board of editors. However, Philip Werner Amram, a Jewish student whose father was a member of the law faculty, publicly objected to the dean's actions, and he prevailed.[327] Alexander took her place on the law review. Dean Mikell's move to bar Alexander from the law review perhaps was due more to her gender than her race, because Robert Burke Johnson, Alexander's black classmate, was elected to the law review without protest.[328]

Sadie T. M. Alexander practiced law with her husband,[329] became an active member and officer of the National Bar Association[330] and the first black woman lawyer to work in the solicitor's office in Philadelphia. She also was an important scholar of the history of American black women lawyers.[331]

In the same year Raymond Pace Alexander was admitted to the Pennsylvania bar, Homer S. Brown and Richard F. Jones graduated from the University of Pittsburgh School of Law. Jones was the law school's first black member of the Order of the Coif, a national legal honor society. He formed a law partnership with his classmate, Homer S. Brown.[332]

Brown was a political activist as well as an outstanding lawyer. He became the president of the Pittsburgh chapter of the NAACP, a position that he held from 1924 to 1944.[333] In 1934, Brown was elected to the Pennsylvania House of Representatives from the First District of Pittsburgh, and served there with distinction for several years. Among his several accomplishments in the legislature was an amendment to the Pennsylvania Labor Relations Act that made exclusion from union membership on account of race, creed, or color illegal.[334]

In 1936, Brown filed an impeachment petition in the Pennsylvania State Legislature against a Lancaster County judge who had stated that blacks accused of raping white women should be lynched. Brown premised his petition on the grounds that the judge's statement defiled the due process guarantee of the United States Constitution. The judge was not impeached, but because of Brown's assertive action, he was required to make a public apology before the legislature.[335]

In 1924 Philadelphia witnessed the appointment of Amos Scott as its "first Negro magistrate."[336] Eugene Washington Rhodes, a 1925 graduate of Temple Law School, followed as the first black appointed assistant United States attorney for the Eastern District of Pennsylvania,[337] and he was followed in 1934 by Walter Arthur Gay, Jr., a 1929 graduate of the University of Pennsylvania's law school.[338] In 1928, John Cornelius Asbury, an 1884 graduate of Howard University law school, became the "first colored man" to serve as assistant district attorney in the local court system in Philadelphia,[339] and he was succeeded by William "Bill" Humphreys.[340]

By the 1930s, the black lawyer continued to face great odds in Pennsylvania, despite the gains made by such lawyers as Raymond Pace Alexander. Alexander continued to assert that the "future of the Negro lawyer, notwithstanding the difficulties he [would] face, is . . . very bright,"[341] even though few, if any, blacks passed the Pennsylvania bar examination between 1934 and 1943.[342] During this period black lawyers continued to be strong advocates for black civil rights, and they broke new ground in Pennsylvania politics. Robert Nix, Sr., "had no fewer than twenty Philadelphia policemen arraigned and punished for maltreating their prisoners and for entering the premises without warrants."[343] Wilbur C. Douglass, a 1920 graduate of the University of Pittsburgh Law School, served as assistant city solicitor for Pittsburgh from 1934 to 1935, and as assistant county solicitor for Allegheny County for more than ten years.[344] John C. Sparks and William Harvey Fuller both served as assistant district attorneys in Philadelphia prior to 1935.[345] And in the late 1930s Fitzhugh Lee Styles, a 1925 graduate of Howard University law school, published *Negroes and the Law*, the first comprehensive book about black lawyers.[346]

By 1944 J. Austin Norris, a 1917 Yale law graduate, was serving as the first black member of the Philadelphia and Pittsburgh boards for revision of taxes.[347] Norris had been slated for a federal judgeship but was pressured into accepting the lesser job on the boards. Norris, a highly respected lawyer, had also served in the Pennsylvania attorney general's office. He had encouraged and witnessed the admission of eight black lawyers to the Allegheny County–Pittsburgh Bar Association[348] and the appointment of Wendell S. Stanton, Jr., a second-generation black lawyer, to the position of assistant United States attorney in 1941.[349]

Between 1920 and 1944, nineteen black lawyers were admitted to the bar in Philadelphia. Of these, one was a woman. Each of these lawyers, as well as others admitted to the bar in different parts of the state, defied the odds and demonstrated with remarkable skill that black lawyers had gained a lasting prominence in the Commonwealth of Pennsylvania.[350]

Rhode Island

On June 3, 1874, John Henry Ballou became the first black citizen admitted to the bar in Rhode Island.[351] Ballou commenced his legal studies at age eighteen, after a comprehensive secondary education. He studied law in the office of Edward T. Ames for three years prior to his admission to the Rhode Island Supreme Court.[352] Ballou did not remain in Rhode Island for long, but before he left to practice law in Florida, he was instrumental in securing the repeal of the antimiscegenation law in Rhode Island.[353]

Ballou was followed to the Rhode Island bar by Maurice Baumann on January 1, 1877, Frederick Clayton Olney on March 8, 1889, Joseph

H. Monroe on June 3, 1893, and William Aaron Heathman on May 20, 1898.[354] Baumann practiced in Rhode Island for five years before relocating to Chicago, Illinois, where he was admitted to the bar on November 16, 1883.

During the next quarter of a century, only a few black lawyers were admitted to the practice in Rhode Island: Julius Linoble Mitchell,[355] an 1894 graduate of Allen University Law Department, on June 25, 1904; John B. Edwards[356] on November 12, 1913; Joseph Gray LeCount on May 5, 1914; Thomas H. Brown on June 7, 1915; and James Matamora Stockett on June 7, 1915.[357]

Frederick Clayton Olney, "part Narragansett Indian and Negro," was graduated from the University of Michigan Law School in 1889.[358] Olney practiced law in Rhode Island for thirty years and was well respected. When he died, a statement of praise for Olney by judges and the Washington County Bar Association "was adopted and ordered spread upon the records of the court."[359]

Reportedly, students at Boston University School of Law in the mid-1890s had sponsors. These sponsors supplemented the student's legal education for which they were paid a fee. While it is not entirely clear what role in legal education these sponsors played, William Aaron Heathman, an 1898 graduate of Boston University's law school, reported that he turned a portion of his wages over to his sponsor, who "would remit the money to the law school."[360] After Heathman graduated from law school, he took the Rhode Island bar examination. At the time, Heathman said that he had "heard indirectly there were some who had said that the Rhode Island Bar 'was not ready' for a Negro lawyer."[361] Under extreme pressure to prove that blacks were capable of passing the bar examination, Heathman passed.[362] He may have been the first black lawyer to appear before the Rhode Island Supreme Court[363] and is the first black to be appointed to the State Returning Board.[364] He was also the first to be elected by the judges of the Superior Court of Providence, Rhode Island, as master in chancery.[365]

In 1912, Joseph Gray LeCount graduated from Howard University's law school and returned to Rhode Island, where he was admitted to the bar in 1914. Prior to LeCount's admission to the bar, he served a clerkship with William A. Heathman.[366] LeCount was followed to Rhode Island by James Matamora Stockett, Jr., a 1914 law graduate of Howard University. Soon thereafter, he opened a law practice and "figured in several locally famous court trials" in Providence.[367] He followed Heathman to the State Returning Board, where he was a Republican member, and held that position for ten years.[368]

No black women were admitted to the Rhode Island bar prior to 1945.

Summary

Connecticut is one of the few states in this study to admit black lawyers who had graduated from schools within the state. Yale University's law school graduated its first black student in 1880. Though many Yale graduates did not remain in Connecticut, instead returning to or seeking states with a larger black population, George Williamson Crawford, a 1903 law graduate of Yale University, did remain in Connecticut and became a successful and respected lawyer. A 1908 Yale University law graduate, Harry Griffy Tolliver, also remained in Connecticut, and was later elected as alderman in the city of New Haven. Other black lawyers, educated at law schools such as Howard University, went to Connecticut to practice law. W. Arvey Wood, who practiced in Hartford, may have been Connecticut's first black judicial officer. Wood was elected justice of the peace in 1926, three years after being admitted to the bar.

The first known black lawyer in Delaware, Louis Lorenzo Redding, was educated at Harvard University's law school. He had difficulty in gaining admission to the bar because he could find no preceptor under whom to study (a condition at the time required of all bar applicants in Delaware). It was Redding's father, a mailman active in state Republican politics, who persuaded Daniel O. Hastings, a U.S. Senator from the state, to act as his son's preceptor. Unlike his white counterparts, however, Redding could not study in the senator's office.

In the District of Columbia, Howard University School of Law produced most of the black lawyers (as it did for the nation as a whole) between 1869, the year Howard University opened its law department, and 1944. However, the Columbian University and the National University schools of law (both of which subsequently merged into what is now George Washington University) also produced a small number of black lawyers.

In 1869 George Boyer Vashon became the first black lawyer admitted to the bar of the District of Columbia. Vashon never practiced law in the District of Columbia, though he did practice in New York, where, in 1848, he became the state's first black lawyer.

In 1873, Charles N. Thomas tried the first criminal case by a black lawyer in the District of Columbia. Criminal law remained the predominant area of practice for black lawyers because white clients used white lawyers in civil cases, and many blacks, too, used white lawyers, hoping for favorable verdicts from white juries. Racism in the court system—that is, the exclusion of blacks from the jury and the overly zealous arrests of blacks by white police forces—prompted black lawyers to use stereotypical trial tactics in the representation of their clients. Such tactics, while often successful and brilliantly executed, did little to enhance the image of the black lawyer as a real player in the legal system.

Cognizant of the plight of black lawyers and of the need for them, the black press in the District of Columbia rebuilt the image of the black bar, which had often been seen as ineffectual in light of the lack of opportunity for blacks in the legal profession. Black lawyers not only fought to emancipate black people in the District of Columbia from the vestiges of slavery, but also to emancipate themselves professionally. They had to force the District of Columbia Bar Association to allow them to use the bar library that was housed in the Federal Court House. Faced with public embarrassment, since they were joint land-lords of the Federal Court House, the attorney general of the United States and the chief justice of the United States Supreme Court inter-vened to stop the bar from such race-based conduct.

Black lawyers in the District of Columbia gradually entered the judicial system, beginning with John A. Moss's appointment as justice of the peace in 1873. Years later Robert Herberton Terrell became the first municipal judge in the District of Columbia, and William Henry Hastie's appointment by President Roosevelt to the District Court of the Virgin Islands in 1937 made him the first federal judge in the nation's history.

As the nation's capital, the District of Columbia offered the oppor-tunity for black lawyers to work for the federal government, but many of these lawyers were denied appointments to legal jobs. Many worked in the post office by day and operated their law offices at dusk. There were exceptions, however. James Adlai Cobb was appointed special assistant to the attorney general of the United States in 1907, while in 1938 Louis Rothschild Mehlinger was one of the first black lawyers in the claims division of the Department of Justice to co-file a brief, on behalf of the Department of Justice, before the United States Supreme Court.

Black women share much of the rich legal history of the District of Columbia. Charlotte E. Ray's admission to the bar in 1872 set the stage for the subsequent admission of black women lawyers across the coun-try. She was the first woman to graduate from Howard University's law school or any law school in the world and to enter the general practice of law and specialize in corporation law.

Maryland's history of barring blacks from becoming lawyers prior to the end of the Civil War demonstrates how difficult it is to determine which individual can lay claim to being this state's first black lawyer. There is no doubt that Edward Garrison Draper was the first black person to receive a certificate from Maryland to practice law, but he was not allowed to practice in Maryland. Draper was examined in open court and found qualified in all respects to be admitted to the Maryland bar, had he been a white man. Instead, Draper received a certificate of competence from the state of Maryland in 1857, and only because he was leaving the state to pursue a legal career in Liberia. The exclusion of blacks from the Maryland bar continued after the Civil War when two black men, one admitted to the Federal Circuit Court of Maryland, the other to the Federal District Court of Maryland, were deemed not qualified to become lawyers in Maryland.

The establishment of black lawyers in Maryland is due to the relentless efforts of a black Baptist minister, Reverend Harvey Johnson, the pastor of Union Baptist Church in Baltimore. Reverend Johnson formed a group called the Brotherhood of Liberty to agitate for the admission of a black lawyer to the bar. Johnson and his supporters believed that if full emancipation of blacks was to be achieved in Maryland, it had to be at the hands of black lawyers. Johnson and the Brotherhood of Liberty won their fight to have a black lawyer admitted without condition in 1885, the year Everett J. Waring was examined and admitted to the court in Baltimore, Maryland.

Everett J. Waring lived up to almost every expectation of the black community, becoming, with Joseph S. Davis, the first black lawyers to argue a case before the United States Supreme Court. Davis and Waring were graduated from Howard University School of Law in 1884 and 1885, respectively.

The Maryland Law School (now the University of Maryland Law School) trained its first two black lawyers in the late 1880s, but due to the protests of white law students, subsequent black students were barred from admission by 1890. It would take Charles Hamilton Houston and Thurgood Marshall (the latter of whom was himself found ineligible to attend the Maryland Law School) to sue the state of Maryland and break the color bar. As a result of Houston and Marshall's victory in the Maryland Court of Appeals in 1935, Donald G. Murray and many other black students after him received their education at the law school.

Black lawyers in Maryland became influential in local and state politics. In 1890, they won terms on the Baltimore city council. William Ashbie Hawkins ran for the United States Senate in 1920 as an independent. By 1944, the black male lawyer was no longer an experiment in Maryland, though no black women had been admitted to the Maryland bar.

New Jersey's first black lawyer, George Jackson, was admitted to the bar in 1893 but left the state soon afterward. Although the number of black lawyers in the state of New Jersey remained small, Isaac Henry

Nutter, Robert S. Hartgrove, and Robert Queen broke new ground in civil rights. The importance of Nutter, Hartgrove, and Queen cannot be emphasized enough. Nutter won praise from the governor of New Jersey in 1918 for his civil rights work. Hartgrove won a significant case in the New Jersey courts which outlawed Jim Crow laws that prohibited black students from using swimming pools in public schools. And Queen won a landmark victory in the New Jersey courts which outlawed the separate but equal doctrine in public education in 1944, ten years before the United States Supreme Court decided *Brown v. Board of Education.*

In Pennsylvania, Jonathan Jasper Wright, the state's first black lawyer, was not admitted to the bar until 1865. Similarly, George Boyer Vashon had tried to gain admission as early as 1847 but was denied because of his race. Wright chose not to remain in Pennsylvania. He went to South Carolina, where he later served on the supreme court from 1870 to 1877, the first black man in the nation to do so.

The entry of black lawyers to the bar in Pennsylvania initially had little impact on the legal system, since the courts were controlled by whites. However, several outstanding black lawyers emerged to emancipate their people from shadows of slavery.

A core group of black lawyers, which included John Daniel Lewis, broke ground by representing the poor. Lewis, a Columbia University law graduate, is the first black lawyer known to have left money in his will to establish a bureau to protect and secure the civil rights of blacks.

Raymond Pace Alexander, a 1923 Harvard University law graduate, reformed the black law firm by hiring law clerks and delegating routine matters to his secretaries. This freed Alexander to work on more complicated matters, particularly civil rights cases. Alexander took on racism root and branch: He was fearless. Sensing his strength and determination, black people sought him out to represent them. Alexander's forceful legal advocacy for the civil rights of his people—while resented by the business establishment that saw a brilliant black lawyer on the loose—won verdicts from white juries.

The University of Pennsylvania, the University of Pittsburgh, and Temple University's law school all admitted blacks around the beginning of the twentieth century. The University of Pennsylvania graduated Aaron Albert Mossell, Jr., its first black student, in 1888. Mossell's daughter, Sadie Tanner Mossell Alexander, was also graduated from the University of Pennsylvania's law school in 1927. Sadie Alexander and Robert Burke Johnson were the first black students on the law review at the law school. Alexander was also the first black woman admitted to the Pennsylvania bar, and the first black woman to work in the solicitor's office in Philadelphia.

Robert Lee Vann, a graduate of the University of Pittsburgh, won fame as the founder and publisher of the *Pittsburgh Courier*. He was also successful in law. President Roosevelt appointed him special assistant attorney general of the United States after the presidential election of 1932. In law and politics, black lawyers succeeded, particularly after Harry W. Bass became the first black elected to the Pennsylvania legislature in 1896.

Few black lawyers practiced in Rhode Island, but John Henry Ballou was admitted to the bar in 1874, becoming Rhode Island's first black lawyer. Black lawyers from the University of Michigan and Boston University's law school migrated to Rhode Island and from black law schools such as Allen University. The outstanding advocacy of John B. Edwards, who (with William Henry Lewis) represented two black men in the famous Mohr murder trial, has previously been highlighted.

All the evidence demonstrates that the black lawyer in the Atlantic states turned the clock forward in both law and politics in order to emancipate the progeny of slavery.

NOTES

1. Letter to author from Nicholas J. Cimmins, chief clerk, Connecticut Superior Court, New Haven, Dec. 29, 1986.
2. Charles S. Brown, "The Genesis of the Negro Lawyer in New England," Part II, 22 *The Negro History Bulletin* 171, 175 (May 1959).
3. "Walter J. Scott of Virginia," *The New York Age*, Dec. 13, 1884, at 1, col. 2.
4. *Ibid.*
5. *New Haven Evening Register*, June 29, 1881.
6. "Walter J. Scott of Virginia," *New York Age*, Dec. 13, 1884, at 1, col. 1.
7. *Ibid.*
8. R. A. Warner, *New Haven Negroes: A Social History* 175–76 (1940); letter from George W. Crawford to Charles Sumner Brown, Sept. 16, 1958.
9. *Ibid.* (Crawford letter).
10. Vol. 1 *Who's Who of the Colored Race* 80 (F. L. Mather ed. 1915).
11. Ramsey, "George W. Crawford," *George W. Crawford Law Association Newsletter*, July 1979, at 1.
12. *Yale Law School Alumni Directory* 106 (1949).
13. Ramsey, "George W. Crawford," *George W. Crawford Law Association Newsletter*, July 1979, at 2.
14. Vol. 1 *Who's Who in Colored America* 203 (J. J. Boris ed. 1927).
15. *Id.* at 227. *Virginia's Contribution to Negro Leadership* 73 (W. Cooper ed. 1937) (mimeo).
16. "Call for Organizing a Negro Bar Association," *New York Age*, Feb. 21, 1925.
17. *Who's Who Among Negro Lawyers* 13 (S. T. M. Alexander ed. 1945).
18. Drew, "Former Track Star Goes Literary," *Baltimore Afro-American*, Dec. 20, 1930.
19. Only one other black lawyer is known to have been practicing in New

Haven, Connecticut, in 1932: Earley E. Caple. *National Bar Association Directory* 127 (1932). In 1940, there were three. *The Sixteenth Census: Population*, Vol. III, *The Labor Force*, Part 2, Table 13, at 458 (1943).

20. *Id.* at 462 (*Sixteenth Census*).

21. Hays, "Louis Redding's Fight for Dignity and Decency," 86 *Brown Alumni Monthly* 38, 40 (Feb. 1986).

22. *Id.* at 38.

23. "First Delaware Negro Lawyer in Making," *Wilmington Star*, July 1, 1928; "Negro Registers for Del. State Bar," *Every Evening*, July 2, 1928.

24. Hays, "Louis Redding's Fight for Dignity and Decency," 86 *Brown Alumni Monthly* 38, 40 (Feb. 1986).

25. "Louis L. Redding, Civil Rights Attorney," 15 *Harvard Law School Record* 2 (Nov. 13, 1952).

26. *Ibid.*; "Delaware City to Get First Race Lawyers," *Baltimore Afro-American*, March 23, 1929. Redding also applied to another lawyer, Robert H. Richards, who, along with Senator Hastings, agreed to sponsor him. Hays, "Louis Redding's Fight for Dignity and Decency," 86 *Brown Alumni Monthly* 38, 40 (Feb. 1986).

27. *Id.* at 41 (*Brown Alumni Monthly*).

28. *Id.* at 38.

29. Hanchett, "George Boyer Vashon, 1824–1878: Black Educator, Poet, Fighter for Equal Rights," 68 *The Western Pennsylvania Historical Magazine* 333, 340, n.27 (1985). Prior to his admission to the District of Columbia bar, Vashon had been admitted to the bars of New York in 1848 and Ohio in 1868.

30. Vashon may have been retained by the Freedman's Bureau in the District of Columbia in 1867. *Dictionary of American Negro Biography* 617 (R. Logan and M. Winston eds. 1982).

31. See *Autographs of Freedom* 44, 60 (J. Griffiths ed. 1854).

32. John Mercer Langston was admitted to the United States Supreme Court bar on January 17, 1867. M. R. Eppse, *The Negro, Too, in America* 457 (1943).

33. "Milton M. Holland, Esq.," *The Indianapolis Freeman*, Dec. 7, 1889, at 2, col. 1. Holland received his law degree from Howard University's law school in 1872. The Medal of Honor was awarded to Sergeant Major Holland on April 6, 1865. *Black Americans in Defense of Our Nation* 56 (Department of Defense, 1982).

34. *Arkansas Daily Gazette*, July 17, 1870.

35. *New National Era and Citizen*, July 20, 1871, at 4.

36. "Charles N. Thomas, Esq.," *New National Era and Citizen*, Sept. 25, 1873. Thomas has erroneously been referred to as the first black lawyer in Washington, D.C.; see *The Twentieth Century Woman League Directory* 60 (A. F. Hilyer compiler, Jan. 1901).

37. *Ibid.* (*New National Era and Citizen*).

38. *Ibid.* Thomas was known also as an effective domestic relations lawyer. *New National Era and Citizen*, Feb. 15, 1872.

39. "John A. Moss, Landmark of Court, Dies, Oldest D.C. Colored Attorney, Called 'Common-Law John' Dead at 77," *The Evening Star*, May 5, 1921. Charles N. Thomas almost shared the distinction of being the first black lawyer appointed justice of the peace with his friend John A. Moss. Thomas was being considered for one of the justice of peace posts by President Rutherford B. Hayes, but his nomination was overshadowed by the *Washington Post*'s charges

of a conflict of interest. The charges may have been based on the fact that Thomas also received federal pay as one of the fire commissioners of the District of Columbia, a position to which he was appointed by Alexander R. Shepherd, the governor of the District of Columbia, in 1873. *Washington Star*, June 17, 1878; *Daily National Republican*, March 26, 1873.

40. *Ibid*. ("Landmark of Court, Dies, Oldest D.C. Colored Lawyer").

41. *Ibid*.

42. W. W. Brown, *The Rising Sun; Or, The Antecedents and Advancement of the Colored Race* 515–16 (1874); "J. P. Sampson," *New York Freeman*, June 19, 1986; *New National Era and Citizen*, Nov. 27, 1873.

43. See *Boyd's Directory of the District of Columbia* 446 (1875) and at 466 (1876). Sampson later became a minister. He also served on the city council in Bordentown, New Jersey. "J. P. Sampson," *New York Freeman*, June 19, 1886.

44. *New National Era and Citizen*, Oct. 8, 1874.

45. "Attorney at Law and Examiner in Chancery," *Washington Bee*, June 22, 1918.

46. *Ibid*.

47. *New National Era and Citizen*, Feb. 16, 1871. The *New National Era and Citizen* was a weekly newspaper designed to "cheer and strengthen [the recently emancipated slaves]." *Dictionary of American Negro Biography* 184 (R. Logan and M. Winston eds. 1982).

48. Letter from Elwood H. Hettrick, dean, Boston University School of Law, to Charles S. Brown, May 21, 1958.

49. "Well-Known Negro Lawyer Is Dead," *Washington Post*, Sept. 21, 1929.

50. "The Colored Lawyer Question," *The New York Freeman*, March 14, 1885, at 2, col. 4.

51. Romaine F. Scott, "The Negro in American History, 1887–1900, as Portrayed in the *Washington Evening Star*" 63 (M.A. Thesis, Howard University, 1948).

52. *Ibid*.

53. *Ibid*.

54. *Ibid*.

55. Hewlett and Holland teamed up in 1889 to defend Robert Logan against charges of murdering his wife. *Indianapolis Freeman*, March 9, 1889.

56. "Judge E. M. Hewlett Is Dead at Home," *Washington Evening Star*, Sept. 21, 1919. Hewlett has at times been erroneously credited as the first black to hold a judicial office in the District of Columbia. See Miller, "D.C.'s First Black Judge," *Washington Post*, April 29, 1976, at A14, col. 3; Miller, "Whither the Black Jurist, a Place in American Law?" 24 *The Hampton Rev.* 28, 36 (Fall 1988).

57. "Well-Known Negro Lawyer Is Dead," *Washington Post*, Sept. 21, 1929.

58. "Houston Tribune Warms Heart of 60-Year Vet," *The Pittsburgh Courier*, Dec. 27, 1952.

59. Meyer and Whitaker, "D.C. Firm a 'School' for Black Jurist," *Washington Post*, April 12, 1976, at A1, col. 5.

60. G. R. McNeil, *Groundwork: Charles Hamilton Houston and the Struggle for Civil Rights* 47, 56, 59, 64 (1983).

61. *The Freeman*, June 5, 1914. Belva A. Lockwood, a white woman, was instrumental in having other black lawyers admitted to American courts, including the United States Supreme Court. In 1873 Lockwood became the second woman admitted to practice in the District of Columbia, and in 1879 the

first woman admitted to practice before the United States Supreme Court. K. B. Morello, *The Invisible Bar* 31–34 (1986).

62. *William H. Heard v. The Georgia Railroad Co.*, 1 I.C.C. 428, 435 (1888). This case was argued before the ICC on December 15, 1887. John Wesley Cromwell and William C. Martin were the first black lawyers *to appear* as lawyers before the ICC. William H. Councill, a black lawyer from Alabama, was the first black American ever *to file a complaint* against a carrier for racial discrimination. Councill, however, was not represented by black lawyers. See *William H. Councill v. The Western and Atlantic Railroad Company*, 1 I.C.C. 399 (1887). Councill's case was argued before the ICC on July 23, 1887. See also, Vol. 1 *Who's Who of the Colored Race* 81 (F. L. Mather ed. 1915): Cromwell's biographical sketch does not mention William C. Martin as his co-counsel in the *Heard* case, a possible oversight. Cromwell went on to author a book entitled *The Negro in American History* (1914). Martin was later described as a "Chesterfieldian member of the [D.C.] bar." Highly respected, Martin was also characterized as "a hard student, logical, concise and pointed." See "The Colored Bar Lawyers," *Washington Bee*, March 6, 1915.

63. "W. L. Houston Appears Before the I.C.C.," *Washington Bee*, Oct. 9, 1920. This article erroneously reports that Houston was "the only colored attorney who has ever appeared and argued a case before the [ICC]." John Wesley Cromwell and William C. Martin had preceded Houston as counsel before ICC by thirty-three years. Years later, William L. Houston would be joined by his son, Charles H. Houston, and William Henry Hastie to fight the Jim Crow practices of railroads in the South. Henderson, "FEPC and the Southern Railway Case: An Investigation into the Discriminatory Practices of Railroads During World War II," 56 *J. of Negro History* 173, 179 (April 1976).

64. "Houston to Retire from Att'y General Office," *Chicago Defender*, Aug. 29, 1942, at 3, col. 1. In all, Houston served in government in various jobs for twenty-four years.

65. H. Elsie Austin, "Above All Barriers—The Story of Louis G. Gregory" 3 (1955) (Baha'i pamphlet).

66. Fountain Peyton was graduated from Howard University's law school in 1890. Harry L. Tignor was graduated from Howard University's law school in 1909.

67. "Colored Lawyers," *The Washington Bee*, March 27, 1915; "The Colored Lawyers," *The Journal and Guide*, Oct. 24, 1914.

68. "The Colored Lawyers," *The Journal and Guide*, Oct. 24, 1914.

69. "Colored Lawyers," *The Washington Bee*, March 27, 1915.

70. *Ibid.*

71. Vol. 1 *Who's Who of the Colored Race* 58 (F. L. Mather ed. 1915).

72. "Attorney at Law and Examiner in Chancery," *Washington Bee*, June 22, 1918.

73. Vol. 1 *Who's Who in Colored America* 115 (J. J. Boris ed. 1927). Robert I. Miller, a 1911 graduate from the National University School of Law (George Washington University School of Law), was by 1920 an effective criminal lawyer in the District of Columbia. A staunch Republican, Miller in 1916 "won the honor of delegate to the Republican National Convention." "Robert I. Miller," *Washington Bee*, June 22, 1918. By 1920, black lawyers in the District of Columbia were growing in numbers and influence. Among these lawyers were John H. Wilson, a 1907 graduate of Howard University law school, described

as "a fine examiner and forceful pleader"; Thomas L. Jones, "one of the brightest lawyers at the bar . . . respected by both white and colored . . . a good criminal lawyer"; William C. Martin, "a good civil lawyer and pension attorney . . . a good writer"; Laudros Melendez King, Clarence W. Tignor (a 1908 graduate of Howard University's law school), and Harry Tignor, all described as "good civil lawyers"; Joseph H. Stewart, described as extremely capable and "one who defends [his cases] without the assistance of others"; E. B. Hubert, a 1909 graduate of Howard University's law school and "a successful member of the bar"; Peter W. Finley, "shrewd [and] good in criminal cases"; Royal A. Hughes, an 1897 graduate of Howard University's law school—"not only a good criminal lawyer, but a good civil lawyer, also"; Augustus W. Gray—"one of the best civil pleaders"; Emanuel D. M. Hewlett was "manly and does not bite his tongue"; William L. Houston, who had "been handling some very large cases"; James M. Ricks, who knew "how to get a fee"; and Benjamin Gaskins, a 1905 graduate of Howard University Law School, described as "a most brilliant lawyer." See "The Colored Bar," *Washington Bee*, Nov. 20, 1920. Other black newspapers, like the *Washington Eagle*, bent over backward to extol the virtues and skills of the black lawyer. See "Attorney John Wilson Wins Again—Local Boy Now Great Criminal Lawyer," *Washington Eagle*, Jan. 25, 1929.

74. Meyer, " 'The Only Colored Man . . .' at Justice," *Washington Post*, April 11, 1976, at A18, col. 1.

75. Robertson, "Honorable William B. Bryant's Reflections on the Legal Profession over the Years," *The Barrister* (Howard Law School student newspaper), Feb. 1984, at 3, col. 1.

76. "Legal Advance Clinic for Washington?" *Norfolk Journal and Guide*, Dec. 16, 1939.

77. "Seek to Move White Barristers," *Norfolk Journal and Guide*, Feb. 11, 1939.

78. "Disbarment Fails Against Dobbins," *Norfolk Journal and Guide*, June 10, 1943. After this victory, black lawyers were not immediately appointed to the grievance committee. However, some white lawyers, believing the exclusionary policy to be unfair, joined forces with the black lawyers to overturn the *de facto* race-based policy. One such lawyer was James J. Laughlin, who filed a petition in court to force "the appointment of a Negro lawyer to the committee." "Capital Court Bars Negro Lawyers," *Savannah Tribune*, Nov. 16, 1944.

79. For example, James A. Cobb had served for some years as municipal judge in the District of Columbia, Perry W. Howard was a national committeeman of the Republican Party, and George E. C. Hayes was the general counsel of Howard University. All three men were highly respected in the community. See "Three of Nation's Best Legal Minds Form Partnership in D.C.," *Norfolk Journal and Guide*, March 7, 1936. Perry W. Howard's central importance to the birth of this firm cannot be overemphasized. His Republican political connections greatly expanded the legal influence of the firm, particularly in 1936, when he urged blacks not to abandon the Republican Party. "Republican Party Should 'Stand Pat' for 1940, Declares Perry Howard—'It Needs No Revamping,' " *Pittsburgh Courier*, Jan. 16, 1937, at 2, col. 3.

80. Tureaud, "Experiences and Observations of Negro Lawyers," circa 1940, A. P. Tureaud Collection, Amistad Research Center, New Orleans, Louisiana. Tureaud's account is based on responses to a survey of black lawyers that he conducted in the late 1930s. Tureaud lived and practiced law in New Orleans.

81. *Ibid.*

82. "Milton M. Holland, Esq.," *The Indianapolis Freeman*, Dec. 7, 1889, at 2, col. 1.

83. Vol. 1 *Who's Who in Colored America* 2 (J. J. Boris ed. 1927).

84. *Id.* at 91; Vol. 6 *The Booker T. Washington Papers, 1901–2*, at 345 (L. R. Harlan, R. W. Smock, and B. S. Kraft eds. 1977).

85. "Milton M. Holland, Esq.," *The Indianapolis Freeman*, Dec. 7, 1889, at 2, col. 1.

86. J. H. Paynter, *Horse and Buggy Days with Uncle Sam* 155, 166 (1943). Wilson and Brown were graduates of Howard University's law school in 1907 and 1913, respectively: Wilson had entered the Internal Revenue Service as a clerk and Brown as a messenger.

87. *Id.* at 166.

88. *Who's Who of the Colored Race* 122 (F. L. Mather ed. 1915). See also the biography of Louis G. Gregory by G. Morrison, *To Move the World* 18 (1982). Gregory later became a spiritual leader to the Baha'is of the United States.

89. Smith, "Black Lawyers in the Federal Government: 1844–1940," 32 *Fed. Bar News-Journal* 193, 195 (April/May 1985).

90. Letter to author from Ruth Weyand, March 23, 1986; "Arthur Christopher, 54, New D.C. Judge, Dies," *The Sunday Washington Star*, Dec. 10, 1967.

91. "Brilliant Career of Young OPA Lawyer Halted by War," *Chicago Defender*, Oct. 9, 1943.

92. Hart may have received this appointment through the influence of Senator William M. Evarts of New York, for whom Hart had worked as a private secretary during his law school days. Hart, a very able law student at Howard University, received his LL.M. degree there in 1891. *Dictionary of American Negro Biography* 294 (R. Logan and M. Winston eds. 1982).

93. "Cobb Is Tenth Colored Judge to Sit on Bench," *Baltimore Afro-American*, July 31, 1926. Cobb's father, who was white, was a lawyer in Louisiana. Vol. 7 *The Booker T. Washington Papers, 1903–4*, at 379 (L. R. Harlan and R. W. Smock eds. 1977). Cobb gained a reputation for his effective prosecution of cases arising out of the new congressionally enacted food and drug law. "Judge James A. Cobb, Howard Ex-Dean, Dies," *Washington Star*, Oct. 15, 1958; "Credit to Race, Bar and Community," *Washington Bee*, June 22, 1918. During Cobb's nine-year stay at the Department of Justice, he worked for four attorney generals: Charles J. Bonaparte, George W. Wickersham, James C. McReynolds, and Thomas W. Gregory. He also worked under three United States attorneys for the District of Columbia: Daniel W. Baker, Clarence R. Wilson, and John E. Laskey. Letter from James A. Cobb to Newton D. Baker, Jan. 9, 1918. For a history of the Department of Justice during the years of Cobb's service, see H. Cummings and C. McFarland, *Federal Justice* 336–51 (1937).

94. See e.g., *Cohen v. United States*, 38 App. D.C. 123 (1912) (with Clarence R. Wilson), on the authority of a U.S. attorney to bring actions on behalf of the United States; *United States v. Von Jenny*, 39 App. D.C. 377 (1912) (with Clarence R. Wilson), on forfeiture of recognizance; *Hartranft v. Mullowny*, 43 App. D.C. 44 (1915) (with Clarence R. Wilson), on the selling of adulterated food, *appeal dismissed* 247 U.S. 296 (1917); *United States v. Walter*, 43 App. D.C. 468 (1915) (with John E. Laskey), on recognizance in a criminal case; *Goode v. United States*, 44 App. D.C. 162 (1915) (with John E. Laskey and Charles W. Arth), on misbranding of food under the Pure Food Law.

95. A. Buni, *Robert L. Vann of Pittsburgh Courier* 181 (1974); *Dictionary of American Negro Biography* 330, 331 (R. Logan and M. Winston eds. 1982).

96. Meyer, "'The Only Colored Man . . .' at Justice," *Washington Post*, April 11, 1976, at A18, Col. 1.

97. Letter to author from Ruth Weyand, March 23, 1986.

98. See, *Southern Pacific Company v. United States*, 87 Court of Claims Rpts. 442, cert. granted, 306 U.S. 625 (1939), *aff'd.*, 307 U.S. 393 (1939). Mehlinger's victory in this case was widely reported by the black press. See "Race Attorney for Government Upheld by Court," *Norfolk Journal and Guide*, June 10, 1939.

99. "D.C. Lawyer Is Named for U.S. Attorneyship," *St. Louis Argus*, May 29, 1925.

100. "Assistant DA," *Baltimore Afro-American*, Oct. 30, 1943.

101. The firm of Lynch and Terrell existed for two years. The firm came to an end in 1898, when President William McKinley appointed Lynch "a Major and Paymaster of Volunteers to serve as such during the Spanish-American War." *Reminiscences of an Active Life: The Autobiography of John Roy Lynch* 369 (J. H. Franklin ed. 1970). After Lynch completed this military service, he went to Chicago, Illinois; he was admitted to the bar there in 1915 and subsequently developed a real estate business. *Id.* at 502.

John Roy Lynch was admitted to the Mississippi bar in 1896, having served as that state's first black United States congressman from 1873 to 1882. President Benjamin Harrison appointed Lynch to a position in the Fourth Auditors Division of the United States Treasury in 1889, the same year Robert Herberton Terrell received an appointment to the division. See Vol. 1 *Who's Who of the Colored Race* 260 (F. L. Mather ed. 1915); "Milton M. Holland, Esq.," *The Indianapolis Freeman*, Dec. 7, 1889, at 2, col. 1; *Dictionary of American Negro Biography* 408 (R. Logan and M. Winston eds. 1982).

102. The influence of Booker T. Washington in the appointment of Terrell as justice of the peace is noteworthy. Washington worked behind the scenes to have Terrell appointed to a judicial post, even though other capable black lawyers were vying for the job. Washington urged Philander Chase Knox, the attorney general, and other officials in the Roosevelt administration not to make his suggestions for the judicial post known, as "I have . . . three letters from various colored lawyers [in Washington, D.C.] insisting that I endorse them." At least five black lawyers were known to be interested in being appointed justice of the peace: Reuben L. Smith, Joseph H. Stewart, Fountain Peyton, L. O. Posey, and Emanuel Hewlett, the incumbent. As it turned out, President Roosevelt reappointed Hewlett and appointed Terrell to the judicial post, an action that brought much praise from blacks. Vol. 6 *The Booker T. Washington Papers, 1901–2*, at 332 (L. R. Harlan, R. W. Smock, and B. S. Kraft eds. 1977). The gains signified by these appointments, however, were short-lived. Within a year Congress reduced the number of justice of the peace positions in the District of Columbia, and Hewlett lost his post. M. Sammy Miller, "Robert Herberton Terrell 1857–1925: Black Lawyer and Community Leader" 114 (Ph.D. diss., Catholic University, 1977), citing letter from Booker T. Washington to Whitefield McKinlay, Oct. 31, 1901, and *id.* at 116. See also, Vol. 6 *The Booker T. Washington Papers, 1901–2*, at 266–67 (L. R. Harlan, R. W. Smock, and B. S. Kraft eds. 1977). In October 1901, Booker T. Washington personally left the names of six "colored men with the Attorney General for appointment to the local court in the District of Columbia." Heading the list were Jesse Lawson, Robert H. Terrell, and Reuben S. Smith. The names at the bottom of the list included James F. Bundy, Joseph H. Stewart, and Fountain Peyton; *Dictionary of American Negro Biography* 585, 586 (R. Logan and M.

Winston eds. 1982). Some black lawyers in the District of Columbia were opponents of Washington and those who espoused Washington's conciliatory views on the race question. Washington's two most vocal critics were Lafayette M. Hershaw and William Calvin Chase, both black lawyers. Chase was also the publisher of the *Washington Bee*. He attended Howard University's law school for a while and was a member of the Virginia and District of Columbia bars. *Id.* at 99; see also, C. R. Gibbs, "Brief Life, Bitter End for Parade," *Washington Post*, April 11, 1985, at D.C. 1, col. 1, (mentions Chase). Chase had wanted the judicial post and had sought Booker T. Washington's support. When Chase discovered that Washington had supported Robert H. Terrell for the post, he "turned against Washington for five years." Vol. 4 *The Booker T. Washington Papers, 1895–98*, at 247 (L. R. Harlan, S. B. Kaufman, B. S. Kraft, and R. W. Smock eds. 1975).

103. "Colored Jurist Visits Here," *Philadelphia Bulletin*, Nov. 3, 1914.

104. Previously, this court had been called the Supreme Court of the District of Columbia. *The Court-House of the District of Columbia* 82 (second edition, 1939). Despite the criticism of William Calvin Chase, Lafayette M. Hershaw, and other noted black citizens in the District of Columbia in the early 1900s, Booker T. Washington managed to work through other black lawyers, including James Adlai Cobb. In 1909, Cobb and Washington visited the White House to discuss with President William H. Taft the dearth of blacks being appointed to federal jobs, particularly those who had opposed his election because of the Republicans' (President Theodore Roosevelt's) handling of the "Negro riot" in Brownsville, Texas, in 1906. See J. H. Franklin, *From Slavery to Freedom* 441–42 (1967). Reportedly, no major appointment of a black lawyer was made by Taft, except for the reappointment of Judge Robert H. Terrell. L. R. Harlan, *Booker T. Washington: The Wizard of Tuskegee* 53, 342–43 (1983).

105. "Armond Scott Gives Credit to President Taft for Recognition Given the Colored Lawyers," *Washington Bee News* (n.d.), (from Armond W. Scott's scrapbook, courtesy Ms. Armond W. Scott in 1975). The Taft administration had appointed other black lawyers to federal posts: J. C. Napier of Tennessee was appointed registrar of the treasury; and Henry Lincoln Johnson, Sr., of Georgia, was named recorder of deeds for the District of Columbia. President Taft also retained James A. Cobb as special assistant to the United States district attorney in Chicago. In 1911, President Taft named William Henry Lewis of Massachusetts assistant attorney general of the United States, the highest appointment to a federal post of any black citizen in the history of the nation. *Ibid*; and see Robinson, "Robert Morris, John S. Rock, William H. Lewis, and Edgar P. Benjamin," *Occasional Paper No. 4*, Afro-American Studies Program, Boston University, 1975, at 57, 71–72.

106. Osborn, "Woodrow Wilson Appoints a Negro Judge," 24 *J. of Southern History* 481, 484 (Nov. 1958).

107. Miller, "Woodrow Wilson and the Black Judge," 84 *Crisis* 81, 83 (Feb. 1977). Miller quotes the *Washington Evening Post*: "Can a Black judge know the law? Are proud white men who violate the city ordinances or who cheat and steal to be compelled to hear a Negro judge define their misdemeanors and pass sentence upon them?"

108. *Id.* at 83: The drama surrounding Judge Terrell's nomination was so intense that the key senators blocked all other pending nominations until the Terrell matter was favorably resolved.

109. Judge Terrell's decisions on the court, even those against prominent

white citizens, were frequently upheld on appeal. "Upholds Judge Terrell in Denying Mileage," *Afro-American*, April 26, 1918; *The Negro Year Book, 1918–1919*, at 54 (M. Work ed. 1919) Judge Terrell dies in office in 1925. By that time his annual salary as a judge was $5,400.

110. "Cobb Is Tenth Colored Judge to Sit on Bench," *Baltimore Afro-American*, July 31, 1926.

111. Miller, "The Advocacy of the Negro Lawyer," *Norfolk Journal and Guide*, March 20, 1926.

112. Judge Terrell had hired black law clerks during his terms on the municipal court.

113. Frank W. Adams served as Judge Cobb's law clerk from 1926 to 1929. Thereafter, he was hired as a prosecutor in Police Court, where he served from 1929 to 1933. Thomas, "Biographical Bits About Terrell Teachers," Vol. 1, No. 8, The Barrister (Robert H. Terrell Law School magazine) 9, 12–13 (May 2, 1941).

114. "Judge Cobb Once Made Senator Pay $186 Debt," *Washington Afro-American*, Oct. 18, 1958.

115. "Judge James A. Cobb, Howard Ex-Dean Dies," *Washington Star*, Oct. 15, 1958. This article notes that Judge Cobb won widespread approval from Washington lawyers and the District of Columbia Bar Association on his handling of cases and his treatment of lawyers and their clients. In 1930, one hundred lawyers signed a petition urging his reappointment to another term on the bench.

116. "Judge Scott Metes Justice with Candor," *The Washington Post and Times Herald*, Dec. 9, 1957, at A13; "Three-Time D.C. Municipal Court Judge," *Pittsburgh Courier*, Jan. 26, 1946, at 1, col. 3; Thomas, "Biographical Bits About Terrell Teachers," Vol. 1, No. 8, *The Barrister* (Robert H. Terrell Law School magazine) 9, 10 (May 2, 1941). Armond Scott, like other black lawyers, often represented parties in intra-church disputes in the black community. See *Taylor v. Jackson*, 50 App. D.C. 381, 273 F. 345 (D.C. Cir. 1921) (with Royal A. Hughes and Thomas L. Jones, both black lawyers).

117. G. Ware, *William Hastie: Grace Under Pressure* 85–86 (1984); D. J. Bailey, "Black and Hispanic Federal Judges: 1900 to Present," *Issue Brief*, Congressional Research Service No, MB81239, at 2.

118. *Id.* at 86 (*Grace Under Pressure*).

119. Congressman Arthur Wergs Mitchell of Chicago, Illinois, himself a lawyer, played a key role in assuring that a black lawyer was appointed to the judgeship of the Virgin Islands. William Henry Hastie was not the only name under consideration for the judicial vacancy. The governor of the Virgin Islands recommended that Charles Hamilton Houston of Howard University School of Law be appointed. Homer S. Cummings, the attorney general, said that he would "make an investigation of other possible colored candidates." In all instances, Congressman Mitchell was consulted by President Franklin D. Roosevelt, Attorney General Cummings, and Acting Attorney General Stanley Reed. Letter from Governor Paul Pearson to Secretary Harold L. Ickes, March 22, 1935; letter from Governor Paul Pearson to Congressman Arthur W. Mitchell, Aug. 26, 1935; letter from President Franklin D. Roosevelt to Congressman Arthur Mitchell, Aug. 28, 1935; letter from Mitchell to the President, Sept. 4, 1935. The National Bar Association also played a key role in Hastie's Senate confirmation, according to George W. Lawrence, the president of NBA. Attorney General Cummings wired Lawrence that he would consider

any lawyer recommended by the NBA to the judicial post in the Virgin Islands. According to Lawrence, "upon learning that Mr. Hastie had been nominated . . . and that efforts were being made to block the confirmation by the Senate, every association member was requested to urge his Senator to vote for the confirmation. The result was Judge Hastie is now in the Virgin Islands." "Tells How Lawyers Helped Secure Hastie Appointment," *Baltimore Afro-American*, Aug. 14, 1937.

120. G. Ware, *William Hastie: Grace Under Pressure* 86 (1984).

121. Smith, "In the Shadow of Plessy: A Portrait of McCants Stewart, Afro-American Legal Pioneer," 73 *Minn. L. Rev.* 495, 500 (1988). Hilyer was the first black to be graduated from the University of Minnesota in 1882. He attended Howard University's law school, where he received his LL.B. in 1884 and his LL.M in 1885. *Twentieth-Century Negro Literature* 373 (D. W. Culp ed. 1902); Vol. 1 *Who's Who of the Colored Race* 139 (F. L. Mather ed. 1915).

122. John H. Butler was a law graduate of Howard University in 1873. See also, *New National Era and Citizen*, June 4, 1874.

123. Vol. 1 *Who's Who in Colored America* 86 (J. J. Boris ed. 1927). Mr. Harris was graduated from Howard University's law school in 1916.

124. *Id.* at 82.

125. "Graduates Who Served as Member of the Board of Education," (undated notes of Ollie May Cooper, in author's files).

126. Garland Mackey, "Benjamin L. Gaskins to Take Oath as Member of Education Board" (no date, source unknown, new article on file with author).

127. Daniel, "Is W. Point for All Americans?" *The McDowell Times* (Keystone, West VA), July 30, 1915. Mr. Daniel was graduated from Howard University's law school in 1909.

128. Daniel, "Mob Violence in the South," *The McDowell Times* (Keystone, West VA), Aug. 27, 1915.

129. *Ibid*; Daniel, "Civilization in Georgia," *The McDowell Times* (Keystone, West VA), Aug. 6, 1915. Daniel also urged the Congress to take action to protect blacks from mob rule.

130. Daniel, "Strayed from Straight Road," *The McDowell Times* (Keystone, West VA), June 25, 1915; Daniel, "Mr. Oswald G. Villard," *The McDowell Times* (Keystone, West VA), Sept. 17, 1915. In these articles Daniel criticized efforts by whites to control the people of color of the world, and cautioned against granting citizenship too soon to immigrants without evidence of loyalty.

131. Among the black lawyers at the conference were James Madison Nabrit, Jr., Charles Hamilton Houston, Helen Elsie Austin, Matthew Bullock, Perry W. Howard, Armond W. Scott, Robert Vann, Louis R. Mehlinger, and Belford V. Lawson.

132. *Proceedings of the Second National Conference on the Problems of the Negro and Negro Youth*, Jan. 12–14, 1939, at 102–3.

133. *Id.* at 107. See also, N. L. Grant, *TVA and Black Americans* 119–20 (1990). Houston had personally visited the Tennessee Valley Authority sites in 1934 in response to a host of racial discrimination claims.

134. See McGuire, "Desegregation of the Armed Forces: Black Leadership, Protest, and World War II," 68 *J. Negro History* 147, 152 (1983); McGuire, "Judge Hastie, World War II, and Army Racism," 62 *J. Negro History* 351 (1977).

135. Letter from James R. Angell, educational counselor, NBC, to William H. Hastie, June 8, 1940. Hastie consented to Angell's request on June 18, 1940.

136. Letter from Jean Blackwell Hutson, curator, Schomburg Center for

Research in Black Culture, New York Public Library, to Charles S. Brown, July 16, 1958. Hutson's letter quotes from Phoeba A. Hannaford's *Daughters of America* 669 (1882). One author writes that Charlotte E. Ray's admission to the D.C. bar "was secured by a clever ruse, her name being sent in with those of her classmates, as C. E. Ray. . . . She was thus admitted although there was some commotion when it was discovered that one of the applicants was a woman." Robinson, "Women Lawyers in the United States," 2 *The Green Bag* 10, 28 (1890). Charlotte E. Ray and Alta M. Hulett of Illinois appear to hold the joint distinction in 1872 of being the first woman to practice law in the United States. K. B. Morello, *The Invisible Bar* 21 (1986).

137. *New National Era and Citizen*, Aug. 13, 1874. Ray advertised as an attorney-at-law and gave her address as "L Box 81, Washington, D.C."

138. M. A. Majors, *Noted Negro Women* 183–84 (1893).

139. *Ibid.* See also, K. B. Morello, *The Invisible Bar* 146 (1986), referring to Charlotte B. [*sic*] Ray.

140. See *In re Miss Lavinia Goodell*, 39 Wis. 232, 239 (1875).

141. Vol. 3 *Notable American Women, 1607–1950*, at 121 (D. Thomas and E. T. James eds. 1971), quoting the *Chicago Legal News*, Oct. 23, 1897.

142. *Ibid*; R. L. Watts, "Brief Biographical Sketch of Charlotte E. Ray," (mimeograph) at 1, Feb. 22, 1983 (Moorland-Spingarn Research Center, Howard University). Ray, said to have been born in 1850, must have died before age forty-seven, according to other accounts. Hence, she was probably about twenty-four years old when she received her law degree from Howard University in 1872. See K. B. Morello, *The Invisible Bar* 145 (1986) and "Colored Female Lawyer," *The Cincinnati Enquirer*, Sept. 19, 1897, at 1, col. 4, regarding Ray's death. But see also, Larry Martin, "Charlotte E. Ray," in *Notable Black American Women* 922–24 (Jessie C. Smith ed. 1991), which says that Ray died on Jan. 4, 1911.

143. For example, Marie A. D. Madre-Marshall, an 1897 graduate of Howard University's law school, never practiced. She opted to teach in the public school system of the District of Columbia. Letter from Ollie May Cooper to Charles S. Brown, April 6, 1962. See also, "Teacher Many Years at College," *Washington Post*, April 3, 1976, referring to Etta Lisemby-DeFrantz, who was graduated from Howard University's law school in 1924. In 1935 she received a master's degree in health from Columbia University.

144. "Oldest Law Graduate," Vol. 1, No. 2, *The Jurist* 5 (Howard University's law alumni magazine) (June 1987).

145. "Ms. O. M. Cooper Admitted to District Bar," *Washington Tribune*, Aug. 15, 1926. At the time Cooper was admitted, she was employed at Howard University School of Law as an administrative clerk.

146. "Nigerin Ollie M. Cooper Wurde in Washington zum Rechtsanwalt gewahlt," *Der Feuerreiter*, Dec. 4, 1926, at 1.

147. *Washington Tribune*, Nov. 8, 1929. The law firm operated during the afternoon and evening hours, as both women held full-time jobs. Cooper was employed at Howard University School of Law in an administrative capacity and Letcher was employed as an examiner in the U.S. Treasury Department.

148. "Mrs. Ackiss to Practice Before Court of Appeals," *Washington Tribune*, May 6, 1932; "Court of Appeals Admits Mrs. Ackiss," *Washington Afro-American*, May 6, 1932. Ackiss was graduated from Howard University's law school in 1931. "Mother of Two Passes D.C. Bar Test," *Baltimore Afro-American*, Feb. 27, 1932. Ackiss, an active member of the New Negro Alliance, and others were

enjoined by the local courts in the District of Columbia for picketing a grocery chain for refusing to hire or promote blacks. In 1934, Ackiss assisted in preparing the response to the injunction filed by the grocery chain against the demonstrators, a case that ultimately reached the United States Supreme Court. *New Negro Alliance v. Sanitary Grocery Co.*, 303 U.S. 552 (1938). F. L. Styles, *Negroes and the Law* 41 (1937). Atkiss did not participate in the appellate aspect of this case. Three black lawyers handled the case before the United States Supreme Court: Belford V. Lawson, Thurman L. Dodson, and Theodore M. Berry.

149. T. D. Ackiss, "The Negro and the Supreme Court to 1900" (M.A. thesis, Howard University, June 1936).

150. "Women at the American Bar," *New York Age*, Aug. 26, 1939. Austin was quick to write about the civil rights victories of black lawyers. H. Elsie Austin, "A Backward Glance at Court Actions," 1 *AfraAmerican Woman's Journal* 6 (Spring 1940).

151. Interview with Helen Elsie Austin, Silver Spring, MD, May 14, 1985.

152. "Law Associate," *Washington Tribune*, Oct. 26, 1940.

153. Bogen, "The Transformation of the Fourteenth Amendment: Reflections from the Admission of Maryland's First Black Lawyers," 44 *Maryland L. Rev.* 939, 982 (1985); See G. F. Bragg, Jr., *Men of Maryland* 21 (1925), and commemorative program, *100th Anniversary of the Admission of Everett J. Waring, the First Black Lawyer to be Admitted to the Bar of Maryland* 1–3, 6–8 (May 5, 1985). See also, Simms, "Integration of the Bar and Bench and Civil Rights Litigation (the Bicentennial of the United States District Court for the District of Maryland, 1790–1990)," 50 *Maryland L. Rev.* 40, 57 (1991).

154. This court order was signed by Z. Collins Lee, judge, Superior Court of Baltimore, Maryland, on October 29, 1857, a year after the United States Supreme Court, under the pen of Chief Justice Roger Brooke Taney, held that Americans of African descent, whether slave or free, were not considered as citizens of the United States. *Dred Scott v. Sandford*, 60 U.S. (19 How.) 393 (1856).

155. M. L. Callcott, *The Negro in Maryland Politics, 1870–1912*, at 62 (1969).

156. Slavery was abolished in 1865, according to the U.S. Constitution's Thirteenth Amendment; the Fourteenth Amendment to the U.S. Constitution became law in 1868.

157. A. B. Koger, *The Negro Lawyer in Maryland* 1, 4 (1948) (pamphlet).

158. *In re Charles Taylor*, 48 Md. 28 (1877). The Maryland Court relied upon a United States Supreme Court decision denying Myra Bradwell, a white woman, the right to be admitted to the Illinois bar solely on account of her sex. *Bradwell v. State*, 83 U.S. (16 Wall) 130, 139 (1872), holding that the states did not transfer their rights to regulate the practice of law to the federal government.

159. A. B. Koger, *The Negro Lawyer in Maryland*, 1, 5 (1948).

160. Elaine K. Freeman, "Harvey Johnson and Everett Waring—A Study of Leadership in the Baltimore Negro Community, 1880–1900," at 21 (M.A. thesis, George Washington University 1968), citing J. Brakett, "Notes on the Progress of the Colored People of Maryland Since the War," Vol. 8, Nos. 7–9 *John Hopkins University Studies in Historical and Political Science* 71 (1890). (Hereafter, "Harvey Johnson and Everett Waring . . . A Study of Leadership).

161. *Id* at 21, quoting the *Baltimore Sun*, Feb. 7, 1884.

162. M. L. Callott, *The Negro in Maryland Politics, 1870–1912* at 77, n.16 (1969).

163. W. J. Simmons, *Men of Mark* 729, 730 (1887); "Bar Association Holds Its Banquet," *Baltimore Afro-American*, Sept. 27, 1922; G. F. Braggs, Jr., *Men of Maryland* 30 (1925).

164. The Brotherhood of Liberty was the "forerunner of the [Maryland Chapter] of the National Association for the Advancement of Colored People." A. B. Koger, *The Negro Lawyer in Maryland* 6 (1948).

165. *Ibid.*

166. *Id.* at 7.

167. *Ibid.*

168. *Ibid.*

169. From "1922 Year's Work," Class of 1878, Hampton University Archives; "Bar Association Holds Its Banquet," *Baltimore Afro-American*, Sept. 27, 1922. In this latter article W. Ashbie Hawkins notes that both "Waring and Davis came after the fight to receive admission for colored lawyers and as a natural consequence, they found a field ready for cultivation." The admission of Everett J. Waring to the Baltimore bar was well-received by the black press. Commenting on Waring's admission to the bar, William E. Matthews, a black lawyer in the District of Columbia stated, "I'm glad to see the subject [of bar admission] treated on its merits and not as a social or political question." See "The Colored Lawyer," *New York Freeman*, March 14, 1885, at 2, col. 4. Four years later, probably with the assistance of Waring, the Brotherhood of Liberty published a significant book entitled *Justice and Jurisprudence* (1889). (No specific author of the books is identified, other than the Brotherhood of Liberty.) In the preface, the authors state that "*Justice and Jurisprudence* is intended to be a history, a handbook, a primer to teach all races to uphold and perpetuate the reign of constitutional law . . . the authority of the Fourteenth Amendment, and of their obligation of obedience to its commandments." *Id.* at iii.

170. "Bar Association Holds Its Banquet," *Baltimore Afro-American*, Sept. 27, 1922.

171. *A Documentary History of the Negro People in the United States* 695 (H. Aptheker ed. 1969), quoting article by Everett J. Waring in 8 *The A.M.E. Church Review* 497 (July 1887).

172. Freeman, "Harvey Johnson and Everett Waring—A Study of Leadership" 29, quoting Warner McGuinn, *Brotherhood of Liberty* 18–20 (1907).

173. *Id.* at 30, 15.

174. *Id.* at 30. Ironically, soon after Everett J. Waring's argument, two white lawyers representing a white male unsuccessfully challenged the Bastardy Act on the ground that it was unconstitutional because it did not apply equally to white and black women. The community credited Waring for having laid the foundation for further challenge of the act by white males. *Id.* at 30. The case ultimately reached the Maryland Supreme Court, where the Bastardy Act was upheld. *Plunkard v. State*, 67 Md. 364, 10 A. 225, 10 A. 309 (1887). No black lawyers were involved in this case.

175. 137 U.S. 202 (1890). Actually, all three of the defendants convicted in the United States District Court of Maryland had separate appeals argued by Everett J. Waring before the United States Supreme Court. The cases were consolidated for oral argument. *Smith v. United States* and *Key v. United States*, 137 U.S. 224 (1890).

176. Between 1865 and 1890, several other black lawyers were admitted to the United States Supreme Court, but none had appeared before the court to argue a case. One other black lawyer in Maryland appeared with Everett

Waring before the court in *Jones v. United States*, and therefore must also be credited: Joseph S. Davis, an 1884 Howard University law graduate. Davis died just around the time the United States Supreme Court decided the *Jones* case. Not only had he made history by appearing on the first known brief ever filed by a black lawyer before the United States Supreme Court, but "he established a splendid record in the field of title examination." See "Bar Association Holds Its Banquet," *Baltimore Afro-American*, Sept. 27, 1922. The other lawyers on the brief were white: John Henry Keene, Jr., Archibald Stirling, and J. Edward Stirling. Archibald Stirling took much interest in issues affecting black people. Five years previously, he had won an important case requiring a steamship passenger carrier to pay damages to four black women denied equal accommodations on the *Steamer Sue. The Sue*, 22 F. 843 (D. Md. 1885) (with Hobbs).

177. Navassa Island was forty-five miles from Santo Domingo and seventy-five miles from Jamaica. According to one account, the black laborers on Navassa Island worked under near slave conditions. They "were ruled with rods of iron." A. B. Koger, *The Negro Lawyer in Maryland* 9 (1948).

178. Freeman, "Harvey Johnson and Everett Waring—A Study of Leadership" 53, quoting the *New York Age*, Nov. 14, 1890. Soon after Everett J. Waring and Joseph S. Davis's impressive appearances before the United States Supreme Court, David A. Straker, himself a black lawyer, noted their achievement in a leading church review. Straker, "The Negro in the Profession of Law," 8 *A.M.E. Rev.* 178, 182 (1891).

179. *Ibid.* ("Harvey Johnson and Everett Waring—A Study of Leadership").

180. *Ibid.*

181. Waring was subjected to such harsh criticism that an article appeared in black national newspapers to demonstrate his past commitments to defending his race in legal matters. "Lawyer Waring's Career," *New York Age*, Nov. 14, 1891, at 4, col. 2. Perhaps out of envy, or out of the competitive force he brought to law in Baltimore, other black lawyers continued to downplay Waring's achievements. Describing Waring some years later, William Ashbie Hawkins, a leading black lawyer in Baltimore, found him to be "a brilliant advocate, but he was erratic. Had he been content to remain in the field of advocacy instead of trying to achieve wealth in real estate, for which he was illy fitted, he might have made a great career for himself, and saved his professional brethren, and his race several serious embarrassments." "Bar Association Holds Its Banquet," *Baltimore Afro-American*, Sept. 27, 1922.

182. *Ibid.* ("Lawyer Waring's Career").

183. *Indianapolis Freeman*, June 29, 1889, at 8.

184. *Marcus Garvey, Life and Lessons* 392 (R. Hill and B. Bair eds. 1987); *Virginia's Contribution to Negro Leadership* 28 (W. Cooper ed. 1937) (mimeo on file, Hampton University). In 1892, William Ashbie Hawkins became the ninth black lawyer in Maryland. With the exception of William Ashbie Hawkins and John Frank Wheaton (admitted later in the year) the following lawyers, in order of admission, were practicing law in Baltimore in January 1892: Everett J. Waring, Joseph S. Davis, Charles W. Johnson, Harry S. Cummings, George M. Lane, Warner T. McGuinn, John L. Dozier, William Daniels, and Malachi Gibson. "Our Lawyers in Baltimore," *The New York Age*, Jan. 23, 1892, at 1, col. 1. John Frank Wheaton has been reported erroneously as a graduate of Howard University's law school. Neither was he Maryland's fourth black lawyer. *Progressive Men of Minnesota* 350, 351 (M. D. Shutter and J. S. McLain eds. 1897). Wheaton attended Howard University's law school and apparently

studied privately under Albert A. Small, a white Maryland lawyer, becoming the first black person admitted to the bar in Hagerstown, Maryland. Thereafter, Wheaton was admitted to and received his formal law education at the University of Minnesota Law School, from which he was graduated in 1894. He was the University of Minnesota's first black law graduate. Smith, "In the Shadow of Plessy: A Portrait of McCants Stewart, Afro-American Legal Pioneer," 73 *Minn. L. Rev.* 495, 500 (1988).

185. Freeman, "Harvey Johnson and Everett Waring—A Study of Leadership" at 59, quoting G. Bracket, "Notes on the Progress of the Colored People of Maryland Since the War," Vol. 8, Nos. 7–9 *John Hopkins University Studies in Historical and Political Science* 11–12 (1890).

186. *Id.* at 63 ("Harvey Johnson and Everett Waring—A Study of Leadership").

187. William Ashbie Hawkins later reported that Johnson's career "was marred by indiscretions, partly responsible for his death." "Bar Association Holds Its Banquet," *Baltimore Afro-American*, Sept. 27, 1922.

188. M. L. Callcott, *The Negro in Maryland Politics, 1870–1912* 58, 77, 94 (1969).

189. *Id.* at 153.

190. *Ibid.* Vol. 1 *Who's Who of the Colored Race* 83 (F. L. Mather ed. 1915). "Bar Association Holds Its Banquet," *Baltimore Afro-American*, Sept. 27, 1922.

191. L. R. Harlan, *Booker T. Washington: The Wizard of Tuskegee* 25 (1983).

192. The Poe Amendment, named for its author, Professor John Prentiss Poe of the University of Maryland Law School, was "the first and most serious threat to Negro suffrage in Maryland." M. L. Callcott, *The Negro in Maryland Politics, 1870–1912*, at 115 (1969). See also, *Who's Who in Maryland* 696 (A. N. Marquis ed. 1939), for biographical material on John Prentiss Poe. The Poe Amendment had four provisions that would have disqualified blacks from voting in Maryland, including a grandfather clause that allowed persons to vote if they were qualified to do so "on the first day of January, 1869." *Ibid.* The Poe Amendment was adopted by the Maryland General Assembly in 1904 and submitted to the voters for ratification in 1905. Harry S. Cummings, a Republican, reported his efforts to defeat the Poe Amendment to Booker T. Washington. *Id.* at 122, n.61, 140, n.4. With a sense of urgency, Booker T. Washington asked Frederick L. McGhee, a black Catholic member of the Minnesota bar and one of the few black Democrats in the nation, to lobby the Catholic Diocese of Maryland to oppose the Poe Amendment. A. Meier, *Booker T. Washington: An Interpretation in Black History* 338, 350 (M. Drimmer ed. 1968). The Poe Amendment was defeated by an unexpected coalition of foreign-born whites who feared that they might be disfranchised under the language of the amendment, though they had been promised that the disfranchisement provision would be applied only to blacks. M. L. Callcott, *The Negro in Maryland Politics, 1870–1912*, at 116, 123–25 (1969).

193. The firm later would be joined by a distinguished black Florida lawyer and educator, Thomas de Saile Tucker. "Bar Association Holds Its Banquet," *Baltimore Afro-American*, Sept. 27, 1922. See also, Vol. 1 *Who's Who in Colored America* 88 (J. J. Boris ed. 1927). George W. F. McMechen was a community leader in his own right. He was the national president of the Improved Benevolent and Protective Order of Elks of the World in 1917. *The Negro Year Book, 1918–1919* at 458 (M. Work ed. 1919). William Ashbie Hawkins was the supreme chancellor of the Knights of Pythias, a national fraternal organization

with considerable assets. *Ibid.* Their involvement in these national organizations probably drew clients to Hawkins and McMechen's law firm.

194. "Bar Association Holds Its Banquet," *Baltimore Afro-American*, Sept. 27,
1922.

195. *Ibid.*

196. *Clark v. The Maryland Institute for the Promotion of the Mechanic Arts*, 87
Md. 643, 41 A. 126 (1898) (with John Phelps).

197. See, e.g., *Burton v. Wilmington Parking Authority*, 365 U.S. 715 (1961).

198. Freeman, "Harvey Johnson and Everett Waring—A Study of Leadership," quoting William Ashbie Hawkins's article, "The Achievement of Harvey
Johnson," 6, Baltimore, 1922.

199. *Joseph P. Evans v. Chesapeake and Ohio Railway Co.*, 92 I.C.C. 713 (1924).
William Ashbie Hawkins, representing the Baltimore Branch of the NAACP,
filed an *amicus curiae* brief in the United States Supreme Court in *Buchanan v.
Warley*, 245 U.S. 60, 69 (1917), in which he urged the Court to void restrictive
covenants barring blacks from purchasing real property in white neighbor-
hoods. In 1913, Hawkins and George W. F. McMechen had failed to persuade
the Maryland Court of Appeals that race covenants violated the United States
Constitution. *State v. Gurry*, 121 Md. 534, 88 A. 546 (1913). See also, "Ashbie
Hawkins, Attorney for 50 Years, Dies at 78," *Baltimore Afro-American* April 12,
1941.

200. Vol. 1 *Who's Who of the Colored Race* 132 (F. L. Mather ed. 1915).

201. *Virginia's Contribution to Negro Leadership* 28 (W. Cooper ed. 1937)
(mimeo on file, Hampton University Archives).

202. *Id.* at 42; Vol. 1 *Who's Who of the Colored Race* 190 (F. L. Mather ed. 1915).

203. Freeman, "Harvey Johnson and Everett Waring—A Study of Leadership" 70.

204. *Virginia's Contribution to Negro Leadership* 42 (W. Cooper ed. 1937)
(mimeo on file, Hampton University Archives). *Negro Year Book, 1918–1919*, at
54 (M. N. Work ed. 1919). William L. Fitzgerald, a 1898 law graduate of
Howard University, was "the first colored man to take a written examination
before the State Board of Law Examiners," in Maryland. Vol. 1 *Who's Who in
Colored America* 66 (J. J. Boris ed. 1927).

205. "Bar Association Holds Its Banquet," *Baltimore Afro-American*, Sept. 27,
1922; Koger, *The Negro Lawyer in Maryland* 8 (1948).

206. Vol. 1 *Who's Who of the Colored Race* 51 (F. L. Mather ed. 1915).

207. See "Indorsement of the Candidacy of the Honorable Robert F. Stanton, *Baltimore Afro-American*, Oct. 13, 1917.

208. "Baltimoreans Who Have Made Good Afro-Americans," Dec. 3, 1920
(source unknown); author's files. Jackson was often assigned to these cases by
the judges of the courts because of his knowledge and skills. *Ibid.*

209. Letter from H. D. Subers, of the Free Library of Philadelphia, to
Charles S. Brown, June 17, 1958. Seven years out of law school, William A. C.
Hughes, Jr., appeared before the Maryland Supreme Court to attack private
agreements that restricted blacks from purchasing property in white neighbor-
hoods. See *Meade v. Dennistone*, 173 Md. 295, 196 A. 330 (1938). Hughes lost
this case, as the Maryland Supreme Court was not inclined to modify the principles of *Buchanan v. Warley*, 245 U.S. 60 (1917) and the Fourteenth Amendment to private restrictions on the sale of land to blacks.

210. "Colored Lawyer Sues Attorney General of Maryland," *Baltimore Afro-
American*, May 19, 1918.

211. "Negro Lawyer Scored," *Baltimore Evening Sun*, June 22, 1918. Pendleton was suspended from practicing in the federal court. However, when federal lawyers tried to have him disbarred at the state level, the local bar committee refused to do so. Telephone interview with Judge William H. Murphy, Sr., Jan. 19, 1990. See also, M. V. Tushnet, *The NAACP's Legal Strategy Against Segregated Education, 1925–1950*, at 46 (1987).

212. *Ibid.* (Tushnet). Thurgood Marshall would later be appointed in 1967 as the first black member of the United States Supreme Court. See Bland R. Walton, "An Examination of the Legal Career of Thurgood Marshall Prior to His Elevation to the Supreme Court of the United States, 1934–1964," at 16 (Ph.D. diss., Notre Dame University, 1970).

213. *Pearson v. Murray*, 169 Md. 478, 182 A. 590 (1935). The University of Maryland School of Law was private until 1920. *Id.* at 482. After Thurgood Marshall and Charles H. Houston won this case, the Maryland State Legislature expanded its out-of-state scholarship program, which aided black Maryland citizens seeking a legal education in other states. M. V. Tushnet, *The NAACP's Legal Strategy Against Segregated Education, 1925–1950*, at 57 (1987). While some blacks were subsidized to leave the state to receive their legal training, one unidentified black student was admitted to Maryland's evening law program, while William H. Murphy, Sr., became the "third Negro student admitted" to the day program. "Maryland U. Admits Negro Law Student," 46 *Crisis* 341 (Nov. 1939).

214. *Mills v. Board of Education of Anne Arundel County*, 30 F. Supp. 245 (D. Md. 1939).

215. A. B. Koger, *The Negro Lawyer in Maryland* 1 (1948). Koger was graduated from Howard University's law school in 1924. Other lawyers, such as William G. McCard, an 1896 graduate of Northwestern University School of Law, and James Henry Hammond, were also a part of this tradition, as were many other black lawyers admitted to the bar in Maryland. Vol. 1 *Who's Who of the Colored Race* 187 (F. L. Mather ed. 1915), on McCard; *id.* at 129, on Hammond.

216. On October 29, 1946, Jane Cleo Marshall Lucas, a 1944 law graduate of the University of Michigan, became the first black woman admitted to the Maryland bar. Letter to author from Alexander L. Cummings, clerk, Court of Appeals of Maryland, June 26, 1992, regarding date of admission.

217. *Daily True American*, June 9, 1893; *New York Times*, June 10, 1893.

218. Letter from John H. Gildea, clerk, Supreme Court of New Jersey, to Charles S. Brown, March 9, 1961.

219. Letter from Lois M. Fawcett, head of Reference Department, Minnesota Historical Society, to Charles S. Brown, April 11, 1961.

220. *Newark Daily Advertiser*, June 9, 1896.

221. *Ibid.*

222. *Ibid.*

223. Letter from John H. Gildea, clerk, Supreme Court of New Jersey, to Charles S. Brown, May 28, 1958. Little is known about Spraggins. He was graduated from Howard University law school in 1895.

224. *The Negro Year Book, 1918–1919*, at 481 (M. Work ed. 1919), listing *American and English Law of Title and Record, 1535–1911* (1914). Cosey published his first book prior to entering law school: *Combination of Crisis, or Items of Foreign Countries* (1888). His second book appeared in 1904 and was titled *Great Men and Strong Platforms*.

225. "Negro Lawyer Accused," *New York Evening Journal*, Nov. 1914.

226. "Cosey Disbarred by Supreme Court as Unfit," *New York Times*, June 22, 1916.

227. Vol. 1 *Who's Who in Colored America* 123 (J. J. Boris ed. 1927).

228. "The Colored Lawyer," *Washington Bee*, March 6, 1915; Vol. 1 *Who's Who of the Colored Race* 177 (F. L. Mather ed. 1915).

229. *Id.* at 207; Vol. 1 *The National Cyclopedia of the Colored Race* 216 (C. C. Richardson ed. 1919).

230. "The Colored Lawyers," *The Washington Bee*, March 6, 1915.

231. F. L. Styles, *Negroes and the Law* 42–43 (1937), quoting "Woman Given Liberty After Killing Would-Be Star Boarder," *Philadelphia Tribune*, 1934.

232. *Proceedings of the Nineteenth Annual Meeting, National Business League*, Atlantic City, NJ, Aug. 21–23, 1918, at 177–78 (Charles L. Webb, reporter).

233. "Well Known Attorney Named with Others in Grand Jury Report," *The Chicago Defender*, April 3, 1920.

234. *Ibid.*

235. "Attorney Nutter Proves That He Was 'Framed,'" *The Cleveland Advocate*, May 22, 1920; "Attorney Nutter Freed of Charge," *Atlanta Independent*, June 19, 1920.

236. *Who's Who Among Negro Lawyers* 18 (S. T. M. Alexander ed. 1945); "Yancey Named Asst. U.S. Atty. in New Jersey," *Afro-American*, July 4, 1942, at 21, col. 3.

237. *Patterson v. Board of Education of City of Trenton*, 11 N.J.M. 179, affirmed 112 N.J.L. 99, 164 A. 892 (1933); F. L. Styles, *Negroes and the Law* 37 (1937), citing article from *The Philadelphia Tribune*, 1933.

238. Letter from Robert Queen to Charles S. Brown, Jan. 10, 1959.

239. *Ibid*; Vol. 1 *Who's Who in Colored America* 164 (J. J. Boris ed. 1927).

240. Letter from Robert Queen to Charles S. Brown, Jan. 10, 1959.

241. See *Hedgepth v. Board of Education of City of Trenton*, 131 N.J.L. 153, 35 A.2d 622 (1944).

242. "Biographical Sketch of William A. Dart, Esq., 1890–1967" (courtesy of the Honorable Lawrence W. Pierce, U.S. Circuit Court, 2d Circuit).

243. *Who's Who Among Negro Lawyers* 12 (S. T. M. Alexander ed. 1945).

244. "Young Negro Lawyer Gets Berth on New Jersey Education Board," *Gary American*, Jan. 17, 1931.

245. *Who's Who Among Negro Lawyers* 38 (S. T. M. Alexander ed. 1945). Yancey's appointment as assistant U.S. attorney was delayed for two years, even with the apparent support of New Jersey senator William H. Smathers. Yancey, a former president of the "colored bar association in New Jersey, was a member of the firm of Yancey, McWilson, and Abrams at the time of his appointment." "Yancey Named Asst. U.S. Atty. in New Jersey," *Afro-American*, July 4, 1942, at 21, col. 3.

246. Walter Straton Forward had served as secretary of the treasury under President John Tyler and had once been a United States district judge in Pennsylvania. Hanchett, "George Boyer Vashon, 1824–1878: Black Educator, Poet, Fighter for Equal Rights," 68 *The Western Pennsylvania Historical Magazine* 205, 208 (July 1985).

247. *The Pittsburgh Morning Post*, Feb. 18, 1847.

248. J. R. Sherman, *Invisible Poets* 54 (1974), quoting *Pittsburgh Telegraph* (n.d.).

249. *Ibid.*

250. Hanchett, "George Boyer Vashon, 1824–1878: Black Educator, Poet, Fighter for Equal Rights," 68 *The Western Pennsylvania Historical Magazine* 205, 339 (July 1985).

251. *Pittsburgh Gazette*, Feb. 24, March 30, 1868.

252. Letter from R. J. Blanchard, deputy clerk, United States Supreme Court, to Charles S. Brown, May 6, 1958. John Swett Rock, of Massachusetts, was admitted to the United States Supreme Court in 1865, and John Mercer Langston, of Ohio, in 1867.

253. Woody, "Jonathan Jasper Wright, Associate Justice of the Supreme Court of South Carolina, 1870–1877," 18 *J. Negro History* 114, 115 (1933).

254. *Ibid*; F. L. Styles, *Negroes and the Law* 123 (1937).

255. *Id.* at 124 (*Negroes and the Law*).

256. *Id.* at 115. The exact date on which Jonathan Jasper Wright was admitted to the bar remains in dispute: R. H. Woody, a noted historian, uses the date August 13, 1866; Fitzhugh F. Styles, a Pennsylvania native who authored the first comprehensive history of black lawyers, uses the date August 13, 1865. Woody, "Jonathan Jasper Wright, Associate Justice of the Supreme Court of South Carolina, 1870–77," 18 *J. Negro History* 114, 115 (1933); F. L. Styles, *Negroes and the Law* 124 (1937). Charles H. McKibben, the prothonotary of the Eastern District of the Pennsylvania Supreme Court, reports that Wright was admitted to the bar of that court on January 17, 1859. Letter from Charles H. McKibben to Charles S. Brown, May 7, 1958. Nevertheless, McKibben's letter is the only official document extant on this subject. He says that Wright was sponsored to the bar "on motion of Benjamin W. Cumming."

257. F. L. Styles, *Negroes and the Law* 124 (1937). It is almost universally accepted that Jonathan Jasper Wright was the first black person admitted to practice law in Pennsylvania. See also, C. L. Blockson, *Pennsylvania's Black History* 73 (L. D. Stone ed. 1975). However, a more recent history of black lawyers, citing a social history project, indicates that Henry Johnson and Isaac Parvis were members of the bar in Pennsylvania by 1850. G. R. Segal, *Blacks in the Law* 28 (1983). Neither of these lawyers is mentioned by Fitzhugh Lee Styles in his pioneering work, *Negroes and the Law* (1937).

258. After Wright was admitted to the Pennsylvania bar, other black lawyers followed between 1865 and 1880: John H. Cavenders, Jacob Ballard, John D. Lewis, J. Howard Scott, and Theophilus J. Minton. Among other lawyers admitted to the Philadelphia bar before 1900 were Aaron Mossell, Jr., John S. Durham, John Wesley Parks, John Adams Sparks, M. Luther Nicholas, and George W. Mitchell. G. R. Segal, *Blacks in the Law* 28 (1983).

259. Letter from Whitney S. Bagnall, Columbia University Law School librarian for special collections, to author, Feb. 16, 1987.

260. Letter from Charles H. McKibben, prothonotary, Supreme Court of Pennsylvania, Eastern District, to Charles S. Brown, May 7, 1958. Lewis was admitted to the court on motion of W. B. Mitchell. On February 26, 1876, Lewis was admitted to the Courts of Common Pleas in Philadelphia. Letter from D. Barlow Burke, Prothonotary, Court of Common Pleas, to Charles S. Brown, Dec. 1, 1959.

261. Obituary, *New York Age*, April 11, 1891.

262. *Peoples Advocate*, Jan. 7, 1882.

263. Obituary, *New York Age*, April 11, 1891; *Detroit Plaindealer*, March 25, 1892.

264. *Ibid.* (*New York Age*); Jeremiah H. Scott was graduated from Howard

University law school in 1875 and admitted to the Courts of Common Pleas of Philadelphia on November 12, 1887. Letter from D. Barlow Burke, Prothonotary, Court of Common Pleas, to Charles S. Brown, March 29, 1961.

265. *New York Daily Tribune*, Jan. 1, 1882; *Philadelphia Ledger*, Jan. 2, 1882.

266. *Ibid. (Philadelphia Ledger).*

267. Letter from Leonidas Dodson, archivist, University of Pennsylvania, to Charles S. Brown, May 9, 1961. In 1893, John Adams Sparks was graduated from the University of Pennsylvania Law School. G. R. Segal, *Blacks and the Law* 29 (1983).

268. Mossell, "The Unconstitutionality of the Laws Against Miscegenation" 9 (1888), courtesy of Raymond F. Trent, Biddle Law Library, University of Pennsylvania Law School. In 1967, the United States Supreme Court struck down state anti-miscegenation laws as violative of the Equal Protection Clause of the Fourteenth Amendment. *Loving v. Virginia*, 388 U.S. 1 (1967).

269. Letter from Clarence O. Lewis, Niagara County historian, to Charles S. Brown, April 27, 1961, incorporating material from the *Lockport Daily Journal*, May 14, 1890; letter from Sadie Tanner Mossell Alexander to Charles S. Brown, May 10, 1961.

270. Comment, "The Black 'Philadelphia Lawyer,' " 20 *Villanova L. Rev.* 371, 372 (1974), quoting W. E. B. Du Bois, *The Philadelphia Negro* 114–15 (1899).

271. *Ibid.* ("The Black 'Philadelphia Lawyer' ").

272. *Ibid.*

273. *Ibid.*

274. *Ibid.*

275. B. T. Washington, *The Negro in Business* 285 (1907), quoting a speech by Wanamaker delivered at the 1904 Convention of the National Business League.

276. Ridley studied in the law offices of a white lawyer, Louis H. Richards, for three years. The motion for his admission was made by John T. Reynolds. *Public Ledger*, March 24, 1891.

277. G. R. Segal, *Blacks in the Law* 181 (1983); Walter E. Billows served in the district attorney's office in Allegheny County from 1903 to 1904. However, his career as a lawyer soon faded. Baldwin, "Silhouettes: The Black Bar and the Allegheny County Courts," 12 *Pittsburgh Legal Journal* 3 (Dec., 1988).

278. *Ibid. (Blacks and the Law).* White was the son of former Congressman George H. White, Sr., who had served in Congress during Reconstruction. See A. Buni, *Robert L. Vann of Pittsburgh Courier* 30 (1974).

279. C. F. White, *Who's Who in Philadelphia* 29–30 (1912).

280. *Id.* at 30.

281. Vol. 1 *Who's Who in Colored America* 38 (J. J. Boris ed. 1927).

282. F. L. Styles, *Negroes and the Law* 154 (1937).

283. Vol. 10 *The Booker T. Washington Papers, 1909–11*, at 387 (L. R. Harlan, R. W. Smock, G. McTigue, and N. E. Woodruff eds. 1981); Vol. 1 *Who's Who of the Colored Race* 61 (F. L. Mather ed. 1915).

284. "W. J. Carter Dies, Howard U. Trustee," *The Washington Evening Star*, March 25, 1947.

285. *Dictionary of American Negro Biography* 206 (R. W. Logan and M. R. Winston eds. 1982).

286. *Id.* at 206–7.

287. Vol. 1 *Who's Who of the Colored Race* 252 (F. L. Mather ed. 1915).

288. *Ibid.*

289. *Ibid.*

290. "Cobbs Is Tenth Colored Judge to Sit on Bench," *Baltimore Afro-American*, July 31, 1926; letter from Jonathan R. Stayer, assistant archivist, Pennsylvania Historical and Museum Commission, to author, Aug. 1, 1986.

291. "Virginia's Contribution to Negro Leadership" 21 (W. Cooper ed. 1937), mimeo on file, Hampton University; "Dickerson—Attorney-at-Law," 2 *The Brown American* 4 (May 1937).

292. *Ibid.* ("Dickerson—Attorney-at-Law").

293. *Id.* at 6.

294. *Ibid.*

295. The fugitive Brown was eventually extradited to South Carolina, but Dickerson laid the groundwork for his safe return, without fear of lynching. *Ibid.*

296. *Dictionary of American Negro Biography* 614, 615 (R. Logan and M. Winston eds. 1982); A. Buni, *Robert L. Vann of Pittsburgh Courier* 39 (1974).

297. *Id.* at 41, 47 (*Robert L. Vann of Pittsburgh Courier*).

298. *Id.* at 47–48.

299. *Id.* at 40.

300. *Id.* at 41, 47.

301. *Id.* at 99–100.

302. *Dictionary of American Negro Biography* 614 (R. Logan and M. Winston eds. 1982).

303. A. Buni, *Robert L. Vann of Pittsburgh Courier* 205–6 (1974).

304. *Id.* at 206.

305. *Id.* at 221. Back in Pennsylvania, Herbert E. Millen, a 1920 black law graduate of the University of Pennsylvania, was appointed deputy attorney general by Republican Governor Gifford Pinchot and "later, under [Democratic] Governor Arthur H. James . . . as Secretary of the County Board of Assistance." Hon. Herbert E. Millen, 11 *The Shingle* 27, 28 (Feb. 1948).

306. *Id.* at 285 (*Robert L. Vann of Pittsburgh Courier*).

307. *Id.* at 285–86.

308. *Id.* at 285–86, 323, listing posthumous honors. The death of Robert Lee Vann was memorialized by his alma mater, Virginia Union University. Hancock, "Robert L. Vann," XLI *Virginia Union Bulletin* 1 (Nov. 1, 1940). A high school in Ahanki, North Carolina, was also named for Vann. "R. L. Vann School to Broaden Curriculum," *Pittsburgh Courier*, Sept. 12, 1942, at 2, col. 1.

309. *Smull's Legislative Handbook of the State of Pennsylvania* 1075 (1914). Bass was reelected to the legislature in 1912.

310. G. R. Segal, *Blacks in the Law* 29 (1983). According to Segal, "The 1910 Census reported that there were thirteen black lawyers in Philadelphia." Despite the effective freeze on black admissions to the bar during this period, Charles F. White was graduated from the University of Pennsylvania's law school in 1910 and within two years edited *Who's Who in Philadelphia* (published in 1912). Joshua Robin Bennett, a 1908 law graduate of Howard University, became the first black admitted to practice law before the Luzerne County bar between 1908 and 1910. Bennett was once jailed for writing bad checks. See "Only Negro Member of Luzerne Bar Is Jailed," *Boston Christian Science Monitor*, July 25, 1915. Bennett also practiced in Wilkes-Barre, Pennsylvania.

311. "Alexander Takes New Offices," *Pittsburgh Courier*, Oct. 9, 1926.

312. *Ibid.*

313. *Ibid.*

314. *Ibid.*

315. *Ibid.* Alexander's law office was staffed with "three very competent young ladies who [did] the important secretarial and stenographic work."

316. "Death of Raymond Pace Alexander," 120 *Cong. Rec.* §37484 (Nov. 26, 1974).

317. "Alexander Takes New Offices," *Pittsburgh Courier*, Oct. 9, 1926.

318. "Alexander, Blacks, and the Law," 43 *N.Y.S.B.J.* 15, 18 (Jan. 1971).

319. *Ibid.*

320. *Ibid.*

321. "Alexander Takes New Offices," *Pittsburgh Courier*, Oct. 9, 1926. See *Commonwealth v. Thomas*, 282 Pa. 20, 127 A. 427 (1925) (with Thomas J. Minnick, Jr.).

322. Maceo William Hubbard was graduated from the Harvard University School of Law in 1926. "The Forum Talks with Maceo Hubbard," 7 *The Civil Rights Forum* 1 (Summer/Fall 1984). Hubbard later became counsel to the Fair Employment Practice Committee in Philadelphia in 1943 and was reported as saying that "FEPC gains made during the war are not important if FEPC ends with the war." W. A. Brower, "What They Said and Did at Lawyers' Meet in Baltimore," *Baltimore Afro-American*, Dec. 4, 1943; "Lawyers Name Committee to Cooperate with FEPC," *Baltimore Afro-American*, Dec. 4, 1943. Later, Hubbard became the first black staff lawyer in what is today the Civil Rights Division of the U.S. Department of Justice. "Maceo W. Hubbard, 92, Local Civil Rights Lawyer," *Washington Times*, July 23, 1991, at B4, col. 1.

323. Alexander, "The Negro Lawyer," 9 *Opportunity* 268, 271 (Sept. 1931).

324. "Noted Philadelphian Has Had Brilliant Scholastic and Legal Career in Establishing Negro Rights," *Norfolk Journal and Guide*, Sept. 17, 1932; Fleming, "A Philadelphia Lawyer," 46 *Crisis* 329, 331 (Nov. 1939).

325. "Woman Lawyer Is Named Attorney for AME Bishops," *Nashville Globe and Independent*, June 2, 1944; letter from Sadie T. M. Alexander to Charles S. Brown, May 10, 1961; "College Degree for Negress," *Chronicle Review*, June 15, 1927; "Finished Law at Penn," *Baltimore Afro-American*, June 18, 1927.

326. Alexander, "Blacks and the Law," 43 *N.Y.S.B.J.* 15, 18 (Jan. 1971).

327. *Ibid.* Amram did not mention his courageous act in his memoirs, but he confirms that his father was on the law faculty at the University of Pennsylvania. *Philip Werner Amram, Born March 14, 1900, My Memoir For 1900–1987*, at 40–41 (courtesy of Tanja H. Castro, of Amram and Hahn, Washington, D.C., Oct. 29, 1991). With regard to Dean Mikell, whom Sadie Alexander called "a very prejudiced man," see also, S. Alexander, "The Best of Times and the Worst of Times," 12 *The University of Pennsylvania Law Alumni Journal* 19, 20 (Spring 1977). Philip Werner Amram became the editor-in-chief of the *Pennsylvania Law Review* when Sadie Alexander was elected to the *Review*. Whether Professor David Werner Amram's presence on the law faculty led Dean Mikell to modify his hostile opposition to Sadie Alexander's membership on the *Review* is unknown.

328. See list of students on the *University of Pennsylvania Law Review* between 1926 and 1927, at 75 *University of Pennsylvania Law Review* 61, 154, 247, 349, 447, 544, 760, also indicating that both Alexander and Johnson became editors on the review. For additional information on Johnson, see "Young Negro Lawyer Gets Berth on New Jersey Education Board," *Gary American*, Jan. 17, 1931, and "N.J. Man Named Prosecutor's Aide," *Baltimore Afro-American*, April 3, 1948.

329. Alexander was the first black woman lawyer elected by the bishops of the African Methodist Episcopal Church as attorney for their council, "the highest governing group of the denomination." "Woman Lawyer Is Named Attorney for AME Bishops," *Nashville Globe and Independent*, June 2, 1944.

330. Alexander was first elected national secretary of the NBA on November 26, 1943, and was reelected to that position for many consecutive years. "Roster of National Bar Association Officers," 3 *Nat'l B.A.J.* 303 (1945).

331. Alexander, "The Best of Times and the Worst of Times," 12 *The Pennsylvania Law Alumni Journal* 19, 20 (Spring 1977). Prior to 1930, there was little or no scholarly work on black women lawyers. During the 15th Annual Meeting of the National Bar Association, Alexander delivered a comprehensive paper on black women lawyers. "Women at the American Bar," *New York Age*, Aug. 26, 1939. The paper was subsequently published in the *National Bar Journal*. See S. Alexander, "Women as Practitioners of Law in the United States," 1 *Nat'l B.A.J.* 56 (1941). See also, "Sadie T. M. Alexander, 'First Lady of First,' Dies at 91," *Jet* 52, Nov. 20, 1989; "Sadie T. M. Alexander, Activist," *Washington Post*, Nov. 5, 1989; at B8, col.1; "McKenna Legal Leaders Mourn Loss of Sadie T. M. Alexander," 201 *The Legal Intelligencer* 1, Nov. 3, 1989; St. George, "Lawyer Sadie Alexander, a Black Pioneer, Dies at 91," *Philadelphia Inquirer*, Nov. 3, 1989, at 1, col. 1.

332. G. R. Segal, *Blacks in the Law* 182 (1983); "Homer S. Brown," 17 *Opportunity* 16 (Jan. 1939). The firm catered to "a predominantly ethnic section in Pittsburgh's Hill District." Cunningham, "Homer S. Brown: First Black Political Leader in Pittsburgh," 66 *J. of Negro History* 304, 305 (1981).

333. *Id.* at 305 ("Homer S. Brown: First Black Political Leader in Pittsburgh"). During this period, Homer S. Brown fought against racial segregation in public schools and police brutality, and for higher teachers salaries. In addition, Brown spoke out on national issues such as the lynching of blacks and the use of black labor on chain gangs in the South. *Ibid.*

334. *Id.* at 308; "Homer S. Brown," 17 *Opportunity* 16–17 (Jan. 1939).

335. *Id.* at 307 ("Homer S. Brown: First Black Political Leader in Pittsburgh"), citing, "Pennsylvania Judge Is Censured for Praising Lynching from the Bench," 43 *Crisis* 278, Sept. 1936; *Philadelphia Record*, Aug. 15, 1936, at 1.

336. "Irish Judge Makes Fight on Negro Judge," *Dallas Express*, July 26, 1924. By 1925, Judge Scott was reported to have 781 cases on his calendar. "Scott Court Largest," *Baltimore Afro-American*, Jan. 31, 1925.

337. Vol. 1 *Who's Who in Colored America* 166 (J. J. Boris ed. 1927).

338. F. D. Tucker, *Directory of the Colored Members of the Philadelphia Bar*, May 15, 1970, listing Gay as admitted to the Pennsylvania bar in 1930. During this time three other blacks were admitted to the Pittsburgh bar—Theron B. Hamilton, Thomas E. Barton, and Joseph Givens—all of whom became successful practitioners and public servants. G. R. Segal, *Blacks in the Law* 182 (1983). Philadelphia lawyers like Henry P. Cheatham represented white people in the criminal courts. "Colored Oxford Lawyer Wins Noted Case," *Oxford Public Ledger*, March 26, 1926. In 1929, Lewis T. Moore became the thirtieth practicing black lawyer in Philadelphia. "30 Lawyers in Philadelphia," *Norfolk Journal and Guide*, Oct. 12, 1929.

339. "His Birthday," *Baltimore Afro-American*, April 6, 1929. Raymond Pace Alexander, "The John M. Langston Law Club," 14 *The Shingle* 233 (Dec. 1951); Vol. 1 *The National Cyclopedia of the Colored Race* 309 (C. C. Richardson ed.

1919). Asbury was a spirited leader in Philadelphia and organized the Eden Cemetery for blacks. *Ibid.* His son, David B. Asbury, became a distinguished lawyer and was appointed to various public posts including assistant attorney general assigned to the Pennsylvania State Banking Department." "Attorney Named Zone Warden," *Afro-America*, July 4, 1942, at 12, col. 6.

340. "William Humphreys Started at 54—He Is Arriving Now," *Amsterdam News*, March 23, 1932.

341. R. P. Alexander, "The Negro Lawyer," 9 *Opportunity* 268, 269 (Sept. 1931). Such statements by Alexander no doubt encouraged Theodore O. Spaulding, a 1928 Detroit College of Law graduate, to apply for admission to the Pennsylvania bar. Spaulding was admitted to the Pennsylvania bar in 1931. Letter from H. D. Subers, head, Free Library of Pennsylvania, to Charles S. Brown, Oct. 1, 1958.

342. David Asbury was the last black lawyer to pass the bar in 1934. In 1943, Thomas M. Reed, Herbert Cain, and Roseberry Clay were admitted to the Pennsylvania bar. "Three Race Youths Pass State Bar" Examinations, *Philadelphia Tribune*, May 15, 1943.

343. "Nix the Lawyer," *Palmetto Leader*, Sept. 10, 1932.

344. *Who's Who Among Negro Lawyers* 13 (S. T. M. Alexander ed. 1945).

345. William Harvey Fuller also served four consecutive terms in the Pennsylvania House of Representatives from 1924 to 1930. See R. P. Alexander, "The John Mercer Langston Law Club," 14 *The Shingle* 233 (Dec. 1951); *The Pennsylvania [Legislative] Manual* 1127 (1931).

346. F. L. Styles, *Negroes and the Law* (1937).

347. A. Buni, *Robert L. Vann of Pittsburgh Courier* 297 (1974); "Lawyers Warned Against 'High Hat' Attitude as Bar Association Meets," *Pittsburgh Courier*, Aug. 14, 1937.

348. "Bar Association Lifts Race Barrier," *Norfolk Journal and Guide*, Oct. 16, 1943.

349. "Mr. District Attorney," *Ebony*, March, 1951, at 82, 84; *Who's Who Among Negro Lawyers* 33 (S. T. M. Alexander ed. 1945); "James Austin Norris funeral program," March 6, 1976 (served in Pennsylvania attorney general's office in 1932), *Yale Law School Sesquicentennial Alumni Directory* 202 (1974). Stanton, a 1929 graduate of the University of Pittsburgh law school, handled many cases in the Office of Price Administration during World War II.

350. F. D. Tucker, *Directory of the Colored Members of the Philadelphia Bar*, May 15, 1970. See also, A. Buni, *Robert L. Vann of Pittsburgh Courier* 297 (1974); in 1940, "Edward Henry, a magistrate from Philadelphia, was nominated for a congressional seat" by the Republican caucus, but no one believed that it was a serious effort to put a black man in Congress. For additional information on J. Austin Norris, see, Aaron Porter, "The Career of an Institution: A Study of Norris, Schmidt, Green, Harris, Higginbotham and Associates" (Ph.D. diss., University of Pennsylvania, 1993).

351. C. R. Gross, "Thumb Nail Sketches of the Negro in Law in Rhode Island" 1–2 (1959) (mimeo).

352. Charles S. Brown, "The Genesis of the Negro Lawyer in New England," 22 *The Negro Hist. Bull.* (Part II) 171, 174 (May 1959), quoting *The Providence Journal*, June 6, 1874.

353. Letter from Clarkson A. Collins, III, librarian, the Rhode Island Society, to Charles S. Brown, June 2, 1958, quoting the *Providence Journal*, June 6, 1874. Vol. 1 *Who's Who of the Colored Race* 17–18 (F. L. Mather ed. 1915).

354. C. R. Gross, "Thumb Nail Sketches of the Negro in Law in Rhode Island" 1–2 (1959) (mimeo).

355. *Ibid.*; see also, Vol. 1 *Who's Who of the Colored Race* 194 (F. L. Mather ed. 1915), on Julius Linoble Mitchell.

356. John B. Edwards and William Henry Lewis, Sr., of Massachusetts were co-counsel in the famous Mohr murder case in Rhode Island in 1916. "Wm. H. Lewis and John B. Edwards Dominant Figures in Mohr Murder Trial," *New York Age*, Jan. 27, 1916.

357. C. R. Gross, "Thumb Nail Sketches of the Negro in Law in Rhode Island" 1–2 (1959) (mimeo).

358. "Death of Frederick C. Olney," *The Narragansett Times*, May 24, 1918; *University of Michigan General Catalogue of Officers and Students*, 1837–1911, at 443 (I. N. Demmon ed. 1912).

359. "Funeral Services of F. C. Olney," *The Narragansett Times*, May 31, 1918.

360. Smith, "William A. Heathman, Esq.," 15 *Rhode Island Bar Journal* 3 (June 1967).

361. *Id.* at 16.

362. *Ibid.*

363. *Hart v. Superior Court*, 29 R.I. 513, 71 A. 33 (1909); *Hart v. Superior Court* 29 R.I. 429, 71 A. 1057 (1909).

364. Smith, "William A. Heathman, Esq.," 15 *Rhode Island Bar Journal* 3 (June 1967); Board of Trustees Executive Session, University of Rhode Island, June 5, 1967, Item No. 2 (on file, University of Rhode Island Library). The State Returning Board counted the election returns in state elections.

365. Heathman was appointed as master in chancery by Justice Jeremiah E. O'Connell in 1935. Smith, "William A. Heathman, Esq.," 15 *Rhode Island Bar Journal* 3, 17 (June 1967); "William A. Heathman Dies; Oldest Lawyer," *Providence Journal*, 1968; "Master in Chancery," *Pittsburgh Courier*, Aug. 13, 1938.

366. Popkin, *The Journal-Bulletin*, Oct. 12, 1975; "Oral History Interview No. 15 with Joseph LeCount," May 14, 1976, by the Rhode Island College Ethnic Studies Project.

367. "J. M. Stockett, Jr., Dies in 55th Year," *Providence Journal*, Dec. 4, 1945.

368. *Ibid.*

Chapter 4

The Southeastern States

The southeastern states include Georgia, North Carolina, South Carolina, Virginia, and West Virginia.

Georgia

Immediately after the Civil War, several black lawyers admitted to practice in New England moved to such southeastern states as Georgia and became known as carpetbaggers. Aaron Alpeoria Bradley was one such lawyer. Bradley, in 1856 the third black person admitted to the Massachusetts bar, applied for admission to the United States District Court in Georgia in 1867. His application for admission was denied by Judge John Ersking, ostensibly because Bradley was not grounded on "first principles" of law and lacked "moral and mental qualifications."[1] The denial of Bradley's application to practice law in the federal courts of Georgia was based probably more on his political advocacy than his lack of knowledge of "first principles."

Bradley arrived in Savannah, Georgia, in 1865. He promptly became a vocal critic of the treatment of blacks during slavery and called for reparations for blacks as compensation for years of enslavement. These actions formed the basis of a criminal sedition charge that was brought against Bradley as a consequence of his efforts to organize blacks to protest the rescission of Special Field Order 15.

After General William Tecumseh Sherman captured Savannah, Georgia, in 1864, he issued Special Field Order 15, "which allocated certain coastal [rice] land for black settlement."[2] Thereafter, hundreds of black citizens staked out claims on the coastal land—land which they had farmed and that had been previously owned by their white masters. After the Civil War ended, the Southern landowners returned to reclaim their land, only to discover that blacks were in possession of it. The former owners appealed to President Andrew Jackson, to their former confederate president, Jefferson Davis, and to General O. O. Howard, a Freedmen's Bureau Commissioner, to restore their land. General Howard was reluctant to rescind General Sherman's order. Nevertheless, he gave in to the demands of the former white land owners, perhaps because of Congress's inaction in conveying land to the black freedmen. Howard first tried to persuade the freedmen to voluntarily give up the land, but after failing in this course he "resorted to force."[3] At this point,

Bradley arrived on the scene. . . . Seeing himself as a champion of all blacks' causes, he cast his interest broadly, establishing loose contacts with black churches and soon opening a school. He began agitating for black suffrage, joining forces with the vote campaign. . . . He accused the city police and the mayor's court of discrimination toward blacks [and] charged the Savannah Freedmen's Bureau Court with similar irregularities and requested inauguration of appeal procedures, offering his services as judge. . . . By inclination drawn toward confirmation, he gave special attention to the land claims of the Sherman grantees.[4]

Bradley, who had opened a private school, was ordered to close it because of his public denunciations. Bradley complained directly to President Andrew Johnson, stating that "my private school . . . was ordered discontinued . . . because it spoke against your reconstruction."[5] Soon a telegram was sent from the military district of Washington to General O. O. Howard ordering that Bradley be prosecuted. The telegram stated that

a man named Bradley has been making speeches at S[avannah] to the colored people criticising [sic] President's policy, advising Negroes not to make contracts except at point of bayonet, and to disobey your orders; have arrested him, he does not deny charges, proof conclusive. General Steedmen [the district commander] has ordered him to be tried by Military Commission.[6]

Soon Bradley was brought before a military commission and charged with sedition for a speech he had made in a black church. At the church, he had stated that it was no crime for former slaves to seize the property of their former white masters. According to one account, Bradley argued that the "colored people had earned this property, and it, by right, belonged to them."[7]

Bradley assisted in his own defense during the trial, being "punctually present and extended considerable deference in his demeanor toward the court."[8] However, the court was not sympathetic to Bradley's claim that when Georgia seceded from the Union, blacks became entitled to the property of their masters. Failing to have the charge against him dismissed, Bradley was found guilty and sentenced to hard labor at Fort Pulaski's stockade for one year. In 1867, Bradley was ordered released from custody by Edwin M. Stanton, the Secretary of War.[9]

After Bradley was released from jail, he applied for and was again denied admission to the Georgia bar. Bradley publicly objected to the denial of his application. His objection prompted the *National Intelligencer* to attack Bradley's credibility, alleging that he had been disbarred in Boston "for malpractice,"[10] a charge that appears to have been groundless.[11]

Undeterred by these attempts to thwart his efforts to use his legal skills, Bradley turned to politics. On April 20, 1868, he was elected to the Georgia state senate from the first district and took his seat on July 4, 1868, at the Extra Session.[12] Bradley's qualifications to serve in the senate were immediately attacked, and efforts were made to have him expelled from the senate. His opponents claimed that he had been convicted "for seduction in New York, and sentenced to the penitentiary."[13] To avoid expulsion, Bradley resigned on August 10, 1868, but was reinstated in time to serve in the Adjourned Session from July 20 to December 6, 1870. (This suggests that in the interim Bradley was able to prove that he was not an ex-convict.)[14]

Bradley also served as a member of the 1869 Constitutional Convention. Bradley's membership on the constitution drafting committee gave him a unique opportunity to propose provisions that guaranteed the equality of blacks in Georgia. During the convention, Bradley sponsored a provision that pledged that "no laws shall be made or enforced which shall abridge the privileges or immunities of citizens of the United States, or deny to any person within its jurisdiction the equal protection of its laws."[15]

Bradley, ever the uncompromising—some might say "hotheaded"— senator, crossed swords with other blacks, as well as with white legislators. In the closing days of the Adjourned Session of the Georgia General Assembly of 1870, Aaron Alpeoria Bradley and Charles Wallace, another black senator, locked horns over Bradley's motion to reconsider the nomination of Henry Spring. Spring earlier had been confirmed by the senate as the election manager for the city of Savannah. According to press accounts, the "proceedings occasionally leaked out," including Bradley's arguments that Senator Spring "was not the right sort of a man for election manager [because] he was a gambler [and a] pimp."[16] Senator Wallace challenged Senator Bradley's assertion, and the following exchange nearly brought bloodshed to the floor of the Georgia General Assembly:

Wallace—Did you say that Spring will steal?

Bradley—I said nothing of the kind.

Wallace—Do you think that he will steal?

Bradley—I do not wish to have anything to say to a man who called me
        a goddamn son of a bitch this morning to Senator Crayton.

Wallace—I am ready in or out of this house to be responsible for
        anything that I say.

Bradley—Would you fight right here in the Senate Chamber?

Wallace—Yes . . . right here.[17]

Wallace advanced toward Bradley, and Bradley "drew out a long bowie knife, laid it on the desk, then drew out a pistol, cocked it and laid it by the side of the knife."[18] Senator Wallace stopped and several senators rushed to separate them, helping to avoid what could have been a most disgraceful altercation.[19]

Bradley's stands on race and equality in Georgia were radical for that period. White factions did everything they could to have him criminally charged and convicted of any crime they could propose. They feared this legally trained man, even as most blacks respected and admired him as a fearless leader.[20]

It is clear that the state of Georgia did not want Aaron Alpeoria Bradley practicing in its courts. True to character, Bradley practiced law without a license until 1875, when state authorities caught up with him. Bradley continued his efforts to be admitted to the courts of Georgia until at least 1881, "but was refused."[21] Bradley moved to Beaufort, South Carolina, where he established a law practice, and he no doubt also serviced his Georgia clients from Beaufort.[22]

During the Georgia Constitutional Convention of 1869, blacks, who constituted a majority in several counties, lost an important battle—the battle to have judges elected by the people. Judgeships were determined to be appointive, "eliminating the possibility that blacks could be elected to the bench."[23] However, in 1871, in a move that surprised many, Governor Rufus B. Bullock appointed James M. Simms to a judgeship in the First Senatorial District Court.[24] The appointment was opposed by the local bar association solely because Simms "[happened] to be black and not white."[25] Whites may also have opposed Simms because he had recently been awarded damages of $1,800 in the federal court after the Richmond, Fredericksburg and Potomac Company ejected him from the white section of the steamer *Keyport* between Washington, D.C., and Richmond, Virginia.[26] Governor Bullock demurred at this local opposition. He felt that he had found a "person suitable for appointment, whose character, standing and ability would commend favorably to a majority of the citizens of the district."[27]

Simms was no second-rate appointment. He was well-known and popular among Georgia blacks, he had a fair education, and in 1868 he had been elected, by a sizeable majority, to successive terms as a member of the lower house of the General Assembly.[28] Referring to these qualifications, Governor Bullock proclaimed that he was "forced to the conclusion that no greater disgrace has been cast upon the judiciary of the state by [Simms's] appointment than was cast upon the General Assembly by his election."[29]

Judge Simms assumed the duties of his office and was ridiculed by the local Republicans in Savannah, and by the Southern press who described him as "black as Erebus and loud as fish guano." He resigned his post within one year.[30]

In 1872, Edwin Belcher graduated from Howard University's law school. He was admitted to the bar of the District of Columbia, but he returned to his home state of Georgia. Prior to enrolling in Howard's law school, Belcher, who was light-skinned, had served as an officer in a white Union regiment during the Civil War.[31] He also had worked as an assessor of internal revenue for the third district of Georgia by appointment of President Ulysses S. Grant. After Belcher completed his legal training, he helped to establish the Republican Party in Georgia,[32] and was appointed postmaster of Macon, Georgia, by President Grant.[33]

Henry Lincoln Johnson, Sr., an 1891 graduate of the University of Michigan's law school, became the first black lawyer to practice in Jackson County, Georgia. In 1896, he formed a law firm in Atlanta with William Anderson Pledger, another black lawyer.[34] Johnson divided his attention between law and politics. By 1908, Johnson had been elected as a national Republican committeeman from Georgia, a post to which he was reelected in 1912.[35] Johnson's influence in Georgia and the support he gave to William Howard Taft's candidacy for the presidency won him recognition in the nation's capital. In 1910, President Taft appointed Johnson recorder of deeds for the District of Columbia, which, for reasons unclear, was the premier black post in government. Johnson served honorably as recorder of deeds until his resignation in 1914.[36] Although Johnson was favored by the Republican Party, in 1912 he fought against the efforts of Northern Republicans to reduce the number of Southern delegates to the Republican National Convention. He believed that such a policy would reduce the number of Southern black Republican delegates.[37]

Possibly because of the significant influence and power that he held in Georgia and in national Republican politics, Henry Lincoln Johnson, Sr., enjoyed the confidence and the respect of white and black lawyers, both in Atlanta and outside the state. In 1926 Rudolph O'Hara and Ernest G. Tidrington, two black lawyers from Indiana, organized a political association named the Henry Lincoln Johnson Club.[38] Johnson also helped blacks gain admission to the Georgia bar. One such lawyer was Matthew Washington Bullock, Sr., a Harvard University law graduate. Bullock was admitted to the Georgia bar on the basis of his admission in Massachusetts. He was not required to take the Georgia bar examination.[39]

In 1920 Johnson was subpoenaed to give testimony before the United States Senate's Subcommittee on Privileges and Elections concerning the abuse of campaign expenditures by presidential candidates. Some observers had suspected that Johnson's election as national committeeman from Georgia was engineered by cash contributions supplied to him to ensure his support. This concern reached back to the presidential campaign of 1912. During the Republican National Convention, Johnson allegedly received $9,000 from various sources to aid him in his effort to be elected as a national Republican committeeman. Once elected, he would control nine important votes in the Georgia delegation. He was elected, and he cast his votes to nominate William Howard Taft as the Republican candidate.

Johnson continued to accept such campaign contributions in subsequent presidential elections, again drawing attention to himself and to other campaign functionaries.[40] Johnson testified before the Senate on campaign abuse, but spoke out as well on the disfranchisement and lynching of black voters, though this testimony was perhaps aimed at deflecting attention from his acceptance of campaign funds. Johnson's testimony on the use of campaign funds in a presidential election made him the first black person to testify on that subject before a Senate Committee.[41]

Johnson's legal skills were equal to his political prowess. He was frequently consulted to assist lawyers in and out of Georgia in criminal cases, especially when blacks were charged with crimes against whites. In 1922 Johnson was called to Washington, D.C., to defend a young black man charged with the sexual assault of a white female minor. The offense, if proved, carried a maximum penalty of thirty years in prison or death. During the trial Johnson displayed exceptional skill, especially during cross-examination of the alleged victim. Johnson reportedly delivered one of the most "eloquent and forceful [closing] arguments ever presented in a criminal court" in Washington, D.C.[42] After six hours of deliberation, the jury reported that it was deadlocked: seven members were in favor of acquittal, five for conviction. Judge McCoy discharged the jury. Later, the foreman of the jury "came into the main corridor of the court house . . . and . . . said to the father of the defendant: 'Your son owes his life to the sum-up of Mr. Johnson, some lawyer.' "[43]

In 1896 Henry Moses Porter and Judson Whitlocke Lyons formed a law firm in Georgia. Lyons was an 1884 Howard University law graduate. Porter attended the University of Michigan's law school. Porter also practiced in Augusta and had gained recognition for his aggressive trial advocacy. Porter may have been the first black lawyer to appear before the Georgia Supreme Court. In 1901, he won a new trial for a client charged with assault with intent to murder before the Georgia Supreme Court. His case was based on contested instructions given to the jury by the trial judge.[44]

Porter's concerns for justice for black citizens in the Georgia courts is no doubt the reason that he and T. M. Malone, a black Atlanta lawyer, called upon other black citizens in the state to meet and confer on the future of their race. One of the major complaints of black citizens in the South was the lack of "enjoyment of civil rights of the colored man . . . [and] of jury privileges."[45] Apparently frustrated by the slow rate of progress toward equality in Georgia, Porter left the state in 1908 to practice in Illinois.

Porter's partner, Judson Whitlocke Lyons, became a major player in the Republican Party. In 1896, he was a delegate to the Republican National Convention, where he cast a vote for William McKinley as the Republican presidential candidate. His support for McKinley was later rewarded with an appointment as register of the United States Treasury. Lyons won reappointment to the post in 1901 with the support of Booker T. Washington, but later lost Washington's confidence when he "expressed sympathy for W. Monroe Trotter [a foe of Washington] after the Boston Riots of 1903."[46]

Other black lawyers were admitted to the Georgia bar as the nineteenth century came to a close. In 1888, Charles Henry James Taylor, a former United States minister to Liberia, settled in Atlanta, Georgia, where he "built up a large and lucrative practice in the courts."[47] In a short period of time, Taylor had won sixty-three of his seventy-two civil and criminal cases and earned legal fees "amounting to four or five thousand dollars a year."[48]

John H. Kinckle, Jr., applied for and was admitted to practice before the superior court in Savannah, Georgia, in 1891. Kinckle was one of the first black lawyers to have a successful practice in Savannah.[49] When Kinckle applied to the Savannah bar, the press described the sentiments of the local bar as "intensely against" his admission. Kinckle, an 1886 law graduate of Howard University, received support from Major Peter W. Meldrim, a white Savannah lawyer, and Judge Robert Falligant appointed four white lawyers to examine him. Although several lawyers refused to examine him, Kinckle was given "a severe test." Judge Falligant, however, "who had listened to the examination, was well satisfied and readily admitted him."[50]

Kinckle had a tough time developing a practice in Savannah because, according to one source, "Savannah blacks who had legal problems usually carried them to white lawyers."[51] Other blacks simply did not have the money to afford a lawyer. Nevertheless, Kinckle joined with two other black lawyers, G. H. Miller and A. L. Tucker, to handle criminal and civil cases for members of the black community for many years.[52]

Two black Georgia lawyers, William Anderson Pledger and D. J. Jordan, took their legal training in the fields of politics and education. Pledger, admitted to the Georgia bar in 1894, became a political leader in Georgia.[53] Jordan, an 1892 graduate of the Allen University law department, practiced law in Georgia for a short period and then became a professor of political science and dean of Morris Brown College. Later, he assumed the presidency of Edward Waters College in Jacksonville, Florida.[54]

In 1913, a new generation of black attorneys settled in Savannah, among them James Garfield Lemon. Lemon had attended the University of Chicago law school but apparently completed his legal education through a Chicago correspondence law school. He became an attorney for the Southwestern Claim and Collection Company in Savannah. Lemon gained recognition in Savannah for his eye for detail in legal matters. Judge Henry McAlpin "of the Court of Ordinary" complimented him for his "clear intelligent and concise presentation of evidence" in a will contest.[55] From 1932 to 1933, Lemon and G. C. Williams, then the only black lawyers in Savannah, welcomed black colleagues W. H. Hopkins, Edwin C. Williams,[56] and William S. Jackson[57] to the local bar.

Austin Thomas Walden relocated to Macon County, Georgia, after graduating from the University of Michigan School of Law in 1911.[58] Walden was known at the University of Michigan's law school for his great oratorical gift.[59] For the next twenty-five years, he was a force to be reckoned with in the state of Georgia, both legally and politically.[60] Politically, Walden increased the number of black registered voters from 1,800 in 1910 to 25,000 by 1939. During the same period of time, "he won the admiration of the black community by his continued defense [and assertion] of black rights in numerous legal suits."[61] He continued his advocacy in the courts, except for a short stint during World War I when he served in 1918 as a trial judge advocate in the United States Army.

In the South, the treatment of middle-class blacks before the law was only a shade better than that of the black underclass. Black professionals were persecuted because they refused to be intimidated by or to yield to injustices imposed by whites. In 1927, a noted black Atlanta dentist was beaten while riding on a public streetcar because he refused to vacate the car so that the conductor could have a drinking party. He was charged with disorderly conduct. Fighting "with his back against the wall" Austin T. Walden appeared before a grand jury on behalf of the dentist and successfully had the charges dropped.[62]

In 1929, Walden and A. W. Ricks, also a black lawyer, jointly represented Dr. and Mrs. C. A. Spence in a civil action against the public transportation company for injuries sustained when a streetcar conductor beat them during a dispute over a transfer. The criminal charges against the Spences raised the ire of the black community, which carefully monitored the case and the performance of the black lawyers defending the Spences. After seven months of legal procedures, the Spences were acquitted. Walden and Ricks immediately filed an unprecedented civil action for damages against the streetcar company. Even though the Spences had been advised to retain white lawyers to handle the civil suit for fear that the white judge would not treat their black lawyers in the same manner as in the criminal case, Walden and Ricks won damages in the amount of $1,500.[63]

Walden's influence was felt in other areas. In 1928 he thwarted efforts by white Georgia Republicans to scuttle the nomination of Benjamin Jefferson Davis, Jr., to the Republican National Committee. The white Republicans had urged the nomination of a more "suitable" black candidate without having the matter considered first by the Republican National Committee.[64] The move against Davis had no doubt stemmed from the fact that he, like Perry W. Howard, had been indicted for selling federal jobs, but Davis had been "quickly exonerated by the postmaster general." Two years later Walden became one of the first black lawyers in the South to move for the admission of a black lawyer, John H. Geer, to the United States Supreme Court.[65]

After twenty-five years as a Georgia lawyer, Walden was quoted in the *New York Times* in 1937 about the dearth of black lawyers in the South. Blaming racism in the law and tradition, Walden concluded that the future of black lawyers was "cloudy and even ominous."[66] Yet despite this gloomy prediction, Walden's own career as a politician, as the leader of the Georgia NAACP, and as a lawyer served as a model for black youths in the South.

In the early 1930s, the Communist Party made a significant effort to recruit black professionals into their ranks by pointing persuasively to the increased violence and lynchings of blacks in the South. The case of

Angelo Herndon, a black imprisoned Communist in Georgia, drew more attention to the plight of blacks in the white justice system. Herndon was charged with inciting "Negroes to insurrection," which was a crime under the centuries-old slave codes of Georgia. The Communist-backed International Labor Defense (ILD) retained two black lawyers, Benjamin Jefferson Davis, Jr., a 1928 Harvard University law graduate, and John H. Geer, who practiced in Atlanta, to defend Herndon.[67]

The selection of a black attorney to defend Herndon "infuriated Georgia authorities" and made a hero of Davis, who was smart, articulate, and not a Communist at the time.[68] Davis and Geer waged a rigorous defense of Herndon in the face of great hostility from local whites. During the trial Judge Lee B. Wyatt, the presiding judge, "turned and read newspapers whenever Davis spoke," and Davis and Herndon were referred to as "niggers" and "darkeys" in open court by the prosecuting attorneys.[69] Herndon was found guilty.

Herndon's conviction was overturned by the United States Supreme Court in 1935.[70] But the experience of the trial left Davis bitter, and he joined the Communist Party:

A little less than a year ago . . . I was suspicious of these gift-bearing Reds . . . lest they should rise to power on the backs of American Negroes and then leave them to their fate. Since that time, a lot of water has run under the bridge. . . . The victory thus far of the Communist in the Scottsboro case, the Orphan (Euel Lee) Jones case, the fight they are putting up for colored and white farmers in Alabama and the defense of Angelo Herndon . . . strike forcefully at the fundamental wrongs suffered by the Negro today.[71]

The number of black lawyers admitted to the bar in Georgia between 1930 and 1940 was negligible. In 1931, "there were only [five] Negro lawyers in Atlanta—probably less than a dozen throughout the state."[72] It was reported that during this decade "not a single colored lawyer [was] admitted to the Georgia bar."[73]

Many lawyers who took the bar examination, and who had been trained at the leading law schools in the nation, were failed by the Georgia bar examiners.[74] Many black Georgians suspected that the forceful advocacy of Benjamin Jefferson Davis, Jr., and John H. Geer was the reason that other blacks had been denied admission to the Georgia bar.[75] In 1940, the number of black lawyers in Georgia had dropped to seven—three in Atlanta, two in Savannah, and one each in Macon and Augusta.[76] In 1941, "none of the four colored persons who took the . . . bar examination" passed.[77] Some reports noted that the motto of the white bar might well be "[Blacks] shall not pass!"[78]

In 1943 George Elmer Ross, a 1936 graduate of the Chicago Law

School, failed the Georgia bar examination for the sixth time. He personally appealed to the Georgia Supreme Court to review his examination, arguing that he had been failed on account of his race. Ross's appeal proved futile when it was discovered that the Bar Review Committee had destroyed all of the examination papers, a disclosure that was considered suspect by blacks in the state.[79] But the attention, local and national, given to the Ross case may have aided the efforts of Charles Morgan Clayton, a 1944 graduate of the LaSalle Extension School in Chicago, who passed the Georgia bar examination in the same year.[80]

No more than two black women were admitted to the Georgia bar prior to 1944. In 1919, Estelle A. Henderson, "already admitted to the bar in Alabama," was preparing to take the Georgia bar "after she [had] gone through the usual formalities."[81] At the time, Henderson was a member of the faculty of Morris Brown College. It is not certain whether Henderson was ever admitted to the Georgia bar. What is known is that Rachel E. Pruden-Herndon was admitted to the Georgia bar in 1943.

Prior to 1937, Pruden (her name prior to her marriage) studied law under the tutelage of Austin Thomas Walden.[82] In that year, the Atlanta press noted that Pruden sat for the bar examination. Relying on her knowledge of law, acquired partly from a correspondence course but mainly from books she had read in the library of her employer, A. T. Walden, Pruden was one of the first bar applicants to complete the task of answering the required fifty questions, which took fifteen hours.[83] She did not pass the examination in 1937, and may have failed other attempts to pass the bar until 1943, the year she passed. But as Judge Virlyn B. Moore, who administered the examination, noted, "Miss Pruden was the second colored woman to take the state examination."[84] Since there is no record of the admission of Estelle A. Henderson to the Georgia bar, in 1943 Rachel E. Pruden-Herndon became the first black woman in history of Georgia to be admitted to the bar.[85]

North Carolina

During the Reconstruction era, George Lawrence Mabson from New Hanover County, North Carolina, was aided in his study of law by General Joseph C. Abbott. General Abbott, who had been elected as a U.S. senator in 1868, helped secure a position for Mabson as a policeman at the U.S. Capitol in Washington, "with the understanding that he was to devote his leisure hours to the study of law."[86] In 1869, Mabson enrolled in the newly formed law department at Howard University, from which he graduated in 1871.

Mabson returned to North Carolina to practice law, but many of his friends and supporters had little faith that the bar examination committee would pass a black. Nevertheless, Mabson applied to take the bar examination, which was administered by three justices of the North Carolina Supreme Court including Chief Justice Richmond M. Pearson, Edwin G. Reade, and William B. Rodman. It was reported that, "acting like true and honorable men to their calling, they only demanded of Mr. Mabson what they did of white men—proof of good moral character and sufficient knowledge of the law."[87] Mabson's certificate of moral character, which the law required be signed by three members of the bar, was executed by A. M. Waddell, a member of Congress, Adam Empil, and Griffith J. M. McRea. On June 16, 1871, Mabson was admitted to the North Carolina bar at Raleigh, becoming "the first colored man . . . ever permitted to be a lawyer in North Carolina."[88]

Days after Mabson was admitted to the bar, he defended Wesley Nixon, who had been charged with murder in Edgecombe County, and won an acquittal. Soon thereafter, he took on a second murder case, defending Jemmie Lee in Raleigh. Lee was also acquitted. Mabson's success in these and other cases was evidence of his skill both as a legal technician and an orator.[89]

John Sinclair Leary, an 1873 graduate of Howard University school of law was North Carolina's second black lawyer. Leary was admitted to the bar a year before he graduated from law school. Prior to his admission to Howard University's law school and during his first year in law school, Leary had represented Cumberland County in the North Carolina legislature from 1868 to 1872. In 1876, Leary was elected for one year to the position of alderman in Fayetteville, North Carolina. Thereafter he was elected school committeeman from 1878 to 1879 and from 1880 to 1881. Leary's local public service was capped by a federal appointment. He became deputy collector of internal revenue in North Carolina in 1881 and continued in that position until 1885.[90] In 1888, the Board of Trustees of Shaw University created a law department and appointed Leary as its first dean; he served in this position for about five years. Leary served on the school's law faculty until 1914, the year it was announced that Shaw University's law department was to be discontinued. Shaw's law school graduated nearly sixty law students.[91]

James Edward O'Hara, admitted to the North Carolina bar in 1873, was that state's third black lawyer.[92] O'Hara had studied law without formal training. Once he was admitted to the bar, O'Hara concentrated on his political career. He participated in the 1875 session of the North Carolina Constitutional Convention and also served as chairman of the board of commissioners of Halifax County from 1874 to 1878.[93] Two years later, O'Hara, a Republican, challenged William H. Kitchin, a Democrat, for the second district congressional seat, but lost this contest in the primary.

O'Hara's defeat was attributed to the fact that white Republicans did not think he could beat his Democratic opponent.[94] However, O'Hara asserted that had the Board of Canvassers not excluded votes from the heavily black Edgecombe County, he would have won the election. O'Hara brought a suit contesting the action of the Board of Canvassers and requested a recount. This suit reached the North Carolina Supreme Court in 1879. The court dismissed O'Hara's claim on grounds that it had no jurisdiction to decide the contest, since Kitchin had already been certified by the Board of Canvassers as the winner of the election. The court concluded that O'Hara's remedy was to petition Congress to preclude it from seating Kitchin.[95]

In 1882, O'Hara ran for Congress again, and this time was successful. During his first term, he served on the Mines and Mining Committee and on the Expenditures on Public Building Committee.[96] In 1883, when the United States Supreme Court invalidated the 1875 Civil Rights Act, holding that the public accommodations sections were beyond the power of Congress under the Thirteenth or Fourteenth amendments,[97] O'Hara proposed legislation to restore the civil rights legislation, but without success.

During O'Hara's first term in Congress, he concentrated most of his legislative agenda on issues related to his congressional district. However, during his second term, O'Hara took an aggressive role in legislative matters that had a direct effect on the civil rights of blacks. He is responsible for securing a provision in the Interstate Commerce Act that required "equal accommodations . . . [to] be provided for all without discrimination."[98] O'Hara also proposed passage of public accommodation legislation that prohibited discrimination against blacks in restaurants in the District of Columbia, but this proposal died in committee. Another of O'Hara's main causes in Congress "was given to the fight for dependent and private pensions, in opposition to President [Grover] Cleveland's vetoes."[99]

In 1886, O'Hara, who was a fair-skinned black, was opposed on the Republican ticket by another black candidate, described as being "of a gingercake color." Local blacks seemed to favor a change in their congressional candidate, and they wanted a darker black representing them in Congress. This dissension split the Republican Party in O'Hara's district, and a white Democrat was elected.[100] O'Hara returned to private life and "resumed his law practice in Newbern," until his death in 1905.[101]

George H. White, Sr., read law under Judge William J. Clarke in North Carolina after receiving his undergraduate degree from Howard University in 1877. In 1879, White was admitted to the North Carolina Supreme Court. Soon thereafter, he ran for the post of solicitor and prosecuting attorney in the Second Judicial District (Edgecomb County), but was defeated by John H. Collins, another black lawyer.[102] White then ran for and was elected to the North Carolina State Senate in 1884.

In 1886, White successfully challenged and defeated Collins for the solicitor's post, which he then held for eight years. White was considered an able and competent solicitor, but, despite his competence, his race blurred the view of his performance held by some whites. They did not take well, for example, to the broad powers of a black prosecutor to question "pure and refined white ladies" during court proceedings.[103]

According to the view of the white community, White's effectiveness as a fair and able prosecutor was not proof enough that an honest black lawyer could faithfully execute the commands of the law. This concern poured over into the North Carolina General Assembly in 1891, when "the general assembly . . . tried to prevent future black solicitors by approving a constitutional amendment providing a statewide vote for solicitors, in the same way superior court judges were selected."[104] If adopted, the amendment would have diluted the black vote, making it impossible to elect a black solicitor, even in judicial districts with sizeable black populations. The voters, however, rejected this amendment in the election of 1892.[105]

In 1897, White ran and was elected to Congress, where he served two terms with distinction in the fifty-fifth and fifty-sixth sessions.[106] During his four years in Congress, White was the only black person in that body. He felt himself, therefore, to be the spokesman for nine million black citizens. It was reported that "no matter what the topic under discussion might be, White, like Cato of Rome, could always bring it around to a discussion of Negro rights."[107] He supported all matters involving the defense of the nation and was one of the hawks favoring the invasion of Cuba in 1898. He used the war to advance the need to establish a black artillery regiment, but his proposal was rejected.[108]

Reelected to the fifty-sixth Congress in 1898, White pressed harder for equal rights for blacks. Sensing a growing opposition among whites in his district and the likelihood of defeat in the next election, White fought on to establish a record on racial issues.[109] After completing his term in Congress, White decided not to return to North Carolina, as it was clear to him that there were efforts by the Democrats there to disfranchise blacks. In 1905 White settled in Washington, D.C., where he practiced law and opened a real estate practice. He later founded an all-black town, Whitesboro, New Jersey, before settling in Philadelphia, Pennsylvania.[110]

By 1890, the number of black lawyers in North Carolina had reached fourteen.[111] That number slowly increased as Shaw University's law department graduated more students and as more out-of-state law graduates migrated to North Carolina.

Edward Austin Johnson was the first graduate of the law department of Shaw University in 1890, the same year he published *History of the Negro Race in America*. His penchant for scholarship led him to the law faculty of Shaw University, which he joined in 1892, and he later served as the school's dean. By 1899, he had published another book, *The Negro Soldier in the Spanish American War*, and in 1897 he served a term as alderman in Raleigh, during the Fusion era in North Carolina.[112] Johnson served for several years as an assistant to the United States district attorney for the Eastern District of North Carolina.[113] But, confronted with the difficulty of making ends meet as a lawyer under Jim Crow, Johnson left North Carolina in 1907 and settled in New York.

In 1894, James Youman Eaton was graduated from Shaw University's law school, and he set out to practice law in Henderson, North Carolina. Two years later, he was elected to the North Carolina legislature. After serving his first term in the legislature, Eaton was elected by the Vance County Board of Commissioners to the post of county attorney, a position he held until 1899, when he was again elected to the North Carolina legislature. Eaton was an active member of the legislature, but he was able to get only two of his proposals adopted. He won adoption of an appropriations bill for two black teachers and the abolition of the second week of the May Term of the Vance Superior Court. Of the ten blacks to hold state office in North Carolina between 1894 and 1901, Eaton was the only lawyer.[114]

In 1895, James Sanders Lanier and Raphael O'Hara were graduated from Shaw University's law department. Both Sanders and O'Hara were admitted to the bar in 1895. Lanier "settled down to practice in Winston-Salem,"[115] and O'Hara formed a firm with his father, James Edward O'Hara, thereby becoming the first second-generation black lawyer in the state. Listed among the clients of O'Hara and O'Hara were the New Bern Land and Improvement Company and the Standard Building and Loan Association.[116] Raphael O'Hara practiced in North Carolina for nearly five decades.

The technical skill of the black lawyers in North Carolina in highly complex criminal cases was frequently superior to that of their white counterparts. During the late 1890s, one black lawyer, L. P. White, "told J. D. Bellamy, a white lawyer, after the judge had corrected the latter in a murder case, 'Young man, you have got to go to school again, you are now talking to a lawyer.' "[117] White lawyers in Wilmington, North Carolina, envied the virtual monopoly that black lawyers had on black clients. Black lawyers such as Armond W. Scott, L. P. White, and William A. Moore, handled a substantial portion of the legal business in Wilmington. Each of these men played a key role in opposing the heightened white supremacist activity that preceded the Wilmington race riots of 1898.[118]

Other black lawyers, among them George Henry Mitchell, were graduated from Shaw University's law department at the turn of the century. After Mitchell graduated from law school in 1900, he attended New York University School of Law, receiving his LL.M. degree in 1901. In 1902, Mitchell was admitted to the North Carolina bar and engaged in private practice. He represented several commercial concerns, including the Mountain City Mutual Life Insurance Company, the Union Cooperative and Industrial Association, and the Laborers Building and Loan Association.[119]

Henry Melvin Edmonds and Franklin Walter Williams were admitted to the North Carolina bar around 1913. Williams, a 1911 graduate of New York Law School, blazed many legal trails in North Carolina, as did Edmonds, a 1913 graduate of Shaw University's law school. Black lawyers slowly integrated the legal communities of Rocky Mount, Goldsboro, and Kinston, North Carolina.[120] Some of these lawyers faced violence when they attempted to represent their clients, especially when the victim was white. Armond W. Scott, a graduate of Shaw's law school, was run out of Wilmington in the early part of the twentieth century for defending a black man accused of raping a white woman. He fled to Washington, D.C.[121]

One of the first deaf mutes to practice law in the nation was Roger Demosthenes O'Kelly, a black lawyer from North Carolina.[122] O'Kelly received two law degrees. He completed Shaw University's three-year law course in 1909 and was admitted to the North Carolina bar by examination one year prior to his graduation. For reasons unknown, O'Kelly also applied to Yale University's law school, where he was accepted in 1910. Describing his first days at Yale, O'Kelly recalled that his "experiences . . . were nothing out of the ordinary."[123] He arrived at New Haven in the fall of 1910 with "exactly $88 to meet board and lodging, tuition, and book charges. Tuition alone was $150 a year and $50 of $88 was paid for the first quarter tuition charge and $5 went to deposit fee."[124]

O'Kelly performed as well as the other law seniors at Yale, although it took him two years to graduate. He failed his senior law examination twice, but in this he was in the company of forty-nine other students out of a class of 150. In 1912, O'Kelly passed his examinations, received a law degree from Yale University, and went to work for the T. A. Gillespie Company, which was constructing the Catskill aqueduct. He remained there until 1921, when he opened a law practice in Raleigh.[125]

By 1926 O'Kelly had built "a lucrative business among his own race and [had] business connections with prominent white lawyers and men of affairs."[126] O'Kelly's corporate client base was significant. The Eagle Insurance Company, for which he was general counsel, and the Progressive Real Estate Company, both domestic white corporations, were listed among his clients. O'Kelly overcame his handicap by sheer determination, in his words, "my pencil and pad; they carried me through Shaw and Yale and they have carried me through many important business deals."[127]

Between 1913 and 1921, several other black lawyers were admitted to practice in North Carolina. In 1912, Nereus Deleon White opened a law office in Goldsboro and by 1919 was commissioned as notary public by Governor Thomas W. Bickett. White made his mark in 1920 when he prevailed against five white lawyers in Goldsboro in a civil case and won four out of five other cases in the same week.[128] In 1915, Cleon Whitemarch Brown passed the North Carolina bar examination and settled in Elizabeth City to practice.[129]

In 1921, Robert McCants Andrews was also admitted to the North Carolina bar, thereafter settling in Durham. Andrews had graduated from Howard University's law school in 1918.[130] He became an active and successful civil and criminal lawyer practicing in both the state and federal courts. In 1925, Andrews sued but lost a negligence claim against the Southern Railroad Company in federal court before Judge Isaac M. Melkins. The railroad was represented by several "eminent white counsel of Raleigh," but Andrews stood his ground against these odds.[131] He also made gains in local jurisdictions where no black lawyer had ever appeared. In 1927, Andrews became the first black lawyer to represent a group of blacks in Chester, North Carolina. The courtroom was "crowded with both white and colored people who were curious to see and hear Andrews plead his case [before a white jury]."[132]

Andrews praised the juries of North Carolina as "fairer and more intelligent than juries I have read about in other parts of the country."[133] Such fairness may have been directly related to how the judges managed their courtrooms. Andrews reports that some of the white judges in North Carolina did not tolerate references to race in their courtrooms. In one case Andrews said that "the presiding judge admonished counsel to refer to the Negro defendant by calling him by his name."[134] As in other states, some of the "best men of the bar [took] pride in championing the elemental rights of the race," but there were others who used the word "nigger" and "darky" in trials in North Carolina "to convey a debased opinion of the Negro litigant."[135]

Andrews's superb legal skills saved the lives of several blacks convicted of murder. In 1928, Andrews defended a black man and woman charged with murdering a white man. After a day of trial, Andrews had so weakened the state's case that "a compromise was reached" that allowed the woman to plead guilty to manslaughter "on an agreed verdict of 12 months, and the man was submitted for second degree murder and drew a sentence of 15 years."[136] Prior to the trial, the prosecution had boasted that both defendants would "get the chair."

One of Andrews's great achievements was to use black professionals as expert witnesses before white juries in North Carolina. The use of expert testimony in civil cases brought by black lawyers was difficult because of the paucity of black physicians in North Carolina and because of the reluctance of local white physicians to testify against the establishment. Andrews tenaciously sought and found black experts to testify in many of his negligence cases. In one case, Andrews sued an insurance company to prove that a death claim was within the terms of the policy. Andrews "put on eight experts . . . to support his case, including two Negro surgeons, three Negro physicians, one white clinician, one white specialist, and one white chiropractor."[137] With the assistance of black medical experts, Andrews won a $6,900 verdict—in the context of the late 1920s, the largest ever won by a black lawyer in North Carolina.[138]

Robert McCants Andrews made such a mark as a lawyer in North Carolina that he was invited to deliver a speech at the University of North Carolina in 1931. His speech, entitled "The Negro Lawyer and His Role in Radical Readjustment," outlined the three thirty-year political cycles which governed blacks in the legal profession.[139] The presence of Andrews in North Carolina inspired other young blacks to attend law school, including Charles W. Williamson, whom Andrews had taught in Sunday School. After graduating from Howard University's law school in 1932, Williamson returned to Durham and practiced with Andrews, his mentor, until Andrews's death in 1935. Williamson subsequently opened an office in Henderson, North Carolina.[140]

The Depression hit black lawyers in North Carolina exceedingly hard. Fred J. Carnage, a 1926 graduate of Howard University's law school and one of two black lawyers practicing in Raleigh in 1932, reported that "nobody had very much money and what little they did have they weren't going to spend on a lawyer."[141] Black lawyers also faced conflict with would-be clients in critical civil rights cases. Efforts by these lawyers to desegregate public schools were sometimes criticized by the black community. Conrad Pearson and Cecil McCoy, both black lawyers, faced severe criticism in 1933 for filing a suit that challenged the state's refusal to desegregate publicly supported schools of higher education. Durham's black leaders, many of whom were officers in the local chapter of the NAACP, were cool to the lawsuit, because they feared the white establishment would retaliate by cutting funding for black colleges in the state. Supported by Charles Hamilton Houston, then head of the NAACP's legal staff based in New York, Pearson and McCoy refused to withdraw the suit, which they eventually lost. To aggressive black civil rights lawyers, this experience demonstrated that their agenda in North Carolina would cause tension between themselves and their likely clients.[142]

No black women were admitted to the North Carolina bar until May 30, 1933, the year Ruth Whitehead Whaley gained her admission.[143] She was followed in 1937 by Dorothy Spaulding of Durham.[144]

South Carolina

In 1868 three black lawyers were admitted to practice before the Supreme Court of South Carolina. At that time, any male citizen could qualify for membership to the bar. Even as the status of the newly freed blacks remained uncertain, Robert Brown Elliott, William J. Whipper, and Jonathan Jasper Wright on September 23, 1868, became the first black lawyers admitted to the South Carolina bar, one year after Whipper and Wright had helped to organize the Republican Party in South Carolina.[145] Elliott was a resident of Aiken, South Carolina. Whipper and Wright were residents of Beaufort, South Carolina.

These men were followed to the bar by several other black men. Samuel J. Lee of Bamberg, South Carolina, was admitted to the bar on March 6,1872; David Augustus Straker of Charleston was admitted to the bar on July 15, 1875; and T. McCants Stewart of Sumter was admitted on December 6, 1875.[146] Admission to the South Carolina bar was not without obstacles. Each applicant was required to be examined as a condition of admission. Elliott, Whipper, and Wright successfully passed a bar examination administered by Senator Charles W. Montgomery and South Carolina attorney general Daniel H. Chamberlain.[147] It is not known whether Macon B. Allen, previously admitted to the bar in Massachusetts, was required to take the South Carolina bar examination.

The nucleus of political and legal activities in South Carolina during the Reconstruction era was America's first black law firm: Whipper, Elliott, and Allen.[148] During Elliott's sixteen-year legal career, he formed four law firms, three in South Carolina and one in New Orleans, Louisiana. Elliott's second firm was formed in Columbia, South Carolina, with James D. Treadwell in 1874. Treadwell was the white former mayor of Columbia. The third firm was formed in Orangeburg, South Carolina, in 1875, with David Augustus Straker and T. McCants Stewart. This firm flourished until 1877, the year that marked the end of the Reconstruction era.[149] There is little doubt that Elliott's political connections and those of his associates generated business for the firm and won the respect of black and white citizens in South Carolina.

Elliott studied for the bar examination while serving as a member of the South Carolina legislature. Elliott was elected to the South Carolina constitutional convention in 1867 and to the legislature in 1868, from Barnell County, thus serving in the first elected legislature under the newly drafted Reconstruction Constitution.[150] It was during the constitutional convention that Elliott established himself "as a confident, articulate, and stubborn spokesman for his race," a characterization that would mark his unusual career.[151] In fact, as a member of the Committee on the Bill of Rights, Elliott played a direct role in the drafting of the constitution. During the committee debates, Elliott supported provisions for compulsory education for black and white children. However, he strongly opposed the imposition of an educational tax to support public education, as well as the literacy clause as a qualification to vote. He proposed, but failed to win, adoption of a provision for equal public accommodations.[152]

Elliott held important legislative assignments in the state legislature. He served on the Committee on Railroads, the Committee on Privileges and Elections (a committee that audited the accounts of the legislature), and on a special committee that investigated the activities of the Ku Klux Klan.[153]

After Elliott was admitted to the South Carolina bar, he was frequently appointed by the court to defend blacks charged with crimes. One of his first cases involved a black man charged with murder. The case was tried by Elliott and his law partner William J. Whipper in a Baptist Church at Blackville, South Carolina, in August 1869. Their client was acquitted. This and other cases won the public's respect for Elliott and the members of his law firm, especially for Elliott's "powerful eloquence [and ability to] carry juries."[154] The press grudgingly "admitted that the easy politeness and general bearing of these 'gentlemen' of color (during the murder trial at Blackville) has impressed the community with no feelings other than those of good will and, we may say, respect."[155]

As Elliott's political influence grew,[156] so did his political aspirations. He sought the Republican nomination for Congress as the representative of the Third Congressional District. Elliott won the endorsement and support of Governor Robert K. Scott, who saw to it that Elliott's political effort was funded (some say by the use of public moneys). On July 30, 1870, Elliott was nominated as the Third District's candidate for Congress, and he later defeated his Democratic opponent. At the age of twenty-nine he was sworn in as South Carolina's first black congressman on March 4, 1871.[157]

Ten days after Elliott was sworn in as a member of Congress, he addressed the House. He later described the event in these words:

I shall never forget that day, when rising in my place to address the House, I found myself the center of attraction. Everything was still. Those who believed in the natural inferiority of the colored race appeared to feel that the hour had arrived in which they should exult in triumph over the failure of the first man of "the despised race" whose voice was about to be lifted in that chamber. The countenances of those who sympathized with our cause seemed to indicate their anxiety for my success, and their heartfelt desire that I might prove equal to the emergency. I cannot, fellow citizens, picture to you the emotions that then filled my mind.[158]

During his two terms in Congress, Elliott opposed amnesty legislation which would have removed the political restrictions on Southerners who had rebelled against the Union during the Civil War, and he supported the passage of the Ku Klux Klan Bill (the Enforcement Act), which proposed to make certain conduct by private citizens a federal crime.[159]

Elliott's legal training was quite helpful during the floor debates on the Civil Rights Act of 1875, debates which occurred two years after the *Slaughter-House Cases*.[160] In 1873, the United States Supreme Court had struck down a Louisiana statute granting a monopoly to one company operating a slaughterhouse business in New Orleans. Persons engaged in competing businesses objected to the exclusive legislative grant, but failed to prove in their legal claims that the monopoly assigned them to a state of slavery and denied them rights guaranteed under the Fourteenth Amendment. For Elliott, the Court's decision in the *Slaughter-House Cases* could not have come at a worse time, just as the House of Representatives was considering a new civil rights bill that would guarantee equal public accommodations to all citizens. The court's opinion cast doubt on the power of Congress to pass such legislation, leaving the matter of civil rights protection in the domain of the states.

Among black congressmen the responsibility for the legal argument favoring the pending civil rights bill fell to Elliott. In this connection, Elliott was assigned the formidable task of responding to the speech of

Georgia congressman Alexander H. Stephens, who, relying on the *Slaughter-House Cases* decision, argued against the constitutionality of the civil rights bill. Stephens was the former vice-president of the Confederacy. Elliott's speech was perhaps the most important one of his congressional career, demonstrating his passion for the virtue of equality:

> To arrest its growth and save the nation we have passed through the harrowing operation of internecine war resorted to at the last extremity . . . to extirpate the disease which threatened the life of the nation with the overturn of civil and political liberty on this continent. . . . The results of the war, as seen in reconstruction, have settled forever the political status of my race. The passage of this bill will determine the civil status, not only of the Negro but of any other class of citizens who may feel themselves discriminated against. It will form the capstone of that temple of liberty begun on this continent under discouraging circumstances, carried on in spite of the sneers of monarchists and the cavils of pretended friends of freedom, until at last it stands in all its beautiful symmetry and proportions, a building the grandest which the world has ever seen, realizing the most sanguine expectations and the highest hopes of those who in the name of equal, impartial and universal liberty, laid the foundation stone.[161]

The speech was widely published in the North and by the *Columbia Daily Union Herald* in South Carolina, but it was barely mentioned in the influential *Charleston News and Courier*.[162]

Elliott's appetite for politics grew during his second term in Congress. He decided to seek his party's support for the United States Senate. Elliott received an unexpected endorsement from the *Columbia South Carolinian*, a Democratic newspaper. This support was prompted by the charges of corruption that had been lodged against Governor Robert K. Scott, who also sought the Senate seat. Despite evidence of public wrongdoing by the governor, the Charleston press opposed Elliott: in Charleston, Elliot's race was the issue, not his qualifications. The *Charleston Daily News* reported that "if the matter were left to us, Elliott is not the man who we would want to send to the United States Senate. . . . He is not the candidate of the white people."[163] The South Carolina General Assembly ultimately elected John J. Patterson to the Senate.[164]

With his hopes for higher public office dashed, and faced with rampant political corruption in South Carolina, Elliott resigned from Congress in 1874 and returned to Aiken, South Carolina, to run for the state legislature. He hoped to be elected speaker of the house in the General Assembly and, eventually, governor. This political plan had apparently been formulated by Daniel H. Chamberlain, who was planning to challenge the incumbent governor, Franklin J. Moses, Jr.[165] Elliott was elected to the state legislature and won the position of speaker of the house, becoming the second black lawyer to win this post in South Carolina.[166]

Curiously, during the early months of 1874, Robert B. Elliott was one of two lawyers retained by Governor Moses to represent him on charges of misappropriation of state funds. On May 28, 1874, the Superior Court in Orangeburg held a hearing on the indictment, during which Elliott and none other than Daniel H. Chamberlain sought to have the trial moved to another location, alleging local prejudice against Governor Moses. Their argument was rejected by the court after Governor Moses refused to appear in court. Elliott, a seasoned legal technician, objected to the indictment, which in his view violated the state's constitution. Before the governor could be indicted, Elliott argued, he had to be impeached. The court reluctantly adopted this position, thereby freeing Governor Moses from further criminal liability.[167] But with Governor Moses publicly embarrassed, Daniel H. Chamberlain was elected governor.

It was rumored that Elliott, as speaker of the house, would succeed Chamberlain as governor, but that was not to be. Elliott's aspirations for the governorship were dashed when he broke with Governor Chamberlain's choice for a Charleston judicial slot, supporting instead his former law partner, William J. Whipper, who ultimately was elected.[168] Nevertheless, Elliott's political power remained strong enough in 1876 to garner him the post of attorney general of South Carolina, in an election that, like Governor Chamberlain's re-election, was challenged by the Democrats.[169]

The contest of the election reached the South Carolina Supreme Court with Elliott, who claimed to be attorney general, representing the State Board of Canvassers. Pending the outcome of these challenges, Elliott acted in all respects as attorney general. Elliott's fate was marked by the Hayes-Tilden Compromise of 1877, which antedated the South Carolina Supreme Court decision on the validity of the 1876 elections, popularly referred to as the "Political Cases."[170] President Hayes's withdrawal of federal troops from South Carolina and the voluntary concession of the Chamberlain's election to the Democrats literally doomed Elliott's chances for victory in the South Carolina Supreme Court, though Jonathan Jasper Wright, the black justice on the state supreme court, might have supported him.[171] Elliott withdrew his claim to the office of attorney general, having served a year in that position.[172]

By 1879 Elliott was in dire financial condition. The Republicans were out of office and the black community was facing renewed racial hostility and disfranchisement. Nevertheless, through the intercession of a friend, Elliott was hired by the United States Treasury Office as a special inspector of customs in Charleston. With politics boiling in his blood, Elliott quietly began canvassing in North Carolina for Secretary of the Treasury John Sherman, who was interested in running for president. Elliott surfaced again as a delegate to the 1880 Republican National Convention in Chicago, where he worked to win black support as Sherman's floor manager. Although Sherman's friend, James A. Garfield, won the nomination, Elliott won a promotion to special agent in the customs office and an increase in salary.[173]

In 1881, still struggling to win political rights for the black majority in South Carolina, Elliott led a delegation of black Republicans to Ohio to visit president-elect James A. Garfield. As spokesman for the group, Elliott sought assurances from Garfield that he would protect the civil rights of blacks during his administration.[174]

Later in the year, Elliott was transferred from Charleston to the New Orleans Federal Customs office, where he opened his fourth law firm with Thomas de Saille Tucker, who had recently passed the bar. The firm flourished, with Elliott and Tucker doing criminal work in the local police court. The firm also opened an office in nearby Pensacola, Florida, that was headed by Tucker. The firm continued to do well until Elliott's death in 1884.[175]

Other contemporaries of Robert Brown Elliott made significant contributions to the legal profession in South Carolina. William J. Whipper, also a member of the constitutional convention in 1868, served on the Committee of the Legislative Part of the Constitution.[176] Whipper appears to have handled most of the legal work in the law firm while his partner, Robert Brown Elliott, engaged in politics.[177] Whipper criticized the corrupt leadership of South Carolina, even when his charges involved the Republican Party, of which he was a member. In 1871, Whipper was one of the leaders who called for the impeachment of Governor Robert K. Scott, who had aided Robert Brown Elliott's campaign to be elected to Congress. Whipper, in public disagreement with his law partner, believed that Governor Scott was guilty of misappropriating state funds.[178]

Whipper's technical skills and his friendship with Elliott no doubt prompted the South Carolina legislature to elect him to a vacancy on the circuit court in Charleston in 1874.[179] However, Whipper's election, managed by Speaker of the House Elliott, occurred while Governor Chamberlain was out of the state. When Governor Chamberlain returned to the state he was furious with Elliott over Whipper's election. Chamberlain wanted to reappoint a conservative Charleston lawyer, J. P. Reed, to the post. Indeed, Whipper was no favorite of at least sixteen blacks in the legislature, all of whom voted against him.[180]

Set in his plan to have a say in the Charleston judicial vacancy,

Governor Chamberlain refused "to sign [Whipper's commission, ostensibly] because the terms of the incumbent judges would not expire until after the next legislature had been elected, [and Chamberlain argued] that the next legislature rather than the existing one should choose the new judges."[181] Whipper filed suit to have Reed vacate the office to which Whipper had been elected, but this matter was eventually decided in Reed's favor by the South Carolina Supreme Court in June 1877.[182]

After the Reconstruction era ended, Whipper remained in South Carolina, locating his practice in Beaufort, a town with a sizeable black population. Whipper established a fair practice and was soon appointed probate judge in Beaufort County, which was controlled by black Republicans. He held this post for ten years.[183]

In 1895, Whipper, still a devoted Republican, was elected delegate to the South Carolina constitutional convention. During these sessions, he proposed that the state constitution assure the right of every citizen to vote and to be able to apply to the court if this right was denied. Whipper's proposal was defeated by a vote of 130 to 6. Efforts by Isaiah R. Reed, another black lawyer, to have similar legislation adopted also failed.[184] Whipper continued to practice in Beaufort, South Carolina, through the early part of the twentieth century. He was admitted to practice before the United States Supreme Court in February 1903, the same month in which he argued before the court against the racial exclusion of blacks from juries.[185]

Macon Bolling Allen arrived in South Carolina in the late 1860s from Boston, Massachusetts, and joined Robert B. Elliott and William J. Whipper in the practice of law. Allen was the first black lawyer in the nation, having been admitted to the bar in Maine in 1844. It is reported that Allen "possessed exceptional qualifications," and he was elected as a criminal court judge in Charleston from 1874 to 1875, filling a vacancy left by the death of George Lee, another black lawyer.[186]

Lee had been admitted to the bar in 1870 and earlier had competed against Allen for the judgeship, winning the endorsement of the state legislature where he had served with distinction in 1868.[187] The subsequent election of Allen to Charleston's probate court prompted the *Charleston Courier*, a white newspaper, to suggest that the state legislature eliminate the court. Still, Allen served as a judge in the Charleston probate court from 1876 to 1878.[188] Like his former law partner, Robert Brown Elliott, with whom he practiced for a short period, Allen was nominated as secretary of state of South Carolina by the Reformed Republicans, a splinter group, but he was not elected.[189]

Jonathan Jasper Wright settled permanently in South Carolina after becoming the first black lawyer admitted to practice law in his native state of Pennsylvania. In 1866, Wright opened a law practice in Beaufort, South Carolina. He was soon appointed legal counsel to the Freedman's Bureau by General O. O. Howard. In 1867, Wright was elected as a member of the South Carolina constitutional convention, serving on the important Judiciary Committee.[190] While a member of this committee, Wright made it clear that black lawyers were well-qualified to serve as judges in the state of South Carolina, although there were only a few black lawyers with experience in the state.

Wright did not let inexperience deter him from his objective: the assurance of black representation in the judiciary of South Carolina. To achieve his goal of a diverse judiciary, Wright relied on the "experience [of] liberal men, who are now ready to get upon the reconstruction train [to] advocate the cause of humanity and justice."[191] Wright was likely the first American to call on the Republican Party to place the name of "one of his own race on the next Presidential ticket of the Republican Party."[192] In fact, Wright was successful in having a resolution to this effect passed when the Republican Party was formed in South Carolina in 1867.[193]

Following the constitutional convention, Wright was elected to the state senate from Beaufort, South Carolina. He was highly regarded by his colleagues in the senate, and a statement by the *Charleston Daily News* which described him as a "very intelligent, well-spoken colored lawyer," also boosted his public image.[194] Wright served with distinction in the senate until 1869, when that body elected him to fill an unexpired term on the South Carolina Supreme Court.[195] The following year the legislature elected Wright to a six-year term on the South Carolina Supreme Court, making him the first black lawyer in the nation to serve on the highest court of a state. Naturally, his election to the South Carolina Supreme Court was widely reported.[196] There was opposition to his selection from the press and from Franklin J. Moses, Jr., the son of the chief justice of the Supreme Court of South Carolina, who had supported William J. Whipper for the post. The press was critical of the prospects of any black lawyer serving on the South Carolina Supreme Court, but Whipper was relatively more in favor because of his close ties to the influential Robert Brown Elliott. Still, Wright prevailed, because he was considered better-qualified than Whipper and because his supporters promised to support the opposition's candidate to a vacancy on a lower court. Justice Wright assumed his seat on the South Carolina Supreme Court on December 9, 1870.[197]

The judicial opinions of Justice Wright indicate that he was an active member of the court. During his seven years on the bench, the court issued 361 decisions. Of that number, Justice Wright authored the majority opinion in seventy-six cases, concurred in four, and issued no dissenting opinions.[198]

Justice Wright served on the court with great distinction during periods of corruption in the state government. However, by 1876, with Republican carpetbaggers being run out of the state, efforts by white supremicists were made to reduce the influence of blacks and black office-holders. Justice Wright himself became a target of political attacks. Franklin J. Moses, Jr., the Republican turncoat who had originally opposed Wright's election to the South Carolina Supreme Court, initiated charges against him for allegedly accepting a bribe. During a hearing conducted by the legislature, Moses "testified that [Governor Daniel H.] Chamberlain had once given him money with which to bribe [Justice] Wright . . . in April, 1874, when Moses was governor and Chamberlain [was] a lawyer in private practice."[199] Moses testified that he "took $2,500 from Chamberlain and gave it to Judge Wright, who then swung the court in favor of Chamberlain's client."[200]

The allegation against Justice Wright appears to be groundless, since he did not participate in the initial decision in *Whaley v. Bank of Charleston*,[201] the so-called bribe case.[202] Justice Wright's participation in this case was limited to hearing the petition for a rehearing. He concurred with Chief Justice Moses and denied the bank's motion, a decision reasonably supported by law.[203] Other accounts claim that Justice Wright was being forced to step down from the bench because he was a drunkard.[204]

After Justice Wright's term expired, he continued to claim his innocence of all allegations of misconduct and requested that the legislature "try him" so that he would have "an opportunity to clear his name." However, "the investigating committee merely concluded that Governor Chamberlain [who himself was being run out of South Carolina] was guilty whether Wright was or not."[205]

In 1871, Samuel J. Lee, who had served as a circuit solicitor in Alabama, moved to Charleston, South Carolina. Lee became an able criminal lawyer and a skilled politician. He was unanimously elected in 1872 as speaker of the house in the legislature, becoming at "about thirty years of age" the first black to hold this post.[206] The legislature then elected Lee in 1874, as probate judge in Charleston, in the same year that Democratic forces attempted to oust Republican and black officeholders from power.[207]

During this period, Judge Lee's life was threatened by a mob of Democrats. The *New York Globe* reported, "As bloodshed was imminent, the Probate Judge Hon. Samuel Lee closed his office and went to his home to protect his wife and children. . . . The democrats planted revolvers and shotguns around the door of the probate office and swore vengeance against the judge."[208] Subsequently, trumped-up charges of misconduct brought against Judge Lee were dropped after Robert Brown Elliott entered his case.[209]

Like other black lawyers, David Augustus Straker traveled to South Carolina after his graduation from Howard University's law school in 1872. Straker worked three years for the Treasury Department as a first class clerk and subsequently as a customs inspector at Charleston, South Carolina, before resigning to join the law firm headed by Robert B. Elliott in 1875.[210] Straker gained a reputation as an aggressive and successful criminal defense attorney. This recognition gave the British West Indies-born Straker a platform from which to pursue public office. He was elected to the South Carolina General Assembly in 1876, 1878, and 1880, but on each occasion he was denied his seat by white Democrats on the grounds that he was not a United States citizen.[211]

Reporting on the treatment of black lawyers during Reconstruction in South Carolina, Straker said that the black lawyer was "looked upon in the community . . . as the lawyer for the colored people, and his practice is by arbitrary custom circumscribed to those of his own race."[212] As to the respect accorded to black lawyers by whites, Straker said that "they shun him . . . as one not expected to do their business."[213]

By 1880, Straker's practice was on the rocks, but Robert B. Elliott, his former senior partner, helped to secure a job for him as a customs inspector in Charleston.[214] Straker did not entirely give up his law practice. He continued to develop his practice and became a pioneer in the use of medical expert testimony in criminal defense work before the South Carolina courts.[215] After a short term as dean of the law department of Allen University in Columbia, South Carolina, Straker moved to Detroit, Michigan, to practice law.

John F. Quarles, Straker's classmate at Howard University's law school, followed Eugene R. Belcher, another Howard classmate, to Hamburg, South Carolina, where they opened a law office in 1872.[216] The partnership lasted only for a year, for in 1873 Quarles was appointed by President Ulysses Grant to the United States consulate in Port Mahon, Spain, a position which he held for four years. When Rutherford B. Hayes was elected president, Quarles was appointed to the consulate at Malaga, Spain. He remained at Malaga until 1880, whereupon he returned to the United States to establish a law practice in New York.[217]

Other black lawyers, such as Richard H. Gleaves, F. D. Lawrence, Julius Irwin Washington, and William Trent Andrews, made significant contributions to the law in South Carolina. Gleaves was appointed probate court judge in Charleston in 1870, elected lieutenant governor in 1872 and 1874, and appointed trial justice for Beaufort in 1877.[218] Lawrence became a moderately successful lawyer in Beaufort.[219] Washington, who studied law under William J. Whipper, served in the South Carolina legislature from 1886 to 1887, and from 1888 to 1889,[220] and Andrews, an 1892 Howard University graduate, established a lucrative real estate practice in Sumter in 1894.[221]

Another black lawyer, Isaiah Reed, was elected as a delegate to the 1895 South Carolina constitutional convention. During the convention, Reed introduced a proposal that authorized the governor "to remove and replace any official who allowed personal harm to come to a prisoner in his custody and provided that the militia be called out in the case of a threatened lynching."[222] Reed's proposal was defeated, but it spurred another proposal, "which provided for the removal of sheriffs who were guilty of negligence, permission or connivance in giving up prisoners, and provided punitive damages of [$2,000] to the families of each person lynched."[223]

The integration of the University of South Carolina in 1873 played a direct role in the education of black lawyers in South Carolina. In 1873, the school's board of trustees voted to accept blacks in the university. This action was taken largely because of the efforts of Daniel H. Chamberlain, who was a member of the board of trustees, and Samuel J. Lee, the board president. The move to integrate the University of South Carolina was resisted by students and faculty. Many students withdrew from the University and many faculty members resigned. However, Chamberlain believed that the university was "the common property of all our citizens without distinction of race."[224] Chamberlain's action also attracted black voters to his camp as he eyed the governorship. The refusal by some white students to attend classes with blacks made the university "predominantly black" until 1877, when federal troops were withdrawn from South Carolina.[225]

The University of South Carolina graduated several blacks from its law school in the five-year period during which blacks were admitted to the university.[226] While many of the names of the law graduates are lost to history, a few names have been preserved because of the significant contributions these graduates made to the legal profession.[227]

Thomas Ezekiel Miller entered the University of South Carolina Law School in 1873, one year before he was elected to the state legislature from Beaufort. Miller also received private instruction, perhaps while attending law school, from P. L. Wiggins, state solicitor, and Franklin J. Moses, Sr., chief justice of the South Carolina Supreme Court.[228] Miller graduated from the law school in 1876, while serving as a member of the state legislature. Curiously, Miller was "a member of the committee on credentials that secured a quorum for the [T. J. Mackey faction] in which the electoral votes for [Rutherford B.] Hayes as president were canvassed and declared" in 1877.[229] Miller may not have anticipated that President Hayes would end the Reconstruction that had helped blacks gain political power.

In 1880 Miller was elected to the state senate, where he introduced legislation to allow blacks to teach in the public schools of South Carolina. In one instance, Miller introduced a bill to permit black women to teach in the public schools in Charleston. Miller's efforts met with much opposition. White women teachers apparently feared that they would be replaced by black teachers. Opponents of the measure "raised the hue and cry 'don't legislate white women out of their positions for that Negro, Tom Miller,'"[230] and Miller's efforts failed. Although he was given assurances that "positions would be given to the Negroes,"[231] these promises were not fulfilled for thirty years.

In 1888 Miller was elected to the United States Congress from the seventh congressional district of South Carolina. Miller's Democratic opponent challenged his election, however, thus delaying his being seated in the fifty-first Congress until days before the first session was to adjourn. Prior to adjournment, Miller introduced legislation "to appropriate $1,000,000 for a home for ex-slaves [and] to spend $250,000 for a monument to the Negro soldiers killed in the war."[232] Neither of these measures passed. During the second session of the fifty-first Congress, Miller "distinguished himself in the House by his bitter tirade against the South in general, and South Carolina in particular."[233] In one speech, he said,

There is no people in the world more self-opinionated without cause, more bigoted without achievement, more boastful without a status, no people in the world so quick to misjudge their countrymen and to misstate historical facts of political economy and to impugn the motives of others. History does not record a civilized people who have been contented with so little and who can feed so long on a worthless, buried past. While crying for mercy and attempting to speak as ambassadors of peace, there are no people in the world more vituperative than her leaders.[234]

Such statements won Miller few white friends, yet he was again the Republican nominee for Congress in the 1890 election. This time, however, he was opposed by a white Republican in his own party. The Democratic candidate was elected.[235]

Soon after Miller's defeat for a second term in Congress, he was again reelected to the state legislature. He served in the South Carolina constitutional convention in 1895 and fought against the establishment of a literacy provision as a qualification to vote, a provision that clearly was aimed at the disfranchisement of blacks.

In 1895 Miller sought to persuade his colleagues to charter a second black college that would be located in Orangeburg. Miller obtained the support of the newly elected United States senator, Benjamin R. Tillman, who had the deserved reputation of being anti-black. Senator Tillman's unexpected support for Miller's proposal probably resulted from the legislative assistance Miller had provided to the agricultural and mechanical college that had been transferred from the University of South Carolina to Clemson University, a school Tillman had created while governor. Tillman's support of Miller's proposal, in turn, created conservative support for the black college.

The white faculty at the existing black Claflin University, which was also located in Orangeburg, posed another obstacle to Miller's project. The faculty at Claflin feared that a second black college would eventually produce black teachers who would replace them. Miller prevailed, however, and South Carolina State College in Orangeburg was chartered and placed in the hands of black teachers, under the administration of a black president, Thomas Ezekiel Miller.[236]

Richard Theodore Greener, Harvard University's first black graduate (1870), was graduated from the University of South Carolina's law school in 1876. That same year, Greener was admitted to the bar in South Carolina. He was also admitted in the District of Columbia in 1877. Greener was appointed professor of the Howard University School of Law in 1878; he became dean in 1879 and served in that capacity until 1880.[237] During part of his deanship at Howard University, Greener held the position of clerk to the first comptroller of the United States Treasury from 1880 to 1882. In 1880, Dean Greener served as co-defense counsel in the celebrated courtmartial of Whittley Whitaker, a black cadet at the United States Military Academy at West Point. Whitaker was charged with self-mutilation, although he claimed his injuries resulted from an attack by white cadets. Greener and his co-counsel, former South Carolina governor Daniel H. Chamberlain, argued that Whitaker was the victim of a racist attack and that he should not be discharged from the academy. The case received the attention of the national press, and Congress debated the issue. Whitaker was ultimately vindicated, but he never graduated from West Point.[238] Since Whitaker's courtmartial had been demanded by Greener as a way of proving his client's innocence, the trial established the precedent that a person admitted to the military academy was also a member and officer of the army and, as such, was entitled to due process of law.[239]

Greener's reputation as a "well-known colored lawyer"[240] continued to grow. In 1883, the *New York Evening Post* sought and published Greener's views when the United States Supreme Court struck down the Civil Rights Act of 1875.[241] The Civil Rights Act prohibited persons from violating the rights of others to the "full and equal enjoyment of the accommodations of inns and public conveyances . . . merely upon the race or color of the latter."[242] Greener called the court's decision "the most startling decision . . . since [Dred Scott]."[243]

In the early days of the administration of President William McKinley, Booker T. Washington used his influence to have Greener appointed as United States consul to Bombay, India. Greener later became consul of the United States at Vladivostok, East Siberia, on May 25, 1898, thereby becoming the first black American to represent the interest of his government in Russia. Further,

in [1900] the Chinese government conferred on him the Order of the Double Dragon, for services rendered Chinese merchants and for aid in succoring the Shansi famine suffers. He remained at his Vladivostok post during the Russo-Japanese War, representing officially the British and Japanese and lent what protection he could to those who had chosen to remain in Vladivostok.[244]

On December 11, 1898, *Dalnii Vostok*, a Vladivostok newspaper, reported that on "the previous day the American flag was raised for the first time on Siberian soil at the house of the new American commercial agent, Mr. [Richard T.] Greener."[245] On July 21, 1898, Greener was reclassified by the Department of State at the rank of commercial agent to Russia, and he held that position until he retired from the foreign service in 1905. While in Russia, he represented Americans criminally charged with seal poaching.[246] In 1907, Greener was admitted to practice before the United States Supreme Court, thereafter dedicating himself mostly to literary endeavors.

Thomas McCants Stewart was graduated from the University of South Carolina's law school, receiving both his A.B. and LL.B. degrees in 1875. After he was admitted to the bar in South Carolina, Stewart joined the law firm of Robert Brown Elliott. Elliott took Stewart under his direct supervision and guided him through his first murder case. Of Stewart's representation in criminal matters, *The Clarion* reported "we must admit that Mr. Stewart displayed signal ability in the management of several cases. His respectful manner and modesty have made a favorable impression among the people."[247] In 1877, Stewart left South Carolina, attended Princeton's theology school, became an ordained minister, and pastored the Bethel African Methodist Episcopal Church in New York. From the pulpit, he built a national reputation. He advocated that blacks either pursue an independent political course or support the Democratic Party, both unpopular stands among the black Republican majority in the nation.[248] After a stint teaching history and literature at Liberia College in Africa, Stewart resumed the practice of law in Brooklyn, New York.

Joseph W. Morris entered the University of South Carolina's law school in 1875. His education was supported financially and substantively by Franklin J. Moses, Sr., chief justice of the South Carolina Supreme Court. Morris graduated from the law school in 1876 and admitted to the bar "after passing a most critical and searching examination."[249] After a short time in private practice, Morris abandoned the law "to accept the principalship of Payne Institute" in Alabama.[250] In 1895, he became the third president of Allen University in Columbia, South Carolina.[251]

Other graduates of the University of South Carolina's law school between 1875 and 1877 included J. W. Meyers, who later became a state senator from Collenton County, South Carolina; John Freeman, who entered the practice of law in Charleston; A. Stewart, who settled in Oklahoma and acquired a fortune before he died; and Joseph H. Stuart, who settled in Denver, Colorado, and was elected to the state legislature in 1895.[252]

As the Reconstruction era in South Carolina ended, the prospects for law as a profession for blacks faded for nearly a quarter of a century. In 1900, black males were being convicted of crimes in South Carolina courts 79.6 percent of the time, as opposed to a 59.7 percent rate for white male convictions for comparable crimes. The overall ratio of blacks being tried on criminal matters exceeded whites by "more than 3 to 1 and the ratio of convictions by 4.3 to 1."[253]

By the turn of the century, only a few black lawyers can be identified, though more may have been admitted to the bar. One prominent lawyer was W. T. Andrews, who practiced in Sumter, South Carolina. In 1907 Andrews traveled to Portland, Oregon, to represent a client in a probate case. The case was widely publicized in Portland because the dead man's estate, in which Andrews's client had an interest, was being claimed by his white girlfriend, who was represented by McCants Stewart, the son of Thomas McCants Stewart.[254]

Jacob Moorer and John Adams, Sr., were admitted to the bar in the early part of 1900 and formed a partnership in Orangeburg, South Carolina. These two young black lawyers risked their lives to represent a black man accused of murdering a white man. The victim identified the defendant as his assailant as he lay dying. At the trial, Moorer and Adams sought unsuccessfully to bar the admission of this dying declaration, and they contested the exclusion of blacks from the grand jury as being in violation of the United States Constitution, but their client was convicted. Moorer and Adams appealed this decision before the Supreme Court of South Carolina and the United States Supreme Court, but to no avail: both courts upheld the conviction.[255]

The appearance of Jacob Moorer and John Adams, Sr., before the

United States Supreme Court in 1910 is likely the second time black lawyers from South Carolina appeared before the court. Moorer practiced in Orangeburg for another twenty-five years.[256] Adams, who had attended Yale Divinity School prior to his admission to the bar, moved to Spokane, Washington, and later to Pueblo, Colorado, and Omaha, Nebraska. In Omaha, Adams made his living preaching in the African Methodist Episcopal Church while continuing to practice law.[257]

Nathaniel Jerome Frederick was admitted to the South Carolina bar in 1913. He practiced in Columbia and was for several years state counsel for the Knights of Pythias in South Carolina. He "rendered splendid and self-sacrificing" service to his people as a lawyer. Frederick was involved in one major case that caught the attention of the national black press. It involved a black man who had been convicted of raping a white woman in 1915. In 1928 the white woman admitted she had lied about the rape. During this thirteen-year period, the black man had been incarcerated. Frederick sought and obtained a pardon from the governor, and his client was released from prison. Thereafter, under the threat of a perjury charge, the white woman recanted her story and Frederick's client was again imprisoned. Frederick reportedly appealed the case to the South Carolina Supreme Court, arguing that once a pardon is granted by the governor, it cannot be revoked, a position with which the court agreed.[258]

Harold Richard Boulware, a 1938 graduate of Howard University law school, was admitted to the South Carolina bar in 1940. Boulware was a member of the aggressive new breed of lawyers who aligned themselves with the NAACP in most civil rights cases.[259] In 1941, Boulware became the first black lawyer to argue a case involving a *writ of habeas corpus* before the Fourth Circuit Court of Appeals. The case involved the conviction of two black defendants whose lawyer had been paid $550 but who failed to appear at their trial. The judge proceeded to try the case. The jury found the defendants guilty after only seven minutes of deliberations. Boulware's efforts began after the South Carolina Supreme Court had affirmed the convictions of the defendants. Boulware sought the advice and assistance of Leon Andrew Ransom, his former law teacher at Howard University, who filed a petition for *certiorari* in the United States Supreme Court; this petition was denied.[260]

The first black woman was examined for admission to the South Carolina bar in 1921. The *Atlanta Georgian* reported that a "Negress . . . S. E. Benjamin of Columbia, South Carolina," was one of nineteen candidates to take the bar.[261] It is possible that Benjamin did not pass the examination. Twenty years later the *Pittsburgh Courier* and other newspaper reported that for the first time in the history of the state of

South Carolina, a black woman, Cassandra E. Maxwell, had passed the examination for admission to the bar.[262] Maxwell, a 1938 graduate of Howard University law school, was joined at the swearing-in ceremony by Walter Frederick Robinson, a 1939 Howard University law graduate. It was noted that "little comment was made because of her presence and the customary procedure was followed without deviation."[263]

Virginia

A month after being graduated from Howard University's law school and his admission to the bar of the District of Columbia, Wathal G. Wynn was admitted to the Hustings Circuit Court of Richmond on March 9, 1871. Wynn was admitted to the bar on the motion of Judge Alfred Mortan, becoming Virginia's first black lawyer. Wynn, however, remained in Virginia for only six months and then moved to Arkansas. He practiced in Arkansas for only a short time before he was murdered by whites.[264] (Wynn's murder is discussed further in Chapter 6.)

Other blacks followed Wynn to the Virginia bar. William N. Stevens commenced the practice of law in Suffolk, Virginia, in 1871, becoming the first member of his race to practice there. He subsequently represented Sussex and Greensville counties in the Virginia State Senate. He was described as one of the ablest and scholarly men in that chamber.[265] In 1873, Robert D. Ruffin was elected sheriff of Alexandria, Virginia,[266] and William C. Roane, an 1875 Howard University law graduate, was admitted to the circuit court of Richmond on June 3, 1876,[267] as was Henry B. Fry, an 1875 law graduate of Howard.[268]

A few law students from Virginia received financial support, albeit modest, from their parents. Robert Peel Brooks, an 1875 graduate of Howard University's law school, was one such student. It is reported that from childhood through law school Brooks's father, who had purchased his son's freedom, had financially supported his son's education.[269] After receiving his law degree, Brooks practiced for a short time in the District of Columbia before settling in Richmond, where he hung out his shingle in 1876, "and soon found himself overcrowded with work."[270]

From time to time, William C. Roane served as commonwealth attorney, a role that often found him prosecuting black criminals who were represented by black lawyers. In 1879 Roane, for the Commonwealth of Virginia, and Robert Peel Brooks, for the defense, squared off in the local court of Richmond. It was said to be a "sign of progress that in the capital of the Old Dominion a prisoner can be prosecuted and defended by colored lawyers."[271]

After Edwin Archer Randolph completed his studies at Yale University's law school in 1880, he returned to Richmond and established a law practice. Within a year Randolph was elected to the common council in Richmond, a post that he held from 1881 to 1883. He then served on the board of aldermen from 1883 to 1886 and on Virginia's commission for the World's Exposition in New Orleans from 1884 to 1885. Randolph maintained his practice for years and also founded a black newspaper, *The Richmond Planet*.[272]

James Apostler Fields, an 1882 graduate of Howard University's law school, became a very successful lawyer and property owner in Virginia. The year Fields entered law school he was completing a term in the Virginia House of Delegates.[273] He also served as a justice of the peace, thereby becoming Virginia's first black judicial officer.[274] Fields soon opened his office to other blacks, allowing them to study law under his tutelage for three nights a week, except in July and August. Drawing on his formal legal training at Howard University, Fields taught his students the practice and theory of law. They all passed the bar examination on their first attempts.[275]

In 1887, Fields served as commonwealth attorney for Newport News and Warwick counties. He continued at these posts until 1889, when he was again elected to the Virginia General Assembly. Fields and John H. Robinson, another black lawyer, were the last two blacks to serve in the Virginia General Assembly for many years to come.[276]

In the late 1870s, William Micaijah Reid and Booker T. Washington commenced private law study in Virginia under J. A. M. Johns, "a scholarly West Indian."[277] They also "obtained the promise of [James Apostler Fields], practicing law in Hampton, to give [them] instruction and bought and paid for a copy of Robinson's *Elementary Law* and a set of *Kents Commentaries*."[278] Apparently, Booker T. Washington never completed his legal studies, choosing instead to become a great educator. He founded Tuskegee Institute in 1881. Reid became a lawyer— Portsmouth's first black lawyer—in 1885. Describing his first days as a member of the bar in Portsmouth, Reid wrote,

Business came very slowly at first, but gradually grew, the first in criminal matters, in which I attained marked success; but civil business being more suited to my disposition, I made the most of it and gradually acquired sufficient business to occupy all of my time.[279]

In 1893, Governor Philip W. McKinney appointed Reid to the state Board of Curators to oversee Hampton University.[280] The high regard for Reid among his peers was evident at the time of his death. Judge K. A. Bain, of the Court of Hustings, appointed a committee of the local bar to draft a resolution to be read on the record before the Norfolk County circuit court. The resolution read in part:

[Reid] stood at the head of his race . . . and was respected by all people, white and colored alike. . . . In the practice of his profession he observed scrupulously its ethics, and while he was diligent in the interests of his clients, he was unfailing in his courtesy towards opposing attorneys and officers of the court.[281]

Williams Micaijah Reid lived to see his son, Thomas Harris Reid, become an active practitioner in Portsmouth after he graduated from Howard University's law school in 1915. Joining his father's firm, the younger Reid became one of the first black second-generation lawyers in Virginia.[282] After Thomas H. Reid was admitted to the bar in 1917, he became a respected leader in the community and the bar. In 1925 Thomas H. Reid was one of the charter members of the Virginia Colored Bar Association.[283] In the 1930s, he initiated a successful, precedent-setting litigation that required election officials to permit blacks to vote in the Democratic primaries.[284]

Between 1881 and 1887 Alfred W. Harris, John Cornelius Asbury, James M. Ricks, Thomas Calhoun Walker, and Giles Beecher Jackson were admitted to the bar in Virginia. Harris had studied law privately in the office of George W. Mitchell, a black lawyer who practiced in Alexandria, Virginia, before he enrolled in the Howard University School of Law. Upon graduating from Howard in 1881, Harris opened a law office in Petersburg in 1882 and was elected to the Virginia legislature in 1883. Harris formed a partnership with Walter J. Scott, an 1881 graduate of Yale University's law school, and "[did] a good business."[285]

John Cornelius Asbury was graduated from Howard University's law school in 1884 and received his LL.M. there the following year. He was admitted to the Virginia bar in 1885, and two years later he became the commonwealth attorney for Norfolk County, a position he held until 1891. During his term as commonwealth attorney he tried eleven murder cases. In 1892, Asbury was elected as a delegate to the Republican National Convention at Minneapolis, Minnesota, representing the second congressional district of Virginia.[286] Asbury later left Virginia and relocated to Pennsylvania to practice law.[287]

James M. Ricks, an 1886 graduate of Howard University's law school, was successfully examined by Judge John A. Kelly and admitted to the bar in Marion, Virginia. Ricks was "the first black attorney in Southwest Virginia." After a short period in practice, he relocated his business to Washington, D.C.[288]

Thomas Calhoun Walker began his law studies in 1883 under Major Benjamin F. Bland, a Confederate soldier who lived in Gloucester County, Virginia. After doing odd jobs for Major Bland, Walker requested Bland's permission to study under his supervision. Walker studied law under Bland's tutelage for three years. In 1887, Walker

changed instructors, and began to study with General William B. Taliaferro, "another white citizen of Gloucester [who was considered] one of
the most liberal men in the South."[289] Walker had difficulty gaining
access to law books, but he reports that he "was given freedom to go to
the General's house any day and night, into his private office which was
a large library filled with legal volumes. There, he and I would read,
study and talk over my problem."[290]

After four years of study under Bland and Taliaferro, the day arrived for Walker to take the bar examination. There were forty lawyers
in the courtroom on the day Walker was to be examined by the circuit
court judges, some of whom opposed the admission of a black man to
the bar.[291] The presiding judge, recognizing that some lawyers opposed Walker's application on account of his race, announced that he
would examine Walker privately. Walker described the examination:

Well, we sat there in the jury room for three-and-a-half hours, he asking me
questions, I answering every one. I know I fumbled over one or two. . . . The
judge then went back on the bench and said: "I have examined this young man
as thoroughly as I have ever examined anyone in my life. Furthermore, I was
more critical with him than I would be with a white boy because I know you are
all going to criticize me for what I am going to say but—he passed a better
examination than anybody I have tested in forty years."[292]

Walker was admitted to practice law in Gloucester County in May 1887.

Immediately after Walker was admitted to the bar he defended a
man indicted for destroying a line stake. Walker was assisted in his first
trial by General Bland, who passed him notes but did not speak.
Walker's client was acquitted.[293] Although he had demonstrated his
considerable legal skills in Gloucester County, Walker was denied permission to represent blacks in other Virginia counties because, in the
county judges' view, "it was 'against the custom for Negro lawyers to
qualify'" for bar admission. Walker saw such restraints as "a complete
obstruction" of justice,[294] and was thus inspired to fight harder to gain
rights for himself and other blacks of Virginia. In time, Walker succeeded in being admitted to practice in other counties. His presence at
the bar evened the odds of his clients in most legal contests.[295]

A rape case involving a black man in Virginia presented Walker with
his greatest challenge, as "[such] an accusation always struck terror to
our hearts."[296] It became a general practice that when a black man was
accused of rape, other blacks in the community, fearing a lynching,
would hide the accused until Walker arrived to personally escort him to
jail. On occasion, Walker sought and obtained the armed protection of
local black men to protect himself and the accused from mob violence
on a twenty-four hour basis.[297] Walker's bravery and his demonstrated

technical skills helped to shatter the stereotypical notion that only a white lawyer could obtain justice for blacks in Virginia.

Word of Walker's reputation as a lawyer reached the White House during the administrations of presidents William McKinley and Franklin D. Roosevelt. In 1896, President McKinley appointed Walker as the Commonwealth of Virginia's first black collector of customs at Tappahannock. Under Roosevelt, Walker in 1934 was appointed advisor and consultant for Negro affairs for the Virginia Emergency Relief Administration.[298] This recognition prompted black Virginians to refer to Walker as the "black governor."[299] Among his many achievements, Walker was also elected justice of the peace in Gloucester County for four successive terms.

Walker also recognized early the importance of education to his people, noting that there was "no way out for my people except through education and property."[300] He contributed his "own limited funds for a down payment on a building that eventually became the Gloucester Training School."[301]

Thomas Calhoun Walker's success as a lawyer in Gloucester County is no doubt attributable to the uncanny way by which he was able to bridge the gap between whites and blacks, a skill that brought severe criticism from some blacks who considered him too accommodating. Nevertheless, Walker was able to maintain the respect of many blacks as he fought against legislation that discriminated against black barbers and oystermen (an important issue for local blacks) and publicly spoke out against whites who favored the deportation of blacks to Africa.[302]

In 1887 Giles Beecher Jackson was admitted to the Virginia bar, and he opened a law office in Richmond. Jackson, a former slave, came to the attention of Booker T. Washington as a result of his pioneering work writing charters for black-owned banks.[303] In 1900, when Washington formed the National Negro Business League, he endorsed Jackson as one of its vice-presidents. He also pushed Jackson to undertake "the legal fight against the Jim Crow Law in Virginia."[304] Jackson was cut from a conservative mold and opposed the more progressive efforts of James H. Hayes, another black Virginia lawyer, who had attacked the "Republicans along with the men who framed the Constitution" that disfranchised blacks.[305] Jackson, no doubt influenced by the views of Booker T. Washington, believed that the "speedy path to recognition and enfranchisement" would be secured when blacks acquired the ownership of property and were viewed as having good character.[306]

One of Jackson's greatest achievements was the formation of the Negro Development and Exhibition Company. He also promoted the Jamestown Negro Exhibition of 1907. At Jackson's urging, President

Theodore Roosevelt supported the Negro Exhibition with $100,000 in federal money. Jackson traveled throughout the nation to extol the virtues of blacks and their significant contributions to the industrial development of the nation, a subject more comprehensively covered in his book, *The Industrial History of the Negro Race in the United States.*[307]

Between 1865 and 1895, several black lawyers in Virginia held state office. This period may be considered the high-water mark of black political representation in Virginia until the present. For example, William H. Brisky was a member of the Virginia House of Delegates from 1869 to 1871 and of the Board of Supervisors from 1880 to 1882. He was justice of the peace from 1870 to 1910.[308] William W. Evans served as a member of the House of Delegates from 1887 to 1888.[309] James Apostler Fields received his first legislative exposure when he was elected doorkeeper in the House of Delegates during the 1879–1880 legislative session.[310] Ten years later, Fields was elected to that body as a representative, serving from 1889 to 1890.[311]

Alfred W. Harris served as a member of the House of Delegates from 1883 to 1888 and was a member of the city council in Petersburg, Virginia. Harris represented Dinwiddie County in the General Assembly and is remembered for introducing a measure to fund the Virginia Normal and Collegiate Institute (now Virginia State University), the black state normal school at Petersburg.[312] He was regarded as one of the most able debaters in the house.[313]

Richard G. L. Paige served as an assistant postmaster and a member of the House of Delegates from 1871 to 1875 and from 1879 to 1882. He became a lawyer in 1879. Paige represented Norfolk County in the House of Delegates. He was described as "among the principal leaders of the House and [there were] few . . . men in that House, whether democrats or republicans, who could outrank [him] in oratory or public debate."[314] He enjoyed "an extensive law practice among both races."[315]

Robert D. Ruffin served in the House of Delegates from 1887 to 1888, and William N. Stevens served four terms in the general assembly, from 1871 to 1878 and from 1881 to 1882.[316] Stevens represented the senatorial district of Sussex and Greenville counties and was an "able and scholarly" man and a "speaker of much elegance and grace."[317] William H. Ash, a native of Loudoun County, served in the House of Delegates from 1887 to 1888. He later taught school in Tennessee.[318] Another black lawyer, M. D. Wright, served as commissioner of revenue in the 1880s.[319]

John Mercer Langston was the first black citizen elected to the United States Congress from Virginia, serving in the fifty-first Congress. Langston won the admiration and respect of the citizens of the fourth congressional district, but had to combat the negative campaigning, sometimes race-based, of both his Republican opponent during the primary, General William Mahone, and his Democratic opponent during the general election, E. C. Venerable. As a former dean of Howard University's law school and past president of the Virginia Normal and Collegiate Institute, Langston was well-qualified to represent Virginia in Congress.[320]

The vote for the congressional seat was so close that no clear winner emerged, and there were claims of voter fraud. Virginia overwhelmingly had supported the election of President Grover Cleveland who, like Langston, was a Republican, so it was hard to believe that the majority of fourth congressional district voters had rejected Langston's candidacy by not voting a "straight" Republican ticket. Langston's chances of establishing his victory seemed bleak as the legal fees that white lawyers wanted to charge him to litigate the contested congressional seat were beyond his means.[321] Langston turned to three black lawyers whose efforts were instrumental in his ultimate certification as the legitimate victor of the congressional seat. James H. Hayes, of the Richmond bar, and Matt N. Lewis and Scott Wood, of the Petersburg bar, were "[a]mong the colored lawyers employed by Mr. Langston."[322] Not only did Lewis assist in Langston's case, he also offered testimony before Congress "which covered thirteen full days."[323]

The contest was considered by a congressional committee which recommended and resolved that John M. Langston had won the election.[324] The resolution was adopted by a majority vote of the House of Representatives in September 1890, nine months after the election.[325] Because of the lengthy contest to seat Congressman Langston, he served in the House until 1891; this year-long service did not give Langston sufficient time to establish a significant legislative record.[326]

Toward the end of the nineteenth century, blacks continued to be admitted to the bar in Virginia. In 1889, the *Indianapolis Freeman* reported that "four colored men" were admitted to the Virginia bar.[327] In the same year, "three colored lawyers were practicing law in Petersburg, Virginia."[328] William Calvin Chase, who later founded the provocative *Washington Bee* in Washington, D.C., was one of three blacks admitted to the Virginia bar in 1889.[329] By 1890, there were thirty-eight non-white and 1,649 white lawyers in Virginia.[330]

In 1890 George Washington Fields was graduated from Cornell University Law School, and he returned to Virginia, his native state, to practice law. Washington, who had been blind since 1878, practiced law "on the Lower Peninsula and was considered a leader of his race."[331] In one case, Fields represented Patrick Henry, a black mail carrier charged with shooting his son. Based on the testimony of Mr. Henry,

Fields was able to get the charge reduced to carrying a concealed weapon, for which his client was fined thirty-two dollars.[332] George Washington Fields is likely the first black lawyer in Virginia whose daughter followed him into the legal profession. In 1922, Inez C. Fields was graduated from Boston University School of Law, and later admitted to the Massachusetts and Virginia bars. She practiced with her father until his death in 1932,[333] and later continued to practice on her own.

The *New York Globe* reported that Charlottesville, Virginia, admitted its first black lawyer, R. C. O. Benjamin, some time prior to 1891, for in that year people came from miles around to witness the admission of Harrison H. Ferrell, the "second colored admitted [on] court day."[334] In 1899, J. Thomas Newsome, a graduate of Howard University's law school, returned to Sussex, Virginia, to be "admitted to the bar on motion of Judge R. W. Arnold, his mother's former master."[335] Newsome had previously passed a rigorous written bar examination, and he had been admitted to the bar in the District of Columbia.[336] During the next forty years, Newsome served as a respected member of the bar, handling a broad range of criminal and civil matters. In 1917, several black people were even prepared to support Newsome's candidacy for attorney general of Virginia if he decided to seek that office.[337] As counsel to the *Newport News Star*, he successfully defended the paper in a libel suit "which covered a week in trial."[338] In 1940 the seasoned Newsome was appointed without objection to the post of commissioner in chancery by Judge Herbert Smith, thereby becoming the second black lawyer in Virginia to win such recognition by the court.[339] The appointment of Newsome to the chancery post in Virginia was noted throughout the South as evidence of the "character and ability of the [black] lawyer."[340]

Newsome's progress as a lawyer in Virginia was not diminished by his civil rights advocacy. In the late 1920s, Newsome and Andrew William Ernest Bassette, Jr., also black, filed a lawsuit challenging the election laws that precluded blacks from voting in the Democratic primaries. After failing to reverse the race-based election laws on their first try, they later sought and obtained a favorable decision in the Virginia Supreme Court of Appeals. The appeals case was filed when the plaintiff, W. E. Davis, was denied the right to register because he allegedly failed the literacy test.[341]

In the last decade of the nineteenth century, William Justin Carter, James Montgomery Morris, and Winston Bell began their practice of law in Virginia. In 1892, the year Carter graduated from Howard University's law school, he was appointed assistant district attorney in Dauphin County, Virginia. Carter remained in this position for only a year; he relocated to Harrisburg, Pennsylvania, where he practiced for more than fifty years.[342] Morris, an 1894 graduate of Howard University's law school, was admitted to the Virginia bar in 1896. He practiced in Stanton, Virginia, where he served black and white clients, and was appointed as counsel for the general receiver of the corporation court of the city of Stanton in the early 1900s.[343] Bell was an 1896 Harvard University law graduate who opened law offices in both Lynchburg and Waynesboro, Virginia. Bell was a person of means, owning "about $1000 in real estate and personal property," before he entered law school. He later became president of the United Endowment Society of Virginia.[344]

At the beginning of the twentieth century, bright, new and aggressive lawyers, such as Boston University law graduates Thomas H. Hewin and Joseph R. Pollard, were admitted to the Virginia bar in Richmond. They developed respectable practices and litigated a fair number of civil rights cases in Virginia courts.[345] The public-minded Ferdinand D. Lee, an 1887 Howard University law graduate, led a national effort in 1916 to pass congressional legislation to erect a memorial in Washington, D.C., honoring the valor of black soldiers and sailors in all foreign wars and the Civil War.[346] William Roscoe Walker, a 1907 graduate of Howard University's law school, served many years as legal counsel to the Crown Savings Bank in Newport News, Virginia. In 1933, the black Elks of Virginia appointed Walker to head the civil liberties committee of Virginia to protect the rights of Virginia's black citizens.[347]

In 1922, William F. Denny, a black lawyer, moved for the admission of B. F. Harris to practice in the Supreme Court of Appeals of Virginia.[348] Harris, a second-generation lawyer from Petersburg, had passed a credible examination held at the University of Virginia and was the only one of five blacks to pass.[349] In the mid-1920s, one lawyer, Frederick M. Burrows, of Eastville, Virginia, expressed concern over the "fraud and intimidation" of blacks that occurred in Southern elections. The situation seemed calculated to reduce the number of black elected officials in the region.[350]

In 1920, around the time that J. Thomas Newsome and Andrew W. E. Bassette, Jr., were challenging the voting restrictions placed on blacks in Virginia, Joseph R. Pollard, a noted black lawyer from Richmond, became the first member of his race from Virginia to make a serious bid for the United States Senate. Pollard, a Republican, opposed Carter Glass, a Democrat, for the Senate seat. Pollard lost the campaign, but made a respectable showing, receiving 17,576 (8.7 percent) of the votes to Glass's 184,646 (91.3 percent).[351] Pollard's showing was aided by the support of women in Richmond, Norfolk, Portsmouth, Lynchburg, and Newport News who had been empowered to vote by the newly ratified Nineteenth Amendment.[352]

Pollard's impressive showing may have influenced the Virginia General Assembly to adopt a race-neutral voting statute in 1924. Although the statute did not bar blacks from voting in the primary elections, it did not preclude political parties from doing so. In 1929, Pollard, acting on behalf of a black client, sued public authorities for damages when they refused to allow a black man to vote. Pollard won the suit in federal court on constitutional grounds.[353]

Still, in the mid-1920s the black lawyer continued to be underrepresented in Virginia, even in northern Virginia. After 1907, no black lawyers appeared before the Corporation Court of Alexandria, Virginia, until A. H. Collins defended two youths charged with assault and robbery in 1922. Collins's performance prompted commendations from the judge of the court, a tribute that was reported by the press.[354] Lawyers such as Richmond's Josiah Curtis Robertson continued to win recognition as masters in chancery in 1928.[355] Other signs of progress were demonstrated in 1932, when three Howard University law graduates and one Ohio State University law graduate passed the Virginia bar.[356]

The trial in 1933 of a black man charged with the murder of a white woman in Loudoun County, Virginia, established the importance and the vulnerability of the black lawyer in the region. George Crawford, the accused, was to be tried in Loudoun County, a county in which no blacks served on juries and where no black lawyer practiced. The sensationalism surrounding the case led blacks in Virginia to welcome the outside legal assistance of Charles Hamilton Houston, Leon Andrew Ransom, Edward P. Lovett, and James G. "Pete" Tyson, all of whom were black. Houston, who was counsel to the NAACP in New York, Ransom, a Howard University law professor, and Lovett and Tyson, Howard law graduates, formed Crawford's defense team. No white lawyer in Virginia would take the case or assist in Crawford's defense because of the emotionally charged atmosphere surrounding the trial. The black defense team faced great danger as they traveled in and out of Virginia to represent Crawford. These lawyers received little financial or other assistance from the blacks in Loudoun County, who feared reprisals.[357]

During the pretrial hearings, the trial judge denied motion after motion challenging procedural irregularities, including the exclusion of blacks from the jury. The hostile setting of the trial drew national attention, and it appeared to be a foregone conclusion that Crawford would be convicted and executed. The prediction of conviction was correct, but the jury recommended that Crawford receive a life sentence.[358] Given the nature of the crime—committed against a white woman in a Southern state—the life sentence was viewed as a victory. News of the sentence was received by the black community as if it had been an acquittal. For the black lawyers in charge of the case, the sentence seemed to be a real recognition of their skills.[359] Yet, perhaps predictably, even this tempered success was criticized.[360]

Whether the Crawford case, and the dangers it presented to the black lawyer, slowed the admission of blacks to the Virginia bar is not altogether clear. Nevertheless, the tide of admissions slowed, though it did not stop. Indeed, the notoriety of the case may have inspired young blacks to consider law as a profession. William Davis Butts, for example, returned to Newport News after being graduated from New York University School of Law in 1931. Butts specialized in criminal law and "won the respect of the profession throughout [Virginia]."[361]

In 1940, three of eight black applicants passed the Virginia bar examination, settling in Richmond and Norfolk, Virginia.[362] One of the three lawyers admitted in 1931 caused a stir in 1941 that reached the attention of the Supreme Court of Virginia Court of Appeals. An assistant law librarian in the Virginia Court of Appeals ordered Frederick Charles Carter to relocate his seat to a "corner alcove," out of the general sight of other library users. When Carter refused this request, the librarian loudly demanded that Carter see him in private. Carter still refused. A policeman was summoned. Carter informed the officer that he was a member of the bar and was thus entitled to occupy any seat in the library that he chose and to speak to whom he chose. The officer refused to arrest him. Subsequently, Carter reported the incident to the newly formed Old Dominion Bar Association, a black bar group. Oliver W. Hill, J. Byron Hopkins, and Carter met with Preston White Campbell, the chief justice of the Supreme Court of Virginia Court of Appeals, to inquire whether the court had authorized the racial segregation of the law library, which was under Campbell's supervision. Chief Justice Campbell informed the group that the court "had made no Jim Crow rules and stated that no further difficulty would come up."[363]

Oliver W. Hill, a 1933 Howard University law graduate, was fast making a name for himself in Richmond, where he practiced law. Hill and Thurgood Marshall had been classmates at Howard University's law school and both had graduated with honors. Hill and Marshall had been students of Howard's resident vice-dean, Charles Hamilton Houston, and later befriended professors William Henry Hastie and Leon Andrew Ransom. By 1940, Hill had become the NAACP's contact in Virginia and part of Houston's new breed of civil rights attorneys in the South.

In the late 1930s, the Norfolk Teacher's Association, an all-black organization, retained Hill to challenge the local school board's policies, which fixed the salaries of black teachers at a lower rate than that paid to white teachers, on constitutional grounds. The lawsuit drew wide attention to a general discriminatory practice of local school boards across the South.[364] The local federal court dismissed the suit, but Hill appealed the decision to the Fourth Circuit Court of Appeals. Hill, joined by Marshall, Hastie, and Ransom, prevailed on appeal, on the basic principal "that the fixing of salary schedules for the teachers is action by the state which is subject to the limitations prescribed by the Fourteenth Amendment."[365]

Hill and Houston also went before the Virginia Supreme Court of Appeals in 1943, this time to save the life of a black man charged with raping a white woman in Loudoun County. Samuel Legions was convicted of rape on the basis of some bizarre testimony. The victim and her husband testified that Legions had broken into their apartment and committed the rape on the kitchen table in plain view of the husband while he cared for their crying child and watched the crime. The court set aside the conviction as preposterous, stating that "common sense and knowledge of human nature tells us that which the prosecutrix and her husband have related did not occur."[366]

In 1943, Attorney General Francis Biddle appointed Martin A. Martin, of Danville, Virginia, as an associate attorney in the trial section of the criminal division of the Department of Justice. At the time of his appointment, Martin represented the Danville Savings Bank, "the oldest Negro banking institution in Virginia," and other significant business clients. Martin was "the first Negro attorney" appointed to the criminal division.[367]

In December 1924, two black women were among the 111 candidates taking the Virginia bar examination.[368] Lavina Marian Fleming-Poe was one of these candidates, but the other female candidate has not been identified. Apparently, neither woman passed the bar in 1924, because it was not until March 27, 1926, that reports mention Fleming-Poe as the first woman of her race to pass the Virginia bar.[369] The fact that Fleming-Poe had passed the Virginia bar was also featured in *The Law Student*, a magazine circulated to law schools throughout the nation.[370] She settled in her native town of Newport News, Virginia, where she practiced law and was frequently called upon to address women's groups.[371]

Two other women were admitted to the Virginia bar shortly after Fleming-Poe. The second black woman admitted to the Virginia bar was Bertha L. Douglass, who gained admission on December 20, 1926, and apparently practiced in Norfolk, Virginia. In 1935, Douglass was listed among several other black lawyers who practiced in Norfolk.[372]

The third black woman admitted to the Virginia bar was Inez C. Fields, a 1922 Boston University law graduate. Fields was admitted to the bar on November 7, 1928, and practiced law in Hampton, Virginia, with her lawyer father, George Washington Fields (see above).[373]

West Virginia

Booker T. Washington seems likely to have been the first black person to study law in the state of West Virginia. In the mid-1870s Washington read law under the direction of Romeo H. Freer, a prosperous white man in Charleston, West Virginia. Washington never completed his law studies, probably because of his greater interest in his educational work at Hampton Institute in Virginia.[374]

In 1882, John H. Hill returned to West Virginia and was admitted to the bar of Jefferson County.[375] Hill was trained as a lawyer in Maine, becoming that state's second black lawyer in 1879, after two years of study in the law offices of Tallman and Larrabee.[376] Hill was also admitted to the Virginia bar in 1882. Thereafter, he enlisted and served in the 10th United States Calvary in the campaign against Geronimo. Hill later served as president of West Virginia State College, a state-supported college for blacks.[377] There is no evidence that Hill actively practiced law.

John Robert Clifford became an early catalyst in the advancement of civil rights among blacks in West Virginia. Clifford studied law under J. Nelson Wisner in Martinsburg, West Virginia, in 1885,[378] and was admitted to practice before the West Virginia Supreme Court of Appeals on September 13, 1887, on the motion of William H. Wilson.[379] Six days later he was admitted to practice in the circuit court of Berkeley County.[380]

Clifford, a member of the bar, enrolled in and was graduated from the Shaw University School of Law in North Carolina in 1893 and returned to West Virginia to practice law.[381] He is likely the first black lawyer ever to appear before the West Virginia Supreme Court of Appeals. In 1898 Clifford represented a black schoolteacher in his defense of a trial court verdict before the West Virginia Supreme Court. The teacher had been denied three months' pay because the school board of Tucker County had shortened the school term of the "colored school" in the district by three months. Clifford's client claimed that she was entitled to pay for a full term in the district, despite the shorter school term for the "colored school." In *Williams v. Board of Education of Fairfax District,*[382] the court declined to permit any distinction in the same district between white and black teachers, stating that "discrimination against the colored people, because of color alone, as to privileges, immunities, and equal legal protection, is contrary to public policy and the law of the land."[383] Clifford's victory in the *Williams* case set in motion a trend toward equal pay for black teachers in West Virginia that many states would be forced to adopt some years later.

Clifford's admission to the bar was followed in 1889 by that of Christopher H. Payne. Payne, who had read law, was soon thereafter appointed deputy collector of internal revenue, a position he held from 1889 to 1893, before opening his law office.[384] In 1891, Moses H. Jones, a recent graduate of Howard University's law school, began his career as an attorney in Charleston, but closed his practice in 1898 in order to enlist in the army at the outbreak of the Spanish-American War.[385]

The number of Howard University law graduates from West Virginia steadily increased toward the turn of the century, particularly after Gabriel Holland was denied admission to the University of West Virginia Law School in 1895. The regents of the university claimed that Holland could not be admitted because the constitution of the state precluded members of the colored race from attending the school.[386]

After James Monroe Ellis graduated from Howard University's law school in 1898, he was hired for a year by a white law firm, Almstead and Goldsberry of Lynchburg, Virginia, before settling in Fayette County, West Virginia, in 1900.[387] Ellis built an excellent practice in Fayette County and represented that county for three terms in the West Virginia state legislature from 1903 to 1909.[388] Ellis also served as school land commissioner of the county. His political activities did not interfere with, but rather strengthened, his law practice among black and white clients. Still, black lawyers like Ellis continued to face dangers as they sought to represent their clients. In 1915, Ellis was threatened with bodily harm while attempting to obtain information about a client from a probation officer.[389] In the same year, Ellis and Thomas L. Sweeney, another Howard University law graduate practicing in Fayetteville, became the first black lawyers to oppose each other before the West Virginia Supreme Court of Appeals.[390] Ellis became an expert in insurance law, and by 1939 he served as the local counsel to the Knights of Pythias, a national black fraternal group that offered life insurance to its members.[391]

One of the most noted black lawyers in West Virginia in the early part of the twentieth century was Thomas Gillis Nutter, an 1899 Howard University law graduate and the brother of Isaac Henry Nutter, a lawyer in New Jersey. In 1903, Nutter opened a law office in Charleston, three years after his initial admission to the bar in Marion County, Indiana.[392] Nutter had been asked to come to West Virginia by another black lawyer, R. S. King, in order to help King defend "the famous Grice murder case." Many blacks assumed that the jury would sentence the defendant to death, but "the brilliant defense of [Nutter and King] reduced [Grice's] offense to voluntary man-slaughter."[393] Nutter's reputation was founded on this case and on the subsequent defense of a black man charged with raping a white woman. The rape case, involving Campbell Clark, lasted four days under mob conditions. Reportedly, "only one poor white man in the entire town dared face the mob, aside from Nutter."[394] Due to Nutter's superior skills, his client was convicted only of attempted assault.

Soon after Nutter started his practice in Charleston, another Howard University law graduate, Emory Rankin Carter, opened a law office in Charleston and practiced there until 1905. He then relocated to McDowell County, becoming its first black lawyer.[395] Nutter, however, remained in Charleston and specialized in civil cases, and Republican politics.

In 1918 and 1919 Nutter was elected by the citizens of Kanawha County to the West Virginia legislature, where he served on the judiciary committee—"one of the most important committees in American legislative bodies,"[396] since it had jurisdiction over all legislative matters governing the courts of West Virginia. During his term in the legislature, he fought for the establishment of a mental hospital for blacks and for an industrial school for boys and girls.[397] Thereafter, Nutter was employed by the state as assistant clerk in the office of state auditor, but he also maintained his practice. He represented several commercial businesses, such as the Midland Brick and Cement Company and the S. W. Starks Improvement Company, as well as the People's Exchange Bank and the Mutual Savings and Loan Company of Charleston (the latter the only black-owned bank in the state).[398] Nutter and James Monroe Ellis often handled cases together, and at times they joined with white law firms to present cases before the Supreme Court of Appeals of West Virginia.[399] In 1929, Nutter's commercial law expertise more than qualified him to challenge, though unsuccessfully, a deed restricting the conveyance of real property "to any person of [the] Ethiopian race or descent for a period of fifty years."[400]

In 1938 Nutter, after thirty-five years as a lawyer, was hired by whites to represent them in a twelve-million-dollar land dispute in West Virginia. He may have been hired, in part, because most local white lawyers had conflicts of interest with one or more of the multiple parties involved in the litigation.[401] The case was appealed to the United States Supreme Court. The appeal, however, was handled by two black Chicago lawyers.[402]

Tyler Edward Hill was admitted to West Virginia bar in Keystone, West Virginia, in 1910. He was counsel to the Keystone Supply Company, and also published a newspaper. Hill's writings on racial discrimination, labor, and mining conditions attracted considerable attention among blacks and whites. These articles, as well as the stand that he took in 1913 against the discriminatory practices of the police force in Bluefield, West Virginia, almost cost him his life.[403]

During the 1920s, Hill, then the director of the West Virginia Bureau of Negro Welfare, reopened the issue of the exclusion of blacks from the University of West Virginia Law School. Hill reported that "Negro citizens of the states who desire to study law must . . . leave the state and pay tuition at Howard University [School of Law] or some other school."[404] He criticized a licensing system that allowed West Virginia's law graduates to be admitted to the bar without examination. Blacks, who were forced to be educated outside of their native state's school, were required to take the bar examination. Hill did not let these issues rest. He asked West Virginia Governor Howard W. Gore "to provide that Negro citizens of the state who graduate from any law school of the same class as that of the West Virginia University be admitted [without examination]."[405] No action was taken.

The decade between 1910 and 1920 brought other black lawyers to West Virginia. In 1910, Robert Roy Cheeks, a 1906 graduate of the Cleveland Law School, was first admitted to practice in 1906 in Ohio and later in McDowell County. He claimed to be the second black lawyer to appear before the Supreme Court of Appeals of West Virginia.[406] James Elijah Graham, Jr., a 1910 graduate of Howard University's law school, was admitted to practice in Wheeling in 1911. Graham's clients included the Defender Publishing Company. He also filed a suit against the school board of Hancock County in an attempt to desegregate the schools.[407]

Graham's classmate, Brown Wesley Payne, also returned to West Virginia to practice law, settling in Beckley. He was the town's first black lawyer.[408] Payne and James M. Ellis are responsible for two decisions by the Supreme Court of Appeals of West Virginia holding that it is unconstitutional to exclude "all persons of the African race" from serving on petit and grand juries.[409] Brown's personal philosophy was that no free government should limit the level of achievement of its citizens. The West Virginia edition of the *History of the Negro* reports that Brown

believed that the term "Social Equality" is mis-applied and has no place in the solution of the race relationship in this country; that if the Negro be not hindered in his self-development along any and every line of his inclination toward uplift, the race problem will take care of itself; that free government cannot obtain in the United States, unless the Negro be permitted to take part in it, unhampered by any preconceived notions of his place and destiny.[410]

In 1913, Governor William G. Conly appointed Payne to an advisory council on education in West Virginia. During his term on the council, Payne attempted to expand the state's purchase of books to include textbooks "dealing more largely with Negro life and history."[411] Later, Payne challenged the authority of the West Virginia legislature to abolish the state board of education, an action which "deprived the colored citizens . . . [of] a voice in the administration of their schools."[412] Payne's position won wide support among blacks.

In 1913, Harry Jheopart Capehart, Sr., opened a law office in Keystone, West Virginia, just after his graduation from Howard University's law school. Five years later, Capehart was elected to the West Virginia state legislature from McDowell County, serving three consecutive two-year terms. He also served three terms on the Keystone city council. As a member of the legislature, Capehart sat on several important committees, including the tax and finance, claims and grievances, human institutions and public buildings, education, railroads, and corporations committees.[413] Capehart authored West Virginia's anti-lynching legislation in 1921, although before it could be adopted, he had to modify its more stringent provisions in order to win the support of his Republican colleagues.[414] Capehart's two law partners, Arthur G. Froe and Leon P. Miller, were also highly talented black lawyers.[415] Capehart and Froe were both well-connected in national Republican circles and highly respected among blacks in McDowell County. In 1925, president Calvin Coolidge appointed Froe recorder of deeds of the District of Columbia, the premier appointment for blacks in the national government.[416]

In 1920, West Virginia had twenty-three black lawyers, none of whom were women. By 1930, that figure had declined to twenty. Nevertheless, in 1923 the editor of West Virginia's edition of the *History of the American Negro* indicated that in "proportion to population, one finds more colored lawyers in West Virginia than the states of the South [and] most . . . are well equipped and are meeting with success."[417] This success was hard won, as black citizens in West Virginia frequently resorted to hiring white lawyers in instances where blacks were excluded from serving on the jury.[418]

Between 1922 and 1928, the number of black lawyers in West Virginia had increased to twenty-five, spread across fourteen cities in eight counties. And yet, as one report noted, "Negro lawyers [were] needed at several places in the state where none [were] located."[419]

In 1934, while the number of black lawyers remained small, J. S. Butts, a graduate of the Detroit College of Law, won the primary election on the Republican ticket for the West Virginia House of Representatives.[420] In 1939, several black lawyers held significant posts in the public sector: Harry J. Capehart was a member of a public committee on employment; Fleming A. Jones, Jr., and Thomas G. Nutter served on a public committee at Bluefield State Teachers College, a black institution; and C. E. Kimbrough, Jr., was the superintendent of the Huntington, West Virginia, Home for Aged and Infirm Colored Men and Women.[421]

According to one record by 1941, there were twenty-three black lawyers in West Virginia, including Fleming Adolphus Jones, Jr., who represented McDowell County in the state legislature. (Jones served in that body from 1933 to 1943, the longest period served by any black legislator in West Virginia since its first black member was seated in 1897.[422]) This total of twenty-three black lawyers is somewhat misleading, however, since four of the lawyers listed in this account had departed the state or died. Five other black lawyers—William L. Lonesome, George W. Crockett, Jr., Willard L. Brown, Abishi C. Cunningham, and Joseph G. Travis—though not listed in the same record, had also joined the ranks in West Virginia.[423]

Even with the sustained and demonstrated success of black lawyers in West Virginia, the future appeared dim. There were only two black students enrolled in pre-law courses at West Virginia State College between 1930 and 1940;[424] there were no prospective black women lawyers enrolled at that time.

Summary

Georgia was one of the southeastern states to which black lawyers migrated after the Civil War. Aaron Alpeoria Bradley, a black lawyer from Massachusetts, was one of the first black professionals to move to Georgia. Bradley became a champion of the newly freed former slaves when he argued that Georgia's secession from the Union voided its citizens' property titles, which black people could then claim.

Because Bradley's activism aroused the political awareness and passions of the newly freed blacks, it concerned even such Union generals as O. O. Howard, the head of the Freedman's Bureau. Bradley's advocacy is no doubt the reason that his application for admission to the Georgia bar was denied. In fact, the Reconstruction generals, with the blessing of President Andrew Johnson, charged Bradley with sedition, and he was subsequently imprisoned. After his release from prison, Bradley, a black hero, was elected to the Georgia state senate in 1868.

Georgia's first-known black lawyer, James M. Simms, who in 1871 became its first judicial officer, was all but run out of office in Savannah. White people, apparently, were unwilling to take the law from a black judge.

Black lawyers achieved power in politics, and it was in this domain that they excelled. Black lawyers such as Edwin Belcher helped to establish the Republican Party in Georgia during the dawn of Reconstruction. Henry Lincoln Johnson, Sr., became a powerful national committeeman in both the local and national Republican parties.

Black lawyers formed law firms to combine their financial and intellectual resources and talents. These firms trained and prepared many black lawyers for the Georgia bar prior to 1900. Despite the efforts of black lawyers to emancipate their people from racism, black people in places like Savannah often sought out white lawyers to represent them: They believed that white judges and juries would listen to white lawyers, not black lawyers.

Black people in Atlanta held black lawyers to a higher standard than white lawyers; the white lawyers' influence and competence before the bench was presumed, but black lawyers such as Austin Thomas Walden and A. W. Ricks were closely monitored by the black community to see if they made any mistakes. Still, when it came to civil rights advocacy and the risks associated with it, blacks in Georgia looked to black lawyers to protect their rights, despite the personal risks and lack of salary guarantees they would have to withstand.

Many of the pioneer black lawyers in Georgia were self-made, but several were graduates of black law schools, such as Howard University and Allen University, and a few were educated at Northern schools, such as the University of Michigan.

The progress of the black lawyer in Georgia had slowed by 1937. Indeed, Austin Thomas Walden predicted that their future was "cloudy, even ominous." Even as the future looked cloudy, the prospects for women lawyers improved in 1943, the year Rachel E. Pruden-Herndon became the first black woman admitted to the Georgia bar.

North Carolina's first black lawyer, George Lawrence Mabson, studied law under a Union Army general and was admitted to the bar in 1871. Mabson entered private practice and specialized in criminal law.

Black lawyers in North Carolina entered politics almost out of necessity. They saw politics as a vehicle to win the emancipation of their people. John Sinclair Leary served in the North Carolina legislature from 1868 to 1872 and was later elected alderman in Fayetteville. James Edward O'Hara served as a member of the North Carolina constitutional convention in 1875, and in 1882 became the state's first black congressman. North Carolina's second black lawyer, George H. White, Sr., was elected to Congress in 1897. White, then the only black congressman in the nation, declared himself the spokesman for nine million people.

Politics and law practice combined to build respect for black lawyers in the North Carolina black community. In Wilmington, North Carolina, black lawyers were preferred over white lawyers, as they fearlessly stood up to defend their clients. The black community supported black lawyers because they looked to the positive example of two black congressmen, both of whom were lawyers. In addition, they witnessed the first black second-generation lawyer's entry into the law in North Carolina in 1895.

The presence of a black law school with scholarly black law teachers in North Carolina gave black lawyers more status and standing in both the white and black communities. The black community was also exposed to a number of black law graduates from other black law schools, including Shaw University, Howard University, and Allen University, and from white law schools, such as Yale University, Harvard University, New York Law School, and South Carolina University. This mix of talent in the state made North Carolina rather unusual in the South, though it did not have any black women lawyers before 1945.

South Carolina was one of the first Southern states to admit three black lawyers on the same day. William J. Whipper, Jonathan Jasper Wright, and Robert Brown Elliott were all admitted to the bar on September 23, 1868. These lawyers would become three of the most influential men in South Carolina, black or white.

The first black law firm was formed by Elliott, Whipper, and Macon Bolling Allen in 1868. The firm would train and hire many black lawyers who also became influential in South Carolina. Elliott would form four law firms during a span of sixteen years. The law firm of Whipper, Elliott, and Allen thrived because of the combined legal talents and political influence of its principals. Whipper was one of the founding members of the Republican Party in South Carolina, and Elliott served as a member of the state constitutional convention in 1867 and the state legislature in 1868. Allen was America's first black lawyer, having been admitted to the bar in Maine in 1844 and to the Massachusetts bar in 1845.

Whipper, Elliott, and Allen were as skillful in the law as they were in politics. This made them attractive to black people and to the white political world they entered at the beginning of the Reconstruction era.

Elliott's political career was exceptional. In 1871, at twenty-nine years of age, he was elected to Congress as South Carolina's first black congressman. Elliott was later elected to the legislature of South Carolina, becoming speaker of the house of that body from 1874 to 1876. He also was elected attorney general of the state.

William J. Whipper and Jonathan Jasper Wright, who both served as members of the 1868 South Carolina constitutional convention, would later compete to become the first black lawyer elected by the legislature to serve on the South Carolina Supreme Court. Wright was ultimately selected. Samuel B. Thompson, who in 1868 held the post of justice of the peace, was South Carolina's first black judicial officer.

Wright, who was the first person known to call on the Republican Party to nominate a black for the presidential ticket, served with distinction as the nation's first state court justice of a supreme court. Whipper became a local probate judge in Charleston, and is likely the first black lawyer from South Carolina to appear before the United States Supreme Court, as he did, in 1903.

In 1888 Thomas Ezekiel Miller, a black lawyer, was elected to Congress. Miller had previously distinguished himself as a member of both houses of the South Carolina legislature. Richard H. Gleaves, also a black lawyer, served as lieutenant governor of South Carolina from 1872 to 1874.

It appears that most of the lawyers in South Carolina during the Reconstruction era studied law under the supervision of a lawyer, with the exception of a few who obtained formal training at black law schools such as Howard University and South Carolina's Allen University. Others attended the University of South Carolina's law school, during a short period when the University admitted blacks. After the Reconstruction era, most of the lawyers admitted to the bar in South Carolina were Howard University law graduates. There were periods between 1900 and 1944 when the star of the black lawyer waned, perhaps due to policies of racial exclusion in the state. However, the few who were admitted to the bar, like Harold Richard Boulware, a 1938 law graduate of Howard University, formed the new breed of black legal emancipators.

Cassandra E. Maxwell became South Carolina's first black woman lawyer in 1938, but little more is known about her.

The state of Virginia admitted its first black lawyer, Wathal G. Wynn, a Howard University law graduate, in 1871, but soon thereafter Wynn left Virginia.

Black lawyers entered politics in Virginia in great numbers between 1865 and 1895. William N. Stevens, Alfred W. Harris, Edwin Archer Randolph, and James Apostler Fields are black lawyers who served in both houses of the state legislature and on the Common Council of Richmond, Virginia. In 1889 John Mercer Langston was elected as Virginia's first black congressman. He served one term after his seat was challenged by his white opponent. In 1920 Joseph R. Pollard ran unsuccessfully as an independent for the United States Senate. He received 5 percent of the vote.

Prior to 1900, black lawyers were admitted to practice in a number of counties in Virginia. For this reason, perhaps, a significant number of black lawyers were elected to a variety of local offices in these counties. By 1879, two black lawyers representing black clients had even opposed each other in a court of law, while James A. Fields had served as justice of the peace. Fields was Virginia's first black judicial officer.

Thomas Calhoun Walker, a black lawyer in Gloucester County, became a folk hero in Virginia after being admitted to the bar in 1887. He fearlessly represented several black men who had been charged with raping white women. In this emotionally charged atmosphere, Walker sometimes required the assistance of armed black citizens to protect him and his clients from white hate groups. After President Roosevelt appointed Walker consultant to the Virginia Emergency Relief Administration in 1934, the title of "black governor" was conferred upon him by Virginia's black citizens.

Many law schools were represented among Virginia's law graduates. New York University, the University of Michigan, Howard University, Yale University, Harvard University, Boston University, Cornell University, and Ohio State University each had law graduates in the state. A few lawyers also received law degrees from the LaSalle University Extension Law School located in Chicago, Illinois.

After 1915 black lawyers began to question the exclusion of blacks from the political process, and they began to file the first voting rights lawsuits in Virginia. Thomas Harris Reid, J. Thomas Newsome, and Andrew William Ernest Bassette, Jr., filed some of these early voting rights suits in order to put an end to the white-dominated primaries.

By the 1930s, a new breed of black lawyers would enter the state, among them Oliver W. Hill, a classmate of Thurgood Marshall at Howard University School of Law. Hill and Marshall co-filed the first equalization-of-pay cases in Virginia.

Lavina Marian Fleming-Poe became Virginia's first black woman lawyer in 1924. She entered the private practice of law in Newport News, Virginia. She was followed to the bar by Bertha L. Douglass and Inez C. Fields. Both women practiced law—Douglass in Norfolk and Fields in Hampton, where she joined her father's law firm.

Booker T. Washington could have been West Virginia's first black lawyer, had his interest not been redirected to the field of education. Instead, in 1881, John H. Hill, already admitted to the bar of Maine, became the state's first black lawyer.

From 1903 to the 1920s, there were at least five black lawyers who served in the West Virginia legislature. One of these lawyers, Harry Jheopart Capehart, Sr., introduced anti-lynching legislation that ultimately became law. One of the earliest cases decided on the issue of the unconstitutionality of disparate pay for white and black public schoolteachers was won by John Robert Clifford in 1898, before the West Virginia Court of Appeals.

Excluded from attending the University of West Virginia Law School, black lawyers admitted to practice in West Virginia came from a number of white law schools, such as Iowa State University, Detroit College of Law, Cleveland Law School, Howard University, and Shaw University (the last two being black).

As early as 1915, two black lawyers opposed each other in the West Virginia Supreme Court of Appeals. And while this seemed to be a sign of progress, Thomas Gillis Nutter faced mob violence at the courthouse door for defending a black man charged with raping a white woman.

Black lawyers in the southeastern states made remarkable names for themselves in politics and law against seemingly unsurmountable odds. They excelled in every area in which they were allowed to participate, and agitated for entrance into those from which they were excluded. These black lawyers—men and women—fully charted the course of liberation in the southeastern region.

NOTES

1. *Savannah Daily Republican*, Feb. 16, 1867. Another reason given by the court for denying Bradley's application was his "impudence and egotism." *Savannah Daily Republican*, Feb. 11, 16, 1867.

2. Joseph P. Reidy, "Aaron A. Bradley: Voice of Black Labor in the Georgia Lowcounty," in *Southern Black Leaders of the Reconstruction Era* 285 (H. N. Rabinowitz ed. 1981). See text of Special Order No. 15, issued on Jan. 16, 1865, in W. L. Fleming, Vol. 1 *Documentary History of Reconstruction* 350–52 (reprint, 1960).

3. *Ibid* (*Southern Black Leaders*). See also, J. M. McPherson, *Battle Cry of Freedom* 841–42 (1988), for discussion of Special Order No. 15 and the reluctance of Congress to exercise its powers under the Thirteenth Amendment.

4. *Id.* at 285, 289 (*Southern Black Leaders*).

5. W. S. McFeely, *Yankee Stepfather* 202 (1968), quoting letter of A. A. Bradley to Andrew Johnson, Dec. 7, 1865.

6. *Id.* at 203, quoting letter from Davis Tillson to O. O. Howard, received Dec. 8, 1865.

7. *Savannah Daily Republican*, Dec. 13, 1865.

8. *Ibid.*

9. *Savannah Daily Republican*, Jan. 21, 1867.

10. *National Intelligence*, Feb. 20, 1867.

11. In 1962, Chester A. Dolan, Jr., clerk of the Supreme Judicial Court of Massachusetts, confirmed that "no charges were ever brought against [Bradley]." Letter from Dolan to Charles S. Brown, June 5, 1962.

12. Letter from Lillie M. Hawes, director, Georgia Historical Society to Charles S. Brown, Aug. 12, 1963.

13. I. H. Avery, *The History of the State of Georgia* 400 (1881). See also, Vol. 1 *Dictionary of Georgia Biography* 109 (K. Coleman and C. S. Gurr, eds. 1983).

14. Letter from Lillie M. Hawes, director, Georgia Historical Society, to Charles S. Brown, Aug. 12, 1963. It is not altogether clear why Aaron Alpeoria Bradley was granted reinstatement as a state senator, unless the claims against him were proven to be groundless, an explanation that has gone wanting by historians critical of Bradley. See E. M. Coulter, *Negro Legislators in Georgia During the Reconstruction Period* 37, 56, 59, 67 (1968).

15. E. L. Drago. *Black Politicians and Reconstruction in Georgia* 44 (1982).

16. "A Lively Scene in the Georgia Senate," *Nashville Republican Banner*, Dec. 9, 1870.

17. *Ibid.*

18. *Ibid.*

19. During the 1870 Adjourned Session of the General Assembly, Senator Bradley called for the admission of blacks to the state militia on the same basis as whites (E. M. Coulter, *Negro Legislation in Georgia During the Reconstruction Period* 84 [1968]). He also announced his intention to run again for the state senate from the First District. This announcement was met with a negative article in a Tennessee newspaper which referred to Senator Bradley as an "irresponsible darky orator." *Nashville Republican Banner*, Dec. 15, 1870.

20. E. M. Coulter, *Negro Legislators in Georgia During the Reconstruction Period* 40–43, 52–53 (1968); E. L. Drago, *Black Politicians and Reconstruction in Georgia* 41–41 (1982).

21. "42 Years Ago," *Savannah Tribune*, April 20, 1933.

22. E. M. Coulter, *Negro Legislators in Georgia During the Reconstruction Period* 114–15, 118 (1968); "42 Years Ago," *Savannah Tribune*, April 20, 1933.

23. E. L. Drago, *Black Politicians and Reconstruction in Georgia* 43 (1982).

24. This appointment had been paved by a decision of the Georgia Supreme Court holding that blacks were eligible to hold public office in Georgia. *White v. Clements*, 39 Ga. 232 (1869); Smith, "Toward a Pure Legal Existence: Blacks and the Constitution," 30 *How. L.J.* 921, 932 (1987).

25. *New National Era*, Feb. 16, 1871.

26. *New Orleans Commercial Bulletin*, May 19, 1871.

27. *Ibid.*, quoting letter from Governor Rufus B. Bullock to Thomas R. Mills, Jr. Mills, a Savannah lawyer, opposed Governor Bullock's appointment, probably because he, as the governor's newly appointed district attorney, would have to frequently appear before Judge Simms. E. L. Drago, *Black Politicians and Reconstruction in Georgia* 60–62 (1982). Mr. Mills returned his commission to the governor, calling Judge Simms's appointment a disgrace (*Savannah Daily Republican*, Feb. 1, 1871 and Jan. 26, 1871, listing the names and reasons why members of the Chatham County Bar Association opposed the appointment).

28. James M. Simms was a member of the House of Representatives from Chatham County during the Extra Session, July 4–October 6, 1868, the General Session of January 13–March 18, 1869, and the Extra Session of January 10–October 25, 1870.

29. *Ibid.* (Governor Bullock's letter to Mills).

30. See, e.g., "A Reconstructed Court," *New Orleans Commercial Bulletin*, March 18, 1871.

31. J. T. Glatthaar, *Forged in Battle* 249 (1990). Edwin Belcher "served as an officer in a white regiment," but no one, at first, knew he was black. When his

ancestry was discovered, he merely proclaimed that he had done his duty at war like any other soldier, including twice being taken prisoner.

32. H. Walton, Jr., *Black Republicans: The Politics of the Black and Tans* 50–51 (1975).

33. "A Prominent Man Dead—Capt. Edwin Belcher," *The New York Globe*, Jan. 20, 1883, at 1, col. 5.

34. H. Walton, Jr., *Black Republicans: The Politics of the Black and Tans* 57 (1975); J. T. Glatthaar, *Forged in Battle* 249 (1991), regarding Belcher's service in the Union Army.

35. Vol. 1 *Who's Who of the Colored Race* 156 (F. L. Mather ed. 1915); *General Catalogue of the University of Michigan, 1837–1911*, at 442 (I. N. Demmon ed. 1912).

36. Telephone interview with James H. Bohannan, deputy recorder of deeds of the District of Columbia, Nov. 21, 1988.

37. W. F. Nowlin, *The Negro in American Politics* 60–61, 71–72 (1931).

38. D. E. Bingham, *We Ask Only a Fair Trial: A History of the Black Community in Evansville, Indiana* 211 (1987).

39. "The Passing of M. Waterloo Bullock," *The Atlantic Guardian*, Sept. 14, 1915. His actual full name was Matthew Washington Bullock. Bullock became special counsel for the Grand District Lodge No. 18, Odd Fellows, and an attorney for the Standard Life Insurance Company. Bullock found greater opportunities in the South than in Boston, where there were "no suitable opportunities" for him. H. Elsie Austin, "Pioneering All the Way: Matthew W. Bullock, Sr.," 3 (mimeo, n.d.); see also, Vol. 1 *Who's Who of the Colored Race* 49 (F. L. Mather ed. 1915).

40. Interview with Henry Lincoln Johnson, Jr., by author on Aug. 15, 1989. Mr. Johnson said that the contribution to his father by Taft forces was referred to as "the $9,000-Georgia Peach." Johnson stated that Theodore Roosevelt, who had become disenchanted with Taft, had offered to make Johnson independently wealthy if he supported his bid for the Republican nomination. According to Johnson, Perry W. Howard encouraged the senior Johnson to take the money to secure his family forever. However, Henry Lincoln Johnson, Sr., refused the money because he had pledged his support to Taft. As a result of the Taft-Roosevelt split, Woodrow Wilson, a Democrat, was elected president in 1912.

41. Vol. 1 *Hearing Before Subcommittee of the Committee on Privileges and Elections*, U.S. Senate, 66th Cong., 2d Sess., 945–65, July 8, 1920. Eight years later, two other black lawyers, Benjamin Jefferson Davis, Jr., of Atlanta, Georgia, and Perry W. Howard, of Mississippi, testified on campaign expenditure during President Herbert Hoover's campaign. At the time Davis and Howard were both Republican National Committeemen from their respective states. *Hearing Before Special Committee Investigating Presidential Campaign Expenditures*, 70th Cong., 1st Sess., 691–93, May 29, 1928 (Davis); *id.* at 722–23 (Howard) (courtesy of Dr. Hanes Walton, Jr., Savannah State College). Some scholars have seen Johnson as the "dispenser of federal patronage jobs to blacks as a member of The Republican National Committee." A. Buni, *Robert L. Vann of Pittsburgh Courier* 178 (1974). During these hearings, Johnson was named Georgia Republican national committeeman. According to one source, "Warren G. Harding, in an attempt to attract black votes, used Johnson to help arrange speaking engagements before black groups. Harding rewarded him by appointment to his old post as recorder of deeds in Washington. Johnson's appointment,

however, was blocked by Georgia Senator Tom Watson." Vol. 9 *The Booker T. Washington Papers, 1906–8*, at 569 (L. R. Harlan, R. W. Smock, and N. E. Woodruff eds. 1980). Johnson never forgave Watson and "went to his grave and spit on it after Watson died." Personal interview by author with Henry Lincoln Johnson, Jr., Washington, D.C., Aug. 15, 1989. Tom Watson was initially elected to Congress with the support of blacks. Watson, a populist, appealed to both poor blacks and whites. Subsequently, the Democrats, fearing black rule, used the racial "specters of rape and corruption" to run Watson out of office. Watson, sensing the winds of change, later turned against blacks, in a betrayal that was never forgotten by Henry Lincoln Johnson, Sr., according to Johnson's son. See also, C. L. Weltner, *Southerner* 132 (1966).

42. "Link Johnson Scores Victory," *Savannah Tribune*, March 23, 1922.

43. *Ibid.*

44. See *Heard v. State*, 114 Ga. 90, 39 S.E. 909 (1901); Vol. 1 *Who's Who of the Colored Race* 221 (F. L. Mather ed. 1915); *General Catalogue of the University of Michigan, 1837–1911*, at 837 (I. N. Demmon ed. 1912), listing Porter as attending but not graduating from the law school.

45. *Georgia Equal Rights Convention Program* 4, 8, 12, 16 (Feb. 13–14, 1906).

46. Vol. 4 *The Booker T. Washington Papers, 1895–98*, at 394 (L. R. Harlan, S. B. Kaufman, B. S. Kraft, and R W. Smock eds. 1975).

47. L. M. Hershaw, "Black Demosthenes," *Indianapolis Freeman*, April 27, 1889, at 1, col. 1.

48. I. G. Penn, *The Afro-American Press, and Its Editors* 187 (1891).

49. "J. H. Kinckle Buried," *Savannah Press*, March 7, 1922.

50. "42 Years Ago," *Savannah Tribune*, April 20, 1933; *New York Age*, April 25, 1891. For additional information on Robert W. Meldrim and Judge Robert Falligant, both of whom fought for the Confederate army during the Civil War, see "Judge Meldrim Passes Away," *The Savannah Press*, Dec. 9, 1933, and "Death of Judge Robert Falligant," *The Savannah Press*, Jan. 9, 1902.

51. R. E. Perdue, *The Negro in Savannah, 1865–1900*, at 130 (1973).

52. *Dictionary of American Negro Biography* 496–97 (R. Logan and M. Winston eds. 1982).

53. *Twentieth-Century Negro Literature* 129 (D. W. Culp ed. 1902).

54. Vol. 1 *Who's Who of the Colored Race* 175 (F. L. Mather ed. 1915); Vol. 1 *Who's Who in Colored America* 122 (J. J. Boris ed. 1927).

55. "Judge Commended Lawyer J. G. Lemon," *The Savannah Tribune*, Dec. 11, 1920.

56. "Two Young Savannahians Pass Bar," *Savannah Tribune*, July 14, 1932.

57. "Local Colored Lawyer Admitted in U.S. Court," *Savannah News*, Nov. 19, 1942.

58. *General Catalogue of the University of Michigan, 1837–1911*, at 524 (I. N. Demmon ed. 1912).

59. *Dictionary of American Negro Biography* 610 (R. Logan and M. Winston eds. 1982).

60. H. Walton, Jr., *Black Politics* 67 (1972).

61. *Ibid.*

62. "Dixie Lawyer Gives Police First Setback," *Chicago Defender*, May 21, 1927.

63. "Two Southern Court Cases," 37 *Crisis* 16–17 (Jan.–Dec. 1930).

64. A. Buni, *Robert L. Vann of Pittsburgh Courier* 181 (1974); W. F. Nowlin, *The Negro in American Politics* 64–65 (1931).

65. "Negro Admitted to Practice Before U.S. Supreme Court on Motion of Negro Attorney," *Atlanta Independent*, Nov. 6, 1930. Geer, a self-taught lawyer, had a deep commitment to assisting poor, working black people of Georgia. He risked his life on several occasions to represent black defendants. Sometimes his offer to help black defendants was rejected because they believed "it was too great a risk to have Negro lawyers defend them." B. J. Davis, Jr., *Communist Councilman from Harlem* 47–48 (1969).

66. "Future Cloudy," *N.Y. Times*, Aug. 16, 1937.

67. For an account of the Herndon trial see A. Herndon, *Let Me Live* 351–54 (reprint, 1969), for closing argument to jury in defense of Angelo Herndon by Benjamin Davis, Jr., and C. H. Martin, *The Angelo Herndon Case and Southern Justice* 34, 35–61 (1976); see also, *Harvard Law Quinquennial* 121 (F. S. Kimball ed. 1948) and M. Naison, *Communists in Harlem During the Depression* 75 (1983).

68. *Ibid. (Communists in Harlem)*.

69. *Dictionary of American Negro Biography* 160 (R. Logan and M. Winston eds. 1982).

70. *Herndon v. State*, 178 Ga. 832, 174 S.E. 597 (1934) (John H. Geer, Benjamin H. (*sic*) Davis, Jr., and Ewing C. Baskette for Herndon), reversed *Herndon v. Georgia*, 295 U.S. 442 (1935). No black lawyers made an appearance in this case before the U.S. Supreme Court. The case was handled by Whitney North Seymour.

71. M. Naison, *Communists in Harlem During the Depression* 75 (1983), quoting C. H. Martin, *The Angelo Herndon Case and Southern Justice* 36–61 (1976); B. J. Davis, Jr., *Communist Councilman from Harlem* 81 (1969). Regarding the Euel Lee case, see *Lee v. State*, 164 Md. 550, 165 A. 614 (1933). Bernard Ades and David Levinson, both white lawyers, handled this case. In the same year, Ades was almost disbarred. The circumstances of the disbarment proceeding were said to be based on Ades's legal participation in unpopular causes and representation of unpopular groups. Charles Hamilton Houston represented Ades for a period during his disbarment proceeding, an apparent repayment for Ades's efforts to save the life of Euel Lee, who was black. G. R. McNeil, *Groundwork: Charles Hamilton Houston and the Struggle for Civil Rights* 95–99 (1983). Regarding the Scottsboro case, see D. T. Carter, *Scottsboro: A Tragedy of the American South* 249, 313–14, 318 (1969), for mention of the involvement of Benjamin J. Davis, Jr., in the Herndon case.

72. B. J. Davis, Jr., *Communist Councilman from Harlem* 45 (1969).

73. Cook, "6 Take Georgia Bar Exams and All 6 Flunk," *Baltimore Afro-American*, Oct. 12, 1940.

74. "Test Georgia Ban on Lawyer in High Court," *Chicago Defender*, June 12, 1943.

75. Cook, "6 Take Georgia Bar Exams and All 6 Flunk," *Baltimore Afro-American*, Oct. 12, 1940.

76. *Ibid.*

77. "Four Fail to Pass Georgia Bar Exams," *Atlanta Daily World*, July 12, 1941.

78. Cook, "6 Take Georgia Bar Exams and All 6 Flunk," *Baltimore Afro-American*, Oct. 12, 1940.

79. "Governor Gets Protest Over Failure to Qualify Lawyers," *Atlanta Daily World*, Jan. 1, 1944; "Appeal Is Lost by Negro in Augusta," *Savannah News*, Sept. 11, 1943; Lee, "Ga. Court Rejects Negro Plea to Practice Law," *Daily Worker*, Feb. 15, 1944; "Prospective Negro Lawyers in Georgia Declared Victims of Bar Examiners," *Pittsburgh Courier*, Jan. 15, 1944. Ross argued his own

case before the Georgia Supreme Court, but without the examination paper, he was unable to prove his claim. *Ex Parte Ross*, 196 Ga. 499, 26 S.E. 2d 880 (1943); 197 Ga. 257, 28 S.E. 2d (1944).

80. "Admit Clayton to Georgia Bar," *Atlanta Daily World*, Dec. 29, 1944.

81. "Negro Woman Will Ask for Admission to Georgia Bar," *Atlanta Constitution*, March 1919.

82. Bell, "News of Atlanta's Negro Community," *Atlanta Journal*, Dec. 27, 1942.

83. "One of Eighty Taking State Law Examination Wednesday Is Miss R. E. Pruden," *Atlanta Daily World*, July 1, 1937.

84. *Ibid.*

85. "First Negro Woman Passes Georgia Bar," *Pittsburgh Courier*, Jan. 30, 1943; "Mrs. Herndon Got Law Education the Hard Way," *Atlanta Daily World*, April 5, 1943.

86. *New National Era*, June 29, 1871; *Biographical Directory: United States Congress* 507 (1989). Abbott served in U.S. Senate from July 14, 1868 to March 3, 1871.

87. *Ibid.* (*New National Era*).

88. *Ibid.*

89. *Ibid.*

90. W. J. Simmons, *Men of Mark* 433 (1887). Booker T. Washington's reference to John S. Leary as "the first man in North Carolina to be admitted to the bar" is in error. B. T. Washington, *The Story of the Negro* 203–4 (1909).

91. Letter from Martha W. Wheeler, registrar, Shaw University, to Charles S. Brown, June 3, 1958, quoting from the "old catalogue."

92. S. D. Smith, *The Negro in Congress, 1870–1901*, at 117 (1940). O'Hara attended Howard University's law school for a short time, but did not graduate. *Dictionary of American Negro Biography* 474 (R. Logan and M. Winston eds. 1982); E. Anderson, "James O'Hara of North Carolina: Black Leadership and Local Government," in *Southern Black Leaders of the Reconstruction Era* 102 (H. N. Rabinowitz ed. 1981).

93. *Id.* at 117 (*Negro in Congress*); *id.* at 101; E. Anderson, *Race and Politics in North Carolina, 1872–1901: The Black Second*, at 63 (1981).

94. *Id.* at 118 (*Negro in Congress*); E. Anderson, "James O'Hara of North Carolina: Black Leadership and Local Government," in *Southern Black Leaders of the Reconstruction Era* 114 (H. N. Rabinowitz ed. 1981).

95. *O'Hara v. Powell*, 80 N.C. 104 (1879).

96. S. D. Smith, *The Negro in Congress, 1870–1901*, at 118 (1940); B. A. Ragsdale and J. D. Treese, *Black Americans in Congress, 1870–1989*, at 105 (1990).

97. *Id.* at 119 (*Negro in Congress*). See also, *The Civil Rights Cases*, 109 U.S. 3 (1883).

98. *Id.* at 119–20 (*Negro in Congress*).

99. *Id.* at 120.

100. *Id.* at 121.

101. *Ibid.*

102. E. Anderson, "James O'Hara of North Carolina: Black Leadership and Local Government," in *Southern Black Leaders of the Reconstruction Era* 125 (H. N. Rabinowitz ed. 1981). Collins is said to have been an "inexperienced black lawyer." It was also believed that the solicitor's position was too important a job for a black, particularly since the solicitor had responsibility over nine

counties. E. Anderson, *Race and Politics in North Carolina, 1872–1901: The Black Second*, at 64 (1981). In fact, "white Democrats were shocked by the victory of an obscure . . . Negro [lawyer]" (*Id.* at 317). Some had even suggested that "Collins may have been . . . a figurehead, guided by a white lawyer [J. C. L. Harris] who helped him capture the Republican nomination" (*ibid.*). Such observations are not based in fact. Collins may have been inexperienced when he won the post of solicitor, but if his inexperience had adversely affected his performance, he likely would have been run out of office. Collins must have had great persuasive powers, as an unknown candidate, to beat O'Hara, who was described by some white lawyers as knowing more than they (*id.* at 63). J. C. L. Harris, the white lawyer who assisted Collins in legal matters, could be described as Collins's mentor. But it is unlikely that a white lawyer would take such an interest in a black lawyer if Collins needed Harris to transact "most of the business for him" (*id.* at 317).

103. E. Anderson, *Race and Politics in North Carolina, 1872–1901: The Black Second*, at 207 (1981).

104. *Ibid.*

105. *Ibid.*

106. Vol. 1 *Chronicle of Black Lawyers in North Carolina* 6 (D. E. Terry ed. 1981), pamphlet; *Who's Who in Philadelphia* 86–88 (C. F. White ed. 1912); *Twentieth-Century Negro Literature* 224 (D. W. Culp ed. 1902); B. A. Ragsdale and J. D. Treese, *Black Americans in Congress, 1870–1989*, at 159 (1990).

107. S. D. Smith, *The Negro in Congress, 1870–1901*, at 126 (1940).

108. *Ibid.* See also, E. Anderson, *Race and Politics in North Carolina, 1872–1901: The Black Second*, at 282 (1981), for other legislative measures that Congressman White sought, all of which failed.

109. *Id.* at 126–27 (*Negro in Congress*); *id* at 292 (*Race and Politics*).

110. Reid, "The Post-Congressional Career of George H. White," 61 *J. Negro History* 362, 363 (Oct. 1976). Another source states that White settled in Philadelphia, Pennsylvania, after he retired from Congress. Vol. 1 *Who's Who of the Colored Race* 282 (F. L. Mather ed. 1915).

111. Lewis, "The History of Black Lawyers in North Carolina," *North Carolina Bar Association Notes* 9 (Dec. 1987), referring to F. Logan, *The Negro in North Carolina, 1876–1894*, at 108 (1974).

112. H. G. Edmonds, *The Negro and Fusion Politics in North Carolina, 1894–1901*, at 126 (1951).

113. *New York State Black and Puerto Rican Legislators: 1917–1977*, at 6 (J. A. Stewart ed. 1977); *Dictionary of American Negro Biography* 349 (R. Logan and M. Winston eds. 1982); G. Osofsky, "Come Out from Among Them," in *Black History* 381 (M. Drimmer ed. 1968). Johnson was one of the first black lawyers to proclaim "that the word *Negro* is written with a capital *N*. It . . . will . . . magnify the race." E. A. Johnson, *History of the Negro Race in America and the Negro Soldier in the Spanish American War* v (1891) (original emphasis).

114. H. G. Edmonds, *The Negro and Fusion Politics in North Carolina, 1894–1901*, at 108, 111 (1951).

115. Vol. 1 *Chronicle of Black Lawyers in North Carolina* 8 (D. E. Terry ed. 1981), pamphlet.

116. *Id.* at 11.

117. H. G. Edmonds, *The Negro and Fusion Politics in North Carolina, 1894–1901*, at 164 (1951).

118. *Id.* at 165.

119. Vol. 1 *Who's Who of the Colored Race* 193 (F. L. Mather ed. 1915).

120. In 1904, Champ F. Rich became Rocky Mount's first black lawyer; in 1912 Nereus Deleon White became Goldboro's, and in 1929 McKinley Battle became Kinston's. Vol. 1 *Chronicle of Black Lawyers in North Carolina* 14–15 (D. E. Terry ed. 1981), pamphlet.

121. Groom, "No Place for Black Judge's Portrait," *Washington Star*, May 9, 1976, at E1, col. 2. Interview by author with Mrs. Armond W. Scott in February 1965.

122. "N.C. Has Only Deaf Mute Lawyer of Race in America" (source unidentified), July 31, 1926 (newspaper article in author's files).

123. *Ibid.* Letter to Charles S. Brown from Martha W. Wheeler, registrar, Shaw University, June 3, 1958, regarding O'Kelly's graduation from Shaw University's Law School.

124. *Ibid.* ("N.C. Has Only Deaf Mute Lawyer").

125. "N.C. State Bar Association," *Supreme Circle News*, Dec. 10, 1921.

126. "N.C. Has Only Deaf Mute Lawyer of Race in America" (source unidentified), July 31, 1926 (newspaper article in author's files).

127. *Ibid.*

128. Bryant, "Colored Lawyer of Goldsboro Wins Fame," *The Raleigh Independent*, Feb. 21, 1920.

129. Vol. 1 *Who's Who of the Colored Race* 41 (F. L. Mather ed. 1915); *The Chicago Defender*, April 24, 1915. Clarence Benjamin Curley, a 1914 Howard University law graduate, also was admitted to the North Carolina bar around 1914.

130. *Harvard Law Quinquennial* 34 (F. S. Kimball ed. 1948).

131. "Young Colored Lawyer Makes Brilliant Plea in Railway Damage Suit," *Pittsburgh Courier*, March 27, 1925.

132. "Probably First Colored Attorney to Appear Here," *Chester News*, April 15, 1927.

133. Calvin, "North Carolina Has Finest Set of Judges, Says Durham Attorney," *Pittsburgh Courier*, Sept. 1, 1928.

134. *Ibid.*

135. *Ibid.*

136. *Ibid.*

137. *Ibid.*

138. *Ibid.*

139. "U. of North Carolina Hears Atty. Andrews" (source unknown), 1931 (newspaper article in files of author).

140. "Biographical Profile—Charles W. Williamson" (author's files).

141. Selby, "For Lawyer Carnage, Giving in a Little Accomplishes a Lot," *Raleigh Times*, April 1987, at 1B, col. 3.

142. Houston, "The Need for Negro Lawyers," 4 *J. of Negro Ed.* 49, 52 (1935); M. V. Tushnet, *The NAACP's Legal Strategy Against Segregated Education, 1925–1950*, at 52–53 (1987).

143. "North Carolina Licenses Negro Woman Attorney," *Atlanta Constitution*, May 31, 1933.

144. "Negro Takes Bar Exam," *Atlanta Constitution*, Aug. 4, 1937; "Durham Negro Woman First to Take Bar Exam," *Durham Sun*, Aug. 3, 1937.

145. Letter from T. C. Callison, attorney general, South Carolina, to Charles S. Brown, Oct. 4, 1948; letter from J. B. Westbrook, clerk, Supreme Court of South Carolina, to Charles S. Brown, May 21, 1958: "[T]he white man's basic

view of the Negro as an inferior caste led to restrictions that treated the freeman oppressively." See also, P. Lamson, *The Glorious Failure* 35 (1973); J. S. Reynolds, *Reconstruction in South Carolina, 1865–1877*, at 59 (reprint, 1969), on Whipper and the Republican party. See also, J. R. Oldfield, "A High and Honorable Calling: Black Lawyers in South Carolina, 1868–1915," 23 *Journal of American Studies* 395 (Great Britain, 1989), reprinted in, 10 *African Americans and the Legal Profession in Historical Perspective* 281 (P. Finkelman ed. 1992).

146. *Ibid.* (Westbrook's letter).

147. *Charleston Daily Courier*, Sept. 24, 1868.

148. P. Lamson, *The Glorious Failure* 75–76 (1973).

149. *Id.* at 145 (starred footnote), 172, 182, 205, 271; S. D. Smith, *The Negro in Congress, 1870–1901*, at 52 (1940); Miller, "Robert Brown Elliott: Reconstruction Leader," 80 *Crisis* 267, 268 (Oct. 1973).

150. Straker, "Brief Sketch of the Political Life of Hon. Robert Browne Elliott of South Carolina," 9 *The A.M.E. Church Rev.* 376, 381 (April 1893); P. Lamson, *The Glorious Failure* 51 (1973); J. S. Reynolds, *Reconstruction in South Carolina, 1865–1877*, at 77 (reprint, 1969).

151. P. Lamson, *The Glorious Failure* 73 (1973). Elliott may have studied law in England, where he attended Eton College in the early 1860s. See F. L. Styles, *Negroes and the Law* 121 (1937).

152. *Id.* at 51 (starred footnote), 56, 58–60, 73 (*The Glorious Failure*).

153. *Id.* at 75, 82. In 1869, Robert Brown Elliott also was elected to the state board, which oversaw the "Lunatic Asylum." J. S. Reynolds, *Reconstruction in South Carolina, 1865–1877*, at 123 (reprint, 1969).

154. "General R. B. Elliott: Statesman, Jurist and Orator—His Brilliant Career in South Carolina During the Reconstruction Period," *N.Y. Globe*, Aug. 16, 1884.

155. P. Lamson, *The Glorious Failure* 76–77 (1973), quoting the *Charleston Daily News*, Sept. 1, 1869.

156. For example, Robert Brown Elliott was one of two lawyers retained in 1870 by the managers of the impeachment proceedings against circuit judge T. O. W. Vernon. Brown received a fee of $1,000 for his services. J. S. Reynolds, *Reconstruction in South Carolina, 1865–1877*, at 152 (reprint, 1969).

157. P. Lamson, *The Glorious Failure* 96, 118 (1973). See also, B. A. Ragsdale and J. D. Treese, *Black Americans in Congress, 1870–1989*, at 45 (1990).

158. *Id.* at 122, quoting Elliott's speech in the *Columbia Daily Union*, Feb. 23, 1874 (*The Glorious Failure*).

159. *Id.* at 123, 128.

160. *Id.* at 174–76; the *Slaughter-House Cases*, 83 U.S. (16 Wall.) 36 (1873).

161. *Id.* at 181, quoting 2 Cong. Rec. 407, 410, 43rd Cong., 1st Sess., Jan. 6, 1874 (*The Glorious Failure*); see also, S. D. Smith, *The Negro in Congress, 1870–1901*, at 55 (1940).

162. *Id.* at 182 (*The Glorious Failure*).

163. *Id.* at 164–71 (1973), quoting the *Charleston Daily News*, Dec. 10, 1872; *id.* at 168.

164. John J. Patterson's victory over Robert Brown Elliott for the United States Senate seat was decisive. Patterson received ninety votes to Elliott's thirty-three. Elliott beat Scott, however, who received only seven votes. The remaining votes were scattered among other candidates. J. S. Reynolds, *Reconstruction in South Carolina, 1865–1877*, at 162 (reprint, 1969).

165. *Id.* at 200.

166. Elliott served as speaker of the house in the Fifty-first General Assembly, Nov. 24, 1874–April 14, 1876. Vol. 1 *The Biographical Directory of the South Carolina House of Representatives, 1692–1973* (Sessions List), at 420 (W. B. Edgar ed., 3d. ed. 1974). During the time in which Elliott campaigned for the legislature, he held the position of high sheriff in one of the counties in South Carolina. F. L. Styles, *Negroes and the Law* 121 (1937). The first black speaker of the house was Samuel J. Lee, who is discussed later in this chapter.

167. P. Lamson, *The Glorious Failure* 196–98 (1973).

168. R. N. Current, *Those Terrible Carpetbaggers: A Reinterpretation* 334, 340 (1988).

169. Initially, Robert Brown Elliott had opposed D. H. Chamberlain's bid to win the nomination for governor, but his efforts failed after a bitter fight. Yet Elliott was able to muster enough votes to win a place on Chamberlain's ticket for the post of attorney general. Chamberlain later wrote that he had "made a grave mistake" by refusing to run on the same ticket with Elliott, because he "gave offense to some honest men of both races." J. S. Reynolds, *Reconstruction in South Carolina, 1865–1877*, at 367 (reprint, 1969), quoting letter of D. H. Chamberlain to William Lloyd Garrison, June 11, 1877.

170. *Statement of Political Cases*, 8 S.C. 365 (1876). So important was the issue of these elections that the reporter of the South Carolina Supreme Court took the unprecedented step of writing a summary of the circumstances giving rise to the instant litigation. Robert B. Elliott's name is mentioned.

171. *State ex rel. Wallace v. Hayne and Mackey*, 8 S.C. 367 (1876). This was a key political case, in which Justice Jonathan Jasper Wright concurred with the court's majority against Governor Daniel H. Chamberlain's slate. *Id.* at 380.

172. P. Lamson, *The Glorious Failure* 254–67 (1973); Straker, "The Negro in the Profession of Law," 8 *The A.M.E. Church Rev.* 178, 182 (1891).

173. *Id.* at 278 (*The Glorious Failure*).

174. *A Documentary History of the Negro People in the United States* 678, 684 (H. Aptheker ed. 1969).

175. F. L. Styles, *Negroes and the Law* 123 (1937).

176. P. Lamson, *The Glorious Failure* 51 (starred footnote) (1973).

177. Whipper and Elliott seemed to have spent a considerable amount of their time in politics. In 1871 Whipper served as a member of the South Carolina State Orphan Asylum, earning an annual salary of $3,500. R. S. Reynolds, *Reconstruction in South Carolina, 1865–1877*, at 118 (reprint, 1969).

178. *Id.* at 133, 144. Elliott himself was accused of accepting a $10,500 fee to assist in defeating efforts to impeach Governor Scott, "an allegation . . . Elliott himself flatly denied." *Id.* at 141.

179. One scholar of the Reconstruction era who was critical of blacks described Whipper: "W. J. Whipper was said by some of his party to be easily among the very ablest colored men in public life in [South Carolina]. He showed considerable shrewdness, but was not generally thought to be either capable or well informed. . . . Corrupt to the core, always insolent, fond of flaunting his stolen money in the faces of white men . . . a coward . . . and a perjurer, he was a good specimen of the leaders whom the Republican party raised up for the Negroes in South Carolina." J. S. Reynolds, *Reconstruction in South Carolina, 1865–1877*, at 333 (reprint, 1969). In 1882, a white citizen of Beaufort praised Whipper for "a good many qualities," including his defense before a colored jury of a white youth accused of murdering a black youth and

for the protection of two white men facing a black mob. G. B. Tindall, *South Carolina Negroes, 1877–1900*, at 146 (1966).

180. R. N. Current, *Those Terrible Carpetbaggers: A Reinterpretation* 340 (1988).

181. *Id.* at 340, 341. Governor Chamberlain also did not believe that Whipper was qualified to serve on the circuit court. J. S. Reynolds, *Reconstruction in South Carolina, 1865–1877*, at 322 (reprint, 1969).

182. *Whipper v. Reed*, 9 S.C. 5 (1877). In a note to this case, the court reporter discloses that "he has not been furnished with the pleadings nor with a brief containing a statement of the facts, and that he has been compelled to gather them from another source. He also regrets that he has not been furnished with the arguments of the counsel for the defense nor even their names." It is clear from the case that Whipper represented himself before the court. Hence, the court ruled against Whipper based upon facts not before the court and with no briefs filed by lawyers on behalf of Reed or the state (*id.* at 5–6). For racial sentiments of the times, see W. L. Fleming, Vol. 2 *Documentary History of Reconstruction* 405–6 (reprint, 1960).

183. P. Lamson, *The Glorious Failure* 284 (1973).

184. *A Documentary History of the Negro People in the United States* 780 (H. Aptheker ed. 1969), referring to the *Journal of the Constitutional Convention of the State of South Carolina*, at 89, 412–13, Sept. 10–Dec. 4, 1895.

185. Letter from Amelia C. Beck, assistant clerk, United States Supreme Court, to Charles S. Brown, April 5, 1962. See *Brownfield v. South Carolina*, 189 U.S. 426 (1903) (with J. L. Mitchell and E. M. Hewlett).

186. Brown, "The Genesis of the Negro Lawyer in New England," 22 *The Negro Hist. Bull.* (Part I), 147–49 (April 1959). See also, *The Beaufort Republican*, March 6, 1873, which describes Allen as "a colored man of light complexion and . . . said to have Scotch blood in his veins"; letter from Virginia Rugheimer, librarian, Charleston Library Society, to Charles Sumner Brown, Sept. 23, 1958. In 1872, Macon B. Allen was respected enough to win the nomination for secretary of state on an alternative slate. He opposed F. J. Moses, Jr., who won the governorship. J. S. Reynolds, *Reconstruction in South Carolina, 1865–1877*, at 223 (reprint, 1969).

187. *Columbia Daily Union*, Feb. 20, 1873; *National Roster of Black Judicial Officers* 2 (M. Kancewick ed. 1980); *Charleston Daily Courier*, March 14, 1872, Feb. 27, 1873. Lee was the nephew of Robert Morris, Sr., of Suffolk County, Massachusetts, the nation's second black lawyer. *New National Era*, March 28, 1872.

188. Letter from Eleanor M. Richardson, reference librarian, University of South Carolina, to Charles S. Brown, Feb. 21, 1977.

189. *Ibid.*

190. F. L. Styles, *Negroes and the Law* 124 (1937); J. S. Reynolds, *Reconstruction in South Carolina, 1865–1877*, at 77 (reprint, 1969).

191. R. H. Woody, "Jonathan Jasper Wright, Associate Justice of the Supreme Court of South Carolina, 1870–77," 18 *J. of Negro History* 114, 116–117 (1833), citing *Proceedings of the South Carolina Constitutional Convention* 599–600 (1868).

192. J. S. Reynolds, *Reconstruction in South Carolina, 1865–1877*, at 61 (reprint, 1969).

193. *Ibid.*

194. *Id.* at 117, quoting the *Charleston Daily News*, July 26, 1867.

195. Vol. 20 *Dictionary of American Biography* 558 (1936).

258 The Southeastern States

196. *Arkansas Daily Gazette*, Feb. 20, 1870.

197. R. H. Woody, "Jonathan Jasper Wright, Associate Justice of the Supreme Court of South Carolina, 1870–77," 18 *J. of Negro History* 119–20 (1933). In 1868, the legislature appointed Samuel B. Thompson, who had served as a delegate to the constitutional convention as justice of the peace for eight years. Little is known about Thompson's legal training, but he is the first known black judicial officer in the state of South Carolina. *Afro-American Encyclopedia; Or, The Thoughts, Doings and Sayings of the Race* 568 (J. T. Haley ed. 1895).

198. Justice Wright's first opinion appeared in volume 3 of the South Carolina Supreme Court reports in 1871. His last opinion appeared in volume 9 in 1876. Justice Wright's opinions covered a broad range of doctrines, such as those involving master-servant relations, trespass, damages, larceny, evidence, torts, corporations, as well as several opinions on technical procedural matters. A critic of the Reconstruction era has asserted that Justice Wright's opinions were written by a ghostwriter, suggesting that the subjects they dealt with were "beyond Wright's capacity." J. S. Reynolds, *Reconstruction in South Carolina, 1865–1877*, at 128 (reprint, 1969). Reynolds's assertion is unsupported by fact or by any scholar of the Reconstruction era. See R. N. Current, *Those Terrible Carpetbaggers: A Reinterpretation* 363–364 (1988); E. Foner, *Reconstruction, 1863–1877*, at 326 (1988).

199. R. N. Current, *Those Terrible Carpetbaggers: A Reinterpretation* 365 (1988).

200. *Ibid.* A review of Associate Justice Wright's opinions and the cases in which he participated does not indicate that Daniel H. Chamberlain appeared before the South Carolina Supreme Court between 1870 and 1877 as a private lawyer. But it may be theorized that Chamberlain was a member of one of the numerous law firms that made appearances before the court, and, perhaps, in this position he could have offered a bribe to Justice Wright. However, it is highly doubtful that Chief Justice Franklin J. Moses, Sr., and Associate Justice A. J. Williard, both seasoned judges and lawyers, could have been duped or swayed by Associate Justice Wright. See Vols. 5–6 *South Carolina Reports.* And yet a document has been published purporting to implicate Justice Wright in a bribery attempt. W. L. Fleming, Vol. 2, *Documentary History of Reconstruction* 41–42 (reprint, 1960).

201. 5 S.C. 189 (1873) (Willard, A. J., dissenting).

202. J. S. Reynolds, *Reconstruction in South Carolina, 1865–1877*, at 492 (reprint, 1969).

203. *Whaley v. Bank of Charleston*, 5 S.C. 262 (1874) (April Term).

204. P. Lamson, *The Glorious Failure* 271 (1973).

205. R. N. Current, *Those Terrible Carpetbaggers: A Reinterpretation* 365 (1988); G. B. Tindall, *South Carolina Negroes, 1877–1900*, at 17–18 (1966).

206. *Aiken Tribune*, Nov. 30, 1872; Lee was speaker of the house during the Fiftieth General Assembly, November 26, 1872–March 17, 1874. Vol. 1 *The Biographical Dictionary of the South Carolina House of Representatives, 1692–1973* (Sessions List), at 416 (W. B. Edgar ed. 1974).

207. P. Lamson, *The Glorious Failure* 255–57 (1973).

208. "General R. B. Elliott: Statesman, Jurist, and Orator—His Brilliant Career in South Carolina During the Reconstruction Period," *New York Globe*, Aug. 16, 1884.

209. *Ibid.* For additional information on Samuel J. Lee, see, J. R. Oldfield, "A High and Honorable Calling: Black Lawyers in South Carolina, 1868–1915,"

23 *Journal of American Studies* 395, 400 (Great Britain, 1989), reprinted in 10 *Race, Law and American History, 1700–1900: African Americans and the Legal Profession in Historical Perspective* 281, 286 (P. Finkelman ed. 1992).

210. *The College of Life or Practical Self Educator: A Manual of Self Improvement for the Colored Race* 150 (H. D. Northrop, J. R. Gay, and I. G. Penn eds. 1896).

211. G. R. Richings, *Evidence of Progress Among Colored People* 287 (1904).

212. Miller, "David Straker and Other Reconstruction Jurists," 81 *Crisis* 314 (Nov., 1974), quoting Straker (no source cited).

213. *Ibid.*

214. P. Lamson, *The Glorious Failure* 280 (1973).

215. See, e.g., *State v. Coleman*, 20 S.C. 441 (1884), discussed extensively by Dorothy D. Hawkshawe in "David Augustus Straker, Black Lawyer and Reconstruction Politician, 1842–1908," at 56–69 (Ph.D. diss., Catholic University, 1974).

216. White, "The Rev. William J. White Makes Some Needful Corrections to [John F.] Quarles Life and Work," *New York Freeman*, Feb. 4, 1885.

217. *Ibid.*

218. Letter from J. B. Westbrook, clerk, Supreme Court of South Carolina, to Charles S. Brown, May 21, 1958; Vol. 1 *Biographical Directory of the South Carolina Senate, 1776–1985*, at 574 (N. L. Bailey, M. L. Morgan, and C. R. Taylor eds. 1985).

219. E. M. Coulter, *Negro Legislators in Georgia During the Reconstruction Period* 115 (1968).

220. Miller, "David Straker and Other Reconstruction Jurists," 81 *Crisis* 314 (Nov. 1974); Vol. 1 *Biographical Directory of the South Carolina House of Representatives* (Session List) 443–47 (W. B. Edgar 3d ed. 1974). Washington was erroneously credited as being South Carolina's first black lawyer in a letter from T. C. Callison, attorney general of South Carolina, to Charles S. Brown, Oct. 4, 1948.

221. Vol. 1 *Who's Who of the Colored Race* 15 (F. L. Mather ed. 1915).

222. M. Berry, *Black Resistance, White Law* 115 (1971).

223. *Ibid.*

224. R. N. Current, *Those Terrible Carpetbaggers: A Reinterpretation* 328 (1988) (no sources are cited regarding Chamberlain's statement); J. S. Reynolds, *Reconstruction in South Carolina, 1865–1877*, at 234 (reprint, 1969).

225. *Ibid.* (*Those Terrible Carpetbaggers*).

226. F. L. Styles, *Negroes and the Law* 138 (1937). The number of black students at the University of South Carolina was so significant that "it soon exceeded 200—more than nine-tenths being Negroes." J. S. Reynolds, *Reconstruction in South Carolina, 1867–1877*, at 236 (reprint, 1969).

227. In 1873, after the resignation of several white trustees who opposed the enrollment of black students at the University of South Carolina, Samuel J. Lee was made responsible for the admission of the first group of black students to the law school. They were C. M. Wilder, Joseph D. Boston, Lawrence Cain, and Paris Simkins, in addition to those mentioned in the text. Three white students were also admitted. In 1874, F. L. Cardozo, a black student, was admitted to the law school. J. S. Reynolds, *Reconstruction in South Carolina, 1865–1877*, at 234 (reprint, 1969). All of the blacks admitted to law school had already served in professional positions in government. C. M. Wilder was the postmaster at Columbia, Joseph D. Boston was in the state legislature, as were Lawrence Cain and Paris Simkins. F. L. Cardozo was state treasurer of South Carolina. *Ibid.* See also, E. L. Green, *A History of the University of South Carolina* 409–15 (1916).

228. *Dictionary of American Negro Biography* 439 (R. Logan and M. Winston eds. 1982).

229. F. L. Styles, *Negroes and the Law* 138 (1937).

230. *Id.* at 140.

231. *Ibid.*

232. S. D. Smith, *The Negro in Congress, 1870–1901*, at 104 (1940).

233. *Ibid.*

234. *Ibid.*, quoting 22 *Cong. Rec.* 2691, 51st Cong., 2nd Sess., Feb. 14, 1891.

235. *Id.* at 105; F. L. Styles, *Negroes and the Law* 139–40 (1937).

236. *Dictionary of American Negro Biography* 439 (R. Logan and M. Winston eds. 1982).

237. R. W. Logan, *Howard University: The First One Hundred Years, 1867–1967*, at 86 (1968).

238. Vol. 1 *Who's Who of the Colored Race* 121 (F. L. Mather ed. 1915); *Dictionary of American Negro Biography* 651–52 (R. Logan and M. Winston eds. 1982).

239. *Id.* at 121 (*Who's Who of the Colored Race*).

240. "The Civil Rights Act, a Negro Lawyer on the Court's Decision," *New York Evening Post*, Oct. 16, 1883, at 4, col. 1.

241. *The Civil Rights Cases*, 109 U.S. 3 (1883).

242. *Id.* at 7.

243. "The Civil Rights Act, a Negro Lawyer on the Court's Decision," *New York Evening Post*, Oct. 16, 1883, at 4, col. 1. Greener, of course, was referring to Chief Justice Roger B. Taney's opinion which held, in part, that a black man had no rights that a white man was bound to respect. *Dred Scott v. Sandford*, 60 U.S. (19 How.) 393, 407 (1857).

244. "Richard T. Greener: The First Black Harvard College Graduate," in *Varieties of Black Experience at Harvard* 35 (W. Sollors, T. A. Underwood, and C. Titcomb eds. 1986); A. Blakely, *Russia and the Negro* 47 (1986); *The National Cyclopedia of the Colored Race* Vol. 1, 530 (C. Richardson ed. 1919).

245. Blakely, "Richard T. Greener and the 'Talented Tenth's' Dilemma," 59 *J. of Negro History* 305 (Oct. 1974).

246. A. Blakely, *Russia and the Negro* 47 (1986). See also, *Diplomatic and Consular Service of the United States* 29, 39 (Dec. 1903); C. S. Johnson, *The Negro College Graduate* 333 (1938); *Dictionary of American Negro Biography* 267–68 (R. Logan and M. Winston eds. 1982). In all, Greener "spent more than seven years as U.S. consul at Vladivostok, [Russia]." Vol. 2 *The Booker T. Washington Papers, 1860–89*, at 291 (L. R. Harlan and P. Daniel ed. 1972). Greener left the foreign service under rumors (spread by the Department of State) of extramarital affairs and drunkenness. Greener claimed that these rumors were slanderous and offered testimony from American citizens in Russia to refute these claims. *Id.* at Vol. 9 *The Booker T. Washington Papers*, at 10. At the urging of Booker T. Washington, Samuel Laing Williams, a black lawyer from Chicago, was considered but not appointed as Greener's replacement at Vladivostok. *Id.* at Vol. 8 *The Booker T. Washington Papers*, at 532.

247. F. L. Styles, *Negroes and the Law* 128–29 (1937), quoting *The Clarion* (no date); G. R. Richings, *Evidence of Progress Among Colored People* 291, 293 (1904); Wynes, "T. McCants Stewart: Peripatetic Black South Carolinian," 80 *South Carolina Historical Magazine* 311, 312 (Oct. 1979).

248. William L. England, Jr., "The Condition of Southern Negroes 1886–1889 as Viewed by the *New York Age*," at 30–31 (M.A. thesis, Butler University, June 17, 1972).

249. W. J. Simmons, *Men of Mark* 163 (1887).

250. *Id.* at 164.

251. F. L. Styles, *Negroes and the Law* 183 (1937); Charles Metze, "The History of Allen University," in *African Methodism in South Carolina* 52 (1987).

252. *Ibid*; *Afro-American Encyclopedia; Or, The Thoughts, Doings and Sayings of the Race* 569 (J. T. Haley ed. 1895). Stuart attended law school with T. McCants Stewart and Richard T. Greener.

253. Hemingway, "Prelude to Change: Black Carolinians in the War Years, 1914–1920," 65 *J. of Negro History* 212 (1980).

254. "White Girl Wants to Share Porter's Estate," *The Evening Telegram*, May 1, 1907. The estate was valued at $2,655. "Claims a Negro's Estate," *The Morning Oregonian*, May 1, 1907.

255. *State v. Franklin*, 80 S.C. 332, 60 S.E. 953 (1908); *aff'd Franklin v. State of South Carolina*, 218 U.S. 161 (1910), popularly referred to as the "Pink Franklin Case."

256. *Directory of Members of the National Bar Association* 140, appended to *Eight Annual Convention Proceedings*, 1932 (lists Jacob Moorer).

257. Letter to author from John Adams, Jr., Dec. 20, 1988. The Pink Franklin case was known throughout the South. It was one of the few cases in which both the NAACP and Booker T. Washington had cooperated. After the South Carolina Supreme Court upheld the conviction of Pink Franklin, both blacks and whites believed that a white lawyer, former attorney general Charles J. Bonaparte, should have handled the case before the United States Supreme Court. However, Adams and Moorer were determined to demonstrate that black lawyers were as capable of arguing the case as Bonaparte. Although the Supreme Court affirmed the conviction, there is no evidence that Adams and Moorer failed in any way to adequately represent their client. For a short statement on the Pink Franklin case, see Vol. 10 *The Booker T. Washington Papers, 1909–11*, at 362–63 (L. R. Harlan, R. W. Smock, G. McTigue, and N E. Woodruff eds. 1981). The record indicates that Booker T. Washington was cool to the legal fight in the case, leaning more toward a political resolution. *Id.* at 364. See also, *Who's Who in Colored America* 3 (G. J. Fleming and C. E. Burckel eds. 7th ed. 1950).

258. "Two Southern Court Cases," 37 *Crisis* 16, 17 (Jan.–Dec. 1930). See also, Vol. 1 *Who's Who in Colored America* 702 (J. J. Boris ed. 1927).

259. M. V. Tushnet, *The NAACP's Legal Strategy Against Segregated Education, 1925–1950*, at 87 (1987); "Harold R. Boulware, Lawyer, Was a Pioneer in Civil Rights," *New York Times*, Jan. 30, 1983, at 26, col. 4.

260. "Crack Barrister," *Norfolk Journal and Guide*, July 25, 1942. See also, *State v. Grant*, 199 S.C. 412, 19 S.E. 2nd 638 (1941), *cert. denied*, 316 U.S. 662 (1942).

261. "Negro Woman Takes S.C. Bar Examination," *Atlanta Georgian*, Nov. 4, 1921.

262. "South Carolina Admits First Colored Woman to State Bar," *Pittsburgh Courier*, Dec. 27, 1941; "S.C. Admits Negro Woman to Bar," *Philadelphia Tribune*, Nov. 10, 1938; "Woman Lawyer Takes Examination for Bar in South Carolina," *New York Age*, Nov. 19, 1938.

263. *Id.* (*Pittsburgh Courier*).

264. "G. W. [*sic*] Wynn, a Colored Lawyer of Chicot County Brutally Murdered," *Arkansas Daily Republican*, Dec. 15, 1871.

265. L. P. Jackson, *Negro Officeholders in Virginia, 1865–1895*, at 40 (1946); G. F. Bragg, Jr., "Documents," 5 *J. Negro History* 242 (1920).

266. *New National Era*, Oct. 23, 1873.

267. Letter from E. M. Edward, deputy clerk, Circuit Court of the City of Richmond, to Charles S. Brown, Dec. 2, 1959.

268. W. H. Bryson and E. L. Shepard, "The Virginia Bar, 1870–1900," in *The New High Priest* 173 (G. W. Gawalt ed. 1984). On Robert Peel Brooks, the authors refer to *The Richmond Daily Dispatch*, Jan. 13, 1876, at 1 and Jan. 14, 1876, at 1.

269. *The New York Freeman*, Feb. 14, 1885.

270. *Ibid.*

271. *People's Advocate*, Sept. 27, 1879.

272. Williams, "Edwin Archer Randolph, LL.B., Rediscovered," 3 *The Richmond Quarterly* 46 (Spring 1981); *Biographies of Graduates of the Yale Law School, 1824–1899*, at 404 (R. W. Tuttle ed. 1911); letter from Barbara D. Simison, assistant reference librarian, Yale University Library, to Charles S. Brown, Oct. 15, 1958.

273. L. P. Jackson, *Negro Officeholders in Virginia* 16 (1945); Bragg, "Documents," 5 *J. Negro History* 244 (1920).

274. "William Micaijah Reid—A Biographical Sketch" 2, on file at Hampton University Archives (n.d.).

275. *Ibid.* Bragg, "Documents," 5 *J. Negro History* 235, 244 (1920).

276. L. P. Jackson, *Negro Officeholders in Virginia* 36, 81 (1946); R. F. Engs, *Freedom's First Generation* 159, 185, 192 (1979).

277. "William Micaijah Reid—A Biographical Sketch," 2–3, on file at Hampton University Archives (n.d.).

278. *Ibid.*

279. *Id.* at 2.

280. "The Industrial Condition, and Securing of Homes," 22 *The Southern Workman* 119, July, 1893. In the same year Booker T. Washington referred to Reid as "a successful lawyer, of excellent standing in Portsmouth, Va." Vol. 7 *The Booker T. Washington Papers, 1903–4*, at 30 (L. R. Harlan and R. W. Smock eds. 1977).

281. F. D. W., "Williams M. Reid," Vol. 1, No. 3 *Hampton Alumni Journal* 3–4 (Dec. 1924), quoting the *Portsmouth Star*, a leading white daily, under the caption "Bar Adopts Resolution on Death of Colored Lawyer."

282. "William Micaijah Reid—A Biographical Sketch," 3–4, Hampton University Archives (n.d.); "William M. Reid," 53 *The Southern Workman* 441, Oct. 1924; "Thomas Reid Dies in Virginia," *Afro-American*, Feb. 14, 1961.

283. Smith, "Whither the Black Lawyer in Virginia?" 34 *Virginia Bar News*, 8, 9 (Aug. 1985). Other co-founders of the Virginia Colored Bar Association were Harry Green, of Richmond, and Harry D. Dolphin, of Roanoke.

284. *Virginia's Contribution to Negro Leadership* 53 (W. M. Cooper ed. 1937) (mimeo). Reid was appointed by "the governor of Virginia to oversee the [Virginia] school's use of land grant funds." He was one of three curators of Hampton Institute. R. F. Engs, *Freedom's First Generation* 156 (1979).

285. *New York Globe*, May 5, 1883; L. P. Jackson, *Negro Officeholders in Virginia* 20 (1946).

286. Vol. 1 *The National Cyclopedia of the Colored Race* 309 (C. C. Richardson ed. 1919).

287. Vol. 1 *Who's Who in Colored America* 6–7 (J. J. Boris ed. 1927); Alexander, "The John M. Langston Law Club," 14 *The Shingle* 233 (Dec. 1951); Bragg, "Documents," 5 *J. of Negro History* 235, 244 (1920).

288. Presgraves, "Careers of Two Ex-Slaves," 7 *Wythe County Historical Rev.* 15–16 (July 1974).

289. T. C. Walker, *The Honey-pod Tree* 66–67 (1958).

290. *Id.* at 67.

291. *Id.* at 68.

292. *Id.* at 68–69.

293. *Id.* at 69.

294. *Id.* at 70.

295. *Ibid.*

296. *Id.* at 71.

297. *Id.* at 72–77.

298. Johnson, "School Is Named for T. C. Walker Again," *Gloucester-Matthews Gazette-Journal*, April 10, 1986, at 1, col. 3; MacInnis, "Marker to Honor Lawyer Who Shaped County's History," *Daily Press*, Feb. 12, 1986, at B2, col. 1; Cooper, "A Saucy Servant," *The Hampton Alumni Journal* 7 (May 1932); *Virginia's Contribution to Negro Leadership* 66 (W. Cooper ed. 1937) (mimeo).

299. "Honoring T. C. Walker," *Daily Press*, June 16, 1986, at A4, col. 1.

300. "T. C. Walker, Among Virginia Negroes," 49 *The Southern Workman* 421, 424 (Sept. 1920); Doggett, "From Slave Farm to County Training School," 55 *The Southern Workman* 500, Nov. 1926.

301. Boyd, "The Legend of Gloucester County," *Washington Post*, Feb. 26, 1984, at C1, col. 1.

302. Cooper, "A Saucy Servant," *The Hampton Alumni Journal* 7, 8–9 (May 1932); Davis, "T. C. Walker," *Journal and Guide*, May 9, 1936.

303. G. R. Segal, *Blacks in the Law* 187 (1983).

304. A. Meier, "Booker T. Washington: An Interpretation," in *Black History* 338, 351 (M. Drimmer ed. 1968). See also, *A Documentary History of the Negro People in the United States* 846 (H. Aptheker ed. 1969), citing the *Indianapolis Freeman*, Sept. 7, 1901.

305. A. Buni, *The Negro in Virginia Politics, 1902–1965*, at 40 (1967); Vol. 7 *The Booker T. Washington Papers, 1903–4*, at 30 (L. R. Harlan and R. W. Smock eds. 1977). In 1904, Hayes fought against efforts in Virginia to disfranchise blacks, a movement that was taking on a more subtle face in the United States Congress. Hayes and Harry S. Cummings, of Baltimore, met with President Theodore Roosevelt in 1904 to object to proposed legislation that would establish a quota for black congressional districts in the most heavily populated black communities in the South. Hayes believed that such legislation was misplaced. He favored instead the outright enforcement of the Fifteenth Amendment, which guaranteed the right to vote for all. Vol. 8 *The Booker T. Washington Papers, 1904–6*, at 168–71 (L. R. Harlan, R. W. Smock, and G. McTigue eds. 1979). See also, *id.* at 164–66.

306. *Ibid.* (*The Negro in Virginia Politics*).

307. Jackson co-authored this book with D. Webster Davis. See also, *The Official Blue Book of the Jamestown Ter-Centennial Exposition* 241, 675 (1907); Ossofer, *Miami Times*, Nov. 18, 1982.

308. L. P. Jackson, *Negro Officeholders in Virginia, 1865–1895*, at 6 (1946).

309. *Id.* at 15.

310. *Id.* at 16.

311. *Id.* at 66.

312. Bragg, "Documents," 5 *J. Negro History* 235, 243 (1920).

313. L. P. Jackson, *Negro Officeholders in Virginia, 1865–1895*, at 20 (1946).

314. Bragg, "Documents," 5 *J. Negro History* 235, 241–43 (1920).
315. L. P. Jackson, *Negro Officeholders in Virginia, 1865–1895*, at 32 (1946).
316. *Id.* at 36, 40.
317. Bragg, "Documents," 5 *J. Negro History* 235, 241 (1920).
318. From "1922 Years' Work," Class of 1882, Items of Interest File, Hampton University Archives; "The Condition of School Houses," 22 *The Southern Workman* 117, July 1893. *General Assembly of Virginia, July 30, 1619–January 1, 1978*, at 546 (C. M. Leonard ed. 1978), representing Amelia County.
319. L. P. Jackson, *Negro Officeholders in Virginia, 1865–1895*, at 67 (1946).
320. J. M. Langston, *From the Virginia Plantation to the National Capitol* 482 (1894).
321. *Id.* at 488–89.
322. *Id.* at 490. John H. Hayes and Scott Wood were graduated from Howard University's law school in 1885 and 1886, respectively. The legal background of Matthew N. Lewis is unknown. In 1886, Hayes succeeded Edwin Randolph, a black lawyer, on the Richmond City Council, and he held that post until 1890 (Michael B. Chesson, "Richmond's Black Councilmen," 187–96, in *Southern Black Leaders of the Reconstruction Era* 202 and unnumbered page following page 202 [H. N. Rabinowitz ed. 1981]). In 1902, Virginia disfranchised many of its black citizens by adopting an "understanding clause" (requiring persons registering to vote to be able to read, quote from, or explain provisions of the United States Constitution), and a poll tax measure. James H. Hayes made a bold protest against these measures and initiated court actions to have them declared unconstitutional. Hayes sought funds from groups in New Jersey and Massachusetts to support the litigation. A. Buni, *The Negro in Virginia Politics, 1902–1965*, at 35, 36, 39 (1967). (The author has "A" as Hayes's middle initial, but it is actually "H.") Hayes later practiced law in Washington, D.C. In 1914, he issued a call for a National Negro congress to address such issues as "should the Negro return to the Republican Party . . . the Democratic Party [or] the Progressive Party, if so, why?" The lynching of blacks was also to be on the agenda. Hayes's call to form the National Negro Congress received coverage as far away as California. Henderson, "The National Negro Congress," *The California Eagle*, Feb. 14, 1914, at 1, col. 3.
323. *Id.* at 493. (*From the Virginia Plantation to the National Capitol*).
324. *Id.* at 498; Cheek, "A Negro Runs for Congress: John Mercer Langston and the Virginia Campaign of 1888," 52 *J. of Negro History*, 14, 33 (Jan. 1967).
325. *Ibid.* (*From the Virginia Plantation to the National Capitol*).
326. However, Congressman Langston took a leading role in the effort to place the American merchant marine, engaged in the foreign trade, on par with that of other nations. See speech of Hon. John M. Langston, "The American Merchant Marine," in the House of Representatives, Friday, Feb. 27, 1891. See also, *Dictionary of American Negro Biography* 382 (R. Logan and M. Winston eds. 1982). Actually, Langston was nominated in 1891, "by a popular Republican conference," to run for a second term. The Virginia State Republican Congressional Committee had refused to convene a regular nominating convention in 1891, apparently to block Langston's chances of being renominated. Although he was elected by a decisive margin in the popular Republican conference, he faced another contest for the seat from his Democratic opponent. Langston chose not to take his seat in Congress "because the Democratic party, holding a majority in that Congress," would contest the validity of his election without a proper nomination by convention. The ex-

pense associated with such a fight probably played a role in Langston's decision not to take the congressional seat. J. M. Langston, *From the Virginia Plantation to the National Capitol* 518 (1894).

327. "Race Notes," *Indianapolis Freeman*, July 13, 1889, at 8, col. 4.

328. "The Black Congressional District," *Indianapolis Freeman*, Dec. 7, 1889.

329. I. G. Penn, *The Afro-American Press, and Its Editors* 287 (1891).

330. W. H. Bryson and E. L. Shepard, "The Virginia Bar, 1870–1900," in *The New High Priests* 173 (G. W. Gawalt ed. 1984), referring to Andrew Boyd & Co., *Virginia State Business Directory, 1871–1872* (Richmond, 1871); see also, *Chataigne's Virginia Gazetteer and Classified Business Directory, 1890–1891*, at 286, 372, 517–20, 773 (Richmond, 1890).

331. "Deaths," 61 *The Southern Workman* 430 (Oct. 1932); "Rites for George Fields, Hampton Negro Lawyer," *Virginia Pilot*, Aug. 21, 1931; "The Armstrong League," 46 *The Southern Workman* 182 (March 1917); "Silver Wedding," 47 *Southern Workman* 46 (Jan. 1918). See also, R. F. Engs, *Freedom's First Generation* 175 (1979).

332. "Patrick Henry," *Daily Press*, Oct. 31, 1916; "Patrick Henry Is Fined Total of $32," *Daily Press*, Nov. 1, 1916.

333. "Graduates and Ex-Students," 47 *The Southern Workman* 606 (Dec. 1918). Fields entered Boston University's law school in 1918. See also, "Hold Funeral Services for Religious and Civil Leader," *Chicago Defender*, Aug. 27, 1932.

334. "Court Day in Virginia," *New York Globe*, Dec. 19, 1891, at 1, col. 1.

335. Scott, "Mr. J. Thomas Newsome," Vol. 1 *Alexander's Magazine* 30–31 (April 1906).

336. *Id.* at 30.

337. A. Buni, *The Negro in Virginia Politics, 1902–1965*, at 71 (1967).

338. Scott, "Mr. J. Thomas Newsome," Vol. 1 *Alexander's Magazine* 30–31 (April 1906).

339. "Has Been Lawyer 42 Years," *Norfolk Journal and Guide*, Jan. 27, 1940.

340. "Deserved Recognition to Deserving Lawyer," *The Norfolk Journal and Guide*, Feb. 3, 1940.

341. *Newport News Daily Press*, July 5, 1951; *Davis v. Allen*, 157 Va. 84, 160 S.E. 85 (1931). Only Bassette's name appears as counsel before the Supreme Court of Appeals of Virginia. Andrew W. E. Bassette, Jr., was graduated from Howard University's law school in 1906. See A. Buni, *The Negro in Virginia Politics, 1902–1965*, at 125–26 (1967) (discussing case). Bassette was a second-generation lawyer. His father, A. W. E. Bassette, Sr., was admitted to the bar in the early 1880s and served as "a magistrate of the Chesapeake District in 1883." Flannary, "What's in a Name?" *Tide Lines* 1, 2 (Winter 1970–71). The senior Bassette is best known for his significant contribution to the education of blacks in Elizabeth City County and Hampton, Virginia. "A. W. E. Bassettes Brought Professionalism to City," *Daily Press*, July 7, 1985 at 19, col. 1; C. W. Weaver, *The History of Negro Schools in Elizabeth City County* 2 (Aug. 6, 1938) (mimeo): "[A. W. E. Bassette, Sr.], once an outstanding figure in the Reconstruction Days of Elizabeth City County, has filled practically every office in Hampton government except Mayor of the town."

342. *Virginia's Contribution to Negro Leadership* 16 (W. Cooper ed. 1937) (mimeo).

343. Vol. 1 *Who's Who of the Colored Race* 200 (F. L. Mather ed. 1915).

344. From "22 Years' Work" Class of 1879, Items of Interest File, Hampton

University Archives; *Quinquennial Catalogue of the Law School of Harvard University, 1817–1914*, at 184 (R. Ames ed. 1915).

345. G. R. Segal, *Blacks in the Law* 187 (1983); *Twentieth Century Negro Literature* 110 (D. W. Culp ed. 1902); *Who's Who Among Negro Lawyers* 19 (S. T. M. Alexander ed. 1945).

346. The governors of several states appointed black commissioners to represent their states in this effort. Virginia Governor H. C. Stewart, for example, appointed John Thomas Hewin from Richmond, Virginia. "Flashlights on Recent Graduates," 52 *The Southern Workman* 361, 363 (July 1923). Reference to Hewin's appointment appears in promotional material on file in Hampton University's Archives for the National Memorial Association, with which Ferdinand D. Lee was associated. Hewin was a 1900 graduate of Boston University Law School.

347. *Virginia's Contribution to Negro Leadership* 16, 67 (W. Cooper ed. 1937) (mimeo).

348. "Colored Lawyers Gaining Recognition in the Courts," *Richmond Planet*, Nov. 25, 1922.

349. "Passes Virginia Bar Examination," *New York Age*, Sept. 13, 1919. B. F. Harris joined the firm of his father, Alfred W. Harris, in Petersburg.

350. From "1922 Years' Work," Class of 1895, Items of Interest File, Hampton University Archives.

351. *Congressional Quarterly's Guide to U.S. Elections* 634 (2d ed., J. L. Moore ed., 1985).

352. H. Walton, Jr., *Black Republicans: The Politics of the Black and Tans* 97 (1975); A. Buni, *The Negro in Virginia Politics, 1902–1965*, at 77 (1967); A. Heard and D. S. Strong, *Southern Primaries and Elections, 1920–1949*, at 192, 198 (1950).

353. *West. v. Bliley*, 33 F.2d 177, 180 (E.D. Va. 1929), *affirmed* 42 F.2d 101 (4th Cir. 1930) (with Alfred E. Cohen).

354. "Alexandria Lawyer First in Fifteen Years to Try Case in Corporation Court," *Washington Tribune*, April 29, 1922.

355. "Has Been Lawyer 42 Years," *Norfolk Journal and Guide*, Jan. 27, 1940. Robertson was graduated from Shaw University's law department in 1894 and was admitted to the Virginia bar in the same year. W. H. Bryson, *Legal Education in Virginia, 1779–1979*, at 549 (1982).

356. "Pass Virginia Bar Examination," *Norfolk Journal and Guide*, Dec. 24, 1932. The Howard University graduates were Charles L. Elliott, of Norfolk, Wilbur O. Watts, of Portsmouth, and J. Byron Hopkins, of Alexandria. Thomas W. Young, of Norfolk, was the Ohio State University law graduate. In 1935, Norfolk had a sizeable black legal community—namely, J. E. Diggs, W. L. Davis, F. J. Torogood, L. A. Howell, W. W. Forman, William Thomas, B. J. Barnes, J. N. Williams, Robert C. Smith, R. S. L. Paige, J. M. Harrison, and Jerry O. Gilliam. "Judge [Armond W.] Scott Accepts Invitation to Speak in Norfolk," *Norfolk Journal and Guide*, Nov. 2, 1935 and Nov. 23, 1935.

357. R. Kluger, *Simple Justice* 149 (1975).

358. *Ibid.*

359. *Id.* at 153.

360. One commentator was critical of Charles H. Houston's handling of the Crawford case, asserting that it was poorly investigated and calling attention to Houston's decision not to appeal the case, despite the number of constitutional

issues raised during the trial. Gruening, "The Truth About the Crawford Case," *New Masses*, Jan. 8, 1935, at 9, col. 1.

361. "Lawyer Butts Admitted to Appeals Court," *Norfolk Journal and Guide*, Oct. 9, 1937.

362. "3 Lawyers Pass State Bar Exams," *Norfolk Journal and Guide*, Aug. 10, 1940. The three new admittees were Frederick Charles Carter, of Richmond, who attended the University of Michigan Law School; Roland D. Ealey, of Richmond, a 1939 Howard University law graduate; and William James Kemp, of Norfolk, a graduate of the LaSalle Extension University Law School in Chicago.

363. "Lawyer Says Circuit Court Candidate Displayed Bias," *Baltimore Afro-American*, Nov. 8, 1943. See also, Miles, Lee, and Smith, "The Black Lawyer in Virginia," 37 *Virginia Lawyer* 28, 30 (Oct. 1988), on the same subject as reported by Petersburg attorney Robert H. Cooley, Jr., a 1937 Howard University law graduate.

364. See, e.g., M. V. Tushnet, *The NAACP's Legal Strategy Against Segregated Education, 1925–1950*, at 78–81 (1987); R. Kluger, *Simple Justice* 131, 215–17 (1975).

365. *Alston v. School Board of City of Norfolk*, 112 F.2d 992, 994 (4th Cir. 1940).

366. *Legions v. Commonwealth*, 181 Va. 89, 23 S.E. 2d 764, 765 (1943).

367. "Named Trial Lawyer for Dep't of Justice," *Atlanta Daily World*, June 7, 1943.

368. "Negro Women Take Bar Examination," *Richmond Times Dispatch*, Dec. 9, 1924.

369. "Virginia Admits First Woman Attorney to Bar," *Chicago Defender*, March 27, 1926. It is likely that Fleming-Poe passed the bar examination given in December 1925, and was sworn in on March 1926. "First Colored Woman Passes Virginia Bar," *The Indianapolis Freeman*, Dec. 26, 1925.

370. "Virginia Admits Colored Woman to Bar," 3 *The Law Student* 18 (Feb. 15, 1926).

371. "Virginia's Only Negro Woman Lawyer to Be 'Womanhood' Speaker for Zeta Chapter," *Norfolk Journal and Guide*, Feb. 16, 1929; Dark and Moye, "L. Marian Poe: A Model of Public Service," 38 *Virginia Lawyer* 32, 33 (March 1990).

372. "Judge Scott Accepts Invitation to Speak in Norfolk," *Norfolk Journal and Guide*, Nov. 2, 1935, Nov. 23, 1935.

373. "Rites for George Fields, Hampton Negro Lawyer," *Virginia Pilot*, Aug. 21, 1932. Inez C. Fields's married name was Scott.

374. B. T. Washington, *The Story of My Life and Work* 70 (1899); L. R. Harlan, *Booker T. Washington: The Making of a Black Leader, 1856–1901*, at 95 (1972).

375. Letter from W. M. Jones, clerk, Circuit Court of Jefferson County, West Virginia, to Charles S. Brown, July 14, 1958.

376. John H. Hill was admitted to the Sagadahoc County bar before the Maine Supreme Judicial Court on April 11, 1879 (letter from Esther L. Brawn, clerk, Supreme Judicial Court–Superior Court, Sagadahoc County, Maine, to Charles S. Brown, June 27, 1958). D. Withrow, *West Virginia State College (1891–1991): From the Grove to the Stars* 10 (1991).

377. "John H. Hill, Former President of West Virginia State, Laid to Rest at Institute," 7 *The Yellow Jacket* 1, Oct. 23, 1936; J. C. Harlan, *History of West Virginia State College, 1890–1965* 15 (1968).

378. W. J Simmons, *Men of Mark* 275 (1887).

379. Letter from Kenneth E. Hines, clerk, State of West Virginia Supreme Court of Appeals, to Charles S. Brown, June 19, 1958; letter to author from Paul I. Clifford, March 5, 1990.

380. Letter from John M. McBride, clerk, Circuit Court of Berkeley County, West Virginia, to Charles S. Brown, July 1958.

381. Vol. 1 *Who's Who of the Colored Race* 69 (F. L. Mather ed. 1915) (Clifford's name appears as Cilford, an apparent error).

382. 45 W. Va. 199, 31 S.E. 985 (1898) (with A. G. Dayton). Clifford was the perfect person to bring this lawsuit, having been a principal of the public school in Martinsburg, West Virginia, prior to his admission to the bar. *Afro-American Encyclopedia; Or, The Thoughts, Doings and Sayings of the Race* 352 (J. T. Haley ed. 1895).

383. *Williams v. Board of Education of Fairfax District*, 45 W. Va. 199, 31 S.E. 985 (1898).

384. Vol. 1 *Who's Who of the Colored Race* 212 (F. L. Mather ed. 1915).

385. "Active Career of Moses H. Jones Is Brought to Close," *Dayton Journal*, Jan. 21, 1920.

386. Romaine F. Scott, "The Negro in American History, 1877–1900, as Portrayed in *The Washington Evening Star* 37" (M.A. thesis, Howard University, 1948).

387. Vol. 7 *History of the American Negro: West Virginia Edition* 61–62 (A. B. Caldwell ed. 1923).

388. *First Annual Report of Bureau of Negro Welfare and Statistics, 1921–1922*, at 67 (T. Edward Hill ed. 1922).

389. "Fred O. Blue Threatened by Damage Suite" (source unknown), 1915 (newspaper article in author's files). Blue was a lawyer in Fayette County. See *State ex rel. White Oak Fuel Co. v. Davis*, 74 W. Va. 261, 262, 82 S.E. 207 (1914).

390. *Chambers v. Great State Council, I.O.R.M.* 76 W. Va. 614, 86 S.E. 467 (1915). This case involved the right of entitlement under a life insurance policy; see also, "Colored Lawyers in W. Va. Supreme Court," *The New York Age*, Oct. 14, 1915. Thomas L. Sweeney graduated from Howard University's law school in 1896, established a successful practice in Fayetteville, and acquired a significant amount of real estate and personal property. Vol. 7 *History of the American Negro: West Virginia Edition* 234 (A. B. Caldwell ed. 1923).

391. *West Virginia Bureau of Negro Welfare and Statistics Biennial Report, 1939–1940*, at 87 (I. M. Carper ed. 1941).

392. *The National Cyclopedia of the Colored Race* 319 (C. C. Richardson ed. 1919); Vol. 7 *History of the American Negro: West Virginia Edition* 180 (A. B. Caldwell ed. 1923).

393. *Ibid.* (*The National Cyclopedia*).

394. *Ibid.*

395. *Id.* at 49–50. *West Virginia Bureau of Negro Welfare and Statistics Biennial Report, 1925–1926*, at 51 (T. Edward Hill ed. 1927). About the same time James Knox Smith opened a law office in Keystone, West Virginia. *Ibid.*

396. Vol. 7 *History of the American Negro: West Virginia Edition* 181 (A. B. Caldwell ed. 1923).

397. Vol. 1 *Who's Who in Colored America* 150 (J. J. Boris ed. 1927).

398. Vol. 7 *History of the American Negro: West Virginia Edition* 180 (A. B. Caldwell ed. 1923).

399. *Mullens v. County Court of Greenbrier County*, 112 W. Va. 593, 166 S.E. 116 (1932).

400. *White v. White*, 108 W. Va. 128, 150 S.E. 531 (1929).

401. "Nutter Counsel in $12,000,000 Property Case," *Baltimore Afro-American*, Oct. 29, 1938 (the case involved *Thomas A. Cook v. Jennie Lewis, et al.*); "Negro Attorneys File $100,000 Suit for Whites," *St. Louis Argus*, Jan. 13, 1939.

402. *Cook v. Lewis*, 306 U.S. 636 (1939) (denying certiorari), *rehearing denied*, 306 U.S. 668 (1939). Samuel A. T. Watkins and James E. White handled the case before the United States Supreme Court. "Chicago Attorneys Retained by White Litigants in Ten Million Dollar Law Suit," *Pittsburgh Courier*, Oct. 31, 1936.

403. Vol. 1 *Who's Who of the Colored Race* 138 (F. L. Mather ed. 1915).

404. *West Virginia Bureau of Negro Welfare and Statistics Biennial Report, 1925–1926*, at 51 (T. Edward Hall ed. 1926).

405. *Ibid.* The official records of the West Virginia Supreme Court of Appeals appear to be neutral on the question of the race of out-of-state applicants. All out-of-state applicants seemed to have been required to take the bar examination after 1923, and the rules do not indicate that students graduating from West Virginia's law school were admitted without taking the bar examination. Vol. 113, "West Virginia Reports" (front pages) (1933). However, as a matter of court practice "graduates of the College of Law of West Virginia were required to sit for the bar examination for the first time in the history of the state" in 1989. Ramey, "The July 1989 West Virginia Bar Examination," 4 *The Bar Examiner* 4 (Aug. 1990).

406. Vol. 1 *Who's Who of the Colored Race* 63–64 (F. L. Mather ed. 1915).

407. *Id.* at 118. The case referenced is *Steel v. Board of Education of Hancock County*, which apparently did not reach the West Virginia Supreme Court of Appeals.

408. Vol. 7 *History of the American Negro: West Virginia Edition* 189 (A. B. Caldwell ed. 1923); "West Virginia Lawyer Put on State Education Board," *Chicago Defender*, July 18, 1931.

409. *State v. Cook*, 81 W. Va. 686, 95 S.E. 792 (1918) (with John M. Anderson); *State v. Young*, 82 W. Va. 714, 97 S.E. 134 (1918).

410. Vol. 7 *History of the American Negro: West Virginia Edition* 109 (A. B. Caldwell ed. 1923).

411. "Brilliant W. Va. Barrister Wins Legal Victory," *Pittsburgh Courier*, Dec. 17, 1932.

412. *Ibid.* Whether Payne participated as counsel or as one of several parties in the challenge abolishing various school boards is uncertain, since no case is reported in 1932 bearing his name before the West Virginia Supreme Court of Appeals. However, Payne may have participated in some manner in *Leonhart v. Board of Education of Charleston Independent School District*, 114 W. Va. 9, 170 S.E. 418 (1933). In *Leonhart*, the citizens and taxpayers of Charleston sued "to enjoin the board of education of Charleston Independent School District from surrendering to the newly created board of education" of that county the "control and management of the schools and the school properties" pursuant to a recently passed state statute. The effect of such legislation in black school districts could have shifted the control of education out of the hands of blacks. Several suits on this issue were filed across the state.

413. Vol. 7 *History of the American Negro: West Virginia Edition* 9 (A. B. Caldwell ed. 1923); *First Annual Report of Bureau of Negro Welfare and Statistics Biennial, 1921–1922*, at 67 (T. Edward Hill ed. 1922). Capehart succeeded E. Howard Harper, a black lawyer, to the West Virginia legislature. Harper had

served from 1917–1919, representing McDowell County. *Ibid.* See also, Vol. 1 *Who's Who in Colored America* 36 (J. J. Boris ed. 1927).

414. J. H. Chadbourn, *Lynching and the Law* 26 (1933).

415. The firm handled many complex civil cases. See, e.g., *Bean v. County Court*, 85 W. Va. 186, 101 S.E. 254 (1919).

416. *West Virginia Bureau of Negro Welfare and Statistics Biennial Report, 1925–1926*, at 135 (T. Edward Hill ed. 1926) and the 1927–1928 edition, at 44 (J. W. Robinson ed. 1928).

417. Vol. 7 *History of the American Negro: West Virginia Edition* 48 (A. B. Caldwell ed. 1923); *West Virginia Bureau of Negro Welfare and Statistics Biennial Report, 1933–1934*, at 29 (I. M. Carper ed. 1934).

418. Vol. 7 *History of the American Negro: West Virginia Edition* 155–56 (A. B. Caldwell ed. 1923).

419. *West Virginia Bureau of Negro Welfare and Statistics Biennial Report, 1925–1926*, at 51 (T. Edward Hill ed. 1926). In 1928, the following twenty-five black lawyers were practicing law in eight West Virginia counties: *Berkeley County:* J. R. Clifford, Martinsburg; *Cabell County:* D. W. Ambrose, Huntington; *Fayette County:* J. M. Ellis, Oak Hill; John Love, Montgomery; T. L. Sweeney, Fayetteville; *Kanawha County:* C. W. Dickerson, Charleston; C. E. Kimbrough, Sr., Charleston; Julius H. Love, Charleston; T. G. Nutter, Charleston; *McDowell County:* Stewart S. Calhoun, Keystone; H. J. Capehart, Welch; B. E. Carter, Kimball; A. G. Froe, Welch; E. H. Harper, Keystone; T. E. Harris, Northfork; Fleming Jones, Welch; Leon P. Miller, Welch; S. B. Moon, Wilcoe; Cecil H. Riley, Northfork; Robert D. Tomlinson, Welch; *Marion County:* Richard W. Tompkins, Fairmont; *Mercer County:* J. P. D. Gardner, Bluefield; James S. Redman, Bluefield; *Raleigh County:* J. S. Butts, Beckley; Brown W. Payne, Beckley. Between 1922 and 1928 the names of a few of the earlier black lawyers were no longer listed as practicing in West Virginia: E. J. Graham, Jr., of Wheeling; G. H. Irish, of Charleston; James Knox Smith and Cecil H. Riley of Northfork. See *West Virginia Bureau of Negro Welfare and Statistics Biennial Report, 1921–1922*, at 77, 99 (T. Edward Hill ed. 1922), and the 1925–1928 report, at 52–53 (listing lawyers).

420. "Beckley Attorney Is Nominated for W. Va. House of Delegates," *Pittsburgh Courier*, Aug. 25, 1934, at 3.

421. *West Virginia Bureau of Negro Welfare and Statistics Biennial Report, 1939–1940*, at 71, 118, 121 (I. M. Carper ed. 1940).

422. *Id.* at 81. Jones, a 1922 Howard University law graduate, had been elected to another term (to commence in 1941) by the time this report was published; Vol. 1 *Who's Who in Colored America* 110 (J. J. Boris ed. 1927); *West Virginia Bureau of Negro Welfare and Statistics Biennial Report, 1939–1940*, at 81 (I. M. Carper ed. 1940).

423. Lonesome was a 1936 Howard University law graduate. See "Bill Lonesome Remembered," 2 *Stinger* 3 (Spring 1983). George W. Crockett, Jr., was a 1934 graduate of the University of Michigan's law school. Brown received a J.D. degree from Boston University School of Law in 1932 and an LL.M. degree in 1936. "Brown W. Payne Program Pamphlet," Mountain State Bar Association 4 (Oct. 1972). Cunningham was a 1941 Iowa University law graduate and its first black graduate to settle in West Virginia. Travis was graduated from Howard University's law school in 1931.

424. *West Virginia Bureau of Negro Welfare and Statistics Biennial Report, 1941–1942*, at 43 (C. F. Hopson ed. 1942).

Chapter 5

The Southern States

The Southern states include Alabama, Florida, Louisiana, and Mississippi.

Alabama

After Moses Wenslydale Moore graduated from Howard University School of Law in 1871, he went to Mobile, Alabama, and applied for admission to the bar. In November 1871, he appeared before Judge John Elliott. The following account of Moore's admission to the bar appeared in the *Mobile Daily Register*:

> Moses Wenslydale Moore, a Negro as black as the ace of spades . . . presented himself for examination, stating that he had been admitted to the bar in the District of Columbia. The court requested Judge Gibbons to examine him, and examination was conducted in open court. A great deal of interest was manifested on the part of the bar . . . from the fact of the applicant's color. He passed a very satisfactory examination, and an order was made by the Court admitting him to the bar. This is the first negro ever admitted to the bar in Mobile.[1]

Four months later, Moore was admitted to the Alabama Supreme Court; he was the first black admitted to practice in that court.[2] His admission was hailed by the *Montgomery Daily State Journal* as inaugurating "an age of progress, [for] ten years ago who would have believed that a Negro was capable of learning the laws sufficiently to practice in the Supreme Court."[3]

James Thomas Rapier, who had read law, followed Moses W. Moore to the Alabama bar around 1872. Within months of his admission, Rapier was elected to the Forty-third Congress, serving from March 4, 1873, to March 3, 1875.[4] Roderick B. Thomas was admitted to the

Alabama bar on December 17, 1876. Prior to Thomas's admission, he had gained considerable respect in the community. On July 7, 1873, the city council of Selma, Alabama, appointed Thomas and two other men to a committee that considered affairs involving the railroads.[5] During this appointment, Thomas proposed an ordinance "creating the office of Commissioners of Railroads for the City of Selma, providing for the election of the same."[6] He also served as secretary for the forty-man Central City Fire Company No. 2.[7] Samuel R. Lowry was admitted to the Alabama bar in 1875 after private law study.[8] Lowry was more a businessman than a lawyer, but he holds the distinction of becoming, in 1883, one of the first black lawyers in the nation—and the first black lawyer from the state of Alabama—to be admitted to the United States Supreme Court.[9]

Prior to 1945, there were hardly any black law firms in Alabama. In 1891, John Henry Ballou left Jacksonville, Florida, and joined the law firm of R. C. O. Benjamin and Henry Clay Smith, which was located in Birmingham, Alabama. This partnership was likely the first black law firm in Alabama.[10] Smith left the firm in 1893 when President Grover Cleveland appointed him (as his first black appointee) United States consul at Santos, Brazil.[11]

P. L. M. Watkins broke ground for black lawyers in Courtland, Alabama. He became an applicant for the post of United States marshal of his district in 1881.[12] William Hooper Councill, a former member of the Alabama House of Representatives, was first admitted to the Alabama Supreme Court in 1882,[13] after reading law for several years. Though he may never have practiced law, Councill in 1887 was the first black lawyer to file a test case before the newly created Interstate Commerce Commission. Councill filed an administrative action against a railroad carrier for discrimination against him on the basis of race.[14] Yet, while Southern whites "encouraged black teachers and farmers, [by 1895] they regarded black . . . lawyers as threats to social peace."[15] For example, A. A. Garner, a black lawyer in Montgomery, Alabama, was given twenty-four hours to leave town after defending Jesse C. Duke, an editor of a black newspaper who had written an article suggesting that white women desired black men.[16]

In 1890 Thomas A. Harris passed the bar examination in Montgomery, Alabama. Harris's sponsors to the bar were "leading conservative lawyers of [Tuskegee, Alabama]."[17] Harris was not popular in either the black or white community in Tuskegee. He was described by a white Tuskegee newspaper as having a "rather . . . seditious character."[18] Harris's decision to practice law in Tuskegee in 1895 triggered a "chain of events that [led] to the attempt on his life by an angry mob of white men [who] did not want any Negro lawyer [in Tuskegee]."[19] The white citizens of Tuskegee, Alabama, "organized a lynch mob and chased . . . Harris out of the city for establishing a law practice."[20] Harris, shot in the leg, survived, but never again practiced in Tuskegee.[21] Later in the year, Harris identified his assailants as "Old Tip Huddleson" and others in a letter to Booker T. Washington. Washington, who was president of the Tuskegee Institute, had hidden Harris when Huddleson tried to kill him. Harris inquired of Washington whether "the grand jury tried to get a true bill against any of them. I would have come before the grand jury if I had been offored [*sic*] any protection." No indictments were ever brought against Harris's assailants.[22]

Even though assaults against black lawyers were prevalent in Alabama before 1895, it did not stop lawyers such as William Francis Crockett, an 1888 University of Michigan law graduate, from going to Montgomery, Alabama, to practice law. Crockett practiced law in Montgomery from 1888 to 1899, during which time he also worked as an assistant in the passenger department of the Southern Railroad and taught a commercial law course at the Tuskegee Institute. In 1900, he left Alabama and went to Wailuku, Maui, Hawaii to practice law.[23]

The first significant voting rights cases appealed to the United States Supreme Court were brought in 1903 and 1904 by Wilford Horace Smith, an 1883 black graduate of Boston University's School of Law. Smith's suits challenged a newly created provision of the Alabama constitution prohibiting black citizens from voting. (As a black lawyer in the South during this period, Smith's litigation schedule must have been hectic. He had cases pending simultaneously before the Alabama Supreme Court and the United States Supreme Court in 1903.) In *Giles v. Harris*,[24] the United States Supreme Court, speaking through Justice Oliver Wendell Holmes, refused to interfere with the racial disfranchisement of black voters in Alabama, choosing instead to decide that case on jurisdictional grounds. However, Smith's appeal drew three dissenting opinions in support of his view that the court had jurisdiction to decide and to adjudge the state constitution as discriminatory, under the Fourteenth and Fifteenth Amendments to the United States Constitution.[25]

Wilford H. Smith was not only a skilled constitutional lawyer but also an exceptional criminal lawyer. In 1904, Smith appealed the Alabama Supreme Court decision not to quash an indictment against a client of Smith who was charged with murder, on grounds that it was unconstitutional to exclude blacks from a grand jury solely on the basis of race. This time, Justice Oliver Wendell Holmes held that a state violated the equal protection clause of the Fourteenth Amendment by excluding blacks from the grand jury on account of race.[26]

Montgomery and Birmingham, Alabama, drew most of the black lawyers in the state, even though they were few in number. Luther L. Chambliss, a 1907 Howard University law graduate, was admitted to practice after passing a written examination in Montgomery. Chambliss opened a practice in Birmingham with another black lawyer, Edward Austin Brown.[27] Brown, who had been previously admitted to the Ohio bar, was admitted to the Alabama bar in 1898. He settled in Birmingham and established a civil practice. He refused to handle any criminal matters, leaving those matters to Chambliss. In 1917 Brown, an "able lawyer," took a leading role in opposing a proposed local ordinance that would have established restrictive covenants.[28]

In 1918, Nathan B. Young, a Yale University law graduate, was admitted to practice in Birmingham. However, Young's experience as a lawyer differed significantly from those of Brown and Chambliss, perhaps because he publicly supported the NAACP. As Young reports, it "was dangerous" for blacks to openly support the NAACP, and his outspoken advocacy for the rights of his people did not play well in the courts. His practice failed, and Young relocated to St. Louis, Missouri.[29] Other black lawyers, such as Charles D. Kline, who practiced in Anniston, Alabama, were less vocal, and called upon white lawyers to assist them in murder cases.[30]

Between 1925 and 1937, the need for black lawyers in Alabama was so great that black citizens organized the Protective National Detective Association. The association furnished legal services, passed on all papers, deeds, and abstracts, and advertised that it would represent black members in any court, civil or criminal, in the state of Alabama without charge. The members of the association paid a fee for membership. One advertisement indicated that "hundreds of poor colored people are hard labor prisoners today, because they did not have a lawyer to represent them."[31]

In 1937, the admission of black lawyers in Alabama eased when Arthur Davis Shores was admitted to the Alabama bar on October 4, 1937, followed by Arthur H. Madison, who was admitted to the bar on March 10, 1938.[32] With the admission of these lawyers, there were four black lawyers in the state of Alabama. Shores, a schoolteacher, was unable to attend Kansas University School of Law because it was too expensive for him; thus he "enrolled in the LaSalle Extension University . . . which allow[ed] students to complete a program of training through correspondence" and short summer sessions.[33] In 1935, Shores received a law degree from LaSalle, but passing the Alabama bar examination presented special difficulties for him, since all of the bar refresher courses barred black applicants. But fate was on Shores' side. His father worked for and maintained the facility in which Judge Walter B. Jones conducted a bar refresher course. Judge Jones, at the request of Shores' father, "made arrangements to review the basis of law with Shores in his chambers," apart from his other white students.[34]

Shores passed the bar exam on his second attempt and almost immediately set to work filing civil rights lawsuits. The filing of civil rights cases by black lawyers in Alabama was still a dangerous activity at that time, and for a good amount of time since. In 1944, Shores reported that "he was physically abused 'while in the corridor of the Courthouse' during a trial in the late 1930s or early 1940s."[35]

Arthur H. Madison, another black Alabama lawyer, was not able to keep the hounds off his back. In 1944, while trying to help blacks register to vote, he was arrested under an Alabama statute that made it a misdemeanor to represent a person without his or her consent. Madison had taken appeals for eight blacks who had been denied the right to vote, but "five [of the eight blacks] made affidavits that they had not employed Madison or authorized him to take the appeals."[36] Madison attempted to obtain a legal decision that the restrictive registration law in Alabama was unconstitutional,[37] but the white power structure, led by United States Senator Lister Hill, was adamant that Madison's efforts to register black voters be stopped by whatever means necessary.[38] As a result of Senator Hill's influence and the pressure brought to bear on the Montgomery County Board of Registrars, Madison was disbarred on July 24, 1945.[39] He relocated to New York City.

Estelle A. Henderson was admitted to the Alabama bar prior to 1920, according to *The Atlanta Independent*.[40] Little else is known about Henderson. In 1944 Jane Cleo Marshall (Lucas), a law graduate of the University of Michigan, joined the firm of Arthur Davis Shores in Birmingham, stating "that opportunities [were] diversified and numerous" in Alabama.[41]

Florida

Harvey S. Harmon was the first black lawyer admitted to practice in the state of Florida. Harmon, who does not appear to have had formal legal training, applied and was admitted to the Fifth Judicial Circuit in the city of Alachua, Florida, on May 13, 1869, by Judge Jesse H. Goss.[42] Two white lawyers, Archibald Banks and George Arnow, vouched for Harmon's character. Upon receiving Harmon's petition to practice law, Judge Goss appointed a committee to examine him. The committee "examined Harmon touching his knowledge of the law on his application for license . . . in the Courts of [Florida]."[43] The committee found him "competent and recommend[ed] that he be admitted to practice in [Florida]."[44]

Harmon was an important Republican figure in Alachua County even before he was admitted to the bar. In 1868, he had been elected to the Alachua County executive committee of the Republican Party and elected to the first session of the general assembly under the newly adopted state constitution.[45] Shortly after Harmon's admission to the bar, he attended the National Negro Labor Convention held in Washington, D.C., and was elected assistant secretary.[46] Harmon was described as "one of the shrewdest colored men in the state" during his run for the Florida state senate in 1872.[47]

A black man named James Dean was elected county judge in Monroe County, Florida, in 1870.[48] Judge Dean was described as "a good-natured fellow but not strong by any means."[49] In 1889, much excitement was stirred in Monroe County when Judge Dean was suspended from his judgeship by Florida Governor Francis P. Fleming. According to the claim of a white lawyer, Dean had issued a license to Antonio Gonzales, a mulatto, to marry Annie Maloney, a Cuban black woman.[50] Despite a sworn statement by Mr. Gonzales that he was not white, Florida's first black judge was removed from office.[51]

The third black lawyer admitted to practice in Florida was an 1873 law graduate of Howard University, Joseph E. Lee. Admitted to the Florida Supreme Court in 1873, Lee was the first black lawyer to practice in Jacksonville, Florida, and the first in the state admitted to practice with a law degree.[52] A year after his admission to the Florida bar, Lee was elected to the lower house of the Florida state legislature, where he served until 1880.[53] Lee's talent came to the attention of Senator Simon B. Conover who, in 1876, selected Lee to run for the lieutenant governorship of Florida, joining Conover on a ticket that had broken away from the Republican Party. The campaign, however, never got off the ground, but Lee made history as the first black person considered for the second highest elected post in Florida.[54]

Lee was employed as a federal tax collector from 1873 to 1913.[55] In 1880, Lee was elected to the Florida state senate, where he served until 1882 as a member of the judiciary, privileges, and election committees.[56] Two years after Lee left the Florida state senate, he was elected as a delegate to the Republican National Convention held in Chicago.

During the Chicago convention, Joshia Walls, Florida's first black congressman, also sought election as a national Republican committeeman, but he had not sought Lee's prior consent or endorsement. As a result, Lee opposed Walls's efforts and prevailed in denying him a seat as committeeman. Lee, however, remained committed to the other members of the slate, who were all white.[57] Perhaps because Lee "was ultra-conservative and . . . careful to give no offense to . . . white people,"[58] he was elected as a municipal judge in Jacksonville, Florida, on April 3, 1888, defeating two white candidates.[59] Lee also served as chairman of the Duval County Republican Party and as secretary of the state Republican Party for thirty years.[60]

In 1873 William F. Thompson was appointed justice of the peace in Tallahassee, Florida. Four years later, he was elected to the Florida state legislature, and he served as a delegate to the Florida constitutional convention in 1885. During the period Thompson served in the state legislature, he also worked as "an attorney at law and school-teacher."[61] In 1912, Thompson, whose practice was in Jacksonville, Florida, fought to eliminate racial discrimination in the selection of juries. He believed that the right to trial by jury implied a jury of one's peers. With great skill, Thompson "showed fully the use of the word 'peer,' and for what purpose it was incorporated into our law."[62] However, he failed to persuade the court that "a jury of one's peers" included black jurors.

A decade later, Joseph E. Lee was followed to the Florida bar by another Howard University law graduate, Rueben S. Smith. Smith was first exposed to the law while working as an office boy in the law office of James C. McLean of Marianna (Jackson County), Florida. Smith was admitted to the District of Columbia bar in 1882, and he returned to Florida as a special agent of the Eleventh Census in 1890. He was assigned to collect data on the recorded indebtedness of Florida.[63]

In 1882 John H. Ballou, a member of the Rhode Island bar, arrived in Jacksonville, Florida, to practice law. For six years Ballou's professional life was split between working in a small law practice and teaching physics and mathematics at Cookman Institute in Jacksonville. In 1888 Ballou was elected justice of the peace of the Eleventh District of Duval County, Florida, and served with distinction until 1892, the year he relocated to Birmingham, Alabama, to practice law.[64]

Thomas de Saille Tucker, an 1882 graduate of Straight University, was admitted to the Louisiana bar in 1882. He opened a branch of his Louisiana firm in Pensacola (Escambia County), Florida, on January 10, 1883, the day that he was admitted to the Florida bar. Tucker and Robert Brown Elliott, a former congressman from South Carolina, were anxious "to establish a branch" of their Louisiana firm in Florida.[65] Their business flourished immediately and, upon the death of Elliott in 1884, James D. Thompson joined the firm.[66] Renamed Tucker and Thompson, the firm continued to prosper in Florida and Louisiana.[67] The client base of the firm was both white and black, and "gave promise of a very brilliant and lucrative practice."[68] In 1887, Tucker left the practice of law and became president of the Florida Agricultural and Mechanical College for blacks, a position he held for years.[69] Many years later, he joined a black law firm in Baltimore, Maryland.

Isaac Lawrence Purcell left his law studies at the University of South Carolina in 1877, when blacks were being forced out because of newly imposed state segregation statutes.[70] Purcell continued to study law privately in Palatka County, Florida, and qualified for admission to the Florida bar on October 8, 1889. Purcell gained admission to the Florida Supreme Court in 1891, and on January 19, 1897, he was admitted to the United States Circuit and District Courts. He was admitted to practice before the United States Supreme Court on November 8, 1901.[71] Purcell practiced throughout the state of Florida, concentrating most of his energies in Jacksonville and Pensacola.

According to Purcell, at the time he was admitted to the Florida bar, blacks were not likely to receive fair treatment before white judges and juries in state courts.[72] However, the appellate courts, which probably were eager to apply the law consistently so as not to prejudice whites in similar cases, "meted out to the Negro even against the white man a lenient form of justice."[73] Purcell reports that this was not the case "when [the Negro's] life, his liberty, reputation or citizenship [were] at stake" before local courts.[74] Black criminal defendants were often "protected" from harsh sentences or execution when their victims were black.[75] If the victim was white, a black defendant was "seldom, if ever, protected" from execution.[76] When blacks were charged with crimes against whites, Purcell stated,

it is not justice that is the object of our courts, but the impeachment and condemnation of a fellow man, giving vent to a vindictive racial prejudice. Be the crime of the Negro ever so trivial, when against the white man, the sheriff, having to carry out the oath; the jury, their party plans; the judge, his selfish means; and, therefore, no evidence, however palpable, however substantial and convincing can shield the Negro under such instances.[77]

Despite the manner in which Purcell's clients were treated, Booker T. Washington, a close observer of the Southern court system, reported in 1907 that Purcell, C. H. Alston, and George W. Parker "seem to have the entire respect of the members of the bar and are accorded the same courtesies in the courts that are shown to white lawyers."[78]

Between 1900 and 1915, Isaac Purcell, Samuel Decatur McGill, and Judson Douglas Wetmore often teamed up to litigate the constitutional rights of blacks in Florida and to vigorously defend blacks in criminal matters. In 1905 Purcell and Wetmore brought the first test cases challenging the constitutionality of the Florida Jim Crow transportation laws.[79] Their advocacy brought down the separate but equal provision relating to streetcar accommodations in both Jacksonville and Pensacola.[80] Purcell and McGill appealed every conviction of a black man sentenced to death.[81] Purcell's dogged and successful advocacy to enjoin the sheriff of Duval County from excluding blacks from juries may have been his greatest single achievement.[82]

James Weldon Johnson—who later wrote "Lift Every Voice and Sing," popularly referred to as the "negro national anthem"—began his study of law in 1896. Johnson studied law in Florida under the tutelage of Thomas A. Ledwith, a white lawyer. Johnson learned fast. Six months after his first lesson, Ledwith allowed Johnson to draft most of the pleadings in the practices' divorce cases, his specialty.[83] Ledwith "gave [Johnson] a good deal of his time in discussing knotty questions and in quizzing [him] in various legal subjects."[84] At the end of eighteen months of study, Johnson applied for admission to take the bar examination in Duval County, Florida. Fortunately for Johnson, R. M. Call, "a very fair man," was selected to chair the examination committee.[85] Because Johnson was one of the first black applicants to be examined in open court, this event took on "the aspect of a spectacle."[86] The other examiners were E. J. L'Engle, "a son of one of Florida's leading families,"[87] Major W. B. Young, "a 'bad' white man,"[88] and Duncan U. Fletcher, one of the outstanding members of the Jacksonville bar, "a fair and just man."[89]

Johnson prepared for and took the bar examination while faced with the possibility that racism rather than his knowledge of the law would govern its outcome. Johnson described his ordeal as follows:

The examination started. The questions were fired at me rapidly; little time being allowed for consideration. . . . As the examination proceeded I gained confidence. Before it was over Major Young took up a copy of *The Statutes of Florida* and began examining me therefrom. It was my impression that the unfairness of this unprecedented procedure was regarded with disapproval by the other members of the committee. . . . After two hours there was a lull in the questioning. A lawyer named W. T. Walker, sitting near the committee leaned over and asked, "Well, what are you going to do about it?" Mr. Fletcher answered, "He's passed a good examination. . . ." Major Young commented . . . for his words blurted out in my face . . . "Well, I can't forget he's a nigger and I'll be damned if I'll stay here to see him admitted."[90]

Upon the motion of Duncan U. Fletcher, who later became a United States senator, James Weldon Johnson was admitted to practice law in Duval County in 1898. His knowledge of the law and dogged determination had won out over racism.[91]

In 1899, the year after James Weldon Johnson's admission, Judson Douglas Wetmore, who had completed one year of formal law study at the University of Michigan Law School, was also admitted to the Florida bar, apparently with little difficulty. He and Johnson formed a law firm in Jacksonville, and their practice "pick[ed] up business from the start."[92] (Their first murder case, however, was lost, and their client ultimately was hanged.) Wetmore and Johnson were both admitted to the Florida Supreme Court on the motion of Frank T. Clark, a white Jacksonville lawyer who later became a United States congressman.[93]

In 1901, Johnson became a supporter of Booker T. Washington. Johnson's influence with Washington, and Washington's influence with President Theodore Roosevelt, won Johnson an appointment as consul to Puerto Cabello, Venezuela, and Corinto, Nicaragua, in 1901.[94] Wetmore ran the firm for a short time after Johnson's departure, and was elected to the Jacksonville city council on the Democratic ticket in 1905.[95] Later, he went to New York to practice law. Wetmore was a very skillful lawyer and served as co-counsel with Isaac Lawrence Purcell and Samuel Decatur McGill in several landmark civil rights decisions before the Florida Supreme Court.

Another lawyer in Florida at the turn of the century was John Wallace, from Tallahassee, who also practiced in Jacksonville, Florida.[96] Wallace had had "scant formal education" and studied law "while plowing his farm near Tallahassee,"[97] but his lack of education did not hinder his legal practice.

Two of Florida's most remarkable black lawyers were Samuel Decatur McGill, a 1908 graduate of Boston University School of Law,[98] and his brother Nathan Kellogg McGill, a 1912 graduate of the same law school. Both practiced in Jacksonville for a number of years, but it was S. D. McGill who laid the foundation for a diversified practice among black lawyers in Florida.

S. D. McGill handled numerous high-profile cases. Unlike many of his black counterparts, S. D. McGill represented corporate clients, the leading one being the Knights of Pythias, a black fraternal organization that also issued life insurance policies to its members. Black and white lawyers cooperated in suing the Knights of Pythias on behalf of black clients. Sometimes blacks retained white lawyers to sue the Knights. In other cases, it is unclear whether the lawyer was black or white.

With a substantial corporate retainer, S. D. McGill had more latitude to handle complex civil and criminal cases that required appeals to the Florida Supreme Court. There is little doubt that during the first century of the genesis of the black lawyer, S. D. McGill appeared in more cases before a state supreme court than any other black lawyer.[99]

In the early 1940s, S. D. McGill sparred with the new wave of young, up-and-coming activists from the NAACP who were attempting to assert control over race litigation in the South. McGill, for example, resisted the efforts of Charles Hamilton Houston and Thurgood Marshall to advise him on legal strategy in race cases in Florida. McGill had assumed responsibility, since 1908, for the major civil rights litigation developed in Florida, and he had done so without the advice of outsiders. Despite McGill's stellar thirty-year performance as a civil rights attorney, however, the architects of the modern legal civil rights movement began closing in on him.[100]

In 1937, Charles H. Houston and Thurgood Marshall began filing test cases throughout the South that dealt with the issue of pay equalization for black teachers. Florida was selected as the site for one such test case. The need for coordination of these cases was essential, since Houston and Marshall had learned how to avoid the dismissal of their cases by the courts on technical grounds. S. D. McGill, the local NAACP counsel, was instructed by Houston and Marshall on such technical matters, but McGill refused to comply with their instructions, and his cases faltered. In one case, several black schoolteachers who wanted their pay increased by the state objected to McGill's handling. McGill's stubbornness made it exceedingly difficult for Houston and Marshall, who had to rely on local counsel, to achieve their litigative objectives. With the pay cases dangerously close to being dismissed, Lawson Edwarde Thomas, a young black Florida lawyer, assumed responsibility for the suits.[101]

While McGill may have had differences with Charles H. Houston and Thurgood Marshall, he sought the assistance of Marshall and Leon A. Ransom, a Howard University law faculty member, to help appeal a murder case, *Chambers v. Florida*,[102] to the United States Supreme Court. For nearly six years McGill and several other black lawyers kept their clients in the Chambers case from being hanged, arguing that their convictions had been based on coerced confessions in violation of the constitution's protection against self-incrimination. The cooperative efforts of McGill, Ransom, and Marshall won reversals of the death sentences in the United States Supreme Court.[103]

Black lawyers in Florida progressed in spite of political efforts to have them barred from the state. In 1913, the lower house of the Florida state legislature voted in favor of a bill barring blacks from practicing law in the state,[104] an action opposed by the *Tampa Tribune*.[105] As the legislature debated the action, D. W. Perkins and H. P. Baily appeared before the Florida Supreme Court to contest the lily-white juries in Tampa, Florida,[106] and helped defeat the discriminatory legislation.[107] Nevertheless, the Jim Crow laws barred blacks from attending Florida law schools until after World War II.[108]

Although the Sixteenth Census (1940) records the existence of one black woman lawyer in Florida, her identity remains a mystery.[109]

Louisiana

Louis A. Bell was graduated from Howard University's law school in 1871. He went to New Orleans, Louisiana, where he was admitted to the bar in the same year.[110] Bell was the class orator at the first law graduation exercises at Howard University School of Law.[111] Prior to Bell's admission to the Louisiana bar, only one other black person was known to have been admitted, C. Clay Morgan, about whom little more is known.[112] Upon Bell's admission, a Louisiana newspaper reported that "the admission to the bar . . . by the Supreme Court, of a colored man, is remarkable only for its entire novelty here."[113] Recognizing the racial prejudice toward other pioneer lawyers, the article continued to note that because of such prejudice "colored lawyers will for a long time be 'few and far between' and for obvious reasons their field of practice must be limited."[114] Prior to his death at age thirty-two, Bell was responsible for the development of plans for the Straight University Law Department and served as chief clerk of the surveyor's office.[115]

Thomas Morris Chester was admitted to practice in Louisiana in 1873.[116] Chester studied law in London, England, at the Middle Temple Inn and was called to the English bar in 1870, becoming the first known black American admitted to the English bar.[117] He practiced law "at the old Bailey and the civil courts" before returning to the United States and settling in Louisiana.[118]

Chester's formal legal training made him a formidable opponent against less-educated white lawyers in New Orleans. In one of his first cases, Morris defended a man charged with murder in the First District Court. The trial lasted two days and resulted in acquittal. Chester's success against the prosecution was attributed to his superior education.[119] During the mid-1870s Chester received two significant political appointments: one as aide-de-camp to the staff of Louisiana Governor William Pitt Kellogg and the other as United States commissioner. The latter appointment was made by Judge Edward Coke Billings.[120] The position of United States commissioner, a judicial post similar to the present-day United States magistrate, made him the first black judicial officer in the federal court system. In this position, Chester's salary was paid by the filing fees of the parties. Chester's popularity as a commissioner brought some embarrassment to Judge Billings in that he drew more fees than the other two commissioners, both of whom were white. To save face, Judge Billings asked Chester to resign.[121] Unfortunately, the record concerning T. Morris Chester's further practice as a lawyer is incomplete.[122]

In 1874 Straight University, an institution sponsored by the American Missionary Association, opened its law department (which, as noted above, had been helped into existence by Louis A. Bell). For the next twelve years, the law department graduated several black and white law students, including Louis André Martinet, its "first Negro graduate," in 1876.[123] He paid for his legal education by moonlighting as a part-time French teacher. Martinet was elected to the Louisiana state legislature representing St. Martin Parrish, where he served from 1876 to 1878.[124]

As was usual in many states, law students in Louisiana were permitted to take the bar at the end of their first year in law school. Martinet took advantage of this opportunity, passed the examination, and was a member of the Louisiana bar when he graduated from Straight University.[125] Two years after Martinet's graduation, the Hayes-Tilden Compromise was reached, and the federal troops that had protected blacks during the Reconstruction era were withdrawn from the South. This left educated lawyers like Martinet and T. Morris Chester "on the scene at a time when the fortunes of the Negro were fast running out."[126]

Martinet's efforts to obtain employment after leaving law school were hard-fought. On August 6, 1877, he applied for a full-time teaching position at Straight University as a professor of Latin and French. In his letter seeking the professorship, Martinet wrote, "I am also one of the graduates of the law class of 1876, though I was admitted previously to the Bar, after a credible examination, by the Supreme Court."[127] At the time Martin applied for an appointment, he was also "one of the directors of the public schools for [New Orleans]."[128] By August 20, 1877, having received no response to his earlier letter, Martinet wrote that he had waited long enough for a reply to his "petition asking for a teachership in Straight University. I leave tomorrow for the country."[129]

Martinet did not remain in the country for very long. He soon returned to New Orleans to practice law. On June 2, 1885, Martinet was admitted to practice in the United States District Court for the Eastern District of Louisiana, though rigid segregation laws were meanwhile being enacted throughout the South. In an effort to inform the New Orleans black community about news and current political issues, Martinet began to publish the *Daily Crusader* around 1890, the same year in which the Louisiana state legislature passed a series of Jim Crow laws. The paper was used as a tool to help fight the violence toward and political repression of his people. One target of the paper was the "separate car law" passed by the Louisiana legislature in 1890. The separate car law required that blacks and whites ride in separate coaches in all public transportation in the state. Martinet publicly denounced the separate car law in the *Daily Crusader* and quickly became the leader of the protest movement to have the Jim Crow laws in Louisiana declared unconstitutional.

A strategy for a legal challenge against the legality of the separate car law had to be formulated by the lawyers, and the black community had to be mobilized. Martinet called upon "Eugene Luscy, R[udolph] L[ucien] Desdunes and other graduates of [Straight University's] law school [who] took an active part in organizing the Citizens Committee for the Annulment of Act No. 111, commonly known as the separate car law."[130] In 1890, Martinet became one of the first black lawyers to use the term "test case" in planning a litigation strategy to repeal the Louisiana Jim Crow laws.[131] Financial support to pay Martinet and his colleagues for what was to be a long legal fight, was raised by the Citizens Committee.[132]

In the early 1890s, Martinet declared "We'll make a case, a test case, and bring it before Federal courts on the grounds of the invasion of the right [of] a person to travel through the states unmolested."[133] In the first test case, Daniel L. Desdunes was arrested when he refused to vacate a seat reserved for whites in a public streetcar in New Orleans. Desdunes was brought before a local judge, who dismissed the charges against him.[134] The Desdunes decision gave the black community confidence that their cause was just, and another test case was planned.

Homer Adolph Plessy was next used as the guinea pig to test the separate car law.[135] Plessy was arrested and criminally charged for refusing to vacate a coach on a passenger train reserved for whites. An urgent call went out to Albion Winegar Tourgée, a white lawyer living in New York, and to James C. Walker, another white lawyer, to represent Plessy. Tourgée was a Union Army veteran and former "carpetbag" North Carolina judge during Reconstruction.[136] Despite the fact that there were black lawyers in the South, many of them practiced "almost exclusively in the police courts,"[137] and thus were not considered to appeal Plessy's case. In addition, an experienced appellate lawyer was needed to take the case to the United States Supreme Court after the Supreme Court of Louisiana denied Plessy's writ of prohibition in 1892.[138]

As the case worked its way to the United States Supreme Court, the nation waited for what may have been the most important race case to be determined by the court since the Dred Scott decision of 1857. On May 18, 1896, Justice Henry Billings Brown, writing for the majority of the court, held that state-imposed separate but equal car statutes on interstate railroad travel did not violate the Thirteenth or Fourteenth Amendments to the United States Constitution.[139]

Albion W. Tourgée's efforts to have the Supreme Court strike down the separate car law in *Plessy* cannot be given enough credit, but the courageous efforts of Louis André Martinet, who laid the groundwork for the test case, deserves as much credit. It was Martinet who mobilized the community effort, shaped the case, selected the lawyers, and edited a key document in the appeal.[140]

Robert Brown Elliott relocated to New Orleans in 1881 after a distinguished career in South Carolina as a lawyer and the state's first black United States congressman. After his political influence had waned, Elliott was appointed as a customs clerk in Charleston, and then to the Federal Customs Office in New Orleans in 1881. Elliott resigned from the customs office in 1882 and entered private practice in New Orleans with another black lawyer, Thomas de Saille Tucker, who had recently been admitted to the bar.[141] Tucker had read law on his own.[142] Elliott and Tucker specialized in criminal law matters before the police courts of New Orleans.[143] Tucker, a native of Pensacola, Florida, opened up a branch of the firm in that city in 1883.

The law firm of Elliott and Tucker has the distinction of being one of the first black firms in the nation to have offices in more than one state. Tucker described their practice as "lucrative,"[144] and the firm's clients "were equally divided between the two races."[145] Black and white clients were drawn to Elliott and Tucker because their skills were superior to those of many of their white counterparts. They also won their cases in all of the local courts. Several of their clients in New Orleans and Pensacola were "foreigners of Southern Europe, who as a class care nothing for the color of the attorney."[146] Because they had white clients, Elliott and Tucker gained the respect of white judges.

Initially, Elliott's status as a former United States congressman also helped the firm. In fact, it appears that Elliott was highly regarded in Louisiana. It is reported "that whenever [he] appeared before the Supreme Court of Louisiana all of the other divisions of the court would adjourn in order to enable members of the bench and bar to attend the arguments in the Supreme Court."[147] When Elliott died in 1884, the New Orleans law office was closed, reducing the number of practicing black lawyers in the city to four.[148]

Between 1885 and 1886, however, the number of black lawyers increased by four, with the admission to the Louisiana bar of Pinckney Benton Stewart Pinchback, John Francis Patty, René Carl Metoyer, and James Madison Vance, Jr. Pinchback was well known in Louisiana because from 1871 to 1872 he had served as Louisiana's first black lieutenant governor. He had also served as governor for forty-three days in 1872.[149] Pinchback did not study law until after his political career had ended. In 1886, at the age of forty-eight, Pinchback graduated from Straight University's law school and was admitted to the Louisiana bar.[150] Little more is known about his career as a lawyer, but

Pinchback later moved to Washington, D.C., and practiced law there until his death in 1921.[151]

John Francis Patty entered Straight University's law department after serving as a naval officer. Patty graduated in 1885 and was immediately admitted to the Louisiana bar. He practiced "principally in the courts of the Nineteenth Judicial District composed of Terrebonne and St. Mary parishes."[152] Three years later, he was nominated in Louisiana "by acclamation for the position of Secretary of State."[153]

René Carl Metoyer graduated from Straight University's law department in 1886. Prior to attending law school, he had worked as a law clerk "in the [law] office of Rouse and Grant."[154] Metoyer practiced in New Orleans for forty years. On June 27, 1917, Louisiana Governor Ruffin G. Pleasant appointed Metoyer notary public, an honor that had been bestowed on only one other black lawyer—Louis A. Martinet, in 1898.[155]

James Madison Vance, Jr., a classmate of René C. Metoyer, graduated from Straight University's law department in 1886.[156] Vance had championed black causes since 1877, when the Hayes-Tilden Compromise accelerated the enactment of Jim Crow laws in the South.[157] In addition to being an eloquent orator "without peer,"[158] Vance was also a fearless advocate for the civil rights of his people, as is evidenced by the role he played in the "Bonseigneur incident."

In 1893, blacks in New Orleans were outraged when Paul Bonseigneur, a black man, was threatened by whites because he refused to sell them his valuable beach property in Maudeville. Bonseigneur, a wealthy gentleman, was respected by blacks and whites alike, but many whites were jealous of his success. Unable to affect his wealth, these whites attempted to interfere with Bonseigneur's domestic tranquility. The harassment of the Bonseigneur family coincided with the enactment of Jim Crow laws, which had been passed by the Louisiana legislature in the early 1890s.

In 1893, Bonseigneur retained two black lawyers associated with the militant Citizen's Committee—James Madison Vance, Jr., and Louis A. Martinet—to help him keep his property. Since Martinet was heavily involved in formulating the strategy to attack the separate car law legislation, Vance took the lead in fending off the attempt to seize Bonseigneur's property. During a rally in August 1893, Vance spoke out on the Bonseigneur case: "We have not assembled as a race or as a class, but as citizens to protect against a wrong, an invasion of our rights by an assault on the rights of a fellow-citizen."[159] Public efforts such as this drew black support to Vance's political initiatives in the Louisiana Republican Party and to his law practice.[160] Vance's strong support for the Republican Party was rewarded in 1895 when he was given the honor of seconding the nomination of William McKinley for president of the United States during the Republican National Convention at St. Louis, Missouri.[161]

Between 1927 and 1941 few if any black lawyers were admitted to the Louisiana bar.[162] During this period, the responsibility for legal advocacy for black rights fell principally on the shoulders of Alexander Pierre Tureaud, the last black admitted to the bar during this period.

Tureaud had excelled as a law student at Howard University. During his senior year his academic achievements were noted in *The Law Student*, a national magazine published by the American Law Book Company.[163] Graduating from law school in 1925, Tureaud returned to Louisiana and was admitted to the bar in 1927.[164] After his admission to practice, Tureaud began to participate in civic activities, while developing a criminal and civil rights case load. His popularity grew, and so did his practice.

Tureaud was also a legal scholar, a fact that went unrecognized by the white bar in Louisiana. He published many articles concerning United States Supreme Court decisions that affected the rights of black people. His articles were circulated widely to black citizens throughout the South.[165]

After ten years had passed without a single black lawyer being admitted to practice in Louisiana, Tureaud encouraged two graduates of Xavier University to apply to Howard University's law school in 1936. Tureaud not only wrote to acting dean William E. Taylor and former dean Charles H. Houston to admit Archie T. LeCesne and Vincent R. Malveaux, but he also requested financial assistance and student employment for them as well.[166] Because black students were locked out of publicly funded law schools in the state of Louisiana due to race restrictions, Tureaud tried to persuade Xavier University, a private, integrated Catholic institution in New Orleans, to establish a law school. This effort was unsuccessful, although Sister M. Agatha Ryan, the president of Xavier University, informed Tureaud that she had "not given up the hope that some day Xavier will have a school of law."[167]

Tureaud specialized in civil law, although he also handled criminal matters from time to time. According to Tureaud, by the 1940s no black lawyer had "appeared in any outstanding criminal case since the late James Madison Vance [, Jr.], who was so outstanding and so highly respected at the criminal bar that his race made no difference to the court."[168] Tureaud received many court appointments to represent blacks involved in civil disputes. These appointments, along with his walk-in clients, kept him in court seventy-five percent of his working time.[169]

Tureaud handled many civil rights cases as local counsel for the

NAACP in the 1940s. Because such claims (teacher equalization pay cases, for example) involved a number of people and support groups, Tureaud was able to generate a fairly sizeable fee for his services, since fees were not paid by the NAACP. However, Tureaud and Joseph A. Thornton,[170] another black lawyer in New Orleans, were often paid less than they charged because the community was not used to paying black lawyers "large sums" for their services.[171] Indeed, the NAACP leadership in New York was sometimes asked to verify Tureaud and Thornton's fees. In one instance, Tureaud complained about his fees to Thurgood Marshall, who apparently supported a lower fee for services provided in one of the teacher pay cases in Louisiana.[172] Still, despite minor fee differences and disputes over who would control the litigation, Tureaud, Thornton, and Marshall pursued the teacher equalization cases through the state and federal courts,[173] and Tureaud seems to have been lead counsel on most of these cases.

In 1941 Tureaud successfully argued the first teacher salary equalization case against the Orleans Parish School Board. This was followed by similar victories against the school boards in Iberville, Jefferson, and East Baton Rouge parishes.[174] Perhaps the most celebrated civil rights victory was achieved when Tureaud, Marshall, and Thornton persuaded an appellate federal court to reverse a voting rights case which had held that discriminatory voting procedures in the Louisiana Constitution were not reviewable by the federal courts.[175] The decision meant that at least one federal court in this region would not rubber-stamp a state law that restricted the voting rights of blacks.

The establishment of social and political rights for black citizens in Louisiana prior to 1945 can be traced directly to the dogged persistence of the black lawyer. However, outside of New Orleans, it is doubtful that these efforts caught the attention of federal authorities. Local parish governments looked the other way when violence occurred against blacks; they also maintained segregated communities and frustrated their political freedom. In 1944, Thurgood Marshall complained to the chief of the newly created civil rights section of the Department of Justice about the police brutality against blacks affiliated with the NAACP in New Iberia, Louisiana,[176] and then waited for federal authorities to act; but they did not.

No black women were admitted to the Louisiana bar until 1956.[177]

Mississippi

During the Reconstruction era in Mississippi, the political climate was very favorable for the admission of blacks to the bar. The provisional military governor of Mississippi, General Adelbert Ames of the Union

Army, had the power to appoint the members of the Mississippi Supreme Court and several other lower state courts. These "judges were friendly to the Negro or at least were not so hostile to him that they would not admit him to the bar."[178] In exceptional instances, "it could be arranged in advance to pass the applicant," as it was for the whites.[179]

James Henry Piles, a graduate of Oberlin College in Ohio, may have been the first black admitted to the Mississippi bar. Piles studied law in the offices of an Ohio lawyer named Shellabarger. He was admitted to the Ohio Supreme Court prior to 1869[180] and settled in Panola County, Mississippi. He was admitted to the Mississippi Supreme Court in the same year.[181] Elected to the Mississippi state legislature in 1870, Piles served under the new Mississippi Constitution that was assembled that year in Jackson, Mississippi. He also served for one year as assistant secretary of state.[182] In 1873, he ran for sheriff of Penola County, losing to a Judge Ozanne by a small number of votes. Piles's defeat prompted black voters to appeal to Governor Ames. Piles, they said, should "be made the first colored judge in Mississippi."[183]

John Roy Lynch, a twenty-one year old black Republican, was appointed by Governor Adelbert Ames to the office of justice of the peace in Natchez, Mississippi. Lynch took office in 1869. A justice of the peace in Mississippi "exercised considerable judicial authority and power."[184] Although Lynch was not admitted to the bar until 1896, he was Mississippi's first black judicial officer.[185] Between 1869 and 1896, Lynch became one of the most successful politicians in the state of Mississippi, as well as a force in national Republican Party politics.[186] In 1896, the year the United States Supreme Court decided *Plessy v. Ferguson*,[187] Lynch, then fifty years old, applied for admission to the Mississippi bar. The exact reason why Lynch wanted to become a lawyer is uncertain. The law, however, was a natural profession for him to pursue, given his broad experience in state and national politics. But as Lynch was applying to take the bar examination, the standards for admission were becoming more rigid in Mississippi. Examination by a court-appointed committee was replaced by a written examination that was graded by the members of the Mississippi Supreme Court.

Lynch failed the bar on his first attempt. Thereafter, he visited with Tim E. Cooper, the chief justice of the Mississippi Supreme Court, to ascertain why he had failed the examination. Lynch reported, perhaps tongue in cheek, that he had informed the judge: "I flatter myself that I know as much about the law as the average Mississippi lawyer. Consequently, I cannot understand why I was turned down in the examination."[188] Lynch believed that he might not have been afforded the same treatment in the grading of his paper as all other applicants. Nevertheless, he passed the examination on his second attempt. A few years later, with the local political environment souring for blacks, Lynch left Mississippi to take a job with the federal government in the District of Columbia.[189]

Two black lawyers, Abram W. Shadd and Hiram Rhodes Revels, arrived in Mississippi shortly after John Roy Lynch was appointed justice of the peace. Shadd, an 1871 graduate of Howard University's law school, hired himself out as an attorney in Washington County around 1872.[190] He was immediately appointed clerk of the court in Washington County and later in Issaquena County, Mississippi. Shadd also served in the Mississippi state legislature.[191]

In the late 1860s, Hiram Rhodes Revels, a minister, "and ambitious well-trained lawyer" who had been admitted to the Indiana bar, settled in Mississippi.[192] Revels's political ambitions were realized when he was elected "Alderman in Natchez in 1868 and was elected to the Mississippi state senate in 1869."[193] After an unsuccessful challenge to his election to the United States Senate, Revels was seated by a senate vote of forty-eight to eight on February 25, 1870, becoming Mississippi's and the nation's first black senator. Senator Revels served until March 3, 1871. No state would elect another black lawyer to the United States Senate until 1966.[194] The extent of Revels's practice as a lawyer in Mississippi or elsewhere remains unclear.

The occasion of a black man being admitted to the bar in Mississippi was noted by the *Hinds County Gazette* in 1872: "A Negro was admitted to the bar in Okolona [Chickasaw County] a few days since. His examination was highly creditable."[195] In the next three years, several other black lawyers, two of whom were educated outside the United States, were admitted to the bar in various Mississippi counties. In 1872 John D. Werles, educated in Canada and a former clerk of the chancery and circuit court of Washington County, "passed a creditable examination."[196] Werles practiced in Greenville, Mississippi. J. D. Ferrire, a Louisiana lawyer, was educated in London. Ferrire was admitted to the bar in Mayersville (Issaquena County), Mississippi, in 1874.[197] John H. Harris was admitted to the bar in Greenville. Harris, however, had had little formal education; reportedly, he "carried a saw under one arm and a Mississippi Code under the other" while preparing for the bar examination.[198]

Between 1875 and 1900, a few liberal white lawyers helped black men to qualify for the bar by allowing them to study in their offices.[199] But during this same period the Democrats increased the admissions regulations "which made it more difficult for Negroes to be admitted to the bar."[200] With few opportunities available for formal training and with increased hostility toward blacks, the legal profession was beyond reach for many.[201]

Despite the political changes that threatened them, both prior to and after the Hayes-Tilden Compromise of 1877, blacks who had been admitted to the bar prior to that time flourished. Black lawyers served their people in the black regions of Mississippi, with few venturing out to practice law in the white regions.[202] Colonel George F. Bowles is one lawyer who persevered during this period. Near the end of the Civil War, Colonel Bowles was admitted to the bar of Tennessee. In 1871 he relocated to Natchez, Mississippi, because he believed he could prosper there as a lawyer. Bowles soon became known as an outstanding civil and criminal lawyer. He was admitted to the bar in Mississippi in 1875.[203] In Natchez, Bowles held several positions of trust. He was a member of the school board and a city attorney. He also was elected to the Mississippi House of Representatives from Adams County, serving consecutive terms from 1887 to 1891.[204]

In 1875, with two state bar memberships to his credit, and having been admitted to the United States Supreme Court, George Boyer Vashon was admitted to the Mississippi bar, winning a "complimentary recommendation" from his examiners.[205] The scope of Vashon's practice in Mississippi is unknown. Also in 1875, Josiah Thomas Settle was admitted to the bar in Jacksonville, Mississippi. Settle was graduated from Howard University's law school in 1872. He had already been admitted to the bar of the District of Columbia. Settle practiced law in Sardis, Mississippi, with another lawyer, D. T. J. Matthews.[206] In 1875, Settle was "unanimously nominated by the [Mississippi] Republican convention for the position of district attorney of the then 12th Judicial District of Mississippi."[207] But Settle and all the other Republicans on the ticket were defeated, since the political winds of the Reconstruction era had changed.[208] In 1883, however, Settle won a seat in the state legislature, where he "command[ed] the attention of the entire House."[209] He was once considered as a likely candidate for Congress in the Second Congressional District in Mississippi, but the convention declined to nominate him.[210] At the end of more than a decade in politics and law, and upon completion of his term in the Mississippi state legislature in 1885, Settle left the state, relocating to Shelby County, Tennessee, to practice law.[211]

In 1879, Willis E. Mollison commenced the study of law under the tutelage of a former Mississippi Supreme Court justice, E. Jeffords.[212] While studying law under Justice Jeffords, Mollison also served as clerk of the circuit chancery court of Issaquena County, a position to which he was elected in 1883 and re-elected in 1887. Mollison was also admitted to the Mississippi bar in 1887. Although a clerk of the chancery court, Mollison practiced law in Mayerville, Mississippi, his birthplace. In 1889 he made an unsuccessful attempt to win the nomination for secretary of state of Mississippi during the Republican state convention.[213] It was during this convention that Mollison and John Roy Lynch encouraged black Republicans to join forces with the moderate Democrats. When their efforts collapsed, Lynch called his own convention, and a slate of blacks were nominated to head state offices "with . . . Mollison as its candidate for the office of secretary of state."[214] Mollison was not elected, but his political activity may have been influential in his appointment as district attorney *pro tem* by a Democratic judge in Vicksburg, Mississippi, in 1892. The appointment of a black Republican lawyer as a district attorney in Mississippi was so unusual that, when Mollison was called to the bench to be sworn in, audible whispers and mutterings could be heard in the courtroom.[215]

Respect was not always accorded to black lawyers like Willis E. Mollison. Indeed, some white lawyers tried to humiliate him. In one instance, Mollison reports that he was involved in a case with a white lawyer as co-counsel. They were opposed by a white lawyer, who throughout the trial referred to Mollison as "Mr. Mollison," perhaps assuming that Mollison's white co-counsel would be offended if he was disrespectful. After the court record was completed, however, Mollison's white co-counsel "went through the record and drew his pencil through the word 'mister' whenever he found it."[216]

In other cases, Mollison's skills, particularly when he defended whites, were praised by local lawyers. A judge in Vicksburg, Mississippi, appointed Mollison to defend a white man charged with murder in the early 1890s. The judge "insisted his wife and quite a number of his personal friends take seats within the railings of his court to hear what he afterward termed 'the best presentation of a murder case he had ever been permitted to hear.'"[217]

In the early years of the twentieth century, Mollison, a supporter of Booker T. Washington, became a successful businessman in Vicksburg. He was president of the Lincoln Savings Bank and owner and publisher of *The National Star*, a black newspaper.[218] Mollison continued in his practice of law, business, and politics. In 1904, he and John Roy Lynch worked closely with Mississippi Republicans to elect President Theodore Roosevelt.[219]

Mollison argued one of his last and possibly most significant cases of his career before the Mississippi Supreme Court in 1911. During the opening arguments in the trial of a black man charged with the murder of another black citizen, the prosecuting attorney had stated, "This bad nigger killed a good nigger; the dead nigger was a white man's nigger, and these bad niggers like to kill these kind; the only way you can break up this pistol toting among these niggers is to have a neck-tie party."[220] Such arguments were not unusual in the South. The remarks were frequently even more prejudicial when blacks were accused of crimes against whites.[221] The Mississippi Supreme Court determined that the statement by the prosecuting attorney was improper and prejudicial to Mollison's client, who had been convicted. Reversing the conviction, Justice William C. McLean wrote:

Those who are at all familiar with the favor, indeed, we may say affection, that the white man entertains for a 'white man's nigger,' can well and justly appreciate the effect that such an unwarrantable statement, made by an officer of the law, will have before the ordinary jury of the land. The [accused] may be a bad Negro, and a very undesirable member of society, yet he is entitled to go before the jury of the land untrammeled by voluntary epithets, the occasion for which is not shown justified [in this case].[222]

Willis E. Mollison's son, Irvin C. Mollison, followed in his father's footsteps. He graduated from the Chicago Law School in the early part of the twentieth century.[223]

Several other outstanding black lawyers were admitted to the Mississippi bar before the close of the nineteenth century. They made significant contributions both to the state of Mississippi and to the nation as a whole. In 1881, John H. Burris was admitted to the bar after reading law. In 1883 he became the president of Alcorn Agricultural and Mechanical College in Rodney, Mississippi, where he introduced and taught a course in constitutional law.[224]

Wilford Horace Smith, a native of Leota, Mississippi, was graduated from Boston University School of Law in 1883 and admitted to the Mississippi bar in Washington County in the same year. He was one of Boston University law school's first black graduates, and one of the most successful private practitioners in Mississippi prior to 1900. He received significant income representing widows and heirs in pension cases involving claims from the Civil War. In the mid-1890s Smith moved to Galveston, Texas, where he became a successful and widely respected lawyer. He later traveled to New York, where he became one of the first black admiralty lawyers in the nation as counsel for Marcus Garvey's *Black Star Line*.[225]

Wilford H. Smith was one of the first black lawyers in Mississippi to argue a case before the United States Supreme Court. In 1895, Smith challenged an 1890 provision of the Mississippi constitution which required, as a qualification to serve on a jury, the juror's ability to read and write. Smith sought to overturn the conviction of a black defendant on the grounds that while there were "7000 black colored citizens [in Washington County] competent for jury service . . . and 1500 whites," not a single black person was selected to sit on the defendant's jury. This, Smith claimed, was a violation of the Fourteenth Amendment to the United States Constitution. He argued that the case should have been removed from the state court to a federal circuit court. Justice John Marshall Harlan, speaking for the majority of the court in *Gibson v. Mississippi*,[226] ruled against Smith's claim, finding no violation of the United States Constitution.

On the same day that Wilford H. Smith argued *Gibson v. Mississippi* before the United States Supreme Court, Cornelius J. Jones, another black Mississippi lawyer, argued *Smith v. Mississippi*,[227] which challenged the racial exclusion of blacks from a Mississippi grand jury. As in the *Gibson* case, Justice Harlan ruled against Jones's client. The arguments of both the *Gibson* and *Smith* cases on December 13, 1895, marked the first time in American legal history that more than one black lawyer had been heard before the United States Supreme Court on different cases on the same day.[228]

Cornelius J. Jones and Wilford H. Smith were admitted to the Mississippi bar at about the same time. Jones was both an active practitioner and a politician, serving one term in the Mississippi state legislature in the 1890s. Jones was one of the first blacks to oppose the James K. Vardaman's efforts to disfranchise black voters in Mississippi,[229] and he challenged the exclusion of blacks from juries on the basis of state regulations that barred them from registering to vote. In 1898, however, the United States Supreme Court rejected Jones's claim.[230]

Jones was a persistent advocate for the rights of blacks. In 1915, while based in Memphis, Tennessee, he brought a class claim against the United States, seeking reparations for persons who labored in the production of cotton while enslaved in the South. The suit was brought against William G. McAdoo, United States Secretary of the Treasury, in the local courts of the District of Columbia. Jones asked for $68,000,000 on behalf of his clients and a putative class of black Americans, claiming that the United States had wrongfully benefited from revenues collected from slave owners through a tax on raw cotton. The relief sought was to compensate the blacks who picked raw cotton between 1859 to 1868 and "their ancestors, 'subject to a system of involuntary servitude' in states of the South."[231] The District of Columbia Court of Appeals rejected Jones's claim on procedural grounds, holding that Secretary McAdoo was merely the custodian of the treasury, leaving as "[t]he real defendant . . . the United States . . . [which] cannot be made a party to this suit without its consent," a ruling upheld by the United States Supreme Court.[232]

Subsequently, the United States brought an indictment for fraud against Jones. The government alleged that Jones was the leader of a conspiracy to swindle blacks throughout the South. The indictment was based on a general letter signed by Jones and sent through the mails to several blacks which requested $1.75 contributions to support the cotton tax reparation cases.[233] Jones promised that they would share in any monetary award if the test case prevailed. There is little doubt that the action against Jones was intended to restrain his advocacy among those he had so fearlessly represented before the United States Supreme Court. The outcome of the action is unknown. In 1918, Jones left Mississippi and Tennessee and relocated to Oklahoma to practice law.[234]

By 1885, with the institution of higher standards in several counties in Mississippi, bar admission became almost impossible for blacks, even for those who had white sponsors. A few blacks satisfied the standards and were admitted, but not without difficulty. In 1884 Samuel A. Beadle applied for admission to the bar in Brandon, Mississippi. He was sponsored by Anselm J. McLaurin, who later became a United States senator. When McLaurin made the motion that Beadle be admitted to the bar by examination, the "chancellor said that he did not examine 'niggers' in [his] court."[235] Beadle was later permitted to be examined after McLaurin became governor of Mississippi, and with the favorable intercession of Mississippi congressman Patrick Henry.[236]

Beadle's bar examination drew a crowd, possibly because of McLaurin and Henry's well-publicized support. Almost half of the thirty-six lawyers in Jackson, Mississippi were in the courtroom when Beadle was examined. The court examined Beadle on the legal principles contained in *Blackstone*, and he also answered questions posed by the lawyers observing the examination. According to Beadle's account, it was as though "[I] was being tried for [my] life or liberty."[237] Beadle's performance was so exceptional that when the examination ended, the lawyers "carried [Beadle] around on their shoulders in recognition of his triumph."[238]

Beadle was admitted to the bar in 1884, but because of racism he could not practice in the cities of Yazoo, Columbus, Greenwood, Winona, or Hattiesburg, Mississippi. Judges in these cities refused to allow him to enter their courtrooms and threatened his life if he tried to represent clients there. In the cities in which he practiced, Beadle prospered, and he was particularly successful in Vicksburg. In Vicksburg, Jackson, Natchez, and Canton, Beadle obtained or sought charters for several banks and, along with other black lawyers including Perry W. Howard and Willis E. Mollison, he became counsel to these banks.[239] Beadle also represented J. B. Hart and Company, a large white merchant firm from which he drew a five-hundred-dollar retainer and payment for all of his office expenses each year. Beadle also handled some of J. B. Hart's personal affairs, until white racists leaned on Hart to drop Beadle, because Hart's employment of a black lawyer "was not in accordance with his ordained status."[240]

The situation in Mississippi did not deter Dave Temple, an 1885 Straight University law graduate, from returning to his home state and practicing in Vicksburg, Mississippi[241]; and M. D. Fleming also practiced there. Fleming was admitted to the Mississippi bar in 1888, but worked there for only three years before moving to Memphis, Tennessee. Fleming was one of the few black lawyers to be examined by the members of the Mississippi Supreme Court "sitting as a body."[242] Julian Talbot Bailey was also listed as being successfully "engaged in the practice of law in Mississippi" near the end of the nineteenth century.[243] But by the turn of the century, James K. Vardaman, who had been elected governor of Mississippi in 1904, managed to foment such broad anti-black sentiments in the state that liberal white lawyers began to withdraw the assistance they had extended to "the Negro law student."[244]

In the early twentieth century, the number of black lawyers admitted to practice in Mississippi declined as new standards for admission to the bar favored applicants with a formal legal education.[245] James Albert Burns, however, was admitted in Biloxi,[246] and other lawyers from the Southern black and Northern white law schools were also admitted to the Mississippi bar. For example, William J. Latham, a graduate of Central Tennessee Law School at Walden University, was admitted to the Mississippi bar in 1902. Nathan S. Taylor, who claimed that he attended the University of Michigan's law school, and Benjamin Allen Morris Green, a 1914 graduate of Harvard University's law school, were both admitted to the Mississippi bar in about 1915.[247]

The dearth of black lawyers and the apparent racial restrictions imposed on black citizens in Mississippi did not seem to deter the open and active practice of law by William J. Latham. Latham was recognized by white and black lawyers for his expertise in insurance law. He served as counsel to the Knights of Pythias, a black fraternal organization, in Mississippi. The representation of various black fraternal groups that contested their members' insurance benefits took Latham to the Mississippi Supreme Court on a number of occasions. The appeals, often won by Latham and another black lawyer named Louis Kossuth Atwood, established several significant precedents favoring insurance companies between 1908 and 1915.[248]

Despite his apparent success as a lawyer in Mississippi, Latham, like many other black lawyers, left the state in 1917 and relocated to Chicago, where he formed the Underwriters Insurance Company, a company that flourished until the Depression.[249] Latham's departure from

Mississippi was not based on any mistreatment by the courts, for in 1915 he stated that "while I have had points decided against me, in cases where I thought my theory was the correct one, as all lawyers have, I cannot truthfully charge that such adverse decisions were made simply because I was colored."[250]

Other black lawyers in Mississippi did not share this experience. Between 1904 and 1915, the lives of lawyers were sometimes threatened when they were called upon to represent clients charged with crimes in Mississippi cities. For example, the local sheriff in Greenville, Mississippi, barred Nathan S. Taylor from sitting inside the bar or railing of a local courtroom, which was his right as a member of the bar. The sheriff required Taylor to sit in the gallery—from which he argued his cases—while the prosecution had the complete attention of the judge and jury on the first floor of the courthouse.[251]

On one occasion, a white lawyer objected to Taylor's treatment, stating that as a member of the bar he was entitled to represent his clients like any other lawyer. However, the judge and sheriff turned a deaf ear to such pleas for fairness, even from the mouth of a white lawyer. The same sheriff reportedly attempted to murder Taylor near or in the courthouse, but his life was saved by "lawyers seeing him in danger."[252] The local judge ignored the sheriff's conduct. Taylor soon left Mississippi and settled in Chicago to practice law.

The effects of hostile racial attitudes caused the black community in Mississippi to doubt the effectiveness of black lawyers as a class. Out of necessity, then, black lawyers in Mississippi were frequently dumped for white lawyers.[253]

Perry W. Howard, a 1904 graduate of the Illinois College of Law (De Paul), was admitted to the Mississippi bar in 1905. He was associated with Samuel A. Beadle.[254] Upon his admission to the bar he reported that "he was considered not only a rascal, [but] a thief and enemy of society and good government, an abettor of crime, and an undesirable citizen on general principles."[255] This perception, however, did not take hold in his political career. By 1914 the Republican state convention had elected Howard as national committeeman, making him one of the most powerful men in Mississippi.[256] In 1921, Howard's political influence landed him a presidential appointment in Washington, D.C. He became special assistant to the attorney general of the United States. When Howard left the Department of Justice he formed a law practice in Washington, D.C., which, with his significant political contacts, flourished even after his death in 1961.[257]

The hostility toward black lawyers described by Perry W. Howard is supported by other accounts. In 1904 P. F. Williams, a graduate of Straight University School of Law, set up practice in Brookhaven,

Mississippi. His practice failed because "the courts decided every case against him, regardless of its merits."[258] Black lawyers in Mississippi also faced physical abuse. When John C. Hill, an early twentieth-century Mississippi lawyer, appeared in the Lauderdale County Court House in Mississippi to be examined for admission to the bar, whites "sprinkled 'high life' down his back . . . a mixture of coarse horse hair and cayenne pepper."[259] Even after suffering this humiliation, Hill managed to pass the examination. He practiced in Meridian, Mississippi, for seven years before moving on.[260]

Some bright spots appeared in the 1920s under Governor Henry L. Whitfield, who broke with the anti-black policy of prior administrations. He appointed Taylor G. Ewing, a black lawyer practicing in Vicksburg, Mississippi, as notary public. Ewing's appointment was considered particularly significant given the nearly fifteen years of anti-black sentiments in Mississippi. When criticized, Governor Whitfield defended his appointment on the "separate but equal" grounds: "Negroes have their separate churches, theaters . . . lawyers . . . why . . . not notaries of their own race."[261] Initially, Ewing, a highly capable lawyer, had to plead his cases through white lawyers.[262] Ewing later left Mississippi and relocated to Memphis, Tennessee, but he continued to practice in Mississippi, winning significant cases before the Mississippi Supreme Court for black brakemen employed by the Yazoo, Mississippi Valley Railroad Company.[263]

Around 1910, Sidney Dillon Redmond, a medical doctor, switched to the legal profession in Hinds County, Mississippi. As a lawyer, Redmond's efforts on behalf of black citizens often put him at odds with the white establishment, and at times with his own people. In 1915 Redmond was disbarred for stirring up litigation against a bankrupt fraternal organization. He was reinstated to practice in 1920.[264] In 1926, Redmond was joined in the practice of law by his son, Sidney Revels Redmond, a Harvard University law graduate.[265]

Between 1926 and 1930, both these men were riddled with charges of legal misconduct by the white legal establishment; many of these accusations likely were intended to embarrass S. D. Redmond, who held important positions in the Mississippi Republican Party. In 1929 both Redmonds were charged with several counts of misconduct, including false testimony during a peonage trial. The charges against Sidney Revels Redmond were dropped on the condition that he leave Mississippi and practice elsewhere.[266]

S. D. Redmond remained in Mississippi to fight the charges leveled against him. But the adverse findings of the local disciplinary bar committee were, after a hearing, affirmed by the chancellor, V. J. Stricker. Redmond filed a motion for a new hearing, alleging "that the chancellor was actuated by prejudice," and citing evidence of racial prejudice in the language of Judge Stricker's summary.[267] Redmond's motion also challenged the state constitution and apparently made reference to the anti-black views of the framers of the document. The members of the disciplinary committee construed the content of Redmond's legal argument "as an attack upon the constitution of Mississippi and its framers."[268] For his statements, the court cited Redmond for criminal contempt, holding that the content of his motion was contrary to law; he was fined five hundred dollars.

Disbarred and cited for criminal contempt, which also carried a penalty of imprisonment, Redmond petitioned the Mississippi Supreme Court through his white lawyers to review his case. Redmond's case, challenging solely the criminal contempt issue, was heard by the Mississippi Supreme Court twice, on various points of law, between 1930 and 1931. In both instances the court ruled in his favor.[269]

Redmond's ultimate fate regarding the disbarment order is not altogether certain. It is unknown whether he was charged again after the Mississippi Supreme Court reversed the Hinds County Circuit Court decision that had disbarred him. The local bar authorities may have ceased in their efforts to rid themselves of Redmond, given his other difficulties. In 1929, S. D. Redmond and Perry W. Howard were indicted by federal authorities in Mississippi for selling federal jobs. These charges resulted in two trials and acquittals for both men. The acquittals came as a surprise to government prosecutors who had said they had a "water tight" case against Howard and Redmond. Republicans, influential white Democrats, and others who may have benefited from Howard and Redmond's alleged misdeeds testified on their behalf. According to one scholar's interpretation of the trial, Howard's conviction would have embarrassed the Democrats in particular, since Howard had lined their pockets with federal jobs.[270]

Nevertheless, the Republican Party was eager to remove these two influential black lawyers from the Republican state executive committee, and so their support waned. Both men were brought before a court-appointed disciplinary committee on charges growing out of the federal indictments.[271] As a result of the disciplinary charges, and despite the pleas of 30,000 blacks on his behalf, Redmond left Mississippi and moved to Washington, D.C., where he joined his friend, Perry W. Howard, in the practice of law.[272]

By 1935 the number of black lawyers in Mississippi had been reduced to five. The exodus of black lawyers from Mississippi was due in large measure to the negative treatment they received in the courts. Judges ruled against them, the bar excluded them from its circles, and black people, observing this treatment, flocked to white lawyers out of necessity.[273] In 1944, W. L. Mhoon, of Jackson, and Taylor G. Ewing, of Vicksburg, were the only blacks listed as lawyers practicing in the state of Mississippi.[274]

No black woman lawyers are known to have practiced in Mississippi before 1945. However, Mary Ann Shadd (Carey), an 1883 graduate of Howard University's law school, was the first black woman lawyer to enter the state. On March 14, 1885, Shadd delivered a speech entitled "Race, Pride, and Cooperation" at the courthouse in Mayersville which reportedly "ruffled the dead-sea level of life in [Mississippi]."[275]

Summary

The state of Alabama admitted its first black lawyer, Moses Wenslydale Moore, in 1871. Moore was a graduate of Howard University's law school, whereas other black lawyers admitted to the Alabama bar during the Reconstruction era appear instead to have read law. During Reconstruction, black lawyers participated in the political processes of Alabama: William Hooper Councill, for example, served in the Alabama state legislature, and Alabama's first black congressman, James Thomas Rapier, was elected to Congress in 1873.

The first black law firm of note was formed in 1891 in Birmingham by John Henry Ballou, R. C. O. Benjamin, and Henry Clay Smith. The firm had ties to national Republican politics, and Henry Clay Smith became, in 1893, President Grover Cleveland's first black appointee. Smith also was appointed to the United States Consulate in Santos, Brazil.

One aim of the black lawyer in Alabama was to expand the civil rights of blacks at the state and federal levels. William Hooper Councill, as a party to an action, filed the first test case before the newly created Interstate Commerce Commission in 1887. He challenged the lawfulness of the railroads' discrimination against black passengers. Wilford Horace Smith and other black lawyers filed the first significant voting rights cases in Alabama in the early days of the twentieth century, and these lawsuits reached the United States Supreme Court in 1903.

All-white juries in Alabama made the color-blind practice of law difficult, particularly in criminal law. Black lawyers constantly challenged the unconstitutionality of the blacks' exclusion from juries. Wilford Horace Smith carried one such jury exclusion case to the United States Supreme Court in 1904, and won.

The sacrifices made by black lawyers challenging the system in Alabama were enormous. Some were run out of town, disbarred on dubious charges, or physically attacked. Black lawyers supporting the

NAACP became marked men. Between 1925 and 1937, the number of black lawyers had declined significantly because of the hostile racial environment in the state. Private groups were formed to provide funds to help black citizens pay for legal services.

The admission of Arthur Davis Shores to the Alabama bar in 1938 opened a new era in civil rights in the state. For years, Shores was the only black lawyer in Alabama. He received his law degree through the LaSalle Extension University in Chicago. Other law schools represented during this new era included the University of Michigan, Yale University, Howard University, and Straight University.

Estelle Henderson is reported to be the first black woman admitted to the Alabama bar. She was admitted in 1919.

Harvey S. Harmon became Florida's first black lawyer in 1869, followed by James Dean, who became the first black in Florida to hold a judicial post. Racial distinctions were so strict in Florida that Dean was removed from his judicial post for issuing a marriage license to a black Cuban woman and a fair-skinned black man who looked white.

During and after the Reconstruction era, black lawyers participated in Florida politics. Joseph E. Lee, the first formally trained black lawyer in the state, was elected to the Florida legislature in 1874. He became the highest-ranking judicial officer in the state in 1888, when he was elected municipal judge in Jacksonville.

Black lawyers in Florida fought for seminal civil rights litigation. As early as 1873, William F. Thompson, a member of the Florida state legislature, attempted to pass legislation making the exclusion of blacks from juries unlawful. However, it was the systematic battle for civil rights litigation waged by Isaac Lawrence Purcell, Samuel Decatur McGill, and Judson Douglas Wetmore that broke most new ground in the state. These lawyers won several civil rights cases before the Florida Supreme Court, and they appealed every death sentence to that court.

Samuel Decatur McGill modernized the private practice of law in black firms in Florida. He represented black corporate clients and handled a significant number of civil rights cases. Prior to 1945, McGill appeared before the Florida Supreme Court in more cases than any other black lawyer in the state.

While many of the pioneer black lawyers in Florida were not formally trained, several were graduates of law schools, such as Boston University and Howard University. No black women are known to have been admitted to the bar prior to 1945.

After the Civil War ended, many in Louisiana predicted that the practice of black lawyers would be limited. And yet the first identifiable black lawyer, C. Clay Morgan, was practicing law in Louisiana in 1860.

And when Louis A. Bell received his law degree from Howard University in 1871, he settled in New Orleans to practice. He also developed plans for the creation of the law program at Straight University.

Thomas Morris Chester, who had been trained at the Middle Temple Inn in London, became a commissioner in the federal court system in the 1870s. However, it was Louis André Martinet who, after serving a term in the Louisiana state legislature, laid the legal groundwork for *Plessy v. Ferguson*, which was decided by the United States Supreme Court in 1896. This case unsuccessfully challenged the separate car law. Martinet and other civil rights lawyers, including James Madison Vance, Jr., and Alexander Pierre Tureaud, organized and waged valiant legal battles to further the rights of black citizens in Louisiana.

Alexander Pierre Tureaud, a 1925 law graduate from Howard University, was one of the "new breed" of civil rights lawyers. Tureaud was the most important black lawyer in Louisiana between 1927 and 1941, when black lawyers were generally denied admission to the Louisiana bar. He and Thurgood Marshall, who was chief counsel for the NAACP, were responsible for the first pay equalization and voting rights cases in Louisiana.

Evidence of heightened participation in politics by black lawyers is not as apparent in Louisiana as it is in other Southern states during the Reconstruction and Post-Reconstruction eras. However, John Francis Patty was nominated for secretary of state in 1888, and John Madison Vance, Jr., seconded the nomination of William McKinley for president during the Republican National Convention of 1896.

No women were admitted to the Louisiana bar before 1945.

After the Civil War, black lawyers were admitted to the bar in the state of Mississippi without incident. James H. Piles, a black man previously admitted to the Ohio bar, was admitted to the bar in Mississippi in 1869. Abram W. Shadd and Josiah Thomas Settle, both trained at Howard University's law school, were part of the first wave of formally trained black lawyers in Mississippi.

The participation of black lawyers in Mississippi and in national Republican politics is noteworthy. One black lawyer, Hiram Rhodes Revels, who practiced more as a minister than a lawyer, was elected to the United States Senate in 1869. He was the first black American to serve in that body. Josiah T. Settle served in the state legislature in 1883, and Willis E. Mollison made an unsuccessful bid to be his party's nominee for secretary of state during the same period.

The progress of the black lawyer in Mississippi began to slow in 1875, just before federal troops were pulled out of the South by President Rutherford B. Hayes. By 1900, their plight had worsened as a result of the anti-black campaign of Governor (and later U.S. Senator) James K. Varadaman.

With few exceptions, the private practice of law by black lawyers was limited to criminal law and to black male clients. Some black defendants appeared without representation in county courts that barred black lawyers. Liberal white businessmen were told not to use black lawyers—it was against white tradition—and this caused black citizens to question the black lawyers' professional validity. Many black lawyers left the state or went into other professions, such as teaching. However, several lawyers, some of whom doubled as politicians, were able to maintain a presence in Mississippi. Among this group of lawyers were Perry W. Howard, who became the most powerful black man in the nation, and Sidney D. Redmond, who became one of the wealthiest.

Men like Cornelius J. Jones plugged along, bringing many civil rights cases to the courts during the 1890s. Jones sued the United States for reparations on behalf of former slaves. His case was based on the fact that the United States had received tax money derived directly from the fruits of slavery. Jones's Cotton Tax case reached the United States Supreme Court, but was lost on technical grounds. The United States then sought an indictment against Jones for soliciting money from blacks to prosecute the claim.

Wilford Horace Smith and Cornelius J. Jones were credited with the first legal assaults on the exclusion of blacks from juries. They won at least one case before the Mississippi Supreme Court, on the grounds that racist language was used before the jury in a murder case.

A few black lawyers, including Louis Kossuth Atwood, staked out ground as specialists in insurance law. In this area, Atwood established several precedents before the Mississippi Supreme Court.

Many law schools were represented in Mississippi during and after the Reconstruction era. Two lawyers of this period were trained in Canada and London; others attended black law schools, such as Central Tennessee University and Howard University, and white law schools, such as De Paul University, Boston University, and Chicago Law School. No black women were admitted to the Mississippi bar prior to 1945.

Black lawyers in the Southern states broke new ground in the law and politics that emancipated their people.

Notes

1. *Mobile Daily Register*, Nov. 22, 1871.
2. *Montgomery Daily State Journal*, Jan. 5, 1872.

3. *Ibid.* Moses W. Moore, then living in Selma, Alabama, was admitted to the Supreme Court of Alabama on January 4, 1872. Letter from J. Render Thomas, clerk, Alabama Supreme Court, to Charles S. Brown, Nov. 30, 1959.

4. Letter from George H. Jones, Jr., register, Circuit Court of Montgomery County, Alabama, to Charles S. Brown, Oct. 15, 1958. James T. Rapier "was admitted to the Alabama Bar but we find no record of dates or any practice in the courts." See also, L. Schweninger, *James T. Rapier and Reconstruction* xviii (1978), which states that Rapier was never admitted to the bar; *History of Alabama and Dictionary of Alabama Biography* 1412 (T. M. Owen ed. 1921).

5. W. M. Jackson, *The Story of Selma* 152 (1954).

6. *Id.* at 153.

7. *Id.* at 272.

8. *The College of Life or Practical Self Educator: A Manual of Self Improvement for the Colored Race* 156 (H. D. Northrop, J. R. Gay, and I. G. Penn eds. 1896).

9. W. J. Simmons, *Men of Mark* 145 (1887); *The Black Book* 124 (M. Levitt, R. Furman, and E. Smith eds. 1974). Lowry was sponsored to the bar by Belva Ann Lockwood, the first woman admitted to the United States Supreme Court in 1879. K. B. Morello, *The Woman Lawyer in America: 1638 to the Present—The Invisible Bar* 35 (1986).

10. *Detroit Plaindealer*, July 1, 1892.

11. Letter from S. Jessie Harris, Dept. of Southern History and Literature, to Charles S. Brown, July 31, 1959; *Register of the Department of State* 20, 49 (1894). Henry Clay Smith was confirmed by the Senate to this position on August 25, 1893, serving until October 8, 1896.

12. *People's Advocate*, March 5, 1881.

13. W. J. Simmons, *Men of Mark* 393 (1887); letter from J. Render Thomas, clerk, Alabama Supreme Court, to Charles S. Brown, May 26, 1958; *People's Advocate*, May 16, 1883. Thomas states that Hooper, from Huntsville, Alabama, was admitted to the bar on May 17, 1882.

14. *Dictionary of American Negro Biography* 138 (R. Logan and W. Winston eds. 1982). See *William H. Councill v. The Western and Atlantic Railroad Company*, 1 I.C.C. 399 (1887).

15. L. R. Harlan and P. Daniel, "A Dark and Stormy Night in the Life of Booker T. Washington," 3 *Chronicle* 4, 6 (Feb. 1970).

16. William L. England, Jr., "The Condition of Southern Negroes, 1886–1889, As Viewed by the *New York Age*," 98–99, (M.A. thesis, Butler University, June 17, 1972).

17. L. R. Harlan and P. Daniel, "A Dark and Stormy Night in the Life of Booker T. Washington," 3 *Chronicle* 4, 6 (Feb. 1970).

18. L. R. Harlan, *Booker T. Washington: The Making of a Black Leader, 1856–1901*, at 171–72 (1972).

19. *Id.* at 171.

20. Marable, "Tuskegee and the Politics of Illusion in the New South," 18 *The Black Scholar* 13, 16 (May 1977).

21. *Ibid.* See also, L. R. Harlan, *Booker T. Washington: The Making of a Black Leader, 1856–1901*, at 171–75 (1972).

22. Vol. 4 *The Booker T. Washington Papers, 1895–98*, at 52 (L. R. Harlan, S. B. Kaufman, B. S. Kraft, and R. W. Smock eds. 1975).

23. Vol. 5 *Men of Hawaii* 157 (G. F. Nellist ed. revised ed. 1937); *Virginia's Contribution to Negro Leadership* 19 (W. Cooper ed. 1937), mimeo; *General Catalogue of the University of Michigan, 1837–1911*, at 431 (I. N. Demmon ed. 1912).

24. 189 U.S. 475 (1903).

25. Justices David Josiah Brewer, Henry Billings Brown, and John Marshall Harlan were the dissenting votes in *Giles v. Harris* (*id.* at 488, 493). Justice Harlan voiced concern that the case "was submitted [to the Court] without oral argument," despite the fact that it presented "questions of considerable importance" (*id.* at 494). It is interesting to note that Justice Brown was the author of *Plessy v. Ferguson*, 163 U.S. 537 (1896), which held that the Fourteenth Amendment was not violated by a state statute requiring separate car accommodations for white and colored persons on railroads. Justice Harlan issued a strong dissent in *Plessy*; Justice Brewer did not participate in *Plessy* (*id.* at 552). In 1904, Wilford H. Smith appealed two actions to the United States Supreme Court that had been adversely decided by the Alabama Supreme Court. See *Giles v. Harris*, 189 U.S. 475 (1903); see also, *Giles v. Teasley*, 136 Ala. 164, 33 So. 819 (1903) and *Giles v. Teasley*, 136 Ala. 228, 33 So. 820 (1903). These cases were consolidated on appeal by the United States Supreme Court in *Giles v. Teasley*, 193 U.S. 146 (1904). The result was the same, except that Justice William R. Day wrote the majority opinion, Justice Joseph McKenna concurred, and Justice John Marshall Harlan dissented without issuing an opinion (*id.* at 193 U.S. 167). Justice Day was appointed to the United States Supreme Court after the court issued its opinion in *Giles v. Harris*. For a general discussion of the case in the black press, see "The Alabama Decision," 6 *The Colored American Magazine* 536 (July 1903).

26. The grand jury exclusion cases had been brought before the United States Supreme Court by black lawyers on at least two previous occasions. In 1896, Emanuel D. M. Hewlett, of the District of Columbia, and Cornelius J. Jones, of Mississippi, had established that such racial exclusion from grand juries was a violation of the Fourteenth Amendment in *Gibson v. Mississippi*, 162 U.S. 565 (1896). During the October 1899 term of the United States Supreme Court, Wilford H. Smith and Emanuel D. M. Hewlett won a similar case in *Carter v. Texas*, 177 U.S. 442 (1900). Faced with these precedents, the majority of the court apparently determined that in non-political areas the interpretation of the Fourteenth Amendment was settled. The Alabama Supreme Court, following the mandate of the United States Supreme Court, reversed its opinion in *Rogers* and remanded the case to the local trial court for a new trial (*Rogers v. State*, 139 Ala. 666, 36 So. 1044 [1903]).

27. Letter from Robert G. Esdale, clerk, Supreme Court of Alabama, to Prince C. Chambliss, Jr., March 26, 1987 (with copy of order admitting L. L. Chambliss to the bar). Edward Austin Brown was admitted to the Ohio bar in the late 1890s. He studied law in Cleveland, Ohio, under Judge Henry McKinney. Brown went to Birmingham to practice law shortly before the start of the Spanish-American War in 1898. Vol. 1 *The National Cyclopedia of the Colored Race* 21 (C. C. Richardson ed. 1919). One author's account is that Brown was "the first black man to pass the Alabama bar exam" is apparently in error (Lynda Dempsey Cochran, "Arthur Davis Shores: Advocate for Freedom," 26 [M.A. thesis, Georgia Southern College, 1977]).

28. *Ibid.* (*The National Cyclopedia*).

29. Chambers, "At 95, He's a Model for All Lawyers," *Nat'l. L.J.*, April 24, 1989, at 13, col. 4.

30. "Judge Allen to Aid in Negro's Defense," *The Montgomery Advertiser*, Jan. 13, 1919. Kline was assisted by former judge Basil M. Allen in the defense of Edgar Caldwell, who was charged with murder.

31. "Something New Under the Sun by Negroes," *Birmingham Reporter*, Oct. 24, 1925.

32. Listing of black lawyers from J. Render Thomas, clerk, Alabama Supreme Court, May 6, 1958; *Who's Who Among Negro Lawyers* 32 (S. T. M. Alexander ed. 1945), regarding Shores. "Passes Test," *Pittsburgh Courier*, Oct. 23, 1937.

33. Lynda Dempsey Cochran, "Arthur Davis Shores: Advocate for Freedom," 22 (M.A. thesis, Georgia Southern College, 1977).

34. *Id.* at 24.

35. Shores, "The Negro at the Bar," 2 *Nat'l. B.A.J.* 266, 270 (1944). Arthur Davis Shores' admission to the United States Supreme Court in 1943 was hailed by the black press. "Admitted to Practice by Highest Court," *Atlanta Daily World*, Nov. 13, 1943.

36. "Negro Vote Lawyer Put in Jail Here," *Montgomery Advertiser*, April 9, 1944; LaFlore, "Attorney Loses Round 2 in Ala. Disbarment Case," *Chicago Defender*, June 10, 1944.

37. *Ibid.* (both articles).

38. "Illegal Practice Laid to Negro Attorney," *Birmingham News Appeal*, April 11, 1944. The Montgomery County Board of Registrars retained a law firm tied to the family of Senator Lister Hill to prosecute Madison.

39. Listing of lawyers from J. Render Thomas, clerk, Supreme Court of Alabama, May 6, 1958.

40. "Law in Georgia," *The Atlanta Independent*, May 12, 1919.

41. "Woman Opens Ala. Legal Office," *Chicago Defender*, Nov. 4, 1944. Telephone interview by author with Arthur Davis Shores, Sept. 28, 1989, confirming that Jane Cleo Marshall (Lucas) was a lawyer.

42. Minutes of Alachua County Court Recorder, May 13, 1869, at p. 11; vol. 9 *Harper's Encyclopedia of United States History from 458 A.D. to 1902*, at 304 (B. J. Lossing ed. 1902). Judge Goss is referred to as a "scalawag" by one Southern historian of the Reconstruction era. William W. Davis, "The Civil War and Reconstruction in Florida," 493, 494, n.2, 509 (Ph.D. diss., Columbia University, 1913).

43. Letter from Guyte P. McCord, clerk, Supreme Court of Florida, to the Julien Young Library, Oct. 31, 1958.

44. *Ibid.*

45. P. D. Klingman, *Josiah Walls, Florida's Black Congressman of Reconstruction* 20–21 (1976).

46. *Id.* at 95.

47. *Id.* at 57.

48. "Cobb Is Tenth Colored Judge to Sit on Bench," *Baltimore Afro-American*, July 31, 1926.

49. *Ibid.*

50. "Judge Dean's Removal," *New York Age*, Aug. 17, 1889.

51. *Ibid.*

52. Isaiah J. Williams III, "Joseph E. Lee: A Man of Power, 1849–1920," at 1 (1974) (paper).

53. *Id.* at 2.

54. P. D. Klingman, *Josiah Walls, Florida's Black Congressman of Reconstruction* 111–12 (1976).

55. Isaiah J. Williams III, "Joseph E. Lee: A Man of Power, 1849–1920," at 3 (1974) (paper). Lee's service as a Federal tax collector continued until 1931

(letter from W. C. Almand, city recorder, City of Jackson, to Charles S. Brown, June 16, 1958).

56. *Id.* at 2 ("Joseph E. Lee: A Man of Power").

57. P. D. Klingman, *Josiah Walls, Florida's Black Congressman of Reconstruction* 130–31 (1976). See also, Isaiah J. Williams III, "Joseph E. Lee: A Man of Power, 1849–1920," at 2, n.7 (1974) (paper). In 1878, Henry Wilkens Chandler was admitted to the Florida bar. He was also elected to the Florida state legislature in 1880 and 1884. C. S. Johnson, *The Negro College Graduate* 333 (1938). Chandler was a native of Ocala, Florida. He was admitted to the bar in the Circuit Court of Marion County, Florida (letter from Guyte P. McCord, clerk, Supreme Court of Florida, to Charles S. Brown, July 7, 1958; *Florida State Government, 1885: An Official Directory* 10 [J. B. Whitfield ed. 1885], listing Chandler).

58. "Cobb Is Tenth Colored Judge to Sit on Bench," *Baltimore Afro-American*, July 31, 1926.

59. Isaiah J. Williams III, "Joseph E. Lee: A Man of Power, 1849–1920," at 3 (1974), citing E. N. Akin, *When a Majority Becomes the Minority: Blacks in Jacksonville Municipal Politics, 1887–1889*, at 6 (1972).

60. *Ibid.* ("Joseph E. Lee: A Man of Power"). Mr. Lee also became a minister in the African Methodist Episcopal Church in 1881 (*People's Advocate*, Nov. 19, 1881).

61. *Florida State Government, 1885: An Official Directory* 11 (J. B. Whitfield ed. 1885).

62. F. L. Styles, *Negroes and the Law* 26–27 (1937).

63. R. S. Smith, *Indianapolis Freeman* (March 1889); *Twentieth Century Negro Literature* 92 (D. W. Culp ed. 1902).

64. Brown, "The Genesis of the Negro Lawyer in New England," 22 *The Negro History Bulletin* (Part II) 171, 174 (May, 1959), referring to *The New York Age*, April 13, 1889; Vol. 1 *Who's Who of the Colored Race* 17–18 (F. L. Mather ed. 1915).

65. "Florida Lawyers," *New York Freeman*, March 12, 1887, at 1, col. 4.

66. *Ibid.*

67. *Ibid.*

68. *Ibid.*

69. Letter from Lucia M. Tyron, librarian, Pensacola Public Library, to Charles S. Brown, May 27, 1958; letter from Guyte P. McCord, clerk, Supreme Court of Florida, to Charles S. Brown, Aug. 18, 1958.

70. *Twentieth Century Negro Literature* 103–4 (D. W. Culp ed. 1902).

71. *Ibid.*

72. I. L. Purcell, "Is the Criminal Negro Justly Dealt with in the Courts of the South?" in *Twentieth Century Negro Literature* 104, 106 (D. W. Culp ed. 1902).

73. *Ibid.*

74. *Ibid.*

75. *Ibid.*

76. *Ibid.*

77. *Ibid.*

78. B. T. Washington, *The Negro in Business* 233 (1907).

79. *The Black Experience in America* 102–4 (J. C. Curtis and L. L. Gould eds. 1970).

80. *State v. Patterson*, 50 Fla. 127, 39 So. 398 (1905) (with Judson Douglas Wetmore) (DuVal County); *Crooms v. Schad*, 51 Fla. 168, 40 So. 497 (1906) (with

Judson Douglas Wetmore) (Pensacola, Florida); *Patterson v. Taylor*, 51 Fla. 275, 40 So. 493 (1906) (with Judson Douglas Wetmore) (Jacksonville, Florida). All three cases dealt with civil rights.

81. See, e.g., *Weaver v. Florida*, 58 Fla. 135, 50 So. 539 (1909) (with S. D. McGill).

82. *Bonaparte v. Florida*, 65 Fla. 287, 61 So. 633 (1913), on racial discrimination in jury selection.

83. J. W. Johnson, *Along This Way* 141 (1933).

84. *Ibid.*

85. *Id.* at 142.

86. *Ibid.* According to Johnson, there were two to three other black lawyers in Jacksonville at the time, "but each of these, I believe, had been admitted in the Federal Courts during or shortly after the Reconstruction period, and were admitted to practice in the state courts through comity."

87. *Ibid.*

88. *Id.* at 143.

89. *Ibid.*

90. *Id.* at 143–44.

91. Johnson's experience sitting for the bar and the Jim Crowism of the South influenced his thinking on how blacks should be educated. In 1902, Johnson stated, "If the Negro is to remain in this country a separate and distinct race, and is, as such to reach the highest development of his powers, he ought to be given an education different from that given to the whites; in that, in addition to whatever instruction he may receive, those virtuous traits and characteristics which are peculiarly his should be developed to the highest degree." J. W. Johnson, "Should the Negro Be Given an Education Different from that Given to the Whites?" in *Twentieth Century Negro Literature* 72, 74 (D. W. Culp ed. 1902).

92. Concerning Judson Douglas Wetmore, see *Dictionary of American Negro Biography* 354 (R. L. Logan and M. R. Winston eds. 1983). Wetmore is referred to as "D———" in James Weldon Johnson's autobiography *Along This Way* 145 (1933). See also, *General Catalogue of the University of Michigan, 1837–1911*, at 920 (I. N. Demmon ed. 1912), which indicates that Wetmore attended the University of Michigan's law school from 1896 to 1897.

93. L. R. Harlan, *Booker T. Washington: The Wizard of Tuskegee* 18–19 (1983). See also, R. T. Kerlin, *Negro Poets and Their Poems* 90 (1923).

94. L. R. Harlan, *Booker T. Washington: The Wizard of Tuskegee* 18–19 (1983).

95. H. Walton, Jr., *Black Politics* 103 (1972). Judson Douglas Wetmore went to New York and became active in Republican politics, but he kept some of his political contacts in Florida. It is reported that Wetmore attempted "to break up the [1908 Republican convention in] Florida when it tried to endorse President [William H.] Taft" (Vol. 10 *The Booker T. Washington Papers, 1909–11*, at 86 [L. R. Harlan, R. W. Smock, G. McTigue, and N. E. Woodruff eds. 1981]).

96. F. L. Styles, *Negroes and the Law* 61 (1937).

97. *Ibid.*

98. *Id.* at 159–63.

99. Between 1915 and 1939, S. D. McGill—alone or with co-counsel—carried over twenty appeals to the Florida Supreme Court on a variety of legal issues involving corporate, civil, and criminal matters. McGill appeared before the Florida Supreme Court in the following ten cases between 1923 and 1937: *Washington v. State*, 86 Fla. 519, 98 So. 603 (1923); *Washington v. Dowling*, 92 Fla.

601, 109 So. 588 (1926); *Washington v. State*, 92 Fla. 740, 110 So. 259 (1926) (all involving the same murder case); *Curry v. Wright*, 101 Fla. 1489, 134 So. 508 (1931) (*rehearing denied*, 101 Fla. 1489, 136 So. 643 (1931) (partnership and bills and notes); *Florida East Coast Railway Company v. Urolia*, 109 Fla. 384, 147 So. 585 (1933) (a civil case); *General Accident, Fire and Life Assurer Corp. v. Colyer*, 111 Fla. 771, 151 So. 717 (1933) (insurance policy contest); *Afro-American Life Insurance Co. v. Jones*, 113 Fla. 158, 151 So. 405 (1933) (insurance policy contest); *Chambers v. State*, 111 Fla. 707, 151 So. 499 (1933), (with D. W. Perkins), *error granted*, 113 Fla. 786 (with Robert Crawford), 152 So. 437 (1934) (criminal procedure); *Chambers v. State*, 136 Fla. 568, 187 So. 156 (1939) (criminal procedure); *ExParte Knights of Pythias*, 128 Fla. 315, 174 So. 464 (1937) (insurance policy contest).

S. D. McGill and his brother N. K. McGill appeared before the Florida Supreme Court at least six times between 1915 and 1933 in *Williams v. Bellelini*, 69 Fla. 193, 67 So. 857 (1915) (real estate); *Phillips v. Howell*, 88 Fla. 280, 102 So. 157 (1924) (real estate); *Floyd v. Floyd*, 91 Fla. 910, 108 So. 896 (1926) (divorce); *Gray v. Gray*, 91 Fla. 103, 107 So. 261 (1926) (civil procedure); *Blount v. State*, 102 Fla. 1100, 138 So. 2 (1931) (seduction of unmarried woman); *Prince Hall Masonic Building Assn. v. Lee*, 104 Fla. 439, 140 So. 193 (1932) (per curiam; civil matter). N. K. McGill's efforts to obtain a political appointment as state attorney in Florida were foiled because of his race. A Chicago newspaper wrote that "if he were white, he would be a state's attorney" in Florida ("Mr. Crowe Gets Another Assistant," *Chicago Defender*, May 2, 1925). N. K. McGill eventually relocated to Chicago, Illinois, to practice law.

There are at least five cases between 1919 and 1934 in which S. D. McGill appeared as co-counsel on the brief with unconfirmed non-black lawyers: *Knights of Pythias v. Morgan*, 77 Fla. 95, 80 So. 739 (1919) (with Tom B. Stewart) (civil matter); *Grand Lodge Knights of Pythias v. Taylor*, 79 Fla. 441, 84 So. 609 (1920) (with Nathan P. Bryan) (beneficial societies); *Knights of Pythias v. Henry*, 87 Fla. 209, 99 So. 557 (1924) (with Burdine and Small) (rights of infant); *Washington v. State*, 95 Fla. 289, 116 So. 470 (1928) (with W. H. Harwick) (criminal procedure); *Holsey v. Atlantic National Bank*, 115 Fla. 604, 155 So. 821 (1934) (with Walter F. Rogers) (decedents estates).

S. D. McGill was often lauded by the black national press for his "able argument . . . learning and skill" ("Florida Bar Lauds Attorney S. D. McGill," *Chicago Defender*, July 3, 1926; "Clever Work by Attorney Stuns State," *Chicago Defender*, Feb. 13, 1926). More on McGill appears in Vol. 1 *Who's Who in Colored America* 131 (J. J. Boris ed. 1927).

100. M. V. Tushnet, *The NAACP's Legal Strategy Against Segregated Education, 1925–1950*, at 94–96 (1987), quoting letter from Lawson Edwarde Thomas to Walter White, Sept. 28, 1942.

101. *Ibid.* Quoting Lawson Edwarde Thomas, Professor Tushnet described the situation involving McGill as follows:

The handling of this case by the local committees and local counsel has resulted in utter confusion. In the first place, Mr. J. L. Williams, head of the Steering Committee, is highly emotional, an alarmist, and has a temper that often gets out of control. It is said that he threatened Counsel McGill with bodily harm, on one occasion. The committees have constantly consulted with the Board of Education without counsel being present. Also, they have talked with counsel for the defendants without Mr. McGill's being present.

There are rumors abroad that the lawyer for the School Board is an associate of Fleming & Fleming, attorneys who have been associated with Mr. McGill in several cases, and that there had been a general sell-out concerning the way the teachers would be rated. McGill's version is that the teachers and the several committees have tried to settle the case without his advice, and have held meetings and conferences without his knowledge; that the teachers have conferred with the lawyer for the School Board more than they have conferred with him. On the other hand, the teachers say that McGill has never met with them at any time, even when they have requested him to do so; and that McGill has refused to answer their questions concerning the case, replying in every instance that he was the lawyer and that they had no business inquiring about legal procedures.

Apparently the teachers do not trust themselves, or him, or any of their committees. Some of the citizens claim that Williams, too, has sold out the teachers. Generally, it appears that none of the teachers have any confidence in McGill. On the day that I arrived in Jacksonville, Sept. 23, Mr. McGill said that he could not be present for the final hearing on the case because he had to go to Tallahassee on a criminal case. I announced this at a meeting of the Steering Committee on that night. I understand that the chairman of the Citizens' Committee called McGill and told him that the opinion was general that he was selling out the teachers, and that his leaving town would confirm this rumor. (*Id.* at 95–96, quoting letter from Thomas to Walter White, Sept. 28, 1942.)

Thomas was graduated from the University of Michigan Law School in 1923 and had been admitted to the Michigan bar in 1926. He was admitted to the Florida bar in 1935 (letter from Thomas to Charles Sumner Brown, June 17, 1958).

102. *Chambers v. Florida*, 309 U.S. 227–28, n.2 (1940), *reversing*, *Chambers v. State*, 123 Fla. 734, 167 So. 697 (1936).

103. *Id.* at 240–42.

104. "Would Bar Negro Lawyer," *The Freeman*, June 26, 1915.

105. The *Tampa Tribune* wrote: "There is no valid reason why an honest colored man should not be allowed to practice law . . . in Florida" ("Favors Colored Lawyers," *The Amsterdam News*, May 28, 1915, quoting *Tampa Tribune*).

106. See *Haynes v. State*, 71 Fla. 585, 72 So. 180 (1916), on racial exclusion from juries. Perkins practiced many years in Broward County, Florida, appearing before the Florida Supreme Court on other occasions. In 1933, D. W. Perkins won a stay of execution for a black man charged with murder. He argued that the defendant had confessed to the crime after being tortured and treated brutally for seven consecutive nights. "Supreme Court Stays Execution," *Pittsburgh Courier*, Aug. 12, 1933, at 2, col. 1; "Snatches Four Men from Electric Chair," *Pittsburgh Courier*, Aug. 19, 1933, at 5, col. 2. See *Chambers v. State*, 111 Fla. 707, 151 So. 499 (1933) (death penalty case).

107. "Negro Attorney Highly Honored in Farthest South," South Eastern News Bureau, 1917 (author's files). The legislation to bar black lawyers from Florida was never expected to pass. The fact that it was defeated with the support of whites is evidence both of the political and social influence of black lawyers in the South and the absurdity of the proposal ("Would Bar Negro Lawyer," *The Freeman*, June 26, 1915). This Jim Crow legislation did not stop Howard University law graduate Robert P. Crawford from successfully seeking

admission to the Florida bar after his graduation from law school in 1918 (Vol. 1 *Who's Who in Colored America* 48 [J. J. Boris ed. 1927]). Indeed, the white population in some areas in Florida appeared eager to have black lawyers in their community. For example, Richard E. S. Toomey began to practice law in 1912 in Miami "upon the invitation of the Miami Chamber of Commerce." He became the first black lawyer in Miami (Reeves, "Toomey Was Dade's First Black Lawyer," *The Miami Times*, Nov. 11, 1982, at 17, col. 5).

108. "Florida Posthumously Reinstates Disciplined Black Lawyer to Bar," *New York Times*, Oct. 21, 1988, at A15, col. 1. This article indicates that the University of Florida School of Law was not admitting blacks as late as 1949. Cooper, "Brown v. Board of Education and Virgil Darnell Hawkins: Twenty-Eight Years and Six Petitions to Justice," 64 *J. of Negro History* 1 (1979); see also, Paulson and Hawkes, "Desegregation and the University of Florida Law School: Virgil Hawkins v. The Florida Board of Control," 12 *Fla. St. U. L. Rev.* 59 (1984).

109. *The Sixteenth Census, Population*, Vol. III, 652 (1943).

110. Letter from V. J. Courville, clerk, Supreme Court of Louisiana, to Charles S. Brown, May 20, 1958; letter from Doris B. Bell, Dilliard University, to Charles S. Brown, Aug. 13, 1959.

111. "Obituary, Louis A. Bell," *New Orleans Weekly Louisianian*, Oct. 10, 1874.

112. C. Clay Morgan, a free black man, was listed as a lawyer in New Orleans in 1860. D. C. Rankin, "The Origins of Negro Leadership in New Orleans During Reconstruction," in *Southern Black Leaders of the Reconstruction Era* (second unnumbered page following) 161 (H. N. Rabinowitz ed. 1981).

113. "A Colored Attorney," *New Orleans Semi-Weekly Louisianian*, June 22, 1871.

114. *Ibid.*

115. Donegan, "The Black Lawyer in Louisiana," *The Public Defender*, March 1983, at 2. Bell died before the first class graduated ("Obituary, Louis A. Bell," *New Orleans Weekly Louisianian*, Oct. 10, 1874; *New National Era and Citizens*, May 22, 1873; letter from Harold A. Moise, Jr., deputy clerk, Supreme Court of Louisiana, to Charles S. Brown, June 2, 1958).

116. *New National Era and Citizen*, May 22, 1873.

117. "A Colored Barrister," *Daily Mississippi Pilot*, Aug. 25, 1871; "Obituary, Thomas Morris Chester," *Indianapolis Freeman*, Oct. 29, 1892. See also, R. J. M. Blackett, *Thomas Morris Chester* 37 (1989). Chester may have received his law training earlier than 1870.

118. W. J. Simmons, *Men of Mark* 674 (1887).

119. *New National Era and Citizen*, May 22, 1873: "Early studies gave [Chester] advantages which shone brightly in contrast with efforts of some who had local educations." Prior to his law studies in England, Chester had attended the Thetford Academy in Vermont.

120. C. G. Woodson, *A Century of Negro Migration* 124–25 (1918); W. J. Simmons, *Men of Mark* 674 (1887). Judge Billings, an 1856 law graduate of Yale University, was appointed to the Federal District Court in Texas in 1876. 30 *Federal Cases* 1363 (1897) (biography).

121. *Ibid.* (*Men of Mark*).

122. A. P. Tureaud says that Chester was "the reporter who scooped the assassination of Abraham Lincoln in 1864 [*sic*]" (A. P. Tureaud, "The Negro at the Louisiana Bar" 1 [n.d.]). In 1865 Morris, age thirty-five, was a correspondent for the *Philadelphia Press*, writing under the name "Rollin." He covered

the Post–Civil War victory celebration in Richmond, Virginia. B. Quarles, *Lincoln and the Negro* 236, 238 (1962).

123. A. P. Tureaud, "The Negro at the Louisiana Bar" 1 (n.d.); Nils R. Douglas, "Who Was Louis A. Martinet" 1 (n.d.) (both on file in the Amistad Collection at Tulane University).

124. *Who's Who in Colored Louisiana* 51 (A. E. Perkins ed. 1930); C. Vincent, *Black Legislators in Louisiana During Reconstruction* 192 (1976).

125. "P. B. S. Pinchback, Reconstruction, and Its Aftermath," *Guide to ARC Light* 43 (Amistad Research Center, 1983).

126. Nils R. Douglas, "Who Was Louis A. Martinet" 16 (n.d.) (Nils R. Douglas Papers, Amistad Collection, Tulane University). Martinet also graduated from Flint Medical College and probably practiced medicine, before he entered Straight University's law department (*ibid.*).

127. Letter No. 46739 of the American Missionary Association Papers, Amistad Collection, Tulane University.

128. *Ibid.*

129. *Ibid.*

130. A. P. Tureaud, "The Negro at the Louisiana Bar" 1 (n.d.) (on file in the Amistad Collection at Tulane University).

131. Letter from "Red" to A. P. Tureaud, Aug. 1, 1935. Other correspondence identifies "Red" as Professor E. M. Coleman, Department of History, Morgan State College, Baltimore, MD.

132. *Ibid.*

133. C. Lofren, *The Plessy Case* 29 (1987).

134. Letter from "Red" (E. M. Coleman) to A. P. Tureaud, Aug. 1, 1935.

135. *Ibid.*

136. See generally, O. H. Olsen, *Carpetbagger's Crusade: The Life of Albion Winegar Tourgée* (1965); R. N. Current, *Those Terrible Carpetbaggers: A Reinterpretation* 46–67, 107–8 (1988).

137. C. Lofren, *The Plessy Case* 31 (1987).

138. *Exparte Plessy*, 45 La. Ann. 80, 11 So. 948 (1893).

139. *Plessy v. Ferguson*, 163 U.S. 537 (1896). The United States Supreme Court relied on another case brought before the Massachusetts Supreme Council by Robert Morris, Sr., America's second black lawyer, to desegregate the public schools in Boston in 1849 (a case Morris had lost). *Id.* at 543, citing *Roberts v. City of Boston*, 5 Cush 198, 59 Mass. 158 (1849). The court distinguished a case which had also been lost by two black lawyers one month before its decision in *Plessy*: *Gibson v. Mississippi*, 162 U.S. 565 (1896), on exclusion of blacks from juries. This case had been handled by Emanuel D. M. Hewlett, of the District of Columbia, and Cornelius J. Jones, of Mississippi.

140. The struggle of Homer Adolph Plessy and other black citizens was recorded by the Citizens' Committee in 1893 in a pamphlet entitled *The Violation of a Constitutional Right*, at 1 (L. A. Martinet ed. 1893).

141. P. Lamson, *The Glorious Failure* 60, 288 (1973); Florida Lawyers, *New York Freeman*, March 2, 1887.

142. *Twentieth Century Negro Literature* 418 (D. W. Culp ed. 1902).

143. P. Lamson, *The Glorious Failure* 288 (1973).

144. "Florida Lawyers," *New York Freeman*, March 2, 1887.

145. *Ibid.*

146. *Ibid.*

147. A. P. Tureaud, "The Negro at the Louisiana Bar" 1 (n.d.).

148. Romaine F. Scott, "The Negro in American History, 1877–1900," as portrayed in the *Washington Evening Star*" 65 (M.A. thesis, Howard University, 1948).

149. In 1871, Governor Henry Clay Warmoth "arranged to have the mulatto P. B. S. Pinchback elected president pro tem of the Louisiana senate." Pinchback and Governor Warmoth later crossed political swords, resulting in Warmoth's impeachment; Pinchback became governor. R. N. Current, *Those Terrible Carpetbaggers: A Reinterpretation* 276, 280 (1988); W. E. B. Du Bois, *Black Reconstruction in America, 1860–1880*, at 470 (reprint, 1973); *Who's Who in Colored Louisiana* 49, 53 (A. E. Perkins ed. 1930); "Freed Slave Was the First . . . Black Governor," *Washington Post*, Jan. 7, 1990, at A16, col. 1.

150. J. Haskins, *Pinckney Benton Stewart Pinchback* 251 (1973).

151. Matthews, "Black Because He Wanted to Be," *Washington Post*, Oct. 24, 1982, at B5, col. 3.

152. "Hon. John Francis Patty," *Indianapolis Freeman*, Aug. 24, 1889, at 1, col. 6.

153. *Ibid.*

154. "Rene Metoyer, 79, Expires at Home," *New Orleans Picayune*, Oct. 28, 1937.

155. *Ibid.* The article erroneously states that Metoyer was the first black lawyer appointed as notary public. Metoyer served as notary public from 1917 to 1937. Biography of Alexander Pierre Tureaud (one page, n.d.), in Alexander P. Tureaud Files, Armistad Collection, Tulane University.

156. Vol. 1 *Who's Who of the Colored Race* 272 (F. L. Mather ed. 1915).

157. The Hayes-Tilden Compromise and its effects caused James Madison Vance, Jr., to join in an "appeal to Congress [in 1879] to enact . . . laws as will remedy the present outrages upon the civil and political rights of Republican citizens of the South . . . to the judiciary to punish without distinction of position, wealth or pedigree . . . lawless men. . . . Our motto is, 'The Constitution; order and good government.'" *A Documentary History of the Negro People in the United States* 678, 682–3 (H. Aptheker ed. 1969), quoting the *New York Daily Tribune*, Jan. 1, 1879.

158. A. P. Tureaud, "The Negro at the Louisiana Bar" 1 (n.d.). Letter from Harold A. Moise, Jr., deputy clerk, Supreme Court of Louisiana, to Charles S. Brown, June 2, 1958, regarding admission to the bar.

159. *The Violation of Constitutional Right* 5–7, 14 (L. A. Martinet ed. 1893).

160. Vance was a consistent supporter of Republican presidential candidates. W. F. Nowlin, *The Negro in American Politics* 53 (1931).

161. *Who's Who in Colored Louisiana* 58 (A. E. Perkins ed. 1930).

162. "Why Has Louisiana Bar Exam Stymied Lawyers Since '25?" *Baltimore Afro-American*, April 19, 1941; "Louisiana Bar on Colored Lawyers Unfortunate; What's the Matter?" *Philadelphia Tribune*, April 24, 1941. While most black lawyers practiced in New Orleans, lawyers like Charles M. Roberson practiced in Shreveport. Roberson received his law degree from Chicago Law School in 1912 and was admitted to the Louisiana bar two years later. Roberson carried the burden of representing and defending the rights of blacks in the northwestern region of Louisiana for several years. *Who's Who in Colored Louisiana* 117 (A. E. Perkins ed. 1930); W. Burton, *On the Black Side of Shreveport* 20 (1983).

163. Vol. 3 *The Law Student* 9, Oct. 1, 1925.

164. Biographical notes, Alexander Pierre Tureaud, 1899–1972, Amis-

tad Research Center, Tulane University; *Who's Who Among Negro Lawyers* 35 (S. T. M. Alexander ed. 1945). Tureaud was admitted to the United States District Court, eastern district of Louisiana, in 1926.

165. See, e.g., A. P. Tureaud, "The United States Supreme Court and Its Decisions Affecting Negroes," Vol. 1 *Civic Leader* 6 (No. 1) and at 7 (No. 2) (1929).

166. Letter from A. P. Tureaud to William E. Taylor, March 5, 1936; letter from A. P. Tureaud to Charles Hamilton Houston, Sept. 20, 1937. Archie T. LeCesne and Vincent R. Malveaux were both graduated from Howard University's law school in 1939. Neither man returned to Louisiana to practice law. Both had distinguished careers: LeCesne went to Chicago, Illinois, and Malveaux went to New York City to practice law.

167. Letter from Sister M. Agatha Ryan to Alexander P. Tureaud, Jan. 27, 1936. In 1990, Louisiana State University named a building on the Baton Rouge campus in honor of Mr. Tureaud and in recognition of his efforts to desegregate public universities in the state. "For First Time, LSU Names Building to Honor a Black," *Jet*, May 28, 1990, at 24; "Alexander P. Tureaud Hall," 3 *Amistad Reports* 1, March, 1990.

168. "Experiences and Observations of Negro Lawyers" (a National Bar Association survey), circa 1940, A. P. Tureaud Files, Amistad Research Center, Tulane University (copy of Tureaud's response to questionnaire).

169. *Ibid.*

170. Joseph A. Thornton was graduated from Howard University School of Law in 1913 and was admitted to the Louisiana bar in 1914. *Who's Who Among Negro Lawyers* 35 (S. T. M. Alexander ed. 1945). Thornton died in 1946.

171. M. V. Tushnet, *The NAACP's Legal Strategy Against Segregated Education, 1925–1950*, at 98 (1987).

172. Thurgood Marshall relied heavily on A. P. Tureaud in Louisiana. Tureaud was well-respected, an alumnus of the same law school as Marshall, and well-known by the local judges. Tureaud also was known to local whites with whom he had worked for many years. This dual association caused a conflict with Thurgood Marshall in 1942 when Tureaud proposed to allow a local school board more time than the NAACP thought appropriate to equalize a court-ordered pay increase for black teachers. Marshall supported a two-year compliance period and Tureaud a three-year period. Marshall's compliance proposal prevailed. *Id.* at 98.

173. *Id.* at 99.

174. Biographical note, Alexander P. Tureaud, 1899–1972, Amistad Research Center, Tulane University. The unreported cases referred to in the biography are: *McKelpin v. Orleans Parish School Board*; *Lee v. Jefferson Parish School Board*.

175. *Hall v. Nagel*, 154 F.2d 924 (5th Cir. 1946) Tureaud, Marshall, and Thornton successfully objected to the Louisiana Constitution, which, after trial by jury on voter rights, provided that the citizen had no right to a further appeal in "any other court." For years, blacks had no recourse for judicial relief in voting disqualification matters until the *Nagel* opinion.

176. Letter from Thurgood Marshall, special counsel, NAACP, to Victor Rotnem, chief, Civil Rights Section, Department of Justice, July 5, 1944. The Civil Rights Section, the forerunner of the Civil Rights Division of the Department of Justice, was established in 1939. During the unit's early days, few criminal prosecutions resulted when the civil rights of blacks were threatened

or denied. "The Forum Talks with Maceo Hubbard," 7 *The Civil Rights Forum* 1, 4 (Summer/Fall 1984).

177. Telephone interview of Revis Ortigue, of New Orleans, by author, Nov. 1, 1988. Ortigue and Gloria Wilson Lawson were both graduated from Southern University Law School in 1956 and were admitted to the bar on June 12, 1956.

178. Mollison, "Negro Lawyers in Mississippi," 15 *J. Negro History* 38, 43–44 (1930).

179. *Id.* at 44.

180. *New National Era and Citizen*, Nov. 20, 1873.

181. Letter to author from Sue Gordon, clerk, Mississippi Supreme Court, Nov. 10, 1987.

182. V. L. Wharton, *The Negro in Mississippi, 1865–1890*, at 173 (1947). According to a letter from Donald M. Love, secretary of Oberlin College, to Charles S. Brown, June 22, 1961, Piles lived in Mississippi for seven years, returning to Springfield, Ohio, where he died in 1918.

183. *New National Era and Citizen*, Nov. 20, 1873.

184. Mollison, "Negro Lawyers in Mississippi," 15 *J. Negro History* 38, 60 (1930).

185. *Reminiscences of an Active Life: The Autobiography of John Roy Lynch* 43 n.2, 59–65 (J. H. Franklin ed. 1970). One author has concluded that John Roy Lynch "was admitted to the bar in 1869 . . . [and] was justice of the peace until December 31, when he resigned to serve four years in the state legislature." S. D. Smith, *The Negro in Congress, 1870–1901*, at 85–86 (1940). The year given for Lynch's admission to the bar (1869) is in error.

186. Lynch was elected to the Mississippi state legislature in 1869. He was elected speaker of the house in 1872. V. L. Wharton, *The Negro in Mississippi, 1865–1890*, at 162, 173 (1947); W. W. Brown, *The Rising Sun; Or, The Antecedents and Advancement of the Colored Race* 491, 493 (1874). During his speakership, Lynch was respected by both Republican and Democratic representatives. In 1873, a public testimonial was given in his honor, and the press recorded the event: "His bearing in office had been so proper, and his rulings in such marked contrast to the partisan conduct of the ignoble whites of his party who have aspired to be leaders of the blacks, that the conservatives cheerfully joined in the testimonial." W. E. B. Du Bois, "Reconstruction and Its Benefits," in *Black History* 273, 289 (M. Drimmer ed. 1981), quoting the *Mississippi Clarion*, April 24, 1873. It was this popularity that helped John Roy Lynch win election to the United States Congress in November 1872. Although his election was contested, Congress finally seated him in 1873, making him the "youngest man ever elected to Congress." V. L. Wharton, *The Negro in Mississippi, 1865–1890*, at 162, 173 (1947). One of the most pressing issues faced by Lynch during his term in Congress was the exodus of blacks seeking to escape the oppression of Southern life after the Hayes-Tilden Compromise of 1877. *Id.* at 113–14. Blacks migrated to the middle-western states to gain political rights. So serious was the issue of black migration that blacks convened a convention in Nashville, Tennessee, to discuss the matter. Congressman Lynch presided over the meeting and, interestingly, gave his approval "to the Exodus, and asked Federal aid to the extent of $500,000," which was never granted (*ibid.*).

A storm of violence raged in parts of Mississippi shortly after the Hayes-Tilden Compromise, with a number of lynchings and public calls for the disfranchisement of blacks. Some black leaders advocated the abandonment of traditional political parties and even revolution. Lynch openly opposed the identification "with any organization that seeks the accomplishment of its purposes through a resort to lawlessness and violence." *A Documentary History of the Negro People in the United States* 652 (H. Aptheker ed. 1969), quoting Vol. 3 *The A.M.E. Church Rev.* 165, 161 (1886).

By 1884, John Roy Lynch was an active and influential member of the Republican Party. However, he opposed efforts by northern Republicans to reduce the number of delegates attending the national Republican convention on the basis of the number of persons voting by congressional district. His opposition was based on his fear that white Republicans would manipulate local voting to the disadvantage of blacks. Lynch asserted this position as temporary chairman of the National Republican Committee, the highest position ever held by a black in the history of the Republican Party. W. F. Nowlin, *The Negro in American Politics* 70–71, 75, 77 (1931). The historic election of John Roy Lynch to the post of temporary chairman was not without opposition. Norris Wright Cuney, a powerful black Republican from Galveston, Texas, objected to Lynch's designation. L. D. Rice, *The Negro in Texas, 1874– 1900*, at 40 (1971).

187. 163 U.S. 537 (1896).

188. *Reminiscences of an Active Life: The Autobiography of John Roy Lynch* 368 (J. H. Franklin ed. 1970). Chief Justice Tim E. Cooper informed Lynch that he had failed the examination because he was weak in the areas of pleading and Mississippi statutes. Cooper encouraged Lynch to take the examination again after studying more diligently on these subjects (*ibid.*).

189. *Id.* at 369.

190. Letter from A. D. Brooks, chancery clerk, Greenville, Mississippi, to Charles Sumner Brown, Nov. 20, 1959.

191. Mollison, "Negro Lawyers in Mississippi," 15 *J. Negro History* 38, 60, 62 (1930).

192. J. W. Lyda, *The Negro in the History of Indiana* 68 (1953). Revels's training as a lawyer in Indiana appears to be a fact lost on most historians of the Reconstruction era. In Mississippi, Revels was known as "a Negro Methodist minister and teacher." B. A. Ames, *Adelbert Ames, 1835–1933*, at 288 (1964).

193. *Ibid.* (*Adelbert Ames, 1835–1933*).

194. Blanche Kelso Bruce, who was not a lawyer, served a regular term in the United States Senate. Elected from the state of Mississippi in 1874, he served from 1875 to 1881. Edward W. Brooke, a black lawyer from Massachusetts, was elected to the United States Senate in 1966. See E. W. Brooke, *The Challenge of Change* ix–xv (1966).

195. *Hinds County Gazette*, Aug. 14, 1872, by courtesy of Mississippi Dept. of Archives and History.

196. *New National Era and Citizen*, Oct. 17, 1872. See also, Mollison, "Negro Lawyers in Mississippi," 15 *J. Negro History* 38, 42, 46 (1930).

197. *Id.* at 45 ("Negro Lawyers in Mississippi").

198. *Id.* at 42, 46.

199. *Id.* at 50, quoting interview with Willis E. Mollison.

200. *Id.* at 45.

201. *Ibid.*

202. *Id.* at 43.

203. *Id.* at 47; "Col. G. F. Bowles," *Indianapolis Freeman*, May 18, 1889.

204. *Detroit Plaindealer*, April 5, 1892.

205. Hanchett, "George Boyer Vashon, 1824–1878: Black Educator, Poet, Fighter for Equal Rights," 68 *The Western Pennsylvania Historical Magazine* 333, 346, n.48 (Oct. 1985). Vashon was examined by notable people—Col. Ethelbert Barksdale, J. R. Chalmers, and General W. S. Featherton.

206. W. J. Simmons, *Men of Mark* 541 (1887); Vol. 1 *Who's Who of the Colored Race* 240 (F. L. Mather ed. 1915).

207. "Hon. J. T. Settle, An Eminent Colored Barrister," *Indianapolis Freeman*, Feb. 2, 1889, at 1, col. 1.

208. *Ibid.*

209. *Afro-American Encyclopedia; Or, The Thoughts, Doings and Sayings of the Race* 46 (J. T. Haley ed. 1895).

210. *Ibid.*

211. "Hon. J. T. Settle, An Eminent Colored Barrister," *Indianapolis Freeman*, Feb. 2, 1889, at 1, col. 1.

212. Justice E. Jefford had served on the Mississippi Supreme Court during the October term, 1868.

213. Mollison, "Negro Lawyers in Mississippi," 15 *J. of Negro History* 38, 40, 42 (1930); Vol. 1 *Who's Who of the Colored Race* 195 (F. L. Mather ed. 1915).

214. V. L. Wharton, *The Negro in Mississippi, 1865–1890*, at 209 (1947).

215. *Report of the Tenth Annual Convention of the National Negro Business League* (Louisville, KY), Aug. 18–20, 1909, at 107.

216. Mollison, "Negro Lawyers in Mississippi," 15 *J. Negro History* 38, 57 (1930), quoting interview with Willis E. Mollison.

217. *Report of the Tenth Annual Convention of the National Negro Business League* (Louisville, KY), Aug. 18–20, 1909, at 107. Mollison reported that he represented both white and black clients: "I had some of my white clients tell me to let no white men be finally upon the jury to try their cases, and, on the other hand, some of the clients of my own race have pled with me to 'leave no Negroes on the jury.'"

218. B. T. Washington, *The Negro in Business* (unnumbered page before) 127 (1907). *Negro Year Book, 1918–1919*, at 469 (M. N. Work ed. 1919): Mollison's middle initial appears as an "H," but this is an error.

219. L. R. Harlan, *Booker T. Washington: The Wizard of Tuskegee* 11 (1983).

220. *Collins v. State*, 100 Miss. 435, 436, 56 So. 527 (1911) (quoting Mollison's brief).

221. See *Gore v. State*, 155 Miss. 306, 124 So. 361 (1929), where a similarly prejudicial race argument was made at trial. In this case, the victim was white. The precedent set by Mollison in *Collins v. State* was completely ignored by the court. In fact, the court, citing no cases to support its rulings, held that the use of the word "nigger" throughout the trial was not prejudicial, since the trial judge admonished the prosecutor to stop using the term.

222. *Collins v. State*, 100 Miss. 435, 436, 56 So. 527, 528 (1911).

223. "Detroit Swamped with Legal Talent During Meeting of National Bar Ass'n," *Amsterdam News*, Aug. 7, 1929.

224. W. J. Simmons, *Men of Mark* 281, 283 (1887).

225. Mollison, "Negro Lawyers in Mississippi," 15 *J. Negro History* 38, no. 63 (1930) (interview with Willis E. Mollison).

226. *Gibson v. Mississippi*, 162 U.S. 565, 567 (1896).

227. 162 U.S. 592 (1896). Jones was joined on the brief by a black lawyer from the District of Columbia, Emanual D. M. Hewlett.

228. The decisions in both the *Gibson* and *Smith* cases were also issued on the same day, April 13, 1896.

229. "Fighting the Battles of the Negro Claimants," *The Topeka Kansas Plaindealer*, June 30, 1916; M. F. Berry and J. W. Blassingame, *Long Memory: The Black Experience in America* 348 (1982).

230. *Williams v. Mississippi*, 170 U.S. 213 (1898).

231. *Johnson v. McAdoo*, 45 App. D. C. 440, 441 (1916), *aff'd* 244 U.S. 643 (1917).

232. *Ibid.*

233. "Negro Lawyer Sought Gigantic War Claims," *Memphis Appeal*, Dec. 1, 1917; "Lawyer in Toils," *The Advocate*, Dec. 29, 1917.

234. In 1920 Cornelius J. Jones, described as "chief counsel of the Civil War revenue cotton tax claimants," purchased some choice property in the District of Columbia "for these claimants" with which to construct a "historical home" for them. "The Eminent Oklahoma Lawyer Makes Larger Realty Purchase in This City," *Washington Bee*, July 10, 1920.

235. Mollison, "Negro Lawyers in Mississippi," 15 *J. Negro History* 38, 44 (1930), quoting interview with Samuel A. Beadle.

236. *Id.* at 44.

237. *Id.* at 45.

238. *Ibid.*

239. *Id.* at 53, 64.

240. *Ibid.*

241. *Id.* at 46; Tureaud, "The Negro at the Louisiana Bar," 2 (n.d.).

242. G. P. Hamilton, *The Bright Side of Memphis* 65 (1908).

243. "Prof. J. T. Bailey, A. M., Journalist, Lawyer, Scholar and Educator," *Indianapolis Freeman*, Feb. 2, 1889, at 1, col. 6.

244. Mollison, "Negro Lawyers in Mississippi," 15 *J. Negro History* 50–51 (1930); R. Cruden, *The Negro in Reconstruction* 74 (1969). Vardaman's power was based on the provision of the Mississippi Constitution of 1890, which all but wrote black rights out of its protections. It was a piece of legislation that would take nearly one hundred years to correct. "Mississippi Begins Analyzing Its Racist Constitution of 1890," *New York Times*, Dec. 12, 1985, at B25, col. 1.

245. *Reminiscences of an Active Life: The Autobiography of John Roy Lynch* 366 (J. H. Franklin ed. 1970).

246. Vol. 1 *Who's Who of the Colored Race* 51 (F. L. Mather ed. 1915).

247. Mollison, "Negro Lawyers in Mississippi," 15 *J. Negro History* 38, 41 (1930). Green practiced in Mound Bayou, Mississippi. Vol. 1 *Who's Who of the Colored Race* 120 (F. L. Mather ed. 1915); *Harvard Law Quinquennial* 186 (F. S. Kimball ed. 1948).

248. See, e.g., *Colored Knights of Pythias v. Tucker*, 92 Miss. 501, 46 So. 51 (1908) (won); *Independent Order of Sons and Daughters of Jacob of America v. Moncrief*, 96 Miss. 419, 50 So. 558 (1909) (won). The Independent Order of Sons and Daughters of Jacob was organized by Louis Kossuth Atwood, an 1875 graduate of Lincoln University's law department (Pennsylvania). Atwood was admitted to the Mississippi bar in 1879 and was elected to the Mississippi state legislature from Hinds County in 1883. He was a major force in the insurance industry in Mississippi and was considered one of "the most capable civil lawyers at the Jackson bar." M. S. Stuart, "Accomplishments of Negro Lawyers," *Pittsburgh Courier*, June 17, 1944. In 1904, Atwood organized the American Trust and Savings Bank at Jackson, Mississippi. Two years later, he organized

and became president of the Southern Bank. Vol. 1 *The National Cyclopedia of the Colored Race* 519 (C. C. Richardson ed. 1919). Atwood was one of the first black lawyers in the nation to hold the position as a commissioner in the federal court of Mississippi. Mollison, "Negro Lawyers in Mississippi," 15 *J. Negro History* 38, 42, 62 (1930). In 1899, Atwood was appointed United States collector of revenue for the states of Mississippi and Louisiana. *The National Cyclopedia of the Colored Race* 519 (C. C. Richardson ed. 1919). W. J. Latham also handled appeals in the following cases: *Woodson v. Colored Grand Lodge of Knights of Honor of America*, 97 Miss. 210, 52 So. 457 (1910) (won); *Grand Lodge Colored Knights of Pythias v. Jones*, 100 Miss. 467, 56 So. 458 (1911) (lost); *Grand Lodge of Colored Knights of Pythias v. Seay*, 106 Miss. 264, 63 So. 571 (1913) (won); *Foote v. Grand Lodge of Colored Knights of Pythias*, 109 Miss. 119, 67 So. 901 (1915) (won); *Grand Lodge of Colored Knights of Pythias v. Harris*, 109 Miss. 173, 68 So. 75 (1915) (lost); *Grand Lodge of Colored Knights of Pythias v. Barlow*, 108 Miss. 663, 67 So. 152 (1915) (lost); *Grand Lodge of Colored Knights of Pythias v. Hill*, 110 Miss. 249, 70 So. 347 (1915) (won).

249. "William J. Latham to Practice in Chicago," *Chicago Defender*, June 30, 1917; A. H. Spear, *Black Chicago: The Making of a Negro Ghetto, 1890–1920*, at 182 (1967).

250. *Southern Christian Advocate*, April 8, 1915.

251. Mollison, "Negro Lawyers in Mississippi," 15 *J. Negro History* 38, 54 (1930) (from interview of Nathan S. Taylor).

252. *Id*. at 55.

253. *Id*. at 59.

254. Actually, Perry W. Howard started to study law on his own in 1900, while chairman of the mathematics department at Alcorn University in Mississippi. During the summer months, he attended the Illinois College of Law (now De Paul Law School), in Chicago, receiving his law degree in 1904. Vol. 1 *The National Cyclopedia of the Colored Race* 518 (C. C. Richardson ed. 1919). See also, Vol. 1 *Who's Who of the Colored Race* 144 (F. L. Mather ed. 1915); Vol. 1 *Who's Who in Colored America* 97 (J. J. Boris ed. 1927); M. S. Stuart, "Accomplishments of Negro Lawyers," *Pittsburgh Courier*, June 17, 1944.

255. *Report of the National Business League, Eighteenth Annual Meeting* (Chattanooga, Tennessee), at 153 (Aug. 1917), William H. Davis, reporter.

256. W. F. Nowlin, *The Negro in American Politics* 59 (1931).

257. Personal interview with Julian Riley Dugas, Washington, D.C., April 10, 1988; Vol. 1 *Who's Who in Colored America* 97 (J. J. Boris ed. 1927).

258. Mollison, "Negro Lawyers in Mississippi," 15 *J. Negro History* 38, 55 (1930).

259. *Id*. at 56, from interview with Willis E. Mollison.

260. *Ibid*.

261. "Negro Notary Public," *Commercial Appeal*, May 8, 1924.

262. S. L. Lightfoot, *Balm in Gilead* 51 (1988).

263. *Yazoo & M. V. R. Co. v. Sideboard*, 161 Miss. 4, 133 So. 669 (1931). Ewing had been a member of the Tennessee bar since 1886. H. F. Kletzing and W. H. Crogman, *Progress of a Race* 534 (1901).

264. "Lawyer Wins Fight to Practice Again," *Chicago Defender*, Jan. 17, 1920.

265. *Harvard Law Quinquennial* 362 (F. S. Kimball ed. 1948). The *St. Louis Argus* indicated that Sidney Revels Redmond was a direct descendant of United States Senator Hiram Rhodes Revels. "Honored for Distinguished Service," *St. Louis Argus*, Jan. 27, 1939.

266. The evidence points to mistreatment of S. D. Redmond. In 1927, Redmond and Perry W. Howard complained to President Calvin Coolidge and the Department of Justice about peonage in Mississippi. There was no response and no action taken against peonage. P. Daniel, *The Shadow of Slavery: Peonage in the South, 1901–1969*, at 153–54 (1972). S. R. Redmond had recently passed the Illinois bar. Because of the hostilities he had experienced after joining his father's law office, he left Mississippi and went to Illinois, but only for a very short period. He soon became one of the leading black lawyers in St. Louis, Missouri. In St. Louis, Redmond formed a law firm with Henry P. Espy ("Heads Local Bar Ass'n.," *St. Louis Argus*, Jan. 17, 1930; "Attorney Sidney Redmond Elected to Presidency of National Bar Association in Convention Here," *New York Age*, Aug. 26, 1939; "Negro Is Disbarred as Mississippi Lawyer," *Atlanta Constitution*, Jan. 30, 1929).

267. "Mississippi Negro G.O.P. Chairman Disbarred and Sentenced by Court," *Montgomery Advertiser*, Feb. 3, 1929; "Redmond Sentenced to Month in Prison," *Memphis Commercial Appeal*, Feb. 3, 1929.

268. *Ibid.*

269. *Ex Parte Redmond*, 156 Miss. 582, 126 So. 485 (1930); *Ex Parte Redmond*, 159 Miss. 449, 132 So. 328 (1931).

270. H. Walton, Jr., *Black Republicans: The Politics of the Blacks and Tans* 135 (1975).

271. Hudson, "Negro's Disbarment Approved by Court," *Memphis Commercial Appeal*, Jan. 30, 1929.

272. "Redmond Leaves Jackson," *Pittsburgh Courier*, Jan. 25, 1930. It remains unclear whether S. D. Redmond was suspended or disbarred from Mississippi or whether his decision to relinquish his political influence among thousands of blacks was all the local whites were after. In 1932, S. D. Redmond was co-counsel in an appeal before the Mississippi Supreme Court. He was unsuccessful in his efforts to reverse a murder conviction, partly because the prosecuting attorney used "inflammatory remarks . . . tending to arouse race prejudice" (*Pruitt v. State*, 163 Miss. 47, 55, 139 So. 861 [1932]). See also, V. O. Key, Jr., *Southern Politics* 286, n.8 (1949). Quoting a Southern newspaper, Key writes that "the late Dr. S. D. Redmond, believed to have been the wealthiest Negro in Mississippi history, left an estate of $604,801.09" (*Birmingham Age-Herald*, Aug. 13, 1948).

273. N. R. McMillen, *Dark Journey: Black Mississippians in the Age of Jim Crow* 169 (1989).

274. Stuart, "Accomplishments of Negro Lawyers," *Pittsburgh Courier*, June 17, 1944.

275. *New York Freeman*, April 11, 1885. For further information on Mary A. Shadd (later Cary), see S. Dannett, Vol. 1, *Profiles of Negro Womanhood* 151–57 (1964).

Chapter 6

The Southwestern States

The southwestern states include the states of Arkansas, Kentucky, Missouri, Tennessee, and Texas.

Arkansas

Thomas P. Johnson is likely the first black lawyer admitted to practice in Arkansas. He began his law career in Little Rock, Arkansas, in about 1866,[1] but little more is known about him. Johnson's entry into the legal profession occurred about the time William H. Gray, a member of the Arkansas state legislature, was elected to the 1868 Arkansas Constitutional Convention from Phillips County. It was in that year, too, that Gray seconded the nomination of Ulysses S. Grant for the presidency at the Republican National Convention.[2] On April 6, 1869, Gray was admitted to the Arkansas bar.[3]

Gray was one of the most eloquent and forceful speakers for black rights in Arkansas. He was also a respected member of the state legislature, where he vigorously fought against the efforts of whites to limit the voting privileges of Arkansas's black citizens. In an 1868 speech, Gray stated the issue plainly: "Give us the franchise, and if we do not exercise it properly, you have the numbers to take it away from us. It would be impossible for the Negro to get justice in a state whereof he was not a full citizen."[4] The extent to which Gray practiced law is unknown.

Mifflin Wistar Gibbs first studied law under a barrister in Victoria, British Columbia, in 1866, while amassing a fortune in the Harbor Bay Company territory. Gibbs completed his legal training at Oberlin College in 1870, about the time his brother, Jonathan Gibbs, was elected lieutenant governor of Florida. Gibbs settled in Little Rock, Arkansas, where he studied for the bar examination in the law offices of Benjamin and Barnes, a white firm. He passed the bar in 1870 and "was appointed County Attorney of Pulaski County, the capital county of the State."[5] Gibbs's legal career appears to have been successful. By 1873 Gibbs had been elected "to the Office of the City Judge, being the first colored man elected to such a position in the United States."[6] He also served in 1873 as a delegate to the National Convention of Colored Men at New Orleans. In 1876, as the curtain fell on the Reconstruction era, Gibbs's reputation came to the attention of President Rutherford B. Hayes, who appointed him register of the United States Land Office at Little Rock, a position he held for thirteen years.[7]

In 1885 Gibbs and three other black supporters of Booker T. Washington—J. C. Napier, of Nashville, Ferdinand Lee Barnett, of Chicago (both of whom were lawyers), and P. B. S. Pinchback (who was about to be admitted to the bar in New Orleans)—were among those calling for a conference on industrial schools for black children.[8] Gibbs's reputation and his association with Washington led President William McKinley to appoint him to the United States consulate to Tamatave, Madagascar, in 1897.[9] In 1903, Gibbs founded the second black-owned bank in Arkansas. The bank thrived until 1908, when it failed due to poor management. In the wake of the bank's failure, Gibbs narrowly escaped jail.[10]

Wathal G. Wynn settled in the city of Lake Village in Chicot County, Arkansas, in the fall of 1871. Earlier in the year, Wynn had graduated from Howard University's law school and was admitted to the bar of the District of Columbia. He was also admitted to the Hustings Circuit Court at Richmond, Virginia, on March 9, 1871, becoming Virginia's first black lawyer.[11] Upon his admission to practice in Arkansas on September 25, 1871,[12] Wynn became the first black lawyer in the nation licensed to practice law in three jurisdictions.

About the time Wynn settled in Chicot County, a referendum was held to determine a taxation issue: "on the proposition to subscribe $100,000 to each of the two railroads—the L. R. P. B. and N. O. road and the M. O. & R. R. road."[13] The local citizenry was greatly divided as to whether they should pay a tax to support the railroads. In December 1871, while visiting a store belonging to Curtis Garrett in Lake Village, Wynn got into a heated argument with John M. Sanders on the taxation question, and a fight ensued. Sanders killed Wynn with a knife. Three white men—Sanders, Garrett, and a man named Jasper Duggan, who stood at the door to prevent Wynn's escape—were all arrested and charged with conspiracy to commit murder.[14]

Anger erupted among the black citizens of Chicot as the details of Wynn's murder spread throughout the county. At the time, James W.

Mason, a black man who had been educated in Paris, was the county and probate judge of Chicot.[15] The three men accused in connection with Wynn's murder appeared before Judge Mason and were placed in the county jail. The black citizens rioted, and many clamored to have Wynn's body viewed in public, a request that was granted by Judge Mason. Fearing for their lives, every white person able to leave Chicot County did so.[16] Wynn's body was placed on view in the county court-house, and the anger of the black citizens grew. A mob of demonstrators formed to demand that the county sheriff release the white prisoners into their custody. Fearing violence, the sheriff "placed a guard of fifty men around the jail," but the "colored people . . . demanded the three prisoners, . . . procured the keys, opened the jail, took out the prisoners, and shot them dead."[17]

Not long after these violent events, Abram W. Shadd followed his classmate Wathal G. Wynn to Chicot County and was admitted to practice there on March 25, 1872,[18] while also practicing law in nearby Greenville, Mississippi.

During the Reconstruction era, black people and particularly black lawyers from the North were not welcomed by many Southern whites. However, C. A. Otley managed to be elected city attorney in Phillips County,[19] and George Napier Perkins served as a delegate to the Arkansas Constitutional Convention in 1874. Perkins was elected to the city council of Little Rock at about the same time.[20]

Shortly after being admitted to the bar in Illinois in 1869, Lloyd G. Wheeler settled in Little Rock (Pulaski County), Arkansas, to practice law. Richard A. Dawson, admitted to the Illinois bar in 1870, settled in Pine Bluff (Jefferson County), Arkansas.[21] In 1871, *The Little Rock Morning Republican*[22] reported that Wheeler was elected by the justices of the peace to the position of county attorney for Pulaski at a salary of $1,000 a year. Wheeler is also listed as one of the attorneys that had matters before the United States Circuit Court in 1871.[23] After his admission to the bar, Wheeler's annual earnings were probably equal to those of the white lawyers in Little Rock. Wheeler is reported to have served for a short while as county attorney in Chicot County, perhaps during the time he held the Pulaski County post.[24]

Wheeler's influence among the leaders of his race was significant. During the 1872 state Republican convention, he was nominated by J. C. Corbin to run for attorney general of Arkansas. But Wheeler declined the nomination, "knowing perhaps that his chances [of election] were remote."[25] He instead stumped for Ulysses S. Grant's presidential campaign, serving as an elector in 1872.[26]

The presence of Shadd and Wheeler in Chicot County; Gibbs, Perkins, and Wheeler in Little Rock; and Gray and Otley in Phillips

County, threatened local whites. They viewed this professional and educated group of black Americans as a threat to their customs and way of life. Of particular concern was the leadership capabilities of these lawyers. Commenting on this influence, the *Arkansas Gazette* wrote, "In view of it, the colored people of this country, if they are fit for suffrage at all, can form their own opinions on political and all other subjects, without the influence of either [Lloyd G.] Wheeler, [Richard A.] Dawson, [or William H.] Gray."[27]

Wheeler and Dawson were targets of constant criticism by the white press. In 1871, Wheeler took the *Arkansas Daily Republican* to task for referring to Dawson as a pettifogger, a description that he said would not have been applied to a white man with Dawson's education and intelligence. Further, he answered those who criticized Dawson because he was from the North by saying, "You cannot run us out; we have come here to stay."[28] As his income dwindled and he received less support from the local Republicans, and as white opposition against him grew, Wheeler returned to Chicago in 1879. There, he took over the operations of a successful tailor shop owned by John Jones, who had recently died.

In 1887 J. Gray Lucas, an honors graduate of Boston University's law school, returned to Arkansas and applied for admission to the bar. Lucas's performance on the bar exam was exceptional; he did not miss a single question.[29] Professionally, Lucas specialized mostly in criminal defense work, and his practice thrived. In 1890 Lucas was appointed assistant prosecuting attorney in Pine Bluff. He was elected a year later to the Arkansas state legislature where he served as a forceful and influential legislator whose legal training placed him above many of his peers. As one historian noted, "In terms of educational qualifications and forensic skills . . . Lucas . . . was the most impressive member of the black delegation in the Arkansas House of Representatives."[30] He was also the youngest member in the house and fought vigorously against Senator J. N. Tillman's efforts to pass Jim Crow legislation. During this period, Lucas became "the first Negro to serve as United States commissioner in the Eastern District of Arkansas."[31] At that time, United States commissioners had broad and important powers similar to present-day United States magistrates. Although he had accomplished much in the state, Lucas left Arkansas in 1893, "probably because of the deteriorating racial situation," and thereafter settled in Chicago.[32]

Other lawyers, such as John E. Patterson, Daniel Webster Lewis, and Lewis Jenks Brown also practiced in Arkansas. Patterson was admitted in 1873,[33] but little more is known about him. Lewis was admitted to the Arkansas bar about 1880, after studying law under Judge R. F. Crittenden and S. P. Swepton of Marion, Arkansas, both of whom were white. Lewis served in the Arkansas legislature from 1880 to 1882. Thereafter, he was elected judge of the Crittenden County probate court, where he served until 1888.[34] Lewis Jenks Brown, an 1886 graduate of Howard University's law school, was the first black lawyer examined by and admitted to practice before the Arkansas Supreme Court in 1887.[35] Two years later, he was admitted to the United States District Court in Arkansas.[36]

Scipio Africanus Jones began the practice of law in Arkansas "at a time when the Negro lawyer was a strange creature."[37] Jones was admitted to the Pulaski Circuit Court on June 15, 1889, after reading law in the office of a white lawyer.[38] He was admitted to the Arkansas Supreme Court in 1900, to the United States District Court for the Western Division of the Eastern District of Arkansas in 1901, and to the United States Supreme Court in 1905.[39] Soon after Jones was admitted to the bar, he and another black attorney, J. A. Hibbler, used their skills to oppose a pending "separate car bill" in the Arkansas state legislature.[40]

In 1901, Jones won two important criminal law cases before the Arkansas Supreme Court: one arising in Perry County, the other in Pulaski County. In these cases, Jones objected to the all-white composition of grand juries selected by the jury commissioners; it was also established that no black citizen had been selected to serve on the grand jury in these counties for almost twenty years, even though a number of blacks were qualified to serve. Racism was so entrenched in the grand jury selection process that a jury commissioner in the Perry County case testified that he would not select a black to serve on the grand jury so long as there was a white man qualified to serve. The court overturned the conviction in the Pulaski County case because the trial court had refused to hear Jones's motion challenging the exclusion of blacks from the grand jury. However, in the Perry County case, the court found no discrimination, apparently discounting the testimony of the racist jury commissioner (although the case was reversed on other grounds).[41]

In 1902, Jones again raised objections to the exclusion of blacks from juries in a pending criminal case. Jones's objections courageously and directly challenged white supremacy in Little Rock. The presiding judge adopted Jones's view and allowed blacks to serve on the jury.[42]

In 1905, Jones waged a successful court fight to expose the unfairness of the county convict labor system, which extended a prisoner's term for days lost from work. Prisoners were required to work for fifty cents a day, and they were charged for each day they could not work. Their sentences would be extended until they worked off whatever debt they had incurred. As a result of litigation brought by Jones, "the court rule[d] that prisoners sent to the county jail were entitled to 75 cents a day whether they worked or not."[43]

In 1915 Jones, who had won the respect of the bench and bar because of his demonstrated excellence in trial advocacy, was named special judge in a case. (Special judges were elected by attorneys present in court, a procedure commonly followed when a judge was disqualified from hearing a case.) Jones's election as a special judge was reportedly "one of the first instances in the history of Little Rock, if not the entire state, that a Negro has acted as a [special] judge."[44] Some questioned why a white lawyer had not been elected to hear the case instead of Jones. The presiding judge noted, "I announced I would not try the case. The case was against a Negro and the offense alleged had been committed against Negroes and all witnesses were Negroes . . . originating . . . in a colored neighborhood row. . . . Scipio Jones was nominated by the city attorney and voted for by [the] deputy prosecuting attorney and all the lawyers in attendance."[45] Hence, Jones's election as a special judge in this instance was influenced mainly by his race.

During the summer of 1919, race riots erupted in several cities in the United States, including Elaine, Arkansas, in Phillips County. Blacks who had tried to oppose racial injustice were charged with various crimes arising from these riots. The Elaine riots drew national attention when former Arkansas attorney general George W. Murphy, a white lawyer retained by the NAACP to represent twelve black defendants, died and was replaced by his co-counsel, Scipio A. Jones. Prior to Murphy's death, Jones and Murphy had won new trials for their clients on grounds that their convictions were void because of the exclusion of blacks from the jury and because of other procedural irregularities.[46] The group of black defendants were retried, convicted, and sentenced to death by a white jury.[47]

The efforts of Scipio A. Jones to free his black clients can be described only as indefatigable. The riot defendants' case finally reached the United States Supreme Court, which set aside the convictions of six of the riot victims. Although Scipio A. Jones's name did not appear on the briefs before the United States Supreme Court, the legal community knew that it was because of his zealous efforts that the lives of these black defendants had been spared, at least temporary.[48]

Jones's private practice also received considerable business. As counsel to the Knights of Pythias, a black fraternal group, and other black-owned insurance companies, he appeared before the Arkansas Supreme Court on several matters between 1913 and 1925. Other black lawyers, among them J. R. Booker, did business for the Knights,[49] as did Thomas J. Price, who prevailed in cases against black and white lawyers.[50]

In 1924, Scipio A. Jones was elected once again to a judgeship in the courts of Arkansas. However, this time he was elected chancellor in the Pulaski County court, "the second highest court" in Arkansas, becoming one of the first black lawyers in the South to ever occupy a judicial post at such a level, albeit temporarily.[51]

Scipio A. Jones did not allow his apparent success within the white bar or his success as a lawyer to sidetrack his civil rights and criminal defense advocacy. In fact, six months prior to his election as chancellor, he was involved in a hotly contested murder case in which he won a stay of execution.[52] In 1929, Jones was honored again by an appointment to the Legal Advisory Board of Pulaski County, an appointment influenced by President Woodrow Wilson.[53] In light of this success, Jones proclaimed that the city of Little Rock was a "good place as any to hang out a shingle."[54]

In 1889, about the time Scipio A. Jones was admitted to the bar in Little Rock, S. H. Scott broke ground as one of the first black lawyer in Fort Smith, Arkansas.[55] Edward D. Dobbins was admitted to the bar at Fort Smith, Arkansas, in 1920,[56] and Julian Talbot Bailey had been admitted to the Little Rock bar in 1891. (Bailey became editor of *The Little Rock Sun* in the same year.[57]) J. D. Royce, of Hot Springs, Arkansas, was an active criminal lawyer in 1895.[58]

Thomas J. Price was admitted to the bar in Little Rock in 1908. Price practiced before all the courts of the state of Arkansas and became an active supporter of Booker T. Washington. Like Scipio A. Jones, Price encouraged black lawyers to migrate south, stating that "reputable and competent colored lawyers [were] treated nicely . . . by white[s] and black[s]."[59] While cities such as Little Rock remained the area in which most black lawyers practiced, others set up their offices elsewhere. G. A. Johnson, for example, located his practice in Huttig, Arkansas.[60]

Although some black lawyers in Little Rock were affluent, a large number were not. In 1923, when the city imposed an occupational tax on the practice of law, black lawyers—as well as some white lawyers—saw this as a threat to their existence. The tax was challenged by W. McIntosh, a black lawyer in Little Rock. McIntosh argued that this practice amounted to double taxation, since he had to pay taxes to the state on the same income. McIntosh appealed his claim to the Arkansas Supreme Court, which ruled against him.[61]

In 1937, William Harold Flowers, Sr., who became an active lawyer in Arkansas, graduated from the Robert H. Terrell Law School. He and his wife, Ruth Caves Flowers, a 1946 Terrell law graduate, returned to Pine Bluff to practice law,[62] but there is no evidence that Ruth C. Flowers practiced law in Arkansas.[63]

The entry of women into the legal profession in Arkansas prior to

1944 is obscure. However, Zanyze H. Hill, the first black woman to be graduated from the University of Nebraska in 1929, became legal counsel for the Woodmen of Union Insurance Company located in Hot Springs, Arkansas, in about 1932. At the time, Woodmen of Union Insurance Company was the largest black-owned insurance company in the nation. Hill's association with the company ended in 1935, the year of her death.[64] She was never admitted to the Arkansas bar.

Kentucky

Nathaniel R. Harper commenced the study of law in 1860, under the instruction of George H. Penniman. George A. Griffith studied law while employed as a storekeeper in Daviess County, Kentucky.[65] Harper and Griffith "were examined by Judges [Henry J.] Stites and [Horatio W.] Bruce" in Louisville, Kentucky, on November 23, 1871, "and found well qualified" to be admitted to the bar "in all the courts of Kentucky, [becoming] the first Negroes . . . admitted to the Kentucky bar."[66] When Harper and Griffith were admitted to practice, the *Louisville Courier-Journal* reported that they would receive the "kindest treatment from the white members of their profession."[67]

Griffith settled in Owensboro, Kentucky, where he soon became deeply involved in the Republican politics of Daviess County. Reportedly, he often "addressed meetings in [the county] at which blacks and whites sat on the same platform."[68] In 1870, the central committee of the Republican Party appointed Griffith "to canvass the state and explain to the blacks their newly acquired rights and duties."[69]

Shortly after Nathaniel Harper was admitted to the bar, he recognized the need for black lawyers to receive formal legal training and thus established the Harper Law School. His law school flourished for several years and produced several lawyers until 1890, when Simmons University, a black college in Louisville, opened Central Law School and absorbed the Harper School. From 1890 to 1935, Central trained many students under the aegis of three black deans: John H. Lawson (1890–1896), Albert S. White (1896–1911), and William C. Brown, a 1903 graduate who became dean in 1911. Brown served until the school closed in 1940.[70]

Harper was the first black lawyer in Kentucky to receive a commission as notary public and the first to be appointed judge in a Louisville court. He was appointed in 1888 by Judge R. N. Thompson. During the same period, Governor William O. Bradley appointed Harper to the post of commissioner of the Kentucky Bureau of Agriculture, Labor, and Statistics of Colored People.[71]

Harper was one of the few successful black attorneys of the state who was engaged in private practice; most other black lawyers failed to attract a broad client base.[72] Indeed, the prospects for black lawyers in the early days of their Kentucky experience was bleak. In 1892, W. H. Perry, a member of the first graduating class of Central Law School, in response to an inquiry from the *Courier-Journal*, stated that although the practice of law for blacks did "not look prosperous or inviting," he was encouraged by "those of our race who have already begun to practice [and who are] overcoming the prejudices that exist."[73] Perry was no doubt referring to lawyers such as Harper, who had represented "three or four . . . white people."[74]

Other black lawyers, such as Yale University law graduate James Robert Spurgeon, located their practices in cities outside of Louisville. In 1892, Spurgeon opened the first law office in Maysville, Kentucky, "the first . . . colored man [to do so] in Northern Kentucky."[75] Spurgeon practiced in Maysville for a short time before assuming the post of principal at the local black high school. In 1896, Spurgeon became active in Republican politics, and in 1898 President William McKinley appointed him secretary of the U.S. legation to Monrovia, Liberia.[76] During his five-year term, Spurgeon gave speeches and wrote several articles on Africa and the possibilities for trade there. He later settled in New York City.[77]

At the outset of the twentieth century, the separate but equal policy was lodged in the statutory laws of Kentucky. State law made it "unlawful for any person . . . to maintain or operate any college . . . where persons of the white and Negro races are both received as pupils for instruction."[78] This statute effectively prohibited blacks from seeking or securing a legal education in a public or private college in Kentucky, except at Central Law School, or perhaps under the instruction of a lawyer willing to provide instruction. By 1897, there were approximately 40,000 black inhabitants in Kentucky, but only a handful of black lawyers.[79]

Despite the apparent impossibility of maintaining a successful law practice in Kentucky, a few black lawyers tried to beat the odds. For example, Shelby James Davidson was admitted to the Kentucky bar at Lexington in 1900. Little more is known about his legal career, except that in 1912 he was admitted to the bar of the United States Supreme Court on motion of Belva Ann Lockwood, a progressive white woman lawyer. Davidson was also an inventor and a specialist in adding machines. He authored several articles on business machines that were published in *Burroughs Journal*.[80] Louis A. Lavelle was admitted to the bar at Lancaster, Kentucky, in 1901. He relocated to New York after practicing in Kentucky for four years.[81] In 1902, Edgar Seward Foreman, a graduate of Walden University Law School in Tennessee, was admitted to the bar at Hopkinsville, Kentucky, where he practiced law and operated a coal company. William Hilliard Wright, a 1902 Howard University law graduate, organized "the first Negro Insurance Company of Kentucky."[82]

Black lawyers in Kentucky continued to face dangers in the early 1930s, especially when they represented black clients charged with crimes against whites in the rural parts of the state. C. Eubank Tucker, a "prominent clergyman and attorney," was assaulted in Elizabethtown, Kentucky, while defending a black client who was charged with murdering a white farmer.[83] Paradoxically, when Jesse B. Colbert, who was also a clergyman and attorney, died in Louisville, "the flag on the Jefferson County court house remained at half-mast" for a full day in his honor.[84]

Charles W. Anderson, Jr., was graduated from Howard University's law school in 1930. He immediately entered private practice in Louisville, Kentucky. On January 7, 1936, Anderson became the first black to be elected to the Kentucky legislature (from Jefferson County).[85] Anderson served four terms in the legislature and made a name for himself by demonstrating his keen political acumen. One of Anderson's first pieces of legislation was known as the Anderson-Mayer State Aid Act. The act authorized the annual appropriation of $17,000 "to assist Negro boys and girls to pursue courses of higher educaton outside of Kentucky."[86] Perhaps because the legislation reduced the tension of integration at Kentucky's public colleges, the act was passed thirty-three days after Anderson was seated.

Anderson was also responsible for the abolition of the public hanging law and fought against a proposal to require blacks using public common carriers to sit behind a glass partition. He was also successful in curtailing the cab companies' practice of refusing to pick up black passengers at the train station in Louisville.[87] During his four terms in the Kentucky state legislature, Anderson served on several key committees, including the committees on Cities of First Class, Juvenile Courts and Childrens Homes, Municipalities,[88] Codes of Practice, Education No. 2, Kentucky Statutes No. 2, State Fair, Teachers Colleges,[89] Appropriations No. 1-A, Statute Properties,[90] Interurban and City Railways, Social Security, Suffrage and Elections Claims,[91] Judicial Council,[92] and Courts and Legislative Research.[93]

Anderson became one of the leading civil rights lawyers in Kentucky in the early 1940s. Along with Prentice Thomas, he mounted the first major challenges to desegregate public education in Kentucky. Thomas brought considerable skill to this effort, since he had previously served "an informal internship with [Charles H.] Houston and [Thurgood] Marshall" in the New York-based national office of the NAACP.[94]

Coleman C. Moore graduated from the Central Law School in 1940, the year it closed its doors. He passed the bar examination and was admitted to the Kentucky Courts of Appeal in 1940. Moore entered the law firm of William C. Brown, who had served as the dean of the Central Tennessee Law School for nearly thirty years.[95]

No black women were admitted to the Kentucky bar prior to 1945.

Missouri

Though bitter about their defeat after the Civil War, some secessionists, drawing a distinction between the political and social equality of blacks, supported the admission of blacks to the bar as a political right. One outcome of such thinking was demonstrated in St. Louis, Missouri, in 1871, when A. J. P. Garesche, a "bitter Democrat and secessionist," moved for the admission of John H. Johnson, a black lawyer, to the Supreme Court of St. Louis in December 1871. In doing so Garesche stated,

But while I will maintain ever the distinction between political and social equality, I shall necessarily deny that they are synonymous terms, but the law has granted to the people of color political equality and however I may depreciate the manner in which it has been brought about, still it is an accomplishment.[96]

Johnson, likely the first black lawyer in Missouri, entered the private practice of law and became a leader in the Colored Emigration Aid Society, a group that gave support to black people who had been uprooted following the Civil War. So serious was the condition of these black refugees that Johnson went to Washington, D.C., in 1880 to testify before a special Senate committee on the flight of blacks from the South.[97] Johnson's testimony was based on information he had gathered as secretary of the refugee organization. He described the poor conditions of the people arriving in St. Louis from Mississippi and other Southern states. Johnson testified that if the black "had his rights under the Constitution he would remain" in the South. However, he claimed that the inhuman treatment by white Southerners was driving blacks away.[98] At the time of this testimony, Johnson was thirty-four years old. He had been a member of the St. Louis bar for nine years, and had been employed in the post office since 1874.[99]

In 1877 Albert Burgess graduated from the University of Michigan's law school. He was admitted to the Michigan bar before relocating to St. Louis. Burgess, like John H. Johnson, was active in the Colored Emigration Aid Society. In fact, it was Burgess who filed the articles of incorporation of the society in April 1879 while serving as its secretary.

Burgess practiced law in St. Louis for several years, serving as city counselor of the Carondelet Police Court in that city in 1887.[100]

Between 1885 and 1890, Hale Giddings Parker and Walter Moran Farmer were graduated from privately operated law schools in Missouri. In 1885, Parker graduated from the St. Louis University Law School and was admitted to the bar in the same year. He was later appointed by President Benjamin Harrison to the position of alternate commissioner-at-large for the Chicago World's Fair of 1893. Parker later relocated to Ottawa, Illinois, to practice law.[101]

In 1889, Walter Farmer became the first black graduate from Washington University's law school, an event that was widely reported by the black press.[102] Farmer's experiences as a law student at Washington University were difficult. White students attempted to force him to leave the University, but he was encouraged to stay by Dean William G. Hammond, with whom he marched on graduation day when other students refused to march with him.[103] Farmer was admitted to the St. Louis bar and entered private practice after he completed his law studies. He handled several major murder trials and probate cases, and became the first black lawyer to argue a case before the Missouri Supreme Court in 1893.[104] Judge William Zachritz appointed him special judge in the municipal court of St. Louis at the beginning of the twentieth century.[105] In 1905, Farmer left St. Louis and moved to Chicago, Illinois, to practice law.

Farmer's appointment by Judge Zachritz made him the first black to serve in a judicial capacity in Missouri. However, in 1922 it was Crittenden Clark who became the first black lawyer elected justice of the peace in Missouri.[106] By 1916, Crittenden had made a name for himself among the general population of St. Louis when he filed suit for five thousand dollars against the United Railways Company "to test the company's right to route passengers on a transfer system according to the dictates of the conductor," rather than according to the shortest route.[107]

D. D. Sledge was admitted to the bar of Missouri in 1894, after studying law in Mississippi under Judge J. C. Longstreet and A. H. Whitfield, chief justice of the Mississippi Supreme Court. Sledge completed his studies in Missouri. He practiced law in St. Louis for three years before relocating to Memphis, Tennessee, where he became "honorably connected with the local bar."[108]

Amasa Knox, an 1897 Howard University law graduate, was admitted to the bar at Kansas City, Missouri, in 1898,[109] and was followed by Charles Henry Calloway. Calloway studied law in the offices of William R. Morris, a black lawyer in Minneapolis, Minnesota, while attending the University of Minnesota's law school. He graduated from the University of Minnesota in 1905 and went to Kansas City, Missouri, where he was admitted to practice in 1906. Calloway became involved in the movement to organize the National Bar Association in 1924, and he became its second president.[110]

Silas E. Garner graduated from Walden University's law department in 1908 and soon thereafter began to practice in St. Louis. He later formed a law firm with George L. Vaughn. Garner became a highly respected lawyer and also did some civil rights work. In 1923 Garner was summoned from a YMCA banquet to save a young black man from being returned by the authorities to Houston, Mississippi, on an unsubstantiated charge of obtaining money under false pretense. Upon leaving the banquet, Garner called Governor Arthur M. Hyde to seek his support. Garner filed a writ of habeas corpus and won the young man's release.[111] In the early 1940s, after years in private practice, Garner was appointed special assistant to the attorney general of Missouri.[112]

Other black citizens of Missouri made names for themselves in the law. Joseph P. Harris was appointed deputy clerk of the probate court in St. Louis in 1913, serving in that post for more than twenty years.[113] Homer G. Phillips, a 1903 Howard University law graduate and one-time candidate for Congress from St. Louis, succeeded Charles H. Calloway as president of the National Bar Association in 1927.[114]

While few stories about the struggles of black lawyers in Missouri have been discovered, the history behind the admission of George B. Jones to the St. Louis bar in the 1920s may be typical of others. Jones passed the Missouri bar in 1920, though his early basic education was marginal. Jones completed his law studies by taking a correspondence law course that took him six years to complete. While studying law, he was employed as a janitor in the city hall. He later served in a clerical position in the office of the deputy sheriff. Eventually, he became an assistant clerk in the circuit attorney's office. A few years after Jones passed the bar, he was hired by Howard Sideway as assistant circuit attorney, making him the highest-ranking black public official in the history of St. Louis. He earned an annual salary of $3,600.[115]

By 1924 there were twenty-eight black lawyers in St. Louis, and in 1925 one of them, N. A. Mitchell, became "the first Negro attorney known to represent a white client."[116] In 1928, Joseph L. McLemore, six years out of Howard University's law school, won the endorsement of the Missouri Democratic Congressional Committee to oppose the Republican incumbent Leonidas C. Dyer in the local congressional election. McLemore beat his white opponent in the primary by nearly two thousand votes.[117] Dyer, who had proposed legislation making lynching a federal crime, was popular among blacks in his congressional district,[118] though others believe that his motive for introducing such legislation was to secure the large Republican black vote.[119] McLemore won the primary election with 1,500 white votes. Because of his white support, McLemore's candidacy posed a dilemma for black Republicans. However, during McLemore's campaign "scarcely a Negro could be induced to make a fight or some statements concerning his candidacy."[120] In the end, McLemore failed in his attempt to unseat Congressman Dyer, but many more black Republicans crossed over to vote for McLemore than was expected. Oddly, Dyer won a majority of the black votes, while McLemore won a majority of the white votes.[121]

During the same period, John Albert Davis, a 1921 Howard University law graduate, was elected to the Fifty-fourth General Assembly.[122] During his term, Davis introduced an anti-lynching bill and served on the Judiciary, Private Corporations, Civil, and Criminal Procedure committees.[123] During the 1930s, an anti-black climate emerged in Missouri, perhaps in response to black demands for political and social rights. Black lawyers, among them David Marshall Grant, were even agitating for proper health care for blacks in Missouri.[124]

Incidents of racial violence against black lawyers were reported in Missouri. William A. Cole was beaten by a mob near the Arkansas state line in Permiscot County, for defending a black client. He was "chased out of the courtroom and . . . beaten for representing Negro defendants who had formed an organization to improve conditions of Negro sharecroppers."[125] The volatile atmosphere interfered so significantly with Cole's ability to represent his clients that he filed a writ of habeas corpus in the Missouri Supreme Court to bring the violence to the court's attention.[126]

By 1939 the number of black lawyers in Missouri had grown to fifty-one. However, because the state-supported law schools refused to admit black students, most of the lawyers were educated outside of the state. Like some Southern states, Missouri paid tuition stipends to many of its black citizens to attend law school elsewhere.[127] The discrimination against blacks seeking a legal education was scaled back in 1938 when Charles H. Houston, Sidney R. Redmond, and Leon A. Ransom prevailed in a case before the United States Supreme Court. The lawyers proved that Missouri's state-supported segregation in higher education was unconstitutional.[128]

In 1939 the state appropriated funds to open a separate but equal law school at Lincoln University, a black college in Jefferson City, Missouri. The law school's first dean was an Iowa University honors law graduate and former Howard University law professor, William E. Taylor. The school was so underfunded that the NAACP decided to reopen a United States Supreme Court case in order to claim that the law school was "blatantly unequal," but Lloyd Gaines, the client in the case who had applied for admission to the University of Missouri law school, "had disappeared without a trace."[129]

By 1943, Lincoln University's law school had graduated ten students; of these, three were women, and eight of the ten passed the bar.[130] On November 7, 1942, Dorothy L. Freeman became the first black woman admitted to practice in Missouri. She was followed by Margaret B. Bush (Wilson), who was admitted on March 27, 1943.[131] After passing the bar, Freeman entered the private practice of law. Bush was appointed "junior attorney with the local branch of the Rural Electrification Administration." Lula M. Howard, who also passed the bar in 1943, became a professor and law librarian at Lincoln University.[132]

Tennessee

Black lawyers began their entry into the profession of law in Tennessee in about 1868. At that time, the requirements for admission were not rigid.[133] An applicant for admission to the bar had only to show that he or she was over twenty-one years old "and of good standing."[134] Compliance with these requirements entitled a person to practice "before any Justice or Justices of the Peace [and] before the County Court of his county."[135]

A number of black lawyers qualified for admission to the Tennessee bar in 1868, and although the economic base of black citizens was meager, some of these lawyers were able to sustain a practice. The cities of Memphis and Nashville drew most of the lawyers, but a few ventured out into other cities as well.

Alfred Menefee became a prominent black lawyer in Nashville in the late 1860s. In fact, it was reported that Menefee was "the first colored man to be admitted to practice at the Nashville bar [and was] elected magistrate several times."[136] Edward Shaw was elected to the city council of Memphis. William Henderson Young opened a law office, also in Memphis, and William Francis Yardley was admitted to practice in Knoxville.[137]

Edward Shaw was admitted to the Tennessee bar in the late 1860s, whereupon he entered politics. By 1880, he was a candidate for sheriff of Shelby County. Shaw lost his bid for sheriff because "the local Democratic Press . . . waged a vicious smear campaign against [him]." Still, Shaw was praised by some Republicans and Democrats as "a man of strong force" and as "a very bright and able colored man."[138] Shaw's defeat made him more pragmatic, but no less controversial.

In 1881, Shaw persuaded some black Republicans to join forces with the low-tax Democrats, a moved that was opposed by major black politicians in Tennessee.[139] Shaw abandoned the Republicans to fully support the "fusion" movement of the Bourbon Democrats. He campaigned "enthusiastically for Governor [William] Bates . . . in the election of 1884."[140] Support of the fusion movement made Shaw the object of severe and personal criticism by white Republicans and Democrats. Shaw was branded a communist and a criminal. The Bourbon Democrats defended Shaw to the extent that they could, and blacks denounced the white press's efforts to destroy him.[141] Shaw, who was under consideration for appointment to state office, was forced to defend himself against false claims that he was disrespectful to white women. Shaw "urged black voters to . . . 'shake off the yoke of Republicanism,'" becoming one of the few black members of the Democratic Party prior to 1900.[142]

Alfred A. Froman, a black lawyer from Memphis, also supported the fusion movement in Tennessee. In 1884 he toured the country to campaign for Grover Cleveland and was later praised by Democrats "for his conciliatory efforts."[143] Froman's support for the Democrats may have caused him embarrassment when Governor Bates reneged on a campaign promise to fill an assistant superintendentship in education with a black. Despite this slap in the face, Froman did not abandon the Democratic Party, holding to the belief that to be a Republican in the South "reaped only 'blood, slaughter and death.'"[144]

William H. Young, a black lawyer from Davidson County, was meanwhile making a name for himself in Tennessee.[145] In 1880, Young was selected as temporary chairman of the state Republican convention in Tennessee. Young stood with the Republicans during the fusion movement and was nominated to run for Congress from the Sixth Congressional District in 1888, when blacks "wrestled control of the congressional nominating convention from whites."[146] This move by black Republicans made white Republicans furious. The *Nashville American* portrayed Young's nomination as "the most violent race upheaval that has occurred in Tennessee since the Negro was set free."[147] Young's nomination "drew racial lines . . . in Davidson County and provoked a movement among white Republicans to disassociate themselves from blacks."[148] Young, a moderate branded as a radical, lost the general election by a vote of 12,677 to 18,956. He carried only Davidson and Montgomery counties, both heavily black.[149]

In 1888, Young and Joseph H. Dismukes, another black lawyer, denounced "mob" law, asserting that the Republican Party was "the only refuge" against lynchings and ballot-box stuffing. Dismukes claimed that mob law went into the jury box. "No black man could be tried in the Nashville courthouse," he said, "except before a white jury who would rather see the Negro dead than alive."[150]

William Francis Yardley, born a freeman, was the first black judicial officer of Tennessee, having served as justice of the peace in Knoxville around 1874.[151] In September 1876 Yardley announced his candidacy for governor of Tennessee:

I hereby announce myself as a candidate for the Office of Governor of this Commonwealth for the next two years. In taking this step, I am aware of the grave responsibilities I assume. . . . I ask of all good citizens a patient hearing of my cause. . . . I am for honest and economical government.[152]

Yardley's announcement "was the street sensation,"[153] but nothing more came of his bid for the governorship.

G. F. Bowles also was admitted to the Tennessee bar in 1868. Bowles, like many of the first black lawyers in Tennessee, studied law on his own. He was twenty-four years of age when he was admitted to practice. Bowles practiced law in Tennessee until 1871, the year he moved to Natchez, Mississippi.[154] W. H. Morse decided that he would study law when, in 1868, he was discharged from a streetcar for smoking a cigar in the presence of women.[155] Morse, an assertive black professional who was determined to challenge the status quo, often found that his determination brought him before the courts. In 1869, Morse was charged with compounding a felony.[156] The following year, he was brought before a United States commissioner for conducting a business without a license.[157]

After the first black jury was impaneled in Nashville in 1869, more blacks began to have faith in the judicial system.[158] Other black lawyers, such as P. A. Ewing, settled in Nashville to practice law. Ewing studied under Edward Baxter, a white Nashville lawyer. He was subsequently elected justice of peace for the Fourth Civil District and also served a four-year term as judge pro tem of the inferior court of Davidson County.[159]

In 1872 James Carroll Napier graduated from Howard University's law school and was admitted to the bar at Nashville.[160] Napier practiced law, but spent a portion of his time engaged in local Republican politics. Just as the Reconstruction era was ending and the shadows of slavery were reappearing, Napier and others, possibly to court favor with President Rutherford B. Hayes, invited him to Nashville for a reception in his honor on September 19, 1877.[161] The next year Napier was elected to the city council of Memphis, a post he held until 1885.[162]

While a member of the city council, Napier voiced his opposition to the black fusion movement led by Governor William B. Bates. Napier opposed the Bourbon Democrats because they supported the separate car policy. Napier also fought for federal and state funds to support equal education for blacks. He complained to Congress when federal appropriations were disproportionately allotted to the black community by the state of Tennessee.[163]

Napier was also a supporter of Booker T. Washington. In 1911, Washington used his influence with President William H. Taft to obtain a federal post for Napier in the United States Treasury Department.[164] Four years later, Napier, clearly having won the respect of the "Washington camp," was elected to succeed Washington as president of the National Negro Business League when Washington died in 1915.[165]

In 1873 John Sinclair Leary, a Howard University law graduate, went to Fayetteville, Tennessee, "where he was admitted to practice before the Tennessee Supreme Court."[166] Leary was one of the first black lawyers to settle in Fayetteville. Robert Charles O'Hara Benjamin, already a member of the bar of Charlottesville, Virginia, studied law under Memphis lawyer Josiah Patterson, with whose "influence he was . . . admitted to the bar [in Memphis] in 1880."[167]

Thomas Frank Cassell, admitted to practice around 1876,[168] became one of the most influential lawyers in west Tennessee. In fact, he was the first black lawyer admitted to practice before the Tennessee Supreme Court in west Tennessee. Though his practice was almost exclusively in Shelby County, his political influence reached beyond the county limits. In 1878, Cassell became the first black appointed assistant attorney general of Tennessee, and he was the second black elected to the Tennessee General Assembly, where he served from 1881 to 1883.[169]

Cassell was an active legislator. He introduced legislation that made it a crime for white persons to have unlawful carnal intercourse with blacks; the bill never passed. Cassell also served on the Claims and Penitentiary Committee in the general assembly. In 1887, Cassells was co-counsel before the Tennessee Supreme Court, opposing the state's separate car law. Ida B. Wells, a progressive black woman, was the plaintiff. Although Cassell lost the case, the fight waged by black lawyers to overturn the separate car law in Tennessee continued. Cassell's civil rights activities did not hurt him politically: In 1888, a year after appearing before the Tennessee Supreme Court, he was certified as a presidential elector.[170]

Cassell influenced, assisted, and trained several lawyers. He was "the lawyer to know" in Memphis. When Benjamin F. Woodson left Jackson County, Ohio, around 1881, he joined Cassell's firm.[171] Samuel Asbury Thompson Watkins studied law under Cassell's tutelage during his term as assistant attorney general of Tennessee. Watkins was admitted to the Tennessee bar in 1891, and thereafter he joined Cassell's firm. He remained there until 1893, when he relocated to Chicago, Illinois.[172] Cassell made a significant mark on the legal profession in

Tennessee. He was appropriately described as "one of the craftiest, most resourceful, and most learned lawyers, regardless of race, that ever practiced at the Memphis bar."[173]

The opportunity for blacks to study law in Tennessee expanded immeasurably in 1879 when Central Tennessee College, located in Nashville, opened its law department. Central Tennessee Law School, as it came to be known, was the second law school established for blacks in the South. During its twenty-one years in existence, it educated several black lawyers who were admitted to the bar in Tennessee. In 1900, Walden University absorbed Central Tennessee University, though the law department continued to be called Central Tennessee Law School.[174]

In 1885 Samuel Allen McElwee graduated from Central Tennessee's law school. In 1883, while still a student in law school, McElwee had been elected from Haywood County to serve three terms in the Tennessee General Assembly. During his second term, he was nominated as speaker of the house.[175] While serving in the general assembly, McElwee fought for equality of education in Tennessee and for equal pay for black teachers. Although a Republican, McElwee tried to gain Democratic support for these measures by suggesting that the Democrats might attract more black Republican voters to their party. His efforts to win support failed, but McElwee was able to obtain a state grant for Fisk University.[176]

The lynching of blacks in Tennessee was of great concern to McElwee. As a result of the lynching of two black men and one black woman in 1886, McElwee introduced legislation "calling for stricter penalties against lawmen who were negligent in defending their prisoners":[177]

[Grant] for the sake of argument, that these parties were guilty, does that make it right and in accord with our principles [to lynch them?] When the citizens of Madison, Dyersburg, and Carroll go to judgment with the blood of Eliza Wood, Matt Washington and Charles Dinwiddie on their garments, it will be more tolerable for Sodom and Gomorrah in that day than it will be for Jackson, Dyersburg and McKenzie. . . . I stand here today and demand a reformation in Southern society.[178]

McElwee's bill was tabled.[179]

McElwee retired from the General Assembly in 1887. One year later, he was elected delegate-at-large to the Republican National Convention. At the convention, McElwee "assumed leadership" of the Tennessee delegation, "representing Tennessee on the important credentials committee. He nominated William A. Moore for vice-president."[180] On January 1, 1890, McElwee delivered a speech commemorating the Emancipation Proclamation in Nashville, Tennessee. By then, McElwee had a lucrative law practice in Nashville, but he chose not to remain there. Near the turn of the century, he moved to Chicago and practiced law.[181]

George T. Robinson, an 1892 law graduate of Central Tennessee University, and H. R. Saddler, another graduate, both became successful lawyers. Robinson opened a law office in Nashville, while Saddler opened one in Memphis. Saddler "was honored by the County Court of Shelby . . . with the appointment of notary public."[182] In 1900, Saddler became the dean of the law department at Lane University, a black college located in Jackson, Tennessee. He served in this position until 1903.[183] T. J. Johnson transferred to Central Tennessee's law school from Shaw University's School of Law and graduated in 1898.[184] In 1900, just as Central Tennessee was merging with Walden University, Edgar L. Webber, one of Central's law professors, was hired by Booker T. Washington to assist in ghostwriting his first autobiography.[185] In 1903, James Bumpass, a graduate of Walden University's law school, opened a law practice in Nashville. He later became a director of the Peoples Savings and Trust Company in Nashville and counsel to the Knights of Peter Claver, a fraternal group.[186]

In 1886, Benjamin Franklin Booth was admitted to the bar in Memphis, Tennessee.[187] Booth studied law under Colonel William M. Inge, "one of the ablest lawyers in the state of Mississippi," who had served at one time as speaker of the Mississippi House of Representatives.[188] Booth became one "of the most resourceful lawyers at the bar," especially in criminal matters.[189] Booth and Josiah Thomas Settle, an 1875 Howard University law graduate, were pioneering civil rights lawyers in Tennessee. In 1905, Booth and Settle appeared before the Tennessee Supreme Court to challenge as unconstitutional the separate but equal common carrier law. The Tennessee Supreme Court ruled against them.[190] By 1908, Booth's legal acumen and the demand for his services made him one of the highest-paid lawyers in Tennessee.[191]

In 1885 Josiah Thomas Settle arrived in Memphis from Mississippi, where he had practiced law and had been involved in politics since 1875. Upon his arrival, Settle was appointed assistant attorney general of the criminal court of Shelby County. Judge A. H. Douglas reported that "[Settle's] uniform attention to official business, his manly courtesy and amiability, won him the esteem and respect of the bench [which] went far to break down the existing prejudices against his color in the profession."[192] Settle was respected by black and white lawyers alike. From time to time, Settle also handled cases in Mississippi and Arkansas. He practiced in Memphis until his death in 1915.[193]

In 1891 M. D. Fleming followed Settle to Memphis. Fleming had previously been admitted to the Mississippi bar after passing an examination administered by the Mississippi Supreme Court in 1888. Since Fleming was a member of the Mississippi bar, the Tennessee Supreme Court waived its rules and admitted him without examination.[194] Robert Lee Mayfield, a member of the District of Columbia bar, was not accorded this waiver privilege in Nashville, perhaps because of his more assertive nature.

The exclusion of blacks from juries in Nashville inhibited the success of black lawyers, and many black clients thus hired white lawyers to present their cases before all-white juries. Even when the victims were black, the juries were white. In 1905, Robert Lee Mayfield, an 1899 Howard University law graduate, moved to dismiss an indictment against his client because blacks had been excluded from the jury; Mayfield argued that this practice was unconstitutional. In support of his motion, Mayfield filed nine affidavits—one of which was signed by James Carroll Napier, who had practiced in Nashville for thirty years—stating that no black citizen had served on a jury there for over a decade. The Tennessee Supreme Court ruled against Mayfield.[195] Mayfield's efforts encouraged John H. Early, a white lawyer from Chattanooga, to raise the same issue on behalf of a white client, but to no avail.[196]

In 1905, Mayfield challenged the Louisville and Nashville Railroad to provide equal accommodations to black passengers traveling between Cincinnati and Nashville. Specifically, Mayfield attempted to negotiate a settlement to obtain equal lavatory or smoking sections for himself in the "colored section" to conform with the separate but equal guarantee. Mayfield filed and lost the lawsuit in trial court. When he appealed this decision to the Tennessee Supreme Court, the court refused to review the appeal "on the grounds that the discrimination was not 'harmful' to Mayfield in that he continued to smoke despite the regulation of the car."[197]

Despite Mayfield's efforts to win equal rights in the courts, racial distinctions in the judicial system still led blacks to hire white lawyers. In 1910 the National Baptist Convention was strongly criticized by the black press for securing a white lawyer to represent its interests instead of hiring Mayfield. One newspaper "ran afoul of one [of its] subscribers" when it criticized the National Baptist Convention for "'always preaching race solidarity' but employing a white lawyer" when it needed legal advice.[198] Mayfield apparently continued to press his civil rights agenda, though a white Nashville lawyer sought to have Mayfield disbarred.[199] Mayfield, claiming that "he was disbarred from practice in . . . Tennessee through prejudice," applied for reinstatement in Knoxville, Tennessee.[200] However, when word of Mayfield's efforts to gain readmission reached Nashville, white lawyers obtained an order which held that the Knoxville court did not have power to readmit him.[201]

In 1892 Charles Warner Causler was admitted to the bar at Knoxville. Causler was a mathematician who combined his legal education and his knowledge of figures by lecturing across the country on subjects such as "lighting calculators." In 1894 Causler authored a book entitled *Short Methods in Arithmetic.*[202] In 1894, T. W. Bradford gained admission to the bar at Memphis in an unorthodox proceeding. The court required Bradford to be examined in open court by all the lawyers present.[203]

By 1900 black lawyers were still able to read law under a few white lawyers in Tennessee. Sandy Southern Carter had the good fortune to study law under W. H. Carroll and Casey Young. Both of these white men were considered deans of the Memphis bar.[204]

Myles Vandahurst Lynk founded the University of West Tennessee in 1900. He established a law program there and was awarded a law degree in 1902, after completing an appropriate course of study. Lynk, who had previously graduated from the Meharry Medical College, was the first black lawyer in Tennessee to hold dual degrees in law and medicine.[205]

The new decade witnessed a decline in the number of black lawyers in Tennessee. In 1908, there were only twelve black lawyers in Memphis.[206] Still, in 1909, despite the state's Jim Crow environment, black lawyers Noah W. Parden and Styles L. Hutchins were able to represent a black defendant accused of raping a white woman. These courageous lawyers won a stay of execution from Justice John Marshall Harlan of the United States Supreme Court, but their client was "taken from the Hamilton County jail . . . and lynched."[207] Justice Harlan held five members of the lynching mob in contempt of court. They each served jail terms in the federal penitentiary. This punishment stirred the community's anger, and Parden and Hutchins received death threats. Both men fled with their families to Oklahoma.[208]

Physical danger remained a constant threat for black lawyers. Arthur Davis Shores, a black Alabama lawyer, described one instance of abuse in 1940: "An attorney for the [NAACP] was struck, without provocation, by a white deputy sheriff in a courtroom in Tennessee. The lawyer, who was from Washington, D.C., had just finished arguing a case to compel Tennessee officials to admit a Negro to the University of Tennessee."[209]

In 1944 Thurgood Marshall complained to the chief of the civil rights section of the Department of Justice about police brutality against blacks in New Iberia, Louisiana, and Brownsville, Tennessee: "On my way back from Louisiana I stopped by Brownsville, Tennessee, and [found] that Negroes in that community are completely cowered and remain in fear of Tip Hunter to such an extent that they hesitate to exercise any of their basic civil rights."[210] Though some black lawyers were threatened and physically assaulted in Tennessee, there is no hard evidence that the courts condoned such conduct, or, conversely, that the court spoke out against it.

Stephen A. Burnley of Nashville, one of a handful of blacks admitted to practice in Tennessee in the 1920s, passed the bar in 1922 after sitting through a rigorous examination. Burnley was the first black to pass the new state bar examination, which was conducted by a Board of Law Examiners established in 1912.[211] Burnley later became active in the National Bar Association.[212]

Zephaniah Alexander Looby was graduated from Columbia University's law school in 1925 and was one of the first black lawyers to earn the Doctor of Juridical Science degree, the highest academic degree awarded in law. He received his degree from New York University in 1926.[213] Looby returned to Nashville, Tennessee, and, after being admitted to the bar, opened a law office in 1928.[214] Looby also became active in civil rights; he was one of the NAACP's progressive civil rights lawyers in the South. Looby and Carl A. Cowan, a 1930 graduate of Howard University's law school, often assisted Thurgood Marshall in handling NAACP cases in Tennessee.[215]

In one instance, Looby and Marshall themselves nearly became victims as a result of their civil rights activities in Tennessee. Marshall reported that a mob went after a black youth for some minor infraction in a black section of town called Mink Slide, in Columbia, Tennessee. The state troopers pursued the youth with machine guns and "shot up . . . Mink Slide."[216] Marshall and Looby were called in to represent the youth. According to Marshall, at one point the car Marshall and Looby were driving was stopped by white police and Marshall was charged with drunk driving.

"I haven't had a drink in three days," Marshall recalled telling the officer. At the hearing, Marshall recalled, "The magistrate said 'Boy!' I said, 'Yes Sir.' 'Are you willing to take my test?' I said, 'What's your test?' He said, 'I am a teetotaler, but I can tell whether you have had a drink or not.' He said, 'Blow your breath in my face.'" Marshall complied. He said, "That man is not drunk, he hasn't had a drink." Back in Mink Slide, Marshall was warned to leave town and change cars. The man who drove the [other] car was beaten badly.[217]

In addition to his civil rights advocacy, Looby represented the Sunday Union of the African Methodist Episcopal Church.[218]

After Robert E. Lillard graduated from Kent College of Law in Nashville in 1935, he went to Tennessee in spite of the rumors of prejudice against black lawyers.[219] William H. Foote was admitted to the United States District Court of Tennessee in 1934 *nunc pro tunc*, having been previously admitted to the Tennessee bar at Shelby County on February 10, 1912.[220]

Lutie A. Lytle, an 1897 graduate of Central Tennessee Law School, was the first black woman to be licensed to practice law in Tennessee and in the South, apparently after taking an oral bar examination.[221] She was twenty-three years old when, on September 8, 1897, "with all the aplomb of an old practitioner," she was admitted to the Criminal Court in Memphis, Tennessee.[222] Lytle went to Topeka, Kansas, and became the first black woman admitted to practice in Kansas in 1897.[223] After her admission to the Kansas bar, Lytle returned to Central Tennessee's law school, where she was appointed professor of law. Later, she was reported to be "the only woman law instructor in the world."[224] She taught "the law of domestic relations, evidence, and criminal procedure."[225]

Lytle apparently married twice. Her first husband was a minister in the African Methodist Episcopal church[226] who may have been assigned to a church in New Paltz, New York, where Lytle reportedly moved after leaving Tennessee. It is uncertain what career path she chose in New York. Her second marriage was to a lawyer, Alfred C. Cowan. In 1913, she and Cowan attended the annual convention of the National Negro Bar Association in Philadelphia. The participation of Lytle-Cowan in the bar association is historically significant on two grounds: She was the first black female member of a national bar group, and she was the first to participate in such a group on equal footing with a lawyer spouse.[227]

In 1939, C. Vernette Grimes was admitted to the Tennessee bar. She was "the first Negro woman to pass [a written] Tennessee State Bar Examination."[228] Grimes had become interested in the law while working as a secretary in a firm of black lawyers in Muskogee, Oklahoma. She also received formal training at the Kent College of Law in Nashville, "an accredited evening school of which Dr. Z. Alexander Looby [was] dean."[229] Grimes was the first woman graduated from Kent's law school[230] and the second black woman graduated from a law school in Tennessee.

Texas

The early history of black lawyers in Texas is uncertain. The paucity of information available may simply mean that black lawyers did not enter the legal profession during, or immediately after, the Reconstruction era, as was the case in other Southern states. However, a few black lawyers were admitted to the various district courts that had authority to license attorneys in Texas.[231]

In 1873 A. W. Wilder combined teaching and the law to make ends meet. Wilder also entered politics and was elected to the Texas legislature.[232] In 1876, Wilder was nearly elected to the Texas senate, an office for which he again ran, unsuccessfully, in 1878.[233]

In some sections of Texas, white Democrats encouraged blacks to enter the legal profession and made their law libraries available to them.[234] As the Reconstruction era closed, the "number of Negro lawyers in [Texas] was relatively small, but they seemed to have been readily admitted to practice upon qualification."[235] W. A. Price, of Fort Bend County, Texas, was admitted there in 1876, and later to the bar of Matagorda County, Texas, in 1878.[236]

The first black lawyers in Texas tended to concentrate their practices on criminal rather than civil law matters. This trend was "not due to any innate or racial criminal tendency but is much better accounted for by inequities before the law."[237] Faced with laws that barred black citizens from serving on juries, black lawyers in Texas were effectively limited in their practices. In 1883 a group of "colored men" convened in Austin, Texas, to discuss and plan a strategy that would void the unlawful exclusion of blacks from juries. Their platform stated that "the previous practice among sheriffs and jury commissioners of summoning jurors exclusively white or nearly so, is in direct violation of the laws of [Texas] for no person is disqualified as a juror on account of his color."[238]

A year before the "colored men's convention," Thomas Morris Chester, then living in Delta, Louisiana, was appointed "as a special assistant to the U.S. Attorney for the Eastern District of Texas" by Benjamin Brewster, the United States attorney general.[239] This special assignment was an important one. It located federal authority in the person of a black lawyer on Texas soil. It was also an "extremely dangerous" assignment, since Chester was investigating "alleged violations of federal electoral laws through [the] manipulation of Negro votes."[240]

In 1886 Joseph E. Wiley graduated from the Union College of Law (Northwestern) in Chicago. He traveled to Dallas, Texas, to open a law office. Wiley was one of the first black lawyers in Texas to receive a formal legal education.[241] The presence of lawyers such as Wiley no doubt inspired other blacks. Frederick K. Chase, an 1888 Howard University law graduate, became a member of the bar in Dallas, Texas, in 1892.[242] John L. Turner, Sr., became a lawyer under the tutelage of Wiley. At about the turn of the century, Turner completed his law studies at the Kent College of Law in Chicago and then returned to Dallas. He was that city's only black lawyer in 1900.[243] John L. Turner,

Jr., later joined his father in the practice of law, becoming one of the first second-generation black lawyers in Texas.[244]

In 1888 William Henry Twine, who had read law while teaching school in Texas, became the "first colored man [to] ever [pass the bar] examination . . . in Limestone County, Texas."[245] After practicing in Groesbeck, Texas, for three years, he moved to Oklahoma.

In 1892 J. J. Oliver, who practiced in San Antonio, Texas, was considered "one of the most prominent colored attorneys in . . . Texas,"[246] as was W. O. Lewis, of Denison, Texas. Oliver and Lewis were involved in state Republican politics during this period, but when the Republican Party began to turn its back on blacks, they supported the movement for "fusion" of black Republicans and Democrats.[247] Around 1893 Joseph Cuney opened a law office in Galveston, Texas, after serving as chief clerk in the United States Customs Service.[248] By 1895 several other black lawyers had begun to establish practices in Galveston.[249]

Around 1895 Wilford Horace Smith arrived in Galveston, Texas. Smith had practiced law in Greenville, Mississippi, for eight years after graduating from Boston University's law school in 1883. Smith represented a new kind of lawyer in Texas, as he was not only formally educated, but extremely skilled in pleading and practice in both civil and criminal matters as well. He also handled a large number of probate matters. "Even when compared to the practice of many white lawyers," Smith's law practice was impressive.[250] Smith, like other black and white lawyers in Galveston, drew business by advertising in local newspapers. He settled several personal injury claims against corporate defendants, winning awards as high as five hundred dollars.[251]

Smith also represented the interests of black businesses before the courts. In 1897, Smith defended the *Galveston City Times* in a libel suit before the Texas Criminal Court of Appeals. Smith, likely the first black lawyer before this court, lost both of these cases.[252] In 1899, he was involved in litigation before the Texas Court of Civil Appeals concerning an internal property dispute in a black church. The case was either settled or determined by the court in favor of his clients.[253]

Wilford Smith's reputation as an outstanding lawyer and a strong advocate for racial equality must have come to the attention of Booker T. Washington. In 1901, Smith became Booker T. Washington's personal attorney and, with Washington's encouragement and support, he was designated by Washington as the legal strategist to challenge the laws of Alabama that excluded blacks from voting.[254] Smith, who had previously qualified to practice before the Alabama Supreme Court while practicing in Mississippi, brought two lawsuits that challenged Alabama's grandfather clause. The clause, Smith argued, violated the Fourteenth Amendment to the United States Constitution.[255] Smith lost both these cases on technical grounds, and he was harshly criticized by blacks for doing so. Despite the public criticism, Booker T. Washington urged Smith to press on in other cases, "to 'at least, put the Supreme Court in an awkward position'" on the race question.[256]

In addition to Smith's practice in Galveston, Texas, his travels to and from Tuskegee, Alabama, to consult with Booker T. Washington, and his civil rights litigation in Alabama, he also found the time in 1903 to write a chapter for a book edited by Washington.[257] Smith's chapter, entitled "The Negro and the Law," provided a rare glimpse of a black lawyer's view of white justice. In it, Smith praised former chief justice J. A. P. Campbell, of the Mississippi Supreme Court, and Chief Justice Christopher C. Garrett, of the Court of Civil Appeals of Texas. The two men, according to Smith, were able and fair jurists.[258] Smith may have held the same high regard for justices on the United States Supreme Court in 1904. In that year, he finally won a case before the court, which held that the exclusion of blacks from grand juries solely on the basis of their African ancestry was unconstitutional.[259]

In 1905 Smith left Galveston, Texas, and the South to become counsel to Marcus Garvey, the head of the Universal Negro Improvement Association (UNIA) based in New York. In 1922 Smith left the UNIA, resigning as Garvey's counsel not too long before Garvey was indicted for mail fraud by federal authorities. Smith returned to Texas, where he resumed his law practice in the cities of Galveston, Houston, and Beaumont.[260] Smith opened his law office in Houston in 1925 and formed a partnership with Joseph G. Wimberly, a 1914 Howard University law graduate who had also practiced law in San Antonio, Texas.[261] Smith's establishment in Texas frequently brought him face to face with "the movements and machinations of the infamous Ku Klux Klan."[262]

The black law firm was slow to develop in Texas. In 1897 Cornelius J. Williams and Alexander Green formed a law firm in Galveston, Texas. However, Green was soon disbarred for client neglect and fraud in a divorce matter.[263] The threat of disbarment seemed to plague some black lawyers in Galveston, particularly Joseph Vance Lewis. Lewis was almost disbarred on several occasions. In one instance, Lewis was charged with forging signatures in several divorce matters; Lewis claimed that his white and black competitors, conspiring to run him out of the practice of law, had forged the signatures. According to Lewis,

There was a little two-by-four colored lawyer, and one or two low class white ones in Houston, who made a living out of the little cases, especially the divorce cases which were now coming to [black lawyers]. When not drunk, they watched our success with ever-increasing envy and finally reported to Judge Charles E.

Ashe and also to Judge W. P. Hamblen that there was some irregularity in the citation of every case I had on file.[264]

The judge found some irregularities in Lewis's pleadings but they were not significant enough for disbarment. Lewis, however, was suspended from practicing law for six months, and subsequently disbarred altogether for "swindling an elderly black couple—Lewis's clients—out of real estate worth $1,500."[265]

With the departure of Wilford H. Smith from Galveston in 1905, Cornelius J. Williams, Allen G. Perkins, and Joseph Cuney assumed the burden of civil rights litigation in the area. They fought a local ordinance excluding blacks from riding white streetcars. Because of the prevailing laws of the time, Williams and Perkins did not attempt to have the law declared unconstitutional. Instead, they filed civil actions on behalf of their clients, seeking damages for violation of the ordinance that required railway cars to be equal, though separate. The case lingered without resolution for years and became highly publicized in the national black press. Eventually, it was dismissed by the court on what appears to have been a procedural ploy. Motions by the railway attorneys to delay the trial increased the security bond to Williams and Perkins, a cost they were unable to meet.[266]

After the turn of the century, the progress of the black lawyer in Texas slowed. Few law firms were formed, but lawyers such as Walter R. Hill of Galveston handled the business of the Knights of Pythias and other black fraternal groups.[267] M. H. Broyles, another black lawyer, complained to the black press that the black American was hiring white lawyers to "the exclusion of lawyers of his own race."[268] Charles D. MacBeth used the National Business League's chapter in Fort Worth, Texas, to explain to black businessmen why it was important to retain black lawyers.[269] The more affluent black lawyers continued to place advertisements in the local newspaper. In 1915 Allen G. Perkins placed the following advertisement in the *Galveston City Times*:

LAW-Bonds, Deeds, Bills of Sale, Releases, Deeds of Trust, Chattel Mortgages, Collections of all Debts (new and old), Wills, Contracts, Articles of Co-Partnership, Permits and Applications for Charters of Corporations, Guardianships, Administration of Estates, both Civil and Criminal Cases in all Courts, etc., given prompt satisfactory attention.[270]

Richard D. Evans was admitted to the bar in Waco, Texas, after graduating from Howard University's law school in 1912. He returned to Washington, D.C., in 1916 to be admitted to the United States Supreme Court on the motion of Robert H. Terrell, a black municipal judge in the District of Columbia.[271] Evans became one of the first black lawyers in Texas to develop a systematic legal attack against the exclusion of blacks from voting in primary elections (which were popularly referred to as white primaries). In 1919, Evans tried one of the first voting cases in Waco, securing a "perpetual injunction enjoining the City Democratic Committee from . . . voting [discrimination]."[272] Evans also sued to end white primaries in other cities in Texas, and appealing one case to the United States Supreme Court. The case was dismissed because the election had already been held by the time it reached the court.[273] The courageous and pioneering efforts of Evans in the voting rights area were soon aided by three other black lawyers in Houston: Carter Walker Wesley, James Madison Nabrit, Jr., and Jasper Alston Atkins.

Wesley, Nabrit, and Atkins received their legal training in white law schools. In 1922, Wesley graduated from Northwestern University's law school. He practiced for a short while in Muskogee, Oklahoma, with Atkins, a 1922 graduate of Yale University School of Law. In 1925, or thereabouts, Wesley and Atkins left Muskogee, Oklahoma, and opened a law office in Houston, Texas. In 1931 Nabrit joined Wesley and Atkins to form a three-man firm. Nabrit had been an honors graduate of Northwestern University School of Law, and the first black at that law school to be elected to the Order of the Coif.

While Richard Evans fought as a solo practitioner in the courts of Texas to void the white primary, Welsey, Nabrit, and Atkins brought the power of a firm to civil rights litigation. For five years, these lawyers filed suit to enjoin the Democratic executive committee in Houston from barring blacks from the primary election.[274] This important work in the voting rights area was eventually taken up by Thurgood Marshall, the NAACP's chief counsel.[275]

In 1936 Nabrit joined the faculty of Howard University's law school. At Howard, Nabrit, Harvard-trained professor William Henry Hastie, and other members of the law faculty formulated the strategy which eventually convinced the United States Supreme Court to strike down the white primary as unconstitutional in 1944.[276]

In 1920 James F. Dawkins, among the first black lawyers in Austin, Texas, was admitted to the bar. He was actively engaged in the practice of law in Austin for at least ten years.[277] Harvard University law graduate Francis Scott Key Whittaker opened a law office in Houston, Texas, in 1923.[278] And George W. White, Jr., opened an office in Beaumont, Texas. Like many black lawyers, these men faced hostilities in their efforts to advance the civil rights of black citizens. But White's life always hung in the balance in Beaumont. White would probably have been killed had he been more assertive on civil rights matters in Beaumont.[279] White was humiliated in court before his clients. The judges refused to call him by any name other than "George." White and his clients had to use the bathroom at his office five blocks away from the courthouse, since such facilities were not made available to black people in the Beaumont courthouse.[280] White was the only black lawyer in Beaumont until Frank Evans was admitted to the Texas bar. Evans amassed a considerable fortune in real estate before he died.[281]

Other black lawyers in Texas took a different approach on the race question. In 1925, T. M. Betts, a black lawyer in Fort Worth, Texas, was reported to have recommended a more cooperative approach "with the best white people" in developing the city. He advised blacks "to quit drifting and buy property. . . . Go back to the farms and help develop the agricultural resources of Texas."[282] Few blacks followed Betts's recommendation.

By 1930, there were only twenty black lawyers in Texas.[283] These lawyers played a significant role in enhancing the quality of life of the black population. A. S. Wells kept blacks in the eyes of the public by running for the Texas state legislature in 1935 from Dallas County. Although Wells failed in his election bid, he made the best showing by a black since 1895, the last time a black was elected to the Texas state legislature. Wells's defeat was partially due to racism, as the Ku Klux Klan campaigned against him.[284]

In 1939 only a few black lawyers continued to read law in white law offices. For example, James H. Hart and Arthur Mitchell of Austin, Texas, tutored Kenneth R. Lampkin prior to his successful admission to the Texas bar. Lampkin entered the private practice of law and later assisted Thurgood Marshall in the early development of *Sweatt v. Painter*,[285] the case that required the University of Texas to admit its first black law student.[286]

Although the Sixteenth Census (1940) records the existence of one black woman lawyer in Texas, her identity remains a mystery.[287]

Summary

The state of Arkansas admitted its first black lawyer, Thomas P. Johnson, in 1866. Those that followed him would enter politics, open law offices, and assume the responsibilities of civil rights lawyers. In 1871 Arkansas also became the first state in which a black lawyer, Wathal G. Wynn, was murdered by whites.

In 1869 William H. Gray was serving in the Arkansas legislature when he was admitted to the bar, as was Daniel Webster Lewis in 1880. George Napier Perkins contributed to the state of Arkansas as a delegate to the Arkansas Constitutional Convention in 1874 and as a member of the city council of Little Rock.

The heavily populated black counties of Arkansas helped to elect Lloyd G. Wheeler to the position of county attorney in Pulaski County in 1871 and C. A. Otley to city attorney in Phillips County in 1872. J. Gray Lucas was appointed assistant prosecutor in Pine Bluff. He, too, served in the Arkansas legislature in 1891.

In 1873, Mifflin Wistar Gibbs became the first black elected municipal judge in Arkansas. In 1897 he served as United States consul at Tamatave, Madagascar. Lloyd G. Wheeler was nominated for attorney general during a Republican state convention.

Scipio Africanus Jones was the black Arkansas lawyer most associated with the early history of the civil rights movement. Jones opposed the separate car law while it was being considered in the Arkansas state legislature. He successfully appealed cases to the United States Supreme Court between 1913 and 1925.

While it appears that the majority of lawyers in Arkansas between 1866 to 1944 read law, law graduates of Boston University, Howard University, and the Robert H. Terrell Law School also were represented in the state. No black women were admitted to the Arkansas bar prior to 1945.

The state of Kentucky admitted its first black lawyers, Nathaniel R. Harper and George A. Griffith, in 1871. The *Louisville Courier-Journal* seemed excited about the prospects of black lawyers in Kentucky and predicted that black lawyers would be treated with kindness by the white bar.

Black lawyers like Harper and Griffith competed in court against white lawyers, despite the fact that blacks were deemed incompetent by state law to testify against white people. For this reason, among others, W. H. Perry, a black lawyer, declared in 1892 that, because of prejudice, the practice of law in Kentucky did not look prosperous or inviting.

Nevertheless, Harper and Griffith, and the black lawyers who followed them to the Kentucky bar, helped to erase white prejudice through their participation in politics and law. By 1888, Harper held a judicial post, the first by a black lawyer in the state. Unable to establish a client base among blacks or whites due to the racial environment of the court system, black lawyers entered low-level state government jobs in Kentucky.

Black lawyers who chose private practice or pursued civil rights claims for their people faced danger in the rural areas of Kentucky. Yet William Hilliard Wright, who practiced corporate law, made progress when he organized the first black-owned insurance company in Kentucky.

Although black lawyers had been elected to state legislatures in other states after the Civil War, Charles W. Anderson, Jr., Kentucky's first black legislator, was not elected until 1936. Anderson is one of the most important black lawyers in Kentucky history. He and Prentice Thomas, also black, were the first to mount a legal challenge to desegregate public schools in Kentucky. As a legislator, Anderson also fought to obtain state aid for black citizens of Kentucky who wanted to attend colleges outside of the state.

Black law schools, such as Harper Law School, Central Law School, Howard University, and Walden University, produced a number of black lawyers in Kentucky. A Yale University graduate, James Robert Spurgeon, was appointed by President William McKinley to the legation at Monrovia, Liberia. No black women were admitted to the Kentucky bar prior to 1945.

The state of Missouri admitted its first black lawyer, John H. Johnson, in 1871. Johnson became a leader in the Colored Emigration Aid Society, which helped blacks fleeing racial repression in the South, and he testified about this issue before Congress in 1880.

Initially, black lawyers in Missouri entered private practice, but it is reported that a black lawyer did not represent a white in the state until 1925. However, the University of Washington's first black law graduate, Walter Moran Farmer, became moderately successful, appearing before the Missouri Supreme Court in 1893, just four years after receiving his law degree.

Prior to 1900, several black lawyers were admitted to the Missouri bar from white law schools. They graduated from St. Louis University, University of Michigan, University of Minnesota, and Washington University. Black law schools such as Howard University, Walden University, and Lincoln University also produced a number of black lawyers.

Political and civil rights concerns made the black lawyer visible in both black and white communities. During the 1920s, John Albert Davis served in the Missouri state legislature, while Homer G. Phillips was a candidate for Congress on the Republican ticket. In 1928, Joseph McLemore ran a spirited campaign for the legislature as a Democrat. His opponent was a white incumbent, Leonidas C. Dyer, who was popular with blacks because he had introduced anti-lynching legislation in Congress. The white people voted for the black Democrat, McLemore, and black people for the white Republican, Dyer, and Dyer was reelected.

Black lawyers arguing civil rights cases in some parts of Missouri were physically assaulted by white mobs. One lawyer, William A. Cole, was beaten by a mob of whites in Permiscot County, Missouri, while defending a black man who had organized black sharecroppers. A significant civil rights victory came in 1938 when Charles Hamilton Houston, Sidney R. Redmond, and Leon Andrew Ramsom won a case before the United States Supreme Court, *Missouri ex rel. Gaines v. Canada*, which declared *de jure* segregation unconstitutional.

Only two black women were admitted to the bar prior to 1945 in Missouri: Dorothy L. Freeman and Margaret B. Bush (Wilson). Freeman entered private practice, while Bush worked in the federal government.

In Tennessee, five black lawyers were admitted to the bar in 1868—Alfred Menefee, Edward Shaw, William H. Young, William F. Yardley, and G. F. Bowles. Except for Bowles, who left Tennessee soon after being admitted to the bar, each of the others made a mark in politics and law. Menefee was elected magistrate in Nashville, Shaw was elected to the Nashville city council, Young was nearly elected to Congress, and Yardley announced his candidacy for governor of Tennessee.

There were other prominent black lawyers who worked in both politics and law. James Carroll Napier was elected to the Memphis city council in 1878, and Samuel Allen McElwee was elected to the Tennessee General Assembly in 1883. McElwee was once nominated to the position of speaker of the house.

Politics, as opposed to private practice, may have been a better career choice for black lawyers, since black clients more often used white lawyers; as in other states, blacks in cities such as Nashville were excluded from serving on juries. Joseph H. Dismukes, a black lawyer, once said that white "mob law" controlled decisions in the jury box in Tennessee.

However, mob rule did not deter Benjamin Franklin Booth, Thomas Frank Cassell, or Robert Lee Mayfield from filing civil rights lawsuits in Tennessee. Booth and Cassell appealed cases to the Tennessee Supreme Court. They sought to have the state separate car laws overturned. Mayfield also fought valiantly before the Tennessee Supreme Court to stop the exclusion of blacks from juries. Lawyers defending black men charged with rape in Tennessee were, on occasion, forced to flee the state after their clients were lynched.

The majority of blacks in Tennessee were formally trained in black law schools such as the University of West Tennessee, Kent College of Law (Nashville), Howard University, Central Tennessee College, Lane University Law School, and Walden University. One black lawyer was educated at Columbia University.

The fourth woman in the nation to be formally trained in law, and the first black woman licensed to practice law in Tennessee and the South, is Lutie A. Lytle. Lytle attended Central Tennessee Law School. After she graduated, she was admitted to the Tennessee bar, and became a law professor at Central—reportedly the first woman law professor in the nation. Forty-two years later, Professor Lytle was followed to the Tennessee bar by C. Vernette Grimes, a Kent College of Law graduate.

In the state of Texas, A. W. Wilder was the first black admitted to the bar. He was admitted in 1873. By the mid-1870s, Wilder was a member of the Texas legislature. Between 1873 and 1900, black lawyers were practicing law in cities as geographically disparate as Dallas, Limestone, Groesbeck, Beaumont, Austin, Denision, San Antonio, Galveston, and Fort Worth, Texas.

Wilford Horace Smith arrived in Galveston in about 1895. He was the first black lawyer in Texas to appear before the United States Supreme Court (although the case he argued arose in Alabama). Smith later relocated to New York to become counsel to the Universal Negro Improvement Association headed by Marcus Garvey.

Civil rights litigation began early in Texas. During the first decade of 1900, Cornelius J. Williams, Allen G. Perkins, and Joseph Cuney challenged, and challenged again, the laws in Galveston, Texas, where blacks were required to ride in separate streetcars. The lawyers in this case did not prevail; nor did Richard D. Evans, in his attempts to void the "white primary" in federal court. Evans was a pioneer voting rights lawyer in Texas, as were Carter Walker Wesley, James Madison Nabrit, Jr., and Jasper Alston Atkins.

Several law schools were represented in Texas prior to 1945, including Boston University, Kent College of Law (Chicago), Northwestern University, Yale University, Harvard University, and Howard University. But the white bar was not interested in black legal education. In Beaumont, Texas, the judges demeaned black lawyers before their clients and juries by referring to them only by their first names.

No black women have been identified as being admitted to practice in Texas before 1945.

Black lawyers in the southwestern states broke new ground, made new laws, and resisted Jim Crow between 1866 and 1944. Each step, whether collective or by individual effort, emancipated the black citizens of the southwestern states from the shameful legacy of slavery and racial discrimination.

NOTES

1. Letter from John L. Ferguson, Arkansas History Commission, to author, Sept. 22, 1986.

2. *Ibid.*

3. Letter from C. R. Stevenson, clerk, Supreme Court of Arkansas, to Charles S. Brown, July 11, 1958.

4. Speech of William H. Gray, during Arkansas Constitutional Convention, 1868, 5 *J. of Negro Hist.* 239, 240 (1920).

5. "Hon. Mifflin W. Gibbs," *Indianapolis Freeman*, May 11, 1889, at 1, col. 1; Vol. 1 *Who's Who of the Colored Race* 114 (F. L. Mather ed. 1915).

6. Gibbs said that he was elected to the judicial post "from a population of 16,000, a large majority of which were not of my race." S. B. Thurman, *Pioneers of Negro Origin in California* 50, 63 (1949).

7. *Dictionary of American Negro Biography* 258–59 (R. Logan and M. Winston eds. 1982).

8. *A Documentary History of the Negro People in the United States* 651 (H. Aptheker ed. 1969).

9. *Dictionary of American Negro Biography* 258, 259 (R. Logan and M. Winston eds. 1982).

10. Dillard, "Perseverance: Black History in Pulaski County, Arkansas—An Excerpt," 31 *Pulaski County Historical Rev.* 62 (Winter 1983).

11. Letter from E. M. Edwards, deputy clerk, Circuit Court of the City of Richmond, to Charles S. Brown, Sept. 29, 1958; "Walthal G. Wynn," *The Richmond Whig*, March 10, 1871.

12. Letter from Irene Parrish, circuit clerk, Lake Village, AR, to Charles S. Brown, 1958; see also, *The Fort Smith Weekly New Era*, Dec. 29, 1871.

13. *Ibid.* (*The Fort Smith Weekly New Era*).

14. *Ibid.* See also, "G. W. [sic] Wynn, A Colored Lawyer of Chicot County, Brutally Murdered," *Arkansas Daily Republican*, Dec. 15, 1871.

15. Letter from Margaret Ross, *Arkansas Gazette*, to Charles S. Brown, July 28, 1958, quoting letter dated Oct. 7, 1868, from Professor A. Butler, who was "a minister and member of the 1868 legislature with Mason." Charles S. Brown indicates that Mason was the owner of a plantation in Chicot County and served as county judge and judge of the probate court from 1871 to 1872 and as sheriff from 1872 to 1874 (letter from Charles S. Brown to office clerk, Chicot County, AR, July 15, 1958). However, Margaret Ross, of the *Arkansas Gazette*, doubts that Mason was a judge (*ibid*).

16. *Arkansas Daily Republican*, Dec. 22, 1871.

17. "Wathal G. Wynn," *The Richmond Whig*, March 10, 1871; see also, T. S. Staples, *Reconstruction in Arkansas* 367 (1923).

18. Letter from Clara Henry, clerk, Chicot County Circuit Court, to Charles S. Brown, June 8, 1961.

19. *Arkansas Daily Gazette*, Nov. 12, 1872.

20. Vol. 1 *Who's Who of the Colored Race* 214 (F. L. Mather ed. 1915).

21. Letter from M. V. Mead, clerk, Circuit Court of Pine Bluff, AR, to Charles S. Brown, July 11, 1958. Dawson was admitted to the bar on December 16, 1870.

22. Unidentified clipping and notes from files of Charles S. Brown, 1958. See also, Bradwell, "The Colored Bar of Chicago," 5 *Mich. L.J.* 385, 386 (1896).

23. *Ibid.* (clippings); *Arkansas Daily Gazette*, April 11, April 13, 1871.

24. *Arkansas Daily Republican*, April 11, 1871, at 4.

25. Notes of Charles S. Brown, "On Lloyd Wheeler," 1958, at 1.

26. Bradwell, "The Colored Bar of Chicago," 5 *Mich. L.J.* 385, 386 (1986).

27. *Arkansas Gazette*, Aug. 31, 1871.

28. "Lloyd G. Wheeler," *Arkansas Daily Republican*, Aug. 30, 1871.

29. Gatewood, "Negro Legislator in Arkansas, 1891: A Document," 31 *The Arkansas Historical Quarterly* 220, 232 (1972).

30. *Id.* at at 220, 232–33.

31. *Id.* at 224.

32. *Ibid.*; *Simms' Blue Book and Directory* 101 (1923); letter from John L. Ferguson, Arkansas History Commission, to author, Sept. 22, 1986; Ellis, "The Chicago Negro in Law and Politics," 1 *The Champion Magazine* 349, 358 (March 1917).

33. *New National Era*, Oct. 23, 1873.

34. *Twenty-seventh Annual Session, Oklahoma Jurisdiction, St. John Grand Lodge, Ancient, Free and Accepted Masons* (frontispiece), Aug. 13–15, 1918.

35. Letter from John L. Ferguson, Arkansas Historical Commission, to author, Sept. 22, 1986.

36. Vol. 1 *Who's Who of the Colored Race* 43 (F. L. Mather ed. 1915).

37. *The National Bar Association: Proceedings of the Sixth Annual Convention* 30, 31, Aug. 7, 1930 (statement of Scipio A. Jones).

38. "A Special Judge," *The Dallas Express*, April 17, 1915; M. W. Ovington, *Portraits in Color* 92 (1927).

39. "'Study Law,' Says Scipio Jones," *Pittsburgh Courier*, Feb. 25, 1929.

40. Letter from John L. Ferguson, Arkansas History Commission, to author, Sept. 22, 1986.

41. Perry County case: *Eastling v. State*, 69 Ark. 189, 62 S.W. 584 (1901) (Scipio A. Jones and J. H. Carmichael); Pulaski county case: *Castleberry v. State*, 69 Ark. 346, 63 S.W. 670 (1901) (same).

42. Dillard, "Perseverance: Black History in Pulaski County Arkansas—An Excerpt," 31 *Pulaski County Historical Rev.* 62 (Winter 1983), citing *Arkansas Gazette*, May 2, 1902.

43. "'Study Law,' Says Scipio Jones," *Pittsburgh Courier*, Feb. 25, 1929.

44. "A Special Judge," *The Dallas Express*, April 17, 1915.

45. *Ibid.*

46. *Banks v. State*, 143 Ark. 154, 219 S.W. 1015 (1920); *Ware v. State*, 146 Ark. 321, 225 S.W. 626 (1920); *Hicks v. State*, 143 Ark. 158, 220 S.W. 308 *cert. denied*, 254 U.S. 630 (1920); *State ex rel. Attorney General v. Martineau*, 149 Ark. 237, 232 S.W. 609, *appeal dismissed*, 257 U.S. 665 (1921).

47. Dillard, "Perseverance: Black History in Pulaski County Arkansas—An Excerpt," 31 *Pulaski County Historical Rev.* 62, 67 (Winter 1983).

48. *Moore v. Dempsey*, 261 U.S. 86 (1923). U. S. Bratton and Moorefield Storey, both white lawyers, represented the Elaine riot defendants before the United States Supreme Court on behalf of the NAACP. A brief that Scipio Jones prepared in defense of the black men in the Elaine and Hoop Spur riot cases was printed in *Crisis* magazine and widely disseminated, throughout the nation, to the black community. See "Brief of Scipio A. Jones—The Arkansas Peons," 23 *Crisis* 72 (Dec. 1921) and 23 *Crisis* 115 (Jan. 1922). For an account of the Elaine Riots, see R. C. Cortner, *A Mob Intent On Death: The NAACP and the Arkansas Riot Cases* 48–55 (1988). Cortner mentions J. A. Booker, Thomas J. Price, and J. A. Hibbler, black lawyers, who were also involved in the defense.

49. See, e.g., *Knights of Pythias of North America v. Bond*, 109 Ark. 543, 160 S.W. 862 (1913); *Grand Camp of Colored Woodmen of Arkansas v. Johnson*, 109 Ark. 527, 160 S.W. 400 (1913); *Knights of Pythias of North America v. Reinberger*, 168 Ark. 77, 269 S.W. 41 (1925).

50. See, e.g., *Knights of Pythias of North America v. Long*, 117 Ark. 136, 174 S.W. 1197 (1915).

51. "Scipio Jones Elected Chancellor in Arkansas Court," *Baltimore Herald*, Sept. 10, 1924; Pickens, "Arkansas and Scipio A. Jones," *New York Amsterdam*

News, Sept. 17, 1924; "Scipio A. Jones Presides in Arkansas Divorce Suit," *Chicago Defender*, Sept. 20, 1924. The case Jones heard was styled *Eason v. Eason*.

52. "Scipio Jones Appeals for Doomed Negroes and Stays Execution," *Pittsburgh American*, Feb. 22, 1924.

53. "'Study Law,' Says Scipio Jones," *Pittsburgh Courier*, Feb. 25, 1929.

54. *Ibid.*

55. Scott's presence as a lawyer in Fort Smith, Arkansas, must have faded. In 1920, the press erroneously reported that Edward D. Dobbins was the first black lawyer "in the history of this city [Fort Smith, Arkansas] . . . admitted to the local bar." "First Lawyer in Fort Smith," *Chicago Defender*, Oct. 23, 1920.

56. *Ibid.*

57. I. G. Penn, *The Afro-American Press, and Its Editors* 240, 243 (1891).

58. Letter from John L. Ferguson, Arkansas History Commission, to author, Sept. 22, 1986.

59. *Fifteenth Annual Report—National Negro Business League* (Boston, MA) 135, Aug. 18–20, 1915.

60. "Negro Lawyer Will Speak at Colored Church Here," *Monroe Louisiana News Star*, March 13, 1929.

61. *McIntosh v. Little Rock*, 159 Ark. 607, 252 S.W. 605 (1923); "Income Tax Law Tested," *Commercial Appeal*, May 2, 1923.

62. "Southern Lawyer," *Ebony* 67, 68, Nov., 1949; "W. Harold Flowers Lawyer and Minister," *Washington Post*, April 9, 1990, at B4, col. 1; "W. Harold Flowers, 78, Arkansas Rights Figure," *New York Times*, April 9, 1990, at D10, col. 6.

63. Ms. Flowers did attempt the Arkansas bar examination, but, according to Mr. Flowers, she failed the bar by one-half of a point. Ms. Flowers was admitted to the bar of the District of Columbia in 1946. Telephone interview by author with William Harold Flowers, Sr., March 15, 1989. Ms. Flowers passed the District of Columbia bar and she had won "her third criminal case" before graduating from law school. "Ex-Tutor's Plea Frees Woman," *Washington Tribune*, May 14, 1946.

64. "Death Claims First Negro Nebraska Woman Lawyer," *Kansas City Call*, April 19, 1935. Hill actually died in Yazoo, Mississippi, causing some to believe, erroneously, that she worked in Hot Springs, Mississippi. "Miss Zanzye Hill Dies in Mississippi," *Lincoln Star*, April 15, 1935, at 4, col. 3.

65. "Kentucky's Negro Lawyers," *New National Era and Citizen*, Dec. 7, 1871; *The Frankfort Commonwealth* Nov. 30, 1871, at 2, col. 4.

66. G. D. Wilson, *A Century of Negro Education in Kentucky* 107 (rev. 1986) (manuscript).

67. "Colored Lawyers in Kentucky," *The Louisianian*, Dec. 10, 1871; R. H. Collins, Vol. 1 *History of Kentucky* 221 (1874). It is difficult to imagine how Harper and Griffiths could practice law in Kentucky, where black people were determined by state law to be incompetent to testify against whites. V. B. Howard, *Black Liberation in Kentucky* 131–45 (1983).

68. *Id.* at 155.

69. *Id.* at 156.

70. G. D. Wilson, *A Century of Negro Education in Kentucky* 107–8 (rev. 1986) (manuscript). This author lists some of the first graduates from Central Law School: John P. Jetton, of Louisville; Isaac W. Thomas, of Hemphill, Texas; Charles W. Mason, of Evansville, Indiana; and W. H. Perry, of Louisville. The

first commencement was held on May 10, 1892, at the Masonic Temple Theater in Louisville. In about 1896, the legislature granted Kentucky Normal University (formerly Simmons University) the sole franchise to educate blacks and to award degrees to blacks in law and medicine. Thereafter, Central Law School became affiliated with Kentucky Normal University. G. Wright, *Life Behind the Veil: Blacks in Louisville, Kentucky, 1865–1930*, at 127 (1985).

71. H. C. Weeden, *History of the Colored People of Louisville* 44 (1897); R. H. Collins, Vol. 1 *History of Kentucky* 221 (1874); A. A. Dunnigan, *The Fascinating Story of Black Kentuckians: Their Heritage and Traditions* 350 (1982).

72. *New York Freeman*, May 16, 1885.

73. G. D. Wilson, *A Century of Negro Education in Kentucky* 108 (rev. 1986) (manuscript quoting *The Courier Journal*, May 11, 1892).

74. *Id.* at 108, referring to *The Courier Journal*, Jan. 22, 1893.

75. "Wants to Go to Tamatave as Consul," *The Courier Journal*, July 8, 1897; "Hampton School Record," 26 *The Southern Workman* 154 (Oct. 1892).

76. "Graduates' Department," 27 *The Southern Workman* 67 (April 1898).

77. Spurgeon, "The Basis of a Nation's Permanency," 1 *The New Africa* 7 (Dec. 1899); Spurgeon, "New York and Liberia Steamship Company, Or, The Commercial Possibilities of the Trade of West Africa with America," 7 *The Colored American Magazine* 735 (1904). Spurgeon practiced law in New York after he left the foreign service and devoted a great deal of time to "the organization of the Boy Scouts of America." *New York Negro Lawyers* 14, 15 (S. H. Lark ed. 1915).

78. Ky. Laws, Chap. 85, Sec. 1, approved, March 22, 1904. See *Berea College v. Kentucky*, 211 U.S. 45 (1908), upholding the state's right to separate races in higher education as being constitutional.

79. H. C. Weeden, *History of the Colored People of Louisville* 44 (1897), listing Nathaniel R. Harper, Isaac E. Black, A. S. White, L. C. Townsend, and T. R. Hammonds.

80. Vol. 1 *Who's Who of the Colored Race* 86 (F. L. Mather ed. 1915).

81. "Petition in Circulation for Colored Magistrate," *Bronx Home News*, Feb. 11, 1925.

82. Vol. 1 *Who's Who of the Colored Race* 106 (F. L. Mather ed. 1915).

83. "Atty. Tucker Appeals for New Trial," *Chicago Defender*, Sept. 5, 1931, on Foreman; Vol. 1 *The National Cyclopedia of the Colored Race* 178 (C. C. Richardson ed. 1919), on Wright.

84. "Colored Lawyer Honored in Ky.," *Kentucky Record*, Jan. 3, 1937.

85. "Lee Brown Opposes Rep. C. W. Anderson for 58th District Post," *Atlanta Daily World*, July 7, 1939; A. A. Dunnigan, *The Fascinating Story of Black Kentuckians: Their Heritage and Traditions* 356 (1982).

86. "Heads Lawyers," *Baltimore Afro-American*, 1943.

87. "Anderson New Head National Bar Ass'n," *Norfolk Journal and Guide*, Dec. 18, 1943; obituary, *Howard University Magazine* 27 (Nov. 1960).

88. *Kentucky Directory* 199, 256, 259–60 (F. K. Kavanaugh ed. 1936).

89. *Kentucky Directory* 168, 228–29, 231, 234 (F. K. Kavanaugh ed. 1938).

90. *Kentucky Directory* 169, 228, 230, 236 (F. K. Kavanaugh ed. 1940).

91. *Kentucky Directory* 170, 237–38, 242–43 (F. K. Kavanaugh ed. 1942).

92. *Kentucky Directory* 172, 207–8, 210 (F. K. Kavanaugh ed. 1944).

93. *Kentucky Directory* 140, 176 (F. K. Kavanaugh ed. 1946).

94. M. V. Tushnet, *The NAACP's Legal Strategy Against Segregated Education, 1925–1950*, at 86, 90 (1987).

95. Telephone interview, Coleman C. Moore (Indianapolis, Indiana), Oct. 3, 1987.

96. *New National Era*, Dec. 14, 1871.

97. *Negro Exodus from Southern States*, Senate Report 693, 46th Cong., 2d Sess., Part II, at 288–302 (1880).

98. *Id.* at 294; see also, *A Documentary History of the Negro People in the United States* 722 (H. Aptheker ed. 1969).

99. *Id.* at 288, 298 (*Negro Exodus from Southern States*).

100. *Id.* at 296 (Burgess mentioned in testimony of John H. Johnson); Vol. 1 *Who's Who of the Colored Race* 50–51 (F. L. Mather ed. 1915); Young, "Early Black Lawyers in St. Louis," 30 *St. Louis B.J.* 6, 11 (Spring 1984); *General Catalogue of the University of Michigan, 1837–1911*, at 401 (I. N. Demmon ed. 1912).

101. Bradwell, *The Colored Bar of Chicago*, 5 *Mich. L.J.* 385, 393 (1896).

102. See, e.g., Bray, *Indianapolis Freeman*, June 29, 1889 at 1, col. 5; *The Seventy-fifth Anniversary of the School of Law, Washington University, St. Louis, 1867–1942*, at 27 (1942).

103. Young, "Early Black Lawyers in St. Louis," 30 *St. Louis B.J.* 6, 11–12 (Spring 1984). Dean Hammond previously had experience with a black student during his tenure as dean at Iowa University's law school. During that time, the law school graduated Alexander G. Clark, Jr., Iowa's first black law graduate. Clarke, "The History of the Black Bar," 30 *St. Louis B.J.* 17, 18 (Spring 1984); Ware, "Contributions of Missouri's Black Lawyers to Securing Equal Justice," 45 *J. of Missouri Bar* 251, 252 (June 1989).

104. *State v. Duncan*, 116 Mo. 288, 304, 22 S.W. 699, 703 (1893) (with G. W. Royse). Vol. 1 *Who's Who in Colored America* 64 (J. J. Boris ed. 1927).

105. *Simms' Blue Book and Directory* 102 (1923); letter from Barbara J. Weston, Washington University School of Law, to author, July 22, 1987.

106. Clarke, "The History of the Black Bar," 30 *St. Louis B.J.* 17, 18 (Spring 1984); L. J. Greene, G. R. Kremer, and A. F. Holland, *Missouri's Black Heritage* 114 (1980). In 1942, Frank S. Bledsoe, a 1922 Howard University law graduate, was appointed judge of the magistrate court in St. Louis. "Judges," *Howard University Bulletin* 13, July 15, 1958.

107. "Negro to Test U.R.'s Right to Route Passengers," *St. Louis Globe-Democrat*, Jan. 18, 1916.

108. G. P. Hamilton, *The Bright Side of Memphis* 75 (1908).

109. *Virginia's Contribution to Negro Leadership* 37 (W. Cooper ed. 1937) (mimeo); Vol. 1 *Who's Who in Colored America* 116 (J. J. Boris ed. 1927).

110. *Id.* at 35 (*Who's Who*); *Alumni Directory of the Law School, University of Minnesota, 1889–1986*, at 1903 (1986); Vol. 1 *Who's Who of the Colored Race* 57 (F. L. Mather ed. 1915).

111. "Attorney S. E. Garner Saves Man from Miss.," *St. Louis Argus*, Nov. 30, 1923. It was not unusual for black lawyers to seek assistance from the governor on civil rights matters, especially if blacks were being returned to a state where peonage was practiced. In 1921, Amasa Knox and Charles H. Calloway sought and won the governor's support in a similar case. "Lawyers L. A. Knox and C. H. Calloway Win Peonage Suit," *Kansas City Sun*, Dec. 17, 1921.

112. *Who's Who Among Negro Lawyers* 16 (S. T. M. Alexander ed. 1945).

113. "Martin Heads Local Negro Bar Ass'n," *St. Louis Argus*, Jan. 14, 1933.

114. "National Bar Assoc. Elects," *Baltimore Afro-American*, Aug. 13, 1927; Young, "Early Black Lawyers in St. Louis," 30 *St. Louis B.J.* 6, 12 (Spring 1984).

115. "Negro, Former Courthouse Janitor, Gets $3,600 Job," *St. Louis Post Dispatch*, March 30, 1926; "George B. Jones Assistant Circuit Attorney," *St. Louis Argus*, April 2, 1926.

116. "First Negro Having White Client Appears in Court," *St. Louis Star*, June 19, 1925; "Head of St. Louis Bar Association Protests to Governor," *The Freeman*, Feb. 16, 1924, listing the following lawyers: E. H. Taylor, Hutchins Inge, George L. Vaughn, Joe Smith, Homer Phillips, Daniel W. Bowles, Robert N. Owens, N. W. Parden, N. A. Mitchell, S. E. Garner, Freeman L. Martin, George W. Wade, John A. Davis, Frank S. Bledsoe, W. R. Hill, Jr., Roy Lowe, J. H. Roberts, Harvey V. Tucker, Emanuel Williams, Graves M. Allen, George B. Jones, Edwin S. Kinswil, Joseph L. McLemore, Frank Clegg, A. C. Davis, and Albert L. Eagland.

117. All twenty members of the committee were white. W. F. Nowlin, *The Negro in American Politics* 101 (1931); Vol. 5 *A History of Missouri* 73 (R. S. Kitkendall ed. 1986).

118. J. H. Chadbourn, *Lynching and the Law* 118 (1933); Zangrando, "The NAACP and a Federal Anti-Lynching Bill, 1934–1940," 50 *J. Negro History* 106 n.3 (1965); C. L. Ferrell, *Nightmare and Dream: Anti-Lynching in Congress, 1917–1922*, at 111–22 (1986).

119. Interview with Margaret Bush Wilson, of Missouri, in Provo, Utah, March 4, 1989.

120. W. F. Nowlin, *The Negro in American Politics* 102 (1931).

121. *Ibid.*

122. "Two Negro Law Makers Take Seats," *St. Louis Argus*, Jan. 7, 1927. Walthall M. Moore, who was not a lawyer and had previously been elected to the general assembly, was also reelected to the Fifty-fourth General Assembly of Missouri. A description of John A. Davis's activities in the general assembly appears in *State of Missouri Official Manual for Years 1927 and 1928* 73 (C. U. Becker ed. 1928).

123. *Ibid.* (*State of Missouri Official Manual*).

124. Pearson, "Lawyer Recalls Fight 50 Years Ago for Blacks' Health Care," *St. Louis Globe-Democrat*, Oct. 16–17, 1982, at 2C, col. 3. Grant was graduated from Howard University School of Law in 1930.

125. Shores, "The Negro at the Bar," 2 *Nat'l. B.A.J.* 266, 270 (1944).

126. F. L. Styles, *Heroes and the Law* 49–50 (1937), quoting "Missouri Court Frees Negroes Convicted by Unfair Trial," *Philadelphia Intelligencer*, Sept. 19, 1934.

127. Stokes, "Decision of the Missouri Supreme Court on the Admission of Negroes to State Universities," 48 *School and Society* 726, 727 (Dec. 1939); see also, Bertha J. McMurdock, "The Development of Higher Education for Negroes in Missouri" 88 (M.A. thesis, Howard University, 1939).

128. *Missouri ex rel. Gaines v. Canada*, 305 U.S. 337 (1938).

129. *Constitutional Law* 459 (G. R. Stone, L. M. Seidman, C. R. Sunstein, and M. V. Tushnet eds. 1986).

130. "Lula Morgan Howard and Scotti Mayo Admitted to Mo. Bar," *New York Age*, Aug. 14, 1943, listing Margaret B. Bush (Wilson), Dorothy L. Freeman, Lula Morgan Howard, Charles H. Blagburn, Richard E. Burns, John W. Harvey, Aguianaldo A. Lenoir, and Scotti R. Mayo.

131. Telephone conversation with Margaret B. Bush Wilson, June 11, 1986. One newspaper has reported that "Miss Dorothy Freeman . . . is the second woman to pass the Missouri State Bar," but does not identify the first ("Portia-

Dorothy Freeman," *Kansas City Call*, Jan. 13, 1943). However, given the history of racial exclusion from higher education in Missouri and the fact that Freeman was the only woman in the graduating class at Lincoln University's law school, it is unlikely that another woman preceded her to the bar.

132. Telephone conversation with Margaret B. Bush Wilson, March 1989 (regarding Freeman); "Lady Barrister Appointed," *Pittsburgh Courier*, Nov. 27, 1943 (regarding Bush); *Who's Who Among Negro Lawyers* 20 (S. T. M. Alexander ed. 1945) (regarding Howard).

133. A. A. Taylor, *The Negro in Tennessee, 1865–1880*, at 289, n.59 (1941). According to one scholar, "There were probably no Black men practicing law in Tennessee prior to the Civil War. This was caused by two reasons: (1) severe restrictions were placed on the actions of freedmen, and (2) educational opportunities were virtually non-existent. In the ante-bellum period, free Negroes were required to register with the county clerk and carry registration papers at all times. They could sue and be sued but were ineligible to hold office. As social and economic outcasts, freedmen could not associate with whites nor keep the company of slaves without their master's permission." Lewis L. Laska, "A History of Legal Education in Tennessee, 1770–1970," at 684 (Ph.D. diss., George Peabody College of Teachers, May 1978), citing C. Patterson, *The Negro in Tennessee, 1790–1865*, at 161, 197 (1968). See also, *State v. Claiborne*, 19 Tenn. 331, 337 (1838). This case held that free blacks were not citizens of the United States within the meaning of Art. 4, Sec. 2 of the U.S. Constitution.

134. *Ibid.* (A. A. Taylor, *The Negro in Tennessee, 1865–1880*).

135. *Ibid.*

136. *Nashville Republican Banner*, April 3, 1897, at 2.

137. C. Patterson, *The Negro in Tennessee, 1790–1865*, at 161, 298, n.13 (1968); R. E. Corlew, *Tennessee* 361 (1981).

138. J. H. Cartwright, *The Triumph of Jim Crow* 25 (1976).

139. *Ibid.* Other black lawyers, such as Thomas F. Cassells, a Republican, opposed Shaw's low-tax views. During this period Cassells was a member of the Tennessee General Assembly. *Id.* at 29.

140. *Id.* at 49.

141. *Id.* at 50–51.

142. *Id.* at 57.

143. *Id.* at 58.

144. *Id.* at 59.

145. *Id.* at 92.

146. *Ibid.* Joseph H. Dismukes, another black lawyer, agreed with William H. Young's view. He opposed the fusion between the Bourbon Democrats and black Republicans because he was skeptical about the Democrats' political agenda regarding blacks. *Id.* at 48.

147. *Ibid.*

148. *Id.* at 93.

149. *Id.* at 95. Young's opponent was Joseph E. Washington, an incumbent Democrat. Young won 38.3 percent of the vote; Washington won fifty-seven percent. See *Congressional Quarterly's Guide to U.S. Elections* 817 (2d ed., John L. Moore ed. 1985).

150. *Id.* at 92 (*The Triumph of Jim Crow*).

151. M. Scott, Jr., *The Negro in Tennessee Politics and Governmental Affairs, 1865–1965* 51 (1964), quoting *Nashville Daily American*, Sept. 3, 1876.

152. *Ibid.* (*The Negro in Tennessee Politics*).

153. *Ibid.*

154. "Col. G. F. Bowles," *Indianapolis Freeman*, May 18, 1889.

155. *Nashville Republican Banner*, April 6, 1868.

156. *Nashville Republican Banner*, May 15, 1869.

157. *Nashville Republican Banner*, Dec. 25, 1870.

158. *Nashville Republican Banner*, May 18, 1869.

159. D. D. Buck, *The Progress in the Race in the United States and Canada* 381 (1907).

160. Letter from Clara Mae Brown to Charles S. Brown, Sept. 18, 1958. Napier entered Howard University's law school in 1870 with distinction, having been appointed in 1865 by Tennessee Governor W. G. Brownlow to the post of county claims commissioner of Davidson County. While a student in Howard University's law school, Napier was invited to become an auditor in the United States Treasury Department. After graduating from law school in 1872, Napier was appointed internal revenue agent and "gauger for the Fifth Collection District of the State of Tennessee." M. Scott, Jr., *The Negro in Tennessee Politics and Governmental Affairs* 33 (1964).

161. *Id.* at 235 (*The Negro in Tennessee Politics*).

162. *Dictionary of American Negro Biography* 470, 471 (R. Logan and M. Winston eds. 1982).

163. L. C. Lamon, *Black Tennesseans, 1900–1930*, at 95, 98 (1977); J. H. Cartwright, *The Triumph of Jim Crow* 47–48 (1976), referring to the *Nashville American*, July 25, 1885.

164. *Dictionary of American Negro Biography* 471 (R. Logan and M. Winston eds. 1982).

165. *The Negro Year Book* 145 (Tuskegee Institute ed. 1952). In fact, even prior to Washington's death, Napier was Washington's choice to succeed him as president of the National Business League. He desired a "man of [Napier's] temperament and standing." Vol. 7 *The Booker T. Washington Papers, 1903–04*, at 199, 200 (L. R. Harlan and R. W. Smock eds. 1977).

166. C. S. Johnson, *The Negro College Graduate* 333 (1938). Daniel Lapsley is reported to have been admitted to the bar in Nashville in 1873, but the extent of his practice in Nashville has not been determined. In 1890 Lapsley moved to Omaha, Nebraska. *Souvenir Album and Directory of the Colored Voters in Omaha, Nebraska* 21 (W. B. Walker ed. 1891).

167. W. J. Simmons, *Men of Mark* 993 (1887); I. G. Penn, *The Afro-American Press, and Its Editors* 324 (1891); *Dictionary of American Negro Biography* 39 (R. Logan and M. Winston eds. 1982).

168. Letter to Charles S. Brown from Mary Davant, head, Memphis Public Library, June 2, 1962.

169. Cassell was elected to the Tennessee General Assembly from Shelby County. Sampson W. Keeble was the first black to serve in the general assembly in 1872. J. H. Cartwright, *The Triumph of Jim Crow* 75 (1976); see also, letter from Bessie Buffaloe, clerk, Tennessee Supreme Court, to Charles S. Brown, April 12, 1961; letter from Mary Davant, head, Memphis Public Library, to Charles S. Brown, June 2, 1962. (Both letters provide different dates as to Cassell's initial admission to practice in Tennessee. Davant's letter states that Cassell was admitted in 1876, while Buffaloe's letter states that he was admitted to the circuit court of Shelby County on May 17, 1886. In view of the fact that Cassell served as assistant attorney general in Tennessee in 1878, it appears that he was admitted to a court inferior to the circuit court prior to 1886.)

170. M. Scott, Jr., *The Negro in Tennessee Politics and Governmental Affairs, 1865–1965*, at 48–49, 87 (1964); *Memphis Avalanche*, Nov. 22, 1878; *Gibson County Herald*, May 18, 1886; *Memphis Commercial Appeal*, Jan. 31, 1899 (courtesy Tennessee State Library and Archives). See also, *Chesapeake, Ohio & Southwestern Railroad Company v. Wells*, 85 Tenn. 613, 4 S.W. 5 (1887) (with Greer and Adams). Ida B. Wells, who later married a black lawyer, Ferdinand Barnett, in Chicago, established a national reputation as a civil rights advocate. See *The Autobiography of Ida B. Wells* 18–19 (A. M. Duster ed. 1970).

171. Letter from John Q. Taylor King, president, Houston-Tillotson College, to Rodman Turner, Nov. 14, 1986.

172. Bradwell, "The Colored Bar of Chicago," 5 *Mich. L.J.* 385, 393 (1896); H. F. Gosnell, *Negro Politicians: The Rise of Negro Politics in Chicago* 199 (1935); Vol. 1 *Who's Who of the Colored Race* 278 (F. L. Mather ed. 1915).

173. G. P. Hamilton, *The Bright Side of Memphis* 59 (1908).

174. L. Merriam, *Higher Education in Tennessee* 27 (1893).

175. Vol. 2 *Biographical Directory, Tennessee General Assembly, 1861–1901*, at 572 (R. M. McBride ed. 1979). McElwee served in the 43rd–45th general assemblies, from 1883–1887.

176. J. H. Cartwright, *The Triumph of Jim Crow* 108, 111, 113 (1976).

177. *Id.* at 116.

178. *Ibid.*

179. *Id.* at 117.

180. *Id.* at 90.

181. *The College of Life or Practical Self Educator: A Manual of Self Improvement for the Colored Race* 140 (H. D. Northrop, J. R. Gay, and I. G. Penn eds. 1896); R. E. Corlew, *Tennessee* 362–63 (1981); *Indianapolis Freeman*, Jan. 11, 1890, at 4, col. 1; R. W. T., "The Brilliant Orator and Barrister, Hon. S. A. McElwee," *Indianapolis Freeman*, March 2, 1889; Ellis, "The Chicago Negro in Law and Politics," 1 *The Champion Magazine* 349, 351 (March 1917).

182. *Afro-American Encyclopedia; Or, The Thoughts, Doings and Sayings of the Race* 620–21 (J. T. Haley ed. 1895) (Robinson); G. P. Hamilton, *The Bright Side of Memphis* 72 (1908) (Saddler).

183. *Ibid.* (*The Bright Side of Memphis*).

184. *Id.* at 68–69.

185. L. R. Harlan, *Booker T. Washington: The Making of a Black Leader*, 186–90, 244 (1972).

186. Vol. 1 *Who's Who of the Colored Race* 50 (F. L. Mather ed. 1915). William Henry Harrison, who also graduated from Walden University's law school, became a noted lawyer in Tennessee. "Negro Lawyer Will Talk Here Tonight," *Selma Times Journal*, April 14, 1939.

187. Vol. 1 *Who's Who in Colored America* 18 (J. J. Boris ed. 1927).

188. G. P. Hamilton, *The Bright Side of Memphis* 62 (1908). Booth was subsequently admitted to the bar at Bolivar, Tennessee, in 1888. He was also admitted to the United States District Court of the Western District of Tennessee in 1889. He was admitted to the Tennessee Supreme Court on May 12, 1890. Letter from Bessie Buffaloe, clerk, Tennessee Supreme Court, to Charles S. Brown, April 12, 1961; letter from E. P. Harrington, deputy clerk, U.S. District Court, to Charles S. Brown, April 10, 1961.

189. *Ibid.* (*The Bright Side of Memphis*).

190. *Morrison v. State*, 116 Tenn. 534, 95 S.W. 494 (1906).

191. G. P. Hamilton, *The Bright Side of Memphis* 63 (1908). Booth also trained

several lawyers. After Edward Johnson, Jr., received legal training from Judge Bigelow in Memphis, Thomas F. Cassell and Benjamin F. Booth were the mentors who gave him his final instruction. He successfully passed the Tennessee bar in 1898. *Id.* at 67–68. H. M. Bomar commenced the study of law under Judge E. L. Bullocks, of Jacksonville, Tennessee, but completed his study under Booth in 1897, the year he was admitted to the bar. *Id.* at 60–61.

192. H. F. Kletzing and W. H. Crogman, *Progress of a Race* 523 (1901).

193. G. P. Hamilton, *The Bright Side of Memphis* 74 (1908); Vol. 1 *Who's Who of the Colored Race* 240 (F. L. Mather ed. 1915); "Hon. J. T. Settle, an Eminent Colored Barrister," *Indianapolis Freeman*, Feb. 2, 1889, at 1, col. 1; L. C. Lamon, *Black Tennesseans, 1900–1930*, at 32 (1977); *Fifteenth Annual Report, National Negro Business League* (Boston, MA) 136, Aug. 18–20, 1915.

194. G. P. Hamilton, *The Bright Side of Memphis* 65 (1908).

195. *Ransom v. State*, 116 Tenn. 355, 96 S.W. 953 (1905).

196. *Rivers v. State*, 117 Tenn. 235, 96 S.W. 956 (1906). See L. C. Lamon, *Black Tennesseans, 1900–1930*, at 9 (1977).

197. *Id.* at 7, Lamon, *Black Tennesseans*, citing Tennessee Supreme Court of Errors and Appeals Index No. 4210.

198. L. C. Lamon, *Black Tennesseans, 1900–1930*, at 175 (1977), quoting the *Nashville Globe*, Feb. 18; March 3, 11; April 8, 1910.

199. "Nashville Court Orders Atty. Mayfield Disbarred," *Chicago Defender*, March 1, 1919.

200. "Disbarred Attorney Seeks to Be Reinstated," *Chicago Defender*, Feb. 14, 1919; "Mayfield Asks for Reinstatement to Bar," *Nashville Tennessean*, Feb. 26, 1919; "Nashville Court Orders Atty. Mayfield Disbarred," *Chicago Defender*, March 1, 1919.

201. *Ibid.* ("Nashville Court Orders Atty. Mayfield Disbarred").

202. Vol. 1 *Who's Who of the Colored Race* 62 (F. L. Mather ed. 1915).

203. G. P. Hamilton, *The Bright Side of Memphis* 64 (1908).

204. *Id.* at 65.

205. Vol. 1 *Who's Who in Colored America* 127 (J. J. Boris ed. 1927).

206. G. P. Hamilton, *The Bright Side of Memphis* 59–60 (1908).

207. L. C. Lamon, *Black Tennesseans, 1900–1930*, at 10 (1977), referring to Henry M. Wiltse, Vol. 2 *The History of Chattanooga* 164 (n.d. unpublished manuscript).

208. *Ibid.*

209. Shores, "The Negro at the Bar," 2 *Nat'l B.A.J.* 266, 270, n.3 (1944). It is believed that the lawyer was Howard University law professor Leon A. Ransom, who was involved in the trial of *Witham v. State* in Knox County, Tennessee. The case was appealed to the Tennessee Supreme Court, where the court upheld the separation of races in public schools. *State ex rel. Michael v. Witham*, 179 Tenn. 250, 165 S.W.2d 378 (1942). Ransom was one of three black lawyers involved in this case. The other two lawyers were Carl A. Cowan and Z. Alexander Looby, both of Tennessee.

210. Letter from Thurgood Marshall, special counsel, NAACP, to Victor Rotnem, chief, Civil Rights Section, Department of Justice, July 5, 1944.

211. "A Young Colored Man Passes the Bar Examination," *Nashville Globe*, Dec. 22, 1922.

212. Roberts, "National Bar Association Ends Sessions," *Chicago Defender*, Aug. 11, 1928.

213. *Who's Who Among Negro Lawyers* 24 (S. T. M. Alexander ed. 1945); letter to author from Dorothea Hutchinson, Columbia University, May 8, 1989; "A Record of the Negro College," 32 *Crisis* 167 (Aug. 1926). Looby, who was from Parham, British West Indies, spent a year at Howard University School of Law, from 1920 to 1921.

214. *Ibid.* (*Who's Who Among Negro Lawyers*).

215. M. V. Tushnet, *The NAACP's Legal Strategy Against Segregated Education, 1925–1950,* at 53, 55 (1987), Tushnet reports that Cowan was a Harvard University law graduate. In fact, Cowan received his law degree from Howard University in 1930.

216. Trescott, "Making Marshall's Night," *Washington Post,* Sept. 15, 1988, at C1, col. 4.

217. *Id.* at C10.

218. See, e.g., *Sunday School Union of African Methodist Episcopal Church v. Walden,* 121 F.2d 719 (6th Cir. 1941) (with Albert Williams and Joe Brown Cummings).

219. Letter from Waverly D. Crenshaw, Jr., president, Napier-Looby Bar Association, to author, June 12, 1986.

220. Letter from E. P. Harrington, deputy chief, U.S. District Court, Western District of Tennessee, to Charles S. Brown, April 10, 1961. Foote was admitted on March 14, 1934. Letter from Joe N. Pless, clerk, Circuit Court, Shelby County, to Charles S. Brown, April 7, 1961.

221. R. W. Logan, *The Betrayal of the Negro* 316–17 (1969); G. Lerner, *Black Women in White America* 324 (1972); *Catalogue for Central Tennessee College, 1896–1897,* at 44 (1897).

222. "Only Colored Female Lawyer," *The Cincinnati Enquirer,* Sept. 9, 1897, at 1, col. 4.

223. "First Colored Woman Admitted to the Practice of Law," *Topeka Daily Capital,* Sept. 15, 1897.

224. *Topeka Daily Capital,* Oct. 27, 1898.

225. *Ibid.*

226. Her name at this time was Lutie Lytle-McNeil. Letter from P. Harp to Charles S. Brown, April 28, 1961. Lytle-McNeil moved to New Paltz, New York, around the turn of the century.

227. *Report of the National Negro Business League* 230 (Philadelphia, PA), Aug. 20–22, 1913.

228. "To Practice Law," *Norfolk Journal and Guide,* Sept. 30, 1939; "Becomes First Woman to Pass Tennessee Bar," *Washington Tribune,* Oct. 7, 1939.

229. *Ibid.* ("Becomes First Woman to Pass Tennessee Bar").

230. *Ibid.*

231. Letter from George Templin, clerk, Supreme Court of Texas, to Charles S. Brown, May 23, 1958.

232. J. M. Brewer, *Negro Legislators of Texas* 126 (1935).

233. L. D. Rice, *The Negro in Texas, 1874–1900,* at 102 (1971).

234. *Id.* at 194.

235. *Ibid.*

236. *Id.* at 91, 94, 194.

237. *Id.* at 246.

238. *A Documentary History of the Negro People in the United States* 690–91 (H. Aptheker ed. 1969), quoting *Proceedings of the State Convention of Colored Men of Texas,* held in Austin, Texas, July 10–12, 1883.

239. *Dictionary of American Negro Biography* 107 (R. Logan and M. Winston eds. 1982).

240. *Ibid.*

241. Bradwell, "The Colored Bar of Chicago," 5 *Mich. L.J.* 385, 398 (1896).

242. *Memorial and Biographical History of Dallas County, Texas* 203 (1892).

243. *Ibid.* In Chicago, Turner also studied law under Ferdinand Lee Barnett and Samuel Laing Williams prior to his admission to the Kent College of Law in 1896. *Ibid.*

244. Letter from Margaret B. Pratt, head, Texas Local History and Genealogy Department, to Charles S. Brown, Oct. 16, 1958.

245. Vol. 1 *Who's Who of the Colored Race* 270–71 (F. L. Mather ed. 1915).

246. *Indiana Freeman*, Dec. 3, 1892.

247. L. D. Rice, *The Negro in Texas, 1874–1900* 73, 74 (1971).

248. Vol. 1 *Who's Who of the Colored Race* 83 (F. L. Mather ed. 1915).

249. M. Bloomfield, "From Deference to Confrontation: The Early Black Lawyers of Galveston, Texas, 1895–1920," in *The New High Priest* 151 (G. W. Gawalt ed. 1984). Bloomfield is one of the few scholars who has reviewed old court dockets and identified specific pleadings of black lawyers. Bloomfield lists the following lawyers as practicing in Galveston, Texas, between 1895 and 1920: Cornelius J. Williams, Joseph Cuney, Allen G. Parkins, J. Vance Lewis, Wilford H. Smith, George O. Burgess, Walter R. Hills, Charles D. McBeth, Alex Green, Henry H. Swanson, Allen D. Bridge, Webster Wilson, M. G. Lewis, M. H. Broyles, John H. Barbour, and Thomas H. Dent. The exact dates these lawyers were admitted to the bar are unclear. Even where dates are available, they often prove to be undependable. For example, Thomas H. Dent was graduated from Howard University's law school in 1884. As Bloomfield suggests, it is likely that he settled in Galveston, Texas, soon after he graduated. Yet, other evidence points to Dent's admission to the bar in Galveston, Texas on April 5, 1926 (letter from Mildred Stevenson, Rosenberg Library, Galveston, Texas, to Charles S. Brown).

250. M. Bloomfield, "From Deference to Confrontation: The Early Black Lawyers of Galveston, Texas, 1895–1920," in *The New High Priest* 159 (G. W. Gawalt ed. 1984).

251. *Ibid.*

252. See *Jones v. State*, 38 Tex. Crim. Rep. 364, 43 S.W. 78 (1897); *Noble v. State*, 38 Tex. Crim. Rep. 368, 43 S.W. 80 (1897). See also, M. Bloomfield, "From Deference to Confrontation: The Early Black Lawyers of Galveston, Texas, 1895–1920," in *The New High Priest* 160–61 (G. W. Gawalt ed. 1984).

253. *Id.* at 159–60. Bloomfield cites *Hubbs v. Perkins*, a case that was apparently settled at the appeals level, or for which the court rendered no opinion.

254. *The Marcus Garvey and UNIA Papers* 426 (R. A. Hill and B. Blair eds. 1987).

255. *Giles v. Harris* 189 U.S. 475 (1903); and *Giles v. Teasley*, 193 U.S. 147 (1904).

256. L. P. Harlan, *Booker T. Washington: The Wizard of Tuskegee* 247 (1983), quoting letter from Washington to Smith, Feb. 24, 1904.

257. Wilford H. Smith, "The Negro and the Law," in *The Negro Problem* (B. T. Washington ed. 1903).

258. *Id.* at 127, 150.

259. *Rogers v. Alabama*, 192 U.S. 226 (1904). See also, *Rogers v. State*, 139 Ala. 666, 36 So. 1044 (1903). Here again, Smith, apparently still a resident of

Galveston, Texas, was litigating cases in Alabama that were secretly funded by Booker T. Washington. L. R. Harlan, *Booker T. Washington: The Wizard of Tuskegee* 247 (1983).

260. "Wilford H. Smith to Locate Permanently at Galveston," *New York Age*, April 15, 1922.

261. "San Antonio Lawyer Joins Local Attorney," *Houston Informer*, July 11, 1925. When Wimberly took the bar after graduating from Howard University's law school, he scored highest "in the class taking the [Texas] bar." All of the others taking the exam were whites.

262. *Ibid.*

263. M. Bloomfield, "From Deference to Confrontation: The Early Black Lawyers of Galveston, Texas, 1895–1920," in *The New High Priest* 155–56 (G. W. Gawalt ed. 1984).

264. *Id.* at 157, quoting from Lewis's autobiography, *Out of a Ditch: A True Story of an Ex-Slave* 84 (1910).

265. *Ibid.* Lewis himself describes the circumstances of his indictment for allegedly swindling elderly people but never says one way or another whether the allegations were true. The evidence at the preliminary hearing was mixed. J. V. Lewis, *Out of a Ditch: A True Story of an Ex-Slave* 91–99 (1910). Apparently, Lewis was re-admitted to the bar. He describes handling criminal cases later in Liberty, Texas. *Id.* at 109, 112. Lewis was a skilled lawyer and appeared at times before the Texas Criminal Court of Appeals. See, e.g., *Pollard v. State*, 58 Tex. Crim. Rep. 299, 300, 125 S.W. 390, 391 (1910), in which he argued unsuccessfully that a murder conviction should be overturned because of the racial composition of the jury. Lewis claimed that he was graduated from the University of Michigan's law school in 1894; however, there is no record available to support this claim. See *General Catalogue of the University of Michigan, 1837–1911*, at 777, 1034 (I. N. Demmon ed. 1912). Lewis states in his autobiography that he "went to Ann Arbor, and after graduation in 1894 was admitted to the Supreme Court of Michigan. But there were some things yet to learn and another course still. This time it was at the Chicago College of Law. I graduated there in 1896 and was admitted to all of the courts of Illinois." *Id.* at 31.

266. *Id.* at 162–63.

267. *Id.* at 156.

268. "Broyles Critical of Race," *The Dallas Express*, April 17, 1915.

269. *First Annual Banquet Program of the Fort Worth Negro Business League*, Aug. 15, 1906, at 3.

270. M. Bloomfield, "From Deference to Confrontation: The Early Black Lawyers of Galveston, Texas, 1895–1920," in *The New High Priest* 156 (G. W. Gawalt ed. 1984), quoting *Galveston City Times*, Aug. 28, 1915.

271. "Admitted to U.S. Court," *Chicago Defender*, April 15, 1916.

272. F. L. Styles, *Negroes and the Law* 22 (1937).

273. *Love v. Griffith*, 266 U.S. 32 (1924). In 1928 Evans brought a suit in Harris County (Houston, Texas) challenging the constitutionality of the Texas state law that excluded blacks from participating in primary elections. He lost. *Grisby v. Harris*, 27 F.2d 942 (S.D. Tex. 1928). His efforts to appeal this decision were denied on technical grounds. *Grisby v. Harris*, 27 F.2d 945 (S.D. Tex. 1928).

274. *Dictionary of American Negro Biography* 639 (R. Logan and M. Winston eds. 1982) (Wesley and Atkins); "A New President Takes Office," 3 *The Howard University Magazine* 4–5 (Nov. 1960) (Nabrit); *Yale Law School Sesquicentennial*

Alumni Directory 10 (1974) (Atkins); "Made Attempt to Break Down Texas Primary Color Bar," *The National World*, Jan. 24, 1931, at 2, col. 3.

275. Thurgood Marshall was a student at Howard University's law school during the period that Wesley, Nabrit, and Atkins were litigating the voting rights cases in Houston. Marshall graduated from Howard University's law school in 1933, while Charles H. Houston was dean. In 1935, Houston praised Wesley and Atkins for their work in the white primary cases (Houston, "Need for Negro Lawyers," 4 *J. of Negro Education* 49, 52 [1935]). In 1935, after joining the NAACP to head its legal office in New York, Houston initiated a strategy to attack a broad range of racial barriers in the South. When Houston assumed the leadership of the NAACP's office, he threw the entire weight of the NAACP against the Texas white primary, until it was determined by the United States Supreme Court to be unconstitutional.

276. *Smith v. Allwright*, 321 U.S. 649 (1944).

277. Simond, "History of Community Misses Tale of Attorney," *Austin American Statesmen*, May 17, 1984. Dawkins's name appears in the Austin City Directory from 1920 to 1929.

278. *Who's Who Among Negro Lawyers* 37 (S. T. M. Alexander ed. 1945); *Harvard Law Quinquennial* 467 (F. S. Kimball ed. 1948).

279. Telephone conversation with Dr. Desra White, of Houston, TX (son of George W. White, Jr.), Oct. 13, 1986.

280. Letter to author from Professor Kirkland Jones, Lamar University, Beaumont, Texas, Jan. 11, 1986.

281. *Ibid.* Professor Jones reports that Evans attended the University of Indiana Law School at Bloomington. However, the records office at the law school could not verify that Frank Evans attended the law school.

282. "Negro Mass Meeting," *Sweetwater Reporter*, April 12, 1925.

283. Letter from Llerena Friend, librarian, University of Texas, Barker Texas History Center, to Charles S. Brown, May 27, 1958.

284. J. M. Brewer, *Negro Legislators of Texas* 118–19 (1935).

285. 339 U.S. 629 (1950).

286. Simond, "History of Community Misses Tale of Attorney," *Austin American Statesman*, May 17, 1984.

287. Vol. III, *The Sixteenth Census, Population*, 492 (1943).

Robert Morris, Sr., of Boston, Massachusetts, was admitted to the Massachusetts bar at Suffolk County on February 2, 1847, becoming the second black
lawyer to practice in the United States. Morris was the first black lawyer to try a
case before a jury. (Courtesy of Moorland-Spingarn Research Center, Howard
University; by permission of The Associated Publishers, Inc.)

In 1865 Jonathan Jasper Wright became the first black to gain admission to the Pennsylvania bar. Wright served on the South Carolina Supreme Court from 1870 to 1877, marking the first time a black lawyer had reached this high state office. (Courtesy of the Moorland-Spingarn Research Center, Howard University.)

William J. Whipper was admitted to the South Carolina state bar in 1868. A key organizer for the Republican Party in South Carolina, Whipper was also one of the principal partners in the nation's first black law firm, Whipper, Elliott and Allen. (Courtesy of Charles Sumner Brown.)

In 1880, Edwin Archer Randolph became Yale University law school's first black graduate and the first black admitted to the Connecticut bar. (Courtesy of Charles Sumner Brown.)

In 1857, Edward Garrison Draper received a certificate of legal competence from the Superior Court in Baltimore, Maryland, but was denied admission to the state bar because of his race. He left Maryland to practice law in Liberia, West Africa. (Courtesy of Charles Sumner Brown.)

George Lewis Ruffin became Harvard University's first black law graduate in 1869. (Courtesy of Ollie May Cooper and Mr. and Mrs. Paul F. Cooper.)

Joseph H. Stuart, an 1877 graduate of the University of South Carolina School of Law, became Colorado's second black lawyer in 1891, and its first black state legislator in 1893. (Courtesy of the Denver Public Library Western Collection.)

Thomas Calhoun Walker was admitted to the state bar of Virginia in 1887. After President William McKinley appointed Walker to the office of collector of customs at Tappahannock, black Virginians came to refer to him as the "black governor." (Courtesy of Hampton University Archives.)

In 1889, Silas Robbins became the first black lawyer to be
admitted to the Nebraska bar. (From author's files.)

The black lawyers of Baltimore pictured here had gathered at the home of the Reverend Harvey Johnson (1923 Druid Hill Avenue), circa 1910. Johnson had been instrumental in securing the admission of the Maryland bar's first black lawyer. In the doorway (*center*): Rev. Harvey Johnson. *From left to right*, top row: U. Grant Tyler (Howard University, 1894) and C. C. Fitzgerald (Howard University, 1892); second row: John L. Dozier (Howard University, 1891), Hugh M. Burkett (Howard University, 1898), Warner T. McGwinn (Yale University, 1887), and H. R. White (layman); third row: George L. Pendleton (Howard University, 1896) and William Chester McCard (Wisconsin and Northwestern universities, 1896); fourth row: W. Ashbie Hawkins (Howard University, 1892); bottom row: William H. Daniels, Harry S. Cummings (University of Maryland, 1889), and J. W. Parker. (Courtesy of Ollie May Cooper and Mr. and Mrs. Paul F. Cooper.)

McCants Stewart, son of lawyer T. McCants Stewart, was the University of Minnesota's second black law graduate (1899) and the first black to receive a master of laws degree there (1901). In 1904 he became the state of Oregon's first black lawyer. (Courtesy of the Moorland-Spingarn Research Center, Howard University.)

James Adlai Cobb was appointed special assistant to the attorney general of the United States in 1907. With the backing of Booker T. Washington, Cobb was appointed municipal judge for the District of Columbia in 1926 by President Calvin Coolidge. Cobb also taught at Howard University School of Law. He taught Thurgood Marshall constitutional law. (Courtesy of Ollie May Cooper and Mr. and Mrs. Paul F. Cooper.)

In 1909, Robert Herberton Terrell was appointed to the municipal court of the District of Columbia by President Robert H. Taft. In 1931, a black law school in Washington, D.C., was named for him. (Courtesy of Ollie May Cooper and Mr. and Mrs. Paul F. Cooper.)

Gertrude Elzora Durden Rush was the state of Iowa's first black woman lawyer. Rush, who was admitted to the bar in 1918, was a co-founder in 1925 of the National Bar Association. (Courtesy of the History Committee of the National Bar Association.)

S. Joe Brown was the first president of the Iowa Colored Bar Association (1918). He co-founded the National Bar Association in 1925. (Courtesy of the History Committee of the National Bar Association.)

Henry Lincoln Johnson, Sr. (*left*), an influential Republican from Georgia, also practiced law in the District of Columbia. Gilchrist Stewart (*right*), son of T. McCants Stewart, was a lawyer in New York. Photo circa 1920. (Courtesy of Henry Lincoln Johnson, Jr.)

Charles Hamilton Houston served as resident vice-dean of Howard University School of Law from 1930 to 1934. Houston was the first black to sit on the editorial board of the *Harvard Law Review* (1921), and the first special counsel to the NAACP (1935). Photo circa 1940. (Courtesy of Moorland-Spingarn Research Center, Howard University.)

Third-year law class, Howard University, 1923. (Courtesy of Ollie May Cooper and Mr. and Mrs. Paul F. Cooper.)

George H. Woodson, an 1895 Howard University law graduate, became the National Bar Association's first president in 1925. (Courtesy of the History Committee of the National Bar Association.)

William Henry Hastie served as dean of Howard University School of Law from 1941 to 1946 and was the second black student on the *Harvard Law Review* (1928). (Courtesy of Moorland-Spingarn Research Center, Howard University.)

George Marion Johnson, the first black student to earn the doctor of juridical science degree at Boalt Hall Law School at the University of California (1930), taught law at Howard University in the 1930s and succeeded William Henry Hastie as law dean in 1946. (Courtesy of Professor Jeanus B. Parks, Jr.)

Helen Elsie Austin was appointed assistant attorney general of the state of Ohio in 1937, becoming the first black woman in the nation to hold such a post. Austin was also the first black female law graduate of the University of Cincinnati (1930). (Courtesy of Helen Elsie Austin and the Moorland-Spingarn Research Center.)

Jane Matilda Bolin, the first black woman to graduate from Yale
University's law school (1931), was also the first black female judge in
the nation. Judge Bolin was appointed to the New York City Domestic
Relations Court in 1939 by Mayor Fiorello H. LaGuardia. (Courtesy
of the Library of Congress Collections.)

Howard University Moot Court Class, 1932. Judge Nathan Cayton (behind desk), a white judge, taught the class. To Judge Cayton's right is James G. "Pete" Tyson (sitting in witness chair against the wall). Also pictured are Edward P. Lovett (front row, far left); Ollie May Cooper (third row, second from left), a 1921 Howard University graduate and secretary to Howard law dean Charles Hamilton Houston; Oliver W. Hill (third row, third from left); and Thurgood Marshall (next to last row, second from left, with mustache). (Courtesy of Ollie May Cooper and Mr. and Mrs. Paul F. Cooper.)

Howard University law class of 1938. At the far left is Joel D. Blackwell; at center (eighth person from left) is Cassandra A. Maxwell (Birney); second from right is Joseph C. Waddy; and at far right is Thomas W. Wallace, Jr. Waddy later became a distinguished federal district judge in Washington, D.C. (Courtesy of Thomas W. Wallace, Jr.)

Group photograph of the 1938 annual meeting of the National Bar Association. Thurgood Marshall, then the outgoing national secretary of the NBA, is fifth from the left in the front row. Helen Elsie Austin, third from the right in the front row, was reelected national vice-president of the NBA, and Isadora Letcher, fourth from the left in the front row, was elected national secretary. (Courtesy of Ollie May Cooper and Mr. and Mrs. Paul F. Cooper.)

Ollie

Dora

New York City - Aug 1939

Ollie May Cooper (*left*) and Isadora Letcher attending the 1939 National Bar Association Convention in New York City. (Courtesy of Ollie May Cooper and Mr. and Mrs. Paul F. Cooper.)

John Mercer Langston, the first black admitted to the Ohio bar (1854), organized Howard University School of Law in 1868 and became its first law dean in 1869. In 1890, Langston became the first black to represent Virginia in Congress. (Courtesy of the Library of Congress Collections.)

In 1942, William Henry Hastie (*left*), on leave from his position as dean of Howard University School of Law, served as assistant to the Secretary of War. Here, Hastie consults with Robert P. Patterson, another assistant to the Secretary of War. (Courtesy of the Library of Congress Collections.)

In 1911, President William Howard Taft nominated William Henry Lewis, an 1895 law graduate of Harvard University, to the position of assistant attorney general of the United States. Lewis was confirmed by the Senate on June 14, 1911. (Courtesy of the Library of Congress Collections.)

Negro lawyers of Mississippi, 1909. (Courtesy of the Library of Congress Collections.)

The signboard for Ollie May Cooper's practice, circa 1930. (The sign is wooden block with gold lettering.) Cooper was one of the first black women to practice law in the District of Columbia, and in the nation. (From author's files.)

The Northeastern States

The northeastern states include Illinois, Indiana, New York, and Ohio.

Illinois

Black lawyers in Illinois prospered and grew in number more rapidly than in most states. This phenomenon may be attributed to the number of law schools in Chicago that admitted blacks prior to 1900. There does not appear to have been a broad racial exclusionary policy in Chicago law school admissions. The old University of Chicago law department graduated its first black student in 1870, and the Chicago College of Law graduated its first in 1889. Other law schools, such as Union College of Law (Northwestern) and John Marshall Law School, also graduated blacks prior to 1900.

It is generally accepted that Lloyd G. Wheeler was the first black lawyer admitted to the bar in Illinois. He was admitted on April 20, 1869.[1] Wheeler did not receive a formal legal education. In 1868, he was listed in the *Chicago City Directory* as a law student in the office of George G. Bellows. Wheeler was apparently known throughout the northwest region prior to and during the days he studied law. He was described as "one of the most conspicuous characters in the northwest [and the] first colored U.S. mail carrier in Chicago."[2] Chicago's second black lawyer, Richard A. Dawson, was the first black graduated from the law department of the old University of Chicago, in June 1870.[3] He was admitted to the Illinois bar on July 11, 1870. In 1871, Wheeler and Dawson left Chicago to practice law in Little Rock and Pine Bluff, Arkansas, respectively.[4] Eventually, both lawyers returned to Chicago, after the close of the Reconstruction era, to practice law.

In 1878 Ferdinand Lee Barnett was graduated from Northwestern University's law school. He was admitted to the bar on June 18, 1878, and "immediately entered upon work of his profession." He also founded Chicago's first black newspaper, *The Chicago Conservator*.[5] As a lawyer, Barnett was an advocate for the rights of his people in Chicago; as a publicist, he was one of the first blacks to publicly criticize the white press for failing to spell the word Negro with a capital *N*.[6] Barnett's combined professions made him a force in Chicago city politics and a leader in the black community. In 1880, Barnett urged his people to "forget the past so far as we can, and unite with other men upon issues liberal, essential, and not dependent upon color of skin or texture of hair."[7]

By 1890, Barnett's stature in the Chicago black community had been matched by two other black lawyers, John G. Jones and Edward H. Morris. These men were highly respected lawyers and businessmen whose influence reached deep within the inner circles of Chicago's Republican political machine. These lawyers have been credited with designing the political blueprint that assured black elected representatives in the state legislature, the Chicago city council, and other public offices. Barnett, Jones, and Morris also formed local groups such as the Prince Hall Masons, the Odd Fellows, and the Knights of Pythias.[8]

Barnett's own political destiny was apparently part of his blueprint for change. In 1896, he became the first black lawyer to be appointed assistant state's attorney in the state of Illinois. In this post, Barnett was assigned to handle extradition and habeas corpus proceedings. He soon became an expert in these areas.[9] Barnett remained in the state's attorney office until 1913. He was succeeded first by James A. Scott, who served in the state's attorney office for four years, and then by Edward E. Wilson.[10]

During Barnett's years in the state's attorney office, he remained active in Chicago Republican politics. In 1904 he and Ida Wells Barnett, his outspoken wife, helped to turn back Booker T. Washington's effort to gain influence among blacks in Chicago. In the 1880s, Washington had managed to win Lloyd G. Wheeler (after Wheeler returned to Chicago from Arkansas) and a few other black Chicago lawyers to his camp. Wheeler assisted Washington in 1901 by establishing a Chicago chapter of the National Negro Business League. Soon thereafter, Wheeler moved to Tuskegee, Alabama, to work at the Tuskegee Institute, headed by Washington.[11]

But there was no love lost between Washington and Barnett. In apparent retaliation against Barnett for locking him out of Chicago, Washington later tried, without success, to block Barnett's appointment "as head of the Chicago branch of the Negro Bureau in the 1904 Republican presidential campaign."[12]

In 1906 Barnett became the first black lawyer in Illinois to run for a judicial post. He launched his candidacy for the municipal court of Chicago while serving as assistant state's attorney. Barnett was well-qualified for the judgeship. By 1906, he had lived in Chicago for thirty-seven years, had been legally trained in the state, and had acquired ten years of experience in the state's attorney office. Barnett, however, was not a professional politician. He was a leader, a black man who could get his people out to vote. Perhaps the Republican leadership placed Barnett's name on the ticket to aid the party—more than to aid Barnett, who needed white as well as black votes. Barnett had sterling qualifications, but the white press painted him as a black man who was stepping outside of his place by running for a judicial post: "White people will never willingly submit to receiving the law from a Negro."[13] Barnett was the only member of the Republican ticket to lose his election. His defeat, surprisingly, was by a margin of 304 votes—out of a total of 200,000 for the office. This narrow margin was evidence that the black political blueprint was more than a notion. It was a reality.[14]

After Barnett left public service in 1913, he returned to private practice. By all accounts, he became very successful, in spite of one judicial reprimand for failing to appear in court when his case was called for trial.[15]

Edward H. Morris was admitted to the Illinois bar on June 13, 1879.[16] Morris studied law under a prominent white Chicago lawyer, Edward A. Fisher. Morris opened a law practice in Chicago and became known as the "defendant attorney for the gambling fraternity."[17] From 1890 to 1892, he served in the Illinois State Legislature,[18] where, as an active member, he introduced a bill to appropriate money for pensions for schoolteachers and a bill legalizing slave marriages for the purpose of inheritance. He also helped draft the first Australian ballot law.[19] He was admitted to practice before the United States Supreme Court in 1885.[20]

Morris became one of the most popular lawyers in the nation, as well as a respected leader of his race.[21] By 1935, he had helped so many black lawyers enter the practice of law that he had won the epithet "dean of the black lawyers."[22] Among those that he assisted was his brother, William Richard Morris, who was admitted to the Illinois bar in 1888 and to the Minnesota bar in 1889.[23] Edward Morris also hired and trained several black lawyers after he was appointed city attorney for South Chicago in 1892.

After Morris's appointment ended, he returned to private practice, where his reputation as a criminal lawyer came to the attention of blacks and whites alike. In 1912 he represented former United States Senator William Lorimer of Illinois, who had been indicted in connection with the collapse of the LaSalle Bank of Chicago. Several other whites were indicted along with Senator Lorimer. All of the defendants were convicted, except Senator Lorimer, the only defendant represented by Morris.[24]

In 1917 the joint defense of Oscar DePriest by Edward H. Morris and Clarence Darrow made an important and lasting mark on Chicago's political history. DePriest was a powerful alderman in Chicago and a staunch supporter of Mayor William Hale Thompson, who was popular among blacks. In an apparent effort to discredit Mayor Thompson's relationship with DePriest, the mayor's opponents filed bribery charges against DePriest. The government asserted that DePriest had accepted a bribe from the gambling syndicate in return for permitting illegal activities in DePriest's ward. Edward Morris and Clarence Darrow argued that the alderman had accepted no bribe, and they won DePriest's acquittal.

While the criminal proceedings were pending against DePriest, Louis Bernard Anderson, another black lawyer, held DePriest's seat on the city council.[25] After his acquittal, DePriest regained the political support of the black people in his ward. Eleven years later, DePriest, a Republican, became the first black in the North to be elected to the House of Representatives, thanks to the superb skills of Morris and Darrow.[26]

John W. E. Thomas was admitted to the Illinois bar in 1880 after reading the law on his own. Thomas probably studied law while serving as the first black in the Illinois legislature, a position to which he was elected from South Chicago in 1876. He served in the legislature during three sessions: 1876–1878, 1882–1884, and 1884–1886.[27] As a member of the Judiciary Committee, Thomas authored the first civil rights law adopted in Illinois.[28] In 1886 the provisions of the law were first invoked when a black woman was denied a seat in the white section of a theater, though she had a ticket of general admission. In defense, the proprietor claimed that the policy of the theater was to separate the races by row, which satisfied the separate but equal doctrine. The civil rights laws of Illinois, however, protected all citizens and provided a penalty for the violation of such rights. The woman sought the assistance of Edward H. Morris, who sued for damages under the civil rights statute and won a verdict for one hundred dollars. The verdict was appealed by the theater to the Illinois Supreme Court, giving Morris an opportunity not only to argue for the rights of his client, but also to urge the court to uphold the civil rights bill authored by John W. E. Thomas. This was probably the first appearance of a black lawyer before the Illinois Supreme Court. In 1889 the court upheld the "comprehensive and sweeping language" of the civil rights act of Illinois and affirmed the judgment in favor of Morris's client.[29]

After leaving the state legislature in 1886, John W. E. Thomas was selected South Town clerk in Chicago. He served in this position for one term. Thomas practiced law in Chicago in what was described as a "lucrative" practice. He supplemented his practice with a successful business as bondsman, which drew both white and black clients.[30]

In 1885, nine black lawyers were engaged in the active practice of law in Chicago: Edward H. Morris, Fedinand Lee Barnett, John G. Jones, John W. E. Thomas, Maurice Baumann, James G. Jones, Lewis Washington, Alexander Clark, Sr., and Frederick L. McGhee. The names of these attorneys appeared in a "colored men's" professional directory which asserted that the "legal profession . . . will . . . produce . . . distinguished and able colored men, who are to become the leading lights of future years."[31]

Maurice Baumann, admitted to the Illinois bar in 1883, was indeed considered one of the "leading lights" of the Chicago bar. He is reported to have had "knowledge of jurisprudence and quick conception of the most difficult questions arising in legal proceedings."[32] In 1892 the press reported that Baumann did "more work for white than colored people."[33] Chicago also had great hopes for Frederick L. McGhee. McGhee studied law at Union Law School (Northwestern) and in the law office of Edward H. Morris, who tutored McGhee for the Illinois bar. He passed the examination in 1885. McGhee, however, did not remain in Chicago, relocating instead to St. Paul, Minnesota, where he continued to practice law.

John G. Jones joined Ferdinand Lee Barnett's law firm immediately after he passed the Iowa and Illinois bars in 1884. By 1884, Jones was well established in Chicago, having been appointed a special United States commissioner to Cuba in 1870 by Ulysses S. Grant. Jones's mission was "to investigate the complaints [of] colored people of the United States being captive and sold there as slaves."[34] The firm of Barnett and Jones lasted for more than twenty years, continuing throughout Barnett's days in public service. The practice was devoted almost exclusively to criminal defense work, a specialization for which Jones won praise from both the bench and bar, and the respect of both white and black clients.[35]

John G. Jones was an outspoken black lawyer in Chicago. His advocacy for black rights won him the nickname "Indignation Jones." Jones opposed any movement that called for race separatism, even the establishment of a separate YMCA. In 1891, he also opposed the establishment of a hospital exclusively for blacks and joined the protest of Ferdinand Lee Barnett, his law partner, against a segregated school system in Chicago.[36] Because of his public opposition to separation, Jones was frequently consulted by public officials on questions pertaining to the "civil and political welfare" of his people.[37] Near the close of the nineteenth century, Jones had become a leader in the Ancient Arabic Order of Nobles of the Mystic Shrine of North and South America, a masonic group. He apparently abandoned his law practice to travel throughout the nation promoting Freemasonry.[38]

Between 1883 and 1900 several distinguished black lawyers continued the legal tradition established by their predecessors. For example, James H. Lott read law in the office of Alfred Sample in Paxton, Illinois. Lott was admitted to the bar in 1884 and opened a private practice. He became the first black lawyer "to regularly represent a railroad in the United States."[39] He acted as counsel for the Wabash Railroad Company in Ford County, Illinois, and as city attorney for Paxton City, Illinois, from 1887 to 1889. In 1894 Lott prevailed in a suit against the Northern Railroad, challenging its segregated car policy under the Commerce Clause of the United States Constitution.[40]

Samuel Laing Williams applied for admission to the Columbian University Law School (George Washington University) in 1882. At the time of his admission and during the time of his matriculation in the law school, Williams worked in the adjudicating department of the United States Pension Bureau.[41] As Columbian University Law School's first black student, he was initially scorned by his white peers. However, Williams excelled and garnered the respect of the law faculty and students, winning second prize in a thesis competition. He graduated from the Columbian University Law School in 1884.[42]

On June 18, 1885, Columbian University's first black law graduate was admitted to the District of Columbia bar. Williams subsequently enrolled in Columbian University's graduate law program and became the first black to earn a master of laws degree in 1886. He then moved to Chicago, Illinois, where he was admitted to the bar. For a short time, he joined Ferdinand Lee Barnett's law firm, but he was soon hired by Judge Lewis Rinaker, becoming one of the first black lawyers to gain experience as an inheritance tax lawyer.[43]

Williams won recognition as a leader among Chicago's black elite. In the mid-1880's, he came to the attention of Booker T. Washington and later became his main contact in Chicago. Washington's respect—or perhaps his need to win the support of a talented Chicago lawyer like Williams to counteract the opposing forces of Ferdinand Lee Barnett—probably influenced Washington's decision to invite Williams to deliver the commencement address at Tuskegee Institute in 1895.[44] Thereafter, their friendship grew to a point where Williams privately reported to Washington on the political activities of Chicago's black leadership.[45] In 1904, "Williams dutifully informed Washington of the activities of the Niagara group in Chicago [and] told Washington [that two black lawyers, Edward H. Morris and Ferdinand Lee Barnett,] were aspiring to gain control of the Negro Bureau of the Republican presidential campaign."[46]

Williams also enabled Washington to win favorable press coverage among black newspapers in Chicago. Reciprocal favors between these men ensued. In 1904, Williams sought Washington's support in a campaign for the chairmanship of the Chicago branch of the Republican Party's Negro Bureau. Williams, however, faced so much opposition from Ferdinand Lee Barnett, John G. Jones, and Edward H. Morris that he was not appointed.[47]

Much of the opposition to Williams was ideological: that is, anti–Booker T. Washington.[48] Despite the decline in Williams's popularity among key black leaders, he became, with the help of Washington, the first black lawyer in Illinois to win an appointment from President William H. Taft. In 1908, he became assistant United States attorney for the Northern District of Illinois and the Eastern District of Wisconsin. He held this position for four years, losing it finally "on a claim that he lacked energy and practicality."[49] By 1914 Williams had altered his political views somewhat and was representing the NAACP in various civil rights claims against Chicago.[50]

Robert Sengstacke Abbott was graduated from the Kent College of Law (Chicago) in 1899.[51] After graduating, he practiced law in Gary, Indiana, and Topeka, Kansas. In 1905, Abbott returned to Chicago and founded the *Chicago Defender*, a newspaper which by 1915 had become one of the best-run black-owned businesses in the nation. Abbott did not practice law after he founded the newspaper, but his legal training made him an exemplary watchman at the local courts. Black lawyers were often featured in Abbott's paper and publicity about their cases was often beneficial.

When the Booker T. Washington–W. E. B. Du Bois debate on education erupted, Abbott refused to align himself with either side. He disliked the "talented tenth" position of Du Bois, considering it to be haughty and aristocratic. However, Abbott also refused requests by Samuel Laing Williams to use the *Chicago Defender* to editorialize on behalf of Booker T. Washington, who favored industrial training of blacks.[52] Abbott did take a strong stand against Marcus Garvey's movement in 1919. In fact, "when Abbott learned that Garvey planned to sell stock in his Black Star Line in Chicago, he engaged a private detective who trapped [Garvey] into selling stock in violation of Illinois law."[53]

Franklin A. Denison enrolled in the Union College of Law (Northwestern) in 1888. He "surprised the faculty by taking [the Illinois bar] examination and being admitted to the bar" a year before he graduated.[54] Denison completed his law study at Union College in 1890, graduating as the class valedictorian—a first for a black student at the law school.[55] Immediately after Denison finished his legal studies, Chicago Mayor Hempstead Washburn appointed him assistant to the city prosecutor based on "his brilliant academic record."[56] He was retained in this position by mayors Carter Henry Harrison, Sr., and John Patrick, and was promoted in 1895 to chief assistant prosecuting attorney by Mayor George Bill Swift.[57] Denison, a Republican, also ran a law firm with Samuel Asbury Thompson Watkins, a Democrat, while serving in government. The political partnership of the two men worked well. Each was appointed assistant city attorney when his party was in power. They were law partners until about 1915.[58]

Samuel Asbury Thompson Watkins was first admitted to the Tennessee bar in 1891. He moved to Illinois in 1893 and was admitted to practice there. He was appointed prosecuting attorney of Chicago in 1898, and he held that position until 1907. In 1911 Watkins was appointed assistant corporation counsel. In 1915 Watkins became "the first . . . Afro-American attorney [to plead] before [the United States Supreme] Court for a municipality."[59] In 1919, Denison, Watkins, and James E. White organized a law firm to formalize what had previously been a firm in name only.[60]

The backgrounds of Denison, Watkins, and White were impressive. Denison had served as an inheritance tax appraiser in the Office of the Corporation Counsel of Chicago and in the state's attorney general's office. As assistant corporation counsel, Denison was responsible for the track elevator department. He had also served as a colonel in the 370th United States Infantry and in the American Expeditionary Forces; he was one of the first black army officers to be trained at Fort Des Moines, Iowa.[61] S. A. T. Watkins also served as an inheritance tax appraiser in the Office of the Corporation Counsel. As an assistant corporation counsel, Watkins "had charge of the admiralty department."[62] He also served for a period as an assistant United States district attorney. James E. White was general counsel for the Railroad Men's Association and had "the reputation of being one of the best civil lawyers in the state."[63]

The reputations of these three men were also known outside of Illinois. In 1938 Watkins and White assisted a black West Virginia lawyer, Thomas G. Nutter, in litigating a twelve-million dollar land dispute in West Virginia that was eventually appealed to the United States Supreme Court.[64] White was the firm's lawyer in its representation of black secret societies and fraternal organizations. In 1918 White successfully defended the Knights of Pythias against an injunction filed by the White Shriners, who alleged that the Knights were wrongfully using their materials and symbols.[65]

In 1886 Alexander Clark, Sr., arrived in Chicago from Iowa University's law school, from which he had graduated in 1884. There he found anarchists trying to persuade the black community to overthrow the government. Denouncing "the plot of anarchists and other evil designing men," Clark urged "African-Americans [to] remain standing face to face . . . in that genius of American liberty."[66] Clark practiced law in Chicago until 1890, when President Benjamin Harrison appointed him minister and consul to Monrovia, Liberia, a position he held until 1891. He died in office.[67]

Edward H. Wright was admitted to the Illinois bar in 1896 and soon got involved in politics. He landed a seat on the county commission in the same year he was admitted to the bar. In 1919 Wright waged an unsuccessful campaign for the Chicago city council "but polled enough votes to demonstrate the potential strength of a Negro candidate on the South Side."[68] It was Wright's campaign that helped lay the foundation for the election of Oscar DePriest to the city council in 1915,[69] the same year Wright was appointed assistant corporation counsel by Mayor William Hale Thompson.[70] Four years later, Wright succeeded Congressman Martin Madden as Republican committeeman in the Second Ward,[71] a post that he used to help secure the election of Oscar DePriest to Madden's congressional seat in 1929. In 1919 Wright was also appointed as special attorney for the Traction Commission by ordinance of the city council.[72]

Albert Bailey George earned a law degree from Northwestern University's law school in 1897. George initially read law from 1894 to 1896 in the offices of Nicholas P. Morevine, of Altoona, Pennsylvania. He also served as a clerk for his brother-in-law, James B. Raymond, who was an alderman in Altoona.[73] After one year at Northwestern University's law school, George was admitted to the Illinois bar and entered the private practice of law. He soon was retained as counsel to the *Chicago Defender* and the Knights of Pythias in Illinois. He represented the fraternal group before the Illinois Supreme Court in 1916.[74]

George was well-respected in the community and was seen as a man who was "bound to succeed," because he was "honest and straight forward."[75] These characteristics enabled him to become the first black lawyer elected to the municipal court of Chicago in 1925.[76] Judge George served on the bench with distinction for six years. At the conclusion of his term, the Chicago Bar Association praised Judge George for his "prompt, industrious, and diligent . . . dispatch of his judicial duties and referred to him as an able lawyer."[77] He was one of the first black lawyers to use radio as a medium for public outreach.[78]

Louis Bernard Anderson, an 1897 Kent College of Law (Chicago) graduate, became one of Chicago's most outstanding lawyers. A year after being admitted to the bar, he was appointed assistant attorney for Cook County, a post that he held from 1898 to 1914. In 1915, he was appointed assistant corporation counsel by Mayor William Hale Thompson. He served in that position until 1917, when he succeeded Oscar DePriest on the city council. (DePriest chose not to seek reelection at that time because of pending bribery charges.)[79]

During the mid-1880s, black lawyers were just beginning to carve out a niche in the state of Illinois. Only a few white law firms—Meech, Asay, and Rice, among them—permitted blacks to study in or have access to their law libraries. Lewis W. Cummings began his law studies in the Meech firm before he entered the first law class of Chicago College of Law in 1887. The opportunity to work and read law in this firm probably eased the preliminary challenges of law study for Cummings. He graduated from the Chicago College of Law in 1889. Admitted to the bar in 1891, Cummings practiced law by day and worked in the post office at night.[80]

William Lewis Martin was graduated from the Chicago College of Law in 1898. Martin entered law school after serving for six years, from 1893 to 1895, as a clerk in Cook County government. He was also elected South Town clerk of Chicago in 1895. Martin served as a member of the Illinois state legislature from 1897 to 1899 while simultaneously studying law. Martin practiced law in Chicago until his death in 1938.[81]

Edward E. Wilson, an 1894 graduate of Howard University's law school, succeeded James A. Scott as assistant state's attorney. Wilson was well known for his opposition to Booker T. Washington and his supporters in Chicago. In 1910 Wilson stated his position clearly:

Separation, where it does not bring a lessening of one's rights and privileges, is not to be frowned upon; but this so seldom happens that it is a dangerous experiment; and wherever there is a tendency to the curtailment of civic rights, or where such separation is an entering wedge for further discrimination, it should be fought without apology and without truce.[82]

Wilson was also known for his participation in the prosecution of Richard Loeb and Nathan F. Leopold, Jr., for the murder of Bobby Franks in 1924.[83]

In 1896 Beauregard Fritz Moseley was admitted to the Illinois bar.[84] He first studied law in Louisiana, in the office of F. B. Earhart, the United States district attorney in New Orleans. Moseley subsequently became a member of the Chicago Law Institute. He maintained a lucrative law practice in Chicago during the first quarter of the twentieth century, and as counsel for the Olivet Baptist Church, he drew a number of clients.[85] Moseley was also an astute businessman. Prior to World War I, when the white establishment excluded black athletes from playing professional baseball in Chicago, "Moseley called together a group of Negro baseball officials from throughout the Midwest and the South to organize a National Negro Baseball League [stating,] 'let those who would serve the Race and assist it in holding its back up . . . organize an effort to secure . . . the best club of ball players possible.' "[86] Between his law practice and business interests, Moseley earned an annual income of fifteen thousand dollars prior to 1915.[87]

Black lawyers who were excluded from the white business and professional directories were listed in directories published by blacks as early as 1909.[88] These listings enabled them to be known throughout the community. In 1909 the *Colored People's Blue Book* and the *Chicago Negro Business Directory* listed forty-eight black lawyers in Chicago.[89] In 1921, seventy black lawyers were listed in *Black's Blue Book*.[90]

The onset of the twentieth century brought a number of new lawyers to Chicago and into its political power base. In 1906 Adelbert H. Roberts, an 1893 graduate of Northwestern University's law school, was appointed deputy clerk in the municipal court. Roberts was also elected to the Illinois General Assembly in 1918 and in 1922, and to the Illinois State Senate in 1924. He held his clerkship and his legislative positions simultaneously.[91] Augustus Lewis Williams, a 1905 graduate of the Illinois College of Law, became the attorney for and a director of the Allen Derrigible Air Ship Co.[92] Williams handled many of the lawsuits that grew out of the race riots of 1919. He "brought twenty lawsuits against the city" for damages resulting in injury to black citizens, obtaining "judgments in their favor . . . in the sum of . . . $113,000.00."[93] During these riots, black leaders such as Arthur C. MacNeal, then the executive director of the Chicago NAACP, criticized the courts for failing to protect the rights of blacks charged with crimes while white misconduct was forgiven.[94]

The migration of black people to Northern cities between 1910 and 1920 created black pockets in these communities. These enclaves generated a host of civil and criminal matters, thereby demonstrating the need for black lawyers. During this same period, the black middle class emerged, generating a greater interest among blacks in business, politics, and civil rights protection.[95]

George Washington Ellis was one of the new generation of black lawyers. He was admitted to the Illinois bar in 1910. An 1893 graduate of the University of Kansas Law School and a former secretary of the

United States legation at Liberia, West Africa, Ellis became one of the first black members of the American Society of International Law, an association founded in 1906. He authored several books on international subjects, including *The Negro Culture in West Africa*, *Liberia in the Political Psychology of West Africa*, and *The Dynamic Factors in the Liberian Situation*.[96]

Richard Hill, Jr., a 1911 graduate of the University of Michigan's law school, organized the Victory Insurance Company.[97] In 1932 Hill became the first black lawyer to run for a judgeship in a Chicago Democratic primary election.[98]

James G. Cotter was graduated from the Illinois College of Law in 1912. He entered private practice, winning recognition throughout the city of Chicago for his exemplary trial skills. His talents came to the attention of the attorney general of Illinois, Edward J. Brundage, who appointed him assistant attorney general in 1917. He held the position for two years, during which Cotter "handled the prosecution of violators of the Medical Practice Act and miscellaneous assignments of cases involving contracts."[99] In 1921 Cotter was appointed assistant United States attorney in Illinois by U.S. Attorney General Harry M. Daugherty, a position that had not been held by a black lawyer since the appointment of Samuel Laing Williams in 1908.

In the federal courts, Cotter handled several complex cases involving the Internal Revenue Code and federal shipping statutes. In one case in which he represented the United States, Cotter opposed former Supreme Court Chief Justice Charles Evans Hughes.[100] In 1928 Nathan S. Taylor succeeded Cotter. In 1929, Herbert T. Dotson succeeded Taylor by appointment of Attorney General John T. Sargent. Dotson served in the post of assistant United States attorney until 1936.[101]

In 1939 William Sylvester White, Jr., a 1937 University of Chicago law graduate, was appointed assistant United States attorney; in this post, he handled food and drug cases.[102] Three years later, White prosecuted Charles Newby, the head of the Colored American's National Organization, for un-American activities. Newby had referred to Adolph Hitler as "'the light of the world' and [to] the Japanese as 'blood brothers of the Negro.'" White was assigned to prosecute Newby because he, like Newby, was black. The prosecution could thereby "remove any suspicion of anti-Negro sentiment" on the part of the federal government. Newby was convicted and sentenced to three years in a federal penitentiary.[103]

William L. Offord, a 1914 Howard University law graduate, served as a special investigator for the United States Department of Labor. Later he was appointed assistant corporation counsel in Chicago.[104] William E. King, a 1915 graduate of the John Marshall Law School who also held this post from 1919 to 1923, was admitted to the Illinois bar in 1916. He was later appointed assistant state's attorney of Cook County. In 1924 King was elected to the Illinois state senate, where he served several terms.[105]

In 1918 Joseph D. Bibb, a black Yale University law graduate, moved to Chicago and co-founded *The Chicago Whip* with Arthur C. MacNeal, a 1916 Yale University graduate. Their newspaper became the chief competitor of the *Chicago Defender*. Bibb and MacNeal took editorial positions supporting Marcus Garvey, while Robert S. Abbott's *Chicago Defender* was highly critical of Garvey. *The Chicago Whip* praised Garvey for "awakening a new race consciousness and creating a new race solidarity."[106] Bibb was one of the first blacks appointed by the mayor of Chicago to the city's library board.[107]

By the 1920s, the black lawyer was firmly established in Illinois. Herman Emmons Moore arrived in Chicago in 1921. Moore, a 1917 graduate of Howard University's law school, received his master of laws degree at Boston University School of Law in 1919. Prior to relocating to Chicago, Moore had established himself as a brief writer for various firms in Boston. He also "served as attorney for the Boston Fraction Company."[108] Moore practiced with William L. Dawson, William L. Hayes, Irving C. Mollison, and J. Ernest Wilkens until 1934, when Governor Henry Horner appointed him to a five-year term as assistant commissioner on the Illinois Commerce Commission, which regulated the electricity, water, gas, and transportation industries of the state. During his term Moore was responsible for the Chicago Traction division's universal transfer case. Moore authored the opinion that legalized the issuance of transfers from elevated trains to streetcars and buses, and vice versa.[109] He was on an Illinois Commerce Commission panel that allocated the division of $30,000,000 in fares. In 1939, President Franklin D. Roosevelt appointed Moore to the United States District Court of the Virgin Islands. Moore succeeded William Henry Hastie in this post, making him the nation's second black federal district court judge.[110]

Charles L. Rice was one of the first black lawyers to practice law in southern Illinois. He practiced in the cities of Cairo and Mounds. Rice reportedly studied law under a white attorney in Mounds, his hometown.[111] Rice was "a prominent member of the Pulaski County bar" in 1920, when he ran as a candidate for state's attorney on the Republican ticket. He was later appointed master in chancery in the local courts.[112]

In 1920 Earl B. Dickerson became the first black law graduate of the new University of Chicago. He was immediately hired by a black firm headed by Edward H. Morris and James B. Cashin,[113] and remained associated with that firm until 1933, when he was appointed assistant attorney general of Illinois.[114] In 1942, Dickerson was appointed by President Franklin Roosevelt to the United States Fair Employment Practice Committee. As the first black person appointed to this committee, Dickerson spoke out against all forms of discrimination by employers:

Today the right to a job cannot be denied because of union membership. The policy to recognize that right as against encroachments of racial prejudice has received national definition in Executive Order No. 8802. The next step is to make the right to a job without regard to race, color or religion a reality in American life.[115]

Wendell Elbert Green also was admitted to the Illinois bar in 1920. He then entered private practice, where he remained until 1942. Though he kept his law practice during these years, Green worked as a staff attorney in the Cook County public defender's office from 1929 to 1930 and as a Civil Service commissioner from 1935 to 1942. During one three-year period, Green reportedly won more than seventy-one murder acquittals. He was dubbed one of the most brilliant criminal lawyers in Chicago. In 1942, Green was elected to the municipal court of Chicago.[116]

It was during the mid-1920s that "the Negro lawyers in Chicago received their greatest recognition [under State's Attorney Robert E. Crow, who hired] ten colored assistant state's attorneys."[117] This was also a period of political violence. In 1926 Octavius C. Grannady, a 1912 Howard University law graduate who was running for ward committeeman in Chicago, was murdered "by a gang of hoodlums engaged in a campaign of terrorism."[118] Two years later, another black lawyer, William H. Haynes, was appointed to investigate crime and election fraud in Chicago by Oscar E. Carlstrom, the attorney general of Illinois.[119]

As the 1920s came to a close, the black lawyer in Chicago remained at the forefront of the legal world, protecting the civil rights of black people. In 1927 Samuel Kennedy, a black man who was "wanted" in Madison, Georgia, for allegedly "slapping" a white woman, had been traced to Chicago by Georgia authorities. Three black lawyers sought a writ of *habeas corpus* when it was learned that a Georgia sheriff had put Kennedy on a southbound train out of Illinois to stand trial in Georgia. Before the train left the state, the writ of *habeas corpus* was served on the Georgia sheriff, and Kennedy was returned to Chicago and spared from Georgia's justice.[120]

By 1928, at least one black lawyer, Nathan Kellogg McGill, a former assistant state's attorney, earned a salary of one hundred dollars per day as general counsel for the *Chicago Defender*;[121] and Alva Lee Bates, a former assistant state's attorney, became counsel for the Lincoln State Bank in 1930.[122]

Milton Jacob Sampson, a 1925 Chicago-Kent Law School graduate, became the legal advisor for the Great Lakes Lodge of the Elks about 1930.[123] Willis Valentine Jefferson, an 1892 University of Michigan law graduate, and Warren B. Douglas, a former member of the Illinois General Assembly, were both appointed assistant attorneys for the Sanitary District of Chicago.[124] The number of black law firms increased during this period, as did their concentration in civil law matters. In 1937 a firm of six black men "was fifth in point of the number of estates opened in the Probate Court," according to the Metropolitan Trust Company of Chicago.[125]

In 1938 the United States Supreme Court decided a significant civil rights case brought by Congressman Arthur Wergs Mitchell and Richard E. Westbrooks, two prominent black Chicago lawyers. Mitchell was elected to Congress in 1934, after defeating Congressman Oscar DePriest. Mitchell was the first black Democrat elected to Congress, and he served until 1942. In 1937 Congressman Mitchell was a victim of discrimination while traveling interstate on a train enroute to Hot Springs, Arkansas. While the train was passing through Arkansas, a conductor, complying with the Arkansas separate car law, forced Congressman Mitchell to sit in a car for "colored passengers." Mitchell and Richard E. Westbrooks later filed a claim against the Chicago and Rock Island Railroad before the Interstate Commerce Commission (ICC), alleging racial discrimination and violation of federal law; their claim was denied.[126] The United States Supreme Court, however, reversed the ICC decision, interpreting the Interstate Commerce Act as prohibiting discrimination under the facts of this case.[127]

In 1940 five black lawyers again faced the United States Supreme Court, this time to challenge the constitutionality of restrictive covenants. (Restrictive covenants were clauses in deeds transferring real property that restricted the sale or use of the land by an excluded group, usually blacks and Jews.) This claim was won on a procedural point. The victory was achieved by a team of Chicago's most talented lawyers: Earl B. Dickerson, Truman K. Gibson, Jr., C. Francis Stradford, Loring B. Moore, and Irvin C. Mollison.[128]

In 1942 Euclid Louis Taylor, Archibald Carey, Jr., A. Morris Burroughs, James Simpson, Jr., and C. Francis Stradford, all black, represented black lawyer Patrick B. Prescott, Jr., in an effort to have him seated on the municipal court of Chicago. Governor Dwight H. Green had appointed Prescott to the bench, an act which won considerable praise from the black community. However, Prescott had been appointed to an unexpired term left vacant by the death of the chief justice of the court and the elevation of a sitting judge to chief justice. When Prescott presented his appointment credentials to the court, the new chief justice refused to recognize the commission. He considered it null and void on procedural grounds. The lawyers representing Prescott argued that the municipal court was without authority to determine whether a commission from the governor was invalid, a claim supported by the Illinois Supreme Court.[129] Prescott was subsequently seated as a judge on the municipal court of Chicago.

In 1894 Ida G. Platt became the first black woman admitted to the bar in Illinois. Prior to her admission, Platt had worked for several years as a legal stenographer in the law office of a white lawyer named Jesse Cox. She attended the Chicago College of Law and graduated on June 15, 1894,[130] becoming the third black woman in the nation to receive a formal legal education and to be admitted to the bar. The court, cognizant of the historic occasion of Platt's admission to the bar, announced at her swearing in that "we have done to-day what we never did before—admitted a colored woman to the bar; and it may now be truly said that persons are admitted to the Illinois bar without regard to race, sex or color."[131] Platt entered the law office of Joseph W. Errant, a "well known lawyer and member of the [Chicago] Board of Education."[132] Whether Platt actually practiced law or continued in her profession as a stenographer remains uncertain; however, she was listed as a lawyer in *Black's Blue Book* in 1921, which is some evidence that she indeed may have practiced.[133]

In 1920 Violette Neatly Anderson graduated from Chicago Law School and became the first black woman to be admitted to the bar by examination of the state board of examiners.[134] She was reportedly one of "the first . . . women [to engage] in active practice" of law in Illinois.[135] Prior to her admission to the bar, Anderson operated a court reporting agency. It was through this avenue that she became interested in the law. One of the first murder cases successfully defended by a black woman in the nation was handled in Chicago by Anderson in 1922. The defendant was charged "with killing her common-law husband [claiming] self-defense."[136] Anderson's victory in this case brought much praise for her skill and determination, especially since great pressure had been exerted on her "to allow her client to plead guilty."[137] Conducting the "entire case alone," Anderson said that she preferred "to trust [her] 'woman's intuition' rather than man's skill in the breaking down of the apparently impassable wall of evidence against her client."[138]

Soon after Anderson won her first murder case, she became the first black woman in Illinois appointed to the position of assistant prosecuting attorney in Chicago. It was during Anderson's service in the prosecutor's office that she became the first black woman lawyer admitted to practice in the United States District Court, Eastern Division of Illinois. In 1923 Anderson was the only black woman lawyer listed in *Simms's Blue Book*, among the eighty-one black lawyers in Chicago.[139] In 1926 Anderson broke another record: she became the first black woman lawyer in the history of the nation to be admitted to the United States Supreme Court, an achievement that received wide coverage by the press.[140]

In 1925 Georgia Huston Jones Ellis graduated from John Marshall's law school and was admitted to the Illinois bar. While she attended the evening division of the law school, Ellis worked in the Recorder's Office in Chicago. After being admitted to the bar, Ellis became "an attaché of the domestic relations branch of the municipal court." She was the "first black woman of her race to hold a quasi-judicial position in the courts of Chicago."[141] During her service as attaché, "only one of her decisions was reversed by a judge."[142] Ellis's fame as a lawyer soon reached beyond the borders of Illinois.[143] In 1941 she followed Violette Anderson's precedent, and was admitted to practice before the United States Supreme Court.[144]

In the early 1940s, Ellis was one of two women associated with Richard E. Westbrooks's law firm in Chicago. Westbrooks, a 1911 graduate of John Marshall's law school, operated one of the few law firms in Chicago that hired women lawyers. Westbrooks's practice was diverse. He served as consul at Chicago for the Republic of Liberia, a position he held for twenty years. It is likely therefore that Ellis also handled matters for the Liberian government.[145]

In 1942 Lucia Theodosia Thomas, a 1940 graduate of the Robert H. Terrell Law School in Washington, D.C., also joined Westbrooks's firm. Thomas had no difficulty finding work at the firm. Westbrooks was a friend of her mother, and he was eager to help her.[146] It was Westbrooks who "encouraged [Thomas] to enroll in the graduate law evening program at John Marshall School of Law, while working in his firm during the day."[147] According to Thomas, "I knew Mr. Westbrooks did not discriminate against women lawyers before I joined the firm because both Georgia Jones Ellis and Barbara [Watts] Goodall were associated with his firm."[148] Thomas completed her first master of laws degree in 1942. She received a second master of laws degree in 1943 from the John Marshall Law School, thereby becoming the first black woman to earn two graduate law degrees. Her second graduate law degree was in copyright law, the subject on which she wrote her thesis. This was a field in which few women practiced.[149]

Thomas recalls that the performance of black women lawyers in court often brought praise from the judges. For example, she remarked on "Judge Joseph Sabath's embarrassing gallantry when she first [began to practice law]. He stopped the whole prosecution to whisper, 'Young lady, you're acquitting yourself *very well!*' He was heard throughout the whole courtroom."[150]

Edith Sampson, a classmate of Georgia Jones Ellis, was graduated from John Marshall's law school in 1925.[151] Both women were described as "among the most efficient and well trained in the graduating class."[152] However, it was Sampson who graduated first in a class of ninety-five students and received a special commendation from Dean Edward T. Lee.[153] Sampson attended law school in the evenings and worked at the YMCA and the Illinois Children's Home and Society during the day.[154]

After Sampson left John Marshall's law school, she worked as a probation officer in the juvenile court system in Chicago and assisted her husband, Joseph E. Clayton, Jr., in his law practice.[155] She soon enrolled in the graduate law program at Loyola Law School in Chicago. In 1927 she became the first black woman to receive a master of laws degree from Loyola and perhaps the first black woman to receive a graduate law degree from a white American law school.[156] She was also admitted to the Illinois bar in 1927. In 1930 Sampson was appointed attaché of the juvenile court in Chicago, where she adjudicated minor civil claims until 1940. In that year, she was appointed "special commissioner . . . by [Cook County Circuit] Judge Frank H. Bicek, [who] stepped forward to champion the cause of qualified Race women in Chicago."[157] This quasi-judicial appointment made Sampson the first black woman to be appointed commissioner in the court system in Chicago.

Sophie Boaz and Alice E. A. Huggins were admitted to the bar in 1925 and 1926, respectively.[158] In 1944 five black women lawyers were actively practicing law in Illinois: Georgia Jones Ellis, Barbara Watts Goodall, Alice E. A. Huggins, Mabel H. Johnson, and Edith S. Sampson.[159]

Indiana

After the Civil War ended, blacks in Northern states such as Indiana were "so accustomed to entrusting [their] meager legal business to men of the dominant race . . . that [they] hesitated to employ a Negro lawyer."[160] The dearth of blacks in Indiana, and the impression that law was a profession for white men only, may have inhibited blacks from entering the legal profession in Indiana. In the 1860s there "were so few Negroes in Indiana . . . that the well-trained Negro lawyer with ambition to win high elective state and national offices did not as a rule remain [there]."[161] Hiram Rhodes Revels, an "ambitious and well-trained [lawyer], left Indiana for the South," but it is unclear when he was admitted to the bar.[162] Nevertheless, by 1880 black lawyers had become a part of the professional class in the state.

James T. V. Hill was admitted to the circuit court of Marion County on January 22, 1879.[163] Hill was apparently admitted to the bar prior to the completion of his legal training at Central Law School (Indianapolis), from which he graduated in 1882.[164] From available accounts of Hill's life, it is apparent that he was a successful and respected member of the Indiana bar who served four years as "a deputy prosecuting attorney of Marion County" in the 1890s.[165] He was the second black appointed to a Marion County grand jury in 1890.[166] The respect accorded Hill by black lawyers outside Indiana is evident in the praise conferred on him during a memorial service conducted by the National Bar Association in 1928.[167]

Charles Henry James Taylor, who is reported to have attended the law department of the University of Michigan "for a while," was admitted to the Indiana bar at about the same time as James T. V. Hill. He may even have preceded Hill's admission by a year.[168] Other evidence indicates that Taylor was admitted to the Marion County circuit court on March 18, 1882.[169] Prior to relocating to Kansas, Taylor served as deputy district attorney of the Nineteenth Judicial District of Indiana.[170]

Hill and Taylor were followed to the bar by other black lawyers. Silas Robbins studied law and "was admitted to the county bar in 1885 and the Indiana Supreme Court . . . in 1888," before relocating to Omaha, Nebraska, in about 1889, to practice law.[171] In 1894 Isador Darius Blair, an 1893 University of Michigan law graduate, opened a law office in Indianapolis, as did Octavius Royall and James H. Lott.[172] Blair practiced in Indianapolis for several years and was admitted to practice before the Indiana Supreme Court on November 25, 1902. He later relocated to Los Angeles, California.[173] Royall practiced law in Indianapolis from 1894 to 1903. Lott had migrated in 1890 from Chicago to Indianapolis, where he opened a law practice and was admitted to the local court. He was admitted to the Indiana Supreme Court on June 28, 1901.[174]

During the same period, Alexander E. Manning and John T. V. Hill were described as two of the lawyers "stamping ground" in the local court in Indianapolis. Robert Bagby was also a force in the state. Though Manning and Bagby were both engaged in private practice, "the law was merely [their] part-time occupation."[175] In 1890 Manning was reportedly "the only colored man holding a commission as a notary public."[176] James Buchanan Rush was admitted to the Marion County bar on February 14, 1891; he practiced there until 1894, when he relocated to Des Moines, Iowa, to practice law.[177]

The climate in Indiana for law as practiced by blacks was apparently not inviting. This is especially evident in the number of black lawyers who left the state after a short time.[178] By the close of the nineteenth century, fewer than ten black lawyers remained in Indianapolis. During this early period most of the black lawyers in the state had settled in Indianapolis, though a few did manage to maintain law practices in other cities with black populations. One lawyer, Jeremiah H. Scott, an 1875 Howard University law graduate, practiced law in Evansville, Indiana, and became "the first Negro in the state to try a case before a federal court in 1892,"[179] four years after he was admitted to the Indiana Supreme Court.[180] When George Washington Bryant Conrad was graduated from the University of Michigan's law school in 1902, he settled in Richmond, Indiana, where he worked with the claims department of the railroad system.[181]

The new century brought Frank Williams, a 1906 Howard University law graduate, to Indianapolis. In 1910, he became one of the first black lawyers to run for justice of the peace.[182] In the same year, two other black lawyers from Indianapolis, Freeman Bailey Ransom and Robert Lee Brokenburr, who were struggling to maintain a law practice, agreed to provide free legal advice to Madame C. J. Walker, the founder of a beauty supply company for black women. Madame Walker later became the nation's first black female millionaire with the assistance of Ransom, who gave up his practice to serve as general manager of the C. J. Walker Manufacturing Company until his death in 1947.

In 1908 Ransom graduated from Walden University's law department in Tennessee. He associated with John Browder, a 1909 Howard University law graduate. The two practiced together until 1911, the year Browder was appointed deputy prosecuting attorney of Marion County.[183] Thereafter, Ransom practiced alone, representing the Colored YMCA and Dr. E. N. Perkin's Cream Float Soap Manufacturing Co., until he joined Madame C. J. Walker's company.[184] In 1939, Ransom was elected as a member of the Indianapolis city council.[185]

Robert Brokenburr graduated from Howard University's law school in 1909. He started a general law practice and handled a number of civil rights matters. Brokenburr divided his time between his law practice and an assistant managerial position at the C. J. Walker Company. He helped to establish markets for Walker's products in Panama, Cuba, and the West Indies,[186] and eventually became chairman of the board of the company.[187] During World War I, Brokenburr served as assistant food administrator in Indiana.[188]

In 1920, Brokenburr successfully challenged Indianapolis's segregation ordinances and won a case against whites who had sued his client for damages because "colored persons purchased . . . property next to them."[189] In that year, Brokenburr was appointed Marion County's deputy prosecuting attorney specializing in bond forfeiture, a post he held for eleven years. While serving as prosecutor, Brokenburr won respect in the community. He was appointed judge pro tem in Marion County by Judge Louis B. Eubank—a first for a black lawyer in the state.[190] In 1940 Brokenburr was elected to the Indiana State Senate, where he served until 1947. During his terms, Brokenburr was the ranking member on several committees, and he chaired the Commission on Election Rights and Privileges in 1941 and 1943.[191]

Indiana was like many Southern states when it came to cases that involved allegations of rape of white women by black men. The defendants' families had to find black lawyers to defend them. In 1920 Joseph Kent Brown, a 1906 Howard University law graduate, defended a black man charged with raping a white woman. Brown's client was convicted and given the death penalty, but Brown, unyielding in his belief that his client was innocent, won a retrial. His client was ultimately acquitted.[192]

Robert Lieutenant Bailey graduated from the University of Indiana Law School at Indianapolis in 1912. Bailey entered private practice and quickly won the respect of the bar when he published a pamphlet entitled "The Vexing Question as to What Constitutes an Accident Within the Terms of an Accident Policy."[193] Bailey handled several civil rights cases in Indiana while serving as local counsel to the NAACP. He was one of the first blacks admitted to the Indianapolis Bar Association. In 1937 Russell Wilson, the president of the Indianapolis Bar Association, announced Bailey's appointment to its Special Legislative Committee.[194] From time to time, Bailey served as a special judge on the Marion County court. He teamed up with Robert L. Brokenburr to win reversals in several criminal matters before the Indiana Supreme Court.[195]

In the 1920s and 1930s, black lawyers were highly visible in Indiana. They practiced in five cities in the state: Gary, Michigan City, Richmond, South Bend, and Indianapolis.[196] As a result of their visibility and effectiveness, a modest demand for black lawyers had begun to grow outside this area as well. For example, in 1917 Clarence Howard Thurston appeared in the local courts of Kokomo, Indiana, representing a defendant charged with assault and battery.[197]

Still, attempts by black lawyers to practice in other parts of Indiana were resisted by the white bar. In 1920 the Evansville Bar Association filed a court action to block a black lawyer, Ernest G. Tidrington, from becoming a member. The action would have precluded him from practicing law in Vanderburgh County.[198] The association claimed that he was a person of unsavory character, a claim that was eventually rejected by Judge Robert Tracewell.[199] Tidrington's fight to practice his profession in southern Indiana and the judge's refusal to give in to local pressure were noted by the *Chicago Defender*: "The fight waged by Attorney Tidrington in contending for representation in the association was a decisive victory for our Race in [Indiana] in that it crumbled all color barriers and destroyed all attempts on the part of white lawyers to force themselves into important cases gained by lawyers of our Race."[200] Tidrington "was sworn in as a member of the bar a few days after the verdict."[201] In contrast to the difficulty Tidrington faced in southern Indiana, Arthur Alonzo Greene, a 1923 Howard University law graduate, was admitted to the bar in Brazil, Indiana (the seat of Clay County in 1925), in southwestern Indiana, and George W. White was granted permission by Judge James S. Drake to practice in Elkhart County in northern Indiana.[202]

William Carroll Hueston left Kansas City, Kansas, in 1920 and relocated to Gary, Indiana, where he opened a law office. Hueston was interested in the economics of "Negro sports" and helped to organize the National Negro Baseball League. He served as president of the league from 1925 to 1930. Hueston was appointed as Gary, Indiana's first black judge in 1922, and he served in this post until 1930, the year he became assistant solicitor for the United States Post Office Department in Washington, D.C.[203]

In 1921, Peter Boult became "the first colored man" ever appointed deputy prosecuting attorney in that city.[204] In the same year, Cornelius Richardson was appointed special judge in Richmond, Indiana, to try three white men for violating liquor laws.[205] In 1934 Richardson, amid opposition from the white bar, was appointed city prosecutor of Richmond. Richardson's position as vice-chairman of President Calvin Coolidge's Virgin Island Commission may have helped him stem the opposition to his appointment.[206]

Upon being graduated from Indiana University's law school in 1928, Henry J. Richardson, Jr., initiated the fight to integrate the public schools in Indianapolis—a fight he waged until 1948, when the schools finally were integrated.[207] Within three years of receiving his law degree, Richardson was appointed judge pro tem in the Marion County Superior Court.[208] In 1932 Richardson became the first black person since 1900 to be elected to the Indiana General Assembly. While serving in the state assembly, Richardson sponsored legislation that amended the "state constitution so that the state militia, now the Indiana National Guard, could be integrated."[209] He authored welfare legislation and one of the first fair employment practice laws in the nation. This law made employment discrimination on public works projects unlawful.[210]

In 1935 Richardson became the target of the Ku Klux Klan when he introduced a civil rights bill providing for equal public accommodations in Indiana. The Klan issued an opposition resolution identifying Richardson as "a [N]egro [who] has introduced" a bill that would "interfere with the comfortable and convenient enjoyment by white people operating such places as service entertainment."[211] On the day the civil rights bill was debated in the Indiana General Assembly, several thousand people, black and white, converged on the state capitol. This was the first time since 1885 that the legislature had debated a civil rights bill, and tension and expectation filled the air. When the vote was called, the public accommodations bill was defeated by opposition from "rural communities and Southern Indiana."[212]

During this period, other black lawyers were also trying to make advances in Indiana. Mercer Montgomery Mance, a 1934 Harvard University law graduate, joined the criminal defense staff of the public defender's office in Marion County,[213] while Charles H. Wills was elected justice of the peace in Portage Township.[214] In 1938, Elijah L. Johnson, Jr., a 1915 Howard University law graduate, was appointed by George M. Beamer, Indiana's attorney general, as deputy prosecutor in Marion County. He later became deputy attorney general in 1942.[215]

Another black lawyer, Frank B. Ryan served two terms as prosecutor in Lake County, Indiana, in the early 1940s.[216] In 1939 Willard Blystone Ransom, a 1939 Harvard University law graduate and the son of Freeman Bailey Ransom, passed the Indiana bar, becoming one of the first second-generation black lawyers in Indiana. Soon thereafter, Ransom was appointed deputy attorney general of Indiana. He served in the post from 1940 to 1941, when he entered the military. After World War II, Ransom returned to Indianapolis to enter private practice.[217]

In 1940 there were fifty-six black lawyers in Indiana, half of whom were located in Indianapolis.[218] There was only one female lawyer: Helen Elsie Austin. Austin, in 1930 the University of Cincinnati School of Law's first black female graduate, entered into a law partnership with Henry J. Richardson, Jr., who was then serving in the Indiana General Assembly. The partnership lasted for only two years, but it was the first time that a black woman and black man had practiced law together in Indiana. After the firm dissolved, Austin, who was a member of the Ohio bar, returned to that state to practice law.[219]

New York

In 1847 George Boyer Vashon's application for admission to the Allegheny County, Pennsylvania, bar was denied because of his race.[220] He moved to New York shortly thereafter. Vashon, who had studied law in Pennsylvania under Judge Walter Forward,[221] was determined to be admitted to the New York bar. Vashon's application for admission was accepted, and he was orally examined on January 10, 1848, along with twenty other applicants. He passed the examination and was admitted to practice before the First Judicial District of New York City on the same day, becoming New York's first black lawyer.[222]

Vashon opened a law office in Syracuse, New York, where he handled several criminal cases. He soon discovered that the practice of law presented exceptional challenges, even for a light-skinned black man. The difficulty of finding white clients, even in an anti-slavery state like New York, led Vashon's white father, John Vashon, to write,

I made a *woeful* mistake in educating my son a lawyer. . . . I then was simple enough to believe, that if a young man [were] of good natural ability, *well*-educated in the law, and with a good moral character, the Antislavery friend would encourage and put all the business in his hand they could. . . . He is [in] a suffering condition, notwithstanding he is located in the *best* Antislavery district of the State of New York; and some have said it is the best in the country.[223]

By 1854 Vashon's efforts to build a law practice in Syracuse had collapsed. Vashon then turned his attention to newspaper work and other literary endeavors, until July 19, 1869, when he was admitted to practice law in the District of Columbia.[224]

In 1864 Henry W. Johnson, a resident of Canandigua, New York, was admitted to the New York bar. Faced with insurmountable obstacles in his efforts to practice law in New York, Johnson sailed for Liberia, West Africa, to practice his profession. Prior to his departure, Johnson acquired a letter of recommendation from Judge James C. Smith, who described him as follows:

By his own efforts, in spite of the hindrances of poverty and race, he has educated himself and his family, acquiring a respectable knowledge of the law and made himself one of the finest speakers in the State. . . . This testimony is endorsed by Honorable Francis Granger, ex-governor Myron H. Clark, and over twenty members of the bar of Ontario County.[225]

James Campbell Matthews began his study of law in 1864 in the law offices of Eugene Callahan and Jacob I. Wirner of Albany, New York. He completed his law studies at Albany Law School in 1870, the year he was admitted to the New York bar.[226] Matthews's early enrollment in law school probably gives him the distinction of being the first black person to complete a formal legal education in New York. Matthews's first major lawsuit was against the Albany School Board in 1872. He brought suit to desegregate the public schools, a move that was opposed by the Republican members of the school board but favored by the Democrats. Matthews succeeded in obtaining the admission of black children to the public schools, and the question of integration in Albany "was sealed forever."[227] Twelve years later, Matthews was instrumental in persuading the New York city council to adopt a law to protect against the closing of "colored schools," because such action would "[throw] out of employment a large number of educated and cultivated ladies and gentlemen."[228]

Matthews seems to have been successful in building a fairly successful law practice in Albany. In 1884 it was reported that his "clientage is extensive and it is well-known that the colored population of Albany does not afford much profitable litigation," which suggests that most of Matthews's clients were white.[229] It was Matthews's legal skill that sealed his appointment to the post of "judge of the Recorder's Court in . . . Albany."[230]

Matthews was one of only a handful of black Democrats in the nation in the 1880s. In 1886 Matthews's nomination by President Grover Cleveland to replace Frederick Douglass, a Republican, as recorder of deeds of the District of Columbia created quite a controversy, since this would entail the replacement of a black Republican with a black Democrat in a period when the Republicans were in control of Congress.[231] Although Matthews was a Democrat, his nomination for recorder of deeds was opposed by the Jefferson Democratic Association of the District of Columbia, which favored the appointment of a resident of the District of Columbia. His civil rights advocacy for blacks was questioned by Senator Isham G. Harris, a member of the Senate Committee on the District of Columbia. Senator Harris requested that Matthews present his views on "mixed or separate schools for colored andd white children."[232] Matthews's civil rights advocacy, coupled with a smear campaign that claimed he bought votes in local elections in Albany, scuttled his confirmation.[233] On July 31, 1886, the Senate voted on the Matthews nomination with fourteen senators in favor and thirty-eight against; the opposing votes included both Republican senators from New York.[234]

The rejection of President Cleveland's black Democratic nominee for recorder of deeds "caused great excitement among the colored people" across the nation and at the *Washington Bee*, a paper run by Calvin Chase, a black lawyer. Matthews's rejection solely because he was a Democrat prompted black Republicans to denounce the Senate's action. They noted "that in this country any man had a right to think as he pleased [and] that Republicans were not the keepers of the Negro conscience."[235] During the four-month congressional debate over his nomination, Matthews had been performing the duties of the recorder of deeds by interim appointment. President Cleveland, pointing to this service and the new support of local business and black leaders, once again nominated Matthews to the recorder of deeds post on December 21, 1886.[236] On January 26, 1887, the Senate again rejected the nominee by a vote of thirty-one to seventeen.[237] James Monroe Trotter, a black Democrat from Hyde Park, Massachusetts, was subsequently confirmed as recorder of deeds for the District of Columbia.[238] Matthews returned to Albany, where he practiced law for forty-four years; in 1898, the citizens of Albany elected him recorder of deeds.[239]

John Francis Quarles graduated from Howard University's law school in 1872. Admitted to the bar in Georgia, Quarles practiced law for a few months[240] and came to the attention of President Ulysses Grant. In 1872 President Grant appointed Quarles consul to Port Mahon, Spain (the chief city of Minorca, one of the Balearic Islands). Subsequently, President Rutherford B. Hayes transferred Quarles to Malaga, Spain. After Quarles retired from foreign service, he was admitted to the New York bar on May 13, 1880.[241]

Quarles was one of the lawyers who provided advice to Whittley Whitaker, a black West Point cadet charged with self-mutilation by President Rutherford B. Hayes. Quarles's role in Whitaker's defense is undocumented, but may have been overshadowed by the participation of two other prominent members of the defense team—Richard T. Greener, who at the time was dean of Howard University School of Law, and former South Carolina governor Daniel H. Chamberlain, the lead counsel in the Whitaker case. There is no doubt that Greener was among the first black lawyers to become involved in a court-martial conducted under the Code of Military Conduct.[242]

Quarles became very active in the presidential campaign of 1880, opposing the candidacy of James A. Garfield; he favored James G. Blaine. Prior to leaving office in 1881, Secretary of Treasury John Sherman made Quarles a special commissioner. His job was to consult with the United States consul on the Spanish Main.[243]

Between 1882 and 1900, only a few black lawyers were engaged in the active practice of law in New York. Though few in number, they continued to break new ground in the legal profession. In 1882 Samuel Warren Gibson, a graduate of the law department of Union University (Albany Law School), was admitted to the bar in Troy, New York, becoming "the first-known colored lawyer in that part of the state."[244] Gibson's career as a lawyer, however, apparently faltered. He was subsequently listed in the Troy city directory as a bookkeeper and later as a porter.[245]

Albert Morris Thomas, Jr., was admitted to the bar in Buffalo, New York, in 1884. Thomas made his way to Yale University's law school from Tennessee after first studying law under Judge Heiskell of Memphis. He had already been admitted to the Tennessee bar when he entered Yale University in 1883.[246] A year later, when Thomas graduated from law school, he was admitted to the Connecticut bar. He went on to work in Buffalo, New York, where he specialized in tax and title searching with the Abstract Guaranty Company until 1906.[247] He was engaged in private practice on a part-time basis during his employment at the abstract company. His law practice drew both white and black clients.[248] In 1906 Thomas served as special deputy clerk at the municipal court in Buffalo.[249] He died shortly after establishing a law firm in New York City.[250]

Jacob H. Simms was admitted to the New York bar in 1884. He had handled eighty cases by 1885.[251] Charles P. Lee was admitted to the bar in 1886, in Rochester, New York, after studying law under Anson S. McNab. Lee held two positions simultaneously—clerk of the local civil service examining board and librarian at the Powers Block Law Library. Though Lee's practice was limited, it increased steadily over a ten-year period.[252]

In 1886 Thomas McCants Stewart, who later would become one of the most celebrated lawyers in the nation, was admitted to the Supreme Court in General Term in New York. He settled in Brooklyn. Stewart was admitted to the bar on the motion of Algermon S. Sullivan and A. M. Keily. Stewart had already been certified by the South Carolina Supreme Court.[253] Appearing "in several important cases, he became one of the most active black lawyers in New York."[254] In 1889 Stewart represented a contestor in a probate matter. After a long and hotly contested trial, the court wrote an opinion that praised Stewart's legal acumen, though he ultimately lost the case. In what might have been the first time a black lawyer appeared before the Surrogate's Court of New York, the judge wrote,

The masterly argument of counsel for the contestant greatly impressed me. . . . His conduct of this proceeding has been so admirable that I feel it to be my duty to commend him. . . . He is animated by motives resting on perfect good faith in the commencement of the contest, and his methods throughout have been honest . . . and in his person we find complete refutation of the popular notion that the colored race are incapable in all walks of life. . . . The gentleman here referred to . . . may be the subject of these remarks because of his race, and the universal spectacle of a colored man.[255]

In 1890 Stewart gained widespread attention when he represented T. Thomas Fortune, the fiery editor of the *New York Freeman*. Fortune had retained Stewart to sue a saloon proprietor who had refused to serve him because of his race and for ejecting him from the premises by force. Stewart used his closing argument to present his theory on the separate but equal doctrine as it related to public accommodations and social mixing of the races:

The intelligent Afro-American does not bother his head any more about social equality than you do about the man in the moon. What he rightly insists upon, gentlemen, is that he shall enjoy without let or hindrance every public, every civil, and every political right guaranteed him by the Constitution and the law of the land.[256]

Because of T. Thomas Fortune's national reputation, his lawsuit was carefully followed by the national black press. Indeed, even prior to the selection of Stewart as counsel, the Afro-American League, a press group based in New York, had consulted with several prominent black lawyers before settling on Stewart to handle the case.[257] Twelve white jurors returned a verdict in Fortune's favor and assessed damages at $1,016. This was a stunning victory for Stewart, who received praise from all over the nation.

In 1890 Stewart prevailed in another case known as *Robinson v. Farren*. His black client, William H. Robinson, sued a white defendant, Miles H. Farren, for false imprisonment, a civil tort in New York. The defendant was represented by H. M. Goldfogle, a part-time judge of the Fifth Judicial District and partner in the firm of Goldfogle and Cohn. The press reported that the case was fought hard and long. Stewart ultimately won a verdict in the amount of one thousand dollars. The press noted that "the verdict showed that a man's color has nothing to do with litigation, at least in our higher courts, when the case is properly conducted."[258]

In 1891 Stewart became the first black appointed to the Brooklyn Board of Education. During his four-year term, Stewart "was successful in having removed the word 'colored' entirely from the school system, and was instrumental in having colored teachers teach mixed classes of white and colored children."[259] By 1893 Stewart's reputation as an outstanding lawyer had brought more business in criminal defense work to his firm. He was also one of the few black lawyers in New York to appear before and receive recognition from the appellate courts of the state. In 1893 Stewart appealed the murder conviction of a black man to the New York Court of Appeals. Stewart lost the appeal, but the court commended his "courage and zeal" and cited his "professional ability [which was] worthy of commendation."[260]

During President Grover Cleveland's second term, Stewart, a Republican, joined the Democratic Party. Like James Campbell Matthews of Albany, New York, Stewart believed that blacks "should not blindly cling to the Republican Party out of sentiments and misguided loyalty."[261] Denied a political appointment by the Cleveland administration, and sensitive to the public criticism heaped on him for switching parties, Stewart returned to the Republican Party in 1895.[262] In 1898 Stewart had begun to question whether black people like himself would ever be given equal opportunities in America. He moved to Maui, Hawaii, to practice law, just as Hawaii was being annexed by the United States.[263]

Toward the close of the century, other black lawyers were being admitted to the finest law schools. Edward Ulysses Brooks graduated from Cornell's law school in 1892. He received a master of laws degree and was admitted to the New York bar in the following year. He practiced in Elmira, New York, from 1894 to 1901, before abandoning the legal profession for the ministry.[264]

In 1900 Francis Fenard Giles graduated from New York Law School. After being admitted to the bar, he opened a law office in Brooklyn, New York, and was soon elected to the board of directors of the King's County Lawyers Association.[265] Like Giles, Louis A. Lavelle was admitted to the New York bar in 1901. He practiced law in Harlem for over a quarter of a century. In 1925 Lavelle was one of the first serious black candidates to seek election to a judicial post in New York City. He collected 745 signatures to qualify for his campaign for the position of magistrate.[266] His bid was unsuccessful.

In 1901 Wilford H. Smith relocated to New York from Galveston, Texas. He became Booker T. Washington's "eyes and ears" in New York City and in the New England states. So sensitive was the correspondence between Smith and Washington that both men used aliases so that if their mail was intercepted by white Southerners they would not be able to identify the authors.[267] Smith later became a trusted advisor to Marcus Garvey and general counsel to the UNIA before returning to Galveston, Texas, in 1922.[268] In 1904 Charles Ellis Toney graduated from Syracuse University School of Law and opened a law office in Harlem.[269] Toney hired a New York Law School graduate, Stephen Alexander Bennett, to clerk for him from 1908 to 1911. In 1911 Bennett passed the New York bar.[270]

In 1906 Edward Austin Johnson, who had been admitted to the North Carolina bar in 1891, moved to New York. Admitted to the New York bar in 1907, Johnson opened a law office and became active in New York politics. In 1917 Johnson, a Republican, was "elected to the assembly at Albany, New York, [from the Twenty-first District], being the first colored representative ever sent to Albany."[271] Although Johnson served only one two-year term, he was an active and productive legislator. He was able to forge a coalition of influential legislators in order to obtain an amendment to the existing civil rights law. The amendment broadened the law's provisions to include equal accommodations in hotels, restaurants, and theaters for all races and religions. It also contained criminal sanctions and civil liabilities for violators. Johnson was also responsible for the passage of legislation that provided free state employment bureaus to help reduce discrimination in publicly supported hospitals. Thirty thousand dollars was appropriated to fund this law.[272]

After Johnson retired from the general assembly, his political agenda there was carried on by his successors, John Clifford Hawkins, Henri W. Shields, and Pope Barrow Billups, all black lawyers.[273] Hawkins was an astute politician. He was elected to the New York Board of Alderman in 1917, the same year Edward A. Johnson was elected to the general assembly.[274] After Johnson lost his reelection bid in the fall of 1917, Hawkins began to organize a campaign for Johnson's seat, which he captured in the fall of 1918. Hawkins won two successive terms in the general assembly. Because he was appointed as associate counsel to the United States Shipping Board, he did not seek a third term.[275] Shields, a 1909 graduate of Howard University's law school, was elected to the New York State Assembly in 1923, becoming "the first colored man to be elected to the legislature of any state by the Democratic Party."[276] Billups, a 1916 graduate of New York University Law School, was admitted to the New York bar in 1917. He had worked as an elevator operator at nights while in law school. Billups later became counsel for the Longshoremen's Union. He was elected to the New York general assembly in 1925.[277]

In 1908 Cornelius W. McDougal graduated from New York University Law School. Two years later, he was appointed assistant district attorney in New York County by Charles S. Whitman, the district attorney. He held the position until 1915, when he entered private practice.[278] In 1923 McDougal's name was recommended to Marcus Garvey when it became evident that federal authorities were about to indict Garvey for mail fraud. McDougal undertook Garvey's representation but was dismissed as counsel soon after the trial began. McDougal was replaced by a Jewish lawyer, Armin Cohn, because Garvey was "dissatisfied with McDougal's method of defense."[279] Elie Garcia, a codefendant in the Garvey mail fraud case, was represented by Henry Lincoln Johnson, Sr., a black lawyer from Washington, D.C. Johnson's shrewd and eloquent defense resulted in the dismissal of the charges against Garcia, who was the UNIA's auditor general. Garvey was convicted, sentenced to five years' imprisonment, and fined one thousand dollars.[280] In 1924 McDougal became the first black lawyer appointed special deputy attorney general of New York. The appointment, made by Carl Sherman, the New York attorney general, carried an annual salary of six thousand dollars.[281]

Rufus Lewis Milford Hope Perry, an 1891 graduate of New York University Law School, was one of the first black lawyers of King's County, New York, to be appointed assistant district attorney. He was admitted to the New York bar in 1891. In 1912 Perry prosecuted John T. Atkins, a black lawyer, for defrauding black citizens out of their property. Perry obtained a conviction against Atkins, who was sentenced to one year in prison and fined five hundred dollars. Atkins's business had been valued at one million dollars.[282]

In 1915 charges were brought against Perry by the Grievance Committee of the Brooklyn Bar Association. The charges included fraud and deceit in the alleged alteration of Perry's father's deed. Perry was disbarred for six years because of this conduct. The black citizens of Brooklyn in turn accused the bar association of racism.[283] By 1926 Perry had been reinstated and had regained the public's confidence. At a tribute on his behalf, the press reported that Perry had "won a high place in the legal world throughout his twenty years of legal practice."[284] In the mid-1920s, Perry was accepted into the Jewish faith. By 1927 he was writing a Hebrew grammar.[285]

In 1915 an intra-racial dispute erupted in New York over the use of white and Jewish lawyers by black women. The dispute arose from an editorial published in the New York Age which urged "the people of their race" to support "worthy colored lawyer[s]" and instructed "colored women . . . [to] employ a lawyer not because he is white, but because he is competent, be he white or black."[286] The same editorial was critical of black women because they "invariably employ Jewish lawyers and pay them exorbitant fees in preference to their own."[287] One black woman who had been criticized for using Jewish lawyers justified her choice in a letter to the editor with a string of examples, ranging from poor service to black lawyers' love affairs with their clients. In response, the editor sided with black lawyers: "The statements contained in this letter may be true, but they are not sufficient to warrant a wholesale condemnation of the colored lawyers. White lawyers are equally as bad."[288] While the public debate on the use of Jewish lawyers appears to have lasted for only a year, the general criticism of this practice continued to surface. In 1939, for example, Albert C. Gilbert, the president of the Harlem Lawyer's Association, decried the "habit of Negroes . . . employing white lawyers in preference to men of their own race."[289]

The number of black lawyers in New York who represented white corporate clients appears to have been negligible during the first quarter of the twentieth century. Two black lawyers, however, practiced on Wall Street. Charles Berrian attended Columbia University's law school between 1879 and 1880. Although Berrian did not receive a law degree, he passed the New York bar and enjoyed "the cream of the practice . . . in the Wall Street section."[290] D. Macon Webster was also a successful Wall Street lawyer. His expertise as an import-export lawyer attracted "Messrs. Lord and Taylor, Tiffany and Company" and other leading corporate clients to Webster's law firm.[291]

In the early 1920s, black lawyers had begun to diversify their practices, but their main income was still predominantly derived from criminal defense. Clarence M. Maloney, Julian J. Evans, and Robert A. Burrell, all of Buffalo, New York, defended several black men in extradition hearings. The defendants had fled to Buffalo from various Southern states.[292] Other black lawyers joined the government service as prosecutors. In 1927 Thomas Benjamin Dyett, a 1920 graduate of Howard University's law school, was appointed assistant district attorney of New York, and he served in that post for ten years.[293]

On the federal side, James C. Thomas, Jr., was one of the first black lawyers appointed assistant United States attorney in the Southern District of New York. He assumed the post in 1921. Thomas was assigned to defend the authority of the government to limit the number of immigrants seeking to enter the United States.[294] Other black lawyers—Gilchrist Stewart and Robert P. Lattimore among them—represented immigrants seeking to enter the country. In 1924 Gilchrist Stewart, the son of T. McCants Stewart, successfully defended two Italians who were barred from reentering the United States on a technicality.[295] In 1925 Robert P. Lattimore from Westchester County prevailed in an immigration exclusion case before the appeals bureau of the United States Department of Labor. The case involved a West Indian who was at the time of the case already being deported.[296] After leaving his federal post, James C. Thomas, Jr., also built a respectable practice representing immigrants in deportation proceedings.[297] And Thomas's experience as an assistant United States attorney was one of the reasons Augustus N. Hand, a noted United States District judge, appointed Thomas as a receiver for the bankrupt estate of a major New York company.[298]

One of Thomas's most famous clients was Major Baker, known as Father Divine, a popular evangelical minister.[299] Father Divine held open tent services in New York and in major cities in the South.[300] In 1932 Father Divine held services in Sayville, New York, that drew hundreds of black and white worshippers. Driven by racial prejudice—due in part to the fact that whites attended the prayer services—the city of Sayville brought criminal charges against Father Divine, claiming that his religious services amounted to a public nuisance.[301] Thomas was outraged. He believed that the city of Sayville was violating Father Divine's freedom of speech:

To allow an incident of this nature to go unchallenged is to weaken the foundations of democracy in the United States and to single out the Negro group as one not entitled to full enjoyment of every right, privilege and immunity guaranteed by the Constitution. Such a situation is the concern of every Negro man, woman, and child in the United States, for if it is permitted to go unnoticed, who can say but that tomorrow these and other constitutional rights and privileges will not be denied to each of us?[302]

Thomas was able to have Father Divine's trial moved from Sayville to the city of Mineola, in Nassau County, in order to avoid the racial hostility in Sayville. But the situation in Mineola was not much different. There, Thomas appeared before Judge Lewis J. Smith, who was described as "the most implacable racist in the courtroom."[303] Despite Thomas's efforts, Father Divine was convicted, partly because of the biased conduct of the presiding judge.[304] The conviction was reversed by the Appellate Division of the New York Supreme Court.[305]

In 1926 Hubert Thomas Delany graduated from New York University Law School. He taught school for a year before Charles H. Tuttle, the United States attorney for New York, appointed him assistant United States attorney; he held this post until about 1933.[306] In 1929 Delany, apparently on leave from his federal post, waged his first serious campaign for the United States Congress, and the black lawyers of the nation rallied to support him. Political contributions were sent from Chicago, Illinois, by Earl B. Dickerson; from St. Louis, Missouri, by Ambrose A. Page; from Des Moines, Iowa, by Samuel Joe Brown; and from New Orleans, Louisiana, by Alexander P. Tureaud.[307] Delany lost his bid against a white opponent, Joseph A. Gavagan, with some blacks voting against him, but he garnered 26,666 votes of the 70,000 cast.[308]

After Delany left his federal post in 1933, he joined Mintzer, Todarelli, and Kleid, a white law firm. While employed at the firm, Delany also served as the taxes and assessment commissioner for New York City. Delany left the law firm in 1937 to become a solo practitioner. In 1942 Mayor Fiorello H. LaGuardia appointed him to the Domestic Relations Court of New York. On the bench, Delany's advice on juvenile issues was "eagerly sought by many individuals and organizations."[309]

Francis Ellis Rivers graduated from Columbia University's law school in 1922, and was admitted to the New York bar in 1923. Unlike many of his white classmates, Rivers had difficulty finding a legal job because of his race. Eventually, Rivers was hired by Jonah J. Goldstein, a Jewish lawyer. He remained associated with the firm of Goldstein and Goldstein[310] for two years, before joining the firm of Finkelstein and Welling, where he remained for one year. In 1925 Rivers opened his own office, in space that he rented from N. William Welling.[311]

Rivers's legal skills as a lawyer were immediately hailed by the bar. His exemplary academic record at Yale University, his law degree from Columbia University, and his demonstrated legal acumen made him the ideal choice to break the color bar of the New York State Bar Association (NYSBA), founded in 1876. Rivers's application for membership in the NYSBA was rigorously opposed by some members but publicly endorsed by eight influential association members, including Louis Marshall. Marshall, a respected constitutional lawyer and a member of the national board of the NAACP, and Underhill Moore, a Columbia University law professor, were Rivers's chief sponsors. He was admitted.

In 1929 Rivers was admitted to the Association of the Bar of the City of New York (ABCNY), becoming its first black member since its founding in 1870.[312] The publicity associated with his election to the ABCNY won Rivers even greater respect from black people in New York's Nineteenth District. In 1930 Rivers was elected to the New York general assembly, where he served one term. During his term, Rivers, a Republican, was ultimately responsible for passage of legislation that created a new judicial district for Harlem. Pope Barrow Billups had originally proposed the legislation in 1925.[313] First opposed but later endorsed by Governor Franklin D. Roosevelt, the legislation was eventually passed. It almost assured the historic election of two black lawyers to the bench.[314] Prior to the creation of the new and predominately black Tenth District, the election of black lawyers to the bench in New York had been impossible, even with the endorsement of white groups.

Immediately after the legislation creating the Tenth Judicial District of New York became law, James Samuel Watson and Charles Ellis Toney, both Democrats, were elected to the municipal court. Watson graduated from New York Law School in 1913 and had managed the law firm of House, Grossman, and Vorhaus in 1914.[315] Toney, a 1904 law graduate of Syracuse University, had gained the public's confidence as a private practitioner for twenty-five years.[316] By 1940 the legislative initiatives of Billups and Rivers had paved the way for the election and appointment of two other black judges in the Tenth Judicial District: Myles A. Paige and Jane Matilda Bolin.[317]

Rivers was appointed assistant district attorney for New York County in 1938. He served in that post until 1943, when Governor Thomas Dewey appointed him to fill an unexpired term in the "old New York [municipal] court."[318] He was subsequently elected to a full ten-year term in that court, becoming the first black lawyer elected to the municipal court outside of the Tenth District in Harlem.[319]

Francis E. Rivers's acceptability to the white legal community was not unique to him. During the 1920s in New York the academic credentials of black lawyers were uniformly impressive. In the black law firm of Dyett, Hall, and Patterson, Thomas B. Dyett had a master of laws degree from Boston University, William L. Patterson was a law graduate of the University of California, and Thomas C. Hall was completing the requirement for the Doctor of Juridical Science degree at New York Law School.[320] In 1924 the talent of this firm was retained by the Harlem branch of the Chelsa Exchange Bank to recover money that had been fraudulently taken from the bank. These lawyers became the "only Negroes in charge of the legal affairs of any white banking institution in the country."[321] During the same period, Oliver D. Williams opened a law firm on Wall Street.[322]

After Stanley Moreland Douglas graduated from Fordham University's law school in 1923, he settled in Brooklyn, New York, and became active in the Brooklyn branch of the NAACP. Douglas, however, did not limit his civil rights activities to Brooklyn. He and Perry Wilson Howard, a prominent black lawyer in Washington, D.C., used their influence to raise sizable sums of money for the NAACP.[323] In the next five years, black lawyers such as Douglas and Charles H. Houston of the NAACP raised questions as to why the public defender's office had hired no black lawyers.[324]

Horace I. Gordon, who practiced in Harlem, also complained about discriminatory treatment by local white judges, who refused to appoint black lawyers to represent indigent black defendants. In 1936 Gordon wrote that

the Negro lawyer has viewed with serious apprehension the practice which has grown up in certain quarters of assigning white attorneys to defend Negroes who are without aid of counsel and who request that counsel be assigned for the defense. Many times there are five or more experienced, able and capable Negro attorneys present . . . and not one of them is asked . . . to appear on behalf of the Negro defendant. . . . No Negro attorney is ever asked to defend a white defendant.[325]

Perhaps because of the growing agitation by the NAACP and the black bar, Mayor Fiorello H. LaGuardia finally made a black appointment. He appointed Columbia University law graduate Myles A. Paige to New York City's magistrate court in 1936.[326]

Even with the Paige appointment, it was not until 1940 that a black lawyer was "assigned to help defend a white man accused of murder." The appointment of Vernon Williams by General Sessions Judge Jonah J. Goldstein was "important news to the one hundred colored lawyers in

Harlem."[327] Francis E. Rivers, then assistant district attorney in New York, saw the appointment of Williams as breaking the ice for the black lawyer.[328]

Some whites also aided the cause of black lawyers. A few liberal, white law professors at various law schools in New York tutored blacks for the bar examination. In 1938 Jawn A. Sandifer, a graduate of Howard University's law school, studied for the New York bar examination under the tutelage of professors Harold Medina, of Columbia University, and A. L. Sainer, of New York University.[329] In 1942 Sandifer became the first black to join the Phillip Morris Company as a sales representative.[330]

As 1944 approached, Thomas C. Hall won appointment as assistant attorney in the office of the New York solicitor general, replacing Ralph E. Mizelle (who was also black),[331] and Benjamin Jefferson Davis, Jr., was elected to the New York City council under a Communist banner.[332] In the same year, Thomas E. Dewey became the first governor to appoint three black lawyers to the staff of the attorney general. As Lamar Perkins, Stanley M. Douglas, and Conrad A. Johnson assumed their posts in the attorney general's office, a new day dawned for black lawyers in New York.[333]

On June 7, 1922, Anna Jones Robinson and Enid Foderingham Thorpe became the first black women to graduate from the New York University Law School. In 1923 Robinson became the first black woman admitted to the New York bar. It is reported that "she [planned] to open an office in Harlem" with H. Eustice Williams, also black.[334] Robinson was followed to the bar by Ruth Whitehead Whaley, who had been encouraged by her husband to attend law school. Whaley was the first black woman to enter Fordham University's law school. However, she apparently faced difficulties at the school, owing to what the black press called "alleged race prejudice." Nevertheless, Whaley was graduated from Fordham in 1925. She passed the New York bar and entered the private practice of law in the same year.[335] Commenting on her intention to practice law, she stated, "I felt that I was going to practice law, and looked for no obstacles; maybe it was my naive attitude that helped me through the first years. I got a case the first day after I had settled in my office. The case was settled out of court. And it has gone on from there."[336]

In 1928 Whaley was the only active practicing female lawyer in New York. Whaley made headlines when she filed suit against a steamship company for violating the New York civil rights law. She alleged that the ship had confined her and her husband to the segregated section of the ship.[337] After her law school experiences at Fordham University, Whaley knew that men did not perceive the law as a profession for women. In fact, she said, "the attitude of the man toward a woman lawyer is generally skeptical . . . until they are convinced of her ability and integrity, [but] women generally prefer a man's . . . handling of legal matters . . . due . . . to custom."[338] Whaley said that the woman lawyer had "to be careful of her actions," lest "men get the notion that because she has more freedom than the woman who makes her name her career, she is just as free in her morals."[339] Whaley surely had more difficulty establishing a law practice, precisely for the reasons she gave. Women lack "the contacts that a man acquires easily [and they lack] the avenues for making these contacts that men enjoy."[340]

Whaley's status as a woman lawyer was of interest to the press, especially when she was retained by men to represent them in criminal matters. She was often mistaken for the client, until local judges got used to seeing a black woman appear before them.[341] She later made a name for herself representing black city and state government employees in administrative discharge proceedings.[342] In about 1944, Ruth Whitehead Whaley left private practice after being appointed to the powerful New York City Board of Estimates. When Whaley assumed this post, she transferred her cases to Pauli Murray, another black woman lawyer.[343]

Florence Lucas, also a black woman, found it difficult to participate in the Queens County Women's Bar Association because it met in restaurants that barred blacks.[344] The same sort of discrimination probably was experienced by Clara Burrill Bruce, the first black to be elected editor-in-chief of the *Boston University Law Review* and of any other law review in the nation.[345]

After graduating from New York University School of Law in the 1920s, Lucille Edwards Rohlehr Chance was admitted to the New York bar, and she formed the firm of Chance and Gray.[346]

One of the most well-known women lawyers in New York during the 1930s was Jane Matilda Bolin, the first black woman to graduate from Yale University Law School (1931). She was also a second-generation lawyer. Both her father, Gaines C. Bolin, Sr., who was admitted to the New York bar in about 1897, and her brother, Gaines C. Bolin, Jr., practiced law in Poughkeepsie, New York.[347] In 1937, Jane Bolin became "the first Negro woman lawyer" in the Corporation Counsel's Office in New York City.[348] After her appointment to this post, Bolin remarked,

My main interest has always been the uplift of our race. Since I conceive the bases of the Negro's plight to be purely economic, I have been particularly interested in propagandizing and educating white people to give Negroes jobs without discrimination . . . on the theory that as soon as Negroes are given equal economic opportunity, they will no longer have to live in slums; their health will improve; and the ratio of crime and juvenile delinquency . . . will greatly decrease.[349]

Bolin married Ralph Mizelle, a lawyer, but she did not change her name throughout her professional career. Apparently, both lawyers had full and productive careers. Bolin was elected vice-president of the Harlem Lawyers' Association in the mid-1930s, shortly before Mayor LaGuardia appointed her to the Domestic Relations Court on July 22, 1939. This appointment made Bolin, at age thirty-one, the first woman of her race in the nation's history to be appointed to a judicial post. Four years later, Judge Bolin also became the first black woman elected to membership in the Association of the Bar of the City of New York.[350]

Eunice Hunton Carter studied law at Fordham University's law school while "a housewife and . . . the mother of a young son."[351] After she received her law degree in 1932, she entered private practice and represented women criminally charged for prostitution before the Women's Day Court of New York. These experiences taught Carter a great deal about the criminal racketeers of New York. She was thus a natural candidate for the anti-racketeering legal team assembled in 1935 by New York's district attorney, Thomas E. Dewey. Dewey's appointment of Carter to assistant district attorney made her the "first colored woman" in New York to be appointed to this post. Because of this honor and others, Smith College, Carter's alma mater, awarded her an honorary degree in 1938. And with an annual salary of $5,500 a year, Carter had become one of the highest paid black lawyers in the nation.[352]

As one of twenty lawyers in Dewey's anti-racketeering unit, Carter was given wide-ranging authority in criminal matters in Harlem. She supervised a staff of white lawyers. She became so good in uncovering crime in New York City that she became known as "a woman on the scent."[353] Her prior experience defending prostitutes in the local courts of New York made her the first to recognize that there was "a racket in prostitution," a fact that had eluded Dewey.[354] By careful investigation and through the use of wire-taps, Carter's theory prevailed: busting prostitution eventually revealed the big-time racketeers.

In 1937 Sarah Pelham Speaks was admitted to the bar and entered the practice of law specializing in criminal matters. Pelham practiced in Manhattan, Brooklyn, and Queens, and there discovered how the criminal justice system mistreated blacks. She openly criticized discrimination in the courts. She was principally responsible for getting the Harlem Lawyers Association to take a stand on the mistreatment of blacks on the New York criminal justice system.[355]

It appeared that, as Ruth Whitehead Whaley said in 1931, "the future of the woman lawyer [was] . . . [as] bright as that of the man,"[356] especially in New York City at the close of 1944.

Ohio

The history of the black lawyer in Ohio begins with John Mercer Langston. In 1849, after completing his studies at Oberlin College, Langston became the first known black to apply to an American law school.[357] However, his applications—to a New York law school and the University of Cincinnati Law School—were both rejected in 1850 because he was black.[358] Convinced that the legal profession was closed to him, Langston entered Oberlin's school of theology, from which he graduated in 1853. But Langston's interest in the law did not end. In 1853, he applied to study law privately under Philemon Bliss in the city of Elyria (Lorain County), Ohio.[359] Bliss, an ardent opponent of slavery, agreed to tutor Langston, who had gained an excellent reputation at Oberlin. Langston's course of study under Bliss was personalized—and exacting. Bliss was careful to inform Langston that the bar examination would be "vexatious," advice that Langston heeded.[360]

After completing his studies, Langston received a certificate from Bliss that attested to his "character and attainments in the law, and [which] moved the court to appoint a special committee to examine him for admission to practice as an attorney and counsellor at law and solicitor in chancery."[361] On September 13, 1854, the District Court of Ohio appointed three members of the bar to examine Langston, none of whom immediately favored the admission of a black man to the bar. The first question posed to Langston was, "What is law?" Langston drew upon the knowledge he had gained from reading *Kent* and *Blackstone* to answer this query and a battery of other questions on a wide range of legal issues. Langston's performance turned a doubting committee into one that made a favorable recommendation to the court.[362]

September 13, 1854, was the day that the motion on Langston's admission to the bar was made, and the courtroom was filled to capacity. Langston's fate was in the hands of five judges; among them were Democrats who raised the issue of whether a man of color was qualified to be admitted to the Ohio bar. The report of the examining committee had been careful not to identify Langston's race. Langston was a fair-skinned man whose father was a white Virginian and whose mother was part Native American and part black.[363] The court assumed that Langston had qualified for admission on the basis of his light skin, taking no account of his mother's mixed heritage. After several hours of discussion and deliberation by the judges, John Mercer Langston was admitted to the Ohio bar.[364]

It was the opinion of the court that Langston's admission to the bar was merely symbolic, and Langston himself doubted that he would actually practice law. However, within ten days of his admission, Hamilton Perry, a white lawyer, requested his assistance in a case involving title to real property. The case was to be tried in Brownhelm Township.[365] When this matter came to trial, so many people were in attendance that the court had to be moved to another location to accommodate the crowd. Perry, deferring to Langston's skill, allowed him to handle most of the six-hour trial, including the closing argument. The jury returned a verdict in favor of Perry and Langston's client, marking one of the first cases in the history of American law that involved a black lawyer.[366]

Following Langston's impressive showing, his legal business, made up mostly of white Democrats, grew in numbers.[367] Langston was also retained by white clients in other Ohio counties, but he was not received with the same respect in these counties as in Lorain County. Indeed, in other counties, Langston received "threatening looks . . . and mincing words" when he appeared to represent a client. A citizen of Huron County remarked that "the community had reached a pitiable condition when a *nigger* lawyer goes in pompous manner about the town."[368]

By 1855 Langston's association with Ohio's Liberty Party had won him respect in Brownhelm Township. In the same year, Langston was elected town clerk of Brownhelm, becoming "the first colored man ever nominated in the United States to an office, and who was elected on a popular vote."[369] The election of Langston enhanced both his law practice and his public standing. He became the *ex-officio* attorney of the township.[370] This election gave Langston immediate national stature among Abolitionists. Soon Langston was invited to address the American Anti-Slavery Society, where he met prominent Abolitionists William Lloyd Garrison, Wendell Phillips, and John G. Whittier.

Langston moved to Ohio's Russia Township, where he was elected clerk and attorney and designated secretary of the Board of Education. Langston demonstrated such proficiency in local government that he was elected to the city council of Oberlin, Ohio, in 1857. Three years later, Langston was elected to Oberlin's Board of Education. He held his position there for several years.[371]

Langston's law practice flourished in Oberlin. William Wells Brown, a noted black historian, gave a rare glimpse of a trial in which Langston participated in 1857:

Being at Oberlin a few years since and learning that suit was to be tried in which Langston was counsel for the defence, I attended. Two white lawyers—one from Elyria, the other residing at Oberlin—were for the plaintiff. One day was consumed in the examination and cross-questioning of witnesses, in which the colored lawyer showed himself more than a match for his antagonists. The plaintiff's counsel moved an adjournment to the next day. The following morning the court room was full before the arrival of the presiding justice and much interest was manifested on both sides. Langston's oratory was a model for the students at the college and all who could leave their studies or recitations were present. . . . In vigor of thought, in imagery of style, in logical connection, in vehemence, in depth, in point and in beauty of language, Langston surpassed his opponents, won . . . the jury and the audience, and . . . gained the suit.[372]

One of Langston's most celebrated cases involved the defense of Mary Edmonia Lewis, who was arrested for the attempted murder of two of her Oberlin College classmates. In 1862, Lewis, who was of black and Native American extraction, gave two white women "a drink of hot spiced wine" minutes before the women went on a joint date with some male companions.[373] Apparently, the wine was mixed with "cantharides, the aphrodisiac popularly known as Spanish Fly."[374] Hours later, both women became seriously ill and were rushed home by their companions. Rumors soon spread that the women had been poisoned by Lewis.

John Mercer Langston was retained to represent Lewis. Because the women may have known they were drinking more than wine, it was a difficult case to investigate. And further, the times did not invite public attention to the sex lives of young women, especially young white women. Langston's investigation of the case took him to the city of Birmingham, Ohio, where one of the critically ill women lived. As Langston was interviewing an attending doctor, the father of one of the women fired his rifle at Langston, but missed hitting him because "a bystander deflected the gun barrel upward."[375]

During the preliminary hearing on the Lewis case, Langston appeared before a panel composed of two justices of the peace.[376] Since no direct evidence was presented to the court to establish that the women had been poisoned, the prosecution's case was weak. At the close of the prosecutor's presentation, Langston shrewdly moved to have the pending case dismissed "on the ground that the *corpus delicti* had not been proved."[377] The case against Lewis was dismissed, but not before racial aspersions were cast on Langston by an Oberlin newspaper.[378]

On January 17, 1867, James Garfield, then a member of Congress from Ohio, moved for Langston's admission to the United States Supreme Court.[379] In the same year, General O. O. Howard appointed Langston general inspector of schools under the Freedman's Bureau, a position that he continued to hold even after he became Howard University's first law dean in 1868.[380]

In 1868 John Patterson Green began to read law in the offices of Judge Jesse P. Bishop and Seymour F. Adams. Green graduated from the Ohio Union Law School of Cleveland in 1870, after one year of formal law study, and was admitted to the bar on September 20, 1870.[381] Green soon left Cleveland and traveled to South Carolina, where he was admitted to the bar in 1871. After two years of practice there, Green returned to Cleveland and opened a law office.[382]

In 1873 Green was "elected a justice of the peace for Cuyahoga County by a majority of 3000 votes," and he served in that position for three consecutive terms, deciding more than twelve thousand cases.[383] Green's election made him the first black judicial officer in the state of Ohio and one of the first blacks to hold a judicial post in the North.[384]

In 1882 Green was elected to the Ohio General Assembly, where he served until 1884. Green served on the Corporations and Library Committees and was an active member of the assembly. Green was reelected to the Ohio General Assembly in 1890. It was during this term that Green sponsored the "Labor Day" law, which recognized the contributions made by working people in Ohio. Green's Labor Day legislation was one of the first of its kind in the nation; it predated the national Labor Day legislation passed by Congress in 1894. Thus Green has been referred to as the "Father of Labor Day" in Ohio.[385] During his 1890 term in the General Assembly, Green also secured an appropriation of $16,000 to lay the foundation for the industrial department of Wilberforce University.[386]

John P. Green is one of the few black lawyers to practice continuously for a substantial number of years in Cleveland despite being "cut off from social and commercial relations with the class who owns property."[387] Green was a highly successful criminal lawyer, reportedly losing only one of fifty-five murder cases in his sixty-year career.[388] Among his clients were several Irish and German immigrants. Indeed, Green enjoyed the distinction of being the first black lawyer in Ohio to train a white Irishman, George P. Phibbs, in the law. Phibbs later passed the Ohio bar and joined Green's law firm.[389]

In 1897 Green's support for the Republican Party was rewarded when President William McKinley appointed him as "postal stamp agent for the United States," with a salary of $2,200 a year. Green supervised "the printing and distribution of postage stamps for the entire nation."[390] In 1905 he was also appointed to the position of acting superintendent of finance for the United States Post Office Department. Both of John P. Green's sons, William and Theodore, became lawyers. William was admitted to the Ohio bar in 1894, but not much more is known about him.[391] Theodore Bliss Green was graduated from Howard University's law school in 1902; he returned to

Cleveland to practice law and was admitted to practice around 1911. Theodore Green became a member of the Cuyahoga County Bar Association.[392] In 1937, at ninety-two years of age and after sixty-seven years at the bar, John Green received the honor of the mayor of Cleveland, who proclaimed April 4, 1937, to be "John P. Green Day" in the city of Cleveland.[393]

According to one historian, Major Travis was the first black person to pass the Cincinnati bar. It is not known how long Travis remained in Cincinnati.[394] In 1874 William H. Parham graduated from the University of Cincinnati Law School after a career as principal of Gaines High School in Cincinnati. He was the first black graduate of the University of Cincinnati Law School and the first black man to be nominated to the Ohio legislature.[395] From 1896 to 1897, Parham served in the Ohio legislature from Hamilton County, serving one two-year term. Parham served on the Judiciary and Revision committees and was an active member of the legislature.[396]

Until George Washington Williams was admitted to the Ohio bar in 1881, William H. Parham was the only black lawyer in Cincinnati. Williams studied law under Alphonso Taft. At the time of his admission to the Ohio bar, Williams was a member of the Ohio State legislature, to which he had been elected from Hamilton County in 1879. As Ohio's first black legislator, he served on the Library, University and Colleges, and Municipal Corporations committees. He served in the Ohio legislature until 1882.[397] After Williams was admitted to the bar, he served as judge advocate in the Ohio Grand Army of the Republic (GAR), a veterans' organization with chapters in several states. Among his accomplishments in the GAR was the revision of its courts-martial rules. Williams later became one of the first noted historians of the black experience in the America.[398]

Benjamin F. Woodson was admitted to the district court of Jackson County, Ohio, in 1879 by William H. Horton, the clerk of the court. He practiced law in Jackson County for a short period before relocating to Memphis, Tennessee, where he was admitted to the bar.[399]

Charles Waddell Chesnutt, like George Washington Williams, had a diverse career. Chesnutt was so fair-skinned that he had to affirmatively declare his African-American heritage. In 1883 Chesnutt arrived in Cleveland, Ohio, and worked "as a clerk and later as a stenographer for [the Nickel Plate Railroad Company's] legal counsel, Judge Samuel Williamson."[400] While employed in Williamson's firm, Chesnutt studied law and in 1887 passed the Ohio bar "with the highest grade in his group."[401] His practice in Cleveland was of short duration, for Chesnutt shifted his profession from law to the literary realm, becoming one of the most accomplished fiction writers of his time. He sometimes wrote short stories drawing on his legal knowledge.[402] Chesnutt's talent was nationally recognized in 1928, when the NAACP presented the Spingarn Medal to him for his pioneering work as a literary artist.[403]

In 1888 Richard Stewart graduated from the University of Cincinnati Law School. He passed the Ohio bar in the same year and opened a law practice in Youngstown specializing in immigration law. From 1896 to 1900, he served two consecutive terms in the Ohio House of Representatives. Stewart's knowledge of immigration law and his defense of aliens under United States treaties secured him several important clients. He became the first black lawyer in America to represent a foreign consulate. Among his clients were the Royal Italian Consul, the Imperial Russian Consulate, and the Imperial and Royal Consul of Austria-Hungary. In 1914 Stewart won the largest judgment recorded in the United States District Court at Cleveland, against the Carnegie Steel Company. Stewart was a member of both the Ohio State Bar Association and the Mahoning County Bar Association. He was also a member of the Youngstown Law Library Association, and in 1915 he reportedly had the "largest law library in Youngstown."[404]

Abraham L. Dalton, an 1893 graduate of Howard University's law school, and William Arthur Carter, an 1898 law graduate of Howard University, were both admitted to the Cincinnati bar. Dalton was inspired to study law after "being robbed by a white lawyer" who had given him some bad advice in a real estate matter. Carter initiated a "movement [to allow] colored men in Cincinnati to take the firemen's examination."[405] In 1893 John T. Oatheral, a 1893 law graduate of Shaw University's law school, was also admitted to the Ohio bar.[406]

In 1898 Western Reserve University's Frank Thomas Backus Law School graduated Alexander Hamilton Martin, perhaps its first black graduate. Martin had passed the Ohio bar a year before he graduated. He practiced law in Ohio throughout his career. In 1924 Martin was appointed special assistant to the United States attorney general.[407] In 1904 Harrington Simpson also graduated from Western Reserve University's law school. A year later, after being admitted to the Ohio bar, Simpson settled in Akron, Ohio, becoming its first black lawyer.[408]

In 1900 Moses H. Jones became one of the first lawyers to practice in Dayton, Ohio. Jones "gained considerable prominence throughout the state" and served as the state legal advisor for the Knights of Pythias, a national black fraternal group.[409] Prior to his death in 1920, the Ohio State Bar Association invited Jones to serve "as a member of the reception committee for the mid-winter meeting."[410]

In 1901 Sully James was graduated from the University of Michigan's law school, as was George Washington Bryant Conrad, a year later.[411] Both men were admitted to the Ohio bar. James became coun-

sel and secretary to the Independent Chattel and Mortgage Loan
Company. On several occasions, he was appointed by the court to act as
defense counsel in a murder case. James's standing at the bar and in
political circles came to the attention of United States Senator Atlee
Pomerene, who in 1914 endorsed him for the position of recorder of
deeds for the District of Columbia. However, the appointment was
never made.[412] Conrad was hired as an assistant in the bureau of claims
of a railroad company's law department. He represented the company
"a number of times in court."[413]

For several years, Robert B. Barcus and Wilbur E. King were active
practitioners in Columbus, Ohio. Barcus, a 1904 graduate of Howard
University's law school, was admitted to the Ohio bar in 1905. He then
opened a law office in Columbus and served as counsel to the Ohio
Lodge of the Knights of Pythias. He was admitted to the Franklin
County Bar Association and to the Ohio State Bar Association, and he
practiced in the local courts in Columbus. Barcus was admitted to
practice in the United States District Court in 1913. Barcus's skills no
doubt led to his appointment in 1919 to the office of special counsel
under John G. Price, the attorney general of Ohio. He was reappointed
to this position in 1923 by Ohio Attorney General Charles C. Crabbe.
Barcus remained special counsel until 1937.[414] Wilbur E. King in 1902
became one of the first black lawyers in Ohio to serve as assistant
prosecutor in Franklin County, a position to which he was successively
appointed for nearly twenty-five years.[415]

Albertus Brown was graduated from Howard University's law school
in 1904. He moved to Lucas County, Ohio, after being admitted to the
bar of the District of Columbia. He was soon admitted to practice in
Ohio, where he became a member of the Lucas County Bar Association. Brown had the distinction of becoming one of the first black
lawyers to join the professional staff of a Republican United States
senator, Charles William Frederick Dick of Ohio. Dick served in the
Senate from 1904 to 1911. Brown handled special pension bills and
administrative inquiries into military records for veterans in Ohio. In
1916, for two days, Brown was appointed to the office of police judge
by the mayor of Toledo, a significant honor for a black lawyer in that
period. Brown also organized the Toledo branch of the NAACP.[416]

In 1905 Albert Lee Beaty was graduated from the University of
Cincinnati's law school. In the same year, Leroy H. Godman received
his degree from Howard University's law school. Beaty made a reputation not only as a lawyer but also as a member of the Ohio General
Assembly, to which he was elected in 1917 and 1919. During his first
term in the legislature, Beaty served on the Civil Service Soldiers' and
Sailors' Orphans' Home Committee. During Beaty's second term, he

served on the Judiciary, Benevolent, and Penal Institutions commit-tees,[417] and led the fight to strengthen Ohio's civil rights laws.[418] After serving in the legislature, Beaty became (by appointment of Haveth Mau, the United States attorney), assistant United States attorney for the Southern District of Ohio—a first for a black lawyer in the state.[419] Leroy H. Godman opened a law practice in Columbus. A superb lawyer, Godman in 1913 was appointed by Timothy S. Hogan, the attorney general of Ohio, as special counsel.[420]

Thomas Edward Greene, Jr., also served as special counsel to the attorney general of Ohio around the same time as Leroy Godman. After Greene was graduated from Western Reserve University's Frank Thomas Backus Law School in 1908, he practiced in Youngstown for a short time. He secured the appointment as special counsel when Edward C. Turner became Ohio's attorney general in 1915.[421] After leaving this position, Green settled in Akron, Ohio, becoming one of "the first Negro attorneys to practice in Summit County."[422] In the late 1930s William T. McNight, a 1927 Yale University law graduate, followed in the footsteps of Barcus, Godman, and Greene, becoming assistant attorney general (formerly called special counsel) of Ohio.[423]

Leroy Godman was among the first black officers trained at Fort Des Moines, Iowa, to serve in World War I.[424] Promoted to captain during the war, Godman defended black servicemen before courts-martial during and after he was discharged from the army. After Godman returned to Columbus, he defended several black officers who were charged with cowardice during the war. Godman discovered, however, that the "colored troops" had been sent into battle against German machine guns without having been trained to use grenades. Retreating under fire, they were "arrested and sent to prison for cowardice."[425] Godman's appeal to the War Department won the "release and exoneration" of the officers.[426] Other black soldiers who were unable "to secure a good colored lawyer . . . were simply condemned as inefficient, and removed, without being given a chance for defense."[427] Unlike Godman, who was a line officer, Major A. E. Patterson served as "the only colored judge advocate in the Army" during World War I. After the war, Patterson settled in Cleveland, and like Godman, he continued to defend soldiers "sentenced to death at Camp Grant."[428]

Thomas Wallace Fleming studied in the evening division of the Cleveland Law School, graduating in 1906. He also passed the bar in 1906. Fleming entered the private practice of law and became involved in Republican politics. He was elected to a two-year term on the Cleveland City Council in 1909—the first black to serve there. During his term, he served as a member of the Finance-Judiciary Commission.[429] Fleming was later reelected to Cleveland's city council in 1917, but he lost political influence when he was suspended from practice for unlawfully accepting money from a private source while in public office. He was jailed for the offense. Fleming was readmitted to the bar in 1934.[430]

A historical event occurred at the United States Supreme Court in October of 1914. William R. Stewart, a black lawyer from Youngstown, Ohio, accompanied Emil J. Anderson, a white lawyer, also from Youngstown, to Washington, D.C., where Anderson was scheduled to argue his first case before the United States Supreme Court. Stewart previously had been admitted to the United States Supreme Court, but Anderson had not. It fell to Stewart to move for Anderson's admission to the court. This was the "first time in the history of the Supreme Court [that] a Negro introduced a white man as qualified to practice before that court."[431] Several Mississippi lawyers who were sponsored for admission to the United States Supreme Court immediately after Anderson's admission were reported to be highly indignant that a black lawyer was responsible for conferring this status on a white man.[432] The press also reported that Stewart's "name will now go down into history as one who had added a remarkable item for the archives of the Supreme Court."[433]

In 1921 Harry E. Davis, a 1908 graduate of Western Reserve University's Frank Thomas Backus Law School, was elected to the Ohio General Assembly. He was reelected by Cleveland voters for three terms. He stepped down in 1926 to become "the first Negro member of the city's Civil Service Commission."[434] In the same year, Chester Karl Gillespie, a 1920 graduate of the law department of Baldwin-Wallace College (Ohio State University Law School) was named assistant law director of the city of Cleveland,[435] while black lawyer Ray Hughes was appointed assistant prosecuting attorney in Columbus, a position that he held for ten years.[436] Gillespie became one of Cleveland's most aggressive black civil rights lawyers. But unlike Harry E. Davis, Gillespie was unsuccessful in his attempts to be elected to the Ohio General Assembly. He built a successful practice and won several cases under Ohio's public accommodations law, which prohibited racial discrimination. In fact, "Gillespie got so many court orders against the Hippodrome that the manager threw up his hands and put a man on the sidewalk to welcome Negroes inside."[437]

One of the best known lawyers in Ohio during the 1920s and 1930s was Perry Brooks Jackson, a 1922 graduate of Western Reserve University's Frank Thomas Backus Law School. Soon after his graduation, Jackson entered private law practice in Cleveland and became a member of the Cleveland Bar Association. In 1928 Jackson was elected to the Ohio General Assembly from Cuyahoga County, serving until 1930, when he was appointed special assistant to Edward C. Turner, the attorney general of Ohio. While in the legislature, Jackson won appropriations for scholarships for one hundred students attending Wilberforce University. During the period he was associated with the Ohio attorney general's office, he headed a firm with John E. Ballard. In 1933 Jackson was appointed to fill an unexpired term on the Cleveland City Council. He then became assistant police prosecutor, by appointment of Mayor Harry L. Davis; he held this position from 1935 to 1940, after which he was named the chief prosecutor.[438]

The need for more black judges was as evident in Cleveland as elsewhere. In 1937 Armond W. Scott, a black municipal judge from Washington, D.C., delivered a speech to this effect before the Cleveland NAACP. He asked, "Why cannot [blacks] secure the representation on a municipal bench to which we are justly entitled?"[439] Scott's speech came at a time when the Harlan Club, a black bar group in Cleveland, was trying to secure the appointment of a black to the bench in Cleveland. Judge Samuel H. Eilbert, a member of the municipal bench, was impressed with Scott's message. While Judge Scott was in town, Eilbert invited him to sit on the bench with him while he conducted a criminal trial. According to press accounts, this "was the first time in the history of Cleveland courts that a Negro judge [had] ever sat on the Bench."[440] Five years later, this symbol became a reality when Governor John W. Bricker appointed Perry B. Jackson to the municipal bench of Ohio.[441]

In 1922 Jesse S. Heslip, a 1923 Harvard University law graduate, was admitted to the Ohio bar. He was followed by Charles W. White, a 1924 Yale University law graduate. Heslip practiced in Toledo, where he became a member of the Toledo Bar Association. He was also a member of the Lucas County and the Ohio State bar associations.[442] Heslip became, by appointment of Ohio Attorney General John W. Bricker, a special counsel from 1936 to 1939. Later, he was the first black professor on the faculty of the University of Toledo School of Law.[443]

In 1931 Theodore Moody Berry was graduated from the University of Cincinnati's law school. He was admitted to the Ohio bar on February 21, 1932. Almost immediately after being admitted to the bar, Berry, who had been a student editor of the law review, was retained to try his first major criminal case. Berry's client, a black man, had confessed to conspiracy to murder a white prison guard in an escape attempt. The defendant had been sentenced to die in the electric chair.[444] Berry appealed the case to the Ohio circuit court of appeals, claiming that his client had been tricked into a plea bargain by his former lawyer, who was white. The defendant had pled guilty because he believed he would be given a life sentence. Based on the facts, the court ordered a new trial to be held in Mansfield, Ohio, where the dead guard had lived;[445] the town was primarily white.

During the trial, Berry "pointed out the flaws in [his client's] confession."[446] Some of the most damaging statements in the confession were not even in his client's handwriting. The case ended with a hung jury. The prosecution hastily prepared to retry the case. As the day of the trial approached, some members in the community became hostile. Berry reported that "there were rumors that I would be run out of town."[447] At the trial Berry "objected to the all-white jury, but to no avail." "I wasn't scared," Berry recalled, "but I was uptight—after all, I was 250 miles away from my home base, Cincinnati."[448] At the close of the week-long trial, Berry won an acquittal.

Berry, a public-spirited man, led Cincinnati's NAACP for several years and established a second law firm in Washington, D.C., with Belford V. Lawson. He also reportedly "dabbled in Cincinnati's politics."[449] In 1939 Berry, supported by the NAACP, brought suit to enjoin the Board of Education of the Wilmington School District from establishing a segregated school district. Although Berry lost the case, he carried an appeal to the Ohio Supreme Court, where, with the aid of Thurgood Marshall, he won.[450] In the early 1940s, Berry was appointed to a position at the Office of Facts and Figures, a department of the War Information Office. He held the post until 1942. Later, he returned to Cincinnati to develop a labor law practice with William A. McClain, another black lawyer.[451]

In 1933 Charles W. White, by appointment of Mayor Harry L. Davis, assumed the post of assistant law director for the city of Cleveland.[452] Norman Leroy McGhee, a 1922 Howard University law graduate, acted as counsel to the Empire Savings and Loan Company, also in Cleveland.[453]

In 1922 Artee Fleming and Samuel Kelly broke ground in lawsuits against the Ku Klux Klan. They restricted the Klan from holding various public meetings within the limits of Summit County, Ohio.[454] In 1942, Fleming became the first black judge appointed to the Court of Common Pleas in Ohio. After Governor John W. Bricker announced Fleming's appointment, the Cuyahoga County Bar Association passed a resolution recommending that Governor Bricker also appoint Perry B. Jackson to the municipal court in Cleveland. The next month Jackson was appointed to this post.[455] As the need for black lawyers in ohio grew, the Works Progress Administration began to include law as a career in its vocational guidance book that was directed at black youths.[456]

In 1919, Daisy D. Perkins became the first black woman admitted to the Ohio bar. Perkins studied law under the supervision of Judge M. B. Earnhart in Columbus, Ohio. After Perkins was admitted to the bar, she joined the prosecutor's office in Columbus, where she won several criminal convictions. She also "built up an extensive practice with clients of both races," and in 1924 she became the first black woman to seek election to the Ohio General Assembly.[457] Perkins fought hard to establish herself in what was, in Ohio, a man's profession. In 1929 she was brought before the Ohio grievance committee on a charge of insubordination or perjury;[458] the charge subsequently was dropped.

In 1926 Jane Hunter passed the Ohio bar exam. Hunter, born an orphan, overcame great odds in order to graduate from the evening division of Cleveland's law school. To make ends meet while she attended school, she worked as a nurse during the day.[459]

In 1930 Helen Elsie Austin graduated from the University of Cincinnati's law school, becoming its first black woman graduate. Austin entered the private practice of law, and her cases drew the immediate attention of the press. In 1933 Austin sued a dancing company for back pay for a female dancer. She was also appointed as special receiver in one case. She uniformly won short sentences when her clients were convicted of crimes.[460] On January 2, 1937, Herbert S. Duffy, the attorney general of Ohio, appointed Austin assistant attorney general of Ohio, making her the first black woman to hold such a position.[461] Austin was highly respected by the black male members of the National Bar Association. In 1938 she addressed the association's annual meeting in a speech that focused on the "anti-Negro propaganda" that she said was "one of the gravest and most fraught-with-danger problems of our day."[462] Apparently, Austin's popularity among local affiliates of the NBA was also high. On May 9, 1940, she was the keynote speaker at the Tenth Annual Banquet of the Washington Bar Association.[463]

At least two other women were admitted to the bar in Ohio before 1944—Eva Crosby, Ohio State University's first female graduate in 1936, who practiced in Oberlin for a short time, and Clara Christopher, who practiced in Cleveland.[464]

Summary

The state of Illinois admitted its first black lawyer, Lloyd G. Wheeler, in 1869. Wheeler and Richard A. Dawson, who was admitted to the bar in 1870, left Illinois for Arkansas during the Reconstruction era, but returned after Reconstruction ended.

In Illinois, the fusion of law and politics for the black lawyer was almost coterminous with his admission to the bar. In 1876 John W. E. Morris, a lawyer, became the first black elected to the Illinois legislature. He served several terms and authored the first civil rights law enacted there. Among members of the black bar, politics became something of a science, due to the leadership of such astute people as Edward H. Morris and John G. Jones, both of Chicago.

Edward H. Morris won the respect of the legal community through his skillful criminal defense work. Morris and Clarence Darrow won an acquittal for Oscar DePriest, who had been charged with taking bribes while serving on the Chicago city council. DePriest later became the first black person in the North to be elected to Congress.

John G. Jones, also a popular lawyer and fraternal figure in Chicago, established, along with Edward Morris, a political blueprint that would see to it that black people played a role in the political affairs of Chicago and the state of Illinois for years to come. The political plan also was beneficial to black lawyers. Black lawyers were appointed to positions in the state's attorneys office, the corporation counsel's office, and the assistant United States attorneys' office in Northern Illinois. Morris's political blueprint ultimately launched the first black candidate for judicial office in 1906, elected several black lawyers to the state legislature, limited the influence of Booker T. Washington in Chicago, and helped to elect the first black judge in the state in 1925.

Although most black lawyers were Republicans, a few, like Richard Hill, Jr., were Democrats. Prior to the election of Franklin D. Roosevelt, however, black Republicans dominated the black political scene.

The legal field drew black lawyers to Chicago from a number of law schools: Kent College of Law (Chicago), Northwestern University, the old and new Universities of Chicago, the Chicago Law School, Loyola University (Chicago), Howard University, George Washington University, Illinois College of Law, Northern Illinois School of Law, John Marshall Law School, Yale University, and Harvard University.

Most of the black lawyers in Illinois practiced in Chicago, but in smaller numbers they dotted the entire state—as far away as Cairo, Illinois, to the south. The law practices of these lawyers were diverse. For example, at one time James H. Lott represented and worked for the Wabash Railroad Company, while Beauregard Fritz Moseley founded and promoted the black National Baseball League. In the 1930s, Earl B. Dickerson, the first black to graduate from the new University of Chicago Law School, trained many black lawyers.

Women lawyers also made dramatic advances in Chicago. Ida G. Platt, the third black woman to receive a formal legal education in the nation, was admitted to the bar in 1894. She entered private practice. Platt was followed to the bar by Violette Neatly Anderson, and more black woman lawyers would follow later. In Chicago, Violette Neatly Anderson won distinction in at least four categories: she was the first woman to try a murder case, to be appointed as a prosecutor, to practice in the United States District Court, and to be admitted to practice before the United States Supreme Court.

The initial entry of the black lawyer in Indiana is difficult to ascertain.

It appears that, during his early preaching career, Hiram R. Revels was admitted to the bar in Indiana. There is far more certainty about James T. V. Hill's legal career. He was admitted to the Indiana bar in 1879.

Many blacks, unlike Hill, left Indiana after being admitted to the bar, because the law was not an inviting profession for blacks in the state. However, between 1879 and 1900 at least six black lawyers were admitted to the bar in Indiana. Some were modestly successful. In 1892 one lawyer, Jeremiah H. Scott, tried the first case by a black lawyer in a federal court.

Most significant progress by black lawyers in Indiana occurred after 1910, when John Browder, Freeman Bailey, and Robert Lee Brokenburr opened law practices in the state. These lawyers and those that followed broke new ground in the law and politics. Freeman B. Ransom and Robert L. Brokenburr represented and became financial advisors to Madame C. J. Walker's multimillion-dollar cosmetics business, which specialized in products for black women. Brokenburr helped establish markets for Madame Walker's products in Panama, Cuba, and the West Indies. Both Ransom and Brokenburr were elected to public office: Ransom, to the Indianapolis city council in 1939, and Brokenburr, to the state senate in 1940.

As in other states, black lawyers like Brokenburr, Robert L. Bailey, and Henry J. Richardson, Jr., brought most of the civil rights litigation to the courts. Brokenburr and Bailey handled civil rights cases for the NAACP, and in 1928 they initiated the first school desegregation cases. As a member of the Indiana state legislature, Richardson also authored anti-discrimination laws in the employment and public accommodations area; these laws were not enacted, however, because of opposition from the Ku Klux Klan.

Law schools represented in Indiana's legal community included the University of Indiana at Indianapolis, Harvard University, Howard University, Central Law School of Indianapolis, Walden University, and the University of Cincinnati. Helen Elsie Austin, a 1930 law graduate of the University of Cincinnati, was the first black woman admitted to practice in the state. Austin and Henry J. Richardson, Jr., opened a law firm in Indianapolis in 1930.

The state of New York admitted its first black lawyer, George Boyer Vashon, in 1848. In 1847 Vashon had been denied admission to the bar in Pennsylvania because he was black, even though his father was a prominent white lawyer in Pennsylvania. Vashon's father recommended that he enter the private practice of law in Syracuse, New York, believing that the Abolitionists in the region would give his son business. But the anti-slavery groups did not support young Vashon's legal enterprise, which led to his decision to pursue literature and teaching.

Henry W. Johnson, perhaps recognizing that a black man could not succeed in the law in New York, left northern New York for Africa in the 1860s. Meanwhile, James Campbell Matthews, the first black graduated from a law school in New York, launched the first school desegregation litigation in Albany, New York, around 1870. Matthews is best remembered for his unsuccessful bid to succeed Frederick Douglass as recorder of deeds of the District of Columbia. In 1886 President Grover Cleveland's nomination of Matthews was twice rejected by the United States Senate.

Other black lawyers of New York were active Democrats between 1886 and 1923. One such lawyer, Henri W. Shields, was the first black Democrat elected to the New York state legislature (1923). He was also the first black Democrat elected to any legislature in the nation. Thomas McCants Stewart was both a Republican and a Democrat at different times in his career. He was one of the most active lawyers in New York in the 1880s. Stewart was often lauded by the courts for his brilliant presentations in both the civil and criminal areas.

The black lawyer broke ground in New York state politics in 1917, the year that Edward Austin Johnson became the first black elected to the state assembly. Under the Republican banner, he was able to broaden the civil rights laws in New York to include an equal public accommodations provision. Ten years after Johnson was elected to the New York State Assembly, Hubert Thomas Delany, also a black lawyer, waged the first serious (albeit unsuccessful) campaign for Congress.

Several law schools were represented in New York between 1870 and 1944, among them Albany Law School, Howard University, Cornell University, Columbia University, Syracuse University, New York Law School, New York University, Brooklyn University, Yale University, Harvard University, and Boston University. Many of the graduates of these law schools were appointed to positions as county and city prosecutors in New York. Some even became assistant United States attorneys.

Black lawyers found it difficult to build private practices in New York. As elsewhere, black people mainly used white lawyers, a practice some black lawyers publicly decried. Yet a few black lawyers had white clients. In 1915, D. Macon Webster broke ground on Wall Street when he was retained by businesses such as Lord and Taylor and Tiffany and Company.

Black women were not admitted to the New York bar until 1922, the year Anna Jones Robinson was graduated from New York University's law school. Robinson, like most of the women that followed her to the bar, entered private practice. She opened a law office with a black male lawyer. Other women, such as Eunice Hunton Carter, Florence Lucas, and Sarah Pelham Speaks, became pioneers in private practice and government. Jane Matilda Bolin broke ground for all women when, in 1939, she became the first black woman judge in American law.

In the state of Ohio, John Mercer Langston was the first black lawyer. He became one of the first black lawyers in the nation to be elected to public office when he assumed the post of town clerk in Brownhelm Township in 1855. Langston was nearly murdered in Birmingham, Ohio, while investigating a case for a black female client.

After John Mercer Langston left Ohio in 1868 to become the first law dean at Howard University, other black lawyers followed him to the Ohio bar. John Patterson Green, admitted to the Ohio bar in 1870, became Ohio's first judicial officer in 1873. Green later followed George Washington Williams to the Ohio state legislature in 1882. He authored the Ohio "Labor Day" legislation, four years before Congress designated Labor Day as a national day of celebration.

Several black lawyers had been admitted to the Ohio bar by the beginning of the twentieth century. They routinely participated in law and politics. Richard Stewart specialized in immigration law while other black lawyers represented Irish and German immigrants in a variety of matters. Some black law firms represented the Knights of Pythias, a nationally affiliated black fraternal group, and a few served as assistant attorneys general in Ohio beginning in 1919.

John Patterson Green is probably the first black lawyer to train a white lawyer in his office. William R. Stewart, meanwhile, was the first black lawyer to sponsor the admission of a white lawyer before the United States Supreme Court.

Black lawyers were involved in local politics as well. For example, in 1909 Thomas Wallace Fleming was the first black elected to Cleveland's city council. Perry Brooks Jackson accomplished the same feat in 1933, and he became the first black municipal judge in that city in 1942.

Black lawyers in Ohio represented several law schools: Walker Law School, Union Law School, Western Reserve University's Frank Thomas Backus Law School, the University of Cincinnati, Howard University, Shaw University, John Marshall Law School, Harvard University, Yale University, Ohio State University, and the University of Michigan.

The first woman was admitted to the Ohio bar in 1919: Daisy D. Perkins became a part-time private practitioner and a full-time prosecutor. Helen Elsie Austin, who in 1930 became the University of Cincinnati's first black woman law graduate, was the first woman in the nation to be appointed to the office of assistant state attorney general.

The black lawyer in the northeastern states made significant breakthroughs in both law and politics. From local to state politics, from private practice to the judiciary, these lawyers achieved professionally, even as they emancipated blacks from old and new forms of racial discrimination.

NOTES

1. Letter from Earle Benjamin Searcy, clerk, Illinois Supreme Court, to Charles S. Brown, June 5, 1958; Bradwell, "The Colored Bar of Chicago," 29 *Chi. Legal News*, Oct. 31, 1896, at 75 col. 1. One historical source states that Joseph M. Burrows, who was also black, was admitted to the Illinois bar on November 22, 1867. However, no other information is available on Burrows (Reference Report on Burrows-Simms, Illinois State Historical Society, April 6, 1961).

2. "Lloyd G. Wheeler Dead," *New York Age*, Sept. 9, 1909. Geographically, the state of Illinois is in the northwestern region of the United States, but in the legal system it falls under the northeastern region.

3. Letter from John L. Ferguson, Arkansas History Commission, to author, Sept. 22, 1986; Bradwell, "The Colored Bar of Chicago," 5 *Mich. L.J.* 385, 387 (1896). The University of Chicago was opened in 1857 by a leading Baptist in the Chicago area. Richard A. Dawson was graduated from its law department in 1870. *Twelfth Annual Catalogue, University of Chicago, 1870–1871*, at 48. The old university closed in 1886, and the new University of Chicago was opened in 1902, through the efforts of John D. Rockefeller. Vol. 5 *The New International Encyclopedia* 173 (2d. 1925); R. J. Storr, *Harper's University: The Beginnings* 3–6 (1966); telephone conversation with Richard Popp, archivist, University of Chicago, Nov. 1, 1989.

4. *Id.* at 386, 387 ("The Colored Bar of Chicago").

5. "Ferdinand Lee Barnett," reference report, by Paul M. Angle, director, Chicago Historical Society, March 29, 1961, citing *The Bench and Bar in Chicago* 419 (n.d.). Lee founded *The Conservator* in 1878.

6. *A Documentary History of the Negro People in the United States* 744 (H. Aptheker ed. 1969), referring to *The Chicago Conservator*, 1878; quoted by Ralph N. Davis, "The Negro Newspaper in Chicago," (M.A. thesis, University of Chicago, 1939) at 13.

7. A. H. Spear, *Black Chicago: The Making of a Negro Ghetto, 1890–1920*, at 53, 60 (1967), quoting S. Drake and H. Clayton, *Black Metropolis* 51 (1945).

8. *Id.* at 77, 107 (*Black Chicago*).

9. Ellis, "The Chicago Negro in Law and Politics," Vol. 1 *The Champion Magazine* 349, 350 (March 1917); H. F. Gosnell, *Negro Politicians: The Rise of Negro Politics in Chicago* 85, 106 (1935).

10. *Id.* at 350 ("Chicago Negro in Law and Politics"). Edward E. Wilson was an 1894 Howard University law school graduate.

11. A. H. Spear, *Black Chicago: The Making of a Negro Ghetto, 1890–1920*, at 66 (1967).

12. *Id.* at 61, 67.

13. *Id.* at 119, quoting *The Chicago Chronicle*, Nov. 8, 1906.

14. "Ferdinand Lee Barnett," reference report, by Paul M. Angle, director, Chicago Historical Society, March 29, 1961, citing H. F. Gosnell, *Negro Politicians: The Rise of Negro Politics in Chicago* 85 (1935).

15. "Negro Lawyer Roils Landis," *Chicago Tribune*, April 27, 1915: "Barnett

kept [the judge], a jury, and the government attorney waiting while he leisurely went out and bought a handkerchief. [Barnett] finally appeared after Judge Landis had sent a scouting party in search of him."

16. Another black lawyer, Louis (sometimes spelled "Lewis") Washington, was admitted to the Chicago bar in 1879. He attended the Union College of Law (Northwestern) and was graduated in 1879. H. F. Kletzing and W. H. Crogman, *Progress of a Race* 532 (1901).

17. "Ed. Morris—Lawyer, Shingle Went Up in '79 to Begin 63 Yrs. Service," *Chicago Defender*, Nov. 28, 1942; Vol. 1 *Who's Who of the Colored Race* 199 (F. L. Mather ed. 1915).

18. *Illinois Blue Book* 767 (L. L. Emmerson, secretary of state, ed. 1925–1926).

19. Vol. 1 *Who's Who in Colored America* 145 (J. J. Boris ed. 1927).

20. *The College of Life or Practical Self Educator: A Manual of Self Improvement for the Colored Race* 158 (H. D. Northrop, J. R. Gay, and I. G. Penn eds. 1896).

21. Morris's reputation was noted by the Oregon press in 1906. "Plan Big Celebration," *The Daily Oregonian*, Sept. 9, 1906.

22. Several of the lawyers that Edward H. Morris assisted in his more than sixty-four years at the bar are referred to in this work. "Ed. Morris—Lawyer, Shingle Went Up in '79 to Begin 63 Years Service," *Chicago Defender*, Nov. 28, 1942. Morris died in 1943. See also, H. F. Gosnell, *Negro Politicians: The Rise of Negro Politics in Chicago* 66, 206 (1935); "Harris Wins Fame as Counsel for Metropolitan," *Chicago Defender*, Feb. 12, 1944. Thomas P. Harris was employed by Edward Morris after he graduated from the University of Chicago School of Law in 1932. Two years later, the Metropolitan Funeral System of America hired Harris away from Morris. Harris was elected vice-president and legal counsel of Metropolitan.

23. Vol. 3 *History of Minneapolis* 816–17 (M. Shutter ed. 1923).

24. F. L. Styles, *Negroes and the Law* 142 (1937).

25. A. H. Spear, *Black Chicago: The Making of a Negro Ghetto, 1890–1920*, at 189–90 (1967).

26. *Ibid*. In 1928 Oscar DePriest was elected to Congress from the First Congressional District. He polled 24,479 votes (47.8 percent). His Democratic opponent polled 20,664 (40.3 percent), and William Harrison polled 5,861 (11.4 percent) of the vote. *Guide to U.S. Elections* 917 (2d ed., J. L. Moore ed. 1985).

27. *Journal of the House of Representatives of the Thirty-fourth General Assembly: Legislative Directory* 55 (D. W. Lusk ed. 1885). Thomas won his first election to the Illinois General Assembly by more than ten thousand votes. In 1885, he served on the Judiciary, Education, Public Charities, and Manufactures committees. *Id.* at 204, 205.

28. On February 3, 1985, J. W. E. Thomas "introduced a bill, House Bill No. 45, for 'An act to protect all citizens in their civil and legal rights.'" *Id.* at 113. House Bill No. 45 passed the House after its third reading, on April 2, 1885, and the Senate on June 4, 1885. *Id.* at 445, 866. It was signed into law by Governor Richard J. Oglesby, a Republican, on June 10, 1885 (*Id.* at 888), and was enacted as Section 471–72 of the Illinois Criminal Code, as a provision "To Protect in Their Civil Rights and Legal Rights, and Fixing a Penalty for Their Violation," on July 1, 1885. *All the Laws of the State of Illinois Passed by the Thirty-fourth General Assembly* 65 (M. Bradwell ed. 1885).

29. *Baylies v. Curry*, 128 Ill. 287, 289, 292, 21 N.E. 595, 596 (1899). See also, Edward B. Toles, *Chicago Negro Judges, 1900–1965*, at 4, June 19, 1965 (pamphlet). Regarding J. W. E. Thomas as a member of the Illinois State Legislature, see *Illinois Legislative Manual . . . 30th General Assembly* 131 (1877).

30. *Indianapolis Freeman*, June 11, 1892; Bradwell, "The Colored Bar of Chicago," 5 *Mich. L.J.* 385, 389 (1896); "John W. E. Thomas Dead," *The Chicago Daily Tribune*, Dec. 19, 1899, at 7; Vol. 1 *Intercollegian Wonder Book—1779–The Negro in Chicago—1927*, at 128 (F. H. Robb ed. 1927).

31. *The Colored Men's Professional and Business Directory of Chicago* 22 (1885).

32. *Ibid.*

33. *Indianapolis Freeman*, June 11, 1892.

34. *The College of Life or Practical Self Educator: A Manual of Self Improvement for the Colored Race* 154 (H. D. Northrop, J. R. Gay, and I. G. Penn eds. 1896).

35. A. H. Spear, *Black Chicago: The Making of a Negro Ghetto, 1890–1920*, at 62 (1967); biographical material on John G. Jones, Chicago Historical Society; and letter from Sara L. McGill to author, Oct. 21, 1986.

36. *Id.* at 62, 84 (*Black Chicago*).

37. *The Colored Men's Professional and Business Directory of Chicago* 25 (1885).

38. Letter from Robert C. Morris, Schomburg Center for Research in Black Culture, to author, Sept. 16, 1986. Among the speeches that have survived is one from the annual session held at Providence, Rhode Island, Oct. 25 and 28, 1897.

39. Vol. 1 *Who's Who of the Colored Race* 179 (F. L. Mather ed. 1915).

40. *Ibid.* See *Anderson v. Louisville & N. R. Co.*, 62 F. 46, 48 (D. Ky. 1894) (with John Feland).

41. Bradwell, "The Colored Bar of Chicago," 5 *Mich. L.J.* 385, 391 (1896).

42. *Ibid.*; see also, letters from Elizabeth Brown to author, May 7, 1987; *The George Washington University Alumni Directory* 236 (1938); H. F. Gosnell, *Negro Politicians: The Rise of Negro Politics in Chicago* 217 (1935).

43. Ellis, "The Chicago Negro in Law and Politics," 1 *The Champion Magazine* 349, 350 (March 1917); A. H. Spear, *Black Chicago: The Making of a Negro Ghetto, 1890–1920*, at 66–67 (1967).

44. *Ibid.* Vol. 3 *The Booker T. Washington Papers, 1889–95*, at 518 (L. R. Harlan and B. S. Kaufman eds. 1974).

45. The friendship between Samuel Laing Williams and Booker T. Washington continued to grow. Williams became a supporter of the National Negro Business League headed by Washington. In 1905, Williams was elected compiler of the league. Clifford Plummer, another black Chicago lawyer, was used by Washington to spy on local black leaders organizing the Niagara Movement. L. R. Harlan, *Booker T. Washington: The Wizard of Tuskegee* 86–87 (1983); B. T. Washington, *The Negro in Business* 276, 288–89 (1907).

46. A. H. Spear, *Black Chicago: The Making of a Negro Ghetto, 1890–1920*, at 67 (1967).

47. *Id.* at 63.

48. One historian reports that "Williams lacked personal force, bordered on incompetence as a lawyer, according to some." L. R. Harlan, *Booker T. Washington: The Wizard of Tuskegee* 19, 29, 76–77 (1983). Williams failed to persuade Edward H. Morris to support the Washington camp because Morris believed that Washington's accommodationist policies were "largely responsible for the lynchings in this country." A. H. Spear, *Black Chicago: The Making of a Negro*

Ghetto, 1890–1920, at 61 (1967), referring to *The Cleveland Gazette*, Aug. 18, 1903. See also, Vol. 7 *The Booker T. Washington Papers, 1903–4*, at 226, 390, 391–92, 420–21 (L. R. Harlan and R. W. Smock eds. 1977).

49. Vol. 3 *The Booker T. Washington Papers, 1889–95*, at 518–19 (L. R. Harlan and B. S. Kaufman eds. 1974); A. H. Spear, *Black Chicago: The Making of a Negro Ghetto, 1890–1920*, at 68–69 (1967); letter from Edward B. Toles, president, Cook County Bar Association, to Charles S. Brown, May 25, 1961; H. F. Gosnell, *Negro Politicians: The Rise of Negro Politics in Chicago* 217 (1935).

50. *Id.* at 69 (*Black Chicago*).

51. The Kent College of Law later merged with the Chicago College of Law and the law department of Lake Forest University, forming what is today the Chicago-Kent Law School. Rowe, "To the Chicago-Kent Alumni," 1 *The Chicago-Kent Rev.* 3 (1923).

52. A. H. Spear, *Black Chicago: The Making of a Negro Ghetto, 1890–1920*, at 81 (1967); *Dictionary of American Negro Biography* 1 (R. Logan and M. Winston eds. 1982).

53. *Id.* at 194 (*Black Chicago*); *Marcus Garvey: Life and Lessons* 354 (R. A. Hill and B. Bair eds. 1987).

54. *The College of Life or Practical Self Educator: A Manual of Self Improvement for the Colored Race* 127 (H. D. Northrop, J. R. Gay, and I. G. Penn eds. 1896). Denison was admitted to the Illinois bar on March 29, 1898.

55. P. M. Angle, reference report, Chicago Historical Society, March 31, 1961.

56. Paul M. Angle, reference report on Franklin A. Denison, Chicago Historical Society, March 31, 1961.

57. Bradwell, "The Colored Bar in Chicago," 5 *Mich. L.J.* 385, 392 (1896).

58. H. F. Gosnell, *Negro Politicians: The Rise of Negro Politics in Chicago* 198–99 (1935).

59. "Lawyer Watkins Pleads Before U.S. Supreme Court," *The Guardian*, May 15, 1915. See *City of Chicago v. Chicago Transportation Company*, 238 U.S. 626 (1915); "Men of the Month," 19 *Crisis* 272 (March 1920).

60. "Denison, Watkins, and White Form Law Firm," *Chicago Defender*, May 24, 1919.

61. *Ibid.*

62. *Ibid.*

63. *Ibid.*

64. *Cook v. Lewis*, 306 U.S. 636 (1939), *reh. denied*, 306 U.S. 668 (1939); "Chicago Attorneys Retained by White Litigants in Ten Million Dollar Law Suit," *Pittsburgh Courier*, Oct. 31, 1936.

65. "Chicago Attorneys to Plead for Rights of Secret Order," *The Chicago Defender*, Dec. 14, 1918; Bell, "D. C. Knights of Pythias Hope to Eliminate Color Barrier," *Washington Post*, Feb. 22, 1990, at D.C. 1, col. 1 (mentions lawsuit).

66. *A Documentary History of the Negro People in the United States* 651 (H. Aptheker ed. 1969), quoting 3 *The A.M.E. Rev.* 53–54 (July 1886).

67. *Dictionary of American Negro Biography* 112 (R. Logan and M. Winston eds. 1982).

68. A. H. Spear, *Black Chicago: The Making of a Negro Ghetto, 1890–1920*, at 78 (1967).

69. *Id.* at 122.

70. *Id.* at 124.

71. *Id.* at 190.

72. *Simms's Blue Book and Directory* 100 (1923).

73. Vol. 1 *Who's Who of the Colored Race* 114 (F. L. Mather ed. 1915).

74. *Knights of Pythias v. Davis*, 203 Ill. App. 131 (1916) (with R. A. J. Shaw, also black). Ralph Alexander Shaw was one of the early graduates of Kent College of Law in Chicago and was apparently highly educated in fields other than law. Ellis, "The Chicago Negro in Law and Politics," 1 *The Champion Magazine* 349, 358 (March 1917). However, the claim by George W. Ellis that he received a Ph.D. from the University of Michigan is unsubstantiated. He did, however, pursue graduate studies at Michigan in 1906–7. *General Catalogue of the University of Michigan, 1837–1911*, at 867 (I. N. Demmon ed. 1912).

75. Ellis, "The Chicago Negro in Law and Politics," 1 *The Champion Magazine* 349, 358 (March 1917).

76. H. F. Gosnell, *Negro Politicians: The Rise of Negro Politics in Chicago* 86, 88 (1935). In 1921, 1922, and 1923, James A. Scott, Richard E. Westbrooks, and Edward H. Morris, respectively, made unsuccessful bids for the bench. *Ibid.*; see also, "Prominent Lawyer Looms Up as Judge," *Chicago Whip*, March 25, 1922.

77. *Ibid.* (*Negro Politicians*); Daly, "Brother Albert B. George," 11 *The Sphinx* 9 (Dec. 1925).

78. "A Successful Educational Campaign," 11 *The Sphinx* 4 (June 1925). George also served on the Illinois Parole Board from 1931 to 1932. Letter from Irene H. Peterson, chief of social sciences and business, Chicago Public Library, to Charles S. Brown, June 24, 1958.

79. A. H. Spear, *Black Chicago: The Making of a Negro Ghetto, 1890–1920*, at 189–90 (1967); Vol. 1 *Who's Who of the Colored Race* 9 (F. L. Mather ed. 1915); Vol. 1 *Intercollegian Wonder Book—1779—The Negro in Chicago—1927*, at 113 (F. H. Robb ed. 1927); *Virginia's Contribution to Negro Leadership* 2 (W. Cooper ed. 1937) (mimeo). In 1917 Chicago had a number of lawyers who had been in practice between five to thirty-three years: Edward H. Morris (33 years), Ferdinand L. Barnett (30 years), C. J. Waring (25 years), Samuel Laing Williams (25 years), Walter M. Farmer (24 years), Frederick A. Denison (23 years), S. A. T. Watkins (23 years), Louis B. Anderson (20 years), H. G. Parker (19 years), James A. White (18 years), Henry M. Porter (18 years), Edward H. Wright (17 years), T. Webster Brown (16 years), Thomas Pearson (16 years), Lawrence A. Newby (16 years), James A. Scott (15 years), Albert B. George (15 years), William L. Martin (15 years), J. Gray Lucas (15 years), Edward E. Wilson (15 years), W. G. Anderson (15 years), R. A. J. Shaw (7 years), James N. Simms (7 years), Arthur Simms (7 years), George W. Blackwell (7 years), Thomas G. Maxwell (6 years), Richard E. Westerbrooks (6 years), James G. Cotter (6 years), Richard Hill, Jr. (6 years), A. L. Bates (6 years), Chester DeArmond (6 years). See, Ellis, "The Chicago Negro in Law and Politics," 1 *The Champion Magazine* 349 (March 1917). George W. Ellis, the author of this article, was also a black lawyer.

80. Bradwell, "The Colored Bar of Chicago," 5 *Mich. L.J.* 385, 393 (1896).

81. Notes of Charles Sumner Brown, compiled from files in the Secretary's Office, Oberlin College, May 4, 1961.

82. A. H. Spear, *Black Chicago: The Making of a Negro Ghetto, 1890–1920*, at 48, 62 (1967).

83. "Negro Lawyer in Franks Case," *Afro-American*, Aug. 15, 1924. See N. F. Leopold, Jr., *Life Plus 99 Years* 61–69 (1958), a trial account of the murder.

84. Bradwell, "The Colored Bar of Chicago," 5 *Mich. L.J.* 385, 398 (1896).

85. A. H. Spear, *Black Chicago: The Making of a Negro Ghetto, 1890–1920*, at 79 (1967).

86. *Id.* at 117–18, quoting *Broad Ax*, Dec. 31, 1910. In the early 1900s, Moseley promoted "the first successful baseball team on the South Side [of Chicago], the Leland Giants." *Ibid.* He also advocated the need to form the National Negro Baseball League in 1910. D. Rogosin, *Invisible Men* 10 (1987).

87. Vol. 1 *Who's Who of the Colored Race* 201 (F. L. Mather ed. 1915). Other black lawyers, not as successful as Moseley, made significant contributions to the law between 1893 and 1900. For example, Moses A. Mardis, an 1893 Northwestern University law graduate, developed a police court and bail bondsman practice in Chicago. "Chicago Lawyer, 95, Funeral Rites Held," *Washington Afro-American*, Jan. 2, 1962. This article erroneously reports that Mardis was the "first black of his race to practice law in the state of Illinois." James Alexander Ross read law under Illinois judge J. C. Nermille. He practiced law in Chicago before forming a partnership with a white lawyer, James O. Herbold, of Buffalo, New York. Vol. 1 *Who's Who of the Colored Race* 234 (F. L. Mather ed. 1915). Arthur Alexander Lowry was graduated from Northern Illinois School of Law in Dixon, Illinois, in 1900. He became a pioneer black lawyer in Pontiac, Illinois. Vol. 1 *Who's Who in Colored America* 126 (J. J. Boris ed. 1927).

88. Starting as early as 1909, and perhaps before then, black lawyers were listed in *The Colored People's Blue Book and Business Directory*, *The Chicago Negro Business Men and Women, and Where They Are Located*, *Scotts Blue Book*, *Simms's Blue Book*, and *Black's Blue Book*. Lawyers also carried advertisements in these listings.

89. *Colored People's Blue Book and Business Directory* 127–29 (1909). The same number of black lawyers were listed in 1912 in *The Chicago Negro Business Men and Women, and Where They Are Located* 10–11 (L. W. Washington ed. 1912).

90. *Black's Blue Book* 37–38 (1921). Another source indicates that in 1920 there were ninety-five black lawyers in Chicago. M. S. Goldman, *A Portrait of the Black Attorney in Chicago* 9–10 (1972).

91. H. F. Gosnell, *Negro Politicians: The Rise of Negro Politics in Chicago* 202–3 (1935). See also, *Blue Book of the State of Illinois, 1919–1920*, at 176 (L. L. Emmerson ed. 1920); *Blue Book . . . 1921–1922*, at 116 (L. L. Emmerson ed. 1922); *Blue Book . . . 1925–1926*, at 128 (L. L. Emmerson ed. 1926); *Blue Book . . . 1927–1928*, at 2,216 (L. L. Emmerson ed. 1928). Adelbert H. Roberts served on several committees during his time in the Illinois State Legislature: the Industrial Affairs Committee (per *Journal of the House of Representatives of the Fifty-first General Assembly, Regular Biennial Sess., Jan. 8, 1919–June 30, 1919*, at 61); the Education, Industrial Affairs, Judiciary, Military Affairs, Senatorial Appointment, and Uniform Laws committees (*Journal . . . Fifty-second General Assembly, Regular Biennial Sess., Jan. 5, 1921–June 30, 1921*, at 96–98); the Reapportionment, State University, and Normal Schools committees (*Journal . . . Fifty-fourth General Assembly, Regular Biennial Sess., Jan. 7, 1925–June 30, 1925*, at 84); and the Reapportionment Congressional Committee (*Journal . . . Fifty-fifth General Assembly, Regular Biennial Sess., Jan. 5, 1927–June 30, 1927*, at 158).

92. Vol. 1 *Who's Who of the Colored Race* 282 (F. L. Mather ed. 1915).

93. *Simms's Blue Book and Directory* 99 (1923).

94. A. H. Spear, *Black Chicago: The Making of a Negro Ghetto, 1890–1920*, at

218 (1967). Arthur C. MacNeal was not a lawyer. See, generally, W. M. Tuttle, Jr., *Race Riot* 32–66 (1970).

95. E. F. Frazier, *Negro Family in the United States* 291–324 (1939); M. S. Goldman, *A Portrait of the Black Attorney in Chicago* 8–9 (1972).

96. Vol. 1 *Who's Who of the Colored Race* 99 (F. L. Mather ed. 1915). Mr. Ellis's accomplishments in international law and his scholarly contributions to this field were recognized beyond American borders. In recognition of Ellis's contributions to ethnological studies, "[he was] elected Fellow of the Royal Geographical Society of Great Britain." Vol. 1 *The National Cyclopedia of the Colored Race* 145 (C. C. Richardson ed. 1919).

97. Vol. 1 *Who's Who in Colored America* 93 (J. J. Boris ed. 1927); *General Catalogue of the University of Michigan, 1837–1911*, at 522 (I. N. Demmon ed. 1912).

98. H. F. Gosnell, *Negro Politicians: The Rise of Negro Politics in Chicago* 89 (1935). Hill also represented a "number [of] Greek and Italian corporations, banking and business houses." Vol. 1 *Who's Who of the Colored Race* 138 (F. L. Mather ed. 1915).

99. Vol. 1 *Intercollegian Wonder Book—1779—The Negro in Chicago—1927*, at 109 (F. H. Robb ed. 1927).

100. *Ibid.* The editor erred in his statement that Cotter was the first black appointed assistant United States attorney in the western region. See also, H. F. Gosnell, *Negro Politicians: The Rise of Negro Politics in Chicago* 213 (1935); "Cotter Wins Big Case for the United States," *Chicago Whip*, Dec. 20, 1924.

101. *Id.* at 217, n. 53 (*Negro Politicians*); "Wants [Alva L.] Bates to Head Bar Association," *Chicago Defender*, Dec. 5, 1931 (Taylor). Both Taylor and White were appointed by Attorney General John T. Sargent.

102. "Mr. District Attorney," *Ebony*, March 1951, at 82.

103. *Ibid.*

104. Vol. 1 *Who's Who in Colored America* 151 (J. J. Boris ed. 1927).

105. *Simms's Blue Book and Directory* 103 (1923); "Black Rulers of White Folk," 37 *Crisis* 14, 16 (Jan.–Dec. 1930); H. F. Gosnell, *Negro Politicians: The Rise of Negro Politics in Chicago* 109 (1935). King was elected to the Illinois General Assembly in 1924 and was reelected in 1928, 1930, and 1932. He was elected to the Illinois State Senate in 1934. *Blue Book of the State of Illinois, 1935–1936*, at 139 (E. J. Hughes ed. 1936). Charles J. Jenkins, another black lawyer, served in the Fifty-ninth Illinois General Assembly in 1935. Jenkins, a graduate of the Chicago-Kent College of Law, was admitted to the Illinois bar in 1922. He practiced law with former judge Albert B. George. *Ibid.*

106. A. H. Spear, *Black Chicago: The Making of a Negro Ghetto, 1890–1920*, at 198, 186 (1967); letter from Morris Cohen, librarian, Yale University Law School, to author July 22, 1987 (regarding Bibb). Henry H. Proctor and George W. Lawrence joined the legal staff of the corporation counsel in 1927. "Att'y Proctor Named Assistant City Attorney Council [*sic*]," *Chicago Whip*, Sept. 10, 1927; Brooks, "Lawrence Beats Obstacles to Rise to Top in Law," *Chicago Defender*, June 26, 1943. In 1935 Frederick Wyman "Duke" Slater, a 1928 graduate of Iowa University's law school, was appointed to the position of assistant corporation counsel by Mayor Edward J. Kelly. "Slater Named Corporation Counsel in Chicago," *The Black Dispatch*, Nov. 16, 1935.

107. H. F. Gosnell, *Negro Politicians: The Rise of Negro Politics in Chicago* 201 (1935).

108. "Herman E. Moore Sat in Case Involving Thirty Million," *Kansas Plain-*

dealer, Aug. 4, 1939. The Boston Tractor Company ran the elevated railway. Moore was the first black lawyer to work for the Company.

109. *Ibid*. See also, *Eighteenth Annual Report of Illinois Commerce Commission*, July 1, 1934, to June 30, 1935, listing Moore as an assistant commissioner and reporting the universal transfer opinion, at 42; *Nineteenth Annual Report of Illinois Commerce Commission*, July 1, 1935–June 30, 1936, at 52.

110. In 1939 William Henry Hastie became dean of the Howard University School of Law. G. Ware, *William Hastie: Grace Under Pressure* 93–94 (1984); "Transfer Slip Is Memento of Island Judge," *Chicago Tribune*, Jan. 14, 1940. Herman Emmons Moore served with distinction on the federal bench in the Virgin Islands from August 4, 1939, to November 15, 1957. His scholarly opinions appear in Vol. 2 *Virgin Island Reports* 3–352 (1940–1953), and Vol. 3 *Virgin Island Reports* 3–272 (1954–1958).

111. Interview with a black citizen on the street in Cairo, Illinois, in 1971.

112. "Prominent Attorney Seeks State's Attorney Office," *The Chicago Defender*, May 15, 1920.

113. Letter from Earl B. Dickerson to Charles S. Brown, July 8, 1960.

114. *Ninth Annual Convention Program of the National Bar Association*, Aug. 3–5, 1933, at 1.

115. Dickerson, "The Participation of Negro Labor in Our War Effort," 2 *Lawyers Guild Rev.* 24, 32 (May 1942). See also, "Ask Use of Negro Lawyers in War," *Daily Worker*, July 7, 1942.

116. Letter from Ruth C. Francis, Chicago Public Library, to Charles S. Brown, Sept. 29, 1958; Vol. 1 *Intercollegian Wonder Book—1779—The Negro in Chicago—1927* at 117 (F. H. Robb ed. 1927); Adams, "Four New Freedoms Outlined by Leading Chicago Attorney," *Amsterdam News*, Jan. 27, 1944. Green was graduated from the University of Chicago Law School in the early 1920s. See Green, "Stare Decisis and the Supreme Court of the United States," 4 *Nat'l B.A.J.* 191 (1946).

117. H. F. Gosnell, *Negro Politicians: The Rise of Negro Politics in Chicago* 207–8 (1935).

118. *Id*. at 59.

119. "Attorney William H. Haynes Aids Prosecution," *Chicago Defender*, June 9, 1928.

120. The lawyers were Harold M. Tyler, David H. Geter, and James T. Lorick of the firm of Lorick and Geter. "Chicago Lawyers Win Hot Tilt with Georgia Sheriff," *Chicago Defender*, Sept. 10, 1927. By the 1940s, black lawyers such as William Henry Huff were still defending blacks who had slipped away from peonage in the South. "Fugitives from Dixie," *Ebony*, Feb. 1950, at 68. See also, *The Autobiography of Ida B. Wells* 335–44 (A. M. Duster ed. 1970), for other instances where black lawyers assisted in stopping sheriffs from the South from taking black men to be tried or lynched for alleged crimes. P. Daniel, *The Shadow of Slavery: Peonage in the South, 1901–1969*, at 175–76 (1972), on Huff and anti-peonage activities.

121. "Gets New Post," *Chicago Defender*, March 17, 1928. McGill worked for the *Chicago Defender* until 1934. "Abbott Ousts N. K. McGill," *Pittsburgh Courier*, Sept. 22, 1934, at 7, col. 3.

122. "Alva L. Bates to Go on Two Month Cruise," *Chicago Whip*, Jan. 18, 1930. Bates was graduated from Howard University's law school in 1914.

123. *Virginia's Contribution to Negro Leadership* 58 (W. Cooper ed. 1937) (mimeo).

124. H. F. Gosnell, *Negro Politicians: The Rise of Negro Politics in Chicago* 211 (1935). Warren B. Douglas was graduated from Chicago-Kent Law School in 1915 and admitted to the Illinois bar in the same year. He served in the Illinois General Assembly from 1919 to 1923 and from 1925 to 1929. He was elected to the Fifty-ninth General Assembly in 1934, but died before he took office. See *Blue Book of the State of Illinois, 1919–1920*, at 176 (L. L. Emmerson ed. 1920). During Douglas's 1919–20 term he served on the Civil Service Committee. See *Journal of the House of Representatives of the Fifty-first General Assembly of Illinois, Regular Biennial Session, Jan. 8, 1919–June 30, 1919*, at 61. He also served on the Efficiency and Economy, Insurance, Judiciary, and Uniform Law committees (*Journal . . . Fifty-second General Assembly, Regular Biennial Sess., Jan. 5, 1921–June 30, 1921*, at 96–98); the Judicial Department and Practice and Municipalities committees (*Journal . . . Fifty-fourth General Assembly of Illinois, Regular Biennial Sess., Jan. 7, 1925–June 30, 1921*, at 84–85); and the Congressional Apportionment and Senatorial Appointment committees (*Journal . . . Fifty-fifth General Assembly, Regular Biennial Sess., Jan. 5, 1927–June 30, 1927*, at 158–96).

125. "Firm of Negro Lawyers Gets High Ratings," *Chicago Bee*, March 6, 1938. The firm consisted of Sydney P. Brown, Oscar C. Brown, Bendley C. Cyrus, William H. Brown, Ernest A. Green, and Marcus A. Mahone.

126. *Mitchell v. Chicago, Rock Island & Pacific Railway Company*, 229 I.C.C. 703 (1938).

127. *Mitchell v. United States*, 313 U.S. 80, 94 (1941) Congressman Mitchell represented himself before the United States Supreme Court. He was joined by Richard E. Westbrooks. The ICC opposed Mitchell's appeal, as did the attorney generals of Arkansas, Alabama, Florida, Georgia, Kentucky, Louisiana, Mississippi, Tennessee, Texas, and Virginia, who each filed briefs in opposition. *Black Americans in Congress, 1870–1989*, at 93–94 (B. A. Ragsdale and J. D. Treese ed. 1990). Francis Biddle, the solicitor general of the United States, sided with Congressman Mitchell. See Crockett, "Comments on *Mitchell v. United States*," 1 *Nat'l B.A.J.* 157 (1941); "Brief of the United States in *Mitchell v. United States*," *id.* at 185; and "Attorney General Francis Biddle," *id.* at 146. See also, Jones, "The Supreme Court's Role in Jim Crow Transportation," 3 *Nat'l B.A.J.* 114, 123–125, (June 1945). It is interesting to note that Chief Justice Charles Evans Hughes, speaking for the court, relied on *Councill v. Western & Atlanta R. Co.*, 1 I.C.C. 339 (1887), the first case brought by a black person challenging racial discrimination by a common carrier traveling in interstate commerce. *Id.* at 95. William H. Councill, the claimant in that case, was also a black lawyer. However, Councill did not prevail in his claim before the Interstate Commerce Commission.

128. It should be noted here that in 1940 Truman K. Gibson, Jr., a 1935 University of Chicago law graduate, became William Henry Hastie's assistant at the Department of War and succeeded Hastie as civilian aide to the secretary of war when Hastie's resignation became effective in 1943 (biographical sketch of Truman K. Gibson, Jr., provided by Gibson to the author in 1986). As a private lawyer, Gibson became one of the first black lawyers to practice entertainment law, along with Aaron H. Payne, a 1926 Howard University law graduate. "Frank Capra, Who Filmed 'The Negro Soldier' in 1944, Dies at 94," *Jet*, Sept. 23, 1991, at 14 (Gibson); "Norman L. McGhee and Aaron H. Payne," 37 *Howard University Bulletin* 23, July 15, 1958. Payne represented such personalities as Nat "King" Cole and Josephine Baker.

129. *The People ex rel. Prescott v. Scheffler*, 381 Ill. 173, 45 N.E. 2d 36 (1942). At

least two of the lawyers who represented Prescott before the Illinois Supreme Court were members of the same law firm—Euclid Louis Taylor and A. Morris Burroughs. Both of these men were skilled lawyers. Taylor attended Chicago-Kent's law school from 1924 to 1926. In 1930 Taylor had gained considerable experience in labor relations as a special attorney for Armour and Company. He also served on the state's attorney's staff. "Euclid L. Taylor Elected Head of Bar Association," *Nashville Globe and Independent*, Aug. 29, 1941; "W. H. Huff, Negro Lawyer to Lecture at John Marshall Law Inst.," *Oklahoma Black Dispatch*, June 3, 1939.

130. Bradwell, "The Colored Bar of Chicago," 29 *Chi. Legal News*, Oct. 31, 1896, at 75, col. 1. Charlotte E. Ray and Mary Ann Shadd Carey were graduated from Howard University School of Law in 1872 and 1883, respectively. Lutie A. Lytle graduated from Central Tennessee Law School in 1897.

131. Bradwell, "The Colored Bar of Chicago," 5 *Mich. L.J.* 385, 397 (1896).

132. *Ibid.*

133. *Black's Blue Book* 38 (1921).

134. "Mrs. Violett Anderson Admitted to Bar," *Chicago Defender*, June 5, 1920.

135. "Miss Anderson Honored: Named as Prosecutor," *Chicago Defender*, Dec. 30, 1922.

136. "It Couldn't Be Done, but She Did It," *Chicago Defender*, July 29, 1922.

137. "Woman Lawyer Wins Her First Murder Case," *Chicago Whip*, July 9, 1922.

138. *Ibid.*

139. *Simms's Blue Book and Directory* 90–92 (1923).

140. "Negro Woman Lawyer Member of Supreme Court," *New York Sun*, Jan. 29, 1926; "Colored Woman U.S. Court Lawyer," *New York City News*, Jan. 20, 1926; "First Negress Practices in U.S. Supreme Court," *Brooklyn Eagle*, Feb. 4, 1926; "First Colored Woman Admitted to Practice in U.S. Supreme Court," *St. Louis Argus*, Feb. 5, 1926. Anderson was admitted to practice before the United States Supreme Court on motion of James A. Cobb, a black municipal judge in the District of Columbia. Vol. 1 *Who's Who in Colored America* 5–6 (J. J. Boris ed. 1927).

141. "Noted Attorney Portia Member," *Chicago Defender*, March 24, 1928.

142. H. F. Gosnell, *Negro Politicians: The Rise of Negro Politics in Chicago* 201–2 (1935).

143. "Negro Lawyers Name Officers at Sessions End," *Nashville Banner*, Aug. 4, 1935.

144. *Who's Who Among Negro Lawyers* 14 (S. T. M. Alexander ed. 1945).

145. *Id.* at 36. See *Foreign Consular Offices in the United States* 29 (GPO, 1932) (listing Westbrooks).

146. Telephone interview of Lucia T. Thomas, Chicago, IL, Oct. 3, 1986.

147. *Ibid.*

148. *Ibid.* Barbara Watts Goodall graduated from the Chicago School of Law in 1926. "Granted Degree at Law College," *Chicago Defender*, June 19, 1926.

149. *Ibid.* (telephone interview, Lucia T. Thomas).

150. "Lady Lawyer," *Ebony* 18 (Aug. 1947) (original emphasis).

151. *Current Biography* 511–12 (A. Rothe ed. 1950).

152. "Two Chicago Women Finish Law Course," *Chicago Defender*, July 4, 1925.

153. *Current Biography* 511–12 (A. Rothe ed. 1950).

154. *Ibid.*

155. *Ibid.*

156. "Race Woman Attorney on Bench in Chicago Juvenile Court," *Chicago Defender*, June 1, 1940. Sampson maintained her maiden name throughout her career. Some sources cite Sampson as having received her master of laws degree from John Marshall Law School, but this is not the case. She was awarded the master of laws degree during the fifty-seventh annual commencement of Loyola University of Chicago. "Courier Columnist Receiving Masters Degree in Law," *Pittsburgh Courier*, June 18, 1927; Funeral Program, Oct. 11, 1979; Vol. 1 *Intercollegian Wonder Book—1779—The Negro in Chicago—1927*, at 120 (F. H. Robb ed. 1927), which states that Sampson was the first black woman "in the country" to receive a master of laws degree.

157. "Race Woman Attorney Serves on Bench in Chicago," *Chicago Defender*, June 1, 1940.

158. "Out to Get $25,000," *Norfolk Journal and Guide*, Sept. 22, 1925 (Boas); "A Graduate of Marshall Law School," *Chicago Whip*, June 19, 1926 (Huggins).

159. *Scott's Business and Service Directory* 216–18 (1947).

160. J. W. Lyda, *The Negro in the History of Indiana* 68 (1953).

161. *Ibid.*

162. *Ibid.* Recent autobiographical works on Revels make no mention of his admission to the Indiana bar or any other bar. See Julius E. Thompson, "Hiram R. Revels, 1827–1901: A Biography" (Ph.D. diss., Princeton University, 1973), published in book form under the same title by Arno Press in 1982.

163. Letter from H. Dale Brown, Marion County clerk, to Charles S. Brown, (n.d., circa 1960).

164. One noted Indiana historian reports that James T. V. Hill was admitted to the bar in 1885. E. L. Thornbrough, *The Negro in Indiana Before 1900*, at 365–66 (1957).

165. Letter from Caroline Dunn, librarian, Wm. Henry Smith Memorial Library, to Charles S. Brown, Oct. 28, 1959, quoting the *Indianapolis News*, Feb. 20, 1928.

166. *Indianapolis Freeman*, Jan. 11, 1890, at 1, col. 1.

167. Roberts, "National Bar Association Ends Session," *Chicago Defender*, Aug. 11, 1928.

168. *The College of Life or Practical Self Educator: A Manual of Self Improvement for the Colored Race* 141 (H. D. Northrop, J. R. Gay, and I. G. Penn eds. 1896), indicating that Taylor was admitted to the bar in 1878. The text, however, is inconclusive as to Taylor's legal training at Michigan. A review of the early graduates of the University of Michigan's law department indicates that a Charles H. Taylor from Orange, New Jersey, was graduated in 1862. *General Catalogue of the University of Michigan, 1837–1911*, at 371 (I. N. Demmon ed. 1912). However, Charles Henry James Taylor was born in Perry County, Alabama, in 1857. Hence, available information does not support accounts that Taylor ever attended or graduated from the University of Michigan's law school as reported in Vol. 5 *The National Cyclopedia of American Biography* 551–52 (reprint, 1967).

169. Letter from H. Dale Brown, Marion County clerk, to Charles S. Brown, (n.d., circa 1960); *Indianapolis Freeman*, Sept. 15, 1886, referring to Taylor as a member of the Indiana bar.

170. Letter from Carolene Dunn, librarian, Wm. Henry Smith Memorial Library, to Charles S. Brown, Oct. 28, 1959, quoting *The Indianapolis News*, Feb. 20, 1928.

171. *Souvenir Album and Directory of the Colored Voters in Omaha, Nebraska* 1 (W. B. Walker ed. 1891).

172. E. L. Thornbrough, *The Negro in Indiana Before 1900*, at 366 (1957).

173. *Id.* at 365–66; letter from Mabel E. Lyons, clerk, Supreme Court of Indiana, to Charles S. Brown, Aug. 5, 1958; *University of Michigan General Catalogue of Officers and Students, 1837–1911*, at 450 (I. N. Demmon ed. 1912).

174. *Ibid.* (letter from Mabel E. Lyons); Vol. 5 *The Booker T. Washington Papers, 1899–1900*, at 464 (L. R. Harlan, R. W. Smock, and B. S. Kraft eds. 1976); *id.*, Vol. 8, at 73 (reference to Lott's involvement in Indiana politics).

175. "The Court House," *Indianapolis Freeman*, Jan. 11, 1890, at 5, col. 1. Manning was also respected by his people. In 1890, he was elected by the local chapter of the Afro-American League to attend the national convention of that group in Chicago, Illinois (*ibid.*, col. 2).

176. *Ibid.*

177. Letter from H. Dale Brown, Marion County clerk, to Charles S. Brown (n.d., circa 1960).

178. For example, Hugh Burkett Mason, an 1898 Howard University law graduate, was admitted to the Indiana bar in that year. By 1899, he had relocated to Baltimore, Maryland. Vol. 1 *Who's Who in the Colored Race* 51 (F. L. Mather ed. 1915).

179. E. L. Thornbrough, *The Negro in Indiana Before 1900*, at 365–66 (1957), citing *The Indianapolis Freeman*, May 14, 1892. A history of the city of Evansville does not mention Scott. D. W. Sprinklers, *The History of Evansville Blacks* 54 (1974) (listing lawyers).

180. Letter from Mabel E. Lyons, clerk, Supreme Court of Indiana, to Charles S. Brown, Aug. 5, 1958.

181. Vol. 1 *Who's Who of the Colored Race* 75 (F. L. Mather ed. 1915).

182. *Virginia's Contribution to Negro Leadership* 71 (W. Cooper ed. 1937) (mimeo).

183. *Id.* at 12.

184. Vol. 1 *Who's Who of the Colored Race* 225 (F. L. Mather ed. 1915); Smith, "The Marion County Lawyers' Club: 1932 and the Black Lawyer," 8 *Black L.J.* 170, 172 (Howard Law School Edition, 1983).

185. "Woman Lawyer Speaks at Bar Assn. Meeting," *Philadelphia Tribune*, Aug. 10, 1939.

186. Smith, "The Marion County Lawyers' Club: 1932 and the Black Lawyer," 8 *Black L.J.* 170, 172 (Howard Law School Edition, 1983). One source reports that in 1919, Ransom, as counsel to the C. J. Walker Manufacturing Co., was one of the highest paid black lawyers in the nation. Vol. 1 *The National Cyclopedia of the Colored Race* 145 (C. C. Richardson ed. 1919).

187. "Ransom Becomes C. J. Walker 'GM,'" *Pittsburgh Courier*, Jan. 15, 1955.

188. "Race Lawyer Wins Unusual Distinction," *The Norfolk Journal and Guide*, Dec. 13, 1919. The same year that Brokenburr graduated from Howard University's law school, another black student, Samuel Saul Dargan, graduated from Indiana University's law school in Bloomington. Dargan became the curator of the law library at Indiana University. F. V. H. Gilliam, *A Time to Speak: A Brief History of the Afro-Americans of Bloomington, Indiana, 1865–1965*, at 73 (1985).

189. *Virginia's Contribution to Negro Leadership* 10 (W. Cooper ed. 1937) (mimeo).

190. "Race Lawyer Wins Unusual Distinction," *The Norfolk Journal and Guide*, Dec. 13, 1919; "Men of the Month," 19 *Crisis* 272–73 (March 1920); Brokenburr, "A Lawyer's Uphill Climb," 52 *The Southern Workman* 317, 318 (July 1923).

191. Vol. 2 *Biographical Directory of Indiana General Assembly, 1900–1984*, at 52 (E. Walsh ed. 1984). Senator Brokenburr's assignments by year were as follows: Aviation, 1945, 1947 (ranking member); Benevolent Institutions, 1941; City of Indianapolis, 1941, 1943 (ranking member of both), 1945, 1947; Congressional Apportionment, 1945, 1947; Corporations, 1947; Constitutional Revision, 1941, 1943, 1945; Elections, 1941 (ranking member), 1943 (chairman), 1945 (ranking member); Judiciary B, 1941, 1943, 1945, 1947 (latter two as ranking member); Labor, 1945, 1947; Legislative Apportionment, 1941; Organization of Courts and Criminal Code, 1943, 1945, 1947 (latter two as chairman); Public Policy, 1941, 1943; Rights and Privileges, 1941, 1943 (chairman of both); Soldiers and Sailors Monument, 1941, 1943, 1945, 1947 (latter two as ranking member). Letter to author from Martha E. Wright, reference librarian, Indiana State Library, Nov. 3, 1989.

192. *Virginia's Contribution to Negro Leadership* 12 (W. Cooper ed. 1937) (mimeo).

193. Vol. 1 *Who's Who in Colored America* 8 (J. J. Boris ed. 1927).

194. "Bailey Named to Special Legislative Committee," *Indianapolis Recorder*, Feb. 6, 1937.

195. See, e.g., *Harris v. State of Indiana*, 203 Ind. 505, 181 N.E. 33 (1932). Brokenburr and Bailey successfully challenged death sentences conferred on two black hobos. The lawyers argued that the defendants had been denied the right to counsel under the Bill of Rights of the Indiana State Constitution.

196. Smith, "The Marion County Lawyers' Club: 1932 and the Black Lawyers," 8 *Black L.J.* 170, 171 (Howard Law School Edition, 1983).

197. "Colored Lawyer Breaks Ice in Indiana Courts," *New Jersey Informer*, Sept. 27, 1917.

198. "Bar Association Stops Fight on Tidrington," *Chicago Defender*, Feb. 14, 1920.

199. "Bar Association Is Still Fighting Negro," *Louisville Times*, Feb. 7, 1920; "Tidrington Wins in Law Practice Battle," *Chicago Defender*, Jan. 24, 1920.

200. *Ibid.* ("Tidrington Wins in Law Practice Battle"). One author has written that Tidrington was admitted to the bar "by virtue of an order of the Indiana Supreme Court," with the aid of Phil Gould, a leading Republican judge. D. E. Bingham, *We Ask Only a Fair Trial: A History of the Black Community of Evansville, Indiana* 168 (1988). Tidrington and another black lawyer, Rudolph O'Hara, opened a law practice in 1924; the firm lasted until Tidrington died in 1930. *Id.* at 165, 166. At the time of Tidrington's death, President Calvin Coolidge had been considering him for an appointment as register of the treasury. *Id.* at 211.

201. "Tidrington wins in Law Practice Battle," *Chicago Defender*, Jan. 24, 1920.

202. R. E. Greene, *They Did Not Tell Me True Facts* 279 (1992); "Colored Lawyer Admitted," *Goshon Indiana Democrat*, March 10, 1925.

203. *The National Bar Association, Proceedings of the Sixth Annual Convention* 4, 14 (Aug. 7, 1930); "Bar Ass'n. Convention Hits Evils," *St. Louis Argus*, Aug. 15, 1930; "W. C. Heuston, 81 Dies; Former Postal Aide," *Washington Star*, 1961.

204. "Boult Is Appointed Dep. Pros. Attorney," *New York Age*, Jan. 15, 1921.

205. "Colored Judge Convicts," *Indianapolis News*, Jan. 14, 1921.

206. "Indiana Attorney Is Named Prosecutor," *Afro-American*, Jan. 20, 1934.

207. Balika, "Henry J. Richardson, Jr. Dies; Rights Leader," *Indianapolis Star*, Dec. 6, 1983, at 16, col. 1.

208. *Ibid*; "Presiding Judge," *Chicago Defender*, Feb. 28, 1931.

209. Balika, "Henry J. Richardson, Jr. Dies; Rights Leader," *Indianapolis Star*, Dec. 6, 1983, at 16, col. 1.

210. *Ibid*; "Henry Richardson, Jr.," *Washington Post*, Dec. 7, 1983, at C17, col. 2. "Equal Rights Bill Approved," from scrap book of H. Elsie Austin (copy in author's files).

211. "Here's the Klan's Official Ultimatum Against Rep. Richardson's Rights Bill," *Pittsburgh Courier*, March 9, 1935, at 7, col. 5.

212. "5,000 in Gallery as Richardson Bill Is Beaten," *Pittsburgh Courier*, March 2, 1935, at 6, col. 5.

213. Biographical sketch of Mercer Montgomery Mance obtained from the National Bar Association.

214. *Opportunities for Negroes in Law* (H. E. Grove ed. 1967) (pages unnumbered).

215. Biographical sketch of Elijah L. Johnson, Jr., obtained from the National Bar Association.

216. W. H. Huff, "Negro Lawyer to Lecture at John Marshall Law Inst.," *Oklahoma Black Dispatch*, June 3, 1939.

217. Biographical sketch of Willard B. Ransom obtained from the National Bar Association.

218. J. W. Lyda, *The Negro in the History of Indiana* 69 (1953).

219. Interview with H. Elsie Austin on May 14, 1985; Thomas, "Biographical Bits About Terrell Teachers," Vol. 1, No. 8 *The Barrister* 9, 13–14 (May 2, 1941). H. Elsie Austin's name appears in the Law Directory of the National Bar Association 132 (appended to proceedings of the seventh and eighth annual conventions, Aug. 6, 1931 and Aug. 4, 1932).

220. Hanchett, "George Boyer Vashon, 1824–1878: Black Educator, Poet, Fighter for Equal Rights," 68 *The Western Pennsylvania Historical Magazine* 205, 208 (July 1985).

221. Judge Forward had previously served as secretary of the treasury under President Martin Van Buren from 1841 to 1843.

222. "George Boyer Vashon," *Pittsburgh Gazette*, Jan. 17, 1848; letter from James McGurrin, county clerk and clerk of the Supreme Court of New York, to Charles S. Brown, May 26, 1958. The list of admittees appears in the January 12, 1848, edition of the *New York Herald*, where "George B. Vashon (Colored)" is noted. See also, W. Armistead, *A Tribute for the Negro* 140–41 (1848). By 1850, there were a total of four black lawyers in New York City. *Negro Population in the United States, 1790–1915*, at 511 (S. L. Rogers Direc. 1918), table 14.

223. Hanchett, "George Boyer Vashon, 1824–1878: Black Educator, Poet, Fighter for Equal Rights," 68 *The Western Pennsylvania Historical Magazine* 205, 212 (July 1985), quoting letter from John Vashon to Gerrit Smith, (original emphasis), Oct. 4, (or 11), 1852. On January 19, 1852, George Vashon had written to Gerrit Smith saying that his law practice had not developed.

224. "Syracuse Lawyer Was First Negro Admitted to Bar," *Syracuse Post Standard*, July 18, 1919.

225. *The New Orleans Tribune*, Sept. 20, 1865.

226. Hamilton, "James Campbell Matthews," *New York Freeman*, Dec. 6, 1884, at 1, col. 1.

227. *Ibid.* William A. Dietz retained Matthews to initiate a lawsuit so that his children could attend school with whites. It is likely that Matthews was retained by Mr. Dietz as a consultant in *People ex rel. Dietz v. Easton*, 13 Abb. Prac. (N.S.) 159 (1872). Dietz's desegregation suit does not list Matthews as counsel of record.

228. W. J. Simmons, *Men of Mark* 963, 968 (1887), quoting letter from James C. Matthews to Thomas J. White, April 20, 1886.

229. Hamilton, "James Campbell Matthews," *New York Freeman*, Dec. 6, 1884, at 1, col. 1.

230. Letter from Erastus Corning II, mayor, Albany, New York, to Charles S. Brown, April 24, 1961.

231. W. J. Simmons, *Men of Mark* 964, 966 (1887).

232. *Ibid.*, referring to the extracts from the minutes of the Committee of the District of Columbia, March 22, 1886, and April 9, 1886.

233. *Id.* at 968–70, referring to extracts from the minutes of the Committee of the District of Columbia, April 30, 1886, May 5, 7, 21, 1886, and extract from the *Executive Journal of the Senate*, May 28, 1886, June 11, 25, 1886 and July 3, 1886.

234. *Id.* at 971, extract from the *Executive Journal of the Senate*, July 31, 1886.

235. *Id.* at 972.

236. *Id.* at 973; document by President Grover Cleveland, Dec. 21, 1886, nominating "James C. Matthew of New York, to be recorder of deeds in the District of Columbia."

237. In rejecting the Matthews nomination, the Senate passed a resolution making it clear that the Republicans took umbrage at the nomination. Frederick Douglass was forced to resign as recorder of deeds. The resolution also denied any knowledge of "whether Matthews is white or black," perhaps a slap at the fair-skinned Matthews. *Id.* at 974–75.

238. *Id.* at 977; W. J. Simmons, *Men of Mark* 833, 838 (1887). James Monroe Trotter was the father of the more progressive, Harvard-educated William Monroe Trotter. The younger Trotter later became a foe of Booker T. Washington's accommodationist policies. Winch, "Geraldine Pindell Trotter," 2 *Trotter Institute Rev.* 10 (Winter 1988).

239. Letter from Eratus Corning II, mayor, Albany, New York, to Charles S. Brown, June 20, 1961. (Matthews served as recorder of deeds under two mayors, John Boyd Thacher and Thomas J. Van Alstyne).

240. "The Rev. William J. White Makes Some Needful Corrections to Mr. Quarles Life and Work," *New York Freeman*, Feb. 4, 1885.

241. Letter from James McGurrin, county clerk and clerk of the Supreme Court, to Charles S. Brown, May 19, 1958.

242. "Obituary," *The New York Freeman*, Jan. 31, 1885 (Quarles's obituary states that after Whitaker's court-martial he lived with Quarles); W. J. Simmons, *Men of Mark* 330–31 (1887). For a full account of the Whitaker trial see, J. F. Marszalek, Jr., *Court-Martial: A Black Man in America* 64, 147, 158, 175–76 (1972). (Marszalek's book does not mention John Francis Quarles.)

243. *Ibid.* (obit.)

244. *People's Advocate*, Feb. 25, 1882; letter from William M. Gibson to Charles S. Brown, May 30, 1961.

245. Letter from Fanny C. Howe, librarian, Troy Public Library, to Charles S. Brown, April 20, 1961.

246. *The New York Globe*, July 5, 1884.

247. *Biographies of Graduates of Yale Law School, 1824–1899*, at 499 (R. W. Tuttle ed. 1911).

248. "Albert Morris Thomas, Jr., Attorney at Law, Buffalo, N.Y.," *Indianapolis Freeman*, April 20, 1889.

249. Letter from Ridgway McNallie, Buffalo and Erie County Public Library, to Charles S. Brown, March 10, 1961.

250. *Biographies of Graduates of Yale Law School, 1824–1899*, at 499 (R. W. Tuttle ed. 1911).

251. *New York Freeman*, June 20, 1885.

252. "Lee," *Union and Advertiser*, May 17, 1894, at 6, col. 4.

253. G. R. Richings, *Evidence of Progress Among Colored People* 294–95 (1904).

254. *Ibid.*

255. *In re Bush's Will*, 5 N.Y. Supp. 23–24 (1889). The opinion of the court was written by Judge S. Ransom. Stewart was opposed in this case by the New York firm of Wilson and Wallis.

256. Justice, "Suit Against Hotel Keeper Trainor Won," *New York Age*, Nov. 14, 1891.

257. Other black lawyers consulted in the case included John Mercer Langston, then a member of Congress, Jacob H. Simms, of New York, and Edward H. Morris, of Chicago. I. G. Penn, *The Afro-American Press, and Its Editors* 535 (1891).

258. "Progress in the Courts," *New York Age*, April 19, 1890.

259. F. L. Styles, *Negroes and the Law* 128, 131 (1937).

260. *New York v. Johnson*, 140 N.Y. 350, 355 (1893).

261. Wynes, "T. McCants Stewart: Peripatetic Black South Carolinian," 80 *South Carolina Historical Magazine* 311, 315 (Oct. 1979).

262. Vol. 2 *The Booker T. Washington Papers, 1860–89*, at 255 (L. R. Harlan and P. Daniels eds. 1972). It is unknown what political appointment Stewart sought, but he failed to be appointed to any federal post. *Dictionary of American Negro Biography* 571, 572 (R. Logan and M. Winston eds. 1982). One of the national black leaders who publicly criticized Stewart's participation in the Democratic Party was his friend and former client, Richard Theodore Greener, a black lawyer and publisher of the *New York Age*. Greener, "M'Cants Stewart Flayed, Richard T. Greener Replies to Stewart's Scurrilous Attack in the *New York Age*," *Indianapolis Freeman*, Jan. 25, 1896, at 1, col. 1.

263. Wynes, "T. McCants Stewart: Peripatetic Black South Carolinian," 80 *South Carolina Historical Magazine* 311, 316 (Oct. 1979).

264. Vol. 1 *Who's Who of the Colored Race* 38 (F. L. Mather ed. 1915).

265. *Id.* at 115.

266. "Petition in Circulation for Colored Magistrate," *Bronx Home News*, Feb. 11, 1925; "Petition for Negro Judge," *New York Evening World*, March 13, 1925.

267. *The Marcus Garvey and UNIA Papers* 426 (R. A. Hill and B. Bair eds. 1987); A. Meier, "Booker T. Washington: An Interpretation," in *Black History* 350–51 (M. Drimmer ed. 1968). Wilford H. Smith's alias was J. C. May. *Id.* at 50, n.19. See also, Vol. 14 *The Booker T. Washington Papers* (index), at 131, 137 (L. R. Harlan and R. W. Smock eds. 1989), listing other aliases.

268. "Wilford H. Smith to Locate Permanently at Galveston," *New York Age*, April 15, 1922. E. D. Cronon, *Black Moses: The Story of Marcus Garvey and the Universal Negro Improvement Association* 98 (2d ed. 1972). Smith, who was counsel to the *Black Star Line*, returned to Galveston, Texas, just before the BSL

began to crumble. See also, *Marcus Garvey: Life and Lessons* 426 (R. A. Hill and B. Bair eds. 1987). Other notable black lawyers became involved in Marcus Garvey's crusade, among them, Louis A. Lavelle, of New York City; William C. Matthews, of Boston; J. Austin Norris, of Philadelphia; and Vernal J. Williams, of New York. *Id.* at 402, 408, 414–15, 443. Lavelle was interested "in forming the UNIA into a political club," a goal opposed by Garvey. The ambitious Lavelle "was an unsuccessful progressive candidate for a seat in the New York assembly from the twenty-first district; and in 1922 and 1924 he was a Democratic nominee for U.S. Congress from the Third Congressional District of the Bronx." *Id.* at 402. He apparently polled less than 5 percent of the vote in both campaigns for Congress. *Guide to U.S. Elections* 904, 909 (2d ed., J. L. Moore ed., 1985).

269. Vol. 1 *Who's Who in Colored America* 203 (J. J. Boris ed. 1927).

270. Vol. 1 *Who's Who of the Colored Race* 24 (F. L. Mather ed. 1915).

271. Vol. 1 *Who's Who in Colored America* 106 (J. J. Boris ed. 1927); R. Ottley and W. J. Weatherby, *The Negro in New York* 195, n.1 (1967); C. V. Hamilton, *Adam Clayton Powell, Jr.* 112 (1991).

272. F. L. Styles, *Negroes and the Law* 20 (1937); *Dictionary of American Negro Biography* 349, 350 (R. Logan and M. Winston eds. 1982). Johnson was not elected to a second term in 1918 because he favored prohibition, a position that proved unpopular with the voters. E. R. Lewinson, *Black Politics in New York City* 59 (1974). In 1929 Johnson ran for Congress in the Twenty-first Congressional District of New York. His attempt was historical but not successful. He complained that although "[colored citizens] had a much larger vote of registered voters than ever before, yet the full strength of the colored vote did not come out." Johnson, "A Congressional Campaign," 36 *Crisis* 118 (Jan. 1929). Johnson apparently was seeking the same votes as the more popular Hubert T. Delany, who was also a candidate. Delany lost to a white Democrat. *Guide to U.S. Elections* 921 (2d ed., J. L. Moore ed. 1985).

273. *Ibid.* (*Black Politics in New York City*). John Clifford Hawkins served in the New York State Assembly from 1918 to 1920, and Pope Barrow Billups served in the Assembly in 1925. *Id.* at 20–21; *Dictionary of American Negro Biography* 349, 350 (R. Logan and M. Winston eds. 1982); *NYS Black and Puerto Rican Legislators: 1917–1977*, at 3 (J. A. Stewart ed. 1977).

274. E. R. Lewinson, *Black Politics in New York City* 59 (1974).

275. *Id.* at 59, 63.

276. Vol. 1 *Who's Who in Colored America* 249 (J. J. Boris ed. 1927).

277. *Id.* at 14.

278. "M'Dougald's [*sic*] Announcement," *New York News*, May 20, 1915. McDougal left office just as Charles S. Whitman was elected governor of New York. *New York Negro Lawyers* 10 (S. H. Lark ed. 1915). Ferdinand Quintin Morton, who attended Boston University School of Law, succeeded McDougal as New York county assistant district attorney, serving from 1916 to 1921. He ultimately succeeded in heading the Indictment Bureau. Morton's political destiny was influenced by Charles F. Murphy, who was impressed with Morton because he had never met a graduate of Phillips Exeter Academy and Harvard College. It was Murphy who "secured an appointment for him as Assistant District Attorney." E. R. Lewinson, *Black Politics in New York City* 61 (1974). In 1921 Morton was appointed to the Municipal Civil Service Commission of New York City. Vol. 1 *Who's Who in Colored America* 146 (J. J. Boris ed. 1927). Morton's political appointments may have resulted from the fact that he

"headed the United Colored Democracy (UCD), a black division of Tammany Hall." Martin Kilson, "Adam Clayton Powell, Jr.: The Militant as Politician," in *Black Leaders of the Twentieth Century* 261 (J. H. Franklin and A. Meir eds. 1982).

279. R. Ottley and W. J. Weatherby, *The Negro in New York* 220 (1967).

280. *Id.* at 221. For more on the Garvey case, see Hobbs and Fitch, "The Marcus Garvey Case: A Law and Power Theory Analysis of Political Suppression of Human Dignity," 2 *Geo. Mason Univ. Civil Rights L.J.* 15 (1991).

281. "M'Dougald [*sic*] Given Big Appointment," *Chicago Defender*, May 17, 1924; "N.Y.'s New Asst. State's Attorney," *Afro-American*, May 16, 1924.

282. "Negro Lawyer to Prison; Atkins Given Jail Sentence," April 1912 (source unknown, on file with author); "Negro Company in Trouble," Feb. 24, 1911; "$1,000,000 Company Fails," *New York Press*, Feb. 24, 1911 (courtesy of Hampton University Archives).

283. "Rufus L. Perry Is Disbarred," *New York Times*, Oct. 6, 1917; "Disbarred for Signing Name to Father's Will," *New York News*, Oct. 11, 1917. Perry's disbarment must have caused much embarrassment to the black bar, especially since the newly elected governor of New York, Charles S. Whitman, had appointed him state commissioner for the National Negro Exposition. *New York Negro Lawyers* 8, 10 (S. H. Lark ed. 1915). "Rufus L. Perry, Negro Re'nstated as Lawyer," *New York Journal*, Dec. 5, 1922.

284. "Business Magazine Pays Tribute to Rufus L. Perry," *New York Age*, Sept. 30, 1915.

285. "Lawyer Rufus L. Perry, Brooklyn Lawyer, Is Writing Hebrew Grammar," *New York Age*, Jan. 29, 1927.

286. Holder, "Colored Women Employing Jewish Lawyers," *New York Age*, Sept. 30, 1915.

287. *Ibid.*

288. "Colored Women Employing Jewish Lawyers," *New York Age*, Oct. 28, 1915. The unsigned letter from the black businesswoman also drew a sharp response from Robert Lewis Waring, a black New York lawyer, who wrote, "First: I did not know that there is a colored woman in New York City whose legal business is of such volume that it has caused the business death of three colored lawyers. . . . Second: I am amazed that a colored woman who has brains enough to develop a business that calls for the service of even a colored lawyer, should display such amazing ignorance of the ordinary methods of gauging people." "Re: Colored Women Employing Jewish Lawyers," *New York News*, Nov. 14, 1915.

289. "Celebrate Negro Lawyers' Day in Harlem Churches," *Amsterdam News*, April 22, 1939. By the time the dispute arose about the use of black lawyers in New York, the number and influence of black lawyers had increased significantly. Among the black lawyers practicing in New York City were James D. Carr, who worked in the corporation counsel's office, Samuel A. Pease, a 1906 graduate of the Brooklyn Law School and an expert in real estate law, N. B. Marshall, A. Q. Morton, James L. Curtis, Judson Douglas Wetmore, Louis A. Levelle, Robert L. Waring, Philip Throne, Samuel F. Edmead, and Robert H. Latimore. During this period, Frederick Chew and Francis T. Giles were practicing in Troy and Brooklyn, New York, respectively. *New York Negro Lawyers* 10, 12, 15 (S. H. Lark ed. 1915).

290. *New York Negro Lawyers* 14 (S. H. Lark ed. 1915); *Columbia Alumni Register, 1754–1931*, at 67 (1932).

291. *Id.* at 12.

292. Lillian S. Williams, "The Development of Black Community: Buffalo, New York, 1900–1940," at 305, 310, 315 (Ph.D. diss., State University of New York at Buffalo, 1979).

293. G. R. Segal, *Blacks in the Law* 172 (1983). Dyett received a master of laws degree in 1921 from Boston University School of Law.

294. "U.S. Attorney J. C. Thomas Wins Laurels in Court," *New York Age*, Sept. 17, 1921.

295. "Colored Attorney Defends Italians," *Amsterdam News*, Nov. 26, 1924. Gilchrist Stewart had been active in New York for at least twenty years. In the late 1890s, Stewart headed the New York Vigilance Committee, "which investigated cases of discrimination against blacks in greater New York." He was so successful in winning anti-discrimination cases that his work later became "instrumental in shaping the NAACP's aggressive legal work on behalf of black citizens." Vol. 3 *The Booker T. Washington Papers, 1889–95*, at 456–57 (L. R. Harlan and B. S. Kaufman eds. 1974). In 1906 Senator Joseph B. Foraker assigned Stewart "to investigate the Brownsville [Texas] affray." Stewart concluded that "the two black regiments dismissed from the army for alleged misconduct (rioting) were innocent." *Id.* at 455. See also, Vol. 9 *The Booker T. Washington Papers, 1906–8*, at 224, 487 (L. R. Harlan, R. W. Smock and N. E. Woodruff eds. 1980), for other references to Gilchrist Stewart.

296. "Race Lawyer Admitted to U.S. Supreme Court," *St. Louis Argus*, May 1, 1925.

297. F. L. Styles, *Negroes and the Law* 43 (1937), quoting "Aged Williams, Walker Agent Not Deported," *Afro-American*, June 1, 1934.

298. "Attorney J. C. Thomas Appointed Receiver for Big Jewish Firm," *New York Age*, July 31, 1926. Richard L. Baltimore was appointed assistant United States district attorney in 1927. Vol. 1 *Who's Who in Colored America* 9 (J. J. Boris ed. 1927).

299. In the 1930s, Father Divine retained and consulted with other noted black lawyers, including Myles Paige and Arthur Madison. He was also supported by a liberal Jewish judge named Jonah Goldstein. R. W. Weisbrot, *Father Divine* 66, 76, 78, 162 (1983).

300. *Id.* at 51.

301. *Ibid.*

302. *Ibid.*

303. *Ibid.*

304. *Id.* at 53.

305. *Id.* at 54. See *People v. Devine* [*sic*], 237 A.D. 890, 261 N.Y.S. 989 (1933). Here the Appellate Division, Second District, reversed the conviction of Father Divine and ordered a new trial because it thought "that prejudice against the defendant was excited in the minds of the jurors by comments, rulings and questions by the court throughout the trial." *Id.* at 990. Although one author has surmised that Father Divine's real name was George Baker, the official caption of the case indicated that his first name was Major. See R. W. Weisbrot, *Father Divine* 9, 16 (1983).

306. Adams, "Justice Delany Active in and out of Court," *Amsterdam News*, Feb. 5, 1944; "Colored Lawyer to Speak Here for Fogarty," *Yonkers Record*, Oct. 27, 1935.

307. "Negroes Everywhere Interested in Delany-for-Congress Fight," *The Negro World*, Oct. 12, 1929, at 1, col. 1; "Delany Must Win—Must Be Made Real," *The Negro World*, Oct. 12, 1929, at 4, col. 3.

308. LaFourche, "Delany, Was He a Victim of Circumstance," Vol. 1 (No. 7) *New Orleans Civic Leader* 4 (1930). Delany, a Republican, ran in a special election for the twenty-first congressional district in New York. Gavagan, a Democrat, polled 39,893 votes, or 56 percent, to Delany's 37.9 percent of the vote. Frank Crosswaith, a Socialist, polled 3,561 (5.1 percent). *Guide to U.S. Elections* 921 (2d ed., J. L. Moore 1985). The black vote appears to have been split between Delany and another black candidate named Edward Austin Johnson, also a lawyer. See Johnson, "A Congressional Campaign," 36 *Crisis* 118 (Jan. 1929).

309. Adams, "Justice Delany Active in and out of Court," *Amsterdam News*, Feb. 5, 1944; "Delany Gets Judgeship at $12,000 a Yr.," *Afro-American*, Aug. 6, 1942, at 1, col. 1; James, "Hubert T. Delany, 89, Ex-Judge and Civil Rights Advocate Dies," *New York Times*, Dec. 31, 1990, at 24, col. 1.

310. Fowle, "Francis E. Rivers Dies—Black City Judge Was 82," *New York Times*, July 29, 1975, at 32, col. 2.

311. Adams, "A 'Profile' of the Latest Judge Elected," *New York Age*, Feb. 19, 1944. Rivers received his undergraduate degree from Yale University in 1915.

312. "Negro Joins Bar Assoc'n," *Savannah Tribune*, Feb. 28, 1929. Fowle, "Francis E. Rivers Dies—Black City Judge Was 82," *New York Times*, July 29, 1975, at 32, col. 2; *Year Book, Association of the Bar, City of New York, 1943*, at 54. For general history of ABCNY, see M. J. Powell, *From Patrician to Professional Elite* 74 (1988). The under-representation of black lawyers in white law firms limited the membership base in ABCNY through the 1970s.

313. In 1925 Pope Barrow Billups, a black lawyer, sponsored legislation to change the political boundaries of the Seventh Municipal Court District in Manhattan. Such a change would have assured the election of two black judges in Harlem. Some white assemblymen objected to Billups's proposal because they feared it would be "impossible to ever elect a white man in the Seventh District as a Municipal Court Justice if this change [was] made." Billups's bill was defeated, but the seed was planted. "Add Three Justices to Municipal Courts," *New York Times*, March 25, 1925, at 6, col. 3. The bill was reintroduced in the following legislative session by a white assemblyman, Abraham Grenthal, of the Ninth District. Grenthal asked Billups, who had retired from the assembly, to come to Albany to argue for the bill. Billups responded to Grenthal's request, asserting "that a representative of his race was entitled to a place on the bench of the poor man's court." While Billups also demonstrated that a new district with two additional judges would reduce the court's backlog of cases, he made it clear that blacks "are for this bill because it will open the way for a colored lawyer to be elected a Justice of the Municipal Court." The Grenthal bill failed because of opposition by Governor Al Smith. "Governor Charges Republicans Assist City Treasury Raid," *New York Times*, April 3, 1927, at 1, col. 1.

314. Rivers, "The Lawyer and Legislation," *The National Bar Association Proceedings of the Six Annual Convention* 24 (Aug. 7, 1930); Rivers, "The Manhattan City Court Election of 1943," 2 *Nat'l. B.A.J.* 38, 40 (1944). The tenth judicial district was created by the adoption of Assembly Bill 2211, which amended Sections 1 and 5 of the New York City Municipal Code by altering the political boundaries of the seventh judicial district and creating the new tenth judicial district. *New York Legislative Record and Index* 252 (1930).

315. Vol. 1 *Who's Who of the Colored Race* 278 (F. L. Mather ed. 1915); *New York Law School—1891 to 1991—A Heritage* 10 (1991). The New York County Lawyers' Association, a white lawyers' group, "endorsed [James S.] Watson when he

ran for judicial office in 1930." Letter from Joseph L. Maged, executive director, NYCLA, to Charles S. Brown, Aug. 26, 1959.

316. Vol. 1 *Who's Who in Colored America* 203 (J. J. Boris ed. 1927); Shipp, "'Family Party' Is Staged at N.Y.U. for the Black Judges in New York," *New York Times*, Dec. 13, 1981, at 55, col. 1. Charles Toney and Ferdinand Q. Morton had practiced together for many years. E. R. Lewinson, *Black Politics in New York City* 67 (1974).

317. "New York's Fourth Negro Judge, Now on the Bench," *New York Age*, July 29, 1939.

318. *Ibid*; Fowle, "Francis E. Rivers Dies; Black City Judge Was 82," *New York Times*, July 29, 1975, at 32, col. 2. Rivers's salary was $17,500 per annum.

319. *Ibid.* ("Francis E. Rivers Dies").

320. "Negro Law Firm Engaged by Bank," *Baltimore Herald*, July 19, 1924.

321. *Ibid.*

322. "Race Lawyer on Wall Street," *Baltimore Afro-American*, Aug. 7, 1926. Williams's office was located at 67 Wall Street.

323. Personal records of Stanley Moreland Douglas, Douglas Papers, Amistad Collection, Tulane University, New Orleans, Louisiana; letter from Stanley M. Douglas to Perry W. Howard, May 3, 1929; *Virginia's Contribution to Negro Leadership* 21 (W. Cooper ed. 1937) (mimeo).

324. Allen, "Negro Lawyers Needed," *New York Age*, July 18, 1936.

325. Gordon, "The Problem of the Negro Lawyer," 2 *Education* 4 (April 1936).

326. *New York Times*, Sept. 2, 1936; "Tall, Likeable; That's Justice Myles A. Paige," *Amsterdam News*, Jan. 22, 1944. Paige was appointed magistrate in 1936 and served in that capacity until 1945. Prior to his appointment, Paige had served as president of the Harlem Lawyers' Association.

327. Lawrence, "Harlem Lawyer Assigned to White Man's Defense," *Amsterdam News*, Dec. 21, 1940.

328. *Ibid.*

329. "Sandifer Rise to Bar in New York an Alger Story," *Norfolk Journal and Guide*, Sept. 5, 1942.

330. *Ibid.*

331. "Hall Becomes Solicitor General's Aide," *Washington Tribune*, Nov. 13, 1943. Hall was a graduate of New York University Law School.

332. M. Naison, *Communists in Harlem During the Depression* 313 (1983); B. J. Davis, *Communist Councilman from Harlem* 101–44 (1969).

333. Lamar Perkins was graduated from Harvard University's law school in 1922; Conrad A. Johnson was a practicing lawyer in Harlem; and Stanley Moreland Douglas was a 1923 Fordham University law graduate. They were all paid four thousand dollars a year. "Dewey Appoints Colored Lawyer to High Office," *Nashville Globe and Independent*, June 9, 1944; letter from Nathaniel L. Goldstein, attorney general of New York, to Stanley Moreland Douglas, April 4, 1944.

334. "Woman Given Place at Bar; First of Race," *Chicago Defender*, Jan. 27, 1923; "Colored Woman Lawyer Admitted N.Y. Bar," *Amsterdam News*, June 13, 1923; "First Girl to Pass Bar," *Chicago Whip*, Jan. 29, 1923. In 1932, Robinson practiced law at 101 West 141st Street in New York. H. Eustice Williams practiced at 200 West 135th Street. *Law Directory of the National Bar Association* 137 (1933) (appended to *Proceedings of the Seventh and Eighth Annual Conventions of the National Bar Association*, Aug. 6, 1931 and Aug. 4, 1932). Robinson and

Enid Foderingham Thorpe were graduates of Hunter College. "First Colored Girls to Receive Degrees in Law," *New York Age*, June 17, 1922, at 1, col. 3.

335. "Ruth Whitehead Whaley," *Afro-American*, Sept. 5, 1924. The article implies that Whitehead did not graduate from Fordham University Law School. "Colored Girl Enters Fordham Law School," *New York Age*, Oct. 1, 1921, at 1, col. 5. More recent articles confirm that Whaley was the first woman graduated from Fordham Law School. "Ruth W. Whaley, Lawyer in New York," *Washington Post*, Dec. 29, 1977, at C9, col. 1. On February 22, 1989, the Fordham Law School registrars' office confirmed that Whaley was graduated on May 25, 1925.

336. "N.Y. Woman Lawyer Takes Off Her Hat to Argue Her Cases," *Baltimore Afro-American*, July 25, 1931.

337. "N.Y. Woman Lawyer to Test Civil Rights," *Washington Tribune*, April 6, 1928.

338. "N.Y. Woman Lawyer Takes Off Her Hat to Argue Her Cases," *Baltimore Afro-American*, July 25, 1931.

339. *Ibid.*

340. *Ibid.*

341. *Ibid*; "Ruth Whaley Creates Stir," *Amsterdam News*, Oct. 26, 1927.

342. "Atty. Ruth Whitehead Whaley Wins Notable Victory For L. I. Client," *New York Age*, Dec. 2, 1939.

343. P. Murray, *Song in a Weary Throat* 277, 294 (1987).

344. K. B. Morello, *The Woman Lawyer in American: 1638 to the Present—The Invisible Bar* 153 (1986).

345. Bruce graduated from Boston University Law School in 1926 and first settled in Washington, D.C. She is listed as practicing in New York City in 1932. *Law Directory of the National Bar Association* (appended to the *Proceedings of the Seventh and Eighth Annual Convention*, Aug. 6, 1931, and Aug. 4, 1932, at 137).

346. "Lucille Chance, Leader in Harlem and Lawyer," *New York Times*, April 8, 1987, at D30, col. 6.

347. "A Sepia Portia—Jane Bolin," 9 *Apex News* 13 (Sept. 1937); Davis, "Judge Bolin Hopes Choice Will Inspire Other Women," *Philadelphia Tribune*, Aug. 17, 1939; "New York's Fourth Negro Judge, Now on Bench," *New York Age*, July 29, 1939.

348. "Miss Jane Bolin Appointed Asst. to Corporation Counsel," *New York Age*, April 27, 1937; "Miss Jane Bolin," *Richmond Planet*, April 17, 1937.

349. "A Sepia Portia—Jane Bolin," 9 *Apex News* 13 (Sept. 1937).

350. Davis, "Judge Bolin Hopes Choice Will Inspire Other Women," *Philadelphia Tribune*, Aug. 17, 1939 (on her marriage to Ralph Mizelle); "New York's Fourth Negro Judge, Now on Bench," *New York Age*, July 29, 1939; "Election to Bar Association," *New York Age*, April 24, 1943. No mention of Judge Bolin's historic admission to this bar group is made in the centennial history of the Association of the Bar of New York City. See G. Martin, *Causes and Conflicts: The Centennial History of the Association of the Bar of the City of New York, 1870–1970*, at 244–45 (1970). Ralph Mizelle was a distinguished lawyer in his own right. In the early 1940s, Mizelle was an assistant attorney in the office of the New York solicitor general. He vacated this post in 1943 and was succeeded by Thomas C. Hall, a black New York University Law School graduate. "Hall Becomes Solicitor General's Aide," *Washington Tribune*, Nov. 13, 1943.

351. "I Earn $5,500 Per Year," *Afro-American*, March 5, 1938.

352. "Negro Woman Lawyer Named Aide in Harlem Racket Inquiry," *New*

York Herald, Aug. 6, 1935; "I Earn $5,500 Per Year," *Afro-American*, March 5, 1938; "Four Women Get Honors at Smith," *New York Times*, June 21, 1938; "Eunice Hunton Carter," 16 *Opportunity* 261 (Sept. 1938).

353. H. Powell, *Ninety Times Guilty* 89 (1970).

354. *Ibid*.

355. "Sara Pelham Speaks!" *The Union*, Jan. 7, 1937, at 1, col. 1; "Bias Against Negro Charged to Courts," *New York Times*, April 19, 1943.

356. "N.Y. Woman Lawyer Takes Off Her Hat to Argue Her Cases," *Baltimore Afro-American*, July 25, 1931.

357. J. M. Langston, *From the Virginia Plantation to the National Capitol* 104 (1894).

358. *Id.* at 109–10. One legal historian has noted that, with the aid of Judge Philemon Bliss, Langston was "allowed to pursue his studies within the walls of [Judge Timothy] Walker's Law School in Cincinnati, Ohio." Daniel, "The Law Library of Howard University, 1867–1956," 51 *Law Library Journal* 202, 204 (1958). However, Langston's autobiography states that "Judge Walker [wrote] to him that he could not receive him, 'because his students would not feel at home with him, and he would not feel at home with them.' " J. M. Langston, *From the Virginia Plantation to the National Capitol* 110 (1894).

359. *Id.* at 117 (*From the Virginia Plantation*).

360. *Id.* at 121. See also, Vol. 1 *Dictionary of American Biography* 375 (A. Johnson ed., 1936) (on Bliss).

361. *Id.* at 123 (*From the Virginia Plantation*).

362. *Id.* at 123–24.

363. W. J. Simmons, *Men of Mark* 510–11 (1887).

364. J. M. Langston, *From the Virginia Plantation to the National Capitol* 125 (1894).

365. *Id.* at 130–31.

366. *Id.* at 132–33.

367. *Id.* at 134–35.

368. *Id.* at 164.

369. *Id.* at 144–45.

370. *Id.* at 145.

371. *Id.* at 168; *Afro-American Encyclopedia; Or, The Thoughts, Doings and Sayings of the Race* 42 (J. T. Haley ed. 1895); F. L. Styles, *Negroes and the Law* 119 (1937).

372. J. M. Langston, *From the Virginia Plantation to the National Capitol* 169–70 (1894), quoting W. W. Brown, *The Black Man* 236–37 (1863).

373. Blodgett, "John Mercer Langston and the Case of Edmonia Lewis: Oberlin, 1862," 53 *J. Negro History* 201, 205 (1968).

374. *Ibid*. W. Cheek and A. L. Cheek, *John Mercer Langston and the Fight for Black Freedom* 303 (1989).

375. *Id.* at 303.

376. Blodgett, "John Mercer Langston and the Case of Edmonia Lewis: Oberlin, 1862," 53 *J. of Negro History* 210 (1968).

377. *Id.* at 213.

378. *Ibid*. After she was cleared of the alleged poisoning incident, Lewis continued to have difficulties at Oberlin. She soon left Oberlin for Boston and later moved to Rome, Italy, where she became "the pride of her race in her profession." "Edmonia Lewis, Sculptress," in *Afro-American Encyclopedia; Or, The Thoughts, Doings and Sayings of the Race* 413 (J. T. Haley ed. 1895).

379. *Addresses and Ceremonies at the New Year's Festival to the Freeman on Arlington Heights—And Statistics and Statements of the Educational Condition of the Colored People in the Southern States, and Other Facts* 48 (1867); *Afro-American Encyclopedia; Or, The Thoughts, Doings and Sayings of the Race* 42 (J. T. Haley ed. 1895).

380. Letter of Mary J. Safford, M.D., New York, April 5, 1869, printed in the *National Anti-Slavery Standard*, April 17, 1869, at 3, col. 3 (courtesy of Dorothy B. Porter-Wesley); Straker, "The Negro in the Profession of the Law," 8 *The A.M.E. Rev.* 178–79 (1891).

381. "John P. Green 'First Lawyer' Is Still Active," *Chicago Whip*, June 21, 1930.

382. Vol. 1 *Who's Who in Colored America* 79 (J. J. Boris ed. 1927); G. W. Williams, *Negro Race in America* 447 (1885); F. L. Styles, *Negroes and the Law* 141 (1937). Throughout Green's career, he took moderate positions on the race question. This "won him influential friends in Cleveland and in Washington." K. Kusmer, *A Ghetto Takes Shape: Black Cleveland, 1870–1930*, at 120 (1976).

383. *Id.* at 447 (*Negro Race in America*).

384. *Dictionary of American Negro Biography* 265–66 (R. Logan and M. Winston eds. 1982). According to the *Dictionary*, "The office, comprising a part of the Court of Common Pleas and including among its duties jurisdiction to hear and decide certain civil actions, constituted the first level in the judicial system of the day."

385. *Ibid*; Vol. 1 *Who's Who in Colored America* 79 (J. J. Boris ed. 1927).

386. *Ibid.* (*Who's Who*).

387. "An Ohio Lawyer," *Indianapolis Freeman*, March 9, 1889.

388. "Green, Dean of Cleveland Bar Ends 60th Year," *Washington Tribune*, Oct. 17, 1930.

389. "Hon. John P. Green," *New York Globe*, Feb. 24, 1883, at 1, col. 2.

390. *Dictionary of American Negro Biography* 264, 266 (R. Logan and M. Winston eds. 1982).

391. K. Kusmer, *A Ghetto Takes Shape: Black Cleveland, 1870–1930*, at 144, n.52 (1976).

392. *Ibid*; Vol. 1 *Who's Who of the Colored Race* 120–21 (F. L. Mather ed. 1915). William and Theodore Green practiced law together in Cleveland around 1911. Vol. 10 *The Booker T. Washington Papers, 1909–11*, at 435 (L. R. Harlan, R. W. Smock, G. McTigue, and N. E. Woodruff eds. 1981).

393. "Mayor's Proclamation," *Cleveland Eagle*, April 2, 1937.

394. W. P. Dabney, *Cincinnati's Colored Citizens* 203 (1926).

395. *Id.* at 108–9, 116, 201.

396. Vol. 92 *Journal of the House of Representatives of the State of Ohio, Seventy-second General Assembly*, 52, 53, 74, Jan. 6, 1896.

397. Vol. 76 *Journal of the House of Representatives of the State of Ohio, Sixty-fourth General Assembly* 34, 46, 1,019, Jan. 5, 1880.

398. J. H. Franklin, *George Washington Williams* 56, 138, 170 (1985); *The College of Life or Practical Self Educator: A Manual of Self Improvement for the Colored Race* 134 (H. D. Northrop, J. R. Gay, and I. G. Penn eds. 1896); Franklin, "George Washington Williams," 31 *J. of Negro History* 60, 64 (Jan. 1946). Williams was admitted to practice in the Supreme Circuit of Ohio on June 7, 1881, in Columbus. He was later admitted to practice before the Supreme Judicial Court of Boston.

399. Letter from John Q. Taylor King, president, Houston-Tillotson College, to Redman Turner, Nov. 14, 1986.

400. *The Short Fiction of Charles W. Chesnutt* 9 (S. L. Render ed. 1974); Vol. 1 *Who's Who of the Colored Race* 64 (F. L. Mather ed. 1915).

401. *Ibid.* (*Short Fiction of Charles W. Chesnutt*).

402. Chesnutt wrote a short story, "A Miscarriage of Justice," and an anecdote entitled, "Busy Day in a Lawyer's Office." *Id.* at 73, 357 (*Short Fiction of Charles W. Chesnutt*).

403. F. L. Styles, *Negroes and the Law* 136 (1937). After Chesnutt was admitted to the bar, he remained somewhat aloof to the civil rights movement in Cleveland. K. Kusmer, *A Ghetto Takes Shape: Black Cleveland, 1870–1930*, at 128 (1976). In 1913, on one of the few occasions at which he showed a deep interest in civil rights, Chesnutt "used his influence with Newton D. Baker to help defeat an Ohio anti-intermarriage bill." Later, in 1915, "he fought to have the racist film 'Birth of a Nation' banned from the state." *Ibid.* But see Vol. 7 *The Booker T. Washington Papers, 1903–4*, at 136 (L. R. Harlan and R. W. Smock eds. 1977). Chesnutt's interest in national civil rights may have exceeded his local interests. For example, in 1903 Chesnutt expressed deep regret to Booker T. Washington regarding the denial of black political rights in the South. He made these remarks in light of the United States Supreme Court's ruling in *Giles v. Harris*, 189 U.S 475 (1903).

404. Vol. 1 *Who's Who of the Colored Race* 255 (F. L. Mather ed. 1915).

405. W. P. Dabney, *Cincinnati's Colored Citizens* 256, 342 (1926).

406. *Virginia's Contribution to Negro Leadership* 48 (W. Cooper ed. 1937) (mimeo).

407. Vol. 1 *Who's Who in Colored America* 137 (J. J. Boris ed. 1927).

408. Shirla R. McClain, "The Contribution of Blacks in Akron: 1825–1975," at 131 (Ph.D. diss., University of Akron, 1975).

409. "Active Career of Moses H. Jones Is Brought to Close," *Dayton Journal*, Jan. 21, 1920.

410. *Ibid.*

411. *University of Michigan General Catalogue of Officers and Students, 1837–1911*, at 485, 488 (I. N. Demmon ed. 1912).

412. Vol. 1 *Who's Who of the Colored Race* 153 (F. L. Mather ed. 1915).

413. W. P. Dabney, *Cincinnati's Colored Citizens* 242 (1926).

414. *Virginia's Contribution to Negro Leadership* 4 (W. Cooper ed. 1937) (mimeo); Vol. 1 *Who's Who of the Colored Race* 19 (F. L. Mather ed. 1915); Vol. 1 *Who's Who in Colored America* 9 (J. J. Boris ed. 1927); "Robert B. Barcus," *Chicago Defender*, Oct. 14, 1922. See also, Vol. 1 *Attorney General Opinions, Ohio* 4 (1919), listing Barcus as special counsel; *id.* at 4 (1923), listing Barcus.

415. "Wilbur E. King Again on Prosecutor's Staff," *Columbus Journal*, March 20, 1924.

416. Vol. 1 *Who's Who in Colored America* 25 (J. J. Boris ed. 1927).

417. Vol. 107 *Journal of the House of Representatives of the State of Ohio, Eighty-second General Assembly* 41, 45, Jan. 16, 1917; Vol. 108 *Journal of the House of Representatives of the State of Ohio, Eighty-third General Assembly* 45, 47, 1909, Jan. 6, 1919.

418. See flyer entitled "Do You Want This Bill to Pass?" H.B. 139 was passed by the Ohio General Assembly in 1919. When the bill reached the Ohio State Senate, handbills were circulated identifying Mr. Beaty, the bill's sponsor, as "Colored" (on file, Cincinnati Historical Society).

419. W. P. Dabney, *Cincinnati's Colored Citizens* 344 (1926); letter from Tom Gerety, dean, University of Cincinnati Law School, to author, Feb. 25, 1988.

420. "Dems Claim 'First' " (no source), circa Jan., 1937 (article from H. Elsie Austin's scrapbook). See Vol. 1 *Attorney General Opinions, Ohio* iii (1915), listing Godman as special counsel.

421. Vol. 1 *Attorney General Opinions, Ohio* iii (1915), listing Green as special counsel.

422. "Diefenback & St. T. Kelly, Atty. Ted Green," *Akron Legal News*, Sept. 6, 1951.

423. Biographical sketch of William T. McKnight, National Bar Association files.

424. *History of the American Negro in the Great World War* 119–30 (W. A. Sweeney ed. 1919), listing Lt. Leroy H. Godman.

425. A. W. Hunton and K. M. Johnson, *Two Colored Women with the American Expeditionary Forces* 49 (1920).

426. *Ibid.*

427. *Id.* at 61.

428. "Noted Attorney Locate in Cleveland," *The Cleveland Advocate*, Aug. 16, 1919. Patterson entered the military as a resident of Chicago, Illinois.

429. Vol. 1 *Who's Who of the Colored Race* 104 (F. L. Mather ed. 1915); Vol. 1 *Who's Who in Colored America* 66 (J. J. Boris ed. 1927).

430. *Dictionary of American Negro Biography* 224–25 (R. Logan and M. Winston eds. 1982). Fleming was probably convicted for accepting a bribe soon after Ohio Governor Frank B. Willis appointed him deputy state oil inspector in 1914. Vol. 1 *The National Cyclopedia of the Colored Race* 319 (C. Richardson ed. 1919).

431. Thompson, "Negro Puts White Man Before Supreme Court," *Atlanta Constitution*, Oct. 29, 1914. Stewart moved for Anderson's admission to the Supreme Court prior to Anderson's oral argument in *Erie Railroad Co. v. Solomon*, 237 U.S. 427, 429 (1915).

432. *Ibid.*

433. "White Admitted by Black Lawyer," *The Freeman*, Nov. 7, 1914; Thompson, "Negro Puts White Man Before Supreme Court," *Atlanta Constitution*, Oct. 29, 1914.

434. K. Kusmer, *A Ghetto Takes Shape: Black Cleveland, 1870–1930*, at 248 (1976); R. H. Davis, *Memorable Negroes in Cleveland's Past* 49 (1969).

435. Vol. 1 *Who's Who in Colored America* 75 (J. J. Boris ed. 1927).

436. G. R. Segal, *Blacks in the Law* 145 (1983).

437. K. Kusmer, *A Ghetto Takes Shape: Black Cleveland, 1870–1930*, at 249–50 (1976), quoting *The Cleveland Advocate*, n.d., circa 1921.

438. Vol. 1 *Who's Who in Colored America* 102 (J. J. Boris ed. 1927); letter from Martha O. Leslie to Charles S. Brown, June 9, 1958.

439. "Capital Jurist Spurs Movement to Elect Colored Judge Here," *The Cleveland News*, Jan. 12, 1937.

440. "Cleveland Sees Negro Judge Ascend Bench," Jan. 15, 1937 (no source; article in Armond Scott's scrapbook, on file at National Portrait Gallery, Washington, D.C.).

441. Vol. 1 *Who's Who in Colored America* 102 (J. J. Boris ed. 1927). Jackson was also a Phi Beta Kappa graduate from Western Reserve University's Franklin Thomas Backus Law School; letter from Martha O. Leslie to Charles S. Brown, June 9, 1958; "Judge Perry B. Jackson," 53 *The Cleveland Bar J.* 115 (March 1982); "A Salute to Judge Perry Jackson," Vol. 131 *Cong. Rec.* E5097, Nov. 12, 1985; "Assist Students," *New York Age*, Oct. 17, 1931.

442. "Indianapolis Lawyer Ready for Big Meet," *Indianapolis Record*, July 23, 1932.

443. *Who's Who Among Negro Lawyers* 19 (S. T. M. Alexander ed. 1945).

444. Personal interview of Theodore Moody Berry, of Cincinnati, by author, June 9, 1989, in Washington, D.C.

445. See *Allen v. State*, 38 Ohio Law Reporter 99 (Ohio App. 1933).

446. Interview of Theodore Moody Berry by author, June 9, 1989.

447. *Ibid.*

448. *Ibid.*

449. *Ibid.*

450. *Lewis v. Board of Education of Wilmington School District*, 137 Ohio 145, 28 N.E. 2d 496 (1940) (with Belford V. Lawson, Herbert T. Delany, and William A. McClain). The opinion drew a dissent (without opinion) from Associate Justice Arthur H. Day. *Id.* at 149, 498.

451. "Berry Quits Off; Favors Legal Work," *Chicago Defender*, Aug. 1, 1942, at 5, col. 5; "Soldier Sues Bus Line in J. C. Case," *Afro-American*, Aug. 29, 1942, at 5, col. 6.

452. Letter from Martha O. Leslie to Charles S. Brown, Oct. 7, 1958. Around the time of White's appointment, several black lawyers were appointed to public posts: Charles V. Carr, a 1928 graduate of John Marshall Law School, was appointed assistant law director in the Cleveland prosecutor's office, where he served until 1941. George Corinth Lacy, a 1925 John Marshall law graduate, became an assistant prosecutor in Cleveland. Chester H. Crumpler, a 1916 Howard University law graduate, was appointed prosecutor in Mahoning County, a position he held until 1945; and William B. Saunders was appointed assistant prosecutor and utility-adjuster in Cleveland. See "A Salute to Charles V. Carr," 127 *Cong. Rec.* E3984, Aug. 4, 1981; *Virginia's Contribution to Negro Leadership* 37 (W. Cooper ed. 1937) (mimeo); *Who's Who Among Negro Lawyers* 11 (S. T. M. Alexander ed. 1945); "Attends Bar Meet," *Afro-American*, Aug. 14, 1937.

453. *Who's Who in Colored America* 131 (J. J. Boris ed. 1927). See also, "Norman L. McGhee and Aaron H. Payne," 37 *Howard University Bulletin* 23, July 15, 1958.

454. Shirla R. McClain, "The Contribution of Blacks in Akron: 1825–1975," at 174–75, 204 (Ph.D. diss., University of Akron, 1975), citing Case No. 41857, Summit County Court of Common Pleas, 1922; "Biography in Brief: Samuel Thomas Kelly," *Akron Beacon Journal*, Dec. 24, 1950.

455. "Frontiers Win Negro Judge for Cleveland," *Chicago Defender*, July 11, 1942, at 6, col. 5; "Negro Named to Judgeship," *Amsterdam New York Star-News*, July 4, 1942, at 24, col. 6.

456. *Job Opportunities for Negro Youth in Columbus, Ohio* 42 (C. J. Gray ed. 1938).

457. "Race Woman Lawyer Candidate for Ohio State Legislature," *Pittsburgh Courier*, May 28, 1924.

458. "May Disbar Colored Woman Lawyer," *Norfolk Journal and Guide*, March 30, 1929.

459. "Jane Hunter," *Baltimore Afro-American*, Jan. 9, 1926.

460. See "Woman Lawyer Wins Case for Brown and Marguerite" and "Receiver Appointed for Smith Bros. Printing Co." (Source, page, and dates of these two articles unknown. The articles are from the scrapbook of H. Elsie Austin, copy on file with the author).

461. *Pittsburgh Courier*, Jan. 16, 1937, at 1, col. 5; Vol. 1 *Attorney General Opinions, Ohio* 1 (1937) and *id.* at 4 (1938), listing Elsie Austin as assistant attorney general of Ohio.

462. "Nation's Lawyers End Conference at Durham," *Norfolk Journal and Guide*, Aug. 13, 1938.

463. Tenth Annual Banquet Program, Washington Bar Association, May 9, 1940.

464. G. R. Segal, *Blacks in the Law* 146 (1983); telephone conversation with Chester J. Gray, of Cleveland, Jan. 23, 1989.

Chapter 8

The Northwestern States

The northwestern states include Iowa, Michigan, Minnesota, Nebraska, North and South Dakota, and Wisconsin.

Iowa

In 1868 A. H. Watkins, a schoolteacher, left Nashville, Tennessee, for Fort Madison, Iowa, where he opened a barbershop. Watkins's real aim, however, was to become a lawyer. It is not known whether Watkins was self-taught or whether he studied under a lawyer. What is known is that in 1874, six years after he arrived in Keokut, Iowa, a newspaper announced that Judge Drayer had admitted Watkins to the bar after the "examining committee . . . found [him] better posted than the average of law students admitted to practice."[1] Watkins was followed to the Iowa bar on April 23, 1875, by Samuel K. Adams[2] and later, in 1877, by John Lewis Waller. Adams apparently was the first black admitted to practice before the Supreme Court of Iowa.[3]

John Lewis Waller received his early training in Toledo, Iowa. Waller was politically active in Iowa in the mid-1870s. His political activities may have led him to the law. And perhaps his prominence in the community led him to Judge N. M. Hubbard, the senior partner in Hubbard, Clark, and Deacon who invited Waller to study law under his tutelage in 1874. Waller reportedly "proved to be a diligent and capable student," and he was described as "a young man of good character, industrious and energetic."[4] Judge Hubbard's law firm was located in Cedar Rapids, Iowa, where Waller completed his law studies in 1877. In that year, he was admitted to the bar in Marion, Iowa. But Waller did not stay in Iowa for long. He moved to Kansas in 1878 to practice law there,[5] as did Turner W. Bell, an early Drake University Law School graduate who was admitted to the Iowa bar in 1886.[6]

The admission of John G. Jones to the Iowa bar in 1883 made news in Washington, D.C., though the *Washington Bee* erroneously reported that Jones was "believed to be the first of his kind [admitted to the Iowa bar]."[7] Jones was admitted to the Iowa bar after a rigorous examination conducted by W. K. White, Fred Heinz, and George Preston. Jones "passed the exam very creditably"[8] with the preparatory assistance of a black Chicago lawyer, Ferdinand Lee Barnett.[9]

In 1896 James Buchanan Rush, who had attended Howard University School of Law, settled in Des Moines, Iowa, after having been admitted to the Indiana bar in 1892 and to the bar at Fort Smith, Arkansas, in 1895.[10] Perhaps one of Rush's most significant contributions was to the legal education of his wife, Gertrude Elzora Durden Rush. Gertrude Rush commenced the study of law under her husband's instruction, though she also studied in 1908 at Des Moines College.[11] In 1914, she completed her third year of law study by correspondence at LaSalle Extension University of Chicago.[12] With the combined assistance of her husband and Vernice Opal Boling, a recent white female graduate of Drake University School of Law,[13] Rush passed the Iowa bar examination in 1918, becoming "the first colored woman admitted to practice law in . . . Iowa."[14] After the death of her husband, Rush, who had helped James Rush in his law office for years, took over her husband's practice.[15] Three years after being admitted to the bar, she was elected president of the Iowa Colored Bar Association, becoming the first woman of color in the nation to head such a group.[16]

Under William G. Hammond, Iowa University College of Law's first dean, that public law school became one of the first in the nation to admit and to graduate black American students. Alexander G. Clark, Jr., graduated from Iowa University's law school in 1879. It is believed that he became a prominent lawyer in Des Moines, Iowa.[17] Alexander G. Clark's father, after whom he was named, graduated from Iowa University's law school in 1884 at the age of 58.[18] Prior to his admission to law school, Alexander G. Clark, Sr., had been a nationally recognized black leader.[19] He had participated in many national conventions on issues relating to blacks, having "served as a delegate from Iowa to the meeting in Rochester, [New York,] in 1853, and the one in Washington [D.C.,] in 1869."[20] After graduating from Iowa University's law school, the senior Clark opened a firm in Chicago, but kept close ties to Iowa.[21] The year that Alexander Clark, Sr., received his law degree he became the sole owner of a black Chicago newspaper, *The Conservator*. He sold the paper in 1887.[22] In 1890 Alexander G. Clark, Sr., a lifelong

Republican, was appointed United States minister and consul-general to Liberia by President Benjamin Harrison. He served in this post for a year and died in office.[23]

George H. Woodson, an 1895 graduate of Howard University's law school, settled in Oskaloosa, Iowa, soon after he left Howard. Woodson was admitted to the Iowa bar and began his practice in the Second District of the Iowa State Bar Association. Woodson qualified for membership to the Iowa State Bar Association soon after it was established in 1894.[24] He later opened a law practice in the all-black town of Buxton, Iowa, where he practiced for several years.[25] In 1898 Woodson became the first black lawyer in Iowa to be nominated to the office of county attorney by the Republican Party.[26] During the early days of World War I, Woodson addressed the annual meeting of the Iowa State Bar Association, asking for the

aid of this Association and of all the lawyers and patriotic people of this country, to the end that we may have a full, fair chance to do what we want to do in this war. We want you to see to it, as long as we are going to have one hundred thousand colored soldiers, that we have the right to have an independent and separate Chapter of the Red Cross of our people who are taking training in various schools and hospitals of our country.[27]

In support of his argument, Woodson reminded the association that "fifty [black] lawyers, graduates from Harvard, Yale, and other great institutions," were in officer-training at Fort Des Moines, Iowa, "to help save this Anglo-Saxon civilization. . . . Men with black blood . . . we expect to stand throughout our lives . . . to see that the best man rules."[28]

In 1924 James J. Davis, the Secretary of Labor, appointed Woodson to "the first all-Negro commission . . . to investigate industrial and economic conditions in the Virgin Islands."[29] In 1925 Woodson's name was a household word among black lawyers in the nation when he cofounded the National Bar Association.[30] Woodson's popularity and influence in Republican circles helped to win him a post as deputy collector of United States Customs for the port of Des Moines, which he held from 1921 to 1933.[31]

In 1898 Drake University's law school graduated John Lay Thompson, who was soon after elected file clerk for the Iowa State Senate for a term of three years.[32] Thompson served as deputy county treasurer of Polk County from 1903 to 1908. He also held a position in the state's Hall of Archives in Des Moines until 1912.[33] Thompson, a supporter of Booker T. Washington's philosophy of self-sufficiency, was elected treasurer of the National Negro Press Association during the thirteenth annual meeting of the National Business League.[34]

In 1901 Iowa University's law school graduated another black student, Herbert Richard Wright, a native of Marshalltown, Iowa. Two years later, Wright was appointed to the United States consulate, "serving at Utilla, Honduras . . . [until] 1908 and [later] at Puerto Cabello, Venezuela, where he served until 1918."[35]

Samuel Joe Brown was also a law graduate of the University of Iowa. Brown was admitted to practice in Albia, Iowa,[36] but he began his law practice in Buxton, Iowa, with George H. Woodson. Their firm also established offices at Muchakinock and Albia, Iowa.[37] Brown's appetite for additional education inspired him to pursue a master of arts degree from the University of Iowa in 1902. He wrote his thesis on "A Constitutional View of the Recent Abridgment of the Rights of Negro Citizens by Certain of the Southern States of the Union."[38]

In 1905, soon after receiving his master of arts degree, Brown took his first case to the Iowa Supreme Court. Brown's client, a juror, had been denied dining accommodations with his fellow jurors at a boarding house because of his race. Brown sued for damages, arguing that the boarding house was covered by Iowa's anti-discrimination laws. Brown prevailed before the court, in what may be the first case presented to the Iowa Supreme Court by a black lawyer.[39]

Among Brown's many achievements was his appointment in 1908 as a member of the commission that drafted a government charter for the city of Des Moines. He was the first known member of color of the Polk County Bar Association, and, in 1916, he became the first black lawyer to run for a judicial post in Iowa. His bid for this post, however, was unsuccessful. During the early 1900s, "Brown was considered one of the seven or eight most important Negro lawyers in America."[40] In 1928 Brown, with the assistance of Charles Preston Howard, another black lawyer, ran unsuccessfully for a municipal judgeship in Des Moines, promising that he would "not make his campaign along racial lines, but [would] seek the support of all races."[41]

Brown organized the Iowa Colored Bar Association in 1916, serving as its first president from 1916 to 1917. In the early 1930s, Brown was appointed to the staff of the city solicitor. He was assigned the "special duty of collecting, revising . . . and codifying the ordinances" of the city of Des Moines.[42]

Charles Preston Howard graduated from Drake University's law school in 1922.[43] Howard became a political force in Des Moines, frequently giving speeches for Republican candidates.[44] Howard believed that black lawyers around the nation, who were barred from most bar groups, should form their own national bar group, and in 1925 he co-founded the National Bar Association.[45] One black newspaper reported in 1925 that a total of thirty-six men and two women of the Negro race [had] been admitted to practice [in Iowa]."[46]

In 1924, six years after Gertrude Elzora Durden Rush was admitted to the bar, Beulah Wheeler, "the first Negro woman ever to have been graduated from Iowa University School of Law, was admitted to the Iowa bar."[47] Other black lawyers, such as Luther T. Glanton, Jr., and Dupree D. Davis, graduated from Iowa law schools in the early 1940s. In 1942, after Glanton graduated from Drake University's law school, he studied for a period at the Sorbonne in Paris.[48] Davis graduated from Iowa University's law school in 1944. He served as a research assistant to acting dean Percy Bordwell, also of Iowa University.[49]

Michigan

The nondiscriminatory policy of the University of Michigan Law School is apparently one of the reasons for the early entry of black lawyers into the profession in Michigan. Michigan's first black lawyer, however, was not a University of Michigan graduate.

In 1870 John C. McLeod was an active practitioner in Detroit, and he appears to have been the first black lawyer in the state. In 1870, according to the *Detroit Free Press*, McLeod represented a black client in a civil action. His client accused three white men of assault and battery. The case received wide press coverage and generated much public interest because it was heard by a jury composed entirely of black citizens, the first such jury in Michigan.[50] The fact that the plaintiff's lawyer was black also heightened the public's attention to this trial. McLeod called witnesses, and then reportedly "proceeded with a long and rambling harangue in the midst of which he was cut off by one of the jurors, who informed the court that they were not disposed to listen to sentimental platitudes concerning their race, color or condition."[51] The black jurors acquitted the white defendants.[52]

Though the end of the Reconstruction era closed the door in the face of Southern blacks seeking a legal education, Michigan appears to have opened its doors to these students in the North. In 1877 Thomas Ralph Crispus and Albert Burgess graduated from the University of Michigan Law School.[53] After graduation, Crispus and Burgess opened a law office together in Detroit. It was a partnership that did not last long, for Burgess soon relocated to St. Louis, Missouri. Crispus remained in Detroit. He handled his first major murder case in 1879, and others followed. In 1890 Crispus defended "one Clemmie Francis who was charged with the murder of her husband." Due to the "high credible manner" with which Crispus handled the defense, the defendant was acquitted.[54] Prior to his death in 1895, Crispus gained an enviable reputation as the "most promising constitutional lawyer in the state."[55]

As black lawyers began to graduate from the University of Michigan Law School,[56] other lawyers appear to have migrated to the state. In the mid-1880s, David Augustus Straker, an 1872 graduate of Howard University's law school, moved to Detroit, having recently served as the dean of the Allen University department of law in Columbia, South Carolina. Straker gained recognition for both his scholarship and legal advocacy. In 1888 he published a book entitled *The New South Investigated.*[57]

In 1890 Straker won the first case ever argued by a black lawyer before the Michigan Supreme Court. Straker argued, and the court ruled, in *Ferguson v. Gies*[58] that black citizens were entitled to the same accommodations as whites in public places. Two years later, he was elected to the post of Wayne County commissioner, becoming the first black judicial officer in Michigan. Straker had received a number of votes from white citizens.[59] Straker's duties included carrying out of all acts, powers, and trusts which a judge of the circuit court performed. He had the authority to take testimony in cases pending in the Wayne County Circuit Court, and to determine landlord and tenant cases and property foreclosures.[60] However, Straker's reelection efforts failed, "owing to factional strife among the colored citizens [resulting in the election of] a white man."[61]

In 1893 Robert Jones Willis graduated from the University of Michigan's law school and began to practice in Detroit with two other black classmates, Benjamin Franklin Lester and William Cyrus Swan.[62] Initially, Willis, Lester, and Swan were only loosely associated. In 1910 Lester and Willis formed a law partnership.[63]

A year after Robert Jones Willis graduated from law school, he was elected as a delegate to the Trade and Labor Council, which subsequently became known as the American Federation of Labor. Between 1894 and 1913, as a delegate to that group, Willis fought to get "black motormen . . . employed on street cars and blacks employed in the post office and fire departments." He also called for other municipal appointments for blacks.[64] In 1914 Willis testified before the Michigan State Senate against a bill prohibiting interracial marriage. This legislation was never adopted by the Michigan legislature.[65] Although Willis became a respected lawyer in Detroit, he was never accorded full respect by white judges, who in open court called him "Willis or Bob."[66]

One of the first cohesive black law firms in Michigan was formed in 1895 by Walter Haslip Stowers and Robert Christopher Barnes. Barnes was admitted to the Michigan bar in 1889. He had originally practiced with David Augustus Straker, in an association that lasted until 1893.[67]

Barnes practiced by himself for two years before he opened the office with Stowers, an 1895 graduate of the Detroit College of Law.[68] The firm was stable in part because it represented corporate firms, such as the White Sewing Machine Co., the Villa Amusement Co., Zelah Amusement Co., and Dorl-Wiley Top Co.[69] In the twenty-year life of the firm, the office drew other Detroit College of Law graduates, like William Hayes McKinney, a 1915 graduate of the law school.[70] Stowers held several positions in Detroit (Wayne County), including deputy sheriff, assessors' clerk, and deputy county clerk; these high-visibility posts brought public attention to his firm.[71]

On the eve of the twentieth century, Oscar William Baker, Sr., and George Washington Bryant Conrad graduated from the University of Michigan Law School.[72] Upon graduation, Baker entered the law offices of L. E. Joslyn, a white lawyer in Bay City, Michigan. Joslyn later became a referee in bankruptcy at the United States District Court for the Eastern District of Michigan.[73] After leaving Joslyn's firm, Baker entered private practice in Bay City, where he served a mostly white clientele.[74] He was soon appointed commissioner in the circuit court of Bay City, a position that he held for one term.[75] Baker's appointment to the Board of Commerce and his subsequent appointment, by Governor Woodbridge N. Ferris, to the delegation attending the National Half-Century Anniversary of Negro Freedom boosted Baker's reputation among both blacks and whites in Bay City, and his law practice prospered.[76]

Some lawyers made significant advances toward breaking down racial barriers in government service. One such lawyer was Francis H. Warren, a 1903 graduate of the Detroit College of Law. Warren was hired by the county treasurer soon after he graduated from law school. While in government, Warren became interested in politics and formulated positions on the need "for public ownership of public utilities and other economic reforms."[77] He also wrote articles on the theory of a single tax and other economic subjects.[78]

Aside from Warren's pioneering and more conservative concentration on utility and economic issues of the time, he became one of the first black lawyers in Michigan to act as local counsel for the NAACP.[79] In that role he opposed police abuse of blacks and antimiscegenation legislation, prosecuted several race discrimination cases for the NAACP, and edited the *Detroit Informer*. Nevertheless, black people—mostly Republicans—openly criticized Warren for his affiliation with the Democratic Party.[80] He was also held up for close scrutiny by white jurors. Prior to one trial, "a discussion arose as to whether [Warren] was a white man. The jury, despite the fact that he was a mulatto, voted him white and the trial proceeded."[81]

Between 1900 and 1915, Detroit College of Law appears to have increased the number of its black graduates, many of whom remained in Detroit to serve in a variety of public and private roles.[82] Other lawyers settled outside of the city. Eugene Joseph Marshall, for example, a 1903 graduate of the University of Michigan's law school, put down roots in Kalamazoo, Michigan, where he enjoyed "a liberal practice."[83]

In the early 1900s, black lawyers were denied rental office space in certain sections of Detroit. When Lindsay E. Johnson was admitted to the bar in 1910, he attempted to rent office space in the center city of Detroit, but he was not allowed to because of his race. He "was . . . forced as a last resort to take a high-priced office" in another part of the city.[84] He later formed a partnership with Charles Henry Mahoney. Mahoney, a 1911 graduate of the University of Michigan's law school, received his first opportunity to practice law in the offices of Francis H. Warren, with whom he practiced until 1913. When the law firm of Johnson and Mahoney was formed, its principal partners were technically experienced, politically astute, and socially aware. Mahoney was the first black lawyer to serve on the city planning committee, which coordinated the future development of private and commercial enterprises in Detroit.[85] Johnson and Mahoney thwarted efforts by the Ypsilanti school board to segregate the public school system. They brought suit against the board in order to force it to close racially separate schools, and they won the case.[86]

Charles Anthony Roxborough, Jr., a second-generation lawyer, graduated from the Detroit College of Law in 1914. Roxborough was a savvy lawyer who used his political connections with the governor to win clients.[87] In 1931 Elvin L. Davenport, a 1929 Howard University law graduate, joined Roxborough in establishing a firm in Detroit. It was tough going for both men,[88] but Roxborough maintained his political and social interests in racial issues, helping to organize the Young Negroes' Progressive Association and working for the local chapter of the Urban League.[89]

In 1931 Roxborough decisively defeated a white opponent to win a seat in the Michigan state senate.[90] In the mid-1930s, Roxborough and H. B. Taliaferro formed a firm that was quite successful. In 1940 the firm played an important role in the defense of one of the Scottsboro boys, Olen Montgomery. Montgomery and the other Scottsboro boys had been convicted in an Alabama court in a racially charged and much-publicized case concerning the alleged rape of a white woman. After his release from prison, Montgomery went to Detroit and soon was charged with raping a black woman. Word of this new allegation, whether proved or disproved, could have jeopardized the pending court appeals and delayed the release of the Scottsboro boys, who were still incarcerated in Alabama. Therefore, it was important to the NAACP and to other leading black groups that the allegation against Montgomery be resolved quickly. The investigation into the Detroit rape charges was skillfully handled by Roxborough and Taliaferro. The charges were dropped when the alleged victim admitted that she was drunk at the time of the sexual encounter and could not recall what had happened.[91]

Black women were admitted to the Michigan bar as early as 1923, but it is not certain which one was the first to receive a formal legal education in Michigan.[92] Barbara F. Keene was probably the first black woman to graduate from the Detroit College of Law. She graduated in 1922.[93] Grace G. Costavas Murphy graduated from the Detroit College of Law in 1923[94] and was one of the first black women to qualify to practice law in Michigan. Murphy's admission to the Michigan bar, on September 10, 1923, was followed by that of a 1925 Howard University law school graduate, Isadora Augusta Jackson Letcher. In 1926 Letcher received "the highest grade of the 400 persons taking the [bar] examination."[95] Letcher returned to Washington, D.C., and entered government service, where she remained until her retirement in 1948.[96] In 1927, Hazel Amanda Lyman Roxborough graduated from the University of Detroit Law School, and she was admitted to the Michigan bar in 1929. Hazel Roxborough, the wife of Charles A. Roxborough, Jr., worked as a probation officer in the Wayne County court system for nearly thirty years.[97]

In 1941 Jeanne Cole-Harbour graduated from the University of Detroit Law School. Admitted to the Wayne County Bar on August 22, 1941, she joined the law firm of Loomis, Jones, Piper, and Calden.[98] The sexual discrimination Cole-Harbour encountered may have redirected her early career to the private practice of law. Just prior to or soon after she graduated from law school, Cole-Harbour wrote to her congressman to seek his assistance in her search for employment. She received no assistance; in fact, she received a few unwelcome words. The congressman "wrote back that there were no jobs for women lawyers, and he also enclosed a . . . cookbook."[99]

Black citizens in Michigan also witnessed the rise of one of the most distinguished members of the Michigan bar, Harold E. Bledsoe, a 1925 graduate of the Detroit College of Law. In 1932 Bledsoe was appointed by the governor to the Michigan State Corrections Commission,[100] and the following year he was appointed assistant attorney general of Michigan, a first for a black lawyer in that state.[101]

Minnesota

On July 17, 1889, Frederick L. McGhee became the first black lawyer admitted to the Minnesota bar.[102] McGhee received his law training in Chicago, Illinois, at Union Law School (Northwestern), and studied law in the office of a black lawyer named Edward H. Morris. He was admitted to the bar of Illinois in 1885, after three years of law study.[103] McGhee is credited with "being the first lawyer of his race in the country west of Illinois," a credit more accurate if narrowed somewhat to one of the first black lawyers admitted to practice in the North-western territory.[104]

McGhee earned a reputation as an aggressive criminal defense and civil rights lawyer in the twin cities of Minneapolis and St. Paul, Minnesota. After his admission to the bar, McGhee's "first case was the securing of [a] pardon of . . . Lewis Carter, who had been sentenced by court-martial to 99 years' imprisonment . . . on the charges of assault, robbery, attempted rape, and desertion."[105] Carter had served five years in prison before McGhee was retained. McGhee located the woman who had accused Carter, "and his unexcelled shrewdness secured evidence to establish Carter's innocence."[106] Based on this evidence, Carter was granted a pardon by the governor.

The success of the Carter case brought other clients, both white and black, to McGhee.[107] McGhee later "[distinguished] himself in the defense of three white persons charged with abducting a delicate 14-year old girl for the purpose of prostitution."[108] Although accounts of actual trials conducted by black lawyers in the northwest region of the nation in the 1890s are rare, the following report of McGhee's defense of the child abductors vividly describes his courtroom skills:

At 2 P.M., F. L. McGhee, the colored attorney, arose to present the argument for the defendants of the jury. It was apparent then that he had a difficult task before him, as it seemed that not only the sentiment of those in the courtroom but of the jury as well was against him. But nothing daunted, he soon warmed up to his cause. Notwithstanding his declaration to speak only an hour, he passed out his illustrations and philippics of oratory for two hours, and grew more eloquent as he progressed. . . . He soon had the undivided attention of the entire jury. . . . The defendant, Ida Shenk, sat with tear-streaming eyes during the address. Watson [another defendant] frequently shed tears, and the powerful frame of the man often trembled with emotion whilst the muscles of this face and throat twitched in his efforts to subdue perceptible sobs.[109]

McGhee won their acquittal. By 1906 McGhee was "considered one of the best criminal lawyers in [Minnesota]."[110] He was known for his craftsmanship in cross-examination and for his powerfully persuasive closing arguments. With these superb skills, McGhee "successfully defended men charged with the most atrocious murders known to the northeast."[111] Despite his success and his apparent acceptance by white clients, some white lawyers objected to having to deal with a black lawyer. On one occasion, McGhee, defending his honor, spat in the face of a white lawyer when he "objected to doing business with a 'damned nigger.'"[112]

Politically, McGhee was one of the few blacks in the nation to join the Democratic Party. He was thus occasionally at odds with many blacks in Minnesota, who often supported the "party of Lincoln."[113] However, McGhee's alignment with the Democratic Party does not appear to have diminished his national influence among blacks. At the close of the nineteenth century, Frederick L. McGhee was the director of the legal bureau of the National Afro-American Council (NAAC). McGhee described the legal bureau's purpose as doing

whatever seems to us best for the purpose of enforcing the law as it now exists and obtaining such remedial legislation as will best enhance the good of the race. So that whenever a case is pending of which we have knowledge that we can render any assistance to, we do so, and also seek to secure briefs of counsel used in the arguments and in the presenting of questions to the Supreme Court of the states and the Supreme Court of the U.S. wherein is involved points that bear upon any phase of the status of our race in matters of law.[114]

The NAAC's legal bureau filed suits against persons that discriminated against black citizens. The NAAC was later used as the model for the National Association for the Advancement of Colored People (NAACP), which was formed in 1909.[115] In fact, it has been stated that the NAAC and the Niagara Movement find their origins in the ideas of Frederick L. McGhee.[116]

McGhee's reputation as an aggressive lawyer on civil rights matters came to the attention of Booker T. Washington. In 1904 Washington sought the assistance of McGhee, a black Catholic, in lobbying the Catholic diocese of Maryland to oppose the state's pending disfranchisement legislation.[117] Although he responded to the call of Booker T. Washington, McGhee later signed a petition condemning him for a speech Washington had given in Europe that claimed the condition of "Negro-Americans . . . [was] satisfactory."[118]

At age thirty-five, William Richard Morris was admitted to the bar in Minnesota shortly after Frederick L. McGhee, in the latter part of 1889.[119] Morris was first admitted to the Tennessee bar in the early 1880s, after studying law privately. Morris had considerable ability, having earned two degrees at Fisk University.[120] From Tennessee, Morris went to Chicago, Illinois, where in 1888 he was admitted to the Illinois bar. (His older brother, Edward H. Morris, was admitted to the bar in Illinois in 1879.)[121] When William Richard Morris was admitted to the Minnesota bar, he became "the first Negro lawyer to appear before the courts of Hennepin County," though Frederick McGhee had been admitted to the bar a year before.[122] Morris made an instant reputation in the practice of criminal law.[123] His defense of Thomas Lyons in the Harris murder trial was particularly notable. A historian has reported that in the Harris trial, as well as in other murder cases, Morris "displayed keen discernment in the solution of intricate problems of law, and few lawyers have made a more lasting impression upon the bar of [Minneapolis]."[124]

Recognizing the importance of black lawyers in defending and fighting for the civil rights of black people in Minnesota, William R. Morris was instrumental "in setting up a state branch of the Afro-American Law Enforcement League [in 1898]."[125] The objective of the local league was "to secure moral and legal rights for Negroes, to suppress lawlessness among them, and 'to seek larger opportunities and more varied avenues of employment' for Negroes."[126]

John Frank Wheaton was the third black lawyer admitted to practice in Minnesota. He was admitted to the Minnesota bar on June 8, 1894, the day he graduated from the University of Minnesota Law School.[127] Wheaton, who had first attended Howard University's law school and had been admitted to the Maryland bar in 1893,[128] was the University of Minnesota law school's first black graduate.[129] Wheaton was appointed deputy clerk of the Minneapolis Municipal Court, a position that he held from 1895 to 1899.[130]

In 1898 Wheaton, a Republican, became the first black person elected to the Minnesota state legislature.[131] While serving in the legislature, Wheaton "strongly supported all civil rights proposals" and made great efforts "to have Black soldiers commissioned as officers during the Spanish-American war."[132] It is not clear exactly why Wheaton, whose career looked so promising, left Minnesota just twelve years after graduating from the University of Minnesota's law school. He moved to New York, where he formed a law firm with another black lawyer, James L. Curtis, who had practiced law in Minneapolis from 1899 to 1906.[133]

Charles William Scrutchin was another pioneering black lawyer in white Minnesota. Scrutchin received his LL.B. and master of laws degrees from the University of Michigan in 1893 and 1894, respectively.[134] After his admission to the Michigan bar on June 10, 1893, Scrutchin, like other black lawyers before him, went to Chicago, where he was admitted to the bar. In 1894 he worked as an "assistant south town attorney under Hon. [Edward] H. Morris, [an] eminent colored lawyer."[135] After a brief period in Chicago, Scrutchin went to Bemidji,

Minnesota, where he "built up an extensive practice"[136] in a "community of 8,000 persons, four of whom [were] Negroes."[137] He was invited back to the University of Michigan in 1900 to speak informally to the graduating law class.[138]

In 1899 McCants Stewart became the second black graduated from the University of Minnesota Law School, and in 1901 the first to receive a master of laws degree from that school.[139] Admitted to the Minnesota bar in 1899, Stewart, one of the first second-generation lawyers in the nation,[140] moved to Portland, Oregon, to practice law.[141]

In 1904, William Trevanne Francis was one of the first blacks graduated from the St. Paul College of Law (William Mitchell College of Law) in St. Paul, Minnesota.[142] Thereafter, Francis was hired by the Northern and Pacific Railroad, initially as a stenographer and later as a lawyer in the legal department.[143] He worked for the railroad company until 1912, when he entered private practice. Francis's practice provided him with the freedom to fight against racial discrimination. In 1913 Francis and William R. Morris appeared before the Minnesota House Judiciary Committee to protest against proposed miscegenation legislation. The legislation never passed.[144] In 1917 Francis also served both as a member of the Minnesota Public Safety Commission and as an "observer of the draft board in the Eighth Ward, and of Division 7's Draft Appeals Board in St. Paul."[145] Francis became well known beyond the borders of the State of Minnesota. In 1927 President Calvin Coolidge appointed Francis United States Minister to Liberia, West Africa, a position that he held until his death in 1929.[146]

John Louis Ervin, Gale Pillsbury Hilyer, and Lena Olive Smith were all admitted to the Minnesota bar after 1900. Ervin was admitted in 1907. He entered into private practice, specializing in criminal law. In 1917, Ervin successfully defended a black man against charges of murdering a white saloon owner in a highly publicized case. His client "had allegedly refused to pay for a drink when served."[147] At the trial, Ervin established "that [his client] had paid for the drink but had been locked in the saloon and attacked by three white men while the proprietor fired at him with a revolver."[148] The black man was acquitted. Reportedly, this was "the first [case] in the history of St. Paul where a Negro accused of killing a white man was defended by a Negro attorney unaided by a white attorney."[149]

In 1915 Gale Pillsbury Hilyer graduated from the University of Minnesota School of Law.[150] Hilyer was the son of the University of Minnesota's first black graduate, Andrew F. Hilyer, an 1884 graduate.[151] (Andrew Hilyer also attended Howard University law school.[152]) After graduating from law school, Gayle P. Hilyer practiced with a white law firm, Hall and Tautges.[153] He became a leading lawyer of the Hennepin County Bar "representing . . . a number of automobile companies."[154] In 1925 Hilyer became the first black lawyer in Minnesota to seek election as a municipal court judge.[155]

Lena Olive Smith, a 1921 graduate of Northwestern College of Law (William Mitchell), was the only black woman admitted to the bar in Minnesota prior to 1945. After being admitted to the bar in 1921, she "devoted herself almost entirely to civil rights law."[156]

Nebraska

In 1889 Silas Robbins became the first black lawyer admitted to practice in Nebraska—sixteen years after the Nebraska Supreme Court held that blacks per se could not be excluded from a jury, and ten years before the Nebraska State Bar Association was created.[157] Robbins entered the private practice of law. Nine years after his admission to the bar, he became the second black man to run for the Nebraska state legislature. His campaign for the legislature won a favorable endorsement from *The Omaha World Herald*, a white newspaper:

Mr. Robbins is a lawyer, and his standing at the bar of Douglas County is high. . . . Mr. Robbins commands the respect of the best lawyers in Douglas County. . . . His struggle upward has been hard. . . . He has doubly earned the honor given him by the three conventions and will not discredit those conventions. As a member of the legislature he will command respect and attention.[158]

After his defeat, Robbins continued to practice law in Omaha[159] until the turn of the century. When the Populist Party took power in Omaha, he became a clerk in the tax commissioner's office. He held this political job from 1900 to 1901 and from 1903 to 1905. Robbins then returned to his practice, concentrating primarily on real estate matters.[160] He was described as "one of [Omaha's] best known colored attorneys."[161]

Harrison J. Pinkett was admitted to the Nebraska bar in 1905. Pinkett, a 1906 law graduate of Howard University, became one of Omaha's most prominent black citizens.[162] In 1939, he was listed as "the oldest Negro attorney in Nebraska."[163]

The University of Omaha law department graduated several blacks. These lawyers were admitted to the bar and practiced law in Omaha. Jesse Hutton, Saybet Hanger, Amos Scruggs, and John Guilford Pegg were all products of Omaha University's department of law in the 1920s and 1930s.[164] John G. Pegg passed the Nebraska bar in 1928, and he associated with another black lawyer, Charles F. Davis, who was admitted to the Nebraska bar in 1927.[165] Pegg became active in the

NAACP and in the Urban League, providing legal assistance to fight racial prejudice in Omaha.[166]

In 1923 the University of Nebraska School of Law graduated one of its first black students, David H. Oliver. Oliver financed his legal education with federal disability payments for injuries he suffered while serving in the United States Army during World War I.[167] Oliver wanted to practice law in Omaha but found it difficult to finance a private practice in that city:

> After graduation I went to Omaha . . . and got a job as typesetter and sportswriter for the *Omaha Guide*, a newspaper, to earn enough money to establish my law practice. This job folded with the 1929 Wall Street crash and I obtained employment as a dining car waiter.[168]

Oliver left Omaha and settled in Ogden, Utah, to practice law.

In 1922 John Adams, Sr., was admitted on motion to practice in Nebraska. He had already been admitted to practice in several other states. Adams was first admitted to the bar in South Carolina during the early 1900s.[169] Although there is no evidence that he was formally trained as a lawyer, Adams's lack of formal education did not make him less competitive. He practiced law in Orangeburg, South Carolina, for several years, forming a firm with another black lawyer, Jacob Moorer.[170] Adams left South Carolina after he and Moorer failed to convince the South Carolina and United States supreme courts of the injustice of black exclusion from grand and petite juries.[171] Adams traveled to Washington state and practiced law there before relocating to Pueblo, Colorado. He finally settled in Omaha, Nebraska, in the early 1920s.[172]

In 1929, John Adams, Jr., became the first second-generation black lawyer in Nebraska when he graduated from the University of Nebraska School of Law and passed the bar.[173] Less than two years out of law school, Adams appeared before the Nebraska Supreme Court in a *habeas corpus* matter.[174] Zanzye H. A. Hill also graduated from the University of Nebraska's law school in 1929, becoming its first black woman graduate and the first black woman admitted to the bar of Nebraska.[175] Hill did not remain in Nebraska but joined the faculty at the Tuskegee Institute in Alabama.[176] Subsequently, Hill "became legal counsel for the Woodmen of Union Insurance Company at Hot Springs, Arkansas, the largest insurance company for colored people in the nation."[177]

A few years after his graduation from the University of Nebraska Law School, John Adams, Jr., was elected to the Nebraska state legislature.[178] In 1934 he was first elected to the Nebraska House of Representatives, during the final days of the bicameral legislature in Nebraska. In 1936 Adams was elected state senator to the unicameral legislature.[179] While serving there, Adams introduced legislation to make lynching a crime[180] and supported legislation for unemployment compensation[181] and fair pensions.[182] Adams also led the fight against legislation that would have required criminal defendants to give notice of alibis twenty-four hours in advance of a trial.[183] Adams served on the Labor, Railroad, Arrangement, and Phraseology committees in the legislature. He was also a partner in the black Omaha law firm of Davis, Adams, and Adams.[184]

Adams was also significantly involved in national Republican politics. In 1936 he appeared before the Credential Committee of the Republican National Convention in Cleveland, Ohio. His efforts to seat a black delegation from Louisiana proved unsuccessful.[185] In 1943 Adams joined the armed forces to fight in World War II. His father, John Adams, Sr., "ran for [his] seat . . . and was elected" to the Nebraska state legislature in 1944.[186]

North Dakota and South Dakota

Prior to 1945, there were few black people in North and South Dakota, perhaps too few to draw black lawyers to practice in these states. Although the clerk of the North Dakota Supreme Court has stated that "no Negro [lawyers were] ever admitted to practice" in North Dakota prior to 1945,[187] the *Twelfth Census* reported in 1900 that, for the first time, there was a black lawyer in the state.[188] The identity of this lawyer remains a mystery. In 1905, the black population in South Dakota was 166; in 1915, it had grown to 229. In 1925, the black population was 493, but it dropped to 187 in 1935 and to 154 by the end of 1944.[189]

The South Dakota bar admitted Will F. Reden, its first black lawyer, in about 1908, although members of the bar may not have known that Reden was black.[190] Reden, a fair-skinned black man, graduated from the University of Iowa School of Law in 1908 and opened a law office in Sioux Falls, South Dakota. Although Reden lived in a white community, he participated in the National Bar Association after its founding in 1925. He became a regional director of the NBA in 1936.[191]

Wisconsin

The history of black lawyers in Wisconsin is traced to Everett E. Simpson, who in 1888 became the University of Wisconsin Law School's first black graduate. Admitted to the state bar, Simpson soon left Wisconsin to practice in the state of Washington.[192] William T. Green, an 1892 University of Wisconsin law graduate, is probably the second black admitted to the bar of that state.[193] In 1890, during his first year in law school, Green attended the convention of the Afro-American League held in Chicago, Illinois. That meeting inspired him to "draft a comprehensive civil rights bill for [Wisconsin]."[194] The bill was introduced in the Wisconsin legislature in January 1891 and eventually passed in 1895, though it was considerably watered down.[195]

During Green's professional career in Milwaukee, he handled most of the local cases involving blacks.[196] He was described 'as a bright and capable lawyer."[197] Green was credited with saving the life of Arthur Hunter, "a burly Negro, accused of having committed several brutal murders."[198] Green skillfully argued for Hunter's insanity, and prevailed. Hunter was committed to a hospital for the insane in Oshkosh, Wisconsin.[199] With Green's death in 1911, only one black lawyer remained in Wisconsin.[200] At the time of his death, the State Bar Association of Wisconsin stated that Green "represented practically all of his race in their trials and tribulations both in the criminal and civil courts, and was a worker for the betterment of conditions among his people."[201]

Before his death, Green saw to it that James G. Thurman was admitted to the Wisconsin bar in 1907. Thurman first practiced in Superior, Wisconsin, but moved to Milwaukee in 1915. Thurman developed a respectable law practice, drawing clients from both races, until his death in 1927.[202] Between 1913 and 1923 other black lawyers—namely, George Heriot DeReef, A. B. Nutt, James Weston Dorsey, and Mabel Raimey—migrated to Milwaukee and became "the most successful members of the new [Negro community]."[203]

In 1913 George Heriot DeReef also began a law practice in Milwaukee. DeReef had graduated from Howard University's law school in 1905. After DeReef completed his legal studies, Judge Robert H. Terrell, a black member of the municipal court in the District of Columbia, hired him as a law clerk, a position DeReef held from 1907 to 1909. DeReef later served as deputy clerk of the district's municipal court until he relocated to Milwaukee.[204] For several years after William T. Green's death, George H. DeReef, James G. Thurman, and A. B. Nutt were the only black lawyers in Milwaukee.

DeReef was a progressive force in the community, and he fought to advance the rights of blacks in Milwaukee. He was also business-minded, owning interests in both the *Milwaukee Enterprise* (later the *Wisconsin Enterprise Blade*) and the Community Drug Store.[205] In 1924 DeReef won the Republican primary election to the state legislature from Milwaukee's Sixth District. However, as a result of postwar racism, he "failed to advance beyond the primary."[206] DeReef's leadership of the Milwaukee chapter of the NAACP also proved important to the black community. However, he was a moderate on most issues, and proved lukewarm in his support of Marcus Garvey. In time, DeReef joined with the more progressive civil rights advocates of the black community.[207]

In 1928 James Weston Dorsey joined George H. DeReef's law firm. Dorsey graduated from Montana State University School of Law (now the University of Montana) in 1927.[208] He succeeded DeReef as president of the NAACP and immediately demanded that the Schlitz and Pabst breweries—located in the Sixth Ward of Milwaukee—end their employment discrimination against blacks. Although unsuccessful in his initial efforts to win employment for blacks at these breweries, Dorsey's demands opened a new era of militancy in Milwaukee.[209] In 1932 Dorsey ran for a position as alderman on the Milwaukee city council. He failed in this and other attempts to be elected in 1940 and 1944. However, in each of these campaigns, he illustrated the increasing importance of the black vote. The strength of this constituency ultimately proved vital for Leroy Simmons, another black man, who won a seat in the Wisconsin General Assembly in 1944.[210]

Dorsey's NAACP presidency lasted through the election of President Franklin D. Roosevelt. During the Roosevelt administration, Dorsey renewed his crusade against employment discrimination, especially at companies that held federal government contracts. In January 1942 Dorsey appeared at a hearing in Chicago, Illinois, at which he presented sworn statements documenting discrimination by federal contractors in Milwaukee. Dorsey's efforts, and those of others, resulted in a finding of racial discrimination against several government contractors. Because of Dorsey's valiant fight, these companies were ordered by the federal government to establish a policy against racial discrimination or face termination of their contracts.[211]

In 1923, one black woman, Mabel Watson Raimey, entered the evening law program at Marquette University. She did not graduate, however, because "the evening program was closed by February 1924."[212] Nevertheless, Raimey was admitted to the Wisconsin bar, no doubt the first black woman to be so admitted, "on October 15, 1927, [after] passing the Wisconsin bar [exam]."[213] Raimey became a private practitioner in Milwaukee, Wisconsin, and she practiced there for many years. In 1941 she was listed as one of fifty-eight black women lawyers in the United States.[214]

Summary

In the state of Iowa, A. H. Watkins appears to be the first black lawyer to have been admitted to the bar; Alexander G. Clark, Jr., was Iowa

University's first black law graduate in 1879. Iowa University is likely the first law school in the nation to graduate the father of its first black graduate after his son. Alexander G. Clark, Sr., was graduated from the law school in 1884.

In 1895 the Iowa bar admitted George H. Woodson, who would become one of the nation's most respected black lawyers. In 1898 Woodson became the first black lawyer in Iowa to be nominated as county attorney. In 1924 he was nominated for a seat in the Iowa state legislature. He is best known as one of the founding members in 1925 of the National Bar Association. He was the black bar group's first president.

Between 1879 and 1900, several black lawyers were admitted to the Iowa bar, many of whom left the state to practice elsewhere. These lawyers were graduated from law schools such as Drake University, LaSalle Extension School of Law (Chicago), Des Moines College of Law, Howard University, and Iowa University.

Samuel Joe Brown remained in Des Moines, Iowa, after he graduated from Iowa University's law school in 1901. He handled several civil rights cases, some of which reached the Iowa Supreme Court as early as 1905. Brown also was a respected lawyer in Des Moines, although its citizens twice declined to elect him to a judicial post. Brown made his mark in 1908 as one of the draftsman of the commission form of government for the city of Des Moines.

Gertrude Elzora Durden Rush, Iowa's first black woman lawyer, was admitted to the bar in 1918. She and her husband, James B. Rush, practiced law together until he died, after which Gertrude Rush assumed responsibility for the firm. At least one other woman, Beulah Wheeler, was admitted to the Iowa bar prior to 1945, but Rush, who was elected president of the Iowa Colored Bar Association in 1921, is the most well known.

The state of Michigan admitted its first black lawyer, John C. McLeod, in 1870. Seven years later, the University of Michigan graduated its first black law graduates, Thomas R. Crispus and Albert Burgess. McLeod was a private practitioner who may hold the distinction of trying and losing his first case to an all-black jury. Cripus and Burgess formed a law firm in 1877. Other black law firms were formed in the state, including one headed by Walter Haslip Stowers and Robert Christopher Barnes, in 1895. Oscar William Baker, Sr., practiced in a nearly all-white community, where he handled the legal work of many whites.

One of Michigan's first nationally known lawyers was David Augustus Straker, formerly the dean of Allen University's law school in South Carolina. He was admitted to the Michigan bar in 1888. Straker is likely the first black lawyer in Michigan to author a book and to win a civil rights case before the Michigan Supreme Court.

Most of the first black lawyers in Michigan were Republicans. Francis H. Warren was often criticized for being a Democrat, but he won the respect of the community by exposing police brutality in Detroit as an NAACP lawyer. Charles Henry Mahoney, the first black lawyer to serve on Detroit's city planning committee, and Lindsay E. Johnson led the fight to desegregate the public schools in Ypsilanti, Michigan.

During the 1930s Charles A. Roxborough, Jr., was elected to the Michigan state senate. Harold E. Bledsoe, meanwhile, was appointed assistant attorney general of Michigan.

Black lawyers in Michigan were graduated from such law schools as the University of Michigan, University of Detroit, Detroit College of Law, and Howard University. Detroit College of Law appears to have graduated most of the early black women lawyers in Michigan, including Grace G. Costavas (Murphy), Michigan's first black female lawyer (admitted to practice in 1923).

In the state of Minnesota, Frederick L. McGhee, the state's first black lawyer, was admitted to the bar in 1889. He was one of the first black lawyers in the Northwest Territory. McGhee, a Democrat, was nationally respected by such black leaders as Booker T. Washington. In 1899 McGhee established the National Afro-American Council (NAAC), a civil rights group that became the prototype for the NAACP. In fact, McGhee is credited for first suggesting the Niagara Movement, the forerunner of the NAACP.

Minnesota was one of the first states in which civil rights litigation was planned by a group formed specifically for that purpose. In 1898 William Richard Morris, the first black lawyer to practice in Hennepin County, established the Afro-American Law Enforcement League to secure the rights of blacks. Four years earlier, John F. Wheaton, a black lawyer, was the first black elected to the Minnesota state legislature. He supported all civil rights initiatives in the legislature.

Black lawyers in Minnesota were graduates of law schools such as the University of Minnesota, University of Michigan, and Northwestern University law school (which later merged into the William Mitchell Law School). Graduates of these schools, such as Charles W. Scrutchin and William T. Francis, entered the private practice of law—Scrutchin in Bemidji, Minnesota, and Francis in St. Paul.

Lena Olive Smith, a graduate of Northwestern Law School (William Mitchell) was Minnesota's first black woman law graduate and lawyer. She was admitted to the bar in 1921 and devoted her life to civil rights law.

The state of Nebraska admitted its first black lawyer, Silas Robbins, in 1889. Robbins entered private practice in Omaha, Nebraska, where most black Nebraskans lived. He became a well-known and respected lawyer in both the black and white communities.

Though black lawyers were few in number, they entered the private practice of law, engaged in state and national politics, and appeared before the Nebraska Supreme Court during the early part of the twentieth century. Most of Nebraska's lawyers were educated out of state, but the University of Nebraska and the law department of Omaha University each graduated a few black lawyers. In 1934, for example, John Adams, Jr., a 1929 law graduate of the University of Nebraska, became the second black person to be elected to the state legislature. He was also elected to the unicameral legislature when it was formed in 1936. Adams introduced legislation to make lynching a crime. In 1944, his father, John Adams, Sr., also a lawyer, succeeded him in the legislature.

Zanzye H. A. Hill holds the dual distinction of being the first black woman to be graduated from the University of Nebraska's law school and to be admitted to the Nebraska bar.

In the state of North Dakota, Will F. Reden is the first known black admitted to the bar. Reden, a 1908 graduate of Iowa University's law school, settled in Sioux Falls, South Dakota, and was active in the National Bar Association in 1936.

In the state of Wisconsin, Everett E. Simpson was the first black to graduate from the University of Wisconsin's law school and to be admitted to the bar. Simpson left the state, but was soon followed to the state bar by William T. Green in 1892. Reportedly Green, while still a student in law school, drafted a civil rights bill that was introduced in the state legislature. The bill, though watered down, ultimately became law in 1895. A Howard University law graduate, George H. DeReef, was elected to the Wisconsin legislature in 1924. He undertook civil rights cases in the state.

James Weston Dorsey ushered in a new era of militancy in Milwaukee. Dorsey, the first black law graduate of Montana State University, succeeded DeReef as president of the NAACP. He demanded that the Schlitz and Pabst breweries cease employment discrimination against black workers.

Mabel Watson Raimey, the first black woman admitted to the Wisconsin bar in 1924, spent her entire legal career in private practice in Milwaukee, Wisconsin.

The number of lawyers admitted to the northwestern states was small, but their achievements and contributions to the law were significant. In every respect, the black lawyers in the northwest substantially helped to emancipate their people.

NOTES

1. Bergmann, "The Negro in Iowa," 46 *Iowa J. of History and Politics* 38 (Jan. 1948), quoting *The Weekly Gate City*, April 22, 1874. A. H. Watkins was admitted to the bar of Lee County, Iowa, on April 9, 1874. Letter from Raymon Trisdale to Charles Sumner Brown, April 1961. See also *Circuit Court Book Records*, Lee County, Iowa, at 338.

2. Letter from Margaret L. Hoit, Public Library at Des Moines, Iowa, to Charles S. Brown, April 13, 1961.

3. Letter from Helen M. Lyman, clerk, Supreme Court of Iowa, to Charles S. Brown, March 10, 1961.

4. R. B. Woods, *A Black Odyssey: John Lewis Waller and the Promise of American Life, 1878–1900*, at 8 (1981); I. G. Penn, *The Afro-American Press, and Its Editors* 190 (1891); "John L. Waller," *New York Age*, May 9, 1891.

5. "Veteran Lawyer Praised as a Great Race Leader," *Chicago Defender*, Dec. 26, 1936.

6. "Some Little Stories of Racial Progress," *Chicago Defender*, Feb. 23, 1918.

7. *Washington Bee*, Feb. 24, 1883.

8. *Ibid.*

9. *Ibid.*

10. Vol. 1 *Who's Who of the Colored Race* 235 (F. L. Mather ed. 1915).

11. "When Negro Lawyer Dies, Wife Takes Over Practice in City," *Des Moines Iowa News*, Oct. 8, 1918.

12. *Ibid.*

13. *Ibid.* Vernice Opal Boling was graduated from Drake University School of Law in 1917. She ultimately became Drake's law librarian. Boling was the first woman in Iowa to argue a case before the Iowa Supreme Court (telephone interviews with William Stoppal, director of libraries, Drake University, by author, Jan. 12 and 18, 1989). Boling probably studied with Rush in preparation for the Iowa bar exam.

14. Vol. 1 *Who's Who in Colored America* 175 (J. J. Boris ed. 1927).

15. "When Negro Lawyer Dies, Wife Takes Over Practice in City," *Des Moines Iowa News*, Oct. 8, 1918.

16. "Made Bar President," *Chicago Defender*, Feb. 5, 1921.

17. Letters to author from Professor Gregory H. Williams, Iowa University College of Law, Nov. 9, 1988, and from Dennis J. Shields, director of admissions, Dec. 6, 1988.

18. *Id.* (Professor Gregory H. Williams). Sixteen years before the elder Clark graduated from Iowa University's law school, he was a party to a lawsuit which challenged the discretion of the local school district of Muscatine, Iowa. The state, Clark's side held, had no authorization to assign black students to "colored schools," under state law. Clark took his case to the Iowa Supreme Court, which ruled in his favor. *Clark v. Board of Directors*, 24 Iowa 266 (1868). See also, "A Father and Son—The First Two Black Graduates of the University of Iowa Law School," undated document provided to the author on March 11, 1989, by Dennis J. Shields, director of admissions, Iowa University School of Law.

19. W. J. Simmons, *Men of Mark* 1097 (1887).

20. J. C. Miller, *The Black Presence in American Foreign Affairs* 9, 15 (1978).

21. In 1887 it was reported that Clark "in his old age graduated from law school, and is now a practicing lawyer in the city of Chicago" (W. J. Simmons,

Men of Mark 1097, 1100 [1887]). See also *Dictionary of American Negro Biography* 112 (R. Logan and M. Winston eds. 1982).

22. See I. G. Penn, *The Afro-American Press, and Its Editors* 262 (1891), discussing *The Conservator*; *Dictionary of American Negro Biography* 112, 113 (R. Logan and M. Winston eds. 1982).

23. *Principal Officers of the Department of State and United States Chiefs of Mission, 1778–1988*, at 72 (1988).

24. *Proceedings of the Thirteenth Annual Meeting of the Iowa State Bar Association*, July 11–12, 1907, at 3, listing date of the establishment of the Iowa State Bar Association; at 196, listing George H. Woodson as a member. Membership to the Iowa State Bar Association was contingent upon admission to the bar. Ostensibly, there were no racial or gender barriers to qualifying for membership. *Id.* at 20 (Const., Iowa State Bar Assn., Rule VII, sec. 1).

25. *Stenographic Report of the Proceedings of the National Business League Convention*, at Topeka, Kansas, Aug. 14–16, 1907, at 326 (William H. Davis, reporter), report of Lewis E. Johnson, Buxton, Iowa. In 1907 Booker T. Washington noted that "two Negro Justices of the Peace, Spencer Carry and George Terrell," helped to govern Buxton, Iowa. B. T. Washington, *The Negro in Business* 77 (1907). See *Proceedings of the Iowa State Bar Association, Twenty-second Session*, June 29–30, 1916, at 275, listing Woodson as living in Buxton, Iowa.

26. Brown, "Our Founder," 2 *Nat'l B.A.J.* 263, 264 (Dec. 1944). Woodson ran for county attorney in Mahaska County, where he resided; Bergmann, "The Negro in Iowa," 46 *Iowa J. of History and Politics* 38, 43 (Jan. 1948).

27. *Proceedings of the Iowa State Bar Association, Twenty-third Session*, June 28–29, 1917, at 159.

28. *Ibid.* Woodson was referring to Camp Des Moines, which had been established on June 15, 1917 "for the purpose of training black soldiers to hold officers' rank." By "October 14, 1917, 639 black soldiers were commissioned as 2d Lieutenants." *The Negro Almanac* 165 (H. A. Ploski and W. Marr II, third ed. 1976). Woodson practiced law in Iowa for several years and continued his support of the Republican Party. In 1924 Woodson "was nominated as the regular Republican candidate for state representative" for Monroe County, "being the only Negro ever nominated by Republicans to this office in the history of the state." Brown, "Our Founder," 2 *Nat'l B.A.J.* 263, 264 (Dec. 1944).

29. "Negroes to Form Bar Association to Cover Nation," *Spartanburg Sun*, Feb. 28, 1925; Brown, "Our Founder," 2 *Nat'l B.A.J.* 263, 264 (Dec. 1944).

30. *Ibid.* ("Negroes to Form Bar Association").

31. *Ibid.*

32. Vol. 1 *Who's Who of the Colored Race* 262–63 (F. L. Mather ed. 1915).

33. Vol. 1 *Who's Who in Colored America* 201 (J. J. Boris ed. 1927).

34. *Report of the Thirteenth Annual National Negro Business League*, Chicago, Illinois, Aug. 21–23, 1912, at 168–69. At least ten other black lawyers were admitted to the Iowa Supreme Court between 1875 and 1900: S. L. Smith (1880), Fred L. Smith (1894), William Foster (1895), W. G. Mott (1896), S. L. Marsh (1891), R. G. Posten (1882), Rev. A. H. Higgs (1884), Albert Bell (1891), J. E. Williamson (1895), and Rev. George I. Holt (1896) (National Bar Association's history committee).

35. Vol. 1 *Who's Who of the Colored Race* 293 (F. L. Mather ed. 1915); Bergmann, "The Negro in Iowa," 56 *Iowa J. of History and Politics* 3, 84 (Jan. 1948).

36. Vol. 1 *Who's Who in Colored America* 28 (J. J. Boris ed. 1927).

37. Vol. 1 *Who's Who of the Colored Race* 45 (F. L. Mather ed. 1915); Brown, "Our Founder," 2 *Nat'l B.A.J.* 263 (Dec. 1944).

38. Vol. 1 *Who's Who in Colored America* 28 (J. J. Boris ed. 1927).

39. See *Humburd v. Crawford*, 128 Iowa 743, 105 N.W. 330 (1905). However, four years later S. Joe Brown and George H. Woodson lost a civil rights case before the Iowa Supreme Court. There, a concessionaire leased a booth to a company that refused to serve coffee to blacks. The court determined that the lessee was not a business covered by the Iowa Civil Rights Act, a decision that drew a sharp dissenting opinion from the chief justice. *Brown v. J. H. Bell Co.*, 146 Iowa 89, 123 N.W. 231, 237 (1909).

40. Bermann, "The Negro in Iowa," 56 *Iowa J. of History and Politics* 3, 82 (Jan. 1948); "Brown to Be Candidate for Municipal Judge," *The Tribune*, Jan. 11, 1928. Brown received more than seven thousand votes in the final election. "Des Moines Negro Lawyer to Codify City Ordinances," *Oklahoma Black Dispatch*, May 16, 1936.

41. "Brown to Be Candidate for Municipal Judge," *The Tribune*, Jan. 11, 1928; Vol. 1 *Who's Who of the Colored Race* 45 (F. L. Mather ed. 1915).

42. "Des Moines Negro Lawyer to Codify City Ordinances," *Oklahoma Black Dispatch*, June 16, 1936; "Atty. Brown City Legal Staff," *Iowa Bystander*, May 15, 1936.

43. Drake University Commencement Day program, June 1, 1922.

44. Telephone interview with Judge Joseph C. Howard, Baltimore, MD, Nov. 29, 1988.

45. "Negroes to Form Bar Association to Cover Nation," *Spartanburg Sun*, Feb. 28, 1925.

46. *Ibid.*

47. *Ibid.*

48. Letter from Richard M. Calkins, dean, Drake University School of Law, to author, May 15, 1986. A letter from Margaret L. Hoit, public library of Des Moines, to Charles S. Brown, April 13, 1961, stating that Glanton graduated from Northwestern University School of Law, is in error.

49. *Who's Who Among Negro Lawyers* 12 (S. T. M. Alexander ed. 1945).

50. "The Law's Equality—The First Colored Jury in Michigan," *Detroit Free Press* April 6, 1870.

51. *Ibid.*

52. The first black jurors in Michigan were John D. Richards, Alexander Moore, S. C. Watson, George DeBaptiste, James H. Binge, and Richard Gordon. *Ibid.*

53. *University of Michigan General Catalogue of Officers and Students, 1837–1911*, at 401, on Burgess and Crispus (I. N. Demmon ed. 1912).

54. *People's Advocate*, June 19, 1890.

55. *Ibid.* See also, letter from James M. Babcock, chief, Burton Historical Collection, to Charles S. Brown, June 3, 1959; *Detroit Free Press*, March 27, 1877, indicating that there were seventy-seven law graduates in the Michigan law class of 1877. All were admitted to the bar by Judge George M. Huntington of the Fourth Circuit.

56. In 1879 John Hiram Fox completed his studies at the University of Michigan's law school and returned to his native city of Ypsilanti, Michigan, to practice law. He died at age thirty-one in 1886. *University of Michigan General Catalogue of Officers and Students, 1837–1911*, at 407 (I. N. Demmon ed. 1912).

57. G. R. Richings, *Evidence of Progress Among Colored People* 290 (1904); McCargo, "Emancipation in Michigan," 64 *Mich. B.J.* 518, 523 n.8 (1985). He would publish other books on practice, procedure, and evidence. Dorothy D. Hawkshawe, "David Augustus Straker, Black Lawyer and Reconstruction Politician, 1842–1908" at 123–24. (Ph.D. diss., Catholic University, 1974).

58. *Ferguson v. Gies*, 82 Mich. 358, 46 N.W. 718 (1890). The plaintiff in the case, William W. Ferguson, became "one of the pioneer Afro-American lawyers of the Detroit Bar." F. H. Warren, *Michigan Manual of Freedmen's Progress* 50 (1915). Ferguson attended the Detroit College of Law. He was listed as a special student in 1896. *Detroit College of Law Announcement* 24 (1896–1897). Thus he was not yet a lawyer at the time he retained Straker to sue Gies. See also, Dorothy D. Hawkshawe, "David Augustus Straker, Black Lawyer and Reconstruction Politician, 1842–1908" at 109 (Ph.D. diss., Catholic University, 1974). However, he probably was admitted to the Michigan bar shortly after serving two terms in the Michigan legislature. Ferguson was Michigan's first black legislator. He served in that body from 1893 to 1896. Vol. 1 *Michigan Biographies* 287 (1924) (compiled by Michigan Historical Commission).

59. McCargo, "Emancipation in Michigan," 65 *Mich. B.J.* 518, 523 (1985), citing J. M. Green, *Negroes in Michigan History* 35 (reprint, 1985).

60. Letter from F. Clever Bald of the Michigan Historical Collection, to Charles S. Brown, June 3, 1958.

61. Vol. 4 *The Booker T. Washington Papers, 1895–98*, at 236 (L. R. Harlan, S. B. Kaufman, B. S. Kraft, and R. W. Smock eds. 1975), quoting Straker; *Dictionary of American Negro Biography* 574, 575 (R. Logan and M. Winston eds. 1982). Straker returned to private practice and continued to publish articles on a variety of subjects, such as "The Larceny of Dogs." G. R. Richings, *Evidence of Progress Among Colored People* 290 (1904).

62. *University of Michigan General Catalogue of Officers and Students, 1837– 1911*, at 453 (Lester), 454 (Swan received an LL.M.), and 455 (Willis) (I. N. Demmon ed. 1912); U. M. Boykin, *A Handbook on the Detroit Negro* 121 (1943). In 1940, Swan became the first black lawyer nominated to the Democratic ticket for circuit court commissioner in Detroit, Michigan. *Id.* at 89 (*A Handbook on the Detroit Negro*). Lester's association with Willis and Swan was short-lived. He left for Baltimore, Maryland, to practice for a period, returning to practice law in Detroit in 1912. F. H. Warren, *Michigan Manual of Freedmen's Progress* 48 (1915).

63. *Id.* at 120 (*A Handbook on the Detroit Negro*). Willis would later open his office to another Michigan Law School graduate, Charles E. Williams. Williams graduated from law school in 1900. *University of Michigan General Catalogue of Officers and Students, 1837–1911*, at 483 (I. N. Demmon ed. 1912); F. H. Warren, *Michigan Manual of Freedmen's Progress* 50–51 (1915).

64. G. R. Segal, *Blacks in the Law* 149–51 (1983).

65. U. M. Boykin, *A Handbook on the Detroit Negro* 121 (1943).

66. Littlejohn and Hobson, "Black Lawyers, Law Practice, and Bar Associations—1844 to 1970: A Michigan History," 33 *Wayne L. Rev.* 1625, 1642 (1987), quoting interview with Ernest Goodman.

67. Vol. 1 *Who's Who in Colored America* 10 (J. J. Boris ed. 1927).

68. Vol. 1 *Who's Who of the Colored Race* 256 (F. L. Mather ed. 1915); F. H. Warren, *Michigan Manual of Freedmen's Progress* 46–47 (1915).

69. *Ibid.* (*Who's Who*); Vol. 1 *Who's Who of the Colored Race* 20 (F. L. Mather ed. 1915).

70. F. H. Warren, *Michigan Manual of Freedmen's Progress* 47 (1915); Vol. 1 *The National Cyclopedia of the Colored Race* 617 (C. C. Richardson ed. 1919).

71. *Id.* at 49 (*Michigan Manual of Freedmen's Progress*); U. M. Boykin, *A Handbook on the Detroit Negro* 127 (1943).

72. Not much is known about Conrad. He was admitted to the Michigan, Ohio, and Indiana bars, which suggests that he practiced law in states other than Michigan. Vol. 1 *Who's Who in Colored America* 46 (J. J. Boris ed. 1927); *University of Michigan General Catalogue of Officers and Students, 1837–1911*, at 488 (I. N. Demmon ed. 1912); letter from F. Clever Bald, Michigan Historical Collections, to Charles S. Brown, June 3, 1958.

73. F. H. Warren, *Michigan Manual of Freedmen's Progress* 45 (1915).

74. Robinson and Stephens, "Blacks in the Law," 64 *Mich. B.J.* 517 (1985).

75. Vol. 1 *Who's Who of the Colored Race* 16–17 (F. L. Mather ed. 1915); F. H. Warren, *Michigan Manual of Freedmen's Progress* 45 (1915).

76. *Id.* at 45 (*Michigan Manual of Freedmen's Progress*). Baker practiced law in Bay City, Michigan, for fifty years. His son, Oscar William Baker, Jr., graduated from Michigan's law school in 1935, and his grandson, James W. Baker, Sr., in 1951. Proffitt, "Baker and Baker (and Baker)," 29 *Law Quadrangle Notes* 24 (Summer 1985).

77. F. H. Warren, *Michigan Manual of Freedmen's Progress* 33 (1915).

78. Vol. 1 *Who's Who of the Colored Race* 276–77 (F. L. Mather ed. 1915).

79. *Id.* at 276.

80. F. H. Warren, *Michigan Manual of Freedmen's Progress* 33 (1915).

81. *Negro Year Book, 1918–1919*, at 112 (M. N. Work ed. 1919).

82. For example, Leonard C. Thompson, a 1905 graduate of the Detroit College of Law, "was employed by the Union Trust Co. as an abstractor." F. H. Warren, *Michigan Manual of Freedmen's Progress* 50 (1915). Ira J. Pettiford entered the private practice of law after graduating from the Detroit College of Law in 1908 (*id.* at 49), as did Charles A. Roxborough, Jr., a 1914 graduate (*ibid.*).

83. F. H. Warren, *Michigan Manual of Freedmen's Progress* 48–49 (1915); *University of Michigan General Catalogue of Officers and Students, 1837–1911*, at 494 (I. N. Demmon ed. 1912).

84. *Ibid.* (*Michigan Manual of Freedmen's Progress*).

85. U. M. Boykin, *A Handbook on the Detroit Negro* 124 (1943).

86. *Ibid.*

87. F. H. Warren, *Michigan Manual of Freedmen's Progress* 49 (1915). Charles A. Roxborough, Sr., was graduated from Straight University in New Orleans, Louisiana, in 1885. A. P. Tureaud, *The Negro at the Louisiana Bar* 2 (n.d.).

88. Littlejohn and Hobson, "Black Lawyers, Law Practice, and Bar Associations—1844–1970: A Michigan History," 33 *Wayne L. Rev.* 1625, 1651 (1987). Other active black lawyers, such as Samuel G. Thompson, an 1899 Howard University law graduate who was admitted to the Michigan bar around 1908, are said to have "achieved considerable success at the Bar in Detroit." F. H. Warren, *Michigan Manual of Freedmen's Progress* 50 (1915).

89. U. M. Boykin, *A Handbook on the Detroit Negro* 85–87 (1943). In the late 1930s, Roxborough and Robert J. Willis were active in the United Voters' League, in "an attempt to register every eligible colored voter in [Detroit]."

90. *Michigan Official Directory and Legislative Manual* 106 (compiled by H. H. Dignan, secretary of state, 1943).

91. D. T. Carter, *Scottsboro: A Tragedy of the American South* 401 (1969).

92. It has been reported that between 1920 and 1923 Mozelle Goins "was the first Black woman to attend the University of Detroit School of Law." She did not graduate. Another woman, Abigail E. Ross, graduated from Wayne State University Law School in 1940. Littlejohn and Hobson, "Black Lawyers, Law Practice, and Bar Associations—1844 to 1970: A Michigan History," 33 *Wayne L. Rev.* 1625, 1673, nn. 173–74 (1987).

93. Telephone interview with Patrice Bukowitz, director of external relations, Detroit College of Law, April 10, 1989.

94. *Ibid.*

95. "Negro Woman Passes Michigan Bar," *Savannah Tribune*, Oct. 17, 1926; Arnold, "Atty. Letcher Retired from Treasury Dept.," *Atlanta Daily World*, Oct. 2, 1948.

96. "Woman Retires, 46 Years at Treasury," *Washington Post*, July 1, 1948, at 17, col. 3. Despite her legal training, Letcher was employed as an examiner in the Bureau of Engraving and Printing of the Treasury Department. "She was hired at Treasury in 1902 at a salary of $1.25. She attended Howard University's evening law program, but received no pay increase or promotion after she graduated in 1925. When she retired in 1948 her salary was 'two cents' more than that—an hour."

97. Telephone interview with Ms. Roxborough, Nov. 12, 1988. See also, Littlejohn and Hobson, "Black Lawyers, Law Practice, and Bar Associations—1844 to 1970: A Michigan History," 33 *Wayne L. Rev.* 1625, 1642, 1673 (1987).

98. "Lady Lawyer," 2 *Ebony* 18, 19 (Aug. 1947).

99. Littlejohn and Hobson, "Black Lawyers, Law Practice, and Bar Associations—1844 to 1970: A Michigan History," 33 *Wayne L. Rev.* 1625, 1642, 1673 (1987), quoting interview of Jeanne Cole-Harbour.

100. U. M. Boykin, *A Handbook on the Detroit Negro* 126 (1943).

101. McCree, "The Negro Renaissance in Michigan Politics," *The Michigan Chronicle*, Feb. 9, 1963, at 7, col. 1.

102. Letter from John McCarty, deputy clerk, Minnesota Supreme Court, to Charles S. Brown, March 20, 1961. McGhee's sponsor to the Minnesota Supreme Court was H. G. Stone. *Past and Present of St. Paul, Minnesota* 632 (W. B. Hennessy ed. 1906).

103. Knox, "Frederick L. McGhee," *Detroit Plaindealer*, April 22, 1892; "Frederick L. McGhee," *St. Paul Appeal*, Sept. 21, 1912, at 3.

104. The claim that McGhee was the first black lawyer west of Illinois, as stated by E. Spangler in his book, *The Negro in Minnesota*, at 68 (1961), is overbroad. A Minnesota Historical Society scrapbook news article more accurately credits McGhee as one of the first colored lawyers "admitted to practice in the Northwestern territory." "Leaders Among the Colored Men of St. Paul," *St. Paul Globe*, Oct. 19, 1902 (found in the Minnesota Historical Society Scrapbook, vol. 22, at 91–92). See also, "Biographies of Black Pioneers," 23 *Gopher Historian* 18 (Winter 1968–1969).

105. Knox, "Frederick L. McGhee," *Detroit Plaindealer*, April 22, 1892. Another report states that McGhee tried his first case in the St. Paul Municipal Court in 1889. "Frederick L. McGhee," *St. Paul Appeal*, Sept. 21, 1912, at 3.

106. *Ibid.* (Knox, "Frederick L. McGhee").

107. "The McGhees of St. Paul," 40 *Crisis* 130 (June 1933).

108. Knox, "Frederick L. McGhee," *Detroit Plaindealer*, April 22, 1892.

109. *Ibid.*

110. *Past and Present of St. Paul, Minnesota* 632 (W. B. Hennessy ed. 1906).

111. "Frederick L. McGhee," *St. Paul Appeal*, Sept. 21, 1912, at 3.

112. E. Spangler, *The Negro in Minnesota* 68 (1961).

113. *Ibid.*

114. Vol. 6 *The Booker T. Washington Papers, 1901–2*, at 425 (L. R. Harlan, R. W. Smock, and B. S. Kraft eds. 1977).

115. When the NAACP was founded, one author notes "there were no more than several hundred even marginally trained black lawyers throughout the nation, and few black men in trouble had enough money to hire competent counsel." R. Kluger, *Simple Justice* 100–101 (1975). Much of what Kluger says may be true, but it must be remembered that many white lawyers in 1909 had less training than their black counterparts.

116. W. L. Katz, *The Black West* 302 (1973). Katz states that "according to Dr. [W. E. B.] Du Bois ' the honor of founding the [Niagara Movement] belongs to F. L. McGhee, who first suggested it.'" For further evidence for this claim, see *Past and Present of St. Paul, Minnesota* 632 (W. B. Hennessy ed. 1906), and Vol. 5 *The Booker T. Washington Papers, 1899–1900*, at 649 (L. R. Harlan, R. W. Smock, and B. S. Kraft eds. 1976).

117. A. Meier, "Booker T. Washington: An Interpretation," in *Black History* 338, 350 (M. Drimmer ed. 1968).

118. *A Documentary History of the Negro People in the United States* 884 (H. Aptheker ed. 1969). McGhee was joined in a petition condemning Booker T. Washington's European speech by five other black lawyers from around the nation: George W. Crawford, of New Haven, Connecticut; N. B. Marshall, of Texas; Clement G. Morgan, of Cambridge, Massachusetts; Edward H. Morris, of Chicago, Illinois; and B. S. Smith, of Kansas. These lawyers opposed Booker T. Washington's statements abroad because of "the willful miscarriage of justice in the courts" in America. *Id.* at 885–86.

119. E. Spangler, *The Negro in Minnesota* 68 (1961).

120. "Biographies of Black Pioneers," 23 *Gopher Historian* 18 (Winter 1968–1969).

121. Telephone interview with Earl B. Dickerson, Chicago, IL, Aug. 24, 1986; Vol. 1 *Who's Who in Colored America* 145 (J. J. Boris ed. 1927).

122. E. Spangler, *The Negro in Minnesota* 68 (1961).

123. *Progressive Men of Minnesota* 446–47 (M. D. Shutter and J. S. McLain eds. 1897).

124. Vol. 3 *History of Minneapolis* 816, 817 (M. Shutter ed. 1923).

125. E. Spangler, *The Negro in Minnesota* 79 (1961).

126. *Ibid.*

127. Letter from John McCarthy, deputy clerk, Minnesota Supreme Court, to Charles S. Brown, March 20, 1961.

128. *Progressive Men of Minnesota* 350, 351 (M. D. Shutter and J. S. McLain eds. 1897).

129. Smith, "In the Shadow of Plessy: A Portrait of McCants Stewart, Afro-American Legal Pioneer," 73 *Minn. L. Rev.* 495, 500 (1988).

130. Vol. 1 *Who's Who of the Colored Race* 281 (F. L. Mather ed. 1915).

131. "Biographies of Black Pioneers," 23 *Gopher Historian* 18 (Winter 1968–1969). By 1898, Wheaton had made a name for himself in Minnesota Republican politics. In 1896 he "was elected by acclamation as alternate delegate from the Fifth Minnesota congressional district to the Republican national convention at [St. Louis, Missouri], another first for a black person in Minnesota." *Progressive Men of Minnesota* 350, 351 (M. D. Shutter and J. S. McLain eds. 1897).

132. *Ibid.* ("Biographies of Black Pioneers").

133. James L. Curtis graduated from Northwestern University's law school in 1894. He practiced in Columbus, Ohio, until 1899. Vol. 11 *The Booker T. Washington Papers, 1911–12*, at 49 (L. R. Harlan, R. W. Smock, and G. McTigue eds. 1988), J. Frank Wheaton became an effective civil rights and criminal lawyer in New York. He filed some of the early lawsuits against restrictive covenants. He was the co-founder of the Equity Congress, a group that raised money to finance such litigation. Although Wheaton was a criminal defense lawyer, he also fought against the spread of vice in Harlem and encouraged black people to "patronize black businesses." Vol. 10 *The Booker T. Washington Papers, 1909–11*, at 76 (L. R. Harlan, R. W. Smock, G. McTigue, and N. E. Woodruff eds. 1981). He even may have represented Jack Johnson, the heavyweight champion of the world in 1909. *Id.* at 75. Vol. 1 *Who's Who of the Colored Race* 281 (F. L. Mather ed. 1915); *New York Negro Lawyers* 10 (S. H. Lark ed. 1915). James L. Curtis was the only black appointee confirmed by the United States Senate during Woodrow Wilson's first term. In 1915, he was appointed minister to Liberia, and he died in office shortly thereafter. Wolgemuth, "Woodrow Wilson's Appointment Policy and the Negro," 24 *J. of Southern History* 457, 465–66 (Nov. 1958).

134. *General Catalogue of the University of Michigan, 1837–1911*, at 454 (I. N. Demmon ed. 1912).

135. Vol. 2 *History of the Bench and Bar of Minnesota* 187 (H. F. Stevens ed. 1904).

136. *Ibid*; "Biographies of Black Pioneers," 23 *Gopher Historian* 18, 19–20 (Winter 1968–1969); Vol. 1 *Who's Who of the Colored Race* 239 (F. L. Mather ed. 1915). Scrutchin may have tried his luck in the state of Washington prior to relocating to Bemidji, or vice-versa, See E. H. Mumford, *Seattle's Black Victorians, 1852–1901*, at 141 (1980). Mumford states that Scrutchin was practicing in Washington state in 1903.

137. "Charles W. Scrutchin," *New York Age*, May 16, 1918; E. Spangler, *The Negro in Minnesota* 70 (1961).

138. Vol. 2 *History of the Bench and Bar of Minnesota* 187 (H. F. Stevens ed. 1904). Stevens reports, "It is a noteworthy fact that [Scrutchin] was invited to deliver the graduating address to the class of 1900, at his alma mater at Ann Arbor, Michigan." If true, such an invitation to a black alumnus would have been a high honor. However, graduation records at the University of Michigan do not show Scrutchin's name "for the 1900 Department of Law commencement exercises" (letter to author from Sharon Wick, Dec. 13, 1989). He may have been among the unlisted law alumni who addressed a luncheon reunion on June 20, 1900, alumni day (letter to author from Sharon Wick, May 8, 1990).

139. Smith, "In the Shadow of Plessy: A Portrait of McCants Stewart, Afro-American Legal Pioneer," 73 *Minn. L. Rev.* 495, 503 (1988).

140. *Id.* at 496.

141. *Id.* at 504.

142. Vol. 1 *Who's Who of the Colored Race* 107 (F. L. Mather ed. 1915).

143. "Biographies of Black Pioneers," 23 *Gopher Historian* 18, 20 (Winter 1968–1969).

144. E. Spangler, *The Negro in Minnesota* 92 (1961).

145. *Id.* at 70. Around 1916, Francis was nominated over a white opponent for a state post in the Republican district. (12 *Crisis* 199 [June 1916]).

146. J. C. Miller, *The Black Presence in American Foreign Affairs* 41, 292 (1978).

147. E. Spangler, *The Negro in Minnesota* 71 (1961).

148. *Ibid.*

149. *Ibid.*

150. "Negro Attorney in Race for Minneapolis Bench," *St. Louis Argus*, April 17, 1925; *Alumni Directory of the University of Minnesota School of Law, 1889–1986* 103 (ninth ed., 1986).

151. Smith, "In the Shadow of Plessy: A Portrait of McCants Stewart, Afro-American Legal Pioneer," 73 *Minn. L. Rev.* 495, 500, n.20 (1988). Andrew F. Hilyer received LL.B. and LL.M. law degrees from Howard University School of Law in 1884 and 1885, respectively.

152. "Son of Dead Howard Trustee Stars in West," *Washington Eagle*, Jan. 17, 1925.

153. *Ibid.*

154. *Ibid.*

155. "Negro Attorney in Race for Minneapolis Bench," *St. Louis Argus*, April 17, 1925.

156. K. B. Morello, *The Woman Lawyer in America: 1638 to the Present—The Invisible Bar* 153 (1986). Smith's "most famous [civil rights case] was the Arthur Lee Housing Discrimination Case . . . in the 1930s in . . . Minneapolis. . . . There were attempts to terrorize Mr. Lee and he suffered acts of vandalism against his property in an attempt by some of the neighbors to make him move. Lena Smith . . . convinced him to stay. The case went to court and Ms. Smith, his attorney, won the case and set the tone for this area on cases of this type." Biographical Sketch of Lena O. Smith, written by James Griffin, former deputy chief of police, St. Paul, Minnesota 2 (n.d.) (courtesy of Professor Ann Juergens, William Mitchell College of Law). Lena O. Smith served as president and general counsel to the Minneapolis NAACP chapter from 1931 to 1942 ("Who's Who in U.S.," *Pittsburgh Courier*, Feb. 3, 1962, at 14).

157. 28 Neb. 4 (1891) (Sept. Term, 1889–Jan. Term, 1890); *Brittle v. The People*, 2 Neb. 198 (1873). "Silas Robbins Kills Self: Ill Health Cause," *Omaha World Herald*, Sept. 12, 1916, at 3, col. 2; *Souvenir Album and Directory of the Colored Voters in Omaha, Nebraska* 1 (W. B. Walker ed. 1891); "Well-Known Attorney Commits Suicide," *The Monitor*, Sept. 16, 1916, at 1, col. 4, which indicates that Robbins had previously been admitted to practice law in the states of Indiana and Mississippi; "Nebraska Lawyer Commits Suicide," *New York News*, Sept. 21, 1916; F. Dixon, *The Negroes of Nebraska* 36 (W.P.A. Writers' Project, 1939); *Legacies '89, NSBA Family Album, 1899–1989*, at 6 (Oct. 1989).

158. "Silas Robbins," *Omaha World Herald*, Sept. 21, 1898, at 4, col. 2. Robbins was not elected.

159. Silas Robbins was listed as a member of the Douglas County Bar Association in 1892. J. W. Savage and J. T. Bell, *History of the City of Omaha, Nebraska* 227 (1894).

160. Letter from Dale Portschy, head reference librarian, Omaha Public Library, to Charles S. Brown, May 29, 1961.

161. "Silas Robbins Kills Self; Ill Health Cause," *Omaha World Herald*, Sept. 12, 1916, at 3.

162. "Who's Who in City Race," *Omaha World Herald*, April 1, 1933. See also, 64 *Nebraska Repts.* (v) (1905).

163. F. Dixon, *The Negroes of Nebraska* 35 (W.P.A. Writers' Project, 1939).

164. Telephone conversation with John Adams, Jr., Berkeley, CA, Oct. 17, 1988.

165. Letter from Elizabeth Davis Pittman to author, May 13, 1985. See, Vol. 115 *Nebraska Repts.* (v) (1927), and Vol. 116 *Nebraska Repts.* (v) (1928).

166. Letter from Mrs. John G. Pegg to author, May 20, 1982. Mr. Pegg later relocated to Cleveland, Ohio. Other students, DeWitte T. Lawson among them, graduated from the University of Nebraska's law school in 1925. "A Record of the Negro at College," 32 *Crisis* 167, 174 (Aug. 1926).

167. D. H. Oliver, *A Negro on Mormonism* 7 (1963).

168. *Ibid.*

169. Telephone conversation with Joan Adams Davis, Oct. 17, 1988. See Vol. 108 *Nebraska Repts.* (v) (1922).

170. "Law Directory, National Bar Association," appended to the *Proceedings of the National Bar Association at Its Eighth Annual Session* 140, Aug. 4, 5, and 6, 1932.

171. *State v. Franklin*, 80 S.C. 332, 60 S.E. 953, *affirmed, Franklin v. South Carolina*, 218 U.S. 161 (1910) (with Jacob Moorer). According to John Adams, Jr., "my father was driven out of town by whites because of his unyielding advocacy for the rights of black people." Telephone interview by author with John Adams, Jr., Oct. 17, 1988.

172. Telephone interview by author with John Adams, Jr., Oct. 17, 1988.

173. *Ibid.* Newbert, "Reflections from the 'Class' of '29," 17 *The Nebraska University Law School Transcript* 20 (Dec./Jan. 1983). Adams's name is listed among the newly admitted members of the Nebraska Supreme Court at Vol. 117 *Supreme Court of Nebraska Reports* (v) (1929).

174. *Ex parte Darling v. Fenton*, 120 Neb. 829, 235 N.W. 582 (1931).

175. "First Woman Lawyer Passes Nebraska Exams," *Baltimore Herald Commonwealth*, July 13, 1929. "Interesting Items About Home Folks," *Scribner Rustler*, June 20, 1929, at 1, col. 6. See also, Vol. 117 *Supreme Court of Nebraska Reports* (v) (1929), listing Hill as a new member of the Nebraska bar. Hill was not the first woman admitted to the Nebraska bar. That honor apparently goes to Ada M. C. Bittenbinder, who was admitted in 1881. K. B. Morello, *The Woman Lawyer in America: 1638 to the Present—The Invisible Bar* 37 (1986).

176. Telephone interview with Thelma Rutherford, May 14, 1985.

177. "Miss Zanzye H. Hill Dies in Mississippi," *Lincoln Star*, April 5, 1935, at 4, col. 3.

178. Matthew Oliver Ricketts, a physician, was the first black elected to the Nebraska legislature, where he served from 1892 to 1894, and from 1894 to 1896. D. M. Polk, *Black Men and Women of Nebraska* 41 (1981); telephone interview with John Adams, Jr., Berkeley, CA, Oct. 17, 1988. He represented a district on the north side of Omaha, which had a sizeable black population. By this time, Fred A. Wachter had become an active black practitioner in Omaha, Nebraska. "Who's Who in City Race," *Omaha World Herald*, April 1, 1933. Letter to author from John Adams, Jr., Dec. 20, 1988.

179. Letter to author from John Adams, Jr., Dec. 20, 1988.

180. J. H. Chadbourn, *Lynching and the Law* 27 (1933).

181. "Adams Makes Fight for Unemployment Insurance," *The Informer*, April 1936, at 1, col. 3.

182. "Adams Fights Lien Clause in Old Age Pension Bill," *The Informer*, April 1936, at 3, col. 2.

183. "Would Demand 24-Hr Notice Prior to Trial Start," *The Informer*, April 1936, at 3, col. 4.

184. "Educated in Nebraska," *The Informer*, April, 1936, at 1, col. 2. John Adams, Jr., practiced with his father, John Adams, Sr., and Charles F. Davis. Davis was "the first black lawyer in Omaha to support the candidacy of Franklin D. Roosevelt. After Roosevelt won the presidency, the Democrats gave Davis legal work, such as doing abstracts and the like." Telephone interview with John Adams, Jr., Berkeley, CA, Feb. 11, 1989.

185. Telephone interview with John Adams, Jr., Berkeley, CA, June 15, 1990. Adams was not the only attorney in Cleveland arguing for the rights of the black delegates from Louisiana. A. T. Walden and Benjamin Davis, Jr., both of Atlanta, Georgia, and Perry W. Howard and Sidney D. Redmond, from Mississippi, were also present to represent black delegations from their states. "G.O.P. Convention Closes in Cleveland—Record Gains by Race" (partial clipping provided to author by John Adams, Jr., from unidentified newspaper). See also, H. Walton, Jr., *Black Republicans: The Politics of the Black and Tans* 161–62 (1975).

186. Letter from John Adams, Jr., to author, Dec. 20, 1988.

187. Letter from J. H. Newton, clerk, Supreme Court of North Dakota, to Charles S. Brown, May 22, 1958.

188. *The Twelfth Census, Special Reports: Occupations* 356 (1900); Vol. 4, *The Thirteenth Census: Population* 434–613 (1914) (reporting one "Negro" lawyer). (See Appendix.)

189. Letter from Will G. Robinson, secretary, South Dakota State Historical Society, to Charles S. Brown, June 4, 1958.

190. Letters to the author from South Dakota have stated that as late as 1985 no black lawyers had ever been admitted to the South Dakota Bar. Letter from Leonard B. Williams, Aug. 20, 1985; letter from James T. Brick, professor of law, University of South Dakota Law School, Sept. 17, 1985; letter from William K. Sahr, secretary-treasurer, State Bar of South Dakota, Sept. 16, 1985.

191. Personal interview with Charles P. Howard, Jr., in Washington, DC, May 27, 1986. Howard, whose father was one of the first black lawyers in Iowa and a 1922 graduate of Drake University Law School, remarked that "Reden was known to be black." He said that Reden visited their home "when he came through," and that he "attended meetings of the Iowa Colored Bar Association." Howard said that it was his recollection, and his father's, that "Reden practiced law in Sioux Falls, South Dakota."

192. Letter to author from Marilyn L. Graves, clerk of the Wisconsin Supreme Court, Oct. 4, 1991; letter from Edward J. Reisner, assistant dean, University of Wisconsin Law School, Dec. 2, 1987; letter from Scott F. Burson, reference librarian, University of Washington Law Library, March 6, 1986, referring to *Martindale American Law Directory* 1112 (1930).

193. A recent history of Wisconsin has reported, erroneously, that William T. Green was the first black graduate of the University of Wisconsin School of Law, an honor that actually belongs to Everett E. Simpson. See R. C. Nesbit, *The History of Wisconsin, 1878–1893*, at 44 (1985).

194. J. W. Trotter, Jr., *Black Milwaukee* 26 (1985); Reneau and Barbee, "Black Lawyers—A Brief History," 57 *Wisconsin Bar Bulletin* 55 (1984): "Attorney Green's draft of Wisconsin's first Civil Rights Law, Chapter 223 Session Laws of 1895, is one of his lasting achievements." See also, William T. Green, "Negroes in Milwaukee," in *The Negro in Milwaukee: A Historical Survey* 5 (1968)

(published by the Milwaukee Historical Society with an introductory note by Harry H. Anderson).

195. *Ibid.* (*Black Milwaukee*).

196. *Ibid*; letter from Leslie H. Fishel, Jr., to Charles S. Brown, March 11, 1964.

197. "Attorney Green Is Dead," *Milwaukee Sentinel*, Dec. 4, 1911, at 9, col. 1.

198. *Ibid.*

199. *Ibid.*

200. *Ibid.*

201. *Proceedings, State Bar Association of Wisconsin* 33 (1912–1914), quoted in letter from Margaret Gleason, reference librarian, State Historical Society of Wisconsin, to Charles S. Brown, Feb. 27, 1961).

202. J. W. Trotter, Jr., *Black Milwaukee* 83 (1985).

203. *Id.* at 103. See also, Locke, "Enter New Negro," 6 *Survey Graphic* 631 (March 1925).

204. Vol. 1 *Who's Who of the Colored Race* 89 (F. L. Mather ed. 1915); *Who's Who in Colored America* 56 (J. J. Boris ed. 1927). Another lawyer known to have practiced law in Milwaukee during the same period is G. H. Hamilton. See, "Law Directory, National Bar Association," appended to the *Proceedings of the National Bar Association at Its Eighth Annual Session* 142, Aug. 4, 5, and 6, 1932.

205. J. W. Trotter, Jr., *Black Milwaukee* 86, 104 (1985). A. B. Nutt was the owner of a car-washing service.

206. *Id.* at 121.

207. *Id.* at 126.

208. *Id.* at 103.

209. *Id.* at 160.

210. *Id.* at 210–11.

211. *Id.* at 166.

212. *Marquette University, Part-Time Evening School, 1923–1924*, at 27 (1924); letter to author from John L. LeDoux, Marquette University archivist, Dec. 12, 1990.

213. Letter to author from Marilyn L. Graves, clerk of the Wisconsin Supreme Court, Dec. 11, 1990. (Graves misspells her last name as "Rainey.") This letter is strong evidence that Mabel Watson Raimey did not graduate from a law school in Wisconsin, since all in-state graduates were admitted without taking the bar. Only nongraduates of Wisconsin law schools, out-of-state law graduates, or non-law graduates were required to take the bar examination in 1927.

214. Alexander, "Women as Practitioners of Law in the United States," 1 *Nat'l B.A.J.* 56, 64 (July 1941); Clevert, "Woman Lawyer, 77, Reminisces About Her Firsts," *The Milwaukee Journal*, Nov. 9, 1976. Clevert states that Raimey "believes she was . . . the first black woman to graduate from [the University of Wisconsin and] from the [Milwaukee University] Law School." See also, Williams, "A Black Woman's Voice: The Story of Mabel Raimey, 'Shero,'" 74 *Marquette L. Rev.* 345 (1991).

Chapter 9

The Pacific States

The Pacific states include the states of Arizona, California, Colorado, Hawaii, Kansas, Montana, New Mexico, Oklahoma, Oregon, Utah, and Washington.

Several states or American territorial possessions in the Pacific region of the nation have had no known history of black lawyers or report one prior to 1945; they include Alaska, Idaho, Nevada, and Wyoming.[1] In large part this phenomenon may be due to the small population of blacks in these states, racism, and the lack of economic opportunities available to black lawyers in regions with little or no exposure to black professionals.[2]

Arizona and Utah

Nevertheless, black lawyers were admitted to the bar in other Pacific states that had small black populations. For example, on April 30, 1921, Robert Lee Fortune was admitted to practice in the state of Arizona.[3] And in 1931 David H. Oliver was admitted to the bar in Utah.[4] Although little is known about Fortune, he probably studied for the bar in his native state of Oklahoma, while serving as a deputy United States marshal in Wilkerton, Oklahoma. Fortune began to practice law in the local courts of Phoenix, Arizona, in 1916. Between 1921 and 1936, he appeared before the Arizona Supreme Court on six occasions. According to one source, when Fortune died, "the Maricopa County Bar Association conducted memorial services for him in the chambers of Judge J. C. Niles."[5] David H. Oliver, a 1923 Nebraska University law graduate, was admitted to the Utah bar on April 30, 1931, and practiced in Ogden, Utah, for over thirty years.[6]

California

In California, "the pioneer Negro fought all of his legal battles through the services of white attorneys."[7] Black people were prohibited from admission to the California bar until 1878.[8] In that year, the California State Assembly passed legislation lifting the bar against women[9] and striking from the Code of Civil Procedure the words "white male" from all sections, thus permitting persons of color to qualify for the bar examination.[10] However, even after the race bar was lifted and the first black was appointed to a grand jury in 1878,[11]

the prejudice was so great that a Negro boy could not be admitted [to the California bar], notwithstanding he had read law under good instructors who had personally examined and considered him qualified for admittance, as was the case of James Wilson, the first Negro boy to apply for admittance to the bar in Alameda County, California [in the pioneer days].[12]

Despite the elimination of the race bar in the law, the practice of excluding blacks from the legal profession in California continued until 1887, nearly a decade after Clara Shortridge Foltz, a white woman, was admitted to the bar after spearheading the fight to eliminate sex- and race-based restrictions in the state.[13] In 1887 Robert Charles O'Hara Benjamin became the first black to be admitted to the California bar.[14] Benjamin, who had first been admitted to the Virginia bar at Charlottesville in the 1880s, had moved around the country. He was reported to have been a member of the bar in "twelve different states."[15] After Benjamin was admitted to the bar in San Francisco, he shared an office in a well-known white law firm,[16] but he spent most of his time editing various newspapers in California.[17]

Shortly after Benjamin's admission, Harrison H. Ferrell became "the second colored lawyer admitted to the court upon oath."[18] Although the state of California authorized the creation of its first public university with a law school in 1878,[19] it was not until 1915 that James M. Alexander became the first black in California to "matriculate in a law school in California, in the University of Southern California."[20]

Charles S. Darden, a 1904 Howard University law graduate, went to California to practice law; two years later he "was nominated by the Prohibition party for the office of judge of the police court," making him the first black lawyer in California to seek a judgeship. For reasons unknown, Darden withdrew from the nomination.[21] Darden's interests in real estate made him a foe of the racially restrictive covenants that appeared on deeds of sale. Darden was the first black lawyer to successfully challenge the legality of such deeds, a fact that was "not . . . commented upon except in few papers beyond the Rocky Mountains,"[22] probably because it was a decision of a local court in Los Angeles. The court decision, however, established "a real precedent, it being the first decision obtained directly upon the question involved in a Court of Justice in the United States."[23]

One case Darden undertook, that of a black woman's claim to title by grant from a white woman, reached the California Supreme Court in 1911 in the first-known case presented to that court by a black lawyer.[24] The case set a precedent for women in California. According to state law, a woman holding or to whom title to real property was transferred, though married, was presumed to have good title. In such a case, Darden argued, a woman could transfer such title, independent of her husband, to another, even if the grantee was a black woman. Darden won his case on this point of law.[25] Darden practiced law in California for many years and joined with other black lawyers in civil and criminal appeals before the Supreme Court of California.[26]

In 1908 Hugh Ellwood Macbeth, Sr., and Willis Oliver Tyler graduated from Harvard University's law school.[27] Macbeth went to Baltimore, Maryland, where he founded the *Baltimore Times*. He continued to practice law there until 1912, when he relocated to Los Angeles, California.[28] Tyler practiced law in Illinois until 1911, when he, too, relocated to Los Angeles. In 1912 Macbeth and Tyler founded a law firm in Los Angeles, which Macbeth's brother, Gobert Eliot Macbeth, a 1919 Howard University law graduate, later joined.[29] It is unknown how long Macbeth and Tyler's association lasted, but both lawyers practiced in Los Angeles for several years, were active in civil rights, and made several appearances before the Supreme Court of California.[30]

In 1918 Tyler publicly criticized Congress for failing to appoint black Americans to the West Point Military and Naval academies. Tyler believed that until America permitted blacks to demonstrate their ability as military leaders, whites would continue to question their loyalty.[31]

In 1927 Macbeth served as president of the Blackstone Club, a bar group. The Blackstone Club included black and Jewish lawyers who were barred from membership in the Los Angeles Bar Association and the California State Bar Association.[32] During this period, the California State Assembly considered a bill which, if adopted, would place the California Bar Association, then a private group, under the jurisdiction of the state judiciary. Black lawyers, among them Macbeth, E. M. McCullough, and W. E. Conegys, formed a coalition with Jewish lawyers in an effort to assure that their groups would not be excluded from membership in the California State Bar Association under the new plan. Macbeth appeared before the California State Assembly and argued for a "stipulation" which insured that if the courts assumed a supervisory role over the California State Bar, "there will be but one common American program for all."[33] Macbeth, on behalf of black and Jewish lawyers, won this stipulation. The members of the Blackstone Club therefore withdrew their opposition to the bill.[34]

In 1931 Macbeth was elected to the Board of Governors of the Lawyers Club of Los Angeles, a post to which he was reelected for seven consecutive years. He was the first black lawyer to hold such an office.[35] Macbeth also participated in the California Bar Association after it was formed in 1927 under the supervision of the California Supreme Court. In 1932 Macbeth was the only black delegate in attendance at the fifth annual meeting of the association. At the meeting, Macbeth issued a minority report after the Committee on Trust Deeds sought to have the bar "stamp its approval on existing mortgages and loan practices which had . . . fleeced . . . workers and small homeowners of their property."[36] In addition to Macbeth's domestic interests, he helped found in 1939 the United Races of the World, a group whose purpose was to advance brotherhood among all races of the world. In 1936 he was appointed consul (at Los Angeles) by the Republic of Liberia, and he held this post for twelve years.[37]

Willis O. Tyler also won recognition for his fight to have restrictive covenants banned in Los Angeles. In fact, in 1920 he secured a verdict in the local courts "to the effect that a private individual could not insert a clause in a deed which prohibited a future sale to persons of African descent."[38] In 1928 Tyler won another verdict involving the restriction of land sales to non-whites, but the verdict was reversed by the California Supreme Court.[39] Later, Tyler joined with Loren Miller, a 1928 graduate of Washburn University's law school, to blaze a trail that would ultimately dismantle all race-based restrictive covenants.[40] Tyler devoted virtually his entire legal career to the problem of restrictive covenants. In 1948, he was rewarded: The covenants were declared unconstitutional when the United States Supreme Court decided *Shelly v. Kraemer*.[41]

In 1910 Edward Burton Ceruti graduated from St. Lawrence University at Canton, New York. He later attended Brooklyn Law School[42] and was admitted to the California bar in 1912. Ceruti opened a law office in Los Angeles, where he received a retainer to handle the collection business for the Enterprise Collection Agency.[43] Ceruti also became the "official attorney" of the Southern California branch of the NAACP. In 1914, he became the second black lawyer to appear before the California Supreme Court.[44] Through Ceruti's efforts as counsel to the NAACP, he was successful in getting black women admitted to the nurse-training programs operated by the county hospital in Los Angeles. He also won damages against restaurants and public entertainment houses that refused to admit blacks in Santa Monica, Santa Barbara, and Pasadena, California.[45] Ceruti and Willis Tyler often tried murder cases together, and these cases were well noted by the press.[46]

In 1911 Oscar Hudson was admitted to practice by the Appellate Court of the First District of California in Los Angeles.[47] In the same year Hudson, who apparently had ties to New Mexico, was elected a delegate-at-large to the first Republican state convention ever held in that state. In 1912, William C. McDonald, governor of New Mexico, appointed Hudson as a delegate to the Negro National Educational Congress held in St. Paul, Minnesota.[48] He was also the first black lawyer in California to be appointed as a notary public by the governor. Fluent in Spanish and other languages, Hudson was appointed foreign consul for Liberia at the port of San Francisco by President Woodrow Wilson.[49] Although blacks were generally barred from becoming members of the California State Bar Association until 1927, Hudson was admitted to the San Francisco Bar Association in 1916, the first black so admitted by any private white bar association in the state.[50] He specialized in criminal law in San Francisco for most of his life and appeared before the Supreme Court of California on both criminal and civil matters.[51]

Another black lawyer, John Merwin, did not immediately use the legal training that he received at the University of California in the 1920s. After receiving his law degree, Merwin served as an assistant coach at the University of California for several years. In 1943 Merwin was appointed to the California Board of Prison Terms and Paroles.[52]

As in other states, black lawyers, because of their skills in criminal law, were retained in California to represent whites charged with serious crimes. In 1924, Sheadrick B. Turner won acclaim in the federal court at Los Angeles when a jury acquitted Nettie C. Bowen, a white woman, of conspiring with David Pashkow, a white man, to conceal $60,000 in a bankruptcy case. Through Turner's skillful representation, the evidence established that Pashkow had been robbed and forced to leave town by a group of thugs, which in turn established that Pashkow and Bowen had not concealed the money from their creditors. Turner's performance was so outstanding that the prosecuting attorney and the jurors praised him "for his masterly argument in defense of his clients."[53]

The use of black lawyers by whites was not limited to the criminal area. Curtis Taylor, of Los Angeles, considered "one of the ablest lawyers on the coast, was retained in 1927 by a wealthy white woman as counsel in a divorce suit involving property worth $25,000."[54] A. W. Hammond, too, served an "attractive interracial clientele" in San Diego because of his knowledge of several foreign languages.[55]

In 1929, George Marion Johnson received his law degree from Boalt

Hall Law School at the University of California. He then pursued the doctor of juridical science degree, the highest degree awarded in law. After Johnson received his degree from Boalt Hall, he joined the state's tax department. In 1935 Johnson became the first black lawyer to publish a law review article on tax law in the *California Law Review*, and he returned to the subject again in 1939[56] when he joined the faculty of Howard University's law school in Washington, D.C.

In the early 1930s, a few black lawyers, such as John Wesley Bussey, Leon Whittaker, and Ivan J. Johnson, were hired by the federal government in the California area. Bussey, a 1931 Harvard University law graduate, was hired as counsel for the Office of Price Administration in Los Angeles.[57] Whittaker, a 1928 law graduate of Boalt Hall Law School at the University of California, became in 1930 the first black lawyer "west of Chicago" appointed to the office of assistant federal district attorney.[58] Seven years later, Johnson became an assistant United States attorney.[59]

In the 1930s Edwin L. Jefferson and David W. Williams were admitted to the California bar. Both were graduates of the University of Southern California's law school. After Jefferson graduated from law school in 1931, he entered private practice in Los Angeles. Ten years later, Governor Culbert L. Olson appointed Jefferson to the municipal court of Los Angeles, making him the first black judge west of the Mississippi. In 1937 Williams opened a law practice in "the ghetto in Los Angeles."[60]

Thomas L. Griffith, a 1931 law graduate of Southwestern University's law school, also entered private practice in Los Angeles.[61] In 1935 just after Congress passed the Communications Act of 1934, Charles H. Matthews, deputy district attorney in Los Angeles, began to broadcast a weekly radio program entitled "The Jury's Verdict" over station KFAC-AM. Matthews, a 1930 graduate of Boalt Hall Law School at the University of California, was one of the first black lawyers to use the public airwaves to report on trials conducted in the Los Angeles courts.[62]

By 1944 Loren Miller, who had been admitted to the California state bar ten years earlier, won the respect of his people for the valiant efforts he and Willis O. Tyler waged in litigating race covenant cases. Miller even explored the possibility of running for Congress, a prospect that excited many in the black community.[63]

At least seven black women lawyers were admitted to the California bar prior to 1945. Virginia Stephens, a graduate of the University of California, was admitted to the bar in 1928, becoming California's first black woman lawyer. At the time of Stephens's admission, she "was . . . secretary and business manager of the famous Stephens Cafe, owned and operated by her father in . . . Oakland."[64] Shortly after being admitted to the bar, Stephens joined another black lawyer, J. W. Bussey, in the practice of law in San Francisco, but she later took a job with the state of California in Sacramento. In 1930 Stephens was followed to the bar by Zephyr Abigail Moore-Ramsey, a 1922 Howard University law graduate. Moore-Ramsey entered the private practice of law in Los Angeles, returning later to Washington, D.C., to work in the Federal Emergency Relief Administration. After World War II, she moved back to Pasadena, California, to practice law.[65]

In 1933 Tabytha Anderson and Myrtle B. Anderson were admitted to the California bar. Tabytha Anderson was a 1931 graduate of Howard University's law school. She practiced for only three years before her death in 1936, but during this time she defeated Leland S. Hawkins, a leading black lawyer, for the presidency of the San Francisco chapter of the NAACP.[66] Little more is known about her law career, but her activities on behalf of religious groups and youth organizations are better documented.[67]

Martha Malone Williams, who began her career as a legal secretary, was a 1943 honors graduate of the Southwestern University Law School of Los Angeles. Williams entered the private practice of law in Los Angeles, and is often erroneously referred to as California's first black woman lawyer.[68] In 1944, Pauli Murray, a 1944 graduate of Howard University's law school, went to California after being denied admission to Harvard University's graduate program in law. Instead, she enrolled in the graduate program of Boalt Hall Law School at the University of California. In 1944 Murray began to research a pioneering article on equal employment opportunities. She later broke ground as the first black woman lawyer to publish a lead article in a major law review. Murray was admitted to the California bar in 1946.[69]

Colorado

On June 7, 1883, Edwin Henry Hackley, who had attended law school at the University of Michigan for one year, was admitted to the Colorado bar.[70] Little is known about Hackley: he practiced law, worked for the city of Denver as clerk in the recorder's office, and founded the *Colorado Statesman*. In 1901 Hackley relocated to Media, Pennsylvania, "to devote his time to dramatic composition," and he resided there until his death in 1940.[71]

On December 1, 1891, Joseph H. Stuart became the second black lawyer admitted to practice in Colorado. Stuart graduated from the University of South Carolina in 1877, just as the Reconstruction era ended. Since Stuart had previously been admitted to the Kansas bar in

1883, he was admitted to the Colorado bar without examination. Stuart entered the private practice of law and became involved in local politics in Arapahoe County. Within five years, he was elected to the Ninth and Tenth Colorado General Assemblies as a representative from Arapahoe County. He served in this capacity from 1893 to 1897. Among Stuart's major achievements in the Colorado legislature was the sponsorship of a bill to strengthen the state's existing civil rights legislation.[72]

Shortly after Stuart's admission to the bar, William Bolden Townsend settled in Pueblo, Colorado. Townsend, in 1891 the first black to graduate from the University of Kansas Law School, had practiced in Kansas since 1891. Townsend moved to Denver in around 1905 to practice law and to represent the Knights of Pythias, a black fraternal group.[73]

Thomas Campbell, who was previously admitted to the bars of Missouri and Oklahoma, settled in Denver, Colorado, in 1903. Campbell, an 1893 Howard University law graduate who was considered "one of the leading lawyers of the race," believed that Denver offered great opportunities for the black lawyer. He indicated that the black lawyer in Denver was being patronized by black property owners as well as by non-property owners of the city.[74] However, he criticized the "few wealthy Negroes and organizations that have not the confidence in the integrity and skill of the Negro to give them consideration in the matter of legal work."[75] Campbell practiced law in Colorado for more than fifty years.[76]

George Gallious Ross, Jr., arrived in Denver in 1904, the year that he graduated from Howard University's law school. Ross practiced law and published the *Denver Star*.[77] Sam Cary followed Ross to the Denver bar in 1919 or soon thereafter. Cary, a 1909 graduate of Washburn University's law school, opened a law office in Denver in 1919. He specialized in criminal law. His clients "were made up of people whom the white lawyers shun: Blacks, Orientals, Indians and poor whites[78] . . . [who] could ill afford to pay him."[79] Cary practiced law until 1926, when he was reportedly disbarred for neglecting his clients. According to some sources, Cary's disbarment may have had racial overtones. He was reinstated to the Colorado bar in 1935.[80]

The history of the black lawyer in Colorado becomes vague in the 1930s. However, W. J. Dixon was active in Colorado, and is reported to have successfully opposed a government case involving the ownership of oil shale lands in 1931.[81] In 1939 Archie Williard McKinney was the first black to graduate from the University of Denver's law school.[82] He was followed by Howard Jenkins, Jr., in 1941.[83]

No black women were admitted to practice in the state of Colorado prior to 1945.

Hawaii

Thomas McCants Stewart relocated to Hawaii from New York in November 1898. He was admitted to the bar of Hawaii in the same year.[84] Stewart, Hawaii's first black lawyer, arrived in what was then a territorial possession of the United States with several letters of recommendation from white New York lawyers,[85] and one from ex-president Grover Cleveland.[86]

The economic opportunities available under the auspices of Manifest Destiny may have prompted Stewart to settle in Hawaii.[87] Between 1889 and 1898, the United States acquired the Samoas, Hawaii, Puerto Rico, Guam, and the Philippine Islands.[88] Stewart, an 1875 law graduate of the University of South Carolina, was familiar with economic expansionism. He had personally witnessed it during his travels to Africa in 1883–1885. He may have desired to start a new life in a land devoid of the racial limitations he faced in the United States.[89]

After his arrival in Hawaii, Stewart became immersed in local politics as well as in the practice of law. He is credited with much of the initial effort to obtain self-government in Hawaii. This movement led eventually to Hawaii's statehood. In 1900 Stewart served on the Republican Territorial Central Committee. Stewart and four other members of the committee drafted the Municipal Act of Honolulu. The purpose of the proposed municipal act was to obtain self-government for the citizens of Honolulu. The act was introduced in the Hawaii Senate by Senator Clarence L. Crabbe, but the proposal failed.

Stewart was then charged with drafting the Long Municipal Act. It too was designed to give self-governance to Honolulu. In 1903 this proposal was introduced in the Hawaii legislature by Representative Carlos Long. This legislation passed but was vetoed by Governor Sanford B. Dole. The veto stirred the people of Hawaii to action, and their demands for control of the local government increased. Stewart advised Governor Dole to establish a commission to continue the study on home rule and the taxation issues associated with it. H. E. Cooper and Stewart were appointed to a subcommittee, and a bill prepared by them was finally submitted to the legislature in 1904. However, George R. Carter, the newly elected governor, opposed the plan for home rule and, again, it failed.[90]

Stewart's legal contributions to Hawaii were no less significant than his political accomplishments. Stewart was an active and distinguished lawyer during his six-year stay in Hawaii. On June 20, 1899, T. McCants Stewart became the first black American to appear before the Hawaii Supreme Court.[91] Between June 1899 and November 1904, Stewart appeared before the Hawaii Supreme Court sixteen times. But seldom did Stewart handle criminal matters in Hawaii; he handled mostly civil cases, sometimes with white lawyers as co-counsel. It is evident that Stewart was a respected member of the Hawaii bar, and was sought after by clients and other members of the bar.[92] The respect the Hawaii Supreme Court accorded to Stewart was underscored on July 7, 1900, when Stewart appeared before the court to eulogize the death of Albert Francis Judd, chief justice of that judicial body. In all likelihood, this was the first time that a black American lawyer ever participated in such a ceremony.[93]

Between 1900 and 1903, Stewart argued five cases before the United States District Court of Hawaii. In 1900 the United States Congress established a federal court in Hawaii with jurisdiction over all criminal and civil matters. Stewart became the first lawyer in Hawaii to litigate a case in the newly established federal court. Because the decisions in federal district court cases in which black lawyers appeared during this period are so rare, these cases are few in number, but provide a clearer picture of Stewart's skills as a lawyer, the types of cases he litigated, the frequency with which he appeared before the court, the racial makeup of his clients, and the significant damage awards he won for them.

Shortly after the federal court was established, Stewart represented a Chinese laborer in a deportation case. Although he lost this case,[94] in 1901 Stewart successfully prosecuted a negligence action involving a wrongful death on board the schooner *Robert Lewers*. The award for the case was in the amount of $1,577.[95] In the same year, Stewart lost another deportation case, this one involving a Chinese woman.[96] In 1903 Stewart prevailed in a libel case in admiralty for injuries to a seaman on board the barkentine *James Tuft*. His client received an award of $2,500.[97] In the same year, Stewart won another case in admiralty for injuries to a seaman on board the *Erskine M. Phelps*. Stewart's client won an award of $1,800.[98]

In 1906, Stewart, perhaps dissatisfied with his progress in Hawaii, or lured by the romance of Africa, left Hawaii for Liberia. Stewart had visited Liberia twenty-three years earlier, but this time he went to Liberia to make a life for himself. Stewart's talents came to the attention of Edward Wilmot Blyden, president of Liberia. A close relationship formed between these men, and Stewart's political career advanced rapidly. He was first appointed deputy attorney general, then acting attorney general, and, finally, attorney general of Liberia.

In 1907 apparently bewildered by the slow progress of black people in America, Stewart stated in an article, "I watch with great interest the fight which you are making in the United States for equality of opportunity. . . . I regard it as a hopeless struggle."[99] In 1911 T. McCants Stewart was appointed associate justice of the Supreme Court of Liberia, a position that he held until 1914.[100] It is a post he never would have attained in the United States.

Stewart was not the only black lawyer in Hawaii between 1900 and 1906. William Francis Crockett, an 1888 graduate of the University of Michigan's law school, arrived in Wailuku, Maui, in 1900 from Montgomery, Alabama, where he had practiced law. Crockett worked for the Hawaiian Commercial and Sugar Company in Puunene, Maui, from 1901 to 1903. Thereafter Crockett "returned to the practice of law . . . soon [becoming] one of the leading attorneys of the Valley Island."[101] He appeared before the Hawaii Supreme Court in 1908,[102] and later became district magistrate of Wailuku and deputy county attorney for Maui. In 1915 he was elected to the Territorial House of Representatives. Crockett held several other public positions. He served on the Board of Registration for Maui and was appointed to the Industrial Accident Board by Governor Wallace R. Farrington in 1925, a position to which he was reappointed by Governor Lawrence Judd in 1930.[103]

In 1917 William F. Crockett's son, Wendell, was graduated from the University of Michigan's law school. Wendell Crockett returned to Maui, Hawaii, where he practiced law for several years. He was elected to the Territorial Senate and served as a circuit judge.[104]

No black women practiced law in Hawaii prior to 1945.

Kansas

In 1871, John H. Morris became the first black person admitted to the Kansas bar. In a rare report by the bar examining committee, the decision to admit Morris was printed in *The Louisianian*. The examining committee concluded that "[Morris] has passed a very creditable exam." The committee was impressed with his "individual effort backed by industry and persuasion" and expressed pride that Morris, a barber, had advanced himself in spite of little formal education. Morris showed "the world that the unfortunate race to which he belongs is capable of being admitted into all the higher walks of life."[105]

Charles Henry James Taylor was admitted to the bar at Leavenworth, Kansas, soon after Morris's admission. Taylor had previously practiced law in Indiana and had served as deputy district attorney of the Nineteenth Judicial District of Indiana. He arrived in Leavenworth, Kansas, about 1878, opened a law practice, and engaged in politics. Taylor also practiced law in Kansas City, Missouri, serving for a time as the state's first black assistant city attorney.[106] Taylor's political influence was apparently significant. President Grover Cleveland, a Democrat, appointed him as consul-general to Liberia in 1887, the year after New Hampshire senator Henry W. Blair, a Republican, had moved for his admission to the United States Supreme Court.[107] Taylor later returned to Kansas, where he again practiced law. He became an advocate for segregated schools, believing that integrated schools would expose black students to racist instructors and eliminate jobs for black teachers.[108] According to available accounts, Taylor was devoted to the cause of his people and successfully defended black squatters from eviction efforts.[109]

In 1894 Taylor was confirmed as recorder of deeds for the District of Columbia, a job then considered to be the key political domestic appointment for blacks. During Taylor's three-year term as recorder of deeds, it was rumored that he had been invited to the White House for lunch by President Cleveland, a rumor Cleveland never denied. In 1903 President Theodore Roosevelt dined with Booker T. Washington, thereby causing quite a stir in the South, because Southerners believed "the President had broken bread with a man whom God had not made his social equal."[110] During the uproar that followed President Roosevelt's lunch with Washington, Congressman Charles F. Scott, from Kansas, and Congressman Edwin Y. Webb, from North Carolina, gave speeches on the floor of the House that cited Cleveland's lunch with Taylor. These speeches forced Cleveland to disavow publicly that he had eaten lunch with Taylor in order to please the Southerners.[111] Whether Cleveland ate lunch with this black lawyer remains officially unverified, though the press in Kansas reported that the meal had taken place. Unfortunately, Taylor could neither confirm nor deny the story. He had passed away before the uproar.[112]

In 1878 John Lewis Waller, recently admitted to the bar at Marion, Iowa, "hung out his shingle" in the First Judicial District of Leavenworth, Kansas. Waller had read law prior to his admission to the Iowa bar. He was examined and admitted to the Kansas bar by Judge Robert Crozier.[113] Initially, Waller's law practice did not flourish. White people did not retain his services and blacks questioned his legal qualifications. The most direct challenge to Waller's qualifications was made by a black man, Charles H. Langston, the brother of John Mercer Langston, Howard University's first law dean. Langston's challenge to Waller may have been caused by envy. As assistant sergeant-at-arms in the Kansas House of Representatives of Kansas,[114] Waller was politically secure. Waller was also a critic of President Chester A. Arthur, whom Langston apparently supported.[115]

Waller later moved to Topeka, Kansas, where he was appointed deputy city attorney on June 28, 1887.[116] He arrived in Topeka just in time to play a direct role in the 1888 presidential election of Benjamin Harrison. Waller was selected to cast the vote for Kansas in the electoral college, the only black person in the nation with such authority.[117] In

Topeka, Waller had apparently begun to publish *The Western Recorder* in Leavenworth, Kansas, a paper that folded in 1885. The year that Waller arrived in Topeka he established *The American Citizen*[118] and formed an association with Turner W. Bell, another black lawyer. In 1889 Waller formed a law firm with two other black lawyers, William Abram Price and Albert M. Thomas.[119]

During Waller's first years of practice in Topeka, he represented three black men charged with "slitting the throat" of a white man. The crime, which occurred in Leavenworth, Kansas, aroused antiblack passions among whites in that city. On the day of the trial, Waller entered a hostile courtroom of white spectators. He not only averted a lynching, he won his clients' acquittal as well.[120] Waller was one of the first black lawyers in the West to sue a private eating establishment for refusing to serve blacks: in 1888 he represented several blacks who claimed that their rights had been violated when they were refused service at a lunch counter in Topeka, Kansas. The case was about to be tried when the "chief witness for the plaintiffs was bought off and left town."[121] Waller, along with William Abram Price, also fought diligently to desegregate the public school system in Topeka. Waller and Price publicly disavowed the reasons for segregation advanced by Charles H. J. Taylor.

In 1891 John Lewis Waller became consul at Tamatave, Madagascar by appointment of President Benjamin Harrison.[122] Three years after his appointment, Waller ran into serious legal difficulties while serving his consulship. He became involved in a complicated land deal known as Wallerland. Pressure from the French government made it difficult for Waller to carry out the venture. Waller retained John Mercer Langston, of the District of Columbia, and Warner T. McGuinn, a leading black lawyer in Baltimore, Maryland, to lobby officials at the State Department and members of the United States Senate to support his venture and his release from a French prison.[123]

The exact date that black lawyers settled in Graham County, Kansas, is uncertain. However, in 1882 D. Hinchman, a black lawyer practicing in Hill City (Graham County), Kansas, became one of the first black judges in the state.[124] By 1889, another black lawyer in Hill City, G. W. Jones, was an active commercial lawyer. Jones was counsel "for the Equitable Mortgage Company, whose capital [amounted to] $2,000,000." The income received from Jones's private practice was substantial enough for him to decline a draft for the position of assistant county attorney.[125]

In around 1914 Will L. Sayers settled in Hill City. Sayers, like Hinchman and Jones, became known county-wide as a superb attorney. In the 1920s, there were few if any black lawyers in Kansas representing white corporate clients. Yet Raymond Jordan Reynolds, a 1929 black graduate of Washburn University's law school, reported that Will Sayers was one of the first black lawyers to represent the interests of a white insurance company.[126] According to Reynolds,

A white insurance company went to the local bank in Hill City, Kansas, and asked the bank's president to recommend the best lawyer in Graham County to represent the company. The bank president recommended Will Sayers, but did not identify him as being black. When the insurance company discovered that Will Sayers was black, it balked. The insurance company's representative returned to the bank president complaining about Sayers race. The bank president responded, "You asked me to recommend the best lawyer in the county. You didn't ask me to recommend the best white lawyer in the county." I believe that Sayers qualifications prevailed. He got the work.[127]

On June 7, 1883, Joseph H. Stuart "signed the roll of attorneys" in Topeka, Kansas, six years after being graduated from South Carolina University's School of Law.[128] Stuart had witnessed the resegregation of public education in South Carolina at the end of the Reconstruction era. Perhaps this experience formed the basis for his first lawsuit, which intended to desegregate the public schools of Topeka. He was not successful in this suit, but its precedent endured eighty years, serving as the model for one of the most important Supreme Court decisions in American history, *Brown v. The Board of Education of Topeka, Kansas.*[129]

Brown Sylvester Smith settled in Kansas City, Kansas, just after graduating from the University of Michigan's law school in 1886. Smith was admitted to the Kansas bar on motion, since he had previously been admitted to both the Michigan and Missouri bars in 1886. Smith practiced law in Kansas City even as he served on the City Council of Kansas City from 1892 to 1896. In 1899 Smith was appointed first assistant county attorney of Wyandotte County, a position that he held with distinction until 1907. Thereafter, he relocated to his native state of Minnesota, where he opened a law practice in Minneapolis.[130]

In 1887 Isaac Franklin Bradley, Sr., graduated from the University of Kansas's law school. He was among the first black students to do so, and was soon after admitted to the bar. Two years later, Bradley was elected justice of the peace in Kansas City, Kansas, a position that he held until 1891. In 1894 he was appointed second assistant county attorney of Wyandotte County, becoming in the process one of the "pioneer Negro [lawyers]" of Kansas. By 1900, Bradley had advanced to first assistant prosecuting attorney. Eight years later, Bradley "was nominated on the Independent [Hearst] ticket for attorney general of Kansas, but received less than enough votes to elect."[131] Isaac Franklin Bradley, Jr., was graduated from the Kansas University's law school in

1917, becoming one of the first second-generation black lawyers in the state.

Turner W. Bell arrived in Leavenworth, Kansas, in 1887, after graduating from Iowa's Drake University Law School. Bell "consulted a prominent white lawyer, who advised him to leave town at once or . . . starve to death."[132] Bell chose to remain in Leavenworth, Kansas, though he knew of the difficulties John Lewis Waller had faced less than ten years before.[133] Bell quickly earned a reputation as a smart criminal lawyer. His expertise in winning the release of prisoners from the federal prison at Leavenworth was widely publicized in Kansas and beyond. In 1911 Bell won the release of Charles Stevens (alias Charles Savage), a black mail clerk who had been convicted in 1908 of robbing a mail pouch of $78,000. In 1917 Bell represented Stevens again on a similar charge. After Stevens was convicted, Bell appealed the conviction to the federal appeals court in Minneapolis, Minnesota, but was not successful in obtaining a reversal. Bell was, however, able to win reduced sentences for eight other clients.[134]

Between 1915 and 1918, Bell reportedly tried "more than 1,400 cases," either at the federal district court level or on appeal in the Eighth Federal Circuit,[135] including the post-conviction appeal of black soldiers involved in the Houston Riots of 1917.[136] In 1912 Bell's criminal defense and appeal skills again came to the attention of the public. On appeal he defended three white men convicted of conspiracy in the famous iron workers' dynamiting cases. The dynamiting cases involved "the destruction of the Times building in Los Angeles," and other buildings in several cities in the United States.[137] The defendants, who had been convicted in Indianapolis, Indiana, were serving their sentences at the federal prison in Leavenworth when they heard about Turner W. Bell. Bell sought a writ of *habeas corpus* on technical grounds before the United States District Court. He lost the case, and the defendants were not released. The press covered the trial not only because of its notoriety but because "a Negro attorney, a one-time slave" was representing white defendants.[138]

Bell's practice was not solely in criminal law. He also assisted J. Coody Johnson, a black Oklahoma lawyer, in oil claim cases.[139] Bell practiced in Kansas for more than fifty years. In 1935, his career as a lawyer was praised by Governor Alfred M. Landon and several members of the Kansas State Supreme Court, during a special celebration in Bell's honor.[140]

William Bolden Townsend, "finding the treatment of his people so inhuman," went to Kansas to work for change. He decided that he could best effect change in society by studying law.[141] Townsend enrolled in the University of Kansas's law school, from which he was graduated in 1891. One of his first cases involved a civil rights issue in which he joined John Lewis Waller and William Abram Price as co-counsel. A light-skinned black man and a darker black woman were refused seats in a general auditorium reserved for whites only, though they had paid for tickets in that section. They were told to sit in the colored section. Townsend, Waller, and Price sued the theater, claiming that their clients' civil rights had been violated. However, the court held that the plaintiffs had merely been inconvenienced, and that the owners were within their rights to "exclude any manner of clientele they considered detrimental to their business."[142] Townsend practiced law in Leavenworth, Kansas, until 1901. He then moved to Colorado, where he continued his legal practice.[143]

In 1899 Topeka, Kansas, had a black justice of the peace by the name of W. I. Jamison. Jamison had read law under Horace H. Harrison. He was elected justice of the peace in 1882 and again in 1886. In 1889, the national press reported that two special prosecutors in Topeka, Kansas, John Lewis Waller and Albert M. Thomas, had represented the state in the case of *State v. George Lacy* before Judge Jamison.[144] It was the first known case in Kansas where two black special prosecutors appeared before a black judge. Jamison, though a justice of the peace, was not admitted to the bar until 1891. After his admission to the bar, he practiced law in Topeka, Kansas. He became assistant county attorney in 1900.[145]

In 1893 George Washington Ellis was graduated from the University of Kansas School of Law. He practiced in Lawrence, Kansas, until 1900, when he was appointed clerk in the United States Census Department in Washington, D.C. In 1902 President Theodore Roosevelt appointed Ellis secretary of the United States legation to the Republic of Liberia, a post that he held for eight years. When Ellis returned to the United States from his assignment in Africa, he went to Chicago, Illinois, and practiced law with Richard E. Westbrooks until 1917, the year he was elected assistant corporation counsel of Chicago.[146]

At the turn of the century, Dorsey Green and Sam Cary were each admitted to the Kansas bar. Green was admitted to the bar in 1901 and opened a law practice in Kansas City, Kansas. Green became active in the NAACP and chaired its Legal Redress Committee in Kansas. He also chaired the Kansas Political State League for several years.[147] Sam Cary, who was admitted to practice in Kansas in about 1909, joined Will L. Sayers's firm in Russell Springs, Kansas. He was later elected city attorney in Russell Springs. He served for a short period before relocating to Denver, Colorado, to practice law.[148]

In 1916 Elisha Scott, Sr., was graduated from Washburn University's law school. After passing the Kansas bar, he entered the law offices of

James H. Guy, a black lawyer, before opening his own law office[149] in Topeka, Kansas. During the early 1920s, Scott was active "protecting the civil rights and property rights of hundreds of colored clients throughout [the Midwest], and in all these cases he obtained splendid results."[150] In 1922 Geraldine Hemmett, "the second richest colored girl in the world," dropped her white attorney, Edward McKeever, and hired Scott to represent her in an oil claim dispute in Oklahoma. McKeever threatened "to bring disbarment proceedings against . . . Scott for usurping . . . his client."[151] Scott reportedly made "plenty money and he spent as much, too."[152]

William McKinley Bradshaw and Albert M. Thomas were contemporaries of Scott, though Thomas had been admitted to the Kansas bar in 1880.[153] In 1924 Bradshaw (a 1920 Washburn University law school graduate) and Thomas became celebrities when they appeared before the Kansas Supreme Court to represent a white woman who wanted her husband jailed for failing to pay child support. This client had also dropped Edward McKeever for Bradshaw. The court affirmed the lower court's refusal to imprison the "trifling" father, but it held that he was not relieved from the contempt order.[154] Bradshaw also represented a woman whose husband claimed that she was insane in an attempt to win custody of his child. Bradshaw promptly filed a $15,000-suit alleging damages for malicious prosecution.[155]

In 1919 William Henry Towers was admitted to the Kansas Supreme Court, one year after graduating from the University of Kansas School of Law.[156] Towers practiced law in Kansas City, Kansas, until 1931, when he was appointed first assistant city attorney of Kansas City. In 1930, Towers defended local blacks against a property sale covered by a racially restrictive covenant. A former owner of the land filed suit to enjoin the sale. In one of the first cases of its kind in Kansas, the Kansas Supreme Court refused to grant the injunction. The case was not defended by Towers on constitutional grounds, but solely on equitable principles of law.[157]

Towers's success as a city attorney heightened his interest in other areas of public service. In 1937 the citizens of Wyandotte County elected him to the Kansas state legislature. It is there that Towers—one of the first blacks to serve in the state legislature—made his mark. Among other important legislative initiatives, Towers sponsored a law forbidding labor unions from excluding blacks from the craft unions.[158] Towers served six distinguished two-year terms in the Kansas state legislature. The inroads that he made to expand employment opportunities set a precedent for equality in the workplace far beyond Kansas.

In 1929 Raymond Jordan Reynolds was graduated from Washburn University's law school. He joined his brother, Earl Thomas Reynolds, at his law firm in Topeka, Kansas. E. T. Reynolds was himself a 1923 graduate of Washburn University's law school. The Reynolds brothers practiced together until the mid-1930s, when E. T. Reynolds moved to Coffeyville, Kansas, to practice law. When Walter A. Huxman was elected governor of Kansas in 1937, he appointed E. T. Reynolds to the Kansas state highway department. He was the first black lawyer to hold the post. Governor Huxman was a Democrat, and it was perhaps R. J. Reynolds's public support of Franklin D. Roosevelt that led to this appointment.[159]

When R. J. Reynolds graduated from Washburn University's law school, there were at least three black lawyers, excluding his brother, practicing law in Topeka, Kansas: William McKinley Bradshaw, Elisha Scott, Sr., and James H. Guy.[160] Reynolds became active in civil rights activities and was elected president of the Topeka chapter of the NAACP for seven terms.[161] In about 1940, R. J. Reynolds ran for judge of the Topeka municipal court. Reynolds states, "I couldn't get *elected* because I was black. I did, however, win some white votes."[162] In addition to his law and civil rights work, Reynolds wrote a column for the *Topeka Daily Capital* on a variety of race issues.[163] During the mid-1940s Reynolds left Topeka and associated with John Adams, Jr., a black lawyer in San Francisco, California.

By the early 1930s, Washburn University and the University of Kansas School of Law fielded some of the most distinguished graduates in the state. However, some Washburn University law graduates, left the state. Loren Miller relocated to Los Angeles, California, in 1930, two years after his graduation. There he opened a law office and began to publish the *Los Angeles Sentinel*, a black weekly newspaper.[164] Even as some black lawyers left Kansas, Howard law graduates, such as Alwynne B. Howard, settled there to practice law. In 1935 Howard was appointed assistant attorney of Wyandotte County, Kansas, a position that he held until 1940. Thereafter, he returned to private practice.[165]

Lutie A. Lytle became the third black woman admitted to the bar in the United States and the first black woman admitted to the Kansas bar in 1897, the year she graduated from Central Tennessee Law School. Lytle first "thought of preparing herself for the profession of law while working as a compositor on a colored newspaper in Topeka."[166] Her newspaper job "brought her into contact with politicians, so her ideas of life were much broader than those entertained by the average young girl."[167] After Lytle graduated from law school, she planned to open a law office in Topeka, Kansas. However, she was understandably uncertain about her future as a woman in private practice. In 1897 Lytle was appointed professor of law at Central Tennessee Law School, becoming the first black woman lawyer in the South and the first woman in the United States to teach law at a chartered law school.[168]

Prior to 1945, at least two other women were graduated from the University of Kansas School of Law: M. Jeane Mitchell and Mildred M. Alexander. Little information about these women is available. Alexander became active in the National Bar Association and served on its Professional Ethics Committee in 1944.[169]

Montana

On July 23, 1890, a year after Montana became a state, John D. Posten, previously admitted to the Missouri bar, was admitted to practice before the Montana Supreme Court.[170] Posten lived and practiced law in Libby (Lincoln County), Montana, until his death in 1924.[171] Posten gained the respect of the citizens of Libby from the moment he arrived. He was responsible for taking the 1890 census,[172] and thereby managed to meet nearly everyone in the township.

His legal ability must have been evident to Hiram Knowles, Montana's first United States District Judge,[173] because he appointed Posten United States commissioner to the District Court (located in the ninth judicial circuit) on June 10, 1893.[174] This appointment made Posten the first black lawyer in the Pacific region to hold a position of trust in the federal judicial system. Posten served as United States commissioner in the federal court until June 30, 1917.[175]

Posten earned a comfortable living as a lawyer in Libby, even though he was its only black citizen.[176] He was accepted as "one of us at Libby," and Southern transplants who tried to discriminate against him because of his race were rebuffed by local citizens.[177] He is remembered fondly by a local historian:

> The most prominent of Libby's early legal advisors was John D. Posten, a graduate of Grinnell College [1882], Iowa, and an authority on land and land locations. He was Libby's dependable attorney and U.S. Land Commissioner from the settlement of the town until his death in 1924. He served as clerk of the school board in the early years, in 1910 as local census enumerator. He did a bit of prospecting in West Fisher, but mostly he lived quietly in his Libby homes (the second one in South Libby). An old-timer says that "John Posten knew more secrets than anybody else in town; and he never told." Half the townspeople brought him their troubles. He took care of all legal and business deals for F. N. Plummer, who had such confidence in him that no written record was ever kept of their transactions. As the Libby Women's Club history phrases it, "He was a friend indeed to all in need."[178]

Three other black lawyers resided in Montana prior to 1945: James P. Ball, Jr., a Mr. Bairpaugh (first name unknown), and James Weston Dorsey. According to one historian of the northwestern region, James P. Ball, Jr., was admitted to the bar in Helena, Montana, during the early part of the 1890s. Ball was a lawyer, but apparently earned his living as a photographer. He studied law in Seattle, Washington, between 1894 and 1896 and returned to Montana, where he resided until 1901.[179] Little is known about Mr. Bairpaugh. He is said to have "practiced law on a full-time basis" in Great Falls, Montana, and "in other cities in Montana" in the mid-1920s.[180] James Weston Dorsey has the distinction of being the first black student graduated from Montana University School of Law. He was admitted to the Montana Supreme Court on June 7, 1927, the same day he graduated from the law school.[181] Dorsey later left Montana and practiced in Wisconsin for several years.[182]

New Mexico

At least two black lawyers were admitted to practice law in New Mexico prior to 1945. Fred Simms, "a Negro stenographer and calligrapher, later became an attorney" in the late 1880s or early 1890s, several years prior to statehood.[183] As a stenographer, Simms may have worked in Judge Rodney's courtroom in Albuquerque, New Mexico, where he studied law. The extent of Simms's practice is unknown; however, the legal documents associated with the founding of the University of New Mexico in 1889 were reported to have been notarized by Simms.[184]

No other black lawyer is known to have been admitted to the bar of New Mexico until 1916, when George W. Malone gained admission to practice before the New Mexico Supreme Court. Malone was a graduate of the Central Law School of Walden University, a black institution located in Nashville, Tennessee. He was first admitted to the State Chancery Court of Bolivar (Coahoma County), Mississippi, in 1910. He practiced in the South until 1914, the year he was admitted to practice before the Supreme Court of Mississippi.[185] Malone then moved to Blackdom (Chaves County), New Mexico, which was a black town. He applied to the New Mexico Supreme Court for a "permanent license" to practice law. Malone's application was supported by Harold Hurd, of Roswell, New Mexico, who vouched for Malone's integrity and informed the clerk of the court that "most of the colored population" called upon him for assistance.[186] Malone signed the roll of the New Mexico Supreme Court on August 8, 1916.[187] He then moved to "Albuquerque and opened an office at Broadway and Tijeras," but died soon thereafter.[188]

Oklahoma

Black lawyers (some perhaps of mixed Creek Indian ancestry) practiced law in what is now Oklahoma when it was an Indian Territory governed by the Indian Nations. In 1875, fifteen years before the Oklahoma Territory was formed and thirty-two years before Oklahoma gained statehood, a black man named Sugar George (probably of mixed heritage), was paid a salary of twenty-five dollars to act as the prosecuting attorney in Fort Smith, Arkansas. George prosecuted criminals in Arkansas rather than in the Indian Territory because at the time all "[c]riminal cases involving United States citizens [in the Indian and Oklahoma territories] were under the jurisdiction of the Federal court," the nearest of which was located the Western Federal District at Fort Smith, Arkansas.[189] George held several elected positions in the Oklahoma Territory. He was an elected member of the House of Kings, "similar to the Senate," and a judge of the Muskogee District.[190]

In the mid-1880s, William Henry Twine moved to the Indian Territory from Texas. Already a member of the Texas bar, he found no difficulty gaining admission to practice before the United States Court for the Indian Territory. Twine opened a law office in Guthrie, Oklahoma, with two other black lawyers, E. L. Saddler and G. W. E. Sawner; together they became known as the "Three Musketeers."[191] The firm specialized in criminal law.

In 1897 Twine defended a man accused of murder in the United States Court for the Northern District of the Indian Territory sitting at Vinita, Oklahoma. His client was convicted and sentenced to death. On February 11, 1898, Twine filed a petition for a writ of error before the United States Supreme Court, but the case was dismissed for lack of jurisdiction.[192] Twine's appearance before the United States Supreme Court was historic, for no other black lawyer from Oklahoma or any other Pacific state had done this before. Twine was also a publisher. He edited the *Muskogee Cimeter*, "the first Negro paper in [the] Indian Territory."[193] He inspired three of his sons to become lawyers, setting a precedent in American law.[194]

In 1891 Daniel Webster Lewis opened a law office in Kingfisher, Oklahoma. Lewis had previously been admitted to the bar in the state of Arkansas. Soon thereafter, he was appointed clerk of the probate court by Judge T. B. McGee, who no doubt was aware that Lewis had served for six years as judge of the probate court at Crittenden, Arkansas. In the early 1900s, Lewis went to Washington, D.C., to work as a clerk in the Census Office, returning to Oklahoma in 1903 to handle legal work for a black fraternal group.[195] Lewis practiced in Oklahoma until his death in 1932.

The respect Lewis commanded from members of the bar was significant. Upon his death, the Kingfisher County Bar Association entered a
resolution into the records of the local court that praised Lewis for his
honesty and service to the bar. The resolution also noted that Lewis's
admission to the Oklahoma bar in 1891 "was a real accomplishment . . .
and reflected great credit upon him for the effort made by him under
unfriendly and adverse conditions."[196]

Byron M. Henderson arrived in Oklahoma at about the same time
as Lewis. In 1891, Henderson graduated from the Chicago's Union
Law School (Northwestern University). Two years later, he was appointed assistant United States Attorney in Guthrie, Oklahoma, a post
he held until 1897. Henderson subsequently practiced law in Detroit,
Michigan.[197]

The exact date that A. G. W. Sango, a black and Creek freedman, was
admitted to the bar in Oklahoma is unknown, but all available sources
indicate that he was probably admitted to practice about 1890. Sango
was first admitted to practice law by the Creek Nation tribal government. The requirements for admission to the bar were minimal. As
Sango reported, "it was only necessary to read, write, cipher, and have
good character."[198] According to Booker T. Washington, Sango "was
elected to the position of district attorney" in Muskogee in 1890.[199]
Washington became familiar with Sango in 1904, when he organized
the Creek Citizens Realty Bank and Trust Co.[200] Sango was also treasurer of the Freedman's Land and Trust Company, a business venture
that he hoped would induce blacks to travel to the Indian Territory. In
1895 Sango "was hired as an attorney for the Creek Nation,"[201] and he
was elected four years later to the House of Warriors, one of the two
constitutional governing bodies of the Creek Council.[202] Sango's popularity with the Creek Nation is probably not unusual, despite his mixed
heritage, since many runaway slaves from the South sought and received refuge in the Creek Nation during the Civil War. A number of
these freedmen later became citizens of the Creek Nation.[203]

The political opportunities for blacks and Indians in Oklahoma were
limited. In 1910, three years after being granted statehood, the Oklahoma state legislature passed a grandfather measure limiting the voting rights of blacks and Indians. The law was similar to those adopted in
many Southern states. It provided that "a person had to be able to read
or write a section of the Oklahoma Constitution, unless he had antecedents who could vote as of January 1, 1866."[204] For five years, A. G. W.
Sango and another black lawyer, J. Coody Johnson, challenged the
constitutionality of the grandfather law in the courts. Their zeal and
persistence kept the issue alive while encouraging other black citizens
to protest against the discriminatory provision.[205] In 1915, the issue of

the Oklahoma provision's constitutionality reached the United States Supreme Court, where it was held to violate the Fifteenth Amendment of the United States Constitution.[206]

J. Coody Johnson was also a leading black lawyer among the Creek Indian tribe. He was described as "a leading spirit of the Indian people."[207] Both Johnson and Sango represented the interests of the Creek Nation and other Indians when oil was discovered on their land in 1900. Their representation saved many blacks and Indians from selling their oil-rich land to unscrupulous white oil barons for little or nothing.[208] Johnson's practice thrived, so much so that he became an oil baron himself. In 1911 Johnson formed the Panther Oil and Gas Company. The company was formed by blacks and Creek Indians who combined their interests. There were several wealthy stockholders in the company. Johnson served both as the chief executive officer and counsel for the company.[209] By 1919 Johnson remained "the only colored man who [had] actually gotten in on the producing end of the [oil] industry." He was also the only colored lawyer in Wewoka, Oklahoma.[210]

Johnson, a native of Oklahoma, may have owed some of his success to political connections. His father was acquainted with John J. Ingalls, the United States senator from Kansas between 1887 and 1891.[211] Johnson's practice was not confined to Oklahoma. He also tried cases with other black lawyers in Kansas, especially when Indian oil and property interests were involved.[212]

The legal needs of Indians and black freedmen drew black lawyers to Oklahoma. The lawyers did not work for free, though their aim was to protect their clients from land-grabbers. Black law firms appeared that specialized in oil matters. In 1906 the firm of John Milton Turner and Sherman Tecumseh Wiggins, located in Ardmore, Oklahoma, was retained to represent the interests of black freedmen in the Choctaw and Chickasaw Nations. On behalf of their clients, Turner, who had served as minister to Liberia between 1871 to 1879, and Wiggins, an 1893 law graduate of the University of Michigan, appeared before Congress and its committees, as well as before various federal departments. Turner and Wiggins may be among the first black lawyers to appear before the Oklahoma Supreme Court. At this appearance, they sought to enforce a fee agreement for services rendered to a black client, and they prevailed.[213]

Other black lawyers relocated to Oklahoma at the turn of the century. In 1898, David A. Lee was listed as practicing in Lee, Oklahoma.[214] Adam Edward Patterson, a 1900 graduate of the University of Kansas Law School, practiced in Muskogee and Fort Gibson, Oklahoma, just about the time Oklahoma gained statehood. In 1913, President Woodrow Wilson named Patterson register of the United States treasury. He was the president's first black appointee, but his nomination was blocked by Southern senators, led by James K. Vardaman of Mississippi. These Southern senators no doubt responded to such antiblack writers as Thomas Dixon, author of *The Clansman* (1905), who, upon hearing of Patterson's appointment, wrote to President Wilson: "I am heartsick over the announcement that you have appointed a Negro to boss white girls as Register of the Treasury."[215] Patterson practiced in Muskogee and Fort Gibson, Oklahoma, for forty years.[216]

Buck Colbert Franklin was another black lawyer who represented Indians in oil matters. Franklin first read law under the supervision of the Sprague School of Law in Detroit, Michigan, in about 1898. Franklin may then have been admitted to practice in Oklahoma, but other sources report that Franklin was admitted to practice before the United States Land Office in Tiskomingo, Oklahoma, in 1903, four years before Oklahoma statehood. He was admitted to the bar of Oklahoma by examination in 1908 and practiced law in Springer, Ardmore, Rentiesville, and Tulsa.[217]

Franklin's efforts to help rebuild the black section of Tulsa following the riots of 1921 demonstrates the importance of black lawyers as leaders in Oklahoma. The riots left many blacks homeless, hostage to a callous city government that was not eager to rebuild the black section of town. As black citizens pitched tents and built shacks for shelter, the Tulsa city government declared that the black section was to be replaced by a railroad terminal. Buck C. Franklin, P. A. Chappelle, I. H. Spears, and S. T. Wiggins filed an injunction and temporarily blocked the city's actions.[218]

Franklin associated with several black lawyers during his legal career in Oklahoma. In 1926 Franklin, Ruffin P. Boulding, and William Neff settled a case for $50,000 involving an "imbecile" who had an interest in some oil leases in Seminole County, Oklahoma. According to press accounts the "attorneys' fee in the case [was] reputed to be $25,000."[219]

In 1903 Henry Augustus Guess, a 1903 Howard University law graduate, was admitted to practice in Tulsa, Oklahoma. He became secretary and attorney for the Oklahoma Realty and Investment Company. He was also one of the first members of the Negro National Bar Association,[220] an affiliate of the National Negro Business League headed by Booker T. Washington. In 1907 Guess and M. W. Guy, a black lawyer practicing in Muskogee, Oklahoma, attended the annual meeting of the National Negro Business League at Topeka, Kansas. During that meeting Guy stated, "We have compelled the white men to respect our Negro lawyers—we have ten of them there [in Muskogee]."[221]

Jacobs J. Jones, a 1906 Howard University law graduate, followed Henry Guess to Muskogee, Oklahoma, where he was appointed "local attorney for the M. V. Railroad Company." He fought to lengthen the school year for black students from seven months to the nine-month program available to white students.[222] By 1908 black law graduates from as far away as North Carolina's Shaw University School of Law had become members of the Oklahoma bar.[223]

On July 20, 1908, T. S. E. Brown of Oklahoma City, Oklahoma, was admitted to practice before the Oklahoma Supreme Court. Brown was among the first black lawyers admitted to the court after statehood in 1907.[224] Brown practiced in Oklahoma City for several years and formed a partnership with Buck C. Franklin. In 1923 Brown "raised a queer point" of law, defending a porter charged with the illegal sale of whiskey in a hotel. The whiskey was purchased from Brown's client by an undercover policeman. At trial, the policeman testified as to his purchase of whiskey from the porter. Brown's defense was "that an . . . officer who purchases whiskey from a person who he later hauls into court, is not a competent [witness] for the reason that said officer is an accomplice." The jury brought in a verdict of not guilty.[225]

Black lawyers in Oklahoma anticipated that the state would adopt Jim Crow laws after Oklahoma was given to statehood. They fought hard to gain assurances that the state would oppose racist policies. In 1904 "a call was issued by the Suffrage League of Indian Territory for a colored Republican mass meeting" to formulate a strategy against Jim Crow policies before and after statehood.[226] Cornelius J. Jones and William Henry Twine helped "to memorialize the Senate of the United States for a speedy passage of the pending Statehood measure [but] emphasized . . . [that] the preservation of the right of suffrage of the citizens of the proposed new state be retained."[227]

William Henry Twine's newspaper, *The Muskogee Cimeter,* carried the fight against Jim Crow to its black subscribers, stating, "We are opposed to Jim Crow no matter where it comes up."[228] Nevertheless, the pro–Jim Crow forces dominated the statehood convention. Black leaders in both territories formed a Negro Protective League, and A. G. W. Sango, of Muskogee, G. W. E. Sawner, of Chandler, and S. T. Wiggins, of Ardmore, all black lawyers, were among the delegates and alternative delegates who were "elected to go to Washington and work for a single statehood bill which insured Negro rights."[229]

As suspected, Jim Crow laws, including laws limiting the right to vote and establishing separate public services, were adopted by the state. A. G. W. Sango, under the banner of the Constitutional League and the Negro Protective League, "took steps 'to wage a war on the legality' on the [grandfather clause] which disfranchised the colored race."[230] Unfortunately, the Oklahoma Supreme Court upheld the provision,[231] which was struck down, as were similar state laws elsewhere, by the United States Supreme Court in 1915.[232]

In 1913 Edwin P. McCabe[233] sought the assistance of William H. Harrison, Edwin O. Tyler, and Ethelbert Barbour to challenge Oklahoma's separate car law. McCabe's lawyers asserted the unconstitutionality of these laws before the United States Supreme Court, but they did not prevail.[234]

William Henry Harrison, a graduate of Walden University's law school, was a respected attorney in Oklahoma among both blacks and whites.[235] Harrison's active participation in civil rights cases enhanced his reputation as a skilled litigator. In 1916 the Oklahoma City Bar Association, "composed almost entirely of white members," honored Harrison with a resolution "setting forth in glowing terms the esteem in which lawyer Harrison [was] held." The resolution was apparently in support of Harrison's efforts to win a state or federal appointment: "Resolved by the Oklahoma City Bar Association of Oklahoma City, Okla., that we recommended Mr. Harrison to our Government as worthy and well qualified to fill any position or do any work which may be called upon by our Government to do [during] this great crisis [of World War I]."[236]

Harrison became a leader, in part, by way of his investment in zinc, lead, and oil companies and real estate. In 1919 he was the only person of color to serve as a member of the Chamber of Commerce.[237] Harrison "was later [in 1934] chosen by the Oklahoma Bar Association . . . to serve as special judge of the Superior Court of Oklahoma County." He served in that position for five years.[238]

Matthew Bullock, George Napier Perkins, and Freeman L. Martin were also contemporaries of William Henry Harrison. Bullock "wandered around through the west" after he graduated from Harvard University's law school in 1907. He reportedly failed in the practice of law—"his clients deserted him as fast as he served them"[239]—and he later moved to Atlanta, Georgia. George Perkins relocated to Guthrie, Oklahoma, after a successful legal career in Arkansas, where, in the 1880s, he had served a four-year term on the City Council of Little Rock. In the early days of Oklahoma statehood, Perkins served a four-year term as a member of the Guthrie city council.[240] Freeman L. Martin was appointed justice of the peace by the city commissioner of Tulsa.[241] Martin's law office became a training ground for other black lawyers, like James Henry Roberts, who joined Martin's firm after his graduation from John Marshall's law school (Chicago) in 1913.[242]

Jasper Alston Atkins and Charles Albert Chandler settled in Muskogee, Oklahoma, after they graduated from Yale University law school in 1922. Atkins and Chandler were honors law graduates and both had been members of the *Yale Law Journal*.[243] They formed a firm with Carter Walker Wesley (a 1922 graduate of Northwestern University's law school) which lasted for five years. Atkins, Chandler, and Wesley engaged in a general practice, but they also represented Indian and black oil claims.[244] In 1927 Atkins and Wesley left Oklahoma and opened a law firm in Houston, Texas.[245] Chandler remained in Oklahoma and fought, as A. G. W. Sango and J. Coody Johnson had done before him, against the disfranchisement of Oklahoma's black citizens.

Desegregating public education and handling voting rights cases occupied much of Chandler's time in 1938. In that year, Chandler filed the first suit in a federal court in Oklahoma that enjoined the local government from using matching federal funds to maintain segregation. The case was widely reported. Chandler sued both the mayor of Muskogee and the attorney general of the state. Chandler's efforts made some difference, but not enough to persuade the United States Supreme Court to give his client the relief requested.[246] In 1939 Chandler, joined by James Madison Nabrit, Jr. (then a member of the Howard University law faculty), successfully sought and won an appeal before the United States Supreme Court to void a discriminatory voting registration law in Oklahoma.[247] Chandler later settled in Cleveland, Ohio, to practice law.

In what appears to have been a difficult period for black people and black lawyers in Oklahoma, Louis C. Taylor was appointed magistrate in the fourth precinct of Okfuskee County in 1923, and he held this post for three years.[248] Between 1935 and 1944, the number of black lawyers in Oklahoma declined, perhaps because of the continued exclusion of blacks from juries in the state. As in the Southern states, such discriminatory practices affected the credibility of black lawyers among their people.

In 1934 a group of NAACP lawyers in Oklahoma obtained the assistance of Charles Hamilton Houston and William L. Houston, both of Washington, to file an appeal to the United States Supreme Court. The appeal was entered on behalf of a black man who had been convicted by a white jury for raping a white woman in Sapulpa, Oklahoma. He had been sentenced to die.[249] The lawyers argued that the conviction was invalid because the mandatory exclusion of blacks from juries was unconstitutional, a position that the United States Supreme Court adopted.[250]

In 1936 Muskogee, Oklahoma, had a population of 32,000 people, of which 7,500 were black. There were eight black lawyers in the city, some of whom were well-off because they represented wealthy black clients who had oil claims.[251] In 1944 Tulsa, Oklahoma, had so few black lawyers that most people knew them by name.[252] One of them, Amos T. Hall, would later join the ranks of the new breed of black civil rights lawyers on the national scene.[253]

There is no record of a black woman having been admitted to the Oklahoma bar prior to 1945.

Oregon

McCants Stewart, a second-generation lawyer,[254] arrived in Portland, Oregon, in 1903 and applied for admission to the bar. *The Oregon Daily Journal*, apparently unaware of Stewart's status as the second black graduate of the University of Minnesota Law School, commented: "Stewart is the only colored law graduate of the University of Minnesota. . . . There has never been a colored man admitted in [Oregon], although one application was made a few years ago."[255] The Supreme Court of Oregon admitted McCants Stewart on March 1, 1904.[256]

McCants Stewart had apparently been admitted to or allowed to practice before local courts in Portland prior to his state bar admission in 1904. In 1903 he was appointed by the court to represent Charles Shanley in a larceny case. Stewart, with little to work with, explained that his client was unemployed and asked the court's mercy. The court, unimpressed by this plea, convicted and sentenced Shanley to nine months "on the rockpile."[257]

Stewart also represented Japanese clients. In 1903 he represented W. Irvane, who had been charged with larceny. Although Irvane's case was hopeless, Stewart waged a spirited defense.[258] In 1904 Stewart represented Viola Reese, who had been charged with assault with a dangerous weapon. The alleged victim claimed that Reese "tried to cut her heart out with a pocketknife because she 'cussed' her for making free with a man and a bucket of beer."[259] The court ignored Stewart's pretrial efforts to subpoena the alleged victim's physician. At trial, he renewed this request. The sheriff testified that the papers had been served on the doctor at the insistence of the prosecuting attorney. Finally, the court ordered the doctor to court. After testimony that the alleged victim had suffered no injury, Stewart's client was acquitted.[260]

The first case argued before the Oregon Supreme Court by a black lawyer was *State v. Browning*,[261] an embezzlement case that Stewart appealed to the court in 1905. In *Browning*, Stewart challenged the Portland Municipal Police Court's jurisdiction over a matter of state law. The Oregon Supreme Court rejected this theory, but not without some difficulty. Although Stewart's artful advocacy had failed, he drew the attention of the white people of Oregon, who had noted that a black lawyer had arrived, fully prepared to do battle.

In the intolerant racial climate of Portland in 1906, McCants Stewart went before the Oregon Supreme Court. In August 1904 Stewart's client, Oliver Taylor, had purchased a general admission ticket to a vaudeville show at Portland's Star Theater. When Taylor, a black citizen, attempted to take a seat on the main floor, he was informed that he would have to sit in the balcony. Claiming a violation of his civil rights, Taylor sued the owner of the theater and alleged, among other things, a breach of contract. The trial judge dismissed Taylor's claims as groundless. McCants Stewart appealed to the Oregon Supreme Court and won a reversal.[262] The public respect Stewart earned for his excellent trial and appellate advocacy, as well as his close association with the Republican Party, probably prompted Oregon Governor George Erie Chamberlain to appoint him as chief commissioner from Oregon to the National Emancipation Commemorative Society, an event organized by President William Howard Taft in 1909.

In 1907 the case of G. L. Joell made headlines in Portland and brought McCants Stewart again into the limelight. Edna Hauz, a white woman, alleged that Joell, a black man, had propositioned her on the streets of Portland. Refusing at first to cooperate with the police,[263] Hauz later accused Joell of defamation. Joell retained McCants Stewart to defend him. When Hauz left Portland before the hearing, certain whites inferred that McCants Stewart had caused her departure.[264] They called Joell a "coon" and a "baboon" in the vulgar local press.[265] Hauz returned to the city to testify. At trial, McCants Stewart was not permitted to offer any evidence regarding the general character of Joell. The press looked unkindly on Stewart's defense, claiming that his cross-examination "subjected [Hauz] to the humiliating questions of a black lawyer who defended the black act of his black client in a black way, viz, by again insulting the [white] girl."[266] Joell was convicted and fined forty dollars.[267]

Also in 1907, McCants Stewart represented an administrator in a hotly contested probate case. In that case, involving the estate of a black hotel porter, a white woman contested the claim of the decedent's father. During the hearing, Stewart conceded that the woman deserved a portion of the estate because she had given money to the decedent, her "Negro friend," to deposit in the bank.[268] The outcome of this case is unknown.

McCants Stewart apparently enjoyed a favorable professional relationship with the white bar of Oregon. In 1908, for example, the Portland firm of Snow and McCamant asked Stewart to review a brief involving a matter similar to one he had argued before the Oregon Supreme Court.[269] Stewart's response to this request indicates technical skill and an eye for detail:

You will never realize how very much I appreciate and thank you for your brief, which you were filing in the [Oregon] Supreme Court in the case of State—vs.—Ross, a copy of which you sent to me a few days ago. I have carefully examined it and mean to go over it again. It is exceptionally strong. The analytical thought, in particular, as shown in all of the arguments display a depth of mind unusually rich, bringing great credit to the Oregon Bar.[270]

McCants Stewart's legal acumen is well illustrated in a 1908 case in which he represented a black man charged with wife beating. His client, who denied the act, was found guilty by a judge authorized to impose fines of up to fifty dollars. Despite the statutory limits of his power, the judge sentenced the client to six months in jail.[271] After Stewart filed a writ of *habeas corpus*, the Circuit Court held that the sentence imposed by the lower court was illegal.[272]

In 1908 Governor George Erie Chamberlain appointed McCants Stewart to represent Oregon at the National Negro Fair in Mobile, Alabama. Stewart joined a select group of "commissioners" chosen to attend the meeting by governors of twenty-four states. According to the Mobile press, the purpose "of the meeting [was] to arouse race interest in the . . . fair" and common issues concerning black people.[273] McCants Stewart figured prominently among the speakers at the fair.[274]

Despite legal victories and public honors, Stewart also experienced hardship. Among the troubles he faced was the destruction of his office by fire in July 1908. Fortunately, the editors of *The Advocate*, a black newspaper in Portland, allowed Stewart to use their offices until his building was restored.[275] This unfortunate and devastating reversal did not dampen Stewart's determination to maintain his practice.

McCants Stewart suffered yet another personal setback when a 1909 streetcar accident necessitated amputation of his left leg.[276] Life slowed for Stewart after his accident. During his convalescence, another black lawyer, L. H. Dawley, began to practice law in Portland. Their court appearances, often on opposing sides, drew public attention.[277]

McCants Stewart had other perplexing moments in Portland. In September 1911, while walking home from a banquet, Stewart stopped at the door of a restaurant to greet friends dining inside. As he stood in the doorway, Officer B. G. Marsh of the Portland Police Department ordered Stewart to move on, threatening arrest if he refused to comply. Stewart, believing that he had violated no law, objected. Officer Marsh, apparently unwilling to have his authority publicly questioned by a black man, arrested Stewart and made him walk a mile to the police station on his prosthetic cork leg. Marsh booked Stewart for drunkenness.[278] Police authorities, however, refused to charge him. The next day, Stewart filed a formal complaint of assault and battery with the district attorney, who issued a warrant against Officer Marsh. Yet Marsh held to his story that Stewart "was much under the influence of alcohol."[279] At the hearing, McCants Stewart "brought numerous witnesses to prove that he had been at a banquet . . . where nothing more arduous than an infusion of leaves of cathay was served to wash down the noodles and chop suey."[280] Nevertheless, the complaint against Officer Marsh was dismissed. McCants Stewart appealed his case to Portland's Mayor Rushlight, asking him to direct the executive board of the city to review the matter. Stewart publicized the incident in a letter to the *Portland Oregon Daily Journal.* The letter alleged that Officer Marsh possessed a "quarrelsome disposition" and that he had "committed a wanton, willful assault and battery upon me, without cause."[281] It is not known whether Mayor Rushlight or the executive board became involved in the matter. It may be, however, that McCants Stewart won his case in the eyes of the public. Even the white press ultimately conceded that Officer Marsh "would take no 'lip' from a colored lawyer."[282]

In the face of public animosity, McCants Stewart was critical of the federal government's failure to protect blacks from physical brutality in Southern states. In 1914 Stewart publicly criticized President Woodrow Wilson's failure to halt the lynching of black citizens in the South. In December of that year, Stewart helped draft a resolution "censuring President Wilson for not interfering when five Negroes [were] lynched in the parish of Shreveport, Louisiana, within 10 days."[283] Stewart also publicly reported that "53 colored men and women have been lynched in this country, and no attention has been given to the matter by National authorities."[284] Even in a far northwestern city like Portland, such words, spoken by a black man, carried extreme risks. In 1914 a black man had been lynched in Portland.[285]

Though far removed geographically from his Southern brothers and sisters, Stewart refused to overlook their plight, their quest for liberty and equal treatment. Stewart constantly sought sympathetic speakers to spread the word at public forums in Portland. For example, Stewart invited Mayor William Hale Thompson of Chicago to Portland in 1915. Mayor Thompson was "considered one of the best friends [of] the colored race . . . in the United States."[286] Stewart telegraphed Mayor Thompson and informed him of a plan by the black population to honor him and asked "him for 15 minutes of his time."[287]

Although McCants Stewart was loyal to the Republican Party and respected by its rank and file, the party provided him with neither legal work nor public position. Nonetheless, he always supported Republican candidates for state offices. In 1916 the secretary of the state of Oregon, Ben W. Olcott, wrote to Stewart seeking his "support and influence in [his] candidacy for reelection."[288]

In 1916 McCants Stewart declined to run for the Oregon House of Representatives. He instead had decided to leave Portland, primarily because its racial climate made survival difficult, even for a black lawyer with demonstrated competency. Whites, who considered him a lawyer of the "colored people," did nothing to help him, and his own people were frequently unable to pay his fees. (In 1917, for example, Stewart sued the black A.M.E. Church for $264 owed for legal services rendered in a condemnation proceeding brought against the church by white residents.[289])

According to *The Advocate*, "the decision of Mr. Stewart to locate elsewhere is not a hasty one, for he has had such a move under advisement for some time."[290] Mary Katherine Stewart-Flippin, Stewart's daughter, reports that her father left Portland because "he simply tired of the great difficulty he faced as a black lawyer in Portland trying to make a living."[291] The departure of Stewart for San Francisco, California, left Portland without a single black lawyer.[292]

The *Vallejo Times*, a San Francisco newspaper, noted the arrival of McCants Stewart in December 1917.[293] A few months after his arrival, Stewart returned to Portland to close his law practice and to finish the appeal in *Allen v. People's Amusement Park*.[294] In *Allen*, Stewart asserted a theory that had prevailed a decade earlier in *Taylor v. Cohn*.[295] He claimed that the owners of the Star Theater had breached a contract with William D. Allen and his wife, a black couple, by refusing to seat them on the main floor of the theater. Although the facts in the cases were indistinguishable, the Oregon Supreme Court sustained a lower court's dismissal of the complaint,[296] plainly ignoring the precedent established in *Taylor v. Cohn*. Ironically, Stewart, who had fought to integrate Oregon's public accommodations, left the state no better than he had found it. The discrimination against blacks in public accommodations continued.[297]

Eugene Minor was admitted to the Oregon bar in 1918, just as McCants Stewart was leaving Portland. Minor graduated from Northwestern College of Law (Lewis and Clark), in Portland, Oregon. He was Oregon's third black lawyer. Minor practiced in Portland for many years, but the level of his practice never matched Stewart's. Minor practiced part-time and was also a librarian and messenger for the federal courthouse.[298]

In 1926, Minor was followed to the Oregon bar by Wyatt Williams. Wyatt "became captain of the bellboys" in a local hotel and "practiced law in his spare time."[299] Ulysses G. Plummer, previously admitted to the Kansas bar, was admitted to the bar in Portland in 1936.[300]

In the fall of 1921 Beatrice Cannady was described as "prominent in club and religious circles and editor of the *Portland Advocate*, the first colored woman to be admitted to the bar [in Oregon]."[301] Cannady graduated from Portland's Northwestern School of Law (Lewis and Clark).[302] Prior to relocating to Los Angeles, California, in 1932, Cannady was successful in her efforts to integrate the public schools in Vernonia, Oregon.[303]

Washington

Everett E. Simpson was admitted to the bar in the state of Washington in 1888, the same year in which he graduated from the University of Wisconsin School of Law.[304] The extent to which Simpson practiced law in Seattle, Washington, is unknown.

Robert O. Lee followed Simpson to the bar in Washington and was admitted in 1889. Lee had attended the South Carolina School of Law in the 1870s. Before relocating to Washington, he attended a "graduate law course at Badden Institute in South Carolina." He ultimately settled in Seattle.[305] The extent to which Lee practiced law is also unknown.

In 1892 Jesse A. Williams completed his law training. He had studied under the tutelage of Daniel W. Henley and William D. Scott, both white lawyers. Williams was admitted to the bar in Spokane, Washington, on October 27, 1890, and to the Washington State Supreme Court on June 30, 1894.[306] Williams was a lawyer in Seattle from 1903 to 1915. Upon completion of his law studies, Williams was immediately recognized as "an able colored lawyer,"[307] and he was elected as a delegate to the Republican National Convention. In fact, upon the recommendation of Judge Turner, a member of the Washington state delegation, Williams, described as a "bright young colored lawyer of his city," became secretary of the state delegation to the convention.[308]

John Edward Hawkins was admitted to practice at the King County bar on May 17, 1895, and to the Supreme Court of Washington eleven days later.[309] Hawkins's capacity to study law came to the attention "of the well-known attorneys W. H. Morris, . . . Judge Hall and W. H. White," who were white. These men observed the businesslike manner in which Hawkins operated a tonsorial parlor in Seattle beneath their law offices.[310] They advised Hawkins to take up the study of law, which he did. Hawkins was described as "an active, aggressive and successful practitioner at the state bar and the United States Circuit Court where he was respected by both judges and attorneys."[311] After Hawkins was admitted to the bar, "he became a favorite of the idle workingmen and curious spectators of the nineties who frequently attended court for their amusement."[312] According to one writer,

Many of [Hawkins's] cases were drawn from sporting-class Blacks, but he was one of the most determined defenders of black people's rights of admission to public baths, restaurants, and theaters. His task was complicated by the [1895] amendment of the state's 1890 Public Accommodations law. . . . The passage of the amendment was followed by several contradictory rulings which virtually left the determination of the rights of Blacks up to proprietors of business establishments.[313]

Such laws hindered the progress of black lawyers, who could get no relief in a state where the courts immunized private businesses that discriminated.

Undaunted, Hawkins won a few cases against those very businesses. Though he lost most of his cases, Hawkins aimed to preserve the principle of equal treatment and not necessarily to obtain damages.[314] Hawkins's inability to demonstrate his legal acumen caused the Republicans to doubt his efficacy. He failed to win an appointment as United States commissioner for Kodiak, Alaska, in 1896 and another, in 1900, as justice of the peace.[315] In 1896 Hawkins was selected by the Washington State Republican Convention as an alternate delegate to the Republican National Convention in St. Louis, Missouri, which nominated William McKinley as its candidate for president of the United States.[316] The influence of Booker T. Washington also reached John Edward Hawkins, who attended the second meeting of the National Negro Business League in 1901.[317]

There were other black lawyers in Washington during the early days of the twentieth century. Edward W. Hart was admitted to the bar in 1902, while Dean Hart was admitted in 1924. It is unknown where the Harts attended law school or under whom they studied law.

The opportunity to attend the University of Washington's law school was apparently not closed to blacks, although only a few blacks matriculated there: William McDonald, Eugene Henry McGee, Clarence Anderson, Elledge Randolph Penland, and John Prim were graduated in 1901, 1902, 1916, 1923, and 1927, respectively.[318] The relative success of most of these law graduates is unknown. Penland, however, was admitted to the bar in Washington in 1923 and elected president of the Seattle branch of the NAACP, a position in which he served from 1924 to 1925.[319]

The name of one other black lawyer has surfaced in Washington during the early days of the twentieth century—Gustave B. Aldridge. Little is known about Aldridge, except that he reportedly practiced in "Tacoma, Washington, during the 1920s and 1930s."[320]

No black women are known to have been admitted to practice law in the state of Washington before 1945.

Summary

Several states and American territorial possessions in the Pacific region of the nation had no known history of black lawyers prior to 1945.

Between 1890 and 1931, at least one black lawyer was admitted to practice in each of the following states: Arizona, Oregon, and Utah. After his 1921 admission to the Arizona bar, Robert Lee Fortune appeared before the Arizona Supreme Court at least six times. David H. Oliver, admitted to the Utah bar in 1931, practiced law in that state for thirty years. Oliver was a University of Nebraska law graduate, and Fortune studied law on his own.

The states of Colorado and Hawaii had black lawyers prior to 1900. Edwin Henry Hackley was admitted to the Colorado bar in 1883, and Joseph H. Stuart in 1891. Stuart was elected to the Colorado state legislature two years later. Hawaii admitted Thomas McCants Stewart, also a graduate of the University of South Carolina's law school, in 1898. By 1906, Stewart had appeared before Hawaii's appellate courts and federal courts at least twenty times.

The states of Montana, New Mexico, and Washington also admitted at least one black lawyer prior to 1900. In 1890, one year after it won statehood, Montana admitted John D. Posten to the bar. In 1893 Posten became a United States commissioner to the federal district court in Montana. He practiced law in Libby until 1924. In 1927 the University of Montana graduated its first black student, James Weston Dorsey. New Mexico's first black lawyer, Fred Simms, was admitted to the bar in the 1880s. In 1916, George W. Malone was the first black lawyer admitted to the New Mexico Supreme Court. Malone was a law graduate of Walden University, a black law school. An 1888 graduate of the University of Wisconsin, Everett E. Simpson, was admitted to the bar of Washington state in the same year.

The state of Oregon's first black lawyer, McCants Stewart, the second black law graduate of the University of Minnesota (and the son of Thomas McCants Stewart), was admitted to the bar in 1904. Stewart won his first case, a civil rights case, before the Oregon Supreme Court in 1906. He practiced law in Oregon for more than a decade.

A number of other law schools were represented in the above-mentioned Pacific states: the state universities of Kansas, Michigan, Minnesota, Washington, and Wisconsin; two black law schools, Howard University and Walden University; and the University of Denver.

Of those mentioned thus far, no state, aside from Oregon, admitted a black woman prior to 1945. Beatrice Cannady, a law graduate of Lewis and Clark University, was admitted to the Oregon bar in 1921. She practiced law in Portland and made efforts to desegregate the schools in Vernonia, Oregon, before relocating to California in the 1930s.

Most of the black lawyers practicing in the Pacific states gravitated to states and cities with sizable black populations. In the state of California, Robert Charles O'Hara Benjamin was the first black lawyer admitted to the bar. He passed the bar exam in 1887. James Wilson, the first black applicant, was denied admission in 1878 because of his race.

One of the first prominent black lawyers in California was Charles S. Darden. Admitted to the bar in 1904, Darden became the first black lawyer in the state to be a candidate for a judgeship, to bring a civil rights case (on restrictive covenants) before the courts, and to appear before the California Supreme Court (in 1911). Willis O. Tyler and Loren Miller also led fights to prohibit restrictive covenants in California, while Edward Burton Ceruti concentrated on suits that dealt with racial discrimination in public accommodations.

In the area of legal education, James M. Alexander, who attended the University of Southern California in 1915, is said to have been the first black student to matriculate in a public university in that state. In 1930, George Marion Johnson became the first black in California to earn a doctorate in law from Boalt Hall Law School, at the University of California. Virginia Stephens, California's first black woman lawyer, was admitted to the bar in 1928.

Among the law schools represented by black lawyers in California were Howard University, Harvard University, Brooklyn Law School, Southwestern University, the University of Southern California, and the University of Michigan.

The state of Kansas admitted its first black lawyer, John H. Morris, in 1871. Black lawyers entered politics in Kansas shortly thereafter. Charles Henry James Taylor entered Democratic politics and became a city attorney. He may also have been the first black American to dine at the White House with the president, during the administration of Grover Cleveland. John Lewis Waller cast the electoral vote for Kansas in the presidential election of Benjamin Harris in 1888. Isaac F. Bradley, Sr., the first black graduate of the University of Kansas, was nominated for attorney general of Kansas on an independent party ticket; William Henry Towers was elected to the Kansas state senate in 1937.

In Kansas the road to *Brown v. The Board of Education of Topeka, Kansas*, decided by the United States Supreme Court in 1954, began in 1883, the year Joseph H. Stuart failed in his attempt to desegregate the public schools of Topeka. By the 1920s, black lawyers such as Elisha Scott, Sr., a 1916 law graduate of Washburn University, were handling civil rights cases throughout the Midwest.

As early as 1889, black lawyers practicing in Hill City, Kansas, were known for their expertise in commercial law. Turner W. Bell, who handled hundreds of criminal law matters in Leavenworth, Kansas, was well known nationally.

In 1897 Lutie A. Lytle became the first woman admitted to the Kansas bar. She soon returned to Tennessee, where she became the nation's first female law professor. She taught at Central Tennessee Law School, her alma mater.

In addition to the law schools mentioned, black lawyers in Kansas were graduated from Drake University, Howard University, the University of Michigan, and the University of South Carolina.

The first known black lawyer in the Oklahoma and Indian Territories was Sugar George, who may have been part Indian. In the mid-1870s, George prosecuted criminal cases in the federal court at Fort Smith, Arkansas, which had jurisdiction over the Indian Territories. A. G. W. Sango, another black thought to be part Indian, emerged as a lawyer for the Creek Nation. He was also a friend of Booker T. Washington.

After Oklahoma became a state in 1907, it adopted laws limiting blacks' and Indians' right to vote. These laws were challenged by J. Coody Johnson and A. G. W. Sango, and a succession of black lawyers continued the struggle against voting rights restrictions. In 1939 two black lawyers, Charles A. Chandler of Oklahoma, and James Madison Nabrit, Jr., a professor of law at Howard University, won a decisive victory in the United States Supreme Court. The court held that Oklahoma's racial voting restrictions violated the Constitution.

Most of the black lawyers in Oklahoma were private practitioners. Black lawyers appear to have held few state or federal posts in Oklahoma prior to 1945. In the 1890s, Daniel Webster Lewis was appointed clerk in the probate court in the vicinity of Kingfisher, Oklahoma, and Byron M. Henderson was appointed an assistant United States attorney for the federal district of Oklahoma. In the private sector, J. Coody Johnson, A. G. W. Sango, and Buck Colbert Franklin all represented the oil interests of black and Indian landowners. Johnson became an oil baron, and Franklin helped settle a large oil claim dispute in 1926.

No women were admitted to the bar in Oklahoma prior to 1945. Black alumni from the following law schools were represented in the state: Howard University, Walden University, Shaw University (all black schools), Union Law School (Northwestern University), Harvard University, Yale University, John Marshall Law School, Oskaloosa College, and the University of Kansas.

Black lawyers in the Pacific states followed the same paths in the law as they did in other states, though fewer black women practiced among them. These lawyers played key roles in the emancipation of blacks from state-imposed and private acts of racial discrimination.

NOTES

1. Alaska was not a state until 1959, and there is no evidence that black lawyers practiced in Alaska prior to 1945. Idaho, admitted to the Union in 1890, reports that no black lawyers were admitted to the bar prior to 1945, as does Nevada (admitted to statehood in 1864), and Wyoming (admitted to statehood in 1890). Letter to Charles S. Brown from L. J. Bidgeganeta, clerk, Supreme Court of Idaho, May 26, 1958. (The first black lawyer admitted to the Idaho bar was Reginald Ray Reeves, of Idaho Falls, on November 3, 1952). Letter to Charles S. Brown from Ned A. Turner, clerk, Supreme Court of Nevada, June 2, 1958. Although Fred Forbes, clerk, Supreme Court of Wyoming, reported by letter that no black lawyer had been admitted to the Wyoming bar, Vol. 4, *The Thirteenth Census, Population* 534 lists one in 1910, as does Nevada (487). The identities of these lawyers are unknown.

2. See W. S. Savage, *Blacks in the West* 19, 147, 189 (1977).

3. Letter from H. B. Daniels, assistant attorney general, Phoenix, Arizona, to Charles S. Brown, April 29, 1958.

4. Telephone conversation with Professor Daily Oliver (D. H. Oliver's nephew), Webster State College, Ogden, Utah, on Oct. 15, 1987. In 1963 D. H. Oliver published *A Negro on Mormonism*, the first known book by a black lawyer that critiqued Mormonism. For bar admission, see letter from L. M. Cummings, clerk, Supreme Court of Utah, to Charles S. Brown, May 28, 1958.

5. Quote from R. E. Harris, *The First Hundred Years: A History of Arizona Blacks* 8–9 (1977). See also *Phoenix City Directory, 1937*, at 194, listing Fortune as a lawyer. Robert L. Fortune is listed as counsel, by himself or with others, in the following cases decided by the Arizona Supreme Court between 1925 and 1936: *Carter v. State*, 27 Ariz. 330, 232 P. 1115 (1925) (murder case—lost); *Dillard v. State*, 32 Ariz. 607, 261 P. 337 (1927) (client convicted of running a house of prostitution—won reversal) (with law firm Baker and Whitney); *White v. Hamilton*, 38 Ariz. 256, 299 P. 124 (1931) (dispute between blacks regarding the control of Palm Chapter No. 3, Order of Eastern Star of Arizona—won reversal) (with law firm of Speakman and Seaman); *Clark v. State*, 39 Ariz. 547, 8 P.2d 1111 (1932) (unspecified criminal matter—lost) (with Thomas J. Croaff); *Hamilton v. White*, 42 Ariz. 170, 22 P.2d 1089 (1933) (the Palm Chapter dispute—won) (with Hess Seaman and William G. Christy); *Most Worshipful Grand Lodge of Free and Accepted Masons of Arizona v. West Temple Lodge No. 425*, 47 Ariz. 57, 53 P.2d 425 (1936) (dispute between two black lodges—lost). (with J. S. Wheeler).

6. Letter from L. M. Cummings, clerk, Supreme Court of Utah, to Charles S. Brown, May 28, 1958. Utah records one black lawyer in 1910 and one in 1920. Vol. 4, *The Thirteenth Census, Population* at 523 (1914); Vol. 4, *The Fourteenth Census*, table 25, at 37 (1920). (See Appendix.)

7. D. L. Beasley, *The Negro Trail Blazers of California* 188 (1919). See also Lapp, "Negro Rights Activities in Gold Rush California," 45 *California Historical Society Quarterly* 4–6 (March 1966); Lapp, *Afro-American in California* 9–11 (N. Hundley, Jr. and J. A. Schutz eds. 1979).

8. Racism in California was so severe that blacks were by law declared

incompetent to give testimony in a court of law. This preclusion lasted until 1873. O. A. Thomas, *The Negro in California Before 1890*, at 41–44 (1945) (mimeo).

9. Babcock, "Clara Shortridge Foltz: 'First Woman,'" 30 *Ariz. L. Rev.* 673, 687, 694, 695, n.112, 697, 714, n.214 (1988). Foltz was the first woman admitted to practice law in California.

10. S. B. Thurman, *Pioneers of Negro Origin in California* 43 (1949).

11. D. L. Beasley, *The Negro Trail Blazers of California* 194 (1919).

12. *Ibid.*

13. Vol. 3 *Appleton's Annual Cyclopedia and Register of Important Events of the Year 1878*, at 71 (N. Series, 1879).

14. Letter from Harold J. Ostly, clerk, Superior Court of Los Angeles, to Charles S. Brown, July 22, 1958.

15. I. G. Penn, *The Afro-American Press, And Its Editors* 320 (1891). See also F. M. Lortie, Jr., *San Francisco Black Community, 1870–1890*, at 46 (1970) (mimeo). One of the black newspapers that R. C. O. Benjamin edited was *The Sentinel*, a San Francisco paper. The paper reportedly "got some heavy opposition from its readers for its advocacy of political conciliation."

16. D. L. Beasley, *The Negro Trail Blazers of California* 195 (1919).

17. *Dictionary of American Negro Biography* 39 (R. Logan and M. Winston eds. 1982).

18. *New York Age*, Dec. 19, 1891.

19. Hastings College of Law at the University of California was established by the California State Assembly in 1878. During the same session, the assembly approved a law allowing women to qualify for admission to the bar. Babcock, "Clara Shortridge Foltz: 'First Woman,'" 30 *Ariz. L. Rev.* 673, 695, n.112, 697 (1988).

20. D. L. Beasley, *The Negro Trail Blazers of California* 194 (1919).

21. "Negro Lawyer up for Election," *The California Eagle*, June 27, 1914, at 1, col. 3. It is possible that black lawyers may have practiced in Allensworth, California, an all-black town founded in 1908; it had "a constable and justice of the peace." Drummond, "Tribute to a Black Utopia," *Washington Post*, Jan. 2, 1992, at C2, col. 1.

22. D. L. Beasley, *The Negro Trail Blazers of California* 197 (1919).

23. *Id.* at 198.

24. *Ibid.*, quoting *The California Eagle*, a black newspaper (no date or page cited). Judge John W. Shenk was the trial judge that made the ruling. The opposing lawyer was Ingall W. Bull.

25. *Randall v. Washington*, 161 Cal. 59, 118 P. 425 (1911); D. L. Beasley, *The Negro Trail Blazers of California* 199 (1919).

26. See, e.g., *In re Morgan's Estate*, 203 Cal. 569, 265 P. 241 (1928) (with Hugh E. Macbeth, Sr.).

27. *Harvard Law Quinquennial* 280, 445 (F. S. Kimball ed. 1948).

28. Vol. 1 *Who's Who of the Colored Race* 182–83 (F. L. Mather ed. 1915).

29. *Id.* at 270; D. L. Beasley, *The Negro Trail Blazers of California* 197 (1919); biographical sketch of Hugh E. Macbeth, circa 1956 (in author's possession).

30. See, e.g., *Connely v. Superior Court of Los Angeles County*, 34 Cal. App. 773, 169 P. 355 (1917) (jurisdictional issue—won) (with George P. Cook); *Hester v. O'Dara*, 206 Cal. 3, 272 P. 1057 (1928) (action for trespass—won); *Stevens v. Stevens*, 215 Cal. 702, 12 P.2d 432 (1932) (domestic relations—won); *Mayock v.*

Kerr, 216 Cal. 171, 13 P.2d 717 (1932) (petition to compel voting registrar to accept petitions to place property issue on ballot—lost).

31. Tyler, "A Plea for Justice," *The California Eagle*, Dec. 7, 1918, at 1, col. 1.

32. "Negro Attorney Addresses Legislators on Insidious Self-Governing Bar Bill," *East Tennessean*, April 24, 1927. Macbeth may have been "the first [black] man to urge admission of Negroes to the Los Angeles Bar Association." W. W. Robinson, *Lawyers of Los Angeles* 235 (1959); C. G. Woodson, *The Negro Professional Man and the Community* 208 (reprint, 1969).

33. "Win Equality at Bar," *East Tennessean*, April 24, 1927.

34. "Opposition to Bar Bill Withdrawn," *Pittsburgh Courier*, April 9, 1927.

35. "Re-Elected Member of Board of Governors on Lawyers Club of California," *Pittsburgh Courier*, Jan. 22, 1938. The Lawyers Club of Los Angeles extended its mission into "liberal discussion of economics and the administration of laws as it touches both the legal profession and the general public." W. W. Robinson, *Lawyers of Los Angeles* 291 (1959).

36. Wheeldin, "The Story of Hugh Macbeth," *Daily People's World*, Dec. 7, 1956, at 10, col. 1. See also *Fifth Annual Meeting Program of the State Bar of California*, Sept. 29, 30 and Oct. 1, 1932, at 50–55 (Macbeth's minority report).

37. Biographical sketch of Hugh E. Macbeth (in author's files). According to Hugh E. Macbeth's son, Hugh E. Macbeth, Jr., his father "was a man whose interests and concerns comprehended all of humanity, and its unconditional entitlement to social, legal, and economic justice, regardless of social, color, creed, religion, national or geographic origin." Letter to author from Hugh E. Macbeth, Jr., Aug. 28, 1990. (Hugh E. Macbeth, Jr., was graduated from the University of California School of Law [Boalt Hall] in 1944.)

38. "Tyler Elected Delegate," *Afro-American*, April 23, 1920.

39. *Wyat v. Patee*, 205 Cal. 46, 269 P. 660 (1928).

40. *Fairchild v. Raines*, 24 Cal. 2d 818, 151 P.2d 260 (1944) (with George Cryer and R. Alston Jones).

41. *Shelley v. Kraemer*, 334 U.S. 1 (1948). In 1892 San Francisco and San Diego had race-restrictive covenants. These cities were among the first in the nation to adopt them. Miller, "Covenants in the Bear Flag State," 53 *Crisis* 138 (May 1946). A black California historian notes, however, that one black lawyer "won a favorable verdict in regard to the purchase of land by [the group] Negroes Against Segregating [on] February 4, 1915," two years before Morefield Story, the lawyer in *Buchanan v. Warley* (245 U.S. 60 [1917]), won this case. (*Buchanan* held that restrictive covenants mandated by ordinance violated the Fourteenth Amendment to the United States Constitution.) D. L. Beasley, *The Negro Trail Blazers of California* 194 (1919).

42. Vol. 1 *Who's Who in Colored America* 40 (J. J. Boris ed. 1927).

43. Vol. 1 *Who's Who of the Colored Race* 62 (F. L. Mather ed. 1915); "Attorney E. Burton Ceruti," *The California Eagle*, Nov. 7, 1914, at 1, col. 3.

44. *People v. Harris*, 169 Cal. 53, 145 P. 520 (1914). Ceruti was a skilled criminal defense lawyer. In this case, he attempted to establish a defense based upon intoxication and insanity. He lost the case, but it took the court nearly twenty pages to dispose of the arguments raised in his appeal.

45. D. L. Beasley, *The Negro Trail Blazers of California* 194, 204 (1919). Around 1914 in northern California, another black lawyer, Walter A. Butler (of Oakland), "was the first president of the . . . NAACP." Butler fought many courageous civil rights battles, including actions to outlaw restrictive covenants and

the showing of *The Birth of a Nation* in Oakland. K. G. Goode, *California's Black Pioneers* 112 (1974).

46. "Ceruti and Tyler Win Big Murder Trial," *The California Eagle*, Jan. 16, 1915, at 1, col. 2.

47. D. L. Beasley, *The Negro Trail Blazers of California* 196 (1919).

48. *Ibid.*

49. *Ibid.* See *Almanach de Gotha Annuaire Genealogique, Diplomatique et Statistique* 620 (Sept. 1920), from the Department of State Library.

50. *Ibid.* (*The Negro Trail Blazers*).

51. See, e.g., *People v. Logan*, 175 Cal. 45, 164 P. 1121 (1917) (murder conviction—reversed) (with Frank J. Murphy and Charles N. Douglas); *People v. Shortridge*, 179 Cal. 507, 177 P. 458 (1918) (murder case—lost); *Ex parte Lockett*, 179 Cal. 581, 178 P. 134 (1919) (criminal/constitutional law matter—won) (with Edwin V. McKenzie, Harry A. McKenzie, and A. S. Newburgh); *Franks v. Cesena*, 192 Cal. 1, 218 P. 437 (1923) (procedural matter—lost) (with Lawrence Sledge).

52. Letter from Thelma Jackman to Charles S. Brown, Oct. 24, 1958.

53. "S. B. Turner Victor in Coast Law Suit," *Chicago Defender*, July 5, 1924.

54. "White Woman Retains Race Attorney in Case," *St. Louis Argus*, July 29, 1927.

55. "Race Lawyer Achieves," *The Guardian*, Aug. 13, 1927.

56. Johnson, "State Sales Taxes and the Commerce Clause," 24 *Cal. L. Rev.* 155 (1935); Johnson, "Multi-State Taxation of Interstate Sales," 27 *Cal. L. Rev.* 547 (1939). See also, "Race Attorney Writes Law for California," *Chicago Defender*, Sept. 9, 1939.

57. *San Francisco Examiner*, June 17, 1958, at 9; letter from Judge John W. Bussey to Charles S. Brown, Nov. 7, 1958. See also, *Harvard Law Quinquennial* 80 (F. S. Kimball ed. 1948).

58. "Colored Lawyer Appointed Assistant District Attorney of Los Angeles, Calif.," *Herald Commonwealth*, March 22, 1930; "Leon Whittaker Is Made Deputy District Attorney," *Chicago Defender*, March 15, 1930.

59. G. R. Segal, *Blacks in the Law* 161 (1983).

60. *Id.* at 162. James A. Fisher, "The Political Development of the Black Community in California, 1850–1950," in *Neither Separate Nor Equal* 41 (California Historical Society, 1971). Oliver, "Pioneer Black Judge Edwin Jefferson Dies," *The Los Angeles Times*, Aug. 22, 1989, at 1, col. 4; *Negro Who's Who in California* 41 (1948); W. W. Robinson, *Lawyers of Los Angeles* 329 (1959). See also, Galanis, "Climbing the Mountain," 75 *A.B.A.J.* 60, 65 (April 1991), on Williams). This article identifies Walter L. Gordan, Jr., who opened a law office in Los Angeles in 1937. *Id.* at 64.

61. Letter from Thelma Jackman, dept. librarian, Los Angeles Public Library, to Charles S. Brown, June 25, 1958; *Negro Who's Who in California* 45 (1948).

62. "A Negro Lawyer Is Radio Star in Los Angeles," *Houston Informer*, Dec. 7, 1935.

63. "West Coast May Send Negro to Congress Seat," *Atlanta Daily World*, April 27, 1944; *Negro Who's Who in California* 46 (1948). Other black lawyers, mostly educated outside of California, were admitted to the California bar between 1914 and 1944. John Henry Kelly, an 1891 Michigan University law graduate, was admitted to the bar in 1891. "Lawyer J. H. Kelly, LL.B.," *The California Eagle*, Nov. 7, 1914, at 1, col. 5; *General Catalogue of the University of*

Michigan, 1837–1911, at 442 (I. N. Demmon ed. 1912). Afue McDowell, a 1911 Howard University School of Law graduate, conducted numerous political campaigns for black lawyers, among them Paul M. Nash's campaign for justice of the peace in Los Angeles in 1914. "Negro Lawyer up for Election," *The California Eagle*, June 27, 1914, at 1, col. 3. Charles Alexander Jones, a 1912 law graduate of Ohio State University, went to California after serving as a prosecutor in Franklin County, Ohio, to head the legal department of the Sidney P. Dones Real Estate Company (letter to author from Edith Jones Boyd, Nov. 2, 1991. Ms. Boyd, Jones's daughter, also reports that her father was admitted to the Supreme Court of Ohio on June 25, 1912. "The Sidney P. Dones Co.," *The California Eagle*, Dec. 5, 1914, at 1, col. 1. Curtis Cavielle Taylor, a 1926 Howard University School of Law graduate, was admitted to the California bar in March 1927. He became a successful criminal lawyer, and "his brilliant defense in the Griffin murder case, popularly referred to as the 'Error Hanging Case' caused the making of a new statute, providing for automatic stay of executions in California murder cases when the death penalty is involved." *Negro Who's Who in California* 41 (1948).

64. Ramsey, "Negro Women Lawyers of State of California," *The California Eagle*, Sept. 14, 1944, at 3, col. 4. Supreme Court of California records do not confirm definitively that Stephens was admitted "between 1920 and 1929," but "the records for this period do not seem complete." Letter to author from John C. Rossi, assistant clerk-administrator, Supreme Court of California, Oct. 8, 1991.

65. *Ibid.* Moore married Fred Douglas Ramsey, also a 1922 Howard University Law School graduate. Smith, "Class Prophecy," *Howard University Professional Schools Yearbook of 1922* (Book V) (pages unnumbered); *Eighth Annual Scholarship Awards Luncheon Program of the Black Women Lawyers Association of Southern California*, May 19, 1984, at 5.

66. Ramsey, "Negro Women Lawyers of State of California," *The California Eagle*, Sept. 14, 1944, at 3, col. 4 (in error, this article spells Anderson's first name as Tobiatha); "28 From S.F. Successful in State Bar Test," *San Francisco Chronicle*, May 2, 1933 (listing Anderson); "Negress *Chronicle* Oratorical Winner, Makes Debut in Court," *San Francisco Chronicle*, March 3, 1934, at 3, col. 2 (errs in stating that Anderson was a UCLA law graduate); "Attorney Tabytha Anderson Wins S.F. NAACP Election in Stormy Meet Over Hawkins," *The Spokesman*, March 15, 1935, at 1, col. 5.

67. "Large Audience Hears Attorney," *Raleigh Times*, March 14, 1933.

68. "First Coast Woman Lawyer," *Chicago Defender*, Oct. 25, 1943; "Widow of Boxer Joe Louis, Martha Louis, 78 Dies," *Jet*, Aug. 19, 1991.

69. Murray, "The Right to Equal Opportunity in Employment," 33 *Cal. L. Rev.* 338 (1945); P. Murray, *Song in a Weary Throat* 262–63 (1987). Murray was admitted to the California bar on January 2, 1946.

70. Letter to author from Cheryl K. Taylor, registration clerk, Colorado Supreme Court, May 18, 1990. Hackley was admitted to the bar on June 7, 1883. Hackley attended the University of Michigan Law School from 1881 to 1882. *General Catalogue of the University of Michigan, 1837–1911* at 721 (I. N. Demmon ed. 1912); "Emancipation Celebration," *Denver Times*, Sept. 23, 1898, at 16, col. 4; *Colorado Graphic*, Oct. 16, 1886, at 1.

71. "Former Denver Publisher Dies," *Colorado Statesman*, July 26, 1940, at 1, col. 5.

72. *Afro-American Encyclopedia; Or, The Thoughts, Doings and Sayings of the Race*

569 (J. T. Haley ed. 1895). Stuart attended the University of South Carolina with T. McCants Stewart and Richard T. Greener. Letter from George A. Trout, clerk, Colorado Supreme Court, to Charles S. Brown, April 3, 1961, regarding admission to bar in Denver and letter from Carolyn Bennett to author, Jan. 16, 1987, regarding admission to Supreme Court of Kansas. See also, letter from John D. Morrison, assistant state historian, to Charles S. Brown, May 6, 1958 (regarding election to Colorado General Assembly); and "J. H. Stuart, Colored Lawyer, Is Dead," *Denver Post*, April 5, 1910, at 5, col. 1. When Stuart died, the *Denver Post* stated that he "was one of the best known men in his profession." See R. G. Dill, *The Political Campaigns of Colorado* 285 (1895); *Portfolio of Tenth General Assembly* 49, 73 (1895); *Laws Passed at the Tenth Session of the General Assembly of the State of Colorado* 139–41 (April 1895).

73. Vol. 1 *Who's Who of the Colored Race* 266 (F. L. Mather ed. 1915).

74. "Says Colored Lawyers Gaining Race Confidence," *Atlanta Daily World*, Aug. 10, 1939.

75. *Ibid.*

76. "Funeral Services Set for Denver Attorney," *Rocky Mountain News*, May 14, 1957, at 19.

77. Telephone conversation with Howard Jenkins, Jr., of Maryland, April 1, 1989.

78. Tucker, "Sam Cary: the Man's Man Black Pioneer of the Legal Profession," *Denver City Blues*, July 25, 1986, at 4, col. 3.

79. *Ibid.*

80. *Ibid.*

81. "Wins Case Against U.S.," *Kansas City Call*, Nov. 27, 1931.

82. "Additional Graduates," 46 *Crisis* 309 (Oct. 1939). McKinney may never have passed the bar; he died at a young age. Telephone conversation with Howard Jenkins, Jr., of Maryland, April 1, 1989.

83. Earley, "Sole Black on NLRB Steps Down," *Washington Post*, Aug. 26, 1983, at A15, col. 1.

84. Letter from Leoti V. Krone, deputy clerk, Hawaii Supreme Court, to Charles S. Brown, July 25, 1958. Stewart was admitted pursuant to Rule 10 of the Hawaii Supreme Court, which required applicants to accompany their petition with a sample of their "handwriting, setting forth their age, birth place, nationality, last place of residence, and character and term of study both liberal and professional." Whether an applicant was examined by the court was discretionary. However, the applicant had to "be a citizen (or denizen) of the Hawaiian Islands, or of the United States of America" (11 *Hawaii Reports* 812 [1899]).

85. Among the persons providing T. McCants Stewart with letters of recommendation were R. Stuart Dodge, chief justice of the New York Supreme Court; General Stewart L. Woodford, former U.S. minister to Spain; Joseph H. Choate, a leader of the New York bar, and C. A. Van Brunt, judge of the First Appellate Division of the Supreme Court of New York. These letters also made it easier for Stewart to enter Republican Party politics in Hawaii. "A New Attorney," *The Pacific Commercial Advertiser*, Nov. 29, 1898, at 6.

86. *Ibid.*

87. T. H. Williams, R. N. Current, and F. Freidel, *A History of the United States* 233, 345 (1960). Hawaii was annexed by the United States on August 12, 1898, during the administration of William H. McKinley.

88. Between 1899 and 1909, black lawyers accompanied black American

army units to help end the insurrection in the Philippines. In 1901 Frank Rudolph Steward, an 1896 law graduate of Harvard University, "served as provost judge in San Pablo." There he organized and presided over the first American-type court. W. B. Gatewood, Jr., *Black Americans and the White Man's Burden, 1898–1903*, at 275 (1975); *Harvard Law Quinquennial* 420 (F. S. Kimball ed. 1948). In 1916, a black lawyer, G. F. Campbell, "formerly of Chicago, was a candidate for election to the municipal board in [Manila]." The civil war in the Philippines had taken Campbell there as a judge advocate of the United Spanish War Veterans (12 *Crisis* 199 [June 1916]).

89. R. B. Woods, *A Black Odyssey: John Lewis Waller and the Promise of American Life, 1878–1900*, at 112 (1981).

90. Sketch of "Long Contest to secure county law" (source unknown, published in Hawaii newspaper in 1904); "County Law Fight by Governor," *The Bulletin* (no date, circa 1904). Both articles are from the McCants Stewart collection, Mooreland Spingarn Research Center, Howard University.

91. *In the Matter of the Application of Charles S. Desky for a Writ of Mandamus Against James A. King*, 12 Hawaii 138 (1899) (with F. M. Hatch). This case concerned police powers of state.

92. *Ibid.*; *Koloa Sugar Co. v. Brown*, 12 Hawaii 142 (1899) (adverse possession); *Republic of Hawaii v. Li Shee*, 12 Hawaii 329 (1900) (with F. J. Berry) (polygamy); *Chilton v. Shaw*, 13 Hawaii 250 (1901) (tax assessment); *Kailikea v. Hapa*, 13 Hawaii 459 (1901) (incompetence of transferor of deed); *Ropert v. Kauai*, 13 Hawaii 637 (1901) (with firm of Holmes & Stanley) (landlord and tenant); *Morgan v. Betters*, 13 Hawaii 685 (1901) (contract for sale of personal property); *Hitchcock v. Humphreys*, 14 Hawaii 1 (1902) (with G. A. Davis, J. A. Magoon, Stewart, and F. M. Hatch) (disqualification of judge); *Harris v. Cooper*, 14 Hawaii 145 (1902) (with firm of Robertson & Wilder) (election laws); *Hitchcock v. Hustace*, 14 Hawaii 232 (1902) (with G. A. Davis, F. M. Hatch, B. L. Marx, J. A. Magoon, T. I. Dillon, and J. Lightfoot) (corporate disclosure of facts to shareholders); *Winslow v. Winslow*, 14 Hawaii 498 (1902) (divorce case); *Proper v. Proper*, 14 Hawaii 596 (1903) (service by publication in divorce cases); *Kellett v. Sumner*, 15 Hawaii 76 (1903) (termination of a trust); *Bolte v. Bellina*, 15 Hawaii 151 (1903) (responsibility of corporate directors); *In re Contested Election of November 3, 1903, for Officers of the County of Oahu*, 15 Hawaii 323 (1903) (with C. W. Ashford); *Ahmi v. Waller*, 15 Hawaii 497 (1904) (with C. W. Ashford) (deed); *Palolo Land and Improvement Co. v. Quai*, 15 Hawaii 554 (1903) (with L. Andrews) (water rights) *rehearing denied*, 16 Hawaii 52 (1904); *Wilcox v. Berrey*, 16 Hawaii 37 (1904) (malicious prosecution); *Mullen v. Walker*, 16 Hawaii 65 (1904) (amendment to a summons); *Boeynaems Zeugma v. Paahao*, 16 Hawaii 345 (1904) (with Antonio Perry).

93. *In re Presentation of Resolutions on the Death of the Late Chief Justice Judd*, 12 Hawaii 427, 435–38 (1900).

94. *United States v. Yong Ho*, 1 Hawaii Repts. 1 (D. Haw. 1900) (with W. A. Whiting).

95. *Kekauoha v. Schooner Robert Lewers Co.*, 1 Hawaii Repts. 75 (D. Haw. 1901).

96. *United States v. Kut Yong*, 1 Hawaii Repts. 104 (D. Haw. 1901).

97. *Langaas v. The Barkentine "James Tuft,"* 1 Hawaii Repts. 420 (D. Haw. 1903).

98. *Schirrmacher v. The Ship "Erskine M. Phelps," R. J. Graham*, 1 Hawaii 444 (D. Haw. 1903) (with J. J. Dunne).

99. Wynes, "T. McCants Stewart: Peripatetic Black South Carolinian," 80

South Carolina Historical Magazine 311, 316 (Oct. 1979), quoting "T. McCants Stewart Writes from Liberia: The Sort of People Needed There," 31 *Liberia* 30, (Nov. 1907).

100. Letter from E. Winfred Smallwood, president, Liberian National Bar Association, to Edward J. Perkins, U.S. Ambassador to Liberia, May 21, 1986.

101. *Virginia's Contribution to Negro Leadership* 19 (W. Cooper ed. 1937) (mimeo). See Vol. 1 *Who's Who in Colored America* 48 (J. J. Boris ed. 1927); "Ex-Errand Boy Returns Home as a Judge," *Baltimore Afro-American*, June 15, 1929.

102. *Robello v. The County of Maui*, 19 Hawaii 168 (1908) (with D. H. Chase), on the method of closing highways.

103. Vol. 5 *Men of Hawaii* 157 (G. F. Nellist, revised ed. 1935); "Ex-Errand Boy Returns Home as a Judge," *Baltimore Afro-American*, June 15, 1929.

104. Telephone conversation with William F. Crockett, of Hawaii, May 13, 1989. (William F. Crockett is the son of Wendell Crockett and the grandson of William F. Crockett.) It is possible that as of 1956 only the University of Michigan School of Law had graduated a third-generation lawyer of African-American descent. William F. Crockett was graduated from the University of Michigan's law school in 1956.

105. "John H. Morris to Kansas Bar," *The Louisianian*, Nov. 2, 1871; *New National Era and Citizen*, Nov. 30, 1871. (The examining committee was composed of three lawyers and one judge: Hiram Griswold, J. L. Pendery, Byron Sherry, and Judge Ide).

106. *Indianapolis Freeman*, Sept. 15, 1886. Charles Henry James Taylor was reported to have attended the University of Michigan School of Law. See *The College of Life or Practical Self-Educator: A Manual of Self Improvement for the Colored Race* 141 (H. D. Northrop, J. R. Gay, and I. G. Penn eds. 1896); Vol. 5 *The National Cyclopaedia of American Biography* 851 (1898). A person named Charles Henry Taylor did attend the University of Michigan Law School, but the schools' records do not confirm that this 1862 graduate and Charles Henry James Taylor are the same person. See *General Catalogue of the University of Michigan, 1837–1911*, at 371 (I. N. Demmon ed. 1912).

107. See also, Hershaw, "Black Demosthenes," *Indianapolis Freeman*, April 27, 1889, at 1, col. 1 (regarding Senator Henry W. Blair); J. C. Miller, *The Black Presence in American Foreign Affairs* 9 (1978).

108. R. B. Woods, *A Black Odyssey: John Lewis Waller and the Promise of American Life, 1878–1900*, at 56 (1981).

109. Hershaw, "Black Demosthenes," *Indianapolis Freeman*, April 27, 1889, at 1, col. 1.

110. "The Disgrace of the Nation," 8 *The Negro History Bulletin* 50, 70 (Dec. 1944). See also W. F. McCaleb, *Theodore Roosevelt* 132–33 (1931).

111. J. M. C., "Cleveland Denies that He Dined Negro," *Public Ledger*, March 4, 1904.

112. *Ibid.*

113. R. B. Woods, *A Black Odyssey: John Lewis Waller and the Promise of American Life, 1878–1900*, at 12–13 (1981); I. G. Penn, *The Afro-American Press, And Its Editors* 190 (1891).

114. "John L. Waller," *New York Age*, May 9, 1891.

115. R. B. Woods, *A Black Odyssey: John Lewis Waller and the Promise of American Life, 1878–1900*, at 12–13 (1981).

116. *Id.* at 15.

117. *Indianapolis Freeman*, Feb. 16, 1889.

118. I. G. Penn, *The Afro-American Press, and Its Editors* 191–92 (1891).

119. Bray, "Western Gleanings," *Indianapolis Freeman*, June 29, 1889, at 1, col. 4. The firm was dissolved in 1889 and reconstituted as Waller and Thomas: "[Mr. Price] having left us, and gone to his home in Peru, Kansas, where he has a farm."

120. R. B. Woods, *A Black Odyssey: John Lewis Waller and the Promise of American Life, 1878–1900*, at 96 (1981).

121. *Id.* at 73.

122. *Id.* at 71–72. A year before this appointment, Waller had urged "opening up the Cherokee Strip and Oklahoma for a Negro state." K. M. Teall, *Black History in Oklahoma: A Resource Book* 154–55 (1971), quoting *Topeka Daily Capitol*, March 9, 1890.

123. *Id.* at 135–36, 156–57. (*Black History in Oklahoma*). John G. Jones, a black Chicago lawyer, once visited the White House on behalf of Waller. Jones tried to persuade U.S. authorities to intervene when Waller was imprisoned by the French as a result of the "Wallerland" scheme. *Id.* at 170; see also, Blakely, "The John L. Waller Affair, 1895–1896," 37 *Negro History Bull.* 216 (Feb.–March 1974).

124. "A New Eldorado," *Indianapolis Freeman*, Jul. 13, 1889, at 8, col. 2.

125. *Ibid.*

126. *Ibid.*

127. *Ibid.*

128. Letter to author from Carolyn Bennett, admissions clerk, Supreme Court of Kansas, Jan. 16, 1987. See also, T. C. Cox, *Blacks in Topeka, Kansas, 1865–1915*, at 87–88, 90 (1982).

129. R. B. Woods, *A Black Odyssey: John Lewis Waller and the Promise of American Life, 1878–1900*, at 57 (1981); *Brown v. The Board of Education of Topeka, Kansas*, 347 U.S. 483 (1954). Efforts to desegregate the secondary public schools in Topeka continued, ultimately reaching the Kansas Supreme Court (*Reynolds v. The Board of Education of Topeka*, 66 Kan. 672, 72 P. 274 [1903]), which upheld *de jure* segregation based on *Plessy v. Ferguson*, 163 U.S. 537 (1896). No black lawyer's name appears as counsel of record before the Kansas Supreme Court in the Reynolds case. See also, T. C. Cox, *Blacks in Topeka, Kansas, 1865–1915*, at 112–13 (1982).

130. *University of Michigan General Catalogue of Officers and Students, 1837–1911*, at 428 (I. N. Demmon ed. 1912); Vol. 2 *History of Minneapolis* 735 (M. D. Shutter ed. 1923); H. F. Kletzing and W. H. Crogman, *Progress of a Race* 539 (1901).

131. Vol. 1 *Who's Who in Colored America* 22 (J. J. Boris ed. 1927); H. F. Kletzing and W. H. Crogman, *Progress of a Race* 539 (1901).

132. "Some Little Stories of Racial Progress," *Chicago Defender*, Feb. 23, 1918.

133. *Ibid.* Bell appeared before every federal court of appeals in the eight states of the Eighth Federal Circuit. "Dynamiters' Plea Is Made by Negro," *Kansas City Sun*, Jan. 20, 1915.

134. *Ibid.*

135. *Ibid.*

136. See *Frazier v. Anderson*, 2 F.2d 36 (8th Cir. 1924); "Habeas Corpus for Release of Soldiers in the Houston Riots," *The California Eagle*, Oct. 26, 1918. Bell was assisted by two other black lawyers, Elisha Scott, Sr., of Topeka, and E. T. Barbour, of El Reno, Oklahoma.

137. "One-Time Slave Wins 41 Out of 61 Appeals Cases," *Chicago Tribune*, Feb. 7, 1915. See also "Former Slave in Strong Plea for White Prisoners," *Chicago Defender*, Jan. 30, 1915; "Lawyer's Hobby Is to Win Appeal Cases," *New York Age*, Feb. 11, 1915.

138. *Ibid.* ("One-Time Slave Wins 41 Out of 61 Appeals Cases"). See also "Dynamiters Plea Is Made by Negro," *Kansas City Sun*, Jan. 20, 1915.

139. "Some Little Stories of Racial Progress," *Chicago Defender*, Feb. 23, 1918.

140. "Veteran Lawyer Praised as a Great Race Leader," *Chicago Defender*, Dec. 26, 1936.

141. I. G. Penn, *The Afro-American Press, and Its Editors* 314 (1891).

142. R. B. Woods, *A Black Odyssey: John Lewis Waller and the Promise of American Life, 1878–1900*, at 73 (1981). Woods indicates that Townsend, who was then a law student at the University of Kansas, assisted Waller and Price in this matter.

143. Vol. 1 *Who's Who of the Colored Race* 266 (F. L. Mather ed. 1915).

144. Bray, "Western Gleanings," *Indianapolis Freeman*, June 29, 1889, at 1, col. 4.

145. Randall B. Woods, Waller's biographer, states that "Jamison was not a lawyer" (letter to author from R. B. Woods, March 18, 1988). This conclusion contradicts a letter from Maria Russell, law librarian, Kansas State Library, to Charles S. Brown, Oct. 2, 1958. Raymond J. Reynolds, a 1929 graduate of Washburn University's law school, also remembers W. I. Jamison as a practicing lawyer in Topeka. In fact, he reported a story about "Jamison almost being held in contempt for failing to show up to represent a client when the case was called. Jamison was summoned to the judge's courtroom by the marshal. When asked why he was not present to represent his client, Jamison responded that 'I am never hired until I am first paid.' Jamison was not held in contempt" (telephone interview with Raymond J. Reynolds, of California, with author, April 7, 1989). See also, Reynolds, "Cheers and Encores," *Topeka Daily Capital*, Jan. 12, 1941, which states that "W. I. Jamison, another Negro attorney, served as an assistant [county attorney in Shawnee County Kansas] under Galen Nichols [and] under Otis E. Hungate (now our very efficient and courageously fair senior judge on the District Court), and John J. Schenck . . . from 1901 to 1911."

146. "Men of the Month," 19 *Crisis* 272, 274 (March 1920); *Dictionary of American Negro Biography* 211 (R. Logan and M. Winston eds. 1982).

147. Vol. 1 *Who's Who in Colored America* 78 (J. J. Boris ed. 1927).

148. Tucker, "Sam Cary The Man's Man Black Pioneer of the Legal Profession," *Denver City Blues*, July 25, 1986, at 4, col. 3.

149. "Noted Topeka Attorney Dies," *Topeka Daily Capital*, April 24, 1963.

150. "Attorney Scott Counsel for Rich Girl," *Topeka Kansas Plaindealer*, Jan. 20, 1922.

151. *Ibid.*

152. Telephone interview with Raymond J. Reynolds, of California, by author, April 4, 1989.

153. 140 *Kansas Reports* xlv (1934). Bradshaw was admitted to the Kansas bar in 1920. *Id.* at lxxxiv (Thomas).

154. *Cooper v. Cooper*, 115 Kan. 500, 223 P. 317 (1924).

155. "Atty. Bradshaw Wins Suit in District Court of Shawnee County, Kansas, Before District Judge [George H.] Whitcomb in the Case of a White Woman," *Topeka Kansas Plaindealer*, May 9, 1924.

156. 110 *Kansas Reports* xxvi (1921); 140 *Kansas Reports* lxxxiv (1934). Both volumes list Towers as being admitted to practice before the Kansas Supreme Court on June 26, 1919.

157. *Clark v. Vaughan*, 131 Kan. 438, 292 P. 783 (1930) (with H. Earl Meade).

158. Gavin, "House Bill No. 27: A Lesson in Democracy," Vol. 2, No. 1 *The Barrister* 4–5 (1941) (student newspaper at the Robert H. Terrell Law School); "William H. Towers," *Kansas City Times*, July 13, 1959. Tower's legislative activities appear in the following numbers of the *House Journal: Proceedings of the House of Representatives of the State of Kansas*: 30th Biennial Sess., Jan. 12 to April 2, inclusive 1042–1043 (1937); Special Sess., Feb. 7 to March 4, inclusive 239 (1938); 31st Biennial Sess., Jan. 10 to April 3, inclusive 1049 (1939); 32nd Biennial Sess., Jan. 14 to April 9, inclusive 980 (1941); 33rd Biennial Sess., Jan. 12 to March 23, inclusive 479 (1943); 34th Biennial Sess., Jan. 14 to April 9, inclusive 557 (1947). See also, *Kansas Legislative Directory* 101–R (1947).

159. Telephone interview with Raymond J. Reynolds, of California, April 14, 1989; N. J. Weiss, *Farewell to the Party of Lincoln* 202, n.72 (1983).

160. James H. Guy had been a member of the Kansas bar for at least thirty years by the time R. J. Reynolds became a lawyer. Guy had served "as a Negro assistant under . . . A. P. Jetmore," the Shawnee County attorney from 1899 to 1901. Reynolds, "Cheers and Encores," *The Topeka Daily Capital*, Jan. 12, 1941. In 1908, Guy's private practice was successful enough for him to afford to hire a stenographer, Carrie Langston (the mother of Langston Hughes, then ten years old). Scott, "Langston Hughes of Kansas," 66 *J. of Negro History* 1, 5 (1981); A. Rampersad, Vol. 1 *The Life of Langston Hughes* 11 (1986). See also, T. C. Cox, *Blacks in Topeka, Kansas, 1865–1915*, at 98, 183 (1982).

161. Telephone interview with Raymond J. Jordan, of California, April 14, 1989; letter from R. J. Reynolds to his daughter, Lurene Pat Reynolds, Aug. 29, 1978.

162. See Reynolds, "Kansas Negro Citizens Keep Pace with State and Nation," *Topeka Daily Capital*, July 26, 1939. Later, R. J. Reynolds wrote a column in *The Topeka Daily Capital* entitled "Cheers and Encores." The column was "dedicated to Negro America."

163. *Ibid.*

164. Smith, "Loren Miller: Advocate for Blacks," 1 *Black L.J.* 7, 8–9 (1971). Ulysses G. Plummer was admitted to practice in Kansas in 1936. After eleven years of practice, he relocated to Portland, Oregon, to practice law. Letter from Arthur S. Benson to Charles S. Brown, May 29, 1958.

165. Letter from Helen Bennett, reference librarian, Public Library of Kansas City, Kansas, to Charles S. Brown, Sept. 30, 1958; *Who's Who Among Negro Lawyers* 20 (S. T. M. Alexander ed. 1945).

166. "First Colored Woman Admitted to the Practice of Law," *The Topeka Daily Capital*, Sept. 15, 1897.

167. *Ibid.*

168. "Lutie Lytle's Luck: Appointed Law Teacher in the Central Tennessee College," *Topeka Daily Capital*, Oct. 27, 1898. This article called Lytle "the only woman law instructor in the world." Lytle was first admitted to the bar in Memphis, Tennessee on September 8, 1897. "Colored Female Lawyer," *The Cincinnati Enquirer*, Sept. 9, 1897, at 1, col. 4. Charlotte E. Ray and Mary Shadd Carey, both Howard University law graduates, and Ida G. Platt, a Chicago Law School graduate, were admitted to bars in 1872, 1883, and 1894, respectively.

169. "Popular Attorney," *Kansas Plaindealer*, April 14, 1939, reports that

M. Jean Mitchell was graduated in 1936 and became a member of the Kansas bar in 1938; *Who's Who Among Negro Lawyers* 3 (S. T. M. Alexander ed. 1945), reports that M. M. Alexander was graduated from Kansas University School of Law. Alexander became active in the National Bar Association. "Standing Committees," 2 *Nat'l B.A.J.* 74, 75 (June 1944); "Plans Activities," *Washington Afro-American*, Nov. 15, 1947.

170. According to court records supplied to the author on October 17, 1990, by Ralph Yeager, John D. Posten signed the roll of the Montana Supreme Court on July 23, 1890, after "previously being admitted in Missouri." According to Inez Herrig, a life-long resident of Libby who knew John D. Posten during her childhood, "he was respected by all" (telephone interview with author, Sept. 8, 1990). Posten's last name was frequently misspelled as "Poston."

171. "John D. Posten Dies in Davenport, Iowa," *Western News and The Libby Times*, Nov. 13, 1924, at 1, col. 1.

172. Letter to author from Dave Walter, Montana Historical Society, Sept. 7, 1990. Posten took the Twelfth Census of the United States of Libby Township, which he certified on June 26, 1890. He listed himself as a lawyer. See Quintard Taylor, Jr., "A History of Blacks in the Pacific Northwest, 1788–1970," at 79 (Ph.D. diss., University of Minnesota, 1977): Posten must be the unidentified black lawyer referred to by Taylor in his dissertation.

173. Judge Knowles, a Harvard University Law School graduate admitted to the bar in 1837, was appointed United States District Court Judge on February 21, 1890. Judge Knowles may have known Posten prior to his appointment to the bench. For additional biographical information about Judge Knowles, see 30 *Federal Cases* 1381 (1897).

174. *Register of the Department of Justice and the Judicial Offices of the United States* 116 (10th ed. 1895).

175. *Register of the Department of Justice and the Courts of the United States* 122 (26th ed. 1918).

176. Posten was listed in the Libby, Montana, city directory as a lawyer and U.S. commissioner. See, e.g., R. L. Polk and Co., *City Directory of Libby* 416 (1909); *id.* at 470 (1913).

177. O. W. Johnson, *Early Libby and Troy, Montana* 68 (1958).

178. *Id.* at 66.

179. E. H. Mumford, *Seattle's Black Victorians, 1852–1901*, at 98 (1980); R. L. Polk and Co., *Helena City Directory* 136 (1896), *id.* at 126 (1901).

180. Telephone interview with Phoebe Novotny Nelson, of Maryland, Feb. 27, 1990. According to Ms. Nelson, Mr. Bairpaugh lived in the 1200 block of 6th Avenue, South, while she lived at 1303 6th Avenue, South. When Nelson left Great Falls, Montana, in 1926, Mr. Bairpaugh was still practicing law. However, a black resident of Bozeman, Montana, says that Mr. Bairpaugh was not a lawyer but a rancher (telephone interview with Lucille W. Thompson, of Bozeman, Montana, Oct. 20, 1990).

181. According to court records supplied to the author by Ralph Yeager on October 17, 1990, James W. Dorsey signed the rolls of the Montana Supreme Court on June 7, 1927.

182. J. W. Trotter, Jr., *Black Milwaukee* 86, 104 (1985).

183. B. J. Richardson, *Black Directory of New Mexico* 26 (1976). *The Twelfth Census* indicates that there were two "Negro" lawyers in New Mexico in 1900. Only Fred Simms has been identified for this period.

184. *Id.* at 46 (*Black Directory of New Mexico*).

185. Malone was admitted to the Supreme Court of Mississippi on May 3, 1915, according to a Western Union night letter from George C. Meyers. (Night letter provided by New Mexico Supreme Court.)

186. *Petition of G. W. Malone in the Supreme Court, State of New Mexico, in re Application of G. W. Malone, for Permanent License*, April 8, 1916. Malone's application was supported by Harold Hurd, a white lawyer from Roswell, New Mexico, as expressed in letters from Harold Hurd to Jose D. Sena, Aug. 5, 1916, and from Maynard Fitzgerald, of Clarksdale (Coahoma County), Mississippi, to Supreme Court of New Mexico, Dec. 10, 1915. (Letters attached to Malone's petition.) For more information on Blackdom, New Mexico, see Gibson, "Blackdom," 64 *New Mexico Magazine* 46, Feb. 1986.

187. Copy of the roll of the Supreme Court of New Mexico provided to author on July 22, 1991. In 1958 the clerk of New Mexico indicated that no black lawyer had ever been admitted to practice in the state (letter to Charles S. Brown from Lowell C. Green, clerk of the Supreme Court of New Mexico).

188. B. J. Richardson, *Black Directory of New Mexico* 56 (1976). Richardson refers to a "W. T. Malone" as the first black admitted to the New Mexico court by examination, an apparent error in Malone's initials but correct in all other accounts.

189. M. T. Bailey, *Reconstruction in Indian Territory* 142 (1972). See also, G. Shirley, *Law West of Fort Smith* 10–11 (1957).

190. K. M. Teall, *Black History in Oklahoma: A Resource Book* 148–49 (1971); G. Aldrich, *Black Heritage of Oklahoma* 107 (1973). The House of Kings "was composed of one representative from each town [in the Creek Nation] who was elected by a vote of the town represented for a term of four years." M. T. Bailey, *Reconstruction in Indian Territory* 109 (1972).

191. "Oklahoma Pioneer Is Dead," *Pittsburgh Courier*, Oct. 21, 1933 at 2, col. 1.

192. *Brown v. United States* and *Curley v. United States*, 171 U.S. 631 (1898). Twine represented George Curley in this consolidated case.

193. Vol. 1 *Who's Who of the Colored Race* 270 (F. L. Mather ed. 1915).

194. "Oklahoma Pioneer Is Dead," *Pittsburgh Courier*, Oct. 21, 1933 at 2, col. 1. The names of two of his three sons are Pliny R. Twine, a 1929 graduate of Howard University's law school, and Harry Thomas Twine, who first enrolled in the Virginia Union Law School but received a certificate of law from Howard University in 1928. See *Virginia Union University Catalogue* 79 (1927).

195. *Twenty-seventh Annual Session, Oklahoma Jurisdiction, St. John Grand Lodge, Ancient, Free and Accepted Masons*, Aug. 13–15, 1918 (frontispiece).

196. Resolution of the Kingfisher County Bar Association, Feb. 24, 1932 (signed by E. M. Bradley, V. D. Firestone, and T. R. Blaine).

197. F. H. Warren, *Michigan Manual of Freedman's Progress* 47 (1915).

198. N. J. Washington, *Historical Development of the Negro in Oklahoma* 18 (1948), quoting from a personal interview with A. G. W. Sango, Feb. 1947.

199. B. T. Washington, *The Negro in Business* 210 (1907).

200. *Id.* at 211.

201. K. M. Teall, *Black History in Oklahoma: A Resource Book* 149 (1971).

202. N. J. Washington, *Historical Development of the Negro in Oklahoma* 18 (1948), citing Oklahoma Historical Society files, nos. 36920, 39367, 33786. Pursuant to the constitution of the Creek Nation, the council consisted of two houses, an upper house (the House of Kings) and a lower house (the House of Warriors). The lower house "was composed of one representative for every two

hundred persons belonging to the town." The term of office was four years. M. T. Bailey, *Reconstruction in Indian Territory* 109 (1972). In 1905 Sango was also elected Republican party central committeeman from the second ward in Muskogee, Oklahoma (*Muskogee Democrat*, March 15, 1905, at 1, col. 1). After the Emancipation Proclamation was issued, the Seminoles, Creeks, and Chickasaws were notified by federal authorities "that Negroes . . . were free." General Sanborn, an official of the Freedman's Bureau in the Indian Territory, instructed "the Indian agents . . . to use every means in their power to impress upon the minds of each individual of the tribes and nations the new relation existing between them and their former slaves." Asa W. Dagley, "The Negro of Oklahoma," 34–36, (M.A. thesis, University of Oklahoma, 1926).

203. J. D. Benedict, *Muskogee and Northern Oklahoma* 228–29 (1922); M. T. Bailey, *Reconstruction in Indian Territory* 122–23 (1972).

204. J. L. Franklin, *The Blacks in Oklahoma* 22 (1988).

205. "Negroes Preparing to Fight Disfranchisement," *The Weekly Chieftain*, Aug. 19, 1910, at 8, col. 2. Sango organized "prominent Negroes throughout the state . . . to wage war on the legality" of the grandfather provision.

206. J. L. Franklin, *The Blacks in Oklahoma* 22 (1980), referring to *Guinn v. United States*, 238 U.S. 347 (1915). Neither Sango's nor Johnson's name appears as counsel in *Guinn*. However, there is little doubt that Sango's and Johnson's early litigative efforts were the reason that the NAACP entered the case.

207. *Topeka Plaindealer*, June 15, 1917.

208. J. D. Benedict, *Muskogee and Northern Oklahoma* 228–29 (1922).

209. "Atty. Johnson Seeks Interest of Creek Indians," *Atlanta Independent*, Sept. 6, 1923.

210. Barnett, "Dead and Courage," *Chicago Defender*, Jan. 25, 1919.

211. Johnson's father was brought to the Oklahoma territory after escaping slavery, and he became the spokesman for the Indians. J. Coody Johnson once "accompanied his father to Washington [where] J. Coody Johnson became a protege of . . . Senator Ingalls. . . . He [attended] Lincoln University [in] Pennsylvania," and returned to Oklahoma. He soon "became a member of the Creek legislature [and] studied law in the office of the United States Circuit judge, then at Little Rock, Ark., and was admitted to the bar" (*ibid.*).

212. "Some Little Stories of Racial Progress," *Chicago Defender*, Feb. 23, 1918. In 1923 Johnson, representing Creek Indians in Washington, D.C., secured twenty-five thousand dollars in fees for R. W. Parmenter, his client. Parmenter was guardian for Martha Jackson, a Creek minor under the jurisdiction of the Department of Interior. "Attorney Johnson Seeks Interest of Creek Indians," *Atlanta Independent*, Sept. 6, 1923.

213. *Cohee v. Turner & Wiggins*, 37 Okla. 778, 132 P. 1082 (1913). Just when and where John Milton Turner became a lawyer is unknown. From 1871 to 1879, Turner had served as U.S. minister resident and consel general at Monrovia, Liberia. Perhaps Turner studied law in his native state of Missouri, to which he returned after serving at Monrovia. However, it is more likely that Turner was admitted to the bar in Oklahoma, where, prior to statehood, the admissions standards were less stringent. See Dillard, "James Milton Turner: A Little Known Benefactor of His People," 19 *J. of Negro History* 372, 408 (1934); J. C. Miller, *The Black Presence in American Foreign Affairs* 9, 32, 39–40 (1978). See also, *General Catalogue of the University of Michigan, 1837–1911*, at 455 (I. N. Demmon ed. 1912), reporting that after Wiggins received his law degree, he earned a master of laws degree in 1894 from Ohio State University.

214. K. M. Teall, *Black History in Oklahoma: A Resource Book* 149 (1971).

215. Wolgemuth, "Woodrow Wilson's Appointment Policy and the Negro," 24 *J. of Southern History* 457, 462 (Nov. 1958).

216. Vol. 1 *Who's Who of the Colored Race* 212 (F. L. Mather ed. 1915).

217. Letter from John Hope Franklin to author, April 30, 1985; J. H. Franklin, *Race and History: Selected Essays, 1938–1988*, at 278 (1989). Lewis, "Pioneer Recalls Early Days on Farm; Disappointments While Reading Law," *Oklahoma Eagle*, March 26, 1959, mentions the Sprague School of Law.

218. S. Ellsworth, *Death in a Promised Land* 87–89 (1982). Elisha Scott, Sr., a black lawyer from Topeka, Kansas, was also involved in these proceedings. "Noted Topeka Attorney Dies," *Topeka Capital*, April 24, 1963.

219. "Franklin, Ruffin, Boulding to Share in $25,000," *Norfolk Journal and Guide*, Dec. 11, 1926.

220. Vol. 1 *Who's Who of the Colored Race* 126 (F. L. Mather ed. 1915).

221. *Stenographic Report of the Eighth Annual Convention of the National Negro Business League* 293, at Topeka, Kansas, Aug. 14–16, 1907 (Wm. H. Davis, reporter, 1907).

222. G. Aldrich, *Black Heritage of Oklahoma* 37 (1973); Vol. 1 *Who's Who in Colored America* 112 (J. J. Boris ed. 1927). A search of the *Oklahoma Reports* found no cases, during the relevant period, in which Jones appeared before the Oklahoma Supreme Court. However in 1923, the Oklahoma Supreme Court did decide a "separate but equal" case involving the public schools of Muskogee. This is likely the case which Gene Aldrich reports Jones initiated. See *State ex rel. Gumm v. Albritton*, 98 Okla. 158, 224 P. 511 (1924). The court held that separate schools for black children within the same district were constitutional.

223. Vol. 1 *Who's Who Among Negro Lawyers* 7 (S. T. M. Alexander ed. 1945), on J. J. Bruce.

224. Letter from Andy Payne, clerk, Supreme Court of Oklahoma, to Charles S. Brown, 1958.

225. "Negro Lawyer Makes History in Oklahoma Court," *Dallas Express*, Oct. 6, 1923.

226. Arthur L. Tolson, "The Negro in Oklahoma Territory, 1889–1907: A Study of Racial Discrimination" 108 (Ph.D. diss., University of Oklahoma, 1966) (hereafter, "The Negro in Oklahoma Territory").

227. *Id.* at 108–9.

228. *Id.* at 109.

229. *Id.* at 110.

230. *Id.* at 114, quoting *Weekly Chieftain*, Aug. 19, 1910.

231. *Id.* at 145. See *Atwater v. Hassett*, 27 Okl. 292, 111 P. 802 (1910). No black lawyers were involved in this case.

232. *Guinn v. United States*, 238 U.S. 347, 360, 363–64 (1915); *Lane v. Wilson*, 307 U.S. 268 (1939).

233. McCabe was not a lawyer, but he was a strong advocate for the rights of black people. Perhaps opposition to McCabe was based on his early attempts "to establish a Negro state in Oklahoma Territory." Arthur L. Tolson, "The Negro in Oklahoma Territory," iii (Ph.D. diss., University of Oklahoma, 1966). "[McCabe's] plan in the beginning was to distribute Negroes so that a majority of black voters would be possible in each representative and senatorial district. Whenever a cabin or house became vacant, a Negro was housed by McCabe's managers. . . . Hundreds of Negro families were arriving daily [in 1891]" (Hill,

"The All-Negro Communities of Oklahoma: The Natural History of a Social Movement," 31 *J. of Negro History* 254, 261–62 [1946]). See also, "Black Oklahomans, Kansas Plan Monument to Pioneer," *Jet*, Oct. 9, 1989.

234. *McCabe v. Atchison, Topeka & Santa Fe Railway Company*, 235 U.S. 51 (1914); F. L. Styles *Negroes and the Law* 29 (1937). It should be noted that these black lawyers may have been encouraged to appeal their case to the United States Supreme Court. Judge Walter H. Sanborn at the Circuit Court of Appeals voiced compelling dissent as to the constitutionality of separate car laws. *McCabe v. Atchison, Topeka & Santa Fe Railway Company*, 186 F. 966, 977–89 (8th Cir. 1911). After the McCabe case was lost, W. E. B. Du Bois criticized (perhaps unfairly) the black lawyers in this case. He felt white lawyers should have been permitted to handle the appeal before the United States Supreme Court. In a critical editorial, Du Bois wrote, "In nine cases out of ten [a black lawyer] cannot bring experience because the color line in the legal profession gives him little chance for experience. . . . Attorney Harrison . . . was warned . . . frankly by lawyers of wide experience to associate with himself [white lawyers] so that this case might be adequately presented." Meier and Rudwick, "Attorneys Black and White: A Case Study of Race Relations Within the NAACP," 62 *J. of American History* 913, 921–22 (March 1976), quoting W. E. B. Du Bois, "NAACP Vitalizing the Fifteenth Amendment," 10 *Crisis* 197, 199–200 (Aug. 1915). See also, "NAACP Annual Meeting Reports," 10 *Crisis* 135, 137 (Jan. 1915). In 1933, Carter G. Woodson, a leading black historian, also criticized McCabe's lawyers, suggesting that they might have prevailed against the white lawyers before the United States Supreme Court if they had had a greater command of the law. C. G. Woodson, *Miseducation of the Negro* 174–75 (1933).

235. H. F. Gosnell, *Negro Politicians: The Rise of Negro Politics in Chicago* 215 (1935).

236. "Wm. H. Harrison Commended," *Nashville Globe*, Dec. 11, 1917. The resolution was signed by E. G. McAdams, president of the Oklahoma City Bar Association.

237. *The National Cyclopedia of the Colored Race* 248 (C. C. Richardson ed. 1919).

238. "Negro Lawyer Will Talk Here Tonight," *Selma Times Journal*, April 14, 1939. See also, "Judge Harrison Speaks to Colored Audience," *Mobile Daily Register*, April 19, 1939.

239. "The Passing of M. Waterloo Bullock," *The Atlanta Guardian*, Sept. 14, 1915.

240. Vol. 1 *Who's Who of the Colored Race* 214 (F. L. Mather ed. 1915).

241. "Negro Court Established," source unknown, Sept. 17, 1951 (article on file with author).

242. Vol. 1 *Who's Who of the Colored Race* 232 (F. L. Mather ed. 1915).

243. Telephone interview with Ruth Bostic (relative of Chandler's), in Washington, D.C., Sept. 6, 1975; Vol. 31 *Yale Law Journal* 299, 408, 514, 635, 747, 869, listing Atkins and Chandler as members of the editorial board. They were the first blacks at Yale University's law school to win seats on its prestigious law review. Certainly, it is unlikely that by 1921 no American law school had had two blacks on their law review at the same time.

244. Telephone interview with Jesse O. Dedmon, July 8, 1985, in Washington, D.C. Mr. Dedmon, a 1935 graduate of Howard University's law school, associated with Charles A. Chandler in the same year. Dedmon was later admitted and practiced law for several years in Washington, D.C.

245. Letter to author from Gloria R. McHugh, executive director of alumni relations, Yale University Law School, July 20, 1987.

246. See *Simmons v. Board of Education of Muskogee*, 306 U.S. 617 (1939) and J. Greenberg, *Staking a Claim* 116–23 (1990).

247. *Lane v. Wilson*, 307 U.S. 268 (1939).

248. Louis C. Taylor received his law degree from Oskaloosa College, located in Mahaska County, Iowa, in 1922. After passing the Kentucky bar, he went to Oklahoma to set up his practice. *Who's Who Among Negro Lawyers* 34 (S. T. M. Alexander ed. 1945).

249. R. Kluger, *Simple Justice* 161 (1977).

250. *Hollins v. Oklahoma*, 295 U.S. 394 (1935).

251. "J. B. Bruce," Muskogee, Oklahoma, general reference information, Oklahoma Historical Society, April 4, 1936.

252. N. J. Washington, *Historical Development of the Negro in Oklahoma* 58 (1948); J. L. Franklin, *Journey Toward Hope* 94 (1982).

253. Interview with Jesse O. Dedmon, April 3, 1985, in Washington, D.C.; "Pioneer Lawyer—Judge, Tulsa, Oklahoma," 7 *National Bar Bulletin* 2 (Aug. 1975).

254. Smith, "In the Shadow of Plessy: A Portrait of McCants Stewart, Afro-American Legal Pioneer," 73 *Minn. L. Rev.* 495, 496 (1988). (Portions of the Oregon section of this chapter are taken from this article with the permission of the *Minnesota Law Review*.)

255. "Colored Attorney May Practice Here," *The Oregon Daily Journal*, May 22, 1903. Before McCants Stewart, only one other Afro-American lawyer was known to have visited Oregon—Robert Charles O'Hara Benjamin, who practiced law in San Francisco. *Dictionary of American Negro Biography* 39, 40 (R. Logan and M. Winston eds. 1982).

256. Supreme Court Clerk J. C. Moreland admitted McCants Stewart to the Oregon bar. Stewart opened a law office at 106½ Third Street in Portland, Oregon. Smith, "In the Shadow of Plessy: A Portrait of McCants Stewart, Afro-American Legal Pioneer," 73 *Minn. L. Rev.* 495, 504 (1988).

257. "Must Labor Now," *The Oregonian*, Sept. 11, 1903. See also E. McLagan, *A Peculiar Paradise: A History of Blacks in Oregon, 1788–1940*, at 115 (1982).

258. "Quibble Fails to Win," *The Morning Oregonian*, May 16, 1903.

259. "On Trial for Assault," *The Telegram*, Oct. 17, 1904.

260. *Ibid.*

261. *State v. Browning*, 47 Or. 470, 82 P. 955 (1905).

262. *Taylor v. Cohn*, 47 Or. 538, 84 P. 388 (1906). See Hill, "The Negro as a Political and Social Issue in the Oregon Country," 33 *J. of Negro Hist.* 130 (1948) (on early history of Oregon and treatment of blacks); L. Davis, "Blacks in the State of Oregon, 1788–1974," at 11 (July 1974, mimeo) (same); Bell, *Forward—An Issue on Race Relations*, 61 *Oregon L. Rev.* 151, 154 (1982) (referring to the attempted exclusion of Afro-Americans from Oregon in its early history: "The presence of exclusion laws did not deter blacks from emigrating to Oregon in slowly increasing numbers throughout the Nineteenth Century, but their activities were strictly circumscribed by law, and their rights were almost nonexistent." See also, E. McLagan, *A Peculiar Paradise: A History of Blacks in Oregon, 1788–1904*, at 23–60 (1982), for a discussion of exclusion laws and slavery in Oregon.

263. "Costs Negro $40 to Insult Woman," *The Evening Telegram*, Apr. 29, 1907; "Negro Editor Follows Girl," *Sunday Mercury*, Apr. 27, 1907.

264. "Girl Must Tell Who Made Threat," *Portland Journal*, Apr. 1907.

265. "Stench Smells to the Heavens," *Welcome*, Apr. 27, 1907; "A Mean Black Hypocritical Howler," *People Press*, Apr. 27, 1907.

266. "Was Treated Unjustly," *The Advocate*, May 44, 1907.

267. "A City's Disgrace," *People Press*, Apr.–May 1907.

268. "White Girl Wants to Share Porter's Estate," *The Evening Telegram*, May 1, 1907; "Claims a Negro's Estate," *The Morning Oregonian*, May 1, 1907.

269. Letter from Wallace McCamant to McCants Stewart, Sept. 26, 1908. At one time, McCamant served as a justice on the Supreme Court of Oregon. See McCamant, "Toasts to Judges Wolverton and Bean," 4 *Ore. L. Rev.* 69 (1924).

270. Letter from McCants Stewart to Wallace McCamant, Oct. 7, 1908. The name of case which was the subject of this brief was *State v. Ross*, 55 Or. 450, 104 P. 596 (1909), *aff'd.* 227 U.S. 150 (1913).

271. "Attorney McCants Stewart Office Burns," *The Charleston, S.C. Southern Reporter*, July 25, 1908. *The Advocate* was the second black-owned newspaper in Portland. It was founded by several local men of Afro-American descent, including McCants Stewart. E. McLagan, *A Peculiar Paradise: A History of Blacks in Oregon, 1788–1940*, at 11 (1982).

272. "Man Weeps as Sentence Is Said," *The Oregon Daily Journal*, July 17, 1908.

273. "Test Case Filed," *The Oregonian*, July 19, 1908. See also "Negro's Sentence Declared Illegal," *The Evening Telegram*, July 22, 1908; "Van Zante Is Reversed," *The Daily News*, July 22, 1908.

274. "For National Negro Fair," *Mobile Register*, Nov. 24, 1908.

275. *Id.* "Honor Portland Lawyer in South," *The Oregon Daily Journal*, Dec. 19, 1908. While in Alabama, "McCants Stewart visited Tuskegee Institute and St. Joseph's College at Montgomery, the only Catholic institution for the higher education of the colored people in this country." At the time there were only four black priests in the world, and one of them was at St. Joseph's College. (Stewart was Catholic.)

276. "Minneapolis Man Suffers," *The Advocate*, May 29, 1909.

277. "Rev. Matthews Not Guilty," *The Advocate*, (n.d.), circa 1910.

278. "Negro Lawyer Aroused," *The Morning Oregonian*, Sept. 20, 1911.

279. "Negro Lawyer and Policeman Fight," *The Evening Telegram*, Sept. 19, 1911.

280. "Chop Suey Court Study," *The Morning Oregonian*, Oct. 3, 1911.

281. "Says Policeman Acted Cruelly," *Portland Daily Journal*, Sept. 20, 1911.

282. *The Morning Oregonian*, Sept. 21, 1911.

283. "Wilson Is Condemned for Recent Lynchings," *The Morning Oregonian*, Dec. 14, 1914. See R. Ginzburg, *100 Years of Lynchings* 93 (1988), regarding Shreveport lynchings. In 1914, there were at least fifty-four lynchings of blacks reported in the United States. *Id.* at 94.

284. *Id.* "Wilson Is Condemned for Recent Lynchings."

285. R. Ginzburg, *100 Years of Lynchings* 267 (1988).

286. "Negroes to Make Gift," *The Morning Oregonian*, Oct. 12, 1915.

287. *Id.* In 1915 McCants Stewart worked successfully to have language excluding blacks from voting removed from the Oregon state statutes. The exclusionary language had remained in Oregon even though such provisions had been expressly invalidated by the ratification of the Fifteenth Amendment to the United States Constitution in 1870. See U.S. Const. amend. XV (1868);

E. McLagan, *A Peculiar Paradise: A History of Blacks in Oregon, 1788–1940*, at 161 (1982).

288. Letter from Ben W. Olcott to McCants Stewart, May 12, 1916. Olcott later became the governor of Oregon. *Id.* at 135.

289. "Attorney Sues Church," *The Advocate*, Jan. 20, 1917. There is no question that McCants Stewart earned his fee. The year before, he had won the church a jury verdict in the amount of $7,296. "A.M.E. Zion Church Awarded Damages," *The Advocate*, Mar. 4, 1916. See also, "Golden Rule Is Shut Out in Condemnation Suit," *The Morning Oregonian*, Feb. 26, 1916.

290. "Attorney McCants Stewart to Leave," *The Advocate*, Sept. 29, 1917.

291. Telephone conversation with Mary Katherine Stewart-Flippin (Mrs. Robert B. Flippin) of San Francisco, CA, Dec. 2, 1987.

292. "Attorney McCants Stewart to Leave," *The Advocate*, Sept. 29, 1917.

293. "Colored Lawyer to Locate in City," *Vallejo Times*, Dec. 5, 1917.

294. 85 Or. 636, 167 P. 272 (1917).

295. "Theater Sued by Negro," *The Morning Oregonian*, Sept. 17, 1917; "Color Line Causes Suit," *The Evening Telegram*, Sept. 16, 1915; "Rights to Any Seat in a Theater," *The Advocate*, Sept. 8, 1917; "Allen Theater Case," *The People's Bulletin*, Sept. 21, 1917.

296. *Taylor v. Cohn*, 47 Or. 538, 84 P. 388 (1906).

297. *Allen v. People's Amusement Co.*, 85 Or. 636, 167 P. 272 (1917); "Allen Loses Suit in Supreme Court," *The Advocate*, Sept. 15, 1917.

298. E. McLagan, *A Peculiar Paradise: A History of Blacks in Oregon, 1788–1940*, at 115 (1982).

299. *Ibid.*; see letter from Arthur S. Benson to Charles S. Brown, May 29, 1958.

300. *Ibid.* (Benson letter).

301. "Portland Woman Admitted to Bar," *East Tennessee News*, Sept. 22, 1921. See also "Oregon Woman Admitted to the Bar," *Afro-American*, Sept. 30, 1921.

302. E. McLagan, *A Peculiar Paradise: A History of Blacks in Oregon, 1788–1940*, at 115 (1982).

303. *Id.* at 141.

304. Letter to author from Edward J. Reisner, assistant dean, University of Wisconsin Law School, Dec. 2, 1987; letter to author from Scott F. Burson, reference librarian, University of Washington Law Library, March 6, 1986, referring to the 1930 *Martindale American Law Directory* 1112.

305. E. H. Mumford, *Seattle's Black Victorians 1852–1901*, at 95 (1980).

306. Letter from Robert Holstein, clerk, the Supreme Court of Washington, to Charles S. Brown, May 1, 1961; letter from Hazel E. Mills, Washington Room librarian, to Charles S. Brown, May 9, 1961, citing letter to Mills from Robert Holstein, concerning the date of William's admission to the Supreme Court of Washington; letter from Elizabeth S. Gilbert, to Charles S. Brown, May 10, 1961.

307. Letter from Hazel E. Mills to Charles S. Brown, May 9, 1961.

308. *Ibid.*, citing the April 14, 1892, editions of the *Seattle Post Intelligencer*.

309. Letter from K. L. Buck, assistant reference librarian, Seattle Washington Public Library, to Charles S. Brown, Oct. 9, 1958, citing *Seattle Press Times*, May 18, 1895; letter from Robert Holstein, clerk, Supreme Court of Washington, to Charles S. Brown, Sept. 25, 1958; letter from Mildred Hill,

reference librarian, Washington State Library, to Charles S. Brown, Oct. 16, 1958, citing the *Daily Olympian*, May 31, 1895, at 3, col. 1.

310. *Who's Who in Religious, Fraternal, Social, and Commercial Life on the Pacific Coast* 148–49 (1926–1927) (posthumous reference).

311. *Ibid.*

312. E. H. Mumford, "Seattle's Black Victorians Revising a City's History," 2 *Portage* 17 (Fall/Winter 1980–1981).

313. *Ibid.*

314. *Ibid.*

315. *Ibid.*

316. *Who's Who in Religious, Fraternal, Social, and Commercial Life on the Pacific Coast* 148–49 (1926–1927). In 1901 Hawkins opened his office to younger black lawyers, such as Andrew R. Black, an 1899 Howard University law graduate. E. H. Mumford *Seattle's Black Victorians, 1852–1901*, at 98 (1980).

317. *Id.* at 148 (*Who's Who*).

318. *Ibid.* Letter to author from Scott F. Burson, Jan. 2, 1986. William McDonald Austin was also a member of the 1902 law class. After he was graduated from the University of Washington's law school, he "went to Manila, the Philippines, to practice law." *Id.* at 141 (*Who's Who*).

319. Vol. 1 *Who's Who in Colored America* 154 (J. J. Boris ed. 1927).

320. Letter to author from United States District Judge Jack E. Tanner, Aug. 15, 1985.

Chapter 10

National White and Black Bar Groups and the State Black Bar Groups

Thus far, this book has focused primarily on the individual role of the black lawyer in the cause of emancipation. Although general reference has been made to the participation of black lawyers in predominantly white state bar groups, this chapter deals directly with the black lawyers' struggles within such groups, and their efforts to forge their own groups when their work from within proved fruitless.

This chapter begins with a discussion of the American Bar Association (ABA) and its official exclusion of black lawyers for sixty-six years. It also discusses the National Association of Women Lawyers and the Federal Bar Association, each of which excluded blacks for decades (for forty-four and twenty years, respectively). Finally, I deal here with the open membership policy of the National Lawyers' Guild.

White Bar Groups

Black lawyers were not present in Saratoga, New York, when the American Bar Association was organized in 1878, one year after the end of Reconstruction and thirty-four years after the first black lawyer was admitted to practice law in the United States. The initial constitution of the ABA contained no race bar, but, the unspoken assumption at the time was that black lawyers would not be able to "advance the science of jurisprudence, promote the administration of justice . . . uphold the honor of the profession of law [or] encourage cordial intercourse among the members of the American Bar."[1] The issue of whether blacks were qualified to join the ABA did not surface officially until 1912, when it was learned that three black lawyers were already members.

Between 1910 and 1911, William Henry Lewis and Butler Roland

Wilson, both of Boston, Massachusetts, and William R. Morris, of Minneapolis, Minnesota, were admitted to membership in the ABA.[2] Each of these lawyers was highly educated and well known beyond the borders of his state. In 1911 President William Howard Taft appointed Lewis, an 1895 Harvard University law graduate, assistant attorney general of the United States. Lewis was not only the first lawyer of his race to hold this position, he was the highest-ranking black public official in the history of the nation. Wilson, meanwhile, an 1884 law graduate of Boston University, was a respected private practitioner in Boston, as was William R. Morris of Minnesota, one of the first black lawyers admitted to the bar in that state.

In 1912 word spread across the ABA that it had admitted three black lawyers. Predictably, opposition to their membership was strongly voiced by Southerners. Asserting that the ABA was a social organization, Southern ABA members claimed that "it was unwise to admit colored men to membership."[3] They also claimed that these black lawyers should be expelled from the ABA for failing to identify themselves as black on their membership applications.[4] Southern opposition to black membership in the ABA grew to such an extent that the executive committee, which had admitted Lewis, Wilson, and Morris, was forced to submit the question of their qualification to the general membership during the 1912 annual convention held in Milwaukee, Wisconsin.

Some members and federal administrators hoped that Lewis, Wilson, and Morris would resign from the ABA to avoid embarrassment. Wilson refused to resign, but Morris complied. Lewis, the most visible of the three, felt pressures from his superiors at the Department of Justice. But he too held firm: "the President of the United States might have his resignation as assistant attorney general, but . . . his resignation from the Bar Association could not be secured at any cost."[5] In an election year, Lewis's refusal to resign from his post presented a most delicate and politically sensitive question for the Taft administration. The eyes of black Republicans throughout the country, and particularly in the South, were on the administration.

In January 1912, eight months before the annual ABA convention was to be held, George Wickersham, the attorney general of the United States, wrote a letter to the ABA expressing opposition to its attempts to disqualify Lewis as a bona fide member. The main reason advanced by Wickersham was that Lewis's status as assistant attorney general of the United States was sufficient basis to qualify for ABA membership. Indeed, how could Wickersham justify his own qualifications for membership, other than on the basis of race, if he denied the superlative qualifications of Lewis? In addition Wickersham stated that "it may be that some of the members of the association prefer not to have a colored man as a fellow member. But the constitution of the association makes no such discrimination."[6] Wickersham threatened to resign from the ABA over the Lewis incident, but not because of the larger race issue. Wickersham simply believed that Lewis had met the minimum qualifications for membership under the association's constitution.[7]

The opposition of Attorney General Wickersham and others did not prevail during the ABA's annual convention in Milwaukee in August 1912. A compromise resolution was adopted requiring black applicants to be identified as black by state officers of the ABA when submitting their applications to the Executive Council. The resolution read:

Whereas, Three persons of the colored race were elected to membership in this Association without knowledge upon the part of those electing them that they were of that race, and are now members of the Association.

Resolved, that as it has never been contemplated that members of the colored race should become members of this Association, the several local councils are directed that, if at any time any of them shall recommend a person of the colored race for membership, they shall accompany the recommendation with a statement of the fact that he is of such race.[8]

Prior to the presentation of the resolution to the assembly, J. M. Dickerson of Tennessee, the presenter, rose to offer his support, reminding the assembly that the race issue was an impending crisis. Dickerson asked the assembly to maintain its "usefulness and honor of the profession"[9] by adopting the resolution.

Dickerson did not directly discuss the admission of the three black lawyers to the ABA, nor did he want the issue discussed. According to his remarks, "the individual members here [would] need no enlightenment to guide them in what they deem to be the right course. Discussion might do much harm."[10] William MacChesney, of Illinois, seconded the resolution, "in the spirit that has been expressed by [Dickerson],"[11] and reminded the assembly that the "Southern view" on race was shared by "some of the gentlemen" of the North. The spirit of the resolution, he said, was not "narrow, partisan or sectional."[12] The resolution was quickly adopted.[13]

The resolution placed a cloud over these three black lawyers' rightful claim to membership. While much credit must be given to Wickersham for his efforts on behalf of the nation's first and highest ranking black official, one historian notes, "What Wickersham did was something less than heroic."[14] The compromise that passed was satisfactory to Southerners who could now veto future applications of black lawyers. Wickersham had helped the ABA to reach a compromise that avoided alienating the South in an election year at the same time that it avoided losing black political support through Lewis's expulsion.[15]

After the ABA's Milwaukee convention, it was generally understood that Lewis, Wilson, and Morris would be the last black lawyers admitted to membership. However, the policy of excluding black lawyers from the ABA was not universally endorsed at the state level. In 1925 George H. Woodson, a prominent black lawyer in Iowa, disclosed that he had "several times [been] extended an invitation . . . to present his application for membership [to the ABA]. Woodson never [did] so because he [was] opposed to arousing the question of race needlessly."[16] At least one black lawyer was admitted to the ABA between 1912 and 1929: T. Gillis Nutter, a black lawyer in West Virginia who was admitted in 1929,[17] although, again, it is not likely that the association was aware that he was black. Except for Lewis and Nutter, then, the ABA remained virtually all-white until 1943.[18]

In 1938 a new generation of Northern white lawyers began to agitate for the admission of black lawyers to the ABA. Joseph C. Thompson, a member of the New York bar, argued that "the American Bar Association ought to admit Negro lawyers or rename itself the American White Bar Association." Arthur Garfield Hays, the general counsel of the American Civil Liberties Union, threatened to resign from the ABA "unless some action is soon taken so that Negroes may be admitted to membership." The positions of these men were widely reported by the press.[19] Ruth Weyand, a white woman lawyer employed at the National Labor Relations Board, lobbied segregationists to support the admission of blacks to the ABA.[20]

In 1942 the ABA's exclusion policy came under renewed criticism from a coalition of white and black lawyers. Meanwhile, the black press continued its almost fifty-year objection to the ABA's racist admissions policy, calling it "the antithesis of democracy and humility," "judicial snobbery," and a "travesty upon Americanism."[21] The ABA insisted that no provision of its constitution barred blacks from membership, but offered no explanation as to why all applications of black lawyers were denied. The real mechanism for the exclusion of blacks from the ABA was its governing process. This process gave the board of governors veto power over any application opposed by two or more governors. The Southern governors voted against any black applicants, and the ABA as a whole did nothing to alter this process. Responding to an invitation to join the ABA, Judge John Beardsley, of Los Angeles, questioned George M. Morris, the president of the ABA, about its Jim Crow policy, which he opposed. In a letter to Beardsley, Morris defended the ABA's policy, noting that the Negro racial problem was of great importance to governors in the South, who could cast two negative votes in the board of governors to prevent membership.[22] When word of Morris's letter reached the black community, *The Pittsburgh Courier*, among others, refused to allow the ABA to shift culpability solely to its white Southern governors. The ABA, the paper pointed out, "is by no means a Southern organization."[23]

In 1942 the stage was set for another dramatic effort to break the ABA's color bar. In that year, Francis Ellis Rivers, a Columbia University law graduate and a respected district attorney in Manhattan, applied for ABA membership. When the ABA declined to act on Rivers's application, the "New York membership committee [of] the Association of the Bar of New York appointed a special committee headed by Samuel Seabury to determine whether race discrimination existed."[24]

Upon hearing of the rejection of his application, Rivers (who, ironically, was vacationing in Saratoga, New York, where the ABA had first organized), stated, "It doesn't surprise me that my application for membership in the American Bar Association has been pigeonholed."[25] In the meantime, however, New York's Governor Thomas Dewey appointed Rivers to fill a vacancy at the city court.[26] The rejection of Rivers's application spurred resignations from within the ABA, among them that of Judge Jonah J. Goldstein, of New York. There were also threats of resignation in Philadelphia.[27] Other resignations by distinguished New York lawyers followed, including those of Arthur Garfield Hays, Herman Hoffman (president of the New York County Criminal Courts Bar Association), and Commissioner William B. Herlands, of the New York Department of Investigations.[28]

The color bar was not broken until the sixty-sixth annual meeting of the ABA in 1943. On August 26, 1943, the ABA, noting no racial exclusionary provision in its constitution, stated: "*Resolved*, that it is the sense of this meeting that membership in the American Bar Association is not dependent upon race, creed or color."[29] The ABA amended its by-laws to require four, instead of two, negative votes to reject membership, thus diluting the voting strength of the Southern governors. The by-law amendment almost assured the admission of blacks to the ABA.[30] After this resolution, Judges Francis Ellis Rivers and Judge James Samuel Watson became the first black lawyers knowingly admitted to the ABA in thirty-one years.[31] However, the Dallas Bar Association sought reconsideration of the new rules, for they believed black membership lowered "the dignity of the bar."[32] The exclusion of blacks from the ABA stigmatized black lawyers in general. The ABA was a center of power and influence, not only in legal circles but in political circles as well. After all, since its founding, most of the justices of the United States Supreme Court and the federal courts had come from the ABA's ranks. Indeed, presidents of the United States, several members of Congress, attorneys general at the federal and state levels, and "most of the leading legislators and judges of the land" were members of the ABA.[33]

Black lawyers, though members of the various bars of their states, were not members of the social circles that influenced their profession. Exclusion from the ABA robbed black lawyers of professional development, for they were not privy to the inside legal and political information disseminated and shared by ABA members of its gatherings; they were denied a forum within which to make critical contacts with white ABA lawyers in other states, and thus could not begin to develop interstate law practices. Finally, since blacks were also excluded from the social clubs to which the judges belonged and because they lived in segregated communities, they were unable to make contact with judges and courthouse personnel outside of the courthouse itself.

In 1944 George Marion Johnson, Howard University's law dean, summed up what was apparent to many: "It was understood throughout the country, that [the ABA] did not want Negro lawyers as members."[34] Although the ABA had opened its doors to white women in 1918,[35] no black women lawyers are known to have been admitted to the bar by the close of 1944.

The National Association of Women Lawyers (NAWL) was founded in New York City in 1899, twenty-seven years after Charlotte E. Ray became the first black woman admitted to the bar in the United States. While there were few black women lawyers in 1899, the paucity of their ranks made no difference: The NAWL simply followed the exclusionary admissions policy of the ABA.

It was not until 1943 that the NAWL admitted its first black members. During the forty-fourth annual meeting held in Chicago, Illinois, "the matter of drafting a new constitution was being considered." Bess Sullivan Heptig, of Chicago,[36] submitted "the historic resolution" that "recommended that all women lawyers who are qualified and in good standing with the bar associations of their states should be admitted to membership . . . without regard to race, creed or color."[37] The NAWL adopted this policy within days of the lifting of the race bar by the ABA.[38]

Heptig's action was taken after Daphne Roberts (Mrs. Robert W. Leeds), of Atlanta, Georgia, succeeded Marguerite Rawalt as president of the NAWL. Rawalt, who was about to become president of the Federal Bar Association, was in the midst of a heated battle to slow the admission of black lawyers in that group.[39] Immediately after the Heptig resolution was adopted, Georgia Jones Ellis, Edith Sampson, and Sophia B. Boaz, all black and all from Chicago, were admitted to national membership in the NAWL.[40]

The Federal Bar Association (FBA) was founded in Washington, D.C., in 1925, for lawyers and judges in the service of the federal government. The FBA's first constitution restricted membership to "any white person of good character."[41] The first discussion of the "color bar" by the Federal Bar Association took place in 1930. During the October 1930 meeting of the executive council, Henry Ward Beer insisted that "further changes [in the FBA constitution] would have to be made to include the membership of colored lawyers."[42]

The real agitation to open the FBA was precipitated not at the national level, but within the local chapters—principally by the FBA chapters of New York, New Jersey, and Connecticut. In the spring of 1931, despite public criticism by the New York chapter, the executive council "unanimously" recommended "not to disturb that provision of the constitution relating to color."[43] In the meantime, the New York chapter had already admitted black lawyers to membership, an action that was criticized by the council. In fact, the council refused to recognize the membership of any black lawyers "accepted in the past or who may be accepted in the future."[44] The actions of the New York chapter led the executive council to recommend that no members "be accepted without first receiving the approval of the Membership Committee of the national body."[45] Indeed, the council threatened reorganization of the New York chapter if it persisted in violating the FBA constitution regarding qualifications for membership.[46]

The threat of reorganization did not deter the New York chapter. In fact, "considerable publicity [was] given out by the New York branch, criticizing the Association for its . . . white members only"[47] policy. New York admitted "several colored attorneys."[48] By June 1931, a chapter "locally known as the Federal Bar Association of New York, New Jersey and Connecticut" was in hot water with the national office. The FBA dissolved the chapter and organized another one.[49] But the race question lingered on through 1936, at which point the executive council determined that all applicants for membership designate their race on the FBA application.[50]

In the spring of 1942, a group of white government lawyers conspired to finish what the New York chapter of the FBA had begun twelve years earlier—to qualify black lawyers for admission to the FBA. As members of the Bill of Rights Subcommittee of the War Work Committee of the FBA, they had an official base from which to push for a change in the FBA's race policy. In 1942 Judge Justin Miller,[51] chairman of the War Work Committee, asked the executive council what its attitude was "on the subject of minorities."[52] The council attempted to avoid the issue, though Judge Miller had made clear that his committee intended to submit the names of black lawyers for membership.[53] The

Bill of Rights Subcommittee of the War Work Committee wasted no time in pressing its demands. The subcommittee membership, made up of eight young but influential lawyers, requested a hearing before the executive council on the admissions questions.[54]

On December 9, 1942, Judge Justin Miller made a formal request to the executive council to hold a hearing concerning the admission of black lawyers. The matter was considered during the December 14, 1942, meeting of the council, which determined that such a matter was "outside of the duties and functions of the Subcommittee" as determined by the council. "No useful purpose," the council went on, "would be served by such hearing at this time."[55] While the FBA executive council was resisting the efforts of the War Work Subcommittee, the subcommittee quietly found a black lawyer at the Department of Justice to apply for membership: Louis Rothschild Mehlinger, a sixty-year-old graduate of Howard University School of Law.[56]

Other black lawyers were also contacted by the subcommittee to apply for membership. These recruitment efforts were difficult, because the number of black lawyers in the federal government could be counted on two hands. However, George W. Crockett, Jr., Louis Rothschild Mehlinger, Sidney Arlington Jones, Jr., and Walter Arthur Gay, Jr., gave their applications to members of the subcommittee. Louis Rothschild Mehlinger, a seventeen-year veteran at the Department of Justice and a captain in World War I, was chosen to be the key "guinea pig" at the FBA.[57] The strategy for Mehlinger's admission was planned by Ruth Weyand and other members of the Bill of Rights Subcommittee in the official dining room of the Department of Justice. Here, Weyand describes the planning session:

Lunch was had in the elegant wood panelled offices at the Department of Justice in the offices of Assistant Attorney General Wendell Berge. . . . In addition to Assistant Attorney General Berge, the committee included four other top Department of Justice officials. . . . At the luncheon we were frank with Captain Mehlinger. We were inviting him to join us in a battle which would most certainly be embarrassing and possibly costly to him while the other of us risked nothing by our endeavor. Although we would do our best to insure success, we couldn't promise it. Captain Mehlinger expressed himself as fully willing to participate in the project.[58]

After the meeting, demands for a hearing on Mehlinger's application for membership were renewed by the subcommittee. In early 1943, a divided executive council agreed to hold a special meeting on the race issue.[59] The stage was set for the hearing in December 1943 when the *Atlanta Daily World* reported that Francis Biddle, attorney general of the United States, threatened to resign his FBA membership if people like Louis Rothschild Mehlinger continued to be turned down.[60] In addition, the Philadelphia branch of the FBA threatened to publicly censure the national leaders of the association if the council refused to act on the application of Walter Arthur Gay, Jr., a 1929 University of Pennsylvania law graduate. Since 1934, Gay had served as assistant United States district attorney in Philadelphia.[61]

On February 14, 1944, John Peter Barnes, Jr., presented the applications of George W. Crockett, Jr.,[62] an attorney in the Department of Labor; Louis Rothschild Mehlinger,[63] an attorney in the Department of Justice; Sidney Arlington Jones, Jr.,[64] an attorney in the Department of Labor; and Walter Arthur Gay, Jr.,[65] an assistant United States attorney, to the executive committee. A hearing was held regarding the admission of these "colored attorneys" to the FBA.[66] After all sides were heard on the issue, a curious statement was entered into the minutes, despite the whites-only qualification stated in the FBA's constitution. Douglas Hartman, a member of the executive council, "pointed out that no question of policy arose in this entire controversy since nothing in the Constitution and By-laws of this Association excluded people because of race. That the only hurdle any colored person had to jump to obtain admission was the individual votes of 75% of the council, a condition precedent to the admission of anyone."[67] No action was taken on the application of the four black lawyers during the February 1944 meeting.

Tom Campbell Clark succeeded Marguerite Rawalt as president of the FBA in 1945.[68] At the time, Clark, who in 1949 would become a member of the United States Supreme Court, was assistant United States attorney general in charge of the criminal division. The applications of the four black lawyers remained in limbo as he assumed office, but other applications by black lawyers, no doubt stimulated by the publicity of the hearings, were submitted to the executive council for approval. That race was still a qualification for FBA membership is evident in Clark's action in returning the application of James W. Johnson, a black lawyer in New York. Johnson, Clark pointed out, failed to "fill in the line where it says 'Race (White, Colored, Other).'"[69] Clark instructed Robert Roy Dann, Johnson's white sponsor, to "fill in 'colored.'"[70]

It is not entirely clear whether all four of the black applicants were eventually admitted to the FBA. However, on January 20, 1945, Tom C. Clark appointed a special committee to determine if Louis Rothschild Mehlinger, a black lawyer of "mixed parentage," qualified for membership.[71] On January 27, 1945, the special committee unanimously determined that Mehlinger was "qualified for membership" and recommended that "his application be accepted and approved,"[72] making Mehlinger the first black member of the Federal Bar Association in 1945.[73] The work of the FBA's subcommittee must be credited with Mehlinger's admission.

Information concerning the early activity of black women in the Federal Bar Association is incomplete. However, Marjorie McKenzie, a 1939 graduate of Robert H. Terrell Law School, was among those critical of the FBA's color bar. In 1943 McKenzie stated that "[i]t is inconceivable that government officials who enact Compliance with the laws of the land . . . should so flaunt its stated democratic principles by continued discrimination in their association."[74] Margaret Bush Wilson appears to be the first black woman to assume membership at a local FBA affiliate. Wilson, a 1943 graduate of Lincoln University School of Law in Jefferson City, Missouri, was hired by the Rural Electrification Administration after completing her legal studies. She became a member of the FBA in 1945.[75]

The National Lawyers' Guild (NLG) was founded in 1937. The NLG was considered a liberal lawyers' group because it accepted members without regard to race. However, a few months after the NLG was organized, its race policy proved ambiguous for William Carroll Hueston, a black lawyer from Washington, D.C. Hueston raised the question of the eligibility of black lawyers for NLG membership during the organization's first annual meeting. The NLG announced that it had no exclusionary race policy. In a letter to Hueston, the NLG's chairman, Frank P. Walsh, clarified the point: "One of the reasons for the formation of the new bar organization was the fact that Negroes were excluded from the American Bar Association."[76]

At least thirteen black lawyers from three cities attended the NLG's first annual meeting. These lawyers were all respected members of the National Bar Association, the black equivalent of the American Bar Association. The extent to which the NLG was open to black lawyers was reported to other black lawyers, including Charles Hamilton Houston, of New York; Thurgood Marshall and Josiah Henry, of Baltimore, Maryland; Raymond Pace Alexander and Fitzhugh Lee Styles, of Philadelphia, Pennsylvania; and Howard University law professor William E. Taylor, of the District of Columbia.[77] And the NLG made good on its pledge to black lawyers. During the first annual meeting, Charles Hamilton Houston was elected second vice-president of the New York chapter. Houston's election made him the first black lawyer to hold office in a nationally affiliated association founded by white lawyers.[78]

Although the NLG's secretary, Mortimer Reimer, was designated to recruit black lawyers to the group, initially few black lawyers sought membership.[79] Such resistance to the NLG may have been due to skepticism about white law organizations, given the history of the ABA and other state bar groups. Black lawyers may also have worried about the NLG's liberal bias and its effect on their legal reputations.[80]

Nevertheless, in 1939 several black lawyers—among them Theodore Moody Berry, of Cincinnati, Ohio; Belford V. Lawson, of Washington, D.C.; and Edward Toles, Will Robinson, and Charles Wilson, of Chicago, Illinois—attended the NLG's third annual meeting.[81] During this meeting the NLG elected Earl B. Dickerson, assistant attorney general of Illinois, and Hubert T. Delany, a member of the New York City Tax Commission, to its national board. The presence of these two black lawyers on the board was a first for a national white law group.[82]

The third annual meeting of the NLG was a significant event for black lawyers. They were not only invited as guests, but participated on panel discussions as well. For example, William Robert Ming, Jr., a professor at Howard University's law school, and Hubert T. Delany led a discussion on public utility law.[83] The meeting closed with a call for "unity of all racial minorities" from Stanley M. Isaac, borough president of Manhattan, and Mortimer Hays, president of the New York chapter of the NLG. Hubert T. Delany, Earl B. Dickerson, and Dean William Henry Hastie were subsequently elected to the NLG's national executive committee.[84]

Between 1941 and 1943, the NLG joined the National Bar Association in its struggle to expose racial discrimination in the Army and Navy.[85] The group also supported President Franklin Roosevelt's appointment of Earl B. Dickerson to the Committee on Fair Labor Practice in the Office of Production Management,[86] and it worked to eliminate the race bar at the Federal Bar Association.[87] Finally, the NLG leadership made efforts to forge a working relationship with such black organizations as the NAACP.[88]

The law faculties of Howard and Lincoln universities supported and participated in the legal activities of the NLG. In 1941 William E. Taylor, the dean of Lincoln University's law school, praised the NLG for its stand "against the fascist powers" and offered NLG "the full cooperation of the staff of my Law School . . . for aiding the President of the United States in his foreign policy."[89] Meanwhile, barred from scholarly participation in virtually all professional legal journals, Earl B. Dickerson, William Henry Hastie, Charles Hamilton Houston, and Thurgood Marshall became associate editors of the *Lawyers' Guild Review*.[90]

The extent to which black women lawyers were drawn to NLG membership is less certain. However, Georgia Jones Ellis, of Chicago, was a member of the NLG in 1943.[91]

Black National Bar Groups

The founding of the National Negro Business League (NNBL) by Booker T. Washington in 1900 offered the first opportunity for black American lawyers to meet as a group on a national basis. Initially, black lawyers, like other black professionals, were drawn to the NNBL because of their beliefs in the ideals of Booker T. Washington, the league's president. The group also offered black lawyers an opportunity to meet black capitalists and to develop corporate law practices. Finally, the NNBL enabled black lawyers to form a network with common aims and objectives on a nationwide basis.

In 1900, during the NNBL's organizational meeting held in Boston, Massachusetts, Giles Beecher Jackson, a black lawyer from Richmond, Virginia, was elected vice-president of the group.[92] Andrew F. Hilyer, a black lawyer-businessman from Washington, D.C., was invited to deliver a paper that was published in the convention proceedings.[93] The NNBL was essentially an association of affiliate groups as well as a convention of individual members. For example, during each annual meeting, various business associations made up of pharmacists, morticians, real estate brokers, and bankers would attend the annual meeting and report on the progress made in their areas. Black lawyers were natural members of the NNBL because many of them doubled as real estate brokers and bankers, and many of them represented non-lawyer members of the NNBL. Still, these men were lawyers first and apparently saw the need to unite to strengthen their professional base and to discuss the special problems associated with being a black lawyer. While it is not altogether clear how a lawyers' auxiliary to the NNBL was formed, it was probably the idea of Josiah Thomas Settle, a respected member of the Tennessee bar and a strong supporter of Booker T. Washington. Settle played a key role in the formation of the first state colored bar association in Greenville, Mississippi, in 1891.[94]

The black lawyers' auxiliary of the NNBL was formed in 1909 at Little Rock, Arkansas. It was named the National Negro Bar Association (NNBA).[95] The initial membership of the NNBA was almost exclusively from the South, although it claimed members from as far west as Tulsa, Oklahoma.[96] Northern black lawyers, such as William Henry Lewis, remained cool to the NNBL and NNBA because they were not comfortable with the racial accommodationist views of Booker T. Washington.[97] Southern lawyers were elected as the NNBA's first officers. Josiah Thomas Settle, assistant attorney general of Shelby County, Tennessee, was elected president; Perry Wilson Howard, of Jackson, Mississippi—a powerful national committeeman of the Republican Party—was elected secretary; and Scipio Africanus Jones, of

Little Rock, Arkansas—one of the most senior black lawyers in the nation—was elected treasurer.[98]

A year after the NNBA was formed, one of its members reported to the NNBL on his experiences as a lawyer in Vicksburg, Mississippi. W. E. Mollison reported that he maintained a private practice and defended many blacks and whites in capital cases.[99] He said that he had "seen many grand juries empaneled [since 1899] in which a majority of the members were Negroes."[100] Mollison's observations concerning the composition of Southern juries gave a rare glimpse of the trial strategy of black lawyers in the South: "I never bank on races in the trial of my criminal cases. I would just as soon have a white man who blinks at me, as a black man who does not like me, on the jury."[101]

From 1909 to 1913, Josiah T. Settle, Perry Wilson Howard, and Scipio A. Jones controlled the direction of NNBA, despite the election in 1911 of J. Madison Vance, of New Orleans, Louisiana, as vice-president, and W. T. Andrews, of Sumter, South Carolina, as treasurer.[102] There is no question that the relationship between the NNBL and the NNBA was mutually beneficial to both groups. The black lawyers' aim was to defend and serve the black businessman. The black businessman's aim was to promote and retain the services of the black lawyer. During the thirteenth annual meeting of the NNBL, Josiah T. Settle justified the interdependence of both groups in a speech:

You are acquiring property rapidly, and you need a Negro lawyer to examine your titles; you need him to say when you put your hard-earned money into land, that the title is perfect. . . . When you engage in corporate business, when your stockholders who make up that corporation put money into it, you want a Negro lawyer to see that your articles of incorporation are properly drawn and filed.[103]

Fourteen black lawyers representing eight states attended the NNBL's annual meeting in 1913. It was during this meeting that the first woman participated in NNBA deliberations. Lutie A. Lytle-Cowan, of New York City, the nation's first female law professor, was well received at the meeting.[104] At the close of the meeting, William H. Harrison of Oklahoma City, Oklahoma, was elected president of the NNBA.[105]

By the 1914 annual meeting of the NNBL-NNBA, the membership of the NNBA had risen to twenty-five. Meeting in Muskogee, Oklahoma, the members "took stock of what little capital we have, and told how well we are getting along in business . . . and practical questions affecting the legal rights and civil rights opportunities of our people."[106] Perry W. Howard, of Jackson, Mississippi, spoke of what appeared to be a broader mission of the NNBA: "We are working together . . . to make ourselves valuable . . . to members of our race who have rights, liberties, and properties to protect, and to be of service to them in all of their business relations. . . . We are helping to organize them in the straight and narrow path of legal requirements." Howard's statement defined the purpose of the affiliation of black lawyers with the NNBL as allowing the individual lawyer to learn about and share information on issues in order to increase his or her economic well-being and to protect the race.

Howard's dual vision of the NNBA's role was clear. The bar group was to be but another extension of the individual lawyer, giving service to the race wherever possible in the nation.[107] At the close of the 1914 meeting, Perry W. Howard was elected president of the NNBA,[108] a post he held until 1923.

By 1915, the NNBL was fifteen years old. The NNBA had been an auxiliary body, meeting during NNBL annual meetings, for six of those years. During that time, the population of black lawyers in America had grown from about 728 in 1900 to 896 in 1915. Perry Howard noted that, in 1900, "the average colored attorney was paying rent and 'riding a hobby,' but to-day . . . they are owning their own homes and in many instances riding to their office in an automobile."[109] Ending its sixth year, the NNBA continued its dual role of helping to keep black lawyers "abreast of the times . . . and . . . [making] conditions better for the businessman, for . . . our race."[110]

As the First World War raged, the NNBL and NNBA discussions about racial discrimination became more probing. A special call went out from Perry W. Howard and William H. Harrison for all to attend the 1916 annual meeting of the NNBL-NNBA to be held in Kansas City, Missouri. Howard and Harrison urged black lawyers to attend the meeting, citing "political, racial, military and economic upheaval [as] a necessity for the activity of the colored bar."[111] The 1917 annual meeting of NNBA was uneventful, except that Perry W. Howard praised the NNBL's strong support of its dual objectives.[112]

In August 1918 another urgent call was issued for black lawyers to attend the NNBL-NNBA annual meeting in New Jersey. The reason for urgency was stated in the *Louisville News*:

At this time when we have an intensified migratory movement going on, international strife, humiliating segregation and proscription by a national party in power in Washington and lynchings and burnings on every hand, not to mention the comparatively tame past time of legislative enactments inimical to our welfare, it behooves us to get together and take counsel.[113]

It was during the NNBA meeting in Atlantic City, New Jersey, that the NNBL first expressed any intent to form an independent bar association.[114] The specific reason for the proposed split was not disclosed, but it was mentioned in the NNBL's formal proceedings of 1919.[115] The likely reason for the split was the realization of black lawyers that they could not function as the auxiliary of a business group, particularly a group whose historical role was not to "rock the boat." NNBA members were unmistakenly more progressive than the NNBL. The NNBA wanted to take action to combat racism in America as progressives, not as gradualists.

The sentiment to form an independent national bar group became so strong among NNBA members that Perry W. Howard appointed a nine-man steering committee to recommend a course of action on the question of severing ties with the NNBL.[116] The steering committee made its report during the 1922 annual meeting of the NNBL-NNBA. It recommended that the lawyers form their own national group. This recommendation was adopted, and the thirteen-year association of the NNBL and the NNBA ended.[117]

Chicago, Illinois, was selected as the site for the organizational meeting of the new national bar group. The black Cook County Bar Association, under the leadership of Champion J. Waring, was designated to host the meeting. The meeting was to take place in 1923. The *Chicago Defender* reported that "the officers [of the National Negro Bar Association] are especially eager to make this meeting the greatest in the history of the organization. It marks a departure. Heretofore the [group] had met at the same time and place and as an auxiliary organization of the National Negro Business League."[118] Perry W. Howard and W. Ashbie Hawkins, chairmen of the steering committee, issued a joint statement highlighting the importance of the meeting. It stated that there were "many vital problems affecting our race group, the successful handling of which is only in the power of trained attorneys, that we should be present in person and participate in the discussions in order that there may be a unanimity of action, purpose and ideas."[119]

The Chicago meeting was subsequently postponed—the date of the meeting conflicted with the trial calendars of several members and prospective members of the group.[120] For the next two years, however, colored state bar groups were organized in anticipation of the formation of a national bar group. Oddly, the focus of much of the discussions and planning for the new national bar group was concentrated in the Midwestern states of Illinois and Iowa. The National Bar Association, the successor of the NNBA, was eventually formed in Des Moines, Iowa, in 1925.

Although Booker T. Washington was not a lawyer, he and lawyer Josiah Thomas Settle must be credited with having the vision that ultimately led to the formation of the NNBA, which set in motion the first black national bar movement in the world. This movement brought the black lawyer and the black businessman together and strengthened both.

The split between the NNBL and the NNBA was unquestionably a reflection of the progressive lawyers' desire to free themselves from the conservative NNBL. After all, the NNBL remained committed to the gradualist ideas of Booker T. Washington, even after his death in 1915. However, the black bar had changed significantly since 1909. There were more black lawyers of influence in the Northern states, more colored state bar groups, more black grduates from white law schools, and more black Howard University law graduates setting up shop in the South. The real reason the NNBA declared its independence from the NNBL may have been provided by Benjamin Jefferson Davis: "Every League ought to have a businessman at its head. . . . Professional men, as a rule are not businessmen."[121]

The formation of the National Bar Association[122] was accomplished by several black lawyers. However, contemporary news accounts indicate that the NBA was formed at "the suggestion of George H. Woodson," an 1895 graduate of Howard University's law school and a leader of the Iowa Negro Bar Association.[123] In February 1925, Woodson spearheaded a resolution at the annual meeting of the Iowa Negro Bar Association which called for the creation of the NBA.[124] A committee was formed consisting of Woodson, S. Joe Brown, of Des Moines, Iowa, and Howard P. Drew, of Hartford, Connecticut. They sent "out an invitation to colored men engaged in the practice of law to meet at Des Moines, Iowa, on August 1, [1925] to organize a National American Bar Association."[125] At this time, there were approximately 1,200 "negro lawyers" in the country, none of whom qualified for membership in the American Bar Association because of their race. The publicity leading to the August meeting noted this exclusion and stated that the aim of the proposed black bar group was "to make available the benefits of the united strength of Negro lawyers in any national emergency."[126]

On August 1, 1925, black lawyers representing seven states and the Virgin Islands met in Des Moines, Iowa, to form the NBA and to elect its first national officers.[127] As expected, George H. Woodson was elected president.[128] To achieve its goal as a national bar group, the NBA was organized into seven geographical regions under the leadership of seven regional directors. These leaders formed the NBA board of directors.[129] Gertrude Elzora Durden Rush, a former president of the Iowa Negro Bar Association, was the only woman in attendance at the first NBA meeting. She was among its charter members.[130] Before the conclusion of the first annual meeting of the NBA, a special committee was formed to plan the second meeting, scheduled to be held in Chicago, Illinois.[131]

On July 29, 1926, the NBA was incorporated in Des Moines, Iowa, by George H. Woodson, S. Joe Brown, and Charles P. Howard. The articles of incorporation declared that the purpose of the NBA as a group was "to advance the science of jurisprudence, uphold the honor of the legal profession, promote social intercourse among the members of the American Bar, and protect the civil and political rights of all citizens of the several states and of the United States."[132] Less than a month after the NBA was incorporated, the group held its second annual meeting in Chicago, Illinois. At this time, nearly one-third of the black lawyers were practicing law in cities of 100,000 or more inhabitants. For its membership drive, the NBA targeted these cities.[133] In 1926, during the second annual meeting, Carl F. Phillips, of Washington, D.C., called on the NBA "to unite themselves in one solid body to fight legally the cause of the Race against unjust discrimination, prejudice and segregation."[134] William Clarence Matthews, then special assistant attorney general of the United States, "lauded the organization for its breadth, saying that unlike the American Bar Association it opens its door to all Americans of whatever creed or color."[135] Several speeches and papers were delivered during the meeting, including one delivered by Judge Albert B. George ("The Citizen and Court") and another by Alva L. Bates ("Race Prejudices and Discriminations"). Judge James A. Cobb, Robert L. Vann, and T. Emmett Stewart also were among the keynote speakers.[136] At the close of the second annual meeting, Charles H. Calloway of Kansas City, Missouri, succeeded George Woodson as the NBA president.[137]

The third annual meeting of the NBA was held in St. Louis, Missouri, in 1927. This meeting drew over one hundred black lawyers from locales as distant as the Republic of Panama. New members from Omaha, Nebraska, Shreveport, Louisiana, San Francisco, California, Newport News, Virginia, and Jacksonville, Florida, attended. Among the attendees were women lawyers Lena Olive Smith, of Minneapolis, Minnesota, and Georgia Jones Ellis and Violette Neatly Anderson, of Chicago.[138] This meeting marked the first time that a white member, John W. Finehout, a municipal court judge in St. Paul, Minnesota, attended the annual meeting.[139] Issues concerning the inequities of workman's compensation laws, discrimination in transportation, and the means to raise funds to assist members appealing cases to the United States Supreme Court dominated the meeting. The NBA established several new committees, including those dealing with "international law, legal education, professional ethics, uniform state laws, jurisprudence, law reform, discriminatory legislation, crime, legal aid, and grievances."[140] At the close of the meeting, Homer G. Phillips, of St. Louis, Missouri, was elected president of the NBA.[141]

The fourth annual meeting of the NBA was held in Chicago, Illinois, in 1928. During the keynote address, President Homer G. Phillips called for a "closer relationship between the businessmen and our lawyers," a statement which may have been made to mend the schism between the black lawyers and the National Negro Business League.[142] However, it was the electrifying speech of Howard University's president, Mordecai Wyatt Johnson, that drove home the need for the NBA and the black lawyer:

We need in the next 25 years great legal minds to carry out every legal decision handed down by the Supreme Court of the United States, protecting the humblest citizens in the smallest communities. We need men who know and interpret the law, and they must have means to carry on the cases to fight the representative battles of the poor in a peaceful way before the courts of the country in a continuous cycle of test cases.[143]

Little did Johnson know that the next twenty-five years of civil rights litigation, spearheaded by black lawyers such as Charles Hamilton Houston and Thurgood Marshall, would result in the reversal of the separate but equal doctrine of *Plessy v. Ferguson*, and in the 1954 landmark decision of *Brown v. The Board of Education*.[144] Johnson also urged the NBA to work for competency as well as status.[145] Among the resolutions passed during the meeting was one "petitioning Congress to make a re-apportionment in the House of Representatives for those states in which Negroes are disfranchised or otherwise denied rights of full citizenship."[146]

The presence of black women in American law was highlighted during the fourth annual meeting by Edith Sampson, of Chicago, Illinois. Speaking "for the 25 women attorneys in the country," Sampson commented "upon their superior preparation [and the] high public honors being conferred upon them."[147] At the close of this meeting C. Francis Stradford, of Chicago, Illinois, was elected president of the NBA, while Georgia Jones Ellis, also of Chicago, was elected assistant secretary, becoming the NBA's first woman officer.[148]

The fifth annual meeting of the NBA was held in Detroit, Michigan, in 1929. Civil rights issues continued to be the primary theme of the keynote addresses by NBA presidents. However, it was clear that the myriad of civil rights cases, the responsibility of which was being carried by black lawyers, was having an economic effect on the law practices of NBA members. The reality of the situation was that there were too few black lawyers to fight and win the war against *de jure* racism.

C. Francis Stradford concluded that it was "not enough to oppose residential segregation, disfranchisement laws and separate schools" on an individual basis.[149] This, Stradford believed, was sapping the strength of the black lawyer and making him ineffective. He urged NBA members return to their communities and to "work incessantly to put on the statute books of every state a comprehensive civil rights law [to] be tested until discrimination in all of its varied forms disappears."[150] Stradford was also quick to criticize blacks who sought the assistance of black lawyers when denied their civil rights but "[placed] their legal affairs in the hands of [white] lawyers who [had] no interest . . . in their welfare."[151]

Former president Homer G. Phillips and Judge James A. Cobb also addressed the annual meeting. Both Phillips and Cobb warned NBA members not to make the NBA a social club. Phillips instructed the group to stick to its historical agenda by providing good service to the black community and by educating them about the evils of segregation. Phillips stated that "the great momentum gained by [the NBA] should be followed through, and [the NBA], like a conquering army, should sweep away those prevalent faults of lethargy, ignorance and false notions about segregation, which faults are the besetting sins of our groups, and . . . service to the Negro Community."[152] Judge Cobb reminded the group that the Jim Crow laws and social conditions of the nation compelled NBA lawyers to be "social engineers." Cobb asserted that black citizens needed the black lawyer to force others to uphold the law and to "protect the weak and oppressed."[153]

The NBA passed resolutions condemning state-imposed restrictive covenants, lynching, peonage laws, and the white primary laws.[154] Perhaps the most important speech of the annual meeting was delivered by a non-lawyer, Bishop B. G. Vernon of the influential African Methodist Episcopal Church, a church that retained black lawyers. Bishop Vernon's praise for black lawyers was surely music to the ears of those assembled. Bishop Vernon echoed the sentiments expressed by C. Francis Stradford: "In every community where there is a first-class Negro lawyer, we are safer."[155] At the close of the fifth annual meeting, Raymond Pace Alexander of Philadelphia, Pennsylvania, was elected president. Georgia Jones Ellis was elected vice-president, becoming the highest-ranking woman in a national bar group.[156]

The sixth annual meeting of the NBA was held in 1930 at Howard University School of Law in Washington, D.C. By then, the NBA's membership had reached 221.[157] The meeting drew an unusually large number of lawyers to what was termed a "volcanic" gathering. Black lawyers attempted to address the indifferent treatment of blacks by President Herbert Hoover. The NBA appealed to its members to fight further erosion of civil rights under the Hoover administration "until all badges of inferiority as a race shall disappear."[158] Raymond Pace Alexander hammered away at the responsibilities of the black bar during his opening remarks at the annual convention:

We lawyers are the conservators of the law. We owe to [black] people, who, more than any other people are in need of our services, a duty to see that there shall be a quick end to the discrimination and segregation they suffer in their everyday activity. . . . And who, may I ask is more able to guard against further and more dangerous encroachments of the rights of the Negro than a body of well trained and well organized lawyers?[159]

Alexander also urged the NBA to establish closer ties with local black bar groups. Prior to this time, the NBA's organizational structure assumed that it spoke for all black lawyers in the nation. However, many black lawyers in the states disagreed. They faced different problems and tenuous political situations. Alexander knew that the influence of the NBA at the national level was essential in order to inform the public about the injustices of the legal system and to shield the local bar against retaliatory conduct. Hence, the NBA reaffirmed the importance of local black bar groups. These groups would stand behind the NBA's national reach, directing its members to "national rather than solely . . . local [issues] in [the] fight for justice."[160]

One of the most important statements of the sixth annual meeting was made by Francis Ellis Rivers, a member of the New York state assembly, who outlined steps for the creation and implementation of legislation to improve the plight of blacks during the Hoover administration:

The Negro lawyer must develop a sensitive and intelligent public opinion. The following technique must be developed: (1) leaders must analyze the needs of respective colored communities and determine which of the needs can be bettered by legislation; (2) leaders must confer with the groups in question and agree on what laws are necessary; (3) they must draft the legislation agreed on, and get it introduced into the legislation; (4) after the bill becomes a law, the leaders should see to it that the direct and indirect benefits of the law are given the widest publicity in order to aid in educating public opinion to that sound perspective.[161]

Here again, a respected black lawyer called upon the NBA membership not only to assess the needs of its communities, but to confer with community groups regarding the proper course of action they needed to follow to achieve their civil rights. Adherence to these steps was essential. Rivers knew that the strength of the black bar as a voice of the people was rooted in the people's understanding of the task they sought to accomplish.

Georgia Jones Ellis, one of the very few black woman lawyers in the nation, took an active role in the debates of the sixth annual meeting. As chairman of the NBA's committee on legislation, she urged the group to oppose Senate Bill 3147, introduced by Senator Arthur Capper of Kansas, which required parties to a marriage to state their nationality under oath. She viewed this as racist legislation and warned that black women "would not secure the proper protection and that illegitimate children would increase."[162] Resolutions were passed urging the federal government to enforce the criminal laws making it a crime to bar blacks from voting in statewide elections in Texas,[163] and others sought to provide apprenticeships for graduates of several law schools.[164]

At the close of the sixth annual meeting, Raymond Pace Alexander was reelected president, while Georgia Jones Ellis was reelected vice-president. The NBA elected a second woman, Louise J. Pridgeon, to the office of national secretary. The election of two women to national office was a progressive step. Yet, the election of Pridgeon was not unexpected, since she had been the first woman president of the Harlan Law Club, Cleveland's local black bar group, and the NBA often drew its leadership from the ranks of local bar leadership. Pridgeon was the second woman to head a local bar group (Gertrude Elzora Durden Rush was president of the Iowa Colored Bar Association in 1921).[165]

The seventh annual meeting of the NBA was held in Cleveland, Ohio, in 1931. This meeting drew "over a hundred prominent colored lawyers from all sections of the country."[166] The meeting and the literature published in preparation for it highlighted the prosecution of the Scottsboro Boys, who faced possible death sentences for the alleged rape of a white woman in Alabama. The case had stirred up serious racial hostility in the South. There were the usual concerns about whether these young black men could get a fair trial. The Scottsboro cases also divided the black bar on the issue of the NAACP's lukewarm financial and moral support for the International Labor Defense (ILD), an ultra-radical group that was handling the case. Some members of the NBA believed that the bar should not declare any allegiance to so-called communist groups like the ILD while others believed that the NAACP was far too meek on critical race issues. The increased number of lynchings in the South was cited as evidence that the judicial system did not protect blacks. At least, some members asserted, the ILD was taking a progressive stand against racism by defending the Scottsboro Boys. Never before had black lawyers as a group publicly declared a lack of confidence in the NAACP. The matter of supporting the NAACP or the ILD was so divisive that the issue had to be put to a vote. By a bare majority, the NBA voted not to break with the NAACP's approach in civil rights matters.[167] Clarence Darrow, a white lawyer who often defended unpopular causes, and Newton D. Baker, a former Secretary of War, were present during the heated debates, though they addressed the group on different issues.[168]

At the close of the seventh annual meeting, Jesse Heslip, of Toledo, Ohio, was elected president. The reasons why Georgia Jones Ellis was not elected are unclear, as is the question of why Louise J. Pridgeon left the leadership of the NBA. Pridgeon was replaced by another prominent woman lawyer, Ollie May Cooper, of Washington, D.C., who was elected national secretary.[169]

The eighth annual meeting of the NBA was held in Indianapolis, Indiana, in 1932. Perhaps because of the narrow vote of support for the NAACP in 1931, Walter White, the executive director of the NAACP, attended the meeting. White spoke about incompetent and unscrupulous lawyers and about the NBA's mandate to weed out such lawyers. His remarks may have been interpreted as a slap at NBA members who had voted to support the ILD the year before. White also proposed that the NBA and the NAACP agree to jointly attack discrimination in interstate commerce, unequal apportionment of school funds, and employment discrimination.[170]

The NAACP and NBA's agreement to work together to fight Jim Crow was met with even greater enthusiasm than the announcement that the popular Charles Hamilton Houston, resident vice-dean of Howard University's law school, had been selected to head the NAACP's national legal committee.[171] This committee was to formulate the uniform strategy to fight Jim Crow. The NAACP also pledged its support for the NBA's efforts to elect black judges and for the NBA's legal aid bureaus, which provided legal assistance to black citizens.[172] The NAACP's effort to win the confidence of black lawyers seems to have been successful, though there is little evidence of any follow-up efforts.

During the eighth annual meeting, the NBA invited Thomas Campbell, of Denver, Colorado, to address his concerns about the exclusion of black workers by private contractors working on the Hoover Dam project.[173] Campbell's presence at the meeting demonstrated the NBA's willingness to allow black lawyers from states with few black lawyers to address local concerns before the group, a policy that had widespread support.

At least five women attended the annual meeting in 1932. Georgia Jones Ellis was featured speaker on the program addressing "The Necessity of Universal Suffrage."[174] Several new women members, including L. Marian Poe and Helen Elsie Austin, attended the meeting, as did Ollie May Cooper, the national secretary of the NBA. At the close of the meeting, Jesse S. Heslip was reelected NBA president.

The ninth annual meeting of NBA was held in St. Louis, Missouri, in 1933. The Depression was having a devastating impact on the nation, and black lawyers were also feeling its effect. Jesse S. Heslip's keynote address was patriotic and emphasized "the need of keeping open the door of hope to every citizen of this great nation."[175] Heslip made a call for the NBA to promote the advancement of science as a way out of poverty for "the rank and file of the common people."[176] Heslip's focus on science was unique, for no other NBA president had urged this approach. Guy H. Parks, the governor of Missouri, also addressed the group,[177] and he, like many other participants, may have been embarrassed by the Jim Crow policy of the hotel at which the annual meeting was held. Because the hotel "would not permit a member of the race to use the guests' elevators," C. Francis Stradford, a former NBA president, canceled a major address that was to have been broadcast from the hotel.[178]

The number of black women at the convention increased at the ninth annual meeting. Helen Elsie Austin and Edith Spurlock Sampson were among the women in attendance. L. Marian Poe, of Newport News, Virginia, gave an address on "Women's Contribution to the Bench and Bar."[179] At the close of the meeting, E. Washington Rhodes, of Philadelphia, was elected president of the NBA.[180]

The tenth annual meeting of the NBA was held in Baltimore, Maryland, in 1934. The events of this meeting are sketchy, though a major speech was given by James C. Thomas, of New York, concerning his defense of the evangelist Father Divine. Father Divine had established a "Kingdom" at Sayville, Long Island, where whites and blacks worshiped, and he had been convicted of causing a public nuisance at this site. However, Thomas won a reversal of the conviction before the Appellate Division of the Supreme Court of New York, a feat that won him the admiration of the NBA.[181] At the close of the annual meeting, E. Washington Rhodes, of Chicago, Illinois, was reelected president.

The eleventh annual meeting of the NBA was held in Nashville, Tennessee, in 1935. Georgia Jones Ellis was the chairman of the convention committee—the first woman in the NBA's history to hold this post.[182]

The progressive membership of the NBA, who previously had voted to disassociate themselves from the NAACP, now faced a political decision of a different dimension. Charles Hamilton Houston, then special counsel to the NAACP, urged the NBA to offer legal aid to a white man under arrest in the South for organizing white and black sharecrop-

pers. In many areas of the South, individuals who attempted to organize blacks to demand higher wages and better working conditions
were considered communists. The NBA, concerned about charges by
Southerners that it was soft on communism, balked at Houston's suggestion. The strongest opposition came from its Southern members.
Webster Porter, of Knoxville, Tennessee, summarized the dilemma: "If
we endorse this plan, we will alienate our good white friends in the
South and good men on the bench who favored us in the past will be
turned against us."[183] Northern lawyers sympathetic to Porter's views
voted the proposal down.[184] This vote was a major victory for the
moderate members of the NBA, who could now count on its black
Southern members to adopt a more moderate approach on civil rights
issues.

Houston must have been perplexed when he left Tennessee, won-
dering whether this could be the same group that had criticized the
NAACP in 1930 as being meek on civil rights. But Houston did not
leave Tennessee empty-handed. He won the support of the NBA on
other matters. Houston's resolution opposing a bill pending in Congress that would establish an industrial commission on Negro affairs
received wide support from NBA members. Houston opposed the bill
because he believed that the proposed commission lacked the power to
subpoena witnesses and to compel the production of books and records
on the plight of blacks. Houston described the bill "as the vehicle for
creating another bureau to which matters vitally affecting the race can
be referred and possibly pigeonholed."[185] Houston also challenged the
NBA to mount a direct attack on segregation in public education:
"Discrimination in education is symbolic of all the more drastic discrimination which [blacks] suffer in American life. And these apparently senseless discriminations in education against [blacks] have a very
definite objective on the part of the ruling whites: to curb the young
[blacks] and prepare them to accept an inferior position in American
life without protest or struggle."[186]

The views of blacks on foreign affairs were rarely publicly articulated
in the 1930s. However, the NBA activated its committee on international law because it considered Africa of special importance to black
Americans, particularly in view of the war then raging between Italy
and Ethiopia. During the annual meeting, the Committee on International Law placed the topic of the war on the floor for debate, urging
that the NBA entreat President Franklin D. Roosevelt to pressure
Benito Mussolini to submit the war issues to arbitration. The committee also discussed Mexico's discriminatory immigration policy, which
made it difficult for blacks to enter Mexico. At the close of the meeting,
George W. Lawrence of Chicago, Illinois, was elected president. Thur-

good Marshall was elected to the post of national secretary.[187] Violette Neatly Anderson, of Chicago, was the only woman to address the group that year. She urged "our colored citizenry" to press harder "for adjudication [of] their civil rights."[188]

The twelfth annual meeting of the NBA was held in Pittsburgh, Pennsylvania, in 1936. Accounts of this meeting are sparse. The lynching of blacks was its focus, and the NBA strongly endorsed the Costigan-Wagner Anti-Lynching Bill pending in Congress. The group reelected George W. Lawrence, of Washington, D.C., to the office of president, and Thurgood Marshall was reelected national secretary.[189]

The thirteenth annual meeting of the NBA was held in Philadelphia at the University of Pennsylvania Law School in 1937. The meeting was highly substantive. The keynote address was given by Robert L. Vann, lawyer and editor of the *Pittsburgh Courier*. Vann urged "the Negro lawyer [to] take leadership in the economic life of the community."[190] Vann's views were forward-looking. He hoped that the black lawyer would advise his client to "interest himself in modest enterprises . . . so that in the next quarter century he may find himself inheriting clients of a new type."[191] Vann's speech, in encouraging more emphasis on economic concerns, reintroduced one of the dual objectives of the association's predecessor, the NNBL. Other speeches on "The Problems Confronting, and the Opportunities of, the Negro Lawyer in the North" and "The Constitutional History of the American Negro" were delivered by Raymond Pace Alexander and Nathan A. Dobbins. A. T. Walden and Earl B. Dickerson conducted a panel discussion on the "Problems Confronting the Negro Lawyer in the South."[192]

In 1937 the *New York Times* reported that an NBA study had found that there were only "1,247 Negro lawyers" in the country, which as a whole had a black population of 11,890,000. The largest number of black lawyers—225—were located in Washington, D.C. Over half of these were "sundowners," that is, professionals who worked at government jobs during the day and practiced law in the evening. New York City had 112 black lawyers, "mostly in Harlem," and the entire South had only 200.[193]

Nearly twenty resolutions were adopted at the NBA meeting in 1937. The NBA formed a legislation committee to monitor Congress on race issues; it condemned the state of Alabama for the injustices surrounding the case of the Scottsboro Boys; it endorsed the Committee on Industrial Organization; it urged black workers to join unions; and it praised the sponsors of the Costigan-Wagner Anti-Lynching Bill and the Van Nuys resolution to investigate lynchings in the United States. NBA resolutions were also passed which committed the group to increasing civil rights litigation, to cooperating with the NAACP's efforts to desegregate public higher education institutions, to condemning the federal government's allowance of restrictive covenants in resettlement projects financed or subsidized by the government, and to condemning the action of a Lancaster, Pennsylvania, common pleas judge "for his injudicious statement condoning mob violence made in open court in the sentencing of a black defendant on June 10, 1936."[194]

At the close of the meeting, William Lepré Houston, of Washington, D.C., was elected president and Thurgood Marshall was again elected as national secretary.[195] Women lawyers Ollie May Cooper, Isadora Augusta Jackson Letcher, and Eunice H. Carter attended the meeting, and Helen Elsie Austin, recently appointed assistant attorney general of Ohio, became the second woman elected vice-president of the NBA.[196]

The fourteenth annual meeting of NBA was held in Durham, North Carolina, in 1938. As usual, the president's keynote address summoned NBA members to do their duty as lawyers and to renew their commitment to the NBA. President William Lepré Houston called the NBA "the only organized force in the land capable of protecting our people, [which] must lead the way out of the darkened Valley of Oppression."[197] The role of the black lawyer as a leader in the nation was the theme of the meeting. This theme was reinforced by the remarks of Judge James Samuel Watson, of New York. Watson's speech called upon black lawyers not to view their duty as "different from any other lawyer." The individual's focus, he said, must be on becoming "the best lawyer that is in him to be." However, he also made it clear that the NBA had a role to play in the liberation of blacks from the Jim Crow world of segregation: "It is for us to open wide the gates of all schools and universities so that from the race will come intellectual achievement [which will] demand recognition of the world."[198]

During the meeting, the NBA went on record condemning the number of police brutality cases in the nation. It also noted the denial of black civil liberties in a number of categories. The NBA publicly condemned anti-Semitism for the first time during this meeting. But perhaps the most important resolution of the annual meeting urged that the president appoint blacks to "federal judgeships [and] that a Negro be appointed to the [United States] Supreme Court."[199] Thurgood Marshall, a member of the NBA and only five years out of Howard University law school, would later be named as the first black member of the high court in 1967.

Women continued to play a role in the NBA. At the close of the fourteenth annual meeting, Helen Elsie Austin was reelected vice-president. Isadora Augusta Jackson Letcher, of the District of Columbia—one of the first black women admitted to the Michigan bar—was elected assistant secretary. William Lepré Houston was reelected president.

The fifteenth annual meeting of the NBA was held in New York City in 1939. The role of the black woman in the law emerged as the major theme of the meeting, probably through the combined efforts of Helen Elsie Austin and Sadie Tanner Mossell Alexander, the first black woman graduate of the University of Pennsylvania's law school. Alexander, the assistant solicitor of Philadelphia, Pennsylvania, and one of only fifty-seven women lawyers in the nation, opened the meeting with an "informative discussion on women as practitioners of law."[200] The fact that the subject of women in law had a prominent place in the program came as no surprise: the NBA had opened its doors to women from its beginnings in 1925. Indeed, the association held the distinction of having a woman as one of its founders. Nevertheless, the subject of women as practitioners and judges had surfaced only twice before at the center stage of an NBA annual meeting.

The NBA had also been successful in extending its reach to black lawyers in Panama. At this meeting, the NBA drew the interest of Haitian lawyers as well. Percival Thoby, dean of the University of Haiti School of Law, and J. Lelio Joseph, the secretary of justice of Haiti and president of the Haitian Bar Association, attended the meeting and formed an association with the NBA.[201]

This annual meeting was generally without controversy, except for an impromptu debate that erupted between Judge James A. Cobb and Charles Hamilton Houston when Cobb resolved that communism and fascism were "just the same." When the dust settled, Charles H. Houston, who offered the view that "communism and fascism [do not] stand on the same basis," prevailed.[202] Sidney Revels Redmond, of St. Louis, Missouri, was elected president of the NBA at the close of the meeting, and women remained leaders of the group as well. Sarah Pelham Speaks, of New York, was elected vice-president, becoming the third woman to hold this post; and Marjorie McKenzie (Lawson), of Washington, D.C., was elected assistant secretary.[203]

The sixteenth annual meeting of NBA was held in Columbus, Ohio, in 1940. Immediately after Sidney R. Redmond's election as president, he broke new ground by lodging his protest against the "colored lawyer" designation printed in the *American Law Directory* published by Martindale and Hubbel. Redmond's protest was more than simply an effort to eliminate yet another race classification. It was a plea that black lawyers be able to compete in the marketplace on the basis of merit. The directory was widely used by individuals and corporations seeking legal advice and assistance, and its designations were therefore crucial. Since it is likely that more white companies than black companies used the directory, striking the race designation would eliminate one barrier for black lawyers eager to compete for corporate clients. Redmond's protest brought a favorable response. He was informed that the 1940 edition of the directory would "appear without any racial appellation."[204]

During his keynote address, Sidney R. Redmond presented an ambitious eleven-point program to confront issues of the moment. In the area of scholarship, Redmond urged the NBA to publish a law journal. He also pressed to increase the number of black lawyers on state and federal government legal staffs; to establish a free legal aid bureau to assist black citizens; to cooperate with allied organizations whose objectives promoted the welfare of blacks; and to agitate against employment discrimination in federal and state governments. Redmond also urged the NBA to wage a vigorous campaign against Jim Crow restrictions in secondary and higher education, to object to the exclusion of blacks from juries, to move to abolish discrimination in public places, and to improve the economic and ethical standards of the bar.

Redmond urged the NBA to take a stand against a segregated military, since black soldiers, like white soldiers, had shed their blood in defense of democracy.[205] The NBA determined that the Navy had the most segregated policies of all the armed services, a point that Redmond later made in a letter to President Franklin D. Roosevelt.[206] Redmond believed that the only way to alter the Navy's racial policy was for President Roosevelt to appoint a "Negro as civilian aide to the secretary of the Navy." The NBA supported Redmond's views, but he reported that no action had been taken by President Roosevelt.[207]

A number of distinguished NBA members addressed the sixteenth annual meeting. S. D. McGill, of Florida, spoke on "The Problems Facing Negro Lawyers in the South"; Joseph L. McLemore, of Missouri, spoke on the "Advantages of Law Firms"; Homer Brown, of Pennsylvania, spoke on "The Unconstitutionality of the Poll Tax." Howard University law professor Leon A. Ransom spoke on "The Role of the Lawyer in Negro Society," while Howard professor William Robert Ming spoke on the "Special Legal Problems Affecting Negro Labor," and Harry J. Capehart, of West Virginia, spoke on the question, "Whose National Labor Relations Act?"[208] Loring B. Moore, of Chicago, one of several black lawyers who compiled a brief before the United States Supreme Court that challenged restrictive covenants, spoke on that issue.[209] At the close of the sixteenth annual meeting, Sidney R. Redmond was reelected president, Sarah P. Speaks was reelected vice-president, and Majorie M. Lawson again became assistant secretary.[210]

The seventeenth annual meeting of the NBA was held in Little Rock, Arkansas, in 1941. During the opening session, Redmond reviewed the ambitious program he had first outlined in 1940. During his first term as president, Redmond had vigorously pressed his campaign to desegregate the armed forces. Redmond reported that he had appointed a special committee on legislation composed of influential black lawyers in Washington, D.C., to lobby for the passage of laws that would ban discrimination in the armed services.[211]

One of the most significant benchmarks of Redmond's administration was the creation of the *National Bar Journal*, a scholarly legal journal. For the first time in American law, black lawyers could express their own views in a scholarly, widely circulated law journal. Their essays on the law and theories of jurisprudence could now be read by and influence a wide audience of lawyers, judges, law professors, and students throughout the nation. The *Journal*, first edited by Freeman Lenore Martin, of St. Louis, Missouri, inspired members of the NBA to write about a variety of subjects that amply demonstrated the legal competence of the black lawyer as a scholar.[212] After the *Journal* was published, Redmond invited NBA members to send briefs on significant civil rights cases to the editor of the *Journal* so that they too could be published. These briefs could also be used by members to write supporting articles, or they could be used by other lawyers litigating similar issues.[213]

Redmond's plan to create free legal bureaus also found a receptive ear in the membership.[214] The legal aid movement was not new; it had existed in states such as New York since 1876.[215] But Redmond's plan to aid the black poor differed somewhat from the services provided by the Legal Aid Society. The new service was to be provided solely on a volunteer basis, by individual members at the local level. This was particularly significant for poor blacks, since most legal aid societies did not handle civil rights cases that challenged race exclusion issues.[216] Redmond's presidency demonstrated to the membership the broader role that the NBA could play in the lives of black people as well as in the area of scholarship. The highlight of the meeting came when one of the sessions "was held in the courtroom of the Supreme Court of Arkansas."[217] At the close of the annual meeting, Euclid Louis Taylor, of Chicago, Illinois, was elected president.[218]

The eighteenth annual meeting of the NBA, scheduled to be held in Chicago, Illinois, in 1942 was canceled, probably due to conditions associated with World War II.[219] However, the work of the NBA continued. During the bar year of 1942, the NBA challenged the exclusion of black lawyers from membership in the American Bar Association, criticized the federal government's failure to hire black lawyers, and continued its quest to integrate the armed services, urging the Department of War to commission black lawyers as judge advocates.

In 1942, the NBA renewed its protest against racist hiring practices within the federal government. The exclusion of black lawyers from federal service both caused economic disadvantage and hindered the black lawyer's ability to help in the war effort. In this regard, Euclid L. Taylor consulted with Earl B. Dickerson, a member of President Roosevelt's Fair Employment Practices Commission, in drawing up a plan for "the employment without discrimination of Negro lawyers in the war effort."[220] The plan was co-authored by Martin Popper, the white executive director of the National Lawyers' Guild. The NBA was careful not to appear solely interested in jobs for black lawyers. It also recommended that the government grant commissions "to Negroes in the newly created Army Specialist Service Corps,"[221] a move that would provide employment opportunities for black professionals as well as black lawyers in the federal government.

When William Henry Hastie, civil aide to the Secretary of War, resigned his post because of continued discrimination in the armed forces, the NBA stepped up pressure to have blacks hired in federal jobs. Particular pressure was applied to the Secretary of War "to place a limited number of Negro judge advocates in designated service commands."[222] The NBA was supported in its efforts by William L. Dawson, a black congressman from Chicago, Illinois.[223] The combined efforts of Earl B. Dickerson, Congressman Dawson, the National Lawyers Guild, and the NBA resulted in some success. Very soon after William Hastie's resignation, Willard B. Ransom, Happy I. Fernandes, Tosh Douglass Davidson, William Robert Ming, Jr., William A. McClain, Samuel M. Huffman, and one woman, Edith S. Sampson, were sworn into the Army Judge Advocate Generals Corps.[224] Although the Euclid L. Taylor NBA presidency was made difficult by the war, it ultimately worked to Taylor's advantage. The war itself provided him with a platform in a year during which no annual meeting was held.

The eighteenth annual meeting of the NBA was held in Baltimore, Maryland in 1943. The postponement of the annual meeting of 1942 and the publicity associated with its activities may have heightened the membership's awareness of the need for the NBA. The eighteenth meeting recorded the "biggest convention in the history of the Association with 151 in attendance, which was over 10% of all the Negro lawyers."[225] Euclid Taylor's keynote address directed the NBA to plan for "The New World and the New Law." He spoke about the new world that blacks were fighting for during World War II, and he challenged the NBA to take up the legal fight to secure equal rights on the domestic scene in the postwar era.[226] Yet the fight to eliminate *de jure* segregation by the United States Supreme Court was not to be achieved until the next decade.

During the eighteenth annual meeting, the NBA criticized the president again, this time for the "systematic exclusion from judicial appointments [of black lawyers] in the Federal Judiciary." They likewise criticized the Department of Justice for failing "to appoint qualified and competent Negro assistants to their staffs."[227] There was a general feeling at the meeting that the Department of Justice was lax in protecting the rights of black citizens, particularly "the safety and rights of Negro soldiers . . . in the southern part of the country."[228] Interestingly, Francis Biddle, the attorney general of the United States, attended the meeting. He reported on the activities of the Department of Justice, among them the appointment of Martin A. Martin, a black Virginia lawyer, to the criminal division.[229] The appointment was a first for a black lawyer.

The speeches during the annual meeting were representative of the mood of the delegates. Thurgood Marshall, speaking in his hometown of Baltimore, talked about the "New Fronts of Attack by Negro Lawyers on the War of Discrimination." Charles Hamilton Houston spoke on "Minority Rights under Fair Labor Practices Statutes," and William Henry Hastie addressed the "Legal Aspects of Racial Discrimination in the Armed Forces." Other distinguished speakers, such as Professor Leon Andrew Ransom and Francis E. Rivers, spoke on similar civil rights issues.[230]

As the meeting drew to an end, an unexpected contest for the NBA presidency emerged between Charles Hamilton Houston of Washington, D.C., and Charles W. Anderson, Jr., of Louisville, Kentucky. Because of the large number of lawyers in attendance from Washington, D.C., a Houston landslide was predicted, but the Washington delegates did not vote for him. This must have been a blow to Houston, for, after all, he was one of the most noted civil rights lawyers in the nation's history and the son of a former NBA president, William Lepré Houston. Charles Anderson, a Howard University law graduate, won the election by a small margin by capitalizing on the fact that the NBA had never elected a president from the South.[231]

Seven black women attended the annual meeting, among them Sadie Tanner Mossell Alexander, who was elected national secretary,[232] and Eunice Hunton Carter, who served as secretary to the resolutions committee.[233] Four of the seven women attending the meeting were from Washington, D.C.[234]

The nineteenth annual meeting of the NBA was held in Chicago, Illinois, in 1944. Although the facts about the meeting are sketchy, the NBA was concerned about the need for a federal voting rights statute to protect black citizens in the Southern states. The NBA pledged to seek a sponsor in Congress to propose legislation "to fix the qualification of voters in federal elections by Constitutional Amendment."[235]

At the close of the annual meeting, Charles W. Anderson, Jr., was reelected as president of NBA. Three women captured significant posts. Georgia Jones Ellis was elected to the influential executive committee; L. Marian Poe, of Newport News, Virginia, was elected assistant secretary, and Sadie Tanner Mossell Alexander was reelected national secretary.[236]

In nineteen years, the National Bar Association, the successor to the National Negro Bar Association, had come of age as an influential force in American law. Unlike other black advocacy groups that fell by the wayside, the NBA had survived by demonstrating that a national bar group was necessary to the interests of its constituents. Although recognition by the general population was slow, the NBA's willingness to take a stand on fundamental rights issues won the admiration of blacks and many whites. There is little doubt that membership in the NBA provided a shield for the black lawyer fighting to establish the civil rights of blacks in both Southern and Northern states. It also provided a nationwide network of lawyers who provided moral support for one another. This network gave greater confidence to black lawyers in localities where the white bar excluded them from the legal academy.

By the close of 1944 the black press, which since 1925 had reported the activities of the NBA in great detail, universally recognized that the NBA and the black lawyer had become a significant force in American law. *The Atlanta Daily World*, a black Republican newspaper, lauded the black lawyer, calling him a "healthy signpost of Negro progress and social advancement."[237]

Black Regional, State, and Local Bar Groups

Between 1890 and 1900, the number of black lawyers in the nation, particularly in the states of Mississippi, Arkansas, Iowa, and Illinois, began to grow and take on the trappings of legal organizations. The Colored Bar Association of Mississippi, the first bar association organized by "colored lawyers," held its annual meeting in the city of Greenville in 1891. Josiah T. Settle, an 1875 Howard University law graduate, made the keynote address at the inaugural meeting.[238] Settle and other lawyers associated with the "Greenville Movement" (the movement to establish black bar groups throughout the states) believed that this meeting would have a permanent impact on a nation that had excluded black lawyers from the mainstream of society and from the legal profession. In his keynote address, Settle stated that the black lawyers in Mississippi were "prepared to meet the demands of the future. . . . I think I may safely say that never in the history of the race has there been a meeting fraught with more significance."[239]

The survival of the black lawyer required association and scholarship. The survival of "colored citizens" required black lawyers capable of judicial agitation and creative jurisprudential thought. Josiah T. Settle's words recognized that

this . . . first annual meeting, marks the advent of the colored citizen into a new field of labor. It evidences the existence of a sufficient number of colored lawyers in Mississippi engaged in active practice of the law to form a State organization to promote their interests individually and collectively, and in doing this they cannot fail to promote the interests of the entire race and to contribute to the general welfare of our common country, for we are as much a part of our composite nationality as any element it contains.[240]

Josiah T. Settle and the lawyers of the Greenville Movement knew that the legal profession would be slow to assimilate blacks. As Settle stated,

Many of our friends and all of our enemies discouraged us by saying that this was one profession in which we could not hope to succeed. . . . We realized in the beginning that the undertaking to become practical lawyers, and to acquire such a mastery of the law as to enter favorably upon its practice, was a serious one and doubly so to us.[241]

Settle concluded that "few men ever reach distinction in the law who were not thorough scholars." The legal profession requires more than an "oily tongue and vivid imagination. It requires real earnest work."[242]

The Greenville Movement was initiated because its participants believed that the established state bar associations were not concerned about the "masses of [black] people." Yet they knew that "the bar has necessarily exercised the whole judicial power of this country."[243] At the close of the Colored Bar Association of Mississippi's first bar meeting, George F. Bowles was chosen as president.[244]

After the Colored Bar Association of Mississippi was formed, the formation of "colored" bar associations began in other states. In fact, these bar associations became the catalysts for civil rights planning and litigation as well as for institutions in which lawyers could have professional discourse and exchange ideas.[245] In 1900 black lawyers in Arkansas, Iowa, and Illinois formed bar groups. The Arkansas bar group was named the Wonder State Bar Association. Lewis Jenks Brown, an 1886 Howard University law graduate, was one of its first presidents.[246] This bar association was active until 1928, when it fell into a decade of inactivity. In 1938 J. R. Booker reactivated the group and was elected as its president. One of the factors leading to the reactivation of the Wonder State Bar Association was the growth of racism in Arkansas. J. R. Booker announced that the bar group would "fight discriminatory legislation and . . . seek passage of laws for the full enforcement of the rights and privileges of citizenship."[247]

In 1901 the Iowa Colored Bar Association was formed at the urging of George H. Woodson, an 1895 Howard University law graduate.[248] Woodson's support and participation in the bar association was one of the principal reasons for its progress. In 1921 Gertrude Elzora Durden Rush, the first black woman admitted to the Iowa bar, was elected president of the Iowa Colored Bar Association, making her the first woman in the nation to head a state bar group composed of men and women.[249] In 1925, when the National Bar Association was organized, the Iowa Colored Bar Association hosted the founders. Five of the twelve founders were members of the Iowa Colored Bar Association: Gertrude E. D. Rush, Charles Preston Howard, George H. Woodson, James B. Morris, and Samuel Joe Brown.[250] To mark the formation of the NBA and the twenty-fifth "silver jubilee" of the Iowa Colored Bar Association, the charter members of the NBA passed a resolution that noted:

There exists in this country no active, effective association . . . uniting any considerable number of the thousands of Negro men and women who are actively engaged in the practice of the . . . legal profession. . . . Lawyers of African descent [should] . . . send representatives . . . to meet at the courthouse in Des Moines . . . on August 1 [1925] to start an association.[251]

In Illinois, black lawyers formed a loosely organized group that campaigned for the election of "Negro judges" in the early 1900s. Later, in 1914, these lawyers formed the Cook County Bar Association.[252] White lawyers objected to and rejected the application of black lawyers seeking to join the Chicago Bar Association; thus the black lawyers banded together instead.[253] The Cook County Bar Association was organized under the leadership of Richard E. Westbrooks, James G. Cotter, and George Washington Ellis.[254] The main objective of the association was to inform black citizens "as to those judges who are unfair and who discriminate in their decisions against Colored people,"[255] so that they might vote against them at election time. It also was formed to mass the political influence of several of its members, who soon won almost as much political favoritism in the disposition of cases as did their white counterparts.[256] The association aided significantly in policing lawyer abuses,[257] and it sent its members to the Illinois state capital to oppose legislation that denied the civil rights of "citizens of color."[258]

Henry M. Porter was elected president of the Cook County Bar

Association in 1918, on the eve of the Chicago race riots of 1919. During the riots the members of the association played a significant role in maintaining peace in the community, and they formed defense teams to represent persons charged with crimes and violence during the riots. The "corps of lawyers representing the association succeeded in keeping many innocent Negroes from being [imprisoned] and succeeded in collecting hundreds and thousands of dollars in damages from the city . . . for damages to their property, injuries to their person and death."[259]

During the presidencies of Willis E. Mollison and Champion J. Waring, the association "strenuously" worked for and succeeded in electing Albert B. George as the first elected black judge in the state of Illinois.[260] It was during Waring's presidency that the groundwork was laid to form the National Bar Association. According to A. Morris Burroughs, a black lawyer and legal historian of the Cook County Bar Association, Waring was credited by George H. Woodson with aiding in "the launching of [the NBA]."[261] The presidency of C. Francis Stradford brought attention to the need for increasing the membership of the association and expanding membership services. Between 1926 and 1928, Stradford increased the membership from sixty-three to two hundred members and published *The Sullivan Law Directory of Chicago*, which listed the names of the members of the association. At the completion of his term, Stradford was elected president of the NBA.[262] A. Morris Burroughs was instrumental in securing a permanent headquarters for the Cook County Bar Association, which housed a law library for the use of its members.[263]

In 1930 Herman Emmons Moore was elected president of the Cook County Bar Association. Moore criticized the Chicago Bar Association for rejecting the applications of blacks. By 1930, many of the various bar groups in Chicago did "not openly deny [blacks] membership," but did require all applicants to identify themselves by race on their applications.[264] The fight for membership for black lawyers in Chicago bar groups continued until after World War II. Blacks were the last group of ethnic lawyers admitted to the Chicago Bar Association.[265] They finally broke the color bar with the assistance of students at the University of Chicago Law School, who in 1944 protested the exclusion of blacks from the all-white association.[266]

The extent to which black women lawyers participated in the Cook County Bar Association is not altogether clear. However, Violette Neatly Anderson served as the first vice-president of the association between 1920 and 1926. She served as chairperson of the entertainment committee in 1923, when the NBA held its annual meeting in Chicago.[267]

Between 1915 and 1920, other black bar groups were formed in

Oklahoma, the District of Columbia, West Virginia, Michigan, Ohio, and North Carolina. The Oklahoma State Negro Bar Association was formed around 1915. In that year, E. L. Saddler, its president, was involved in the fight against the separate car law and against efforts to disfranchise blacks in Oklahoma.[268] While information on this black Oklahoma bar group is scarce, there is evidence that it did not survive for a sustained period of time. Nevertheless, in 1937 several Oklahoma black lawyers met in the city of Muskogee to reactivate a statewide "negro bar association." Chauncey D. Twine, a Muskogee lawyer, was the moving force behind this group. Lawyers from Tulsa, Oklahoma City, Okmulgee, and Wewoka, Oklahoma, attended this meeting.[269]

In the fall of 1916, "a large number of colored lawyers of the District [of Columbia,] met . . . and formed a temporary organization, looking to their mutual benefit and protection."[270] L. Melendez King was elected chairman of the group. King and the other officers of the temporary group were charged with forming the permanent "colored bar association."[271] In 1918, the temporary group met in the office of Emanuel D. Molyneaux Hewlett and, "after exchanging views, organized a bar association."[272] The District of Columbia Colored Bar Association was a fairly close-knit group made up "mostly of the old lawyers in the city, such as William L. Houston and L. Melendez King. The younger lawyers such as [Louis Rothschild] Mehlinger and Charlie Houston were left out."[273]

The exclusivity of the District of Columbia Colored Bar Association prompted the younger lawyers to form the Washington Bar Association in 1925.[274] Charles Hamilton Houston was one of the leaders of the revolt against the old regime, which included his father, William L. Houston. Houston was elected as the third president of the Washington Bar Association in 1930.[275] Between 1925 and 1944, the Washington Bar Association was one of the strongest and most progressive local black bar associations in the country. It was supported by a large number of black lawyers in the nation's capital[276] and drew politically important men to its leadership, such as George E. C. Hayes and, ultimately, William L. Houston, both influential and well-connected black Republicans.

The Washington Bar Association had an active civic program. For example, on Lawyer's Day the members of the WBA visited churches and civic groups to speak on legal subjects. During the celebration of Lawyer's Day in 1933, the WBA announced that the "Negro lawyer bears to the community what the community ought to expect of him, and what he ought to expect from the community."[277]

In 1936 a split occurred in the WBA when the majority of its members endorsed the militant National Negro Congress.[278] The members opposing the endorsement formed the Harlan-Terrell Lawyer's Association and elected Nathan A. Dobbins as their president.[279] A number of WBA members joined the new bar group, including Louis Rothschild Mehlinger, one of the WBA's founders, and Perry W. Howard, a past president.[280] The split between the groups may have been cosmetic. In 1937 the two groups jointly sponsored a resolution at the annual meeting of the NBA "urging President [Franklin D.] Roosevelt, Attorney General [Homer] Cummings and Postmaster General James A. Farley to appoint a Negro to the police court bench in the District of Columbia."[281]

The Washington Bar Association led the fight to give blacks access to the District of Columbia Bar Association Law Library. Use of the law library was contingent on membership in the District of Columbia Bar Association, from which black lawyers were excluded. In 1939 the law library of the District of Columbia Bar Association was located in the United States Courthouse. The law library was used by local and federal judges, their law clerks, the United States attorney and his staff, and the members of the white District of Columbia Bar Association. During a trial, a white lawyer called upon by a judge to support an argument with legal precedent could research the matter in the law library without rushing back to his office library. Black lawyers, therefore, were at a marked disadvantage. With no access to the law library at the courthouse, black lawyers had to argue the law as they thought it should be. Such "seat of the pants" arguments often cost their clients dearly, and sometimes brought the lawyers before the bar's disciplinary bodies. The practice of excluding black lawyers from membership in the District of Columbia Bar Association and from use of its law library had continued for sixty-six years.

In 1939 Huver I. Brown, a member of the Washington Bar Association, attempted to use the law library after a judge had requested scholarly support for an argument made during a pending trial. Brown was refused. Soon thereafter Brown announced his intention to file an injunction in federal court against the District of Columbia Bar Association to enjoin discrimination against black lawyers. Brown claimed that it was unconstitutional for a private bar group to deny black lawyers the use of its law library, which was housed in a federal court building. Brown was immediately criticized by the white bar for "rocking the boat." He was also threatened: Brown reported that one white lawyer said, "You're the nigger that's trying to get in the white association. We're going to get you."[282] Brown turned to the Washington Bar Association for assistance, and James Pete Tyson agreed to handle the case.

The Washington Bar Association's support of Brown's stand was compelling. Exclusion from the law library not only affected its membership, but it affected all black lawyers licensed to practice in the District of Columbia. The WBA also criticized the Department of Justice for its silence on the matter.[283] The litigation drew national attention and won the support of white women lawyers, who also were denied membership in the association.[284]

Huver I. Brown's case against the District of Columbia Bar Association was ultimately settled. The settlement was reached in 1941, when Francis M. Shea, assistant United States attorney, brought the matter to the direct attention of Robert H. Jackson, the United States attorney general. As attorney general, Jackson was one of the official supervisors of the United States Courthouse building, as was Harlan Fiske Stone, the chief justice of the United States Supreme Court. On February 12, 1941, Jackson issued an order prohibiting the District of Columbia Bar Association from denying use of any space to "all members of the bar in good standing without discrimination or account of race, color, religious, or sex."[285] Technically, Jackson's order did not require this private bar association to admit black lawyers to membership. However, the effect of the order sent the message that if the association continued to exclude black lawyers from the law library, it would have to find another location, which would cost several thousand dollars.

Huver I. Brown and the members of the Washington Bar Association were eventually permitted access to the law library, contingent on payment of an eight-dollar annual fee.[286] But until 1958, they were denied membership to the District of Columbia Bar Association.[287] Huver Brown's case also benefited white women lawyers in the District of Columbia, who during his lawsuit were admitted to the District of Columbia Bar Association and were therefore allowed to use the courthouse library.

The dearth of black women lawyers in the district may be the reason that little information about their bar activities exists. However, by 1929, four years after the formation of the Washington Bar Association, Ollie May Cooper and Isadora Augusta Jackson Letcher were both active members of the group. They remained so throughout their careers.[288] In 1940 H. Elsie Austin was also active in the WBA. She was the WBA's representative on one of the National Bar Association's substantive panels.[289]

The Negro Bar Association of West Virginia was formed in 1918. In the years after its organization, it was not unanimously supported by black lawyers. In fact, in 1928 there were some black lawyers who opposed a "strictly Negro Bar Association."[290] However, since the ABA excluded blacks from membership, the majority prevailed in persuading the doubting faction of the need for a black bar group.[291] The first annual meeting of the Negro Bar Association of West Virginia was held in the city of Huntington in 1919. During the meeting, papers were presented on "Abstracting Titles," "Civil Rights," and "The Lawyer's Place in Reconstruction" by C. E. Kimbrough, E. J. Graham, and Harry J. Capehart, respectively. A majority of the bar group's forty-five members, "mostly residents of the southern part of the state," attended the meeting.[292] The members elected J. M. Ellis, of Fayette County, as president, and T. Edward Hill, of McDowell County, as secretary of the bar group. Information is sparse on the extent to which this bar group was sustained.[293] By 1937 the group had been renamed the Mountain State Bar Association, and it was still headed by J. M. Ellis.[294]

In 1918 "twenty four race lawyers . . . formed a club, as yet unnamed," for the betterment of their interests in Detroit, Michigan. The law club elected R. C. Barnes as its president and appointed a committee to draft a constitution and by-laws.[295] Subsequently, the group was named the Harlan Law Club, "in honor of Supreme Court Associate Justice John Marshall Harlan," the author of the dissent in *Plessy v. Ferguson*.[296] The Harlan Law Club was sustained by a succession of strong leaders, including Percival Piper.[297] In the early 1930s, the Harlan Law Club, which essentially had been composed of lawyers from the Detroit area, was renamed the Wolverine Bar Association. It then expanded its membership to black lawyers statewide.

The leaders of the Wolverine Bar Association included Francis Morse Dent, a 1923 Detroit College of Law graduate. Like other such groups throughout the country, the Wolverine Bar Association was opened to all lawyers, regardless of race. It was dedicated to "the unity of its members," to the cause of providing legal assistance to the poor, and to inspiring "full confidence in the general public."[298] It also lobbied for the appointment of black judges, and used its monthly meetings to exchange ideas on trial techniques and political developments in the state.[299]

In 1937 Willis M. Graves, Henry W. Sweet, Jr., and Robert Evans "protested successfully against the formation and continuance of a [Detroit] police squad to handle Negro work exclusively."[300] In 1939 when a judge in the Detroit Probate Court refused to appoint black lawyers to administer estates, the Wolverine Bar Association filed a formal protest against the practice. R. M. Golightly, the president of the law group, and Arthur Randall, Jr., its secretary, conducted a survey "to find out what part of probate political patronage is received by the Negro Lawyer."[301]

The Wolverine Bar Association provided a forum for both political advocacy and continuing legal education programs. The group fielded distinguished speakers from the political and the judicial communities.

For example, Carl V. Weygant, chief justice of the Michigan Supreme Court, addressed the group in 1939. The Wolverine Bar Association was also instrumental in obtaining key appointments for its members with the Michigan State Bar Association.[302] Despite the race restrictions against membership in the American Bar Association, the Wolverine Bar Association continued to recommend that its members apply for ABA membership.[303]

The black lawyers in Cleveland, Ohio, also formed a Harlan Law Club, at about the same time as the Michigan group. Headed by Thomas M. Frey, the club took on all the trappings of a bar association. By 1930 black lawyers may have had full rights to apply for membership in the Cleveland Bar Association, in part because John Patterson Green and a "few [other] Negro[es]" were members of that bar."[304] However, the black bar continued to grow, probably due to the special needs of black lawyers and the particular problems of their clients and community.

In 1931 Louise J. Pridgeon became the first woman in Ohio to head the Harlan Law Club, and thus was one of the few women in the nation to be elected to hear a bar group.[305] The following year, the black lawyers in Franklin County, Ohio, formed the Robert Brown Elliott Law Club, named after a black South Carolina lawyer who was elected to Congress during the Reconstruction era.[306] This club also grew in influence and numbers. In 1940 the club had a membership of thirty lawyers and was headed by David D. White.[307]

The Negro State Bar Association of North Carolina was established in 1920. During its first annual meeting in Wilson, North Carolina, it declared that its purpose was "to cultivate the Science of Jurisprudence," to fight for the political and civil rights of the Race, to facilitate the administration of justice, to elevate the standard of integrity, honor and courtesy in the legal profession."[308] The name of the group was changed in 1935, when "27 Negro lawyers" of North Carolina, supported by the Durham Negro Bar Association, established the statewide Old North State Bar Association.[309] The new group elected F. W. Williams, of Winston-Salem, as president.[310] During its first meeting, the group focused its attention on the exclusion of blacks from juries and the obligation of its members to participate in civic activities around the state.[311]

Between 1921 and 1944, the black bar movement reached the states of Texas, Maryland, Virginia, Missouri, Indiana, Pennsylvania, Kentucky, New York, New Jersey, and Tennessee.

In 1921, five black lawyers organized a colored bar association in San Antonio, Texas. The bar group was headed by L. W. Green.[312] The bar movement among black lawyers in Texas did not expand statewide, as it did in other states, perhaps because of the dearth of black lawyers there.

The Monumental Bar Association was formed in Baltimore, Maryland, in 1921. Ephraim Jackson was elected as its first president.[313] During the first annual meeting of the association, W. Ashbie Hawkins, a senior black member of the Maryland bar, spoke about "the refusal of the State and Federal courts to admit [Charles S.] Taylor to practice [in 1877] on the ground that the law restricted this profession to 'white males only.'"[314] This group thrived under the strong leadership of such lawyers as Roy S. Bond and Josiah F. Henry.[315] The membership of the Monumental Bar Association continued to grow throughout World War II, and beyond.

In Virginia, the bar movement began in the city of Norfolk where, in 1921, ten black lawyers formed the Norfolk Colored Bar Association.[316] With the advent of the National Bar Association in 1925, several black lawyers met in Richmond, Virginia, to form a statewide bar group known as the Old Dominion Bar Association. They elected a Roanoke lawyer, Henry D. Dolphin, as their first president.[317]

Between 1922 and 1930, four black bar associations were organized in the state of Missouri. Excluded from membership in the St. Louis Bar Association on account of race, fourteen black lawyers met in St. Louis in 1922 to form the St. Louis Negro Bar Association.[318] Although the bar groups were separated by race, they sometimes acted jointly in passing resolutions urging authorities to investigate such matters as "ambulance chasing."[319] The St. Louis Negro Bar Association pushed for the appointment of black judges to the local bench. In 1924 the group submitted Daniel W. Bowles's name to the white bar for a judicial appointment. It was customary to publish in the local press the names of all persons submitted by bar groups for judicial consideration, but a controversy arose when Bowles's name was not published. The black lawyers cried foul, and Silas E. Gardner, the president of the St. Louis Negro Bar Association, protested the action to the governor.[320]

In 1927 black lawyers in Missouri formed a new bar group named the Mound City Bar Association. It too was established because "the white bar association wouldn't give [blacks] membership."[321] Joseph L. McLemore was elected the group's first president.[322] Under the leadership of John A. Davis in 1930, the Mound City Bar Association created programs to enhance the image of local black lawyers. Davis, a former member of the Missouri state legislature, asserted that the black community was unaware of the caliber of black lawyers in St. Louis. He knew that unless blacks used black lawyers they would fail, and the rights of blacks would be threatened along with them.[323] Davis also led the fight "to secure jury recognition for the members of our group."[324]

A succession of leaders, including Freeman L. Martin and Robert L. Witherspoon, spurred the bar groups forward until the start of World War II.[325]

In May 1926, "nearly one hundred [black] lawyers who resided in different sections of Missouri gathered [in St. Louis] and organized a state association . . . to be known as the Harlan State Bar Association."[326] The group elected L. Amasa Knox of Kansas City, Missouri, as its president.[327] Within two years after the formation of the Harlan State Bar group, all but two of the nearly fifty members lived in the cities of Kansas City and St. Louis, Missouri.[328] The programs during the early years of the association's annual meetings were substantial and highly applicable to the causes of black lawyers. Under the leadership of Carl Roman Johnson, papers on habeas corpus, political participation of black lawyers, and recent court decisions affecting blacks were presented.[329] In 1930, the Harlan Bar Association was still protesting the exclusion of blacks from juries in St. Louis.[330]

One year after the formation of the Harlan State Bar Association, several lawyers, many of them members of the statewide group, formed the Jackson County Bar Association in Missouri.[331] The group may have been formed to demonstrate its strength and to exert influence in Kansas City. With the Jackson County Bar Association in the western part of Missouri, and the St. Louis Negro Bar Association and Mound City Bar Association in the east, the black lawyers of Missouri consolidated their voices in legal and political matters throughout the state.

The first bar association organized by black lawyers in Indiana was formed in Marion County in 1925. The bar group was known as the Marion County Lawyers' Club. Most of the black lawyers in Indiana resided in Indianapolis. Unlike many other state and city bar groups, the Indianapolis Bar Association is not known to have had a race exclusion policy. It can only be assumed that the Marion County Lawyers' Club was formed to muster the power and influence of black lawyers in the state and to join the growing black bar movement.[332]

In 1932 Paul G. Davis was the white president of the Indianapolis Bar Association and Forrest W. Littlejohn was the black president of the Marion County Lawyers' Club. There were approximately one thousand lawyers in Indianapolis and 3,683 white lawyers in the state. The Indianapolis Bar Association had four hundred members. In contrast, the Marion County Lawyers' Club had approximately fifty members, including at least one black woman lawyer, H. Elsie Austin. There were approximately fifty black lawyers in Indianapolis and a total of sixty-two black lawyers in the state. The Marion County Lawyers' Club served as the base of operation for the black bar until 1942, when it changed its name to the Marion County Bar Association.[333]

Barred from any meaningful participation in the Philadelphia Bar Association, the black lawyers of that city in 1925 formed the John Mercer Langston Law Club, named for the first dean of Howard University School of Law. Describing the conditions existing in 1925 between black and white lawyers in Philadelphia, Raymond Pace Alexander wrote,

There were few if any social relations between Negro and the white lawyers at this great Bar. The lawyers from these two groups—white and colored— rarely, if ever, met on any occasion other than a chance meeting, or sitting next to one another in the criminal courts. Few of the lawyers practiced civil law. Few entered Orphans' Court. We did not attend the meetings of the Philadelphia Bar Association.[334]

The John Mercer Langston Law Club provided a professional and social base for the black legal cadre of Philadelphia. It also formed the base for community action projects. In 1932, under the leadership of John Francis Williams and Sadie Tanner Mossell Alexander (the only black woman lawyer in the group), the club proposed and completed plans for the formation of a legal aid bureau to assist blacks "unable to bear the cost of hiring lawyers."[335] The legal aid bureau was initiated after the Philadelphia Aid Welfare Bureau was abolished. The need for the legal aid bureau was never questioned by the black bar. Several members of the group volunteered their time to assist blacks charged with crimes and those who were in need of lawyers in civil matters.[336]

The exact year that black lawyers in Kentucky formed a bar group is unknown, but in 1927 the "colored lawyers," under the leadership of Ned Williamson, of Louisville, Kentucky, reorganized the preexisting Lincoln Bar Association, which was named for President Abraham Lincoln. The object of the group was in "furtherance of justice, the upholding of legal ethics and advice to the members of our race."[337] The extent to which the black bar movement flourished in Kentucky prior to 1945 remains undocumented.

In 1926 the Harlem Lawyers' Association was founded in New York City, three years before the Bar Association of the City of New York lifted the race bar and admitted Francis Ellis Rivers to membership.[338] The Harlem Lawyers' Association gained influence under programs initiated by Arthur H. Madison, the first president of the bar group, who served as its president for several years.[339] In 1931 Judge James A. Cobb, a leading jurist on the local bench in the District of Columbia, addressed the fifth annual dinner of the Harlem Lawyers' Association. He stated what must have been the consensus of the group: "The Constitution is sufficiently broad to give the Negro every right; the only thing needed is application. . . . The Negro as a minority race must work out his own destiny through education, industry and the arts, and he must have an equal respect for all peoples."[340]

The Harlem Lawyers' Association influenced judicial selections in the city, and in 1936 it fought vigorously to upgrade Harlem's public school system.[341] By 1942 a black woman, Lucille E. Chance, had been elected as a member of the board of directors of the Harlem Lawyers' Association.[342] In 1936 Hutson Leon Lovell, a 1926 graduate of Fordham University's law school, formed the Brooklyn and Long Island Lawyers Association. Lewis S. Flagg was elected its president. The group was active for several years, and it also supported the Harlem Lawyers' Association in its efforts to have black lawyers appointed to the bench.[343]

By 1933 black lawyers in New Jersey had also formed a Negro Lawyers' Association. According to Roger M. Yancey, its president, one of the objects of the group was the establishment of a "defense fund to fight segregation and discrimination." Yancey was assisted in his efforts by William A. Dart and Frank Wimberley, leading lawyers in Atlantic City and Camden, New Jersey.[344]

In Tennessee, it is likely that black lawyers established a bar group before the 1930s, but it was not until then that the loosely organized lawyers formed the James C. Napier Lawyers' Association. Named after one of the early black lawyers in Tennessee, the bar association progressed for a period under the able leadership of Walter S. Walker, of Nashville.[345]

Only one regional bar association was formed by black lawyers prior to 1945. In 1940 black lawyers formed the Southwestern Bar Association. The region included the states of Arkansas, Oklahoma, Texas, and Kansas, with the Oklahoma lawyers taking the lead in the group's formation. The group increased both the political and legal influence of black lawyers in a region where the population of black lawyers was small. The Southwestern Bar Association gave equal representation to each of the states. It elected J. J. Bruce, of Oklahoma, as its first president.[346] The stated purpose of the group was "to effectively assist in carrying out the program of Negro Lawyers in the respective states, and [to] satisfy the needs of Negro citizens of the Southwest area."[347] The group remained a viable force in the southwest for many years.[348]

Summary

For sixty-six years black lawyers were barred from membership in the American Bar Association solely on the basis of race. During this period, from 1878 to 1944, black lawyers played no role in the development of the ABA policy that directly affected them. They were legally outcast. The exclusion was similar at the other national bar groups: in the Federal Bar Association and the National Association of Women Lawyers, blacks were barred between 1925 and 1945, and between 1899 and 1943, respectively.

There were, of course, exceptions. The Jim Crow policies of any bar group were not shared by all of its members. In fact, a small minority of white voices advanced the view that blacks should be made members of these bar groups. Some of these voices may also have become disfranchised. Ultimately, the actions of the legally outcast blacks and whites defeated the Jim Crow policies of the nation's major bar groups. Groups such as the National Lawyers' Guild, founded in 1937, joined the ranks of bar groups that opened their membership to all.

The formation of black bar groups was a direct result of the exclusion of black lawyers from the national and state bar groups. Josiah Thomas Settle's 1891 speech inaugurating the first black bar group in the nation at Greenville, Mississippi, correctly recognized that bar groups exercised "the whole judicial power of this country." The founding of black bar groups throughout the nation at the state level is known as the Greenville Movement.

As the roots of the Greenville Movement took hold, so did the need for black lawyers to organize into national bar groups. They began this process in 1909, as an affiliate group of the National Negro Business League headed by Booker T. Washington. In 1925 black lawyers founded the National Bar Association.

The state and national bar groups founded by black lawyers enhanced their importance in the legal community. In these groups they had a base from which to influence both law and politics. Black bar groups created forums for the exchange of ideas about law and how to change it; about politics, and how to participate in it; about justice, and how to achieve it.

Black women lawyers also benefited from black bar groups, because it was there, to some degree, that they liberated themselves. At the state level, Gertrude Elzora Durden Rush led the black bar in Iowa in 1921. She was also a founder of the National Bar Association in 1925. In 1930, Louise J. Pridgeon, led a black bar group in Ohio; and Georgia Jones Ellis, of Chicago, broke new ground in 1928 when she was elected as an officer of the National Bar Association.

The individual efforts and achievements of black lawyers must be lauded and revered. These lawyers made significant progress in the law in the face of collective exclusion from white bar groups. By forming their own bar groups, individual black lawyers were able to combine their talents and resources in order to reform American law and establish a base from which to emancipate their people.

NOTES

1. Vol. 1 *Reports of the American Bar Association* 16 (1878). See also E. R. Sunderland, *History of the American Bar Association and Its Work* 1, 6 (1953).

2. Actually, Butler Roland Wilson and William R. Morris have the distinction of being the first black lawyers admitted to the ABA. Both lawyers were elected by the executive committee between the 1910 and 1911 annual meetings of the ABA. William Henry Lewis was elected to the ABA after the annual meeting in 1911. Vol. 36 *Report of the Thirty-Fourth Annual Meeting of the American Bar Association* 177, 198 (Wilson), 161, 201 (Morris) (1911).

3. "The Bar Association and the Negro," 111 *The Outlook* 2 (Sept. 7, 1912).

4. Charles S. Brown, "The Genesis of the Negro Lawyer in New England (Part 2)," 22 *The Negro History Bulletin* 171, 173–74 (May 1959) (quoting the *Boston Herald*, Aug. 28, 1912). Apparently, the executive committee of the ABA had admitted Lewis, Wilson, and Morris to membership without knowing they were black. Each of these men was a member in good standing before the bar of his state. Indeed, Lewis's application for membership was "endorsed by the Massachusetts Bar Association." *The National Bar Association: Proceedings of the Sixth Annual Convention* 4, 15 (Aug. 7, 1930) (remarks of Judge James A. Cobb introducing William Henry Lewis); "The Bar Association and the Negro," 111 *The Outlook* 1 (Sept. 7, 1912).

5. *Ibid.* (NBA Proceedings). In a letter to Booker T. Washington regarding the ABA's policy on the admission of blacks to membership, Wickersham stated that he believed William Morris resigned from the ABA in order to embarrass Frank Billings Kellog of St. Paul, Minnesota, who was vying for the ABA presidency. Morris was from the same city. Vol. 12 *The Booker T. Washington Papers, 1912–14*, at 8 (L. R. Harlan and R. W. Smock eds. 1982). See Vol. 37 *Reports of American Bar Association* 175 (1912): Morris is not listed as a member of American Bar Association. Nevertheless, Morris's name remained the subject of the resolution barring blacks from ABA membership in the future. *Id.* at 11.

6. "Wickersham Denounces Attempt to Oust Lewis," *Boston Advertiser*, March 1, 1912.

7. "Wickersham to Resign from American Bar Association," *Boston Advertiser*, March 5, 1912.

8. Vol. 37 *Reports of the American Bar Association* 11–12 (1912). "Federal Lawyer Assn. Reveals ABA Bias," *The People's Voice* (June 5, 1943). Joseph B. David, a white lawyer who was present at the time the vote on the resolution was taken, later reported that he had voted " 'no' amid a wild chorus of 'yes' on a motion thereafter excluding nonwhite barristers from membership in the American Bar Association." "Bar Association Dedicates New $2,000 Law Library," *Chicago Defender*, Sept. 29, 1928.

9. Vol. 37 *Reports of the American Bar Association* 12 (1912).

10. *Ibid.*

11. *Id.* at 13.

12. *Ibid.*

13. *Id.* at 15.

14. L. R. Harlan, *Booker T. Washington: The Wizard of Tuskegee* 350 (1983).

15. *Id.* at 348. Wickersham made no objection to William MacChesney's remarks. He accepted them and stated, "I . . . shall vote for this resolution because *I did not embark upon any wider campaign* than that which finds its

solution in the recognition of the continued membership of [William Henry Lewis, William R. Morris, and Butler R. Wilson]." Vol. 37 *Reports of the American Bar Association* 14 (1912) (emphasis added). Lewis's appointment as assistant attorney general of the United States was made during the final year of the Taft administration. Presumably, Lewis's appointment was made to swing black votes in what was to be a tough primary fight against Theodore Roosevelt. (Woodrow Wilson, a Democrat, was ultimately elected.) Despite Wickersham's efforts to stay the expulsion of Lewis from the ABA, "two months [after the ABA convention he] invited . . . twenty-two attorneys connected with [the Department of Justice] . . . to an official dinner in honor of a new solicitor general from Kentucky." Lewis, however, was excluded, though he ranked higher than most attending the dinner. *Id.* at 350 (*Booker T. Washington: The Wizard of Tuskegee*). This snub, which may have been politically motivated (to win white Southern support on the eve of the election of 1912), prompted one black leader to write, "Such gross discrimination is enough to make anarchists out of peaceful men." *Ibid.*, quoting letter from Ralph Tyler to Emmett Scott, Nov. 19, 1912. Regarding the Wickersham compromise, see Vol. 12 *The Booker T. Washington Papers, 1912–14*, at 8–9 (L. R. Harlan and R. W. Smock eds. 1982).

16. "Negroes to Form Bar Association to Cover Nation," *Spartanburg Sun*, Feb. 28, 1925.

17. Vol. 54 *Report of the Fifty-second Annual Meeting of American Bar Association* 963, 1188, 1403 (1929); letter from T. Gillis Nutter to Charles S. Brown, June 9, 1958. W. Arvey Wood, a black lawyer in Connecticut, was reported to have been a member of the ABA in 1937, but the ABA *Reports* do not support this claim. *Virginia's Contribution to Negro Leadership* 73 (W. Cooper ed. 1937) (mimeo).

18. Ironically, the ABA may have inadvertently, or perhaps purposefully, allowed the local ABA officers to decide whose name should be advanced for membership. On January 1, 1914, Lucien Hugh Alexander, the chairman of the ABA's membership committee, issued a national appeal to increase its membership. In view of the action taken in 1912, the appeal was limited to white male lawyers. There were vice-presidents of the ABA, one for every state, whose main function was to recruit new members. The "membership proposals" form did not ask the applicant to state his race. It merely reminded the proposer that the ABA "constitution declares five years membership, in good standing at State Bar, a prerequisite to election." Based on this form, and because of state bar associations that opposed the exclusionary policies of the ABA, other black lawyers may have been elected to ABA membership, just as Butler R. Wilson, William R. Morris, and William Henry Lewis had been in 1910 and 1911. See *Special Communication in re the Membership Situation* 5, 10 (and attached ABA membership proposals) (1914). Both William Henry Lewis and Butler Roland Wilson remained members of the ABA throughout their legal careers. See, e.g., Vol. 70 *Reports of the American Bar Association* 603 (1945).

19. "American Bar Association Is Urged to Admit Race Lawyers," *Pittsburgh Courier*, Sept. 24, 1938; "Tells U.S. Bar Admit Negroes, or Change Name," *Cleveland Eagle*, Sept. 23, 1938; "Urge Lawyers Association to Admit Negroes," *Atlanta Daily World*, Aug. 26, 1938.

20. Letter from Clifford Langsdale to Ruth Weyand, July 28, 1943; letter to author from Ruth Weyand, March 23, 1986.

21. "The American Bar," *Pittsburgh Courier*, Oct. 3, 1942.

22. "Hays Insists ABA Bars Negroes as Members," *World Telegram*, April 24,

1943. (The process of voting was explained here in a letter from Judge John Beardsley to Arthur Garfield Hays, president of the American Civil Liberties Union).

23. "The ABA Ban," *Pittsburgh Courier*, April 24, 1943.

24. "Color Ban Lifted in Two Bar Associations," *Chicago Defender*, Sept. 4, 1943.

25. Bojack, "Judge Watson Gets ABA Membership Under New Rules," *Pittsburgh Courier*, Sept. 4, 1943.

26. "Rivers Given Judgeship by Dewey," *Chicago Defender*, Sept. 18, 1943. Actually, the appointment by Governor Dewey was to fill an unexpired term which had only two months remaining. Rivers would have been required to stand for election in November 1943. Shipp, "'Family Party' Is Stayed at N.Y.U. for the Black Judges in New York," *New York Times*, Dec. 13, 1981, at 55, col. 1.

27. Threats of resignations from the ABA were voiced by members during a meeting of the Philadelphia Bar Association ("2 Philly Lawyers May Quit the ABA," *Baltimore Afro-American*, June 26, 1943). However, the Philadelphia Bar Association stopped short of publicly condemning the ABA's discriminatory policy. In lieu of such a condemnation, the Philadelphia Bar Association adopted a resolution requesting that the chancellor of the association appoint a committee to "deliberate and report on racial discrimination within the National Association" ("Lead Lawyers Sidestep Mover to Probe Bias," *Philadelphia Tribune*, June 19, 1943).

28. "Judge Goldstein Resigns in Protest as Bar Association Rejects Negro," *The People's Voice*, April 10, 1943.

29. Vol. 68 *Reports of the American Bar Association* 110 (1943). Joseph C. Thompson, of New York, was the mover of the original resolution to break the Jim Crow membership rule.

30. "American Bar Relents," *The Washington Bee* (magazine section), Sept. 5, 1943.

31. "Rivers Admitted to Membership in American Bar Association," *New York Age*, March 4, 1944; Bojack, "Judge Watson Gets ABA Membership Under New Rules," *Pittsburgh Courier*, Sept. 4, 1943. The movement to integrate the ABA spread to affiliates in large metropolitan cities. Several attorneys in Chicago, Illinois, supported black applicants to the Chicago Bar Association. In 1943 Charles Liebman, secretary of the Chicago Bar Association's committee on civil rights, endorsed three black lawyers to membership: Earl B. Dickerson, Euclid Taylor, and W. Sylvester White ("Fight Jim Crow Setup in Local Bar Association," *Norfolk Journal and Guide*, June 5, 1943). However, the Chicago Bar Association continued to exclude blacks from its membership until 1945 (J. P. Heinz and E. O. Laumann, *Chicago Lawyers* 302 [1982]).

32. "ABA's Lowering of Color Bar Splits Dallas Lawyers," *Baltimore Afro-American*, Sept. 11, 1943.

33. "The American Bar," *Pittsburgh Courier*, Oct. 3, 1942.

34. Johnson, "Legal Profession," in *The Integration of the Negro into American Society* 97 (E. F. Frazier ed. 1951).

35. R. Stevens, *Law School* 84 (1983).

36. "Color Ban Lifted in Two Bar Associations," *Chicago Defender*, Sept. 4, 1943.

37. Heptig's resolution may have been adopted because of her local influence in Illinois. From 1939 to 1940, Heptig had been a state vice-president of

the NAWL in Illinois (*75 Year History, National Association of Women Lawyers* 85 [M. H. Zimmerman ed. 1975]).

38. *Ibid.* The history of the NAWL, edited by Mary H. Zimmerman (who ended her term as second vice-president of the NAWL in 1943), is silent on the question of its race restrictions and on the resolution of Bess Sullivan Heptig. *Id.* at 108–10.

39. J. Paterson, *Be Somebody: A Biography of Marguerite Rawalt* 75 (1986). In Rawalt's biography she makes no claim of initiating the move to admit black women during her presidency. (*id.* at 69–70). See also, Vol. 68 *Reports of the American Bar Association* 95 (1943). Rawalt was president of the FBA and was the FBA representative to the ABA House of Delegates in 1943, when the ABA voted to lift its Jim Crow membership restrictions. Roberts was also a member of the House of Delegates, representing the NAWL as its president. See "Leader, Lawyer and Women's Rights Advocate Dies at 94," 37 *Federal Bar News & Journal* 16 (Jan. 1990).

40. Georgia Jones Ellis reportedly "broke the color bar of [the] National Association of Women Lawyers in 1938. "Lady Lawyer," 2 *Ebony* 18, 19 (Aug. 1947). Given the news account of her admission to national membership in the NAWL in 1943, Ellis—perhaps with the assistance of Bess Sullivan Heptig—was probably admitted to membership in the Illinois chapter of the NAWL. At the time, Ellis was a leader in the Northern District Association of the Cook County Bar Association Guild. Sophie Boaz was an assistant probation officer in Chicago. Edith Sampson also was employed by the probation office of the juvenile court and was vice-president of the National Council of Negro Women. "Color Ban Lifted in Two Bar Associations," *Chicago Defender*, Sept. 4, 1943. The NAWL's history does include an article written by Sampson in 1944, but makes no other reference to her or any other black woman's admission to the group (*75 Year History, National Association of Women Lawyers* 126 [M. H. Zimmerman ed. 1975]). Zimmerman's history also notes the death of Ellis (*id.* at 465).

41. Federal Bar Association Constitution and By-Laws, Art. IV, sec. 1, adopted on April 20, 1926.

42. Minutes of FBA Executive Council, Oct. 28, 1930, at 139.

43. Minutes of FBA Executive Council, April, 1931, at 187.

44. *Id.* at 188.

45. *Ibid.*

46. Judge Miller was a member of the Federal Circuit Court of Appeals for the District of Columbia.

47. Minutes of FBA Executive Council, June 22, 1931, at 236.

48. *Ibid.*

49. *Id.* at 237.

50. Minutes of FBA Executive Council, June 3, 1936, at 58.

51. Minutes of FBA Executive Council, Nov. 16, 1942; letter to author from Ruth Weyand, March 23, 1986.

52. *Ibid.*

53. The members of the subcommittee on the Bill of Rights included Robert McKinley (chairman), special attorney, National Labor Relations Board; John P. Barnes, Legal Division, Office of Price Administration; John R. Benney, attorney, Department of Justice; Wendell Berge, assistant United States attorney general; Charles Fahy, solicitor general of the United States; Norman L. Littell, assistant United States attorney general; Henry A. Schweinhaut, special assistant to the United States attorney general; and Ruth Weyand, supervising

attorney, National Labor Relations Board. The names of the subcommittee were listed in the *Report of War Work Committee of the Federal Bar Association*, Oct. 1, 1942, at 3. The initial request for the hearing was supported by Bernard F. Burdick, William R. Vallance, and John T. Vance, members of the FBA executive council, at its November 12, 1942 meeting, but the majority of the council rejected the request. Minutes of FBA Executive Council, Nov. 16, 1942.

54. Minutes of FBA Executive Council, Dec. 14, 1942 (determined by resolution).

55. Letter to author from Ruth Weyand, March 23, 1986.

56. Smith, "Louis Rothschild Mehlinger: The First One Hundred Years," 26 *Howard Law Journal* 359, 363 (1983).

57. *Ibid.*

58. Letter to author from Ruth Weyand, March 23, 1986.

59. Minutes of FBA Executive Council, April 19, 1943.

60. "Biddle Protests Jim Crow in Bar; May Quit Group," *Atlanta Daily World*, Dec. 26, 1943. The attorney general's alleged threat to resign from the FBA because of its Jim Crow policy appeared in other newspapers, but Marguerite Rawalt, the first woman president of the FBA, claimed that Biddle had told her that he had "given no interview and [had] authorized no such statement" about his resignation. Minutes of FBA Executive Council, Dec. 13, 1943. But see, J. Paterson, *Be Somebody: A Biography of Marguerite Rawalt* 75 (1986). In Paterson's biography of Marguerite Rawalt, she confirms that Rawalt knew that "Biddle intended to resign from FBA unless the highly qualified Mehlinger was admitted."

61. *Id.* (FBA minutes). The petition for this hearing was signed by Robert Todd McKinley, John P. Barnes, Jr., Frank Coleman, Wendell Berge, and Ms. Ruth Weyand, all members of the subcommittee.

62. George W. Crockett, Jr., later a member of Congress, wrote, "I have no recollection of having applied in 1944 for membership in the Federal Bar Association; nor do I recall receiving any notice of a hearing on any such application. I must confess, however, that it would have been in character for me to have made such an application since I was aware that the Federal Bar Association, like the American Bar Association at that time, was 'lily-white'" (letter to author from Congressman George W. Crockett, Jr., July 19, 1985).

63. Louis Rothschild Mehlinger was a senior attorney in the Claims Division of the Department of Justice, a post he had held since 1923. Smith, "Louis Rothschild Mehlinger: The First One Hundred Years," 26 *Howard Law Journal* 359, 395 (1983).

64. Sidney A. Jones, Jr., worked in the Wage and Hour Division of the U.S. Department of Labor from 1939 to 1947. Jones remembers "attending several meetings and dinners of the Federal Bar Association, Chicago Chapter, during those years. I think I was a member, but I cannot recall with certainty. Also, I do not recall that black lawyers were excluded from membership" (letter to author from Judge Sidney A. Jones, Jr., July 12, 1985). Judge Jones's letter supports the notion that some local chapters paid little attention to the color bar in the constitution of the FBA. These chapters allowed black lawyers to attend and to participate in its activities.

65. Walter Arthur Gay, Jr., applied for FBA membership in 1936. Gay's application was rejected because of his race, and his check for dues was returned to him by the secretary of the FBA, Kenneth H. Bruner, Sr. The application was dated June 29, 1936. Gay may be the first black lawyer admit-

ted to membership in a state chapter of the FBA. It appears that he was active in the Philadelphia chapter of the FBA in 1936. At that time, Gay was an assistant United States attorney in the United States attorney's office in Philadelphia. Seven years later, the president of the Philadelphia chapter resubmitted Gay's application for membership to the national officers of the FBA, "recommending favorable action . . . and predicting censure by that chapter unless the Council acted [favorably]" at its December 13, 1943, meeting. Minutes of Executive Council FBA, Dec. 13, 1943. Letter to author from Walter Arthur Gay, Jr., Aug. 2, 1985 (in which Gay states, "I do remember that the tension became so great that the Philadelphia branch threatened to disaffiliate and to act independently and possibly with the support of other locals establish a rival Federal Bar Association").

66. Minutes of FBA Executive Committee, Feb. 14, 1944.

67. *Ibid.* Marguerite Rawalt provides a different basis for the race dispute in her biography. J. Paterson, *Be Somebody: A Biography of Marguerite Rawalt* 75–76 (1986). Rawalt resisted Tom Clark's efforts to have black lawyers admitted to the FBA without changing the whites-only provision in the FBA's constitution, which apparently Clark and the executive council believed unnecessary. *Ibid.*

68. *Ibid.*

69. Letter from Tom C. Clark to Robert Roy Dann, April 5, 1945. Dann objected to Clark's instruction, stating, "I would prefer not to cause [Johnson] the embarrassment of returning his application and asking him to fill in the line which was crossed out when he first received it. I would appreciate it if you would inform the Admissions Committee of the above and urge upon them the strong feelings of the more than eighty members in New York whose displeasure will be incurred if Mr. Johnson is barred because of his color." Letter from Robert Roy Dann to Tom C. Clark, April 9, 1945. The Subcommittee on the Bill of Rights members "were assured by Tom Clark that once he got to be president, Mehlinger and all attorneys employed by the federal government would be admitted. Everyone seemed agreed that Tom Clark not only meant it but that he would be able to carry through" (letter to author from Ruth Weyand, March 23, 1986).

70. Letter from Robert Roy Dann to Tom C. Clark, April 9, 1945.

71. Smith, "Louis Rothschild Mehlinger: The First One Hundred Years," 26 *Howard Law Journal* 359, 366–67 (1983).

72. *Id.* at 367, quoting from the special committee report filed with Tom C. Clark on Jan. 27, 1945. The special committee consisted of William G. Hamilton, Robert H. Shields, and Douglas B. Maggs (chairman).

73. Sidney Arlington Jones, Jr., was admitted on December 19, 1945, becoming the second black to be admitted to the FBA. See the FBA Application for Membership Form 9–43, Dec. 19, 1945. The action taken on George W. Crockett's application is uncertain. It is also unclear whether Walter Arthur Gay, Jr., was admitted during this period (letter from George W. Crockett, Jr., to author, July 19, 1985; letter from Walter Gay, Jr., to author, Aug. 2, 1985). Gay eventually gained national membership in 1965, at age sixty, long after the race bar was dropped by the FBA (FBA Application for Membership Form, Feb. 18, 1965).

74. McKenzie, "Pursuit of Democracy," *Pittsburgh Courier*, Nov. 11, 1943.

75. *Who's Who Among Negro Lawyers* 37 (S. T. M. Alexander ed. 1945).

76. "National Lawyers' Guild, in Liberal Move, Opens Its Doors to Negro Barristers," *Washington Tribune*, Feb. 27, 1937.

77. Other black lawyers in attendance at the NLG meeting were J. Howard Payne and Dallas Nichols, of Baltimore, Maryland; Edward P. Lovett, Belford V. Lawson, William L. Houston, and Leon Andrew Ransom, of Washington, D.C. "Nat. Lawyers Guild to Accept Negroes," *Richmond Planet*, Jan. 16, 1937. Years later Howard University law dean George Marion Johnson stated that "from the beginning [the NLG] accepted members without regard to race." George M. Johnson, "Legal Profession," in *The Integration of the Negro into American Society* 99 (E. F. Frazier ed. 1951).

78. *The National Lawyers' Guild: From Roosevelt Through Reagan* 18 (A. F. Ginger and E. M. Tobin eds. 1988); "Name Houston Official," *Amsterdam News*, Aug. 23, 1937.

79. "Durham, N.C. Selected for 1938 Meeting," *Chicago Defender*, Aug. 14, 1937.

80. "Lawyers Guild Closes Third Annual Meet," *Chicago Bee*, Feb. 26, 1939; Glaberson, "F.B.I. Admits Bid to Disrupt Lawyer Group," *New York Times*, Oct. 13, 1989, at B1, col. 6. Because of the liberal stands taken by the NLG, the group was considered suspect by governmental organizations like the FBI.

81. *Ibid.* ("Lawyers Guild Closes Third Annual Meet").

82. *Ibid.*

83. *Ibid.*

84. "Isaac Urges Negro-White Unity at Lawyers Dinner," *Atlanta Daily Worker*, Aug. 19, 1939; See also, "Officers and Directors," 1 *Lawyers' Guild Review* 53 (June 1941).

85. "Charges 'Jim Crow' Tests," *New York Times*, March 17, 1941.

86. "Earl B. Dickerson Appointed to Fair Labor Practice Committee," 1 *Lawyers' Guild Rev.* 29 (Aug. 1941).

87. McKenzie, "Pursuit of Democracy," *Pittsburgh Courier*, Nov. 11, 1943.

88. Letter from the Board of the National Lawyers' Guild to NAACP, 2 *Lawyers' Guild Rev.* 34 (July 1942).

89. Letter from Dean William E. Taylor to Martin Popper, 1 *Lawyers' Guild Rev.* 32 (Aug. 1941). By 1942, every member of the law faculty at Lincoln University School of Law was a member of the NLG. Letter from Dean William E. Taylor to Martin Popper, 2 *Lawyers' Guild Rev.* 24 (Jan. 1942). See also, "Martin Popper, 79, Lawyer in Leftist Causes," *New York Times*, Jan. 29, 1989, at 36, col. 4.

90. See 3 *Lawyers' Guild Rev.* (masthead) (Jan./Feb. 1943); *id.* at 1 (March/April 1943); *id.* at 1 (May/June 1943); *id.* at 1 (July/Aug. 1943); *id.* at 1 (Sept./Oct. 1943); *id.* at 1 (Nov./Dec. 1943); 4 *Lawyers' Guild Rev.* 1 (Jan./Feb. 1944); *id.* at 1 (March/April 1944); *id.* at 1 (July/Aug. 1944); *id.* at 1 (Oct. 1944); *id.* at 1 (Nov./Dec. 1944).

91. "Color Ban Lifted in Two Bar Associations," *Chicago Defender*, Sept. 4, 1943.

92. Report of the First Annual Convention of the National Negro Business League 1, Aug. 23–24, 1900 (Boston, MA).

93. Andrew F. Hilyer, "The Colored American in Business," *id.* at 13.

94. Smith, "The Black Bar Association and Civil Rights," 15 *Creighton L. Rev.* 651 (1982).

95. *Negro Year Book* 455 (M. Word ed. 1919).

96. "To the Colored Attorneys of the Nation," *Louisville News*, July 6, 1918; *Report of the Twelfth Annual Convention of the National Negro Business League* 142, Aug. 16–18, 1911 (Little Rock, AR). Henry Augustus Guess, a 1903 Howard

University law graduate and a practicing lawyer in Tulsa, Oklahoma, since 1903, was one of the NNBA's charter members. Guess was also a businessman. He was secretary and attorney for the Oklahoma Realty and Investment Co. in Tulsa. Vol. I *Who's Who of the Colored Race* 126 (F. L. Mather ed. 1915).

97. *Report of the Sixteenth Annual Convention of the National Negro Business League* 59, Aug. 18–20, 1915 (Boston, MA). Lewis, however, would later become one of Washington's staunchest supporters.

98. Stuart, "Accomplishments of Negro Lawyers," *Pittsburgh Courier*, June 17, 1944.

99. *Report of the Tenth Annual Convention of the National Negro Business League* 104, 106, Aug. 18–20, 1909 (Louisville, KY).

100. *Id.* at 107.

101. *Id.* at 107–8.

102. Josiah T. Settle remained president of the NNBA until 1913. In 1911, Perry W. Howard remained secretary, while Scipio A. Jones was named chairman of the executive committee. New faces at the NBL-NNBA annual meetings included B. F. Booth, of Tennessee, and L. G. Brown and S. Laing Williams, both of Chicago, Illinois. *Report of the Twelfth Annual Convention of the National Negro Business League* 141, Aug. 16–18, 1911 (Little Rock, AR).

103. *Report of the Thirteenth Annual Convention of the National Negro Business League* 172, Aug. 21–23, 1911 (Chicago, IL).

104. Lawyers in attendance from Philadelphia, Pennsylvania, included Charles H. Brooks, George W. White, John A. Sparks, and J. W. Garrett; from Little Rock, Arkansas, Scipio A. Jones; from Richmond, Virginia, Giles Beecher Jackson; from Washington, D.C., J. Arthur Davis and Ferdinand D. Lee; from New York City, Alfred C. Cowan and Lutie A. Lytle-Cowan; from Mississippi, Perry W. Howard; from Oklahoma, William Harrison, George W. Sawner, and C. Elbert Corbett. *Report of the Fourteenth Annual Convention of the National Negro Business League* 230, Aug. 20–22, 1913 (Philadelphia, PA). See also, R. W. Logan, *The Betrayal of the Negro* 317 (1969).

105. The election of Harrison must be viewed with some interest, since he was not from a Southern state. Nevertheless, Harrison was supported by a broad segment of those in attendance, among them Scipio A. Jones, of Arkansas, Giles B. Jackson, of Richmond, and Alfred C. Cowan, of New York. *Report of the Fourteenth Annual Convention of the National Negro Business League* 229–30, Aug. 20–22, 1913 (Philadelphia, PA).

106. *Report of the Fifteenth Annual Convention of the National Negro Business League* 225, Aug. 19–21, 1914 (Muskogee, OK).

107. *Ibid.*

108. *Id.* at 226. Other persons elected to office included Scipio A. Jones, of Little Rock, Arkansas, vice-president; William H. Harrison, of Oklahoma City, Oklahoma, secretary; William T. Andrews, of Sumter, South Carolina, treasurer; and C. Elbert Corbett, of Muskogee, Oklahoma, corresponding secretary. The following persons were elected to the executive committee: R. Emmett Stewart, of Muskogee, Oklahoma, chairman; William H. Twine, of Muskogee, Oklahoma; James C. Napier, of Nashville, Tennessee; W. E. Mollison, of Vicksburg, Mississippi; and S. T. Wiggins, of Wagner, Oklahoma.

109. *Report of the Sixteenth Annual Convention of the National Negro Business League* 133, Aug. 18–20, 1915 (Boston, MA). Perry W. Howard said that "there [were] 1,896 practicing Negro attorneys in the country" in 1915. *Ibid.* He probably intended to cite the figure as 896. In 1910, Vol. 4, *The Thirteenth Census,*

reports that there were no more than 805 black lawyers, Vol. 4, *The Fourteenth Census*, 1920, also reports fewer than 1,000 black lawyers in the nation.

110. *Id.* at 134 (*Report of the Sixteenth Annual Convention*).

111. "Meeting of the National Negro Bar Association," *The Atlanta Independent*, July 8, 1916.

112. *Report of the Eighteenth Annual Convention of the National Negro Business League* 153, Aug. 1917 (William H. Davis, reporter) (Chattanooga, TN). The NNBA also praised the growing number of "our young men . . . now graduating from law departments of some of the leading colleges and universities of our country and [the] greater recognition . . . being accorded Negro attorneys at the bar." *Ibid.*

113. "To the Colored Attorneys of the Nation," *Louisville News*, July 6, 1918.

114. In 1918, the NNBA remained under the presidency of Perry W. Howard. Other officers of the group included James C. Napier, of Nashville, Tennessee, vice-president; S. D. McGill, of Jacksonville, Florida, secretary; and William H. Harrison, of Chicago, Illinois, corresponding secretary. *Negro Year Book, 1918–1919* at 455 (M. N. Work ed. 1919).

115. *Report of the Twentieth Annual Convention of the National Negro Business League* 157, Aug. 13–15, 1919 (William H. Davis, reporter) (St. Louis, MO). The 1919 meeting of the NNBA with the NNBL marked their ten-year anniversary. Again the leadership of the NNBA called on black lawyers to attend the annual meeting in St. Louis, Missouri: "There was never a time when the sober, conservative and united thought of our race attorneys was more needed." "To the Race Members of the Bar," *The Daily Herald*, June 30, 1919.

116. The steering committee was composed of a distinguished group of lawyers representing Northern and Southern cities. The membership on the steering committee included its chairman, W. Ashbie Hawkins, of Baltimore, Maryland; Henry Lincoln Johnson, of Atlanta, Georgia; Cornelius Richardson, of Richmond, Virginia; William C. Matthews, of Boston, Massachusetts; S. D. McGill, of Jackson, Florida; Sidney D. Redmond, of Jackson, Mississippi; W. T. Andrews, of Baltimore, Maryland; D. W. Perkins, of Jacksonville, Florida; and James N. Simms, of Chicago, Illinois. "National Negro Bar Association," *Washington Eagle*, May 19, 1923; "Chicagoans to Welcome Bar Members," *Chicago Defenders*, May 26, 1923.

117. The black lawyers continued to carry the name of the NNBA and associated with the NNBL until 1925. However, the records of the NNBL are unclear as to whether the NNBA ever met again during its annual meeting. The last officers of the NNBA were Perry W. Howard, president; William C. Matthews, of Boston, Massachusetts, secretary; S. D. McGill, of Jacksonville, Florida, corresponding secretary; W. T. Andrews, of Baltimore, Maryland, treasurer; and Scipio A. Jones, of Little Rock, Arkansas, chairman of the executive committee. "National Negro Bar Association to Meet in Chicago," *Atlanta Independence*, Aug. 13, 1925.

118. "Chicagoans to Welcome Bar Members," *The Chicago Defender*, May 26, 1923.

119. "National Negro Bar Association," *Washington Eagle*, May 19, 1923.

120. "Postponed," *St. Louis Argus*, June 1, 1923.

121. Speech of Benjamin Jefferson Davis, Jr., Bar of Public Opinion, *Twenty-second Annual National Negro Business League* 117, 119, Aug. 17–19, 1921 (Atlanta). After the NBA was formed, Charles H. Calloway, the NBA's second

president, publicly disavowed any ties with the NNBA, stating that "[the NBA has] no connection with [the NNBA], which was headed by Mr. Perry Howard. We are free from politics, meet every year, function every day in the year, and have the backing of the majority of legal practitioners in the country." "Lawyers End Chicago Meet," *St. Louis Argus*, Aug. 8, 1926.

122. The National Bar Association, organized by black lawyers in 1925, should not be confused with a bar group with the same name organized by white lawyers in 1888. Brockman, "The National Bar Association, 1888–1893: The Failure of Early Bar Federation," 10 *Am. J. Legal History* 122 (1966); see Vol. 12 *Reports of American Bar Association* 54 (1889) (says that the NBA was founded in 1887).

123. "Negroes to Form Bar Association to Cover Nation," *Spartanburg Sun*, Feb. 28, 1925; "The NBA History and Perspective," in *National Bar Association Membership Directory*, at xiii (1991).

124. "Call for Organizing a Negro Association," *New York Age*, Feb. 21, 1925.

125. *Ibid.*

126. "Negroes to Form Bar Association to Cover Nation," *Spartanburg Sun*, Feb. 28, 1925.

127. The states and districts represented at this meeting included Iowa, Minnesota, Missouri, Kansas, Washington, D.C., Massachusetts, and Illinois. However, S. Joe Brown, one of the founders of the NBA, stated years later that the meeting was attended by lawyers from four states—Iowa, Illinois, Missouri, and Nebraska. Brown, "Our Founder," 2 *Nat'l A.B.J.* 263, 264 (Dec. 3, 1944).

128. Other officers elected included Charles H. Calloway, of Kansas City, Missouri, vice-president; Wendell E. Green, of Chicago, Illinois, assistant secretary; Charles P. Howard, of Des Moines, Iowa, treasurer; Jesse N. Baker, of Chicago, member of the executive committee.

129. Gustove B. Aldrich, of Tacoma, Washington, was elected region 1 director; David B. Henderson, of Kansas City, Kansas, was elected region 2 director; W. T. Francis, of St. Paul, Minnesota, was elected region 3 director; L. Amasa Knox, of Kansas City, Missouri, was elected region 4 director; William H. Hayes, of Chicago, Illinois, was elected region 5 director; and William C. Matthews, of Boston, Massachusetts, was elected region 6 director (this region covered the Virgin Islands). D. Hamilton Jackson, of Christianstead, St. Croix, Virgin Islands, U.S.A., was elected region 7 director. The list of officers and directors was reported across the nation. The above list is gathered from the original NBA articles of incorporation filed at Des Moines, Iowa, on July 29, 1926. The following articles, while helpful, are somewhat inaccurate with respect to the above information: "National Bar Association Is Organized," *Chicago Defender*, Aug. 15, 1925; "Negroes Form Bar Association," *Sedalia Democrat*, Aug. 2, 1925.

130. *Ibid.* ("National Bar Association Is Organized").

131. "National Bar Association Plans Meet Here Next Year," *Chicago Defender*, Aug. 13, 1925.

132. Articles of Incorporation of the National Bar Association, Article II. Object, filed for record, July 29, 1926, at 3:05 P.M., Mrs. E. O. Fleur and P. J. Griffin, record deputies. Brown, "Our Origin," 2 *Nat'l B.A.J.* 161, 163 (Sept. 1944).

133. A breakdown of a few of these cities follows:

CITY:	NO. BLACK LAWYERS:
Chicago, IL	95
New York, NY	50
Detroit, MI	32
Baltimore, MD	27
Indianapolis, IN	26
Boston, MA	16
Columbus, OH	14
Memphis, TN	13
Philadelphia, PA	13
Richmond, VA	12
St. Louis, MO	12
Kansas City, KA	11
Los Angeles, CA	10
Louisville, KY	10
Total	341

There were approximately 58,143 white lawyers total in these cities of 100,000 inhabitants, of which 11,246 practiced in New York City alone. "11,246 Practice Law in New York," *New York Times*, March 14, 1926. Black lawyers, as seen by the figures represented above, made up a small number of lawyers practicing in large urban cities. See also, "Chicago Leads in Lawyers," *Baltimore Afro-American*, Feb. 27, 1926; "Chicago Leads Cities in Number of Lawyers," *Amsterdam News*, Feb. 24, 1926.

134. "Lawyers End Annual Meet in Chicago," *Chicago Defender*, Aug. 4, 1926.
135. *Ibid.*
136. *Ibid*; "National Bar Association to Meet Here," *Chicago Defender*, July 10, 1926. All persons listed here are black. Judge Albert B. George was the first black judge elected in Chicago, Illinois; Alva L. Bates was from Chicago, Illinois; Judge James A. Cobb sat on the municipal court in the District of Columbia; Robert T. Vann was from Pittsburgh, Pennsylvania; and T. Emmett Stewart was from Muskogee, Oklahoma.
137. Most of the original officers were reelected. C. Francis Stradford was elected treasurer. "Lawyers End Annual Meet in Chicago," *Chicago Defender*, Aug. 14, 1926.
138. Omaha, Nebraska, was represented by John Adams, Sr., N. H. Ware, D. H. Oliver, and Amos Scruggs; Shreveport, Louisiana, by Charles M. Robertson; San Francisco, California, by Edward D. Mabson, Leland Hawkins, and Stanford Hawkins; Newport News, Virginia, by E. J. Newsome; and Jacksonville, Florida, by W. W. Parker. William C. Todd, from the Republic of Panama, also was present. "Atty. H. G. Phillips Elected President of Nat'l Bar Ass'n.," *St. Louis Argus*, Aug. 12, 1927; "National Bar Comfab Ends in St. Louis, Mo.," *Chicago Whip*, Aug. 13, 1927.
139. "Atty. H. G. Phillips Elected President of Nat'l Bar Ass'n"; "National Bar Association Plans Effective Drive," *Birmingham Reporter*, May 19, 1928.
140. *Ibid.* ("National Bar Association Plans Effective Drive").
141. John Adams, Sr., of Omaha, Nebraska, was elected vice-president. "National Bar Asso. Elects," *Baltimore Afro-American*, Aug. 13, 1927.
142. Roberts, "National Bar Association Ends Session," *Chicago Defender*, Aug. 11, 1928.
143. *Ibid.*

144. See *Plessy v. Ferguson*, 163 U.S. 537 (1896); *Brown v. The Board of Education of Topeka, Kansas*, 347 U.S. 483 (1954).

145. Johnson's speech was entitled "The Legal Profession and the Future of the Negro." In his speech, Johnson added that "the legal profession was the last to develop among a people who had been slaves, and it is one of the most important for the future of this race." Roberts, "National Bar Association Ends Session," *Chicago Defender*, Aug. 11, 1928.

146. *Ibid.*

147. *Ibid.*

148. "Nat'l Bar Ass'n. Ends Ann'l. Meet," *St. Louis Argus*, Aug. 10, 1928; "Noted Attorney Portia Member," *Chicago Defender*, March 24, 1928.

149. "Detroit Swamped with Legal Talent During Meeting of National Bar Association," *Amsterdam News*, Aug. 7, 1929. (The title of Stradford's speech was "Changes in Law Brought by Social and Economic Forces.").

150. *Ibid.*

151. *Ibid.*

152. *Ibid.*

153. *Ibid.* (The title of Judge Cobb's speech was "The Opportunity of the Negro Lawyer to Make a Real Contribution to American Jurisprudence.")

154. *Ibid.*

155. *Ibid.* Apparently influenced by Bishop B. G. Vernon's keynote address, Raymond Alexander urged that a coalition with the black church be forged in order to fight segregation. Alexander, along with Irving Mollison of Chicago, sent a letter to Rev. L. K. Williams, of Kansas City, and to Dr. J. E. Woods, of Norfolk, Virginia, both leaders of Baptist conventions, urging them to combine forces with the NBA for the "common welfare" of the race. "Bar Association Asks Church Cooperation," *Birmingham Reporter*, Sept. 14, 1929.

156. "Detroit Swamped with Legal Talent During Meeting of National Bar Association Ass'n," *Amsterdam News*, Aug. 7, 1929.

157. The members' support of the NBA did not match its growth. It was reported that the members were not paying their dues. *Id.* at 22 (report of the secretary, Irvin C. Mollison).

158. "Hoover Scored by Nation's Lawyers," *Baltimore Afro-American*, Aug. 16, 1930. During the convention, James J. Davis, Secretary of Labor, and Walter Brown, postmaster general, addressed the NBA. "Bar Ass'n. Convention Hits Evils," *St. Louis Argus*, Aug. 15, 1930. At the close of the sixth annual meeting of the NBA, Emory S. Smith, Sylvester L. McLaurin, W. Justin Carter, R. McCants Andrews, and R. D. Evans issued a statement criticizing "the attitude of the [Hoover] administration toward the appointment of Negroes to responsible positions in the Federal Government" and the enforcement of laws to protect blacks. *NBA Proceedings of the Sixth Annual Convention* 62, Aug. 8, 1930.

159. *Id.* at 7. (The title of Raymond Pace Alexander's speech was "The Negro Lawyer: His Duty in a Rapidly Changing Social, Economic and Political World.")

160. "6th Annual Session of Lawyers End," *Chicago Defender*, Aug. 16, 1930. The need to maintain strong local bar groups was emphasized in an address by A. M. Burroughs of the Cook County Bar Association.

161. "Resumé of Addresses Before the National Bar Association," *Baltimore Afro-American*, Aug. 16, 1930.

162. "Hoover Scored by Nation's Lawyers," *Baltimore Afro-American*, Aug. 16, 1930.

163. "Bar Ass'n Convention Hits Evils," *St. Louis Argus*, Aug. 15, 1930. This resolution was proposed by R. D. Evans, of Waco, Texas.

164. "6th Annual Session of Lawyers End," *Chicago Defender*, Aug. 16, 1930.

165. "Bar Ass'n Convention Hits Evils," *St. Louis Argus*, Aug. 15, 1930; "Hoover Scored by Nation's Lawyers," *Baltimore Afro-American*, Aug. 16, 1930. "Nat'l Bar Association Holds Annual Convention," *Washington Tribune*, Aug. 14, 1931.

166. *Ibid.*

167. D. T. Carter, *Scottsboro: A Tragedy of the American South* 143 (1969).

168. "Newton D. Baker Invited to Address Bar Association," *Chicago Defender*, July 18, 1931.

169. "Nat'l Bar Ass'n. Elects Jesse Heslip of Toledo President at Cleveland Meeting," *Amsterdam News*, Aug. 12, 1931.

170. "Indianapolis Lawyers Ready for Big Meet," *Indianapolis Recorder*, July 23, 1932; "N.A.A.C.P. Bar Asso. United for Action," *Baltimore Afro-American*, Aug. 13, 1932.

171. Louis Lorenzo Redding, of Wilmington, Delaware, and N. J. Frederick, of Columbia, South Carolina, were also members of the NAACP's legal committee. "Cooperation of N.A.A.C.P. Pledged by Sec'y White," *Pittsburgh Courier*, Aug. 13, 1932.

172. "N.A.A.C.P. Bar Asso. United for Action," *Baltimore Afro-American*, Aug. 13, 1932.

173. "Indianapolis Lawyers Ready for Big Meet," *Indianapolis Recorder*, July 23, 1932.

174. Smith, "The Marion County Lawyers' Club: 1932 and the Black Lawyer," 8 *Black L.J.* 170, 175 (Howard Law School ed. 1983); "D.C. Delegation Returns from Bar Assn. Convention," *Washington Tribune*, Aug. 19, 1932.

175. "Stradford Cancels Radio Talk from Jim Crow Hotel," *Chicago Defender*, Aug. 11, 1933.

176. *Ibid.*

177. "National Bar Association Will Meet in St. Louis," *Chicago Defender*, Aug. 11, 1933.

178. "Stradford Cancels Radio Talk from Jim Crow Hotel," *Chicago Defender*, Aug. 11, 1933.

179. "Rhodes Heads Nat. Bar Association," *Baltimore Afro-American*, Aug. 12, 1933.

180. *Ninth Annual Convention Program of the NBA*, Aug. 3–5, 1933, at 3.

181. "Thomas Speaker at Bar Confab," *Pittsburgh Courier*, Aug. 25, 1934.

182. "Lawyers Elect Lawrence Head of National Bar," *Chicago Defender*, Aug. 10, 1935.

183. Matthews, "National Bar Association a Little Pink but Refuses to Turn Red," *Baltimore Afro-American*, Aug. 17, 1935.

184. *Ibid.*

185. "National Bar Acts Against Mitchell Bill," *Chicago Defender*, Aug. 10, 1935.

186. McNeil, "Charles Hamilton Houston," 3 *Black L.J.* 123, 126 (1975), quoting speech by Houston entitled, "Proposed Legal Attacks on Educational Discrimination."

187. "Lawyers Elect Lawrence Head of National Bar," *Chicago Defender*, Aug. 10, 1935.

188. *Ibid.*

189. "National Bar Group Raps Congressman," *Norfolk Journal and Guide*, Aug. 15, 1936; Smith, "The Black Bar Association and Civil Rights," 15 *Creighton L. Rev.* 651, 678 (1982).

190. "Lawyers Warned Against 'High Hat' Attitude as Bar Association Meets," *Pittsburgh Courier*, Aug. 14, 1937.

191. *Ibid.* The title of Vann's speech was "The Legal Influences on Economic Life."

192. *NBA Thirteenth Annual Convention Program*, 1937.

193. "Future Cloudy," *New York Times*, Aug. 16, 1937.

194. "NBA Resolutions Cover Many Topics," *Chicago Defender*, Aug. 14, 1937.

195. Noting a need for "closer cooperation . . . in carrying out the progress of [the NBA,]" Houston moved quickly to enlarge the regions and the directorships to the following eighteen:

REGIONS

1. Massachusetts, Maine, New Hampshire, Connecticut, Rhode Island, Vermont
   Director: Matthew W. Bullock (Boston, MA)
2. New York State
   Director: Albert C. Gilbert (New York City)
3. Pennsylvania
   Director: Robert L. Vann (Pittsburgh, PA)
4. Maryland, Delaware, New Jersey
   Director: George W. Evans (Baltimore, MD)
5. Virginia and West Virginia
   Director: Harry J. Capehart (Welch, WV)
6. North Carolina, South Carolina
   Director: F. W. Williams (Winston-Salem, NC)
7. Georgia, Florida, Alabama
   Director: T. J. Henry (Atlanta, GA)
8. Tennessee, Mississippi, Louisiana, Arkansas
   Director: Webster L. Porter (Knoxville, TN)
9. Michigan, Indiana
   Director: Percival R. Piper (Detroit, MI)
10. Ohio, Kentucky
    Director: Clarence G. Smith (Toledo, OH)
11. Illinois, Wisconsin
    Director: Euclid L. Taylor (Chicago, IL)
12. Minnesota, Iowa, Nebraska
    Director: S. Joe Brown (Des Moines, IA)
13. Kansas, Missouri
    Director: Sidney R. Redmond (St. Louis, MO)
14. Wyoming, Idaho, Utah, Colorado
    Director: Thomas Campbell (Denver, CO)
15. Texas, Oklahoma, New Mexico
    Director: Charles H. Chandler (Muskogee, OK)
16. Southern California, Arizona
    Director: Thomas L. Griffin (Los Angeles, CA)

17. North Dakota, South Dakota, Montana
    Director: Will F. Reden (Sioux Falls, SD)
18. Washington, Oregon
    Director: Walter Gordon (Berkeley, CA)
19. District of Columbia, Insular Possessions
    Director: Thurman L. Dodson (District of Columbia)

See, "Lawyers Warned Against 'High' Attitude as Bar Association Meets," *Pittsburgh Courier*, Aug. 14, 1937.

196. "74 Lawyers from 21 States Attend Meet," *Baltimore Afro-American*, Aug. 14, 1937; Smith, "The Marion County Lawyers' Club: 1932 and the Black Lawyer," 8 *Black L.J.* 170, 175 (Howard Law School ed. 1983).

197. "Nation's Lawyers End Conference at Durham," *Norfolk Journal and Guide*, Aug. 13, 1938.

198. *Ibid.*

199. *Ibid.* The NBA noted the dearth of black lawyers employed by government agencies and "voiced its support of the campaign to get equal salaries and equal educational opportunities." The NBA adopted a resolution condemning the Federal Civil Service for requiring persons to designate their race or color on applications for government jobs.

200. "Negro Lawyers Delegates Reject Red-Baiting Smear," *Atlanta Daily World*, Aug. 18, 1939.

201. *Ibid.* Interview with Dr. Joseph Dejean, professor emeritus, Howard University School of Law, March 1 and 4, 1985. J. Lelio Joseph also addressed the general body.

202. *Ibid.* ("Negro Lawyer Delegates Reject Red-Baiting Smear").

203. "Attorney Sidney Redmond Elected to Presidency of National Bar Association in Convention Here," *New York Age*, Aug. 26, 1939. Other women in attendance at the meeting included Ollie May Cooper, Isadora Augusta Jackson Letcher, both of Washington, D.C., Eunice Hunton Carter, Sally Gatling, and Lucille Chance, all of New York, and Sadie T. M. Alexander, of Philadelphia, Pennsylvania.

204. Bethea, "Lifting Bans on Negroes," *Chicago Tribune*, Nov. 29, 1939.

205. "National Bar Association to Establish Free Aid Bureaus for Needy," *Philadelphia Tribune* Aug. 29, 1940.

206. "Head of National Bar Association Writes President," *Pittsburgh Courier*, Dec. 14, 1940.

207. *Ibid.* While no black civilian aide to the Secretary of the Navy was ever appointed, in 1942, William Henry Hastie, dean of Howard University School of Law, was appointed civilian aide to the Secretary of War, Henry L. Stimson. G. Ware, *William Hastie: Grace Under Pressure* 97 (1984).

208. *NBA 16th Annual Convention Program*, Aug. 1–3, 1940.

209. "Resident Bans to Be Topic at Bar Convention," *Baltimore Afro-American* July 27, 1940. See *Hansberry v. Lee*, 311 U.S. 32 (1940). Other black lawyers on the brief with Miller included Earl B. Dickerson, C. Francis Stradford, and Irving C. Mollison.

210. *NBA 16th Annual Convention Program*, Aug. 1–3, 1940; "Will Publish Law Journal," *Amsterdam News*, Aug. 31, 1940.

211. The committee included Perry W. Howard (chairman), Nathan A. Dobbins, Belford V. Lawson, George A. Parker, Leon A. Ransom, Thurman L. Dodson, Henry Lincoln Johnson, and Emory Smith.

212. "National Bar Journal Pub.," *St. Louis Argus* July 2, 1941; Smith, "The Black Bar Association and Civil Rights," 15 *Creighton L. Rev.* 651, 665 (1982). Credit for the idea that the NBA establish a law journal belongs to Raymond Pace Alexander, who originally had recommended a journal to be established in 1931, when he was president of the NBA, and again in 1938. *Id.* at 665. See also, "Report of Bar Publication Committee," *The National Bar Association: Proceedings of the Seventh Annual Convention* 49 (Aug. 1931). Although Alexander was in his final days as president of the NBA, he served as a member of the Publication Committee, chaired by E. Washington Rhodes. The committee was composed of five people, including Violette N. Anderson, the only woman on the committee. A letter from Alexander to Francis Biddle, attorney general of the United States, appeared in the *Journal*. Alexander's letter called upon the attorney general to "quickly and thoroughly investigate . . . the klan." Alexander, "Attorney General Francis Biddle," 1 *Nat'l B.A.J.* 146, 148 (1941).

213. "Lawyers to Record All Discrimination Cases," *Norfolk Guide and Journal*, Jan. 18, 1941.

214. The free legal aid bureaus were organized throughout the nation by Clark S. Frazier, president of the Mound City Bar Association, and Professor James C. Bush, of Lincoln University School of Law. "Mound City Bar Favors Legal Center," *St. Louis Argus*, April 11, 1941. See also, Smith, "The Black Bar Association and Civil Rights," 15 *Creighton L. Rev.* 651, 653 (1982).

215. E. A. Brownell, *Legal Aid in the United States* xiii (1951).

216. *Id.* at 12–16, 87.

217. Letter from Charles H. Houston to National Lawyers' Guild, 1 *Lawyers' Guild Rev.* 32 (Aug. 1941).

218. Euclid L. Taylor finished law school in Chicago with the aid of Silas N. Strawn, ex-president of the United States Chamber of Commerce and former president of the American Bar Association. Strawn was head of the Chicago law firm of Winston, Strawn and Shaw, the largest firm in the Midwest. Strawn's support came after Taylor was shot five times while riding with Octavius Grannady. Grannady was assassinated in the incident. Strawn was impressed with Taylor's willingness to stand up and testify against Grannady's murderers. "Euclid L. Taylor Elected Head of Bar Association," *Nashville Globe and Independent*, Aug. 29, 1941.

219. Taylor, "The New World and the New Law," *Chicago Defender*, Dec. 19, 1943; "Roster of National Bar Association Officers," 3 *Nat'l B.A.J.* 303 (Sept. 1945).

220. "Ask Use of Negro Lawyers in War," *The New York Daily Worker*, July 7, 1942. See generally, M. R. Davie, *Negroes in American Society* 330–31 (1949).

221. *Ibid.* ("Ask Use of Negro Lawyers in War").

222. "Post for Negro Lawyers," *New York Times*, Aug. 5, 1943, quoting John J. McCloy, assistant secretary of war. See G. Ware, *William Hastie: Grace Under Pressure* 130–33 (1984), regarding Hastie's resignation as civilian aide to the secretary of war. In 1942, "the percentage of Negro lawyers commissioned in the Armed Forces [was] smaller than doctors and dentists, apparently due to their many legal victories in civilian life. In reality, an increased number of Negro attorneys might possibly be a step forward to better racial harmony in the Armed Forces through a more balanced legal justice." *Black Armed Forces Officers* 67 (J. Johnson ed. 1971). After the close of the NBA's 1942 annual meeting, the NLG, in cooperation with the NBA, continued their efforts to increase the number of black lawyers in the judge advocate generals' corps of

602   White and Black Bar Groups

the various services. Letter from the Board of the National Lawyers Guild to National Association for the Advancement of Colored People, 2 *Lawyers' Guild Rev.* 34 (July 1942); Popper, "The Guild Contributes to Victory," 3 *Lawyers' Guild Rev.* 4 (March–April 1943). Despite the NBA and NLG's protest, discrimination against black lawyers continued. As a result of racism in the armed forces, William Henry Hastie, civilian aide to Henry L. Stimpson, the Secretary of War, resigned his post. Martin Popper of the NLG stated that "Hastie's resignation was a service to the country, because it focused national attention upon this serious situation." *Ibid.* ("The Guild Contributes to Victory"). See also, G. Ware, *William Hastie: Grace Under Pressure* 129–31 (1984). Secretary of War Simpson appointed Truman Gibson, Jr., to replace Hastie as his aide. Simpson believed that Hastie had yielded to the pressures of his people. He was more than happy to replace him with Truman K. Gibson, Jr., another, and perhaps more conservative, black. See G. Hodgson, *The Colonel: The Life of Henry Simpson, 1867–1950*, at 250, star note (1990).

223. "War Department Okays Race Lawyers," *Pittsburgh Courier*, Aug. 14, 1943.

224. Willard Ransom, a 1939 Harvard University law graduate, was commissioned while serving as deputy attorney general of Indiana (biographical sketch of Williard B. Ransom, courtesy National Bar Association). Fernandes graduated from Suffolk University's law school in 1941. He acted as defense counsel and handled more than three hundred cases at the rank of captain (*Who's Who Among Negro Lawyers* 15 [S. T. M. Alexander ed. 1945]). Davidson, a member of the District of Columbia bar, served as a trial judge in Europe and the Pacific (*id.* at 12). Ming entered the army as a private, but acted as defense counsel in several courts-martial. On one occasion, Ming was given special permission to participate in a civil rights case before the United States Supreme Court. He had been involved in the case prior to entering the military. "Ming 1st Private to Argue Case Before High Court," *Baltimore Afro-American*, Dec. 25, 1943. See *Smith v. Allwright*, 321 U.S. 649 (1944). (The headline of the article is misleading. Ming, while in the armed services, was a signatory to the brief, along with Thurgood Marshall, William Henry Hastie, Leon A. Ransom, Carter Wesley, W. J. Durham, and George M. Johnson.)

William A. McClain, a 1937 University of Michigan law graduate, was also commissioned (biographical sketch of McClain, courtesy National Bar Association). Edith S. Sampson was designated as a judge advocate of the Women's Army for National Defense in 1942 (*Who's Who, id.* at 32). Cecil Francis Poole, a 1936 law graduate of the University of Michigan, served as a legal officer and trial judge advocate at the Tuskegee Air Field in Alabama after he received his master of laws degree from Harvard University in 1938. Samuel M. Huffman, a 1912 law graduate of Northwestern University law school, was called on to defend black servicemen in general courts-martial at Fort Huachuca, Arizona, in 1944. The interest of black lawyers in the Army Judge Advocates Generals Corps was not new. In 1918, James A. Cobb was perhaps the first black lawyer to seek an appointment as "Judge Advocate for one of the colored divisions, National army, now being organized." Letter from James A. Cobb to Newton D. Baker, secretary of war, Jan. 9, 1918.

225. "Highlights of 18th Annual Convention," 2 *Nat'l B.A.J.* 80 (June 1944).

226. Euclid Taylor, "The New World and the New Law," *Chicago Defender*, Dec. 19, 1943.

227. "Highlights of 18th Annual Convention," 2 *Nat'l B.A.J.* 80, 81 (June 1944).

228. *Ibid.*

229. *Id.* at 80. See, "Named Trial Lawyer for Dep't of Justice," *Atlanta Daily World*, June 7, 1943.

230. *Ibid.* ("Named Trial Lawyer for Dep't of Justice").

231. "Kentucky Legislator New NBA President," *Pittsburgh Courier*, Dec. 4, 1943, at 1, col. 4. Interview by author of Charles S. Brown, July 12, 1986. Brown said that Houston may have been "resented by some because he thought that he was better than we were. He lost the 1943 election because of this." See also, "Kentucky Legislator New NBA President," *Pittsburgh Courier*, 1942, at 1, col. 3: "The narrow victory was etched out over Charles H. Houston, Washington attorney and counsel to the NAACP, whose defeat was directly attributable to the resentment of a large portion of his hometown group." "Anderson New Head National Bar Ass'n.," *Norfolk Journal and Guide*, Dec. 18, 1943. Houston lost by a narrow margin of four votes.

232. "Roster of National Bar Association Officers," 3 *Nat'l B.A.J.* 303 (Sept. 1945).

233. "Highlights of 18th Annual Convention," 2 *Nat'l B.A.J.* 80, 82 (June 1944).

234. Emma Chase, Isadora A. Letcher, Ollie May Cooper, and Marjorie McKenzie were from Washington, D.C.; Sadie T. M. Alexander was from Philadelphia, Pennsylvania; L. Marian Poe was from Newport News, Virginia; and Eunice Hunton Carter was from New York City. "National Bar Association Had Feminine Contingent Too," *Baltimore Afro-American*, Dec. 4, 1943.

235. "Lawyers Pledge Efforts for Federal Voting Law," *The People's Voice*, Dec. 16, 1944.

236. "National Bar Association Fights Bias at Convention," *Baltimore Afro-American*, Dec. 9, 1944; "Lawyers Pledge Efforts for Federal Voting Law," *The People's Voice*, Dec. 16, 1944.

237. "Negro National Bar Week," *The Atlanta Daily World*, May 2, 1944.

238. Settle graduated from the Howard College Department of Law in 1875, and was admitted to the District of Columbia bar before he left the area to practice law in northern Mississippi.

239. Settle, "The Colored Bar Association," in *Afro-American Encyclopedia; Or, The Thoughts, Doings and Sayings of the Race* 60 (J. Haley ed. 1895).

240. *Id.*

241. *Id.* at 51.

242. *Id.* at 52.

243. *Id.* at 55.

244. *Detroit Plaindealer*, April 15, 1892.

245. Smith, "The Black Bar Association and Civil Rights," 15 *Creighton L. Rev.* 651, 658 (1982).

246. *Who's Who of the Colored Race* 43 (F. L. Mather ed. 1915).

247. "Arkansas Lawyers Form Organization," *Oklahoma Black Dispatch*, Nov. 5, 1938. Other officers elected at the 1938 meeting included Theodore X. Jones, of Pine Bluff, vice-president; William A. Singfield, of Little Rock, vice-president; W. Harold Flowers, of Pine Bluff, executive secretary; and Scipio Africanus Jones, of Little Rock, treasurer. Five other lawyers formed the remaining membership of the bar group: J. A. Hibbler, of Little Rock; Wallace L.

Purifoy, Jr., of Forrest City; Joseph Atkins, of Camden; G. H. Green, of Hot Springs; and I. H. Spears, of Eldorado.

248. "Call for Organizing a Negro Bar Association," *New York Age*, Feb. 21, 1925; "Negroes to Form Bar Association to Cover Nation," *Spartanburg Sun*, Feb. 28, 1925.

249. "Made Bar President," *Chicago Defender*, Feb. 5, 1921. Rush was counsel for the Women's Convention Auxiliary of the National Baptist Convention. In addition, she was "a clubwoman, having served as president of the Iowa Federation of Colored Women's Clubs for four years." She was active as a social worker in Des Moines, Iowa, and was a member of the board of directors of several civic organizations, including the Des Moines Playground Association. She also founded the Charity League, an organization for the general welfare of black citizens in Des Moines. "First Race Woman Attorney of Iowa," *Chicago Defender*, Nov. 14, 1925.

250. Only the names of George H. Woodson, Charles Preston Howard, Sr., and Samuel Joseph Brown appear on the articles of incorporation of the National Bar Association. E. B. Toles, *Fifty Years of Progress for Black Lawyers* 25 (1975) (NBA Convention Program, citing articles of incorporation filed with the recorder of Polk County, Document No. 29551).

251. "National Negro Bar Association," *Savannah Tribune*, Feb. 19, 1920.

252. E. B. Toles, *Chicago Negro Judges, 1900–1965*, at 3, June 19, 1965 (pamphlet).

253. H. F. Gosnell, *Negro Politicians: The Rise of Negro Politics in Chicago* 108 (1935).

254. The first officers of the Cook County Bar Association were Edward H. Wright, president; Richard E. Westbrooks, first vice-president; Richard Hill, third vice-president; George W. Ellis, secretary; and Harrison H. Farrel, treasurer. Members of the executive council included William L. Martin, Augustus L. Williams, and James N. Simms. "Hon. E. H. Wright Elected President of Bar Meeting," *Chicago Defender*, Jan. 30, 1915. At the time of his election, Edward H. Wright was an assistant corporation counsel in Chicago under Mayor William Hale Thompson. He was the "first Negro to be appointed a member of the Illinois Commerce Commission." Burroughs, "History of the Cook County Bar Association," *Chicago Defender*, May 24, 1930.

255. Ellis, "The Chicago Negro in Law and Politics," 1 *The Champion Magazine* 349, 358 (March 1917).

256. *Id.* at 359. The organizing members of the Cook County Bar Association were "found in important positions in every one of the political factions." H. F. Gosnell, *Negro Politicians: The Rise of Negro Politics in Chicago* 108 (1935).

257. "Hon. E. H. Wright Elected Pres. of Bar Meeeting," *Chicago Defender*, Jan. 30, 1915.

258. "Cook County Bar Association Holds Interesting Meeting," *Chicago Defender*, April 10, 1915.

259. Burroughs, "History of the Cook County Bar Association," *Chicago Defender*, May 24, 1930. Porter was the second president of the group, followed by James T. Terry, who served from 1920 to 1921, and Richard E. Westbrooks, who served a second term as president from 1921 to 1922.

260. *Ibid.* Mollison was the fifth president (1922–1924) of the group, followed by Waring (1924–1926). Regarding Mollison, see also, "Chicagoans to Welcome Bar Members," *Chicago Defender*, May 26, 1923.

261. *Ibid.* ("History of the Cook County Bar Association").

262. *Ibid.*

263. *Ibid.*

264. *Ibid*; "Lawyers Elect Herman Moore to Head Ass'n.," *Chicago Whip*, Jan. 18, 1930.

265. M. S. Goldman, *A Portrait of the Black Attorney in Chicago* 36 (1972).

266. "Chicago U. Law Group Raps Bar Discrimination," *Chicago Defender*, July 8, 1944. The Cook County Bar Association never excluded whites from membership; in fact, it affirmatively proclaimed a nondiscriminatory membership policy. Burroughs, "History of the Cook County Bar Association," *Chicago Defender* May 24, 1930. A white Chicago judge, Joseph B. David, was a member of the group in 1928. "Bar Association Dedicates New $2,000 Law Library," *Chicago Defender*, Sept. 29, 1928.

267. Vol. 1 *Intercollegian Wonder Book—1779—The Negro in Chicago—1927*, at 115 (F. H. Robb ed. 1927); "National Bar Association to Meet Here," *Chicago Defender*, July 10, 1926; "Chicagoans to Welcome Bar Members," *Chicago Defender*, May 6, 1923.

268. "Negro Bar Association Meet," *The Freeman*, March 20, 1915.

269. During this meeting, Chauncey D. Twine was elected president of the Oklahoma Negro Bar Association. Other officers elected included Primus Wade, of Tulsa, vice president; H. McKinley Rowan, of Oklahoma City, secretary; and E. L. Barbour, of Oklahoma City, treasurer. Other lawyers attending this meeting included Buck Franklin, A. L. J. Meriwether, and J. C. Evans (all of Okmulgee); Ernest Richards, J. J. Bruce, H. T. Walker, R. E. Stewart, J. Bernard Smith, C. E. Robertson, C. E. Colbert, C. P. Kimble, and Harry Twine (all of Muskogee); and Roy Lowe, of Wewoka. "Negro Lawyers in Annual Meeting," *Oklahoma Black Dispatch*, July 3, 1937. Another source adds the names of J. J. Seabrook of Oklahoma City (who served as the group's chaplin), and Charles A. Chandler, of Muskogee, to those elected to office when the Oklahoma Negro Bar Association met in 1939. The other officers remained the same. "Oklahoma Barristers Close First Annual Session After Forming Southwestern Ass'n," *Black Dispatch*, June 9, 1940.

270. "Colored Lawyers Organize," *The Herald*, 1916. Other officers included E. B. Hubert, secretary; Thomas L. Jones, treasurer; and J. E. Collins, sergeant-at-arms. A committee of permanent organizations was appointed, consisting of Joseph H. Stewart, Benjamin L. Gaskins, and J. E. Collins.

271. The names of all the officers in the group are unknown, however, "L. Melendez King was named secretary and he and Attorney Frisby were named a committee on [the] constitution." "Lawyers Organize," *The Washington Bee*, March 23, 1918. In 1920 Royal Hughes was elected president of the Colored Bar Association in Washington, D.C. "The Colored Bar," *The Washington Bee*, Oct. 9, 1920.

272. Personal interview with Louis Rothschild Mehlinger, Oct. 19, 1979, in Washington, D.C.

273. *Ibid.*

274. The following black lawyers founded the Washington Bar Association: Ulysses Simpson Garnes, George E. C. Hayes, Charles Hamilton Houston, Isaiah Lisemby, Louis Rothschild Mehlinger, Charles E. Robinson, and J. Franklin Wilson.

275. The Washington Bar Association was also successful because it had a succession of distinguished presidents from its founding through World War II: George E. C. Hayes (1925–1928), Sylvester McLaurin (1928–1930),

Charles Hamilton Houston (1930–1932), Charles E. Robinson (1932–1933), Augustus Gray (1933–1934), Thurman L. Dodson (1934–1936), William L. Houston (1936–1938), Henry Lincoln Johnson, Jr. (1938–1940), James A. Cobb (1940–1942), and Richard L. Atkinson (1942–1944). *1988 Law Day Program, Washington Bar Association* (compiled by J. C. Smith, Jr.).

276. Members of the Washington Bar Association were frequently invited to address bar groups throughout the nation. See "Philadelphia Judge Speaks to Bar Groups," *Washington World*, May 27, 1931.

277. "Washington Bar Association Will Celebrate Lawyer's Day," *Washington Tribune*, March 24, 1933.

278. The National Negro Congress, headed by A. Philip Randolph, had a membership that "included several known Communists of both races." The congress supported black rights and opposed Jim Crow laws. See E. Peeks, *The Long Struggle for Black Power* 285–86 (1971).

279. Richard R. Horner was elected vice-president, Frederick L. French, secretary, and Phillip W. Thomas, treasurer. "Nathan Dobbins Elected Head of Barristers Ass'n," *Chicago Defender*, April 11, 1936.

280. Other members of the WBA forming the new bar group included William C. Hueston, George E. C. Hayes, Charles K. Brown, J. Flipper Derricotte, George C. Jefferson, Frank W. Adams, James A. Cobb, Andrew Howard, Thomas W. Parks, Jr., and Otho D. Branson (*ibid*).

281. "National Bar Group Urges Negro Judge," *Washington Tribune*, Aug. 7, 1937.

282. "Library Drops Bars After Attorney Sues," *Washington Afro-American*, April 25, 1964, at A4.

283. "Two-Year Fight Ends in Moral Victory for Lawyers," *Washington Tribune*, March 1, 1941; "Bar Library," *Washington Post*, March 14, 1941; "The Washington Bar," *Chicago Defender*, March 8, 1941; "Negro Lawyers Aided by Head of White Bar," *Philadelphia Tribune*, March 20, 1941. Frances W. Hill, the white president of the District of Columbia Bar Association, moved quickly to support the use of the law library by black lawyers. There was little other choice, given the fact that relocation of the library would be very costly to the association.

284. "Library Drops Bar After Attorney Sues," *Washington Afro-American*, April 25, 1964, at A4.

285. *Ibid.*

286. In response to the ruling by the Department of Justice, the District of Columbia Bar Association voted 116 to 54 to permit black lawyers to use the library, provided they paid an eight-dollar annual fee. "White Lawyers Vote Library Open to Negroes," *Nashville Globe and Independent,* March 21, 1941.

287. "District Bar Votes to Admit All Lawyers," *Washington Afro-American*, Oct. 18, 1958, at 2, col. 2.

288. "Robinson Again Heads Bar," *Washington Tribune*, April 26, 1929.

289. *NBA 16th Annual Convention Program*, Aug. 1–3, 1940.

290. Letter to editor from Clinton W. Dickerson, Charleston, West Virginia, *Pittsburgh Courier*, Jan. 21, 1928.

291. *Ibid.*

292. "Negro Bar Assoc. Meets Saturday," *Wheeling West Virginia Intelligence*, June 6, 1919.

293. There is some evidence that the Negro Bar Association of West Virginia continued through the 1920s. In 1913 Jonathan S. Butts, a graduate of the

Detroit College of Law, returned to West Virginia to practice law. He is reported to have been a member of the Negro Bar Association of West Virginia and the Raleigh County Bar Association. Membership in the Raleigh County Bar Association suggests that not all county bar groups in West Virginia excluded black lawyers from membership. Vol. 7 *History of Negro West Virginia* 48–49 (A. B. Caldwell ed. 1923).

294. In 1937 Jonathan S. Butts was elected vice-president of the Mountain State Bar Association. J. R. Redmond became treasurer of the group. In 1939 Daniel W. Ambrose, Jr., was elected president, Harry J. Capehart, vice-president, Willard L. Brown, secretary, and Jonathan S. Butts, treasurer. *West Virginia Bureau of Negro and Statistics Biennial Report, 1937–1938*, at 81 (I. M. Carper ed. 1938); *id., 1939–1940*, at 85.

295. The law club elected Charles A. Roxborough, Jr., vice-president, C. Henry Lewis, secretary, and Frances Warren, treasurer. "Race Lawyers Form Club for Betterment," *Indianapolis Indiana Ledger*, Nov. 2, 1918.

296. *Plessy v. Ferguson*, 163 U.S. 537, 552–564 (1896). Littlejohn and Hudson, "Black Lawyers, Law Practice, and Bar Associations, 1844 to 1970: A Michigan History," 33 *Wayne L. Rev.* 1625, 1682 (1987).

297. "Detroit Swamped with Legal Talent During Meeting of National Bar Ass'n.," *Amsterdam News*, Aug. 7, 1929.

298. Littlejohn and Hudson, "Black Lawyers, Law Practice, and Bar Associations, 1844 to 1970: A Michigan History," 33 *Wayne L. Rev.* 1,625, 1,684 (1987).

299. *Ibid.*

300. Frances M. Dent, *Annual Report of President* (Wolverine Bar Association), Oct. 20, 1937, at 2.

301. Letter from Arthur Randall, Jr., and R. M. Golightly to Francis M. Dent, Oct. 23, 1939.

302. Francis M. Dent, *Annual Report of President* (Wolverine Bar Association), Oct. 28, 1939, at 1.

303. *Id.* (Oct. 20, 1932, at 2).

304. Green, "Dean of Cleveland Bar, Ends 60th Year," *Washington Tribune*, Oct. 17, 1930.

305. "Nat'l Bar Asso. Holds Annual Convention," *Washington Tribune*, Aug. 14, 1931; *The National Bar Association's Seventh Annual Convention Program, Cleveland, Ohio* 4, Aug. 1931.

306. G. R. Segal, *Blacks in the Law* 145 (1983).

307. *National Bar Association Annual Convention Program*, Aug. 1–3, 1940.

308. "N.C. State Bar Association Meets," *Supreme Circle News*, Dec. 10, 1921.

309. *Ibid.* Other officers elected included Glenn S. McBrayer, of Wilson, North Carolina, corresponding secretary; Roger D. O'Kelly, of Raleigh, North Carolina, treasurer.

310. "Negro Lawyers of N.C. Form State-Wide Body," *Charlotte Observer*, Feb. 24, 1935. Other elected officers included Curtis Todd, of Raleigh, secretary; H. O. Bright, of Winston-Salem, treasurer.

311. "Negro Attorneys Hold State Meeting," *Raleigh Observer*, Feb. 23, 1935. P. H. Bell and J. S. Bowser, of Durham, and Fred J. Carnege, of Raleigh, were the presenters at the meeting. In 1936, the Old North State Bar Association elected M. H. Thompson, of Durham, president; Charles Williams, of Henderson, secretary; and Conrad O. Pearson, of Durham, treasurer. "Durham Man Heads Negro Bar Group," *Durham Herald*, June 1, 1936.

312. "Negro Lawyers Organize Bar Association Here," *San Antonio Express*, Feb. 15, 1921. Other officers of the group included D. R. Pickens, R. A. Campbell, and O. W. Johnson.

313. "Bar Association Holds Its Banquet," *Baltimore Afro-American*, Sept. 27, 1922.

314. *Ibid.*

315. Roy S. Bond served as president of the Monumental Bar Association in 1926. Josiah F. Henry succeeded Ulysses Grant Tyler as president in 1929. "Bond Again Heads Bar Association," *Baltimore Afro-American*, March 13, 1926; "Elect Henry Head of Baltimore Lawyers," *Chicago Defender*, Nov. 20, 1929. For years to come, many of the following lawyers would be included among the members of the Monumental Bar Association: W. C. McCard, Daniel Baymen, Arthur Briscoe, G. I. Brown, Norman Bishop, Emory R. Cole, J. Steward Davis, G. W. Evans, C. C. Fitzgerald, W. L. Fitzgerald, L. F. Flagg, Jr., C. S. Frazier, J. M. Hampton, Thomas Knox, L. G. Koger, W. F. McMechen, J. H. Payne, George L. Pendleton, and William E. Thomas.

316. "Norfolk Colored Bar Association," *Norfolk Journal and Guide*, July 30, 1921. The ten members of the group were W. H. Land, V. C. Hodges, W. L. Davis, J. M. Harrison, L. A. Howell, W. H. Thomas, R. G. L. Paige, J. S. Hall, R. C. Stith, and J. E. Diggs.

317. "Roanoke Man Elected Head of Virginia Negro Lawyers," *Washington Eagle*, Sept. 5, 1925. Thomas H. Reid, of Portsmouth, was elected vice-president, and Harry Green, of Richmond, was elected secretary-treasurer.

318. M. V. Tushnet, *The NAACP's Legal Strategy Against Segregated Education, 1925–1950*, at 181 (notes) (1987); Clarke, "The History of the Black Bar," 30 *St. Louis B.J.* 17, 18 (Spring 1984), quoting *St. Louis Argus*, Jan. 13, 1922, at 1.

319. "Bar Association Is for Better Ethics," *St. Louis Argus*, March 24, 1922.

320. "Head of St. Louis Bar Association Protests to Governor," *The Freeman*, Feb. 16, 1924.

321. Chambers, "At 95 He's a Model for All Lawyers," *National Law Journal*, April 24, 1989, at 13, 30, col. 1., quoting Nathan B. Young, one of the founding members of the Mound City Bar Association.

322. "Negro Bar Meeting Opens," *Post Dispatch*, Aug. 4, 1927. Other officers included Nathan B. Young, secretary Harry R. Bracy, assistant secretary, and Harvey Tucker, treasurer.

323. "Head Local Bar Ass'n.," *St. Louis Argus*, Jan. 17, 1930. Other officers of the group included Henry D. Espy, vice-president, Sidney R. Redmond, secretary, J. C. Young, treasurer, and George L. Vaughn, Benjamin F. Wilson, and Silas E. Garner, members of the executive committee.

324. *Ibid.*

325. "Martin Heads Local Negro Bar Assoc'n.," *St. Louis Argus*, Jan. 14, 1933. During Martin's term as president, Joseph P. Harris served as vice-president, Robert L. Witherspoon as secretary, Harvey V. Tucker as treasurer, George W. Wade as historian, and John A. Davis, George L. Vaughn, Sidney R. Redmond, and Robert L. Witherspoon as members of the executive committee. In 1935 Robert L. Witherspoon ascended to the presidency. Other elected officers included Harry Bracy, vice-president, Harvey V. Tucker, secretary, Emmanuel Williams, treasurer, George W. Wade, historian, and Joseph P. Harris, Joseph L. McLemore, and Noah Parden, members of the executive committee. "Witherspoon Heads the Mound City Bar," *St. Louis Argus*, Jan. 10, 1936.

326. "100 Missouri Lawyers Form State Society," *Chicago Defender*, May 29, 1926.

327. *Ibid.* The group elected Freeman L. Martin, of St. Louis, vice-president; Duane B. Mason, of Kansas City, second vice-president; Frank S. Bledsoe, of St. Louis, secretary; Carl Roman Johnson, of Kansas City, assistant secretary; Silas E. Garner, of St. Louis, treasurer; Nathan B. Young, Jr., of St. Louis, historian; Emmanuel Williams, of St. Louis, chaplain; and J. D. Pouncey, of Kansas City, sergeant-at-arms.

328. "Carl Roman Johnson New Head of State Lawyers," *Kansas City Call*, June 1, 1928. George L. Vaughn succeeded L. Amasa Knox as the second president of the group. Carl Roman Johnson became its third president.

329. During the 1929 annual meeting, G. B. Jones presented a paper on "Writs of Habeas Corpus"; John E. Wesson presented a paper on "Recent Decisions Affecting the Negro"; and Silas E. Garner presented a paper entitled "Why Should the Negro Lawyer Take the Leadership in Political Affairs?" "Heads Harlan Bar Ass'n," *St. Louis Argus*, May 31, 1929. At the close of this meeting, Silas E. Garner, of St. Louis, was elected president of the Harlan State Bar Association; John E. Wesson, of Kansas City, became vice-president; Ellis S. Outlaw, of St. Louis, became secretary; Harrison W. Hollie, of St. Louis, became historian. Carl Roman Johnson and L. Amasa Fox, both of Kansas City, and Joseph L. McLemore, of St. Louis, were selected to the executive committee. *Ibid.*

330. *The National Bar Association Proceedings of the Sixth Annual Convention* 4, 11, Aug. 7, 1930 (comments of Albert Burgess).

331. In 1930 the leading lawyers in the Jackson County Bar Association were D. W. White, W. H. Parker, Charles H. Calloway, L. Amasa Knox, W. F. Clark, Herbert Wallace, Marion Johnson, Carl Roman Johnson, J. D. Pouncey, J. A. Curry, J. J. Joseph, John E. Wesson, and George T. Wesson. "Kansas City Bar Association," *Kansas City Call*, May 23, 1930.

332. Smith, "The Marion County Lawyers' Club: 1932 and the Black Lawyer," 8 *Black L.J.* 170–71 (Howard Law School ed. 1983).

333. *Ibid.*

334. R. P. Alexander, "The John M. Langston Law Club," 14 *The Shingle* 233, 234 (Dec. 1951).

335. The following lawyers assisted John F. Williams's efforts to organize the legal aid bureau: Raymond Pace Alexander, Sadie T. M. Alexander, Maceo Hubbard, Fleming Tucker, Tanner Moore, Mercer Lewis, William Fuller, John C. Asbury, Walter Livingston, Fitzhugh L. Styles, Theodore Spaulding, Leslie P. Hill, William T. McKnight, J. Austin Norris, and Rufus Watson. "Noted Philadelphian Has Had Brilliant Scholastic and Legal Career in Establishing Negro Rights," *Norfolk Journal and Guide*, Sept. 17, 1932.

336. *Ibid.*

337. "Lincoln Bar Ass'n. of Louisville Ky. Is Reorganized," *Louisville News*, Sept. 24, 1927. Other officers of the group included W. C. Brown, vice-president, J. E. Buckner, secretary, and H. C. Weeden, treasurer.

338. "Negro Must Achieve His Own Destiny, Jurist Says at Lawyers' Dinner Here," *Amsterdam News*, April 29, 1931; "Negro Joins Bar Assoc'n.," *Savannah Tribune*, Feb. 28, 1929.

339. The Harlem Lawyers' Association was also inspired by Louis A. Lavelle, "the oldest Harlem lawyer in point of practice" at the time the group was

formed. The two succeeding presidents of the bar were William H. Austin and Demerald Williams. *Ibid.* ("Negro Must Achieve His Own Destiny"). See also, "Harlem Lawyers Meet Saturday," *Amsterdam New York Star-News*, July 11, 1942, at 5, col. 2.

340. "Negro Must Achieve His Own Destiny, Jurist Says at Lawyers' Dinner Here," *Amsterdam News*, April 29, 1931.

341. In 1936 the Harlem Lawyers' Association supported the appointment of Oliver D. Williams for a New York City judgeship. Mayor Fiorello LaGuardia disappointed the group by refusing to appoint him. "Lawyers Will Keep Trying," *New York Age*, Aug. 1, 1936.

342. "Harlem Lawyers Meet Saturday," *Amsterdam New York Star-News*, July 11, 1942, at 5, col. 2.

343. *Ibid.* In 1943 Paul W. White, a black attorney, was appointed to two bar committees of the Brooklyn Bar Association, suggesting that black lawyers had begun to have more involvement in some white groups in New York. "Negro Attorney Is Named to Two Bar Assoc. Committees," *New York Age*, Sept. 4, 1943; "In Memoriam Hutson Leon Lovell," *New York Times*, Dec. 16, 1990, at 56, col. 3.

344. "Jersey Lawyers Plan Hard War on Color Bias," *Philadelphia Tribune*, Nov. 2, 1933.

345. "Lawyers Elect Lawrence Head of National Bar," *Chicago Defender*, Aug. 10, 1935.

346. Other officers elected included W. Harold Flowers, of Pine Bluff, Arkansas, vice-president; Roger Q. Mason, of Dallas, Texas, second vice-president; Elisha Scott, Sr., of Topeka, Kansas, third vice-president; Cecil E. Robinson, of Muskogee, Oklahoma, secretary; J. H. Stevens, of Okmulgee, Oklahoma, assistant secretary; and Robert Lowe, of Wewoka, Oklahoma, treasurer. "Oklahoma Barristers Close First Annual Session After Forming Southwestern Ass'n," *Black Dispatch*, June 9, 1940.

347. *Ibid.*

348. *22nd Annual Convention Report of the Resolutions Committee of the Southwestern Bar Association*, June 22, 1962.

Appendix 1. The First Black Lawyers, 1844–1944

The First Black Lawyers, by State/Territory and Year of Bar Admission.

State (Territory)	Name	Year admitted to bar
Alabama	Moses Wenslydale Moore	1871
	Estelle A. Henderson*	1919
Alaska	None identified	
Arizona	Robert Lee Fortune	1921
Arkansas	Thomas P. Johnson	1866
California	Robert Charles O'Hara Benjamin	1887
	Virginia Stephens*	1928
Colorado	Edwin Henry Hackley	1883
Connecticut	Edwin Archer Randolph	1880
Delaware†	Louis Lorenzo Redding	1929
District of Columbia	George Boyer Vashon	1869
	Charlotte E. Ray*	1872
Florida	Harvey S. Harmon	1869
Georgia	James M. Simms	1871
	Rachel E. Pruden-Herndon*	1943
Hawaii	Thomas McCants Stewart	1898
Idaho	None identified	
Illinois	Lloyd G. Wheeler	1869
	Ida G. Platt*	1894
Indiana	Hiram R. Revels	1860s
	Helen Elsie Austin*	1930
Iowa	A. H. Watkins	1874
	Gertrude Elzora Durden Rush*	1918
Kansas	John H. Morris	1871
	Lutie A. Lytle*	1897
Kentucky	George A. Griffith	1871
	Nathaniel R. Harper	1871
Louisiana	C. Clay Morgan	1860
Maine	Macon Bolling Allen	1844

Maryland	Everett J. Waring	1885
Massachusetts	Macon Bolling Allen	1845
	Blanche E. Braxton*	1923
Michigan	John C. McLeod	1870
	Grace G. Costavas*	1923
Minnesota	Frederick L. McGhee	1889
	Lena Olive Smith*	1921
Mississippi	James Henry Piles	1869
Missouri	John H. Johnson	1871
	Dorothy L. Freeman*	1942
Montana	John D. Posten	1890
Nebraska	Silas Robbins	1889
	Zanzye H. A. Hill*	1929
Nevada†	None identified	
New Hampshire†	None identified	
New Jersey	George Jackson	1893
New Mexico	Fred Simms	1890
New York	George Boyer Vashon	1848
	Anna Jones Robinson*	1923
North Carolina	George Lawrence Mabson	1871
	Ruth Whitehead Whaley*	1933
North Dakota†	None identified	
Ohio	John Mercer Langston	1854
	Daisy D. Perkins*	1919
Oklahoma (Territory)	Sugar George	1875
Oregon†	McCants Stewart	1903
	Beatrice Cannady*	1921
Pennsylvania	Jonathan Jasper Wright	1865
	Sadie Tanner Mossell Alexander*	1927
Rhode Island	John Henry Ballou	1874
South Carolina	Robert Brown Elliott	1871
	John P. Green	1871
	William J. Whipper	1871
	Jonathan Jasper Wright	1871
	Cassandra E. Maxwell*	1941
South Dakota	Will F. Reden	1908
Tennessee	Alfred Menefee	1868
	Edward Shaw	1868
	William Henderson Young	1868
	William Frances Yardley	1868
	B. F. Bowles	1868
	Lutie A. Lytle*	1897
Texas	A. W. Wilder	1873
Utah†	David H. Oliver	1931
Vermont†	None located	
Virginia	Walthal G. Wynn	1871
	Lavina Marian Fleming-Poe*	1925
Washington	Everett E. Simpson	1888
Wisconsin	Everett E. Simpson	1888
	Mable Watson Raimey	1927
Wyoming†	None located	

First Black Man and Black Woman Admitted to United States Supreme Court, 1844–1944

State	Name	Year admitted to Supreme Court
Massachusetts	John Swett Rock	1865
Illinois	Violet Neatly Anderson*	1926

*Denotes black women. From 1872 to 1930, twenty-two black female lawyers can be identified. *The Sixteenth Census* (1940) is the first to break down female lawyers by race and state. It indicates that in 1940 there were at least one or more black women lawyers in the states of *Connecticut, Delaware, Florida*, and *Texas*. The existence of these lawyers cannot be confirmed here. See Table 13: "Race and Age of Employed Persons (Except on Public Emergency Work), and of Experienced Workers Seeking Work by Occupation and Sex, for the State, and for Cities of 100,000 or More: 1940," in *The Sixteenth Census: Population*, Vol. 3 at 462 (Connecticut), 525 (Delaware), 652 (Florida), 492 (Texas) (1943). By 1944, therefore, there were at least twenty-five black women who would qualify for inclusion in this list.

†Denotes state census data reporting black lawyers (likely male) not identified here, or that indicate black lawyers for years earlier than listed here. This information suggests the following possibilities: (1) the presence of a black lawyer in the state whose name the author has been unable to determine; (2) that an unidentified black lawyer may have preceded the person herein designated as the first black lawyer; (3) that the census data are in error. *The Twelfth Census* (1900) reports that the states of *North Dakota* and *Oregon* each had one "colored" male lawyer. See Table 41: "Total Males and Females Ten Years of Age and Over Engaged in Selected Group of Occupations, Classified by General Nativity, Color, Conjugal Condition, Months Unemployed, Age Periods and Parentage: 1900," in *The Twelfth Census, Special Reports: Occupations* at 356 (North Dakota), 368 (Oregon) (1904). *The Thirteenth Census* (1910) reports the presence of "Negro" male lawyers in the states of *Delaware, Nevada, North Dakota, Utah*, and *Wyoming*, Table 7: "Total Male and Females 10 Years of Age and Over Engaged in Selected Occupations, by Age Periods and Color or Race, Nativity, and Parentage, by States: 1910," in Vol. 4, *Population (Occupation Statistics)* at 445 (Delaware), 487 (Nevada), 501 (North Dakota), 523 (Utah), 534 (Wyoming) (1914). *The Fourteenth Census* (1920) reports the presence of "Negro" male lawyers in the states of *New Hampshire, Utah*, and *Vermont*. See (unnumbered) Table: "Total Males and Females 10 Years of Age and Over Engaged in Each Selected Occupation, Nativity, and Parentage, and Age Periods for the State: 1920," in U.S. Bureau of the Census (1923), Pamphlet 28: Table 25, p. 30 (New Hampshire); Pamphlet 43: Table 25, p. 37 (Utah); Pamphlet 44: Table 24, p. 31 (Vermont).

Appendix 2. U.S. Census: The Number of Lawyers in Each State/Territory by Race and Sex, 1850–1940

1850

TABLE L.   Professions, Occupations and Trades of the Male Population in the United States, over Fifteen Years of Age, in *The Seventh Census* (1853) at lxxii. (Race, color, nativity, sex not broken down.)

State (Territory)	No. of lawyers
Alabama	570
Arkansas	224
California	191
Connecticut	289
Delaware	46
District of Columbia	99
Florida	131
Georgia	711
Illinois	817
Indiana	924
Iowa	272
Kentucky	995
Louisiana	622
Maine	560
Maryland	535
Massachusetts	1,111
Michigan	560
Minnesota	23
Mississippi	590
Missouri	687
New Hampshire	326
New Jersey	412
New Mexico	11
New York	4,263
North Carolina	399

TABLE L.   *Continued*

State (Territory)	No. of lawyers
Ohio	2,028
Oregon	22
Pennsylvania	2,503
Rhode Island	114
South Carolina	397
Tennessee	725
Texas	428
Utah	5
Vermont	494
Virginia	1,384
Wisconsin	471
Total	23,939

1860

TABLE 6.   "Occupations" in *Eighth Census of the United States: Population* (1864) at 11–590. (Race, color, nativity, sex not broken down.)

State	No. of lawyers
Alabama	763
Arkansas	467
California	894
Connecticut	468
Delaware	87
Florida	173
Georgia	1,168
Illinois	1,602
Indiana	1,211
Iowa	1,161
Kansas	361
Kentucky	1,190
Louisiana	698
Maine	646
Maryland	599
Massachusetts	1,186
Michigan	791
Minnesota	407
Mississippi	620
Missouri	1,187
New Hampshire	375
New Jersey	537
New York	5,592
North Carolina	500
Ohio	2,537
Oregon	104
Pennsylvania	2,414
Rhode Island	96
South Carolina	457
Tennessee	1,037
Texas	904
Vermont	(no listing for lawyers)
Virginia	1,341
Wisconsin	1,133
Territory	
Colorado	89
Dakota	8
Nebraska	130
Nevada	18
New Mexico	23
Utah	8
Washington	22
District of Columbia	189
Total	33,193

1870

TABLE 27(B).   "The Number of Females in the United States Engaged in Each Special Occupation (by States and Territories)," in *The Ninth Census*, Vol. I: *The Statistics of the Population of the United States* (1872) at 686–687.

Female lawyers (white)	Number
Total in U.S.	5
Louisiana	1
Missouri	2
New York	1
Pennsylvania	1

TABLE 29.   "Number of Persons in the United States Engaged in Each Special Occupation, with Distinctions of Age and Sex, and of Nativity," in *The Ninth Census*, Vol. I, at 706.

Lawyers	Number
All Ages	
Total*	40,736 (not broken down by race)
Male	40,731
Female	5
Nativity	
United States	38,412
Germany	513
Ireland	730
England/Wales	443
Scotland	122
Sweden/Norway/Denmark	31
France	58
Other North of Europe	37
Italy	3
Other South of Europe	25
British American	258
China and Japan	0
Other and Unknown	104

*Note: "Other" and "Unknown" not defined in the census.

TABLE 30.   "The Number of Persons of Each State and Territory Engaged in Each Selected Occupation with Distinctions of Age and Sex and of Nativity," in *The Ninth Census*, Vol. I, at 719–65.

State (*Territory*)	No. *of lawyers*
Alabama	758
Arizona (Territory)	21
Arkansas	413
California	1,115
Colorado (Territory)	99
Connecticut	391
Dakota (Territory)	23
Delaware	84
District of Columbia	411
Florida	149
Georgia	851
Idaho (Territory)	42
Illinois	2,683
Indiana	1,685
Iowa	1,456
Kansas	682
Kentucky	1,552
Louisiana	663
Maine	558
Maryland	772
Massachusetts	1,270
Michigan	1,107
Minnesota	449
Mississippi	632
Missouri	3,452
Montana (Territory)	67
Nebraska	204
Nevada	166
New Hampshire	349
New Jersey	888
New York	5,913
New Mexico	48
North Carolina	574
Ohio	2,563
Oregon	194
Pennsylvania	3,253
Rhode Island	163
South Carolina	387
Tennessee	1,126
Texas	1,027
Utah (Territory)	23
Vermont	72
Virginia	1,075
Washington (Territory)	56

TABLE 30. *Continued*

State (*Territory*)	No. of lawyers
West Virginia	400
Wisconsin	785
Wyoming (Territory)	25
Total	40,676*

*This total and the total listed in Table 27, above, are not in agreement, but the discrepancy is not resolvable according to the available census data.

1880

TABLE 31.   "The Number of Persons in the United States Engaged in Twenty
Selected Occupations, with Distinctions of Age and Sex and of
Nativity, by States and Territories," in *The Tenth Census, Statistics of
Population of the United States*: "Lawyers" at 733 (1883). (Race not
broken down.)

	Number
Female lawyers	
California	2
Dakota	1
District of Columbia	3
Florida	1
Georgia	2
Illinois	9
Indiana	1
Iowa	5
Kansas	1
Louisiana	3
Maryland	1
Massachusetts	4
Michigan	7
Missouri	2
Nebraska	1
New Hampshire	3
New Jersey	2
New York	7
North Carolina	3
Ohio	5
Pennsylvania	8
Tennessee	1
Texas	2
Virginia	1
Total	75
Male lawyers	
Total	64,062
Nativity	
United States	60,342
Ireland	1,008
Germany	791
Great Britain	948
Sweden/Norway	89
British America	559
Other Countries	400
States/Territories	
Alabama	798
Arizona	118

TABLE 31.   *Continued*

	Number
States/Territories (continued)	
Arkansas	745
California	1,899
Colorado	807
Connecticut	796
Dakota	300
Delaware	127
District of Columbia	918
Florida	306
Georgia	1,432
Idaho	61
Illinois	4,025
Indiana	2,904
Iowa	2,610
Kansas	1,492
Kentucky	1,981
Louisiana	828
Maine	725
Maryland	1,087
Massachusetts	1,984
Michigan	2,097
Minnesota	906
Mississippi	820
Missouri	2,907
Montana	77
Nebraska	840
Nevada	119
New Hampshire	382
New Jersey	1,557
New Mexico	128
New York	9,459
North Carolina	772
Ohio	4,489
Oregon	311
Pennsylvania	4,992
Rhode Island	237
South Carolina	614
Tennessee	1,506
Texas	2,109
Utah	119
Vermont	424
Virginia	1,355
Washington	113
West Virginia	629
Wisconsin	1,198
Wyoming	34
Total U.S. lawyers	64,137

1890

TABLE 6.   "Total Persons 10 Years of Age and Over in the United States Engaged in Each Specified Occupation, Classified by Sex, General Nativity, and Color: 1890," in *The Eleventh Census: 1890, Special Census Report of the United States* (1896) at 70–71. (Not broken down by state.)

	Number
All Occupations—White	
Male	16,603,147
Female	2,939,041
Total	19,542,188
Lawyers—White	
Male	88,982
Female	208
Total	89,190
All Occupations—Colored	
Male	2,217,943
Female	975,530
Total	3,193,473
Lawyers—Colored	
Male	440
Female	0
Total	440
All occupations—Persons of Negro descent	
Male	2,101,379
Female	971,785
Total	3,073,164
Lawyers—Negro	
Male	431
Female	0
Total	431

1900

TABLE 41.   "Total Males and Females Ten Years of Age and Over Engaged in Selected Group of Occupations, Classified by General Nativity, Color, Conjugal Condition, Months Unemployed, Age Periods and Parentage: 1900," in *The Twelfth Census, Special Reports, Occupations Available* (1904) at 220–420.*

State	White male lawyers	Colored male lawyers†	Negro male lawyers‡	Total no. of lawyers
Alabama	1,587	0	6	1,593
Alaska	No listing			
Arizona	263	0	0	263
Arkansas	1,345	0	27	1,372
California	4,208	4	6	4,218
Colorado	1,611	0	5	1,616
Connecticut	1,070	0	3	1,073
Delaware	214	0	0	214
District of Columbia	1,405	2	38	1,445
Florida	598	0	13	611
Georgia	2,352	0	33	2,385
Hawaii	165	5	0	170
Idaho	344	2	0	346
Illinois	8,863	0	54	8,917
Indiana	4,226	0	19	4,245
Indian Territory	465	56	5	526
Iowa	3,379	0	4	3,383
Kansas	2,318	0	22	2,340
Kentucky	3,106	0	25	3,131
Louisiana	1,293	0	15	1,308
Maine	891	0	0	891
Maryland	2,007	0	22	2,029
Massachusetts	3,391	1	20	3,412
Michigan	3,032	1	10	3,043
Minnesota	2,491	0	6	2,497
Mississippi	999	0	24	1,023
Missouri	5,202	0	22	5,224
Montana	536	3	1	540
Nebraska	1,904	1	2	1,907
Nevada	104	0	0	104
New Hampshire	466	0	0	466
New Jersey	2,833	0	9	2,842
New Mexico	272	0	2	274
New York	14,601	2	32	14,635
North Carolina	1,238	0	25	1,263
North Dakota	450	0	1	451
Ohio	6,557	0	32	6,589
Oklahoma	655	2	8	665
Oregon	1,024	2	1	1,027

TABLE 41.   *Continued*

State	White male lawyers	Colored male lawyers†	Negro male lawyers‡	Total no. of lawyers
Pennsylvania	8,233	0	24	8,257
Rhode Island	365	0	1	366
South Carolina	822	0	29	851
Tennessee	2,643	0	73	2,716
Texas	4,572	0	28	4,600
Utah	433	0	0	433
Vermont	424	0	0	424
Virginia	1,972	0	53	2,025
Washington	1,524	0	3	1,527
West Virginia	1,320	0	14	1,334
Wisconsin	2,225	0	1	2,226
Wyoming	142	0	0	142
Total	112,140	81	718	112,939*

*Table 36, *id.* at 14, indicates that in 1900 there were 718 Negro male lawyers and 10 Negro women lawyers. Table 41 does not indicate the states where these 10 black women lawyers resided. With the addition of 10 black women lawyers, the total number of black lawyers in 1900 is 728, and the total number of lawyers is 112,949. No data are available for white female lawyers.

†"Colored" = persons of Chinese, Japanese, or Indian origin.

‡"Negro" = all persons of Negro descent.

1910

TABLE 7.   "Total Males and Females 10 Years of Age and Over Engaged in Selected Occupations, by Age Periods and Color or Race, Nativity, and Parentage, by States: 1910," in *The Thirteenth Census*, Vol. 4: *Population* (1914) at 434–613.

State	White male lawyers	Negro male lawyers	Indian, Chinese, Japanese, and other lawyers	Total no. of lawyers
Alabama	1,470	12	0	1,482
Alaska	127	0	0	127
Arizona	330	0	3	333
Arkansas	1,328	20	0	1,348
California	4,855	5	11	4,871
Colorado	1,631	3	0	1,634
Connecticut	1,115	2	0	1,117
Delaware	178	1	0	179
District of Columbia	1,455	59	7	1,521
Florida	697	14	0	711
Georgia	2,215	18	0	2,233
Hawaii	98	0	67	165
Idaho	557	0	6	563
Illinois	7,945	60	0	8,005
Indiana	3,572	22	0	3,594
Indian Territory	0	0	0	0
Iowa	2,563	6	0	2,569
Kansas	1,743	22	0	1,765
Kentucky	2,637	27	0	2,664
Louisiana	1,217	13	0	1,230
Maine	854	1	0	855
Maryland	1,968	21	0	1,989
Massachusetts	4,354	27	1	4,382
Michigan	2,807	16	0	2,823
Minnesota	2,383	7	5	2,395
Mississippi	1,196	21	0	1,217
Missouri	4,508	26	1	4,535
Montana	619	1	1	621
Nebraska	1,443	3	2	1,448
Nevada	289	1	2	292
New Hampshire	407	0	0	407
New Jersey	3,200	15	0	3,215
New Mexico	385	0	0	385
New York	17,075	58	5	17,138
North Carolina	1,294	19	0	1,313
North Dakota	661	1	4	666
Ohio	6,090	39	0	6,129
Oklahoma	2,629	61	42	2,732
Oregon	1,302	3	1	1,306

TABLE 7.   *Continued*

State	White male lawyers	Negro male lawyers	Indian, Chinese, Japanese, and other lawyers	Total no. of lawyers
Pennsylvania	7,154	26	0	7,180
Rhode Island	460	4	0	464
South Carolina	890	17	0	907
South Dakota	682	0	7	689
Tennessee	2,053	43	0	2,096
Texas	4,521	33	0	4,554
Utah	443	1	0	444
Vermont	380	0	0	380
Virginia	1,772	37	0	1,809
Washington	2,465	9	6	2,480
West Virginia	1,388	17	0	1,405
Wisconsin	1,862	4	1	1,867
Wyoming	203	1	0	204
Puerto Rico	285	9	0	294
*Total**	113,755	805	172	114,732

*According to the summary information in the 1910 census (Table 6, at 429), there were a total of 107,888 lawyers in the United States in 1910, of which 106,479 were white males, 556 were white females, 777 were black males, 2 were black females, and 74 were Indian, Chinese, Japanese, and other males. The discrepancy between the total number of lawyers cited above and the figure published in said Table 6 is not resolvable according to available census data.

Table 6 gives us a glimpse of two professions associated with the law that could have introduced women and minorities into the legal profession: (1) *Abstractors* summarized legal documents and facts that appeared on the public records that affected title to land. In 1910, 764 white women, 21 black women, 96 black men and 17 Indians, Chinese, Japanese, and others (combined) were abstractors. A total of 4,587 white males were abstractors. (2) Justices of the peace (JPs) handled many legal matters, the jurisdiction over which varied by state law. Some JPs were lawyers, but many were not. JPs were both elected and appointed positions. In 1910, there were 19 black male JPs; 31 Indian, Chinese, Japanese, and all "other" male JPs; and 533 white women JPs. There were 5,268 white male JPs.

1920

The Fourteenth Census (1920) had a separate bulletin for each state; hence, the table numbers and page numbers vary from state to state. In this compilation, the table number and page number are given on which the information for each state was found. The table names and report titles were the same for each state. Data on lawyers in Alaska, Hawaii, and Puerto Rico were found in Volume 4 on *Occupations in the Population Report*, at Table 11, p. 1266, Table 22, p. 1278 and Table 36, p. 1297, respectively. Data on female lawyers were taken from Volume 4 on *Occupations in the Census Population Report* (Chapter 3, Table 5). No state compilation by race is available for female lawyers.

State	White male lawyers	Negro male lawyers	Indian, Chinese, Japanese, or Other male lawyers	Total no. of male lawyers
Alabama	1,388	3	0	1,391
(T.25, p. 51)				
Alaska	80	0	0	80
Arizona	436	1	2	439
(T.24, p. 31)				
Arkansas	1,307	26	0	1,333
(T.25, p. 52)				
California	6,563	19	13	6,595
(T.25, p. 53)				
Colorado	1,511	6	0	1,517
(T.24, p. 48)				
Connecticut	1,322	4	0	1,326
(T.25, p. 38)				
Delaware	167	3	0	170
(T.25, p. 28)				
District of Columbia	2,289	68	0	2,357
(T.20, p. 23)				
Florida	1,113	13	0	1,126
(T.25, p. 48)				
Georgia	2,479	27	0	2,506
(T.25, p. 68)				
Hawaii	122	1	49	172
Idaho	646	0	0	646
(T.24, p. 38)				
Illinois	8,574	103	2	8,679
(T.25, p. 84)				
Indiana	3,231	36	0	3,267
(T.25, p. 66)				
Iowa	2,446	7	1	2,454
(T.25, p. 68)				

State	White male lawyers	Negro male lawyers	Indian, Chinese, Japanese, or Other male lawyers	Total no. of male lawyers
Kansas (T.25, p. 63)	1,615	29	0	1,644
Kentucky (T.25, p. 56)	2,346	22	0	2,368
Louisiana (T.25, p. 44)	1,181	8	0	1,189
Maine (T.25, p. 38)	792	1	0	793
Maryland (T.25, p. 37)	2,070	30	0	2,100
Massachusetts (T.25, p. 64)	4,821	30	0	4,851
Michigan (T.25, p. 67)	2,964	35	0	2,999
Minnesota (T.25, p. 65)	2,578	9	2	2,589
Mississippi (T.24, p. 45)	1,134	14	0	1,148
Missouri (T.25, p. 64)	4,409	23	2	4,434
Montana (T.24, p. 45)	860	3	0	863
Nebraska (T.25, p. 57)	1,500	7	0	1,507
Nevada (T.24, p. 31)	224	0	0	224
New Hampshire (T.25, p. 30)	377	1	0	378
New Jersey (T.25, p. 55)	3,846	19	0	3,865
New Mexico (T.24, p. 36)	341	1	0	342
New York (T.25, p. 91)	18,066	57	6	18,129
North Carolina (T.24, p. 56)	1,537	27	0	1,564
North Dakota (T.24, p. 49)	626	0	0	626
Ohio (T.25, p. 86)	6,347	53	1	6,401
Oklahoma (T.25, p. 53)	2,700	64	31	2,795
Oregon (T.24, p. 40)	1,392	3	3	1,398

State	White male lawyers	Negro male lawyers	Indian, Chinese, Japanese, or Other male lawyers	Total no. of male lawyers
Pennsylvania (T.25, p. 108)	6,685	24	1	6,710
Puerto Rico	372	16	0	388
Rhode Island (T.25, p. 30)	509	3	0	512
South Carolina (T.25, p. 42)	960	14	0	974
South Dakota (T.24, p. 50)	694	0	2	696
Tennessee (T.25, p. 59)	1,986	33	0	2,019
Texas (T.25, p. 90)	5,240	31	0	5,271
Utah (T.25, p. 37)	525	1	0	526
Vermont (T.24, p. 31)	334	1	0	335
Virginia (T.25, p. 56)	1,923	52	0	1,975
Washington (T.25, p. 47)	2,206	2	0	2,208
West Virginia (T.25, p. 43)	1,295	23	0	1,318
Wisconsin (T.25, p. 61)	1,947	2	2	1,951
Wyoming (T.24, p. 32)	265	0	0	265
Total*	120,341	955	117	121,413*

*According to *The Fourteenth Census*, Chapter 3, Table 5, at 356, totals were as follows (the discrepancy in the total [121,413] cited above and the totals at Table 5 is not resolvable according to the available census data):

Total all races	122,519
Total white males	119,767
Total white females	1,734
Total negro males	946
Total negro females	4
Total Indian males	47
Total Chinese males	4
Total Japanese males	13
Total all other males	4

No record of female lawyers from Alaska, Hawaii, or Puerto Rico, or of any Indian, Chinese, or Japanese female lawyers.

1930

The Fifteenth Census (1930) broadened the category of "other races" to include not only "Indians, Chinese and Japanese," but also "filipinos, Hindus, Koreans, and Hawaiians, etc." Compilations regarding the territories of Hawaii and Puerto Rico listed below appear in *The Outlying Territories and Possessions* volume of *The Fifteenth Census* (1932), Table 8, p. 89 (Hawaii) and Table 11, p. 196 (Puerto Rico). No census data on the number of lawyers in Alaska were found. Compilations on "Negro" and white female lawyers are available only for the District of Columbia and the states of Massachusetts and New York. The state compilation of all gender and race categories, other than the "Outlying Territories," appear in Table 11: "Males and Females 10 Years Old and Over in Selected Occupations, by Color, Nativity, and Age, for the State: 1930," in *The Fifteenth Census: 1930, Population*, Vol. 4, pp. 119–1791 (1933).

State	White male lawyers	Negro male lawyers	Male lawyers of other races	Total no. of male lawyers
Alabama	1,579	4	0	1,583
Arizona	520	1	12	533
Arkansas	1,481	16	0	1,497
California	9,763	34	50	9,847
Colorado	1,539	2	1	1,542
Connecticut	1,855	6	0	1,861
Delaware	203	2	0	205
District of Columbia	3,215	94	11	3,320
Florida	2,570	10	0	2,580
Georgia	2,750	14	0	2,764
Idaho	578	0	0	578
Illinois	11,338	187	4	11,529
Indiana	3,683	62	2	3,747
Iowa	2,596	7	0	2,603
Kansas	1,768	28	0	1,796
Kentucky	2,580	25	0	2,605
Louisiana	1,595	8	1	1,604
Maine	747	0	0	747
Maryland	2,697	33	0	2,730
Massachusetts	6,617	38	1	6,656
Michigan	4,349	63	1	4,413
Minnesota	3,089	11	3	3,103
Mississippi	1,225	6	0	1,231
Missouri	5,392	55	1	5,448
Montana	702	0	4	706
Nebraska	1,718	8	0	1,726

State	White male lawyers	Negro male lawyers	Male lawyers of other races	Total no. of male lawyers
Nevada	226	0	0	226
New Hampshire	356	0	0	356
New Jersey	6,443	23	1	6,467
New York	26,676	117	8	26,801
North Carolina	2,335	27	1	2,363
North Dakota	594	0	1	595
Ohio	8,569	94	2	8,665
Oklahoma	3,346	53	62	3,461
Oregon	1,565	2	1	1,568
Pennsylvania	7,922	48	0	7,970
Rhode Island	665	3	0	668
South Carolina	1,108	13	0	1,121
South Dakota	727	0	7	734
Tennessee	2,431	26	1	2,458
Texas	6,455	20	41	6,516
Utah	598	0	0	598
Vermont	321	0	0	321
Virginia	2,334	57	0	2,391
Washington	2,242	3	4	2,249
West Virginia	1,518	20	0	1,538
Wisconsin	2,556	3	1	2,560
Wyoming	295	0	0	295
Total	155,431	1,223	221	156,875*

	White female lawyers	Negro female lawyers	Female lawyers of other races	Total no. of female lawyers
District of Columbia	153	4	0	157
Massachusetts	284	0	0	284
New York	789	3	0	792
Total	1,226	7†	0	1,233†

OUTLYING TERRITORIES AND POSSESSIONS IN *THE FIFTEENTH CENSUS* (TABLE 8).

	White male lawyers	Negro male lawyers	Other races	Total no. of male lawyers
Alaska	(no information)			
Hawaii	134	4	56	194
Puerto Rico	516	31	0	547
Total	650*	35‡	56	741

*The adjusted total (adding in the 650 white males from the outlying territories) of all white males, Negro males, and males of other races is 157,961, according to the author's calculations based on census figures.
†It is assumed that the figure for women lawyers (1,233) is included in the total of 3,385.
‡The adjusted total (adding the 35 black males from the outlying territories) of all Negro males is 1,258, according to the author's calculations based on census figures.

Totals—Lawyers, judges, and justices (from *The Fifteenth Census*, Vol. 4, Table 13, at 33):

All males	157,220
All females	3,385
All Negro males	1,223
All Negro females	24
All other races (male)	222
All other races (female)	1

1940

TABLE 13.   "Race and Age of Employed Persons (Except on Public Emergency Work), and of Experienced Workers Seeking Work, by Occupation and Sex, for the State, and for Cities of 100,000 or More: 1940," in *The Sixteenth Census, Population*, Vol. 3: *The Labor Force* (1943), Part 2: Alabama–Indiana; Part 3: Iowa–Montana; Part 4: Nebraska–Oregon. ("Other races" include Indian, Chinese, Japanese, Korean lawyers, etc.)

State (Territory)	White male lawyers	Negro male lawyers	Male lawyers of other races	Total no. of male lawyers
Alabama	1,605	3	0	1,608
Alaska	(no data available)			
Arizona	550	0	5	555
Arkansas	1,514	8	0	1,522
California	10,294	32	30	10,356
Colorado	1,414	1	0	1,415
Connecticut	2,179	3	0	2,182
Delaware	238	2	1	241
District of Columbia	4,339	73	6	4,418
Florida	2,652	9	2	2,663
Georgia	2,612	8	0	2,620
Hawaii*				
Idaho	509	0	1	510
Illinois	12,843	134	2	12,979
Indiana	3,752	56	1	3,809
Iowa	2,798	11	0	2,809
Kansas	1,920	27	0	1,947
Kentucky	2,591	21	0	2,612
Louisiana	1,847	6	0	1,853
Maine	782	1	0	783
Maryland	3,418	32	1	3,451
Massachusetts	7,006	26	0	7,032
Minnesota	2,995	6	1	3,002
Mississippi	1,276	3	0	1,279
Missouri	5,219	36	0	5,255
Montana	640	1	7	648
Michigan	5,124	61	0	5,185
Nebraska	1,738	4	0	1,742
Nevada	201	0	1	202
New Hampshire	381	0	0	381
New Jersey	7,546	26	1	7,573
New Mexico	373	0	2	375
New York	33,366	120	6	33,492
North Carolina	2,385	26	0	2,411
North Dakota	515	0	3	518
Ohio	8,918	103	0	9,021

TABLE 13.   *Continued*

State (Territory)	White male lawyers	Negro male lawyers	Male lawyers of other races	Total no. of male lawyers
Oklahoma	3,192	25	26	3,243
Oregon	1,546	2	0	1,548
Pennsylvania	8,134	35	0	8,169
Puerto Rico	(no data available)			
Rhode Island	724	3	0	727
South Carolina	1,131	5	0	1,136
South Dakota	603	0	10	613
Tennessee	2,591	16	0	2,607
Texas	7,570	22	0	7,592
Utah	612	1	0	613
Vermont	331	0	0	331
Washington	2,240	1	6	2,247
West Virginia	1,424	17	0	1,441
Wisconsin	3,322	3	1	3,326
Wyoming	261	0	1	262
Virginia	3,108	44	0	3,152
Total	172,329	1,013	114	173,456

State	White female lawyers	Negro female lawyers	Female lawyers of other races	Total no. of female lawyers
Alaska	(no available information)			
Alabama	20	1	0	21
Arizona	11	0	0	11
Arkansas	19	0	0	19
California	317	3	1	321
Colorado	28	0	0	28
Connecticut	43	0	0	43
Delaware	3	0	0	3
District of Columbia	342	1	0	343
Florida	49	1	0	50
Georgia	60	0	0	60
Hawaii†				
Idaho	8	0	0	8
Illinois	293	8	0	301
Indiana	63	2	0	65
Iowa	39	1	0	40
Kansas	42	0	0	42
Kentucky	31	0	0	31
Louisiana	37	0	0	37
Maine	14	0	0	14

Table 13.   *Continued*

State	White female lawyers	Negro female lawyers	Female lawyers of other races	Total no. of female lawyers
Maryland	76	0	0	76
Massachusetts	322	1	0	323
Minnesota	40	1	0	41
Mississippi	21	0	0	21
Missouri	87	0	0	87
Montana	8	0	0	8
Michigan	115	2	0	117
Nebraska	30	0	0	30
Nevada	4	0	0	4
New Hampshire	10	0	0	10
New Jersey	167	0	0	167
New Mexico	9	0	0	9
New York	990	10	0	1,000
North Carolina	28	0	0	28
North Dakota	13	0	0	13
Ohio	207	2	0	209
Oklahoma	50	0	0	50
Oregon	25	0	0	25
Pennsylvania	136	2	0	138
Rhode Island	3	0	0	3
South Carolina	23	0	0	23
South Dakota	9	0	1	10
Tennessee	35	0	0	35
Texas	131	1	0	132
Utah	8	0	0	8
Vermont	12	0	0	12
Washington	46	0	0	46
West Virginia	19	0	0	19
Wisconsin	48	0	0	48
Wyoming	4	0	0	4
Virginia	51	3	0	54
Total	4,146	39	2	4,187

*The compilation from Hawaii (male lawyers and judges) is broken into only two categories: the Territory (196) and Honolulu City (136). The cumulative total of male lawyers and judges is 329. *The Sixteenth Census: Population, Second Series, Characteristics of the Population—Hawaii 16* (1943) (Table 13).

†The compilation from Hawaii (women lawyers and judges) is broken into only two categories: the Territory (5) and Honolulu City (2). The cumulative total of women lawyers and judges is 7. *The Sixteenth Census: Population, Second Series, Characteristics of Population*—Hawaii 16 (1943) (Table 13).

Total lawyers and judges employed by race:

Total male	173,456
Total white male	172,329
Total Negro male	1,013
Total other races—male	114
Total female	4,187
Total white females	4,146
Total Negro females	39
Total other races—female	2

Table 62, "Race of Employed Persons (Except on Public Emergency Work), and of Experienced Workers Seeking Work, by Occupation and Sex, for the United States: 1940," *The Sixteenth Census: Population, Volume 3*, at 88 (1943). The compilation of men and women (by race) "seeking work," and the regional breakdown of employed men and women (by race) is not listed here. It is compiled in Tables 62–63.

Bibliography

PRINCIPAL WORKS CITED

Abel, R. L., *American Lawyers* (1989).
Ackiss, T. D., The Negro and the Supreme Court to 1900 (M.A. thesis, Howard University, June 1936).
A Documentary History of the Negro People in the United States (H. Aptheker ed. 1969).
Afro-American Encyclopedia; Or, The Thoughts, Doings and Sayings of the Race (J. T. Haley ed. 1895).
Afro-American History: Primary Sources (T. R. Frazier ed. 1971).
Akin, E. N., *When a Majority Becomes the Minority: Blacks in Jacksonville, Municipal Politics, 1887–1889* (1972).
Aldrich, G., *Black Heritage of Oklahoma* (1973).
Alexander, R. P., "Attorney General Francis Biddle," 1 *National Bar Association Journal* 146 (1941).
———, "Blacks and the Law," 43 *New York State Bar Journal* 15 (Jan. 1971).
———, "The John M. Langston Law Club," 14 *The Shingle* 233 (Dec. 1951).
———, "The Negro Lawyer," 9 *Opportunity* 268 (Sept. 1931).
———, "Voices from Harvard's Own Negroes," in *Varieties of Black Experience at Harvard* 90 (W. Sollors, T. A. Underwood, and C. Titcomb eds. 1986).
Alexander, S. T. M., "The Best of Times, the Worst of Times," 12 *The University of Pennsylvania Law Alumni Journal* 19 (Spring 1977).
———, "Women as Practitioners of Law in the United States," 1 *National Bar Association Journal* 56 (July 1941).
Almanach de Gotha Annuaire Genealogique Diplomatique Et Statistique (Sept. 1920).
Alumni Directory of the University of Minnesota Law School 1889–1986 (ninth ed. 1986).
All the Laws of the State of Illinois Passed by the Thirty-fourth General Assembly (M. Bradwell ed. 1885).
Ames, B. A., *Adelbert Ames, 1835–1933* (1964).
Anderson, E., "James O'Hara of North Carolina: Black Leadership and Local Government," in *Southern Black Leaders of the Reconstruction Era* 101 (H. N. Rabinowitz ed. 1981).
———, *Race and Politics in North Carolina, 1872–1901: The Black Second* (1981).
Annual Reports of Howard University Law School (passim).
Annual Reports of the President of Howard University (passim).

Appleton's Annual Cyclopedia and Register of Important Events of the Year 1878 (n. Series, 1879).

"The Arkansas Peons," 23 *Crisis* 72 (Dec. 1921).

Armistead, W., *A Tribute for the Negro* (1848).

Association of American Law Schools: Directory of Teachers in Member Schools (1924–1933).

Association of American Law Schools and Proceedings of the Twenty-ninth Annual Meeting, Handbook of (1931).

Austin, H. Elsie, "Pioneering All the Way: Matthew W. Bullock, Sr.," (mimeo, n.d.).

The Autobiography of Ida B. Wells (A. M. Duster ed. 1970).

Autographs of Freedom (J. Griffiths ed. 1854).

Avery, I. H., *The History of the State of Georgia* (1881).

Ayers, E. L., *The Promise of the New South: Life After Reconstruction* (1992).

Babcock, B., "Clara Shortridge Folta, First Woman," 30 *Arizona Law Review* 673 (1988).

Bailey, H. R., "Favoritism in Bar Examination and How to Avoid It," Vol. 45 *Report of the Forty-third Annual Meeting of the American Bar Association* 488 (1920).

Bailey, M. T., *Reconstruction in Indian Territory* (1972).

Baker, W. B., *History of Rust College* (1924).

Baldwin, C. A., "Silhouettes: The Black Bar and the Allegheny County Courts," 12 *Pittsburgh Legal Journal* 3 (Dec. 1988).

"The Bar Association and the Negro," 111 *The Outlook* 2 (Sept. 7, 1912).

Bardolph, R., *The Civil Rights Record* (1970).

Barnes, T. G., *Hastings College of the Law: The First Century* (1973).

Bartlett, J. R., "Americanism Pertaining to Afro-Americans," in *Afro-American Encyclopedia; Or, The Thoughts, Doings and Sayings of the Race* 339 (J. T. Haley ed. 1895).

Beasley, D. L., *The Negro Trail Blazers of California* (1919).

Bell, D., "Forward—An Issue on Race Relations," 61 *Oregon Law Review* 151 (1982).

"The Bench and Bar of the Court of Claims to Judge George W. Atkinson on His Retirement," April 17, 1916, 51 Court of Claims Rpts. XVII (1915).

Benedict, J. D., *Muskogee and Northern Oklahoma* (1922).

Bennett, M. T., *The United States Court of Claims: A History, Part I*, Vol. 1 (1976).

Bergmann, L. N., "The Negro in Iowa," 46 *Iowa Journal of History and Politics* 38 (Jan. 1948).

Berry, M., *Black Resistance, White Law* (1971).

Berry, M., and J. W. Blassingame, *Long Memory: The Black Experience in America* (1982).

Bingham, D. E., *We Ask Only a Fair Trial: A History of the Black Community of Evansville, Indiana* (1987).

Biographical Directory of Indiana General Assembly, 1900–1984 (E. Walsh ed. 1984).

The Biographical Directory of the South Carolina House of Representatives, 1692–1973 (Sessions List) (W. B. Edgar ed., 3d ed. 1974).

Biographical Directory of the South Carolina Senate, 1776–1985 (N. L. Bailey, M. L. Morgan and C. R. Taylor eds. 1985).

Biographical Directory of the Tennessee General Assembly, 1861–1901 (R. M. McBride ed. 1979).

Biographical Directory of the United States Congress (1989).

"Biographies of Black Pioneers," 23 *Gopher Historian* 18 (Winter 1968–69).

Biographies of Graduates of the Yale Law School, 1824–1899 (R. W. Tuttle ed. 1911).

Black Abolitionist Papers, 1830–1865 (G. E. Carter and C. P. Ripley eds. 1981).

Black Americans in Congress, 1870–1989 (B. A. Ragsdale and J. D. Treese eds. 1990).

Black Armed Forces Officers (J. Johnson ed. 1971).

The Black Book (M. Levitt, R. Furman, and E. Smith eds. 1974).

"Black Educator, Poet, Fighter for Equal Rights," 68 *The Western Pennsylvania Historical Magazine* 205 (July 1985).

The Black Experience in America (J. C. Curtis and L. L. Gould eds. 1970).

Black Leaders of the Twentieth Century (J. H. Franklin and A. Meir eds. 1982).

"Black Rulers of White Folk," 37 *Crisis* 14 (Jan.–Dec. 1930).

Blackett, J. M., *Thomas Morris Chester* (1989).

Black's Blue Book (1921).

Blakely, A., "The John L. Waller Affair, 1895–1896," 37 *Negro History Bulletin* 216 (Feb.–March 1974).

———, "Richard T. Greener and the 'Talented Tenth's' Dilemma," 59 *Journal of Negro History* 305 (Oct. 1974).

———, *Russia and the Negro* (1986).

Bledsoe, F. S., "History of Senior Class," in *Howard University Yearbook of 1922* (*Book V*).

Blockson, C. L., *Pennsylvania's Black History* (L. D. Stone ed. 1975).

Blodgett, "John Mercer Langston and the Case of Edmonia Lewis: Oberlin, 1862," 53 *Journal Negro History* 201 (1968).

Bloom, C., "Sadie Alexander Is School's 1st Black Woman Graduate," 7 *The University of Pennsylvania Law Alumni Journal* 19 (Winter 1972).

Bloomfield, M., *American Lawyers in a Changing Society, 1776–1876* (1976).

———, "From Deference to Confirmation: The Early Black Lawyers of Galveston, Texas, 1895–1920," in *The New High Priest* 151 (G. W. Gawalt ed. 1984).

———, "John Mercer Langston and the Training of Black Lawyers," in W. J. Leonard, *Black Lawyers* 59 (1977).

Blue Book of the State of Illinois (passim).

Bogen, D. S., "The First Integration of the University of Maryland School of Law," 84 *Maryland Historical Magazine* 39 (Spring 1989).

———, "The Transformation of the Fourteenth Amendment: Reflections from the Admission of Maryland's First Black Lawyers," 44 *Maryland Law Review* 939 (1985).

The Booker T. Washington Papers [1860–1915], Vols. 1–13 (L. R. Harlan, B. S. Kraft, R. W. Smock, G. McTigue, N. E. Woodruff, J. W. Blassingame, P. Daniel, B. S. Kaufman, S. Valenza, and S. M. Harlan eds. 1972–1984).

Boorstin, D. J., "Tradition and Method in Legal History," 54 *Harvard Law Review* 424 (1941).

Boykin, U. M., *A Handbook on the Detroit Negro* (1943).

Brackett, J., "Notes on the Progress of the Colored People of Maryland Since the War," 8 *Johns Hopkins University Studies in Historical and Political Science* 11 (1890).

Bradwell, J. B., "The Colored Bar of Chicago," 5 *Michigan Law Journal* 385 (1896).

———, "The Colored Bar of Chicago," 29 *Chicago Legal News* 75, Oct. 31, 1896.

Bragg, G. F., Jr., *Men of Maryland* (1925) (pamphlet).

Brandt, N., *The Town That Started the Civil War* (1990).

Brawley, B., *Negro Genius* (1937).

Brewer, J. M., *Negro Legislators of Texas* (1935).

Brockman, N., "The National Bar Association, 1888–1893: The Failure of Early Bar Federation," 10 *American Journal of Legal History* 122 (1966).

Brokenburr, R., "Hampton Men in Professions and Business," 48 *The Southern Workman* 262 (June, 1919).

——, "A Lawyer's Uphill Climb," 52 *The Southern Workman* 317 (July, 1923).

Brown, C. S., "The Genesis of the Negro Lawyer in New England," 22 *The Negro History Bulletin* 147 (April 1959) and Part 2, at 171 (May 1959).

Brown, E. G., "The Initial Admission of Negro Students to the University of Michigan," 2 *The Michigan Quarterly Review* 233 (Autumn 1963).

Brown, S. J., "Our Founder," 2 *National Bar Association Journal* 263 (Dec. 1944).

——, "Our Origin," 2 *National Bar Association Journal* 161 (Sept. 1944).

Brown, W. W., *The Black Man* (1863).

——, *The Rising Sun; Or, The Antecedents and Advancement of the Colored Race* (1874).

Brownell, E. A., *Legal Aid in the United States* (1951).

Bruce, A. A., "Interest of the Public in Legal Education," Vol. 45 *Report of the Forty-third Annual Meeting of the American Bar Association* 480 (1920).

Bryson, W. H., *Legal Education in Virginia, 1779–1979* (1982).

Bryson, W. H., and E. L. Shepard, "The Virginia Bar, 1870–1900," in *The New High Priest* (G. W. Gawalt ed. 1984).

Buck, D. D., *The Progress of the Race in the United States and Canada* (1907).

Bulletin of North Carolina Central University School of Law (1972–1974).

Bullock, H. A., *A History of Negro Education in the South* (1967).

Buni, A., *The Negro in Virginia Politics, 1902–1965* (1967).

——, *Robert L. Vann of the Pittsburgh Courier* (1974).

Burton, W., *On the Black Side of Shreveport* (1983).

Callcott, M. L., *The Negro in Maryland, 1870–1912* (1969).

Carrington, P., "Butterfly Effects: The Possibilities of Law Teaching in a Democracy," 41 *Duke L.J.* 741 (1992).

——, "Teaching Law in the Antebellum Northwest," 23 *U. of Toledo L. Rev.* 3 (1991).

Carter, D. T., *Scottsboro: A Tragedy of the American South* (1969).

Carter, W., *Shaw Universe* (1973).

Carter, W. B., "William Henry Hastie: Jurist, Scholar, Friend," 79 *Harvard Law Record* 3 (Nov. 30, 1984).

Cartwright, J. H., *The Triumph of Jim Crow* (1976).

Catalogue of Allen University, 1899–1900 (1900).

Catalogue for Central Tennessee College, 1896–1897 (1897).

Catalogue of Howard University School of Law (passim).

Catalogue of the Washington College of Law (primarily for women) (1898–1899).

Census of the United States 1850–1940.

Chadbourn, J. H., *Lynching and the Law* (1933).

Chambers, M., "At 95, He's a Model for All Lawyers," *National Law Journal* (April 24, 1989).

Chataigne's Virginia Gazetteer and Classified Business Directory, 1890–1891 (1890).

Cheek, W., and A. L. Cheek, *John Mercer Langston and the Fight for Black Freedom* (1989).

————, "A Negro Runs for Congress: John Mercer Langston and the Virginia Campaign of 1888," 52 *Journal of Negro History* 14 (Jan. 1967).

Chesson, Michael B., "Richmond's Black Councilmen," in *Southern Black Leaders of the Reconstruction Era* (H. N. Rabinowitz ed. 1981).

Chester, R., *Uneasy Access: Women Lawyers in a Changing America* (1985).

The Chicago Negro Business Directory (L. W. Washington ed. 1912).

Chronicle of Black Lawyers in North Carolina Vol. 1 (D. E. Terry ed. 1981) (pamphlet).

Chroust, A. H., *The Rise of the Legal Profession in America* (1965).

Clarke, A. M., "The History of the Black Bar," 30 *Saint Louis Bar Journal* 17 (Spring 1984).

Cleveland, J. M. C., "Denies That He Dined Negro," *Public Ledger* (March 4, 1904).

Cochran, Lynda Dempsey, "Arthur D. Shores: Advocate for Freedom," (M.A. thesis, Georgia Southern College, 1977).

Colbert, D., "Challenging the Challenge: Thirteenth Amendment As a Prohibition Against the Racial Use of Preemptory Challenges," 76 *Cornell Law Review* 1 (1990).

The College of Life or, Practical Self-Educator: A Manual of Self Improvement for the Colored Race (H. D. Northrop, J. R. Gay and I. G. Penn eds. 1896).

Collins, R. H., *History of Kentucky* Vol. 1 (1874).

The Colored Men's Professional and Business Directory of Chicago (1885).

Colored People's Blue Book and Business Directory (1909).

Columbia Alumni Register, 1754–1931 (1932).

Congressional Quarterly's Guide to U.S. Elections (2d ed., J. L. Moore ed., 1985).

Constitutional Law (G. R. Stone, L. M. Seidman, C. R. Sunstein, and M. V. Tushnet eds. 1986).

Contee, C. G., "The Supreme Court Bar's First Member," *Supreme Court Historical Society Yearbook* 82 (1976).

Cooke, A., *Lane College: Its Heritage and Outreach, 1882–1982* (1987).

Cooper, A. R., "*Brown v. Board of Education* and Virgil Darnell Hawkins: Twenty-eight Years and Six Petitions to Justice," 64 *Journal of Negro History* 1 (1979).

Corlew, R. E., *Tennessee* (1981).

Cornell Directory of Alumni and Chronicle (1988).

Cortner, R. C., *A Mob Intent on Death: The NAACP and the Arkansas Riot Cases* (1988).

Cosey, A. B., *American and English Law on Titles of Record, 1535–1911* (1914).

Cottrol, R., "Law, Politics, and Race in Urban America: Towards a New Synthesis," 17 *Rutgers Law Journal* 483 (1986).

Coulter, E. M., *Negro Legislators in Georgia During the Reconstruction Period* (1968).

Cox, T. C., *Blacks in Topeka, Kansas, 1865–1915* (1982).

Crockett, W. H., *The History of Vermont* Vol. 5 (1923).

Cronon, E. D., *Black Moses: The Story of Marcus Garvey and the Universal Negro Improvement Association* (2d ed. 1972).

Cunningham, C. A., "Homer S. Brown: First Black Political Leader in Pittsburgh," 66 *Journal of Negro History* 304 (1981).

Current, R. N., *Those Terrible Carpetbaggers: A Reinterpretation* (1988).

Dabney, W. P., *Cincinnati's Colored Citizens* (1926).

Dagley, A. W., "The Negro of Oklahoma" (M.A. thesis, University of Oklahoma, 1926).

Daly, V. R., "Brother Albert B. George," 11 *The Sphinx* 9 (Dec. 1925).

Daniel, A. M., "The Law Library of Howard University, 1867–1956," 51 *Law Library Journal* 202 (1958).

Daniel, P., *The Shadow of Slavery: Peonage in the South, 1901–1969* (1972).

Daniels, J., *In Freedom's Birthplace: A Study of Boston Negroes* (reprint, 1968).

Dannett, S., *Profiles of Negro Womanhood* Vol. 1 (1964).

Dark, O., and A. R. Moye, "L. Marian Poe, A Model of Public Service," 38 *Virginia Lawyer* 32 (March 1990).

Davie, M. R., *Negroes in American Society* (1949).

Davis, B. J., Jr., "Bar of Public Opinion," in *Twenty-second Annual National Negro Business League* 117 (Aug. 17–19, 1921).

———, *Communist Councilman from Harlem* (1969).

Davis, L., *Blacks in the State of Oregon, 1788–1974* (July 1974, mimeo).

Davis, R. H., *Memorable Negroes in Cleveland's Past* (1969).

Davis, W. T., *Bench and Bar of Massachusetts* Vol. II (1895).

Davis, William W., "The Civil War and Reconstruction in Florida" (Ph.D. diss., Columbia University, 1913).

Delany, M. R., *The Condition, Elevation, Emigration, and Destiny of the Colored People of the United States* (1852).

Dent, Francis M., *Annual Reports of the President* (Wolverine Bar Association), Oct. 20, 1937.

Detroit College of Law Announcement, 1891–1892 and 1896–1897.

Dickerson, E. B., "The Participation of Negro Labor in Our War Effort," 2 *Lawyers Guild Review* 24 (May 1942).

Dictionary of American Biography (A. Johnson and D. Malone eds. 1931).

Dictionary of American Negro Biography (R. Logan and M. Winston eds. 1982).

Dictionary of Georgia Biography Vol. 1 (K. Coleman and C. S. Gurr eds. 1983).

Dill, R. G., *The Political Campaigns of Colorado* (1895).

Dillard, I., "James Milton Turner: A Little Known Benefactor of His People," 19 *Journal of Negro History* 372 (1934).

Dillard, T., "Perseverance: Black History in Pulaski County, Arkansas—An Excerpt," 31 *Pulaski County Historical Review* 62 (Winter 1983).

Diplomatic and Consular Service of the United States (Dec. 1903).

"The Disgrace of the Nation," 8 *The Negro History Bulletin* 50 (Dec. 1944).

Dixon, F., *Negroes of Nebraska* (1939).

A Documentary History of the Negro People in the United States (H. Aptheker ed. 1969).

Donald, D. H., *Charles Sumner* (1960).

Douglas, Nils R., "Who Was Louis A. Martinet?" (n.d.) (manuscript).

Douglass, Frederick, "A Plea for Free Speech in Boston," in Vol. 5 *The World's Best Orations* 1906 (D. J. Brewer ed. 1899).

Dowd, J., *The Negro in American Life* (student's edition, 1926).

Drachman, V. G., "Women Lawyers and the Quest for Professional Identity in Late Nineteenth-Century America," 88 *Michigan Law Review* 2414 (1990).

Drago, E. L., *Black Politicians and Reconstruction in Georgia* (1982).

Drake, S., and H. Clayton, *Black Metropolis* (1945).

Du Bois, W. E. B., *Black Reconstruction in America, 1860–1880* (reprint, 1973).

———, *The Philadelphia Negro* (reprint, 1970).

———, "Reconstruction and Its Benefits," in *Black History* 271 (M. Drimmer ed. 1981).

Dunnigan, A. A., *The Fascinating Story of Black Kentuckians: Their Heritage and Traditions* (1982).

Dyson, W., *Howard University: The Capstone of Negro Education, 1867–1940* (1941).

"Earl B. Dickerson Appointed to Fair Labor Practice Committee," 1 *Lawyers' Guild Review* 29 (Aug. 1941).

Edmonds, H. G., *The Negro and Fusion Politics in North Carolina, 1894–1901* (1951).

Eight Annual Scholarship Awards Luncheon Program of the Black Women Lawyers Association of Southern California, May 19, 1984.

Ellis, G. W., "The Chicago Negro in Law and Politics," 1 *The Champion Magazine* 349 (March 1917).

Ely, M. P., *Amos 'N' Andy* (1991).

Encyclopedia of Black America (W. A. Low and V. A. Clift eds. 1981).

England, William L., Jr., "The Condition of Southern Negroes, 1886–1889, as Viewed by the *New York Age*" (M.A. thesis, Butler University, June 17, 1972).

Engs, R. F., *Freedom's First Generation* (1979).

"Eunice Hunton Carter," 16 *Opportunity* 261 (Sept. 1938).

"Faculty Approves Scholarship to Honor the Memory of H. Claude Hudson," 7 *Loyola Lawyer* 1 (Spring 1989).

"The Failure of Early Bar Federation," 10 *American Journal Legal History* 122 (1966).

Ferguson, C. C., "Group Roles in America Legal History—Blacks," 69 *Law Library Journal* 470 (1969).

Ferrell, C. L., *Nightmare and Dream: Anti-Lynching in Congress, 1917–1922* (1986).

Fifteenth Annual Report of the National Negro Business League (Aug. 18–20, 1915).

Fifth Annual Meeting Program of the State Bar of California, Sept. 29, 30 and Oct. 1, 1932.

Fisher, James A., "The Political Development of the Black Community in California, 1850–1950," in *Neither Separate Nor Equal* 41 (California Historical Society 1971).

Fleming, G. J., "A Philadelphia Lawyer," 46 *Crisis* 329 (Nov. 1939).

Fleming, W. L., *Documentary History of Reconstruction* Vols. 1–2 (reprint, P. Smith ed. 1960).

Florida State Government, 1885: An Official Directory (J. B. Whitfield ed. 1885).

Foner, E., *Reconstruction, 1863–1877* (1988).

Forbes, G. W., *John S. Rock* (n.d.) (manuscript).

Foreign Consular Offices in the United States (1932).

"The Forum Talks with Maceo Hubbard," 7 *The Civil Rights Forum* 1 (Summer/Fall 1984).

Fox, S. R., "W. Monroe Trotter at Harvard," in *Varieties of Black Experience at Harvard* 52 (W. Sollors, T. A. Underwood, and C. Titcomb eds. 1986).

Franklin, J. H., *From Slavery to Freedom* (1967).

———, *George Washington Williams* (1985).

———, "George Washington Williams," 31 *Journal of Negro History* 60 (Jan. 1946).

———, *Race and History: Selected Essays, 1938–1988* (1989).

———, "The South's New Leaders," in *Black History* 307 (M. Drimmer ed. 1968).

Franklin, J. L., *The Blacks in Oklahoma* (1988).
———, *Journey Toward Hope* (1982).
Frazier, E. F., *The Negro Church* (1964).
———, *Negro Family in the United States* (1939).
Free Blacks in America, 1800–1860 (J. H. Bracey, Jr., A. Meier, and E. Rudwick eds. 1971).
Freedom and Citizenship: Selected Lectures and Addresses of Hon. John Mercer Langston (J. E. Rankin ed. 1883).
Freeman, Elaine K., "Harvey Johnson and Everett Waring—A Study of Leadership in the Baltimore Negro Community, 1880–1900" (M.A. thesis, George Washington University, 1968).
Gallagher, B. G., *American Caste and the Negro College* (1966).
Gatewood, W. B., Jr., *Aristocrats of Color* (1991).
———, *Black Americans and the White Man's Burden, 1898–1903* (1975).
———, "Negro Legislator in Arkansas, 1891: A Document," 31 *The Arkansas Historical Quarterly* 220 (1972).
General Assembly of Virginia, July 30, 1619–January 1, 1978 (C. M. Leonard ed. 1978).
General Catalogue of the University of Michigan, 1837–1911 (I. N. Demmon ed. 1912).
The George Washington University Alumni Directory (1938).
Gillett, W., *Retreat from Reconstruction, 1869–1879* (1979).
Gilliam, F., *A Time to Speak: A Brief History of the Afro-American of Bloomington, Indiana, 1865–1965* (1965).
Ginzburg, R., *100 Years of Lynchings* (reprint, 1988).
Glatthaar, J. T., *Forged in Battle* (1991).
Goebel, J., Jr., *A History of the School of Law of Columbia University* (1955).
Goldman, M. S., *A Portrait of the Black Attorney in Chicago* (1972).
Goode, K. G., *California's Black Pioneers* (1974).
Gordon, H. I., "The Problem of the Negro Lawyer," 2 *Education* 4 (April 1936).
Gosnell, H. F., *Negro Politicians: The Rise of Negro Politics in Chicago* (1935).
Grant, N. L., *TVA and Black Americans* (1990).
Green, E. L., *A History of the University of South Carolina* (1916).
Green, J. M., *Negroes in Michigan History* (reprint, 1985).
Green, W., "Stare Decisis and the Supreme Court of the United States," 4 *National Bar Association Journal* 191 (1946).
Green, W. T., "Negroes in Milwaukee," in *The Negro in Milwaukee: A Historical Survey* 5 (1968) (pamphlet).
Greenberg, Jack, *Race Relations and American Law* (1950).
Greenberg, Jonathan, *Staking a Claim* (1990).
Greene, L. J., G. R. Kremer, and A. F. Holland, *Missouri's Black Heritage* (1980).
Greene, R. E., *They Did Not Tell Me True Facts* (1992).
Grimké, A. H., *The Life of Charles Sumner* (1892).
Griswold, E. N., *Law and Lawyers in the United States* (1985).
Gross, C. R., "Thumb Nail Sketches of the Negro in Law in Rhode Island" (1959) (mimeo).
Hale, William H., "The Career Development of the Negro Lawyer in Chicago" (Ph.D. diss., Univ. of Chicago, Sept. 1949).
Hamilton, C. V., *Adam Clayton Powell, Jr.* (1991).
Hamilton, G. H., *The National Bar Association Law Directory* (1931–1932).
Hamilton, G. P., *The Bright Side of Memphis* (1908).

Hanchett, C. M., "George Boyer Vashon, 1824–1878: Black Educator, Poet, Fighter for Equal Rights," 68 *The Western Pennsylvania Historical Magazine* 205 (July 1985).

Hancock, G. B., "Robert L. Vann," 41 *Virginia Union Bulletin* 1 (Nov. 1, 1940).

Harlan, J. C., *History of West Virginia State College, 1890–1965* (1968).

Harlan, L. R., *Booker T. Washington: The Making of a Black Leader, 1856–1901* (1972).

———, *Booker T. Washington: The Wizard of Tuskegee* (1983).

Harlan, L. R., and P. Daniel, "A Dark and Stormy Night in the Life of Booker T. Washington," 3 *Chronicle* 4 (Feb. 1970).

Harper, C., "Some Black Lawyers in the Post-Civil War South," *American Bar Association Litigation* 41 (Spring 1977).

Harper's Encyclopedia of United States History from 458 A.D. to 1902 (B. J. Lossing ed. 1902).

Harris, R. E., *The First Hundred Years: A History of Arizona Blacks* (1977) (pamphlet).

Harvard Law Quinquennial (F. S. Kimball ed. 1948).

Haskins, J., *Pinckney Benton Stewart Pinchback* (1973).

Hastie, W. H., "Negro Officers in Two World Wars," 12 *Journal of Negro Education* 312 (1943).

———, "A Note to the Aspiring Lawyer on His Prospective Profession," 33 *The Fisk Herald* 10 (April 1940).

Hawshawe, Dorothy D., "David Augustus Straker, Black Lawyer and Reconstruction Politician, 1842–1908" (Ph.D. diss., Catholic University, 1974).

Hays, L., "Louis Redding's Fight for Dignity and Decency," 86 *Brown Alumni Monthly* 38 (Feb. 1986).

Heard, A., and D. S. Strong, *Southern Primaries and Elections 1920–1949* (1950).

Hearing Before Senate Subcommittee of the Committee on Privileges and Elections, 66th Cong., 2d. Sess. 945, Vol. 1, July 8, 1920.

Hearing Before Special Committee Investigating Presidential Campaign Expenditures, 70th Cong., 1st Sess., 691, May 29, 1928.

Heinz, J. P., and E. O. Laumann, *Chicago Lawyers* (1982).

Hemingway, T., "Prelude to Change: Black Carolinians in the War Years, 1914–1920," 65 *Journal of Negro History* 212 (1980).

Henderson, A. B., "FEPC and the Southern Railway Case: An Investigation into the Discriminatory Practices of Railroads During World War II," 56 *Journal of Negro History* 173 (April 1976).

Hepburn, C. M., "Organized Co-operation for the Ideals of Legal Education," in Vol. 45 *Report of the Forty-third Annual Meeting of the American Bar Association* 467 (1920).

Herndon, A., *Let Me Live* (reprint, 1969).

Higginbotham, A. L., Jr. *In the Matter of Color: Race and the American Legal Process—The Colonial Period* (1978).

Higgins, C., "The Longest Struggle," *Tony Brown's Journal* (Jan.–March 1984).

"Highlights of 18th Annual Convention," 2 *National Bar Association Journal* 80 (June 1944).

Hill, D., "The Negro as a Political and Social Issue in the Oregon County," 33 *Journal of Negro History* 130 (1948).

Hill, M., "The All-Negro Communities of Oklahoma: The Natural History of a Social Movement," 31 *Journal of Negro History* 254 (1946).

Hilyer, A. F., "The Colored American in Business," in *Proceedings of The National Negro Business League* 1, Aug. 23–24, 1943.

History of Alabama and Dictionary of Alabama Biography (T. M. Owen ed. 1921).
History of the American Negro in the Great World War (W. A. Sweeney ed. 1919).
History of the Bench and Bar of Minnesota Vol. 2 (H. F. Stevens ed. 1904).
History of Minneapolis Vols. 2 and 3 (M. Shutter ed. 1923).
A History of Missouri (R. S. Kitkendall ed. 1986).
History of the American Negro: West Virginia Edition, Vol. 7 (W. Va. edition, A. B. Caldwell eds. 1923).
Hobbs, S. H., and F. Fitch, "The Marcus Garvey Case: A Law and Power Theory Analysis of Political Suppression of Human Dignity," 2 *George Mason University Civil Rights Law Journal* 15 (1991).
Hodson, G., *The Colonel: The Life of Henry Simpson, 1867–1950* (1990).
Holmes, O. W., Jr., "The Places of History in Understanding Law," in *The Life of the Law* 1 (J. Honnold ed. 1964).
"Homer S. Brown," 17 *Opportunity* 16 (Jan. 1939).
Hopkins, P. E., "Famous Men of the Negro Race: Robert Morris," 2 *The Colored American Magazine* 337 (Sept. 1901).
Horack, H. C., and W. Shafroth, "The Law Schools of Tennessee," 15 *Tennessee Law Review* 311 (1938).
Horton, J. O., and L. E. Horton, *Black Bostonians* (1979).
Houston, C. H., "Need for Negro Lawyers," 4 *Journal of Negro Education* 49 (1935).
———, "Survey of Howard University Law Students" (Dec. 21, 1927) (paper).
Howard University Law School Bulletin (1871, 1903–1904, 1919, 1944).
Howard, V. B., *Black Liberation in Kentucky* (1983).
Hunton, A. W., and K. M. Johnson, *Two Colored Women with the American Expeditionary Forces* (1920).
Hurst, J. W., *Law and Social Process in United States History* (1987).
Hutchinson, L. D., *Anna J. Cooper: A Voice from the South* (1981).
Illinois Blue Book (L. L. Emmerson, secretary of state, ed. 1925–1926).
Illinois Legislative Manual Thirtieth General Assembly (1877).
Intercollegian Wonder Book—1779—The Negro in Chicago—1927 Vol. 1 (F. H. Robb ed. 1927).
Jack, R. L., *History of the National Association for the Advancement of Colored People* (1943).
Jackson, L. P., *Negro Officeholders in Virginia, 1865–1895* (1946).
Jackson, W. M., *The Story of Selma* (1954).
Jacobstein, J. M., and R. M. Mersky, *Fundamentals of Legal Research* (3rd ed. 1985).
Jefferson, B. S., "Race Discrimination in Jury Service," 19 *Boston University Law Review* 413 (1939).
———, "The Supreme Court and State Separation and Delegation of Powers," 54 *Columbia Law Review* 1 (1944).
Job Opportunities for Negro Youth in Columbus, Ohio (C. J. Gray ed. 1938).
"John H. Hill, Former President of West Virginia State, Laid to Rest at Institute," 7 *The Yellow Jacket* 1 (Oct. 23, 1936).
Johnson, C. S., *The Negro College Graduate* (1938).
Johnson, E. A., "A Congressional Campaign," 36 *Crisis* 118 (Jan. 1929).
———, *History of the Negro Race in America and the Negro Soldier in The Spanish American War* (1891).
Johnson, G. M., "Legal Profession," in *The Integration of the Negro into American Society* 87 (E. F. Frazier ed. 1951).
———, "The Law School," 1 *Howard Law Journal* 86 (1955).

————, *The Making of a Liberal* (1985) (bound manuscript).

————, "Multi-State Taxation of Interstate Sales," 27 *California Law Review* 547 (1939).

————, "State Sales Taxes and the Commerce Clause," 24 *California Law Review* 155 (1935).

Johnson, J. W., *Along this Way* (1933).

————, "Should the Negro Be Given an Education Different from that Given to the Whites?" in *Twentieth Century Negro Literature* 72 (D. W. Culp 1902).

Johnson, O. W., *Early Libby and Troy, Montana* (1958).

Johnson, W. D., *Biographical Sketches of Prominent Negro Men and Women of Kentucky* (1897).

Jones, S., "The Supreme Court's Role in Jim Crow Transportation," 3 *National Bar Association Journal* 114 (June 1945).

Journal of the House of Representatives of the General Assembly (Illinois) (passim).

Journal of the House of Representatives of the State of Ohio (passim).

Journal Proceedings of the House of Representatives of the State of Kansas (1937–1943) (passim).

"Judge Perry B. Jackson," 53 *The Cleveland Bar Journal* 115 (March 1982).

Justice and Jurisprudence (1889).

The Justices of the United States Supreme Court, 1789–1969: Their Lives and Major Opinions (L. Friedman and F. L. Israel eds. 1969).

Katz, W. L., *The Black West* (1973).

Kent College of Law Bulletin, 1933–1934 (1934).

Kentucky [Legislative] Directory (F. K. Kavanaugh ed. 1936–1946) (passim).

Kerlin, R. T., *Negro Poets and Their Poems* (1923).

Key, V. O., Jr., *Southern Politics* (1949).

Kidd, F., *Profile of the Negro in American Dentistry* (1979).

Kilson, M., "Adam Clayton Powell, Jr.: The Militant as Politician," in *Black Leaders of the Twentieth Century* (J. H. Franklin and A. Mier eds. 1982).

Kletzing, H. F., and W. H. Crogman, *Progress of a Race* (1901).

Klingman, P. D., *Josiah Walls: Florida's Black Congressman of Reconstruction* (1976).

Kluger, R., *Simple Justice* (1975).

Koger, A. B., *The Negro Lawyer in Maryland* (1948) (pamphlet).

Kusmer, K., *A Ghetto Takes Shape: Black Cleveland, 1870–1930* (1976).

"Lady Lawyer," 2 *Ebony* 18 (Aug. 1947).

LaFourche, Delany, "Was He a Victim of Circumstance," Vol. 1 *New Orleans Civic Leader* 4 (1930).

Lamon, L. C., *Black Tennesseans, 1900–1930* (1977).

Lamson, P., *The Glorious Failure* (1973).

Lane, R., *Dorsey's Philadelphia and Ours on the Past and Future of the City in America* (1941).

————, *Roots of Violence in Black Philadelphia, 1860–1900* (1986).

Langston, J. M., *From the Virginia Plantation to the National Capitol* (1894).

Lapp, R. M., *Afro-American in California* (N. Hundley, Jr., and J. A. Schutz eds. 1979).

————, "Negro Rights Activities in Gold Rush California," 45 *California Historical Society Quarterly* 1 (March 1966).

Laska, Lewis L., "A History of Legal Education in Tennessee 1770–1970" (Ph.D. diss., George Peabody College of Teachers, May 1978).

"The Law as a Profession," 2 *The Home Mission College Review* 4 (Jan. 1929).

Law in American History (D. Fleming and B. Bailyn eds. 1971).

Law Directory of the National Bar Association (1933) (appended to *Proceedings of the Seventh and Eighth Annual Conventions of the National Bar Association*, Aug. 6, 1931 and Aug. 4, 1932).

Laws Passed at the Tenth Session of the General Assembly of the State of Colorado (April 1895).

"Leader, Lawyer and Women's Rights Advocate Dies at 94," 37 *Federal Bar News & Journal* 16 (Jan. 1990).

Lee, G. B., V. V. Miles, and G. N. Smith, "The Black Lawyer in Virginia: Reflections Upon a Journey, 1938–1988," 37 *Virginia Lawyer* 29 (Oct. 1988).

"The Legal Needs of Black-Owned Businesses in Los Angeles," 20 *UCLA Law Review* 827 (1973).

Leonard, W. J., *Black Lawyers* (1977).

———, "The Development of the Black Bar," 407 *Annals of the American Academy of Political and Social Science* 134 (May 1973).

Leopold, N. F., Jr., *Life Plus 99 Years* (1958).

Lerner, G., *Black Women in White America* (1972).

Letter from Charles H. Houston to National Lawyers' Guild, 1 *Lawyers' Guild Review* 32 (Aug. 1941).

Letter from Dean William E. Taylor to Martin Popper, 1 *Lawyers' Guild Review* 32 (Aug. 1941).

Letter from Dean William E. Taylor to Martin Popper, 2 *Lawyers' Guild Review* 24 (Jan. 1942).

Letter from the Board of the National Lawyers' Guild to NAACP, 2 *Lawyers' Guild Review* 34 (July 1942).

Levesque, George A., "Black Boston: Negro Life in Garrison's Boston, 1800–1860" (Ph.D. diss., S.U.N.Y., 1976).

———, "Boston's Black Brahmin: Dr. John S. Rock," 26 *Civil War History* 326 (1980).

Levy, L. W., and H. B. Phillips, "The Roberts Case: Source of the 'Separate but Equal' Doctrine," 56 *American Historical Review* 510 (1950).

Lewinson, E. R., *Black Politics in New York City* (1974).

Lewis, K., "The History of Black Lawyers in North Carolina," *North Carolina Bar Association Notes* (Dec. 1987).

Lewis, J. V., *Out of a Ditch: a True Story of an Ex-Slave* (1910).

Lightfoot, S. L., *Balm in Gilead* (1988).

Littlejohn, E. J., and D. L. Hobson, "Black Lawyers, Law Practice, and Bar Associations—1844 to 1970: A Michigan History," 33 *Wayne Law Review* 1625 (1987).

Locke, A., "Enter New Negro," 6 *Survey Graphic* 621 (March 1925).

Lofren, C., *The Plessy Case* (1987).

Logan, F., *The Negro in North Carolina, 1876–1894* (1974).

Logan, R. W., *The Betrayal of the Negro* (1969).

———, *Howard University: The First One Hundred Years, 1867–1967* (1968).

———, *The Negro in American Life and Thought: The Nadir, 1877–1901* (1954).

Lortie, Jr., F. M., *The San Francisco Black Community, 1870–1890* (1970).

"Louis L. Redding, Civil Rights Attorney," 15 *Harvard Law School Record* 2 (Nov. 13, 1952).

Lukingbeal, A., "Cornell Law Students—Change and Continuity," *Cornell Law Forum* (1988 centennial issue).

Lumpkin, K. P., *The Emancipation of Angelina Grimke* (1974).

Lyda, J. W., *The Negro in the History of Indiana* (1953).

Mabee, C., *Black Freedom* (1970).

Major, M. A., *Noted Negro Women* (1893).

Marable, M., "Tuskegee and the Politics of Illusion in the New South," 18 *The Black Scholar* 13 (May 1977).

Marcus Garvey Life and Lessons (R. A. Hill and B. Bair eds. 1987).

The Marcus Garvey and UNIA Papers (R. A. Hill and B. Bair eds. 1987).

Marquette University Part-Time Evening School 1923–1924 (catalogue) (1924).

Marszalek, J. F., Jr., *Court-Martial: A Black Man in America* (1972).

Martin, C., *The Angelo Herndon Case and Southern Justice* (1976).

Martin, G., *Causes and Conflicts: The Centennial History of the Association of the Bar of the City of New York, 1870–1970* (1970).

McCaleb, W. F., *Theodore Roosevelt* (1931).

McCargo, S. E., "Emancipation in Michigan," 64 *Michigan Bar Journal* 518 (1985).

McClain, Shirla R. "The Contribution of Blacks in Akron: 1825–1975," (Ph.D. diss., University of Akron, 1975).

McFeely, W. S., *Frederick Douglass* (1991).

———, *Yankee Stepfather* (1968).

"The McGhee's of St. Paul," 40 *Crisis* 130 (June 1933).

McGinnis, F. A., *History of the A.M.E. Church* (1941).

McGuire, P., "Desegregation of the Armed Forces: Black Leadership, Protest and World War II," 68 *Journal Negro History* 147 (1983).

McLagan, E., *A Peculiar Paradise: A History of Blacks in Oregon, 1788–1940* (1982).

McMillen, N. R., *Dark Journey: Black Mississippians in the Age of Jim Crow* (1989).

McMurdock, Bertha J., "The Development of Higher Education for Negroes in Missouri" (M.A. thesis, Howard University, 1939).

McNeil, G. R., "Charles Hamilton Houston," 3 *Black Law Journal* 123 (1975).

———, *Groundwork: Charles Hamilton Houston and the Struggle for Civil Rights* (1983).

———, "Justiciable Cause: Howard University Law School and the Struggle for Civil Rights," 22 *Howard Law Journal* 283 (1979).

McPherson, J. M., *Battle Cry of Freedom* (1988).

Meier, A., "Booker T. Washington: An Interpretation," in *Black History* 336 (M. Drimmer ed. 1968).

Meier, A., and E. Rudwick, "Attorneys Black and White: A Case Study of Race Relations Within the NAACP," 62 *Journal of American History* 913 (March 1976).

Memorial and Biographical History of Dallas County, Texas (1892).

Men of Hawaii Vol. 5 (G. F. Nellist ed., revised ed. 1935).

Merriam, L., *Higher Education in Tennessee* (1893).

"Message from Dean George A. Parker," Vol. 1, No. 2 *The Barrister* (Robert H. Terrell Law School) 1 (1941).

Metze, Charles, "The History of Allen University," in *African Methodism in South Carolina* 52 (1987).

Michigan Biographies Vol. 1 (compiled by Michigan Historical Commission).

Michigan Official Directory and Legislative Manual (compiled by H. H. Dignan, secretary of state 1943).

Miller, J. C., *The Black Presence in American Foreign Affairs* (1978).

Miller, K., "The Historic Background of the Negro Physician," 1 *Journal of Negro History* 99 (1916).

————, "The Negro's Progress in Fifty Years," 49 *Annals of the American Academy of Political and Social Science* 182 (Sept. 1913).

Miller, L., "Covenants in the Bear Flag State," 53 *Crisis* 138 (May 1946).

Miller, M. S., "David Straker and Other Reconstruction Jurists," 81 *Crisis* 314 (Nov. 1974).

————, "Robert Brown Elliott: Reconstruction Leader," 80 *Crisis* 267 (Oct. 1973).

————, "Robert Herberton Terrell, 1877–1925: Black Lawyer and Community Leader" (Ph.D. diss., Catholic Univ., 1977).

————, "Whither the Black Jurist, a Place in American Law?" 14 *The Hampton Review* 31 (Fall 1988).

————, "Woodrow Wilson and the Black Judge," 84 *Crisis* 81 (Feb. 1977).

Ming, R., "Racial Restrictions and the Fourteenth Amendment: The Restrictive Covenant Cases," 16 *University of Chicago Law Review* 203 (1949).

Mollison, I. C., "Negro Lawyers in Mississippi," 15 *Journal of Negro History* 38 (1930).

Morello, K. B., *The Woman Lawyer in America: 1638 to the Present—the Invisible Bar* (1986).

Morrison, G., *To Move the World* (1982).

Mumford, E. H., *Seattle's Black Victorians, 1852–1901* (1980).

————, "Seattle's Black Victorians: Revising a City's History," 2 *Portage* 17 (Fall/Winter 1980–1981).

Murray, P., "The Right to Equal Opportunity in Employment," 33 *California Law Review* 338 (1945).

————, *Song in a Weary Throat* (1987).

"NAACP Annual Meeting Reports," 10 *Crisis* 135 (Jan. 1915).

Nabrit, J. M., Jr., *Cases and Materials on Civil Rights* (1949) (mimeo).

Naison, M., *Communists in Harlem During the Depression* (1983).

National Bar Association Annual Convention Program, Aug. 1–3, 1940.

The National Bar Association: Proceedings of the Sixth, Seventh and Eighth Annual Conventions (1930, 1931, and 1932).

National Cyclopedia of American Biography (1898 and 1967 issues).

The National Cyclopedia of the Colored Race Vol. 1 (C. C. Richardson ed. 1919).

The National Lawyers' Guild: From Roosevelt Through Reagan (A. F. Ginger and E. M. Tobin eds. 1988).

National Roster of Black Judicial Officers (M. Kancewick ed. 1980).

"The NBA History and Perspective," in *National Bar Association Membership Directory* xiii (1991).

The Negro Almanac (H. A. Ploski and W. Marr II, third ed. 1976).

Negro Exodus from Southern States, Senate Report 693, 46th Cong., 2d Sess., Part 2 (1880).

Negro Population in the United States, 1790–1915 (S. L. Rogers ed. 1918).

Negro Who's Who in California 41 (1948).

The Negro Year Book (Tuskegee Institute ed. 1952).

Negro Year Book, 1918–1919 (M. N. Work ed. 1919).

The Negro Year Book, 1931–1932 (M. N. Work ed. 1931).

The Negroes of Nebraska (Works Progress Administration pamphlet, 1939).

Nelson, Bernard H., "The Fourteenth Amendment and the Negro Since 1920" (Ph.D. diss., Catholic Univ., 1946).

Nesbit, R. C., *The History of Wisconsin, 1878–1893* (1985).

Newbert, D. D., "Reflections from the 'Class' of '29," 17 *The [Nebraska University Law School] Transcript* 20 (Dec./Jan. 1983).

Newbold, "Common Schools for Negroes in the South," 140 *Annals of the American Academy of Political and Social Science* 209 (Nov. 1928).

The New High Priest (G. W. Gawalt ed. 1984).

New Perspectives on Black Educational History (V. P. Franklin and J. D. Anderson eds. 1978).

New York Law School—1891 to 1991—A Heritage (1991).

New York Legislative Record and Index (1930).

New York Negro Lawyers (S. H. Lark ed. 1915).

New York State Black and Puerto Rican Legislators: 1917–1977, (J. A. Stewart ed. 1977).

New York University General Alumni Catalogue (W. J. Maxwell ed. 1916).

Nichols, R. F., "United States v. Davis," 31 *American Historical Review* 266 (1926).

Nieman, D. G., "The Road to Brown," 35 *The American Journal of Legal History* 333 (July 1991).

Ninth Annual Convention Program of the National Bar Association, Aug. 3–5, 1933.

Ninth Edition Alumni Directory University of Minneapolis School of Law (1986).

Notable American Women, 1607–1950 Vol. 3, (D. Thomas and E. T. James eds. 1971).

Notable Black American Women (Jessie C. Smith ed. 1992).

Nowlin, W. F., *The Negro in American Politics* (1931).

The Official Blue Book of the Jamestown Ter-Centennial Exposition (1907).

Oldfield, J. R., "A High and Honorable Calling: Black Lawyers in South Carolina, 1868–1915," 23 *Journal of American Studies* 395 (Great Britain, 1989), reprinted in 10 *African Americans and the Legal Profession in Historical Perspective* 281 (P. Finkelman ed. 1992).

Oliver, D. H., *A Negro on Mormonism* (1963).

Olsen, O. H., *Carpetbagger's Crusade: The Life of Albion Winegar Tourgee* (1965).

Opportunities for Negroes in Law (H. E. Groves ed. 1967).

"Oral History: Justice Bernard S. Jefferson," 14 *Hastings Constitutional Law Quarterly* 225 (1987).

Osborn, G. C., "Woodrow Wilson Appoints a Negro Judge," 24 *The Journal of Southern History* 481 (Nov. 1958).

Osofsky, G., "Come Out from Among Them," in *Black History* 372 (M. Drimmer ed. 1968).

Ottley, R., and W. J. Weatherby, *The Negro in New York* (1967).

Ovington, M. W., *Portraits in Color* (1927).

———, *The Walls Came Tumbling Down* (reprint, 1969).

Past and Present of St. Paul, Minnesota (W. B. Hennessy ed. 1906).

Paterson, J., *Be Somebody: A Biography of Marguerite Rawalt* (1986).

Patterson, C., *The Negro in Tennessee, 1790–1865* (1968).

Paulson, D., and P. Hawkes, "Desegregation at the University of Florida Law School: Virgil Hawkins v. The Florida Board of Control," 12 *Florida State University Law Review* 59 (1984).

Paynter, J. H., *Horse and Buggy Days with Uncle Sam* (1943).

Pease, J. H., and W. H. Pease, *They Who Would Be Free* (1974).

Peeks, E., *The Long Struggle for Black Power* (1971).

Penn, I. G., *The Afro-American Press and Its Editors* (1891).

The Pennsylvania [Legislative] Manual (1937).

Perdue, R. E., *The Negro in Savannah, 1865–1900* (1973).
"Pioneer Lawyer-Judge, Tulsa, Oklahoma," 7 *National Bar Bulletin* 2 (Aug. 1975).
Polk, D. M., *Black Men and Women of Nebraska* (1981).
Popper, M., "The Guild Contribution to Victory," 3 *Lawyers' Guild Review* 4 (March–April 1943).
Porter, Aaron, "The Career of an Institution: A Study of Norris, Schmidt, Green, Harris, Higginbotham and Associates" (Ph.D. diss., University of Pennsylvania, 1993).
Portfolio of Tenth General Assembly [Colorado] (1895).
Powell, H., *Ninety Times Guilty* (1970).
Powell, M. J., *From Patrician to Professional Elite* (1988).
Presgraves, J. S., "Careers of Two Ex-Slaves," 7 *Wythe County Historical Review* 15 (July 1974).
Principal Officers of the Department of State and United States Chiefs of Mission, 1778–1988 (1988).
Proceedings, State Bar Association of Wisconsin (1912–1914).
Proceedings of the Thirteenth Annual Meeting of the Iowa State Bar Association, July 11–12, 1907.
Proctor, J. C., "Belva Ann Lockwood," Vols. 35–36, *The Records of the Columbia Historical Society* 192 (1935).
Proffitt, R. F., "Baker and Baker (and Baker)," 29 *Law Quadrangle Notes* 24 (Summer 1985).
Progressive Men of Minnesota (M. D. Shutter and J. S. McLain eds. 1897).
Purcell, Isaac L., "Is the Criminal Negro Justly Dealt with in the Courts of the South?" in *Twentieth Century Negro Literature* 104 (D. W. Culp ed. 1902).
Quarles, B., *Black Abolitionists* (reprint, 1970).
———, *Lincoln and the Negro* (1962).
Quinquennial Catalogue of the Law School of Harvard University, 1817–1914 (R. Ames ed. 1915).
Ragsdale, B. A., and J. D. Treese, *Black Americans in Congress, 1870–1989* (1990).
Rampersad, A., *The Life of Langston Hughes* (1986).
Ramsey, W. B., "George W. Crawford," *George W. Crawford Law Association Newsletter* (July 1979).
Rankin, D. C., "The Origins of Negro Leadership in New Orleans During Reconstruction," in *Southern Black Leaders of the Reconstruction Era* 155 (H. N. Rabinowitz ed. 1981).
"A Record of the Negro College," 32 *Crisis* 167 (Aug. 1926).
Reed, A. Z., *Review of Legal Education in the United States and Canada for the Year 1930* (1931).
———, *Training for the Public Profession of the Law* (reprint, 1986).
Register of the Department of Justice and the Courts of the United States (26th ed. 1918).
Register of the Department of Justice and the Judicial Offices of the United States (10th ed. 1895).
Register of the Department of State (1894).
Reid, G. W., "The Post-Congressional Career of George H. White," 61 *Journal Negro History* 362 (Oct. 1976).
Reidy, Joseph P., "Aaron A. Bradley: Voice of Black Labor in the Georgia Lowcountry," in *Southern Black Leaders of the Reconstruction Era* 281 (H. N. Rabinowitz ed. 1981).

Reitzes, D. C., *Negroes and Medicine* (1958).

Relief of Professor William H. H. Hart: Papers Relating to the Claim of William H. H. Hart, S. 2233, 68th Cong., 1st Sess. 412 (1924).

R. L. Polk and Co., *City Directory of Libby, Montana* (1909).

Reminiscences of an Active Life: The Autobiography of John Roy Lynch (J. H. Franklin ed. 1970).

Reneau, A., and L. Barbee, "Black Lawyers—A Brief History," 57 *Wisconsin Bar Bulletin* 55 (1984).

Report of Bureau of Negro Welfare and Statistics, 1921–1922 (T. Edward Hill ed. 1922).

Report of War Work Committee of the Federal Bar Association, Oct. 1, 1942 (pamphlet).

Reports and Proceedings of the National Negro Business League Convention (1900–1921) (passim).

Reports of the American Bar Association, Vols. 1–70 (1878–1944) (passim).

"Respecting the Rescue of an Alleged Fugitive Slave at Boston," Vol. 9 *United States Statutes at Large* 1006 (G. Minot ed. 1862).

Reynolds, J. S., *Reconstruction in South Carolina, 1865–1877* (reprint, 1969).

Rice, L. D., *The Negro in Texas, 1874–1900* (1971).

"Richard T. Greener: The First Black Harvard College Graduate," in *Varieties of Black Experience at Harvard* 90 (W. Sollors, T. A. Underwood, and C. Titcomb eds. 1986).

Richardson, B. J., *Black Directory of New Mexico* (1976) (pamphlet).

Richings, G. R., *Evidence of Progress Among Colored People* (1904).

Riddle, A. G., *Law Students and Lawyers: The Philosophy of Political Parties, and Other Subjects* (1873).

Riley, G. H., "Woman at the Bar," 8 *The Law Student* 7 (Jan., 1931).

Rivers, F. E., "The Lawyer and Legislation," in *The National Bar Association Proceedings of the Six Annual Convention* 24 (Aug. 7, 1930).

————, "The Manhattan City Court Election of 1943," 2 *National Bar Association Journal* 38 (1944).

Robbins, D. L., *Suffolk University: A Social History* (1981) (pamphlet).

Robinson, B. G., "Robert Morris, John S. Rock, William H. Lewis, and Edgar P. Benjamin," *Occasional Paper No. 4*, Afro-American Studies Program, Boston University 57 (1975).

Robinson, D., and C. Stephens, "Blacks in the Law," 64 *Michigan Bar Journal* 517 (1985).

Robinson, L. J., "Woman Lawyers in the United States," 2 *Greenbag* 10 (1890).

Robinson, S., "William Henry Hastie—The Lawyer," 125 *University of Pennsylvania Law Review* 8 (1976).

Robinson, W. W., *Lawyers of Los Angeles* (1959).

Rogosin, D., *Invisible Men* (1987).

Rose, A., *Negro in America* (1944).

Rowe, F. A., "To the Chicago-Kent Alumni," 1 *The Chicago-Kent Review* 3 (1923).

"A Salute to Charles V. Carr," 127 *Congressional Record* E3984 (Aug. 4, 1981).

"A Salute to Judge Perry Jackson," Vol. 131 *Congressional Record* E5097 (Nov. 12, 1985).

Saunders, D., "Founded by Feminists," *The American [University Law School] Jurist* 12 (March 1991).

Savage, J. W., and J. T. Bell, *History of the City of Omaha, Nebraska* (1894).

Savage, W. S., *Blacks in the West* (1977).

Schweninger, L., *Black Property Owners in the South, 1790–1915* (1990).

———, *James T. Rapier and Reconstruction* (1978).

Scott, M., "Langston Hughes of Kansas," 66 *Journal of Negro History* 1 (1981).

Scott, M., Jr., *The Negro in Tennessee Politics and Governmental Affairs, 1865–1965* (1964).

Scott, Romaine F., "The Negro in American History, 1877–1900, as Portrayed in the *Washington Evening Star*," (M.A. thesis, Howard University, 1948).

Scott's Business and Service Directory (1947).

Segal, G. R., *Blacks in the Law* (1983).

Settle, Josiah, "The Colored Bar Association," in *Afro-American Encyclopedia; Or, The Thoughts, Doings and Sayings of the Race* 50 (J. Haley ed. 1895).

The Seventy-fifth Anniversary of the School of Law of Washington University, St. Louis, 1867–1942 (1942).

75-Year History, National Association of Women Lawyers (M. H. Zimmerman ed. 1975).

Sewell, G. A., and C. V. Troup, *Morris Brown College: The First One Hundred Years* (1981).

Sherman, J. R., *Invisible Poets* (1974).

Shirley, G., *Law West of Fort Smith* (1957).

Shores, A. D., "The Negro at the Bar," 2 *National Bar Association Journal* 266 (1944).

The Short Fiction of Charles W. Chesnutt (S. L. Render ed. 1974).

Simmons, W. J., *Men of Mark* (1887).

Simms's Blue Book and Directory (1923).

16th Annual Catalogue, Law School of Columbia College, 1873–1874 (1874).

Smith, E. P., "William A. Heathman, Esq.," 15 *Rhode Island Bar Journal* 3 (June, 1967).

Smith, J. Clay, Jr., "The Black Bar Association and Civil Rights," 15 *Creighton Law Review* 651 (1982).

———, "Black Lawyers in the Federal Government: 1844–1940," 32 *Federal Bar News-Journal* 193 (April/May 1985).

———, "Forgotten Hero," (book review of G. R. McNeil's *Charles Hamilton Houston and the Struggle for Civil Rights*), 98 *Harvard Law Review* 482 (1984).

———, "The High Mountain of William Henry Hastie as Witnessed from Howard University School of Law" (commemorative symposium at Harvard Law School, Nov. 16, 1984) (pamphlet).

———, "In the Shadow of Plessy: A Portrait of McCants Stewart, Afro-American Legal Pioneer," 73 *Minnesota Law Review* 495 (1988).

———, "Louis Rothschild Mehlinger: The First One Hundred Years," 26 *Howard Law Journal* 359 (1983).

———, "The Marion County Lawyers' Club: 1932 and the Black Lawyer," 8 *Black Law Journal* 170 (Howard Law School Edition, 1983).

———, "Patricia Roberts Harris: A Champion in Pursuit of Excellence," 29 *Howard Law Journal* 437 (1986).

———, "Profile: Howard University Entering Law Students, 1893–1903, Age and Legal Residence" (Dec. 1985) (unpublished paper).

———, "Profile: Howard University Entering Law Students, 1904–1920, Age, Legal Residence, and Education" (Dec. 1985) (unpublished paper).

———, "Retirement of Herbert Ordre Reid, Sr.," 3 *The Jurist* (Howard Law School Alumni Journal) 18 (Summer 1989).

————, "Toward a Pure Legal Existence: Blacks and the Constitution," 30 *Howard Law Journal* 921 (1987).

————, "Whither the Black Lawyer in Virginia?" 34 *Virginia Bar News* 8 (Aug. 1985).

Smith, J. W., "Class Prophecy," *Howard University Professional Schools Yearbook of 1922* (Book 5) (pages unnumbered).

Smith, S. D., *The Negro in Congress, 1870–1901* (1940).

Smith, W., "Loren Miller: Advocate for Blacks," 1 *Black Law Journal* 7 (1971).

Smith, W. H., "The Negro and the Law," in *The Negro Problem* 127 (B. T. Washington ed. 1903).

Smull's Legislative Handbook of the State of Pennsylvania (1914).

Souvenir Album and Directory of the Colored Voters in Omaha, Nebraska (W. B. Walker ed. 1891).

Spangler, E., *The Negro in Minnesota* (1961).

Spear, A. H., *Black Chicago: The Making of a Negro Ghetto, 1890–1920* (1967).

Special Communication (of the American Bar Association) in re the Membership Situation (1914).

"Speech of William H. Gray Before the Arkansas Constitutional Convention, 1868," 5 *Journal of Negro History* 239 (1920).

Sprinklers, D. W., *The History of Evansville Blacks* (1974).

Spurgeon, J. R., "The Basis of a Nation's Permanency," 1 *The New Africa* 7, Dec., 1899.

————, "New York and Liberia Steamship Company; or, The Commercial Possibilities of the Trade of West Africa with America," 7 *The Colored American Magazine* 735 (Dec. 1904).

Staples, T. S., *Reconstruction in Arkansas* (1923).

State of Missouri Official Manual for Years Nineteen Twenty-seven and Nineteen Twenty-eight (C. U. Becker ed. 1928).

Stevens, R., *Law School: Legal Education in America from the 1850s to the 1980s* (1983).

Stokes, R. R., "Decision of the Missouri Supreme Court on the Admission of Negroes to State Universities," 48 *School and Society* 726 (Dec. 1939).

Storr, R. J., *Harper's University: The Beginnings* (1966).

Straker, D. A., "Brief Sketch of the Political Life of Honorable Robert Browne Elliott of South Carolina," 9 *The A.M.E. Church Review* 376 (April, 1893).

————, "The Negro in the Profession of Law," 8 *The A.M.E. Church Review* 178 (1891).

Styles, F. L., *Negroes and the Law* (1937).

"A Successful Educational Campaign," 11 *The Sphinx* 4 (June 1925).

Sumner, C., *The Works of Charles Sumner* Vol. 9 (1874).

Sunderland, E. R., *History of the American Bar Association and Its Work* (1953).

Taylor, A. A., *The Negro in Tennessee, 1865–1880* (1941).

Taylor, Quintard, Jr. "The History of Blacks in the Pacific Northwest, 1788–1970" (Ph.D. diss., University of Minnesota, 1977).

Taylor, W. E., "Howard's Law School," *Howard University Alumni Journal* 13, Sept., 1935.

Teall, K. M., *Black History in Oklahoma—A Resource Book* (1971).

"Thirteen Negro American Legislators," 21 *Crisis* 120 (Jan. 1921).

Thomas, L. T., "Biographical Bits About Terrell Teachers," Vol. 1, No. 8, *The Barrister* (Robert H. Terrell Law School) 9 (May 2, 1941).

Thomas, O. A., *The Negro in California Before 1890* (1945).

Thompson, J. E., *Hiram R. Revels, 1827–1901: A Biography*, (Ph.D. diss., Princeton University, 1973).

Thornbrough, E. L., *The Negro in Indiana Before 1900* (1957).

Thurman, S. B., *Pioneers of Negro Origin in California* (1949).

Tindall, G. B., *South Carolina Negroes, 1877–1900* (1966).

Tocqueville, A. de, *Democracy in America* (R. D. Heffner ed. 1963).

Toles, E. B., *Chicago Negro Judges, 1900–1965*, June 19, 1965 (pamphlet).

———, "Fifty Years of Progress for Black Lawyers," in *National Bar Association Commemorative Convention Program* 25 (1975).

Tollett, K. S., "Black Lawyers, Their Education, and the Black Community," 17 *Howard Law Journal* 326 (1972).

———, "Universal Education, Blacks, and Democracy," in *Race: Twentieth Century Dilemmas—Twenty-First Century Prognoses* 49 (W. A. Van Horne and T. V. Tonnesen eds. 1989).

Tolson, Arthur L., "The Negro in Oklahoma Territory, 1889–1970: A Study of Racial Discrimination" (Ph.D. diss., University of Oklahoma, 1966).

Triennial Catalogue of Wilberforce University for Academic Year 1872–73 (1873).

Trotter, J. W., Jr., *Black Milwaukee* (1985).

Tucker, F. D., *Directory of the Colored Members of the Philadelphia Bar*, May 15, 1970.

Tureaud, A. P., *The Negro at the Louisiana Bar* (n.d.) (paper).

———, "The United States Supreme Court and Its Decisions Affecting Negroes," Vol. 1 *Civic Leader* 6 (1929).

Tushnet, M. V., *The NAACP's Legal Strategy Against Segregated Education, 1925–1950* (1987).

Tuttle, W. M., Jr., *Race Riot* (1970).

Twelfth Annual Catalogue University of Chicago, 1870–1871.

Twentieth Century Negro Literature (D. W. Culp ed. 1902).

The Twentieth-Century Union League Directory (A. F. Hilyer Compiler, Jan. 1901).

22nd Annual Convention Report of the Resolutions Committee of the Southwest Bar Association, June 22, 1962.

Twenty-seventh Annual Session Oklahoma Jurisdiction, St. John Grand Lodge, Ancient, Free and Accepted Masons, Aug. 13–15, 1918.

"The University of Detroit Law School," 12 *University of Detroit Law Journal* 6 (1948).

University of Michigan General Catalogue of Officers and Students, 1837–1911 (I. N. Demmon ed. 1912).

Vincent, C., *Black Legislators in Louisiana During Reconstruction* (1976).

The Violation of a Constitutional Right (L. A. Martinet ed. 1893).

Virgin Island Reports (1917–1939).

Virgin Island Reports (1954–1958).

"Virginia Admits Colored Woman to Bar," 3 *The Law Student* 18 (Feb. 15, 1926).

Virginia's Contribution to Negro Leadership (W. Cooper ed. 1937) (mimeo).

Virginia Union Bulletin Centennial Issue: A Century of Service to Education and Religion (June 1965).

Virginia Union University Catalogues, 1921–1927 (passim).

Walker, G. H., "Legal Education in Negro Institutions of Higher Learning," 73 *School and Society* 326 (May 26, 1951).

Walker, T. C., "Among Virginia Negroes," 49 *The Southern Workman* 421 (Sept. 1920).

———, *The Honey-pod Tree* (1958).

Walton, H., Jr., *Black Politics* (1972).

———, *Black Republicans: The Politics of the Blacks and Tans* (1975).

Ware, G., *William Hastie: Grace Under Pressure* (1984).

Ware, L., "Contributions of Missouri's Black Lawyers to Securing Equal Justice," 45 *Journal of Missouri Bar* 251 (June 1989).

Warner, R. A., *New Haven Negroes: A Social History* (1940).

Warren, C., *The Supreme Court in United States History, 1836–1918*, Vol. 2 (1926).

Warren, F. H., *Michigan Manual of Freedmen's Progress* (1915).

Washington, B. T., *The Negro in Business* (1907).

———, *The Story of My Life and Work* (1899).

———, *The Story of the Negro* (1909).

Washington, H., "History and Role of Black Law Schools," 18 *Howard Law Journal* 385 (1974).

Washington, N. J., *Historical Development of the Negro in Oklahoma* (1948).

Weaver, C. W., *The History of Negro Schools in Elizabeth City County* (Va.) (Aug. 6, 1938) (mimeo).

Weaver, S. P., *Constitutional Law and Its Administration* (1946).

Weeden, H. C., *History of the Colored People of Louisville* (1897).

Weeks, W., *History of the Law, the Courts, and the Lawyers of Maine* (1863).

Weisberg, D. K., *Women and the Law* (1982).

Weisbrot, R. W., *Father Divine* (1983).

Weiss, N. J., *Farewell to the Party of Lincoln* (1983).

Weltner, C. L., *Southerner* (1966).

West, E. J., "Harvard and the Black Man, 1636–1850," in *Variety of Black Experience at Harvard* 1 (W. Sollors, T. A. Underwood, and C. Titcomb eds. 1986).

West Virginia Bureau of Negro Welfare and Statistics Biennial Reports (1933–1934, 1938–1940) (I. M. Carper ed. 1941).

West Virginia Bureau of Negro Welfare and Statistics Biennial Reports (1921–1922, 1926–1927) (T. Edward Hill ed. 1922, 1926, 1927).

West Virginia Bureau of Negro Welfare and Statistics Biennial Report (1941–1942) (C. F. Hopson ed. 1942).

The West Virginia Heritage Encyclopedia (1976).

Wharton, V. L., *The Negro in Mississippi, 1895–1890* (1947).

White, C. F., *Who's Who in Philadelphia* (1912).

Who's Who Among Negro Lawyers (S. T. M. Alexander ed. 1945).

Who's Who in Colored America Vol. 1 (J. J. Boris ed. 1927).

Who's Who in Colored America (G. J. Fleming and C. E. Burckel eds. 7th ed. 1950).

Who's Who in Colored Louisiana (A. E. Perkins ed. 1930).

Who's Who in Maryland (A. N. Marquis ed. 1939).

Who's Who in Philadelphia (C. F. White ed. 1912).

Who's Who in Religious, Fraternal, Social, and Commercial Life on the Pacific Coast (1926–1927).

Who's Who of the Colored Race Vol. 1 (F. L. Mather ed. 1915).

Wigmore, J. H., *A Panorama of the World's Legal Systems* (Library ed. 1938).

Williams, G. W., *Negro Race in America* (1885).

Williams, Isaiah J., III, "Joseph E. Lee: A Man of Power, 1849–1920" (1974) (paper).

Williams, Lillian S., "The Development of Black Community: Buffalo, New York, 1900–1940" (Ph.D. diss., State University of New York at Buffalo, 1979).

Williams, P., "A Black Woman's Voice: The Story of Mabel Raimey, 'Shero,'" 74 *Marquette L. Rev.* 345 (1991).

Williams, R., "Edwin Archer Randolph, LL.B., Rediscovered," 3 *The Richmond Quarterly* 46 (Spring 1981).

Williams, T. H., R. N. Current, and F. Freidel, *A History of the United States* (1960).

Wilson, G. D., *A Century of Negro Education in Kentucky* (revised manuscript, 1986).

Wilson, J. Q., *Negro Politics* (1969).

Wiltse, Henry M., *The History of Chattanooga* Vol. 2, (n.d.) (manuscript).

Winch, J., "Geraldine Pindell Trotter," 2 *Trotter Institute Review* 10 (Winter 1988).

Wolgemuth, K. L., "Woodrow Wilson's Appointment Policy and the Negro," 24 *Journal of Southern History* 457 (Nov. 1958).

Women at Harvard Law School, 1953–1987, Alumnae Directory (N. Lictenstein and R. W. Tate eds. 1988).

Woods, R. B., *A Black Odyssey: John Lewis Waller and the Promise of American Life, 1878–1900* (1981).

Woodson, C. G., *A Century of Negro Migration* (1918).

———, *Miseducation of the Negro* (1933).

———, *The Negro Professional Man and the Community* (1934 and reprint, 1969).

Woody, R. H., "Jonathan Jasper Wright, Associate Justice of the Supreme Court of South Carolina, 1870–1877," 18 *Journal of Negro History* 114 (1933).

Work, M. N., "The Negro in Business and the Professions," 140 *Annals of the American Academy of Political and Social Science* 138 (Nov. 1928).

Wright, G., *Life Behind the Veil: Blacks in Louisville, Kentucky 1865–1930* (1985).

Wright, M. C., *The Guarantee, P. W. Chavers: Banker, Entrepreneur, Philanthropist in Chicago's Black Belt of the Twenties* (1987).

Wright, R. R., *The Negro in Pennsylvania* (reprint, 1969).

Wynes, C. E., "T. McCants Stewart: Peripatetic Black South Carolinian," 80 *South Carolina Historical Museum* 311 (Oct. 1979).

Yale Alumna Directory (1949).

Yale Law School Sesquicentennial Alumni Directory (1974).

Year Book, Association of the Bar City of New York 1943.

Young, N. B., "Early Black Lawyers in St. Louis," 30 *Saint Louis Bar Journal* 6, (Spring 1984).

Zangrando, R. L., "The NAACP and a Federal Anti-Lynching Bill, 1934–1940," 50 *Journal Negro History* 106 (1965).

INTERVIEWS

Adams, John, Jr., of Berkeley, CA. Telephone interviews, Oct. 17, 1988; Feb. 11, 1989; and June 15, 1990.

Austin, Helen Elsie, of Silver Springs, MD. Personal interview, May 14, 1985.

Berry, Theodore Moody. Personal interview, in Washington, DC, June 9, 1989.

Bohannan, James H., deputy recorder of deeds of Washington, DC. Telephone interview, Nov. 21, 1988.

Bostic, Ruth, of Washington, DC. Telephone interview, Sept. 6, 1975.

Brown, Ellen Eppes, of Washington, DC. Telephone interview, Sept. 17, 1985.

Bukowitz, Patrice, Department of external relations, Detroit College of Law. Telephone interview, April 10, 1989.

Coleman, Luella, of Massachusetts. Telephone interview, Nov. 16, 1988.

Crockett, William F., of Hawaii. Telephone interview, May 13, 1989.

Davis, Joan Adams, of Kansas City, MO. Telephone interview, Oct. 17, 1988.

Dedmon, Jesse O., of Washington, DC. Telephone interviews, April 3 and July 8, 1985.

Dejean, Dr. Joseph, professor of law, emeritus. Personal interviews, Howard University School of Law, March 1 and 4, 1985.

Dickerson, Earl B., of Chicago, IL. Telephone interview, Aug. 24, 1986.

Dugas, Julian Riley, of Washington, DC. Personal interview, April 10, 1988.

Flowers, W. Harold, Sr., of Arkansas. Telephone interview, March 15, 1989.

Gray, Chester J., of Cleveland, OH. Telephone interview, Jan. 23, 1989.

Herrig, Inez, of Libby, MT. Telephone interview, Sept. 8, 1990.

Howard, Charles P., Jr. Personal interview, in Washington, DC, May 27, 1986.

Howard, Judge Joseph C., of Baltimore MD. Telephone interview, Nov. 29, 1988.

Jenkins, Howard, Jr., of Maryland. Telephone interview, in Washington, DC, April 1, 1989.

Johnson, Henry Lincoln, Jr., of Washington, DC. Personal interview, Aug. 15, 1989.

Mehlinger, Louis Rothschild, of Washington, DC. Personal interview, Oct. 19, 1979.

Moore, William Coleman, of Indianapolis, IN. Telephone interview, Oct. 3, 1987.

Nelson, Phoebe Novotny, of Maryland. Telephone interview, Feb. 27, 1990.

Oliver, Daily, Webster State College, Ogden, UT. Telephone interview, Oct. 15, 1987.

Ortigue, Revis, of New Orleans, LA. Telephone interview, Nov. 1, 1988.

Popp, Richard, University of Chicago. Telephone interview, Nov. 1, 1989.

Reynolds, Raymond J., of California. Telephone interviews, April 4, 7, and 14, 1989.

Robinson, G. Bruce, of Massachusetts. Telephone interview, Sept. 3, 1988.

Rutherford, Thelma, of Washington, DC. Telephone interview, May 14, 1985.

Stewart-Flippin, Mary Katherine, of San Francisco, CA. Telephone interview, Dec. 2, 1987.

Stoppal William, Drake University. Telephone interviews, Jan. 12 and 18, 1989.

Thomas, Lucia T., of Chicago, IL. Telephone interview, Oct. 3, 1986.

Thompson, Lucille W., of Bozeman, MT. Telephone interview, Oct. 20, 1990.

White, Dr. Desra, of Houston, TX. Telephone interview, Oct. 13, 1986.

Wilson, Margaret Bush, of St. Louis, MO. Telephone interview, June 11, 1986; personal interview, Provo, UT, March 4, 1989.

Table of Cases

Index

This book was set in Baskerville typeface. Baskerville was designed by John Baskerville at his private press in Birmingham, England, in the eighteenth century. The first typeface to depart from oldstyle typeface design, Baskerville has more variation between thick and thin strokes. In an effort to insure that the thick and thin strokes of his typeface reproduced well on paper, John Baskerville developed the first wove paper, the surface of which was much smoother than the laid paper of the time. The development of wove paper was partly responsible for the introduction of typefaces classified as modern, which have even more contrast between thick and thin strokes.

Printed on acid-free paper.